P9-DWH-656

Perspectives from the Past

PRIMARY SOURCES IN WESTERN CIVILIZATIONS

Sixth Edition

Perspectives from the Past

PRIMARY SOURCES IN WESTERN CIVILIZATIONS

Sixth Edition

VOLUME 2

From the Age of Exploration
through Contemporary Times

JAMES M. BROPHY · JOSHUA COLE · JOHN ROBERTSON

THOMAS MAX SAFLEY · CAROL SYMES

W · W · NORTON & COMPANY NEW YORK · LONDON

W. W. Norton & Company has been independent since its founding in 1923, when William Warder Norton and Mary D. Herter Norton first published lectures delivered at the People's Institute, the adult education division of New York City's Cooper Union. The firm soon expanded its program beyond the Institute, publishing books by celebrated academics from America and abroad. By mid-century, the two major pillars of Norton's publishing program—trade books and college texts—were firmly established. In the 1950s, the Norton family transferred control of the company to its employees, and today—with a staff of four hundred and a comparable number of trade, college, and professional titles published each year—W. W. Norton & Company stands as the largest and oldest publishing house owned wholly by its employees.

Copyright © 2016, 2012, 2009, 2005, 2002, 1998 by W. W. Norton & Company, Inc.

All rights reserved.
Printed in the United States of America

Editor: Jon Durbin
Editorial assistant: Travis Carr
Production Manager: Jane Searle
Composition: Westchester Publishing Services
Manufacturing: Maple Press
Book Design: Jack Meserole

Acknowledgments and copyrights continue on page 633, which serves
as a continuation of the copyright page.

ISBN 978-0-393-26539-2 (v. 1 : pbk.)—**ISBN 978-0-393-26540-8** (v. 2 : pbk.)

W. W. Norton & Company, Inc., 500 Fifth Avenue, New York, N.Y. 10110
www.wwnorton.com

W. W. Norton & Company Ltd., Castle House,
75/76 Wells Street, London W1T 3QT

1 2 3 4 5 6 7 8 9 0

ABOUT THE AUTHORS

JAMES M. BROPHY is the Francis H. Squire Professor of history at the University of Delaware, where he has taught since 1992. He received his B.A. from Vassar College and did his graduate training at Eberhard Karls Universität in Tübingen, Germany, and Indiana University, where he took his Ph.D. in modern European history. He is the author of *Capitalism, Politics, and Railroads in Prussia, 1830–1870* (1998) and *Popular Culture and the Public Sphere in the Rhineland, 1800–1850* (2007). He has also published numerous articles on German and European history, which have appeared in such journals as *Past & Present, Journal of Modern History,* and *Historische Zeitschrift.* He regularly teaches the Western civilization survey as well as courses and seminars on historiography, nationalism, modern European history, print culture, and the Holocaust.

JOSHUA COLE is associate professor of history at the University of Michigan. He received his B.A. from Brown University and his M.A. and Ph.D. from the University of California, Berkeley. The author of *The Power of Large Numbers: Population, Politics, and Gender in Nineteenth-Century France* (2000), he has also published articles on French and German social and cultural history in the modern period. His current research is on the legacy of colonial violence in France, Algeria, and Madagascar, with a focus on the problems created by this history of violence in the postcolonial world. He has enjoyed teaching European history in a global context since 1993.

JOHN ROBERTSON received both his M.A. (1976) and his Ph.D. (1981) in ancient history from the University of Pennsylvania. A specialist in the social and economic history of the ancient Near East, he has published several articles in major scholarly journals and contributed articles to such major reference works as the *Anchor Bible Dictionary, Civilizations of the Ancient Near East,* and the *Blackwell Companion to the Ancient Near East.* His book *Iraq: A History* was published in 2015. He has also participated in archaeological excavations in Syria and Greece as well as the American Southwest. Since 1982, he has been a member of the faculty of the department of history at Central Michigan University, where he has taught the history of Western civilization for both the department of history and the university honors program, as well as more specialized courses in the history of the ancient Near East and the Islamic and modern Middle East.

THOMAS MAX SAFLEY teaches the history of early modern Europe at the University of Pennsylvania. A specialist in economic and social history, he has particular research interests in the history of marriage and the family, of poverty and charity, and of labor and business. In addition to numerous articles and reviews, he is the author of *Let No Man Put Asunder: The Control of Marriage in the German Southwest, 1550–1620* (1984), *Charity and Economy in the Orphanages of Early Modern Augsburg* (1996), *Matheus Miller's Memoir: A Merchant's Life in the Seventeenth Century* (2000), and *The Children of* the *Laboring Poor: Expectation and Experience among the Orphans of Early Modern Augsburg* (2004). He is coeditor of *The Workplace before the Factory: Artisans and Proletarians, 1500–1800* (1993) and *Childhood and Emotion: Across Cultures, 1450–1800* (2013), and he is editor of *The Reformation of Charity: The Secular and the Sacred in Early Modern Poor Relief* (2003), *A Companion to Multiconfessionalism in the Early Modern World* (2011), and *The History of Bankruptcy: Economic, Social and Cultural Implications in Early Modern Europe* (2013). At the University of Pennsylvania, he regularly teaches the introductory survey of European history and advanced lecture courses on the early modern period. He also offers a broad array of undergraduate and graduate seminars.

CAROL SYMES is the Lynn M. Martin Professorial Scholar at the University of Illinois, Urbana—Champaign, where she is an associate professor of history with appointments in theatre and medieval studies. Educated at Yale and Oxford, she trained for an acting career at the Bristol Old Vic Theatre School (England) and continued to work professionally in theatre while earning the Ph.D. at Harvard, and for several years thereafter. Her research deals with the relationships among premodern performance practices and written records, asking fundamental questions about the transmission of knowledge and the development of communication media and technologies. Her book, *A Common Stage: Theatre and Public Life in Medieval Arras* (2007), won four national awards in three different disciplines, including the Herbert Baxter Adams Prize of the American Historical Association and the John Nicholas Brown Prize from the Medieval Academy of America. Her current book project is a study of the embodied, performative, and material conditions in which medieval texts were negotiated and created. She is the founding executive editor of *The Medieval Globe*, the first academic journal to practice a globalized methodology of medieval studies.

CONTENTS

CHAPTER 13 ∽ THE AGE OF DISSENT AND DIVISION, 1500–1564   80

CHAPTER 14 ∽ EUROPE IN THE ATLANTIC WORLD, 1550–1660   114

CHAPTER 15 ⟳ EUROPEAN MONARCHIES AND ABSOLUTISM, 1660–1725   145

CHAPTER 16 ⟳ THE NEW SCIENCE OF THE SEVENTEENTH CENTURY   189

CHAPTER 17 ✑ EUROPE DURING THE ENLIGHTENMENT   225

CHAPTER 18 ✑ THE FRENCH REVOLUTION   287

CHAPTER 19   THE INDUSTRIAL REVOLUTION AND NINETEENTH-CENTURY SOCIETY   324

CHAPTER 22   IMPERIALISM AND COLONIALISM, 1870–1914   428

CHAPTER 23   MODERN INDUSTRIES AND MASS POLITICS, 1870–1914   458

CHAPTER 27 ⤫ THE COLD WAR WORLD: GLOBAL POLITICS, ECONOMIC RECOVERY, AND CULTURAL CHANGE   586

CHAPTER 28 ⤫ A WORLD WITHOUT WALLS: GLOBALIZATION AND THE WEST   610

PREFACE FOR INSTRUCTORS

The authors of this text are very pleased to have the opportunity to design and compile this reader, which is the outgrowth of approximately nine decades of combined experience in teaching the history of Western civilization. In the course of acquiring that experience, we were frustrated by what we perceived as serious shortcomings in most of the available supplementary readers. We noted, for example, a frequent overemphasis on political and intellectual history at the expense of social and economic trends, and on elite culture at the expense of sources relating to the experiences of common people and, especially, of women. There is also a tendency to under represent the experiences and perspectives of European societies east of what is today Germany and a lack of attention to the West's important interactions with non-Western peoples and civilizations. We have also wanted to avoid the common practice of presenting texts so abbreviated or disjointed that students are unable to gain a proper appreciation of their contexts or of the nature of the documents from which they are derived. For ancient and medieval sources, this problem is all too often compounded by the use of translations that are either obsolete or rendered in an antiquated idiom that fails to engage students' interest.

In order to address such concerns, we have worked to produce a text that incorporates the following features:

- Selections consist of complete texts or lengthy excerpts of primary documents, ranging from one to eight pages in length and reproduced in authoritative and accessible translations.

- Since images and artifacts are also meaningful primary sources, most chapters of this edition contain visual features (e.g., photographs, paintings, posters, cartoons, sculptures) intended to help students learn how to analyze and interpret visual sources.

- We strive to achieve an appropriate balance of primary sources from the Western canon—works that are illustrative of the origins and development of Western political institutions, intellectual life, and high culture—as well as those that illustrate aspects of social and economic history and daily life in Western societies.

- Selections reflect the experiences and perspectives of women and the dynamics of gender relations, as well as the experiences of commoners and marginalized peoples.

- Selections focus on western civilizations within a broader, global perspective and include ancient Egyptian and Babylonian literature, the Qur'an, and then works of such figures as Ali ibn al-Athir, Ibn Battuta, Edward Morel, Mohandas Gandhi, Frantz Fanon, and Tadataka Kuribayshi.

- In addition to review questions that assist the students in close reading and analysis of individual texts, we include questions designed to link documents (both within and among chapters) in a coherent, pedagogically useful framework. The documents in this reader can thus be used to explore and discuss overarching issues and thematic trends: What are responsibilities and rights of the individual within a local community or broader society, and how have they changed over time? How have people defined their own communities, and how have they viewed outsiders? Who should have power within society, and why? How have people responded to changes in the material world and the environment?

The pedagogical and critical apparatus provided in this reader has been designed to guide the student to an appreciation of the sources but without imparting too much in the way of historical interpretation. For each chapter we have supplied a brief introduction that provides a historical context for the readings and alerts the student to the thematic threads that link them. Each reading in turn has an introduction that supplies an even more specific context. Finally, each selection is accompanied by several questions intended to stimulate analysis and discussion.

For this edition we have included the following new documents:

- Bartolomeo de Giano, from "A Letter on the Cruelty of the Turks"

- Vasco da Gama, Round Africa to India, 1497–1498 C.E.

- from The Peace of Westphalia

- Thomas Mun, from England's Treasure by Forraign Trade, or The Balance of our Forraign Trade is The Rule of our Treasure

- Margaret Cavendish, from Observations upon Experimental Philosophy. To which is added, the Description of a New Blazing World

- Robert Hooke, from Micrographia

- Lady Mary Wortley Montagu, from *Letters of the Right Honourable Montagu*
- Moses Mendelssohn, "What is Enlightenment?"
- Society of the Friends of Blacks, from Address to the National Assembly in Favor of the Abolition of the Slave Trade
- The Haitian Declaration of Independence
- Edmund Burke and Thomas Paine, Opposing Views of the Revolution
- Jakob Walter, from *The Diary of a Napoleonic Foot Soldier*
- David Ricardo, "On Wages"
- Evidence from the Sandler Report
- George Annesley, Viscount Valentia, from *Voyages and Travels to India, Ceylon, the Red Sea, Abyssinia, and Egypt*
- The Decembrist Revolt
- Joseph de Maistre, "Of Monarchy"
- Pierre-Joseph Proudhon, from *What is Property?*
- Simón Bolívar, from "The Jamaica Letter"
- Percy Bysshe Shelley, "Feelings of a Republican," "Song to the Men of England," and "England in 1819"
- Francis Palacký, from *History of the Czech Nation in Bohemia and Moravia*
- The Imperial Edict of the Rose Chamber
- Alexander II, from Manifesto Emancipating the Serfs
- Lin Tse-hsü, from Letter to Queen Victoria
- Ismāʿīl b. ʿAbd al-Qādir, from The Siege of Khartoum
- J. A. Hobson, from *Imperialism: A Study*
- Gustave Le Bon, from *The Crowd: A Study of the Popular Mind*
- Fritz Stern, from *Five Germanys I Have Known*
- Stanley Hoffmann, from "Obstinate or Obsolete? The Fate of the Nation-State and the Case of Western Europe"
- The Greek Debt Crisis

In addition to these features, this Sixth Edition has also been made more affordable and compact to meet the changing needs of instructors and students. Nearly one hundred instructors participated in our online survey, to identify the most essential and highly teachable primary sources from the previous edition, and to offer suggestions of sources that could be included. We have also brought this Sixth Edition into closer alignment with our best-selling survey texts, *Western Civilizations* Eighteenth Edition and *Western Civilizations* Brief Fourth Edition, by Joshua Cole and Carol Symes

Coordinating a project as complex as this one requires the skills, support, inspiration, and dedication of many people. We therefore wish to express our admiration and profound gratitude to the editorial and marketing staff of W. W. Norton, especially to Travis Carr and Jane Searle, who did a fantastic job of researching sources and pulling the manuscript together; to Bethany Salminen, for her work in securing permissions; and, most especially, to Jon Durbin, who assembled the team, helped us to define and refine our work, organized the project, offered useful insight and judicious criticism, and kept all of us on task and on time. The credit for this reader is as much theirs as ours.

In addition, we would like to thank the following faculty for their valuable input as we developed the Sixth Edition:

- David Adams, Harding University
- Christine Arnold-Lourie, College of Southern Maryland
- Kenneth Atkinson, University of Northern Iowa
- Michelle Barsom, Bainbridge State College
- Jordan Bauer, University of Alabama at Birmingham
- Philippe Beauchamp, Champlain College
- Hilary Bernstein, University of California
- Kurt M. Boughan, The Citadel
- Richard Byington, University of Central Florida
- Amy Colon, SUNY Sullivan
- Trevor Corless, Heritage College
- Christopher Daly, SUNY Albany
- Babette Faehmel, Schenectady County Community College
- Jessica Hammerman, Central Oregon Community College
- David M. Head, John Tyler Community College
- Anthony Heideman, Front Range Community College
- Padhraig Higgins, Mercer County College
- Andrew Kellett, Hartford Community College
- Jacob Latham, University of Tennessee, Knoxville
- John Livingston, William Paterson University
- Marina Maccari-Clayton, University of Tennessee, Knoxville
- Matthew Mingus, University of New Mexico–Gallup
- Aubrey Neal, St. Paul's College
- Stefan Papaioannou, Framingham State University
- Roberta Pergher, Indiana University

- Janet Polasky, University of New Hampshire
- David Porter, Northern Virginia Community College
- Michael Prahl, University of Northern Iowa
- Paula Rieder, Slippery Rock University
- Martin Saltzman, Long Island University
- Wanda L. Scarbro, Pellissippi State Community College
- Kathleen Sheppard, Missouri University of Science and Technology
- Jace Stuckey, Marymount University
- Larissa Taylor, Colby College
- Elisaveta Todorova, University of Cincinnati
- Steven A. Usitalo, Northern State University
- Joseph Western, St. Louis University
- Rebecca Woodham, Wallace Community College

PREFACE FOR STUDENTS

Good Tips for Learning How to Analyze Primary Sources

The purpose of this collection of illustrations and documents is to provide the student with the raw materials of history, the sources, in the form of the objects and written words that survive from the past. Your textbook relies on such documents, known as primary sources, as well as on the works of many past and present historians who have analyzed and interpreted these sources—the secondary literature. In some cases the historians were themselves sources, eyewitnesses to the events they recorded. Authors of textbooks select which facts and interpretations they think you should know, and so the textbook filters what you think about the human past by limiting the information available to you. Textbooks are useful because they provide a coherent historical narrative for students of history, but it is important to remember that they are only an introduction to the rich complexity of human experience over time.

A collection of historical documents and artifacts provides a vital supplement to the textbook, but it also has problems. First, the sources, mostly not intended for us to read and study, exist for the reasons that prompted some people to create them and others to preserve them. These reasons may include a measure of lies, self-deception, or ignorance about what was really happening and being recorded. So we must ask the following questions about any document or object—a treaty, contract, painting, photograph, poem, newspaper article, or sculpture: Why does it exist? What specific purpose did it serve when it was done? Who is its author? What motives prompted the creator to produce this material in this form?

The second major problem is that we, the editors of this collection, have selected, from millions of possible choices, these particular documents and objects, and not others. Even in this process, because of the limitations of space and our own personal experiences, we present a necessarily partial and highly selective view of Western civilization (also because of space limitations, it has been necessary to delete portions from some of the longer sections).* Our purpose is not to repeat what you can find in the textbook but to give you the opportunity to see and discuss how historians, now including you, make history out of documents and objects, and their understanding of why people behave the way they do.

The illustrations in this collection provide a glimpse at the millions of material objects that survive from the past. These churches, buildings, paintings, mosaics, sculptures, photographs, and other items make up an important set of sources for the historian to consider about the past. It is certainly difficult to appreciate an immense building or a small manuscript painting from a photograph. Nevertheless, the editors of this collection include illustrations in the Sixth Edition to make clear the full range of sources that historians utilize. Also, the illustrations in many cases complement the written documents and in every case provide opportunities for a broader discussion of historical questions and the variety of sources that can help answer them.

Before exploring in more detail what documents are, we should be clear about what history is. Simply put, history is what we can say about the human past, in this case about the vast area of Western civilization from its remote origins to the most recent past. We can say, or write, things about the past because people left us their words, in the form of documents, and we can, like detectives, question these sources and then try to understand what happened. Before the written word, there is no history in the strictest sense; instead there are preliterate societies and the tens of thousands of years for which we know only what the anthropologists and archaeologists can tell us from the physical remains of bodies and objects made by human hands. And yet during this time profoundly important human institutions like language, the family, and religion first appeared. History begins with writing because that is when the documentation starts. These accomplishments of our remote ancestors occurred over tens of thousands of years, broken into ages of stone, copper, and bronze. Objects and images, but no words, reveal advances in weapons, art, farming, and other activities.

Although history cannot exist without written documents, we must remember that this evidence is complex and ambiguous. In the first place, it first appears in ancient languages, and the majority of documents in this book were not originally in English. The act of translating the documents into modern English raises another barrier or filter, and we must use our imaginations to recreate the past worlds in which modern words like *liberty, race,* or *sin* had different meanings. One job of the historian is to understand the language of the documents in

---

* We indicate omissions, no matter how brief, with three spaced asterisks (* * *), running them in when the opening, middle, or closing of a paragraph has been deleted and centering them between lines when a full paragraph is dropped. Why asterisks, when ellipsis dots are the standard? Because authors use ellipsis dots, and we want to distinguish our deletions from theirs.

their widest possible contexts. All the authors intended their documents to communicate something, but as time passes, languages and contexts change, and so it becomes more difficult for us to figure out what a document meant then and may mean now. Language is an imperfect way to communicate, but we must make the best of what we have. If we recollect how difficult it is sometimes to understand the events we see and experience, then we can perhaps understand how careful we must be when we interpret someone else's report about an event in the past, especially when that past is far removed in space and time from our experience.

The documents give us the language, or testimony, of witnesses, observers, or people with some point to make. Some documents claim to reveal religious truths and interpreting these claims requires historians to inquire respectfully and sincerely. Historical evidence, like any other, must be examined for flaws, contradictions, lies, and what it tells us that the writer did not necessarily intend to reveal. Like a patient detective, we must question our witnesses with a full awareness of their limited and often-biased perception, piecing together our knowledge of their history with the aid of multiple testimonies and a broad context. Consider the document, whatever it is, as testimony and a piece of a bigger puzzle, many of the remaining pieces of which are missing or broken. It is useful at the beginning to be clear about the simple issues—What type of document is this evidence? Who wrote it? Where and when was it written? Why does it exist? Try to understand the context of the document by relating it to the wider world—how do words by Plato or about the Nazi Party fit with what you already know about ancient Greece or twentieth-century Germany?

When the document, or witness, has been correctly identified and placed in some context, we may then interrogate it further by asking questions about the words before us. Not all documents suggest the same questions, but there are some general questions that apply to nearly every document. One place to begin is to ask, Who or what is left out? Once you see the main point, it is interesting to ask what the documents tell us about people and subjects often left out of the records—women, children, or religious or ethnic minorities, for example. Or, if the document is about a religious minority, we can ask what it tells us about the majority. Take the document and try to turn it inside out by determining the basic assumptions or biases of its author, and then explore what has been intentionally or unintentionally left out. look for anomalies—pieces of evidence that appear out of place or simply weird; they are often clues to understanding the distances between us and the sources. Another way to ask a fresh question of an old witness is to look beneath the surface and see what else is there. For example, if the document in question seems mainly to offer evidence on religion, ask what it tells us about the economy or contemporary eating habits or whatever else might occur to you. Documents frequently reveal excellent information on topics far from their ostensible subjects, if we remember to ask.

Every document in this collection is some kind of story, either long or short. The stories are almost all nonfiction, at least in theory, but they all have characters; a plot, or story line; and above all a point to the story, the meaning. We have suggested some possible meanings in the sample questions at the end of each document, but these questions are just there to help your thinking or get a discussion going, about the many possible meanings of the documents. You can ask what the meaning was in the document's own time, as well as what we might now see as a meaning that makes sense to us of some pieces of the past. The point of the story in a document may often concern a central issue in history, the process of change. If history is what we can say about the human past, then the most important words describe how change occurs, for example, rapidly, as in revolutions and wars, or more slowly, as in marriage customs or family life. Every document casts some light on human change, and the meaning of the story often relates to why something changed.

History is often at its dullest when a document simply describes a static situation, for example, a law or farming. However, even a good description reveals choices and emphasis. If you ask, Why this law now? Why farm in this way? How did these activities influence human behavior? you can see that the real subject of nearly all documents is human change, on some level. You will find that people can and will strongly disagree about the meaning of a story: they can and will use the same evidence from a document to draw radically different meanings. This is one of the challenges of history and what makes it fun, for some explanations and meanings make more sense than others in the broader context of what you know about an episode or period of history. Argue about meaning, and you will learn something about not only your own biases and values but also the process of sifting facts for good arguments and answers. These skills have a value well beyond the study of history.

The documents and objects in this collection, even the most general works of philosophy or social analysis, reveal the particular and contingent aspects of history. Even the most abstract of these documents and objects comes from a specific time, place, and person and sheds some light on a unique set of circumstances. When history is like the other social sciences (anthropology, economics, sociology, political science, and others), it tries to deal with typical or average people, societies, or behavior. When history is like the other humanities (literature, philosophy, religion, art, and others), it stresses individual people, their quirks and uniqueness. The documents and objects also illustrate the contingent aspect of history, which unlike the social or natural sciences but like the humanities, appears to lack rules or laws. History depends on what people did, subject to the restrictions of their natures, resources, climate, and other natural factors—people with histories of their own! Rerunning this history is not like a movie, and it would never turn out the same way twice, for it is specific and contingent to the way it turned out this time. The documents and objects do not tell a story of an orderly progression from simple to complex societies or from bad to good ones. Instead, history continues, and people cope, or not, with the issues of religious faith, family life, making a living, and creating artifacts and documents. These documents and objects collectively provide perspectives on how experiments in living succeeded or failed. We invite you to use them to learn more about the people of the past than the textbooks can say and to use your imaginations to get these witnesses to answer your questions about the process and meaning of human change.

WHERE TO BEGIN?

A Primary Source Checklist

This checklist is a series of questions that can be used to analyze most of the documents and objects in this reader.

✔ What type of document or object is this evidence?

✔ Why does the document or object exist? What motives prompted the author to create the material in this form?

✔ Who created this work?

✔ Who or what is left out—women, children, minorities, members of the majority?

✔ In addition to the main subject, what other kinds of information can be obtained?

✔ How do the subjects of the document or object relate to what we know about broader society?

✔ What was the meaning of the document or object in its own time? What is its meaning for the audience?

✔ What does the document or object tell us about change or stability in society?

Perspectives from the Past

PRIMARY SOURCES IN WESTERN CIVILIZATIONS

Sixth Edition

11 ❧ REBIRTH AND UNREST, 1350–1453

The fourteenth and fifteenth centuries proved to be a crucial turning point for Europe, both internally and externally—a true period of "rebirth and unrest." The Black Death pandemic that swept the continent at mid-century resulted in population losses that had not occurred in a millennium. The immediate results for many were lower costs of living and higher wages. More striking than the loss of life, perhaps, altered social structures and relations created new opportunities in the forms of expanded trade and prosperity, and posed new challenges to traditional authority. Revolts erupted across Europe. Established governments and groups faced unprecedented questions about the legitimacy of their rule. The rising challengers, especially in the Low Countries and northern Italy, used their newly acquired wealth and confidence not only to challenge for political power but also to patronize new forms of cultural expression. The fourteenth century experienced a new realism in the arts and a new inspiration to scholarship. The first expressions of classicism, that is, a new appreciation for and attention to the authors of classical antiquity, emerged at this point in time and expanded eventually into the cultural program that became known as humanism.

The slow, painful centralization of large territorial states that becomes visible in the fourteenth century stands in sharp contrast to the decentralization fostered by the newly rich. The conflicts among and against these new states increased the general unrest of the period. That unrest had spiritual elements as well. The rise of new, prosperous, and powerful social groups, bringing with them new ambitions, priorities, and values, led to a fundamental revival in religious piety. Individuals, such as Catherine of Siena, and groups, such as the beguines, offer evidence of a widespread yearning for spiritual meaning and fulfillment. Proto-reformers, such as John Wyclif and Jan Hus, levied criticism on an established Christian Church that they believed had become separated from the true inspiration and imperative of the Gospels.

All of these developments, economic and social, cultural and political, received further impetus from what social scientists would call an exogenous shock. The rise of a new and aggressive power in Central Asia and the Middle East, the empire of the Ottoman Turks, unleashed a flood of refugees who brought the remnants of ancient Greek culture into the West, closed established trade routes to the bazaars of the East, and inspired European states with horror.

By the end of the fourteenth century, forces worked upon Europe that would inspire scholars to speak of an end to the Middle Ages and the beginnings of the modern world. The Renaissance, or "rebirth," grew out of all these developments. It began as an Italian phenomenon, occurring between c. 1350 and 1520, that spread to the rest of Europe over the course of the 1500s and early 1600s, although we focus on the early Renaissance in this chapter. Its principal manifestations were the revival of classicism and naturalism in arts and literature, the rise of the modern dynastic state as the dominant political structure, and an economic crisis fueled by industrial change and economic contraction. The following selections capture something of these major developments that represent both continuity and change.

GEOFFREY CHAUCER

FROM *The Canterbury Tales:* "*The Pardoner's Tale*"

Geoffrey Chaucer (c. 1340–1400) was an English civil servant and poet who, like Boccaccio, survived the Black Death. He never finished his most famous work, The Canterbury Tales, *framed (like Boccaccio's* Decameron*) as a series of stories, in this case told by a diverse group of pilgrims making their way to the shrine of Saint Thomas Becket at Canterbury. One of these pilgrims is a "pardoner," a contemporary slang term for a priest or cleric who makes his living selling indulgences ("pardons") for sins. Here, the Pardoner introduces himself and his cynical attitude toward the people he dupes, then launches into a story that reveals even more about his character. Although Chaucer's language (known as Middle English) may seem difficult at first, you will find that it is quite easy to understand if you read it aloud.*

From *The Canterbury Tales: Nine Tales and the General Prologue: A Norton Critical Edition*, by Geoffrey Chaucer, edited by V. A. Kolve and Glending Olson, (New York: Norton, 1989), pp. 192–207.

The Prologue

"Lordinges," quod he, "in chirches whan I preche,
I peyne me° to han an hauteyn° speche,   *take pains / elevated*
And ringe it out as round as gooth° a belle,   *sounds*
For I can al by rote° that I telle.   *know all by memory*
My theme° is alwey oon,° and evere was—   *text / always the same*
Radix malorum est Cupiditas.[1]

   First I pronounce° whennes° that I come,   *proclaim / whence, from where*
And thanne my bulles[2] shewe I, alle and somme.°   *one and all*
Oure lige lordes seel[3] on my patente,°   *license*
That shewe I first, my body° to warente,°   *person / authorize*
That no man be so bold, ne preest ne clerk,°   *neither priest nor scholar*
Me to destourbe of Cristes holy werk;
And after that thanne telle I forth my tales.
Bulles of popes and of cardinales,
Of patriarkes,° and bishoppes I shewe,   *heads of churches*
And in Latyn I speke a wordes fewe
To saffron with my predicacioun,[4]
And for to stire° hem to devocioun.   *stir*
Thanne shewe I forth my longe cristal stones,°   *glass cases*
Y-crammed ful of cloutes° and of bones—   *rags*
Reliks been they, as wenen they echoon.[5]
Thanne have I in latoun[6] a sholder-boon
Which that was of an holy Jewes shepe.
'Goode men,' seye I, 'tak of my wordes kepe:°   *heed*
If that this boon be wasshe° in any welle,   *washed, dunked*
If cow, or calf, or sheep, or oxe swelle,°   *swell (up)*
That any worm hath ete, or worm y-stonge,[7]
Tak water of that welle, and wash his tonge,
And it is hool° anon;° and forthermore,   *healed / at once*
Of pokkes° and of scabbe and every sore   *pox*
Shal every sheep be hool,° that of this welle   *healed*
Drinketh a draughte. Tak kepe° eek° what I telle: *heed / also*
If that the good-man that the bestes° oweth°   *animals / owns*
Wol every wike,° er° that the cok him croweth,   *week / before*

---

[1] "Avarice (the love of money) is the root of all evil."
[2] Bulls, writs of indulgence for sin, purchasable in lieu of other forms of penance.
[3] Bishop's seal.
[4] "With which to season my preaching." (Saffron is a yellow spice.)
[5] "They are (saints') relics, or so they all suppose."
[6] Latten, a metal like brass.
[7] "Who has eaten any (poisonous) worm, or whom a snake has stung (bitten)."

Fastinge,° drinken of this welle a draughte—   *(While) fasting*
As thilke° holy Jewe[8] bure eldres taughte—   *that same*
His bestes and his stoor° shal multiplye.   *stock*
    And, sires, also it heleth° jalousye: *heals*
For though a man be falle in jalous rage,
Let maken with this water his potage,[9]
And nevere shal he more his wyf mistriste,°   *mistrust*
Though he the sooth° of hir defaute° wiste°—   *truth / erring / should know*
Al° had she taken° preestes two or three.   *Even if / taken (as lovers)*
    Heer is a miteyn° eek, that ye may see: *mitten*
He that his hond wol putte in this miteyn,
He shal have multiplying of his greyn°   *grain*
Whan he hath sowen, be it whete° or otes,°   *wheat / oats*
So that he offre pens, or elles grotes.[10]
    Good men and wommen, o° thing warne° I yow: *one / tell*
If any wight° be in this chirche now,   *person*
That hath doon sinne horrible, that he
Dar° nat for shame of it y-shriven[11] be,   *Dare*
Or any womman, be she yong or old,
That hath y-maked hir housbonde cokewold,°   *a cuckold*
Swich° folk shul have no power ne no grace   *Such*
To offren° to my reliks in this place.   *To offer (money)*
And whoso findeth him out of swich blame,°   *not deserving such blame*
He wol com up and offre a° Goddes name,   *make an offering in*
And I assoille° him by the auctoritee°   *(will) absolve / authority*
Which that by bulle y-graunted was to me.'
    By this gaude° have I wonne,° yeer° by yeer,   *trick / earned / year*
An hundred mark sith I was pardoner.[12]
I stonde lyk a clerk° in my pulpet,   *scholar*
And whan the lewed° peple is doun y-set,   *ignorant, unlearned*
I preche, so as ye han herd bifore,
And telle an hundred false japes° more.   *tricks, stories*
Thanne peyne I me° to strecche forth the nekke,   *I take pains*
And est and west upon the peple I bekke°   *nod*
As doth a dowve,° sittinge on a berne.°   *dove / in a barn*
Myn hondes and my tonge goon so yerne°   *rapidly*
That it is joye to see my bisinesse.
Of avaryce and of swich° cursednesse   *such*
Is al my preching, for° to make hem free°   *in order / generous*

---

[8] Jacob.
[9] "Have his soup made with this water."
[10] "Provided that he offers (to me) pennies or else groats (coins worth fourpence)."
[11] Confessed and absolved.
[12] "A hundred marks (coins worth thirteen shillings fourpence) since I became a pardoner."

To yeven hir pens, and namely unto me.[13]
For myn entente° is nat but for to winne,°   *intention / profit*
And nothing° for correccioun of sinne: *not at all*
I rekke° nevere, whan that they ben beried,°   *care / buried*
Though that hir soules goon a-blakeberied![14]
For certes,° many a predicacioun°   *certainly / sermon*
Comth ofte tyme of yvel° entencioun: *evil*
Som for plesaunce° of folk and flaterye,   *the entertainment*
To been avaunced by ypocrisye,[15]
And som for veyne glorie,° and som for hate.   *vainglory*
For whan I dar non other weyes debate,[16]
Than wol I stinge him[17] with my tonge smerte°   *sharp*
In preching, so that he shal nat asterte°   *leap up (to protest)*
To been° defamed falsly, if that he   *At being*
Hath trespased to° my brethren[18] or to me.   *wronged*
For, though I telle noght his propre° name,   *own*
Men shal wel knowe that it is the same
By signes and by othere circumstances.
Thus quyte° I folk that doon us displesances;°   *requite / offenses*
Thus spitte I out my venim under hewe°   *hue, coloring*
Of holynesse, to semen° holy and trewe.   *seem*
    But shortly° myn entente I wol devyse:°   *briefly / describe*
I preche of no thing but for coveityse.°   *out of covetousness*
Therfore my theme is yet, and evere was,
Radix malorum est cupiditas.
Thus can I preche agayn° that same vyce   *against*
Which that I use,° and that is avaryce.   *practice*
But though myself be gilty in that sinne,
Yet can I maken other folk to twinne°   *part*
From avaryce, and sore° to repente.   *ardently*
But that is nat my principal entente:
I preche nothing but for coveityse.
Of this matere° it oughte y-nogh suffyse.   *subject*
    Than telle I hem ensamples many oon°   *examples many a one*
Of olde stories longe tyme agoon,°   *past*
For lewed° peple loven tales olde;   *unlearned*
Swich° thinges can they wel reporte° and holde.°   *Such / repeat / remember*
What, trowe ye, the whyles I may preche[19]

---

[13] "In giving their pence, and particularly to me."
[14] Blackberrying, i.e., wandering.
[15] To seek advancement through hypocrisy.
[16] "For when I dare enter into contest (argument) no other way."
[17] Some enemy.
[18] Fellow pardoners.
[19] "What? do you believe (that) as long as I can preach."

And winne° gold and silver for° I teche,   *obtain / because*
That I wol live in povert° wilfully?°   *poverty / willingly*
Nay, nay, I thoghte° it nevere, trewely!   *considered*
For I wol preche and begge in sondry° londes;   *various*
I wol nat do no labour with myn hondes,
Ne make baskettes,[20] and live therby,
By cause I wol nat beggen ydelly.°   *without profit*
I wol non of the Apostles counterfete:°   *imitate*
I wol have money, wolle,° chese, and whete,   *wool*
Al° were it yeven of° the povereste page,°   *Even if / given by / servant*
Or of° the povereste widwe° in a village,   *by / poorest widow*
Al sholde hir children sterve for famyne.[21]
Nay! I wol drinke licour° of the vyne,   *liquor, wine*
And have a joly wenche in every toun.
But herkneth,° lordinges, in conclusioun: *listen*
Youre lyking is that I shall telle a tale.
Now have I dronke a draughte of corny° ale,   *malty*
By God, I hope I shal yow telle a thing
That shal by resoun° been at° youre lyking.   *with reason / to*
For though myself be a ful vicious° man,   *evil, vice-ridden*
A moral tale yet I yow telle can,

Which I am wont to preche for to winne.[22]
Now holde youre pees,° my tale I wol beginne."   *peace*

The Tale

In Flaundres whylom was° a compaignye   *once (there) was*
Of yonge folk, that haunteden folye—
As ryot, hasard, stewes, and tavernes,[23]
Where as° with harpes, lutes, and giternes,°   *There where / guitars*
They daunce and pleyen at dees° bothe day and night,   *dice*
And eten also and drinken over hir might,°   *beyond their capacity*
Thurgh which they doon the devel sacrifyse°   *make sacrifice to the devil*
Withinne that develes temple,[24] in cursed wyse,°   *way*
By superfluitee° abhominable.   *excess*
Hir othes° been so grete and so dampnable,°   *oaths, curses / condemnable*
That it is grisly for to here hem swere.

---

[20] St. Paul was said to have been a basket maker.
[21] "Even though her children should die of hunger."
[22] "Which I am in the habit of preaching, in order to make some money."
[23] "Of young folk who gave themselves up to folly— (such) as excessive revelry, gambling with dice, (visiting) brothels and taverns."
[24] The tavern.

Our blissed Lordes body they totere°—   *tear apart*
Hem thoughte° Jewes rente° him noght y-nough—   *It seemed to them / tore*
And ech° of hem at otheres sinne lough.°   *each / laughed*
And right anon thanne comen tombesteres°   *female tumblers, dancers*
Fetys and smale, and yonge fruytesteres,²⁵
Singeres with harpes, baudes,° wafereres,°   *bawds / girls selling cakes*
Whiche been the verray° develes officeres   *the very*
To kindle and blowe the fyr of lecherye
That is annexed° unto glotonye: *joined (as a sin)*
The Holy Writ take I to my witnesse
That luxurie° is in wyn and dronkenesse.   *lechery*
    Lo, how that dronken Loth° unkindely°   *Lot / unnaturally*
Lay by his doghtres two, unwitingly;°   *unknowingly*
So dronke he was, he niste° what he wroghte.°   *knew not / did*
    Herodes,° whoso wel the stories soghte,°   *Herod / should seek out*
Whan he of wyn was repleet° at his feste,   *replete, full*
Right at his owene table he yaf° his heste°   *gave / command*
To sleen the Baptist John ful giltelees.°   *guiltless (innocent)*
    Senek° seith a good word doutelees: *Seneca*
He seith, he can no difference finde
Bitwix a man that is out of his minde
And a man which that is dronkelewe,°   *drunken*
But that woodnesse, y-fallen in a shrewe,²⁶
Persevereth lenger° than doth dronkenesse.   *Continues longer*
O glotonye,° ful of cursednesse!   *gluttony*
O cause first° of oure confusioun!°   *first cause / ruin*
O original° of oure dampnacioun,   *origin*
Til Crist had boght us with his blood agayn!

Lo, how dere,° shortly for to sayn,°   *costly / to speak briefly*
Aboght was thilke cursed vileinye;²⁷
Corrupt° was al this world for glotonye!   *Corrupted*
Adam oure fader and his wyf also
Fro Paradys to labour and to wo
Were driven for that vyce, it is no drede.°   *doubt*
For whyl that Adam fasted, as I rede,°   *read*
He was in Paradys; and whan that he
Eet of the fruyt defended° on the tree,   *forbidden*
Anon° he was outcast to wo and peyne.°   *Immediately / pain*
O glotonye, on thee wel oghte us pleyne!²⁸
    O, wiste a man° how manye maladyes   *(if) a man knew*

---

²⁵ "Shapely and slender, and young girls selling fruit."
²⁶ "Except that madness, having afflicted a miserable man."
²⁷ "Bought was that same cursed, evil deed."
²⁸ "Oh, gluttony, we certainly ought to complain against
  you."

Folwen of° excesse and of glotonyes,   *Follow on*
He wolde been the more mesurable°   *measured, temperate*
Of his diete, sittinge at his table.
Allas! the shorte throte, the tendre mouth,[29]
Maketh that,° est and west, and north and south, *Causes*
In erthe, in eir,° in water, men to swinke°   *air / labor*
To gete a glotoun deyntee° mete and drinke!   *dainty*
Of this matere,° O Paul, wel canstow trete:°   *subject / canst thou treat*
"Mete° unto wombe,° and wombe eek unto mete, *Meat / belly*
Shal God destroyen bothe," as Paulus seith.[30]
Allas! a foul thing is it, by my feith,
To seye this word, and fouler is the dede,
Whan man so drinketh of the whyte and rede[31]
That of his throte he maketh his privee,°   *privy (toilet)*
Thurgh thilke° cursed superfluitee.°   *that same / excess*
 The apostel,[32] weping, seith ful pitously,
"Ther walken manye of whiche yow told have I"—
I seye it now weping with pitous voys—
"They been enemys of Cristes croys,°   *cross*
Of which the ende is deeth: wombe° is her° god!" *belly / their*
O wombe! O bely! O stinking cod,[33]
Fulfild of donge and of corrupcioun![34]
At either ende of thee foul is the soun.°   *sound*
How° greet labour and cost is thee to finde!°   *What / to provide for*
Thise cookes, how they stampe,° and streyne,° and
grinde,   *pound / strain*
And turnen substaunce into accident,[35]
To fulfille al thy likerous talent!°   *lecherous (here, gluttonous) appetite*
Out of the harde bones knokke they
The mary,° for they caste noght° awey   *marrow / nothing*
That may go thurgh the golet° softe and swote;° *gullet / sweet*
Of spicerye° of leef, and bark, and rote°   *spices / root(s)*
Shal been his sauce y-maked by delyt,°   *to give pleasure*
To make him yet a newer° appetyt.   *renewed*
But certes, he that haunteth swich delyces[36]

---

[29] "The brief pleasure of swallowing, the mouth accustomed to delicacies."
[30] 1 Corinthians 6:13.
[31] Wines.
[32] St. Paul. See Philippians 3:18–19.
[33] "Bag," i.e., the stomach.
[34] "Filled up with dung and with decaying matter."
[35] "And turn substance into accident" (a scholastic joke: *substaunce* means "essence, essential qualities"; *accident*, "external appearances").
[36] "But truly, he that gives himself up to such pleasures."

Is deed, whyl that° he liveth in tho° vyces.   *while / those*
   A lecherous thing is wyn, and dronkenesse
Is ful of stryving° and of wrecchednesse.   *quarreling*
O dronke man, disfigured is thy face,
Sour is thy breeth, foul artow° to embrace,   *art thou*
And thurgh thy dronke nose semeth the soun°   *sound*
As though thou seydest ay° "Sampsoun, Sampsoun";[37]   *ever*
And yet, God wot,° Sampsoun drank nevere no wyn.   *knows*
Thou fallest,[38] as it were a stiked swyn;°   *stuck pig*
Thy tonge is lost, and al thyn honest cure,°   *care for decency*
For dronkenesse is verray sepulture°   *the true tomb*
Of mannes wit° and his discrecioun.°   *understanding / discretion*
In whom that° drinke hath dominacioun,   *In him whom*
He can no conseil° kepe, it is no drede.°   *secrets / doubt*
Now kepe yow fro the whyte and fro the rede—
And namely° fro the whyte wyn of Lepe[39]   *especially*
That is to selle° in Fishstrete° or in Chepe.°   *for sale / Fish Street / Cheapside*
This wyn of Spaigne crepeth subtilly
In othere wynes growinge faste by,[40]
Of° which ther ryseth swich fumositee,°   *From / vapor*
That whan a man hath dronken draughtes three
And weneth° that he be at hoom in Chepe,   *thinks*
He is in Spaigne, right at the toune of Lepe,
Nat at The Rochel,° ne at Burdeux toun;°   *La Rochelle / Bordeaux*
And thanne wol he seye, "Sampsoun, Sampsoun."
  But herkneth,° lordinges, o° word I yow preye,   *listen / one*
That alle the sovereyn actes,° dar I seye,   *supreme deeds*
Of victories in the Olde Testament,
Thurgh verray° God, that is omnipotent,   *true*
Were doon in abstinence and in preyere:
Loketh the Bible, and ther ye may it lere.°   *learn*
  Loke Attila,[41] the grete conquerour,
Deyde° in his sleep, with shame and dishonour,   *Died*
Bledinge ay° at his nose in dronkenesse: *continually*
A capitayn shoulde live in sobrenesse.
And over al this, avyseth yow right wel°   *be well advised*
What was comaunded unto Lamuel°—   *Lemuel*
Nat Samuel, but Lamuel, seye I—
Redeth the Bible, and finde it expresly

---

[37] A witty kind of onomatopoeia—the snoring sound seems to say "Samson," who was betrayed.
[38] Down.
[39] Near Cadiz.
[40] The wines sold as French are often mixed with the cheaper wines of Spain.
[41] The Hun.

Of wyn-yeving to hem that han justyse.[42]
Namore of this, for it may wel suffyse.

    And now that I have spoke of glotonye,
Now wol I yow defenden° hasardrye.°   *forbid / gambling at dice*
Hasard is verray moder° of lesinges,°   *the true mother / lies*
And of deceite and cursed forsweringes,°   *perjuries*
Blaspheme of Crist, manslaughtre, and wast° also   *waste*
Of catel° and of tyme; and forthermo,   *goods*
It is repreve° and contrarie of honour   *a reproach*
For to ben holde a commune hasardour.°   *gambler*
And ever the hyer° he is of estaat°   *higher / in social rank*
The more is he y-holden desolaat:°   *considered debased*
If that a prince useth° hasardrye,   *practices*
In alle governaunce and policye
He is, as by commune opinioun,
Y-holde the lasse in reputacioun.

    Stilbon, that was a wys° embassadour,   *wise*
Was sent to Corinthe in ful greet honour,
For Lacidomie° to make hire alliaunce.°   *Lacedaemon (Sparta) / their alliance*
And whan he cam, him happede par chaunce°   *it happened by chance*
That alle the grettest° that were of that lond,   *greatest (men)*
Pleyinge atte° hasard he hem fond.   *at (the)*
For which, as sone as it mighte be,°   *could be*
He stal him° hoom agayn to his contree,   *stole away*
And seyde, "Ther wol I nat lese° my name,°   *lose / (good) name*
Ne I wol nat take on me so greet defame,°   *dishonor*
Yow for to allye° unto none hasardours.°   *to ally / gamblers*
Sendeth othere wyse embassadours—
For by my trouthe, me were levere dye°   *I would rather die*
Than I yow sholde to hasardours allye.
For ye that been so glorious in honours
Shul nat allyen yow with hasardours
As by my wil, ne as by my tretee."°   *negotiations*
This wyse philosophre, thus seyde he.

    Loke eek° that to the king Demetrius   *also*
The king of Parthes,° as the book seith us,[43]   *Parthia*
Sente him a paire of dees° of gold in scorn,   *dice*
For he hadde used hasard ther-biforn;
For which he heeld his glorie or his renoun°   *renown*
At no value or reputacioun.
Lordes may finden other maner pley

---

[42] Concerning the giving of wine to those responsible for the law (see Proverbs 31.4–5).

[43] The *Policraticus* of John of Salisbury, which also contains the preceding story.

Honeste° y-nough to dryve the day awey.	*Honorable*
Now wol I speke of othes° false and grete	*oaths, curses*
A word or two, as olde bokes trete.	
Gret swering° is a thing abhominable,	*cursing*
And false swering[44] is yet more reprevable.°	*reproachable*
The heighe° God forbad swering at al—	*high*
Witnesse on Mathew—but in special	
Of swering seith the holy Jeremye,°	*Jeremiah*
"Thou shalt swere sooth° thyn othes° and nat lye,	*truly / oaths*
And swere in dome,° and eek in rightwisnesse;"°	*(good) judgment / righteousness*
But ydel° swering is a cursednesse.°	*vain / wickedness*
Bihold and see, that in the first table°	*tablet (of Moses)*
Of heighe Goddes hestes° honurable,	*commandments*
How that the seconde heste of him is this:	
"Tak nat my name in ydel° or amis."°	*in vain / amiss (wrongly)*
Lo, rather° he forbedeth swich° swering	*earlier (in the list) / such*
Than homicyde or many a cursed thing—	
I seye that, as by ordre,° thus it stondeth—	*in terms of the order*
This knoweth, that his hestes understondeth,[45]	
How that the second heste of God is that.	
And forther over,° I wol thee telle al plat°	*moreover / flatly*
That vengeance shal nat parten° from his hous	*depart*
That° of his othes is to° outrageous.	*Who / too*
"By Goddes precious herte," and "By his nayles,"	
And "By the blode of Crist that is in Hayles,[46]	
Seven is my chaunce,[47] and thyn is cink° and treye;"°	*five / three*
"By Goddes armes, if thou falsly pleye,	
This dagger shal thurghout thyn herte go!"	
This fruyt cometh of the bicched bones two—[48]	
Forswering,° ire,° falsnesse, homicyde.	*Perjury / anger*
Now for the love of Crist that for us dyde,	
Lete° youre othes, bothe grete and smale.	*Cease*
But, sires, now wol I telle forth my tale.	
Thise ryotoures° three of which I telle,	*rioters, revelers*
Longe erst er° pryme° rong of any belle,	*before / 9 A.M.*
Were set hem° in a taverne for to drinke;	*Had set themselves down*
And as they sat, they herde a belle clinke	
Biforn a cors° was° caried to his grave.	*corpse / (which) was (being)*
That oon of hem gan callen to his knave,	

---

[44] I.e., Of oaths.
[45] "[He] knows this, who understands His commandments."
[46] An abbey in Gloucestershire supposed to possess (as a high relic) some of Christ's blood.
[47] Throw.
[48] This fruit, i.e., result, comes from the two cursed dice. (Dice were made of bone; hence "bones" here.)

"Go bet," quod he, "and axe redily,[49]
What cors is this that passeth heer forby;°   *by here*
And looke that thou reporte his name wel."[50]
    "Sire," quod this boy, "it nedeth never-a-del.°   *it isn't at all necessary*
It was me told, er° ye cam heer two houres.   *before*
He was, pardee,[51] an old felawe° of youres;   *companion*
And sodeynly he was y-slayn to-night,
For-dronke,° as he sat on his bench upright.   *Dead drunk*
Ther cam a privee° theef men clepeth° Deeth,   *secret / call*
That in this contree° al the peple sleeth,°   *region / kills*
And with his spere he smoot his herte atwo,[52]
And wente his wey withouten wordes mo.°   *more*
He hath a thousand slayn this pestilence.°   *(during) this plague*
And maister, er° ye come in his presence,   *before*
Me thinketh° that it were necessarie   *It seems to me*
For to be war° of swich an adversarie: *aware, careful*
Beth redy for to mete him everemore.°   *always*
Thus taughte me my dame,° I sey namore."   *mother*
"By Seinte Marie," seyde this taverner,°   *tavernkeeper*
"The child seith sooth, for he hath slayn this yeer,
Henne° over a myle, withinne a greet village,   *Hence, from here*
Bothe man and womman, child, and hyne,° and page;°   *laborer / servant*
I trowe° his habitacioun be there.   *believe*
To been avysed° greet wisdom it were,   *forewarned*
Er that° he dide a man a dishonour."   *Before*
    "Ye,° Goddes armes," quod° this ryotour,°   *Aye, yes / said / reveler*
"Is it swich peril with him for to mete?
I shal him seke by wey° and eek° by strete,   *road / also*
I make avow to° Goddes digne° bones!   *avow (it) by / worthy*
Herkneth, felawes, we three been al ones:°   *all of one mind*
Lat ech° of us holde up his hond til other,°   *each / to the other*
And ech of us bicomen otheres° brother,   *the others'*
And we wol sleen° this false traytour Deeth.   *slay*
He shal be slayn, he that so manye sleeth,
By Goddes dignitee,° er it be night."   *worthiness*
    Togidres° han thise three hir trouthes plight°   *Together / plighted their troth*
To live and dyen ech of hem for other,°   *one another*
As though he were his owene y-boren° brother.   *born*

---

[49] The one of them proceeded to call to his servant-boy,
    "Go quickly," he said, "and ask straightway."
[50] Correctly.
[51] A weak form of the oath "by God," based on the French
    par dieu.
[52] "And with his spear he struck his heart in two." (Death
    was often shown in the visual arts as a hideous skele-
    ton menacing men with a spear or arrow.)

And up they sterte,° al dronken in this rage,°	*leaped / passion*
And forth they goon towardes that village	
Of which the taverner hadde spoke biforn,	
And many a grisly ooth thanne han they sworn,	
And Cristes blessed body they to-rente°—	*tore apart*
Deeth shal be deed, if that they may him hente.°	*seize*
Whan they han goon nat fully half a myle,	
Right° as they wolde han troden° over a style,°	*Just / stepped / stile*
An old man and a povre° with hem mette.	*poor (one)*
This olde man ful mekely° hem grette,°	*meekly / greeted them*
And seyde thus, "Now, lordes, God yow see!"°	*may God protect you*
The proudest of thise ryotoures three	
Answerde agayn, "What, carl,° with sory grace!°	*Hey, fellow / confound you*
Why artow al forwrapped save thy face?[53]	
Why livestow° so longe in so greet age?"	*livest thou*
This olde man gan loke in° his visage,	*scrutinized*
And seyde thus, "For° I ne can nat finde	*Because*
A man, though that I walked into Inde,°	*India*
Neither in citee nor in no village,	
That wolde chaunge his youthe for myn age;	
And therfore moot° I han myn age stille,	*must*
As longe time as it is Goddes wille.	
Ne Deeth, allas! ne wol nat han my lyf.	
Thus walke I, lyk° a restelees caityf,°	*like / captive*
And on the ground, which is my modres° gate,	*mother's*
I knokke with my staf bothe erly and late,	
And seye, 'Leve° moder, leet me in!	*Dear*
Lo, how I vanish,° flesh, and blood, and skin!	*waste away*
Allas! whan shul my bones been at reste?	
Moder, with yow wolde I chaunge° my cheste°	*exchange / chest (of clothes)*
That in my chambre longe tyme hath be,°	*been*
Ye, for an heyre clout° to wrappe me!'	*haircloth (for burial)*
But yet to me she wol nat do that grace,	
For which ful pale and welked° is my face.	*withered*
But sires, to yow it is no curteisye[54]	
To speken to an old man vileinye,°	*rudeness*
But° he trespasse° in worde or elles° in dede.	*Unless / offend / else*
In Holy Writ ye may yourself wel rede,°	*read*
'Agayns° an old man, hoor° upon his heed,	*Before / hoary, white*
Ye sholde aryse.' Wherfor I yeve yow reed:[55]	
Ne dooth unto an old man noon harm now,	

---

[53] "Why art thou all wrapped up, except for thy face?"
[54] "But, sirs, it is not courteous of you."
[55] "'You should stand up (in respect).' Therefore I give you (this) advice."

Namore than that ye wolde men did to yow
In age, if that ye so longe abyde.°   *remain (alive)*
And God be with yow, wher ye go° or ryde;   *walk*
I moot° go thider as° I have to go."   *must / thither where*
   "Nay, olde cherl, by God, thou shalt nat so,"
Seyde this other hasardour° anon;°   *gambler / at once*
"Thou partest° nat so lightly, by Seint John!   *departest*
Thou spak right now of thilke° traitour Deeth   *that same*
That in this contree alle oure frendes sleeth.
Have heer my trouthe,° as° thou art his espye,°   *pledge / since / spy*
Telle wher he is, or thou shalt it abye,°   *pay for*
By God, and by the holy sacrament!
For soothly thou art oon of his assent°   *in league with him*
To sleen us yonge folk, thou false theef!"
   "Now, sires," quod he, "if that yow be so leef°   *desirous*
To finde Deeth, turne up this croked° wey,   *crooked*
For in that grove I lafte° him, by my fey,°   *left / faith*
Under a tree, and there he wol abyde:°   *stay*
Nat for youre boost he wole him nothing hyde.[56]
See ye that ook?° right ther ye shul him finde.   *oak*
God save yow, that boghte agayn° mankinde,   *redeemed*
   And yow amende!"° Thus seyde this olde man.   *make you better*
And everich° of thise ryotoures° ran,   *each / revelers*
Til he cam to that tree, and ther they founde
Of florins° fyne of golde y-coyned° rounde   *florins, coins / coined*
Wel ny an° eighte busshels, as hem thoughte.°   *nearly / it seemed to them*
No lenger thanne° after Deeth they soughte,   *No longer then*
But ech° of hem so glad was of that sighte—   *each*
For that the florins been so faire and brighte—
That doun they sette hem by this precious hord.
The worste of hem he spake the firste word.
   "Brethren," quod he, "take kepe° what that I seye: *heed*
My wit° is greet, though that I bourde° and pleye.   *understanding / jest*
This tresor° hath Fortune unto us yiven°   *treasure / given*
In mirthe and jolitee° our lyf to liven,   *merriment*
And lightly as it comth, so wol we spende.
Ey! Goddes precious dignitee!° who wende°   *worthiness / would have supposed*
To-day that we sholde han so fair a grace?°   *favor*
But° mighte this gold be caried fro this place   *If only*
Hoom to myn hous—or elles unto youres—
For wel ye woot° that al this gold is oures—   *know*
Thanne were we in heigh felicitee.°   *supreme happiness*
But trewely, by daye it may nat be:°   *be (done)*

---

[56] "He won't conceal himself at all because of your boasting."

Men wolde seyn that we were theves stronge,°   *flagrant*
And for oure owene tresor doon us honge.°   *have us hanged*
This tresor moste y-caried be by nighte,
As wysly° and as slyly° as it mighte.°   *prudently / craftily / can (be)*
Wherfore I rede° that cut° among us alle   *advise / lots, straws*
Be drawe,° and lat se wher the cut wol falle;   *drawn, pulled*
And he that hath the cut with herte blythe
Shal renne° to the toune, and that ful swythe,°   *run / quickly*
And bringe us breed and wyn ful prively.°   *secretly*
And two of us shul kepen° subtilly°   *guard / carefully*
This tresor wel; and if he wol nat tarie,°   *tarry*
Whan it is night we wol this tresor carie,
By oon assent, where as us thinketh best."[57]

That oon of hem the cut broughte in his fest,°   *fist*
And bad hem drawe, and loke wher it wol falle;
And it fil on the yongeste of hem alle,
And forth toward the toun he wente anon.
And also sone as° that he was agon,   *as soon as*
That oon of hem° spak thus unto that other: *The one of them*
"Thou knowest wel thou art my sworne brother;
Thy profit° wol I telle thee anon.   *Something to thy advantage*
Thou woost° wel that oure felawe is agon,°   *knowest / gone*
And heer is gold, and that° ful greet plentee,   *that (in)*
That shal departed° been among us three.   *divided*
But natheles,° if I can shape° it so   *nonetheless / arrange*
That it departed were among us two,
Hadde I nat doon a freendes torn° to thee?"   *turn*
    That other answerde, "I noot° how that may be: *know not*
He woot how that the gold is with us tweye.
What shal we doon? what shal we to him seye?"
    "Shal it be conseil?"° seyde the firste shrewe;°   *a secret / wretch*
"And I shal tellen in a wordes fewe
What we shal doon, and bringe it wel aboute."
"I graunte,"° quod that other, "out of doute,[58]   *grant (it)*
That, by my trouthe, I wol thee nat biwreye."°   *betray*
    "Now," quod the firste, "thou woost° wel
        we be tweye,°   *knowest / two*
And two of us shul strenger° be than oon.   *stronger*
Looke whan that he is set,° that right anoon°   *has sat down / right away*
Arys° as though thou woldest with him pleye;   *Arise (get up)*
And I shal ryve° him thurgh the sydes tweye°   *stab / through his two sides*
Whyl that thou strogelest° with him as in game,°   *strugglest / as if in play*
And with thy dagger looke° thou do the same;   *take heed*

---

[57] "By common assent, wherever seems to us best."
[58] You can be sure.

And thanne shall al this gold departed° be,   *divided*
My dere freend, bitwixen me and thee.
Thanne may we bothe oure lustes° al fulfille,   *desires*
And pleye at dees° right at oure owene wille."   *dice*
And thus acorded° been thise shrewes° tweye   *agreed / cursed fellows*
To sleen the thridde, as ye han herd me seye.

   This yongest, which that wente unto the toun,
Ful ofte in herte he rolleth up and doun[59]
The beautee of thise florins newe and brighte.
"O Lord!" quod he, "if so were that I mighte
Have al this tresor to myself allone,
Ther is no man that liveth under the trone°   *throne*
Of God that sholde live so mery as I!"
And atte laste° the feend,° our enemy,   *at (the) last / devil*
Putte in his thought that he shold poyson beye,°   *buy poison*
With which he mighte sleen his felawes tweye°—   *two companions*
For-why the feend fond him in swich lyvinge[60]
That he had leve° him to sorwe bringe: *permission (from God)*
For this was outrely° his fulle entente,°   *completely / purpose*
To sleen hem bothe, and nevere to repente.
And forth he gooth—no lenger wolde he tarie—
Into the toun, unto a pothecarie,°   *apothecary, pharmacist*
And preyed° him that he him wolde selle   *asked*
Som poyson, that° he mighte his rattes quelle,°   *so that / kill his rats*
And eek° ther was a polcat° in his hawe,°   *also / weasel / yard*
That, as he seyde, his capouns° hadde y-slawe,°   *capons / killed*
And fayn° he wolde wreke him,° if he mighte,   *gladly / avenge himself*
On vermin, that destroyed° him by nighte.   *were ruining*

   The pothecarie answerde, "And thou shalt have
A thing that, also° God my soule save,   *so (may)*
In al this world ther nis no° creature,   *is not any*
That ete or dronke hath of this confiture°   *mixture*
Noght but the mountance of a corn of whete,[61]
That he ne shal his lyf anon° forlete.°   *at once / lose*
Ye,° sterve° he shal, and that in lasse whyle°   *Yes / die / shorter time*
Than thou wolt goon a paas° nat but° a myle,   *walk at normal pace / only*
This poyson is so strong and violent."

   This cursed man hath in his hond y-hent°   *grasped*
This poyson in a box, and sith° he ran   *afterward*
Into the nexte strete unto a man
And borwed [of] him large botels° three,   *bottles (probably of leather)*

---

[59] Thinks on.
[60] "Because the fiend [the devil] found him living in such a way."
[61] "No more than the quantity of a grain of wheat."

And in the two his poyson poured he—
The thridde he kepte clene for his° drinke—   *his (own)*
For al the night he shoop him° for to swinke°   *was preparing himself / work*
In caryinge of the gold out of that place.
And whan this ryotour, with sory grace,[62]
Hadde filled with wyn his grete botels three,
To his felawes agayn repaireth° he.   *returns*
    What nedeth it to sermone° of it more?   *speak*
For right as they hadde cast° his deeth bifore,   *planned*
Right so they han him slayn, and that anon.°   *immediately*
And whan that this was doon, thus spak that oon:
"Now lat us sitte and drinke, and make us merie,
And afterward we wol his body berie."°   *bury*
And with that word it happed° him, par cas,°   *befell / by chance*
To take the botel ther° the poyson was,   *where*
And drank, and yaf° his felawe drink also,   *gave*
For which anon they storven° bothe two.   *died*
    But certes, I suppose that Avicen
Wroot nevere in no canon, ne in no fen,

Mo wonder signes of empoisoning[63]
Than hadde thise wrecches two, er° hir° ending.   *before / their*
Thus ended been thise homicydes two,
And eek° the false empoysoner° also.°   *also / poisoner / as well*
    O cursed sinne of alle cursednesse!
O traytours° homicyde, O wikkednesse!   *traitorous*
O glotonye, luxurie,° and hasardrye!   *lechery*
Thou blasphemour of Crist with vileinye°   *vile speech*
And othes grete, of usage° and of pryde!   *out of habit*
Allas! mankinde, how may it bityde°   *happen*
That to thy Creatour which that thee wroghte,
And with his precious herte-blood thee boghte,°   *redeemed*
Thou art so fals and so unkinde,° allas!   *unnatural*
    Now, goode men, God forgeve° yow youre trespas,   *may God forgive*
And ware yow fro° the sinne of avaryce.   *make you beware of*
Myn holy pardoun may yow alle waryce°—   *cure*
So that ye offre nobles or sterlinges,[64]
Or elles silver broches, spones,° ringes.   *spoons*
Boweth youre heed° under this holy bulle!   *head*
Cometh up, ye wyves, offreth of youre wolle!°   *wool*

---

[62] Blessed by evil.
[63] "But truly, I would guess that Avicenna—an Arab physician and author—never described, in any treatise or chapter, more terrible symptoms of poisoning."
[64] "As long as you offer nobles [gold coins] or silver pennies."

Youre names I entre heer in my rolle° anon:°   *roll, list / at once*
Into the blisse of hevene shul ye gon.
I yow assoile,° by myn heigh power—   *absolve*
Yow that wol offre°—as clene and eek as cleer°   *make an offering / pure*
As ye were born.—And, lo, sires, thus I preche.
And Jesu Crist, that is our soules leche,°   *healer, doctor*
So graunte° yow his pardon to receyve,   *May He grant*
For that is best; I wol yow nat deceyve.
    But sires, o° word forgat I in my tale: *a, one*
I have relikes and pardon in my male°   *pouch*
As faire as any man in Engelond,
Whiche were me yeven° by the Popes hond.   *given*
If any of yow wol of devocioun°   *out of devotion*
Offren and han myn absolucioun,
Cometh forth anon, and kneleth heer adoun,
And mekely receyveth my pardoun;
Or elles, taketh pardon as ye wende,°   *travel*
Al newe and fresh, at every myles ende—
So that ye offren alwey newe and newe[65]
Nobles or pens,° which that be gode and trewe.   *pence*
It is an honour to everich° that is heer   *every one*
That ye mowe° have a suffisant° pardoner   *may / capable*
T'assoille° yow, in contree as ye ryde,   *To absolve*

For aventures whiche that may bityde.[66]
Peraventure° ther may falle oon or two   *By chance*
Doun of his hors, and breke his nekke atwo.°   *in two*
Look which a seuretee° is it to you alle   *what a security*
That I am in youre felaweship y-falle,
That may assoille yow, bothe more and lasse,°   *great and small*
Whan that the soule shal fro the body passe.
I rede° that oure Host heer shal biginne,   *advise*
For he is most envoluped° in sinne.   *enveloped, wrapped up*
Com forth, sire Hoste, and offre first anon,°   *first now*
And thou shalt kisse the reliks everichon,°   *every one*
Ye, for a grote:° unbokel° anon thy purs."   *groat (four pence) / unbuckle*
    "Nay, nay," quod° he, "thanne have I Cristes curs!   *said*
Lat be," quod he, "it shal nat be, so theech!°   *as I hope to prosper*
Thou woldest make me kisse thyn olde breech°   *breeches*
And swere it were a relik of a seint,
Thogh it were with thy fundement° depeint!°   *fundament (rectum) / stained*
But by the croys° which that Seint Eleyne° fond,   *(true) Cross / St. Helena*

---

[65] "As long as you make offering anew each time (of)."
[66] "In respect to things which may befall."

I wolde I hadde thy coillons° in myn hond   *testicles*
In stede of relikes or of seintuarie.[67]
Lat cutte hem of! I wol thee helpe hem carie.[68]
Thay shul be shryned° in an hogges tord!"°   *enshrined / turd*
   This Pardoner answerde nat a word;
So wrooth° he was, no word ne wolde he seye.   *wroth, angered*
   "Now," quod our Host, "I wol no lenger pleye
With thee, ne with noon other angry man."
But right anon the worthy Knight bigan,
"Whan that he saugh that al the peple lough,°   *laughed*
"Namore of this, for it is right y-nough!°   *quite enough*
Sire Pardoner, be glad and mery of chere;°   *mood*
And ye, sire Host, that been to me so dere,
I prey yow that ye kisse the Pardoner.
And Pardoner, I prey thee, drawe thee neer,
And, as we diden, lat us laughe and pleye."
Anon° they kiste, and riden forth hir weye.°   *At once / (on) their way*

*　　*　　*

REVIEW QUESTIONS

1. How do the character of the Pardoner and the tale he tells reflect contemporary trends and problems within the late medieval Church and society? What can you discern about Chaucer's attitude toward the sale of indulgences or false relics?

2. How does the Pardoner's Tale reflect the realities of life in the world after the Black Death?

3. Did you find that the reading of Middle English became easier as you became more accustomed to it? How different is this language from our own? What words and phrases are still in use today? What might that reveal about continuities over time?

---

[67] Holy things.
[68] "Have them cut off! I'll help thee carry them."

CHRISTINE DE PISAN

FROM *The Book of the City of Ladies*

Christine de Pisan (1365–after 1429) was the highly educated daughter of a Venetian physician at the court of Charles VI of France. Widowed at an early age, Christine became a writer to support her family, becoming the first professional woman of letters. Her most famous work, The Book of the City of Ladies, *is both a historical treatise on women and a defense of them. In this selection, the allegorical figure of Lady Rectitude introduces the subject of virtuous women.*

From *The Book of the City of Ladies*, by Christine de Pizan, translated by Earl Jeffrey Richards (New York: Persea Books, 1982), pp. 206–15.

*   *   *

Rectitude Says That Many Women Are Loved for Their Virtues More Than Other Women for Their Prettiness

"If we assumed that women who wished to be loved tried, for this reason, to be pretty, conceited, cute, and vain, then I can show you that such action will not make wise and worthwhile men love them more quickly or better and that, in fact, honest, virtuous, and simple women will more readily and more deeply be loved by men who love honor than pretty women, even if we suppose that these honest women are less beautiful. One could answer that, since women attract men with virtue and integrity and since it is bad that men be attracted, it would be better if women were less good. But of course this argument has no validity at all, for one should not neglect the cultivation and advancement of the good in spite of however much fools abuse it, and everyone must do his duty by acting well regardless of what might happen. I will give you an example to prove that women are loved for their virtue and integrity. First I could tell you about the many women who are saints in Paradise who were desired by men because of their honesty.

"Consider Lucretia, whom I spoke to you about before and who was raped: her great integrity was the reason why Tarquin became enamored, much more so than because of her beauty. For once, when her husband was dining with this Tarquin (who afterward raped her) and with many other knights, the subject of their conversation turned to their wives, and each one claimed that his own was the best. In order to discover the truth and to prove which one of their wives was worthy of the highest praise, they got up and rode home, and those women found occupied in the most honest occupation and activity were to be the most celebrated and honored. Lucretia, of all these wives, turned out to be the most honestly occupied, for her husband found her, such a wise and upright woman, clothed in a simple gown, sitting at home among her women servants, working in wool, and discoursing on various subjects. This same Tarquin, the king's son, arrived there with her husband and saw her outstanding honesty, her smile and fair conduct, and her serene manner. He was so captivated by her that he began to plan the folly which he committed later."

Here She Speaks of Queen Blanche, the Mother of Saint Louis, and of Other Good and Wise Ladies Loved for Their Virtue

"The most noble Queen Blanche, mother of Saint Louis, was similarly loved for great learning, prudence, virtue, and goodness by Thibault, the count of Champagne. Even though she had already passed the flower of her youth, this noble count—hearing the wise and good queen speak to him so judiciously after he had gone to war against Saint Louis, sensibly reproving him, telling him he ought not to have acted this way, considering the good deeds her son had done for him—looked at her intently, amazed by her enormous goodness and virtue, and was so overwhelmed by love that he did not know what to do. He did not dare confess his love for fear of death, for he realized that she was so good that she would never consent to his proposition. From that time onward he suffered much grief because of the mad desire which oppressed him. Nevertheless, he told her then not to fear his continuing to wage war against the king and that he wished to be her subject totally, that she should be certain that everything he possessed, body and soul, was entirely subject to her command. So he loved her all his life, from that hour on, and he never stopped loving her in spite of the slight chance he had of ever winning her love. He made his laments to Love in his poems, where he praised his lady most graciously. These beautiful poems of his were put to music in a charming way. He had them inscribed in his bedroom in Provins and also in Troyes, and they appear there to this day. And so I could tell you about many others."

And I, Christine, replied, "Indeed, my lady, I have seen in my own experience several cases similar to the one you mention, for I know of virtuous and wise women who, from what they have confessed to me in lamenting their distress, have been propositioned more frequently after their peak of beauty and youthfulness than when they were in their greatest flower. Concerning this, they have told me, 'Gods! What can this possibly mean? Do these men see in me some foolish behavior which would give them the slightest glimmer of hope that I would agree to commit such foolishness?' But I realize now, from what you say, that their outstanding goodness caused them to be loved. And this is very much against the opinion of many people who claim that an honest woman who intends to be chaste will never be desired or propositioned unless she herself so wishes."

Christine Speaks, and Rectitude Responds in Her Reply to Those Men Who Claim That Women Are Naturally Greedy

"I do not know what more to tell you, my dear lady, for all my questions are answered. It seems to me that you have disproven the slanders put forth by so many men against women. Likewise, what they so often claim is not true, that greed is, among feminine vices, a very natural thing."

She answered, "My dear friend, let me assure you that greed is no more natural in women than it is in men, and God only knows whether men are less greedy! You can see that the latter is in fact the case because considerably more evil occurs and recurs in the world because of the rapacity of different men than because of the greed of women. But, just as I told you before, the fool sees his neighbor's peccadillo and fails to see his own enormous crime. Since one commonly sees women taking delight in collecting cloth and thread and such trifles which go into a household, women are thought to be greedy. I can, however, assure you that there are many women who, were they to possess anything, would not be greedy or stingy in bestowing honors and giving generously where what they have could be used well, just as one poor person would do for an even poorer person in need. Women are usually kept in such financial straits that they guard the little that they can have, knowing they can recover this only with the greatest pain. So some people consider women greedy because some women have foolish husbands, great wastrels of property and gluttons, and the poor women, who know well that their households need what their husbands spend foolishly and that in the end their poor children will have to pay for it, are unable to refrain from speaking to their husbands and from urging them to spend less. Thus, such behavior is not at all avarice or greed, but is a sign of great prudence. Of course I am referring to those women who act with discretion. One sees so much quarreling in these marriages because the husbands do not like such urging and so blame their wives for something which they should praise them for. It is clear from the alms which these women so freely give that the vice of avarice is not to be found in them. God knows how many prisoners, even in the lands of the Saracens, how many destitute and needy noblemen and others have been and are every day, in this world here below, comforted and helped by women and their property."

And I, Christine, then said, "Indeed, my lady, your remarks remind me that I have seen women show themselves honorable in prudent generosity, and today I am acquainted with women who rejoice when they can say, 'See, the money is put to good use there, and no greedy man can hoard it away in some coffer.' For although Alexander the Great was said to be generous, I can tell you that I never saw any examples of it."

Rectitude then began to laugh and said, "Indeed, my friend, the ladies of Rome were not greedy when their city was gravely afflicted with war, when the public treasury was completely spent on warriors. The Romans had terrible trouble finding money to finance a large army which they had to raise. But the ladies, with their liberality—even the widows—collected all their jewels and property together, sparing nothing, and freely gave them to the princes of Rome. The ladies received great praise for this deed, and afterward their jewels were given back to them, and quite rightly so, for they had saved Rome."

Here She Speaks of the Rich and Generous Lady Named Busa

"In the *Faits des Romains* the generosity of a rich and upright woman named Busa, or Paulina, is described. She lived in Apuleia during the time when Hannibal was ravaging the Romans with fire and arms, despoiling almost all of Italy of men and goods. Many Romans retreated after the great defeat at the battle of Cannae, where Hannibal won such a noble victory, and they fled the battlefield wounded or injured. But this valiant Lady Busa received as many as she could take in, until she sheltered some ten thousand in her household, for she was extremely wealthy and had them cared for at her expense. All of them, having been helped by her wealth as much as by the aid and comfort she afforded them, were able to return to Rome and put the army back on its feet, for which she was highly praised. So do not doubt, dear friend, that I could tell you more about the endless generosity, bounty, and liberality of women.

"And even without going back to look for historical examples, how many other examples of the generosity of ladies from your own time could be mentioned! Was not the generosity great which was shown by the Dame de la Rivière, named Marguerite, who is still alive and was formerly the wife of Monsieur Burel de la Rivière, first chamberlain of the wise King Charles? On one occasion among others it happened that this lady, as she was always wise, valiant, and well-bred, was attending a very fine celebration which the duke of Anjou, later king of Sicily, was holding in Paris. At this celebration there were a large number of noble ladies and knights and gentlemen in fine array. This lady, who was young and beautiful, realized while she watched the noble knights assembled there, that a most noteworthy knight of great fame among those then living, named Emerion de Poumiers, was missing from the company of knights. She, of course, allowed that this Sir Emerion was too old to remember her, but his goodness and valiance made the lady remember him, and she felt there could be no more beautiful an ornament for such an assembly than so noteworthy and famous a man, even if he were old, so she inquired where the missing knight was. She was told that he was in prison in the Châtelet in Paris because of a debt of five hundred francs that he had incurred during his frequent travels in arms. 'Ah!' said the noble lady, 'what a shame for this kingdom to suffer a single hour of such a man imprisoned for debt!' Whereupon she removed the gold chaplet which she was wearing on her rich and fair head and replaced it with a chaplet of periwinkle on her blond hair. She gave the gold chaplet to a certain messenger and said, 'Go and give this chaplet as a pledge for what he owes, and let him be freed immediately and come here.' This was done and she was highly praised for it."

She Speaks Here of the Princesses and Ladies of France

Then I, Christine, spoke again. "My lady, since you have recalled a lady from my own time and since you have come to the history of the ladies of France and of those ladies still living, let me ask you whether you think it is a good idea to lodge some of them in our City. For why should they be forgotten, and foreign women as well?"

She replied, "I can answer you, Christine, that there are certainly a great many virtuous ladies of France, and I would be more than pleased if they were among our citizens. First of all, the noble queen of France, Isabella of Bavaria, will not be refused, reigning now by the grace of God, and in whom there is not a trace of cruelty, extortion, or any other evil vice, but only great love and good will toward her subjects.

"We can equally praise the fair, young, good, and wise duchess of Berry, wife of Duke John, son of the late King John of France and brother of wise King Charles. In the flower of her youth this noble duchess conducted herself so chastely, so sensibly, and so wisely that all the world praised and reputed her for her excellent virtue.

"What could I say about Valentina Visconti, the duchess of Orléans, wife of Duke Louis, son of Charles, the wise king of France, and daughter of the duke of Milan? What more could be said about such a prudent lady? A lady who is strong and constant in heart, filled with devotion to her lord and good teaching for her children, well-informed in government, just toward all, sensible in her conduct, and virtuous in all things—and all this is well known.

"What more could be said concerning the duchess of Burgundy, wife of Duke John, son of Philip, the son of the late King John of France? Is she not extraordinarily virtuous, loyal to her lord, kind in heart and manners, excellent in her morals and lacking a single vice?

"Is not the countess of Clermont, daughter of the duke of Berry mentioned above from his first marriage, and wife of Count John of Clermont, son of the duke of Bourbon and heir to the duchy, is she not everything which every lofty princess must be, devoted to her love, well-bred in everything, beautiful, wise, and good? In short, her virtues shine forth in her good conduct and honorable bearing.

"And what about that one woman among others whom you love singularly as much for the goodness of her virtues as for the favors she has extended to you and to whom you are much beholden, the noble duchess of Holland and countess of Hainault, daughter of the late Duke Philip of Burgundy mentioned above, and sister of the present duke? This lady should be ranked among the most perfect ladies, loyal-hearted, most prudent, wise in government, charitable, supremely devoted to God, and, in short, wholly good.

"Should not the duchess of Bourbon also be recalled among princesses known for their honor and laudability in all things?

"What more shall I tell you? I would need much time to recount all their great virtues.

"The good and beautiful countess of Saint-Pol, noble and upright, daughter of the duke of Bar, second cousin of the king of France, should also be ranked among the good women.

"Similarly the woman whom you love, Anne, daughter of the late count of La Marche and sister of the present duke, married to Ludwig of Bavaria, brother of the queen of France, does not discredit the company of women endowed with grace and praise, for her excellent virtues are well-known to God and the world.

"In spite of the slanderers, there are so many good and beautiful women among the ranks of countesses, baronesses, ladies, maidens, bourgeois women, and all classes that God should be praised who upholds them all. May He correct those women with shortcomings! Do not think otherwise, for I assure you of its truth, even if many jealous and slanderous people say the opposite."

And I, Christine, replied, "My lady, hearing this from you is a supreme joy for me."

She answered, "My dear friend, it seems to me I have now more than adequately executed my office in the City of Ladies. I have built it up with beautiful palaces and many fair inns and mansions. I have populated it for your sake with noble ladies and with such great numbers of women from all classes that it is already completely filled. Now let my sister Justice come to complete the rest, and this should satisfy you."

Christine Addresses Herself to All Princesses and to All Women

"Most excellent, revered, and honored princesses of France and of all lands, and all ladies and maidens, and, indeed, all women who have loved and do love and will love virtue and morality, as well as all who have died or who are now living or who are to come, rejoice and exult in our new City which, thanks to God, is already formed and almost finished and populated. Give thanks to God who has led me to undertake this great labor and the desirable task of establishing for you honorable lodging within city walls as a perpetual residence for as long as the world endures. I have come this far hoping to reach the conclusion of my work with the aid and comfort of Lady Justice, who, in accordance with her promise, will unfailingly help me until the City is finished and wholly completed. Now, my most honored ladies, pray for me."

*   *   *

REVIEW QUESTIONS

1. Christine was outspokenly critical of the ways that women were represented by the male authors of her own day, notably Boccaccio. How might she have responded to the depictions of women in the *Decameron* or even in Dante's *Divine Comedy* from Volume 1, Chapter 10?
2. How does Christine use history to make her case for women?
3. What does Christine see as the correct way for men and women to relate in society?

FROM *The Trial of Jeanne d'Arc*

Jeanne d'Arc appeared on the scene in 1429 as French fortunes in the Hundred Years' War were at their lowest. Taking command of the Dauphin's army, and then lifting the siege of Orleans, she had him crowned as Charles VII at Rheims and revived the French cause. Captured by the Burgundians and then sold to their English allies, Jeanne was tried as a heretic and eventually burned at the stake in Rouen in May of 1431. Although she was dead before the age of twenty, Jeanne's career is a remarkable episode in the history of France and of late medieval women. The following excerpts from her trial include some of Jeanne's own words and reveal the concerns of the prosecutors.

From *The Trial of Jeanne d'Arc*, edited by W. P. Barrett (London: Routledge and Paul, 1931), pp. 50–51, 68–70, 73–74, 125–26, 318–19.

*   *   *

First Inquiry after the Oath

When she had thus taken the oath the said Jeanne was questioned by us about her name and her surname. To which she replied that in her own country she was called Jeannette, and after she came to France, she was called Jeanne. Of her surname she said she knew nothing. Consequently she was questioned about the district from which she came. She replied she was born in the village of Domrémy, which is one with the village of Greux; and in Greux is the principal church.

Asked about the name of her father and mother, she replied that her father's name was Jacques d'Arc, and her mother's Isabelle.

Asked where she was baptized, she replied it was in the church of Domrémy.

Asked who were her godfathers and godmothers, she said one of her godmothers was named Agnes, another Jeanne, another Sibylle; of her godfathers, one was named Jean Lingué, another Jean Barrey: she had several other godmothers, she had heard her mother say.

Asked what priest had baptized her, she replied that it was master Jean Minet, as far as she knew.

Asked if he was still living, she said she believed he was.

Asked how old she was, she replied she thought nineteen. She said moreover that her mother taught her the Paternoster, Ave Maria, and Credo; and that no one but her mother had taught her her Credo.

*   *   *

Asked whether the voice which spoke to her was that of an angel, or of a saint, male or female, or straight from God, she answered that the voice was the voice of St. Catherine and of St. Margaret. And their heads were crowned in a rich and precious fashion with beautiful crowns. "And to tell this," she said, "I have God's permission. If you doubt it, send to Poitiers where I was examined before."

Asked how she knew they were these two saints, and how she knew one from the other, she answered she knew well who they were, and easily distinguished one from the other.

Asked how she knew one from the other, she answered she knew them by the greeting they gave her. She said further that a good seven years have passed since they undertook to guide her. She said also she knows the saints because they tell her their names.

Asked if the said saints are dressed in the same cloth, she answered: "I will tell you no more now; I have not leave to reveal it. If you do not believe me, send to Poitiers!" She said also that there were some revelations made directly to the king of France, and not to those who question her.

Asked if the saints are the same age, she answered that she had not leave to say.

Asked if the saints spoke at the same time, or one after another, she answered: "I have not leave to tell you; nevertheless I have always had counsel from both."

Asked which one appeared first, she answered: "I did not recognize them immediately; I knew well enough once, but I have forgotten; if I had leave I would gladly tell you. It is written down in the register at Poitiers." She added that she had received comfort from St. Michael.

Asked which of the apparitions came to her first, she answered that St. Michael came first.

Asked whether it was a long time ago that she first heard the voice of St. Michael, she answered: "I do not speak of St. Michael's voice, but of his great comfort."

Asked which was the first voice which came to her when she was about thirteen, she answered that it was St. Michael whom she saw before her eyes; and he was not alone, but accompanied by many angels from heaven. She said also that she came into France only by the instruction of God.

Asked if she saw St. Michael and these angels corporeally and in reality, she answered: "I saw them with my bodily eyes as well as I see you; and when they left me, I wept; and I fain would have had them take me with them too."

Asked in what form St. Michael appeared, she answered: "There is as yet no reply to that, for I have not had leave to answer."

Asked what St. Michael said to her the first time, she answered: "You will get no further reply to-day." She said the voices told her to answer boldly. She said she had indeed once told her king everything that had been revealed to her, since it concerned him. She said, however, that she had not yet leave to reveal what St. Michael said. She added that she wished her examiner had a copy of the book at Poitiers, provided that God desired it.

Asked if the voices told her not to tell her revelations without their permission, she answered: "I will not answer you further about that; and what I have permission to, that I will gladly answer. If the voices forbade me, I did not understand."

Asked what sign she gives that this revelation comes from God, and that it is St. Catherine and St. Margaret who speak to her, she answered: "I have told you often enough that it is St. Catherine and St. Margaret; believe me if you will."

Asked if it is forbidden for her to tell, she answered: "I have not quite understood whether that is permitted or not."

Asked how she can distinguish such points as she will answer, and such as she will not, she answered that on some points she had asked permission, and on some points she had received it. Furthermore she said she would rather be torn asunder by horses than have come to France without God's leave.

Asked if God ordered her to wear a man's dress, she answered that the dress is a small, nay, the least thing. Nor did she put on man's dress by the advice of any man whatsoever; she did not put it on, nor did she do aught, but by the command of God and the angels.

Asked whether it seemed to her that this command to assume male attire was lawful, she answered: "Everything I have done is at God's command; and if He had ordered me to assume a different habit, I should have done it, because it would have been His command."

Asked if she did it at the order of Robert de Baudricourt she said no.

Asked if she thought she had done well to take man's dress, she answered that everything she did at God's command she thought well done, and hoped for good warrant and succour in it.

Asked if, in this particular case, by taking man's dress, she thought she had done well, she answered that she had done nothing in the world but by God's commands.

Asked whether, when she saw the voice coming to her, there was a light, she answered that there was a great deal of light on all sides, as was most fitting. She added to the examiner that not all the light came to him alone!

*   *   *

Asked whether, when she went to Orleans, she had a standard or banner, in French *estandart ou banière,* and what colour it was, she answered she had a banner, with a field sown with lilies; the world was depicted on it, and two angels, one at each side; it was white, of white linen or boucassin, and on it were written, she thought, these names, JHESUS MARIA; and it was fringed with silk.

Asked if these names JHESUS MARIA were written above, or below, or at the side, she answered, at the side, she believed.

Asked which she preferred, her standard or her sword, she answered she much preferred her standard to her sword.

Asked who persuaded her to have this painting on her standard, she answered: "I have told you often enough that I have done nothing but by God's command." She said also that she herself bore the standard, when attacking the enemy, so as not to kill anyone; she never has killed anyone, she said.

Asked what force her king gave her when he set her to work, she answered that he gave her 10 or 12,000 men; and she went first to Orleans, to the fortress of Saint-Loup, and then to the fortress of the Bridge.

Asked to which fortress she ordered her men to retire, she says she does not remember. She added that she was confident of raising the siege of Orleans, for it had been revealed to her, and she had told the king so before going there.

Asked whether, when the assault was to be made, she did not tell her men that she would receive arrows, crossbolts and stones hurled by catapults or cannons, she answered no; there were a hundred wounded, or more. But she had indeed told her men not to fear and they would raise the siege. She said also that at the assault upon the fortress of the Bridge she was wounded in the neck by an arrow or crossbolt; but she received great comfort from St. Margaret, and was better in a fortnight. But she did not on account of that give up her riding or work.

Asked if she knew beforehand that she would be wounded, she answered that she did indeed, and she had told her king so; but that notwithstanding she would not give up her work. And it was revealed to her by the voices of the two saints, namely the blessed Catherine and Margaret. She added that she herself was the first to plant the ladder against the said fortress of the Bridge; and as she was raising the ladder she was wounded in the neck with the crossbolt, as she had said.

*   *   *

Asked on the subject of the woman's dress offered her so that she might hear Mass, she answered that she would not put it on till it should please Our Lord. And if it be that she must be brought to judgment she requests the Lords of the Church to grant her the mercy of a woman's dress and a hood for her head; she would die rather than turn back from what Our Lord commanded her; she firmly believed God would not let her be brought so low, or be presently without His help or miracle.

Asked why, if she wore man's dress at God's bidding, she asked for a woman's robe in the event of her death, she answered: "It is enough for me that it be long."

Asked if her godmother, who saw the fairies, was held to be a wise woman, she answered that she was held and reputed to be an honest woman, and not a witch or sorceress.

Asked whether her saying she would take a woman's dress if they would let her go would please God, she answered that if she were given permission to go in woman's dress she would immediately put on man's dress and do what Our Lord bade her. So she had formerly answered: and nothing would induce her to swear not to take up arms or to wear man's dress, to accomplish our Lord's will.

Asked about the age of the garments worn by St. Catherine and St. Margaret, she answered: "You already have my reply on this matter, and you will get none other from me. I have answered you as best I can."

Asked if she did not believe heretofore that the fairies were evil spirits, she answered she knew nothing of that.

Asked how she knew that St. Catherine and St. Margaret hated the English, she answered: "They love those whom God loves, and hate whom He hates."

Asked if God hated the English, she answered that of God's love or His hatred for the English, or of what He would do to their souls, she knew nothing, but she was certain that, excepting those who died there, they would be driven out of France, and God would send victory to the French and against the English.

Asked if God was for the English when they were prospering in France, she answered that she knew not whether God hated the French, but she believed it was His will to suffer them to be beaten for their sins, if they were in a state of sin.

*   *   *

The Trial for Relapse

On Monday following, the day after Holy Trinity Sunday, we the said judges repaired to Jeanne's prison to observe her state and disposition. * * *

Now because the said Jeanne was wearing a man's dress, a short mantle, a hood, a doublet and other garments used by men (which at our order she had recently put off in favour of woman's dress), we questioned her to find out when and for what reason she had resumed man's dress and rejected woman's clothes. Jeanne said she had but recently resumed man's dress and rejected woman's clothes.

Asked why she had resumed it, and who had compelled her to wear it, she answered that she had taken it of her own will, under no compulsion, as she preferred man's to woman's dress.

She was told that she had promised and sworn not to wear man's dress again, and answered that she never meant to take such an oath.

Asked for what reason she had assumed male costume, she answered that it was more lawful and convenient for her to wear it, since she was among men, than to wear woman's dress. She said she had resumed it because the promises made to her had not been kept, which were to permit her to go to Mass and receive her Saviour, and to take off her chains.

Asked whether she had not abjured and sworn in particular not to resume this male costume, she answered that she would rather die than be in chains, but if she were allowed to go to Mass, if her chains were taken off and she were put in a gracious prison and were given a woman as companion, she would be good and obey the Church.

As we her judges had heard from certain people that she had not yet cut herself off from her illusions and pretended revelations, which she had previously renounced, we asked her whether she had not since Thursday heard the voices of St. Catherine and St. Margaret. She answered yes.

Asked what they told her, she answered that they told her God had sent her word through St. Catherine and St. Margaret of the great pity of this treason by which she consented to abjure and recant in order to save her life; that she had damned herself to save her life. She said that before Thursday they told her what to do and say then, which she did. Further her voices told her, when she was on the scaffold or platform before the people, to answer the preacher boldly. The said Jeanne declared that he was a false preacher, and had accused her of many things she had not done. She said that if she declared God had not sent her she would damn herself, for in truth she was sent from God. She said that her voices had since told her that she had done a great evil in declaring that what she had done was wrong. She said that what she had declared and recanted on Thursday was done only for fear of the fire.

Asked if she believed her voices to be St. Catherine and St. Margaret, she answered yes, and they came from God.

Asked to speak truthfully of the crown which is mentioned above, she replied: "In everything, I told you the truth about it in my trial, as well as I could."

*   *   *

REVIEW QUESTIONS

1. Why do the prosecutors seem preoccupied with the issues of Jeanne's dress and appearance?
2. On what grounds is Jeanne being tried for heresy? What are her crimes, according to the tribunal?
3. In what other ways can legal testimony such as this be used as a historical evidence source? What are the potential pitfalls and limitations of such sources?

LEON BATTISTA ALBERTI

FROM *I Libri della Famiglia*

Leon Battista Alberti (1404–1474) embodied the Renaissance universal man. Born the illegitimate son of a Florentine merchant, he was an athlete, polymath, and artist. He earned a degree in canon law at the University of Bologna in 1428 and migrated to Rome, where he entered papal service. It was there, in 1438, that he began to write On the Family. *Written in the form of a dialogue among the members of the Alberti family, gathered at the deathbed of Leon Battista's father in 1421, it examines the ideal family as a unit for the begetting and rearing of children, for the amassing and maintaining of fortunes, and for the accumulation and exercise of power. It was also a sly exercise in satire, insofar as it indirectly criticizes his brothers and uncles for violating his father's dying wish that Leon Battista be treated as a legitimate member of the family.*

From *I Libri della Famiglia*, translated by Renée Neu Watkins (Columbia: University of South Carolina Press, 1969).

*   *   *

XIII

Lionardo: If I had children, you may be sure I should think about them, but my thoughts would be untroubled. My first consideration would only be to make my children grow up with good character and virtue. Whatever activities suited their taste would suit me. Any activity which is not dishonest is not displeasing to an honorable mind. The activities which lead to honor and praise belong to honorable and wellborn men. Certainly I will admit that every son cannot achieve all that his father might wish. If he does something he is able to do, however, I like that better than to have him strike out in a direction where he cannot follow through. I also think it is more praiseworthy for a man, even if he does not altogether succeed, to do his best in some field rather than sit inactive, inert, and idle. There is an old saying which our ancestors often repeated: "Idleness is the mother of vice." It is an ugly and hateful thing to see a man keep himself forever useless, like that idle fellow who when they asked him why he spent all day as if condemned to sit or lie on public benches, answered "I am waiting to get fat." The man who heard him was disgusted, and asked him rather to try to fatten up a pig, since at least something useful might come of it. Thus quite correctly he showed him what an idle fellow amounts to, which is less than a pig.

I'll go further, Adovardo. However rich and noble a father may be, he should try to have his son learn, besides the noble skills, some occupation which is not degrading. By means of this occupation in case of misfortune he can live honestly by his own labor and the work of his hands. Are the vicissitudes of this world so little or so infrequent that we can ignore the possibility of adverse circumstances? Was not the son of Perseus, king of Macedonia, seen sweating and soiled in a Roman factory, employed in making his living with heavy and painful labor? If the instability of things could thus transport the son of a famous and powerful king to such depths of poverty and need, it is right for us private citizens as well as for men of higher station to provide against every misfortune. If none in our house ever had to devote himself to such laboring occupations, thank fortune for it, and let us make sure that none will have to in the future. A wise and foresightful pilot, to be able to survive in adverse storms, carries more rope, anchors, and sheets than he needs for good weather. So let the father see that his sons enjoy some praiseworthy and useful activity. In this matter let him consider first of all the honesty of the work, and then adapt his course to what he knows his son can actually accomplish, and finally try to choose a field in which, by applying himself, the young man can hope to earn a reputation.

*   *   *

Battista: Whatever you think. The only question we have is what are the things that make a family fortunate. Go on with what you have to say and we shall listen.

*   *   *

Lionardo: In our discussion we may establish four general precepts as sound and firm foundation for all the other points to be developed or added. I shall name them. In the family the number of men must not diminish but augment; possessions must not grow less, but more; all forms of disgrace are to be shunned—a good name and fine reputation is precious and worth pursuing; hatreds, enmities, rancor must be carefully avoided, while good will, numerous acquaintances, and friendships are something to look for, augment, and cultivate.

*   *   *

If a family is not to fall for these reasons into what we have described as the most unfortunate condition of decline, but is to grow, instead, in fame and in the prosperous multitude of its youth, we must persuade our young men to take wives. We must use every argument for this purpose, offer incentive, promise reward, employ all our wit, persistence, and cunning. A most appropriate reason for taking a wife may be found in what we were saying before, about the evil of sensual indulgence, for the condemnation of such things may lead young men to desire honorable satisfactions. As other incentives, we may also speak to them of the delights of this primary and natural companionship of marriage. Children act as pledges and securities of marital love and kindness. At the same time they offer a focus for all a man's hopes and desires. Sad, indeed, is the man who has labored to get wealth and power and lands, and then has no true heir and perpetuator of his memory. No one can be more suited than a man's true and legitimate sons to gain advantages by virtue of his character, position, and authority, and to enjoy the fruits and rewards of his labor. If a man leaves such heirs, furthermore, he need not consider himself wholly dead and gone. His children keep his own position and his true image in the family. Dido, the Phoenician, when Aeneas left her, his mistress, cried out with tears, among her great sorrows no desire above this one: "Ah, had I but a small Aeneas now, to play beside me." As you were first poisoned, wretched and abandoned woman, by that man whose fatal and consuming love you did embrace, so another little Aeneas might by his similar face and gestures have offered you some consolation in your grief and anguish.

*   *   *

When, by the urging and counsel of their elders and of the whole family, young men have arrived at the point of marriage, their mothers and other female relatives and friends, who have known the virgins of the neighborhood from earliest childhood and know the way their upbringing has formed them, should select all the well-born and well-brought-up girls and present that list to the new groom-to-be. He can then choose the one who suits him best. The elders of the house and all of the family shall reject no daughter-in-law unless she is tainted with the breath of scandal or bad reputation. Aside from that, let the man who will have to satisfy her satisfy himself. He should act as do wise heads of families before they acquire some property—they like to look it over several times before they actually sign a contract. It is good in the case of any purchase and contract to inform oneself fully and to take counsel. One should consult a good number of persons and be very careful in order to avoid belated regrets. The man who has decided to marry must be still more cautious. I recommend that he examine and anticipate in every way, and consider for many days, what sort of person it is he is to live with for all his years as husband and companion. Let him be minded to marry for two purposes: first to perpetuate himself in his children, and second to have a steady and constant companion all his life. A woman is needed, therefore, who is likely to bear children and who is desirable as a perpetual mate.

*   *   *

To sum up this whole subject in a few words, for I want above all to be brief on this point, let a man get himself new kinsmen of better than plebeian blood, of a fortune more than diminutive, of a decent occupation, and of modest and respectable habits. Let them not be too far above himself, lest their greatness overshadow his own honor and position. Too high a family may disturb his own and his family's peace and tranquillity, and also, if one of them falls, you cannot help to support him without collapsing or wearing yourself out as you stagger under a weight too great for your arms and your strength. I also do not want the new relatives to rank too low, for while the first error puts you in a position of servitude, the second causes expense. Let them be equals, then, and, to repeat, modest and respectable people.

*   *   *

We have, as I said, made the house numerous and full of young people. It is essential to give them something to do now, and not let them grow lazy. Idleness is not only useless and generally despised in young men, but a positive burden and danger to the family. I do not need to teach you to shun idleness, when I know you are hard workers and active. I do encourage you to continue as you are doing in every sort of activity and hard discipline that you may attain excellence and deserve fame. Only think this matter over and consider whether any man, even if he is not necessarily ambitious of gaining glory but merely a little shy of falling into disgrace, can ever be, in actuality or even if we merely try to imagine him, a man not heartily opposed to idleness and to mere sitting. Who has ever dreamed he might reach any grace or dignity without hard work in the noblest arts, without assiduous efforts, without plenty of sweat poured out in manly and strenuous exertions? Certainly a man who would wish for the favor of praise and fame must avoid and resist idleness and inertia just as he would do major and hateful enemies. There is nothing that leads more quickly to dishonor and disgrace than idleness. The lap of the idler has always been the nest and lair of vice. Nothing is so harmful and pestilent in public and private life as the lazy and passive citizen. From idleness springs lasciviousness; from lasciviousness comes a contempt for the law; from disobedience to law comes ruin and the destruction of the country itself. To the extent that men tolerate the first resistance of men's will to the customs and ways of the country, their spirits soon turn to arrogance, pride, and the harmful power of avarice and greed. Thieves, murderers, adulterers, and all sorts of criminals and evil men run wild.

*   *   *

To this I might add that man ought to give some reward to God, to satisfy him with good works in return for the wonderful gifts which He gave to the spirit of man exalting and magnifying it beyond that of all other earthly beings. Nature, that is, God, made man a composite of two parts, one celestial and divine, the other most beautiful and noble among mortal things. He provided him with a form and a body suited to every sort of movement, so as to enable him to perceive and to flee from that which threatened to harm and oppose him. He gave him speech and judgment so that he would be able to seek after and to find what he needed and could use. He gave him movement and sentiment, desire and the power of excitement, so that he might clearly appreciate and pursue useful things and shun those harmful and dangerous to him. He gave him intelligence, teachability, memory and reason, qualities divine in themselves and which enable man to investigate, to distinguish, to know what to avoid and what to desire in order best to preserve himself. To these great gifts, admirable beyond measure, God added still another power of the spirit and mind of man, namely moderation. As a curb on greed and on excessive lusts, he gave him modesty and the desire for honor. Further, God established in the human mind a strong tie to bind together human beings in society, namely justice, equity, liberality, and love. These are the means by which a man can gain the favor and praise of other men, as well as the mercy and grace of the creator. Beyond this, God filled the manly breast with powers that make man able to bear fatigue, adversity, and the hard blows of fortune. He is able to undertake what is difficult, to overcome sorrow, not even to fear death—such are his qualities of strength, of endurance and fortitude, such can be his contempt for transitory things. These are qualities which enable us to honor and serve God as fully as we should, with piety, with moderation, and with every other perfect and honorable deed. Let us agree, then, that man was not born to languish in idleness but to labor and create magnificent and great works, first for the pleasure and glory of God, and second for his own enjoyment of that life of perfect virtue and its fruit, which is happiness.

*   *   *

Let men seek their own happiness first, and they will obtain the happiness of their family also. As I have said, happiness cannot be gained without good works and just and righteous deeds. Works are just and good which not only do no harm to anyone, but which benefit many. Works are righteous if they are without a trace of the dishonorable or any element of dishonesty. The best works are those which benefit many people. Those are most virtuous, perhaps, which cannot be pursued without strength and nobility. We must give ourselves to manly effort, then, and follow the noblest pursuits.

It seems to me, before we dedicate ourselves to any particular activity, it would be wise to think over and examine the question of what is our easiest way to reach or come near to happiness. Not every man easily attains happiness. Nature did not make all men of the same humor, or of the same intelligence or will, or equally endowed with skill and power. Rather nature planned that where I might be weak, you would make good the deficiency, and in some other way you would lack the virtue found in another. Why this? So that I should have need of you, and you of him, he of another, and some other of me. In this way one man's need for another serves as the cause and means to keep us all united in general friendship and alliance. This may, indeed, have been the source and beginning of republics. Laws may have begun thus rather than as I was saying before; fire and water alone may not have been the cause of so great a union among men as society gives them. Society is a union sustained by laws, by reason, and by custom.

Let us not disgress. To decide which is the most suitable career for himself, a man must take two things into account: the first is his own intelligence, his mind and his body, everything about himself; and the second, the question requiring close consideration, is that of outside supports, the help and resources which are necessary or useful and to which he must have early access, welcome, and free right of use if he is to enter the field for which he seems more suited than for any other. Take an example: if a man wished to perform great feats of arms while he knew he was himself but a weak fellow, not very robust, incapable of bearing up through dust and storm and sun, this would not be the right profession for him to pursue. If I, being poor, longed to devote my life to letters, though I had not the money to pay the considerable expenses attached to such a career, again this would be a poor choice of career. If you are equipped with numerous relatives, plenty of friends, abundant wealth, and if you possess within yourself intelligence, eloquence, and such tact as to keep you out of any rough or awkward situations, and you decide to dedicate yourself to civic affairs, you might do extremely well.

*   *   *

We should also consider at this point how much reward and profit, how much honor and fame, you can gain from any work or achievement you undertake to perform. The only condition is that you surpass everyone else in the field. In every craft the most skilled master, as you know, gains most riches and has the best position and the greatest stature among his companions. Think how even in so humble a profession as shoemaking men search out the best among the cobblers. If it is true of the humblest occupations that the most skilled practitioners are ever most in demand and so become most famous, consider whether in the highest professions the opposite suddenly holds true. In fact you will find it still more to the point to be the best in these, or at least one of the best. If you succeed in these fields, you know that you have been given a greater portion of happiness than other men. If you are learned, you realize the misfortune of the ignorant. You know, in addition, that the unhappiest lot falls to those who, being ignorant, desire still to appear learned.

*   *   *

Consider in your own mind what a boon to know more than others and to put the knowledge to good use at the right time and place. If you think it over, I am sure you will realize that in every field a man who would appear to be valuable must be valuable in fact. Now we have stated this much: that youth should not be wasted but should be directed to some honorable kind of work, that a man should do his utmost in that work, and that he should choose the field which will be most helpful to his family and bring him most fame. A career should suit our own nature and the state of our fortunes, and should be pursued in such a way that we may never, by our own fault at least, fall short of the first rank.

Riches, however, are for nearly everyone the primary reason for working at all. They are also most useful in making it possible to persevere in our undertakings until we win approval and attain public favor, position, and fame. This is the time, therefore, to explain how wealth is acquired and how it is kept. It was also one of the four things which we said were necessary to bring about and to preserve contentment in a family. Now, then, let us begin to accumulate wealth. Perhaps the present moment, as the evening grows dark, is just right for this subject, for no occupation seems less attractive to a man of large and liberal spirit than the kind of labor by which wealth is in fact gathered. If you will count over in your imagination the actual careers that bring great profits, you will see that all basically concern themselves with buying and selling or with lending and collecting the returns. Having neither petty nor vulgar minds, I imagine you probably find these activities, which are solely directed to making a profit, somewhat below you. They seem entirely to lack honor and distinction.

*   *   *

Those who thus dismiss all mercenary activities are wrong, I believe. If the pursuit of wealth is not as glorious as are other great pursuits, yet a man is not contemptible if, being unsuited by nature to achieve anything much in other finer fields of work, he devotes himself to this kind of activity. Here, it may be, he knows he is not inadequately equipped to do well. Here everyone admits he is very useful to the republic and still more to his own family. Wealth, if it is used to help the needy, can gain a man esteem and praise. With wealth, if it is used to do great and noble things and to show a fine magnanimity and splendor, fame and dignity can be attained. In emergencies and times of need we see every day how useful is the wealth of private citizens to the country itself. From public funds alone it is not always possible to pay the wages of those whose arms and blood defend the country's liberty and dignity. Nor can republics increase their glory and their might without enormous expenditure.

*   *   *

Why have I gone on at length on these topics? Only to show you that, among occupations, there are quite a few, both honorable and highly esteemed, by means of which wealth in no small measure may be gained. One of these occupations, as you know, is that of merchant. You can easily call to mind other similar careers which are both honorable and highly profitable. You want to know, then, what they are. Let us run through them. We shall spread out all the occupations before us and choose the best among them, then we shall try to define how they make us wealthy and prosperous. Occupations that do not bring profit and gain will never make you rich. Those that bring frequent and large profits are the ones that make you rich. The only system for becoming rich, by our own industry and by the means that luck, friends, or anyone's favor can give us, is to make profits. And how do men grow poor? Ill fortune certainly plays a part, this I admit, but excluding fortune, let us speak here of industry. If riches come through profits, and these through labor, diligence, and hard work, then poverty, which is the reverse of profit, will follow from the reverse of these virtues, namely from neglect, laziness, and sloth. These are the fault neither of fortune nor of others, but of oneself. One grows poor, also, by spending too much. Prodigality dissipates wealth and throws it away. The opposite of prodigality, the opposite of neglect, are carefulness and conscientiousness, in short, good management. Good management is the means to preserve wealth. Thus we have found out that to become rich one must make profits, keep what one has gained, and exercise rational good management.

*   *   *

REVIEW QUESTIONS

1. What, according to Alberti, is the role and nature of a father?
2. How is a father's authority different from other kinds of authority?
3. What is the role of education in the formation of human nature?
4. How does this view differ from that of other authors?
5. What is Alberti's definition of honor?
6. What is its relationship to the family? Why is it so important to Alberti?
7. How might Alberti define the family?

JAN HUS

FROM *The Church*

Jan Hus (c. 1373–1415) was a Czech preacher and writer active in Prague. Influenced by the writings of the English theologian John Wyclif (c. 1330–1384), he called for radical reforms in the Church. Summoned under safe conduct to the Council of Constance, he was nevertheless accused of heresy, convicted, and burned at the stake. Hus thus became a national martyr in his native Bohemia, which remained for decades in rebellion against the Catholic Church. This chapter from his book The Church *expresses his opinions on the papacy.*

From *The Church by John Hus*, edited by David S. Schaff (New York: Scribner's, 1915).

Chapter XII
Christ the True Roman Pontiff upon Salvation Depends

To the honor of our Lord Jesus Christ, which honor and also Christ the aforesaid doctors nowhere mention in their writing, this conclusion is proved, namely, "to be subject to the Roman pontiff is necessary for salvation for every human being."[1] From this it is clear, that no one can be saved unless he is meritoriously subject to Jesus Christ. But Christ is the Roman pontiff, just as he is the head of the universal church and every particular church. Therefore the conclusion is a true one. The consequence is clear from the major premise. And the minor premise is clear from the things said above and from what is said in I Peter 2:25, "For ye were sometime going astray like sheep but are now returned unto the shepherd and bishop of your souls," and also from Heb. 7:22: "By so much also hath Jesus become the surety of a better covenant and they indeed have been made free, many in number, according to the law because that by death they are hindered from continuing. But this man, because he continueth forever, hath his priesthood

---

[1] From Boniface VIII's bull *Unam sanctam*. The expression in the next sentence, "meritoriously," refers to the mediæval doctrine of merit in proportion to our good works.

unchangeable, wherefore also he is able to save to the uttermost, drawing near through himself to the Lord and always living to intercede for us. For such a high priest became us holy, guileless, undefiled, separated from sinners and made higher than the heavens, who needeth not daily like those priests, to offer up sacrifices first for his own sins and then for the sins of the people, for this he did once for all when he offered himself."

Truly this is the most holy and chief Roman pontiff, sitting at God's right hand and dwelling with us, for he said: "And lo, I am with you all the days, even unto the consummation of the age," Matt. 28:20. For that person, Christ, is everywhere present, since he is very God whose right it is to be everywhere without limitation. He is the bishop, who baptizes and takes away the sins of the world, John 1:29. He is the one who joins in marriage so that no man may put asunder: "What God hath joined together let not man put asunder," Matt. 19:6. He is the one who makes us priests: "He made us a kingdom and priests," Rev. 1:6. He performs the sacrament of the eucharist, saying: "This is my body," Luke 22:19. This is he who confirms his faithful ones: "I will give you a mouth of wisdom which all your adversaries will not be able to withstand or gainsay," Luke 21:15. He it is who feeds his sheep by his word and example and by the food of his body. All these things, however, he does on his part indefectibly, because he is a holy priest, guileless, undefiled, separated from sinners and made higher than the heavens. He is the bishop holding supreme guardianship over his flock, because he sleeps not nor is he, that watches over Israel, weary. He is the pontiff who in advance makes the way easy for us to the heavenly country. He is the pope—*papa*—because he is the wonderful Prince of Peace, the Father of the future age. For, indeed, such a pontiff became us who, since he was in the form of God, did not think it robbery to be equal with God but emptied himself, taking upon him the form of a servant, because he humbled himself by being made obedient unto death, even the death of the cross. Wherefore God hath highly exalted and given him a name which is above every name, that at the name of Jesus every knee should bow, of

things in heaven, of things on the earth, and things in hell [Phil. 2:6 *sqq.*].

To this the conclusion follows, namely: "To be subject to the Roman pontiff is necessary for salvation for every human being." But there is no other such pontiff except the Lord Jesus Christ himself, our pontiff. . . .

Chapter XIII
The Pope Not the Head of the Church but Christ's Vicar

Further, the aforesaid doctors lay down in their writing that "the pope is head of the Roman church and the college of cardinals the body, and that they are very successors and princes of the apostle Peter and the college of Christ's other apostles in ecclesiastical office for the purpose of discerning and defining all catholic and church matters, correcting and purging all errors in respect to them and, in all these matters, to have the care of all the churches and of all the faithful of Christ. For in order to govern the church throughout the whole world it is fitting there should always continue to be such manifest and true successors in the office of Peter, the prince of the apostles, and of the college of the other apostles of Christ. And such successors cannot be found or procured on the earth other than the pope, the existing head, and the college of cardinals, the existing body, of the aforesaid Roman church." . . .

I assume that the pope stands for that spiritual bishop who, in the highest way and in the most similar way, occupies the place of Christ, just as Peter did after the ascension. But if any person whatsoever is to be called pope—whom the Western church accepts as Roman bishop—appointed to decide as the final court ecclesiastical cases and to teach the faithful whatever he wishes, then there is an abuse of the term, because according to this view, it would be necessary in cases to concede that the most unlettered layman or a female, or a heretic and antichrist, may be pope. This is plain, for Constantine II, an unlettered layman, was suddenly ordained a priest and through ambition made pope and then was deposed and all the things which he ordained were declared invalid, about A.D. 707. And the same is plain from the case of Gregory, who was unlettered and consecrated another in addition to himself. And as the people were displeased with the act, a third pope was super-induced. Then these quarrelling among themselves, the emperor came to Rome and elected another as sole pope. As for a female, it is plain in the case of Agnes, who was called John Anglicus,[2] and of her Castrensis, 5:3, writes: "A certain woman sat in the papal chair two years and five months, following Leo. She is said to have been a girl, called Agnes, of the nation of Mainz, was led about by her paramour in a man's dress in Athens and named John Angli-cus. She made such progress in different studies that, coming to Rome, she read the trivium to an audience of great teachers. Finally, elected pope, she was with child by her paramour, and, as she was proceeding from St. Peter's to the Lateran, she had the pains of labor in a narrow street between the Colosseum and St. Clement's and gave birth to a child. Shortly afterward she died there and was buried. For this reason it is said that all the popes avoid this street. Therefore, she is not put down in the catalogue of popes."

As for a heretic occupying the papal chair we have an instance in Liberius, of whom Castrensis writes, . . . that at Constantius's command he was exiled for three years because he wished to favor the Arians. At the counsel of the same Constantius, the Roman clergy ordained Felix pope who, during the sessions of a synod condemned and cast out two Arian presbyters, Ursacius and Valens, and when this became known, Liberius was recalled from exile, and being wearied by his long exile and exhilarated by the reoccupation of the papal chair, he yielded to heretical depravity; and when Felix was cast down, Liberius with violence held the church of Peter and Paul and St. Lawrence so that the clergy and priests who favored Felix were murdered in the church, and Felix was martyred, Liberius not preventing.

As for antichrist occupying the papal chair, it is evident that a pope living contrary to Christ, like any other perverted person, is called by common consent antichrist. In accordance with John 2:22, many are become antichrists. And the faithful will not dare to deny persistently that it is possible for the man of sin to sit in the holy place. Of him the Saviour prophesied when he said: "When ye see the abomination of desolation, which is spoken of by Daniel, standing in the holy place." Matt. 24:15. The apostle also says: "Let no man beguile you in any wise, for it will not be except the falling away come first and the man of sin be revealed, the son of per-dition; he that opposeth and exalteth himself against all that is called God or is worshipped; so that he sitteth in the temple of God setting himself forth as God," II Thess. 2:3–4. And it is apparent from the *Chronicles* how the papal dignity has sunk. . . .

. . . No pope is the most exalted person of the catholic church but Christ himself; therefore no pope is the head of the catholic church besides Christ. The conclusion is valid reasoning from description to the thing described. Inasmuch as the head of the church is the capital or chief person of the church, yea, inasmuch as the head is a name of dignity and of office—dignity in view of predesti-nation, and office in view of the administration of the whole church—it follows that no one may rea-sonably assert of himself or of another without revelation that he is the head of a particular holy church, although if he live well he ought to hope that he is a member of the holy catholic church, the bride of Christ. Therefore, we should not contend in regard to the reality of the incumbency whether any one, whoever he may be, living with us is the head of a particular holy church but, on the ground of his works, we ought assume that, if he is a supe-rior, ruling over a particular holy church, then he is the superior in that particular church, and this ought to be assumed of the Roman pontiff, unless his works gainsay it, for the Saviour said: "Beware of false prophets which come unto you in sheep's clothing but inwardly they are ravening wolves. By their fruits ye shall know them." Matt. 7:15. Also John 10:38: "Believe the works." . . .

---

[2] The alleged female Pope Agnes (John VIII, about 855), whom Hus refers again and again in his writings.

In the same way, it is not of necessity to salvation for all Christians, living together, that they should believe expressly that any one is head of any church whatsoever unless his evangelical life and works plainly moved them to believe this. For it would be all too much presumption to affirm that we are heads of any particular church which perhaps might be a part of holy mother church. How, therefore, may any one of us without revelation presume to assert of himself or of another that he is the head, since it is said truly, Ecclesiasticus 9, that "no one knows, so far as predestination goes, whether one is worthy of love or hatred."

Likewise, if we examine in the light of the feeling and influence with which we influence inferiors and, on the other hand, examine by the mirror of Scripture, according to which we should regulate our whole life, then we would choose rather to be called servants and ministers of the church than its heads. For it is certain that if we do not fulfil the office of a head, we are not heads, as Augustine, *de decem chordis* says: that a perverse husband is not the head of his wife, much less is a prelate of the church, who alone from God could have a dignity of this kind, the head of a particular church in case he fall away from Christ.[3]

Therefore, after Augustine has shown that a truly Christian wife ought to mourn over the fornication of her husband, not for carnal reasons, but out of love and for the chastity due to the man Christ—he says consequentially that Christ speaks in the hearts of good women, where the husband does not hear, and he goes on to say: "Mourn over the injuries done by thy husband, but do not imitate them that he may rather imitate you in that which is good. For in that wherein he does wrong, do not regard him as thy head but me, thy Lord." And he proves that this ought to be the case and says: "If he is the head in that wherein he does wrong and the body follow its head, they both go over the precipice. But that the Christian may not follow this bad head, let him keep himself to the head of the church, Christ, to whom he owes his chastity, to whom he yields his honor, no longer a single man but now a man wedded to his mother, the church." Blessed, therefore, be the head of the church, Christ, who cannot be separated from his bride which is his mystical body, as the popes have often been separated from the church by heresy.

But some of the aforesaid doctors say that the pope is the bodily head of the church militant and this head ought always to be here with the church, but in this sense Christ is not the bodily head. Here is meant that the same difficulty remains, namely, that they prove the first part of the statement. For it remains for them to prove that the pope is the head of holy church, a thing they have not proved. And, before that, it remains for them to prove that Christ is not the bodily head of the church militant, inasmuch as Christ is a bodily person, because the man who is the head of the church militant, who is Christ, is present through all time with his church unto the consummation of the age, in virtue of his divine personality. Similarly, he is present by grace, giving his body to the church to be eaten in a sacramental and spiritual way. Wherefore, is not that bridegroom, who is the head of the church, much more present with us than the pope, who is removed from us two thousand miles and incapable of influencing of himself our feeling or movements? Let it suffice, therefore, to say, that the pope may be the vicar of Christ and may be so to his profit, if he is a faithful minister predestinated unto the glory of the head, Jesus Christ.[4]

*   *   *

---

[3] Not an exact quotation. The inference is drawn by Hus. The Sermon on the Ten Strings, Psalms 144:9, has much to say on the relation of husband and wife on the basis of "Thou shalt not commit adultery."

[4] The same thought is expressed in Reply to Palecz, *Mon.*, 1:321: "God gave Christ to be the head over the militant church, that he might preside over it most excellently without any hindrance of local distance . . . and pour into it, as the head pours into the body, movement, feeling and a gracious life whether there be no pope or a woman be pope."

REVIEW QUESTIONS

1. What sources of authority in the Church does Hus accept? Which does he deny?
2. How do Hus's arguments compare with those that Gregory VII and Boniface VIII raised in defense of papal authority (see Volume 1, Chapters 8 and 10)?
3. In what ways was Hus a threat to the organized Church? In what ways was he an asset?

BARTOLOMEO DE GIANO

FROM "A Letter on the Cruelty of the Turks"

We know very little of the life of Bartolomeo de Giano, a Franciscan friar of the mid-fifteenth century. What little we do know must be derived from the letter that preserves his name in history. The dates of his birth and death are unknown, though he is generally assumed to have been born at the end of the fourteenth century in or near the town of Giano, in Umbria. At some point in early life, Bartolomeo entered the Order of Friars Minor as a Conventual, because he is listed by Bernardino of L'Aquila among the famous men of his country. In 1402, he seems to have become an Observant Franciscan, following the example of the great preacher, Bernardino of Siena. Bartolomeo seems to have spent the early portion of his career at Foligno, where he became a Master of Theology and is reported to have preached regularly on the necessity of Christian peace and modesty. All of this changed in 1431, when he and five other friars, including Albert of Sarteano, the addressee of his letter, were chosen by Pope Eugenius IV for a mission to Constantinople. There he was to negotiate with the Byzantine Emperor John VIII Paleologus to facilitate the participation of Orthodox Christians in the coming Council of Florence. Due to his erudition and eloquence, it is reported, Bartolomeo convinced both the Byzantine Emperor and the Greek patriarch Joseph II to attend the council. He is reported to have accompanied them to Italy in 1437–1438, then returned to Constantinople to found a Franciscan friary. In 1444, Eugenius named Bartolomeo Vicar to the Minister General of the Eastern province of the Franciscan Order. At this point, the historical record ceases but for a rumor that he spent the final years of his life in the Franciscan convent of S. Francesco del Monte in Perugia to which he is said to have brought books written in Greek and translated into Latin. In 1438, during or shortly after his first mission to Constantinople, he wrote to his companion, Albert of Sarteano, at that time preaching in Venice, to urge the necessity of a crusade to counter the growing threat posed to Christendom by the expansion of the Ottoman Turks.

From "A Letter on the Cruelty of the Turks," by Bartolomeo de Giano, translated by W. L. North, in *Patrologia Graeca*, Vol. 158, edited by J. P. Migne (Paris: J. P. Migne, 1857–66), cols. 1055–68.

To the venerable religious and my outstanding brother, Friar Abbot of Sartiano of the order of the Friars who preaches to the Venetians and is his father in Christ Jesus, who should be greatly beloved.

For a long time now, my venerable father, I have longed to see, to speak, and to embrace your person but this grace has not yet been granted to me. For when I am traveling in the West, you head for the East, and when I seek you in the East, you return to your homeland in the West. But all this, I suppose, has happened through God's plan, since, as I have heard, your preaching—as usual—brought no small benefit this year in Venice. But now I would wish with fervent desire that when, with the Lord's favor, the union of both churches is celebrated, you visit these and farther distant regions with your usual lessons of preaching, knowledge, and life. Indeed, we think that a tremendous harvest of souls can be accomplished by the friars. For although Greece has been lost as has all of Turkey (which is elsewhere called Asia where the seven churches mentioned in the Apocalypse are and where Teucer, the enemy of Christ, reigns), at the present time innumerable Christian peoples still remain beyond the Black Sea, governing themselves under the Greek rite to this very day. First, there is to the East of Trebizond the not insignificant kingdom of the Georgians, i.e., of Georgia, where King Alexander rules today. And who can traverse under the open sky the homeland of the Russians and the Ruthenians to the marshes of Meotis (which is called the Sea of Habbakuk when interpreted)? I leave out Circasia, Vogaria, Mingrillia, Wallachia, Patras on the sea, though at present these are under the Greek rite. I'll say nothing about the Armenians, whom, I hope, you will soon see coming to Italy along with our father Jacob so as to be led back to the Catholic faith. They are far more eager than other nations for ready conversion and for receiving the truth and most favorably inclined to the Latins. Furthermore, you know from experience that innumerable Christians are scattered in the Caesian mountains and here and there in Persia and Scythia, where the houses of our brethren stand devoid of friars, and that some are still living even among the Tartars. I therefore think that your personality and others like yours would be not without benefit—indeed, they would be most appropriate in those regions—once the sacred union is celebrated, if God should permit it.

Oh, but why do I recall these things when it is far more pleasant to weep than to hope for anything good for the aforementioned peoples? It is far more pleasing to weep, I say, and to shout to the stars, that the ever merciful Most High may look down upon these regions that should be liberated—in the midst of which we almost are—and not instead gaze upon the peoples' sins for so long that the name of Christianity is snuffed out in the North and East. Alas! each day Christians are lost and the Devil's followers grow in number and strength of arms. For in Turkey and in Greece there is scarcely a city, fort, or village in which—and scarcely a day on which—the most holy name of Christ is denied and Muhammad, the son of the devil, exalted. And this happens not only because of fear and threats but also because of delights and honor. And this will perhaps surprise you: this is done by those who concern themselves with wealth, honor, and with the prudence of the world! But passing over past evils in silence—since I believe no tongue capable of recounting them—I shall touch briefly on what I have recently seen with my own eyes so that you may know and lament it with me and so that if you find anyone not utterly devoid of piety, you may compel them to weep as well.

I think you can recall, beloved Father, that when we left Venice, destined for these parts by our Lord Pope, at the same time that you arrived there, having just returned from Jerusalem, news spread there over the next few days that the Hungarians had burned some Turkish ships and killed many of them. These things, I declare, were all true. But I do not know if you later heard that the Turk himself, enraged by this, came there in person with a great army and carried off, it is said, more than sixty thousand souls from the kingdom of Rascia, Hungary's neighbor. It is uncertain as to whether any of them now remember Christ. Does this surprise you? You should instead wonder and lament much more what has for the last twenty-five or thirty years been reckoned to our own shame and no small damage: that each year the Turk seizes no less than ten to fifteen thousand souls (and I am stating a lower number so that you may believe it)? And if you would believe it, I would say that the Turk has compelled five hundred thousand to deny Christ Jesus with threats and blandishments. Truly I would be not a little surprised if even one Christian is still found in these parts. For the city of Corinth alone gains thousands and thousands of ducats each year as the toll for the captives passing from Gallipoli into Turkey. Oh sins of Christians, where are you heading? Where are you taking yourselves? To what servitude, to what shame do you compel yourselves to be subject?

*   *   *

Three great mountains of heads have been made there from the dead men who refused to give themselves up peacefully. Their bodies, meanwhile, have been rolled up upon the slopes of the mountains—a horrific food for wolves, dogs, and birds. Priests and monks, young and old, were led away in iron fetters tied to the backs of horses, at least as long as they were able to walk. But the rest of the crowd, including women and children, were herded by dogs without any mercy or piety. If one of them slowed down, unable to walk further because of thirst or pain, O Good Jesus! she immediately ended her life there in torment, cut in half. So great was the multitude of the dead, as I learned from the aforementioned brother who told me with his conscience as his witness, that this brother, after deliberating within himself over whether or not to recite the *De profundis* for each of the dead and being unable to do so because of the multitude of the dead, finally said, weeping, the prayer *Inclina*. Nor did this perhaps happen just in one place, as one might think, but over the entire course of the twenty days' journey that the aforementioned captives had made and especially in Adrianople where outside the dwellings so great a quantity of bodies lay consumed, partially rotted, partially devoured by dogs, that it would seem unbelievable to anyone who had not seen it with their own eyes. Meanwhile, some of the dying are cast out in the sight of the Latin merchants, and if any of them did try to

bury or remove them from there it was more because of the stench than their piety, and not was even this allowed on any conditions, unless they paid first. Oh!! I shall call these people blessed unless they died in despair! For they were crying out loud with weak wailing as children and infants, youths and virgins, men and women, were captured, driven along, and killed. Thou Who art in Heaven, are You seeing all this? Are You moved even a little by piety? O blessed Virgin, O holy men and women of God, where is our hope, our trust in you? Or perhaps we were deceived, because our faith is empty and false? No! Blessed I would call these people, I say, if they should have patiently endured hunger, thirst, travail, pain, servitude, and death. Yet why should I call them blessed when they constantly deny the faith of Christ, especially youths of both sexes who are turned from the faith and converted to a hostility towards Christians with such great ease that they may almost begin to believe, if it is possible, even the elect are led into error. Oh the depths of God's wisdom and knowledge! How incomprehensible are His judgments and untraceable are His ways! Oh, how many and what great people are in the world, I believe, who seem in both fact and name to be Christians but who, if this coal of persecution should heat them—or rather the mild sweetness of the flesh should entreat them—would deny Christ and say with Peter: *I do not know him.* Oh, would that we not encounter such a testing, such an experience, such a furnace, and if it is going to consume, let it not make its trial in our age, saving God's will! Indeed, many who believe that they will be immoveable columns and are believed by others to be so, we shall see, or perhaps be seen, to be in a wretched state of ruined wretchedly. I am a liar if I do not know many religious persons of diverse orders who most fervently preach Christ today but tomorrow shall foully renounce Him. This is why I think that no one should trust in themselves but all should be afraid. But let us return to our initial theme.

*   *   *

Often do we say these things, often do we lament them, and on these and similar lamentable deeds we consume no small portion of our time, although we would rather die than see the latest evils that each day consume more and more of our race. But what arouses and confirms even greater sorrow is the fact that we have absolutely no one with whom we can share these things and [thereby] lighten the punishment. For if any Christians either stay in or visit these parts, they burn with so much lust for temporal gain that they either do not give any thought to these things or—horrible to say—they secretly desire them. Behold! They fill their purses from Turkish profits and enrich themselves on the blood of Christians.

*　　*　　*

For you see, it just was two hundred years or so ago that all of Asia down to Antioch and beyond was inhabited by Christian peoples. Now, little by little this fire has consumed Asia so that now you shall find but few Christians there unless they be Slavs dedicated to the service of the Turks. I exclude Syria, the Holy Land, Armenia, Arabia, and the surrounding countries up to Alexandria which obviously have not been Christian by and large for a long time now. Nor shall I speak of Egypt, Ethiopia, Persia and—greater than all the rest—all of Africa, where you shall find hardly a single Christian except perhaps some merchants. And yet it is asserted that all the aforementioned were Christian countries. But these [Christian nations] have now been laid to rest by the length of time [under Muslim rule].

It was only eighty years ago or so that not a single Turk was found in Greece. They even crossed over carried by the Christians themselves and have filled that entire country. Indeed, unless it is provided with some swift remedy, Greece shall soon become like Arabia or Egypt. I am speaking of a broad and populous country adorned by the most glorious cities which have all been, for the time being at least, reduced to nothingness, so to speak, since they have been emptied of their inhabitants. It is the land where Alexander the Great ruled, and where there are the cities of Athens, Corinth, Sparta, Thessalonika, and Philippi . . . cities that now it is painful to see.

What I have described is nothing in comparison with the following deeds that have or will occur

there unless someone pays attention and offers help. Where, I ask you, are the countries now of Dalmatia, Croatia, Bosnia, Rascia, Bulgaria, Albania, and Wallachia—not insignificant kingdoms that were despoiled of their inhabitants in just a few years? I come now to Hungary from which, it is said, three hundred thousand (though I would say more truly six hundred thousand) souls have been carried off in just a few days.

Don't you believe that what I fear could happen, namely that by the just judgment of God this fire shall advance so far that it could occupy the border of [European] Christians? What then are those wretched Christians doing now? What are their princes doing? What about the pastors of the Church? Do they not sleep or do they suffer instead from lethargy so that they simply await Christendom to be consumed bit by bit? They play around—or rather hurt themselves—with lances and dances! And in the meantime, the Turk snuffs out the name of Christ and has already sworn, has already vowed himself to his own God, not to remain at peace under any agreement, unless he hears the praises of Muhammad sung in all of Hungary as soon as possible.

*　　*　　*

Now, venerable father, wait to hear something else amazing and not a little delightful: it is said that the Turks do not have weapons! And if you consider this to be impossible when they have despoiled so many Christians countries, take a look at the merchants from Italy—Latins, Venetians, Genoese, and others. Because of their great piety and grace and contrary to what is just and unjust, these merchants bring galleys and ships there loaded not with iron but with steel in such great abundance that I can scarcely believe that steel would be found in any Italian city at such a good price and in such great quantities as it is found in Gallipoli, Pera, and Adrianople! I am a liar if I have not seen it with my own eyes and in the galleys on which it came. But hear how they excuse themselves—they do not sell it to the Turks but only to the Jews and the Greeks. It is they, therefore, who later give the steel to the Turks with their own hands. And this, so that the Turks may make sharper swords to spill the guts of Christians!

O how much God's piety endures! How long do you intend to delay your vengeance?! You are perhaps amazed at how troubled are Venice, Genoa, and the other Italian cities? Surely you should wonder more why they are not completely destroyed. Indeed, over the last forty days we have seen mules loaded with steel led from this city to Adrianople where the Turks themselves foully mock the Christians, saying openly: *Look at your blindness, you wretches: you offer us arms so that we may completely destroy you!* What do you think of that, beloved brother!? On this point alone why do you not openly proclaim this disaster to those in the city in which you preach? But I know without a doubt what you are doing. You cry out but are not heard. But the scourge of God is at hand which justly whips sinners. But you want us now to return to the Tartars.

In this very year around the month of August when the Turk was destroying Hungary, many here claimed that a new emperor was elected, though I do not confirm this because I have not seen it. You are more familiar with these matters because, when fighting with the Poles for the kingdom of Hungary, he conquered them and killed innumerable people—I mean Christians. Then, the Tartars, who are the Poles neighbors, perceived that the Christian peoples were involved in wars and invaded Poland. What they did there, I have no words to describe. Ask them yourself, if some people have come from there.

Such are the princes' fortifications! Such are their plans! Such is their warfare against the infidel! Alas, for the wretches who should and can help but do not do so. Nor did they lack advance notice. For I sent brethren [to them] on behalf of the majority and wrote more than thirty letters long before the month of December when that man was preparing an army against them. And these letters I sent to the emperor and the dukes—they had them, they read them but they did not care, as the results themselves show. That trumpet of God, Friar James, was also proclaiming this before the kings and princes and was declaring these injuries to their faces, saying: *Behold, you wretches, foreigners despoil your homeland, dishonor your wives in your presence, and lead your brothers and sons off in chains—and yet you do not care.* But when they heard these words and the like, they laughed and seemed without feeling. And what is more, our lord, the most holy Pope, even sent them eternal gifts, namely the indulgence of their sins, if any would take up arms against the infidel.

When, oh when, therefore, shall these miserable Christians be roused [to action]? When shall that time come? Shall I see it with mine own eyes before I die? This is my hope but it is a very weak one and has truly waned and is now all but despair. Where is the glorious kingdom of the Franks now, which in ancient times drove the Saracens from Hispania? Where is the great power of the English? These two have been consumed [fighting] against one another. Where now is the king of Aragon, terror of the infidel? Where are the other powers and Christian princes? . . .

*   *   *

But, really, the most important reason that moved me to write these things to you is this: so that you, who burn with the piety of Christ and a zeal for souls and who blossom with learning and eloquence, may shape and adorn this letter that I have prepared for you, and compose it with due piety and gravity so that it may be worthy to stand in the sight of kings and princes, if they perchance should hear and at some point be turned to avenge the injury done to Jesus Christ. But unless you shall decide the opposite, anyone will recognize that a text is all the more likely to lend itself to believability as it has been written not with carefully composed and ornate eloquence but in a simple style. But this matter I leave entirely to your judgment. . . .

*   *   *

It therefore seems abundantly clear—to conclude this summary briefly—that the time is now unmistakably upon us when he shall destroy the Christians or be utterly destroyed by them. I am profoundly afraid of the first of these; may God Himself grant the other instead. Yet we should not give up hope. For a rumor is said to be widespread among the Saracens and Turks that the time of their destruction is at hand, indeed already past, as certain of their prophets say. But because of their alms and piety towards the poor—and this is true—it has been delayed for the moment and shall yet be deferred a little longer.

*   *   *

Why delay any longer? Look, here is what you seek. But why do I waste time and breath on such things? Since no one but God Himself can illuminate their eyes and move their hearts, all human exhortation is rendered void. Yet on this matter, fathers and brothers, when this news comes to your ears, rouse God, I beg you, with your cries, rouse Him with your sighs, disturb the saints, male and female alike, with your prayers, hasten through cities and towns, call the people, gather an assembly and pierce the hearts of small and great alike concerning these events. For thus these people may abstain from sin for a time, persist in diligent prayer, and set their minds to works of piety, so that pious and merciful God, who is now roused to anger because of man's sins, may be calmed by these good works and may look down briefly upon the Christian people, infuse love into their hearts, and give holy union and peace to prelates and princes. For when the Devil, the inventor and kindler of all evils who has hitherto sown so many stumbling blocks in Christ's Church, is dragged off to Tartarus, confounded, then the Church's faithful shall be exultant and the infidel shall blush for shame, be confounded, and give way: the Turks who today deride and mock Christ and the Christians. And if with the Lord's favor, this sacred union is celebrated, cross the sea, my brothers, in safety (I mean those who are suitable and willing) for within your gaze there shall be much land overflowing with eternal fruits. And beloved brother, I invite you all the more confidently as I know the secrets of your heart. Amen.

From Constantinople, 12 December 1438

Yours completely,
Brother Bartholomew de Jano of the order of Friars Minor, although unworthy.

REVIEW QUESTIONS

1. What threat do the Ottoman Turks pose to Christians in the East?
2. Given that many, even most, eastern Christians are Greek and offer no obedience to the Pope in Rome, why is Bartolomeo so concerned about them?
3. What is the importance of Constantinople in Bartolomeo's eyes?
4. What should western Christians do to support their co-religionaries in the East?
5. What makes this "crusade" different from those intended to reclaim the Holy Land for Christianity?

12 &ens; INNOVATION AND EXPLORATION, 1453–1533

This chapter takes up both the Renaissance at its height and the intensification of contact between Europe and the rest of the world. We have already witnessed the impact that closer relations between Europeans and Muslims around the Fall of Constantinople had on launching the early Renaissance. Equally important was the rise of the printing press that would enable the cultural and intellectual transmissions that took place during this period, which included maps, geographies, and histories, to be shared widely around Europe. Ultimately, the transmission and spread of this information spurred explorations along the western coast of Africa, the Atlantic Ocean, and around the globe leading to encounters and exchanges that would forever change Europe and all the regions of the world.

As noted in Chapter 11, scholars have traditionally viewed the Renaissance as a period of great change and have identified the following several characteristics: 1) scholars and artists revived classical antiquity as a subject of study and emulation; 2) the state emerged as a subject that could be studied and used by those seeking power; 3) the notion that the ideal ("universal") man was well rounded in physical and intellectual endeavors; and 4) the notion that achievement mattered more than lineage. Scholars in recent decades, however, argue that while there were indeed some new cultural and intellectual developments during this period, much of the political, cultural, and social changes that took place were part of longer developments that had been underway for centuries. Many of the selections in this chapter take on the characteristics of the Renaissance in a longer context.

Exploration, expansion, and exploitation intensified and increased as a result of these short and long term historic developments, leading to what historians refer to as the "Age of Exploration." One recalls the well-known stories of the attempt in 1492 of Christopher Columbus to find a sea route to East Asia by sailing west across the Atlantic Ocean only to reach the islands of the Caribbean, a truly "new world," or the voyage of Vasco da Gama around the Cape of Good Hope on the southern tip of Africa and across the Indian Ocean to make landfall in 1497 on the Coromandel coast of South Asia. These discoveries and their consequences had an impact that cannot be overestimated. They utterly transformed, directly or indirectly, every single aspect of European society and culture, and the lives of the peoples encountered as well. They brought Europe into more immediate contact with non-European cultures and civilizations. Direct sea routes to Europe's most important trading partners, whether in new worlds or old ones, resulted in intensified trade relations, exotic consumable goods, and vast new wealth. Contact with different, often less advanced civilizations led to conquest and colonization, creating vast empires that forcibly exported European culture, often provoking desperate resistance and brutal oppression, and radically changing the balance of power both within Europe and across the globe. That contact likewise unleashed a flood of new knowledge that would alter the perceived understanding Europeans had of themselves and their world.

The discoveries that followed prompted humanistically trained philosophers such as Thomas More to reconsider fundamental European values and assumptions. The states that underwrote the voyages of exploration, and those that soon followed in their paths, pursued real political power as well as moral or ideological goals. The kingdom of Portugal and the united kingdoms of Aragon and Castile had recently completed the Reconquista of the Iberian peninsula, in the process of which they had subjugated and converted or expelled Muslim and Jewish communities that had resided there since at least the tenth century. The states had experienced a radical increase in their power, authority, and prestige. When they sponsored voyages into the southern and western Atlantic, therefore, they did so not only in the hope of converting non-believers to Christianity and spreading the benefits of European society, but also with the clear intention of further expanding their supremacy and stature.

Thus briefly described, the expansion of European power and influence beyond its own boundaries to a wider world, which begins at the end of the fifteenth century and shapes global history to the present day, has roots in a more distant past. Crucial to that longer term is the transformation of Europe that began with the unrest and rebirth of the fourteenth century. Conquest, commerce, and colonization in what would become the first global economy created further currents of change in Europe that would shape all aspects of its history.

VASCO DA GAMA

Round Africa to India, 1497–1498 C.E.

Vasco da Gama (c. 1460–23 December 1524) was a Portuguese explorer, the first European to reach India by sea. His voyage to India via Cape Horn, which occurred between 1497 and 1499, created a sea route that linked Europe and Asia. It is widely credited with making possible an age of European political and economic expansion that resulted in the first exercise in global imperialism on the part of the West with the establishment by the Portuguese of a trading empire in Asia. It is also credited with beginning a long-term shift in the economic and political balance of power in Europe away from the Mediterranean, which gradually declined to the status of a backwater, and toward the Atlantic economies. For centuries, Asian luxury goods, especially textiles and spices, had reached Europe via land and sea routes that terminated on the eastern shores of the Black and Mediterranean Seas. From there, merchants, especially Italians, transshipped them to various entrepôts in Europe. By the late fourteenth century the most valuable luxury commodities from Asia were spices, pepper and cinnamon above all. When da Gama landed near Calicut on the western coast of India, he placed the Portuguese in a position to bring much of this trade into their own hands. It improved the Portuguese economy, which had hitherto depended upon trade with northern and western Africa, by giving it a virtual commercial monopoly of the Asian spice trade. It also inspired competition. Within a century of da Gama's achievement, the Netherlands, England, and France would rise to the point where they could challenge, and ultimately break, Portugal's maritime superiority and commercial dominance in the Indian Ocean basin. This, in turn, would transform and expand European imperialism in Asia and Africa. Rewarded with noble titles in his lifetime and celebrated in the Portuguese epic poem Os Lusíadas, *da Gama remains a key figure in the history of exploration, and his trip marks a turning point in the historical processes of globalization and multiculturalism.*

From *The Library of Original Sources.* Vol. V: 9th to 16th Century, edited by Oliver J. Thatcher (Milwaukee: University Research Extension, 1907), pp. 26–40.

1498. Calicut. [Arrival.] That night (May 20) we anchored two leagues from the city of Calicut, and we did so because our pilot mistook Capna, a town at that place, for Calicut. Still further there is another town called Pandarani. We anchored about a league and a half from the shore. After we were at anchor, four boats (*almadias*) approached us from the land, who asked of what nation we were. We told them, and they then pointed out Calicut to us.

On the following day (May 22) these same boats came again alongside, when the captain-major sent one of the convicts to Calicut, and those with whom he went took him to two Moors from Tunis, who could speak Castilian and Genoese. The first greeting that he received was in these words: "May the Devil take thee! What brought you hither?" They asked what he sought so far away from home, and he told them that we came in search of Christians and of spices. They said: "Why does not the King of Castile, the King of France, or the Signoria of Venice send thither?" He said that the King of Portugal would not consent to their doing so, and they said he did the right thing. After this conversation they took him to their lodgings and gave him wheaten bread and honey. When he had eaten he returned to the ships, accompanied by one of the Moors, who was no sooner on board, than he said these words: "A lucky venture, a lucky venture! Plenty of rubies, plenty of emeralds! You owe great thanks to God, for having brought you to a country holding such riches!" We were greatly astonished to hear his talk, for we never expected to hear our language spoken so far away from Portugal.

The city of Calicut is inhabited by Christians. [The first voyagers to India mistook the Hindus for Christians.] They are of tawny complexion. Some of them have big beards and long hair, whilst others clip their hair short or shave the head, merely allowing a tuft to remain on the crown as a sign that they are Christians. They also wear moustaches. They pierce the ears and wear much gold in them. They go naked down to the waist, covering their lower extremities with very fine cotton stuffs. But it is only the most respectable who do this, for the others manage as best they are able. The women of this country, as a rule, are ugly and of small stature. They wear many jewels of gold round the neck, numerous bracelets on their arms, and rings set with precious stones on their toes. All these people are well-disposed and apparently of mild temper. At first sight they seem covetous and ignorant.

*   *   *

On the following morning, which was Monday, May 28th, the captain-major set out to speak to the king, and took with him thirteen men. On landing, the captain-major was received by the alcaide,[1] with whom were many men, armed and unarmed. The reception was friendly, as if the people were pleased to see us, though at first appearances looked threatening, for they carried naked swords in their hands. A palanquin was provided for the

captain-major, such as is used by men of distinction in that country, as also by some of the merchants, who pay something to the king for this privilege. The captain-major entered the palanquin, which was carried by six men by turns. Attended by all these people we took the road of Calicut, and came first to another town, called Capna. The captain-major was there deposited at the house of a man of rank, whilst we others were provided with food, consisting of rice, with much butter, and excellent boiled fish. The captain-major did not wish to eat, and as we had done so, we embarked on a river close by, which flows between the sea end the mainland, close to the coast. The two boats in which we embarked were lashed together, so that we were not separated. There were numerous other boats, all crowded with people. As to those who were on the banks I say nothing; their number was infinite, and they had all come to see us. We went up that river for about a league, and saw many large ships drawn up high and dry on its banks, for there is no port here.

When we disembarked, the captain-major once more entered his palanquin. The road was crowded with a countless multitude anxious to see us. Even the women came out of their houses with children in their arms and followed us. When we arrived (at Calicut) they took us to a large church, and this is what we saw: The body of the church is as large as a monastery, all built of hewn stone and covered with tiles. At the main entrance rises a pillar of bronze as high as a mast, on the top of which was perched a bird, apparently a cock. In addition to this, there was another pillar as high as a man, and very stout. In the center of the body of the church rose a chapel, all built of hewn stone, with a bronze door sufficiently wide for a man to pass, and stone steps leading up to it. Within this sanctuary stood a small image which they said represented Our Lady. Along the walls, by the main entrance, hung seven small bells. In this church the captain-major said his prayers, and we with him.

*   *   *

May 28. The king was in a small court, reclining upon a couch covered with a cloth of green velvet, above which was a good mattress, and upon this

---

[1] Governor.

again a sheet of cotton stuff, very white and fine, more so than any linen. The cushions were after the same fashion. In his left hand the king held a very large golden cup (spittoon), having a capacity of half an almude (8 pints). At its mouth this cup was two palmas (16 inches) wide, and apparently it was massive. Into this cup the king threw the husks of a certain herb which is chewed by the people of this country because of its soothing effects, and which they call atambor. On the right side of the king stood a basin of gold, so large that a man might just encircle it with his arms: this contained the herbs. There were likewise many silver jugs. The canopy above the couch was all gilt.

The captain-major, on entering, saluted in the manner of the country: by putting the hands together, then raising them towards Heaven, as is done by Christians when addressing God, and immediately afterwards opening them and shutting fists quickly. The king beckoned to the captain-major with his right hand to come nearer, but the captain-major did not approach him, for it is the custom of the country for no man to approach the king except only the servant who hands him the herbs, and when anyone addresses the king he holds his hand before the mouth, and remains at a distance. When the king beckoned to the captain-major he looked at the others [i.e., da Gama's men], and ordered them to be seated on a stone bench near him, where he could see them. He ordered that water for their hands should be given them, as also some fruit, one kind of which resembled a melon, except that its outside was rough and the inside sweet, whilst another kind of fruit resembled a fig, and tasted very nice. There were men who prepared these fruits for them; and the king looked at them eating, and smiled; and talked to the servant who stood near him supplying him with the herbs referred to.

Then, throwing his eyes on the captain-major, who sat facing him, he invited him to address himself to the courtiers present, saying they were men of much distinction, that he could tell them whatever he desired to say, and they would repeat it to him (the king). The captain-major replied that he was the ambassador of the King of Portugal, and the bearer of a message which he could only deliver to him personally. The king said this was good, and

immediately asked him to be conducted to a chamber. When the captain-major had entered, the king, too, rose and joined him, whilst the rest remained where they were. All this happened about sunset. An old man who was in the court took away the couch as soon as the king rose, but allowed the plate to remain. The king, when he joined the captain-major, threw himself upon another couch, covered with various stuffs embroidered in gold, and asked the captain-major what he wanted. And the captain-major told him he was the ambassador of a King of Portugal, who was Lord of many countries and the possessor of great wealth of every description, exceeding that of any king of these parts; that for a period of sixty years his ancestors had annually sent out vessels to make discoveries in the direction of India, as they knew that there were Christian kings there like themselves. This, he said, was the reason which induced them to order this country to be discovered, not because they sought for gold or silver, for of this they had such abundance that they needed not what was to be found in this country. He further stated that the captains sent out traveled for a year or two, until their provisions were exhausted, and then returned to Portugal, without having succeeded in making the desired discovery. There reigned a king now whose name was Dom Manuel, who had ordered him to build three vessels, of which he had been appointed captain-major, and who had ordered him not to return to Portugal until he should have discovered this King of the Christians, on pain of having his head cut off. That two letters had been intrusted to him to be presented in case he succeeded in discovering him, and that he would do so on the ensuing day; and, finally, he had been instructed to say by word of mouth that he [the King of Portugal] desired to be his friend and brother.

In reply to this the king said that he was welcome; that, on his part, he held him as a friend and brother, and would send ambassadors with him to Portugal. This latter had been asked as a favor, the captain-major pretending that he would not dare to present himself before his king and master unless he was able to present, at the same time, some men of this country. These and many other things passed between the two in this chamber, and as it was already late in the night, the king asked the captain-major with whom he desired to lodge, with Christians or with Moors? And the captain-major replied, neither with Christians nor with Moors, and begged as a favor that he be given a lodging by himself. The king said he would order it thus, upon which the captain-major took leave of the king and came to where the men were, that is, to a veranda lit up by a huge candlestick. By that time four hours of the night had already gone.

*   *   *

May 30. On Wednesday morning the Moors returned, and took the captain-major to the palace. The palace was crowded with armed men. Our captain-major was kept waiting with his conductors for fully four long hours, outside a door, which was only opened when the king sent word to admit him, attended by two men only, whom he might select. The captain-major said that he desired to have Fernao Martins with him, who could interpret, and his secretary. It seemed to him that this separation portended no good. When he had entered, the king said that he had expected him on Tuesday. The captain-major said that the long road had tired him, and that for this reason he had not come to see him. The king then said that he had told him that he came from a very rich kingdom, and yet had brought him nothing; that he had also told him that he was the bearer of a letter, which had not yet been delivered. To this the captain-major rejoined that he had brought nothing, because the object of his voyage was merely to make discoveries, but that when other ships came he would then see what they brought him; as to the letter, it was true that he had brought one, and would deliver it immediately. The king then asked what it was he had come to discover: stones or men? If he came to discover men, as he said, why had he brought nothing? Moreover, he had been told that he carried with him the golden image of a Santa Maria. The captain-major said that the Santa Maria was not of gold, and that even if she were he would not part with her, as she had guided him across the ocean, and would guide him back to his own country. The king then asked for the letter. The captain-major said that he begged

as a favor, that as the Moors wished him ill and might misinterpret him, a Christian able to speak Arabic should be sent for. The king said this was well, and at once sent for a young man, of small stature, whose name was Quaram. The captain-major then said that he had two letters, one written in his own language and the other in that of the Moors; that he was able to read the former, and knew that it contained nothing but what would prove acceptable; but that as to the other he was unable to read it, and it might be good, or contain something that was erroneous. As the Christian was unable to read Moorish, four Moors took the letter and read it between them, after which they translated it to the king, who was well satisfied with its contents.

The king then asked what kind of merchandise was to be found in his country. The captain-major said there was much corn, cloth, iron, bronze, and many other things. The king asked whether he had any merchandise with him. The captain-major replied that he had a little of each sort, as samples, and that if permitted to return to the ships he would order it to be landed, and that meantime four or five men would remain at the lodgings assigned them. The king said no! He might take all his people with him, securely moor his ships, land his merchandise, and sell it to the best advantage. Having taken leave of the king the captain-major returned to his lodgings, and we with him. As it was already late no attempt was made to depart that night.

REVIEW QUESTIONS

1. How would you characterize the first encounter of the Portuguese with non-European indigenous peoples?
2. What technological limits influence both the progress of the Portuguese and their relations with indigenous peoples?
3. How do the Portuguese contend with the problem of communication?
4. What do the Portuguese seek in Calicut and why?
5. Do the Portuguese truly encounter Christians in Calicut?

CHRISTOPHER COLUMBUS

Letter on His First Voyage

Christopher Columbus (c. 1450–1506) was born somewhere around Genoa and made his living as a sailor from an early age. Columbus saw much of the Mediterranean and Atlantic world and acquired real skill as a mapmaker and navigator. Self-taught in geography, Columbus developed an erroneous theory of the globe's size that made sailing across the Atlantic to China and Japan a daring but plausible adventure. After he had spent years looking for a patron among the rulers of Europe, Isabella of Castile took the lead (along with her husband Ferdinand of Aragon) in sponsoring Columbus's first voyage. This letter is one of his earliest accounts of this trip in 1492.

From *Selected Documents Illustrating the Four Voyages of Christopher Columbus*, translated and edited by Cecil Jane (London: Hakluyt Society, 1930), pp. 3–18.

Sir, As I know that you will be pleased at the great victory with which Our Lord has crowned my voyage, I write this to you, from which you will learn how in thirty-three days, I passed from the Canary Islands to the Indies with the fleet which the most illustrious king and queen, our sovereigns, gave to me. And there I found very many islands filled with people in-numerable, and of them all I have taken possession for their highnesses, by proclamation made and with the royal standard unfurled, and no opposition was offered to me. To the first island which I found, I gave the name *San Salvador,* in remembrance of the Divine Majesty, Who has marvellously bestowed all this; the Indians call it "Guanahani." To the second, I gave the name *Isla de Santa María de Concepción;* to the third, *Fernandina;* to the fourth, *Isabella;* to the fifth, *Isla Juana,* and so to each one I gave a new name.

When I reached Juana, I followed its coast to the westward, and I found it to be so extensive that I thought that it must be the mainland, the province of Catayo. And since there were neither towns nor villages on the seashore, but only small hamlets, with the people of which I could not have speech, because they all fled immediately, I went forward on the same course, thinking that I should not fail to find great cities and towns. And, at the end of many leagues, seeing that there was no change and that the coast was bearing me northwards, which I wished to avoid, since winter was already beginning and I proposed to make from it to the south, and as moreover the wind was carrying me forward, I determined not to wait for a change in the weather and retraced my path as far as a certain harbour known to me. And from that point, I sent two men inland to learn if there were a king or great cities. They travelled three days' journey and found an infinity of small hamlets and people without number, but nothing of importance. For this reason, they returned.

I understood sufficiently from other Indians, whom I had already taken, that this land was nothing but an island. And therefore I followed its coast eastwards for one hundred and seven leagues to the point where it ended. And from that cape, I saw another island, distant eighteen leagues from the former, to the east, to which I at once gave the name "Española." And I went there and followed its northern coast, as I had in the case of Juana, to the eastward for one hundred and eighty-eight great leagues in a straight line. This island and all the others are very fertile to a limitless degree, and this island is extremely so. In it there are many harbours on the coast of the sea, beyond comparison with others which I know in Christendom, and many rivers, good and large, which is marvellous. Its lands are high, and there are in it very many sierras and very lofty mountains, beyond comparison with the island of Teneriffe. All are most beautiful, of a thousand shapes, and all are accessible and filled with trees of a thousand kinds and tall, and they seem to touch the sky. And I am told that they never lose their foliage, as I can understand, for I saw them as green and as lovely as they are in Spain in May, and some of them were flowering, some bearing fruit, and some in another stage, according to their nature. And the nightingale was singing and other birds of a thousand kinds in the month of November there where I went. There are six or eight kinds of palm, which are a wonder to behold on account of their beautiful variety, but so are the other trees and fruits and plants. In it are marvellous pine groves, and there are very large tracts of cultivatable lands, and there is honey, and there are birds of many kinds and fruits in great diversity. In the interior are mines of metals, and the population is without number. Española is a marvel.

The sierras and mountains, the plains and arable lands and pastures, are so lovely and rich for planting and sowing, for breeding cattle of every kind, for building towns and villages. The harbours of the sea here are such as cannot be believed to exist unless they have been seen, and so with the rivers, many and great, and good waters, the majority of which contain gold. In the trees and fruits and plants, there is a great difference from those of Juana. In this island, there are many spices and great mines of gold and of other metals.

The people of this island, and of all the other islands which I have found and of which I have information, all go naked, men and women, as their mothers bore them, although some women cover a single place with the leaf of a plant or with a net of cotton which they make for the purpose. They have no iron or steel or weapons, nor are they fitted to use them, not because they are not well built men and of handsome stature, but because they are very marvellously timorous. They have no other arms than weapons made of canes, cut in seeding time, to the ends of which they fix a small sharpened stick. And they do not dare to make use of these, for many times it has happened that I have sent ashore two or three men to some town to have speech, and countless people have come out to them, and as soon as they have seen my men approaching they have fled, even a father not waiting for his son. And this, not because ill has been done to anyone; on the contrary, at every point where I have been and have been able to have speech, I have given to them of all that I had, such as cloth and many other things, without receiving anything for it; but so they are, incurably timid. It is true that, after they have been reassured and have lost their fear, they are so guileless and so generous with all they possess, that no one would believe it who has not seen it. They never refuse anything which they possess, if it be asked of them; on the contrary, they invite anyone to share it, and display as much love as if they would give their hearts, and whether the thing be of value or whether it be of small price, at once with whatever trifle of whatever kind it may be that is given to them, with that they are content. I forbade that they should be given things so worthless as fragments of broken crockery and scraps of broken glass, and ends of straps, although when they were able to get them, they fancied that they possessed the best jewel in the world. So it was found that a sailor for a strap received gold to the weight of two and a half *castellanos*, and others much more for other things which were worth much less. As for new *blancas*, for them they would give everything which they had, although it might be two or three *castellanos'* weight of gold or an *arroba* or two of spun cotton. . . . They took even the pieces of the broken hoops of the wine barrels and, like savages, gave what they had, so that it seemed to me to be wrong and I forbade it. And I gave a thousand handsome good things, which I had brought, in order that they might conceive affection, and more than that, might become

Christians and be inclined to the love and service of their highnesses and of the whole Castilian nation, and strive to aid us and to give us of the things which they have in abundance and which are necessary to us. And they do not know any creed and are not idolaters; only they all believe that power and good are in the heavens, and they are very firmly convinced that I, with these ships and men, came from the heavens, and in this belief they everywhere received me, after they had overcome their fear. And this does not come because they are ignorant; on the contrary, they are of a very acute intelligence and are men who navigate all those seas, so that it is amazing how good an account they give of everything, but it is because they have never seen people clothed or ships of such a kind.

And as soon as I arrived in the Indies, in the first island which I found, I took by force some of them, in order that they might learn and give me information of that which there is in those parts, and so it was that they soon understood us, and we them, either by speech or signs, and they have been very serviceable. I still take them with me, and they are always assured that I come from Heaven, for all the intercourse which they have had with me; and they were the first to announce this wherever I went, and the others went running from house to house and to the neighbouring towns, with loud cries of, 'Come! Come to see the people from Heaven!' So all, men and women alike, when their minds were set at rest concerning us, came, so that not one, great or small, remained behind, and all brought something to eat and drink, which they gave with extraordinary affection. In all the island, they have very many canoes, like rowing *fustas,* some larger, some smaller, and some are larger than a *fusta* of eighteen benches. They are not so broad, because they are made of a single log of wood, but a *fusta* would not keep up with them in rowing, since their speed is a thing incredible. And in these they navigate among all those islands, which are innumerable, and carry their goods. One of these canoes I have seen with seventy and eighty men in her, and each one with his oar.

In all these islands, I saw no great diversity in the appearance of the people or in their manners

and language. On the contrary, they all understand one another, which is a very curious thing, on account of which I hope that their highnesses will determine upon their conversion to our holy faith, towards which they are very inclined.

I have already said how I have gone one hundred and seven leagues in a straight line from west to east along the seashore of the island Juana, and as a result of that voyage, I can say that this island is larger than England and Scotland together, for, beyond these one hundred and seven leagues, there remain to the westward two provinces to which I have not gone. One of these provinces they call "Avan," and there the people are born with tails; and these provinces cannot have a length of less than fifty or sixty leagues, as I could understand from those Indians whom I have and who know all the islands.

The other, Española, has a circumference greater than all Spain, from Colibre, by the seacoast, to Fuenterabia in Vizcaya, since I voyaged along one side one hundred and eighty-eight great leagues in a straight line from west to east. It is a land to be desired and, seen, it is never to be left. And in it, although of all I have taken possession for their highnesses and all are more richly endowed than I know how, or am able, to say, and I hold them all for their highnesses, so that they may dispose of them as, and as absolutely as, of the kingdoms of Castile, in this Española, in the situation most convenient and in the best position for the mines of gold and for all intercourse as well with the mainland here as with that there, belonging to the Grand Khan, where will be great trade and gain, I have taken possession of a large town, to which I gave the name *Villa de Navidad,* and in it I have made fortifications and a fort, which now will by this time be entirely finished, and I have left in it sufficient men for such a purpose with arms and artillery and provisions for more than a year, and a *fusta,* and one, a master of all sea-craft, to build others, and great friendship with the king of that land, so much so, that he was proud to call me, and to treat me as, a brother. And even if he were to change his attitude to one of hostility towards these men, he and his do not know what arms are and they go naked, as I have already said, and are the most timorous people that there are in the world, so that the men whom I have left there alone would suffice to destroy all that land, and the island is without danger for their persons, if they know how to govern themselves.

In all these islands, it seems to me that all men are content with one woman, and to their chief or king they give as many as twenty. It appears to me that the women work more than the men. And I have not been able to learn if they hold private property; what seemed to me to appear was that, in that which one had, all took a share, especially of eatable things.

In these islands I have so far found no human monstrosities, as many expected, but on the contrary the whole population is very well-formed, nor are they Negroes as in Guinea, but their hair is flowing, and they are not born where there is intense force in the rays of the sun; it is true that the sun has there great power, although it is distant from the equinoctial line twenty-six degrees. In these islands, where there are high mountains, the cold was severe this winter, but they endure it, being used to it and with the help of meats which they eat with many and extremely hot spices. As I have found no monsters, so I have had no report of any, except in an island "Quaris," the second at the coming into the Indies, which is inhabited by a people who are regarded in all the islands as very fierce and who eat human flesh. They have many canoes with which they range through all the islands of India and pillage and take as much as they can. They are no more malformed than the others, except that they have the custom of wearing their hair long like women, and they use bows and arrows of the same cane stems, with a small piece of wood at the end, owing to lack of iron which they do not possess. They are ferocious among these other people who are cowardly to an excessive degree, but I make no more account of them than of the rest. These are those who have intercourse with the women of "Matinino," which is the first island met on the way from Spain to the Indies, in which there is not a man. These women engage in no feminine occupation,

but use bows and arrows of cane, like those already mentioned, and they arm and protect themselves with plates of copper, of which they have much.

In another island, which they assure me is larger than Española, the people have no hair. In it, there is gold incalculable, and from it and from the other islands, I bring with me Indians as evidence.

In conclusion, to speak only of that which has been accomplished on this voyage, which was so hasty, their highnesses can see that I will give them as much gold as they may need, if their highnesses will render me very slight assistance; moreover, spice and cotton, as much as their highnesses shall command; and mastic, as much as they shall order to be shipped and which, up to now, has been found only in Greece, in the island of Chios, and the Seignory sells it for what it pleases; and aloe wood, as much as they shall order to be shipped, and slaves, as many as they shall order to be shipped and who will be from the idolaters. And I believe that I have found rhubarb and cinamon, and I shall find a thousand other things of value, which the people whom I have left there will have discovered, for I have not delayed at any point, so far as the wind allowed me to sail, except in the town of Navidad, in order to leave it secured and well established, and in truth, I should have done much more, if the ships had served me, as reason demanded.

This is enough . . . and the eternal God, our Lord, Who gives to all those who walk in His way triumph over things which appear to be impossible, and this was notably one; for, although men have talked or have written of these lands, all was conjectural, without suggestion of ocular evidence, but amounted only to this, that those who heard for the most part listened and judged it to be rather a fable than as having any vestige of truth. So that, since Our Redeemer has given this victory to our most illustrious king and queen, and to their renowned kingdoms, in so great a matter, for this all Christendom ought to feel delight and make great feasts and give solemn thanks to the Holy Trinity with many solemn prayers for the great exaltation which they shall have, in the turning of so many peoples to our holy faith, and afterwards for temporal benefits, for not only Spain but all Christians will have hence refreshment and gain.

This, in accordance with that which has been accomplished, thus briefly.

Done in the caravel, off the Canary Islands, on the fifteenth of February, in the year one thousand four hundred and ninety-three.

At your orders.   El Almirante.

After having written this, and being in the sea of Castile, there came on me so great a south-south-west wind, that I was obliged to lighten ship. But I ran here to-day into this port of Lisbon, which was the greatest marvel in the world, whence I decided to write to their highnesses. In all the Indies, I have always found weather like May; where I went in thirty-three days and I had returned in twenty-eight, save for these storms which have detained me for fourteen days, beating about in this sea. Here all the sailors say that never has there been so bad a winter nor so many ships lost.

Done on the fourth day of March.

REVIEW QUESTIONS

1. What can we learn about Columbus's personality and motives from this letter?
2. Columbus provides here the first Western account of the people he called Indians. What do we learn about his interests and abilities as an ethnographer?
3. Compare this account to those of William of Rubruck (see Volume 1, Chapter 10) and Bartolomeo de Giano (pp. 38–43). What can you conclude from their similiarities and differences?

LEONARDO DA VINCI

FROM *The Notebooks*

Leonardo da Vinci (1452–1519) was born in the countryside of Florence, the illegitimate son of a notary in the town of Vinci. He was self-taught and could read Latin only poorly. He was left-handed, a condition viewed by contemporaries as a deformity. Sometime around 1481, he moved to Milan, where his patrons were the dukes Gian Galeazzo (1476–94) and Ludovico Sforza (1494–1500). During the French invasion of 1499, Leonardo fled Milan and led a peripatetic existence until 1508, when he returned to the city. In 1513, he was taken to France, where he lived the remainder of his days. He is widely acclaimed as a genius, the designer of futuristic machines of many sorts. Among these was a device for grinding concave mirrors and lenses that made possible the invention of the telescope in 1509. He was a great artist in many media as well as a keen observer of nature. His interests ranged from aerodynamics to physics to biology to anatomy to optics. His writings on perspective are drawn from his notebooks, which he wrote backward, in a mirror hand, and in no particular order, and which were never published in his lifetime.

From *Leonardo da Vinci's Notebooks*, translated by Edward MacCurdy (London: Duckworth & Co., 1906).

*   *   *

Principle of Perspective

All things transmit their image to the eye by means of pyramids; the nearer to the eye these are intersected the smaller the image of their cause will appear.

If you should ask how you can demonstrate these points to me from experience, I should tell you, as regards the vanishing point which moves with you, to notice as you go along by lands ploughed in straight furrows, the ends of which start from the path where you are walking, you will see that continually each pair of furrows seem to approach each other and to join at their ends.

As regards the point that comes to the eye, it may be comprehended with greater ease; for if you look in the eye of anyone you will see your own image there; consequently if you suppose two lines to start from your ears and proceed to the ears of the image which you see of yourself in the eye of the other person, you will clearly recognise that these lines contract so much that when they have continued only a little way beyond your image as mirrored in the said eye they will touch one another in a point.

The thing that is nearer to the eye always appears larger than another of the same size which is more remote.

Perspective is of such a nature that it makes what is flat appear in relief, and what is in relief appear flat.

The perspective by means of which a thing is represented will be better understood when it is seen from the view-point at which it was drawn.

If you wish to represent a thing near, which should produce the effect of natural things, it is impossible for your perspective not to appear false, by reason of all the illusory appearances and errors in proportion of which the existence may be assumed in a mediocre work, unless whoever is looking at this perspective finds himself surveying it from the exact distance, elevation, angle of vision or point at which you were situated to make this perspective. Therefore it would be necessary to make a window of the size of your face or in truth a hole through which you would look at the said work. And if you should do this, then without any doubt your work will produce the effect of nature if the light and shade are correctly rendered, and you will hardly be able to convince yourself that these things are painted. Otherwise do not trouble yourself about representing anything, unless you take your view-point at a distance of at least twenty times the maximum width and height of the thing that you represent; and this will satisfy every beholder who places himself in front of the work at any angle whatever.

If you wish to see a proof of this quickly, take a piece of a staff like a small column eight times as high as its width without plinth or capital, then measure off on a flat wall forty equal spaces which are in conformity with the spaces; they will make between them forty columns similar to your small column. Then let there be set up in front of the middle of these spaces, at a distance of four braccia from the wall, a thin band of iron, in the centre of which there is a small round hole of the size of a large pearl; place a light beside this hole so as to touch it, then go and place your column above each mark of the wall and draw the outline of the shadow, then shade it and observe it through the hole in the iron.

In Vitolone there are eight hundred and five conclusions about perspective.

Perspective

No visible body can be comprehended and well judged by human eyes, except by the difference of the background where the extremities of this body terminate and are bounded, and so far as its contour lines are concerned no object will seem to be separated from this background. The moon, although far distant from the body of the sun, when by reason of eclipses it finds itself between our eyes and the sun, having the sun for its background will seem to human eyes to be joined and attached to it.

Perspective comes to aid us where judgment fails in things that diminish.

It is possible to bring about that the eye does not see distant objects as much diminished as they are in natural perspective, where they are diminished by reason of the convexity of the eye, which is obliged to intersect upon its surface the pyramids of every kind of image that approach the eye at a right angle. But the method that I show here in the margin cuts these pyramids at right angles near the surface of the pupil. But whereas the convex pupil of the eye can take in the whole of our hemisphere, this will show only a single star; but where many small stars transmit their images to the surface of the pupil these stars are very small; here only one will be visible but it will be large; and so the moon will be greater in size and its spots more distinct. You should place close to the eye a glass filled with the water mentioned in chapter four of book 113 'Concerning Natural Things', water which causes things congealed in balls of crystalline glass to appear as though they were without glass.

Of the eye. Of bodies less than the pupil of the eye that which is nearest to it will be least discerned by this pupil—and from this experience it follows that the power of sight is not reduced to a point.

But the images of objects which meet in the pupil of the eye are spread over this pupil in the same way as they are spread about in the air; and the proof of this is pointed out to us when we look at the starry heavens without fixing our gaze more upon one star than upon another, for then the sky shows itself to us strewn with stars, and they bear to the eye the same proportions as in the sky, and the spaces between them also are the same.

Natural perspective acts in the opposite way, for the greater the distance the smaller does the thing seen appear, and the less the distance the larger it appears. But this invention constrains the beholder to stand with his eye at a small hole, and then with this small hole it will be seen well. But

since many eyes come together to see at the same time one and the same work produced by this art, only one of them will have a good view of the function of this perspective and all the others will only see it confusedly. It is well therefore to shun this compound perspective, and to keep to the simple which does not purport to view planes foreshortened but as far as possible in exact form.

And of this simple perspective in which the plane intersects the pyramid that conveys the images to the eye that are at an equal distance from the visual faculty, an example is afforded us by the curve of the pupil of the eye upon which these pyramids intersect at an equal distance from the visual faculty.

Of Equal Things the More Remote Appears Smaller

The practice of perspective is divided into two parts, of which the first treats of all the things seen by the eye at whatsoever distance, and this in itself shows all these things diminished as the eye beholds them, without the man being obliged to stand in one place rather than in another, provided that the wall does not foreshorten it a second time.

But the second practice is a combination of perspective made partly by art and partly by nature, and the work done according to its rules has no part that is not influenced by natural and accidental perspective. Natural perspective I understand has to do with the flat surface on which this perspective is represented; which surface, although it is parallel to it in length and height, is constrained to diminish the distant parts more than its near ones. And this is proved by the first of what has been said above, and its diminution is natural.

Accidental perspective, that is that which is created by art, acts in the contrary way; because it causes bodies equal in themselves to increase on the foreshortened plane, in proportion as the eye is more natural and nearer to the plane, and as the part of this plane where it is represented is more remote from the eye.

*   *   *

THE SCHOOL OF ATHENS (1509–1511)

RAPHAEL

The School of Athens, *by Raphael, is one of the most famous frescoes of the Italian Renaissance. Completed between 1509 and 1511, it formed part of a commission to decorate rooms in the Apostolic Palace in the Vatican. The* School of Athens, *representing Philosophy, has long been considered both a great masterpiece by Raphael and the ideal representation the classical spirit of the Renaissance. What do you imagine Raphael's purpose was in painting* The School of Athens? *What makes this painting particularly representative of Renaissance classicism? Why do you imagine Raphael placed Plato and Aristotle at the exact center of the architectural structure? What do you make of the fact that at the center of an image of classical knowledge is a representation of one of its greats pointing upwards? What may Raphael be arguing about the relationship of classical knowledge and Christianity? What does the architectural structure suggest to the viewer? How does Raphael use posture, gesture, and color to link various figures? Would you describe this painting as secular or religious in theme? Given that this painting was commissioned by the pope, why do you imagine Raphael chose philosophy as his theme?*

REVIEW QUESTIONS

1. According to Leonardo, what is the relationship between perspective in nature and perspective in the human eye?

2. What is the relationship between perspective and mathematical principles?
3. Is perspective a constant or contingent?
4. What implications does this have for painting?
5. How might it shape the enterprise of reading?

BALDESAR CASTIGLIONE

FROM *The Book of the Courtier*

Baldesar Castiglione (1478–1529) was born near Mantua and educated in Milan. He entered the service of the duke of Milan in 1496. After the duke was carried to France as a prisoner, Castiglione returned to Mantua. In 1504, he entered the court of Guidobaldo of Montefeltro, duke of Urbino, where he remained until 1524; this is the setting of The Book of the Courtier. *Although he wrote elegant verse in Latin and Italian, this reflection on courtly life was Castiglione's claim to fame. Fashioned as a discourse among courtiers and ladies of the court, it described the ideal courtier and presented the Renaissance man.*

From *The Book of the Courtier*, by Count Baldesar Castiglione, translated by Leonard Eckstein Opdycke (New York: Charles Scribner's Sons, 1903), pp. 22–23, 25–26, 59, 175–77, 247.

*   *   *

"I wish, then, that this Courtier of ours should be nobly born and of gentle race; because it is far less unseemly for one of ignoble birth to fail in worthy deeds, than for one of noble birth, who, if he strays from the path of his predecessors, stains his family name, and not only fails to achieve but loses what has been achieved already; for noble birth is like a bright lamp that manifests and makes visible good and evil deeds, and kindles and stimulates to virtue both by fear of shame and by hope of praise. And since this splendour of nobility does not illumine the deeds of the humbly born, they lack that stimulus and fear of shame, nor do they feel any obligation to advance beyond what their predecessors have done; while to the nobly born it seems a reproach not to reach at least the goal set them by their ancestors. And thus it nearly always happens that both in the profession of arms and in other worthy pursuits the most famous men have been of noble birth, because nature has implanted in everything that hidden seed which gives a certain force and quality of its own essence to all things that are derived from it, and makes them like itself: as we see not only in the breeds of horses and of other animals, but also in trees, the shoots of which nearly always resemble the trunk; and if they sometimes degenerate, it arises from poor cultivation. And so it is with men, who if rightly trained are nearly always like those from whom they spring, and often better; but if there be no one to give them proper care, they become like savages and never reach perfection.

*　　*　　*

"But to return to our subject: I say that there is a middle state between perfect grace on the one hand and senseless folly on the other; and those who are not thus perfectly endowed by nature, with study and toil can in great part polish and amend their natural defects. Besides his noble birth, then, I would have the Courtier favoured in this regard also, and endowed by nature not only with talent and beauty of person and feature, but with a certain grace and (as we say) air that shall make him at first sight pleasing and agreeable to all who see him; and I would have this an ornament that should dispose and unite all his actions, and in his outward aspect give promise of whatever is worthy the society and favour of every great lord.". . .

—"But to come to some details, I am of opinion that the principal and true profession of the Courtier ought to be that of arms; which I would have him follow actively above all else, and be known among others as bold and strong, and loyal to whomsoever he serves. And he will win a reputation for these good qualities by exercising them at all times and in all places, since one may never fail in this without severest censure. And just as among women, their fair fame once sullied never recovers its first lustre, so the reputation of a gentleman who bears arms, if once it be in the least tarnished with cowardice or other disgrace, remains forever infamous before the world and full of ignominy. Therefore the more our Courtier excels in this art, the more he will be worthy of praise; and yet I do not deem essential in him that perfect knowledge of things and those other qualities that befit a commander; since this would be too wide a sea, let us be content, as we have said, with perfect loyalty and unconquered courage, and that he be always seen to possess them. For the courageous are often recognized even more in small things than in great; and frequently in perils of importance and where

there are many spectators, some men are to be found, who, although their hearts be dead within them, yet, moved by shame or by the presence of others, press forward almost with their eyes shut, and do their duty God knows how. While on occasions of little moment, when they think they can avoid putting themselves in danger without being detected, they are glad to keep safe. But those who, even when they do not expect to be observed or seen or recognized by anyone, show their ardour and neglect nothing, however paltry, that may be laid to their charge,—they have that strength of mind which we seek in our Courtier.

"Not that we would have him look so fierce, or go about blustering, or say that he has taken his cuirass to wife, or threaten with those grim scowls that we have often seen in Berto; because to such men as this, one might justly say that which a brave lady jestingly said in gentle company to one whom I will not name at present; who, being invited by her out of compliment to dance, refused not only that, but to listen to the music, and many other entertainments proposed to him,—saying always that such silly trifles were not his business; so that at last the lady said, 'What is your business, then?' He replied with a sour look, 'To fight.' Then the lady at once said, 'Now that you are in no war and out of fighting trim, I should think it were a good thing to have yourself well oiled, and to stow yourself with all your battle harness in a closet until you be needed, lest you grow more rusty than you are;' and so, amid much laughter from the bystanders, she left the discomfited fellow to his silly presumption.

"Therefore let the man we are seeking, be very bold, stern, and always among the first, where the enemy are to be seen; and in every other place, gentle, modest, reserved, above all things avoiding ostentation and that impudent self-praise by which men ever excite hatred and disgust in all who hear them."

*　　*　　*

"I would have him more than passably accomplished in letters, at least in those studies that are called the humanities, and conversant not only with the Latin language but with the Greek, for the sake of the many different things that have been admirably written therein. Let him be well versed in the poets, and not less in the orators and historians, and also proficient in writing verse and prose, especially in this vulgar tongue of ours; for besides the enjoyment he will find in it, he will by this means never lack agreeable entertainment with ladies, who are usually fond of such things. And if other occupations or want of study prevent his reaching such perfection as to render his writings worthy of great praise, let him be careful to suppress them so that others may not laugh at him, and let him show them only to a friend whom he can trust: because they will at least be of this service to him, that the exercise will enable him to judge the work of others. For it very rarely happens that a man who is not accustomed to write, however learned he may be, can ever quite appreciate the toil and industry of writers, or taste the sweetness and excellence of style, and those latent niceties that are often found in the ancients.

"Moreover these studies will also make him fluent, and as Aristippus said to the tyrant, confident and assured in speaking with everyone. Hence I would have our Courtier keep one precept fixed in mind; which is that in this and everything else he should be always on his guard, and diffident rather than forward, and that he should keep from falsely persuading himself that he knows that which he does not know. . . .

Then my lady Duchess said:

"Do not wander from your subject, my lord Magnifico, but hold to the order given you and describe the Court Lady, to the end that so noble a Lady as this may have someone competent to serve her worthily."

The Magnifico continued:

"Then, my Lady, to show that your commands have power to induce me to essay even that which I know not how to do, I will speak of this excellent Lady as I would have her; and when I have fashioned her to my liking, not being able then to have another such, like Pygmalion I will take her for my own.

"And although my lord Gaspar has said that the same rules which are set the Courtier, serve also for the Lady, I am of another mind; for while some qualities are common to both and as necessary to man as to woman, there are nevertheless some others that befit woman more than man, and some are befitting man to which she ought to be wholly a stranger. The same I say of bodily exercises; but above all, methinks that in her ways, manners, words, gestures and bearing, a woman ought to be very unlike a man; for just as it befits him to show a certain stout and sturdy manliness, so it is becoming in a woman to have a soft and dainty tenderness with an air of womanly sweetness in her every movement, which, in her going or staying or saying what you will, shall always make her seem the woman, without any likeness of a man.

"Now, if this precept be added to the rules that these gentlemen have taught the Courtier, I certainly think she ought to be able to profit by many of them, and to adorn herself with admirable accomplishments, as my lord Gaspar says. For I believe that many faculties of the mind are as necessary to woman as to man; likewise gentle birth, to avoid affectation, to be naturally graceful in all her doings, to be mannerly, clever, prudent, not arrogant, not envious, not slanderous, not vain, not quarrelsome, not silly, to know how to win and keep the favour of her mistress and of all others, to practise well and gracefully the exercises that befit women. I am quite of the opinion, too, that beauty is more necessary to her than to the Courtier, for in truth that woman lacks much who lacks beauty. Then, too, she ought to be more circumspect and take greater care not to give occasion for evil being said of her, and so to act that she may not only escape a stain of guilt but even of suspicion, for a woman has not so many ways of defending herself against false imputations as has a man.

"But as Count Ludovico has explained very minutely the chief profession of the Courtier, and has insisted it be that of arms, methinks it is also fitting to tell what in my judgment is that of the Court Lady: and when I have done this, I shall think myself quit of the greater part of my duty.

"Laying aside, then, those faculties of the mind that she ought to have in common with the Courtier (such as prudence, magnanimity, continence, and many others), and likewise those qualities that befit all women (such as kindness, discretion, ability to manage her husband's property and her house and children if she be married, and all those capacities that are requisite in a good housewife), I say that in a lady who lives at court methinks above all else a certain pleasant affability is befitting, whereby she may be able to entertain politely every sort of man with agreeable and seemly converse, suited to the time and place, and to the rank of the person with whom she may speak, uniting with calm and modest manners, and with that seemliness which should ever dispose all her actions, a quick vivacity of spirit whereby she may show herself alien to all indelicacy; but with such a kindly manner as shall make us think her no less chaste, prudent and benign, than agreeable, witty and discreet; and so she must preserve a certain mean (difficult and composed almost of contraries), and must barely touch certain limits but not pass them.

"Thus, in her wish to be thought good and pure, the Lady ought not to be so coy and seem so to abhor company and talk that are a little free, as to take her leave as soon as she finds herself therein; for it might easily be thought that she was pretending to be thus austere in order to hide something about herself which she feared others might come to know; and such prudish manners are always odious. Nor ought she, on the other hand, for the sake of showing herself free and agreeable, to utter unseemly words or practise a certain wild and unbridled familiarity and ways likely to make that believed of her which perhaps is not true; but when she is present at such talk, she ought to listen with a little blush and shame.

"Likewise she ought to avoid an errour into which I have seen many women fall, which is that of saying and of willingly listening to evil about other women. For those women who, on hearing the unseemly ways of other women described, grow angry thereat and seem to disbelieve it and to regard it almost monstrous that a woman should be immodest,—they, by accounting the offence so heinous, give reason to think that they do not commit it. But those who go about continually prying into other women's intrigues, and narrate them so

minutely and with such zest, seem to be envious of them and to wish that everyone may know it, to the end that like matters may not be reckoned as a fault in their own case; and thus they fall into certain laughs and ways that show they then feel greatest pleasure. And hence it comes that men, while seeming to listen gladly, usually hold such women in small respect and have very little regard for them, and think these ways of theirs are an invitation to advance farther, and thus often go such lengths with them as bring them deserved reproach, and finally esteem them so lightly as to despise their company and even find them tedious.

"And on the other hand, there is no man so shameless and insolent as not to have reverence for those women who are esteemed good and virtuous; because this gravity (tempered with wisdom and goodness) is as it were a shield against the insolence and coarseness of the presumptuous. Thus we see that a word or laugh or act of kindness (however small it be) from a virtuous woman is more prized by everyone, than all the endearments and caresses of those who show their lack of shame so openly; and if they are not immodest, by their unseemly laughter, their loquacity, insolence and like scurrile manners, they give sign of being so. . . .

"I think then that the aim of the perfect Courtier, which has not been spoken of till now, is so to win for himself, by means of the accomplishments ascribed to him by these gentlemen, the favour and mind of the prince whom he serves, that he may be able to say, and always shall say, the truth about everything which it is fitting for the prince to know, without fear or risk of giving offence thereby; and that when he sees his prince's mind inclined to do something wrong, he may be quick to oppose, and gently to make use of the favour acquired by his good accomplishments, so as to banish every bad intent and lead his prince into the path of virtue. And thus, possessing the goodness which these gentlemen have described, together with readiness of wit and pleasantness, and shrewdness and knowledge of letters and many other things,—the Courtier will in every case be able deftly to show the prince how much honour and profit accrue to him and his from justice, liberality, magnanimity, gentleness, and the other virtues that become a good prince; and on the other hand how much infamy and loss proceed from the vices opposed to them. Therefore I think that just as music, festivals, games, and the other pleasant accomplishments are as it were the flower, in like manner to lead or help one's prince towards right, and to frighten him from wrong, are the true fruit of Courtiership.

"And since the merit of well-doing lies chiefly in two things, one of which is the choice of an end for our intentions that shall be truly good, and the other ability to find means suitable and fitting to conduce to that good end marked out,—certain it is that that man's mind tends to the best end, who purposes to see to it that his prince shall be deceived by no one, shall hearken not to flatterers or to slanderers and liars, and shall distinguish good and evil, and love the one and hate the other.

*   *   *

REVIEW QUESTIONS

1. What does Castiglione mean by "grace"? How is it created?
2. To what extent is grace the product of birth or nature?
3. How is grace gendered?
4. What does a courtier's conduct tell others about his status?
5. If status was once thought to reside in one's birth and lineage, how does the courtier alter that notion?
6. How does Castiglione's courtier differ from a medieval monk or knight?
7. Is the courtier's virtue the expression of his nature, cultivation, or education?

PORTRAIT OF POPE LEO X AND TWO CARDINALS (1518)   RAPHAEL

This intriguing portrait of Pope Leo X and two of his cardinals, relatives elevated through acts of nepotism, reveals the full sophistication of Raphael's artistry. He created an attractive painting of his patron in full papal regalia. At the same time, he subtly included less attractive hints about the subject's office and character. What might this portrait tell us of Leo's character? What does the portrait tell us about Renaissance values? Is Raphael exercising a subtle criticism of the church through his portrait of its head? If so, what elements of his criticism are explicit in the painting?

GIOVANNI PICO DELLA MIRANDOLA

FROM "Oration on the Dignity of Man"

Giovanni Pico della Mirandola (1463–1494) is a singular figure in the history of Renaissance humanism. Although the corpus of his published works remained small as a result of his early death, the breadth of his learning won him the admiration of scholars past and present. He received a thorough classical education in Greek and Latin, and studied the scholastic tradition of the Middle Ages as well as Jewish and Arabic philosophy. His conception of the dignity of man and harmony among philosophers found expression in his "Oration on the Dignity of Man." In 1486, Pico published his 900 theses, inviting all scholars to a public debate in January 1487. Before it could take place, however, Pope Innocent VIII appointed a commission to examine the theses, some of which were found to be heretical. An attempt to defend the incriminated points plunged Pico into a conflict with ecclesiastical authorities that lasted several years. The oration, never published in its author's lifetime, was written as an introductory speech for the disputation.

From *Reflections on the Philosophy of the History of Mankind*, by J. G. Herder and F. E. Manuel (Chicago: University of Chicago Press, 1968).

I have read in the records of the Arabians, reverend Fathers, that Abdala the Saracen, when questioned as to what on this stage of the world, as it were, could be seen most worthy of wonder, replied: "There is nothing to be seen more wonderful than man." In agreement with this opinion is the saying of Hermes Trismegistus: "A great miracle, Asclepius, is man." But when I weighed the reason for these maxims, the many grounds for the excellence of human nature reported by many men failed to satisfy me—that man is the intermediary between creatures, the intimate of the gods, the king of the lower beings, by the acuteness of his senses, by the discernment of his reason, and by the light of his intelligence the interpreter of nature, the interval between fixed eternity and fleeting time, and (as the Persians say) the bond, nay, rather, the marriage song of the world, on David's testimony but little lower than the angels. Admittedly great though these reasons be, they are not the principal grounds, that is, those which may rightfully claim for themselves the privilege of the highest admiration. For

why should we not admire more the angels themselves and the blessed choirs of heaven? At last it seems to me I have come to understand why man is the most fortunate of creatures and consequently worthy of all admiration and what precisely is that rank which is his lot in the universal chain of Being—a rank to be envied not only by brutes but even by the stars and by minds beyond this world. It is a matter past faith and a wondrous one. Why should it not be? For it is on this very account that man is rightly called and judged a great miracle and a wonderful creature indeed.

But hear, Fathers, exactly what this rank is and, as friendly auditors, conformably to your kindness, do me this favor. God the Father, the supreme Architect, had already built this cosmic home we behold, the most sacred temple of His godhead, by the laws of His mysterious wisdom. The region above the heavens He had adorned with Intelligences, the heavenly spheres He had quickened with eternal souls, and the excrementary and filthy parts of the lower world He had filled with a multitude of animals of every kind. But, when the work was finished, the Craftsman kept wishing that there were someone to ponder the plan of so great a work, to love its beauty, and to wonder at its vastness. Therefore, when everything was done (as Moses and Timaeus bear witness), He finally took thought concerning the creation of man. But there was not among His archetypes that from which He could fashion a new offspring, nor was there in His treasure-houses anything which He might bestow on His new son as an inheritance, nor was there in the seats of all the world a place where the latter might sit to contemplate the universe. All was now complete; all things had been assigned to the highest, the middle, and the lowest orders. But in its final creation it was not the part of the Father's power to fail as though exhausted. It was not the part of His wisdom to waver in a needful matter through poverty of counsel. It was not the part of His kindly love that he who was to praise God's divine generosity in regard to others should be compelled to condemn it in regard to himself.

At last the best of artisans ordained that that creature to whom He had been able to give nothing proper to himself should have joint possession of whatever had been peculiar to each of the different kinds of being. He therefore took man as a creature of indeterminate nature and, assigning him a place in the middle of the world, addressed him thus: "Neither a fixed abode nor a form that is thine alone nor any function peculiar to thyself have we given thee, Adam, to the end that according to thy longing and according to thy judgment thou mayest have and possess what abode, what form, and what functions thou thyself shalt desire. The nature of all other beings is limited and constrained within the bounds of laws prescribed by Us. Thou, constrained by no limits, in accordance with thine own free will, in whose hand We have placed thee, shalt ordain for thyself the limits of thy nature. We have set thee at the world's center that thou mayest from thence more easily observe whatever is in the world. We have made thee neither of heaven nor of earth, neither mortal nor immortal, so that with freedom of choice and with honor, as though the maker and molder of thyself, thou mayest fashion thyself in whatever shape thou shalt prefer. Thou shalt have the power to degenerate into the lower forms of life, which are brutish. Thou shalt have the power, out of thy soul's judgment, to be reborn into the higher forms, which are divine."

O supreme generosity of God the Father, O highest and most marvelous felicity of man! To him it is granted to have whatever he chooses, to be whatever he wills. Beasts as soon as they are born (so says Lucilius) bring with them from their mother's womb all they will ever possess. Spiritual beings, either from the beginning or soon thereafter, become what they are to be for ever and ever. On man when he came into life the Father conferred the seeds of all kinds and the germs of every way of life. Whatever seeds each man cultivates will grow to maturity and bear in him their own fruit. If they be vegetative, he will be like a plant. If sensitive, he will become brutish. If rational, he will grow into a heavenly being. If intellectual, he will be an angel and the son of God. And if, happy in the lot of no created thing, he withdraws into the center of his own unity, his spirit, made one with God, in the solitary darkness of God, who is set above all things, shall surpass them all. Who would not admire this our chameleon? Or who could more greatly admire aught else whatever? It is man who Asclepius of Athens, arguing from his mutability of character and from his self-transforming nature, on just grounds says was symbolized by Proteus in the mysteries. Hence those metamorphoses renowned among the Hebrews and the Pythagoreans.

* * *

REVIEW QUESTIONS

1. How does Pico reorder the hierarchy of creation?
2. What does he claim for human nature that sets it apart?
3. How does Pico conceive of human will?
4. What implications does that conception have?
5. What is Pico's understanding of the relationship of humankind to God?
6. What are its implications?

NICCOLÒ MACHIAVELLI

FROM *The Prince*

Niccolò Machiavelli (1469–1527) was the son of a Florentine lawyer. Little is known of him until 1498, when he entered the service of the Florentine Republic of Pier Soderini as secretary to the second chancery, a minor bureaucratic post he held for fourteen years. From this position, Machiavelli observed the political process of his day. A staunch republican, he lost his position in government in 1512, when Soderini's republic was toppled and the Medici of Florence were restored to power by a papal army. He spent the rest of his days in retirement, possibly trying to restore himself to the graces of the Medici and the pope, but certainly engaged in the scholarly and literary pursuits that would establish his reputation as a political analyst. Among the fruits of these labors was The Prince, *written in 1513. Of the many observations and ideas expressed in this short work, two at least became fundamental truths of modern politics. One was the necessity of national unity based on a common language, culture, and economy. The other was the preservation of national unity through the concentration and exercise of power by the state. As controversial as they were prescient in Machiavelli's day, these ideas encouraged later scholars to number him among the first modern students of politics.*

From *The Prince*, by Niccolò Machiavelli, translated by Robert M. Adams, A Norton Critical Edition, 2d ed. (New York: Norton, 1977), pp. 31–32, 44–50.

How to Measure the Strength of Any Prince's State

There is one other consideration to bear in mind regarding these civil principates; that is, whether a prince is strong enough to stand on his own feet in case of need, or whether he is in constant need of help from others. And to make the matter clearer, let me say that in my opinion princes control their own destiny when they command enough money or men to assemble an adequate army and make a stand against anyone who attacks them. I think princes who need outside protection are those who can't take the field against their foes, but have to hide behind their walls and defend themselves there. I've already mentioned the first class, and will save whatever else I have to say about them till later. As for the others, all I can say is that they should keep their cities well fortified and well supplied, and pay no heed to the surrounding countryside. Whenever a man has fortified his city strongly, and has dealt with his subjects as I described above and will describe further below, people will be slow to attack him; men are always wary of tasks that seem hard, and it can't seem easy to attack a prince whose city is in fine fettle, and whose people do not hate him.

*   *   *

Thus a prince who has a strong city and does not earn his people's hatred cannot be attacked, or if he were, that attacker would be driven off to his own disgrace; because the way things keep changing in this world, it's almost impossible for a prince with his armies to devote an entire year to a siege while doing nothing else. Maybe someone will object: when the people see their possessions outside the walls being burnt up, they will get impatient; a long siege and their own self-interest will make them forget the prince. But to this I answer that a brave, strong prince will overcome all these problems, giving his subjects hope at one minute that the storm will soon pass, stirring them up at another moment to fear the enemy's cruelty, and on still other occasions restraining those who seem too rash. Besides, the enemy will generally do his burning and ravishing of the countryside as soon as he begins the siege, when men's minds are still passionate and earnest for the defense; thus the prince has less reason to worry, because, after a few days, when tempers have cooled, the harm will already have been done, the losses inflicted, and there will clearly be no cure. At that point, the people will rally even more strongly behind their prince, because they will feel he owes them something, since their houses were burnt and their fields ravaged in defense of his cause. Indeed, men are so constructed that they feel themselves committed as much by the benefits they grant as by those they receive. Hence, all things considered, it should not be hard for a prudent prince to keep his subjects in good spirits throughout a siege, as long as he does not run short of food or weapons.

*   *   *

On the Reasons Why Men Are Praised or Blamed—Especially Princes

It remains now to be seen what style and principles a prince ought to adopt in dealing with his subjects and friends. I know the subject has been treated frequently before, and I'm afraid people will think me rash for trying to do so again, especially since I intend to differ in this discussion from what others have said. But since I intend to write something useful to an understanding reader, it seemed better to go after the real truth of the matter than to repeat what people have imagined. A great many men have imagined states and princedoms such as nobody ever saw or knew in the real world, for there's such a difference between the way we really live and the way we ought to live that the man who neglects the real to study the ideal will learn how to accomplish his ruin, not his salvation. Any man who tries to be good all the time is bound to come to ruin among the great number who are not good. Hence a prince who wants to keep his post must learn how not to be good, and use that knowledge, or refrain from using it, as necessity requires.

Putting aside, then, all the imaginary things that are said about princes, and getting down to the truth, let me say that whenever men are discussed (and especially princes because they are prominent), there are certain qualities that bring them either praise or blame. Thus some are considered generous, others stingy (I use a Tuscan term, since "greedy" in our speech means a man who wants to take other people's goods; we call a man "stingy" who clings to his own); some are givers, others grabbers; some cruel, others merciful; one man is treacherous, another faithful; one is feeble and effeminate, another fierce and spirited; one humane, another proud; one lustful, another chaste; one straightforward, another sly; one harsh, another gentle; one serious, another playful; one religious, another skeptical, and so on. I know everyone will agree that among these many qualities a prince certainly ought to have all those that are considered good. But since it is impossible to have and exercise them all, because the conditions of human life simply do not allow it, a prince must be shrewd enough to avoid the public disgrace of those vices that would lose him his state. If he possibly can, he should also guard against vices that will not lose him his state; but if he cannot prevent them, he should not be too worried about indulging them. And furthermore, he should not be too worried about incurring blame for any vice without which he would find it hard to save his state. For if you look at matters carefully, you will see that something resembling virtue, if you follow it, may be your ruin, while something else resembling vice will lead, if you follow it, to your security and well-being.

On Liberality and Stinginess

Let me begin, then, with the first of the qualities mentioned above, by saying that a reputation for liberality is doubtless very fine; but the generosity that earns you that reputation can do you great harm. For if you exercise your generosity in a really virtuous way, as you should, nobody will know of it, and you cannot escape the odium of the opposite vice. Hence if you wish to be widely known as a generous man, you must seize every opportunity to make a big display of your giving. A prince of this character is bound to use up his entire revenue in works of ostentation. Thus, in the end, if he wants to keep a name for generosity, he will have to load his people with exorbitant taxes and squeeze money out of them in every way he can. This is the first step in making him odious to his subjects; for when he is poor, nobody will respect him. Then, when his generosity has angered many and brought rewards to a few, the slightest difficulty will trouble him, and at the first approach of danger, down he goes. If by chance he foresees this, and tries to change his ways, he will immediately be labelled a miser.

Since a prince cannot use this virtue [*virtù*] of liberality in such a way as to become known for it unless he harms his own security, he won't mind, if he judges prudently of things, being known as a miser. In due course he will be thought the more liberal man, when people see that his parsimony enables him to live on his income, to defend himself against his enemies, and to undertake major projects without burdening his people with taxes. Thus he will be acting liberally toward all those people from whom he takes nothing (and there are an immense number of them), and in a stingy way toward those people on whom he bestows nothing (and they are very few). In our times, we have seen great things being accomplished only by men who have had the name of misers; all the others have gone under. Pope Julius II, though he used his reputation as a generous man to gain the papacy, sacrificed it in order to be able to make war; the present king of France has waged many wars without levying a single extra tax on his people, simply because he could take care of the extra expenses out of the savings from his long parsimony. If the present king of Spain had a reputation for generosity, he would never have been able to undertake so many campaigns, or win so many of them.

*   *   *

On Cruelty and Clemency: Whether It Is Better to Be Loved or Feared

Continuing now with our list of qualities, let me say that every prince should prefer to be considered merciful rather than cruel, yet he should be careful not to mismanage this clemency of his. People thought Cesare Borgia was cruel, but that cruelty of his reorganized the Romagna, united it, and established it in peace and loyalty. Anyone who views the matter realistically will see that this prince was much more merciful than the people of Florence, who, to avoid the reputation of cruelty, allowed Pistoia to be destroyed. Thus, no prince should mind being called cruel for what he does to keep his subjects united and loyal; he may make examples of a very few, but he will be more merciful in reality than those who, in their tenderheartedness, allow disorders to occur, with their attendant murders and lootings. Such turbulence brings harm to an entire community, while the executions ordered by a prince affect only one individual at a time. A new prince, above all others, cannot possibly avoid a name for cruelty, since new states are always in danger. And Virgil, speaking through the mouth of Dido, says:

> Res dura et regni novitas me talia cogunt
> Moliri, et late fines custode tueri.[1]

Yet a prince should be slow to believe rumors and to commit himself to action on the basis of them. He should not be afraid of his own thoughts; he ought to proceed cautiously, moderating his conduct with prudence and humanity, allowing nei-

---

[1] "Severe pressures and the newness of the regime compel me to these measures. I must maintain the borders against foreign enemies."

ther overconfidence to make him careless, nor overtimidity to make him intolerable.

Here the question arises: is it better to be loved than feared, or vice versa? I don't doubt that every prince would like to be both; but since it is hard to accommodate these qualities, if you have to make a choice, to be feared is much safer than to be loved. For it is a good general rule about men, that they are ungrateful, fickle, liars and deceivers, fearful of danger and greedy for gain. While you serve their welfare, they are all yours, offering their blood, their belongings, their lives, and their children's lives, as we noted above—so long as the danger is remote. But when the danger is close at hand, they turn against you. Then, any prince who has relied on their words and has made no other preparations will come to grief; because friendships that are bought at a price, and not with greatness and nobility of soul, may be paid for but they are not acquired, and they cannot be used in time of need. People are less concerned with offending a man who makes himself loved than one who makes himself feared: the reason is that love is a link of obligation which men, because they are rotten, will break any time they think doing so serves their advantage; but fear involves dread of punishment, from which they can never escape.

Still, a prince should make himself feared in such a way that, even if he gets no love, he gets no hate either; because it is perfectly possible to be feared and not hated, and this will be the result if only the prince will keep his hands off the property of his subjects or citizens, and off their women. When he does have to shed blood, he should be sure to have a strong justification and manifest cause; but above all, he should not confiscate people's property, because men are quicker to forget the death of a father than the loss of a patrimony. Besides, pretexts for confiscation are always plentiful; it never fails that a prince who starts living by plunder can find reasons to rob someone else. Excuses for proceeding against someone's life are much rarer and more quickly exhausted.

*　　*　　*

Returning to the question of being feared or loved, I conclude that since men love at their own inclination but can be made to fear at the inclination of the prince, a shrewd prince will lay his foundations on what is under his own control, not on what is controlled by others. He should simply take pains not to be hated, as I said.

The Way Princes Should Keep Their Word

How praiseworthy it is for a prince to keep his word and live with integrity rather than by craftiness, everyone understands; yet we see from recent experience that those princes have accomplished most who paid little heed to keeping their promises, but who knew how craftily to manipulate the minds of men. In the end, they won out over those who tried to act honestly.

You should consider then, that there are two ways of fighting, one with laws and the other with force. The first is properly a human method, the second belongs to beasts. But as the first method does not always suffice, you sometimes have to turn to the second. Thus a prince must know how to make good use of both the beast and the man. Ancient writers made subtle note of this fact when they wrote that Achilles and many other princes of antiquity were sent to be reared by Chiron the centaur, who trained them in his discipline. Having a teacher who is half man and half beast can only mean that a prince must know how to use both these two natures, and that one without the other has no lasting effect.

Since a prince must know how to use the character of beasts, he should pick for imitation the fox and the lion. As the lion cannot protect him-self from traps, and the fox cannot defend himself from wolves, you have to be a fox in order to be wary of traps, and a lion to overawe the wolves. Those who try to live by the lion alone are badly mistaken. Thus a prudent prince cannot and should not keep his word when to do so would go against his interest, or when the reasons that made him pledge it no longer apply. Doubtless if all men were good, this rule would be bad; but since they are a sad lot, and keep no faith with you, you in your turn are under no obligation to keep it with them.

*   *   *

REVIEW QUESTIONS

1. What, according to Machiavelli, is the basis of political authority?

2. How does his theory differ from others of his day?

3. When he claims that a prince must assume many guises, what is Machiavelli saying about his understanding of human nature?

4. What is the role of artifice in political authority?

5. What might Machiavelli's prince have in common with Castiglione's courtier?

DESIDERIUS ERASMUS OF ROTTERDAM

FROM *Ten Colloquies*

Desiderius Erasmus of Rotterdam (1476–1536) was one of the greatest scholars of his day, measured in terms of his writings and their influence. Educated at Deventer in the Netherlands and in Paris, he began his career as an editor, translator, and popularizer of classical texts. In the humanistic tradition, he used classical tropes as models for his own society, a practice that made him not only a great scholar but also a great satirist. His chief intellectual commitment, however, was the renewal of Christian piety through the study of Christian literature, the Bible and church fathers above all. In this context he is often viewed as the great exponent of Christian humanism, the northern European variant of classical Italian humanism. His translation of the Bible inspired the biblical scholarship of sixteenth-century reformers. His editions of patristic sources remain authoritative to this day. His Ten Colloquies *were written as popular texts to inculcate elegant Latin and to inspire Christian conduct.*

From *Ten Colloquies of Erasmus*, by Desiderius Erasmus, translated by Craig R. Thompson (New York: The Liberal Arts Press, 1957), pp. 120–29.

"Cyclops, or the Gospel Bearer"

CANNIUS: What's Polyphemus hunting here?

POLYPHEMUS: What could I be hunting without dogs or spear? Is that your question?

CANNIUS: Some wood nymph, perhaps.

POLYPHEMUS: A good guess. Look, here's my hunting net.

CANNIUS: What a sight! Bacchus in a lion's skin—Polyphemus with a book—a cat in a saffron gown!

POLYPHEMUS: I've painted this little book not only in saffron but bright red and blue, too.

CANNIUS: I'm not talking about saffron; I said something in Greek. Seems to be a soldierly book, for it's protected by bosses, plates, and brass clasps.

POLYPHEMUS: Take a good look at it.

CANNIUS: I'm looking. Very fine, but you haven't yet decorated it enough.

POLYPHEMUS: What's lacking?

CANNIUS: You should have added your coat of arms.

POLYPHEMUS: What coat of arms?

CANNIUS: The head of Silenus peering out of a wine jug. But what's the book about? The art of drinking?

POLYPHEMUS: Be careful you don't blurt out blasphemy.

CANNIUS: What, you don't mean it's something sacred?

POLYPHEMUS: The most sacred of all, the Gospels.

CANNIUS: By Hercules! What has Polyphemus to do with the Gospels?

POLYPHEMUS: You might as well ask what a Christian has to do with Christ.

CANNIUS: I'm not sure a halberd isn't more fitting for the likes of you. If I were at sea and met a stranger who looked like this, I'd take him for a pirate; if I met him in a wood, for a bandit.

POLYPHEMUS: Yet this very Gospel teaches us not to judge a man by appearances. Just as a haughty spirit often lurks under an ash-colored cowl, so a cropped head, curled beard, stern brow, wild eyes, plumed cap, military cloak, and slashed breeches sometimes cover a true Christian heart.

CANNIUS: Of course. Sometimes a sheep lurks in wolf's clothing, too. And if you trust fables, an ass in a lion's skin.

POLYPHEMUS: What's more, I know a man who has a sheep's head and a fox's heart. I could wish him friends as fair as his eyes are dark, and a character as shining as his complexion.

CANNIUS: If a man with a sheepskin cap has a sheep's head, what a load *you* carry, with both a sheep and an ostrich on your head. And isn't it rather ridiculous to have a bird on your head and an ass in your heart?

POLYPHEMUS: That hurt!

CANNIUS: But it would be well if, as you've decorated the Gospels with various ornaments, the Gospels in turn adorned you. You've decorated them with colors; I wish they might embellish you with good morals.

POLYPHEMUS: I'll take care of that.

CANNIUS: After your fashion, yes.

POLYPHEMUS: But insults aside, you don't condemn those who carry a volume of the Gospels about, do you?

CANNIUS: I'd be the last person in the world to do that.

POLYPHEMUS: What? I seem to you the least person in the world, when I'm taller than you by an ass's head?

CANNIUS: I don't believe you'd be that much taller even if the ass pricked up its ears.

POLYPHEMUS: Certainly by a buffalo's.

CANNIUS: I like the comparison. But I said "last"; I wasn't calling you "least."

POLYPHEMUS: What's the difference between an egg and an egg?

CANNIUS: What's the difference between middle finger and little finger?

POLYPHEMUS: The middle one's longer.

CANNIUS: Very good! What's the difference between ass ears and wolf ears?

POLYPHEMUS: Wolf ears are shorter.

CANNIUS: That's right.

POLYPHEMUS: But I'm in the habit of measuring long and short by span and ell, not by ears.

CANNIUS: Well, the man who carried Christ was called Christopher. You, who carry the Gospels, ought to be called Gospel-bearer instead of Polyphemus.

POLYPHEMUS: Don't you think it's holy to carry the Gospels?

CANNIUS: No—unless you'd agree that asses are mighty holy.

POLYPHEMUS: How so?

CANNIUS: Because one of them can carry three thousand books of this kind. I should think you'd be equal to that load if fitted with the right packsaddle.

POLYPHEMUS: There's nothing farfetched in thus crediting an ass with holiness because he carried Christ.

CANNIUS: I don't envy you that holiness. And if you like, I'll give you relics of the ass that carried Christ, so you can kiss them.

POLYPHEMUS: A gift I'll be glad to get. For by touching the body of Christ that ass was consecrated.

CANNIUS: Obviously those who smote Christ touched him too.

POLYPHEMUS: But tell me seriously, isn't carrying the Gospel about a reverent thing to do?

CANNIUS: Reverent if done sincerely, without hypocrisy.

POLYPHEMUS: Let monks have hypocrisy! What has a soldier to do with hypocrisy?

CANNIUS: But first tell me what hypocrisy is.

POLYPHEMUS: Professing something other than what you really mean.

CANNIUS: But what does carrying a copy of the Gospels profess? A gospel life, doesn't it?

POLYPHEMUS: I suppose so.

CANNIUS: Therefore, when the life doesn't correspond to the book, isn't that hypocrisy?

POLYPHEMUS: Apparently. But what is it truly to bear the Gospel?

CANNIUS: Some bear it in their hands, as the Franciscans do their Rule. Parisian porters, and asses and geldings, can do the same. There are those who bear it in their mouths, harping on nothing but Christ and the Gospel. That's pharisaical. Some bear it in their hearts. The true Gospel bearer, then, is one who carries it in hands and mouth *and* heart.

POLYPHEMUS: Where are these?

CANNIUS: In churches—the deacons, who bear the book, read it to the congregation, and have it by heart.

POLYPHEMUS: Though not all who bear the Gospel in their hearts are devout.

CANNIUS: Don't quibble. A man doesn't bear it in his heart unless he loves it through and through. Nobody loves it wholeheartedly unless he emulates the Gospel in his manner of living.

POLYPHEMUS: I don't follow these subtleties.

CANNIUS: But I'll tell you more bluntly. If you carry a jar of Beaune wine on your shoulder, it's just a burden, isn't it?

POLYPHEMUS: That's all.

CANNIUS: But if you hold the wine in your throat, and presently spit it out?

POLYPHEMUS: Useless—though, really, I'm not accustomed to doing that!

CANNIUS: But if—as you *are* accustomed—you take a long drink?

POLYPHEMUS: Nothing more heavenly.

CANNIUS: Your whole body glows; your face turns rosy; your expression grows merry.

POLYPHEMUS: Exactly.

CANNIUS: The Gospel has the same effect when it penetrates the heart. It makes a new man of you.

POLYPHEMUS: So I don't seem to you to live according to the Gospel?

CANNIUS: You can best decide that question yourself.

POLYPHEMUS: If it could be decided with a battle-ax—

CANNIUS: If someone called you a liar or a rake to your face, what would you do?

POLYPHEMUS: What would I do? He'd feel my fists.

CANNIUS: What if someone hit you hard?

POLYPHEMUS: I'd break his neck for that.

CANNIUS: But your book teaches you to repay insults with a soft answer; and "Whosoever shall smite thee on thy right cheek, turn to him the other also."

POLYPHEMUS: I've read that, but it slipped my mind.

CANNIUS: You pray frequently, I dare say.

POLYPHEMUS: That's pharisaical.

CANNIUS: Long-winded but ostentatious praying is pharisaical. But your book teaches us to pray without ceasing, yet sincerely.

POLYPHEMUS: Still, I do pray sometimes.

CANNIUS: When?

POLYPHEMUS: Whenever I think of it—once or twice a week.

CANNIUS: What do you pray?

POLYPHEMUS: The Lord's Prayer.

CANNIUS: How often?

POLYPHEMUS: Once. For the Gospel forbids vain repetitions as "much speaking."

CANNIUS: Can you concentrate on the Lord's Prayer while repeating it?

POLYPHEMUS: Never tried. Isn't it enough to say the words?

CANNIUS: I don't know, except that God hears only the utterance of the heart. Do you fast often?

POLYPHEMUS: Never.

CANNIUS: But your book recommends prayer and fasting.

POLYPHEMUS: I'd recommend them too, if my belly did not demand something else.

CANNIUS: But Paul says that those who serve their bellies aren't serving Jesus Christ. Do you eat meat on any day whatever?

POLYPHEMUS: Any day it's offered.

CANNIUS: Yet a man as tough as you are could live on hay or the bark of trees.

POLYPHEMUS: But Christ said that a man is not defiled by what he eats.

CANNIUS: True, if it's eaten in moderation, without giving offense. But Paul, the disciple of Christ, prefers starvation to offending a weak brother by his food; and he calls upon us to follow his example, in order that we may please all men in all things.

POLYPHEMUS: Paul's Paul, and I'm me.

CANNIUS: But Egon's job is to feed she-goats.

POLYPHEMUS: I'd rather eat one.

CANNIUS: A fine wish! You'll be a billygoat rather than a she-goat.

POLYPHEMUS: I said *eat* one, not *be* one.

CANNIUS: Very prettily said. Are you generous to the poor?

POLYPHEMUS: I've nothing to give.

CANNIUS: But you would have, if you lived soberly and worked hard.

POLYPHEMUS: I'm fond of loafing.

CANNIUS: Do you keep God's commandments?

POLYPHEMUS: That's tiresome.

CANNIUS: Do you do penance for your sins?

POLYPHEMUS: Christ has paid for us.

CANNIUS: Then why do you insist you love the Gospel?

POLYPHEMUS: I'll tell you. A certain Franciscan in our neighborhood kept babbling from the pulpit against Erasmus' New Testament. I met the man privately, grabbed him by the hair with my left hand, and punched him with my right. I gave him a hell of a beating; made his whole face swell. What do you say to that? Isn't that promoting the Gospel? Next I gave him absolution by banging him on the head three times with this very same book, raising three lumps, in the name of Father, Son, and Holy Ghost.

CANNIUS: The evangelical spirit, all right! This is certainly defending the Gospel with the Gospel.

POLYPHEMUS: I ran across another member of the same order who never stopped raving against Erasmus. Fired with evangelical zeal, I threatened the fellow so much he begged pardon on both knees and admitted the devil had put him up to saying what he said. If he hadn't done this, my halberd would have bounced against his head. I looked as fierce as Mars in battle. This took place before witnesses.

CANNIUS: I'm surprised the man didn't drop dead on the spot. But let's go on. Do you live chastely?

POLYPHEMUS: I may when I'm old. But shall I confess the truth to you, Cannius?

CANNIUS: I'm no priest. If you want to confess, find somebody else.

POLYPHEMUS: Usually I confess to God, but to you I admit I'm not yet a perfect follower of the Gospel; just an ordinary fellow. My kind have four Gospels. Four things above all we Gospelers seek: full bellies; plenty of work for the organs below the belly; a livelihood from somewhere or other; finally, freedom to do as we please. If we get these, we shout in our cups, "Io, triumph; Io, Paean! The Gospel flourishes! Christ reigns!"

CANNIUS: That's an Epicurean life, surely, not an evangelical one.

POLYPHEMUS: I don't deny it, but you know Christ is omnipotent and can turn us into other men in the twinkling of an eye.

CANNIUS: Into swine, too, which I think is more likely than into good men.

POLYPHEMUS: I wish there were no worse creatures in the world than swine, oxen, asses, and camels! You can meet many men who are fiercer than lions, greedier than wolves, more lecherous than sparrows, more snappish than dogs, more venomous than vipers.

CANNIUS: But now it's time for you to begin changing from brute to man.

POLYPHEMUS: You do well to warn me, for prophets these days declare the end of the world is at hand.

CANNIUS: All the more reason to hurry.

POLYPHEMUS: I await the hand of Christ.

CANNIUS: See that you are pliant material for his hand! But where do they get the notion that the end of the world is near?

POLYPHEMUS: They say it's because men are behaving now just as they did before the Flood overwhelmed them. They feast, drink, stuff themselves, marry and are given in marriage, whore, buy, sell, pay and charge interest, build buildings. Kings make war, priests are zealous to increase their wealth, theologians invent syllogisms, monks roam through the world, the commons riot, Erasmus writes colloquies. In short, no calamity is lacking: hunger, thirst, robbery, war, plague, sedition, poverty. Doesn't this prove human affairs are at an end?

CANNIUS: In this mass of woes, what worries you most?

POLYPHEMUS: Guess.

CANNIUS: That your purse is full of cobwebs.

POLYPHEMUS: Damned if you haven't hit it!—Just now I'm on my way back from a drinking party. Some other time, when I'm more sober, I'll argue with you about the Gospel, if you like.

CANNIUS: When shall I see you sober?

POLYPHEMUS: When I'm sober.

CANNIUS: When will you be so?

POLYPHEMUS: When you see me so. Meantime, my dear Cannius, good luck.

CANNIUS: I hope you, in turn, become what you're called.

POLYPHEMUS: To prevent you from outdoing me in courtesy, I pray that Cannius, as the name implies, may never be lacking a can!

REVIEW QUESTIONS

1. Why does Erasmus use the dialogue form?
2. What might he be saying, not only about his readers but also about voice and perspective?
3. What is the older mode of Christianity that Erasmus parodies?
4. What is wrong with it?
5. What ideal of Christian behavior emerges in the colloquy?
6. How might it differ from the older form?
7. How might it be better suited to the instabilities of life in Renaissance Europe?

SIR THOMAS MORE

FROM *Utopia*

Sir Thomas More (1478–1535) was born on Milk Street, in London, the "brightest star that ever shined in the via lactea," according to Thomas Fuller. His father, John More, was a butler at Lincoln's Inn, later raised to the knighthood and made a judge first in the court of common pleas and later on the king's bench. The son was educated in the household of John Morton, archbishop of Canterbury, and at Christ Church, Oxford. Compelled by his father to study law, More entered New Inn in 1494 and Lincoln's Inn in 1496. He lived with the monks at the London Charterhouse and

developed there the discipline and devotion that would serve him well in later trou-
bles. Yet he decided on married rather than monastic life. He wed Jane Colet in 1505
and they had four children. More was an early advocate of education for women; he
insisted that his son and daughters be taught by the best tutors available. Despite his
many interests—intellectual, religious, and domestic—the law remained his career.
City, monarchy, and church called on his services.

   He was part of a London trade delegation to the cities of the Hanse in 1515. Dur-
ing this service, he wrote Book II of Utopia, *describing a pagan, communist city-state*
in which all policies and institutions were governed by reason. Such a state con-
trasted notably with the polity of Christian Europe with its greed, self-interest, and
violence, as More described it in Book I. The complete work, which drew heavily on
descriptions of the new world as well as passages from classical literature, was pub-
lished in 1516 in Louvain. It established More's international reputation as a man of
letters. But public affairs constantly drew him out of his study. In 1523, he served as
speaker of the House of Commons, and in 1529, he succeeded Cardinal Wolsey as
lord chancellor under Henry VIII. The king favored More, keeping him in atten-
dance, visiting him at home, and enjoying his learned conversation. They fell out
over Henry's growing dispute with the Catholic Church. More resigned his office in
1532, the day after the clergy were deprived of the power to enact constitutions with-
out royal consent. Refusal to swear the Oath of Supremacy in 1534, by which he
would have recognized Henry as the supreme head of the church in England, made
More guilty of treason. He was martyred in 1535, in his own words "the king's good
servant but God's first."

From *Utopia*, by Sir Thomas More, translated by Robert M. Adams, A Norton Critical Edition, 2d ed. (New York: Norton, 1975), pp. 30–33, 40–42, 50–51, 64.

*   *   *

"**B**ut as a matter of fact, my dear More, to tell you what I really think, as long as you have private property, and as long as cash money is the measure of all things, it is really not possible for a nation to be governed justly or happily. For justice cannot exist where all the best things in life are held by the worst citizens; nor can anyone be happy where property is limited to a few, since those few are always uneasy and the many are utterly wretched.

   "So I reflect on the wonderfully wise and sacred institutions of the Utopians who are so well governed with so few laws. Among them virtue has its reward, yet everything is shared equally, and all men live in plenty. I contrast them with the many other nations which are constantly passing new ordinances and yet can never order their affairs satisfactorily. In these other nations, whatever a man can get he calls his own private property; but all the mass of laws old and new don't enable him to secure his own, or defend it, or even distinguish it from someone else's property. Different men lay claim, successively or all at once, to the same property; and thus arise innumerable and interminable lawsuits—fresh ones every day. When I consider all these things, I become more sympathetic to Plato and do not wonder that he declined to make laws for any people who refused to share their goods equally. Wisest of men, he easily perceived that the one and only road to the welfare of all lies through the absolute equality of goods. I doubt whether such equality can ever be achieved where property belongs to individual men. However abundant goods may be, when every man tries to get as much as he can for his own exclusive use, a handful of men end up sharing the whole thing, and the rest are left in poverty. The result generally is two sorts of people whose fortunes ought to be interchanged: the rich are rapacious, wicked, and useless, while the poor are unassuming, modest men who work hard, more for the benefit of the public than of themselves.

"Thus I am wholly convinced that unless private property is entirely done away with, there can be no fair or just distribution of goods, nor can mankind be happily governed. As long as private property remains, by far the largest and the best part of mankind will be oppressed by a heavy and inescapable burden of cares and anxieties. This load, I admit, may be lightened a little bit under the present system, but I maintain it cannot be entirely removed. Laws might be made that no one should own more than a certain amount of land or receive more than a certain income. Or laws might be passed to prevent the prince from becoming too powerful and the populace too unruly. It might be made unlawful for public offices to be solicited, or put up for sale, or made burdensome for the office-holder by great expense. Otherwise, officeholders are tempted to get their money back by fraud or extortion, and only rich men can afford to seek positions which ought to be held by wise men. Laws of this sort, I agree, may have as much effect as good and careful nursing has on men who are chronically or even terminally sick. The social evils I mentioned may be alleviated and their effects mitigated for a while, but so long as private property remains, there is no hope at all of effecting a cure and restoring society to good health. While you try to cure one part, you aggravate the disease in other parts. Suppressing one symptom causes another to break out, since you cannot give something to one man without taking it away from someone else."

"But I don't see it that way," I replied. "It seems to me that men cannot possibly live well where all things are in common. How can there be plenty of commodities where every man stops working? The hope of gain will not spur him on; he will rely on others, and become lazy. If a man is driven by want of something to produce it, and yet cannot legally protect what he has gained, what can follow but continual bloodshed and turmoil, especially when respect for magistrates and their authority has been lost? I for one cannot conceive of authority existing among men who are equal to one another in every respect."

*   *   *

"As for the relative ages of the governments," Raphael replied, "you might judge more accurately if you had read their histories. If we believe these records, they had cities before there were even human inhabitants here. What ingenuity has discovered or chance hit upon could have turned up just as well in one place as the other. As a matter of fact, I believe we surpass them in natural intelligence, but they leave us far behind in their diligence and zeal to learn.

"According to their chronicles, they had heard nothing of men-from-beyond-the-equator (that's their name for us) until we arrived, except that once, some twelve hundred years ago, a ship which a storm had blown toward Utopia was wrecked on their island. Some Romans and Egyptians were cast ashore, and never departed. Now note how the Utopians profited, through their diligence, from this one chance event. They learned every single useful art of the Roman civilization either directly from their guests, or indirectly from hints and surmises on which they based their own investigations. What benefits from the mere fact that on a single occasion some Europeans landed there! If a similar accident has hitherto brought any men here from their land, the incident has been completely forgotten, as it will be forgotten in time to come that I was ever in their country. From one such accident they made themselves masters of all our useful inventions, but I suspect it will be a long time before we accept any of their institutions which are better than ours. This willingness to learn, I think, is the really important reason for their being better governed and living more happily than we do, though we are not inferior to them in brains or resources."

*   *   *

Their Occupations

Agriculture is the one occupation at which everyone works, men and women alike, with no exceptions. They are trained in it from childhood, partly in the schools where they learn theory, and partly through field trips to nearby farms, which make something like a game of practical instruction. On these trips they not only watch the work being done, but frequently pitch in and get a workout by doing the jobs themselves.

Besides farm work (which, as I said, everybody performs), each person is taught a particular trade of his own, such as wool-working, linen-making, masonry, metal-work, or carpentry. There is no other craft that is practiced by any considerable number of them. Throughout the island people wear, and down through the centuries they have always worn, the same style of clothing, except for the distinction between the sexes, and between married and unmarried persons. Their clothing is attractive, does not hamper bodily movement, and serves for warm as well as cold weather; what is more, each household can make its own.

Every person (and this includes women as well as men) learns a second trade, besides agriculture. As the weaker sex, women practice the lighter crafts, such as working in wool or linen; the heavier crafts are assigned to the men. As a rule, the son is trained to his father's craft, for which most feel a natural inclination. But if anyone is attracted to another occupation, he is transferred by adoption into a family practicing the trade he prefers. When anyone makes such a change, both his father and the authorities make sure that he is assigned to a grave and responsible householder. After a man has learned one trade, if he wants to learn another, he gets the same permission. When he has learned both, he pursues whichever he likes better, unless the city needs one more than the other.

The chief and almost the only business of the syphogrants is to manage matters so that no one sits around in idleness, and assure that everyone works hard at his trade. But no one has to exhaust himself with endless toil from early morning to late at night, as if he were a beast of burden. Such wretchedness, really worse than slavery, is the common lot of workmen in all countries, except Utopia. Of the day's twenty-four hours, the Utopians devote only six to work. They work three hours before noon, when they go to dinner. After dinner they rest for a couple of hours, then go to work for another three hours. Then they have supper, and at eight o'clock (counting the first hour after noon as one), they go to bed and sleep eight hours.

The other hours of the day, when they are not working, eating, or sleeping, are left to each man's individual discretion, provided he does not waste them in roistering or sloth, but uses them busily in some occupation that pleases him. Generally these periods are devoted to intellectual activity. For they have an established custom of giving public lectures before daybreak; attendance at these lectures is required only of those who have been specially chosen to devote themselves to learning, but a great many other people, both men and women, choose voluntarily to attend. Depending on their interests, some go to one lecture, some to another. But if anyone would rather devote his spare time to his trade, as many do who don't care for the intellectual life, this is not discouraged; in fact, such persons are commended as especially useful to the commonwealth.

*   *   *

But in all this, you may get a wrong impression, if we don't go back and consider one point more carefully. Because they allot only six hours to work, you might think the necessities of life would be in scant supply. This is far from the case. Their working hours are ample to provide not only enough but more than enough of the necessities and even the conveniences of life. You will easily appreciate this if you consider how large a part of the population in other countries exists without doing any work at all. In the first place, hardly any of the women, who are a full half of the population, work; or, if they do, then as a rule their husbands lie snoring in the bed. Then there is a great lazy gang of priests and so-called religious men. Add to them all the rich, especially the landlords, who are commonly called gentlemen and nobility. Include with them their retainers, that mob of swaggering bullies. Finally, reckon in with these the sturdy and lusty beggars, who go about feigning some disease as an excuse for their idleness. You will certainly find that the things which satisfy our needs are produced by far fewer hands than you had supposed.

And now consider how few of those who do work are doing really essential things. For where money is the standard of everything, many superfluous trades are bound to be carried on simply to satisfy luxury and licentiousness. Suppose the multitude of those who now work were limited to a few trades, and set to producing more and more of those conveniences and commodities that nature really requires. They would be bound to produce so much that the prices would drop, and the workmen would be unable to gain a living. But suppose again that all the workers in useless trades were put to useful ones, and that all the idlers (who now guzzle twice as much as the workingmen who make what they consume) were assigned to productive tasks—well, you can easily see how little time each man would have to spend working, in order to produce all the goods that human needs and conveniences require—yes, and human pleasure too, as long as it's true and natural pleasure.

*   *   *

Their Gold and Silver

For these reasons, therefore, they have accumulated a vast treasure, but they do not keep it like a treasure. I'm really quite ashamed to tell you how they do keep it, because you probably won't believe me. I would not have believed it myself if someone had just told me about it; but I was there, and saw it with my own eyes. It is a general rule that the more different anything is from what people are used to, the harder it is to accept. But, considering that all their other customs are so unlike ours, a sensible man will not be surprised that they use gold and silver quite differently than we do. After all, they never do use money among themselves, but keep it

only for a contingency which may or may not actually arise. So in the meanwhile they take care that no one shall overvalue gold and silver, of which money is made, beyond what the metals themselves deserve. Anyone can see, for example, that iron is far superior to either; men could not live without iron, by heaven, any more than without fire or water. But gold and silver have, by nature, no function that we cannot easily dispense with. Human folly has made them precious because they are rare. Like a most wise and generous mother, nature has placed the best things everywhere and in the open, like air, water, and the earth itself; but she has hidden away in remote places all vain and unprofitable things.

If in Utopia gold and silver were kept locked up in some tower, foolish heads among the common people might well concoct a story that the prince and the senate were out to cheat ordinary folk and get some advantage for themselves. They might indeed put the gold and silver into beautiful plateware and rich handiwork, but then in case of necessity the people would not want to give up such articles, on which they had begun to fix their hearts, only to melt them down for soldiers' pay. To avoid all these inconveniences, they thought of a plan which conforms with their institutions as clearly as it contrasts with our own. Unless we've actually seen it working, their plan may seem ridiculous to us, because we prize gold so highly and are so careful about protecting it. With them it's just the other way. While they eat from pottery dishes and drink from glass cups, well made but inexpensive, their chamber pots and stools—all their humblest vessels, for use in the common halls and private homes—are made of gold and silver. The chains and heavy fetters of slaves are also made of these metals. Finally, criminals who are to bear through life the mark of some disgraceful act are forced to wear golden rings on their ears, golden bands on their fingers, golden chains around their necks, and even golden crowns on their heads. Thus they hold gold and silver up to scorn in every conceivable way. As a result, when they have to part with these metals, which other nations give up with as much agony as if they were being disemboweled, the Utopians feel it no more than the loss of a penny.

*   *   *

Slaves

The Utopians enslave prisoners of war only if they are captured in wars fought by the Utopians themselves. The children of slaves are not automatically enslaved, nor are any men who were enslaved in a foreign country. Most of their slaves are either their own former citizens, enslaved for some heinous offense, or else men of other nations who were condemned to death in their own land. Most are of the latter sort. Sometimes the Utopians buy them at a very modest rate, more often they ask for them, get them for nothing, and bring them home in considerable numbers. These kinds of slaves are kept constantly at work, and are always fettered. The Utopians deal with their own people more harshly than with others, feeling that their crimes are worse and deserve stricter punishment because, as it is argued, they had an excellent education and the best of moral training, yet still couldn't be restrained from wrongdoing. A third class of slaves consists of hardworking penniless drudges from other nations who voluntarily choose to become slaves in Utopia. Such people are treated well, almost as well as citizens, except that they are given a little extra work, on the score that they're used to it. If one of them wants to leave, which seldom happens, no obstacles are put in his way, nor is he sent off empty-handed.

*   *   *

REVIEW QUESTIONS

1. Why did More choose to call the place *Utopia*, literally "Nowhere"?
2. What possibilities created by the discovery of a new world does More explore in *Utopia*?
3. How are More's Utopians different from what medieval Europeans would have considered Christian?
4. How does More's attitude toward the people of Utopia reflect attitudes of the Renaissance?
5. How might *Utopia* be critical of Renaissance society?
6. What do More's Utopians have in common with the kind of Christian Erasmus described in his colloquy "Cyclops, or the Gospel-Bearer"?

13 ❧ THE AGE OF DISSENT AND DIVISION, 1500–1564

The year 1492 marked both the end of the expansion of Christianity in Europe, with the final expulsion of the Jews and Muslims from the Iberian Peninsula, and the beginning of the expansion of European Christianity across the globe. So, too, it marked the nadir of papal ambition, venality, and corruption, and thereby the medieval Christian hierarchy. In that year, the Borgia pope, Alexander VI, whom contemporaries such as Machiavelli knew to be rapacious, murderous, treacherous, and ambitious, was elected.

Within a generation of the Reconquista of Spain, the German lands of the grandson of Ferdinando and Isabella of Spain would be split between two very different understandings of Christianity: what it meant to be a Christian, what the Church was and how it was to be constituted, and what the nature of worship was. In part, the Reformation arose in response to perceptions of papal bellicosity and immorality; it belonged to an older tradition of reformatio. *Equally, however, the Reformation was heir to the Renaissance: the philological skills and discoveries of fifteenth-century humanists enabled new approaches to the study of the Bible, and the humanist emphasis on historical accuracy led to a call for a return to apostolic Christianity. That return to the text of Scripture, along with a new sensitivity to historical periods, brought theologians such as Martin Luther to reconsider not only devotional practices but the very structure of authority of medieval Christendom—the papal hierarchy—and others, such as John Calvin, to return to the Acts of the Apostles for a vision of the true church.*

Even as Christendom divided against itself in Europe, it expanded through the persons of conquistadores to create worlds unimagined in the European tradition. Reformation and expansion both came through bloodshed. In Germany, peasants and artisans fought lords and emperor to institute the godly law they found in the Bible, only to be massacred. In France, the Low Countries, and England, as well as the Holy Roman Empire, Christians executed Christians over questions of the Eucharist, the place of images in worship, and the cult of the

*saints. Churches divided from one another, each defining itself against the others,
even as all confronted worlds for which neither the Bible nor the classical tradition had prepared them.*

MARTIN LUTHER

FROM *The Large Catechism*, 1530

Martin Luther (1483–1546), one of the founders of Protestantism, was born of peasant stock. His father had left his fields for the copper mines of Mansfeld in Saxon, where he flourished economically and rose to the status of town councilor. His son, Martin, received a primary education from the Brethren of the Common Life and enrolled at the University of Erfurt in 1501, where he earned his bachelor of arts in 1502 and his master of arts in 1505. His father hoped that his son would continue the family's rise to prominence by pursuing a legal career. These aspirations were shattered when Luther unexpectedly entered a monastery in 1505. As a member of the order of Augustinian Hermits, he began formal training in theology. Selected for advanced training in theology, he made his way to the University of Wittenberg, where he received his doctorate in 1512 and occupied the chair of biblical theology. Even as his academic career prospered, his inner life suffered. Luther was beset by doubts about his own salvation, the result of a consciousness both of his own weakness and of divine righteousness. Long study and meditation led him to a resolution that became the basis for his theology of justification. Salvation was the result of divine grace, freely given; the forgiven conscience could be at peace; the soul could serve God joyfully. Luther having experienced this new conviction, it is not surprising that the extravagant claims surrounding the sale of indulgences in 1517 provoked him to public protest. The form and text of that protest became known as the "95 Theses." His objection to the claim that the pope could remit the temporal punishment of sins led him deeper and deeper into controversy and ultimately to schism. By 1520, the rift between Luther and the Catholic Church had become irreparable and extended to far more issues than papal power. His The Large Catechism, *whose Preface follows, reveals another dimension of Luther's reform: his engagement in the care of souls. Through catechism, a process of recitation and repetition, young people were to be brought to a proper understanding of God's Will and Word. It reveals Luther's familiarity with the Christian Church's past and his hope for its future.*

From *The Large Catechism of Martin Luther*, translated by Robert H. Fischer (Philadelphia: Augsburg Fortress Press, 1959).

Martin Luther's Preface[1]

It is not for trivial reasons that we constantly treat the Catechism and strongly urge others to do the same. For we see to our sorrow that many pastors and preachers[2] are very negligent in this respect and despise both their office and this teaching itself. Some because of their great and lofty learning, others because of sheer laziness and gluttony, behave in this matter as if they were pastors or preachers for their bellies' sake and had nothing to do but live off the fat of the land all their days, as they used to do under the papacy.

Everything that they are to teach and preach is now available to them in clear and simple form in the many excellent books which are in reality what the old manuals claimed in their titles to be: "Sermons That Preach Themselves," "Sleep Soundly," "Prepared!" and "Treasury."[3] However, they are not so upright and honest as to buy these books, or if they have them, to examine and read them. Such shameful gluttons and servants of their bellies would make better swineherds or dogkeepers than spiritual guides and pastors.

Now that they are free from the useless, bothersome babbling of the Seven Hours,[4] it would be fine if every morning, noon, and evening they would read, instead, at least a page or two from the Catechism, the Prayer Book,[5] the New Testament, or something else from the Bible and would pray the Lord's Prayer for themselves and their parishioners. In this way they might show honor and gratitude to the Gospel, through which they have been delivered from so many burdens and troubles, and they might feel a little shame because, like pigs and dogs, they remember no more of the Gospel than this rotten, pernicious, shameful, carnal liberty. As it is, the common people take the Gospel altogether too lightly, and even our utmost exertions accomplish but little. What, then, can we expect if we are sluggish and lazy, as we used to be under the papacy?

Besides, a shameful and insidious plague of security and boredom has overtaken us. Many regard the Catechism as a simple, silly teaching which they can absorb and master at one reading. After reading it once they toss the book into a corner as if they are ashamed to read it again. Indeed, even among the nobility there are some louts and skinflints who declare that we can do without pastors and preachers from now on because we have everything in books and can learn it all by ourselves. So they blithely let parishes fall into decay, and brazenly allow both pastors and preachers to suffer distress and hunger. This is what one can expect of crazy Germans. We Germans have such disgraceful people among us and must put up with them.

As for myself, let me say that I, too, am a doctor and a preacher—yes, and as learned and experienced as any of those who act so high and mighty. Yet I do as a child who is being taught the Catechism. Every morning, and whenever else I have time, I read and recite word for word the Lord's Prayer, the Ten Commandments, the Creed, the Psalms, etc. I must still read and study the Catechism daily, yet I cannot master it as I wish, but must remain a child and pupil of the Catechism, and I do it gladly. These dainty, fastidious fellows would like quickly, with one reading, to become doctors above all doctors, to know all there is to be known. Well, this, too, is a sure sign that they despise both their office and the people's souls, yes, even God and his Word. They need not fear a fall, for they have already fallen all too horribly. What they need is to become children and begin learning their ABC's, which they think they have outgrown long ago.

Therefore, I beg these lazy-bellies and presumptuous saints, for God's sake, to get it into their heads that they are not really and truly such learned

---

[1] In the German edition of the Book of Concord, 1580, this Longer Preface (which dates from 1530) appeared after the Shorter Preface in accordance with the order observed in the fourth German volume of the Jena edition of Luther's Works (1556).

[2] Preachers (*Prediger*) were limited to preaching; pastors (*Pfarrherren*) exercised the full ministerial office.

[3] Titles of medieval sermon books.

[4] The seven canonical hours, daily prayers prescribed by the medieval Breviary.

[5] Luther published the "Little Prayer Book" (*Betbüchlein*) in 1522 to replace Roman Catholic devotional books.

and great doctors as they think. I implore them not to imagine that they have learned these parts of the Catechism perfectly, or at least sufficiently, even though they think they know them ever so well. Even if their knowledge of the Catechism were perfect (though that is impossible in this life), yet it is highly profitable and fruitful daily to read it and make it the subject of meditation and conversation. In such reading, conversation, and meditation the Holy Spirit is present and bestows ever new and greater light and fervor, so that day by day we relish and appreciate the Catechism more greatly. This is according to Christ's promise in Matt. 18:20, "Where two or three are gathered in my name, there am I in the midst of them."

Nothing is so effectual against the devil, the world, the flesh, and all evil thoughts as to occupy oneself with the Word of God, talk about it, and meditate on it. Psalm 1 calls those blessed who "meditate on God's law day and night."[6] You will never offer up any incense or other savor more potent against the devil than to occupy yourself with God's commandments and words and to speak, sing, and meditate on them. This, indeed, is the true holy water, the sign which routs the devil and puts him to flight.[7]

For this reason alone you should eagerly read, recite, ponder, and practice the Catechism, even if the only blessing and benefit you obtain from it is to rout the devil and evil thoughts. For he cannot bear to hear God's Word. God's Word is not like some empty tale, such as the one about Dietrich of Bern,[8] but as St. Paul says in Rom. 1:16, it is "the power of God," indeed, the power of God which burns the devil and gives us immeasurable strength, comfort, and help.

Why should I waste words? Time and paper would fail me if I were to recount all the blessings that flow from God's Word. The devil is called the master of a thousand arts. What, then, shall we call

God's Word, which routs and destroys this master of a thousand arts with all his wiles and might? It must, indeed, be master of more than a hundred thousand arts. Shall we frivolously despise this might, blessing, power, and fruit—especially we who would be pastors and preachers? If so, we deserve not only to be refused food but also to be chased out by dogs and pelted with dung. Not only do we need God's Word daily as we need our daily bread; we also must use it daily against the daily, incessant attacks and ambushes of the devil with his thousand arts.

If this were not enough to admonish us to read the Catechism daily, there is God's command. That alone should be incentive enough. Deut. 6:7, 8 solemnly enjoins that we should always meditate upon his precepts whether sitting, walking, standing, lying down, or rising, and keep them before our eyes and in our hands as a constant token and sign. Certainly God did not require and command this so solemnly without good reason. He knows our danger and need. He knows the constant and furious attacks and assaults of the devil. So he wishes to warn, equip, and protect us against them with good "armor" against their "flaming darts,"[9] and with a good antidote against their evil infection and poison. O what mad, senseless fools we are! We must ever live and dwell in the midst of such mighty enemies as the devils, and yet we despise our weapons and armor, too lazy to give them a thought!

Look at these bored, presumptuous saints who will not or cannot read and study the Catechism daily. They evidently consider themselves much wiser than God himself, and wiser than all his holy angels, prophets, apostles, and all Christians! God himself is not ashamed to teach it daily, for he knows of nothing better to teach, and he always keeps on teaching this one thing without varying it with anything new or different. All the saints know of nothing better or different to learn, though they cannot learn it to perfection. Are we not most marvelous fellows, therefore, if we imagine, after reading or hearing it once, that we know it all and need

---

[6] Ps. 1:2.

[7] I.e., the Word of God really does what holy water was formerly believed to accomplish.

[8] Luther frequently cited the legend of Dietrich of Bern as an example of lies and fables.

[9] Eph. 6:11, 16.

not read or study it any more? Most marvelous fellows, to think we can finish learning in one hour what God himself cannot finish teaching! Actually, he is busy teaching it from the beginning of the world to the end, and all prophets and saints have been busy learning it and have always remained pupils, and must continue to do so.

This much is certain: anyone who knows the Ten Commandments perfectly knows the entire Scriptures. In all affairs and circumstances he can counsel, help, comfort, judge, and make decisions in both spiritual and temporal matters. He is qualified to sit in judgment upon all doctrines, estates, persons, laws, and everything else in the world.

What is the whole Psalter but meditations and exercises based on the First Commandment? Now, I know beyond a doubt that such lazy-bellies and presumptuous fellows do not understand a single Psalm, much less the entire Scriptures, yet they pretend to know and despise the Catechism, which is a brief compend and summary of all the Holy Scriptures.

Therefore, I once again implore all Christians, especially pastors and preachers, not to try to be doctors prematurely and to imagine that they know everything. Vain imaginations, like new cloth, suffer shrinkage! Let all Christians exercise themselves in the Catechism daily, and constantly put it into practice, guarding themselves with the greatest care and diligence against the poisonous infection of such security or vanity. Let them continue to read and teach, to learn and meditate and ponder. Let them never stop until they have proved by experience that they have taught the devil to death and have become wiser than God himself and all his saints.

If they show such diligence, then I promise them—and their experience will bear me out—that they will gain much fruit and God will make excellent men of them. Then in due time they themselves will make the noble confession that the longer they work with the Catechism, the less they know of it and the more they have to learn. Only then, hungry and thirsty, will they truly relish what now they cannot bear to smell because they are so bloated and surfeited. To this end may God grant his grace! Amen.

Preface[10]

This sermon has been undertaken for the instruction of children and uneducated people. Hence from ancient times it has been called, in Greek, a "catechism"—that is, instruction for children. Its contents represent the minimum of knowledge required of a Christian. Whoever does not possess it should not be reckoned among Christians nor admitted to a sacrament,[11] just as a craftsman who does not know the rules and practices of his craft is rejected and considered incompetent. For this reason young people should be thoroughly instructed in the various parts of the Catechism or children's sermons and diligently drilled in their practice.

Therefore, it is the duty of every head of a household to examine his children and servants at least once a week and ascertain what they have learned of it, and if they do not know it, to keep them faithfully at it. I well remember the time when there were old people who were so ignorant that they knew nothing of these things—indeed, even now we find them daily—yet they come to Baptism and the Sacrament of the Altar and exercise all the rights of Christians, although those who come to the sacrament ought to know more and have a fuller understanding of all Christian doctrine than children and beginners at school. As for the common people, however, we should be satisfied if they learned the three parts[12] which have been the heritage of Christendom from ancient times, though they were rarely taught and treated correctly, so that all who wish to be Christians in fact as well as

---

[10] The Shorter Preface is based on a sermon of May 18, 1528.

[11] This was not only a proposal of Luther, but also a medieval prescription; cf. John Surgant, *Manuale Curatorum* (1502), etc.

[12] Ten Commandments, Creed, Lord's Prayer. From 1525 on catechetical instruction in Wittenberg was expanded to include material on Baptism and the Lord's Supper.

in name, both young and old, may be well-trained in them and familiar with them.

I. THE TEN COMMANDMENTS OF GOD

1. You shall have no other gods before me.
2. You shall not take the name of God in vain.
3. You shall keep the Sabbath day holy.
4. You shall honor father and mother.
5. You shall not kill.
6. You shall not commit adultery.
7. You shall not steal.
8. You shall not bear false witness against your neighbor.
9. You shall not covet your neighbor's house.
10. You shall not covet his wife, man-servant, maid-servant, cattle, or anything that is his.[13]

II. THE CHIEF ARTICLES OF OUR FAITH

I believe in God, the Father almighty, maker of heaven and earth:

And in Jesus Christ, his only Son, our Lord: who was conceived by the Holy Spirit, born of the virgin Mary, suffered under Pontius Pilate, was crucified, dead, and buried: he descended into hell, the third day he rose from the dead, he ascended into heaven, and sits on the right hand of God, the Father almighty, whence he shall come to judge the living and the dead.

I believe in the Holy Spirit, the holy Christian church,[14] the communion of saints, the forgiveness of sins, the resurrection of the body, and the life everlasting. Amen.

III. THE PRAYER, OR OUR FATHER, WHICH CHRIST TAUGHT

Our Father who art in heaven, hallowed be thy name. Thy kingdom come, thy will be done, on earth as it is in heaven. Give us this day our daily bread; and forgive us our debts, as we also have forgiven our debtors; and lead us not into temptation, but deliver us from evil. For thine is the kingdom and the power and the glory, forever. Amen.[15]

These are the most necessary parts of Christian instruction. We should learn to repeat them word for word. Our children should be taught the habit of reciting them daily when they rise in the morning, when they go to their meals, and when they go to bed at night; until they repeat them they should not be given anything to eat or drink. Every father has the same duty to his household; he should dismiss man-servants and maid-servants if they do not know these things and are unwilling to learn them. Under no circumstances should a person be tolerated if he is so rude and unruly that he refuses to learn these three parts in which everything contained in Scripture is comprehended in short, plain, and simple terms, for the dear fathers or apostles, whoever they were,[16] have thus summed up the doctrine, life, wisdom, and learning which constitute the Christian's conversation, conduct, and concern.

When these three parts are understood, we ought also to know what to say about the sacraments which Christ himself instituted, Baptism and the holy Body and Blood of Christ, according to the texts of Matthew and Mark at the end of their Gospels where they describe how Christ said farewell to his disciples and sent them forth.

BAPTISM

"Go and teach all nations, and baptize them in the name of the Father and of the Son and of the Holy Spirit" (Matt. 28:19). "He who believes and is baptized will be saved; but he who does not believe will be condemned" (Mark 16:16).

It is enough for an ordinary person to know this much about Baptism from the Scriptures. The

---

[13] Ex. 20:2–17; cf. Deut. 5:6–21.
[14] The translation of *ecclesiam catholicam* by *eine christliche Kirche* was common in fifteenth-century Germany.
[15] Matt. 6:9–13; cf. Luke 11:2–4.
[16] Luther was not interested in defending the apostolic authorship of the Creed.

other sacrament may be dealt with similarly, in short, simple words according to the text of St. Paul.

THE SACRAMENT [OF THE ALTAR]

"Our Lord Jesus Christ on the night when he was betrayed took bread, gave thanks, and broke it and gave it to his disciples, saying, 'Take and eat, this is my body, which is given for you. Do this in remembrance of me.'

"In the same way also the cup, after supper, saying, 'This cup is the new testament in my blood, which is shed for you for the forgiveness of sins. Do this, as often as you drink it, in remembrance of me'" (I Cor. 11:23–25).

Thus we have, in all, five parts covering the whole of Christian doctrine, which we should constantly teach and require young people to recite word for word. Do not assume that they will learn and retain this teaching from sermons alone. When these parts have been well learned, you may assign them also some Psalms or some hymns,[17] based on these subjects, to supplement and confirm their knowledge. Thus our youth will be led into the Scriptures so that they make progress daily.

However, it is not enough for them simply to learn and repeat these parts verbatim. The young people should also attend preaching, especially at the time designated for the Catechism,[18] so that they may hear it explained and may learn the meaning of every part. Then they will also be able to repeat what they have heard and give a good, correct answer when they are questioned, and thus the preaching will not be without benefit and fruit. The reason we take such care to preach on the Catechism frequently is to impress it upon our youth, not in a lofty and learned manner but briefly and very simply, so that it may penetrate deeply into their minds and remain fixed in their memories.

Now we shall take up the above-mentioned parts one by one and in the plainest possible manner say about them as much as is necessary.

REVIEW QUESTIONS

1. Why is the catechism so important to Martin Luther?
2. To whom is the catechism to be taught, and by whom is it to be taught?
3. What matters, issues, or ideas does the catechism teach?
4. What purposes does the catechism serve in the reformation of Luther?
5. What concerns on the part of Luther do these purposes reflect?

---

[17] Luther himself wrote six hymns based on the parts of the Catechism.

[18] Preaching and instruction on the Catechism especially during Lent.

SEBASTIAN LOTZER

The Twelve Articles of the Peasants of Swabia

The Twelve Articles of the Peasants of Swabia, adopted at the free imperial city of Memmingen in 1525, is one of the signal documents of the great agrarian revolt known as the Peasants' War of 1525. More than any other such document, it specifically linked the social and political grievances of the peasants with the evangelical

THE WITTENBERG ALTARPIECE (1547)

LUCAS CRANACH THE ELDER

Created in 1547 by the German Renaissance painter Lucas Cranach the Elder (1472–1553), the Wittenberg altarpiece stands in the City Church of Wittenberg, Luther's own church. Cranach was a court painter to the Electors of Saxony as well as an important figure, at times serving as both a city councilman and mayor, of the city of Wittenberg. In this context, the work came into being. It shows leading figures of the Lutheran Reformation as they perform the "sacraments." On the left front panel, a minister baptizes an infant into the faith; the right panel depicts a minister hearing confession; the center panel shows communion, depicted as the Last Supper of Christ with the leaders of the Lutheran movement as the apostles. The altarpiece seems to suggest, as seems appropriate, given its content and place, that the Lutheran confession is the true church of Christ. In fact, however, it stands in ambiguous relationship to the reformer. Painted after his death, the altarpiece takes a firmer position on the sacramentality of confession than did Luther himself. How do the frames affect your understanding of the three sacraments? Why is the Supper at center? Why is preaching in the predella, or foundation, of the altarpiece? Considering the composition of each panel, what do the postures and gestures of the various figures tell us about their relationship to one another? As ministers play a central role in the altarpiece, what does it communicate about the function of an ideal minister? Comparing this work of Lutheran art to Rubens's The Miracle of St. Ignatius of Loyola, (see page 101) how would you characterize the intended message of the altarpiece to those people, regardless of confession, who might view it? Why do you think Cranach placed Luther in the Last Supper, and what might be the significance of Luther passing the cup to the knight to our right? Again, comparing the work of Cranach to that of Rubens, why do you suppose the architectural elements are relatively minimal in the former? Are they part of the "message"?

principles of the Reformation. Ironically, this document was not composed by a peas-
ant but by a townsman, the journeyman furrier and lay preacher Sebastian Lotzer.
To do so, he summarized and condensed the long (several hundred articles) list of
demands put forward by the peasants of Baltringen. The Memmingen preacher
Christoph Schappeler added a preamble and supplied biblical references in the mar-
gins. This document acquired its importance because it was quickly printed and
widely disseminated. In many areas of the revolt, it was adopted as the basis for lists
of grievances and proposals for settlement.

From *The Revolution of 1525: The German Peasants' War from a New Perspective*, translated
by Thomas A. Brady Jr. (Baltimore: Johns Hopkins University Press, 1981), pp. 195–201.

The Just and Fundamental Articles of All the Peasantry and Tenants of Spiritual and Temporal Powers by Whom They Think Themselves Oppressed

To the Christian reader, the peace and grace of God through Jesus Christ.

There are many antichrists who, now that the peasants are assembled together, seize the chance to mock the gospel, saying, "Is this the fruit of the new gospel: to band together in great numbers and plot conspiracies to reform and even topple the spiritual and temporal powers—yes, even to murder them?" The following articles answer all these godless, blasphemous critics. We want two things: first, to make them stop mocking the word of God; and second, to establish the Christian justice of the current disobedience and rebellion of all the peasants.

First of all, the gospel does not cause rebellions and uproars, because it tells of Christ, the promised Messiah, whose words and life teach nothing but love, peace, patience, and unity. And all who believe in this Christ become loving, peaceful, patient, and one in spirit. This is the basis of all the articles of the peasants (as we will clearly show): to hear the gospel and to live accordingly. How then can the antichrists call the gospel a cause of rebellion and of disobedience? It is not the gospel that drives some antichrists and foes of the gospel to resist and reject these demands and requirements, but the

devil, the deadliest foe of the gospel, who arouses through unbelief such opposition in his own followers. His aim is to suppress and abolish the word of God, which teaches love, peace, and unity.

Second, it surely follows that the peasants, whose articles demand this gospel as their doctrine and rule of life, cannot be called "disobedient" or "rebellious." For if God deigns to hear the peasants' earnest plea that they may be permitted to live according to his word, who will dare deny his will? Who indeed will dare question his judgment? Who will dare oppose his majesty? Did he not hear the children of Israel crying to him and deliver them out of Pharaoh's hand? And can he not save his own today as well? Yes, he will save them, and soon! Therefore, Christian reader, read these articles diligently, and then judge for yourself.

These are the Articles.

THE FIRST ARTICLE

First of all, we humbly ask and beg—and we all agree on this—that henceforth we ought to have the authority and power for the whole community to elect and appoint its own pastor. We also want authority to depose a pastor who behaves improperly. This elected pastor should preach to us the holy gospel purely and clearly, without human additions or human doctrines or precepts. For constant preaching of the true faith impels us to beg God for his grace, that he may instill in us and confirm in us that same true faith. Unless we have his grace in us, we remain mere, useless flesh and blood. For the Scripture clearly teaches that we may come to God only through true faith and can be saved only through His mercy. This is why we need such a guide and pastor; and thus our demand is grounded in Scripture.

THE SECOND ARTICLE

Second, although the obligation to pay a just tithe prescribed in the Old Testament is fulfilled in the New, yet we will gladly pay the large tithe on grain—but only in just measure. Since the tithe should be given to God and distributed among his servants, so the pastor who clearly preaches the word of God deserves to receive it. From now on we want to have our church wardens, appointed by the community, collect and receive this tithe and have our elected pastor draw from it, with the whole community's consent, a decent and adequate living for himself and his. The remainder should be distributed to the village's own poor, again with the community's consent and according to need. What then remains should be kept in case some need to be called up to defend the country; and then the costs can be met from this reserve, so that no general territorial tax will be laid upon the poor folk.

Wherever one or more villages have sold off the tithe to meet some emergency, those purchasers who can show that they bought the tithe with the consent of the whole village shall not be simply expropriated. Indeed we hope to reach fair compromises with such persons, according to the facts of the case, and to redeem the tithe in installments. But wherever the tithe holder—be he clergyman or layman—did not buy the tithe from the whole village but has it from ancestors who simply seized it from the village, we will not, ought not, and do not intend to pay it any longer, except (as we said above) to support our elected pastor. And we will reserve the rest or distribute it to the poor, as the Bible commands. As for the small tithe, we will not pay it at all, for the Lord God created cattle for man's free use; and it is an unjust tithe invented by men alone. Therefore, we won't pay it anymore.

THE THIRD ARTICLE

Third, it has until now been the custom for the lords to own us as their property. This is deplorable, for Christ redeemed and bought us all with his precious blood, the lowliest shepherd as well as the greatest lord, with no exceptions. Thus the Bible proves that we are free and want to be free. Not that we want to be utterly free and subject to no authority at all; God does not teach us that. We ought to live according to the commandments, not according to the lusts of the flesh. But we should love God, recognize him as our Lord in our neighbor, and willingly do all things God commanded us at his Last Supper. This means we should live according to his commandment, which does not teach us to obey only the rulers, but to humble ourselves before everyone. Thus we should willingly obey our elected and rightful ruler, set over us by God, in all proper and Christian matters. Nor do we doubt that you, as true and just Christians, will gladly release us from bondage or prove to us from the gospel that we must be your property.

THE FOURTH ARTICLE

Fourth, until now it has been the custom that no commoner might catch wild game, wildfowl, or fish in the running waters, which seems to us altogether improper, unbrotherly, selfish, and contrary to God's Word. In some places the rulers protect the game to our distress and great loss, for we must suffer silently while the dumb beasts gobble up the crops God gave for man's use, although this offends both God and neighbor. When the Lord God created man, he gave him dominion over all animals, over the birds of the air, and the fish in the waters. Thus we demand that if someone owns a stream, lake, or pond, he should have to produce documentary proof of ownership and show that it was sold to him with the consent of the whole village. In that case we do not want to seize it from him with force but only to review the matter in a Christian way for the sake of brotherly love. But whoever cannot produce adequate proof of ownership and sale should surrender the waters to the community, as is just.

THE FIFTH ARTICLE

Fifth, we have another grievance about wood-cutting, for our lords have seized the woods for themselves alone; and when the poor commoner needs some wood, he has to pay twice the price for it. We think that those woods whose lords, be they clergymen or laymen, cannot prove ownership by purchase should revert to the whole community. And the community should be able to allow in an orderly way each man to gather firewood for his home and building timber free, though only with permission of the community's elected officials. If all the woods have been fairly purchased, then a neighborly and Christian agreement should be reached with their owners about their use. Where the woods were simply seized and then sold to a third party, however, a compromise should be reached according to the facts of the case and the norms of brotherly love and Holy Writ.

THE SIXTH ARTICLE

Sixth, there is our grievous burden of labor services, which the lords daily increase in number and kind. We demand that these obligations be properly investigated and lessened. And we should be allowed, graciously, to serve as our forefathers did, according to God's word alone.

THE SEVENTH ARTICLE

Seventh, in the future we will not allow the lords to oppress us any more. Rather, a man shall have his holding on the proper terms on which it has been leased, that is, by the agreement between lord and peasant. The lord should not force or press the tenant to perform labor or any other service without pay, so that the peasant may use and enjoy his land unburdened and in peace. When the lord needs labor services, however, the peasant should willingly serve his own lord before others; yet a peasant should serve only at a time when his own affairs do not suffer and only for a just wage.

THE EIGHTH ARTICLE

Eighth, we have a grievance that many of us hold lands that are overburdened with rents higher than the land's yield. Thus the peasants lose their property and are ruined. The lords should have honorable men inspect these farms and adjust the rents fairly, so that the peasant does not work for nothing. For every laborer is worthy of his hire.

THE NINTH ARTICLE

Ninth, we have a grievance against the way serious crimes are punished, for they are constantly making new laws. We are not punished according to the severity of the case but sometimes out of great ill will and sometimes out of favoritism. We think that punishments should be dealt out among us according to the ancient written law and the circumstances of the case, and not according to the judge's bias.

THE TENTH ARTICLE

Tenth, we have a grievance that some people have seized meadows and fields belonging to the community. We shall restore these to the community, unless a proper sale can be proved. If they were improperly bought, however, then a friendly and brotherly compromise should be reached, based on the facts.

THE ELEVENTH ARTICLE

Eleventh, we want the custom called death taxes totally abolished. We will not tolerate it or allow widows and orphans to be so shamefully robbed of their goods, as so often happens in various ways, against God and all that is honorable. The very ones who should be guarding and protecting our goods have skinned and trimmed us of them instead. Had they the slightest legal pretext, they would have grabbed everything. God will suffer this no longer but will wipe it all out. Henceforth no one shall have to pay death taxes, whether small or large.

CONCLUSION

Twelfth, we believe and have decided that if any one or more of these articles is not in agreement with God's Word (which we doubt), then this should be proved to us from Holy Writ. We will abandon it, when this is proved by the Bible. If some of our articles should be approved and later found to be unjust, they shall be dead, null, and void from that moment on. Likewise, if Scripture truly reveals further grievances as offensive to God and a burden to our neighbor, we will reserve a place for them and declare them included in our list. We, for our part, will live and exercise our-selves in all Christian teachings, for which we will pray to the Lord God. For he alone, and no other, can give us the truth. The peace of Christ be with us all.

REVIEW QUESTIONS

1. What do the Twelve Articles tell you about relations between the common man and his lords?
2. What are the priorities of the Twelve Articles?
3. What is most important to the petitioners?
4. Why is it so important?
5. What is second in importance?
6. What changes are the petitioners asking for the tithe?
7. What is Godly Law?
8. What might be its applications?
9. What are the implications of Godly Law for the lords?

JOHN CALVIN

FROM Draft of Ecclesiastical Ordinances, September and October 1541

John (Jean) Calvin (1509–1564) was born of bourgeois parents in the city of Noyon in Picardy. Destined by his father for an ecclesiastical career, he received several benefices to finance his education as early as 1521. In 1523, he transferred to the University of Paris, where he imbibed the spirit of humanism from such teachers as Mathurin Cordier and Guillaume Bude. Calvin earned a master of arts degree at Paris and, without abandoning his study of classical languages and literature, turned to law at Orléans in 1528. By 1532, he had earned a doctorate of law. Sometime during his legal training or shortly thereafter, Calvin converted to Protestantism. The year 1534 was decisive for Calvin. Forced to flee Paris because of the proscription of Protestantism, he made his way to Basel, where he began work on his great systematic theology, Institutes of the Christian Religion *(1536). It was immediately recognized as a superb normative statement of reformed theology and established Calvin's stature as a leader among Protestants despite his youth. As the first edition went to press, Calvin made his way to Geneva, where Guillaume Farel enlisted his aid in the reform of the city. The early years of the Reformation in Geneva were stormy, and the doctrines advocated by Calvin met with considerable opposition. In a dispute over church discipline, the city council banished the*

Protestant pastors. Calvin made his way to Strasbourg, where he remained as a colleague of Martin Bucer and minister to the French refugee church until 1541. Meanwhile, political and religious chaos in Geneva eventually forced the government to seek the return of Calvin. He reluctantly consented, but only with the assurance that his entire original scheme of church polity would be instituted. The ecclesiastical ordinance adopted in 1541 encapsulated that polity and became influential for reformed churches throughout Europe. Written four years later, his Catechism of the Church of Geneva *offers a different vision of the reformer's range of activity. He was no less deeply committed to the inner life of the faithful than he was to the explication of doctrine or the organization of the church. The dedication summarizes the role of education in preserving an embattled and isolated religious community. Calvin remained in Geneva from 1541 until his death in 1564, by which time the city that had accepted reform so reluctantly had been transformed into the center of an international Reformation.*

From *John Calvin*, by G. R. Potter and M. Greengrass (London: Edward Arnold, 1983), pp. 71–76.

First there are four orders of offices instituted by our Saviour for the government of his Church: namely, the pastors, then the doctors, next the elders [*nominated and appointed by the government,*] and fourthly the deacons. If we wish to see the Church well-ordered and maintained we ought to observe this form of government.

The Duty of Pastors

Pastors are sometimes named in the Bible as overseers, elders and ministers. Their work is to proclaim the Word of God, to teach, admonish, exhort and reprove publicly and privately, to administer the sacraments and, with the elders or their deputies, to issue fraternal warnings.

The Examination of Pastors

This consists of two parts. The first concerns doctrine—to find out if the candidate has a good and sound knowledge of the Bible; and, secondly, comes his suitability for expounding this to the people for their edification.

Further, to avoid any danger of his having any wrong ideas, it is fitting that he should profess to accept and uphold the teaching approved by the Church.

Questions must be asked to find out if he is a good teacher and he must privately set forth the teaching of our Lord.

Next, it must be ascertained that he is a man of good principles without any known faults.

The Selection of Pastors

First the ministers should choose someone suitable for the position [*and notify the government*]. Then he is to be presented to the council. If he is approved, he will be accepted and received by the council [*as it thinks fit*]. He is then given a certificate to be produced when he preaches to the people, so that he can be received by the common consent of the faithful. If he is found to be unsuitable and this is demonstrated by evidence, there must be a new selection to find another.

As to the manner of introducing him, because the ceremonies previously used led to a great deal of superstition, all that is needed is that a minister should explain the nature of the position to which he has been appointed and then prayers and pleas should be made that our Lord will give him grace to do what is needed.

After election he must take an oath of allegiance to the government following a written form as required of a minister.

Weekly Meetings to be Arranged

In the first place it is desirable that all ministers should meet together once a week. This is to maintain purity and agreement in their teaching and to hold Bible discussions. Attendance shall be compulsory unless there is good reason for absence. . . . As for the preachers in the villages under the control of the government, it is for the city ministers to urge them to attend whenever possible. . . .

What Should be Done in Cases of Difference About Doctrine

If any differences of opinion concerning doctrine should arise, the ministers should gather together and discuss the matter. If necessary, they should call in the elders and commissioners [*appointed by the government*] to assist in the settlement of any difficulties.

There must be some means available to discipline ministers . . . to prevent scandalous living. In this way, respect for the ministry can be maintained and the Word of God not debased by any minister bringing it into scorn and derision. Those who deserve it must be corrected, but at the same time care must be taken to deal with gossip and malicious rumours which can bring harm to innocent parties.

But it is of first importance to notice that certain crimes are quite incompatible with the ministry and cannot be dealt with by fraternal rebuke. Namely heresy, schism, rebellion against Church discipline, open blasphemy deserving civil punishment, simony and corrupt inducement, intriguing to take over one another's position, leaving the Church without special permission, forgery.

There Follows the Second Order Which We Have Called the Doctors

The special duty of the doctors is to instruct the faithful in sound doctrine so that the purity of the gospel is not corrupted by ignorance or wrong opinion.

As things stand at present, every agent assisting in the upholding of God's teaching is included so that the Church is not in difficulties from a lack of pastors and ministers. This is in common parlance the order of school teachers. The degree nearest the minister and closely joined to the government of the Church is the lecturer in theology.

Establishment of a College

Because it is only possible to profit from such teaching if one is first instructed in languages and humanities, and also because it is necessary to lay the foundations for the future . . . a college should be instituted for instructing children to prepare them for the ministry as well as for civil government.

In the first place suitable accommodation needs to be provided for the teaching of children and others who want to take advantage of it. We also need a literate, scholarly and trained teacher who can take care of the establishment and their education. He should be chosen and paid on the understanding that he should have under his charge teachers in languages and logic, if they can be found. He should also have some student teachers (*bacheliers*) to teach the little ones. . . .

All who are engaged must be subject to the same ecclesiastical ordinances as apply to the ministers.

There is to be no other school in the city for small children, although the girls are to have a separate school of their own as has been the case up to now.

No one is to be appointed without the approval of the ministers—essential to avoid trouble. [*The candidate must first have been notified to the government and then presented to the council. Two members of the 'council of 24' should be present at all interviews.*]

Here Follows the Third Order, or Elders

Their duty is to supervise every person's conduct. In friendly fashion they should warn backsliders and those of disorderly life. After that, where necessary, they should report to the Company [of pastors] who will arrange for fraternal correction. . . .

As our Church is now arranged, it would be most suitable to have two elected from the 'council of 24', four from the 'council of 60' and six from the 'council of 200'. They should be men of good repute and conduct. . . . They should be chosen from each quarter of the city so that they can keep an eye on the whole of it.

Method of Choosing the Elders

Further we have decided upon the machinery for choosing them. The 'council of 24' will be asked to nominate the most suitable and adequate men they can discover. In order to do this, they should discuss the matter with the ministers and then present their suggestions to the 'council of 200' for approval. If they are found worthy [and approved], they must take an oath in the same form as it is presented to the ministers. At the end of the year and after the elections to the council, they should present themselves to the government so that a decision can be made as to whether they shall be re-appointed or not, but they should not be changed frequently and without good cause provided that they are doing their work faithfully.

The Fourth Order of Ecclesiastical Government, Namely, the Deacons

There have always been two kinds of these in the early Church. One has to receive, distribute and care for the goods of the poor (i.e. daily alms as well as possessions, rents and pensions); the other has to tend and look after the sick and administer the allowances to the poor as is customary. [*In order to avoid confusion*], since we have officials and hospital staff, [*one of the four officials of the said hospital should be responsible for the whole of its property and revenues and he should have an adequate salary in order to do his work properly*].

Concerning the Hospital[1]

Care should be taken to see that the general hospital is properly maintained. This applies to the sick, to old people no longer able to work, to widows, orphans, children and other poor people. These are to be kept apart and separate from others and to form their own community.

Care for the poor who are scattered throughout the city shall be the responsibility of the officials. In addition to the hospital for those visiting the city, which is to be kept up, separate arrangements are to be made for those who need special treatment. To this end a room must be set apart to act as a reception room for those that are sent there by the officials. . . .

Further, both for the poor people in the hospital and for those in the city who have no means, there must be a good physician and surgeon provided at the city's expense. . . .

As for the plague hospital, it must be kept entirely separate.

Begging

In order to stop begging, which is contrary to good order, the government should use some of its officers to remove any beggars who are obstinately present when people come out of Church.

And this especially if it should happen that the city is visited by this sourge of God.

Of the Sacraments

Baptism is to take place only at sermon time and is to be administered only by ministers or their assistants. A register is to be kept of the names of the children and of their parents: the justice department is to be informed of any bastard.

Since the Supper was instituted by our Lord to be more often observed by us and also since this was the case in the early Church until such time as

---

[1] The Geneva general hospital had been established in 1535 in one of the series of measures by which the city had broken all connections with the Roman Catholic Church, and which consolidated the various confraternities and eight charitable foundations of the city.

the devil upset everything by setting up the mass in its place, the defect ought to be remedied by celebrating it a little more frequently. All the same, for the time being we have agreed and ordained that it should be administered four times a year, i.e. at Christmas, Easter, Pentecost and the first Sunday in September in the autumn.

The ministers shall distribute the bread in orderly and reverent fashion and no other person shall offer the chalice except those appointed (or the deacons) along with the ministers and for this reason there is no need for many plates and cups.

The tables should be set up close to the pulpit so that the mystery can be more suitably set forth near by.

Celebration should take place only in church and at the most suitable time.

Of the Order Which Must be Observed in Obedience to Those in Authority, for the Maintenance of Supervision in the Church

A day should be fixed for the consistory. The elders should meet once a week with the ministers, on a Thursday, to ensure that there is no disorder in the Church and to discuss together any necessary remedial action.

Since they have neither the power nor the authority to use force, we have agreed to assign one of our officials to them to summon those whom they wish to admonish.

If any one should deliberately refuse to appear, the council is to be informed so as to take action.

If any one teaches things contrary to the received doctrine he shall be summoned to a conference. If he listens to reason, let him be sent back without any scandal or disgrace. If he is obstinate, he should be admonished several times until it is apparent that greater severity is needed: then he

shall be forbidden to attend the communion of the Supper and he shall be reported to the magistrates.

If any one fails to come to church to such a degree that there is real dislike for the community of believers manifested, or if any one shows that he cares nothing for ecclesiastical order, let him be admonished, and if he is tractable let him be amicably sent back. If however he goes from bad to worse, after having been warned three times, let him be cut off from the Church and be denounced to the magistrate. . . .

[*All this must be done in such a way that the ministers have no civil jurisdiction nor use anything but the spiritual sword of the word of God as St Paul commands them; nor is the authority of the consistory to diminish in any way that of the magistrate or ordinary justice. The civil power must remain unimpaired. In cases where, in future, there may be a need to impose punishments or constrain individuals, then the ministers and the consistory, having heard the case and used such admonitions and exhortations as are appropriate, should report the whole matter to the council which, in turn, will judge and sentence according to the needs of the case.*]

*　　*　　*

REVIEW QUESTIONS

1. What is the church according to Calvin?
2. What is its structure?
3. What do the four offices tell us about the function of the church?
4. What is the purpose of the church?
5. What are its goals?
6. What are the practices of the church and the relation of those practices to the process of becoming a Christian?
7. What is the relation between the church and salvation?

JOHN CALVIN

FROM Catechism of the Church of Geneva, Being a Form of Instruction for Children in the Doctrine of Christ, 1545

From *Tracts Relating to the Reformation*, vol. 2, by John Calvin, translated by Henry Beveridge (Edinburgh: The Calvin Translation Society, 1844–1851), pp. 34–37.

Dedication.

JOHN CALVIN TO THE FAITHFUL MINISTERS OF CHRIST THROUGHOUT EAST FRIESLAND, WHO PREACH THE PURE DOCTRINE OF THE GOSPEL.

Seeing it becomes us to endeavour by all means that unity of faith, which is so highly commended by Paul, shine forth among us, to this end chiefly ought the formal profession of faith which accompanies our common baptism to have reference. Hence it were to be wished, not only that a perpetual consent in the doctrine of piety should appear among all, but also that one Catechism were common to all the Churches. But as, from many causes, it will scarcely ever obtain otherwise than that each Church shall have its own Catechism, we should not strive too keenly to prevent this; provided, however, that the variety in the mode of teaching is such, that we are all directed to one Christ, in whose truth being united together, we may grow up into one body and one spirit, and with the same mouth also proclaim whatever belongs to the sum of faith. Catechists not intent on this end, besides fatally injuring the Church, by sowing the materials of dissension in religion, also introduce an impious profanation of baptism. For where can any longer be the utility of baptism unless this remain as its foundation—that we all agree in one faith?

Wherefore, those who publish Catechisms ought to be the more carefully on their guard, lest, by producing anything rashly, they may not for the present only, but in regard to posterity also, do grievous harm to piety, and inflict a deadly wound on the Church.

This much I wished to premise, as a declaration to my readers, that I myself too, as became me, have made it my anxious care not to deliver any thing in this Catechism of mine that is not agreeable to the doctrine received among all the pious. This declaration will not be found vain by those who will read with candour and sound judgment. I trust I have succeeded at least so far that my labour, though it should not satisfy, will be acceptable to all good men, as being in their opinion useful.

In writing it in Latin, though some perhaps will not approve of the design, I have been influenced by many reasons, all of which it is of no use to detail at present. I shall only select such as seem to me sufficient to obviate censure.

First, In this confused and divided state of Christendom, I judge it useful that there should be public testimonies, whereby churches which, though widely separated by space, agree in the doctrine of Christ, may mutually recognise each other. For besides that this tends not a little to mutual confirmation, what is more to be desired than that mutual congratulations should pass between them, and that they should devoutly commend each other to the Lord? With this view, bishops were wont in old time, when as yet consent in faith existed and flourished among all, to send Synodal Epistles beyond sea, by which, as a kind of badges, they might maintain sacred communion among the churches. How much more necessary is it now, in this fearful devastation of the Christian world, that the few churches which duly worship God, and they too scattered and hedged round on all sides by the profane synagogues of Antichrist, should mutually give and receive this token of holy union, that they may thereby be incited to that fraternal embrace of which I have spoken?

But if this is so necessary in the present day, what shall our feelings be concerning posterity, about which I am so anxious, that I scarcely dare to think? Unless God miraculously send help from heaven, I cannot avoid seeing that the world is threatened with the extremity of barbarism. I wish our children may not shortly feel, that this has been rather a true prophecy than a conjecture. The more, therefore, must we labour to gather together, by our writings, whatever remains of the Church shall continue, or even emerge, after our death. Writings of a different class will show what were our views on all subjects in religion, but the agreement which our churches had in doctrine cannot be seen with clearer evidence than from catechisms. For therein will appear, not only what one man or other once taught, but with what rudiments learned and unlearned alike amongst us, were constantly imbued from childhood, all the faithful holding them as their formal symbol of Christian communion. This was indeed my principal reason for publishing this Catechism.

A second reason, which had no little weight with me, was, because I heard that it was desired by very many who hoped it would not be unworthy of perusal. Whether they are right or wrong in so judging is not mine to decide, but it became me to yield to their wish. Nay, necessity was almost laid upon me, and I could not with impunity decline it. For having seven years before published a brief summary of religion, under the name of a Catechism, I feared that if I did not bring forward this one, I should cause (a thing I wished not) that the former should on the other hand be excluded. Therefore if I wished to consult the public good, it behoved me to take care that this one which I preferred should occupy the ground.

Besides, I deem it of good example to testify to the world, that we who aim at the restitution of the Church, are everywhere faithfully exerting ourselves, in order that, at least, the use of the Catechism which was abolished some centuries ago under the Papacy, may now resume its lost rights. For neither can this holy custom be sufficiently commended for its utility, nor can the Papists be sufficiently condemned for the flagrant corruption, by which they not only set it aside, by converting it into puerile trifles, but also basely abuse it to purposes of impure and impious superstition. That spurious Confirmation, which they have substituted in its stead, they deck out like a harlot, with great splendour of ceremonies, and gorgeous shows without number; nay, in their wish to adorn it, they speak of it in terms of execrable blasphemy, when they give out that it is a sacrament of greater dignity than baptism, and call those only half Christians who have not been besmeared with their oil. Meanwhile, the whole proceeding consists of nothing but theatrical gesticulations, or rather the wanton sporting of apes, without any skill in imitation.

To you, my very dear brethren in the Lord, I have chosen to inscribe this work, because some of your body, besides informing me that you love me, and that the most of you take delight in my writings, also expressly requested me by letter to undertake this labour for their sake. Independently of this, it would have been reason sufficient, that what I learned of you long ago, from the statement of grave and pious men, had bound me to you with my whole soul. I now ask what I am confident you will of your own accord do—have the goodness to consult for the utility of this token of my goodwill towards you! Farewell. May the Lord increase you more and more in the spirit of wisdom, prudence, zeal, and fortitude, to the edification of his Church.

GENEVA, *2d December*, 1545.

TO THE READER.

It has ever been the practice of the Church, and one carefully attended to, to see that children should be duly instructed in the Christian religion. That this might be done more conveniently, not only were schools opened in old time, and individuals enjoined properly to teach their families, but it was a received public custom and practice, to question children in the churches on each of the heads, which should be common and well known to all Christians. To secure this being done in order, there was written out a formula, which was called a Catechism or Institute. Thereafter the devil miserably rending the Church of God, and bringing upon it fearful ruin, (of which the marks are still too visible in the greater part of the world,) overthrew this sacred policy, and left nothing behind but certain trifles, which only beget superstition, without any fruit of edification. Of this description is that confirmation, as they call it, full of gesticulations which, worse than ridiculous, are fitted only for apes, and have no foundation to rest upon. What we now bring forward, therefore, is nothing else than the use of things which from ancient times were observed by Christians, and the true worshippers of God, and which never were laid aside until the Church was wholly corrupted.

REVIEW QUESTIONS

1. What is the purpose of catechism for John Calvin, and how does his purpose differ from that of Martin Luther?
2. Who, according to Calvin, should be taught catechism, and who should do the teaching?
3. How did Calvin reconcile the unity of faith, which he hoped his catechism would serve, and the diversity of local circumstances andobservances, which he expected would be the case?
4. What do this hope for unity and this admission of diversity tell us about the Reformation as Calvin understood it?
5. Use the catechism as a measure of the reformers' concerns and goals to explain how had these changed between 1530, when Luther published his *Large Catechism*, and 1545, when Calvin dedicated the *Catechism of the Church of Geneva*. Do the titles reveal anything?
6. Why did Calvin compose his catechism in Latin rather than a vernacular language, as did Martin Luther?

SAINT IGNATIUS OF LOYOLA

FROM *The Spiritual Exercises*

Saint Ignatius of Loyola (1491–1556), the great mystic and founder of the Society of Jesus, was born into a hidalgo family and spent his early manhood in military service to the king of Spain. Wounded in battle, he spent his convalescence reading the lives of saints, which awoke in him a sense of spiritual inadequacy not unlike those which fired the religious engagements of Martin Luther and John Calvin. His early attempts at reconciliation, in the form of physical austerities practiced on pilgrimage to Montserrat and in the hermitage at Manresa, failed to reassure him of his soul's salvation, just as they failed to ease the spiritual torments of the young Luther. The scholastically trained Luther sought solace in the systematic study of the Bible; the uneducated Loyola found it in visions of God. Loyola spent the next decade educating himself and seeking his mission. After a pilgrimage to the Holy Land in 1523, Loyola began his formal education by studying elementary Latin with schoolboys in Barcelona. He attended the universities in Alcalá and Salamanca, preached in the streets, and was arrested by the Inquisition on suspicion of heresy. He attended the University of Paris from 1528 to 1535 and began to gather around him the companions who would form the initial core of the Society of Jesus. In 1534, he and nine companions swore an oath of poverty and chastity and promised either to undertake a crusade to the Holy Land or, failing that, to offer absolute obedience to the pope. At the center of this group was not only the man Loyola but his series of devotions and meditations that would later be published as The Spiritual Exercises *(1548). These exercises offered a practical and ascetic meditation on the life and death of Christ that drew much from the systematic meditations of the* devotio moderna *("modern devotions"). This system instructed those who made or directed a religious retreat in order to stimulate an imitation of Christ that would be expressed in apostolic action as well as religious devotion. In 1535, Loyola and his company left for Italy. He was ordained in Venice in 1537. Finding no passage to the Holy Land, they continued to Rome, where they preached in the streets and ministered to the poor. Introduced to Pope Paul III by Gasparo Contarini, a great advocate of monastic reform, the company received a charter of foundation as the Society of Jesus in 1540. Constituted an order of clerks regular, devoted to educating the young and propagating the faith, sworn to poverty and obedience, the Jesuits grew quickly to become one of the most influential Catholic orders of the early modern period, a model of piety, discipline, education, and service.*

From *The Spiritual Exercises of St. Ignatius of Loyola,* translated from the *Autograph* by Father Elder Mullen, S. J. (New York: P. J. Kennedy and Sons, 1914).

To Have the True Sentiment Which We Ought to Have in the Church Militant

Let the following Rules be observed.

First Rule. All judgment laid aside, we ought to have our mind ready and prompt to obey, in all, the true Spouse of Christ our Lord, which is our holy Mother the Church Hierarchical.

Second Rule. To praise confession to a Priest, and the reception of the most Holy Sacrament of the Altar once in the year, and much more each month, and much better from week to week, with the conditions required and due.

Third Rule. To praise the hearing of Mass often, likewise hymns, psalms, and long prayers, in the church and out of it; likewise the hours set at the time fixed for each Divine Office and for all prayer and all Canonical Hours.

Fourth Rule. To praise much Religious Orders, virginity and continence, and not so much marriage as any of these.

Fifth Rule. To praise vows of Religion, of obedience, of poverty, of chastity and of other perfections of supererogation. And it is to be noted that as the vow is about the things which approach to Evangelical perfection, a vow ought not to be made in the things which withdraw from it, such as to be a merchant, or to be married, etc.

Sixth Rule. To praise relics of the Saints, giving veneration to them and praying to the Saints; and to praise Stations, pilgrimages, Indulgences, pardons, Cruzadas, and candles lighted in the churches.

Seventh Rule. To praise Constitutions about fasts and abstinence, as of Lent, Ember Days, Vigils, Friday and Saturday; likewise penances, not only interior, but also exterior.

Eighth Rule. To praise the ornaments and the buildings of churches; likewise images, and to venerate them according to what they represent.

Ninth Rule. Finally, to praise all precepts of the Church, keeping the mind prompt to find reasons in their defence and in no manner against them.

Tenth Rule. We ought to be more prompt to find good and praise as well the Constitutions and recommendations as the ways of our Superiors. Because, although some are not or have not been such, to speak against them, whether preaching in public or discoursing before the common people, would rather give rise to fault-finding and scandal than profit; and so the people would be incensed against their Superiors, whether temporal or spiritual. So that, as it does harm to speak evil to the common people of Superiors in their absence, so it can make profit to speak of the evil ways to the persons themselves who can remedy them.

Eleventh Rule. To praise positive and scholastic learning. Because, as it is more proper to the Positive Doctors, as St. Jerome, St. Augustine and St. Gregory, etc., to move the heart to love and serve God our Lord in everything; so it is more proper to the Scholastics, as St. Thomas, St. Bonaventure, and to the Master of the Sentences, etc., to define or explain for our times the things necessary for eternal salvation; and to combat and explain better all errors and all fallacies. For the Scholastic Doctors, as they are more modern, not only help themselves with the true understanding of the Sacred Scripture and of the Positive and holy Doctors, but also, they being enlightened and clarified by the Divine virtue, help themselves by the Councils, Canons and Constitutions of our holy Mother the Church.

Twelfth Rule. We ought to be on our guard in making comparison of those of us who are alive to the blessed passed away, because error is committed not a little in this; that is to say, in saying, this one knows more than St. Augustine; he is another, or greater than, St. Francis; he is another St. Paul in goodness, holiness, etc.

Thirteenth Rule. To be right in everything, we ought always to hold that the white which I see, is black, if the Hierarchical Church so decides it, believing that between Christ our Lord, the Bridegroom, and the Church, His Bride, there is the same Spirit which governs and directs us for the salvation of our souls. Because by the same Spirit and our Lord Who gave the ten Commandments, our holy Mother the Church is directed and governed.

Fourteenth Rule. Although there is much truth in the assertion that no one can save himself without being predestined and without having faith and grace; we must be very cautious in the manner of speaking and communicating with others about all these things.

Fifteenth Rule. We ought not, by way of custom, to speak much of predestination; but if in some way and at some times one speaks, let him so speak that the common people may not come into any error, as sometimes happens, saying: Whether I have to be saved or condemned is already determined, and no other thing can now be, through my doing well or ill; and with this, growing lazy, they become negligent in the works which lead to the salvation and the spiritual profit of their souls.

Sixteenth Rule. In the same way, we must be on our guard that by talking much and with much insistence of faith, without any distinction and explanation, occasion be not given to the people to be lazy and slothful in works, whether before faith is formed in charity or after.

Seventeenth Rule. Likewise, we ought not to speak so much with insistence on grace that the poison of discarding liberty be engendered. So that of faith and grace one can speak as much as is possible with the Divine help for the greater praise of His Divine Majesty, but not in such way, nor in such manners, especially in our so dangerous times, that works and free will receive any harm, or be held for nothing.

Eighteenth Rule. Although serving God our Lord much out of pure love is to be esteemed above all; we ought to praise much the fear of His Divine Majesty, because not only filial fear is a thing pious and most holy, but even servile fear—when the man reaches nothing else better or more useful— helps much to get out of mortal sin. And when he is out, he easily comes to filial fear, which is all acceptable and grateful to God our Lord: as being at one with the Divine Love.

*   *   *

THE MIRACLE OF ST. IGNATIUS OF LOYOLA (C. 1620)   PETER PAUL RUBENS

The Miracle of St. Ignatius of Loyola *was painted by Peter Paul Rubens (1577–1640) a pro-*
lific seventeenth-century Flemish Baroque painter, whose works exemplify an exuberant
Baroque style, full of movement, color, and sensuality. He is well-known for his Catholic
altarpieces, portraits, landscapes, and history paintings on mythological and allegorical
themes. In addition to running a large studio in Antwerp, which produced paintings popu-
lar with nobility and art collectors throughout Europe, Rubens was a classically-educated
humanist scholar, art collector, Catholic diplomat and, it has been speculated, a Protestant
spy. This particular painting, commissioned for the Jesuit church in Antwerp, is one of two
treatments of the miracle of Saint Ignatius that were completed sometime around 1620.
They show the saint, Ignatius of Loyola, founder of the Society of Jesus, standing before the
altar and performing miracles, including the casting out of demons to the amazement of his
congregation below. How does Rubens capture the spirit of Catholic reform and its response
to Protestant criticism in his painting? Given that the Council of Trent authorized the use of
images for teaching doctrine, what lessons about doctrine and about the function of saints
in religious life might you take away from this image? What do the positions of the various
bodies, especially the gesturing of the hands, tell us about the relationship of the human
figures to one another? In particular, why did Rubens elevate Loyola above some men and
women, but place a row of figures, all in Jesuit habit alongside him? Given that both the
Cranach and the Rubens are altarpieces, that is, paintings intended to be place over an
altar, what does each tell you about worship in its respective Church? What makes this
painting "baroque"? Contrasting Rubens's religious masterpiece with an early masterpiece,
for example, Raphael's The School of Athens *(p. 57), what sets them apart?*

REVIEW QUESTIONS

1. What do you suppose Loyola means by the *Church Militant?*
2. How might the Jesuits have been soldiers of Christ?

3. Loyola asks the members of his order to "praise" in order to be "thinking with the Church." How does this serve the Church?
4. What specifically does Loyola ask the Jesuits to praise?
5. What do the "Rules for Thinking with the Church" tell us about the Church?

SAINT FRANCIS XAVIER

FROM "Letter from India"

Saint Francis Xavier (1506–1552) was one of the original companions of Saint Ignatius of Loyola and one of the original members of the Society of Jesus. The two became friends during their student years at the University of Paris. Shortly after the founding of the Society, Loyola sent Xavier on a mission to Portugal's mercantile empire in South Asia. After a voyage that lasted more than a year, he arrived in Goa on the Coromandel coast of India, accompanied by the Portuguese governor, Don Martin Alfonso de Sousa, and two fellow missionaries, Father Paul and Francis Mancias, not yet in holy orders. It was at Sousa's behest that Xavier turn his attention to the pearl-fishing villages of Cape Comorin, in an effort to spread Christianity among those peoples and, so, bring them more fully into the Portuguese sphere of influence. It was from Comorin that Xavier wrote the following letter. He would remain there two years before spreading his mission to the East Indies and Japan. He died in 1552, waiting to extend his work to China. His was a life of extraordinary hardship and danger as well as extraordinary activity and achievement. To him belongs credit for extending Roman Christianity and Western ideas to Asian peoples.

From *The Life and Letters of St Francis Xavier*, vol. 1, edited by Henry James Coleridge, 2d ed. (London: Burns and Oates, 1890), pp. 151–63.

To the Society at Rome

May the grace and charity of Christ our Lord always help and favour us! Amen.

It is now the third year since I left Portugal. I am writing to you for the third time, having as yet received only one letter from you, dated February 1542. God is my witness what joy it caused me. I only received it two months ago—later than is usual for letters to reach India, because the vessel which brought it had passed the winter at Mozambique.

I and Francis Mancias are now living amongst the Christians of Comorin. They are very numerous, and increase largely every day. When I first came I asked them, if they knew anything about our Lord Jesus Christ? but when I came to the points of faith in detail and asked them what they thought of them, and what more they believed now than when they were Infidels, they only replied that they were Christians, but that as they are ignorant of Portuguese, they know nothing of the precepts and mysteries of our holy religion. We could not understand one another, as I spoke Castilian and they Malabar; so I picked out the most intelligent and well read of them, and then sought out with the greatest diligence men who knew both languages. We held meetings for several days, and by our joint efforts and with infinite difficulty we translated the Catechism into the Malabar tongue. This I learnt by heart, and then I began to go through all the villages of the coast, calling around me by the sound of a bell as many as I could, children and men. I asembled them twice a day and taught them the Christian doctrine: and thus, in the space of a month, the children had it well by heart. And all the time I kept telling them to go on teaching in their turn whatever they had learnt to their parents, family, and neighbours.

Every Sunday I collected them all, men and women, boys and girls, in the church. They came with great readiness and with a great desire for instruction. Then, in the hearing of all, I began by calling on the name of the most holy Trinity, Father, Son, and Holy Ghost, and I recited aloud the Lord's Prayer, the *Hail Mary*, and the Creed in the language of the country: they all followed me in the same words, and delighted in it wonderfully. Then I repeated the Creed by myself, dwelling upon each article singly. Then I asked them as to each article, whether they believed it unhesitatingly; and all, with a loud voice and their hands crossed over their breasts, professed aloud that they truly believed it. I take care to make them repeat the Creed oftener than the other prayers; and I tell them that those who believe all that is contained therein are called Christians. After explaining the Creed I go on to the Commandments, teaching them that the Christian law is contained in those ten precepts, and that every one who observes them all faithfully is a good and true Christian and is certain of eternal salvation, and that, on the other hand, whoever neglects a single one of them is a bad Christian, and will be cast into hell unless he is truly penitent for his sin. Converts and heathen alike are astonished at all this, which shows them the holiness of the Christian law, its perfect consistency with itself, and its agreement with reason. . . .

*   *   *

The fruit that is reaped by the baptism of infants, as well as by the instruction of children and others, is quite incredible. These children, I trust heartily, by the grace of God, will be much better than their fathers. They show an ardent love for the Divine law, and an extraordinary zeal for learning our holy religion and imparting it to others. Their hatred for idolatry is marvellous. They get into feuds with the heathen about it, and whenever their own parents practise it, they reproach them and come off to tell me at once. Whenever I hear of any act of idolatrous worship, I go to the place with a large band of these children, who very soon load the devil with a greater amount of insult and abuse than he has lately received of honour and worship from their parents, relations, and acquaintances. The children run at the idols, upset them, dash them down, break them to pieces, spit on them, trample on them, kick them about, and in short heap on them every possible outrage.

I had been living for nearly four months in a Christian village, occupied in translating the Catechism. A great number of natives came from all parts to entreat me to take the trouble to go to their houses and call on God by the bedsides of their sick relatives. Such numbers also of sick made their own way to us, that I had enough to do to read a Gospel over each of them. At the same time we kept on with our daily work, instructing the children, baptizing converts, translating the Catechism, answering difficulties, and burying the dead. For my part I desired to satisfy all, both the sick who came to me themselves, and those who came to beg on the part of others, lest if I did not, their confidence in, and zeal for, our holy religion should relax, and I thought it wrong not to do what I could in answer to their prayers. But the thing grew to such a pitch that it was impossible for me myself to satisfy all, and at the same time to avoid their quarrelling among themselves, every one striving to be the first to get me to his own house; so I hit on a way of serving all at once. As I could not go myself, I sent round children whom I could trust in my place. They went to the sick persons, assembled their families and neighbours, recited the Creed with them, and encouraged the sufferers to conceive a certain and wellfounded confidence of their restoration. Then after all this, they recited the prayers of the Church. To make my tale short, God was moved by the faith and piety of these children and of the others, and restored to a great number of sick persons health both of body and soul. How good He was to them! He made the very disease of their bodies the occasion of calling them to salvation, and drew them to the Christian faith almost by force!

I have also charged these children to teach the rudiments of Christian doctrine to the ignorant in private houses, in the streets, and the crossways. As soon as I see that this has been well started in one village, I go on to another and give the same instructions and the same commission to the children, and so I go through in order the whole number of their villages. When I have done this and am going away, I leave in each place a copy of the Christian doctrine, and tell all those who know how to write to copy it out, and all the others are to learn it by heart and to recite it from memory every day. Every feast day I bid them meet in one place and sing all together the elements of the faith. For this purpose I have appointed in each of the thirty Christian villages men of intelligence and character who are to preside over these meetings, and the Governor, Don Martin Alfonso, who is so full of love for our Society and of zeal for religion, has been good enough at our request to allot a yearly revenue of 4000 gold *fanams* for the salary of these catechists. He has an immense friendship for ours, and desires with all his heart that some of them should be sent hither, for which he is always asking in his letters to the King.

*   *   *

We have in these parts a class of men among the pagans who are called Brahmins. They keep up the worship of the gods, the superstitious rites of religion, frequenting the temples and taking care of the idols. They are as perverse and wicked a set as can anywhere be found, and I always apply to them the words of holy David, "from an unholy race and a wicked and crafty man deliver me, O Lord." They are liars and cheats to the very backbone. Their whole study is, how to deceive most cunningly the simplicity and ignorance of the people. They give out publicly that the gods command certain offerings to be made to their temples, which offerings are simply the things that the Brahmins themselves wish for, for their own maintenance and that of their wives, children, and servants. Thus they make the poor folk believe that the images of their gods eat and drink, dine and sup like men, and some devout persons are found who really offer to the idol twice a day, before dinner and supper, a certain sum of money. The Brahmins eat sumptuous meals to the sound of drums, and make the ignorant believe that the gods are banqueting. When they are in need of any supplies, and even before, they give out to the people that the gods are angry because the things they have asked for have not been sent, and that if the people do not take care, the gods will punish them by slaughter, disease, and the assaults of the devils. And the poor ignorant creatures, with the fear of the gods before them, obey them implicitly. . . .

The heathen inhabitants of the country are commonly ignorant of letters, but by no means ignorant of wickedness. All the time I have been here in this country I have only converted one Brahmin, a virtuous young man, who has now undertaken to teach the Catechism to children. As I go through the Christian villages, I often pass by the temples of the Brahmins, which they call pagodas. One day lately, I happened to enter a pagoda where there were about two hundred of them, and most of them came to meet me. We had a long conversation, after which I asked them what their gods enjoined them in order to obtain the life of the blessed. There was a long discussion amongst them as to who should answer me. At last, by common consent, the commission was given to one of them, of greater age and experience than the rest, an old man, of more than eighty years. He asked me in return, what commands the God of the Christians laid on them. I saw the old man's perversity, and I refused to speak a word till he had first answered my question. So he was obliged to expose his ignorance, and replied that their gods required two duties of those who desired to go to them hereafter, one of which was to abstain from killing cows, because under that form the gods were adored; the other was to show kindness to the Brahmins, who were the worshippers of the gods. This answer moved my indignation, for I could not but grieve intensely at the thought of the devils being worshipped instead of God by these blind heathen, and I asked them to listen to me in turn. Then I, in a loud voice, repeated the Apostles' Creed and the Ten Commandments. After this I gave in their own language a short explanation, and told them what Paradise is, and what Hell is, and also who they are who go to Heaven to join the company of the blessed, and who are to be sent to the eternal punishments of hell. Upon hearing these things they all rose up and vied with one another in embracing me, and in confessing that the God of the Christians is the true God, as His laws are so agreeable to reason. Then they asked me if the souls of men like those of other animals perished together with the body. God put into my mouth arguments of such a sort, and so suited to their ways of thinking, that to their great joy I was able to prove to them the immortality of the soul. I find, by the way, that the arguments which are to convince these ignorant people must by no means be subtle, such as those which are found in the books of learned schoolmen, but must be such as their minds can understand. They asked me again how the soul of a dying person goes out of the body, how it was, whether it was as happens to us in dreams, when we seem to be conversing with our friends and acquaintance? (Ah, how often this happens to me, dearest brothers, when I am dreaming of you!) Was this because the soul then leaves the body? And again, whether God was black or white? For as there is so great a variety of colour among men, and the Indians being black themselves, consider their own colour the best, they believe that their gods are

black. On this account the great majority of their idols are as black as black can be, and moreover are generally so rubbed over with oil as to smell detestably, and seem to be as dirty as they are ugly and horrible to look at. To all these questions I was able to reply so as to satisfy them entirely. But when I came to the point at last, and urged them to embrace the religion which they felt to be true, they made that same objection which we hear from many Christians when urged to change their life,— that they would set men talking about them if they altered their ways and their religion, and besides, they said that they should be afraid that, if they did so, they would have nothing to live on and support themselves by.

I have found just one Brahmin and no more in all this coast who is a man of learning: he is said to have studied in a very famous Academy. Knowing this, I took measures to converse with him alone. He then told me at last, as a great secret, that the students of this Academy are at the outset made by their masters to take an oath not to reveal their mysteries, but that, out of friendship for me, he would disclose them to me. One of these mysteries was that there only exists one God, the Creator and Lord of heaven and earth, whom men are bound to worship, for the idols are simply images of devils, The Brahmins have certain books of sacred literature which contain, as they say, the laws of God. The masters teach in a learned tongue, as we do in Latin. He also explained to me these divine precepts one by one; but it would be a long business to write out his commentary, and indeed not worth the trouble. Their sages keep as a feast our Sunday. On this day they repeat at different hours this one prayer: "I adore Thee, O God; and I implore Thy help for ever." They are bound by oath to repeat this prayer frequently, and in a low voice. My friend added, that the law of nature permitted them to have more wives than one, and their sacred books predicted that the time would come when all men should embrace the same religion. After all this he asked me in my turn to explain the principal mysteries of the Christian religion, promising to keep them secret. I replied, that I would not tell him a word about them unless he promised beforehand to publish abroad what I should tell him of the religion of Jesus Christ. He made the promise, and then I carefully explained to him those words of Jesus Christ in which our religion is summed up: "He who believes and is baptized shall be saved." This text, with my commentary on it, which embraced the whole of the Apostles' Creed, he wrote down carefully, as well as the Commandments, on account of their close connection with the Creed. He told me also that one night he had dreamt that he had been made a Christian to his immense delight, and that he had become my brother and companion. He ended by begging me to make him a Christian secretly. But as he made certain conditions opposed to right and justice, I put off his baptism. I don't doubt but that by God's mercy he will one day be a Christian. I charged him to teach the ignorant and unlearned that there is only one God, Creator of heaven and earth; but he pleaded the

obligation of his oath, and said he could not do so, especially as he was much afraid that if he did it he should become possessed by an evil spirit. . . .

REVIEW QUESTIONS

1. What was involved in the conversion of Asian peoples to Christianity?
2. What were the greatest challenges that Xavier and his fellows confronted?
3. How did Xavier's values shape his perception of Asian peoples?
4. How would you describe the reception of Christian missionaries and Christianity among the people of Cape Comorin?
5. How might Xavier and his mission have shaped the interaction and understanding of East and West?

SAINT TERESA OF ÁVILA

FROM *The Life of Teresa of Jesus*

Saint Teresa of Ávila (1515–1582) was a Spanish mystic, spiritual author, and monastic reformer. Her worldly achievements were great, to which the Discalced Carmelites still bear witness; in addition, the beauty of her inner life, as revealed in her writings, earned her recognition as one of the world's great female religious authors. Teresa was born in central Spain, the daughter of a wealthy hidalgo. At age fourteen, she was sent to a boarding school, where she became ill and began to consider her life's vocation. Despite paternal opposition, Teresa became a novice in a Carmelite convent around 1535. Her health collapsed again, leaving her an invalid for three years. During her convalescence, she began the series of meditations that would establish her reputation as a mystic. It took her fifteen years to perfect the prayers and meditations that would lead to her ecstatic visions and conversations with God. Her most celebrated work, The Life, *written in obedience to her confessors and directors, captured this process as the history of a soul, much like Augustine's* Confessions. *They combine religious ardor with human candor, an insistence that her experiences were a gift of God with an unwillingness to claim any spiritual distinction.*

In 1558, Teresa began to consider the restoration of Carmelite life to its original observance of austerity. It required complete separation from the world to promote prayerful meditation, such as was enjoined in the Primitive Carmelite Rule of 1247. In 1562, with the authorization of Pope Pius IV, Teresa and four companions opened the first convent of the Carmelite reform. Despite intense opposition from secular and ecclesiastical officials, her efforts eventually won the approval of the Carmelite general as well as his mandate to extend her reform to men. In 1567, she met a young Carmelite priest, Juan de Yepes, later canonized as Saint John of the Cross, a brilliant friar who helped her initiate the Carmelite reform for men. In her lifetime, she saw sixteen convents and twelve monasteries established. The last decades of her life were given to this work. Forty years after her death, she was canonized; in 1970, she was made a doctor of the Church.

From *The Life of Theresa of Jesus: The Autobiography of Teresa of Avila*, translated by E. Allison Peters (New York: Bantam Doubleday Dell, 1991), pp. 68–71.

*   *   *

I have strayed far from any intention, for I was trying to give the reasons why this kind of vision cannot be the work of the imagination. How could we picture Christ's Humanity by merely studying the subject or form any impression of His great beauty by means of the imagination? No little time would be necessary if such a reproduction was to be in the least like the original. One can indeed make such a picture with one's imagination, and spend time in regarding it, and considering the form and the brilliance of it; little by little one may even learn to perfect such an image and store it up in the memory. Who can prevent this? Such a picture can undoubtedly be fashioned with the understanding. But with regard to the vision which we are discussing there is no way of doing this: we have to look at it when the Lord is pleased to reveal it to us—to look as He wills and at whatever He wills. And there is no possibility of our subtracting from it or adding to it, or any way in which we can obtain it, whatever we may do, or look at it when we like or refrain from looking at it. If we try to look at any particular part of it, we at once lose Christ.

For two years and a half things went on like this and it was quite usual for God to grant me this favour. It must now be more than three years since He took it from me as a continually recurring favour, by giving me something else of a higher kind, which I shall describe later. Though I saw that He was speaking to me, and though I was looking upon that great beauty of His, and experiencing the sweetness with which He uttered those words—sometimes stern words—with that most lovely and Divine mouth, and though, too, I was extremely desirous of observing the colour of His eyes, or His height, so that I should be able to describe it, I have never been sufficiently worthy to see this, nor has it been of any use for me to attempt to do so; if I tried, I lost the vision altogether. Though I sometimes see Him looking at me compassionately, His gaze has such power that my soul cannot endure it and remains in so sublime a rapture that it loses this beauteous vision in order to have the greater fruition of it all. So there is no question here of our wanting or not wanting to see the vision. It is clear that the Lord wants of us only humility and shame, our acceptance of what is given us and our praise of its Giver.

This refers to all visions, none excepted. There is nothing that we can do about them; we cannot see more or less of them at will; and we can neither call them up nor banish them by our own efforts. The Lord's will is that we shall see quite clearly that they are produced, not by us but by His Majesty. Still less can we be proud of them: on the contrary, they make us humble and fearful, when we find that, just as the Lord takes from us the power of seeing what we desire, so He can also take from us these favours and His grace, with the result that we are completely lost. So while we live in this exile let us always walk with fear.

Almost invariably the Lord showed Himself to me in His resurrection body, and it was thus, too, that I saw Him in the Host. Only occasionally, to strengthen me when I was in tribulation, did He show me His wounds, and then He would appear sometimes as He was on the Cross and sometimes as in the Garden. On a few occasions I saw Him wearing the crown of thorns and sometimes He would also be carrying the Cross—because of my necessities, as I say, and those of others—but always in His glorified flesh. Many are the affronts and trials that I have suffered through telling this and many are the fears and persecutions that it has brought me. So sure were those whom I told of it that I had a devil that some of them wanted to exorcize me. This troubled me very little, but I was sorry when I found that my confessors were afraid to hear my confessions or when I heard that people were saying things to them against me. None the less, I could never regret having seen these heavenly visions and I would not exchange them for all the good things and delights of this world. I always considered them a great favour from the Lord, and I think they were the greatest of treasures; often the Lord Himself would reassure me about them. I found my love for Him growing exceedingly: I used to go to Him and tell Him about all these trials and I always came away from prayer comforted and with new strength. I did not dare to argue with my critics, because I saw that that made things worse, as they thought me lacking in humility. With my confessor, however, I did discuss these matters; and whenever he saw that I was troubled he would comfort me greatly.

As the visions became more numerous, one of those who had previously been in the habit of helping me and who used sometimes to hear my confessions when the minister was unable to do so, began to say that it was clear I was being deceived by the devil. So, as I was quite unable to resist it, they commanded me to make the sign of the Cross whenever I had a vision, and to snap my fingers at it so as to convince myself that it came from the devil, whereupon it would not come again: I was not to be afraid, they said, and God would protect me and take the vision away. This caused me great distress: as I could not help believing that my visions came from God, it was a terrible thing to have to do; and, as I have said, I could not possibly wish them to be taken from me. However, I did as they commanded me. I besought God often to set me free from deception; indeed, I was continually doing so and with many tears. I would also invoke Saint Peter and Saint Paul, for the Lord had told me (it was on their festival that He had first appeared to me) that they would prevent me from being deluded; and I used often to see them very clearly on my left hand, though not in an imaginary vision. These glorious Saints were in a very real sense my lords.

To be obliged to snap my fingers at a vision in which I saw the Lord caused me the sorest distress. For, when I saw Him before me, I could not have believed that the vision had come from the devil even if the alternative were my being cut to pieces. So this was a kind of penance to me, and a heavy one. In order not to have to be so continually crossing myself, I would carry a cross in my hand. This I did almost invariably; but I was not so particular about snapping my fingers at the vision, for it hurt me too much to do that. It reminded me of the way the Jews had insulted Him, and I would beseech Him to forgive me, since I did it out of obedience to him who was in His own place, and not to blame me, since he was one of the ministers whom He had placed in His Church. He told me not to worry about it and said I was quite right to obey, but He would see that my confessor learned the truth. When they made me stop my prayer He seemed to me to have become angry, and He told me to tell them that this was tyranny. He used to show me ways of knowing that the visions were not of the devil; some of these I shall describe later.

*   *   *

REVIEW QUESTIONS

1. What distinguishes Teresa's spirituality from that of Ignatius of Loyola?
2. Might we call her spirituality feminine?
3. Is Teresa's piety private or public? In what ways?
4. Are visions portable?
5. Are they entirely private?
6. How does language fail Teresa?

The Council of Trent

The Council of Trent (Latin: Concilium Tridentinum*), held between 1545 and 1563 in the cities of Trent and Bologna in northern Italy, was one of the most important ecumenical councils of the Roman Catholic Church. Prompted by the Protestant Reformation, it has been described as the embodiment of the Counter-Reformation. Yet, its actions were as creative as they were reactive. In a series of 25 sessions that extended from 13 December 1545 until 4 December 1563, it declared anathema a wide range of theological, liturgical, and ecclesiological positions adopted by religious reform movements commonly referred to as Protestant. It also defined standard Catholic doctrine on a wide range of subjects including scripture, the biblical canon, sacred tradition, original sin, justification, salvation, the sacraments, the Mass, and the veneration of saints. In the course of its deliberations, the members of the council declared the Vulgate the official, canonical version of the Bible. A year after the council concluded its deliberations, Pope Pius IV issued the Tridentine Creed, and his successor Pius V issued the Roman catechism, both standard works of the Roman Catholic confession. Along with revisions of the Missal and Breviary, issued in the following years, these codified the Tridentine mass, which remained for the next 400 years the principal form of the mass for the Catholic Church. It would be more than three centuries before the next ecumenical council convened, the First Vatican Council. When Pope John XXIII initiated preparations for the Second Vatican Council, he affirmed the decrees issued at Trent, declaring "What was, still is."*

From *The Canons and Decrees of the Sacred and Ecumenical Council of Trent, Celebrated under the Sovereign Pontiffs Paul III, Julius III, and Pius IV,* translated by Rev. J. Waterworth (London: C. Dolman, 1848), pp. 152–59.

Session the Twenty-Second,

Being the sixth under the Sovereign Pontiff, Pius IV., celebrated on the seventeenth day of September, MDLXII.

DOCTRINE ON THE SACRIFICE OF THE MASS.

The sacred and holy, ecumenical and general Synod of Trent—lawfully assembled in the Holy Ghost, the same Legates of the Apostolic See presiding therein—to the end that the ancient, complete, and in every part perfect faith and doctrine touching the great mystery of the Eucharist may be retained in the holy Catholic Church; and may, all errors and heresies being repelled, be preserved in its own purity; (the Synod) instructed by the illumination of the Holy Ghost, teaches, declares, and decrees what follows, to be preached to the faithful, on the subject of the Eucharist, considered as being a true and singular sacrifice.

CHAPTER I.

ON THE INSTITUTION OF THE MOST HOLY SACRIFICE OF THE MASS.

Forasmuch as, under the former Testament, according to the testimony of the Apostle Paul, there was no perfection, because of the weakness of the Levitical priesthood; there was need, God, the Father of mercies, so ordaining, that another priest should rise, according to the order of Melchisedech, our Lord Jesus Christ, who might consummate, and lead to what is perfect, as many as were to be sanctified. He, therefore, our God and Lord, though He was about to offer Himself once on the altar of the cross unto God the Father, by means of his death, there to operate an eternal redemption; nevertheless, because that His priesthood was not to be extinguished by His death, in the last supper, on the night in which He was betrayed,—that He might leave, to His own beloved Spouse the Church, a visible sacrifice, such as the nature of man requires, whereby that bloody sacrifice, once to be accomplished on the cross, might be represented, and the memory thereof remain even unto the end of the world, and its salutary virtue be applied to the remission of those sins which we daily commit,—declaring Himself constituted a priest forever, according to the order of Melchisedech, He offered up to God the Father His own body and blood under the species of bread and wine; and, under the symbols of those same things, He delivered (His own body and blood) to be received by His apostles, whom He then constituted priests of the New Testament; and by those words, Do this in commemoration of me, He commanded them and their successors in the priesthood, to offer (them); even as the Catholic Church has always understood and taught. For, having celebrated the ancient Passover, which the multitude of the children of Israel immolated in memory of their going out of Egypt, He instituted the new Passover, (to wit) Himself to be immolated, under visible signs, by the Church through (the ministry of) priests, in memory of His own passage from this world unto the Father, when by the effusion of His own blood He redeemed us, and delivered us from the power of darkness, and translated us into his kingdom. And this is indeed that clean oblation, which cannot be defiled by any unworthiness, or malice of those that offer (it); which the Lord foretold by Malachias was to be offered in every place, clean to his name, which was to be great amongst the Gentiles; and which the apostle Paul, writing to the Corinthians, has not obscurely indicated, when he says, that they who are defiled by the participation of the table of devils, cannot be partakers of the table of the Lord; by the table, meaning in both places the altar. This, in fine, is that oblation which was prefigured by various types of sacrifices, during the period of nature, and of the law; in as much as it comprises all the good things signified by those sacrifices, as being the consummation and perfection of them all.

CHAPTER II.

THAT THE SACRIFICE OF THE MASS IS PROPITIATORY BOTH FOR THE LIVING AND THE DEAD.

And forasmuch as, in this divine sacrifice which is celebrated in the mass, that same Christ is contained and immolated in an unbloody manner, who once offered Himself in a bloody manner on the altar of the cross; the holy Synod teaches, that this sacrifice is truly propritiatory and that by means thereof this is effected, that we obtain mercy, and find grace in seasonable aid, if we draw nigh unto God, contrite and penitent, with a sincere heart and upright faith, with fear and reverence.

For the Lord, appeased by the oblation thereof, and granting the grace and gift of penitence, forgives even heinous crimes and sins. For the victim is one and the same, the same now offering by the ministry of priests, who then offered Himself on the cross, the manner alone of offering being different. The fruits indeed of which oblation, of that bloody one to wit, are received most plentifully through this unbloody one; so far is this (latter) from derogating in any way from that (former oblation). Wherefore, not only for the sins, punishments, satisfactions, and other necessities of the faithful who are living, but also for those who are departed in Christ, and who are not as yet fully purified, is it rightly offered, agreebly to a tradition of the apostles.

CHAPTER III.

ON MASSES IN HONOUR OF THE SAINTS.

And although the Church has been accustomed at times to celebrate, certain masses in honour and memory of the saints; not therefore, however, doth she teach that sacrifice is offered unto them, but unto God alone, who crowned them; whence neither is the priest wont to say, "I offer sacrifice to thee, Peter, or Paul;" but, giving thanks to God for their victories, he implores their patronage, that they may vouchsafe to intercede for us in heaven, whose memory we celebrate upon earth.

CHAPTER IV.

ON THE CANON OF THE MASS.

And whereas it beseemeth, that holy things be administered in a holy manner, and of all holy things this sacrifice is the most holy; to the end that it might be worthily and reverently offered and received, the Catholic Church instituted, many years ago, the sacred Canon, so pure from every error, that nothing is contained therein which does not in the highest degree savour of a certain holiness and piety, and raise up unto God the minds of those that offer. For it is composed, out of the very words of the Lord, the traditions of the apostles, and the pious institutions also of holy pontiffs.

CHAPTER V.

ON THE SOLEMN CEREMONIES OF THE SACRIFICE OF THE MASS.

And whereas such is the nature of man, that, without external helps, he cannot easily be raised to the meditation of divine things; therefore has holy Mother Church instituted certain rites, to wit that certain things be pronounced in the mass in a low, and others in a louder, tone. She has likewise employed ceremonies, such as mystic benedictions, lights, incense, vestments, and many other things of this kind, derived from an apostolical discipline and tradition, whereby both the majesty of so great a sacrifice might be recommended, and the minds of the faithful be excited, by those visible signs of religion and piety, to the contemplation of those most sublime things which are hidden in this sacrifice.

CHAPTER VI.

ON MASS WHEREIN THE PRIEST ALONE COMMUNICATES.

The sacred and holy Synod would fain indeed that, at each mass, the faithful who are present should communicate, not only in spiritual desire, but also by the sacramental participation of the Eucharist, that thereby a more abundant fruit might be derived to them from this most holy sacrifice: but not therefore, if this be not always done, does It condemn, as private and unlawful, but approves of and therefore commends, those masses in which the priest alone communicates sacramentally; since those masses also ought to be considered as truly common; partly because the people communicate spiritually thereat; partly also because they are celebrated by a public minister of the Church, not for himself only, but for all the faithful, who belong to the body of Christ.

CHAPTER VII.

ON THE WATER THAT IS TO BE MIXED WITH THE WINE
TO BE OFFERED IN THE CHALICE.

The holy Synod notices, in the next place, that it has
been enjoined by the Church on priests, to mix
water with the wine that is to be offered in the chalice; as well because it is believed that Christ the Lord
did this, as also because from His side there came
out blood and water; the memory of which mystery
is renewed by this commixture; and, whereas in the
apocalypse of blessed John, the peoples are called
waters, the union of that faithful people with Christ
their head is hereby represented.

CHAPTER VIII.

ON NOT CELEBRATING THE MASS EVERYWHERE IN THE
VULGAR TONGUE; THE MYSTERIES OF THE MASS TO BE
EXPLAINED TO THE PEOPLE.

Although the mass contains great instruction for
the faithful people, nevertheless, it has not seemed
expedient to the Fathers, that it should be everywhere celebrated in the vulgar tongue. Wherefore,
the ancient usage of each church, and the rite
approved of by the holy Roman Church, the mother
and mistress of all churches, being in each place
retained; and, that the sheep of Christ may not suffer hunger, nor the little ones ask for bread, and
there be none to break it unto them, the holy Synod
charges pastors, and all who have the cure of souls,
that they frequently, during the celebration of mass,
expound either by themselves, or others, some
portion of those things which are read at mass, and
that, amongst the rest, they explain some mystery
of this most holy sacrifice, especially on the Lord's
days and festivals.

CHAPTER IX.

PRELIMINARY REMARK ON THE FOLLOWING CANONS.

And because that many errors are at this time disseminated and many things are taught and maintained by divers persons, in opposition to this
ancient faith, which is based on the sacred Gospel,
the traditions of the Apostles, and the doctrine of
the holy Fathers; the sacred and holy Synod, after
many and grave deliberations maturely had touching these matters, has resolved, with the unanimous consent of all the Fathers, to condemn, and
to eliminate from holy Church, by means of the
canons subjoined, whatsoever is opposed to this
most pure faith and sacred doctrine.

ON THE SACRIFICE OF THE MASS.

CANON I.—If any one saith, that in the mass a
true and proper sacrifice is not offered to God; or,
that to be offered is nothing else but that Christ is
given us to eat; let him be anathema.

CANON II.—If any one saith, that by those words,
Do this for the commemoration of me (Luke xxii. 19),
Christ did not institute the apostles priests; or, did
not ordain that they, and other priests should offer
His own body and blood; let him be anathema.

CANON III.—If any one saith, that the sacrifice of
the mass is only a sacrifice of praise and of thanks-
giving; or, that it is a bare commemoration of the
sacrifice consummated on the cross, but not a pro-
pitiatory sacrifice; or, that it profits him only who
receives; and that it ought not to be offered for the
living and the dead for sins, pains, satisfactions,
and other necessities; let him be anathema.

CANON IV.—If any one saith, that, by the sacrifice
of the mass, a blasphemy is cast upon the most holy
sacrifice of Christ consummated on the cross; or,
that it is thereby derogated from; let him be
anathema.

CANON V.—If any one saith, that it is an impos-
ture to celebrate masses in honour of the saints,
and for obtaining their intercession with God,
as the Church intends; let him be anathema.

CANON VI.—If any one saith, that the canon of
the mass contains errors, and is therefore to be
abrogated; let him be anathema.

CANON VII.—If any one saith, that the ceremonies, vestments, and outward signs, which the Catholic Church makes use of in the celebration of masses, are incentives to impiety, rather than offices of piety; let him be anathema.

CANON VIII.—If any one saith, that masses, wherein the priest alone communicates sacramentally, are unlawful, and are, therefore, to be abrogated; let him be anathema.

CANON IX.—If any one saith, that the rite of the Roman Church, according to which a part of the canon and the words of consecration are pronounced in a low tone, is to be condemned; or, that the mass ought to be celebrated in the vulgar tongue only; or, that water ought not to be mixed with the wine that is to be offered in the chalice, for that it is contrary to the institution of Christ; let him be anathema.

REVIEW QUESTIONS

1. Why did the council find it necessary to redefine the mass?
2. On the basis of your reading, what makes the work of the council creative, as well as reactive?
3. What does the council emphasize as important within the doctrine of the mass?
4. What does the council consider the proper function of the priest to be, when celebrating the mass, and what is his relationship to the laity?
5. How does the council's formulation about the mass differ from those of Luther and Calvin?
6. How would you describe the nature of God as understood by the council?

14 ⁓ EUROPE IN THE ATLANTIC WORLD, 1550–1660

The challenge to the authority of classical culture that the new worlds posed, combined with the fragmentation of the medieval Christian Church—the "body of all believers"—laid the foundation in the second half of the sixteenth century for profound crises of political and social order and of epistemology, the very foundation of human knowledge. In their efforts to describe what they saw in the Americas, European conquistadores and clergy were forced to adopt analogies: hundreds of species of plants and animals were not to be found in the writings of Pliny, the great and trusted botanist and zoologist of the ancient world, or in the Bible. The cultures of the Americas posed new models of social and political relations, opening new possibilities for the ordering of political relations and calling into question the very nature of political authority.

Within Europe, civil wars arose in the wake of the fragmentation of the Christian Church. The wars of religion in France, 1562–98, led astute observers such as Montaigne to question the claim of each side to know the truth, and to question whether human reason was sufficient to discern the truth. In all the religious wars, beginning with the German Peasants' War of 1525 and culminating in the Thirty Years' War, 1618–48, the social order was overthrown, as peasant killed lord, brother killed brother, son killed father, and neighbor killed neighbor. What was it to be human? To be savage? And where was God while Christian slaughtered Christian?

The crisis of the seventeenth century was not simply intellectual and spiritual but also had real material aspects. The expansion of Europe into new worlds changed patterns of consumption and production, thus contributing to the overthrow of traditional work processes and lifestyles. It created a tremendous influx of wealth that aided the rise of new economic and political powers, both social groups and nation-states, and that contributed to chronic inflation. Changes in society, economy, and politics created tensions that found expression in the violence of the period. Religious wars were seldom entirely religious in cause or in consequence. The almost constant march and countermarch of armies not only destroyed life and property but also disrupted agriculture and spread disease. The struggle for existence, difficult under the best of circumstances in the early modern period, became much more difficult in the age of crisis.

By 1660, peasants had risen in unprecedented numbers against their lords; common Englishmen had executed their king; Europeans had witnessed multiple incidents of cannibalism in their own villages; and the medieval epistemology, that very base by which Europeans could be certain of the veracity of what they knew, had collapsed. New formulations were being tentatively put forward, but they did not yet replace the old certainties that had been irrecoverably lost.

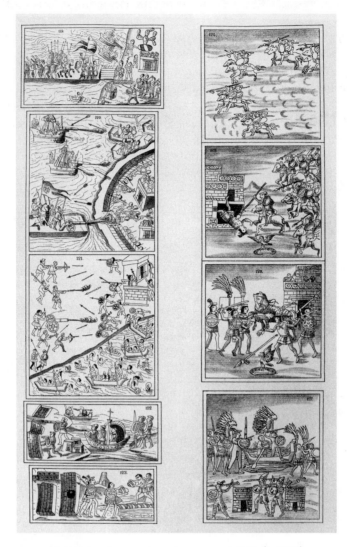

CONQUEST OF MEXICO, FLORENTINE CODEX (C. 1555)

The Franciscan friar Bernardino de Sahagún (d. 1590) directed the team of Nahua artists who produced the Florentine Codex. This book is an account of Cortéz's expedition of 1519, which resulted in the destruction of the Aztec Empire. The story is told in Nahuatl, and is accompanied by over 100 illustrations. Scholars have debated the extent to which the text and pictures allowed the Nahua to express their own views of these events. Sahagún began collecting information in the 1540s, and this chapter may have been composed around 1555. These nine pictures show characteristic battle scenes. Guns and steel certainly played a role in the Spanish conquest of Mexico. What evidence do these pictures provide of this? Perhaps even more striking were the roles of horses. What advantages did these animals provide the Spaniards? Why would indigenous artists have been involved in a project like this? What are the advantages and shortcomings of this historical source?

GIOVANNI MICHIEL

FROM A Venetian Ambassador's Report on the St. Bartholomew's Day Massacre

The struggle for supremacy in northern Italy, which marked the last half of the fifteenth century, gave rise to a new form of diplomacy, including structures and procedures that would be fundamental to relations among all modern states. Requiring continuous contact and communication, Renaissance states turned to permanent diplomacy, distinguished by the use of accredited resident ambassadors rather than ad hoc missions of medieval legates. The tasks of a permanent ambassador were to represent his government at state ceremonies, to gather information, and, occasionally, to enter into negotiations. Nowhere was this system more fully and expertly articulated than by the Republic of Venice in the late fifteenth and sixteenth centuries. Its ambassadors were chosen with unusual care from the most prominent families of the city. They were highly educated, and their duties were carefully defined. Among the latter were weekly dispatches reporting all matters of any interest to Venice. These reports were regularly read and debated in the senate, which replied with questions, instructions, and information of its own. As a result, Venetian ambassadors were among the most skilled and respected in early modern Europe. In this report, Giovanni Michiel interprets the events of St. Bartholomew's Day in 1572. The massacre of Huguenots, instigated by the Queen Mother, Catherine de Medici, outraged Protestant Europe and dashed all hopes for peace in France. Of particular interest is the ambassador's harshly realistic account of the political motives for so violent an act of statecraft.

From *Pursuit of Power: Venetian Ambassadors' Reports on Spain, Turkey and France in the Age of Phillip II, 1560–1600,* by James C. Davis (New York: HarperCollins, 1970), pp. 72–76, 78–79.

*   *   *

Turning to the queen, Admiral de Coligny said, "Madame, the king refuses to involve himself in one war. God grant that he may not be caught up in another which he cannot avoid."

By these words he meant, some say, that if they abandoned the prince of Orange things might go badly for him, and there would be a danger that if the prince failed to win or was actually driven out by the Spanish or for some other reason, then he might enter France with his French and German followers and it might be necessary to drive him out by force. However, everyone understood his words in a very different sense, namely that he was giving notice that he planned to stir up new storms and renew the rioting and civil war. When the queen carefully pondered this it became the chief reason, taken together with the other considerations, why she hurried to prepare that fate for him which he eventually met.

*   *   *

Then, at the dinner hour on Friday, while the admiral was returning on foot from the court to his lodgings and reading a letter, someone fired an arquebus at him. The shot came from a window which faced a bit obliquely on the street, near the royal palace called the Louvre. But it did not strike him in the chest as intended because it so happened that the admiral was wearing a pair of slippers which made walking difficult and, wanting to take them off and hand them to a page, he had just started to turn around. So the arquebus shot tore off a finger on his left hand and then hit his right arm near the wrist and passed through it to the other side near the elbow. If he had simply walked straight ahead it would have hit him in the chest and killed him.

As you can imagine, news of the event caused great excitement, especially at court. Everyone supposed it had been done by order of the duke of Guise to avenge his family, because the window from which the shot was fired belonged to his mother's house, which had purposely been left empty after she had gone to stay in another. When the news was reported to the king, who happened to be playing tennis with the duke of Guise, they say he turned white and looked thunderstruck. Without saying a word he withdrew into his chambers and made it obvious that he was extremely angry.

*   *   *

On Saturday the admiral's dressings were changed and the word was given out—which may or may not have been true—that the wound was not a mortal one and that there was no danger even that he would lose the arm. The Huguenots only blustered all the more, and everyone waited to see what would happen next. The duke of Guise knew he might be attacked, so he armed himself and stuck close to his uncle, the duke of Aumale, and as many relatives, friends and servants as possible.

But before long the situation changed. Late Saturday night, just before the dawn of Saint Bartholomew's Day, the massacre or slaughter was carried out. The French say the king ordered it. How wild and terrifying it was in Paris (which has a larger population than any other city in Europe),

no one can imagine. Nor can one imagine the rage and frenzy of those who slaughtered and sacked, as the king ordered the people to do. Nor what a marvel, not to say a miracle, it was that the common people did not take advantage of this freedom to loot and plunder from Catholics as well as Huguenots, and ravenously take whatever they could get their hands on, especially since the city is incredibly wealthy. No one would ever imagine that a people could be armed and egged on by their ruler, yet not get out of control once they were worked up. But it was not God's will that things should reach such a pass.

The slaughter went on past Sunday for two or three more days, despite the fact that edicts were issued against it and the duke of Nevers was sent riding through the city along with the king's natural brother to order them to stop the killing. The massacre showed how powerfully religion can affect men's minds. On every street one could see the barbarous sight of men cold-bloodedly outraging others of their own people, and not just men who had never done them any harm but in most cases people they knew to be their neighbors and even their relatives. They had no feeling, no mercy on anyone, even those who kneeled before them and humbly begged for their lives. If one man hated another because of some argument or lawsuit all he had to say was "This man is a Huguenot" and he was immediately killed. (That happened to many Catholics.) If their victims threw themselves in the river as a last resort and tried to swim to safety, as many did, they chased them in boats and then drowned them. There was a great deal of looting and pillaging and they say the goods taken amounted to two million because many Huguenots, including some of the richest of them, had come to live in Paris after the most recent edict of pacification. Some estimate the number who were killed as high as four thousand, while others put it as low as two thousand.

The killing spread to all the provinces and most of the major cities and was just as frenzied there, if not more so. They attacked anyone, even the gentry, and as a result all the leaders who did not escape have been killed or thrown in prison. It is true that

Montgomery and some others who were pursued by the duke of Guise escaped to England, but they are not major figures. And the king has terrified them enough so they won't make any trouble.

*   *   *

REVIEW QUESTIONS

1. According to the report, at what level of society did the St. Bartholomew's Day Massacre originate?

2. How was a person identified as Huguenot or Catholic?
3. What does that say about religious identity in early modern France?
4. Do we know from this report who ordered the assassination of Admiral de Coligny?
5. Who caused the massacre?
6. What do we learn about the relation of religion to politics and political action?

REGINALD SCOT

FROM *Discoverie of Witchcraft*

Reginald Scot (1538–1599) was a Kentish squire who witnessed a number of fraudulent accusations of witchcraft in the villages of his shire during the reign of Elizabeth I. In 1584, he wrote his Discoverie of Witchcraft, *which contains a remarkable exposition of magical elements in medieval Catholicism and a protest against the persecution of harmless old women. Scot doubted that God could ever have allowed witches to exercise supernatural powers, much less demand that they be persecuted for it. In this regard, he deserves to be ranked among the skeptics on the question of witchcraft, although he never denied the existence of witches. According to Scot, all "witches" fell into one of four categories. First were the innocent, those falsely accused. Second were the deluded, those convinced through their own misery that they were witches. Third were the malefactors, those who harmed people and damaged property, though not by supernatural means. Fourth were imposters, those who posed as witches and conjurers. Scot denied that any of these "witches" had access to supernatural powers. Malefactors and imposters were, in fact, the witches named in the Bible as not being suffered to live. They were the only witches Scot admitted. His work is said to have made a great impression in the magistracy and clergy of his day. Nonetheless, his remained a minority opinion. Most contemporaries understood as tantamount to atheism any denial of the reality of spirits or the possibility of the supernatural. The persecution of witches continued unabated into the eighteenth century; many thousands, mostly harmless old women, fell victim to the rage.*

From *Discoverie of Witchcraft*, by Reginald Scot, 1584, edited by Brinsley Nicholson (London: E. Stock, 1886).

*   *   *

*T*he inconvenience growing by mens credulitie herein, with a reproofe of some churchmen, which are inclined to the common conceived opinion of witches omnipotencie, and a familiar example thereof. But the world is now so bewitched and over-run with this fond error, that even where a man shuld seeke comfort and counsell, there shall hee be sent (in case of necessitie) from God to the divell; and from the Physician, to the coosening witch, who will not sticke to take upon hir, by wordes to heale the lame (which was proper onelie to Christ: and to them whom he assisted with his divine power) yea, with hir familiar & charmes she will take upon hir to cure the blind: though in the tenth of S. *Johns* Gospell it be written, that the divell cannot open the eies of the blind. And they attaine such credit as I have heard (to my greefe) some of the ministerie affirme, that they have had in their parish at one instant, xvii. or xviii. witches: meaning such as could worke miracles supernaturallie. Whereby they manifested as well their infidelitie and ignorance, in conceiving Gods word; as their negligence and error in instructing their flocks. For they themselves might understand, and also teach their parishoners, that God onelie worketh great woonders; and that it is he which sendeth such punishments to the wicked, and such trials to the elect: according to the saieng of the Prophet *Haggai*, I smote you with blasting and mildeaw, and with haile, in all the labours of your hands; and yet you turned not unto me, saith the Lord. And therefore saith the same Prophet in another place; You have sowen much, and bring in little. And both in *Joel* and *Leviticus*, the like phrases and proofes are used and made. But more shalbe said of this hereafter.

*   *   *

At the assises holden at *Rochester*, Anno 1581, one *Margaret Simons*, the wife of *John Simons*, of *Brenchlie* in *Kent*, was araigned for witchcraft, at the instigation and complaint of divers fond and malicious persons; and speciallie by the meanes of one *John Ferrall* vicar of that parish: with whom I talked about that matter, and found him both fondlie assotted in the cause, and enviouslie bent towards hir: and (which is worse) as unable to make a good account of his faith, as shee whom he accused. That which he, for his part, laid to the poore womans charge, was this.

His sonne (being an ungratious boie, and prentise to one *Robert Scotchford* clothier, dwelling in that parish of *Brenchlie*) passed on a daie by hir house; at whome by chance hir little dog barked. Which thing the boie taking in evill part, drewe his knife, & pursued him therewith even to hir doore: whom she rebuked with some such words as the boie disdained, & yet neverthelesse would not be persuaded to depart in a long time. At the last he returned to his maisters house, and within five or six daies fell sicke. Then was called to mind the fraie betwixt the dog and the boie: insomuch as the vicar (who thought himselfe so privileged, as he little mistrusted that God would visit his children with sicknes) did so calculate; as he found, partlie through his owne judgement, and partlie (as he himselfe told me) by the relation of other witches, that his said sonne was by hir bewitched. Yea, he also told me, that this his sonne (being as it were past all cure) received perfect health at the hands of another witch.

He proceeded yet further against hir, affirming, that alwaies in his parish church, when he desired to read most plainelie, his voice so failed him, as he could scant be heard at all. Which hee could impute, he said, to nothing else, but to hir inchantment. When I advertised the poore woman hereof, as being desirous to heare what she could saie for hir selfe; she told me, that in verie deed his voice did much faile him, speciallie when he strained himselfe to speake lowdest. How beit, she said that at all times his voice was hoarse and lowe: which thing I perceived to be true. But sir, said she, you shall understand, that this our vicar is diseased with such a kind of hoarsenesse, as divers of our neighbors in this parish, not long since, doubted that he had the French pox; & in that respect utterly refused to communicate with him: untill such time as (being therunto injoined by M. D. *Lewen* the Ordinarie) he had brought frō *London* a certificat, under the hands of two physicians, that his hoarsenes proceeded from a disease in the lungs. Which certificat he published in the church, in the presence of the whole congregation: and by this meanes hee was cured, or rather excused of the shame of his disease. And this I knowe to be true by the relation of divers honest men of that parish. And truelie, if one of the Jurie had not beene wiser than the other, she had beene condemned thereupon, and upon other as ridiculous matters as this. For the name of a witch is so odious, and hir power so feared among the common people, that if the honestest bodie living chance to be arraigned thereupon, she shall hardlie escape condemnation.

A Confutation of the Common Conceived Opinion of Witches and Witchcraft, and How Detestable a Sinne It Is to Repaire to Them for Counsell or Helpe in Time of Affliction

But whatsoever is reported or conceived of such manner of witchcrafts, I dare avow to be false and fabulous (coosinage, dotage, and poisoning excepted:) neither is there any mention made of these kind of witches in the Bible. If Christ had knowne them, he would not have pretermitted to invaie against their presumption, in taking upon them his office: as, to heale and cure diseases; and to worke such miraculous and supernaturall things, as whereby he himselfe was speciallie knowne, beleeved, and published to be God; his actions and cures consisting (in order and effect) according to the power of our witchmoongers imputed to witches. Howbeit, if there be any in these daies afflicted in such strange sort, as Christs cures and patients are described in the new testament to have beene: we flie from trusting in God to trusting in witches, who doo not onelie in their coosening art take on them the office of Christ in this behalfe; but use his verie phrase of speech to such idolators, as com to seeke divine assistance at their hands, saieng; Go thy waies, thy sonne or thy daughter, &c. shall doo well, and be whole.

*   *   *

In like manner I say, he that attributeth to a witch, such divine power, as dulie and onelie apperteineth unto GOD (which all witchmongers doo) is in hart a blasphemer, an idolater, and full of grosse impietie, although he neither go nor send to hir for assistance.

A Further Confutation of Witches Miraculous and Omnipotent Power, by Invincible Reasons and Authorities, with Dissuasions from Such Fond Credulitie

If witches could doo anie such miraculous things, as these and other which are imputed to them, they might doo them againe and againe, at anie time or place, or at anie mans desire: for the divell is as strong at one time as at another, as busie by daie as by night, and readie enough to doo all mischeefe, and careth not whom he abuseth. And in so much as it is confessed, by the most part of witchmoongers themselves, that he knoweth not the cogitation of mans heart, he should (me thinks) sometimes appeere unto honest and credible persons, in such grosse and corporall forme, as it is said he dooth unto witches: which you shall never heare to be justified by one sufficient witnesse. For the divell indeed entreth into the mind, and that waie seeketh mans confusion.

The art alwaies presupposeth the power; so as, if they saie they can doo this or that, they must shew how and by what meanes they doo it; as neither the witches, nor the witchmoongers are able to doo. For to everie action is required the facultie and abilitie of the agent or dooer; the aptnes of the patient or subject; and a convenient and possible application. Now the witches are mortall, and their power dependeth upon the analogie and consonancie of their minds and bodies; but with their minds they can but will and understand; and with their bodies they can doo no more, but as the bounds and ends of terrene sense will suffer: and therefore their power extendeth not to doo such miracles, as surmounteth their owne sense, and the understanding of others which are wiser than they; so as here wanteth the vertue and power of the efficient. And in reason, there can be no more vertue in the thing caused, than in the cause, or that which proceedeth of or from the benefit of the cause. And we see, that ignorant and impotent women, or witches, are the causes of incantations and charmes; wherein we shall perceive there is none effect, if we will credit our owne experience and sense unabused, the rules of phi-losophie, or the word of God. For alas! What an unapt instrument is a toothles, old, impotent, and unweldie woman to flie in the aier? Truelie, the divell little needs such instruments to bring his purposes to passe.

It is strange, that we should suppose, that such persons can worke such feates: and it is more strange, that we will imagine that to be possible to be doone by a witch, which to nature and sense is impossible; speciallie when our neighbours life dependeth upon our credulitie therein; and when we may see the defect of abilitie, which alwaies is an impediment both to the act, and also to the pre-sumption thereof. And bicause there is nothing possible in lawe, that in nature is impossible; there-fore the judge dooth not attend or regard what the accused man saith; or yet would doo: but what is prooved to have beene committed, and naturallie falleth in mans power and will to doo. For the lawe saith, that To will a thing unpossible, is a signe of a mad man, or of a foole, upon whom no sentence or judgement taketh hold. Furthermore, what Jurie will condemne, or what Judge will give sentence or judgement against one for killing a man at *Ber-wicke;* when they themselves, and manie other sawe that man at *London,* that verie daie, wherein the murther was committed; yea though the partie confesse himself guiltie therein, and twentie wit-nesses depose the same? But in this case also I saie the judge is not to weigh their testimonie, which is weakened by lawe; and the judges authoritie is to supplie the imperfection of the case, and to mainte-ine the right and equitie of the same.

Seeing therefore that some other things might naturallie be the occasion and cause of such calam-ities as witches are supposed to bring; let not us that professe the Gospell and knowledge of Christ, be bewitched to beleeve that they doo such things, as are in nature impossible, and in sense and rea-son incredible. If they saie it is doone through the divels helpe, who can work miracles; whie doo not theeves bring their busines to passe miraculouslie, with whom the divell is as conver-sant as with the other? Such mischeefes as are imputed to witches, happen where no witches are; yea and continue when witches are hanged and burnt: whie then should we attribute such effect to that cause, which being taken awaie, happeneth neverthelesse?

*   *   *

What Testimonies and Witnesses Are Allowed to Give Evidence against Reputed Witches, by the Report and Allowance of the Inquisitors Themselves, and Such as Are Speciall Writers Heerein

Excommunicat persons, partakers of the falt, infants, wicked servants, and runnawaies are to be admitted to beare witnesse against their dames in this mater of witchcraft: bicause (saith *Bodin* the champion of witchmoongers) none that be honest are able to detect them. Heretikes also and witches shall be received to accuse, but not to excuse a witch. And finallie, the testimonie of all infamous persons in this case is good and allowed. Yea, one lewd person (saith *Bodin*) may be received to accuse and condemne a thousand suspected witches. And although by lawe, a capitall enimie may be chal-lenged; yet *James Sprenger,* and *Henrie Institor,* (from whom *Bodin,* and all the writers that ever I have read, doo receive their light, authorities and arguments) saie (upon this point of lawe) that The poore frendlesse old woman must proove, that hir capitall enimie would have killed hir, and that hee hath both assalted & wounded hir; otherwise she pleadeth all in vaine. If the judge aske hir, whether she have anie capitall enimies; and she rehearse other, and forget hir accuser; or else answer that he was hir capital enimie, but now she hopeth he is not so: such a one is nevertheles admitted for a witnes. And though by lawe, single witnesses are not admittable; yet if one depose she hath bewitched hir cow; another, hir sow; and the third, hir butter: these saith (saith *M. Mal.* and *Bodin*) are no single witnesses; bicause they agree that she is a witch.

The Fifteene Crimes Laid to the Charge of Witches, by Witchmongers, Speciallie by Bodin, in Dæmonomania

They denie God, and all religion.

Answere. Then let them die therefore, or at the least be used like infidels, or apostataes.

They cursse, blaspheme, and provoke God with all despite.

Answere. Then let them have the law expressed in *Levit.* 24. and *Deut.* 13 & 17.

They give their faith to the divell, and they worship and offer sacrifice unto him.

Ans. Let such also be judged by the same lawe.

They doo solemnelie vow and promise all their progenie unto the divell.

Ans. This promise proceedeth from an unsound mind, and is not to be regarded; bicause they cannot performe it, neither will it be prooved true. Howbeit, if it be done by anie that is sound of mind, let the cursse of *Jeremie,* 32.36. light upon them, to wit, the sword, famine and pestilence.

They sacrifice their owne children to the divell before baptisme, holding them up in the aire unto him, and then thrust a needle into their braines.

Ans. If this be true, I maintaine them not herein: but there is a lawe to judge them by. Howbeit, it is so contrarie to sense and nature, that it were follie to beleeve it; either upon *Bodins* bare word, or else upon his presumptions; speciallie when so small commoditie and so great danger and inconvenience insueth to the witches thereby.

They burne their children when they have sacrificed them.

Ans. Then let them have such punishment, as they that offered their children unto *Moloch: Levit.* 20. But these be meere devises of witchmoongers and inquisitors, that with extreame tortures have wroong such confessions from them; or else with false reports have beelied them; or by flatterie & faire words and promises have woon it at their hands, at the length.

They sweare to the divell to bring as manie into that societie as they can.

Ans. This is false, and so prooved elsewhere.

They sweare by the name of the divell.

Ans. I never heard anie such oth, neither have we warrant to kill them that so doo sweare; though indeed it be verie lewd and impious.

They use incestuous adulterie with spirits.

Ans. This is a stale ridiculous lie, as is prooved apparentlie hereafter.

They boile infants (after they have murthered them unbaptised) untill their flesh be made potable.

Ans. This is untrue, incredible, and impossible.

They eate the flesh and drinke the bloud of men and children openlie.

Ans. Then are they kin to the *Anthropophagi* and *Canibals.* But I beleeve never an honest man in *England* nor in *France,* will affirme that he hath seene any of these persons, that are said to be witches, do so; if they shuld, I beleeve it would poison them.

They kill men with poison.

Ans. Let them be hanged for their labour.

They kill mens cattell.

Ans. Then let an action of trespasse be brought against them for so dooing.

They bewitch mens corne, and bring hunger and barrennes into the countrie; they ride and flie in the aire, bring stormes, make tempests, &c.

Ans. Then will I worship them as gods; for those be not the works of man nor yet of witch: as I have elsewhere prooved at large.

They use venerie with a divell called *Incubus,* even when they lie in bed with their husbands, and have children by them, which become the best witches.

Ans. This is the last lie, verie ridiculous, and confuted by me elsewhere.

Of Foure Capitall Crimes Objected against Witches, All Fullie Answered and Confuted as Frivolous

First therefore they laie to their charge idolatrie. But alas without all reason: for such are properlie knowne to us to be idolaters, as doo externall worship to idols or strange gods. The furthest point that idolatrie can be stretched unto, is, that they, which are culpable therein, are such as hope for and seeke salvation at the hands of idols, or of anie other than God; or fixe their whole mind and love upon anie creature, so as the power of God be neglected and contemned thereby. But witches neither seeke nor beleeve to have salvation at the hands of divels, but by them they are onlie deceived; the instruments of their phantasie being corrupted, and so infatuated, that they suppose, confesse, and saie they can doo that, which is as farre beyond their power and nature to doo, as to kill a man at *Yorke* before noone, when they have beene seene at *London* in that morning, &c. But if these latter idolaters, whose idolatrie is spirituall, and committed onelie in mind, should be punished by death; then should everie covetous man, or other, that setteth his affection anie waie too much upon an earthlie creature, be executed, and yet perchance the witch might escape scotfree.

Secondlie, apostasie is laid to their charge, whereby it is inferred, that they are worthie to die. But apostasie is, where anie of sound judgement forsake the gospell, learned and well knowne unto them; and doo not onelie embrace impietie and infidelitie; but oppugne and resist the truth erstwhile by them professed. But alas these poore women go not about to defend anie impietie, but after good admonition repent.

Thirdlie, they would have them executed for seducing the people. But God knoweth they have small store of Rhetorike or art to seduce; except to tell a tale of Robin good-fellow be to deceive and seduce. Neither may their age or sex admit that opinion or accusation to be just: for they themselves are poore seduced soules. I for my part (as else-where I have said) have prooved this point to be false in most apparent sort.

Fourthlie, as touching the accusation, which all the writers use herein against them for their carnall copulation with *Incubus*: the follie of mens credulitie is as much to be woondered at and derided, as the others vaine and impossible confessions. For the divell is a spirit, and hath neither flesh nor bones, which were to be used in the performance of this action. And since he also lacketh all instruments, substance, and seed ingendred of bloud; it were follie to staie overlong in the confutation of that, which is not in the nature

of things. And yet must I saie somewhat heerein, bicause the opinion hereof is so stronglie and universallie received, and the fables thereupon so innumerable; wherby *M. Mal. Bodin, Hemingius, Hyperius, Danaeus, Erastus,* and others that take upon them to write heerein, are so abused, or rather seeke to abuse others; as I woonder at their fond credulitie in this behalfe. For they affirme undoubtedlie, that the divell plaieth *Succubus* to the man, and carrieth from him the seed of generation, which he delivereth as *Incubus* to the woman, who manie times that waie is gotten with child; which will verie naturallie (they saie) become a witch, and such one they affirme *Merline* was.

* * *

By What Meanes the Common People Have Beene Made Beleevein the Miraculous Works of Witches, a Definition of Witchcraft, and a Description Thereof

The common people have beene so assotted and bewitched, with whatsoever poets have feigned of witchcraft, either in earnest, in jest, or else in derision; and with whatsoever lowd liers and couseners for their pleasures heerein have invented, and with whatsoever tales they have heard from old doting women, or from their mothers maids, and with whatsoever the grandfoole their ghostlie father, or anie other morrow masse preest had informed them; and finallie with whatsoever they have swallowed up through tract of time, or through their owne timerous nature or ignorant conceipt, concerning these matters of hagges and witches: as they have so settled their opinion and credit thereupon, that they thinke it heresie to doubt in anie part of the matter; speciallie bicause they find this word witchcraft expressed in the scriptures; which is as to defend praieng to sainets, bicause *Sanctus, Sanctus, Sanctus* is written in *Te Deum.*

And now to come to the definition of witchcraft, which hitherto I did deferre and put off purposelie: that you might perceive the true nature thereof, by the circumstances, and therefore the rather to allow of the same, seeing the varietie of other writers. Witchcraft is in truth a cousening art, wherin the name of God is abused, prophaned and blasphemed, and his power attributed to a vile creature. In estimation of the vulgar people, it is a supernaturall worke, contrived betweene a corporall old woman, and a spirituall divell. The maner thereof is so secret, mysticall, and strange, that to this daie there hath never beene any credible witnes thereof. It is incomprehensible to the wise, learned or faithfull; a probable matter to children, fooles, melancholike persons and papists. The trade is thought to be impious. The effect and end thereof to be sometimes evill, as when thereby man or beast, grasse, trees, or corne, &c; is hurt: sometimes good, as whereby sicke folkes are healed, theeves bewraied, and true men come to their goods, &c. The matter and instruments, wherewith it is accomplished, are words, charmes, signes, images, characters, &c; the which words although any other creature do pronounce, in manner and forme as they doo, leaving out no circumstance requisite or usually for that action: yet none is said to have the grace or gift to performe the matter, except she be a witch, and so taken either by hir owne consent, or by others imputation.

Reasons to Proove That Words and Characters Are But Bables, and That Witches Cannot Doo Such Things as the Multitude Supposeth They Can, Their Greatest Woonders Prooved Trifles, of a Yoong Gentleman Cousened

That words, characters, images, and such other trinkets, which are thought so necessarie instruments for witchcraft (as without the which no such thing can be accomplished) are but bables, devised by couseners, to abuse the people withall; I trust I have sufficientlie prooved. And the same maie be further and more plainelie perceived by these short and compendious reasons following.

First, in that *Turkes* and infidels, in their witchcraft, use both other words, and other characters than our witches doo and also such as are most contrarie. In so much as, if ours be bad, in reason theirs should be good. If their witches can doo anie thing, ours can doo nothing. For as our witches are said to renounce Christ, and despise his sacraments: so doo the other forsake *Mahomet,* and his lawes, which is one large step to christianitie.

It is also to be thought, that all witches are couseners; when mother *Bungie,* a principall witch, so reputed, tried, and condemned of all men, and continuing in that exercise and estimation manie yeares (having cousened & abused the whole realme, in so much as there came to hir, witchmongers from all the furthest parts of the land, she being in diverse bookes set out with authoritie, registred and chronicled by the name of the great witch of *Rochester,* and reputed among all men for the cheefe ringleader of all other witches) by good proofe is found to be a meere cousener; confessing in hir death bed freelie, without compulsion or inforcement, that hir cunning consisted onlie in deluding and deceiving the people: saying that she had (towards the maintenance of hir credit in that cousening trade) some sight in physicke and surgerie, and the assistance of a freend of hirs, called *Heron,* a professor thereof. And this I know, partlie of mine owne knowledge, and partlie by the testimonie of hir husband, and others of credit, to whome (I saie) in hir death bed, and at sundrie other times she protested these things; and also that she never had indeed anie materiall spirit or divell (as the voice went) nor yet knew how to worke anie supernaturall matter, as she in hir life time made men beleeve she had and could doo.

*   *   *

Againe, who will mainteine, that common witchcrafts are not cousenages, when the great and famous witchcrafts, which had stolne credit not onlie from all the common people, but from men of great wisdome and authoritie, are discovered to be beggerlie slights of cousening varlots? Which otherwise might and would have remained a perpetuall objection against me. Were there not three images of late yeeres found in a doonghill, to the terror & astonishment of manie thousands? In so much as great matters were thought to have beene pretended to be doone by witchcraft. But if the Lord preserve those persons (whose destruction was doubted to have beene intended thereby) from all other the lewd practises and attempts of their enimies; I feare not, but they shall easilie withstand these and such like devises, although they should indeed be practised against them. But no doubt, if such bables could have brought those matters of mischeefe to passe, by the hands of traitors, witches, or papists; we should long since have beene deprived of the most excellent jewell and comfort that we enjoy in this world. Howbeit, I confesse, that the feare, conceipt, and doubt of such mischeefous pretenses may breed inconvenience to them that stand in awe of the same. And I wish, that even for such practises, though they never can or doo take effect, the practisers be punished with all extremitie: bicause therein is manifested a traiterous heart to the Queene, and a presumption against God.

*   *   *

REVIEW QUESTIONS

1. What is witchcraft?
2. How does Scot depict it?
3. According to Scot, what characterizes witches and witchcraft?
4. How does Scot confound the very notion of witchcraft?
5. Where does he locate the source of all power to override the laws of nature?
6. What sort of power is left to witches?
7. What, according to Scot, is the relation of witches to the natural world?

THE PLUNDERING AND BURNING OF A VILLAGE, A HANGING, AND

PEASANTS AVENGE THEMSELVES (1633)   JACQUES CALLOT

These three prints, often referred to as The Horrors of War, powerfully reveal commonplace events of the early seventeenth century: the ravages of war on a small village, the punishment of unruly troops, and the violence of the violated. How does Callot portray rural life? What general aspects of the Iron Century does Callot capture in his images? Why do you think Callot decided to reveal the underbelly of seventeenth-century warfare rather than portraying it in more heroic terms?

FROM The Peace of Westphalia

A series of peace treaties signed over a six-month period in 1648, the Peace of West-phalia ended both the Thirty Years' War that ravaged the Holy Roman Empire between 1618 and 1648 and the Eighty Years' War that accompanied the struggle of the Dutch Republic for independence from the Spanish Empire. A complex process and treaty, the Peace of Westphalia involved multiple parties, including the Holy Roman emperor, the king of Spain, the king of France, the king of Sweden, the state-holder of the Dutch Republic, the princes of the Holy Roman Empire, and the repre-sentatives of the free imperial cities. It can be denoted by two major events. With the signing of the Peace of Münster between the Dutch Republic and the kingdom of Spain on 30 January 1648, which was officially ratified in Münster on 15 May 1648, Spain recognized the independence of the Dutch Republic. Two further treaties were signed later in the year, on 24 October 1648: the Treaty of Münster declared peace between the Holy Roman Emperor and France, and their respective allies; the Treaty of Osnabrück declared peace among the Holy Roman Empire, the kingdom of France, the kingdom of Sweden, and their respective allies. Despite their names, the treaties did not immediately restore peace throughout Europe, but they did create a basis for national self-determination and a new system of political order, sometimes referred to as Westphalian sovereignty. Based upon the concept of coexisting sovereign states, military aggression was to be held in check by a balance of power. A principle of noninterference in the internal affairs of other states likewise came into being. As European influence spread across the globe in the course of the seventeenth and eighteenth centuries, these principles became central to international law and the world order.

From Treaty of Westphalia, transcribed by the Avalon Project (Yale Law School, Lillian Goldman Law Library).

In the name of the most holy and individual Trinity: Be it known to all, and every one whom it may concern, or to whom in any manner it may belong, That for many Years past, Discords and Civil Divisions being stir'd up in the Roman Empire, which increas'd to such a degree, that not only all Germany, but also the neighbouring King-doms, and France particularly, have been involv'd in the Disorders of a long and cruel War: And in the first place, between the most Serene and most Puis-sant Prince and Lord, Ferdinand the Second, of famous Memory, elected Roman Emperor, always August, King of Germany, Hungary, Bohemia, Dal-matia, Croatia, Slavonia, Arch-Duke of Austria, Duke of Burgundy, Brabant, Styria, Carinthia, Car-niola, Marquiss of Moravia, Duke of Luxemburgh, the Higher and Lower Silesia, of Wirtemburg and Teck, Prince of Suabia, Count of Hapsburg, Tirol, Kyburg and Goritia, Marquiss of the Sacred Roman Empire, Lord of Burgovia, of the Higher and Lower Lusace, of the Marquisate of Slavonia, of Port Naon and Salines, with his Allies and Adherents on one side; and the most Serene, and the most Puissant Prince, Lewis the Thirteenth, most Christian King of France and Navarre, with his Allies and Adher-ents on the other side. And after their Decease, between the most Serene and Puissant Prince and Lord, Ferdinand the Third, elected Roman Emperor, always August, King of Germany, Hun-gary, Bohemia, Dalmatia, Croatia, Slavonia, Arch-

Duke of Austria, Duke of Burgundy, Brabant, Styria, Carinthia, Carniola, Marquiss of Moravia, Duke of Luxemburg, of the Higher and Lower Silesia, of Wirtemburg and Teck, Prince of Suabia, Count of Hapsburg, Tirol, Kyburg and Goritia, Marquiss of the Sacred Roman Empire, Burgovia, the Higher and Lower Lusace, Lord of the Marquisate of Slavonia, of Port Naon and Salines, with his Allies and Adherents on the one side; and the most Serene and most Puissant Prince and Lord, Lewis the Fourteenth, most Christian King of France and Navarre, with his Allies and Adherents on the other side: from whence ensu'd great Effusion of Christian Blood, and the Desolation of several Provinces. It has at last happen'd, by the effect of Divine Goodness, seconded by the Endeavours of the most Serene Republick of Venice, who in this sad time, when all Christendom is imbroil'd, has not ceas'd to contribute its Counsels for the publick Welfare and Tranquillity; so that on the side, and the other, they have form'd Thoughts of an universal Peace. And for this purpose, by a mutual Agreement and Covenant of both Partys, in the year of our Lord 1641, the 25th of December, N.S. or the 15th O.S. it was resolv'd at Hamburgh, to hold an Assembly of Plenipotentiary Ambassadors, who should render themselves at Munster and Osnabrug in Westphalia the 11th of July, N.S. or the 1st of the said month O.S. in the year 1643. The Plenipotentiary Ambassadors on the one side, and the other, duly establish'd, appearing at the prefixt time, and on the behalf of his Imperial Majesty, the most illustrious and most excellent Lord, Maximilian Count of Trautmansdorf and Weinsberg, Baron of Gleichenberg, Neustadt, Negan, Burgau, and Torzenbach, Lord of Teinitz, Knight of the Golden Fleece, Privy Counsellor and Chamberlain to his Imperial Sacred Majesty, and Steward of his Houshold; the Lord John Lewis, Count of Nassau, Catzenellebogen, Vianden, and Dietz, Lord of Bilstein, Privy Counsellor to the Emperor, and Knight of the Golden Fleece; Monsieur Isaac Volmamarus, Doctor of Law, Counsellor, and President in the Chamber of the most Serene Lord Arch-Duke Ferdinand Charles. And on the behalf of the most Christian King, the most eminent Prince and

Lord, Henry of Orleans, Duke of Longueville, and Estouteville, Prince and Sovereign Count of Neuschaftel, Count of Dunois and Tancerville, Hereditary Constable of Normandy, Governor and Lieutenant-General of the same Province, Captain of the Cent Hommes d'Arms, and Knight of the King's Orders, &c. as also the most illustrious and most excellent Lords, Claude de Mesmes, Count d'Avaux, Commander of the said King's Orders, one of the Superintendents of the Finances, and Minister of the Kingdom of France &c. and Abel Servien, Count la Roche of Aubiers, also one of the Ministers of the Kingdom of France. And by the Mediation and Interposition of the most illustrious and most excellent Ambassador and Senator of Venice, Aloysius Contarini Knight, who for the space of five Years, or thereabouts, with great Diligence, and a Spirit intirely impartial, has been inclin'd to be a Mediator in these Affairs. After having implor'd the Divine Assistance, and receiv'd a reciprocal Communication of Letters, Commissions, and full Powers, the Copys of which are inserted at the end of this Treaty, in the presence and with the consent of the Electors of the Sacred Roman Empire, the other Princes and States, to the Glory of God, and the Benefit of the Christian World, the following Articles have been agreed on and consented to, and the same run thus.

I.

That there shall be a Christian and Universal Peace, and a perpetual, true, and sincere Amity, between his Sacred Imperial Majesty, and his most Christian Majesty; as also, between all and each of the Allies, and Adherents of his said Imperial Majesty, the House of Austria, and its Heirs, and Successors; but chiefly between the Electors, Princes, and States of the Empire on the one side; and all and each of the Allies of his said Christian Majesty, and all their Heirs and Successors, chiefly between the most Serene Queen and Kingdom of Swedeland, the Electors respectively, the Princes and States of the Empire, on the other part. That this Peace and Amity be observ'd and cultivated with such a

Sincerity and Zeal, that each Party shall endeavour to procure the Benefit, Honour and Advantage of the other; that thus on all sides they may see this Peace and Friendship in the Roman Empire, and the Kingdom of France flourish, by entertaining a good and faithful Neighbourhood.

II.

That there shall be on the one side and the other a perpetual Oblivion, Amnesty, or Pardon of all that has been committed since the beginning of these Troubles, in what place, or what manner soever the Hostilitys have been practis'd, in such a manner, that no body, under any pretext whatsoever, shall practice any Acts of Hostility, entertain any Enmity, or cause any Trouble to each other; neither as to Persons, Effects and Securitys, neither of themselves or by others, neither privately nor openly, neither directly nor indirectly, neither under the colour of Right, nor by the way of Deed, either within or without the extent of the Empire, notwithstanding all Covenants made before to the contrary: That they shall not act, or permit to be acted, any wrong or injury to any whatsoever; but that all that has pass'd on the one side, and the other, as well before as during the War, in Words, Writings, and Outrageous Actions, in Violences, Hostilitys, Damages and Expences, without any respect to Persons or Things, shall be entirely abolish'd in such a manner that all that might be demanded of, or pretended to, by each other on that behalf, shall be bury'd in eternal Oblivion.

III.

And that a reciprocal Amity between the Emperor, and the Most Christian King, the Electors, Princes and States of the Empire, may be maintain'd so much the more firm and sincere (to say nothing at present of the Article of Security, which will be mention'd hereafter) the one shall never assist the present or future Enemys of the other under any Title or Pretence whatsoever, either with Arms,

Money, Soldiers, or any sort of Ammunition; nor no one, who is a Member of this Pacification, shall suffer any Enemys Troops to retire thro' or sojourn in his Country.

*   *   *

VI.

According to this foundation of reciprocal Amity, and a general Amnesty, all and every one of the Electors of the sacred Roman Empire, the Princes and States (therein comprehending the Nobility, which depend immediately on the Empire) their Vassals, Subjects, Citizens, Inhabitants (to whom on the account of the Bohemian or German Troubles or Alliances, contracted here and there, might have been done by the one Party or the other, any Prejudice or Damage in any manner, or under what pretence soever, as well in their Lordships, their fiefs, Underfiefs, Allodations, as in their Dignitys, Immunitys, Rights and Privileges) shall be fully re-establish'd on the one side and the other, in the Ecclesiastick or Laick State, which they enjoy'd, or could lawfully enjoy, notwithstanding any Alterations, which have been made in the mean time to the contrary.

*   *   *

XXVIII.

That those of the Confession of Augsburg, and particularly the Inhabitants of Oppenheim, shall be put in possession again of their Churches, and Ecclesiastical Estates, as they were in the Year 1624. as also that all others of the said Confession of Augsburg, who shall demand it, shall have the free Exercise of their Religion, as well in publick Churches at the appointed Hours, as in private in their own Houses, or in others chosen for this purpose by their Ministers, or by those of their Neighbours, preaching the Word of God.

*   *   *

XXXVII.

That the Contracts, Exchanges, Transactions, Obligations, Treatys, made by Constraint or Threats, and extorted illegally from States or Subjects (as in particular, those of Spiers complain, and those of Weisenburg on the Rhine, those of Landau, Reitlingen, Hailbron, and others) shall be so annull'd and abolish'd, that no more Enquiry shall be made after them.

XXXVIII.

That if Debtors have by force got some Bonds from their Creditors, the same shall be restor'd, but not with prejudice to their Rights.

XXXIX.

That the Debts either by Purchase, Sale, Revenues, or by what other name they may be call'd, if they have been violently extorted by one of the Partys in War, and if the Debtors alledge and offer to prove there has been a real Payment, they shall be no more prosecuted, before these Exceptions be first adjusted. That the Debtors shall be oblig'd to produce their Exceptions within the term of two years after the Publication of the Peace, upon pain of being afterwards condemn'd to perpetual Silence.

XL.

That Processes which have been hitherto enter'd on this Account, together with the Transactions and Promises made for the Restitution of Debts, shall be look'd upon as void; and yet the Sums of Money, which during the War have been exacted bona fide, and with a good intent, by way of Contributions, to prevent greater Evils by the Contributors, are not comprehended herein.

*   *   *

XLVI.

As for the rest, Law and Justice shall be administer'd in Bohemia, and in all the other Hereditary Provinces of the Emperor, without any respect; as to the Catholicks, so also to the Subjects, Creditors, Heirs, or private Persons, who shall be of the Confession of Augsburg, if they have any Pretensions, and enter or prosecute any Actions to obtain Justice.

*   *   *

REVIEW QUESTIONS

1. Why does the peace involve separate treaties for the Holy Roman emperor and the Holy Roman Empire?
2. When the peace refers to "entertaining a good and faithful Neighbourhood," what is meant?
3. Why is "restitution" a particularly important issue of the peace?
4. What becomes of the constitution of the Holy Roman Empire as a result of the peace?
5. How does the treaty define sovereignty?
6. What internal affairs of states does the peace specifically address?

MICHEL EYQUEM DE MONTAIGNE

FROM "Of Cannibals"

Michel Eyquem de Montaigne (1533–1592) originated the essay as a literary form. Born of a wealthy family at the Château de Montaigne, near Libourne, he was first educated by a tutor who spoke to him in Latin but no French. Until he was six years old, Montaigne learned the classical language as his native tongue. He was further educated at the Collège du Guyenne, where his fluency intimidated some of the finest Latinists in France, and studied law at Toulouse. In 1554, his father purchased an office in the Cour des Aides of Périgeaux, a fiscal court later incorporated into the Parlement of Bordeaux, a position he soon resigned to his son. Montaigne spent thirteen years in office at work he found neither pleasant nor useful. In 1571, he retired to the family estate. Apart from brief visits to Paris and Rouen, periods of travel, and two terms as mayor of Bordeaux (1581–85), Montaigne spent the rest of his life as a country gentleman. His life was not all leisure. He became gentleman-in-ordinary to the king's chamber and spent the period 1572–76 trying to broker a peace between Catholics and Huguenots. His first two books of the Essais *appeared in 1580; the third and last volume appeared in 1588. These essays are known for their discursive, conversational style, in which Montaigne undertook explorations of custom, opinion, and institutions. They gave voice to his opposition to all forms of dogmatism that were without rational basis. He observed life with a degree of skepticism, emphasizing the limits of human knowledge and the contradictions in human behavior. Indeed, Montaigne's essays are often cited as examples of an epistemological crisis borne of the new discoveries, theological debates, and social tensions that marked the early modern period.*

From *The Complete Essays of Montaigne*, translated by Donald M. Frame (Stanford: Stanford University Press, 1958).

When King Pyrrhus passed over into Italy, after he had reconnoitered the formation of the army that the Romans were sending to meet him, he said: "I do not know what barbarians these are" (for so the Greeks called all foreign nations), "but the formation of this army that I see is not at all barbarous." The Greeks said as much of the army that Flamininus brought into their country, and so did Philip, seeing from a knoll the order and distribution of the Roman camp, in his kingdom, under Publius Sulpicius Galba. Thus we should beware of clinging to vulgar opinions, and judge things by reason's way, not by popular say.

I had with me for a long time a man who had lived for ten or twelve years in that other world which has been discovered in our century, in the place where Villegaignon landed, and which he called Antarctic France. This discovery of a boundless country seems worthy of consideration. I don't know if I can guarantee that some other such discovery will not be made in the future, so many personages greater than ourselves having been mistaken about this one. I am afraid we have eyes bigger than our stomachs, and more curiosity than capacity. We embrace everything, but we clasp only wind.

*   *   *

This man I had was a simple, crude fellow—a character fit to bear true witness; for clever people observe more things and more curiously, but they interpret them; and to lend weight and conviction to their interpretation, they cannot help altering history a little. They never show you things as they are, but bend and disguise them according to the way they have seen them; and to give credence to their judgment and attract you to it, they are prone to add something to their matter, to stretch it out and amplify it. We need a man either very honest, or so simple that he has not the stuff to build up false inventions and give them plausibility; and wedded to no theory. Such was my man; and besides this, he at various times brought sailors and merchants, whom he had known on that trip, to see me. So I content myself with his information, without inquiring what the cosmographers say about it.

*   *   *

Now, to return to my subject, I think there is nothing barbarous and savage in that nation, from what I have been told, except that each man calls barbarism whatever is not his own practice; for indeed it seems we have no other test of truth and reason than the example and pattern of the opinions and customs of the country we live in. *There* is always the perfect religion, the perfect government, the perfect and accomplished manners in all things. Those people are wild, just as we call wild the fruits that Nature has produced by herself and in her normal course; whereas really it is those that we have changed artificially and led astray from the common order, that we should rather call wild. The former retain alive and vigorous their genuine, their most useful and natural, virtues and properties, which we have debased in the latter in adapting them to gratify our corrupted taste. And yet for all that, the savor and delicacy of some uncultivated fruits of those countries is quite as excellent, even to our taste, as that of our own. It is not reasonable that art should win the place of honor over our great and powerful mother Nature. We have so overloaded the beauty and richness of her works by our inventions that we have quite smothered her. Yet wherever her purity shines forth, she wonderfully puts to shame our vain and frivolous attempts:

> Ivy comes readier without our care;
> In lonely caves the arbutus grows more fair;
> No art with artless bird song can compare.
>   Propertius

All our efforts cannot even succeed in reproducing the nest of the tiniest little bird, its contexture, its beauty and convenience; or even the web of the puny spider. All things, says Plato, are produced by nature, by fortune, or by art; the greatest and most beautiful by one or the other of the first two, the least and most imperfect by the last.

These nations, then, seem to me barbarous in this sense, that they have been fashioned very little by the human mind, and are still very close to their original naturalness. The laws of nature still rule them, very little corrupted by ours; and they are in such a state of purity that I am sometimes vexed that they were unknown earlier, in the days when there were men able to judge them better than we. I am sorry that Lycurgus and Plato did not know of them; for it seems to me that what we actually see in these nations surpasses not only all the pictures in which poets have idealized the golden age and all their inventions in imagining a happy state of man, but also the conceptions and the very desire of philosophy. They could not imagine a naturalness so pure and simple as we see by experience; nor could they believe that our society could be maintained with so little artifice and human solder. This is a nation, I should say to Plato, in which there is no sort of traffic, no knowledge of letters, no science of numbers, no name for a magistrate or for political superiority, no custom of servitude, no riches or poverty, no contracts, no successions, no partitions, no occupations but leisure ones, no care for any but common kinship, no clothes, no agriculture, no metal, no use of wine or wheat. The very words that signify lying, treachery, dissimulation, avarice, envy, belittling, pardon—unheard of. How far from this perfection would he find the republic that he imagined: *Men fresh sprung from the gods.*

These manners nature first ordained.

Virgil

For the rest, they live in a country with a very pleasant and temperate climate, so that according to my witnesses it is rare to see a sick man there; and they have assured me that they never saw one palsied, bleary-eyed, toothless, or bent with age. They are settled along the sea and shut in on the land side by great high mountains, with a stretch about a hundred leagues wide in between. They have a great abundance of fish and flesh which bear no resemblance to ours, and they eat them with no other artifice than cooking. The first man who rode a horse there, though he had had dealings with them on several other trips, so horrified them in this posture that they shot him dead with arrows before they could recognize him.

Their buildings are very long, with a capacity of two or three hundred souls; they are covered with the bark of great trees, the strips reaching to the ground at one end and supporting and leaning on one another at the top, in the manner of some of our barns, whose covering hangs down to the ground and acts as a side. They have wood so hard that they cut with it and make of it their swords and grills to cook their food. Their beds are of a cotton weave, hung from the roof like those in our ships, each man having his own; for the wives sleep apart from their husbands.

They get up with the sun, and eat immediately upon rising, to last them through the day; for they take no other meal than that one. Like some other Eastern peoples, of whom Suidas tells us, who drank apart from meals, they do not drink then; but they drink several times a day, and to capacity. Their drink is made of some root, and is of the color of our claret wines. They drink it only lukewarm. This beverage keeps only two or three days; it has a slightly sharp taste, is not at all heady, is good for the stomach, and has a laxative effect upon those who are not used to it; it is a very pleasant drink for anyone who is accustomed to it. In place of bread they use a certain white substance like preserved coriander. I have tried it; it tastes sweet and a little flat.

The whole day is spent in dancing. The younger men go to hunt animals with bows. Some of the women busy themselves meanwhile with warming their drink, which is their chief duty. Some one of the old men, in the morning before they begin to eat, preaches to the whole barnful in common, walking from one end to the other, and repeating one single sentence several times until he has completed the circuit (for the buildings are fully a hundred paces long). He recommends to them only two things: valor against the enemy and love for their wives. And they never fail to point out this obligation, as their refrain, that it is their wives who keep their drink warm and seasoned.

There may be seen in several places, including my own house, specimens of their beds, of their ropes, of their wooden swords and the bracelets with which they cover their wrists in combats, and of the big canes, open at one end, by whose sound they keep time in their dances. They are close shaven all over, and shave themselves much more cleanly than we, with nothing but a wooden or stone razor. They believe that souls are immortal, and that those who have deserved well of the gods are lodged in that part of heaven where the sun rises, and the damned in the west.

They have some sort of priests and prophets, but they rarely appear before the people, having their home in the mountains. On their arrival there is a great feast and solemn assembly of several villages—each barn, as I have described it, makes up a village, and they are about one French league from each other. The prophet speaks to them in public, exhorting them to virtue and their duty; but their whole ethical science contains only these two articles: resoluteness in war and affection for their wives. He prophesies to them things to come and the results they are to expect from their undertakings, and urges them to war or holds them back from it; but this is on the condition that when he fails to prophesy correctly, and if things turn out otherwise than he has predicted, he is cut into a thousand pieces if they catch him, and condemned as a false prophet. For this reason, the prophet who has once been mistaken is never seen again.

*   *   *

They have their wars with the nations beyond the mountains, further inland, to which they go quite naked, with no other arms than bows or wooden swords ending in a sharp point, in the manner of the tongues of our boar spears. It is astonishing what firmness they show in their combats, which never end but in slaughter and bloodshed; for as to routs and terror, they know nothing of either.

Each man brings back as his trophy the head of the enemy he has killed, and sets it up at the entrance to his dwelling. After they have treated their prisoners well for a long time with all the hospitality they can think of, each man who has a prisoner calls a great assembly of his acquaintances. He ties a rope to one of the prisoner's arms, by the end of which he holds him, a few steps away, for fear of being hurt, and gives his dearest friend the other arm to hold in the same way; and these two, in the presence of the whole assembly, kill him with their swords. This done, they roast him and eat him in common and send some pieces to their absent friends. This is not, as people think, for nourishment, as of old the Scythians used to do; it is to betoken an extreme revenge. And the proof of this came when they saw the Portuguese, who had joined forces with their adversaries, inflict a different kind of death on them when they took them prisoner, which was to bury them up to the waist, shoot the rest of their body full of arrows, and afterward hang them. They thought that these people from the other world, being men who had sown the knowledge of many vices among their neighbors and were much greater masters than themselves in every sort of wickedness, did not adopt this sort of vengeance without some reason, and that it must be more painful than their own; so they began to give up their old method and to follow this one.

I am not sorry that we notice the barbarous horror of such acts, but I am heartily sorry that, judging their faults rightly, we should be so blind to our own. I think there is more barbarity in eating a man alive than in eating him dead; and in tearing by tortures and the rack a body still full of feeling, in roasting a man bit by bit, in having him bitten and mangled by dogs and swine (as we have not only read but seen within fresh memory, not among ancient enemies, but among neighbors and fellow citizens, and what is worse, on the pretext of piety and religion), than in roasting and eating him after he is dead.

*   *   *

So we may well call these people barbarians, in respect to the rules of reason, but not in respect to ourselves, who surpass them in every kind of barbarity.

Their warfare is wholly noble and generous, and as excusable and beautiful as this human disease can be; its only basis among them is their rivalry in valor. They are not fighting for the conquest of new lands, for they still enjoy that natural abundance that provides them without toil and trouble with all necessary things in such profusion that they have no wish to enlarge their boundaries. They are still in that happy state of desiring only as much as their natural needs demand; anything beyond that is superfluous to them.

They generally call those of the same age, brothers; those who are younger, children; and the old men are fathers to all the others. These leave to their heirs in common the full possession of their property, without division or any other title at all than just the one that Nature gives to her creatures in bringing them into the world.

If their neighbors cross the mountains to attack them and win a victory, the gain of the victor is glory, and the advantage of having proved the master in valor and virtue; for apart from this they have no use for the goods of the vanquished, and they return to their own country, where they lack neither anything necessary nor that great thing, the knowledge of how to enjoy their condition happily and be content with it. These men of ours do the same in their turn. They demand of their prisoners no other ransom than that they confess and acknowledge their defeat. But there is not one in a whole century who does not choose to die rather than to relax a single bit, by word or look, from the grandeur of an invincible courage; not one who would not rather be killed and eaten than so much as ask not to be. They treat them very freely, so that life may be all the dearer to them, and usually entertain them with threats of their coming death, of the torments they will have to suffer, the preparations that are being made for that purpose, the cutting up of their limbs, and the feast that will be made at their expense. All this is done for the sole purpose of extorting from their lips some weak or base word, or making them want to flee, so as to gain the advantage of having terrified them and broken down their firmness. For indeed, if you take it the right way, it is in this point alone that true victory lies:

It is no victory
Unless the vanquished foe admits your mastery.
Claudian

The Hungarians, very bellicose fighters, did not in olden times pursue their advantage beyond putting the enemy at their mercy. For having wrung a confession from him to this effect, they let him go unharmed and unransomed, except, at most, for exacting his promise never again to take up arms against them.

We win enough advantages over our enemies that are borrowed advantages, not really our own. It is the quality of a porter, not of valor, to have sturdier arms and legs; agility is a dead and corporeal quality; it is a stroke of luck to make our enemy stumble, or dazzle his eyes by the sunlight; it is a trick of art and technique, which may be found in a worthless coward, to be an able fencer. The worth and value of a man is in his heart and his will; there lies his real honor. Valor is the strength, not of legs and arms, but of heart and soul; it consists not in the worth of our horse or our weapons, but in our own. He who falls obstinate in his courage, *if he has fallen, he fights on his knees.* He who relaxes none of his assurance, no matter how great the danger of imminent death; who, giving up his soul, still looks firmly and scornfully at his enemy—he is beaten not by us, but by fortune; he is killed, not conquered.

*   *   *

To return to our story. These prisoners are so far from giving in, in spite of all that is done to them, that on the contrary, during the two or three months that they are kept, they wear a gay expression; they urge their captors to hurry and put them to the test; they defy them, insult them, reproach them with their cowardice and the number of battles they have lost to the prisoners' own people.

I have a song composed by a prisoner which contains this challenge, that they should all come boldly and gather to dine off him, for they will be eating at the same time their own fathers and grandfathers, who have served to feed and nourish his body. "These muscles," he says, "this flesh and these veins are your own, poor fools that you are. You do not recognize that the substance of your ancestors' limbs is still contained in them. Savor them well; you will find in them the taste of your own flesh." An idea that certainly does not smack of barbarity. Those that paint these people dying, and who show the execution, portray the prisoner spitting in the face of his slayers and scowling at them. Indeed, to the last gasp they never stop braving and defying their enemies by word and look. Truly here are real savages by our standards; for either they must be thoroughly so, or we must be; there is an amazing distance between their character and ours.

The men there have several wives, and the higher their reputation for valor the more wives they have. It is a remarkably beautiful thing about their marriages that the same jealousy our wives have to keep us from the affection and kindness of other women, theirs have to win this for them. Being more concerned for their husbands' honor than for anything else, they strive and scheme to have as many companions as they can, since that is a sign of their husbands' valor.

*   *   *

Three of these men, ignorant of the price they will pay some day, in loss of repose and happiness, for gaining knowledge of the corruptions of this side of the ocean; ignorant also of the fact that of this intercourse will come their ruin (which I suppose is already well advanced: poor wretches, to let

THE "ARMADA PORTRAIT" OF QUEEN ELIZABETH (c. 1588)   GEORGE GOWER

The English portraitist George Gower (1540–1596) became Sergeant Painter to Queen Eliz-abeth I of England in 1581. This—his most famous painting—notwithstanding, we know little of the artist or his career. A number of portraits survive from the period before his court appointment. Thereafter, he created portraits of many English aristocrats and supervised the decoration of the royal palace at Hampton Court. The "Armada Portrait" commemorates the defeat of the Spanish Armada in 1588. What elements of the painting indicate the importance of the sea and of naval power for England? Given that warfare was commonly understood to be "man's work," how does Gower handle the apparent contradiction of a warrior queen? How does he signal his patroness's firmness of command without making her masculine? How does he glorify Glorianna?

themselves be tricked by the desire for new things, and to have left the serenity of their own sky to come and see ours!)—three of these men were at Rouen, at the time the late King Charles IX was there. The king talked to them for a long time; they were shown our ways, our splendor, the aspect of a fine city. After that, someone asked their opinion, and wanted to know what they had found most amazing. They mentioned three things, of which I have forgotten the third, and I am very sorry for it; but I still remember two of them. They said that in the first place they thought it very strange that so many grown men, bearded, strong, and armed, who were around the king (it is likely that they were talking about the Swiss of his guard) should submit to obey a child, and that one of them was not chosen to command instead. Second (they have a way in their language of speaking of men as halves of one another), they had noticed that there were among us men full and gorged with all sorts of good things, and that their other halves were beggars at their doors, emaciated with hunger and poverty; and they thought it strange that these needy halves could endure such an injustice, and did not take the others by the throat, or set fire to their houses.

I had a very long talk with one of them; but I had an interpreter who followed my meaning so badly, and who was so hindered by his stupidity in taking in my ideas, that I could get hardly any satisfaction from the man. When I asked him what profit he gained from his superior position among his people (for he was a captain, and our sailors called him king), he told me that it was to march foremost in war. How many men followed him? He pointed to a piece of ground, to signify as many as such a space could hold; it might have been four or five thousand men. Did all his authority expire with the war? He said that this much remained, that when he visited the villages dependent on him, they made paths for him through the underbrush by which he might pass quite comfortably.

All this is not too bad—but what's the use? They don't wear breeches.

*   *   *

REVIEW QUESTIONS

1. What lessons does Montaigne draw from accounts of the New World?
2. Why do you suppose Montaigne chose cannibalism, of all possible topics, to compare European and American cultures?
3. How do Montaigne's ideas reflect the crisis of the iron century?
4. Are there any human constants for Montaigne?
5. Does he believe in a single human nature, a single ideal of virtue?

HUGO GROTIUS

FROM *On the Law of War and Peace*

Hugo Grotius (1583–1645) was a Dutch statesman, jurist, theologian, poet, philologist, and historian, a man of all-embracing knowledge whose writings were of fundamental importance in the formulation of international law. He was born in Delft, the son of the burgomaster and curator at the University of Leiden. Grotius was precocious; he matriculated at the University of Leiden at age eleven. By age fifteen, he had edited the encyclopedia of Martianus Capella and accompanied a diplomatic mission to the king of France, who described Grotius as the "miracle of Holland." He earned his doctorate in law at the University of Orléans and became a distinguished jurist at The Hague. In 1601, he was appointed historiographer of the States of Holland.

He wrote a number of minor but memorable legal treatises before publishing his great work, On the Law of War and Peace, in 1625. Grotius argued that the entire law of humankind was based on four fundamental precepts: neither a state nor an individual may attack another state or individual, neither a state nor an individual may appropriate what belongs to another state or individual, neither a state nor an individual may disregard treaties or contracts, and neither a state nor an individual may commit a crime. In the case of a violation of one of these precepts, compensation might be sought either by war or by individual action. These principles and the arguments that surrounded them significantly aided the development of a theory of state sovereignty and international relations in the early modern period. During the remainder of his life, Grotius remained involved in the political as well as the intellectual affairs of his day. Besides creating a vast corpus of written works, he participated in the government of the United Provinces of the Netherlands. He was eventually imprisoned for his support of Arminianism and managed to escape hidden in a trunk. He spent the rest of his life in exile, honored as one of the great intellectuals of the seventeenth century but unacknowledged by his own country.

From *The Rights of War and Peace*, by Hugo Grotius (Washington and London: M. Walter Dunne, 1901).

*   *   *

VIII

And here is the proper place for refuting the opinion of those, who maintain that, every where and without exception, the sovereign power is vested in the people, so that they have a right to restrain and punish kings for an abuse of their power. However there is no man of sober wisdom, who does not see the incalculable mischiefs, which such opinions have occasioned, and may still occasion; and upon the following grounds they may be refuted.

From the Jewish, as well as the Roman Law, it appears that any one might engage himself in private servitude to whom he pleased. Now if an individual may do so, why may not a whole people, for the benefit of better government and more certain protection, completely transfer their sovereign rights to one or more persons, without reserving any portion to themselves? Neither can it be al-

ledged that such a thing is not to be presumed, for the question is not, what is to be presumed in a doubtful case, but what may lawfully be done. Nor is it any more to the purpose to object to the inconveniences, which may, and actually do arise from a people's thus surrendering their rights. For it is not in the power of man to devise any form of government free from imperfections and dangers. As a dramatic writer says, "you must either take these advantages with those imperfections, or resign your pretensions to both."

Now as there are different ways of living, some of a worse, and some of a better kind, left to the choice of every individual; so a nation, "under certain circumstances, when for instance, the succession to the throne is extinct, or the throne has by any other means become vacant," may choose what form of government she pleases. Nor is this right to be measured by the excellence of this or that form of government, on which there may be varieties of opinion, but by the will of the people.

There may be many reasons indeed why a people may entirely relinquish their rights, and surrender them to another: for instance, they may have no other means of securing themselves from the danger of immediate destruction, or under the pressure of famine it may be the only way, through which they can procure support. For if the Campanians, formerly, when reduced by necessity surrendered themselves to the Roman people in the following terms:—"Senators of Rome, we consign to your dominion the people of Campania, and the city of Capua, our lands, our temples, and all things both divine and human," and if another people as Appian relates, offered to submit to the Romans, and were refused, what is there to prevent any nation from submitting in the same manner to one powerful sovereign? It may also happen that a master of a family, having large possessions, will suffer no one to reside upon them on any other terms, or an owner, having many slaves, may give them their liberty upon condition of their doing certain services, and paying certain rents; of which examples may be produced. Thus Tacitus, speaking of the German slaves, says, "Each has his own separate habitation, and his own household to govern. The master considers him as a tenant, bound to pay a certain rent in corn, cattle, and wearing apparel. And this is the utmost extent of his servitude."

Aristotle, in describing the requisites, which fit men for servitude, says, that "those men, whose powers are chiefly confined to the body, and whose principal excellence consists in affording bodily service, are naturally slaves, because it is their interest to be so." In the same manner some nations are of such a disposition that they are more calculated to obey than to govern, which seems to have been the opinion which the Cappadocians held of themselves, who when the Romans offered them a popular government, refused to accept it, because the nation they said could not exist in safety without a king. Thus Philostratus in the life of Apollonius, says, that it was foolish to offer liberty to the Thracians, the Mysians, and the Getae, which they were not capable of enjoying. The example of nations, who have for many ages lived happily under a kingly government, has induced many to give the preference to that form. Livy says, that the cities under Eumenes would not have changed their condition for that of any free state whatsoever. And sometimes a state is so situated, that it seems impossible it can preserve its peace and existence, without submitting to the absolute government of a single person, which many wise men thought to be the case with the Roman Republic in the time of Augustus Cæsar. From these, and causes like these it not only may, but generally does happen, that men, as Cicero observes in the second book of his offices, willingly submit to the supreme authority of another.

Now as property may be acquired by what has been already styled just war, by the same means the rights of sovereignty may be acquired. Nor is the term sovereignty here meant to be applied to monarchy alone, but to government by nobles, from any share in which the people are excluded. For there never was any government so purely popular, as not to require the exclusion of the poor, of strangers, women, and minors from the public councils. Some states have other nations under them, no less dependent upon their will, than subjects upon that of their sovereign princes. From whence arose that question, Are the Collatine people in their own power? And the Campanians, when they submitted to the Romans, are said to have passed under a foreign dominion. In the same manner Acarnania and Amphilochia are said to have been under the dominion of the Aetolians; Peraea and Caunus under that of the Rhodians; and Pydna was ceded by Philip to the Olynthians. And those towns, that had been under the Spartans, when they were delivered from their dominion, received the name of the free Laconians. The city of Cotyora is said by Xenophon to have belonged to the people of Sinope. Nice in Italy, according to Strabo, was adjudged to the people of Marseilles; and the island of Pithecusa to the Neapolitans. We find in Frontinus, that the towns of Calati and Caudium with their territories were adjudged, the one to the colony of Capua, and the other to that of Beneventum. Otho, as Tacitus relates, gave the cities of the Moors to the Province of Baetia. None of these instances, any more than the cessions of other conquered countries could be admitted, if it were a received rule that the rights of sovereigns are under the controul and direction of subjects.

Now it is plain both from sacred and profane history, that there are kings, who are not subject to the controul of the people in their collective body; God addressing the people of Israel, says, if thou shalt say, "I will place a king over me"; and to Samuel "Shew them the manner of the king, who shall reign over them." Hence the King is said to be anointed over the people, over the inheritance of the Lord, over Israel. Solomon is styled King over all Israel. Thus David gives thanks to God, for subduing the people under him. And Christ says, "the Kings of the nations bear rule over them." There is a well known passage in Horace, "Powerful sovereigns reign over their own subjects, and the supreme being over sovereigns themselves." Seneca thus describes the three forms of government, "Sometimes the supreme power is lodged in the people, sometimes in a senate composed of the leading men of the state, sometimes this power of the people, and dominion over the people themselves is vested in a single person." Of the last description are those, who, as Plutarch says, exercise authority not according to the laws, but over the laws. And in Herodutus, Otanes describes a monarch as one whose acts are not subject to controul. Dion Prusaeensis also and Pausanias define a monarchy in the same terms.

Aristotle says there are some kings, who have the same right, which the nation elsewhere possesses over persons and property. Thus when the Roman Princes began to exercise regal power, the people it was said had transferred all their own personal sovereignty to them, which gave rise to the saying of Marcus Antoninus the Philosopher, that no one but God alone can be judge of the Prince. Dion. L. liii. speaking of such a prince, says, "he is perfectly master of his own actions, to do whatever he pleases, and cannot be obliged to do any thing against his will." Such anciently was the power of the Inachidae established at Argos in Greece. For in the Greek Tragedy of the Suppliants, Aeschylus has introduced the people thus addressing the King: "You are the state, you the people; you the court

from which there is no appeal, you preside over the altars, and regulate all affairs by your supreme will." King Theseus himself in Euripides speaks in very different terms of the Athenian Republic; "The city is not governed by one man, but in a popular form, by an annual succession of magistrates." For according to Plutarch's explanation, Theseus was the general in war, and the guardian of the laws; but in other respects nothing more than a citizen. So that they who are limited by popular controul are improperly called kings. Thus after the time of Lycurgus, and more particularly after the institution of the Ephori, the Kings of the Lacedaemonians are said by Polybius, Plutarch, and Cornelius Nepos, to have been Kings more in name than in reality. An example which was followed by the rest of Greece. Thus Pausanias says of the Argives to the Corinthians, "The Argives from their love of equality have reduced their kingly power very low; so that they have left the posterity of Cisus nothing more than the shadow of Kings." Aristotle denies such to be proper forms of government, because they constitute only a part of an Aristocracy or Democracy.

Examples also may be found of nations, who have not been under a perpetual regal form, but only for a time under a government exempt from popular controul. Such was the power of the Amimonians among the Cnidians, and of the Dictators in the early periods of the Roman history, when there was no appeal to the people, from whence Livy says, the will of the Dictator was observed as a law. Indeed they found this submission the only remedy against imminent danger, and in the words of Cicero, the Dictatorship possessed all the strength of royal power.

It will not be difficult to refute the arguments brought in favour of the contrary opinion. For in the first place the assertion that the constituent always retains a controul over the sovereign power, which he has contributed to establish, is only true in those cases where the continuance and existence of that power depends upon the will and pleasure of the constituent: but not in cases where the power, though it might derive its origin from that constituent, becomes a necessary and fundamental part of the established law. Of this nature is that authority to which a woman submits when she gives herself to a husband. Valentinian the Emperor, when the soldiers who had raised him to the throne, made a demand of which he did not approve, replied; "Soldiers, your election of me for your emperor was your own voluntary choice; but since you have elected me, it depends upon my pleasure to grant your request. It becomes you to obey as subjects, and me to consider what is proper to be done."

Nor is the assumption true, that all kings are made by the people, as may be plainly seen from the instances adduced above, of an owner admitting strangers to reside upon his demesnes on condition of their obedience, and of nations submitting by right of conquest. Another argument is derived from a saying of the Philosophers, that all power is conferred for the benefit of the governed and not of the governing party. Hence from the nobleness of the end, it is supposed to follow, that subjects have a superiority over the sovereign. But it is not universally true, that all power is conferred for the benefit of the party governed. For some powers are conferred for the sake of the governor, as the right of a master over a slave, in which the advantage of the latter is only a contingent and adventitious circumstance. In the same manner the gain of a Physician is to reward him for his labour; and not merely to promote the good of his art. There are other kinds of authority established for the benefit of both parties, as for instance, the authority of a husband over his wife. Certain governments also, as those which are gained by right of conquest, may be established for the benefit of the sovereign; and yet convey no idea of tyranny, a word which in its original signification, implied nothing of arbitrary power or injustice, but only the government or authority of a Prince. Again, some governments may be formed for the advantage both of subjects and sovereign, as when a people, unable to defend themselves, put themselves under the protection and dominion of any powerful king. Yet it is not to be denied, but that in most governments the good of the subject is the chief object which is regarded: and that what Cicero has said after Herodotus, and Herodotus after Hesiod, is true, that Kings were appointed in order that men might enjoy complete justice.

Now this admission by no means goes to establish the inference that kings are amenable to the people. For though guardianships were invented for the benefit of wards, yet the guardian has a right to authority over the ward. Nor, though a guardian may for mismanagement be removed from his trust, does it follow that a king may for the same reason be deposed. The cases are quite different, the guardian has a superior to judge him; but in governments, as there must be some dernier resort, it must be vested either in an individual, or in some public body, whose misconduct, as there is no superior tribunal before which they can be called, God declares that he himself will judge. He either punishes their offences, should he deem it necessary; or permits them for the chastisement of his people.

This is well expressed by Tacitus: he says, "you should bear with the rapacity or luxury of rulers, as you would bear with drought, or excessive rains, or any other calamities of nature. For as long as men exist there will be faults and imperfections; but these are not of uninterrupted continuance, and they are often repaired by the succession of better times." And Marcus Aurelius speaking of subordinate magistrates, said, that they were under the controul of the sovereign: but that the sovereign was amenable to God. There is a remarkable passage in Gregory of Tours, where that Bishop thus addresses the King of France, "If any of us, Sir, should transgress the bounds of justice, he may be punished by you. But if you exceed them, who can call you to account? For when we address you, you may hear us if you please; but if you will not, who can judge you, except him, who has declared himself to be righteousness?" Among the maxims of the Essenes, Porphyry cites a passage, that "no one can reign without the special appointment of divine providence." Irenaeus has expressed this well, "Kings are appointed by him at whose command men are created; and their appointment is suited to the condition of those, whom they are called to govern." There is the same thought in the Constitutions of Clement, "You shall fear the King, for he is of the Lord's appointment."

Nor is it an objection to what has been said, that some nations have been punished for the offences of their kings, for this does not happen, because they forbear to restrain their kings, but because they seem to give, at least a tacit consent to their vices, or perhaps, without respect to this, God may use that sovereign power which he has over the life and death of every man to inflict a punishment upon the king by depriving him of his subjects.

*   *   *

REVIEW QUESTIONS

1. What is the relation between political power and will according to Grotius?
2. How does Grotius define the state? The sovereign state?
3. Where does Grotius locate sovereignty?
4. Does sovereignty have a moral component?
5. What is sovereignty's relation to property? To the good of the people?

FROM The Religious Peace of Augsburg

On September 25, 1555, the Religious Peace of Augsburg officially ended the religious struggle between the Catholic authorities, led by the Holy Roman Emperor Charles V, and the forces of the Schmalkaldic League, an alliance of Lutheran princes. It made permanent the division of Christian church within the Holy Roman Empire by establishing the principle that each ruling authority could determine the official religion of its realm, either Lutheranism in accordance with the Augsburg Confession or Catholicism. This principle was later referred to as cuius regio, eius religio. *Subjects had to submit or migrate.*

From *Select Documents*, edited by E. Reich (London: P. S. King: 1905), pp. 230–32.

*   *   *

15. In order to bring peace to the Holy Roman Empire of the Germanic Nation between the Roman Imperial Majesty and the Electors, Princes and Estates, let neither his Imperial Majesty nor the Electors, Princes, etc., do any violence or harm to any estate of the empire on the account of the Augsburg Confession, but let them enjoy their religious belief, liturgy and ceremonies as well as their estates and other rights and privileges in peace; and complete religious peace shall be obtained only by Christian means of amity, or under threat of punishment of the Imperial ban.

16. Likewise the Estates espousing the Augsburg Confession shall let all the Estates and Princes who cling to the old religion live in absolute peace and in the enjoyment of all their estates, rights, and privileges.

17. However, all such as do not belong to the two above named religions shall not be included in the present peace but be totally excluded from it.

18. And since it has proved to be a matter of great dispute what was to happen with the bishoprics, priories and other ecclesiastical benefices of such Catholic priests who would in course of time abandon the old religion, we have in virtue of the powers of Roman Emperors ordained as follows: where an archbishop, bishop or prelate or any other priest of our old religion shall abandon the same, his archbishopric, bishopric, prelacy and other benefices together with all their income and revenues which he has so far possessed, shall be abandoned

by him without any further objection or delay. The chapter and such [as] are entitled to it by common law or the custom of the place shall elect a person espousing the old religion who may enter on the possession and enjoyment of all the rights and incomes of the place without any further hindrance and without prejudging any ultimate amicable transaction of religion.

19. Some of the abbeys, monasteries and other ecclesiastical estates having been confiscated and turned into churches, schools, and charitable institutions, it is herewith ordained that such estates which their original owners had not possessed at the time of the Treaty of Passau [1552] shall be comprised in the present treaty of peace.

20. The ecclesiastical jurisdiction over the Augsburg Confession, dogma, appointment of ministers, church ordinances, and ministries hitherto practiced (but apart from all the rights of Electors, Princes and Estates colleges and monasteries to taxes in money or tithes) shall from now cease and the Augsburg Confession shall be left to the free and untrammeled enjoyment of their religion, ceremonies, appointment of ministers, as is stated in a subsequent separate article, until the final transaction of religion will take place.

*   *   *

23. No Estate shall try to persuade the subjects of other Estates to abandon their religion or protect them against their own magistrates. Such as had from olden times the rights of patronage are not included in the present article.

24. In case our subjects whether belonging to the old religion or the Augsburg Confession should intend leaving their homes with their wives and children in order to settle in another, they shall be hindered neither in the sale of their estates after due payment of the local taxes nor injured in their honor.

REVIEW QUESTIONS

1. Why do we call this document a "religious peace"?
2. What does the Religious Peace specifically allow?
3. What does the Religious Peace specifically disallow?
4. Does the Religious Peace constitute an act of toleration?
5. What is the particular significance of Article 18, the so-called ecclesiastical reservation?
6. What grounds for future conflicts does this "religious peace" contain?

15 ∽ EUROPEAN MONARCHIES AND ABSOLUTISM, 1660–1725

The word transition *best characterizes the economy and society of early modern Europe. Although the forms of production and exchange remained corporatist and traditional, elements of individualism and capitalism exerted increasingly strong influence. Accordingly, European society, which remained in large part hierarchical and patriarchal, showed signs of an emergent class structure. Evidence of these changes remained regional, being more marked in certain places and times than in others. Nonetheless, the evidence of such a transition can be seen nearly everywhere in Europe, driven by forces that gripped the entire continent.*

For much of this period, the population remained locked in a struggle to survive. Beset by periodic famine and disease, life seemed tenuous and expectancies were short. Given high and early mortality, marriages occurred relatively late in life, and truncated families were commonplace. Beginning in the late seventeenth century, however, mortality began to decline. By the eighteenth century, populations were expanding across Europe.

The principal cause of the change in demographic dynamics was an increase in food supply that can be attributed in turn to a gradual change in agricultural techniques. Throughout the early modern period, traditional agricultural practices gradually yielded to techniques known generally as scientific farming. Landowners who sought gain in the marketplaces of Europe needed more direct control over land use and the ability to respond flexibly to market conditions. As a result, they enclosed communal lands and turned to the kinds of husbandry that would increase harvests and profits. The result was an increased food supply that eventually freed Europe from its age-old cycle of feast and famine.

An increasing population put new pressures on industry by raising the demand for manufactured goods and supplying a ready labor force to produce them. Rural manufacturing in the form of extensive production networks, known as the putting-out system, increased industrial productivity and captured surplus population in industrial work processes. Those who could not find such employment fled to the cities, which also grew rapidly. It is interesting that urban manufacturing remained largely traditional, that is, highly regulated and guild based, throughout the early modern period.

The greatest single force for change between 1500 and 1800 was the expansion of long-distance commerce based on the development of overseas empires and the consolidation of central states. Capitalist practices had existed since the late fourteenth century at least, but the possibility of large profits from direct trade with Asia and the Americas offered new scope for their application. The development of mercantilist theories, which advocated the expansion of trade as a source of political power, combined with capitalist ambitions to facilitate global commerce. As a result, enterprises such as charter companies emerged on a larger scale. The supplies of goods traded and their profitability promoted the refinement of commercial facilities such as commodity exchanges, stock markets, and banking techniques. Moreover, the activities of these enterprises introduced new commodities in such volumes that new tastes emerged and old patterns of consumption were transformed.

Growing populations and expanding economies notwithstanding, the society of early modern Europe remained traditional. It was hierarchical in structure; each individual's place was fixed by birthright. Authority was patriarchal in nature, modeled on the supposedly absolute authority of the father within his family. Yet transition was also evident here. Economic change created mobility. New wealth encouraged social and political aspirations as bourgeois everywhere chafed under the exclusivity of the aristocracy and sought admission to their ranks. New poverty created a class of have-nots that challenged the established order and threatened its security.

Observers and theorists viewed the transformation of Europe's economy and society with some trepidation. In most instances, their responses were reactionary. They returned to notions of fatherhood for a model of authority that could withstand the changing times. As the period progressed, however, more and more theorists turned to philosophical reason to find general laws of human interaction that might be applied to govern economic and social behavior.

Absolutism refers to a particular conception of political authority that emerged in the wake of this transition and its attendant disorders in the later sixteenth century. It asserted order, where Europeans felt order had been undermined in political and social relations, by positing a vision of a society that had its apex in the person of a single ruler. At the center of all conceptions of absolutism was the will of the ruler: For all theorists, that will was absolute, not merely sovereign but determinative of all political relations. Such an understanding of the nature and operation of political power required a number of developments, not the least of which were a military and a bureaucracy to carry out the king's will.

By the end of the period, there would be calls for enlightened absolutism, whereby reason guided the will of the sovereign, but the will of the monarch was still the agent of political life. Among theorists, several emerged who countered the notion of absolute monarchy with that of sovereignty placed in the hands of property owners. Moreover, they argued persuasively that the exercise of sovereignty was limited in accordance with the principles of natural law.

No monarch in this period was truly absolute—such an effective expression of the will of the ruler requires greater technological and military support than any ruler prior to the nineteenth century could have. Many, however, were largely successful in representing themselves as the center of all political life in their states, nurturing courts and bureaucracies that reflected images of omniscient and powerful rulers. These same courts provided both a milieu and the financial support for philosophes such as Voltaire and scientists such as Galileo, even as those intellectuals were calling into question the ethics of and the social bases for absolutism.

JEAN BODIN

FROM *On Sovereignty*

Jean Bodin (1529–1596) was born a bourgeois in Angers. He entered a Carmelite monastery in 1545, apparently set on an ecclesiastical career, but obtained release from his vows around 1549. He pursued a course of study at the royal Collège de Quatre Langues in Paris. By 1550, he was well trained in humanist studies and went on to become one of the greatest scholars of his day. His continual search for religious truth placed him repeatedly under suspicion of heresy, but no clear evidence exists to support a conversion to Calvinism. Bodin continued his studies and attended the University of Toulouse, where he studied law during the 1550s. In 1561, he launched his public career by serving as an advocate before the parliament in Paris. Bodin soon came to the attention of high officials and dignitaries and received special commissions from the king as early as 1570. In 1571, he entered the service of Francis, duke of Alençon, a prince of the blood. During his service to Alençon, and in the aftermath of the St. Bartholomew's Day massacre, Bodin published his great work, Six livres de la république *(1576), a systematic exposition of public law. It included an absolutist theory of royal government, from which the following selection is drawn. Bodin's theory was based on the controversial notion, which proved highly influential in the development of royal absolutism, that sovereignty was indivisible and that high powers of government could not be shared by separate agents or agencies. His notion that all governmental powers were concentrated in the king of France can be seen as a direct response to the anarchy of civil war that gripped the kingdom during the second half of the sixteenth century. In 1576, Bodin was chosen as a deputy for the Third Estate of the Estates-General of Blois. Though a royalist, Bodin opposed the civil wars that raged in France and became a leading spokesperson against royal requests for increased taxation and religious uniformity. It cost him royal favor and high office. With the death in 1584 of his patron, the duke of Alençon, Bodin's career in high politics ended. He retired to Laon, where he died.*

From *On Sovereignty*, by Jean Bodin, edited by Julian H. Franklin (Cambridge: Cambridge University Press, 1992), pp. 46–50.

Book I

*   *   *

CHAPTER 8
ON SOVEREIGNTY

Sovereignty is the absolute and perpetual power of a commonwealth, which the Latins call *maiestas;* the Greeks *akra exousia, kurion arche,* and *kurion politeuma;* and the Italians *segnioria,* a word they use for private persons as well as for those who have full control of the state, while the Hebrews call it *tomech shévet*—that is, the highest power of command. We must now formulate a definition of sovereignty because no jurist or political philosopher has defined it, even though it is the chief point, and the one that needs most to be explained, in a treatise on the commonwealth. Inasmuch as we have said that a commonwealth is a just government, with sovereign power, of several households and of that which they have in common, we need to clarify the meaning of sovereign power.

*   *   *

We shall conclude, then, that the sovereignty of the monarch is in no way altered by the presence of the Estates. On the contrary, his majesty is all the greater and more illustrious when all his people publicly acknowledge him as sovereign, even though, in an assembly like this, princes, not wishing to rebuff their subjects, grant and pass many things that they would not consent to had they not been overcome by the requests, petitions, and just complaints of a harassed and afflicted people which has most often been wronged without the knowledge of the prince, who sees and hears only through the eyes, ears, and reports of others.

We thus see that the main point of sovereign majesty and absolute power consists of giving the law to subjects in general without their consent. Not to go to other countries, we in this kingdom have often seen certain general customs repealed by edicts of our kings without hearing from the Estates when the injustice of the rules was obvious. Thus the custom concerning the inheritance by mothers of their children's goods, which was observed in this kingdom throughout the entire region governed by customary law, was changed without assembling either the general or local estates. Nor is this something new. In the time of King Philip the Fair, the general custom of the entire kingdom, by which the losing party in a case could not be required to pay expenses, was suppressed by an edict without assembling the Estates.

*   *   *

CHAPTER 10
ON THE TRUE MARKS OF SOVEREIGNTY

Since there is nothing greater on earth, after God, than sovereign princes, and since they have been established by Him as His lieutenants for commanding other men, we need to be precise about their status so that we may respect and revere their majesty in complete obedience, and do them honor in our thoughts and in our speech. Contempt for one's sovereign prince is contempt toward God, of whom he is the earthly image. That is why God, speaking to Samuel, from whom the people had demanded a different prince, said "It is me that they have wronged."

To be able to recognize such a person—that is, a sovereign—we have to know his attributes, which are properties not shared by subjects. For if they were shared, there would be no sovereign prince. Yet the best writers on this subject have not treated this point with the clarity it deserves, whether from flattery, fear, hatred, or forgetfulness.

We read that Samuel, after consecrating the king that God had designated, wrote a book about the rights of majesty. But the Hebrews have written that the kings suppressed his book so that they could tyrannize their subjects. Melanchthon thus went astray in thinking that the rights of majesty were the abuses and tyrannical practices that Samuel pointed out to the people in a speech. "Do you wish to know," said Samuel, "the ways of tyrants? It is to seize the goods of subjects to dispose of at his pleasure, and to seize their women and their children in order to abuse them and to make them slaves." The word *mishpotim* as it is used in this passage does not mean rights, but rather practices and ways of doing things. Otherwise this good prince, Samuel, would have contradicted himself. For when accounting to the people for the stewardship that God had given him, he said, "Is there anyone among you who can say that I ever took gold or silver from him, or any present whatsoever?" And thereupon the whole people loudly praised him for never having done a wrong or taken anything from anyone no matter who.

*　　*　　*

We may thus conclude that the first prerogative of a sovereign prince is to give law to all in general and each in particular. But this is not sufficient. We have to add "without the consent of any other, whether greater, equal, or below him." For if the prince is obligated to make no law without the con-sent of a superior, he is clearly a subject; if of an equal, he has an associate; if of subjects, such as the senate or the people, he is not sovereign. The names of grandees that one finds affixed to edicts are not put there to give the law its force, but to witness it and to add weight to it so that the enactment will be more acceptable. For there are very ancient edicts, extant at Saint Denys in France, issued by Philip I and Louis the Fat in 1060 and 1129 respectively, to which the seals of their queens Anne and Alix, and of Robert and Hugh, were affixed. For Louis the Fat, it was year twelve of his reign; for Adelaide, year six.

When I say that the first prerogative of sovereignty is to give law to all in general and to each in particular, the latter part refers to privileges, which are in the jurisdiction of sovereign princes to the exclusion of all others. I call it a privilege when a law is made for one or a few private individuals, no matter whether it is for the profit or the loss of the person with respect to whom it is decreed. Thus Cicero said, *Privilegium de meo capite latum est.* "They have passed," he said, "a capital privilege against me." He is referring to the authorization to put him on trial decreed against him by the commoners at the request of the tribune Clodius. He calls this the *lex Clodia* in many places, and he bitterly protests that privileges could be decreed only by the great Estates of the people as it was laid down by the laws of the Twelve Tables in the words: *Privilegia, nisi comitiis centuriatis irroganto, qui secus faxit capital esto.*[1] And all those who have written of regalian rights agree that only the sovereign can grant privileges, exemptions, and immunities, and grant dispensations from edicts and ordinances. In monarchies, however, privileges last only for the lifetime of the monarchs, as the emperor Tiberius, Suetonius reports, informed all those who had received privileges from Augustus.

*　　*　　*

---

[1] "Let no privileges be imposed except in the *comita centuriata;* let him who has done otherwise be put to death."

Book II

CHAPTER 5
WHETHER IT IS LAWFUL TO MAKE AN ATTEMPT UPON THE TYRANT'S LIFE AND TO NULLIFY AND REPEAL HIS ORDINANCES AFTER HE IS DEAD

Ignorance of the exact meaning of the term "tyrant" has led many people astray, and has been the cause of many inconveniences. We have said that a tyrant is someone who makes himself into a sovereign prince by his own authority—without election, or right of succession, or lot, or a just war, or a special calling from God. This is what is understood by tyrant in the writings of the ancients and in the laws that would have him put to death. Indeed, the ancients established great prizes and rewards for those who killed tyrants, offering titles of nobility, prowess, and chivalry to them along with statues and honorific titles, and even all the tyrant's goods, because they were taken as true liberators of the fatherland, or of the motherland, as the Cretans say. In this they did not distinguish, between a good and virtuous prince and a bad and wicked one, for no one has the right to seize the sovereignty and make himself the master of those who had been his companions, no matter what pretenses of justice and virtue he may offer. In strictest law, furthermore, use of the prerogatives reserved to sovereignty is punishable by death. Hence if a subject seeks, by whatever means, to invade the state and steal it from his king or, in a democracy or aristocracy, to turn himself from a fellow-citizen into lord and master, he deserves to be put to death. In this respect our question does not pose any difficulty.

*   *   *

At this point there are many questions one may ask, such as whether a tyrant, who I said may be justly killed without form or shape of trial, becomes legitimate if, after having encroached upon sovereignty by force or fraud, he has himself elected by the Estates. For it seems that the solemn act of election is an authentic ratification of the tyranny, an indication that the people have found it to their lik-

ing. But I say that it is nevertheless permissible to kill him, and to do so by force unless the tyrant, stripping off his authority, has given up his arms and put power back into the hands of the people in order to have its judgment. What tyrants force upon a people stripped of power cannot be called consent. Sulla, for example, had himself made dictator for eighty years by the Valerian law, which he got published with a powerful army camped inside the city of Rome. But Cicero said that this was not a law. Another example is Caesar, who had himself made permanent dictator by the Servian law; and yet another is Cosimo de Medici who, having an army inside Florence, had himself elected duke. When objections were raised, he set off a volley of gunfire in front of the palace, which induced the lords and magistrates to get on with it more quickly.

*   *   *

So much then for the tyrant, whether virtuous or wicked, who makes himself a sovereign lord on his own authority. But the chief difficulty arising from our question is whether a sovereign prince who has come into possession of the state by way of election, or lot, or right of succession, or just war, or by a special calling from God, can be killed if he is cruel, oppressive, or excessively wicked. For that is the meaning given to the word tyrant. Many doctors and theologians, who have touched upon this question, have resolved that it is permissible to kill a tyrant without distinction, and some, putting two words together that are incompatible, have spoken of a king-tyrant (*roi tyran*), which has caused the ruin of some very fine and flourishing monarchies.

But to decide this question properly we need to distinguish between a prince who is absolutely sovereign and one who is not, and between subjects and foreigners. It makes a great difference whether we say that a tyrant can be lawfully killed by a foreign prince or by a subject. For just as it is glorious and becoming, when the gates of justice have been shut, for someone, whoever he may be, to use force in defense of the goods, honor, and life of those who have been unjustly oppressed—as Moses did when he saw his brother being beaten and mistreated and had no way of getting justice—so is it a most beautiful and magnificent thing for a prince to take up arms in order to avenge an entire people unjustly oppressed by a tyrant's cruelty, as did Hercules, who traveled all over the world exterminating tyrant-monsters and was deified for his great feats. The same was done by Dion, Timoleon, Aratus, and other generous princes, who obtained the title of chastisers and correctors of tyrants. This, furthermore, was the sole cause for which Tamerlane, prince of the Tartars, declared war on Bajazet, who was then besieging Constantinople, Tamerlane saying that he had come to punish him for tyranny and to deliver the afflicted peoples. He defeated Bajazet in a battle fought on the plateau of Mount Stella, and after he had killed and routed three hundred thousand Turks, he had the tyrant chained inside a cage until he died. In this case it makes no difference whether this virtuous prince proceeds against a tyrant by force, deception, or judicial means. It is however true that if a virtuous prince has seized a tyrant, he will obtain more honor by putting him on trial and punishing him as a murderer, parricide, and thief, rather than acting against him by the common law of peoples (*droit des gens*).

But as for subjects, and what they may do, one has to know whether the prince is absolutely sovereign, or is properly speaking not a sovereign. For if he is not absolutely sovereign, it follows necessarily that sovereignty is in the people or the aristocracy. In this latter case there is no doubt that it is permissible to proceed against the tyrant either by way of law if one can prevail against him, or else by way of fact and open force, if one cannot otherwise have justice. Thus the Senate took the first way against Nero, the second against Maximinus inasmuch as the Roman emperors were no more than princes of the republic, in the sense of first persons and chief citizens, with sovereignty remaining in the people and the Senate.

*   *   *

But if the prince is sovereign absolutely, as are the genuine monarchs of France, Spain, England, Scotland, Ethiopia, Turkey, Persia, and Moscovy—whose power has never been called into question and whose sovereignty has never been shared with subjects—then it is not the part of any subject individually, or all of them in general, to make an attempt on the honor or the life of the monarch, either by way of force or by way of law, even if he has committed all the misdeeds, impieties, and cruelties that one could mention. As to the way of law, the subject has no right of jurisdiction over his prince, on whom all power and authority to command depends; he not only can revoke all the power of his magistrates, but in his presence, all the power and jurisdiction of all magistrates, guilds and corporations, Estates and communities, cease, as we have said and will say again even more elaborately in the proper place. And if it is not permissible for a subject to pass judgment on his prince, or a vassal on his lord, or a servant on his master—in short, if it is not permissible to proceed against one's king by way of law—how could it be licit to do so by way of force? For the question here is not to discover who is the strongest, but only whether it is permissible in law, and whether a subject has the power to condemn his sovereign prince.

A subject is guilty of treason in the first degree not only for having killed a sovereign prince, but also for attempting it, advising it, wishing it, or even thinking it. And the law finds this so monstrous [as to subject it to a special rule of sentencing]. Ordinarily, if someone who is accused, seized, and convicted dies before he has been sentenced, his personal status is not diminished, no matter what his crime, even if it was treason. But treason in the highest degree can never be purged by the death of the person accused of it, and even someone who was never accused is considered in law as having been already sentenced. And although evil thoughts are not subject to punishment, anyone who has thought of making an attempt on the life of his sovereign prince is held to be guilty of a capital crime, no matter whether he repented of it. In fact there was a gentleman from Normandy who confessed to a Franciscan friar that he had wanted to kill King Francis I but had repented of this evil wish. The Franciscan gave him absolution, but still told the king about it; he had the gentleman sent before the Parlement of Paris to stand trial, where he was condemned to death by its verdict and thereupon executed. And one cannot say that the court acted from fear, in view of the fact that it often refused to verify edicts and letters patent even when the king commanded it. And in Paris a man, named Caboche, who was completely mad and out of his senses, drew a sword against King Henry II without any effect or even attempt. He too was condemned to die without consideration of his insanity, which the law ordinarily excuses no matter what murder or crime the madman may have committed.

*   *   *

As for Calvin's remark that if there existed in these times magistrates especially constituted for the defense of the people and to restrain the licentiousness of kings, like the ephors in Sparta, the tribunes in Rome, and the demarchs in Athens, then those magistrates should resist, oppose, and prevent their licentiousness and cruelty—it clearly shows that it is never licit, in a proper monarchy, to attack a sovereign king, or defend one's self against him, or to make an attempt upon his life or honor, for he spoke only of democratic and aristocratic states. I have shown above that the kings of Sparta were but simple senators and captains. And when he speaks of the Estates, he says "possible," not daring to be definite. In any event there is an important difference between attacking the honor of one's prince and resisting his tyranny, between killing one's king and opposing his cruelty.

We thus read that the Protestant princes of Germany, before taking up arms against the emperor, asked Martin Luther if it were permissible. He frankly replied that it was not permissible no matter how great the charge of impiety or tyranny. But he was not heeded; and the outcome of the affair was miserable, bringing with it the ruin of some great and illustrious houses of Germany. *Quia nulla iusta causa videri potest,* said Cicero, *adversus patriam arma capiendi.*[2] Admittedly, it is quite certain that the sovereignty of the German Empire does not lie in the person of the emperor, as we shall explain in due course. But since he is the chief, they could have taken up arms against him only with the consent of the Estates or its majority, which was not obtained. It would have been even less permissible against a sovereign prince.

I can give no better parallel than that of a son with respect to his father. The law of God says that he who speaks evil of his father or his mother shall be put to death. If the father be a murderer, a thief, a traitor to his country, a person who has committed incest or parricide, a blasphemer, an atheist, and anything else one wants to add, I confess that the entire gamut of penalties will not suffice for his punishment; but I say that it is not for his son to lay hands on him, *quia nulla tanta impietas, nullum tantum factum est quod sit parricidio vindicandum,*[3] as it was put by an orator of ancient times. And yet Cicero, taking up this question, says that love of country is even greater. Hence the prince of our country, being ordained and sent by God, is always more sacred and ought to be more inviolable than a father.

I conclude then that it is never permissible for a subject to attempt anything against a sovereign prince, no matter how wicked and cruel a tyrant he may be. It is certainly permissible not to obey him in anything that is against the law of God or nature—to flee, to hide, to evade his blows, to suffer death rather than make any attempt upon his life or honor. For oh, how many tyrants there would be if it were lawful to kill them! He who taxes too heavily would be a tyrant, as the vulgar understand it; he who gives commands that the people do not like would be a tyrant, as Aristotle defined a tyrant

---

[2] "Because there can never be a just cause to take up arms against one's country."

[3] "Because there is no impiety so great, and no crime so great that it ought to be avenged by patricide."

in the *Politics;* he who maintains guards for his security would be a tyrant; he who punishes conspirators against his rule would be a tyrant. How then should good princes be secure in their lives? I would not say that it is illicit for other princes to proceed against tyrants by force of arms, as I have stated, but it is not for subjects.

*   *   *

REVIEW QUESTIONS

1. What, according to Bodin, is the definition of *sovereignty*?
2. In describing its prerogatives, would Bodin have agreed with Machiavelli?
3. Can sovereignty be mixed? Why?
4. Is it permissible to resist a tyrant?
5. Can a sovereign ruler be a tyrant?
6. May one resist a sovereign?

THOMAS MUN

FROM *England's Treasure by Forraign Trade. or The Ballance of our Forraign Trade is The Rule of our Treasure*

One of the chief exponents of the economic doctrine known as mercantilism, Sir Thomas Mun (1571–1641) was an English merchant, who served as director of the British East India Company and wrote on economic policy. A strong believer in state support for and direction of commerce, Mun strongly advocated its intervention to relieve the economic depression of the 1620s. He wrote his A Discourse of Trade from England unto the East-Indies *to defend the East India Company and its role in British economic stability. A second pamphlet,* England's Treasure by Forraign Trade, *stands as one of the first expressions of mercantilist principle. In it Mun proposed a set of "means to enrich a kingdom," which centered around ensuring that exports exceeded imports. Mun argued that a positive balance of trade would cause England's wealth steadily to increase. Published posthumously, this concise statement of mercantilist principle made Mun's reputation as a sophisticated economic thinker and became an important contribution to the development of economic theory.*

From *England's Treasure by Forraign Trade*, by Thomas Mun (New York: Macmillan, 1895), pp. ix–13, 22–27, 43–60.

*   *   *

Chapter II

THE MEANS TO ENRICH THIS KINGDOM, AND TO ENCREASE OUR TREASURE.

Although a Kindom may be enriched by gifts received, or by purchase taken from some other Nations, yet these are things uncertaim and of small consideration when they happen. The ordinary means therefore to encrease our wealth and treasure is by Forraign Trade, wherein wee must ever observe this rule; to sell more to strangers yearly than wee consume of theirs in value. For suppose that when this Kingdom is plentifully served with the Cloth, Lead, Tinn, Iron, Fish and other native commodities, we doe yearly export the overplus to forraign Countries to the value of twenty two hundred thousand pounds; by which means we are enabled beyond the Seas to buy and bring in forraign wares for our use and Consumption, to the value of twenty hundred thousand pounds; By this order duly kept in our trading, we may rest assured that this order duly kept in our trading, we may rest assured that the Kingdom shall be enriched yearly two hundred thousand pounds, which must be brought to us in so much Treasure; because that part of our stock which is not returned to us in wares must necessarily be brought home in treasure.

For in this case it cometh to pass in the stock of a Kingdom, as in the estate of a private man; who is supposed to have one thousand pounds yearly revenue and two thousand pounds of ready money in his Chest: If such a man through excess shall spend one thousand five hundred pounds per annum, all his ready mony will be gone in four years; and in the like time his said money will be doubled if he take a Frugal course to spend but five hundred pounds per annum; which rule never faileth likewise in the Common-wealth, but in some cases (of no great moment) which I will hereafter declare, when I shall shew by whom and in what manner this ballance of the Kingdoms account ought to be drawn up yearly,

or so often as it shall please the State to discover how much we gain or lose by trade with forraign Nations. But first I will say something concerning those ways and means which will encrease our exportations and diminish our importations of wares; which being done, I will then set down some other arguments both affirmative and negative to strengthen that which is here declared, and thereby to shew that all the other means which are commonly supposed to enrich the Kingdom with Treasure are altogether insufficient and meer fallacies.

Chap. III.

THE PARTICULAR WAYS AND MEANS TO ENCREASE THE EXPORTATION OF OUR COMMODITIES, AND TO DECREASE OUR CONSUMPTION OF FORRAIGN WARES.

The revenue or stock of a Kingdom by which it is provided of forraign wares is either Natural or Artificial. The Natural wealth is so much only as can be spared from our own use and necessities to be exported unto strangers. The Artificial consists in our manufactures and industrious trading with forraign commodities, concerning which I will set down such particulars as may serve for the cause we have in hand.

1. First, although this Realm be already exceeding rich by nature, yet might it be much encreased by laying the waste grounds (which are infinite) into such employments as should no way hinder the present revenues of other manufactured lands, but hereby to supply our selves and prevent the importations of Hemp, Flax, Cordage, Tobacco, and divers other things which now we fetch from strangers to our great impoverishing.

2. We may likewise diminish our importations, if we would soberly refrain from excessive consumption of forraign wares in our diet and rayment, with such often change of fashions as is used, so much the more to encrease the waste and charge; which vices at this present are more notorious amongst us than in former ages. Yet might they easily be amended by enforcing the observa-

tion of such good laws as are strictly practised in other Countries against the said excesses; where likewise by commanding their own manufactures to be used, they prevent the coming in of others, without prohibition, or offence to strangers in their mutual commerce.

3. In our exportations we must not only regard our own superfluities, but also we must consider our neighbours necessities, that so upon the wares which they cannot want, nor yet be furnished thereof elsewhere, we may (besides the vent of the Materials) gain so much of the manufacture as we can, and also endeavour to sell them dear, so far forth as the high price cause not a less vent in the quantity. But the superfluity of our commodities which strangers use, and may also have the same from other Nations, or may abate their vent by the use of some such like wares from other places, and with little inconvenience; we must in this case strive to sell as cheap as possible we can, rather than to lose the utterance of such wares. For we have found of late years by good experience, that being able to sell our Cloth cheap in Turkey, we have greatly encreased the vent thereof, and the Venetians have lost as much in the utterance of theirs in those Countreys, because it is dearer. And on the other side a few years past, when by excessive price of Wools our Cloth was exceeding dear, we lost at the least half our clothing for forraign parts, which since is no otherwise (well neer) recovered again than by the great fall of price for Wools and Cloth. We find that twenty five in the hundred less in the price of these and some other Wares, to the loss of private mens revenues, may raise above fifty upon the hundred in the quantity vented to the benefit of the publique. For when Cloth is dear, other Nations doe presently practise clothing, and we know they want neither art nor materials to this performance. But when by cheapness we drive them from this employment, and so in time obtain our dear price again, then do they also use their former remedy. So that by these alterations we learn, that it is in vain to expect a greater revenue of our wares than their condition will afford, but rather it concerns us to apply our endeavours to the times with care and diligence to help our selves the best we may, by making our cloth and other manufactures without deceit, which will encrease their estimation and use.

4. The value of our exportations likewise may be much advanced when we perform it our selves in our own Ships, for then we get only not the price of our wares as they are worth here, but also the Merchants gains, the changes of ensurance, and fraight to carry them beyond the seas. As for example, if the Italian Merchants should come hither in their own shipping to fetch our Corn, our red Herrings or the like, in the case the Kingdom should have ordinarily but 25s for a quarter of Wheat, and 20s for a barrel of red herrings, whereas if we carry these wares our selves into Italy upon the said rates, it is likely that wee shall obtain fifty shillings for the first, and forty shillings for the last, which is a great difference in the utterance or vent of the Kingdoms stock. And although it is true that the commerce ought to be free to strangers to bring in and carry out at their pleasure, yet nevertheless in many places the exportation of victuals and munition are either prohibited, or at least limited to be done onely by the people and Shipping of those places where they abound.

5. The frugal expending likewise of our own natural wealth might advance much yearly to be exported unto strangers; and if in our rayment we will be prodigal, yet let this be done with our own materials and manufactures, as Cloth, Lace, Imbroderies, Cutworks and the like, where the excess of the rich may be the employment of the poor, whose labours notwithstanding of this kind, would be more profitable for the Commonwealth, if they were done to the use of strangers.

6. The Fishing in his Majesties seas of England, Scotland and Ireland is our natural wealth, and would cost nothing but labour, which the Dutch bestow willingly, and thereby draw yearly a very great profit to themselves by serving many places of Christendom with our Fish, for which they return and supply their wants both of forraign Wares and Mony, besides the multitude of Mariners and Shipping, which hereby are maintain'd, whereof a long

discourse might be made to shew the particular manage of this important business. Our Fishing plantation likewise in New England, Virginia, Groenland, the Summer Islands and the New-found-land, are of the like nature, affording much wealth and employments to maintain a great number of poor, and to encrease our decaying trade.

7. A Staple or Magazin for forraign Corn, Indico, Spices, Raw-silks, Cotton wool or any other commodity whatsoever, to be imported will encrease Shipping, Trade, Treasure, and the Kings customes, by exporting them again where need shall require, which course of Trading, hath been the chief means to raise Venice, Genoa, the low-Countreys, with some others; and for such a purpose England stands most commodiously, wanting nothing to this performance but our own diligence and endeavour.

8. Also wee ought to esteem and cherish those trades which we have in remote or far Countreys, for besides the encrease of Shipping and Mariners thereby, the wares also sent thither and receiv'd from thence are far more profitable unto the kingdom than by our trades neer at hand: As for example; suppose Pepper to be worth here two Shillings the pound constantly, if then it be brought from the Dutch at Amsterdam, the Merchant may give there twenty pence the pound, and gain well by the bargain; but if he fetch this Pepper from the East-indies, he must not give above three pence the pound at the most, which is a mighty advantage, not only in that part which serveth for our own use, but also for that great quantity which (from hence) we transport yearly unto divers other Nations to be sold at a higher price: whereby it is plain, that we make a far greater stock by gain upon these Indian Commodities, than those Nations doe where they grow, and to whom they properly appertain, being the natural wealth of their Countries. But for the better understanding of this particular, we must ever distinguish between the gain of the Kingdom, and the profit of the Merchant; for although the Kingdom payeth no more for this Pepper than is before supposed, nor for any other commodity bought in forraign parts more than the stranger receiveth from us for the same, yet the Merchant

payeth not only that price, but also the fraight, ensurance, customes and other charges which are exceeding great in these long voyages; but yet all these in the Kingdoms accompt are but commutations among our selves, and no Privation of the Kingdoms stock, which being duly considered, together with the support also of our other trades in our best Shipping to Italy, France, Turkey, and East Countreys and other places, by transporting and venting the wares which we bring yearly from the East Indies; It may well stir up our utmost endeavours to maintain and enlarge this great and noble business, so much importing the Publique wealth, Strength, and Happiness. Neither is there less honour and judgment by growing rich (in this manner) upon the stock of other Nations, than by an industrious encrease of our own means, especially when this later is advanced by the benefit of the former, as we have found in the East Indies by sale of much of our Tin, Cloth, Lead and other Commodities, the vent whereof doth daily encrease in those Countreys which formerly had no use of our wares.

9. It would be very beneficial to export money as well as wares, being done in trade only, it would encrease our Treasure; but of this I write more largely in the next Chapter to prove it plainly.

10. It were policie and profit for the State to suffer manufactures made of forraign Materials to be exported custome-free, as Velvets and all other wrought Silks, Fustians, thrown Silks and the like, it would emply very many poor people, and much encrease the value of our stock yearly issued into other Countreys, and it would (for this purpose) cause the more foraign Materials to be brought in, to the improvement of His Majesties Customes. I will here remember a notable increase in our manufacture of winding and twisting only of forraign raw Silk, which within 35 years to my knowledge did not employ more than 300 people in the City and suburbs of London, where at this present time it doth set on work above fourteen thousand souls, as upon diligent enquiry hath been credibly reported unto His Majesties Commissioners for Trade. and it is certain, that if the raid forraign Commodities might be exported from hence, free

of custome, this manufacture would yet encrease very much, and decrease as fast in Italy and in the Netherlands. But if any man allege the Dutch proverb, Live and let others live; I answer, that the Dutchmen notwithstanding their own Proverb, doe not onely in these Kingdoms, encroach upon our livings, but also in other forraign parts of our trade (where they have power) they do hinder and destroy us in our lawful course of living, hereby taking the bread out of our mouth, which we shall never prevent by plucking the pot from their nose, as of late years too many of us do practise to the great hurt and dishonour of this famour Nation; We ought rather to imitate former times in taking sober and worthy courses more pleasing to God and suitable to our ancient reputation.

11. It is needful also not to charge the native commodities with too great customes, lest by indearing them to the strangers use, it hinder their vent. And especially forraign wares brought in to be transported again should be favoured, for otherwise that manner of trading (so much importing the good of the Commonwealth) cannot prosper nor subsist. But the Consumption of such forraign wares in the Realm may be the more charged, which will turn to the profit of the kingdom in the Ballance of the Trade, and thereby also enable the King to lay up the more Treasure out of his yearly incomes, as of this particular I intend to write more fully in his proper place, where I shall shew how much money a Prince may conveniently lay up without the hurt of his subjects.

12. Lastly, in all things we must endeavour to make the most we can of our own, whether it be Natural or Artificial, And forasmuch as the people which live by the Arts are far more in number than they who are masters of the fruits, we ought the more carefully to maintain those endeavours of the multitude, in whom doth consist the greatest strength and riches both of the King and Kingdom: for where the people are many, and the arts good, there the traffique must be great, and the Countrey rich. The Italians employ a greater number of people; and get more money by their industry and manufactures of the raw Silks of the Kingdom of Cicilia, than the King of Spain and his Subjects have by the revenue of this rich commodity. But what need we fetch the example so far, when we know that our own natural wares doe not yield us so much profit as our industry? For Iron oar in the Mines is of no great worth, when it is compared with the employment and advantage it yields being digged, tried, transported, brought, sold, cast into Ordnance, Muskets, and many other instruments of war for offence and defence, wrought into Anchors, bolts, spikes, nayles and the like, for the use of Ships, Houses, Carts, Coaches, Ploughs, and other instruments for Tillage. Compare our Fleece-wools with our Cloth, which requires shearing, washing, carding, spinning, Weaving, fulling, dying, dressing and other trimmings, and we shall find these Arts more profitable than the natural wealth, whereof I might instance other examples, but I will not be more tedious, for if I would amplify upon this and the other particulars before written, I might find matter sufficient to make a large volume, but my desire in all is only to prove what I propound with brevity and plainness.

REVIEW QUESTIONS

1. Why does Mun emphasize the importance of the state as an economic actor?
2. What qualities comprise the perfect merchant and do these differ from the qualities we expect today?
3. By what means might a state by enriched by trade?
4. What "forraign wares" does Mun consider and what "forraign wares" does he ignore?
5. How might a state increase its exports, and what would the consequences be?
6. Why are export prohibitions and trade barriers futile?
7. Are individuals unimportant in Mun's conception of economic practice?

THOMAS HOBBES

FROM *Leviathan*

Thomas Hobbes (1588–1679) was an English philosopher whose mechanistic and deterministic theories of political life were highly controversial in his own time. Born in Malmesbury, Hobbes attended Magdalen Hall, Oxford, and became tutor to William Cavendish, later the Earl of Devonshire, in 1608. With his student, he undertook several tours of the Continent, where he met and spoke with leading intellectual lights of the day, including Galileo and Descartes. Around 1637, he became interested in the constitutional struggle between Parliament and Charles I and set to work writing a "little treatise in English" in defense of the royal prerogative. Before its publication in 1650, the book circulated privately in 1640 under the title Elements of Law, Natural and Politic. *Fearing arrest by Parliament, Hobbes fled to Paris, where he remained for the next eleven years. While in exile, he served as math tutor to the Prince of Wales, later Charles II, from 1646 to 1648. His great work,* Leviathan *(1651), was a forceful argument for political absolutism. Its title, taken from the horrifying sea monster of the Old Testament, suggested the power and authority Hobbes thought necessary to compel obedience and order in human society. Strongly influenced by mechanical philosophy, he treated human beings as matter in motion, subject to certain physical, rational laws. According to Hobbes, people feared one another and lived in a state of constant competition and conflict. For this reason, they must submit to the absolute, supreme authority of the state, a social contract among selfish individuals moved by fear and necessity. Once delegated, that authority was irrevocable and indivisible. Ironically, these theories found favor neither with royalists nor with antiroyalists. Charles II believed that it was written in justification of the Commonwealth. The French feared its attacks on the papacy. After the Restoration, Parliament added* Leviathan *to a list of books to be investigated for atheistic tendencies. Despite frustrations over the reception of his political theories, Hobbes retained his intellectual vigor. At age eighty-four, he wrote an autobiography in Latin and translated the works of Homer into English. He died at age ninety-one.*

From *Leviathan*, by Thomas Hobbes, edited by E. Hershey Sneath (Needham, Eng.: Ginn Press, 1898).

*   *   *

Of the Causes, Generation, and Definition of a Commonwealth

The final cause, end, or design of men, who naturally love liberty and dominion over others, in the introduction of that restraint upon themselves in which we see them live in commonwealths is the foresight of their own preservation, and of a more contented life thereby; that is to say, of getting themselves out from that miserable condition of war which is necessarily consequent…to the natural passions of men when there is no visible power to keep them in awe and tie them by fear of punishment to the performance of their covenants, and observation of the laws of nature. . . .

For the laws of nature, as "justice," "equity," "modesty," "mercy," and, in sum, "doing to others as we would be done to," of themselves, without the terror of some power to cause them to be observed, are contrary to our natural passions, that carry us to partiality, pride, revenge, and the like. And covenants without the sword are but words, and of no strength to secure a man at all. Therefore, notwithstanding the laws of nature, which every one has then kept when he has the will to keep them, when he can do it safely, if there be no power erected, or not great enough for our security; every man will, and may lawfully rely on his own strength and art, for protection against all other men. And in all places where men have lived by small families, to rob and spoil one another has been a trade, and so far from being reputed against the law of nature that the greater spoils they gained, the greater was their honor; and men observed no other laws therein but the laws of honor; that is, to abstain from cruelty, leaving to men their lives and instruments of livelihood. And as small families did then, so now do cities and kingdoms, which are but greater families, for their own security enlarge their dominions upon all pretenses of danger and fear of invasion or assistance that may be given to invaders, and endeavor as much as they can to subdue or weaken their neighbors by open force and secret arts, for lack of other protection, justly; and are remembered for it in later ages with honor.

Nor is it the joining together of a small number of men that gives them this security, because in small numbers small additions on the one side or the other make the advantage of strength so great as is sufficient to carry the victory; and therefore gives encouragement to an invasion. The multitude sufficient to confide in for our security is not determined by any certain number but by comparison with the enemy we fear; and is then sufficient when the advantage of the enemy is not so visible and conspicuous to determine the event of war as to move him to attempt it.

And should there not be so great a multitude, even if their actions be directed according to their particular judgments and particular appetites, they can expect thereby no defense nor protection, neither against a common enemy nor against the injuries of one another. For being distracted in opinions concerning the best use and application of their strength, they do not help but hinder one another, and reduce their strength by mutual opposition to nothing; whereby they are easily not only subdued by a very few that agree together, but also, when there is no common enemy, they make war upon each other for their particular interests. For if we could suppose a great multitude of men to consent in the observation of justice and other laws of nature without a common power to keep them all in awe, we might as well suppose all mankind to do the same; and then there neither would be, nor need to be, any civil government or commonwealth at all, because there would be peace without subjection.

Nor is it enough for the security which men desire should last all the time of their life that they be governed and directed by one judgment for a limited time, as in one battle or one war. For though they obtain a victory by their unanimous endeavor against a foreign enemy, yet afterwards, when either they have no common enemy or he that by one group is held for an enemy is by another group held for a friend, they must needs, by the difference of their interests, dissolve, and fall again into a war among themselves.

It is true that certain living creatures, as bees and ants, live sociably one with another, which are therefore by Aristotle numbered among political creatures, and yet have no other direction, than their particular judgments and appetites; nor speech whereby one of them can signify to another what he thinks expedient for the common benefit; and therefore some man may perhaps desire to know why mankind cannot do the same. To which I answer:

First, that men are continually in competition for honor and dignity, which these creatures are not; and consequently among men there arises on the ground envy and hatred and finally war, but among these not so.

Secondly, that among these creatures the common good differ not from the private; and being by nature inclined to their private, they procure thereby the common benefit. But man, whose joy consists in comparing himself with other men, can relish nothing but what is eminent.

Thirdly, that these creatures, having not, as man, the use of reason, do not see nor think they see any fault, in the administration of their common business; whereas among men, there are very many that think themselves wiser and abler to govern the public better than the rest; and these strive to reform and innovate, one this way, another that way, and thereby bring it into distraction and civil war.

Fourthly, that these creatures, though they have some use of voice in making known to one another their desires and other affections, yet they lack that art of words by which some men can represent to others that which is good in the likeness of evil; and evil in the likeness of good; and augment or diminish the apparent greatness of good and evil, making men discontented and troubling their peace at their pleasure.

Fifthly, irrational creatures cannot distinguish between "injury" and "damage"; and, therefore, as long as they be at ease they are not offended with their fellows; whereas man is then most troublesome when he is most at ease; for then it is that he loves to show his wisdom and control the actions of them that govern the commonwealth.

Lastly, the agreement of these creatures is natural, that of men is by covenant only, which is artificial; and therefore, it is no wonder if there be somewhat else required besides covenant to make their agreement constant and lasting, which is a common power to keep them in awe and to direct their actions to the common benefit.

The only way to erect such a common power which may be able to defend them from the invasion of foreigners and the injuries of one another, and thereby to secure them in such sort so that by their own industry and by the fruits of the earth they may nourish themselves and live contentedly, is to confer all their power and strength upon one man, or upon one assembly of men that may reduce all their wills, by plurality of voices, unto one will; which is as much as to say, to appoint one man or assembly of men to bear their person; and every one to accept and acknowledge himself to be author of whatsoever he that so bears their person shall act or cause to be acted in those things which concern the common peace and safety, and therein to submit their wills every one to his will, and their judgments to his judgment. This is more than consent or concord; it is a real unity of them all in one and the same person, made by covenant of every man with every man, in such manner as if every man should say to every man, "I authorize and give up my right of governing myself to this man, or to this assembly of men, on this condition, that you give up your right to him and authorize all his actions in like manner." This done, the multitude so united in one person is called a "commonwealth," in Latin *civitas*. This is the generation of that great "leviathan," or rather, to speak more reverently, of that "mortal god," to which we owe, under the "immortal God," our peace and defense. For by this authority, given him by every particular man in the commonwealth, he has the use of so much power and strength conferred on him that, by terror thereof, he is enabled to form the wills of them all to peace at home and mutual aid against their enemies abroad. And in him consists the essence of the commonwealth, which, to define it, is "one person, of whose acts a great multitude, by mutual covenants one with another, have made themselves the author, to the end he may use the strength and means of them all as he shall think expedient for their peace and common defense."

And he that carries this person is called "sovereign" and said to have "sovereign power"; and every one besides, his "subject."

The attaining to this sovereign power is by two ways. One, by natural force, as when a man makes his children to submit themselves and their children to his government, as being able to destroy them if they refuse; or by war subdues his enemies to his will, giving them their lives on that condition. The other is when men agree among themselves to submit to some man or assembly of men voluntarily, on confidence that they will be protected by him against all others. This latter, may be called a political commonwealth, or commonwealth by "institution," and the former, a commonwealth by "acquisition." . . .

*   *   *

Of the Office of the Sovereign Representative

The office of the sovereign, be it a monarch or an assembly, consists in the end for which he was trusted with the sovereign power, namely, the securing of "the safety of the people"; to which he is obliged by the law of nature, and to render an account thereof to God, the author of that law, and to none but him. But by safety here is not meant a bare preservation but also all other contentments of life which every man by lawful industry, without danger or hurt to the commonwealth, shall acquire to himself.

And this is to be done, not by care applied to individuals further than their protection from injuries when they shall complain, but by a general provision contained in public instruction, both of doctrine and example, and in the making and executing of good laws to which individual persons may apply their own cases.

And because, if the essential rights of sovereignty . . . be taken away, the commonwealth is thereby dissolved and every man returns into the condition and calamity of a war with every other man, which is the greatest evil that can happen in this life; it is the office of the sovereign, to maintain those rights entire, and consequently against his duty, first, to transfer to another or to lay from himself any of them. For he that deserts the means deserts the ends; and he deserts the means when, being the sovereign, he acknowledges himself subject to the civil laws and renounces the power of supreme judicature, or of making war or peace by his own authority; or of judging of the necessities of the commonwealth; or of levying money and soldiers when and as much as in his own conscience he shall judge necessary; or of making officers and ministers both of war and peace; or of appointing teachers and examining what doctrines are con-

formable or contrary to the defense, peace, and good of the people. Secondly, it is against his duty to let the people be ignorant or misinformed of the grounds and reasons of those his essential rights, because thereby men are easy to be seduced and drawn to resist him when the commonwealth shall require their use and exercise.

And the grounds of these rights have the need to be diligently and truly taught, because they cannot be maintained by any civil law or terror of legal punishment. For a civil law that shall forbid rebellion (and such is all resistance to the essential rights of the sovereignty), is not, as a civil law, any obligation, but by virtue only of the law of nature that forbids the violation of faith; which natural obligation if men know not, they cannot know the right of any law the sovereign makes. And for the punishment, they take it but for an act of hostility which when they think they have strength enough, they will endeavor by acts of hostility, to avoid.

*   *   *

To the care of the sovereign belongs the making of good laws. But what is a good law? By a good law I mean not a just law; for no law can be unjust. The law is made by the sovereign power, and all that is done by such power is warranted and owned by every one of the people; and that which every man will have so, no man can say is unjust. It is in the laws of a commonwealth as in the laws of gaming; whatsoever the gamesters all agree on is injustice to none of them. A good law is that which is "needed" for the "good of the people" and "perspicuous."

For the use of laws, which are but rules authorized, is not to bind the people from all voluntary actions but to direct and keep them in such a motion as not to hurt themselves by their own impetuous desires, rashness, or indiscretion; as hedges are set not to stop travellers, but to keep them in their way. And, therefore, a law that is not needed, having not the true end of a law, is not good. A law may be conceived to be good when it is for the benefit of the sovereign, though it be not necessary for the people, but it is not so. For the good of the sovereign and people cannot be separated. It is a weak sovereign, that has weak subjects, and a weak people, whose sovereign lacks power to rule them at his will. Unnecessary laws are not good laws but traps for money; which, where the right of sovereign power is acknowledged, are superfluous, and where it is not acknowledged, insufficient to defend the people. . . .

It belongs also to the office of the sovereign to make a right application of punishments and rewards. And seeing the end of punishing is not revenge and discharge of anger, but correction, either of the offender, or of others by his example; the severest punishments are to be inflicted for those crimes that are of most danger to the public; such as are those which proceed from malice to the government established; those that spring from contempt of justice; those that provoke indignation in the multitude; and those which, unpunished, seem authorized, as when they are committed by sons, servants, or favorites of men in authority. For indignation carries men not only against the actors and authors of injustice, but against all power that is likely to protect them; as in the case of Tarquin, when for the insolent act of one of his sons he was driven out of Rome and the monarchy itself dissolved. But crimes of infirmity, such as are those which proceed from great provocation, from great fear, great need, or from ignorance, whether the fact be a great crime or not, there is place many times for leniency without prejudice to the commonwealth; and leniency, when there is such place for it, is required by the law of nature. The punishment of the leaders and teachers in a commotion, not the poor seduced people, when they are punished, can profit the commonwealth by their example. To be severe to the people is to punish that ignorance which may in great part be imputed to the sovereign, whose fault it was that they were no better instructed.

In like manner it belongs to the office and duty of the sovereign, to apply his rewards so that there may arise from them benefit to the commonwealth, wherein consists their use, and end; and is then done when they that have well served the commonwealth are, with as little expense of the common treasure as is possible, so well rec-

ompensed as others thereby may be encouraged both to serve the same as faithfully as they can and to study the arts by which they may be enabled to do it better. To buy with money or preferment from a popular ambitious subject to be quiet and desist from making ill impressions in the minds of the people has nothing of the nature of reward (which is ordained not for disservice, but for service past), nor a sign of gratitude, but of fear; nor does it tend to the benefit but to the damage of the public. It is a contention with ambition like that of Hercules with the monster Hydra which, having many heads, for every one that was vanquished there grew up three. For in like manner, when the stubbornness of one popular man is overcome with reward there arise many more, by the example, that do the same mischief in hope of like benefit; and as all sorts of manufacture, so also malice increases by being salable. And though sometimes a civil war may be deferred by such ways as that, yet the danger grows still the greater and the public ruin more assured. It is therefore against the duty of the sovereign, to whom the public safety is committed, to reward those that aspire to greatness by disturbing the peace of their country, and not rather to oppose the beginnings of such men with a little danger than after a longer time with greater.

*   *   *

When the sovereign himself is popular, that is, revered and beloved of his people, there is no danger at all from the popularity of a subject. For soldiers are never so generally unjust as to side with their captain though they love him, against their sovereign, when they love not only his person but also his cause. And therefore those who by violence have at any time suppressed the power of their lawful sovereign, before they could settle themselves in his place have been always put to the trouble of contriving their titles to save the people from the shame of receiving them. To have a known right to sovereign power is so popular a quality as he that has it needs no more, for his own part, to turn the hearts of his subjects to him but that they see him able absolutely to govern his own family; nor, on the part of his enemies, but a disbanding of their armies. For the greatest and most active part of mankind has never hitherto been well contented with the present.

Concerning the offices of one sovereign to another, which are comprehended in that law which is commonly called the "law of nations," I need not say anything in this place because the law of nations and the law of nature is the same thing. And every sovereign has the same right, in securing the safety of his people that any particular man can have in securing the safety of his own body. And the same law that dictates to men that have no civil government what they ought to do and what to avoid in regard of one another dictates the same to commonwealths, that is, to the consciences of sovereign princes and sovereign assemblies, there being no court of natural justice but in the conscience only; where not man but God reigns whose laws, such of them as oblige all mankind, in respect of God as he is the author of nature are "natural," and in respect of the same God as he is King of kings are "laws."

*   *   *

Review Questions

1. What is Hobbes's view of human nature?
2. What, according to Hobbes, motivates human beings?
3. What, according to Hobbes, is the purpose of the state?
4. Why do human beings come together to form a political society?
5. What are the responsibilities of the sovereign?
6. What is the sovereign's highest obligation?
7. Does Hobbes hold out any hope that the state can improve human nature?

Ambassadeurs Siamois devant Louis XIV

Ambasciatori di Siam dinanzi a Luigi XIV.   Embajadores de Siam delante de Luis XIV.

SIAMESE EMBASSY TO LOUIS XIV, IN 1686 (1686)

This unattributed engraving commemorates the Siamese embassy to the court of Louis XIV in 1686. It may be a copy of a similar image, created by Nicolas III Larmessin (c. 1640–1725), a member of the de Larmessin (also: de L'Armessin) family, a famous French dynasty of engravers, printers, and booksellers who were active during the seventeenth and eighteenth centuries. It portrays at once the increasing range of international relations and diplomacy, and the centrality of European imperial pretentions in the seventeenth century. What might have made this event a fit subject for an engraving? How does the artist glorify the French king? What elements of court ritual in an age of absolutism are readily visible? In a period of burgeoning imperialism, what propaganda purposes might this image have served?

Coffee House Society

Coffee is an example of the impact of overseas trade and colonial empire on the consumption and lifestyle of ordinary Europeans. The bean's historical origins are shrouded in legend. What seems clear is that they were taken to Arabia from Africa during the fifteenth century and placed under cultivation. Introduced into Europe during the sixteenth and seventeenth centuries, they gained almost immediate popularity. Served at coffeehouses, the first of which was established in London around 1650, coffee's consumption became an occasion for transacting political, social, commercial, or literary business. So great was the demand for coffee that European merchants took it from the Arabian Peninsula to Java, Indonesia, and the Americas. The following descriptions by two anonymous authors give some sense of the ways in which colonial products shaped European culture in the seventeenth century.

From *Selections from the Sources of English History*, edited by Charles W. Colby (New York: Longmans, Green, 1899), pp. 208–12.

*   *   *

1673

A coffee-house is a lay conventicle, good-fellowship turned puritan, ill-husbandry in masquerade, whither people come, after toping all day, to purchase, at the expense of their last penny, the repute of sober companions: A Rota [club] room, that, like Noah's ark, receives animals of every sort, from the precise diminutive band, to the hectoring cravat and cuffs in folio: a nursery for training up the smaller fry of virtuosi in confident tattling, or a cabal of kittling [carping] critics that have only learned to spit and mew; a mint of intelligence, that, to make each man his pennyworth, draws out into petty parcels, what the merchant receives in bullion: he, that comes often, saves twopence a week in Gazettes, and has his news and his coffee for the same charge, as at a threepenny ordinary they give in broth to your chop of mutton; it is an exchange, where haberdashers of political small-wares meet, and mutually abuse each other, and the public, with bottomless stories, and headless notions; the rendezvous of idle pamphlets, and persons more idly employed to read them; a high court of justice, where every little fellow in a camlet cloak takes upon him to transpose affairs both in church and state, to show reasons against acts of parliament, and condemn the decrees of general councils.

*   *   *

As you have a hodge-podge of drinks, such too is your company, for each man seems a leveller, and ranks and files himself as he lists, without regard to degrees or order; so that often you may see a silly fop and a worshipful justice, a griping rook and a grave citizen, a worthy lawyer and an errant pickpocket, a reverend nonconformist and a canting mountebank, all blended together to compose an oglio [medley] of impertinence.

If any pragmatic, to show himself witty or eloquent, begin to talk high, presently the further tables are abandoned, and all the rest flock round (like smaller birds, to admire the gravity of the madge-howlet [barn-owl]). They listen to him awhile with their mouths, and let their pipes go out, and coffee grow cold, for pure zeal of attention, but on the sudden fall all a yelping at once with more noise, but not half so much harmony, as a pack of beagles on the full cry. To still this bawling, up starts Capt. All-man-sir, the man of mouth, with a face as blustering as that of Æolus and his four sons, in painting, and a voice louder than the speaking trumpet, he begins you the story of a sea-fight; and though he never were further, by water, than the Bear-garden, . . . yet, having pirated the names of ships and captains, he persuades you himself was present, and performed miracles; that he waded knee-deep in blood on the upper-deck, and never thought to serenade his mistress so pleasant as the bullets whistling; how he stopped a vice-admiral of the enemy's under full sail; till she was boarded, with his single arm, instead of grappling-irons, and puffed out with his breath a fire-ship that fell foul on them. All this he relates, sitting in a cloud of smoke, and belching so many common oaths to vouch it, you can scarce guess whether the real engagement, or his romancing account of it, be the more dreadful: however, he concludes with railing at the conduct of some eminent officers (that, perhaps, he never saw), and protests, had they taken his advice at the council of war, not a sail had escaped us.

He is no sooner out of breath, but another begins a lecture on the Gazette, where, finding several prizes taken, he gravely observes, if this trade hold, we shall quickly rout the Dutch, horse and foot, by sea: he nicknames the Polish gentlemen wherever he meets them, and enquires whether Gayland and Taffaletta be Lutherans or Calvinists? *stilo novo* he interprets a vast new stile, or turnpike, erected by his electoral highness on the borders of Westphalia, to keep Monsieur Turenne's cavalry from falling on his retreating troops: he takes words by the sound, without examining their sense: Morea he believes to be the country of the Moors, and Hungary a place where famine always keeps her court, nor is there anything more certain, than that he made a whole room full of fops, as wise as himself, spend above two hours in searching the map for Aristocracy and Democracy, not doubting but to have found them there, as well as Dalmatia and Croatia.

1675

Though the happy Arabia, nature's spicery, prodigally furnishes the voluptuous world with all kinds of aromatics, and divers other rarities; yet I scarce know whether mankind be not still as much obliged to it for the excellent fruit of the humble coffee-shrub, as for any other of its more specious productions: for, since there is nothing we here enjoy, next to life, valuable beyond health, certainly those things that contribute to preserve us in good plight and eucrasy, and fortify our weak bodies against the continual assaults and batteries of disease, deserve our regards much more than those which only gratify a liquorish palate, or otherwise prove subservient to our delights. As for this salutiferous berry, of so general a use through all the regions of the east, it is sufficiently known, when prepared, to be moderately hot, and of a very drying attenuating and cleansing quality; whence reason infers, that its decoction must contain many good physical properties, and cannot but be an incomparable remedy to dissolve crudities, comfort the brain, and dry up ill humours in the stomach. In brief, to prevent or redress, in those that frequently drink it, all cold drowsy rheumatic distempers whatsoever, that proceed from excess of moisture, which are so numerous, that but to name them would tire the tongue of a mountebank.

*   *   *

Lastly, for diversion. It is older than Aristotle, and will be true, when Hobbes is forgot, that man is a sociable creature, and delights in company. Now, whither shall a person, wearied with hard study, or the laborious turmoils of a tedious day, repair to refresh himself? Or where can young gentlemen, or shop-keepers, more innocently and advantageously spend an hour or two in the evening, than at a coffee-house? Where they shall be sure to meet company, and, by the custom of the house, not such as at other places, stingy and reserved to themselves, but free and communicative; where every man may modestly begin his story, and propose to, or answer another, as he thinks fit. Discourse is *pabulum animi, cos ingenii;*

the mind's best diet, and the great whetstone and incentive of ingenuity; by that we come to know men better than by their physiognomy. *Loquere, ut te videam,* speak, that I may see thee, was the philosopher's adage. To read men is acknowledged more useful than books; but where is there a better library for that study, generally, than here, amongst such a variety of humours, all expressing themselves on divers subjects, according to their respective abilities?

*   *   *

In brief, it is undeniable, that, as you have here the most civil, so it is, generally, the most intelligent society; the frequenting whose converse, and observing their discourses and department, cannot but civilise our manners, enlarge our understandings, refine our language, teach us a generous confidence and handsome mode of address, and brush off that *pudor rubrusticus* (as, I remember, Tully somewhere calls it), that clownish kind of modesty frequently incident to the best natures, which renders them sheepish and ridiculous in company.

So that, upon the whole matter, spite of the idle sarcasms and paltry reproaches thrown upon it, we may, with no less truth than plainness, give this brief character of a well-regulated coffee-house (for our pen disdains to be an advocate for any sordid holes, that assume that name to cloak the practice of debauchery), that it is the sanctuary of health, the nursery of temperance, the delight of frugality, an academy of civility, and free-school of ingenuity.

*   *   *

REVIEW QUESTIONS

1. How would you describe coffeehouse society in the late seventeenth century?
2. What is the attitude of each of our two anonymous authors? How and why do they differ?
3. What is the significance of reading the gazette?
4. What are the virtues of coffee?
5. How could coffee drinking be considered a vice in early modern Europe?

JOHN LOCKE

FROM *Two Treatises of Government*

John Locke (1632–1704) was an English philosopher whose thought contributed to the Enlightenment. He grew up in a liberal Puritan family, the son of an attorney who fought in the civil war against Charles I, and attended Christ Church College, Oxford. He received his bachelor of arts in 1656, lectured in classical languages while earning his master of arts, and entered Oxford's medical school to avoid being forced to join the clergy. In 1666, Locke attached himself to the household of the Earl of Shaftesbury and his fortunes to the liberal Whig Party. Between 1675 and 1679, he lived in France, where he made contact with leading intellectuals of the late seventeenth century. On his return to England, he plunged into the controversy surrounding the succession of James II, an avowed Catholic with absolutist pretensions, to the throne of his brother, Charles II. Locke's patron, Shaftesbury, was imprisoned for his opposition, and Locke went into exile in 1683. Though he was involved to some extent in the Glorious Revolution of 1688, he returned to England in 1689, in the entourage of Mary, Princess of Orange, who would assume the throne with her husband, William. The Two Treatises of Government *(1690) were published anonymously, although readers commonly assumed Locke's authorship. More interesting is the time at which they were written. Most scholars assume that they were written immediately before publication, as a justification of the revolution just completed. Other scholars believe, however, that the treatises were written from exile as a call to revolution, a riskier, much more inflammatory project. The first treatise comprises a long attack on Robert Filmer's* Patriarcha, *a denial of the patriarchal justification of the absolute monarch. The second treatise constructs in the place of patriarchy a theory of politics based on natural law, which provides the foundation of human freedom. The social contract creates a political structure by consent of the governed and designed to preserve those freedoms established in natural law. Locke's treatises inspired the political theories of the Enlightenment.*

From *First Treatise* in *Two Treatises of Government,* by John Locke (London: Whitmore and Fenn, 1821).

*　　*　　*

Chapter VI
Of Paternal Power

It may perhaps be censured an impertinent criticism in a discourse of this nature to find fault with words and names that have obtained in the world. And yet possibly it may not be amiss to offer new ones when the old are apt to lead men into mistakes, as this of paternal power probably has done, which seems so to place the power of parents over their children wholly in the father, as if the mother had no share in it; whereas if we consult reason or revelation, we shall find she has an equal title, which may give one reason to ask whether this might not be more properly called parental power? For whatever obligation Nature and the right of generation lays on children, it must certainly bind them equal to both the concurrent causes of it. And accordingly we see the positive law of God everywhere joins them together without distinction, when it commands the obedience of children: "Honour thy father and thy mother"; "Whosoever curseth his father or his mother"; "Ye shall fear every man his mother and his father"; "Children, obey your parents" etc., is the style of the Old and New Testament.

*　　*　　*

Though I have said above "That all men by nature are equal," I cannot be supposed to understand all sorts of "equality." Age or virtue may give men a just precedency. Excellency of parts and merit may place others above the common level. Birth may subject some, and alliance or benefits others, to pay an observance to those to whom Nature, gratitude, or other respects, may have made it due; and yet all this consists with the equality which all men are in in respect of jurisdiction or dominion one over another, which was the equality I there spoke of as proper to the business in hand, being that equal right that every man hath to his natural freedom, without being subjected to the will or authority of any other man.

Children, I confess, are not born in this full state of equality, though they are born to it. Their parents have a sort of rule and jurisdiction over them when they come into the world, and for some time after, but it is but a temporary one. The bonds of this subjection are like the swaddling clothes they are wrapt up in and supported by in the weakness of their infancy. Age and reason as they grow

PALACE AND GARDENS OF VERSAILLES (1668)   PIERRE PATEL

Patel's famous print of the palace at Versailles captures the grand scale of monarchy in the seventeenth century. Note not only the size of the palace but also its location in the center of carefully planned gardens, boulevards, and buildings. Versailles was truly a theater for the display of political power. Why was such a theater of power necessary? What can be learned from the iconography of power that was built into Versailles, such as the function of gardens or the location of boulevards or alleys or broad open spaces? How might Versailles have functioned not only as a theater of power but also as a prison for the powerful?

up loosen them, till at length they drop quite off, and leave a man at his own free disposal.

Adam was created a perfect man, his body and mind in full possession of their strength and reason, and so was capable from the first instance of his being to provide for his own support and preservation, and govern his actions according to the dictates of the law of reason God had implanted in him. From him the world is peopled with his descendants, who are all born infants, weak and helpless, without knowledge or understanding. But to supply the defects of this imperfect state till the improvement of growth and age had removed them, Adam and Eve, and after them all parents were, by the law of Nature, under an obligation to preserve, nourish and educate the children they had begotten, not as their own workmanship, but the workmanship of their own Maker, the Almighty, to whom they were to be accountable for them.

The law that was to govern Adam was the same that was to govern all his posterity, the law of reason. But his offspring having another way of entrance into the world, different from him, by a natural birth, that produced them ignorant, and without the use of reason, they were not presently under that law. For nobody can be under a law that is not promulgated to him; and this law being promulgated or made known by reason only, he that is not come to the use of his reason cannot be said to be under this law; and Adam's children being not presently as soon as born under this law of reason, were not presently free. For law, in its true notion, is not so much the limitation as the direction of a free and intelligent agent to his proper interest, and prescribes no farther than is for the general good of those under that law. Could they be happier without it, the law, as a useless thing, would of itself vanish; and that ill deserves the name of confinement which hedges us in only from bogs and precipices. So that however it may be mistaken, the end of law is not to abolish or restrain, but to preserve and enlarge freedom. For in all the states of created beings, capable of laws, where there is no law there is no freedom. For liberty is to be free from restraint and violence from others, which cannot be where

there is no law; and is not, as we are told, "a liberty for every man to do what he lists." For who could be free, when every other man's humour might domineer over him? But a liberty to dispose and order freely as he lists his person, actions, possessions, and his whole property within the allowance of those laws under which he is, and therein not to be subject to the arbitrary will of another, but freely follow his own.

The power, then, that parents have over their children arises from that duty which is incumbent on them, to take care of their offspring during the imperfect state of childhood. To inform the mind, and govern the actions of their yet ignorant nonage, till reason shall take its place and ease them of that trouble, is what the children want, and the parents are bound to. For God having given man an understanding to direct his actions, has allowed him a freedom of will and liberty of acting, as properly belonging thereunto within the bounds of that law he is under. But whilst he is in an estate wherein he has no understanding of his own to direct his will, he is not to have any will of his own to follow. He that understands for him must will for him too; he must prescribe to his will, and regulate his actions, but when he comes to the estate that made his father a free man, the son is a free man too.

This holds in all the laws a man is under, whether natural or civil. Is a man under the law of Nature? What made him free of that law? what gave him a free disposing of his property, according to his own will, within the compass of that law? I answer, an estate wherein he might be supposed capable to know that law, that so he might keep his actions within the bounds of it. When he has acquired that state, he is presumed to know how far that law is to be his guide, and how far he may make use of his freedom, and so comes to have it; till then, somebody else must guide him, who is presumed to know how far the law allows a liberty. If such a state of reason, such an age of discretion made him free, the same shall make his son free too. Is a man under the law of England? what made him free of that law—that is, to have the liberty to dispose of his actions and possessions, according to his own will, within the permission of that law? a capacity of knowing that law. Which is supposed, by that law, at the age of twenty-one, and in some cases sooner. If this made the father free, it shall make the son free too. Till then, we see the law allows the son to have no will, but he is to be guided by the will of his father or guardian, who is to understand for him. And if the father die and fail to substitute a deputy in this trust, if he hath not provided a tutor to govern his son during his minority, during his want of understanding, the law takes care to do it: some other must govern him and be a will to him till he hath attained to a state of freedom, and his understanding be fit to take the government of his will. But after that the father and son are equally free, as much as tutor and pupil, after nonage, equally subjects of the same law together, without any dominion left in the father over the life, liberty, or estate of his son, whether they be only in the state and under the law of Nature, or under the positive laws of an established government.

*   *   *

The freedom then of man, and liberty of acting according to his own will, is grounded on his having reason, which is able to instruct him in that law he is to govern himself by, and make him know how far he is left to the freedom of his own will. To turn him loose to an unrestrained liberty, before he has reason to guide him, is not the allowing him the privilege of his nature to be free, but to thrust him out amongst brutes, and abandon him to a state as wretched and as much beneath that of a man as theirs. This is that which puts the authority into the parents' hands to govern the minority of their children. God hath made it their business to employ this care on their offspring, and hath placed in them suitable inclinations of tenderness and concern to temper this power, to apply it as His wisdom designed it, to the children's good as long as they should need to be under it.

But what reason can hence advance this care of the parents due to their offspring into an absolute, arbitrary dominion of the father, whose power reaches no farther than by such a discipline as he finds most effectual to give such strength and health to their bodies, such vigour and rectitude to their minds, as may best fit his children to be most useful to themselves and others, and, if it be necessary to his condition, to make them work when they are able for their own subsistence; but in this power the mother, too, has her share with the father.

Nay, this power so little belongs to the father by any peculiar right of Nature, but only as he is guardian of his children, that when he quits his care of them he loses his power over them, which goes along with their nourishment and education, to which it is inseparably annexed, and belongs as much to the foster-father of an exposed child as to the natural father of another. So little power does the bare act of begetting give a man over his issue, if all his care ends there, and this be all the title he hath to the name and authority of a father. And what will become of this paternal power in that part of the world where one woman hath more than one husband at a time? or in those parts of America where, when the husband and wife part, which happens frequently, the children are all left to the mother, follow her, and are wholly under her care and provision? And if the father die whilst the children are young, do they not naturally everywhere owe the same obedience to their mother, during their minority, as to their father, were he alive? And will any one say that the mother hath a legislative power over her children that she can make standing rules which shall be of perpetual obligation, by which they ought to regulate all the concerns of their property, and bound their liberty all the course of their lives, and enforce the observation of them with capital punishments? For this is the proper power of the magistrate, of which the father hath not so much as the shadow. His command over his children is but temporary, and reaches not their life or property. It is but a help to the weakness and imperfection of their nonage, a discipline necessary to their education. And though a father may dispose of his own possessions as he pleases when his children are out of danger of perishing for want, yet his power extends not to the lives or goods which either their own industry, or another's bounty, has made theirs, nor to their liberty neither, when they are once arrived to the enfranchisement of the years of discretion. The father's empire then ceases, and he can from thenceforward no more dispose of the liberty of his son than that of any other man. And it must be far from an absolute or perpetual jurisdiction from which a man may withdraw himself, having licence from Divine authority to "leave father and mother and cleave to his wife."

*   *   *

Chapter VII
Of Political or Civil Society

God, having made man such a creature that, in His own judgment, it was not good for him to be alone, put him under strong obligations of necessity, convenience, and inclination, to drive him into society, as well as fitted him with understanding and language to continue and enjoy it. The first society was between man and wife, which gave beginning to that between parents and children, to which, in time, that between master and servant came to be added. And though all these might, and commonly did, meet together, and make up but one family, wherein the master or mistress of it had some sort of rule proper to a family, each of these, or all together, came short of "political society," as we shall see if we consider the different ends, ties, and bounds of each of these.

Conjugal society is made by a voluntary compact between man and woman, and though it consist chiefly in such a communion and right in one another's bodies as is necessary to its chief end, procreation, yet it draws with it mutual support and assistance, and a communion of interests too, as necessary not only to unite their care and affection, but also necessary to their common offspring, who have a right to be nourished and maintained by them till they are able to provide for themselves.

For the end of conjunction between male and female being not barely procreation, but the continuation of the species, this conjunction betwixt male and female ought to last, even after procreation, so long as is necessary to the nourishment and support of the young ones, who are to be sustained by those that got them till they are able to shift and provide for themselves. This rule, which the infinite wise Maker hath set to the works of His hands, we find the inferior creatures steadily obey. In those vivaporous animals which feed on grass the conjunction between male and female lasts no longer than the very act of copulation, because the teat of the dam being sufficient to nourish the young till it be able to feed on grass, the male only begets, but concerns not himself for the female or young, to whose sustenance he can contribute nothing. But in beasts of prey the conjunction lasts longer, because the dam, not being able well to subsist herself and nourish her numerous offspring by her own prey alone (a more laborious as well as more dangerous way of living than by feeding on grass), the assistance of the male is necessary to the maintenance of their common family, which cannot subsist till they are able to prey for themselves, but by the joint care of male and female. The same is observed in all birds (except some domestic ones, where plenty of food excuses the cock from feeding and taking care of the young brood), whose young, needing food in the nest, the cock and hen continue mates till the young are able to use their wings and provide for themselves.

And herein, I think, lies the chief, if not the only reason, why the male and female in mankind are tied to a longer conjunction than other creatures—viz., because the female is capable of conceiving, and, *de facto,* is commonly with child again, and brings forth too a new birth, long before the former is out of a dependency for support on his parents' help and able to shift for himself, and has all the assistance due to him from his parents, whereby the father, who is bound to take care for those he hath begot, is under an obligation to continue in conjugal society with the same woman longer than other creatures, whose young, being able to subsist of themselves before the time of procreation returns again, the conjugal bond dissolves of itself, and they are at liberty till Hymen, at his usual anniversary season, summons them again to choose new mates. Wherein one cannot but admire the wisdom of the great Creator, who, having given to man an ability to lay up for the future as well as supply the present necessity, hath made it necessary that society of man and wife should be more lasting than of male and female amongst other creatures, that so their industry might be encouraged, and their interest better united, to make provision and lay up goods for their common issue, which uncertain mixture, or easy and frequent solutions of conjugal society, would mightily disturb.

But though these are ties upon mankind which make the conjugal bonds more firm and lasting in a man than the other species of animals, yet it would give one reason to inquire why this compact, where procreation and education are secured and inheritance taken care for, may not be made determinable, either by consent, or at a certain time, or upon certain conditions, as well as any other voluntary compacts, there being no necessity, in the nature of the thing, nor to the ends of it, that it should always be for life—I mean, to such as are under no restraint of any positive law which ordains all such contracts to be perpetual.

But the husband and wife, though they have but one common concern, yet having different understandings, will unavoidably sometimes have different wills too. It therefore being necessary that the last determination (i.e., the rule) should be placed somewhere, it naturally falls to the man's share as the abler and the stronger. But this, reaching but to the things of their common interest and property, leaves the wife in the full and true possession of what by contract is her peculiar right, and at least gives the husband no more power over her than she has over his life; the power of the husband being so far from that of an absolute monarch that the wife has, in many cases, a liberty to separate from him where natural right or their contract allows it, whether that contract be made by themselves in the state of Nature or by the customs or laws of the country they live in, and the children, upon such separation, fall to the father or mother's lot as such contract does determine.

For all the ends of marriage being to be obtained under politic government, as well as in the state of Nature, the civil magistrate doth not abridge the right or power of either, naturally necessary to those ends—viz., procreation and mutual support and assistance whilst they are together, but only decides any controversy that may arise between man and wife about them. If it were otherwise, and that absolute sovereignty and power of life and death naturally belonged to the husband, and were necessary to the society between man and wife, there could be no matrimony in any of these countries where the husband is allowed no such absolute authority. But the ends of matrimony requiring no such power in the husband, it was not at all necessary to it. The condition of conjugal society put it not in him; but whatsoever might consist with procreation and support of the children till they could shift for themselves—mutual assistance, comfort, and maintenance—might be varied and regulated by that contract which first united them in that society, nothing being necessary to any society that is not necessary to the ends for which it is made.

*   *   *

Let us therefore consider a master of a family with all these subordinate relations of wife, children, servants and slaves, united under the domestic rule of a family, with what resemblance soever it may have in its order, offices, and number too, with a little commonwealth, yet is very far from it both in its constitution, power, and end; or if it must be thought a monarchy, and the paterfamilias the absolute monarch in it, absolute monarchy will have but a very shattered and short power, when it is plain by what has been said before, that the master of the family has a very distinct and differently limited power both as to time and extent over those several persons that are in it; for excepting the slave (and the family is as much a family, and his power as paterfamilias as great, whether there be any slaves in his family or no) he has no legislative power of life and death over any of them, and none too but what a mistress of a family may have as well as he. And he certainly can have no absolute power over the whole family who has but a very limited one over every individual in it. But how a family, or any other society of men, differ from that which is properly political society, we shall best see by considering wherein political society itself consists.

Man being born, as has been proved, with a title to perfect freedom and an uncontrolled enjoyment of all the rights and privileges of the law of Nature, equally with any other man, or number of men in the world, hath by nature a power not only to preserve his property—that is, his life, liberty, and estate, against the injuries and attempts of other men, but to judge of and punish the breaches of that law in others, as he is persuaded the offence deserves, even with death itself, in crimes where the heinousness of the fact, in his opinion, requires it. But because no political society can be, nor subsist, without having in itself the power to preserve the property, and in order thereunto punish the offences of all those of that society, there, and there only, is political society where every one of the members hath quitted this natural power, resigned it up into the hands of the community in all cases that exclude him not from appealing for protection to the law established by it. And thus all private judgment of every particular member being excluded, the community comes to be umpire, and by understanding indifferent rules and men authorised by the community for their execution, decides all the differences that may happen between any members of that society concerning any matter of right, and punishes those offences which any member hath committed against the society with such penalties as the law has established; whereby it is easy to discern who are, and are not, in political society together. Those who are united into one body, and have a common established law and judicature to appeal to, with authority to decide controversies between them and punish offenders, are in civil society one with another; but those who have no such common appeal, I mean on earth, are still in the state of Nature, each being where there is no other, judge for himself and executioner; which is, as I have before showed it, the perfect state of Nature.

And thus the commonwealth comes by a power to set down what punishment shall belong to the several transgressions they think worthy of it, committed amongst the members of that society (which is the power of making laws), as well as it has the power to punish any injury done unto any of its members by any one that is not of it (which is the power of war and peace); and all this for the preservation of the property of all the members of that society, as far as is possible. But though every man entered into society has quitted his power to punish offences against the law of Nature in prosecution of his own private judgment, yet with the judgment of offences which he has given up to the legislative, in all cases where he can appeal to the magistrate, he has given up a right to the commonwealth to employ his force for the execution of the judgments of the commonwealth whenever he shall be called to it, which, indeed, are his own judgments, they being made by himself or his representative. And herein we have the original of the legislative and executive power of civil society, which is to judge by standing laws how far offences are to be punished when committed within the commonwealth; and also by occasional judgments founded on the present circumstances of the fact, how far injuries from without are to be vindicated, and in both these to employ all the force of all the members when there shall be need.

Wherever, therefore, any number of men so unite into one society as to quit every one his executive power of the law of Nature, and to resign it to the public, there and there only is a political or civil society. And this is done wherever any number of men, in the state of Nature, enter into society to make one people one body politic under one supreme government: or else when any one joins himself to, and incorporates with any government already made. For hereby he authorises the society, or which is all one, the legislative thereof, to make laws for him as the public good of the society shall require, to the execution whereof his own assistance (as to his own decrees) is due. And this puts men out of a state of Nature into that of a commonwealth, by setting up a judge on earth with authority to determine all the controversies and redress the injuries that may happen to any member of the commonwealth, which judge is the legislative or magistrates appointed by it. And wherever there are any number of men, however associated, that have no such decisive power to appeal to, there they are still in the state of Nature.

And hence it is evident that absolute monarchy, which by some men is counted for the only government in the world, is indeed inconsistent with civil society, and so can be no form of civil government at all. For the end of civil society being to avoid and remedy those inconveniencies of the state of Nature which necessarily follow from every man's being judge in his own case, by setting up a known authority to which every one of that society may appeal upon any injury received, or controversy that may arise, and which every one of the society ought to obey. Wherever any persons are who have not such an authority to appeal to, and decide any difference between them there, those persons are still in the state of Nature. And so is every absolute prince in respect of those who are under his dominion.

For he being supposed to have all, both legislative and executive, power in himself alone, there is no judge to be found, no appeal lies open to any one, who may fairly and indifferently, and with authority decide, and from whence relief and redress may be expected of any injury or inconveniency that may be suffered from him, or by his order. So that such a man, however entitled, Czar, or Grand Signior, or how you please, is as much in the state of Nature, with all under his dominion, as he is with the rest of mankind. For wherever any two men are, who have no standing rule and common judge to appeal to on earth, for the determination of controversies of right betwixt them, there they are still in the state of Nature, and under all the inconveniencies of it, with only this woeful difference to the subject, or rather slave of an absolute prince. That whereas, in the ordinary state of Nature, he has a liberty to judge of his right, according to the best of his power to maintain it; but whenever his property is invaded by the will and order of his monarch, he has not only no appeal, as those in society ought to have, but, as if he were degraded from the common state of rational creatures, is denied a liberty to judge of, or defend his right, and so is exposed to all the misery and inconveniencies that a man can fear from one, who being in the unrestrained state of Nature, is yet corrupted with flattery and armed with power.

*   *   *

Chapter VIII
Of the Beginning of Political Societies

Men being, as has been said, by nature all free, equal, and independent, no one can be put out of this estate and subjected to the political power of another without his own consent, which is done by agreeing with other men, to join and unite into a community for their comfortable, safe, and peaceable living, one amongst another, in a secure enjoyment of their properties, and a greater security against any that are not of it. This any number of men may do, because it injures not the freedom of the rest; they are left, as they were, in the liberty of the state of Nature. When any number of men have so consented to make one community or government, they are thereby presently incorporated, and make one body politic, wherein the majority have a right to act and conclude the rest.

For, when any number of men have, by the consent of every individual, made a community, they have thereby made that community one body, with a power to act as one body, which is only by the will and determination of the majority. For that which acts any community, being only the consent of the individuals of it, and it being one body, must move one way, it is necessary the body should move that way whither the greater force carries it, which is the consent of the majority, or else it is impossible it should act or continue one body, one community, which the consent of every individual that united into it agreed that it should; and so every one is bound by that consent to be concluded by the majority. And therefore we see that in assemblies empowered to act by positive laws where no number is set by that positive law which empowers them, the act of the majority passes for the act of the whole, and of course determines as having, by the law of Nature and reason, the power of the whole.

And thus every man, by consenting with others to make one body politic under one government, puts himself under an obligation to every one of that society to submit to the determination of the majority, and to be concluded by it; or else this original compact, whereby he with others incorporates into one society, would signify nothing, and be no compact if he be left free and under no other ties than he was in before in the state of Nature. For what appearance would there be of any compact? What new engagement if he were no farther tied by any decrees of the society than he himself thought fit and did actually consent to? This would be still as great a liberty as he himself had before his compact, or any one else in the state of Nature, who may submit himself and consent to any acts of it if he thinks fit.

*   *   *

Whosoever, therefore, out of a state of Nature unite into a community, must be understood to give up all the power necessary to the ends for which they unite into society to the majority of the community, unless they expressly agreed in any number greater than the majority. And this is done by barely agreeing to unite into one political society, which is all the compact that is, or needs be, between the individuals that enter into or make up a commonwealth. And thus, that which begins and actually constitutes any political society is nothing but the consent of any number of freemen capable of majority, to unite and incorporate into such a society. And this is that, and that only, which did or could give beginning to any lawful government in the world.

*   *   *

Every man being, as has been showed, naturally free, and nothing being able to put him into subjection to any earthly power, but only his own consent, it is to be considered what shall be understood to be a sufficient declaration of a man's consent to make him subject to the laws of any government.

There is a common distinction of an express and a tacit consent, which will concern our present case. Nobody doubts but an express consent of any man, entering into any society, makes him a perfect member of that society, a subject of that government. The difficulty is, what ought to be looked upon as a tacit consent, and how far it binds—*i.e.*, how far any one shall be looked on to have consented, and thereby submitted to any government, where he has made no expressions of it at all. And to this I say, that every man that hath any possession or enjoyment of any part of the dominions of any government doth hereby give his tacit consent, and is as far forth obliged to obedience to the laws of that government, during such enjoyment, as any one under it, whether this his possession be of land to him and his heirs for ever, or a lodging only for a week; or whether it be barely travelling freely on the highway; and, in effect, it reaches as far as the very being of any one within the territories of that government.

To understand this the better, it is fit to consider that every man when he at first incorporates himself into any commonwealth, he, by his uniting himself thereunto, annexes also, and submits to the community those possessions which he has, or shall acquire, that do not already belong to any other government. For it would be a direct contradiction for any one to enter into society with others for the securing and regulating of property, and yet to suppose his land, whose property is to be regulated by the laws of the society, should be exempt from the jurisdiction of that government to which he himself, and the property of the land, is a subject. By the same act, therefore, whereby any one unites his person, which was before free, to any commonwealth, by the same he unites his possessions, which were before free, to it also; and they become, both of them, person and possession, subject to the government and dominion of that commonwealth as long as it hath a being. Whoever therefore, from thenceforth, by inheritance, purchases permission, or otherwise enjoys any part of the land so annexed to, and under the government of that commonweal, must take it with the condition it is under—that is, of submitting to the government of the commonwealth, under whose jurisdiction it is, as far forth as any subject of it.

But since the government has a direct jurisdiction only over the land and reaches the possessor of it (before he has actually incorporated himself in the society) only as he dwells upon and enjoys that, the obligation any one is under by virtue of such enjoyment to submit to the government begins and ends with the enjoyment; so that whenever the owner, who has given nothing but such a tacit consent to the government will, by donation, sale or otherwise, quit the said possession, he is at liberty to go and incorporate himself into any other commonwealth, or agree with others to begin a new one *in vacuis locis,* in any part of the world they can find free and unpossessed; whereas he that has once, by actual agreement and any express declaration, given his consent to be of any commonweal, is perpetually and indispensably obliged to be, and remain unalterably a subject to it, and can never be again in the liberty of the state of Nature, unless by any calamity the government he was under comes to be dissolved.

But submitting to the laws of any country, living quietly and enjoying privileges and protection under them, makes not a man a member of that society; it is only a local protection and homage due to and from all those who, not being in a state of war, come within the territories belonging to any government, to all parts whereof the force of its law extends. But this no more makes a man a member of that society, a perpetual subject of that commonwealth, than it would make a man a subject to another in whose family he found it convenient to abide for some time, though, whilst he continued in it, he were obliged to comply with the laws and submit to the government he found there. And thus we see that foreigners, by living all their lives under another government, and enjoying the privileges and protection of it, though they are bound, even in conscience, to submit to its administration as far forth as any denizen, yet do not thereby come to be subjects or members of that commonwealth. Nothing can make any man so but his actually entering into it by positive engagement and express promise and compact. This is that which, I think, concerning the beginning of political societies, and that consent which makes any one a member of any commonwealth.

Chapter IX
Of the Ends of Political Society and Government

If man in the state of Nature be so free as has been said, if he be absolute lord of his own person and possessions, equal to the greatest and subject to nobody, why will he part with his freedom, this empire, and subject himself to the dominion and control of any other power? To which it is obvious to answer, that though in the state of Nature he hath such a right, yet the enjoyment of it is very uncertain and constantly exposed to the invasion of others; for all being kings as much as he, every man his equal, and the greater part no strict observers of equity and justice, the enjoyment of the property he has in this state is very unsafe, very insecure. This makes him willing to quit this condition which, however free, is full of fears and continual dangers; and it is not without reason that he seeks out and is willing to join in society with others who are already united, or have a mind to unite for the mutual preservation of their lives, liberties and estates, which I call by the general name—property.

The great and chief end, therefore, of men uniting into commonwealths, and putting themselves under government, is the preservation of their property; to which in the state of Nature there are many things wanting.

Firstly, there wants an established, settled, known law, received and allowed by common consent to be the standard of right and wrong, and the common measure to decide all controversies between them. For though the law of Nature be plain and intelligible to all rational creatures, yet men, being biased by their interest, as well as ignorant for want of study of it, are not apt to allow of it as a law binding to them in the application of it to their particular cases.

Secondly, in the state of Nature there wants a known and indifferent judge, with authority to determine all differences according to the established law. For every one in that state being both judge and executioner of the law of Nature, men being partial to themselves, passion and revenge is very apt to carry them too far, and with too much heat in their own cases, as well as negligence and unconcernedness, make them too remiss in other men's.

Thirdly, in the state of Nature there often wants power to back and support the sentence when right, and to give it due execution. They who by any injustice offended will seldom fail where they are able by force to make good their injustice. Such resistance many times makes the punishment dangerous, and frequently destructive to those who attempt it.

*   *   *

REVIEW QUESTIONS

1. According to Locke, what is the nature of political society?
2. How does political society come into being?
3. How does Locke's notion of a social contract compare with that of Hobbes?
4. What are the ends of political society?
5. What are the implications of Locke's reasoning for early modern economic thinking?

ADAM SMITH

FROM *The Wealth of Nations*

Though best remembered for his towering system of political economy, An Inquiry into the Nature and Causes of the Wealth of Nations *(1776), Adam Smith (1723–1790) was one of the most important social philosophers of the eighteenth century. His economic writings constitute only a part of his larger view of social and political development. Born the son of a minor government official, he entered the University of Glasgow in 1737, already a center of what became known as the Scottish Enlightenment, where he was deeply influenced by another great moral and economic philosopher, Francis Hutcheson. After completing his education at Oxford, he returned to Scotland, where he embarked on a series of public lectures in Edinburgh. In 1752, he was appointed professor of logic at Glasgow, and in 1754, he assumed the chair in moral philosophy. He would look on his tenure as the happiest and most honorable of his life. It was certainly the most productive. There he made the acquaintance of some of the leading intellectual lights of his day: James Watt, of steam-engine fame; David Hume, the great philosopher; and Andrew Cochrane. The last was the founder of the Political Economy Club and the likely source of much of Smith's information on business and commerce. In 1759, Smith published his first important work,* The Theory of Moral Sentiments, *in which he attempted to describe universal principles of human nature. His answer to the question of moral judgment was the thesis of the "inner man," or "impartial spectator," which is the conscience in each human being and whose pronouncements cannot be ignored. Thus, human beings can be driven by passions and self-interests and simultaneously capable of ethics and generosity. This principle foreshadowed the "invisible hand" that would guide economic behavior in* The Wealth of Nations. *He began work on this classic text after resigning his post at Glasgow to serve as tutor to the young Duke of Buccleuch. When it finally appeared, it continued the themes first addressed in* The Theory of Moral Sentiments, *the resolution of passion and reason in human behavior, and now, human history. According to Smith, society evolves through four broad stages, each with appropriate institutions: simple hunters, nomadic herders, feudal farmers, and commercial workers. The guiding force in this development is human nature, motivated by self-interest but guided by disinterested reason. Most of the book is given over to a discussion of the function of the invisible hand in the final, current stage. Whereas conscience provided the necessary guidance in* The Theory of Moral Sentiments, *competition assumes that function in* The Wealth of Nations. *Competition rendered markets self-regulating and ensured that prices and wages never stray far from their "natural" levels. Much of the book, especially Book IV, where he places his discussion of colonies, is given over to a polemic against restriction, through both regulation and monopoly, in economic life.* The Wealth of Nations *appeared to great acclaim and earned its author fame and fortune. He published nothing more.*

From *An Inquiry into the Nature and Causes of the Wealth of Nations*, by Adam Smith (Edinburgh: Thomas Nelson, 1838).

∗   ∗   ∗

Of the Motives for Establishing New Colonies

The interest which occasioned the first settlement of the different European colonies in America and the West Indies, was not altogether so plain and distinct as that which directed the establishment of those of ancient Greece and Rome.

GREEK COLONIES WERE SENT OUT WHEN THE POPULATION GREW TOO GREAT AT HOME.

All the different states of ancient Greece possessed, each of them, but a very small territory, and when the people in any one of them multiplied beyond what that territory could easily maintain, a part of them were sent in quest of a new habitation in some remote and distant part of the world; the warlike neighbours who surrounded them on all sides, rendering it difficult for any of them to enlarge very much its territory at home. ∗ ∗ ∗

THE MOTHER CITY CLAIMED NO AUTHORITY.

The mother city, though she considered the colony as a child, at all times entitled to great favour and assistance, and owing in return much gratitude and respect, yet considered it as an emancipated child, over whom she pretended to claim no direct authority or jurisdiction.

The colony settled its own form of government, enacted its own laws, elected its own magistrates, and made peace or war with its neighbours as an independent state, which had no occasion to wait for the approbation or consent of the mother city. Nothing can be more plain and distinct than the interest which directed every such establishment.

ROMAN COLONIES WERE SENT OUT TO SATISFY THE DEMAND FOR LANDS AND TO ESTABLISH GARRISONS IN CONQUERED TERRITORIES.

Rome, like most of the other ancient republics, was originally founded upon an Agrarian law, which divided the public territory in a certain proportion among the different citizens who composed the state. The course of human affairs, by marriage, by succession, and by alienation, necessarily deranged this original division, and frequently threw the lands, which had been allotted for the maintenance of many different families into the possession of a single person. To remedy this disorder, for such it was supposed to be, a law was made, restricting the quantity of land which any citizen could possess to five hundred jugera, about three hundred and fifty English acres. This law, however, though we read of its having been executed upon one or two occasions, was either neglected or evaded, and the inequality of fortunes went on continually increasing. The greater part of the citizens had no land, and without it the manners and customs of those times rendered it difficult for a freeman to maintain his independency. . . . The people became clamorous to get land, and the rich and the great, we may believe, were perfectly determined not to give them any part of theirs. To satisfy them in some measure, therefore, they frequently proposed to send out a new colony.

THEY WERE ENTIRELY SUBJECT TO THE MOTHER CITY.

But conquering Rome was, even upon such occasions, under no necessity of turning out her citizens to seek their fortune, if one may say so, through the wide world, without knowing where they were to settle. She assigned them lands generally in the conquered provinces of Italy, where, being within the dominions of the republic, they could never form any independent state; but were at best but a sort of corporation, which, though it had the power of enacting bye-laws for its own government, was at all times subject to the correction, jurisdiction, and legislative authority of the mother city. The sending out a colony of this kind, not only gave some satisfaction to the people, but often established a sort of garrison too in a newly conquered province, of which the obedience might otherwise have been doubtful. A Roman colony, therefore, whether we consider the nature of the establishment itself, or the motives for making it, was altogether different from a Greek one. The words accordingly, which in the original languages denote those different establishments, have very different meanings. The Latin word (*Colonia*) signifies simply a plantation. The Greek word (αποιηια), on the contrary, signifies a separation of dwelling, a departure from home, a going out of the house. But, though the Roman colonies were in many respects different from the Greek ones, the interest which prompted to establish them was equally plain and distinct. Both institutions derived their origin either from irresistible necessity, or from clear and evident utility.

THE UTILITY OF THE AMERICAN COLONIES IS NOT SO EVIDENT.

The establishment of the European colonies in America and the West Indies arose from no necessity: and though the utility which has resulted from them has been very great, it is not altogether so clear and evident. It was not understood at their first establishment, and was not the motive either of that establishment or of the discoveries which gave occasion to it; and the nature, extent, and limits of that utility are not, perhaps, well understood at this day.

THE VENETIANS HAD A PROFITABLE TRADE IN EAST INDIA GOODS.

The Venetians, during the fourteenth and fifteenth centuries, carried on a very advantageous commerce in spiceries, and other East India goods, which they distributed among the other nations of Europe. They purchased them chiefly in Egypt, at that time under the dominion of the Mammeluks, the enemies of the Turks, of whom the Venetians were the enemies; and this union of interest, assisted by the money of Venice, formed such a connection as gave the Venetians almost a monopoly of the trade.

THIS WAS ENVIED BY THE PORTUGUESE AND LED THEM TO DISCOVER THE CAPE OF GOOD HOPE PASSAGE.

The great profits of the Venetians tempted the avidity of the Portuguese. They had been endeavouring, during the course of the fifteenth century, to find out by sea a way to the countries from which the Moors brought them ivory and gold dust across the Desart. They discovered the Madeiras, the Canaries, the Azores, the Cape de Verd islands, the coast of Guinea, that of Loango, Congo, Angola, and Benguela, and finally, the Cape of Good Hope. They had long wished to share in the profitable traffic of the Venetians, and this last discovery opened to them a probable prospect of doing so. In 1497, Vasco de Gama sailed from the port of Lisbon with a fleet of four ships, and, after a navigation of eleven months, arrived upon the coast of Indostan, and thus completed a course of discoveries which had been pursued with great steadiness, and with very little interruption, for near a century together.

COLUMBUS ENDEAVOURED TO REACH THE EAST INDIES BY SAILING WESTWARDS.

Some years before this, while the expectations of Europe were in suspense about the projects of the Portuguese, of which the success appeared yet to be doubtful, a Genoese pilot formed the yet more daring project of sailing to the East Indies by the West. The situation of those countries was at that time very imperfectly known in Europe. The few European travellers who had been there had magnified the distance; perhaps through simplicity and ignorance, what was really very great, appearing almost infinite to those who could not measure it; or, perhaps, in order to increase somewhat more the marvellous of their own adventures in visiting regions so immensely remote from Europe. The longer the way was by the East, Columbus very justly con-cluded, the shorter it would be by the West. He proposed, therefore, to take that way, as both the shortest and the surest, and he had the good fortune to convince Isabella of Castile of the probability of his project. He sailed from the port of Palos in August 1492, near five years before the expedition of Vasco de Gama set out from Portugal, and, after a voyage of between two and three months, discovered first some of the small Bahama or Lucayan islands, and afterwards the great island of St. Domingo.

COLUMBUS MISTOOK THE COUNTRIES HE FOUND FOR THE INDIES.

But the countries which Columbus discovered, either in this or in any of his subsequent voyages, had no resemblance to those which he had gone in quest of. Instead of the wealth, cultivation and populousness of China and Indostan, he found, in St. Domingo, and in all the other parts of the new world which he ever visited, nothing but a country quite covered with wood, uncultivated, and inhabited only by some tribes of naked and miserable savages. He was not very willing, however, to believe that they were not the same with some of the countries described by Marco Polo, the first European who had visited, or at least had left behind him any description of China or the East Indies; and a very slight resemblance, such as that which he found between the name of Cibao, a mountain in St. Domingo, and that of Cipango, mentioned by Marco Polo, was frequently sufficient to make him return to this favourite prepossession, though contrary to the clearest evidence. In his letters to Ferdinand and Isabella he called the countries which he had discovered, the Indies. He entertained no doubt but that they were the extremity of those which had been described by Marco Polo, and that they were not very distant from the Ganges, or from the countries which had been conquered by Alexander. Even when at last convinced that they were different, he still flattered himself that those rich countries were at no great distance, and in a subsequent voyage, accordingly, went in quest of them along the coast of Terra Firma, and towards the isthmus of Darien.

HENCE THE NAMES EAST AND WEST INDIES.

In consequence of this mistake of Columbus, the name of the Indies has stuck to those unfortunate countries ever since; and when it was at last clearly discovered that the new were altogether different from the old Indies, the former were called the West, in contradistinction to the latter, which were called the East Indies.

THE COUNTRIES DISCOVERED WERE NOT RICH.

It was of importance to Columbus, however, that the countries which he had discovered, whatever they were, should be represented to the court of Spain as of very great consequence; and, in what constitutes the real riches of every country, the animal and vegetable productions of the soil, there was at that time nothing which could well justify such a representation of them.

*   *   *

SO COLUMBUS RELIED ON THE MINERALS.

Finding nothing either in the animals or vegetables of the newly discovered countries, which could justify a very advantageous representation of them, Columbus turned his view towards their minerals; and in the richness of the productions of this third kingdom, he flattered himself, he had found a full compensation for the insignificancy of those of the other two. The little bits of gold with which the inhabitants ornamented their dress, and which, he was informed, they frequently found in the rivulets and torrents that fell from the mountains, were sufficient to satisfy him that those mountains abounded with the richest gold mines. St. Domingo, therefore, was represented as a country abounding with gold, and upon that account (according to the prejudices not only of the present times, but of those times), an inexhaustible source of real wealth to the crown and kingdom of Spain.

THE COUNCIL OF CASTILE WAS ATTRACTED BY THE GOLD, COLUMBUS PROPOSING THAT THE GOVERNMENT SHOULD HAVE HALF THE GOLD AND SILVER DISCOVERED.

In consequence of the representations of Columbus, the council of Castile determined to take possession of countries of which the inhabitants were plainly incapable of defending themselves. The pious purpose of converting them to Christianity sanctified the injustice of the project. But the hope of finding treasures of gold there, was the sole motive which prompted to undertake it; and to give this motive the greater weight, it was proposed by Columbus that the half of all the gold and silver that should be found there should belong to the crown. This proposal was approved of by the council.

*   *   *

THE SUBSEQUENT SPANISH ENTERPRISES WERE ALL PROMPTED BY THE SAME MOTIVE.

All the other enterprises of the Spaniards in the new world, subsequent to those of Columbus, seem to have been prompted by the same motive. It was the sacred thirst of gold that carried Oieda, Nicuessa, and Vasco Nugnes de Balboa, to the isthmus of Darien, that carried Cortez to Mexico, and Almagro and Pizzarro to Chile and Peru. When those adventurers arrived upon any unknown coast, their first enquiry was always if there was any gold to be found there; and according to the information which they received concerning this particular, they determined either to quit the country or to settle in it.

*   *   *

IN THIS CASE EXPECTATIONS WERE TO SOME EXTENT REALISED, SO FAR AS THE SPANIARDS WERE CONCERNED.

In the countries first discovered by the Spaniards, no gold or silver mines are at present known which are supposed to be worth the working. The quantities of those metals which the first adventurers are said to have found there, had probably been very much magnified, as well as the fertility of the mines which were wrought immediately after the first discovery. What those adventurers were reported to have found, however, was sufficient to inflame the avidity of all their countrymen. Every Spaniard who sailed to America expected to find an Eldorado. Fortune too did upon this what she has done upon very few other occasions. She realized in some measure the extravagant hopes of her votaries, and in the discovery and conquest of Mexico and Peru (of which the one happened about thirty, the other about forty years after the first expedition of Columbus), she presented them with something not very unlike that profusion of the precious metals which they sought for.

A project of commerce to the East Indies, therefore, gave occasion to the first discovery of the West. A project of conquest gave occasion to all the establishments of the Spaniards in those newly discovered countries. The motive which excited them to this conquest was a project of gold and silver mines; and a course of accidents, which no human wisdom could foresee, rendered this project much more successful than the undertakers had any reasonable grounds for expecting.

BUT THE OTHER NATIONS WERE NOT SO SUCCESSFUL.

The first adventures of all the other nations of Europe, who attempted to make settlements in America, were animated by the like chimerical views; but they were not equally successful. It was more than a hundred years after the first settlement of the Brazils, before any silver, gold, or diamond mines were discovered there. In the English, French, Dutch, and Danish colonies, none have ever yet been discovered; at least none that are at present supposed to be worth the working. The first English settlers in North America, however, offered a fifth of all the gold and silver which should be found there to the king, as a motive for granting them their patents. In the patents to Sir Walter Raleigh, to the London and Plymouth companies, to the council of Plymouth, &c. this fifth was accordingly reserved to the crown. To the expectation of finding gold and silver mines, those first settlers too joined that of discovering a north-west passage to the East Indies. They have hitherto been disappointed in both.

Causes of the Prosperity of New Colonies

The colony of a civilized nation which takes possession either of a waste country, or of one so thinly inhabited, that the natives easily give place to the new settlers, advances more rapidly to wealth and greatness than any other human society.

COLONISTS TAKE OUT KNOWLEDGE AND REGULAR GOVERNMENT.

The colonists carry out with them a knowledge of agriculture and of other useful arts, superior to what can grow up of its own accord in the course of many centuries among savage and barbarous nations. They carry out with them too the habit of subordination, some notion of the regular government which takes place in their own country, of the system of laws which supports it, and of a regular administration of justice; and they naturally establish something of the same kind in the new settlement. But among savage and barbarous nations, the natural progress of law and government is still slower than the natural progress of arts, after law and government have been so far established, as is necessary for their protection.

LAND IS PLENTIFUL AND CHEAP.

Every colonist gets more land than he can possibly cultivate. He has no rent, and scarce any taxes to pay. No landlord shares with him in its produce, and the share of the sovereign is commonly but a trifle. He has every motive to render as great as possible a produce, which is thus to be almost entirely his own. But his land is commonly so extensive, that with all his own industry, and with all the industry of other people whom he can get to employ, he can seldom make it produce the tenth part of what it is capable of producing.

WAGES ARE HIGH.

He is eager, therefore, to collect labourers from all quarters, and to reward them with the most liberal wages. But those liberal wages, joined to the plenty and cheapness of land, soon make those labourers leave him, in order to become landlords themselves, and to reward, with equal liberality, other labourers, who soon leave them for the same reason that they left their first master.

*   *   *

Of the Advantages Which Europe Has Derived from the Discovery of America, and from That of a Passage to the East Indies by the Cape of Good Hope

THE ADVANTAGES DERIVED BY EUROPE FROM AMERICA ARE (1) THE ADVANTAGES OF EUROPE IN GENERAL, AND (2) THE ADVANTAGES OF THE PARTICULAR COUNTRIES WHICH HAVE COLONIES.

Such are the advantages which the colonies of America have derived from the policy of Europe.

What are those which Europe has derived from the discovery and colonization of America?

Those advantages may be divided, first, into the general advantages which Europe, considered as one great country, has derived from those great events; and, secondly, into the particular advantages which each colonizing country has derived from the colonies which particularly belong to it, in consequence of the authority or dominion which it exercises over them.

(1) THE GENERAL ADVANTAGES TO EUROPE ARE (A) AN INCREASE OF ENJOYMENTS.

The general advantages which Europe, considered as one great country, has derived from the discov-ery and colonization of America, consist, first, in the increase of its enjoyments; and secondly, in the augmentation of its industry.

The surplus produce of America, imported into Europe, furnishes the inhabitants of this great continent with a variety of commodities which they could not otherwise have possessed, some for conveniency and use, some for pleasure, and some for ornament, and thereby contributes to increase their enjoyments.

(B) AN AUGMENTATION OF INDUSTRY NOT ONLY IN THE COUNTRIES WHICH TRADE WITH AMERICA DIRECTLY, BUT ALSO IN OTHER COUNTRIES WHICH DO NOT SEND THEIR PRODUCE TO AMERICA OR EVEN RECEIVE ANY PRODUCE FROM AMERICA.

The discovery and colonization of America, it will readily be allowed, have contributed to augment the industry, first, of all the countries which trade to it directly; such as Spain, Portugal, France, and England; and, secondly, of all those which, without trading to it directly, send, through the medium of other countries, goods to it of their own produce; such as Austrian Flanders, and some provinces of Germany, which, through the medium of the countries before mentioned, send to it a considerable quantity of linen and other goods. All such countries have evidently gained a more extensive market for their surplus produce, and must consequently have been encouraged to increase its quantity.

*   *   *

Those great events may even have contributed to increase the enjoyments, and to augment the industry of countries which, not only never sent any commodities to America, but never received any from it. Even such countries may have received a greater abundance of other commodities from countries of which the surplus produce had been augmented by means of the American trade. This greater abundance, as it must necessarily have increased their enjoyments, so it must likewise have augmented their industry. A greater number of new equivalents of some kind or other must have been presented to them to be exchanged for the surplus produce of that industry. A more extensive market must have been created for that surplus produce, so as to raise its value, and thereby encourage its increase. The mass of commodities annually thrown into the great circle of European commerce, and by its various revolutions annually distributed among all the different nations comprehended within it, must have been augmented by the whole surplus produce of America. A greater share of this greater mass, therefore, is likely to have fallen to each of those nations, to have increased their enjoyments, and augmented their industry.

*   *   *

(2) THE PARTICULAR ADVANTAGES OF THE COLONISING COUNTRIES ARE (A) THE COMMON ADVANTAGES DERIVED FROM PROVINCES, (B) THE PECULIAR ADVANTAGES DERIVED FROM PROVINCES IN AMERICA.

The particular advantages which each colonizing country derives from the colonies which particularly belong to it, are of two different kinds; first, those common advantages which every empire derives from the provinces subject to its dominion; and, secondly, those peculiar advantages which are supposed to result from provinces of so very peculiar a nature as the European colonies of America.

The common advantages which every empire derives from the provinces subject to its dominion, consist, first, in the military force which they furnish for its defence; and, secondly, in the revenue which they furnish for the support of its civil government.

*   *   *

(A) THE COMMON ADVANTAGES ARE CONTRIBUTIONS OF MILITARY FORCES AND REVENUE, BUT NONE OF THE COLONIES HAVE EVER FURNISHED MILITARY FORCE.

The European colonies of America have never yet furnished any military force for the defence of the mother country. Their military force has never yet been sufficient for their own defence; and in the different wars in which the mother countries have been engaged, the defence of their colonies has generally occasioned a very considerable distraction of the military force of those countries. In this respect, therefore, all the European colonies have, without exception, been a cause rather of weakness than of strength to their respective mother countries.

AND THE COLONIES OF SPAIN AND PORTUGAL ALONE HAVE CONTRIBUTED REVENUE.

The colonies of Spain and Portugal only have contributed any revenue towards the defence of the mother country, or the support of her civil government. The taxes which have been levied upon those of other European nations, upon those of England in particular, have seldom been equal to the expence laid out upon them in time of peace, and never sufficient to defray that which they occasioned in time of war. Such colonies, therefore, have been a source of expence and not of revenue to their respective mother countries.

(B) THE EXCLUSIVE TRADE IS THE SOLE PECULIAR ADVANTAGE.

The advantages of such colonies to their respective mother countries, consist altogether in those peculiar advantages which are supposed to result from provinces of so very peculiar a nature as the European colonies of America; and the exclusive trade, it is acknowledged, is the sole source of all those peculiar advantages.

THE EXCLUSIVE TRADE OF EACH COUNTRY IS A DISADVANTAGE TO THE OTHER COUNTRIES.

In consequence of this exclusive trade, all that part of the surplus produce of the English colonies, for example, which consists in what are called enumerated commodities, can be sent to no other country but England. Other countries must afterwards buy it of her. It must be cheaper therefore in England than it can be in any other country, and must contribute more to increase the enjoyments of England than those of any other country. It must likewise contribute more to encourage her industry. For all those parts of her own surplus produce which England exchanges for those enumerated commodities, she must get a better price than any other countries can get for the like parts of theirs, when they exchange them for the same commodities. The manufactures of England, for example, will purchase a greater quantity of the sugar and tobacco of her own colonies, than the like manufactures of other countries can purchase of that sugar and tobacco. So far, therefore, as the manufactures of England and those of other countries are both to be exchanged for the sugar and tobacco of the English colonies, this superiority of price gives an encouragement to the former, beyond what the latter can in these circumstances enjoy. The exclusive trade of the colonies, therefore, as it diminishes, or, at least, keeps down below what they would otherwise rise to, both the enjoyments and the industry of the countries which do not possess it; so it gives an evident advantage to the countries which do possess it over those other countries.

*   *   *

REVIEW QUESTIONS

1. How, according to Smith, did the colonial empires of early modern Europe differ from those of the ancient world?
2. What was the motive force of empire?
3. How does Smith explain the eventual success of the colonies in America?
4. What benefits does he think derive from empire? What costs?
5. How do we explain Smith's apparent indifference to the exploitation of native or slave populations?

CATHERINE THE GREAT

FROM Proposals for a New Code of Law

Catherine II (1729–1796), a German princess who became Tsarina of Russia after disposing of her ineffectual husband, was one of the most successful European monarchs of the eighteenth century and one of the most remarkable female rulers of all time. She followed Peter the Great in regarding Russia as a European power. Among her many achievements was the addition of some 200,000 square miles to the territory of the Russian Empire. Nor were her interests limited to expansion. She also took effective measures to modernize the empire's administration and improve its society. In 1767 Catherine summoned an assembly to draft a new code of laws for Russia and gave detailed instructions to the members about the principles they should apply. The proposed code never went into effect, but the proposal breathes the spirit of the Enlightenment.

From *Documents of Catherine the Great: The Correspondence with Voltaire and the Instruction of 1767 in the English Text of 1768*, translated by W. F. Reddaway (Cambridge: Cambridge University Press, 1931), pp. 216–17, 219, 231, 241, 244, 256, 258.

*   *   *

6. Russia is a European State.

7. This is clearly demonstrated by the following Observations: The Alterations which *Peter the Great* undertook in Russia succeeded with the greater Ease, because the Manners, which prevailed at that Time, and had been introduced amongst us by a Mixture of different Nations, and the Conquest of foreign Territories, were quite unsuitable to the Climate. *Peter the First*, by introducing the Manners and Customs of Europe among the European People in his Dominions, found at that Time such Means as even he himself was not sanguine enough to expect. . . .

8. The Possessions of the Russian Empire extend upon the terrestrial Globe to 32 Degrees of Latitude, and to 165 of Longitude.

9. The Sovereign is absolute; for there is no other Authority but that which centers in his single Person, that can act with a Vigor proportionate to the Extent of such a vast Dominion.

10. The Extent of the Dominion requires an absolute Power to be vested in that Person who rules over it. It is expedient so to be, that the quick Dispatch of Affairs, sent from distant Parts, might make ample Amends for the Delay occasioned by the great Distance of the Places.

11. Every other Form of Government whatsoever would not only have been prejudicial to Russia, but would even have proved its entire Ruin.

12. Another Reason is: That it is better to be subject to the Laws under one Master, than to be subservient to many.

13. What is the true End of Monarchy? Not to deprive People of their natural Liberty; but to correct their Actions, in order to attain the *supreme Good*.

14. The Form of Government, therefore, which best attains this End, and at the same Time sets less Bounds than others to natural Liberty, is that which coincides with the Views and Purposes of rational Creatures, and answers the End, upon which we ought to fix a steadfast Eye in the Regulations of civil Polity.

15. The Intention and the End of Monarchy, is the Glory of the Citizens, of the State, and of the Sovereign.

16. But, from this Glory, a Sense of Liberty arises in a People governed by a Monarch; which may produce in these States as much Energy in transacting the most important Affairs, and may contribute as much to the Happiness of the Subjects, as even Liberty itself. . . .

*   *   *

33. The Laws ought to be so framed, as to secure the Safety of every Citizen as much as possible.

34. The Equality of the Citizens consists in this; that they should all be subject to the same Laws.

35. This Equality requires Institutions so well adapted, as to prevent the Rich from oppressing those who are not so wealthy as themselves, and converting all the Charges and Employments entrusted to them as Magistrates only, to their own private Emolument. . . .

*   *   *

37. In a State or Assemblage of People that live together in a Community, where there are Laws, Liberty can only consist *in doing that which every One ought to do*, and *not to be constrained to do that which One ought not to do*.

38. A Man ought to form in his own Mind an exact and clear Idea of what Liberty is. *Liberty is the Right of doing whatsoever the Laws allow:* And if any one Citizen could do what the Laws forbid, there would be no more Liberty; because others would have an equal Power of doing the same.

39. The political Liberty of a Citizen is the Peace of Mind arising from the Consciousness, that every Individual enjoys his peculiar Safety; and in order that the People might attain this Liberty, the Laws ought to be so framed, that no one Citizen should stand in Fear of another; but that all of them should stand in Fear of the same Laws. . . .

*   *   *

123. The Usage of Torture is contrary to all the Dictates of Nature and Reason; even Mankind itself

cries out against it, and demands loudly the total Abolition of it. . . .

*   *   *

180. That Law, therefore, is highly beneficial to the Community where it is established, which ordains that every Man shall be judged by his Peers and Equals. For when the Fate of a Citizen is in Question, all Prejudices arising from the Difference of Rank or Fortune should be stifled; because they ought to have no Influence between the Judges and the Parties accused. . . .

*   *   *

194. (1.) No Man ought to be looked upon as *guilty*, before he has received his judicial Sentence; nor can the Laws deprive him of *their* Protection, before it is proved that he *has forfeited all Right* to it. What Right therefore can Power give to any to inflict Punishment upon a Citizen at a Time, when it is yet dubious, whether he is *Innocent* or *guilty*? . . .

*   *   *

250. A Society of Citizens, as well as every Thing else, requires a certain fixed Order: There ought to be *some to govern*, and *others to obey*.

251. And this is the Origin of every Kind of Subjection; which feels itself more or less alleviated, in Proportion to the Situation of the Subjects. . . .

252. And, consequently, as the Law of Nature commands Us to take as much Care, as lies in *Our* Power, of the Prosperity of all the People; we are obliged to alleviate the Situation of the Subjects, as much as sound Reason will permit.

253. And therefore, to shun all Occasions of reducing People to a State of Slavery, except the *utmost* Necessity should *inevitably* oblige us to do it; in that Case, it ought not to be done for our own Benefit; but for the Interest of the State: Yet even that Case is extremely uncommon.

254. Of whatever Kind Subjection may be, the civil Laws ought to guard, on the one Hand, against the *Abuse* of Slavery, and, on the other, against the *Dangers* which may arise from it. . . .

*   *   *

269. It seems too, that the Method of exacting their Revenues, *newly* invented by the Lords, diminishes both the *Inhabitants*, and the *Spirit of Agriculture* in Russia. Almost all the Villages are *heavily* taxed. The Lords, who seldom or never *reside* in their Villages, lay an Impost on every Head of one, two, and even five Rubles, without the least Regard to the *Means* by which their Peasants may be able to *raise* this Money.

270. It is highly necessary that the Law should prescribe a Rule to the Lords, for a more judicious Method of raising their Revenues; and oblige them to levy *such* a Tax, as *tends least* to separate the Peasant from his House and Family; this would be the Means by which Agriculture would become more extensive, and Population be more increased in the Empire.

REVIEW QUESTIONS

1. Which articles and which instructions, coincide with the liberal or enlightened principles that were spreading across Europe in the late seventeenth and eighteenth centuries?

2. These liberal sentiments notwithstanding, what makes this document a classic exercise in absolute monarchy?

3. Why does Catherine include the curious instruction in Article 6?

4. How does Catherine understand such concepts as "society" and the "laws of nature"?

5. How does Catherine understand monarchy? How do her ideas differ from those of other absolute monarchs you may have studied?

16   THE NEW SCIENCE OF THE SEVENTEENTH CENTURY

The term scientific revolution *is commonly applied to the changes in scientific theory and practice that took root in the early seventeenth century and promoted the advance of science as we know it today. It grew initially out of changes in astronomy and physics, the creation of mechanical philosophy as a general theory of nature, and the adoption of mathematics as a basic language of science. Natural phenomena were conceived to be regular and rational. Because nature was subject to reason, human beings could uncover its laws, which were assumed to be few in number and universal in application, by the right exercise of their own rational capacities. Among these laws were those of mechanics, which altered the scientific vision of the universe. They explained all physical phenomena in terms of matter and assumed that motion was the natural state of the universe. Mechanical philosophy posited that all bodies were composed of a single, universal substance, matter. These natural phenomena, matter and motion, were so defined as to be measurable and translatable into numbers that could be manipulated in mathematical formulas. As a form of reason, therefore, mathematics could become the language of scientific inquiry. Reason and mathematics, scientists believed, could teach reliable truths about nature. Thus the scientific revolution created the basic intellectual milieu for enlightened thinking.*

Nicolaus Copernicus

FROM *Six Books Concerning the Revolutions of the Heavenly Orbs*

The Polish cleric and astronomer Nicolaus Copernicus (1473–1543) is generally cred-ited as the discoverer of the heliocentric solar system. He proposed and demonstrated mathematically how the observed motions of stars and planets might be reconciled by assuming that the sun was a fixed point and that the earth rotated around the Sun while revolving on its own axis. His interest in the heavens probably began dur-ing a period of study at the University of Bologna, where he came into contact with Domenic Maria de Novara, the university's leading astronomer. Although his princi-pal interests were scientific, his career remained ecclesiastical. He served as a church canon, involved in administrative matters, and pursued astronomy in his spare time. Troubled by the discrepancies between theoretical descriptions and direct observa-tions of planetary motion, Copernicus overturned Aristotle's earth-centered universe by proposing instead that the sun remained stationary and that the earth revolved around it. If this were true, it would mean that the remaining planets also revolved around the sun at fixed distances and in mathematically predictable time frames. Though he is thought to have developed his theory between 1508 and 1514, De revo-lutionibus orbium coelestium libri vi *("Six Books Concerning the Revolutions of the Heavenly Orbs") did not appear until the year of his death, 1543. Its full implications as a new theory of the fundamental structure of the universe would not be recognized until Johannes Kepler published his own theories a century later.*

From *On the Revolutions of the Heavenly Spheres*, by Nicolaus Copernicus, translated by Charles Glenn Wallis (Amherst, Mass.: Prometheus Books, 1996), pp. 4–7, 15–19.

*   *   *

Preface and Dedication to Pope Paul III

I can reckon easily enough, Most Holy Father, that as soon as certain people learn that in these books of mine which I have written about the revolutions of the spheres of the world I attribute certain motions to the terrestrial globe, they will immediately shout to have me and my opinion hooted off the stage. For my own works do not please me so much that I do not weigh what judgments others will pronounce concerning them. And although I realize that the conceptions of a philosopher are placed beyond the judgment of the crowd, because it is his loving duty to seek the truth in all things, in so far as God has granted that to human reason; nevertheless I think we should avoid opinions utterly foreign to rightness. And when I considered how absurd this "lecture" would be held by those who know that the opinion that the Earth rests immovable in the middle of the heavens as if their centre had been confirmed by the judgments of many ages—if I were to assert to the contrary that the Earth moves; for a long time I was in great difficulty as to whether I should bring to light my commentaries written to demonstrate the Earth's movement, or whether it would not be better to follow the example of the Pythagoreans and certain others who used to hand down the mysteries of their philosophy not in writing but by word of mouth and only to their relatives and friends—witness the letter of Lysis to Hipparchus. They however seem to me to have done that not, as some judge, out of a jealous unwillingness to communicate their doctrines but in order that things of very great beauty which have been investigated by the loving care of great men should not be scorned by those who find it a bother to expend any great energy on letters—except on the money-making variety—or who are provoked by the exhortations and examples of others to the liberal study of philosophy but on account of their natural stupidity hold the position among philosophers that drones hold among bees. Therefore, when I weighed these things in my mind, the scorn which I had to fear on account of the newness and absurdity of my opinion almost drove me to abandon a work already undertaken.

*   *   *

But perhaps Your Holiness will not be so much surprised at my giving the results of my nocturnal study to the light—after having taken such care in working them out that I did not hesitate to put in writing my conceptions as to the movement of the Earth—as you will be eager to hear from me what came into my mind that in opposition to the general opinion of mathematicians and almost in opposition to common sense I should dare to imagine some movement of the Earth. And so I am unwilling to hide from Your Holiness that nothing except my knowledge that mathematicians have not agreed with one another in their researches moved me to think out a different scheme of drawing up the movements of the spheres of the world. For in the first place mathematicians are so uncertain about the movements of the sun and moon that they can neither demonstrate nor observe the unchanging magnitude of the revolving year. Then in setting up the solar and lunar movements and those of the other five wandering stars, they do not employ the same principles, assumptions, or demonstrations for the revolutions and apparent movements. . . . Moreover, they have not been able to discover or to infer the chief point of all, i.e., the form of the world and the certain commensurability of its parts. But they are in exactly the same fix as someone taking from different places hands, feet, head, and the other limbs—shaped very beautifully but not with reference to one body and without correspondence to one another—so that such parts made up a monster rather than a man. And so, in the process of demonstration which they call "method," they are found either to have omitted something necessary or to have admitted something foreign which by no means pertains to the matter; and they would by no means have been in this fix, if they had followed sure principles. For if the hypotheses they assumed were not false, everything which followed from the hypotheses would have been verified without fail; and though what I am saying may be obscure right now, nevertheless it will become clearer in the proper place.

Accordingly, when I had meditated upon this lack of certitude in the traditional mathematics concerning the composition of movements of the spheres of the world, I began to be annoyed that the philosophers, who in other respects had made a very careful scrutiny of the least details of the world, had discovered no sure scheme for the movements of the machinery of the world, which has been built for us by the Best and Most Orderly Workman of all. Wherefore, I took the trouble to reread all the books by philosophers which I could get hold of, to see if any of them even supposed that the movements of the spheres of the world were different from those laid down by those who taught mathematics in the schools. And as a matter of fact, I found first in Cicero that Nicetas thought that the Earth moved. And afterwards I found in Plutarch that there were some others of the same opinion: I shall copy out his words here, so that they may be known to all:

Some think that the Earth is at rest; but Philolaus the Pythagorean says that it moves around the fire with an obliquely circular motion, like the sun and moon.

Herakleides of Pontus and Ekphantus the Pythagorean do not give the Earth any movement of locomotion, but rather a limited movement of rising and setting around its centre, like a wheel.

Therefore I also, having found occasion, began to meditate upon the mobility of the Earth. And although the opinion seemed absurd, nevertheless because I knew that others before me had been granted the liberty of constructing whatever circles they pleased in order to demonstrate astral phenomena, I thought that I too, would be readily permitted to test whether or not, by the laying down that the Earth had some movement, demonstrations less shaky than those of my predecessors could be found for the revolutions of the celestial spheres.

And so, having laid down the movements which I attribute to the Earth farther on in the work, I finally discovered by the help of long and numerous observations that if the movements of the other wandering stars are correlated with the circular movement of the Earth, and if the movements are computed in accordance with the revolution of each planet, not only do all their phenomena follow from that but also this correlation binds together so closely the order and magnitudes of all the planets and of their spheres or orbital circles and the heavens themselves that nothing can be shifted around in any part of them without disrupting the remaining parts and the universe as a whole.

Accordingly, in composing my work I adopted the following order: in the first book I describe all the locations of the spheres or orbital circles together with the movements which I attribute to the earth, so that this book contains as it were the general set-up of the universe. But afterwards in the remaining books I correlate all the movements of the other planets and their spheres or orbital circles with the mobility of the Earth, so that it can be gathered from that how far the apparent movements of the remaining planets and their orbital circles can be saved by being correlated with the movements of the Earth. And I have no doubt that talented and learned mathematicians will agree with me, if—

as philosophy demands in the first place—they are willing to give not superficial but profound thought and effort to what I bring forward in this work in demonstrating these things. And in order that the unlearned as well as the learned might see that I was not seeking to flee from the judgment of any man, I preferred to dedicate these results of my nocturnal study to Your Holiness rather than to anyone else; because, even in this remote corner of the earth where I live, you are held to be most eminent both in the dignity of your order and in your love of letters and even of mathematics; hence, by the authority of your judgment you can easily provide a guard against the bites of slanderers, despite the proverb that there is no medicine for the bite of a sycophant.

But if perchance there are certain "idle talkers" who take it upon themselves to pronounce judgment, although wholly ignorant of mathematics, and if by shamelessly distorting the sense of some passage in Holy Writ to suit their purpose, they dare to reprehend and to attack my work; they worry me so little that I shall even scorn their judgments as foolhardy. For it is not unknown that Lactantius, otherwise a distinguished writer but hardly a mathematician, speaks in an utterly childish fashion concerning the shape of the Earth, when he laughs at those who have affirmed that the Earth has the form of a globe. And so the studious need not be surprised if people like that laugh at us. Mathematics is written for mathematicians; and among them, if I am not mistaken, my labours will be seen to contribute something to the ecclesiastical commonwealth, the principate of which Your Holiness now holds. For not many years ago under Leo X when the Lateran Council was considering the question of reforming the Ecclesiastical Calendar, no decision was reached, for the sole reason that the magnitude of the year and the months and the movements of the sun and moon had not yet been measured with sufficient accuracy. From that time on I gave attention to making more exact observations of these things and was encouraged to do so by that most distinguished man, Paul, Bishop of Fossombrone, who had been present at those deliberations. But what have I accomplished in this matter I leave to the judgment of Your Holiness in particular and to that of all other learned mathematicians. And so as not to appear to Your Holiness to make more promises concerning the utility of this book than I can fulfill, I now pass on to the body of the work.

*   *   *

7. Why the Ancients Thought the Earth Was at Rest at the Middle of the World as Its Centre

Wherefore for other reasons the ancient philosophers have tried to affirm that the Earth is at rest at the middle of the world, and as principal cause they put forward heaviness and lightness. For Earth is the heaviest element; and all things of any weight are borne towards it and strive to move towards the very centre of it.

For since the Earth is a globe towards which from every direction heavy things by their own nature are borne at right angles to its surface, the heavy things would fall on one another at the centre if they were not held back at the surface; since a straight line making right angles with a plane surface where it touches a sphere leads to the centre. And those things which are borne toward the centre seem to follow along in order to be at rest at the centre. All the more then will the Earth be at rest at the centre; and, as being the receptacle for falling bodies, it will remain immovable because of its weight.

They strive similarly to prove this by reason of movement and its nature. For Aristotle says that the movement of a body which is one and simple is simple, and the simple movements are the rectilinear and the circular. And of rectilinear movements, one is upward, and the other is downward. As a consequence, every simple movement is either toward the centre, i.e., downward, or away from the centre, i.e., upward, or around the centre, i.e., circular. Now it belongs to earth and water, which are considered heavy, to be borne downward, i.e., to seek the centre: for air and fire, which are endowed with lightness, move upward, i.e., away from the centre. It seems fitting to grant rectilinear movement to these four elements and to give the heavenly bodies a circular movement around the centre. So Aristotle. Therefore, said Ptolemy of Alexandria, if the Earth moved, even if only by its daily rotation, the contrary of what was said above would necessarily take place. For this movement which would traverse the total circuit of the Earth in twenty-four hours would necessarily be very headlong and of an unsurpassable velocity. Now things which are suddenly and violently whirled around are seen to be utterly unfitted for reuniting, and the more unified are seen to become dispersed, unless some constant force constrains them to stick together. And a long time ago, he says, the scattered Earth would have passed beyond the heavens, as is certainly ridiculous; and *a fortiori* so would all the living creatures and all the other separate masses which could by no means remain unshaken. Moreover, freely falling bodies would not arrive at the places appointed them, and certainly not along the perpendicular line which they assume so quickly. And we would see clouds and other things floating in the air always borne toward the west.

8. Answer to the Aforesaid Reasons and Their Inadequacy

For these and similar reasons they say that the Earth remains at rest at the middle of the world and that there is no doubt about this. But if someone opines that the Earth revolves, he will also say that the movement is natural and not violent. Now things which are according to nature produce effects contrary to those which are violent. For things to which force or violence is applied get broken up and are unable to subsist for a long time. But things which are caused by nature are in a right condition and are kept in their best organization. Therefore Ptolemy had no reason to fear that the Earth and all things on the Earth would be scattered in a revolution caused by the efficacy of nature, which is greatly different from that of art or from that which can result from the genius of man. But why didn't he feel anxiety about the world instead, whose movement must necessarily be of greater velocity, the greater the heavens are than the Earth? Or have the heavens become so immense, because an unspeakably vehement motion has pulled them away from the centre, and because the heavens would fall if they came to rest anywhere else?

Surely if this reasoning were tenable, the magnitude of the heavens would extend infinitely. For the farther the movement is borne upward by the vehement force, the faster will the movement be, on account of the ever-increasing circumference which must be traversed every twenty-four hours: and conversely, the immensity of the sky would increase with the increase in movement. In this way, the velocity would make the magnitude increase infinitely, and the magnitude the velocity. And in accordance with the axiom of physics that *that which is infinite cannot be traversed or moved in any way,* then the heavens will necessarily come to rest.

But they say that beyond the heavens there isn't any body or place or void or anything at all; and accordingly it is not possible for the heavens to move outward: in that case it is rather surprising that something can be held together by nothing. But if the heavens were infinite and were finite only with respect to a hollow space inside, then it will be said with more truth that there is nothing outside the heavens, since anything which occupied any space would be in them; but the heavens will remain immobile. For movement is the most powerful reason wherewith they try to conclude that the universe is finite.

But let us leave to the philosophers of nature the dispute as to whether the world is finite or infinite, and let us hold as certain that the Earth is held together between its two poles and terminates in a spherical surface. Why therefore should we hesitate any longer to grant to it the movement which accords naturally with its form, rather than put the whole world in a commotion—the world whose limits we do not and cannot know? And why not admit that the appearance of daily revolution belongs to the heavens but the reality belongs to the Earth? And things are as when Aeneas said in Virgil: "We sail out of the harbor, and the land and the cities move away." As a matter of fact, when a ship floats on over a tranquil sea, all the things outside seem to the voyagers to be moving in a movement which is the image of their own, and they think on the contrary that they themselves and all the things with them are at rest. So it can easily happen in the case of the movement of the Earth that the whole world should be believed to be moving in a circle. Then what would we say about the clouds and the other things floating in the air or falling or rising up, except that not only the Earth and the watery element with which it is conjoined are moved in this way but also no small part of the air and whatever other things have a similar kinship with the Earth? whether because the neighbouring air, which is mixed with earthly and watery matter, obeys the same nature as the Earth or because the movement of the air is an acquired one, in which it participates without resistance on account of the contiguity and perpetual rotation of the Earth. Conversely, it is no less astonishing for them to say that the highest region of the air follows the celestial movement, as is shown by those stars which appear suddenly—I mean those called "comets" or "bearded stars" by the Greeks. For that place is assigned for their generation; and like all the other stars they rise and set. We can say that that part of the air is deprived of terrestrial motion on account of its great distance from the Earth. Hence the air which is nearest to the Earth and the things floating in it will appear tranquil, unless they are driven to and fro by the wind or some other force, as happens. For how is the wind in the air different from a current in the sea?

But we must confess that in comparison with the world the movement of falling and of rising bodies is twofold and is in general compounded of the rectilinear and the circular. As regards things which move downward on account of their weight because they have very much earth in them, doubtless their parts possess the same nature as the whole, and it is for the same reason that fiery bodies are drawn upward with force. For even this earthly fire feeds principally on earthly matter; and they define flame as glowing smoke. Now it is a property of fire to make that which it invades to expand; and it does this with such force that it can be stopped by no means or contrivance from breaking prison and completing its job. Now expanding movement moves away from the centre to the circumference; and so if some part of the Earth caught on fire, it would be borne away from the centre and upward. Accordingly, as they say, a simple body possesses a simple movement—this is first verified in the case of circular movement—as long as the simple body remain in its unity in its natural place. In this place, in fact, its movement is none other than the circular, which remains entirely in itself, as though at rest. Rectilinear movement, however, is added to those bodies which journey away from their natural place or are shoved out of it or are outside it somehow. But nothing is more repugnant to the order of the whole and to the form of the world than for anything to be outside of its place. Therefore rectilinear movement belongs only to bodies which are not in the right condition and are not perfectly conformed to their nature—when they are separated from their whole and abandon its unity. Furthermore, bodies which are moved upward or downward do not possess a simple, uniform, and regular movement—even without taking into account circular movement. For they cannot be in equilibrium with their lightness or their force of weight. And those which fall downward possess a slow movement at the beginning but increase their velocity as they fall. And conversely we note that this earthly fire—and we have experience of no other—when carried high up immediately dies down, as if through the acknowledged agency of the violence of earthly matter.

Now circular movement always goes on regularly, for it has an unfailing cause; but [in rectilinear movement] the acceleration stops, because, when the bodies have reached their own place, they are no longer heavy or light, and so the movement ends. Therefore, since circular movement belongs to wholes and rectilinear to parts, we can say that the circular movement stands with the rectilinear, as does animal with sick. And the fact that Aristotle divided simple movement into three genera: away from the centre, toward the centre, and around the

centre, will be considered merely as an act of reason, just as we distinguish between line, point, and surface, though none of them can subsist without the others or without body.

In addition, there is the fact that the state of immobility is regarded as more noble and godlike than that of change and instability, which for that reason should belong to the Earth rather than to the world. I add that it seems rather absurd to ascribe movement to the container or to that which provides the place and not rather to that which is contained and has a place, i.e., the Earth. And lastly, since it is clear that the wandering stars are sometimes nearer and sometimes farther away from the Earth, then the movement of one and the same body around the centre—and they mean the centre of the Earth—will be both away from the centre and toward the centre. Therefore it is necessary that movement around the centre should be taken more generally; and it should be enough if each movement is in accord with its own centre. You see therefore that for all these reasons it is more probably that the Earth moves than that it is at rest—especially in the case of the daily revolution, as it is the Earth's very own. And I think that is enough as regards the first part of the question.

9. Whether Many Movements Can Be Attributed to the Earth, and Concerning the Centre of the World

Therefore, since nothing hinders the mobility of the Earth, I think we should now see whether more than one movement belongs to it, so that it can be regarded as one of the wandering stars. For the apparent irregular movement of the planets and their variable distances from the Earth—which cannot be understood as occurring in circles homocentric with the Earth—make it clear that the Earth is not the centre of their circular movements. Therefore, since there are many centres, it is not foolhardy to doubt whether the centre of gravity of the Earth rather than some other is the centre of the world. I myself think that gravity or heaviness is nothing except a certain natural appetency implanted in the parts by the divine providence of the universal Artisan, in order that they should unite with one another in their oneness and wholeness and come together in the form of a globe. It is believable that this affect is present in the sun, moon, and the other bright planets and that through its efficacy they remain in the spherical figure in which they are visible, though they nevertheless accomplish their circular movements in many different ways. Therefore if the Earth too possesses movements different from the one around its centre, then they will necessarily be movements which similarly appear on the outside in the many bodies; and we find the yearly revolution among these movements. For if the annual revolution were changed from being solar to being terrestrial, and immobility were granted to the sun, the risings and settings of the signs and of the fixed stars—whereby they become morning or evening stars—will appear in the same way; and it will be seen that the stoppings, retrogressions, and progressions of the wandering stars are not their own, but are a movement of the Earth and that they bor-row the appearances of this movement. Lastly, the sun will be regarded as occupying the centre of the world. And the ratio of order in which these bodies succeed one another and the harmony of the whole world teaches us their truth, if only—as they say—we would look at the thing with both eyes.

*   *   *

REVIEW QUESTIONS

1. Why did Copernicus dedicate his great work to Pope Paul III?
2. What assumptions about the nature of scientific knowledge caused Copernicus to revisit and revise the received natural philosophy?
3. How does Copernicus refute in this work the notion that the Earth is at rest in the universe?
4. What does this reveal about his scientific method?
5. What benefits would arise from the establishment of scientific truth?

GALILEO GALILEI

FROM *The Starry Messenger* AND *The Assayer*

Galileo Galilei (1564–1642), an Italian astronomer, mathematician, and physicist, was a major contributor to the shift in scientific practice commonly called the scientific revolution. Born the son of a musician, Vincenzo Galilei, Galileo received his primary education from a tutor in Pisa and later from the monks of Santa Maria at Vallambrosa in Florence. From 1581 to 1585, he studied medicine at the University of Pisa and supplemented his education with private lessons in mathematics. Without formal instruction in that field, Galileo occupied the chair in mathematics at the University of Pisa from 1589 to 1591 and at the University of Padua from 1592 until 1610, when he was appointed court philosopher and mathematician to the grand duke of Tuscany. During his tenure at court, he published The Starry Messenger *(1610) and* The Assayer *(1619). The former presented evidence to confirm the heliocentric theory of the solar system. The latter offered a strong defense of the empirical basis of scientific reasoning. It was his advocacy of*

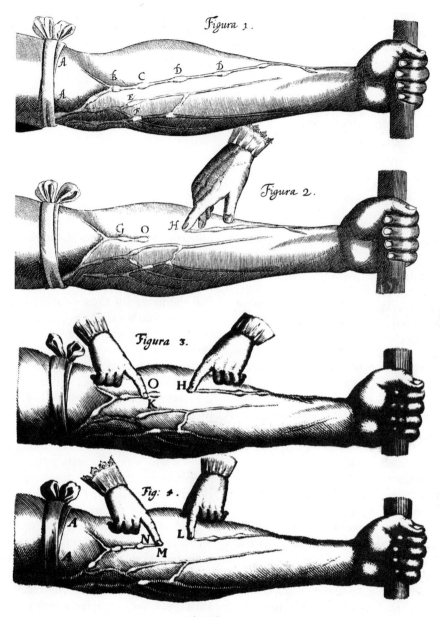

ON THE CIRCULATION OF THE BLOOD (1628)   WILLIAM HARVEY

This illustration depicts one of William Harvey's experiments in his On the Circulation of the Blood (1628). Venal valves had already been discovered, but here Harvey shows that venal blood flows only toward the heart. He ligatured an arm to make obvious the veins and their valves, then pressed blood away from the heart and showed that the vein would remain empty because it was blocked by the valve. How is Harvey's work representative of the revolution in science? What does the image suggest about the connection between advances in scientific discovery and mechanistic philosophy in early modern Europe?

the Copernican theory that led Galileo into conflict with the Roman Catholic Inquisition. Galileo was forced to abjure his scientific findings and was sentenced to perpetual house arrest. His books were burned. His trial, no less than his discoveries, secured his fame, and his books continued to circulate clandestinely throughout Europe.

From *Discoveries and Opinions of Galileo*, translated by Stillman Drake (New York: Bantam Doubleday Dell, 1957), pp. 27–31, 237–38.

FROM *The Starry Messenger*

from ASTRONOMICAL MESSAGE WHICH CONTAINS AND EXPLAINS RECENT OBSERVATIONS MADE WITH THE AID OF A NEW SPYGLASS CONCERNING THE SURFACE OF THE MOON, THE MILKY WAY, NEBULOUS STARS, AND INNUMERABLE FIXED STARS, AS WELL AS FOUR PLANETS NEVER BEFORE SEEN, AND NOW NAMED THE MEDICEAN STARS

Great indeed are the things which in this brief treatise I propose for observation and consideration by all students of nature. I say great, because of the excellence of the subject itself, the entirely unexpected and novel character of these things, and finally because of the instrument by means of which they have been revealed to our senses.

Surely it is a great thing to increase the numerous host of fixed stars previously visible to the unaided vision, adding countless more which have never before been seen, exposing these plainly to the eye in numbers ten times exceeding the old and familiar stars.

It is a very beautiful thing, and most gratifying to the sight, to behold the body of the moon, distant from us almost sixty earthly radii, as if it were no farther away than two such measures—its diameter appears almost thirty times larger, its so that surface nearly nine hundred times, and its volume twenty-seven thousand times as large as when viewed with the naked eye. In this way one may learn with all the certainty of sense evidence that the moon is not robed in a smooth and polished surface but is in fact rough and uneven, covered everywhere, just like the earth's surface, with huge prominences, deep valleys, and chasms.

Again, it seems to me a matter of no small importance to have ended the dispute about the Milky Way by making its nature manifest to the very senses as well as to the intellect. Similarly it will be a pleasant and elegant thing to demonstrate that the nature of those stars which astronomers have previously called "nebulous" is far different from what has been believed hitherto. But what surpasses all wonders by far, and what particularly moves us to seek the attention of all astronomers and philosophers, is the discovery of four wandering stars not known or observed by any man before us. Like Venus and Mercury, which have their own periods about the sun, these have theirs about a certain star that is conspicuous among those already known, which they sometimes precede and sometimes follow, without ever departing from it beyond certain limits. All these facts were discovered and observed by me not many days ago with the aid of a spyglass which I devised, after first being illuminated by divine grace. Perhaps other things, still more remarkable, will in time be discovered by me or by other observers with the aid of such an instrument, the form and construction of which I shall first briefly explain, as well as the occasion of its having been devised. Afterwards I shall relate the story of the observations I have made.

About ten months ago a report reached my ears that a certain Fleming had constructed a spyglass by means of which visible objects, though very distant from the eye of the observer, were distinctly seen as if nearby. Of this truly remarkable effect several experiences were related, to which some persons gave credence while others denied them. A few days later the report was confirmed to me in a letter from a noble Frenchman at Paris, Jacques Badovere, which caused me to apply myself wholeheartedly to inquire into the means by which I might arrive at the invention of a similar instrument. This I did shortly afterwards, my basis being the theory of refraction. First I prepared a tube of lead, at the ends of which I fitted two glass lenses, both plane on one side while on the other side one was spherically convex and the other concave. Then placing my eye near the concave lens I perceived objects satisfactorily large and near, for they appeared three times closer and nine times larger than when seen with the naked eye alone. Next I constructed another one, more accurate, which represented objects as enlarged more than sixty times. Finally, sparing neither labor nor expense, I succeeded in constructing for myself so excellent an instrument that objects seen by means of it appeared nearly one thousand times larger and over thirty times closer than when regarded with our natural vision.

It would be superfluous to enumerate the number and importance of the advantages of such an instrument at sea as well as on land. But forsaking terrestrial observations, I turned to celestial ones, and first I saw the moon from as near at hand as if it were scarcely two terrestrial radii away. After that I observed often with wondering delight both the planets and the fixed stars, and since I saw these latter to be very crowded, I began to seek (and eventually found) a method by which I might measure their distances apart.

Here it is appropriate to convey certain cautions to all who intend to undertake observations of this sort, for in the first place it is necessary to prepare quite a perfect telescope, which will show all objects bright, distinct, and free from any haziness, while magnifying them at least four hundred times and thus showing them twenty times closer. Unless the instrument is of this kind it will be vain to attempt to observe all the things which I have seen in the heavens, and which will presently be set forth. Now in order to determine without much trouble the magnifying power of an instrument, trace on paper the contour of two circles or two

squares of which one is four hundred times as large as the other, as it will be when the diameter of one is twenty times that of the other. Then, with both these figures attached to the same wall, observe them simultaneously from a distance, looking at the smaller one through the telescope and at the larger one with the other eye unaided. This may be done without inconvenience while holding both eyes open at the same time; the two figures will appear to be of the same size if the instrument magnifies objects in the desired proportion.

Such an instrument having been prepared, we seek a method of measuring distances apart. This we shall accomplish by the following contrivance.

Let ABCD be the tube and E be the eye of the observer. Then if there were no lenses in the tube, the rays would reach the object FG along the straight lines ECF and EDG. But when the lenses have been inserted, the rays go along the refracted lines ECH and EDI; thus they are brought closer together, and those which were previously directed freely to the object FG now include only the portion of it HI. The ratio of the distance EH to the line HI then being found, one may by means of a table of sines determine the size of the angle formed at the eye by the object HI, which we shall find to be but a few minutes of arc. Now, if to the lens CD we fit thin plates, some pierced with larger and some with smaller apertures, putting now one plate and now another over the lens as required, we may form at pleasure different angles subtending more or fewer minutes of arc, and by this means we may easily measure the intervals between stars which are but a few minutes apart, with no greater error than one or two minutes. And for the present let it suffice that we have touched lightly on these matters and scarcely more than mentioned them, as on some other occasion we shall explain the entire theory of this instrument.

.   *   *   *

Deserving of notice also is the difference between the appearances of the planets and of the fixed stars. The planets show their globes perfectly round and definitely bounded, looking like little moons, spherical and flooded all over with light;

the fixed stars are never seen to be bounded by a circular periphery, but have rather the aspect of blazes whose rays vibrate about them and scintillate a great deal. Viewed with a telescope they appear of a shape similar to that which they present to the naked eye, but sufficiently enlarged so that a star of the fifth or sixth magnitude seems to equal the Dog Star, largest of all the fixed stars. Now, in addition to stars of the sixth magnitude, a host of other stars are perceived through the telescope which escape the naked eye; these are so numerous as almost to surpass belief. One may, in fact, see more of them than all the stars included among the first six magnitudes. The largest of these, which we may call stars of the seventh magnitude, or the first magnitude of invisible stars, appear through the telescope as larger and brighter than stars of the second magnitude when the latter are viewed with the naked eye. In order to give one or two proofs of their almost inconceivable number, I have adjoined pictures of two constellations. With these as samples, you may judge of all the others.

FROM *The Assayer*

*   *   *

In Sarsi I seem to discern the firm belief that in philosophizing one must support oneself upon the opinion of some celebrated author, as if our minds ought to remain completely sterile and barren unless wedded to the reasoning of some other person. Possibly he thinks that philosophy is a book of fiction by some writer, like the *Iliad* or *Orlando Furioso*, productions in which the least important thing is whether what is written there is true. Well, Sarsi, that is not how matters stand. Philosophy is written in this grand book, the universe, which stands continually open to our gaze. But the book cannot be understood unless one first learns to comprehend the language and read the letters in which it is composed. It is written in the language of mathematics, and its characters are triangles, circles, and other geometric figures without which it is humanly impossible to understand a single word of it; without these, one wanders about in a dark labyrinth.

Sarsi seems to think that our intellect should be enslaved to that of some other man. . . . But even on that assumption, I do not see why he selects Tycho. . . . Tycho could not extricate himself from his own explanation of diversity in the apparent motion of his comet; but now Sarsi expects my mind to be satisfied and set at rest by a little poetic flower that is not followed by any fruit at all. It is this that Guiducci rejected when he quite rightly said that nature takes no delight in poetry. That is a very true statement, even though Sarsi appears to disbelieve it and acts as if acquainted with neither nature nor poetry. He seems not to know that fables and fictions are in a way essential to poetry, which could not exist without them, while any sort of falsehood is so abhorrent to nature that it is as absent there as darkness is in light.

*   *   *

REVIEW QUESTIONS

1. How does a telescope work? What is its relation to human sight?
2. What does Galileo see? What does he discern?
3. What are the two books for Galileo?
4. What is the relation of one to the other?
5. What are the implications of Galileo's assertion that understanding depends on how one reads the book of the universe?

MARGARET CAVENDISH

FROM *Observations upon Experimental Philosophy. To which is added, the Description of a New Blazing World*

Margaret Cavendish, Duchess of Newcastle-upon-Tyne (1623–1673), was an English aristocrat, writer, and scientist. Born Margaret Lucas of a royalist family, she became an attendant of Queen Henrietta Maria and accompanied her into exile in France. She became the second wife of William Cavendish, 1st Duke of Newcastle-upon-Tyne in 1645. Cavendish was a writer who published a wide range of works under her own name at a time when most women writers published anonymously. Her writing addressed a number of topics, including political philosophy and scientific method. She is noteworthy as a female contributor to natural philosophy and early science, and her utopian work The Blazing World *stands as an early example of science fiction. A groundbreaking woman writer and scientific thinker, Cavendish rejected Aristotelian physics and mechanical philosophy, preferring a vitalist model that argued the fundamental difference between animate and inanimate things based on the non-physical or vital element that governed the living. She corresponded critically with the leading political and natural philosophers of her day, including Thomas Hobbes, René Descartes, and Robert Boyle. She has been claimed as an advocate for animals and as an early opponent of animal testing.*

From *Observations upon Experimental philosophy. To which is added, the Description of a New Blazing World*, by Lady Margaret Cavendish (London: A. Maxwell, 1666).

When I was setting forth this Book of *Experimental Observations*, a Dispute chanced to arise between the rational Parts of my Mind concerning some chief Points and Principles in Natural Philosophy; for some New Thoughts endeavoring to oppose and call in question the Truth of my former Conceptions, caused a war in my mind, which in time grew to that height, that they were hardly able to compose the differences between themselves, but were in a manner necessitated to refer them to the Arbitration of the impartial Reader, desiring the assistance of his judgment to reconcile their Controversies, and, if possible, to reduce them to a setled peace and agreement.

The first difference did arise about the question, How it came, that Matter was of several degrees, as Animate and Inanimate, Sensitive and Rational? for my latter thoughts would not believe that there was any such difference of degrees of Matter: To which my former conceptions answered, That Nature, being Eternal and Infinite, it could not be known how she came to be such, no more than a reason could be given how God came to be: for Nature, said they, is the Infinite Servant of God, and her origine cannot be described by any finite or particular Creature; for what is infinite, has neither beginning nor end; but that Natural Matter consisted of so many degrees as mentioned, was evidently perceived by her effects or actions; by which it appeared first, that Nature was a self-moving body, and that all her parts and Creatures were so too: Next, That there was not onely an animate or self-moving and active, but also an inanimate, that is, a dull and passive degree of Matter; for if there were no animate degree, there would be no motion, and so no action nor variety of figures; and if no inanimate, there would be no degrees of natural figures and actions, but all actions would be done in a moment, and the figures would all be so pure, fine and subtil, as not to be subject to any grosser perception such as our humane, or other the like perceptions are. This Inanimate part of Matter, said they, had no self-motion, but was carried along in all the actions of the animate degree, and so was not moving, but moved; which Animate part of Matter being again of two degrees, viz. Sensitive and Rational, the Rational being so pure, fine and subtil, that it gave onely directions to the sensitive, and made figures in its own degree, left the working with and upon the Inanimate part, to the Sensitive degree of Matter, whose Office was to execute both the rational parts design, and to work those various figures that are perceived in Nature; and those three degrees were so inseparably commixt in the body of Nature, that none could be without the other in any part or Creature of Nature, could it be divided to an Atome; for as in the Exstruction of a house there is first required an Architect or Surveigher, who orders and designs the building, and puts the Labourers to work; next the Labourers or Workmen themselves, and lastly the Materials of which the House is built: so the Rational part, faid they, in the framing of Natural Effects, is, as it were, the Surveigher or Architect; the Sensitive, the labouring or working part, and the Inanimate, the materials, and all these degrees are necessarily required in every composed action of Nature.

To this, my latter thoughts excepted, that in probability of sense and reason, there was no necessity of introducing an inanimate degree of Matter; for all those parts which we call gross, said

they, are no more but a composition of self-moving parts, whereof some are denser, and some rarer then others; and we may observe, that the denser parts are as active, as the rarest; for example, Earth is as active as Air or Light, and the parts of the Body are as active, as the parts of the Soul or Mind, being all self-moving, as it is perceiveable by their several, various compositions, divisions, productions and alterations; nay, we do see, that the Earth is more active in the several productions and alterations of her particulars, then what we name Celestial Lights, which observation is a firm argument to prove, that all Matter is animate or self-moving, onely there are degrees of motion, that some parts move slower, and some quicker.

Hereupon my former Thoughts answered, that the difference consisted not onely in the grossness, but in the dulness of the Inanimate parts; and that, since the sensitive animate parts were labouring on, and with the inanimate, if these had self-motion, and that their motion was slower then that of the animate parts, they would obstruct, cross and oppose each other in all their actions, for the one would be too slow, and the other too quick.

The latter Thoughts replied, that this slowness and quickness of motion would cause no obstruction at all; for, said they, a man that rides on a Horse is carried away by the Horses motion, and has nevertheless also his own motions himself; neither does the Horse and Man transfer or exchange motion into each other, nor do they hinder or obstruct one another.

The former Thoughts answer'd, it was True, that Motion could not be transferred from one body into another without Matter or substance; and that several self-moving parts might be joined, and each act a part without the least hinderance to one another; for not all the parts of one composed Creature (for example Man) were bound to one and the same action; and this was an evident proof that all Creatures were composed of parts, by reason of their different actions; nay, not onely of parts, but of self-moving parts: also they confessed, that there were degrees of motion, as quickness and slowness, and that the slowest motion was as much motion as the quickest. But yet, said they, this does not prove, that Nature consists not of Inanimate Matter as well as of Animate; for it is one thing to speak of the parts of the composed and mixed body of Nature, and another thing to speak of the constitutive parts of Nature, which are, as it were, her ingredients of which Nature is made up as one intire self-moving body; for sense and reason does plainly perceive, that some parts are more dull, and some more lively, subtil and active; the Rational parts are more agil, active, pure and subtil then the sensitive; but the Inanimate have no activity, subtilty and agility at all, by reason they want self-motion; nor no perception, for self-motion is the cause of all perception; and this Triumvirate of the degrees of Matter, said they, is so necessary to ballance and poise Natures actions, that otherwise the creatures which Nature produces, would all be produced alike, and in an instant; for example, a Child in the Womb would as suddenly be framed, as it is figured in the mind; and a man would be as suddenly dissolved as a thought: But sense and reason perceives that it is otherwise; to wit, that such figures as are made of the grosser parts of Matter, are made by degrees, and not in an instant of time, which does manifestly evince, that there is and must of necessity be such a degree of Matter in Nature as we call Inanimate; for surely although the parts of Nature are infinite, and have infinite actions, yet they cannot run into extreams, but are ballanced by their opposites, so that all parts cannot be alike rare or dense, hard or soft, dilating or contracting, &c. but some are dense, some rare, some hard, some soft, some dilative, some contractive, &c. by which the actions of Nature are kept in an equal ballance from running into extreams. But put the case, said they, it were so, that Natures body consisted altogether of Animate Matter, or corporeal self-motion, without an intermixture of the inanimate parts, we are confident that there would be framed as many objections against that opinion as there are now against the inanimate degree of Matter; for disputes are endless, and the more answers you receive, the more objections you will find; and the more objections you make, the more answers you will receive; and even shews, that Nature is ballanced by opposites: for, put the case, the Inanimate parts of Matter were self-moving;

then first there would be no such difference between the rational and sensitive parts as now there is; but every part, being self-moving, would act of, and in it self, that is, in its own substance as now the rational part of Matter does: Next, if the inanimate part was of a slower motion then the rational and sensitive, they would obstruct each other in their actions, for one would be too quick, and the other too slow; neither would the quicker motion alter the nature of the slower, or the slower retard the quicker; for the nature of each must remain as it is; or else it would be thus, then the animate part might become inanimate, and the rational the sensitive, &c. which is impossible, and against all sense and reason.

*   *   *

After these and several other objections, questions and answers between the later and former thoughts and conceptions of my mind, at last some Rational thoughts which were not concerned in this dispute, perceiving that they became much heated, and fearing they would at last cause a Faction or Civil War amongst all the rational parts, which would breed that which is called a Trouble of the Mind, endeavoured to make a Peace between them, and to that end they propounded, that the sensitive parts should publickly declare their differences and controversies, and refer them to the Arbitration of the judicious and impartial Reader. This proposition was unanimously embraced by all the rational parts, and thus by their mutual consent this Argumental Discourse was set down and published after this manner: In the mean time all the rational parts of my Mind inclined to the opinion of my former conceptions, which they thought much more probable then those of the later; and since now it is your part, Ingenious Readers, to give a final decision of the Cause, consider well the subject of their quarrel, and be impartial in your judgment; let not Self-love or Envy corrupt you, but let Regular Sense and Reason be your onely Rule, that you may be accounted just Judges, and your Equity and Justice be Remembred by all that honour and love it.

*   *   *

1. Of Humane Sense and Perception.

Before I deliver my observations upon that part of Philosophy which is call'd Experimental, I thought it necessary to premise some discourse concerning the Perception of Humane Sense. It is known that man has five Exterior Senses, and every sense is ignorant of each other; for the Nose knows not what the Eyes see, nor the Eyes what the Ears hear, neither do the Ears know what the Tongue tastes; and as for Touch, although it is a general Sense, yet every several part of the body has a several touch, and each part is ignorant of each others touch: And thus there is a general ignorance of all the several parts, and yet a perfect knowledg in each part; for the Eye is as knowing as the Ear, and the Ear as knowing as the Nose, and the Nose as knowing as the Tongue, and one particular Touch knows as much as another, at least is capable thereof: Nay, not only every several Touch, Taste, Smell, Sound or Sight, is a several knowledg by it self, but each of them has as many particular knowledges or perceptions as there are objects presented to them: Besides, there are several degrees in each particular sense; As for example, some Men (I will not speak of other animals) their perception of sight, taste, smell, touch, or hearing, is quicker to some sorts of objects, then to others, according either to the perfection or imperfection, or curiosity or purity of the corporeal figurative motions of each sense, or according to the presentation of each object proper to each sense; for if the presentation of the objects be imperfect, either through variation or obscurity, or any other ways, the sense is deluded. Neither are all objects proper for one sense, but as there are several senses, so there are several sorts of objects proper for each several sense. Now if there be such variety of several knowledges, not onely in one Creature, but in one sort of sense; to wit, the exterior senses of one humane Creature; what may there be in all the parts of Nature? 'Tis true, there are some objects which are not at all perceptible by any of our exterior senses; as for example, rarified air, and the like: But although they be not subject to our exterior sensitive perception, yet they are subject to our rational perception, which is much purer and subtiler then the sensitive; nay, so pure and subtil a knowledg,

that many believe it to be immaterial, as if it were some God, when as it is onely a pure, fine and subtil figurative Motion or Perception; it is so active and subtil, as it is the best informer and reformer of all sensitive Perception; for the rational Matter is the most prudent and wisest part of Nature, as being the designer of all productions, and the most pious and devoutest part, having the perfectest notions of God, I mean, so much as Nature can possibly know of God; so that whatsoever the sensitive Perception is either defective in, or ignorant of, the rational Perception supplies. But mistake me not: by Rational Perception and Knowledg, I mean Regular Reason, not Irregular; where I do also exclude Art, which is apt to delude sense, and cannot inform so well as Reason doth; for Reason reforms and instructs sense in all its actions: But both the rational and sensitive knowledg and perception being divideable as well as composeable, it causes ignorance as well as knowledg amongst Natures Creatures; for though Nature is but one body, and has no sharer or copartner, but is intire and whole in it self, as not composed of several different parts or substances, and consequently has but one Infinite natural knowledg and wisdom, yet by reason she is also divideable and composeable, according to the nature of a body, we can justly and with all reason say, That, as Nature is divided into infinite several parts, so each several part has a several and particular knowledg and perception, both sensitive and rational, and again that each part is ignorant of the others knowledg and perception; when as otherwise, considered altogether and in general, as they make up but one infinite body of Nature, so they make also but one infinite general knowledg. And thus Nature may be called both Individual, as not having single parts subsisting without her, but all united in one body; and Divideable, by reason she is partable in her own several corporeal figurative motions, and not otherwise; for there is no Vacuum in Nature, neither can her parts start or remove from the Infinite body of Nature, so as to separate themselves from it, for there's no place to flee to, but body and place are all one thing, so that the parts of Nature can onely joyn and disjoyn to and from parts, but not to and from the body of Nature. And since Nature is but one body, it is intirely wise and knowing, ordering her self-moving parts with all facility and ease, without any disturbance, living in pleasure and delight, with infinite varieties and curiosities, such as no single Part or Creature of hers can ever attain to.

REVIEW QUESTIONS

1. How does Cavendish's vitalist principle alter her scientific method?

2. What is the vital spark the animates living things?
3. What proof can Cavendish offer that such a spark actually exists?
4. To what extent are her proofs empirical as opposed to purely rational?
5. Would Cavendish go so far as to say that the principles of physical nature do not apply to animate objects?
6. Why does Cavendish organize her essay in the form of a dialogue?

BLAISE PASCAL

FROM *Pensées*

Blaise Pascal (1623–1662) was the son of a French official. Over the course of his life, he dabbled in many subjects, including science, religion, and literature. His conversion to Jansenism plunged him into controversy with the Jesuits, giving rise to his Lettres provinciales. *These, along with his* Pensées, *from which the following selection is drawn, established his literary fame. His thought contained a fascinating blend of confidence in human reason and consciousness of its limits. Descartes viewed Pascal as the embodiment of a mentality of intellectual and spiritual crisis. Be that as it may, Pascal raised profound questions about the purpose and potential of human knowledge.*

From *Pensées*, by Blaise Pascal, translated by A. J. Krailsheimer (New York: Penguin, 1995), pp. 58–64, 121–25.

*   *   *

XV. Transition from Knowledge of Man to Knowledge of God

DISPROPORTION OF MAN

*   *   *

This is where unaided knowledge brings us. If it is not true, there is no truth in man, and if it is true, he has good cause to feel humiliated; in either case he is obliged to humble himself.

And, since he cannot exist without believing this knowledge, before going on to a wider inquiry concerning nature, I want him to consider nature just once, seriously and at leisure, and to look at himself as well, and judge whether there is any proportion between himself and nature by comparing the two.

Let man then contemplate the whole of nature in her full and lofty majesty, let him turn his gaze away from the lowly objects around him; let him behold the dazzling light set like an eternal lamp to light up the universe, let him see the earth as a mere speck compared to the vast orbit described by this star, and let him marvel at finding this vast orbit itself to be no more than the tiniest point compared to that described by the stars revolving in the firmament. But if our eyes stop there, let our imagination proceed further; it will grow weary of conceiving things before nature tires of producing them. The whole visible world is only an imperceptible dot in nature's ample bosom. No idea comes near it; it is no good inflating our conceptions beyond imaginable space, we only bring forth atoms compared to the reality of things. Nature is an infinite sphere whose centre is everywhere and circumference nowhere. In short it is the greatest perceptible mark of God's omnipotence that our imagination should lose itself in that thought.

Let man, returning to himself, consider what he is in comparison with what exists; let him regard himself as lost, and from this little dungeon, in which he finds himself lodged, I mean the universe, let him learn to take the earth, its realms, its cities, its houses and himself at their proper value.

What is a man in the infinite?

But, to offer him another prodigy equally astounding, let him look into the tiniest things he knows. Let a mite show him in its minute body incomparably more minute parts, legs with joints, veins in its legs, blood in the veins, humours in the blood, drops in the humours, vapours in the drops: let him divide these things still further until he has exhausted his powers of imagination, and let the last thing he comes down to now be the subject of our discourse. He will perhaps think that this is the ultimate of minuteness in nature.

I want to show him a new abyss. I want to depict to him not only the visible universe, but all the conceivable immensity of nature enclosed in this miniature atom. Let him see there an infinity of universes, each with its firmament, its planets, its earth, in the same proportions as in the visible world, and on that earth animals, and finally mites, in which he will find again the same results as in the first; and finding the same thing yet again in the others without end or respite, he will be lost

in such wonders, as astounding in their minuteness as the others in their amplitude. For who will not marvel that our body, a moment ago imperceptible in a universe, itself imperceptible in the bosom of the whole, should now be a colossus, a world, or rather a whole, compared to the nothingness beyond our reach? Anyone who considers himself in this way will be terrified at himself, and, seeing his mass, as given him by nature, supporting him between these two abysses of infinity and nothingness, will tremble at these marvels. I believe that with his curiosity changing into wonder he will be more disposed to contemplate them in silence than investigate them with presumption.

For, after all, what is man in nature? A nothing compared to the infinite, a whole compared to the nothing, a middle point between all and nothing, infinitely remote from an understanding of the extremes; the end of things and their principles are unattainably hidden from him in impenetrable secrecy.

Equally incapable of seeing the nothingness from which he emerges and the infinity in which he is engulfed.

What else can he do, then, but perceive some semblance of the middle of things, eternally hopeless of knowing either their principles or their end? All things have come out of nothingness and are carried onwards to infinity. Who can follow these astonishing processes? The author of these wonders understands them: no one else can.

Because they failed to contemplate these infinities, men have rashly undertaken to probe into nature as if there were some proportion between themselves and her.

Strangely enough they wanted to know the principles of things and go on from there to know everything, inspired by a presumption as infinite as their object. For there can be no doubt that such a plan could not be conceived without infinite presumption or a capacity as infinite as that of nature.

When we know better, we understand that, since nature has engraved her own image and that of her author on all things, they almost all share her double infinity. Thus we see that all the sciences are infinite in the range of their researches, for who can doubt that mathematics, for instance, has an infinity of infinities of propositions to expound? They are infinite also in the multiplicity and subtlety of their principles, for anyone can see that those which are supposed to be ultimate do not stand by themselves, but depend on others, which depend on others again, and thus never allow of any finality.

But we treat as ultimate those which seem so to our reason, as in material things we call a point indivisible when our senses can perceive nothing beyond it, although by its nature it is infinitely divisible.

Of these two infinites of science, that of greatness is much more obvious, and that is why it has occurred to few people to claim that they know everything. 'I am going to speak about everything,' Democritus used to say.

But the infinitely small is much harder to see. The philosophers have much more readily claimed to have reached it, and that is where they have all tripped up. This is the origin of such familiar titles as *Of the principles of things, Of the principles of philosophy,* and the like, which are really as pretentious, though they do not look it, as this blatant one: *Of all that can be known.*

We naturally believe we are more capable of reaching the centre of things than of embracing their circumference, and the visible extent of the world is visibly greater than we. But since we in our turn are greater than small things, we think we are more capable of mastering them, and yet it takes no less capacity to reach nothingness than the whole. In either case it takes an infinite capacity, and it seems to me that anyone who had understood the ultimate principles of things might also succeed in knowing infinity. One depends on the other, and one leads to the other. These extremes touch and join by going in opposite directions, and they meet in God and God alone.

Let us then realize our limitations. We are something and we are not everything. Such being as we have conceals from us the knowledge of first principles, which arise from nothingness, and the smallness of our being hides infinity from our sight.

Our intelligence occupies the same rank in the order of intellect as our body in the whole range of nature.

Limited in every respect, we find this intermediate state between two extremes reflected in all our faculties. Our senses can perceive nothing extreme; too much noise deafens us, too much light dazzles; when we are too far or too close we cannot see properly; an argument is obscured by being too long or too short; too much truth bewilders us. I know people who cannot understand that 4 from 0 leaves 0. First principles are too obvious for us; too much pleasure causes discomfort; too much harmony in music is displeasing; too much kindness annoys us: we want to be able to pay back the debt with something over. *Kindness is welcome to the extent that it seems the debt can be paid back. When it goes too far gratitude turns into hatred.*

We feel neither extreme heat nor extreme cold. Qualities carried to excess are bad for us and cannot be perceived; we no longer feel them, we suffer them. Excessive youth and excessive age impair thought; so do too much and too little learning.

In a word, extremes are as if they did not exist for us nor we for them; they escape us or we escape them.

Such is our true state. That is what makes us incapable of certain knowledge or absolute ignorance. We are floating in a medium of vast extent, always drifting uncertainly, blown to and fro; whenever we think we have a fixed point to which we can cling and make fast, it shifts and leaves us behind; if we follow it, it eludes our grasp, slips away, and flees eternally before us. Nothing stands still for us. This is our natural state and yet the state most contrary to our inclinations. We burn with desire to find a firm footing, an ultimate, lasting base on which to build a tower rising up to infinity, but our whole foundation cracks and the earth opens up into the depth of the abyss.

Let us then seek neither assurance nor stability; our reason is always deceived by the inconsistency of appearances; nothing can fix the finite between the two infinites which enclose and evade it.

Once that is clearly understood, I think that each of us can stay quietly in the state in which nature has placed him. Since the middle station allotted to us is always far from the extremes, what does it matter if someone else has a slightly better understanding of things? If he has, and if he takes them a little further, is he not still infinitely remote from the goal? Is not our span of life equally infinitesimal in eternity, even if it is extended by ten years?

In the perspective of these infinites, all finites are equal and I see no reason to settle our imagination on one rather than another. Merely comparing ourselves with the finite is painful.

If man studied himself, he would see how incapable he is of going further. How could a part possibly know the whole? But perhaps he will aspire to know at least the parts to which he bears some proportion. But the parts of the world are all so related and linked together that I think it is impossible to know one without the other and without the whole.

There is, for example, a relationship between man and all he knows. He needs space to contain him, time to exist in, motion to be alive, elements to constitute him, warmth and food for nourishment, air to breathe. He sees light, he feels bodies, everything in short is related to him. To understand man therefore one must know why he needs air to live, and to understand air one must know how it comes to be thus related to the life of man, etc.

Flame cannot exist without air, so, to know one, one must know the other.

Thus, since all things are both caused or causing, assisted and assisting, mediate and immediate, providing mutual support in a chain linking together naturally and imperceptibly the most distant and different things, I consider it as impossible to know the parts without knowing the whole as to know the whole without knowing the individual parts.

The eternity of things in themselves or in God must still amaze our brief span of life.

The fixed and constant immobility of nature, compared to the continual changes going on in us, must produce the same effect.

And what makes our inability to know things absolute is that they are simple in themselves, while we are composed of two opposing natures of different kinds, soul and body. For it is impossible

for the part of us which reasons to be anything but spiritual, and even if it were claimed that we are simply corporeal, that would still more preclude us from knowing things, since there is nothing so inconceivable as the idea that matter knows itself. We cannot possibly know how it could know itself.

Thus, if we are simply material, we can know nothing at all, and, if we are composed of mind and matter, we cannot have perfect knowledge of things which are simply spiritual or corporeal.

That is why nearly all philosophers confuse their ideas of things, and speak spiritually of corporeal things and corporeally of spiritual ones, for they boldly assert that bodies tend to fall, that they aspire towards their centre, that they flee from destruction, that they fear a void, that they have inclinations, sympathies, antipathies, all things pertaining only to things spiritual. And when they speak of minds, they consider them as being in a place, and attribute to them movement from one place to another, which are things pertaining only to bodies.

Instead of receiving ideas of these things in their purity, we colour them with our qualities and stamp our own composite being on all the simple things we contemplate.

Who would not think, to see us compounding everything of mind and matter, that such a mixture is perfectly intelligible to us? Yet this is the thing we understand least; man is to himself the greatest prodigy in nature, for he cannot conceive what body is, and still less what mind is, and least of all how a body can be joined to a mind. This is his supreme difficulty, and yet it is his very being. *The way in which minds are attached to bodies is beyond man's understanding, and yet this is what man is.*

*   *   *

REVIEW QUESTIONS

1. According to Pascal, what is the relation between universality and infinity?
2. Why does Pascal argue in favor of the former?

3. Why cannot humans know everything? What does Pascal's contention that nature is an infinite sphere teach us about human knowledge?

4. Why does nature hold abysses that human knowledge cannot penetrate?

5. How has Pascal's concept of infinity, which he uses first as a concept by which human beings might approach knowledge of God, changed in this passage?

RENÉ DESCARTES

FROM *Discourse on Method and Meditations on First Philosophy*

René Descartes (1596–1650) was born of a family of the judicial nobility. He graduated in 1612 from the Collège La Flèche and received a law degree in 1616 from the University of Poitiers. From 1616 until 1624, he saw military service in the Thirty Years' War. During the winter of 1620, while quartered near Ulm, Descartes claimed to have achieved the philosophical insights that would form the basis of his entire system of rational thought. In 1628 he left France, for reasons that are not clear, and returned only for relatively brief periods of time. Until 1649, he lived in the United Provinces of the Netherlands. There, with the publication of the Discourse on Method *in 1637, he began to make public the ideas first glimpsed in 1620, the systematic philosophy that would make him famous. His was one of the three great systems of rationalism of the seventeenth century, along with those created by Baruch Spinoza and Gottfried Leibniz. Reacting to the skepticism of the early seventeenth century, represented by the thought of philosophers such as Pascal, Descartes decided to subject every idea to critical scrutiny and retain as true only those ideas that were self-evident. The result was a geometric method of reasoning that consisted of four simple rules: to start only with clear and distinct ideas, to simplify any difficulty in thinking by dividing it into small parts, to think in an orderly process from simplest to most complex, and to make thorough evaluations that overlook no part of the problem. The Cartesian method gained enthusiastic popular support and became an important stimulus for the science of the Enlightenment.*

From *The Philosophical Works of Descartes*, translated by Elizabeth S. Haldane and G. R. T. Ross (Cambridge: Cambridge University Press, 1911).

*   *   *

Part 2

I was then in Germany, to which country I had been attracted by the wars which are not yet at an end. And as I was returning from the coronation of the Emperor to join the army, the setting in of winter detained me in a quarter where, since I found no society to divert me, while fortunately I had also no cares or passions to trouble me, I remained the whole day shut up alone in a stove-heated room, where I had complete leisure to occupy myself with my own thoughts. One of the first of the considerations that occurred to me was that there is very often less perfection in works composed of several portions, and carried out by the hands of various masters, than in those on which one individual alone has worked. Thus we see that buildings planned and carried out by one architect alone are usually more beautiful and better proportioned than those which many have tried to put in order and improve, making use of old walls that were built with other ends in view. . . . And similarly I thought that the sciences found in books—in those at least whose reasonings are only probable and which have no demonstrations, composed as they are of the gradually accumulated opinions of many different individuals—do not approach so near to the truth as the simple reasoning that a man of common sense can quite naturally carry out respecting the things which come immediately before him. Again I thought that since we have all been children before being men, and since it has for long fallen to us to be governed by our appetites and by our teachers (who often enough contradicted one another, and none of whom perhaps counselled us always for the best), it is almost impossible that our judgments should be so excellent or solid as they would have been had we had complete use of our Reason since our birth, and had we been guided by it alone.

It is true that we do not find that all the houses in a town are razed to the ground for the sole reason that the town is to be rebuilt in another fashion, with streets made more beautiful; but at the same time we see that many people cause their own houses to be knocked down in order to rebuild them, and that sometimes they are forced to do so where there is danger of the houses falling of themselves, and when the foundations are not secure. From such examples I argued to myself that there was no plausibility in the claim of any private individual to reform a state by altering everything, and by overturning it throughout, in order to set it right again. Nor is it likewise probable that the whole body of the Sciences, or the order of teaching established by the Schools, should be reformed. But as regards all the opinions which up to this time I had embraced, I thought I could not do better than endeavor once for all to sweep them completely away, so that they might later on be replaced, either by others that were better, or by the same, when I had made them conform to the uniformity of a rational scheme. And I firmly believed that by this means I should succeed in directing my life much better than if I had only built on old foundations, and relied on principles of which I allowed myself to be in youth persuaded without having inquired into their truth. For although in so doing I recognized various difficulties, these were at the same time not unsurmountable, nor comparable to those which are found in reformation of the most insignificant kind in matters which concern the public. . . .

. . . My design has never extended beyond trying to reform my own opinion and to build on a foundation that is entirely my own. If my work has given me a certain satisfaction, so that I here present to you a draft of it, I do not so do because I wish to advise anybody to imitate it. Those to whom God has been most beneficent in the bestowal of His grace will perhaps form designs that are more elevated; but I fear much that this particular one will seem too venturesome for many. The simple resolve to strip oneself of all opinions and beliefs formerly received is not to be regarded as an example that each man should follow, and the world may be said to be mainly composed of two classes of minds neither of which could prudently adopt it. There are those who, believing themselves to be cleverer than they are, cannot restrain themselves from being precipitate in judgment and have not sufficient patience to arrange their thoughts in proper order; hence, once a man of this description had taken the liberty of doubting the principles he formerly accepted, and had deviated from the beaten track, he would never be able to maintain the path which must be followed to reach the appointed end more quickly, and he would hence remain wandering astray all through his life. Secondly, there are those who having reason or modesty enough to judge that they are less capable of distinguishing truth from falsehood than some others from whom instruction might be obtained, are right in contenting themselves with following the opinions of these others rather than in searching better ones for themselves.

For myself I should doubtless have been of these last if I had never had more than a single master, or had I never known the diversities that have from all time existed between the opinions of men of the greatest learning. But I had been taught, even in my College days, that there is nothing imaginable so strange or so little credible that it has not been maintained by one philosopher or other, and I further recognized in the course of my travels that all those whose sentiments are very contrary to ours are yet not necessarily barbarians or savages, but may be possessed of Reason in as great or even a greater degree than ourselves. I also considered how very different the self-same man, identical in mind and spirit, may become, according as he is brought up from childhood amongst the French or Germans, or has passed his whole life amongst Chinese or cannibals. I likewise noticed how even in the fashions of one's clothing the same thing that pleased us ten years ago, and that will perhaps please us once again before ten years are passed, seems at the present time extravagant and ridiculous. I thus concluded that it is much more custom and example that persuade us than any certain knowledge, and yet in spite of this the voice of the majority is valueless as a proof of any truths that are a little difficult to discover, because such truths are much more likely to have been discovered by one man than by a nation. I could not, however, put my finger on a single person whose opinions seemed preferable to those of others, and I found that I was, so to speak, constrained myself to undertake the direction of my procedure.

But like one who walks alone and in the twilight I resolved to go so slowly, and to use so much circumspection in all things, that if my advance was but very small, at least I guarded myself well from falling. I did not wish to set about the final rejection of any single opinion which might formerly have crept into my beliefs without having been introduced there by means of Reason, until I had first of all employed sufficient time in planning out the task which I had undertaken, and in seeking the true Method of arriving at a knowledge of all the things of which my mind was capable.

Among the different branches of Philosophy, I had in my younger days to a certain extent studied Logic; and in those of Mathematics, Geometrical Analysis and Algebra—three arts or sciences which seemed as though they ought to contribute something to the design I had in view. But in examining them I observed in respect to Logic that the syllogisms and the greater part of the other teaching served better in explaining to others those things that one knows (or like the art of Lully, in enabling one to speak without judgment of those things of which one is ignorant) than in learning what is new. And although in reality Logic contains many precepts that are very true and very good, there are at the same time mingled with them so many others that are hurtful or superfluous, that it is almost as difficult to separate the two as to draw a Diana or a Minerva out of a block of marble that is not yet roughly hewn. And as to the Analysis of the ancients and the Algebra of the moderns, besides the fact that they embrace only matters the most abstract, such as appear to have no actual use, the former is always so restricted to the consideration of symbols that it cannot exercise the Understanding without greatly fatiguing the Imagination; and in the latter one is so subjected to certain rules and formulas that the result is the construction of an art that is confused and obscure, and that embarrasses the mind, instead of a science that contributes to its cultivation. This made me feel that some other Method must be found, which, comprising the advantages of the three, is yet exempt from their faults. And as a multiplicity of laws often furnishes excuses for evil-doing, and as a State is hence much better ruled when, having but very few laws, these are most strictly observed; so, instead of the great number of precepts of which Logic is composed, I believed that I should find the four which I shall state quite sufficient, provided that I adhered to a firm and constant resolve never on any single occasion to fail in their observance.

The first of these was to accept nothing as true which I did not clearly recognize to be so: that is to say, carefully to avoid precipitation and prejudice in judgments, and to accept in them nothing more than what was presented to my mind so clearly and distinctly that I could have no occasion to doubt it.

The second was to divide up each of the difficulties that I examined into as many parts as possible, and as seemed requisite in order that it might be resolved in the best manner possible.

The third was to carry on my reflections in due order, commencing with objects that were the most simple and easy to understand, in order to rise little by little, or by degrees, to knowledge of the most complex, assuming an order, even if a fictitious one, among those which do not follow a natural sequence relatively to one another.

The last was in all cases to make enumerations so complete and reviews so general that I should be certain of having omitted nothing.

Those long chains of reasoning, simple and easy as they are, of which geometricians make use in order to arrive at the most difficult demonstrations, had caused me to imagine that all those things which fall under the cognizance of man might very likely be mutually related in the same fashion; and that, provided only that we abstain from receiving anything as true that is not so, and always retain the order that is necessary in order to deduce the one conclusion from the other, there can be nothing so remote that we cannot reach to it, nor so recondite that we cannot discover it. And I had not much trouble in discovering which objects it was necessary to begin with, for I already knew that I must begin with the most simple and most easy to apprehend. Considering also that of all those who have hitherto sought for the truth in the Sciences, it has been the mathematicians alone who have been able to succeed in making any demonstrations, that is to say producing reasons that are evident and certain, I did not doubt that it had been by means of a similar kind that they carried on their investigations. I did not at the same time hope for any practical result in so doing, except that my mind would become accustomed to the nourishment of truth and would not content itself with false rea-

soning. But for all that I had no intention of trying to master all those particular sciences that receive in common the name of Mathematics; but observing that, although their objects are different, they do not fail to agree in this, that they take nothing under consideration but the various relationships or proportions that are present in these objects, I thought it would be better if I only examined these proportions in their general aspect, and without viewing them otherwise than in the objects that would serve most to facilitate a knowledge of them. Not that I should in any way restrict them to these objects, for I might later on all the more easily apply them to all other objects to which they were applicable. Then, having carefully noted that in order to comprehend the proportions I should sometimes require to consider each one in particular, and sometimes merely keep them in mind, or take them in groups, I thought that, in order the better to consider them in detail, I should picture them in the form of lines, because I could find no method more simple nor more capable of being distinctly represented to my imagination and senses. I considered, however, that in order to keep them in my memory or to embrace several at once, it would be essential that I should explain them by means of certain formulas, the shorter the better. And for this purpose it was requisite that I should borrow all that is best in Geometrical Analysis and Algebra, and correct the errors of the one by the other.

*   *   *

But what pleased me most in this Method was that I was certain by its means of exercising my reason in all things, if not perfectly, at least as well as was in my power. And besides this, I felt in making use of it that my mind gradually accustomed itself to conceive of its objects more accurately and distinctly; and not having restricted this Method to any particular matter, I promised myself to apply it as usefully to the difficulties of other sciences as I had done to those of Algebra. Not that on this account I dared undertake to examine just at once all those which might present themselves; for that would itself have been contrary to the order that the Method prescribes.

But having noticed that the knowledge of these difficulties must be dependent on principles derived from Philosophy in which I yet found nothing to be certain, I thought that it was requisite above all to try to establish certainty in it. I considered also that since this endeavor is the most important in all the world, and that in which precipitation and prejudice were most to be feared, I should not try to grapple with it till I had attained to a much riper age than that of three and twenty, which was the age I had reached. I thought, too, that I should first of all employ much time in preparing myself for the work by eradicating from my mind all the wrong opinions that I had up to this time accepted, and accumulating a variety of experiences fitted later on to afford matter for my reasonings, and by ever exercising myself in the Method I had prescribed, in order

more and more to fortify myself in the power of using it.

*   *   *

REVIEW QUESTIONS

1. Why does Descartes reject the received knowledge of the past?
2. Why does Descartes not trust his own mind as a reasoning instrument?
3. What method does he propose, and what relationship does he see between experience and knowledge?
4. How does Descartes's epistemology compare with those of Montaigne (pp. 132–138)?

ISAAC NEWTON

FROM *Mathematical Principles of Natural Philosophy*

Isaac Newton (1642–1727) created the great reformulation of seventeenth-century mechanical philosophy. He was born of yeoman stock. His intellectual gifts were recognized early by a teacher and an uncle, who urged that Newton be prepared for a university education. He entered Trinity College, Cambridge, in 1661 and received his bachelor of arts in 1665 and his master of arts in 1668. The next year, Newton was appointed Lucasian Professor, a position he held until 1701. As a natural philosopher, Newton agreed with Bacon that empiricism, that is, the gathering of experimental data, was the starting point for scientific inquiry. Yet he reserved a role for Cartesian rationalism by demonstrating the theoretical utility of mathematics in mechanical philosophy. In Mathematical Principles of Natural Philosophy, *Newton laid out the quantitative framework of his mechanical philosophy and showed how it was possible, experimentally, to work with invisible bodies. In the following rules of reason, he offered a methodological guide to the study of reality.*

From *Mathematical Principles of Natural Philosophy*, vol. 2, by Isaac Newton, translated by Andrew Motte (London: Sherwood, Neely and Jones, 1919).

*   *   *

Book III

In the preceding books I have laid down the principles of philosophy; principles not philosophical, but mathematical; such, to wit, as we may build our reasonings upon in philosophical enquiries. These principles are the laws and conditions of certain motions, and powers or forces, which chiefly have respect to philosophy; but, lest they should have appeared of themselves dry and barren, I have illustrated them here and there with some philosophical scholiums, giving an account of such things as are of more general nature, and which philosophy seems chiefly to be founded on; such as the density and the resistance of bodies, spaces void of all bodies, and the motion of light and sounds. It remains that, from the same principles, I now demonstrate the frame of the System of the World. Upon this subject I had, indeed, composed the third book in a popular method, that it might be read by many; but afterwards, considering that such as had not sufficiently entered into the principles could not easily discern the strength of the consequences, nor lay aside the prejudices to which they had been many years accustomed, therefore, to prevent the disputes which might be raised upon such accounts, I chose to reduce the substance of this book into the form of propositions (in the mathematical way), which should be read by those only who had first made themselves masters of the principles established in the preceding books: not that I would advise any one to the previous study of every proposition of those books; for they abound with such as might cost too much time, even to readers of good mathematical learning. It is enough if one carefully reads the definitions, the laws of motions, and the first three sections of the first book. He may then pass on to this book, and consult such of the remaining propositions of the *first two books,* as the references in this, and his occasions, shall require.

Rules of Reasoning in Philosophy

RULE I
WE ARE TO ADMIT NO MORE CAUSES OF NATURAL THINGS THAN SUCH AS ARE BOTH TRUE AND SUFFICIENT TO EXPLAIN THEIR APPEARANCES.

To this purpose the philosophers say that Nature does nothing in vain, and more is in vain when less will serve; for Nature is pleased with simplicity, and affects not the pomp of superfluous causes.

RULE II
THEREFORE TO THE SAME NATURAL EFFECTS WE MUST, AS FAR AS POSSIBLE, ASSIGN THE SAME CAUSES.

As to respiration in a man and in a beast; the descent of stones in Europe and in America; the light of our culinary fire and of the sun; the reflection of light in the earth and in the planets.

RULE III
THE QUALITIES OF BODIES, WHICH ADMIT NEITHER INTENSION OR REMISSION OF DEGREES, AND WHICH ARE FOUND TO BELONG TO ALL BODIES WITHIN THE REACH OF OUR EXPERIMENTS, ARE TO BE ESTEEMED THE UNIVERSAL QUALITIES OF ALL BODIES WHATSOEVER.

For since the qualities of bodies are only known to us by experiments, we are to hold for universal all such as universally agree with experiments; and such as are not liable to diminution can never be quite taken away. We are certainly not to relinquish the evidence of experiments for the sake of dreams and vain fictions of our own devising; nor are we to recede from the analogy of Nature, which is wont to be simple, and always consonant to itself. We no other way know the extension of bodies than by our senses, nor do these reach it in all bodies; but because we perceive extension in all that are sensible, therefore we ascribe it universally to all others also. That abundance of bodies are hard, we learn by experience; and because the hardness of the whole arises from the hardness of the parts,

DETAIL FROM THE FRONTISPIECE OF DE HUMANI CORPORIS FABRICA (1543)   ANDREAS VESALIUS

Andreas Vesalius (Andreas van Wesel, 1514–1564) came from a family of physicians. Educated in Leuven, Paris, and Padua, he was appointed explicator chirurgiae (professor of surgery) at the University of Padua in 1537, at twenty-three years of age. There he began teaching, not simply by lecturing but also by demonstrating. He also prepared drawings as aids to memory for his students. De Fabrica, as it is often called, was published in 1543, when Vesalius was only twenty-eight years old. It became not only the most influential book in the history of medicine but also one of the most important books ever published. It overturned fourteen centuries of Galenic teaching and tradition in medicine. It was also the first printed book to integrate every aspect of book design: content, art, layout and typography. What does this image reveal about science and education in the sixteenth century? Why are the architectural elements and figures of animals so prominent? Can you identify Vesalius? Why is he represented, posing and gesturing, as he is? Looking carefully, what can you determine about the corpse? Given what you see, why would this image have been particularly daring? What purpose might that daring have served?

we therefore justly infer the hardness of the undivided particles not only of the bodies we feel but of all others. That all bodies are impenetrable, we gather not from reason, but from sensation. The bodies which we handle we find impenetrable, and thence conclude impenetrability to be an universal property of all bodies whatsoever. That all bodies are moveable, and endowed with certain powers (which we call *vires inertiæ*) of persevering in their motion, or in their rest, we only infer from the like properties observed in the bodies which we have seen. The extension, hardness, impenetrability, mobility, and *vis inertiæ* of the whole, result from the extension, hardness, impenetrability, mobility, and *vires inertiæ* of the parts; and thence we conclude the least particles of all bodies to be also all extended, and hard, and impenetrable, and moveable, and endowed with their proper *vires inertiæ*. And this is the foundation of all philosophy. Moreover, that the divided but continuous particles of bodies may be separated from one another, is matter of observation; and, in the particles that remain undivided, our minds are able to distinguish yet lesser parts, as is mathematically demonstrated. But whether the parts so distinguished, and not yet divided, may, by the powers of Nature, be actually divided and separated from one another, we cannot certainly determine. Yet, had we the proof of but one experiment that any undivided particle, in breaking a hard and solid body, suffered a division, we might by virtue of this rule conclude that the undivided as well as the divided particles may be divided and actually separated to infinity.

Lastly, if it universally appears, by experiments and astronomical observations, that all bodies about the earth gravitate towards the earth, and that in proportion to the quantity of matter which they severally contain; that the moon likewise, according to the quantity of its matter, gravitates towards the earth; that, on the other hand, our sea gravitates towards the moon; and all the planets mutually one towards another; and the comets in like manner towards the sun; we must, in consequence of this rule, universally allow that all bodies whatsoever are endowed with a principle of mutual gravitation. For the argument from the appearances concludes with more force for the universal gravitation of all bodies than for their impenetrability; of which, among those in the celestial regions, we have no experiments, nor any manner of observation. Not that I affirm gravity to be essential to bodies: by their *vis insita* I mean nothing but their *vis inertiæ*. This is immutable. Their gravity is diminished as they recede from the earth.

RULE IV
IN EXPERIMENTAL PHILOSOPHY WE ARE TO LOOK UPON PROPOSITIONS COLLECTED BY GENERAL INDUCTION FROM PHÆNOMENA AS ACCURATELY OR VERY NEARLY TRUE, NOTWITHSTANDING ANY CONTRARY HYPOTHESES THAT MAY BE IMAGINED, TILL SUCH TIME AS OTHER PHÆNOMENA OCCUR, BY WHICH THEY MAY EITHER BE MADE MORE ACCURATE, OR LIABLE TO EXCEPTIONS.

This rule we must follow, that the argument of induction may not be evaded by hypotheses.

*   *   *

REVIEW QUESTIONS

1. Why does Newton take mathematical principles as the principles of philosophy?
2. If nature, as Newton asserts, is "pleased with simplicity," what is the origin of "superfluous causes"?
3. What is the relation between cause and law?
4. How does Newton arrive at the universal?
5. How does his method differ from that of Pascal?

ROBERT HOOKE

FROM *Micrographia*

Robert Hooke (1635–1703) was an English natural philosopher, architect and poly-math. He achieved great wealth and fame in the course of his life, based on his repu-tation for skillful and honest scientific research, but became mired in controversy due to jealousies and illnesses late in life. These problems may explain to some extent his relative obscurity in the history of science. His obscurity might also arise from the range of his interests, which were not confined to a single field. Hooke stud-ied at Wadham College during the Protectorate, where he worked with Thomas Wil-lis and Robert Boyle. Much of Hooke's scientific work was conducted in his capacity as curator of experiments of the Royal Society, a post he held from 1662, or as part of the household of Robert Boyle. In addition to assisting Boyle's physical experiments, he also constructed telescopes to make astronomical observations. His publication of Micrographia *in 1665 inspired the use of microscopes in science. In addition to his active engagement in a wide range of scientific researches, he was at one time simul-taneously the curator of experiments of the Royal Society and a member of its coun-cil, Gresham Professor of Geometry, and a Surveyor to the City of London after the Great Fire of London, in which capacity he appears to have performed more than half of all the surveys after the fire. He was also an important architect of his time and was instrumental in devising a set of planning controls for London whose influ-ence remains today. The controversies that burdened his later life arose likewise from his broad scientific engagement. He came near to an experimental proof that gravity follows an inverse square law, and hypothesized that such a relation governs the motions of the planets, an idea which was subsequently developed by Isaac Newton. His claims resulted in contention with Newton that did neither of them credit.*

From *Micrographia: or Some Physiological Descriptions of Minute Bodies made by Magnify-ing Glasses with observations and Inquiries thereupon,* by Robert Hooke (London: J. Martyn, 1667) pp. 242–46.

To the King.

SIR,

I Do here most humbly lay this small Present at Your Majesties Royal feet. And though it comes accompany'd with two disadvantages, the mean-ness of the Author, and of the Subject; yet in both I am incouraged by the greatness of your Mercy and your Knowledge. By the one I am taught, that you can forgive the most presumptuous Offen-dors: And by the other, that you will not esteem the least work of Nature, or Art, unworthy your Observation. Amidst the many felicities that have accompani'd your Majesties happy Restauration and Government, it is none of the least considerable that Philosophy and Experimental Learning have prosper'd under your Royal Patronage. And as the calm prosperity of your Reign has given us the lei-sure to follow these Studies of quiet and retire-ment, so it is just, that the Fruits of them should, by way of acknowledgement, be return'd to your Majesty. There are, Sir, several other of your Subjects, of your Royal Society, now busie about Nobler matters: The Improvement of Manufactures and Agriculture, the Increase of Commerce, the Advantage of Navigation: In all which they are assisted by your Majesties Incouragement and Example. Amidst all those greater Designs, I here presume to bring in that which is more proportionable to the smalness of my Abilities, and to offer some of the least of all visible things, to that Mighty King, that has establisht an Empire over the best of all Invisible things of this World, the Minds of Men.

Your Majesties most humble and most obedient Subject and Servant,

ROBERT HOOKE.

To the Royal Society.

After my Address to our Great Founder and Patron, I could not but think my self oblig'd, in consideration of those many Ingagements you have laid upon me, to offer these my poor Labours to this MOST ILLUSTRIOUS ASSEMBLY. YOU have been pleas'd formerly to accept of these rude Draughts. I have since added to them some Descriptions, and some Conjectures of my own. And therefore, together with YOUR Acceptance, I must also beg YOUR pardon. The Rules YOU have prescrib'd YOUR selves in YOUR Philosophical Progress do seem the best that have ever yet been practis'd. And particularly that of avoiding Dogmatizing, and the espousal of any Hypothesis not sufficiently grounded and confirm'd by Experiments. This way seems the most excellent, and may preserve both Philosophy and Natural History from its former Corruptions. In saying which, I may seem to condemn my own Course in this Treatise; in which there may perhaps be some Expressions, which may seem more positive then YOUR Prescriptions will permit: And though I desire to have them understood only as Conjectures and Quæries (which YOUR Method does not altogether disallow) yet if even in those I have exceeded, 'tis fit that I should declare, that it was not done by YOUR Directions. For it is most unreasonable, that YOU should

undergo the imputation of the faults of my Conjectures, seeing YOU can receive so small advantage of reputation by the sleight Observations of

YOUR most humble and most faithful Servant
ROBERT HOOKE.

*   *   *

Observ. LX. Of the Moon.

Having a pretty large corner of the Plate for the seven Starrs, void, for the filling it up, I have added one small Specimen of the appearance of the parts of the Moon, by describing a small spot of it, which, though taken notice of, both by the Excellent Hevelius, and called Mons Olympus (though I think somewhat improperly, being rather a vale) and represented by the Figure X. of the 38. Scheme, and also by the Learn'd Ricciolus, who calls it Hipparchus, and describes it by the Figure Y, yet how far short both of them come of the truth, may be somewhat perceiv'd by the draught, which I have here added of it, in the Figure Z, (which I drew by a thirty foot Glass, in October 1664. just before the Moon was half inlightned) but much better by the Reader's diligently observing it himself, at a convenient time, with a Glass of that length, and much better yet with one of threescore foot long, for through these it appears a very spacious Vale, incompassed with a ridge of Hills, not very high in comparison of many other in the Moon, nor yet very steep. The Vale it self ABCD, is much of the figure of a Pear, and from several appearances of it, seems to be some very fruitful place, that is, to have its surface all covered over with some kinds of vegetable substances; for in all positions of the light on it, it seems to give a much fainter reflection then the more barren tops of the incompassing Hills, and those a much fainter then divers other cragged, chalky, or rocky Mountains of the Moon. So that I am not unapt to think, that the Vale may have Vegetables analogus to our Grass, Shrubs, and Trees; and most of these incompassing Hills may be covered with so thin a vegetable Coat, as we may observe the Hills with us to be, such as the short Sheep pasture which covers the Hills of Salisbury Plains.

Up and down in several parts of this place here describ'd (as there are multitudes in other places all over the surface of the Moon) may be perceived several kinds of pits, which are shap'd almost like a dish, some bigger, some less, some shallower, some deeper, that is, they seem to be a hollow Hemisphere, incompassed with a round rising bank, as if the substance in the middle had been digg'd up, and thrown on either side. These seem to me to have been the effects of some motions within the body of the Moon, analogus to our Earthquakes, by the eruption of which, as it has thrown up a brim, or ridge, round about, higher then the Ambient surface of the Moon, so has it left a hole, or depression, in the middle, proportionably lower; divers places resembling some of these, I have observ'd here in England, on the tops of some Hills, which might have been caus'd by some Earthquake in the younger dayes of the world. But that which does most incline me to this belief, is, first, the generality and diversity of the Magnitude of these pits all over the body of the Moon. Next, the two experimental wayes, by which I have made a representation of them.

The first was with a very soft and well temper'd mixture of Tobacco-pipe clay and Water, into which, if I let fall any heavy body, as a Bullet, it would throw up the mixture round the place, which for a while would make a representation, not unlike these of the Moon; but considering the state and condition of the Moon, there seems not any probability to imagine, that it should proceed from any cause analogus to this; for it would be difficult to imagine whence those bodies should come; and next, how the substance of the Moon should be so soft; but if a Bubble be blown under the surface of it, and suffer'd to rise, and break; or if a Bullet, or other body, sunk in it, be pull'd out from it, these departing bodies leave an impression on the surface of the mixture, exactly like these of the Moon, save that these also quickly subside and vanish. But the second, and most notable, representation was, what I observ'd in a pot of boyling Alabaster, for there that powder being by the eruption of vapours reduc'd to a kind of fluid consistence, if, whil'st it boyls, it be gently remov'd besides the fire, the Alabaster presently ceasing to boyl, the whole surface, especially that where some of the last Bubbles have risen, will

appear all over covered with small pits, exactly shap'd like these of the Moon, and by holding a lighted Candle in a large dark Room, in divers positions to this surface, you may exactly represent all the Phænomena of these pits in the Moon, according as they are more or less inlightned by the Sun.

And that there may have been in the Moon some such motion as this, which may have made these pits, will seem the more probable, if we suppose it like our Earth, for the Earthquakes here with us seem to proceed from some such cause, as the boyling of the pot of Alabaster, there seeming to be generated in the Earth from some subterraneous fires, or heat, great quantities of vapours, that is, of expanded aerial substances, which not presently finding a passage through the ambient parts of the Earth, do, as they are increased by the supplying and generating principles, and thereby (having not sufficient room to expand themselves) extreamly condens'd, at last overpower, with their elastick properties, the resistence of the incompassing Earth, and lifting it up, or cleaving it, and so shattering of the parts of the Earth above it, do at length, where they find the parts of the Earth above them more loose, make their way upwards, and carrying a great part of the Earth before them, not only raise a small brim round about the place, out of which they break, but for the most part considerable high Hills and Mountains, and when they break from under the Sea, divers times, mountainous Islands; this seems confirm'd by the Vulcans in several places of the Earth, the mouths of which, for the most part, are incompassed with a Hill of a considerable height, and the tops of those Hills, or Mountains, are usually shap'd very much like these pits, or dishes, of the Moon: Instances of this we have in the descriptions of Ætna in Sicily, of Hecla in Iceland, of Tenerif in the Canaries, of the several Vulcans in New-Spain, describ'd by Gage, and more especially in the eruption of late years in one of the Canary Islands. In all of which there is not only a considerable high Hill raised about the mouth of the Vulcan, but, like the spots of the Moon, the top of those Hills are like a dish, or bason. And indeed, if one attentively consider the nature of the thing, one may find sufficient reason to judge, that it cannot be otherwise; for these eruptions, whether of fire, or smoak, always raysing great quantities of Earth before them, must necessarily, by the fall of those parts on either side, raise very considerable heaps.

Now, both from the figures of them, and from several other circumstances; these pits in the Moon seem to have been generated much after the same manner that the holes in Alabaster, and the Vulcans of the Earth are made. For first, it is not improbable, but that the substance of the Moon may be very much like that of our Earth, that is, may consist of an earthy, sandy, or rocky substance, in several of its superficial parts, which parts being agitated, undermin'd, or heav'd up, by eruptions of vapours, may naturally be thrown into the same kind of figured holes, as the small dust, or powder of Alabaster. Next, it is not improbable, but that there may be generated, within the body of the Moon, divers such kind of internal fires and heats, as may produce such Exhalations; for since we can plainly enough discover with a Telescope, that there are multitudes of such kind of eruptions in the body of the Sun it self, which is accounted the most noble Ætherial body, certainly we need not be much scandaliz'd at such kind of alterations, or corruptions, in the body of this lower and less considerable part of the universe, the Moon, which is only secundary, or attendant, on the bigger, and more considerable body of the Earth. Thirdly, 'tis not unlikely, but that supposing such a sandy or mouldring substance to be there found, and supposing also a possibility of the generation of the internal elastical body (whether you will call it air or vapours) 'tis not unlikely, I say, but that there is in the Moon a principle of gravitation, such as in the Earth. And to make this probable, I think, we need no better Argument, then the roundness, or globular Figure of the body of the Moon it self, which we may perceive very plainly by the Telescope, to be (bating the small inequality of the Hills and Vales in it, which are all of them likewise shap'd, or levelled, as it were, to answer to the center of the Moons body) perfectly of a Sphærical figure, that is, all the parts of it are so rang'd (bating the comparitively small ruggedness of the Hills and Dales) that the outmost bounds of them are equally distant from the Center of the Moon, and consequently, it is exceedingly probable also, that they are equidistant from the Center of gravitation; and indeed, the fig-

ure of the superficial parts of the Moon are so exactly shap'd, according as they should be, supposing it had a gravitating principle as the Earth has, that even the figure of those parts themselves is of sufficient efficacy to make the gravitation, and the other two suppositions probable: so that the other suppositions may be rather prov'd by this considerable Circumstance, or Observation, then this suppos'd Explication can by them; for he that shall attentively observe with an excellent Telescope, how all the Circumstances, notable in the shape of the superficial parts, are, as it were, exactly adapted to suit with such a principle, will, if he well considers the usual method of Nature in its other proceedings, find abundant argument to believe it to have really there also such a principle; for I could never observe, among all the mountainous or prominent parts of the Moon (whereof there is a huge variety) that any one part of it was plac'd in such a manner, that if there should be a gravitating, or attracting principle in the body of the Moon, it would make that part to fall, or be mov'd out of its visible posture. Next, the shape and position of the parts is such, that they all seem put into those very shapes they are in by a gravitating power: For first, there are but very few clifts, or very steep declivities in the ascent of these Mountains; for besides those Mountains, which are by Hevelius call'd the Apennine Mountains, and some other, which seem to border on the Seas of the Moon, and those only upon one side, as is common also in those Hills that are here on the Earth; there are very few that seem to have very steep ascents, but, for the most part, they are made very round, and much resemble the make of the Hills and Mountains also of the Earth; this may be partly perceived by the Hills incompassing this Vale, which I have here describ'd; and as on the Earth also, the middlemost of these Hills seems the highest, so is it obvious also, through a good Telescope, in those of the Moon; the Vales also in many are much shap'd like those of the Earth, and I am apt to think, that could we look upon the Earth from the Moon, with a good Telescope, we might easily enough perceive its surface to be very much like that of the Moon.

Now whereas in this small draught, (as there would be multitudes if the whole Moon were drawn after this manner) there are several little Ebullitions, or Dishes, even in the Vales themselves, and in the incompassing Hills also; this will, from this supposition, (which I have, I think, upon very good reason taken) be exceeding easily explicable; for, as I have several times also observ'd, in the surface of Alabaster so ordered, as I before describ'd, so may the later eruptions of vapours be even in the middle, or on the edges of the former; and other succeeding these also in time may be in the middle or edges of these, &c. of which there are Instances enough in divers parts of the body of the Moon, and by a boyling pot of Alabaster will be sufficiently exemplifi'd.

To conclude therefore, it being very probable, that the Moon has a principle of gravitation, it affords an excellent distinguishing Instance in the search after the cause of gravitation, or attraction, to hint, that it does not depend upon the diurnal or turbinated motion of the Earth, as some have somewhat inconsiderately supposed and affirmed it to do; for if the Moon has an attractive principle, whereby it is not only shap'd round, but does firmly contain and hold all its parts united, though many of them seem as loose as the sand on the Earth, and that the Moon is not mov'd about its Center; then certainly the turbination cannot be the cause of the attraction of the Earth, and therefore some other principle must be thought of, that will agree with all the secundary as well as primary Planets. But this, I confess, is but a probability, and not a demonstration, which (from any Observation yet made) it seems hardly capable of, though how successful future indeavours (promoted by the meliorating of Glasses, and observing particular circumstances) may be in this, or any other, kind, must be with patience expected.

REVIEW QUESTIONS

1. Why does Hooke dedicate the *Micrographia* to the King of England?
2. What are the bases of Hooke's scientific method?
3. How would you describe the tone of Hooke's essay?
4. What is the purpose and significance of Hooke's reference to the Salisbury Plains?
5. How does Hooke makes his claims about gravitation?
6. Why is *Micrographia* about so much more than microscopes, and what does this tell you about Hooke's science?

JOHN LOCKE

FROM *An Essay Concerning Human Understanding*

John Locke (1632–1704) was an English philosopher whose thought contributed to the Enlightenment. He grew up in a liberal, Puritan family, the son of an attorney who fought in the Civil War against Charles I, and attended Christ Church College, Oxford. He received his bachelor of arts in 1656, lectured in classical languages while earning his master of arts, and entered Oxford's medical school to avoid being forced to join the clergy. In 1666, Locke attached himself to the household of the Earl of Shaftesbury and his fortunes to the liberal Whig Party. Between 1675 and 1679, he lived in France, where he made contact with leading intellectuals of the late seventeenth century. On his return to England, he plunged into the controversy surrounding the succession of James II, an avowed Catholic with absolutist pretensions, to the throne of his brother, Charles II. Locke's patron, Shaftesbury, was imprisoned for his opposition, and Locke went into exile in 1683. Though he was involved to some extent in the Glorious Revolution of 1688, he returned to England in 1689, in the entourage of Mary, Princess of Orange, who would assume the throne with her husband William. This was a period of intense political engagement for Locke, the fruits of which would be the publication of the Two Treatises on Government *(1690). Yet he was also engaged in broader philosophical study. Locke's great work on epistemology,* An Essay Concerning Human Understanding, *appeared in the same year. It was a complete account of human knowledge, its source and its reliability. His argument was as simple as it was revolutionary. Rejecting all appeals to authority and theory, he showed that all knowledge derives from sensory perception and experience as considered and elaborated by reason. It was one of the most influential works in all of Western philosophy and had an immediate impact on enlightened thinkers. As Voltaire himself announced, "No Man ever had a more judicious or more methodical Genius . . . than Mr. Locke."*

From *The Works of John Locke* (London: Thomas Tegg et al., 1823).

*   *   *

Book II
Of Ideas

Chapter I
Of Ideas in General, and Their Original

IDEA IS THE OBJECT OF THINKING.

Every man being conscious to himself, that he thinks, and that which his mind is applied about, whilst thinking, being the ideas, that are there, 'tis past doubt, that men have in their minds several ideas, such as are those expressed by the words, *whiteness, hardness, sweetness, thinking, motion, man, elephant, army, drunkenness,* and others: it is in the first place then to be inquired, how he comes by them? I know it is a received doctrine, that men have native ideas, and original characters stamped upon their minds, in their very first being. This opinion I have at large examined already; and, I suppose, what I have said in the foregoing book, will be much more easily admitted, when I have shown, whence the understanding may get all the ideas it has, and by what ways and degrees they

may come into the mind; for which I shall appeal to everyone's own observation and experience.

ALL IDEAS COME FROM SENSATION OR REFLECTION.

Let us then suppose the mind to be, as we say, white paper, void of all characters, without any ideas; how comes it to be furnished? Whence comes it by that vast store, which the busy and boundless fancy of man has painted on it, with an almost endless variety? Whence has it all the materials of reason and knowledge? To this I answer, in one world, from *experience* in that, all our knowledge is founded; and from that it ultimately derives itself. Our observation employed either about *external sensible objects; or about the internal operations of our minds, perceived and reflected on by ourselves, is that, which supplies our understandings with all the materials of thinking.* These two are the fountains of knowledge, from whence all the ideas we have, or can naturally have, do spring.

THE OBJECTS OF SENSATION ONE SOURCE OF IDEAS.

First, *our senses,* conversant about particular sensible objects, do *convey into the mind,* several distinct *perceptions* of things, according to those various ways, wherein those objects do affect them: and thus we come by those ideas, we have of *yellow, white, heat, cold, soft, hard, bitter, sweet,* and all those which we call sensible qualities, which when I say the senses convey into the mind, I mean, they from external objects convey into the mind what produces there those *perceptions.* This great source, of most of the ideas we have, depending wholly upon our senses, and derived by them to the understanding, I call *sensation.*

THE OPERATIONS OF OUR MINDS, THE OTHER SOURCE OF THEM.

Secondly, the other fountain, from which experience furnisheth the understanding with ideas, is the *perception of the operations of our own minds* within us, as it is employed about the ideas it has got; which operations, when the soul comes to reflect on, and consider, do furnish the understanding with another set of ideas, which could not be had from things without; and such are, *perception, thinking, doubting, believing, reasoning, knowing, willing,* and all the different actings of our own minds; which we being conscious of, and observing in ourselves, do from these receive into our understandings, as distinct ideas, as we do from bodies affecting our senses. This source of ideas, every man has wholly in himself: and though it be not sense, as having nothing to do with external objects; yet it is very like it, and might properly enough be called internal sense. But as I call the other *sensation,* so I call this *reflection,* the ideas it affords being such only, as the mind gets by reflecting on its own operations within itself. By *reflection* then, in the following part of this discourse, I would be understood to mean, that notice which the mind takes of its own operations, and the manner of them, by reason whereof, there come to be ideas of these operations in the understanding. These two, I say, *viz.* external, material things, as the objects of *sensation;* and the operations of our own minds within, as the objects of *reflection,* are, to me, the only originals, from whence all our ideas take their beginnings. The term *operations* here, I use in a large sense, as comprehending not barely the actions of the mind about its ideas, but some sort of passions arising sometimes from them, such as is the satisfaction or uneasiness arising from any thought.

ALL OUR IDEAS ARE OF THE ONE OR THE OTHER OF THESE.

The understanding seems to me, not to have the least glimmering of any ideas, which it doth not receive from one of these two. *External objects furnish the mind with the ideas of sensible qualities,* which are all those different perceptions they produce in us: and the *mind furnishes the understanding with ideas of its own operations.*

These, when we have taken a full survey of them, and their several modes, combinations, and relations, we shall find to contain all our whole stock of ideas; and that we have nothing in our minds, which did not come in, one of these two ways. Let anyone examine his own thoughts, and throughly search into his understanding, and then let him tell me, whether all the original ideas he has there, are any other than of the objects of his *senses;* or of the operations of his mind, considered as objects of his *reflection:* and how great a mass of knowledge soever he imagines to be lodged there, he will, upon taking a strict view, see, that he has *not any idea in his mind, but what one of these two have imprinted;* though, perhaps, with infinite variety compounded and enlarged by the understanding, as we shall see hereafter.

OBSERVABLE IN CHILDREN.

He that attentively considers the state of a *child,* at his first coming into the world, will have little reason to think him stored with plenty of ideas, that are to be the matter of his future knowledge. 'Tis by degrees he comes to be furnished with them: and though the ideas of obvious and familiar qualities, imprint themselves, before the memory begins to keep a register of time and order, yet 'tis often so late, before some unusual qualities come in the way, that there are few men that cannot recollect the beginning of their acquaintance with them: and if it were worthwhile, no doubt a child might be so ordered, as to have but a very few, even of the ordinary ideas, till he were grown up to a man. But all that are born into the world being surrounded with bodies, that perpetually and diversely affect them, variety of ideas, whether care be taken about it or no, are imprinted on the minds of children.

Light, and *colours,* are busy at hand everywhere, when the eye is but open; *sounds,* and some *tangible qualities* fail not to solicit their proper senses, and force an entrance to the mind; but yet, I think, it will be granted easily, that if a child were kept in a place, where he never saw any other but black and white, till he were a man, he would have no more ideas of scarlet or green, than he that from his childhood never tasted an oyster, or a pineapple, has of those particular relishes.

MEN ARE DIFFERENTLY FURNISHED WITH THESE, ACCORDING TO THE DIFFERENT OBJECTS THEY CONVERSE WITH.

Men then come to be furnished with fewer or more simple ideas from without, according as the *objects,* they converse with, afford greater or less variety; and from the operation of their minds within, according as they more or less *reflect* on them. For, though he that contemplates the operations of his mind, cannot but have plain and clear *ideas* of them; yet unless he turn his thoughts that way, and considers them *attentively,* he will no more have clear and distinct ideas of all the *operations of his mind,* and all that may be observed therein, than he will have all the particular ideas of any landscape, or of the parts and motions of a clock, who will not turn his eyes to it, and with attention heed all the parts of it. The picture, or clock may be so placed, that they may come in his way every day; but yet he will have but a confused idea of all the parts they are made up of, till he *applies himself with attention,* to consider them each in particular.

IDEAS OF REFLECTION LATER, BECAUSE THEY NEED ATTENTION.

And hence we see the reason, why 'tis pretty late, before most children get ideas of the operations of their own minds; and some have not any very clear, or perfect ideas of the greatest part of them all their lives. Because, though they pass there continually; yet like floating visions, they make not deep impressions enough, to leave in the mind clear distinct lasting ideas, till the understanding turns inwards upon itself, *reflects* on its own *operations,* and makes them the object of its own contemplation. Children, when they come first into it, are surrounded with a world of new things, which, by a constant solicitation of their senses, draw the mind constantly to them, forward to take notice of new, and apt to be delighted with the variety of changing objects. Thus the first years are usually employed and diverted in looking abroad. Men's business in them is to acquaint themselves with what is to be found without; and so growing up in a constant attention to outward sensations, seldom make any considerable reflection on what passes within them, till they come to be of riper years; and some scarce ever at all.

THE SOUL BEGINS TO HAVE IDEAS, WHEN IT BEGINS TO PERCEIVE.

To ask, *at what time a man has first any ideas,* is to ask, when he begins to perceive; having ideas, and perception, being the same thing. I know it is an opinion, that the soul always thinks, and that it has the actual perception of ideas in itself constantly, as long as it exists; and that actual thinking is as inseparable from the soul, as actual extension is from the body; which if true, to inquire after the beginning of a man's ideas, is the same, as to inquire after the beginning of his soul. For by this account, soul and its ideas, as body and its extension, will begin to exist both at the same time.

*   *   *

REVIEW QUESTIONS

1. What, according to Locke, is the source of human knowledge? How does this compare with the philosophy of Descartes?
2. How reliable is human knowledge as a source of truth?
3. What does Locke mean by the "soul"?
4. How does Locke arrive at his epistemology?

17 ❧ EUROPE DURING THE ENLIGHTENMENT

The Enlightenment continued and extended the work begun by the revolution in science by spreading its new ideas to the general reading public and by extending those ideas to new disciplines devoted to the study of human nature. As an intellectual and cultural movement of the eighteenth century, it was characterized by faith in the power of human reason to solve the basic problems of existence. Though centered in Paris, the Enlightenment was international in scope, manifesting itself throughout Europe and North America. Enlightened intellectuals turned critical reason on all received institutions and traditions with an eye to rebuilding human society according to the natural order of things. This natural order was born of three scientific cornerstones: mechanics, reason, and empiricism. Reason provided both an analogy for the universe and a tool for its analysis. Nature was assumed to be rational, to be ordered according to knowable, controllable relations—fundamental laws that could be discovered through observation and experimentation. Confidence in the existence of natural laws encouraged the search for similar laws governing human relations. Knowledge of these laws would benefit humankind by making possible practical reforms at all levels of life.

By popularizing and extending the ideas of the scientific revolution, the Enlightenment encouraged a secular view of the world. In this way, it helped bring Europe into the modern era.

"ENGRAVINGS OF A PRINTSHOP"   DENIS DIDEROT AND JEAN D'ALEMBERT

FROM ENCYCLOPÉDIE, OU DICTIONNAIRE RAISONNÉ DES SCIENCES, DES ARTS ET DES MÉTIERS (1751–72)

Intended to be a systematic dictionary of the sciences, arts and crafts, as the subtitle indicates, the Encyclopédie was innovative as well as ambitious. It was the first compendium of knowledge to include contributions from many named authors, a model that is followed to this day. It was also the first encyclopedia to pay particular attention to the mechanical arts. Its purpose, according to Diderot, who wrote the article on encyclopédie, was "to change the way people think." How might the engravings before you help to achieve that purpose? What do the engravings reveal about their creator's understanding of mechanical arts and mechanics in a world dominated by reason? Why would representations of the mechanical arts, such as printing, have been particularly important to Enlightenment thinkers?

VOLTAIRE

FROM *Letters Concerning the English Nation*

François-Marie Arouet (1694–1778) was the son of a Parisian notary and royal official at the Cour des Comptes and became one of the fathers of the Enlightenment in France. As a youngster, he attached himself to his godfather, the abbé de Chateauneuf, a freethinker who introduced him to progressive circles in the French capital. He attended the Jesuit Collège Louis-le-Grand, where he graduated in 1711 with a degree in philosophy. Though he enrolled in law school, he decided on a literary career and frequented the salons of Paris. His first success came in 1718 with the staging of Oedipus. *At this point, he adopted the pen name of Voltaire. Legal difficulties that followed a brawl with the servants of the chevalier de Rohan resulted in Voltaire's exile to England. From 1726 to 1729 he was brought into direct contact with English philosophy, science, politics, and culture. Voltaire considered English thought and institutions the best in human history and devoted himself to their introduction in France on his return. His* Letters Concerning the English Nation *(1734) brought fame and notoriety. A warrant for his arrest forced him to flee once again. In fact, his career was marked by a series of legal difficulties and exiles: to Circey in Champagne in 1734, to Berlin and the court of Frederick II in 1750, to Geneva in 1752, and to Ferney in 1757. His lifelong commitments to freedom, toleration, reform, and empiricism made Voltaire one of the great figures of the Enlightenment.*

From *Letters Concerning the English Nation*, by F. Arouet, edited by Nicholas Cronk (Oxford: Oxford University Press, 1994), pp. 61–66.

*   *   *

Letter 13
On Mr. Locke

Perhaps no Man ever had a more judicious or more methodical Genius, or was a more acute Logician than Mr. *Locke,* and yet he was not deeply skill'd in the Mathematicks. This great Man could never subject himself to the tedious Fatigue of Calculations, nor to the dry Pursuit of Mathematical Truths, which do not at first present any sensible Objects to the Mind; and no one has given better Proofs than he, that 'tis possible for a Man to have a geometrical Head without the Assistance of Geometry. Before his Time, several great Philos-ophers had declar'd, in the most positive Terms, what the Soul of Man is; but as these absolutely knew nothing about it, they might very well be allow'd to differ entirely in opinion from one another.

In *Greece,* the infant Seat of Arts and of Errors, and where the Grandeur as well as Folly of the human Mind went such prodigious Lengths, the People us'd to reason about the Soul in the very same Manner as we do.

The divine *Anaxagoras,* in whose Honour an Altar was erected, for his having taught Mankind that the Sun was greater than *Peloponnesus,* that Snow was black, and that the Heavens were of Stone; affirm'd that the Soul was an aerial Spirit, but at the same Time immortal. *Diogenes,* (not he who was a cynical Philosopher after having coyn'd base Money) declar'd that the Soul was a Portion of the Substance of God; an Idea which we must confess was very sublime. *Epicurus* maintain'd that it was compos'd of Parts in the same Manner as the Body.

Aristotle who has been explain'd a thousand Ways, because he is unintelligible, was of the Opinion, according to some of his Disciples, that the Understanding in all Men is one and the same Substance.

The divine *Plato,* Master of the divine *Aristotle,* and the divine *Socrates* Master of the divine *Plato,* us'd-to say that the Soul was corporeal and eternal. No doubt but the Demon of *Socrates* had instructed him in the Nature of it. Some People, indeed, pretend, that a Man who boasted his being attended by a familiar Genius, must infallibly be either a Knave or a Madman, but this kind of People are seldom satisfied with any Thing but Reason.

With regard to the Fathers of the Church, several in the primitive Ages believ'd that the Soul was human, and the Angels and God corporeal. Men naturally improve upon every System. St. *Bernard,* as Father *Mabillon* confesses, taught that the Soul after Death does not see God in the celestial Regions, but converses with *Christ's* human Nature only. However, he was not believ'd this Time on his bare Word; the Adventure of the Crusade having a little sunk the Credit of his Oracles. Afterwards a thousand Schoolmen arose, such as the irrefragable Doctor, the subtil Doctor, the angelic Doctor, the seraphic Doctor, and the cherubic Doctor, who were all sure that they had a very clear and distinct Idea of the Soul, and yet wrote in such a Manner, that one would conclude they were resolv'd no one should understand a Word in their Writings. Our *Des Cartes,* born not to discover the Errors of Antiquity, but to substitute his own in the Room of them; and hurried away by that systematic Spirit which throws a Cloud over the Minds of the greatest Men, thought he had demonstrated that the Soul is the same Thing as Thought, in the same Manner as Matter, in his Opinion, is the same as Extension. He asserted, that Man thinks eternally, and that the Soul, at its coming into the Body, is

inform'd with the whole Series of metaphysical Notions; knowing God, infinite Space, possessing all abstract Ideas; in a Word, completely endued with the most sublime Lights, which it unhappily forgets at its issuing from the Womb.

Father *Malbranche,* in his sublime Illusions, not only admitted innate Ideas, but did not doubt of our living wholly in God, and that God is, as it were, our Soul.

Such a Multitude of Reasoners having written the Romance of the Soul, a Sage at last arose, who gave, with an Air of the greatest Modesty, the History of it. Mr. *Locke* has display'd the human Soul, in the same Manner as an excellent Anatomist explains the Springs of the human Body. He every where takes the Light of Physicks for his Guide. He sometimes presumes to speak affirmatively, but then he presumes also to doubt. Instead of concluding at once what we know not, he examines gradually what we wou'd know. He takes an Infant at the Instant of his Birth; he traces, Step by Step, the Progress of his Understanding; examines what Things he has in common with Beasts, and what he possesses above them. Above all he consults himself; the being conscious that he himself thinks.

I shall leave, says he, to those who know more of this Matter than my self, the examining whether the Soul exists before or after the Organization of our Bodies. But I confess that 'tis my Lot to be animated with one of those heavy Souls which do not think always; and I am even so unhappy as not to conceive, that 'tis more necessary the Soul should think perpetually, than that Bodies shou'd be for ever in Motion.

With regard to my self, I shall boast that I have the Honour to be as stupid in this Particular as Mr. *Locke.* No one shall ever make me believe, that I think always; and I am as little inclin'd as he cou'd be, to fancy that some Weeks after I was conceiv'd, I was a very learned Soul; knowing at that Time a thousand Things which I forgot at my Birth; and possessing when in the Womb, (tho' to no Manner of Purpose,) Knowledge which I lost the Instant I had occasion for it; and which I have never since been able to recover perfectly.

Mr. *Locke* after having destroy'd innate Ideas; after having fully renounc'd the Vanity of believing that we think always; after having laid down, from the most solid Principles, that Ideas enter the Mind through the Senses; having examin'd our simple and complex Ideas; having trac'd the human Mind through its several Operations; having shew'd that all the Languages in the World are imperfect, and the great Abuse that is made of Words every Moment; he at last comes to consider the Extent or rather the narrow Limits of human Knowledge. 'Twas in this Chapter he presum'd to advance, but very modestly, the following Words, 'We shall, perhaps, never be capable of knowing, whether a Being, purely material, thinks or not.' This sage Assertion was, by more Divines than one, look'd upon as a scandalous Declaration that the Soul is material and mortal. Some *Englishmen,* devout after their Way, sounded an Alarm. The Superstitious are the same in Society as Cowards in an Army; they themselves are seiz'd with a panic Fear, and communicate it to others. 'Twas loudly exclaim'd, that Mr. *Locke* intended to destroy Religion; nevertheless, Religion had nothing to do in the Affair, it being a Question purely Philosophical, altogether independent on Faith and Revelation. Mr. *Locke*'s Opponents needed but to examine, calmly and impartially, whether the declaring that Matter can think, implies a Contradiction; and whether God is able to communicate Thought to Matter. But Divines are too apt to begin their Declarations with saying, that God is offended when People differ from them in Opinion; in which they too much resemble the bad Poets, who us'd to declare publickly that *Boileau* spake irreverently of *Lewis* the Fourteenth, because he ridicul'd their stupid Productions. Bishop *Stillingfleet* got the Reputation of a calm and unprejudic'd Divine, because he did not expressly make use of injurious Terms in his Dispute with Mr. *Locke.* That Divine entred the Lists against him, but was defeated; for he argued as a Schoolman, and *Locke* as a Philosopher who was perfectly acquainted with the strong as well as the weak Side of the human Mind, and who fought with Weapons whose Temper he knew. If I might presume to give my Opinion on so delicate a Subject after Mr. *Locke,* I would say, that Men have long disputed on the Nature and the Immortality of the Soul. With regard to its Immortality tis impossible to give a Demonstration of it, since its Nature is still the Subject of Controversy; which however must be thoroughly understood, before a Person can be able to determine whether it be immortal or not. Human Reason is so little able, merely by its own Strength, to demonstrate the Immortality of the Soul, that 'twas absolutely necessary Religion should reveal it to us. 'Tis of Advantage to Society in general, that Mankind should believe the Soul to be immortal; Faith commands us to do this; nothing more is requir'd, and the Matter is clear'd up at once. But 'tis otherwise with respect to its Nature; 'tis of little Importance to Religion, which only requires the Soul to be virtuous, what Substance it may be made of. 'Tis a Clock which is given us to regulate, but the Artist has not told us of what Materials the Spring of this Clock is compos'd.

I am a Body and, I think, that's all I know of the Matter. Shall I ascribe to an unknown Cause, what I can so easily impute to the only second Cause I am acquainted with? Here all the School Philosophers interrupt me with their Arguments, and declare that there is only Extension and Solidity in Bodies, and that there they can have nothing but Motion and Figure. Now Motion, Figure, Extension and Solidity cannot form a Thought, and consequently the Soul cannot be Matter. All this, so often repeated, mighty Series of Reasoning, amounts to no more than this; I am absolutely ignorant what Matter is; I guess, but imperfectly, some Properties of it; now, I absolutely cannot tell whether these Properties may be joyn'd to Thought. As I therefore know nothing, I maintain positively that Matter cannot think. In this Manner do the Schools reason.

Mr. *Locke* address'd these Gentlemen in the candid, sincere Manner following. At least confess your selves to be as ignorant as I. Neither your Imaginations nor mine are able to comprehend in what manner a Body is susceptible of Ideas; and do you conceive better in what manner a Substance, of what kind soever, is susceptible of them? As you cannot comprehend either Matter or Spirit, why will you presume to assert any thing?

The superstitious Man comes afterwards, and declares, that all those must be burnt for the Good of their Souls, who so much as suspect that 'tis possible for the Body to think without any foreign Assistance. But what would these People say should they themselves be prov'd irreligious? And indeed, what Man can presume to assert, without being guilty at the same time of the greatest Impiety, that 'tis impossible for the Creator to form Matter with Thought and Sensation? Consider only, I beg you, what a Dilemma you bring yourselves into; you who confine in this Manner the Power of the Creator. Beasts have the same Organs, the same Sensations, the same Perceptions as we; they have Memory, and combine certain Ideas. In case it was not in the Power of God to animate Matter, and inform it with Sensation, the Consequence would be, either that Beasts are mere Machines, or that they have a spiritual Soul.

Methinks 'tis clearly evident that Beasts cannot be mere Machines, which I prove thus. God has given them the very same Organs of Sensation as to us: If therefore they have no Sensation, God has created a useless Thing; now according to your own Confession God does nothing in vain; he therefore did not create so many Organs of Sensation, merely for them to be uninform'd with this Faculty; consequently Beasts are not mere Machines. Beasts, according to your Assertion, cannot be animated with a spiritual Soul; you will therefore, in spight of your self, be reduc'd to this only Assertion, *viz.* that God has endued the Organs of Beasts, who are mere Matter, with the Faculties of Sensation and Perception, which you call Instinct in them. But why may not God if he pleases, communicate to our more delicate Organs, that Faculty of feeling, perceiving, and thinking, which we call human Reason? To whatever Side you turn, you are forc'd to acknowledge your own Ignorance, and the boundless Power of the Creator. Exclaim therefore no more against the sage, the modest Philosophy of Mr. *Locke,* which so far from interfering with Religion, would be of use to demonstrate the Truth of it, in case Religion wanted any such Support. For what Philosophy can be of a more religious Nature than that, which affirming nothing but what it con-

ceives clearly; and conscious of its own Weakness, declares that we must always have recourse to God in our examining of the first Principles.

Besides, we must not be apprehensive, that any philosophical Opinion will ever prejudice the Religion of a Country. Tho' our Demonstrations clash directly with our Mysteries, that's nothing to the Purpose, for the latter are not less rever'd upon that Account by our Christian Philosophers, who know very well that the Objects of Reason and those of Faith are of a very different Nature. Philosophers will never form a religious Sect, the Reason of which is, their Writings are not calculated for the Vulgar, and they themselves are free from Enthusiasm. If we divide Mankind into twenty Parts, 'twill be found that nineteen of these consist of Persons employ'd in manual Labour, who will never know that such a Man as Mr. *Locke* existed. In the remaining twentieth Part how few are Readers? And among such as are so, twenty amuse themselves with Romances to one who studies Philosophy. The thinking Part of Mankind are confin'd to a very small Number, and these will never disturb the Peace and Tranquillity of the World.

Neither *Montagne, Locke, Bayle, Spinoza, Hobbes,* the Lord *Shaftsbury, Collins* nor *Toland* lighted up the Firebrand of Discord in their Countries; this has generally been the Work of Divines, who being at first puff'd up with the Ambition of becoming Chiefs of a Sect, soon grew very desirous of being at the Head of a Party. But what do I say? All the Works of the modern Philosophers put together will never make so much Noise as even the Dispute which arose among the *Franciscans,* merely about the Fashion of their Sleeves and of their Cowls.

Letter XIV

ON *DES CARTES* AND SIR *ISAAC NEWTON.*

A Frenchman who arrives in *London,* will find Philosophy, like every Thing else, very much chang'd there. He had left the World a *plenum,* and he now finds it a *vacuum.* At *Paris* the Universe is seen, compos'd of Vortices of subtile Matter; but nothing like it is seen in *London.* In *France,* 'tis the Pressure of the Moon that causes the Tides; but in *England* 'tis the Sea that gravitates towards the Moon; so that when you think that the Moon should make it Flood with us, those Gentlemen fancy it should be Ebb, which, very unluckily, cannot be prov'd. For to be able to do this, 'tis necessary the Moon and the Tides should have been enquir'd into, at the very instant of the Creation.

You'll observe further, that the Sun, which in *France* is said to have nothing to do in the Affair, comes in here for very near a quarter of its Assistance. According to your *Cartesians,* every Thing is perform'd by an Impulsion, of which we have very little Notion; and according to Sir *Isaac Newton,* 'tis by an Attraction, the Cause of which is as much unknown to us. At *Paris* you imagine that the Earth is shap'd like a Melon, or of an oblique Figure; at *London* it has an oblate one. A *Cartesian* declares that Light exists in the Air; but a *Newtonian* asserts that it comes from the Sun in six Minutes and a half. The several Operations of your Chymistry are perform'd by Acids, Alkalies and subtile Matter; but Attraction prevails even in Chymistry among the *English.*

The very Essence of Things is totally chang'd. You neither are agreed upon the Definition of the Soul, nor on that of Matter. *Descartes,* as I observ'd in my last, maintains that the Soul is the same Thing with Thought, and Mr. *Locke* has given a pretty good Proof of the contrary.

Descartes asserts farther, that Extension alone constitutes Matter, but Sir *Isaac* adds Solidity to it. How furiously contradictory are these Opinions! *Non nostrum inter vos tantas componere lites.*

VIRGIL, Eclogue III.

'Tis not for us to end such great Disputes.

This famous *Newton,* this Destroyer of the *Cartesian* System, died in *March Anno* 1727. His Countrymen honour'd him in his Life-Time, and interr'd him as tho' he had been a King who had made his People happy.

The *English* read with the highest Satisfaction, and translated into their Tongue, the Elogium of

Sir *Isaac Newton,* which Mr. *de Fontenelle,* spoke in the Academy of Sciences. Mr. *de Fontenelle* presides as Judge over Philosophers; and the *English* expected his Decision, as a solemn Declaration of the Superiority of the *English* Philosophy over that of the *French.* But when 'twas found that this Gentleman had compar'd *Des Cartes* to Sir *Isaac,* the whole Royal Society in *London* rose up in Arms. So far from acquiescing with Mr. *Fontenelle's* Judgment, they criticis'd his Discourse. And even several (who however were not the ablest Philosophers in that Body) were offended at the Comparison; and for no other Reason but because *Des Cartes* was a *Frenchman.*

It must be confess'd that these two great Men differ'd very much in Conduct, in Fortune, and in Philosophy.

Nature had indulg'd *Des Cartes* a shining and strong Imagination, whence he became a very singular Person both in private Life, and in his Manner of Reasoning. This Imagination could not conceal itself even in his philosophical Works, which are every where adorn'd with very shining, ingenious Metaphors and Figures. Nature had almost made him a Poet; and indeed he wrote a Piece of Poetry for the Entertainment of *Christina* Queen of *Sweden,* which however was suppress'd in Honour to his Memory.

He embrac'd a Military Life for some Time, and afterwards becoming a complete Philosopher, he did not think the Passion of Love derogatory to his Character. He had by his Mistress a Daughter call'd *Froncine,* who died young, and was very much regretted by him. Thus he experienc'd every Passion incident to Mankind.

He was a long Time of Opinion, that it would be necessary for him to fly from the Society of his Fellow Creatures, and especially from his native Country, in order to enjoy the Happiness of cultivating his philosophical Studies in full Liberty.

Des Cartes was very right, for his Cotemporaries were not knowing enough to improve and enlighten his Understanding, and were capable of little else than of giving him Uneasiness.

He left *France* purely to go in search of Truth, which was then persecuted by the wretched

Philosophy of the Schools. However, he found that Reason was as much disguis'd and deprav'd in the Universities of *Holland,* into which he withdrew, as in his own Country. For at the Time that the *French* condemn'd the only Propositions of his Philosophy which were true, he was persecuted by the pretended Philosophers of *Holland,* who understood him no better; and who, having a nearer View of his Glory, hated his Person the more, so that he was oblig'd to leave *Utrecht. Des Cartes* was injuriously accus'd of being an Atheist, the last Refuge of religious Scandal: And he who had employ'd all the Sagacity and Penetration of his Genius, in searching for new Proofs of the Existence of a God, was suspected to believe there was no such Being.

Such a Persecution from all Sides, must necessarily suppose a most exalted Merit as well as a very distinguish'd Reputation, and indeed he possess'd both. Reason at that Time darted a Ray upon the World thro' the Gloom of the Schools, and the Prejudices of popular Superstition. At last his Name spread so universally, that the *French* were desirous of bringing him back into his native Country by Rewards, and accordingly offer'd him an annual Pension of a thousand Crowns. Upon these Hopes *Des Cartes* return'd to *France;* paid the Fees of his Patent, which was sold at that Time, but no Pension was settled upon him. Thus disappointed, he return'd to his Solitude in *North-Holland,* where he again pursued the Study of Philosophy, whilst the great *Galileo,* at fourscore Years of Age, was groaning in the Prisons of the Inquisition, only for having demonstrated the Earth's Motion.

At last *Des Cartes* was snatch'd from the World in the Flower of his Age at *Stockholm.* His Death was owing to a bad Regimen, and he expir'd in the Midst of some *Literati* who were his Enemies, and under the Hands of a Physician to whom he was odious.

The Progress of Sir *Isaac Newton*'s Life was quite different. He liv'd happy, and very much honour'd in his native Country, to the Age of fourscore and five Years.

'Twas his peculiar Felicity, not only to be born in a Country of Liberty, but in an Age when all scholastic Impertinencies were banish'd from the World. Reason alone was cultivated, and Mankind cou'd only be his Pupil, not his Enemy.

One very singular Difference in the Lives of these two great Men is, that Sir *Isaac,* during the long Course of Years he enjoy'd was never sensible to any Passion, was not subject to the common Frailties of Mankind, nor ever had any Commerce with Women; a Circumstance which was assur'd me by the Physician and Surgeon who attended him in his last Moments.

We may admire Sir *Isaac Newton* on this Occasion, but then we must not censure *Des Cartes.*

The Opinion that generally prevails in *England* with regard to these two Philosophers is, that the latter was a Dreamer, and the former a Sage.

Very few People in *England* read *Descartes,* whose Works indeed are now useless. On the other Side, but a small Number peruse those of Sir *Isaac,* because to do this the Student must be deeply skill'd in the Mathematicks, otherwise those Works will be unintelligible to him. But notwithstanding this, these great Men are the Subject of every One's Discourse. Sir *Isaac Newton* is allow'd every Advantage, whilst *Des Cartes* is not indulg'd a single one. According to some, 'tis to the former that we owe the Discovery of a *Vacuum,* that the Air is a heavy Body, and the Invention of Telescopes. In a Word, Sir *Isaac Newton* is here as the *Hercules* of fabulous Story, to whom the Ignorant ascrib'd all the Feats of ancient Heroes.

In a Critique that was made in *London* on Mr. *de Fontenelle*'s Discourse, the Writer presum'd to assert that *Des Cartes* was not a great Geometrician. Those who make such a Declaration may justly be reproach'd with flying in their Master's Face. *Des Cartes* extended the Limits of Geometry as far beyond the Place where he found them, as Sir *Isaac* did after him. The former first taught the Method of expressing Curves by Equations. This Geometry which, Thanks to him for it, is now grown common, was so abstruse in his Time, that not so much as one Professor would undertake to explain it; and *Schotten* in *Holland,* and *Format* in *France,* were the only Men who understood it.

He applied this geometrical and inventive Genius to Dioptricks, which, when treated of by him, became a new Art. And if he was mistaken in some Things, the Reason of that is, a Man who discovers a new Tract of Land cannot at once know all the Properties of the Soil. Those who come after him, and make these Lands fruitful, are at least oblig'd to him for the Discovery. I will not deny but that there are innumerable Errors in the rest of *Des Cartes*'s Works.

Geometry was a Guide he himself had in some Measure fashion'd, which would have conducted him safely thro' the several Paths of natural Philosophy. Nevertheless he at last abandon'd this Guide, and gave entirely into the Humour of forming Hypotheses; and then Philosophy was no more than an ingenious Romance, fit only to amuse the Ignorant. He was mistaken in the Nature of the Soul, in the Proofs of the Existence of a God, in Matter, in the Laws of Motion, and in the Nature of Light. He admitted innate Ideas, he invented new Elements, he created a World; he made Man according to his own Fancy; and 'tis justly said, that the Man of *Des Cartes* is in Fact that of *Des Cartes* only, very different from the real one.

He push'd his metaphysical Errors so far, as to declare that two and two make four, for no other Reason but because God would have it so. However, 'twill not be making him too great a Compliment if we affirm that he was valuable even in his Mistakes. He deceiv'd himself, but then it was at least in a methodical Way. He destroy'd all the absurd Chimæra's with which Youth had been infatuated for two thousand Years. He taught his Contemporaries how to reason, and enabled them to employ his own Weapons against himself. If *Des Cartes* did not pay in good Money, he however did great Service in crying down that of a base Alloy.

I indeed believe, that very few will presume to compare his Philosophy in any respect with that of Sir *Isaac Newton*. The former is an Essay, the latter a Master-Piece: But then the Man who first brought us to the Path of Truth, was perhaps as great a Genius as he who afterwards conducted us through it.

Des Cartes gave Sight to the Blind. These saw the Errors of Antiquity and of the Sciences. The Path he struck out is since become boundless. *Rohault*'s little Work was during some Years a complete System of Physicks; but now all the Transactions of the several Academies in *Europe* put together do not form so much as the Beginning of a System. In fathoming this Abyss no Bottom has been found. We are now to examine what Discoveries Sir *Isaac Newton* has made in it.

*　　*　　*

REVIEW QUESTIONS

1. How does Voltaire describe the scientific revolution?
2. What are its consequences?
3. What, according to Voltaire, was the particular contribution of John Locke?
4. Why does Voltaire single out Descartes and Newton?
5. What differentiates their methods?
6. Why, according to Voltaire, was Descartes persecuted and Newton not?

DAVID HUME

FROM *A Treatise of Human Nature*

David Hume (1711–1776) was born the younger son of a gentry family in Scotland. Though he attended the University of Edinburgh, he found formal education distasteful and applied himself instead to an intense program of reading. After a nervous breakdown in 1729 and an unsuccessful foray into business, Hume moved to France in 1734. During his stay there, which lasted until 1737, he devoted himself to studying and to writing A Treatise of Human Nature *(1739–1740). Though he later dismissed it as immature, it became his most influential work. In it, he introduced his notion of skepticism, which restricted human knowledge to the experience of ideas and impressions and denied the ability to verify their ultimate truth. Nonetheless, given the cautious, persistent exercise of reason, humankind could gather knowledge that was reliable and useful. As a historian, economist, and essayist, Hume was one of the most influential figures of the middle years of the Enlightenment.*

From *A Treatise of Human Nature*, by David Hume, edited by L. A. Selby-Biggs (Oxford: Clarendon Press, 1888), pp. xvii–xxiii.

Introduction

Nothing is more usual and more natural for those, who pretend to discover any thing new to the world in philosophy and the sciences, than to insinuate the praises of their own systems, by decrying all those, which have been advanced before them. And indeed were they content with lamenting that ignorance, which we still lie under in the most important questions, that can come before the tribunal of human reason, there are few, who have an acquaintance with the sciences, that would not readily agree with them. 'Tis easy for one of judgment and learning, to perceive the weak foundation even of those systems, which have obtained the greatest credit, and have carried their pretensions highest to accurate and profound reasoning. Principles taken upon trust, consequences lamely deduced from them, want of coherence in the parts, and of evidence in the whole, these are every where to be met with in the systems of the most eminent philosophers, and seem to have drawn disgrace upon philosophy itself.

Nor is there requir'd such profound knowledge to discover the present imperfect condition of the sciences, but even the rabble without doors may judge from the noise and clamour, which they hear, that all goes not well within. There is nothing which is not the subject of debate, and in which men of learning are not of contrary opinions. The most trivial question escapes not our controversy, and in the most momentous we are not able to give any certain decision. Disputes are multiplied, as if every thing was uncertain; and these disputes are managed with the greatest warmth, as if every thing was certain. Amidst all this bustle 'tis not reason, which carries the prize, but eloquence; and no man needs ever despair of gaining proselytes to the most extravagant hypothesis, who has art enough to represent it in any favourable colours. The victory is not gained by the men at arms, who manage the pike and the sword; but by the trumpeters, drummers, and musicians of the army.

From hence in my opinion arises that common prejudice against metaphysical reasonings of all kinds, even amongst those, who profess themselves scholars, and have a just value for every other part of literature. By metaphysical reasonings, they do not understand those on any particular branch of science, but every kind of argument, which is any way abstruse, and requires some attention to be comprehended. We have so often lost our labour in such researches, that we commonly reject them without hesitation, and resolve, if we must for ever be a prey to errors and delusions, that they shall at least be natural and entertaining. And indeed nothing but the most determined scepticism, along with a great degree of indolence, can justify this aversion to metaphysics. For if truth be at all within the reach of human capacity, 'tis certain it must lie very deep and abstruse; and to hope we shall arrive at it without pains, while the greatest geniuses have failed with the utmost pains, must certainly be esteemed sufficiently vain and presumptuous. I pretend to no such advantage in the philosophy I am going to unfold, and would esteem it a strong presumption against it, were it so very easy and obvious.

'Tis evident, that all the sciences have a relation, greater or less, to human nature; and that however wide any of them may seem to run from it, they still return back by one passage or another. Even *Mathematics, Natural Philosophy, and Natural Religion,* are in some measure dependent on the science of Man; since they lie under the cognizance of men, and are judged of by their powers and faculties. 'Tis impossible to tell what changes and improvements we might make in these sciences were we thoroughly acquainted with the extent and force of human understanding, and cou'd explain the nature of the ideas we employ, and of the operations we perform in our reasonings. And these improvements are the more to be hoped for in natural religion, as it is not content with instructing us in the nature of superior powers, but carries its views farther, to their disposition towards us, and our duties towards them; and consequently we ourselves are not only the beings, that reason, but also one of the objects, concerning which we reason.

If therefore the sciences of Mathematics, Natural Philosophy, and Natural Religion, have such a dependence on the knowledge of man, what may be expected in the other sciences, whose connexion with human nature is more close and intimate? The sole end of logic is to explain the principles and operations of our reasoning faculty, and the nature of our ideas: morals and criticism regard our tastes and sentiments: and politics consider men as united in society, and dependent on each other. In these four sciences of *Logic, Morals, Criticism, and Politics,* is comprehended almost every thing, which it can any way import us to be acquainted with, or which can tend either to the improvement or ornament of the human mind.

Here then is the only expedient, from which we can hope for success in our philosophical researches, to leave the tedious ling'ring method, which we have hitherto followed, and instead of taking now and then a castle or village on the frontier, to march up directly to the capital or center of these sciences, to human nature itself; which being once masters of, we may every where else hope for an easy victory. From this station we may extend our conquests over all those sciences, which more intimately concern human life, and may afterwards proceed at leisure to discover more fully those, which are the objects of pure curiosity. There is no question of importance, whose decision is not compriz'd in the science of man; and there is none, which can be decided with any certainty, before we become acquainted with that science. In pretending therefore to explain the principles of human nature, we in effect propose a compleat system of the sciences, built on a foundation almost entirely new, and the only one upon which they can stand with any security.

And as the science of man is the only solid foundation for the other sciences, so the only solid foundation we can give to this science itself must be laid on experience and observation. 'Tis no astonishing reflection to consider, that the application of experimental philosophy to moral subjects should come after that to natural at the distance of above a whole century; since we find in fact, that there was about the same interval betwixt the origins of these sciences; and that reckoning from Thales to Socrates, the space of time is nearly equal to that betwixt my Lord Bacon and some late philosophers in *England,* who have begun to put the science of man on a new footing, and have engaged the attention, and excited the curiosity of the public. So true it is, that however other nations may rival us in poetry, and excel us in some other agreeable arts, the improvements in reason and philosophy can only be owing to a land of toleration and of liberty.

Nor ought we to think, that this latter improvement in the science of man will do less honour to our native country than the former in natural philosophy, but ought rather to esteem it a greater glory, upon account of the greater importance of that science, as well as the necessity it lay under of such a reformation. For to me it seems evident, that the essence of the mind being equally unknown to us with that of external bodies, it must be equally impossible to form any notion of its powers and qualities otherwise than from careful and exact experiments, and the observation of those particular effects, which result from its different circumstances and situations. And tho' we must endeavour to render all our principles as universal as possible, by tracing up our experiments to the utmost, and explaining all effects from the simplest and fewest causes, 'tis still certain we cannot go beyond experience; and any hypothesis, that pretends to discover the ultimate original qualities of human nature, ought at first to be rejected as presumptuous and chimerical.

I do not think a philosopher, who would apply himself so earnestly to the explaining the ultimate principles of the soul, would show himself a great master in that very science of human nature, which he pretends to explain, or very knowing in what is naturally satisfactory to the mind of man. For nothing is more certain, than that despair has almost the same effect upon us with enjoyment, and that we are no sooner acquainted with the impossibility of satisfying any desire, than the desire itself vanishes. When we see, that we have arrived at the utmost extent of human reason, we sit down contented; tho' we be perfectly satisfied in the main of

our ignorance, and perceive that we can give no reason for our most general and most refined principles, beside our experience of their reality; which is the reason of the mere vulgar, and what it required no study at first to have discovered for the most particular and most extraordinary phaenomenon. And as this impossibility of making any farther progress is enough to satisfy the reader, so the writer may derive a more delicate satisfaction from the free confession of his ignorance, and from his prudence in avoiding that error, into which so many have fallen, of imposing their conjectures and hypotheses on the world for the most certain principles. When this mutual contentment and satisfaction can be obtained betwixt the master and scholar, I know not what more we can require of our philosophy.

But if this impossibility of explaining ultimate principles should be esteemed a defect in the science of man, I will venture to affirm, that 'tis a defect common to it with all the sciences, and all the arts, in which we can employ ourselves, whether they be such as are cultivated in the schools of the philosophers, or practised in the shops of the meanest artizans. None of them can go beyond experience, or establish any principles which are not founded on that authority. Moral philosophy has, indeed, this peculiar disadvantage, which is not found in natural, that in collecting its experiments, it cannot make them purposely, with premeditation, and after such a manner as to satisfy itself concerning every particular difficulty which may arise. When I am at a loss to know the effects of one body upon another in any situation, I need only put them in that situation, and observe what results from it. But should I endeavour to clear up after the same manner any doubt in moral philosophy, by placing myself in the same case with that which I consider, 'tis evident this reflection and premeditation would so disturb the operation of my natural principles, as must render it impossible to form any just conclusion from the phaenomenon. We must therefore glean up our experiments in this science from a cautious observation of human life, and take them as they appear in the common course of the world, by men's behaviour in company, in affairs, and in their pleasures. Where experiments of this kind are judiciously collected and compared, we may hope to establish on them a science, which will not be inferior in certainty, and will be much superior in utility to any other of human comprehension.

*   *   *

REVIEW QUESTIONS

1. To what does Hume attribute all the disputes in the sciences?
2. According to Hume, what is the science of man? What are its methods and goals?
3. Why must one understand human reason before studying the science of man?

BARON DE LA BRÈDE ET DE MONTESQUIEU

FROM *The Spirit of Laws*

Charles-Louis de Secondat, baron de La Brède et de Montesquieu (1689–1755), was a French philosopher, historian, and satirist. He was born at the family chateau of La Brède near Bordeaux. His great-grandfather, a Calvinist, had been rewarded with a title of nobility for his service to Henry IV. In the next generation, however, the family had converted to Catholicism and had entered the judicial nobility by purchasing offices in the Parlement of Bordeaux. Charles-Louis de Secondat inherited one of these offices, that of presiding judge of the criminal division, in 1712 and held it for eleven years. Montesquieu studied law at the University of Bordeaux and married Jeanne de Lartique, a practicing Calvinist who risked persecution for her faith. This and his own background may explain Montesquieu's lifelong championship of religious toleration. He entered the literary world with the publication of his Persian Letters *(1721). Shortly thereafter Montesquieu moved to Paris and joined the intellectual world of the salon. His most influential work, at least among his contemporaries, was* The Spirit of Laws *(1748). By 1750, twenty-two editions had appeared, and it had been translated into every major European language. Montesquieu explored the role of law in shaping political society and sought theoretical and practical responses to the problem of despotism. He envisioned political order as a human body, possessed of a dynamic balance among its various parts. A healthy political order contained inner mechanisms to maintain its balance. An ideal example of such separation and balance of power was the English system of monarch and Parliament. These ideas made Montesquieu one of the most widely read and influential figures of the Enlightenment.*

From *The Spirit of Laws*, vol. 1, translated by Thomas Nugent (London: Bell, 1901).

Book XII
Of the Laws that Establish Political Liberty, in Relation to the Subject

I. It is not sufficient to have treated of political liberty in relation to the constitution; we must examine it likewise in the relation it bears to the subject.

We have observed that in the former case it arises from a certain distribution of the three powers; but in the latter we must consider it in another light. It consists in security, or in the opinion people have of their country.

The constitution may happen to be free, and the subject not. The subject may be free, and not the constitution. In those cases, the constitution will be free by right, and not in fact; the subject will be free in fact, and not by right.

It is the disposition only of the laws, and even of the fundamental laws, that constitutes liberty in relation to the constitution. But as it regards the subject: manners, customs, or received examples may give rise to it, and particular civil laws may encourage it, as we shall presently observe.

Further, as in most states liberty is more checked or depressed than their constitution requires, it is proper to treat of the particular laws that in each constitution are apt to assist or check the principle of liberty which each state is capable of receiving.

II. Philosophic liberty consists in the free exercise of the will; or at least, if we must speak agreeably to all systems, in an opinion that we have the free exercise of our will. Political liberty consists in securing, or, at least, in the opinion that we enjoy security.

This security is never more dangerously attacked than in public or private accusations. It is, therefore, on the goodness of criminal laws that the liberty of the subject principally depends.

Criminal laws did not receive their full perfection all at once. Even in places where liberty has been most sought after, it has not been always found. Aristotle informs us that at Cumae the parents of the accuser might be witnesses. So imperfect was the law under the kings of Rome, that Servius Tullius pronounced sentence against the children of Ancus Martius, who were charged with having assassinated the king, his father-in-law. Under the first kings of France, Clotarius made a law that nobody should be condemned without being heard, which shows that a contrary custom had prevailed in some particular case or among some barbarous people. It was Charondas that first established penalties against false witnesses. When the subject has no fence to secure his innocence, he has none for his liberty.

The knowledge already acquired in some countries, or that may be hereafter attained in others, concerning the surest rules to be observed in criminal judgments, is more interesting to mankind than any other thing in the world.

Liberty can be founded on the practice of this knowledge only; and supposing a state to have the best laws imaginable in this respect, a person tried under that state, and condemned to be hanged the next day, would have much more liberty than a pasha enjoys in Turkey.

Those laws which condemn a man to death on the deposition of a single witness are fatal to liberty. In reason there should be two, because a witness who affirms, and the accused who denies, make an equal balance, and a third must incline the scale.

The Greeks and Romans required one voice more to condemn; but our French laws insist upon two. The Greeks pretend that their custom was established by the gods; but this more justly may be said of ours.

III. Liberty is in perfection when criminal laws derive each punishment from the particular nature of the crime. There are then no arbitrary decisions; the punishment does not flow from the capriciousness of the legislator, but from the very nature of the thing; and man uses no violence to man.

There are four sorts of crimes. Those of the first species are prejudicial to religion, the second to morals, the third to the public tranquillity, and the fourth to the security of the subject. The punishments inflicted for these crimes ought to proceed from the nature of each of these species.

In the class of crimes that concern religion, I rank only those which attack it directly, such as all simple sacrileges. For as to crimes that disturb the exercise of it, they are of the nature of those which prejudice the tranquillity or security of the subject, and ought to be referred to those classes.

In order to derive the punishment of simple sacrileges from the nature of the thing, it should consist in depriving people of the advantages conferred by religion in expelling them out of the temples, in a temporary or perpetual exclusion from the society of the faithful, in shunning their presence, in execrations, comminations, and conjurations.

In things that prejudice the tranquillity or security of the state, secret actions are subject to human jurisdiction. But in those which offend the Deity, where there is no public act, there can be no criminal matter; the whole passes between man and God, who knows the measure and time of his vengeance. Now, if magistrates confounding things should inquire also into hidden sacrileges, this inquisition would be directed to a kind of action that does not at all require it; the liberty of the subject would be subverted by arming the zeal of timorous as well as of presumptuous consciences against him.

The mischief arises from a notion which some people have entertained of revenging the cause of the Deity. But we must honor the Deity and leave him to avenge his own cause. And, indeed, were we to be directed by such a notion, where would be the end of punishments? If human laws are to avenge the cause of an infinite Being, they will be directed by his infinity, and not by the weakness, ignorance, and caprice of man.

A historian of Provence relates a fact which furnishes us with an excellent description of the consequences that may arise in weak capacities from the notion of avenging the Deity's cause. A Jew was accused of having blasphemed against the Virgin Mary, and upon conviction was condemned to be flayed alive. A strange spectacle was then exhibited: gentlemen masked, with knives in their hands, mounted the scaffold, and drove away the executioner, in order to be the avengers themselves of the honor of the blessed Virgin. I do not here choose to anticipate the reflections of the reader.

The second class consists of those crimes which are prejudicial to morals. Such is the violation of public or private continence—that is, of the police

directing the manner in which the pleasure annexed to the conjunction of the sexes is to be enjoyed. The punishment of those crimes ought to be also derived from the nature of the thing; the privation of such advantages as society has attached to the purity of morals, fines, shame, necessity of concealment, public infamy, expulsion from home and society, and, in fine, all such punishments as belong to a corrective jurisdiction, are sufficient to repress the temerity of the two sexes. In effect these things are less founded on malice than on carelessness and self-neglect.

We speak here of none but crimes which relate merely to morals, for as to those that are also prejudicial to the public security, such as rapes, they belong to the fourth species.

The crimes of the third class are those which disturb the public tranquillity. The punishments ought therefore to be derived from the nature of the thing, and to be in relation to this tranquillity; such as imprisonment, exile, and other like chastisements, proper for reclaiming turbulent spirits, and obliging them to conform to the established order.

I confine those crimes that injure the public tranquillity to things which imply a bare offense against the police; for as to those which by disturbing the public peace attack at the same time the security of the subject, they ought to be ranked in the fourth class.

The punishments inflicted upon the latter crimes are such as are properly distinguished by that name. They are a kind of retaliation, by which the society refuses security to a member who has actually or intentionally deprived another of his security. These punishments are derived from the nature of the thing, founded on reason, and drawn from the very source of good and evil. A man deserves death when he has violated the security of the subject so far as to deprive, or attempt to deprive, another man of his life. This punishment of death is the remedy, as it were, of a sick society. When there is a breach of security with regard to property, there may be some reasons for inflicting a capital punishment; but it would be much better, and perhaps more natural, that crimes committed against the security of property should be punished with the loss of property; and this ought, indeed, to be the case if men's fortunes were common or equal. But as those who have no property of their own are generally the readiest to attack that of others, it has been found necessary, instead of a pecuniary, to substitute a corporal, punishment.

All that I have here advanced is founded in Nature, and extremely favorable to the liberty of the subject.

IV. It is an important maxim that we ought to be very circumspect in the prosecution of witchcraft and heresy. The accusation of these two crimes may be vastly injurious to liberty, and productive of infinite oppression, if the legislator knows not how to set bounds to it. For as it does not directly point at a person's actions, but at his character, it grows dangerous in proportion to the ignorance of the people; and then a man is sure to be always in danger, because the most exceptional conduct, the purest morals, and the constant practice of every duty in life are not a sufficient security against the suspicion of his being guilty of the like crimes.

Under Manuel Comnenus, the Protestator was accused of having conspired against the emperor, and of having employed for that purpose some secrets that render men invisible. It is mentioned in the life of this emperor that Aaron was detected as he was poring over a book of Solomon's, the reading of which was sufficient to conjure up whole legions of devils. Now, by supposing a power in witchcraft to rouse the infernal spirits to arms, people look upon a man whom they call a sorcerer as the person in the world most likely to disturb and subvert society, and of course they are disposed to punish him with the utmost severity.

But their indignation increases when witchcraft is supposed to have the power of subverting religion. The history of Constantinople informs us that in consequence of a revelation made to a bishop of a miracle having ceased because of the magic practices of a certain person, both that person and his son were put to death. On how many surprising things did not this single crime depend!—that revelations should not be uncommon, that the bishop should be favored with one, that it was real, that there had been a miracle in the case, that this miracle had ceased, that there was an art magic, that

magic could subvert religion, that this particular person was a magician, and, in fine, that he had committed that magic act.

The Emperor Theodorus Lascarus attributed his illness to witchcraft. Those who were accused of this crime had no other resource left than to handle a red-hot iron without being hurt. Thus among the Greeks a person ought to have been a sorcerer to be able to clear himself of the imputation of witchcraft. Such was the excess of their stupidity that to the most dubious crime in the world they joined the most dubious proofs of innocence.

Under the reign of Philip the Long, the Jews were expelled from France, being accused of having poisoned the springs with their lepers. So absurd an accusation ought to make us doubt all those that are founded on public hatred.

I have not here asserted that heresy ought not to be punished; I said only that we ought to be extremely circumspect in punishing it.

V. God forbid that I should have the least inclination to diminish the public horror against a crime which religion, morality, and civil government equally condemn. It ought to be proscribed, were it only for its communicating to one sex the weaknesses of the other, and for leading people by a scandalous prostitution of their youth to an ignominious old age. What I shall say concerning it will in no way diminish its infamy, being leveled only against the tyranny that may abuse the very horror we ought to have against the vice.

As a natural circumstance of this crime is secrecy, there are frequent instances of its having been punished by legislators upon the deposition of a child. This was opening a very wide door to calumny. "Justinian," says Procopius, "published a law against this crime; he ordered an inquiry to be made not only against those who were guilty of it, after the enacting of that law, but even before. The deposition of a single witness, sometimes of a child, sometimes of a slave, was sufficient, especially against such as were rich, and against those of the green faction."

It is very odd that these three crimes—witchcraft, heresy, and that against Nature, of which the first might easily be proved not to exist, the second to be susceptible of an infinite number of distinctions, interpretations, and limitations, the third to be often obscure and uncertain—it is very odd, I say, that these three crimes should among us be punished with fire.

I may venture to affirm that the crime against Nature will never make any great progress in society, unless people are prompted to it by some particular custom, as among the Greeks, where the youths of that country performed all their exercises naked; as among us, where domestic education is disused; as among the Asiatics, where particular persons have a great number of women whom they despise, while others can have none at all. Let there be no customs preparatory to this crime; let it, like every other violation of morals, be severely proscribed by the civil magistrate; and Nature will soon defend or resume her rights. Nature, that fond, that indulgent parent, has strewed her pleasures with a bounteous hand, and while she fills us with delights she prepares us, by means of our issue, in whom we see ourselves, as it were, reproduced—she prepares us, I say, for future satisfactions of a more exquisite kind than those very delights.

VI. It is determined by the laws of China that whosoever shows any disrespect to the emperor is to be punished with death. As they do not mention in what this disrespect consists, everything may furnish a pretext to take away a man's life, and to exterminate any family whatsoever.

Two persons of that country who were employed to write the court gazette, having inserted some circumstances relating to a certain fact that was not true, it was pretended that to tell a lie in the court gazette was a disrespect shown to the court, in consequence of which they were put to death. A prince of the blood having inadvertently made some mark on a memorial signed with the red pencil by the emperor, it was determined that he had behaved disrespectfully to the sovereign, which occasioned one of the most terrible persecutions against that family that ever was recorded in history.

If the crime of high treason be indeterminate, this alone is sufficient to make the government degenerate into arbitrary power. I shall descant more largely on this subject when I come to treat of the composition of laws.

VII. It is likewise a shocking abuse to give the appellation of high treason to an action that does not deserve it. By an imperial law it was decreed that those who called in question the prince's judgment, or doubted the merit of such as he had chosen for a public office, should be prosecuted as guilty of sacrilege. Surely it was the cabinet council and the prince's favorites who invented that crime. By another law it was determined that whosoever made any attempt to injure the ministers and officers belonging to the sovereign should be deemed guilty of high treason, as if he had attempted to injure the sovereign himself. This law is owing to two princes remarkable for their weaknesses—princes who were led by their ministers as flocks by shepherds; princes who were slaves in the palace, children in the council, strangers to the army; princes, in fine, who preserved their authority only by giving it away every day. Some of those favorites conspired against their sovereigns. Nay, they did more, they conspired against the empire—they called in barbarous nations; and when the emperors wanted to stop their progress the state was so enfeebled as to be under a necessity of infringing the law, and of exposing itself to the crime of high treason in order to punish those favorites.

And yet this is the very law which the judge of Monsieur de Cinq-Mars built upon when endeavoring to prove that the latter was guilty of the crime of high treason for attempting to remove Cardinal Richelieu from the ministry. He says: "Crimes that aim at the persons of ministers are deemed by the imperial constitutions of equal consequence with those which are leveled against the emperor's own person. A minister discharges his duty to his prince and to his country; to attempt, therefore, to remove him is endeavoring to deprive the former one of his arms, and the latter of part of its power." It is impossible for the meanest tools of power to express themselves in more servile language.

By another law of Valentinian, Theodosius, and Arcadius, false coiners are declared guilty of high treason. But is not this confounding the ideas of things? Is not the very horror of high treason diminished by giving that name to another crime?

Paulinus having written to the Emperor Alexander that "he was preparing to prosecute for high treason a judge who had decided contrary to his edict," the emperor answered that "under his reign there was no such thing as indirect high treason."

Faustinian wrote to the same emperor, that as he had sworn by the prince's life never to pardon his slave, he found himself thereby obliged to perpetuate his wrath, lest he should incur the guilt of *laesa majestas*. Upon which the emperor made answer, "Your fears are groundless, and you are a stranger to my principles."

It was determined by a senatus-consultum that whosoever melted down any of the emperor's statues which happened to be rejected should not be deemed guilty of high treason. The Emperors Severus and Antoninus wrote to Pontius that those who sold unconsecrated statues of the emperor should not be charged with high treason. The same princes wrote to Julius Cassianus that if a person in flinging a stone should by chance strike one of the emperor's statues he should not be liable to a prosecution for high treason. The Julian law requires this sort of limitations; for in virtue of this law the crime of high treason was charged not only upon those who melted down the emperor's statues, but likewise on those who committed any suchlike action, which made it an arbitrary crime. When a number of crimes of *laesa majestas* had been established, they were obliged to distinguish the several sorts. Hence Ulpian, the civilian, after saying that the accusation of *laesa majestas* did not die with the criminal, adds that this does not relate to all the treasonable acts established by the Julian law, but only to that which implies an attempt against the empire, or against the emperor's life.

There was a law passed in England under Henry VIII, by which whoever predicted the king's death was declared guilty of high treason. This law was extremely vague; the terror of despotic power is so great that it recoils upon those who exercise it. In this king's last illness, the physicians would not venture to say he was in danger; and surely they acted very right.

VIII. Marsyas dreamed that he had cut Dionysius' throat. Dionysius put him to death, pretending that he would never have dreamed of such a thing by night if he had not thought of it by day. This was a most tyrannical action, for though it had been the subject of his thoughts, yet he had made no attempt toward it. The laws do not take upon them to punish any other than overt acts.

IX. Nothing renders the crime of high treason more arbitrary than declaring people guilty of it for indiscreet speeches. Speech is so subject to interpretation; there is so great a difference between indiscretion and malice; and frequently so little is there of the latter in the freedom of expression, that the law can hardly subject people to a capital punishment for words unless it expressly declares what words they are.

Words do not constitute an overt act; they remain only in idea. When considered by themselves, they have generally no determinate signification, for this depends on the tone in which they are uttered. It often happens that in repeating the same words they have not the same meaning; this depends on their connection with other things, and sometimes more is signified by silence than by any expression whatever. Since there can be nothing so equivocal and ambiguous as all this, how is it possible to convert it into a crime of high treason? Wherever this law is established, there is an end not only of liberty, but even of its very shadow.

In the manifesto of the late Czarina against the family of the Dolgorukis, one of these princes is condemned to death for having uttered some indecent words concerning her person; another, for having maliciously interpreted her imperial laws, and for having offended her sacred person by disrespectful expressions.

Not that I pretend to diminish the just indignation of the public against those who presume to stain the glory of their sovereign; what I mean is, that if despotic princes are willing to moderate their power, a milder chastisement would be more proper on those occasions than the charge of high treason—a thing always terrible even to innocence itself.

Overt acts do not happen every day; they are exposed to the eye of the public, and a false charge with regard to matters of fact may be easily detected. Words carried into action assume the nature of that action. Thus a man who goes into a public marketplace to incite the subject to revolt incurs the guilt of high treason, because the words are joined to the action, and partake of its nature. It is not the words that are punished, but an action in which words are employed. They do not become criminal but when they are annexed to a criminal action; everything is confounded if words are construed into a capital crime, instead of considering them only as a mark of that crime.

The Emperors Theodosius, Arcadius, and Honorius wrote thus to Rufinus, who was *praefectus praetorio*: "Though a man should happen to speak amiss of our person or government, we do not intend to punish him. If he has spoken through levity, we must despise him; if through folly, we must pity him; and if he wrongs us, we must forgive him. Therefore, leaving things as they are, you are to inform us accordingly, that we may be able to judge of words by persons, and that we may duly consider whether we ought to punish or overlook them."

X. In writings there is something more permanent than in words, but when they are in no way preparative to high treason they cannot amount to that charge. . . .

*   *   *

REVIEW QUESTIONS

1. What kinds of liberty does Montesquieu distinguish?
2. On what basis does he make his distinctions?
3. What is the relation between liberty and reason?
4. What is the relation between crime and nature?
5. What role does a concept of nature play in Montesquieu's differentiation of crimes?

CESARE, MARCHESE DI BECCARIA BONESANA

FROM *An Essay on Crimes and Punishments*

Cesare, marchese di Beccaria Bonesana (1738–1794), was an economist and criminologist and one of the best-known Italian thinkers of the Enlightenment. Born the son of a Milanese aristocrat, he was educated by Jesuits and received a degree in law from the University of Pavia in 1755. He gravitated into the enlightened circle around Count Pietro Verri, who encouraged him in 1763 to take up the study of criminal law. Beccaria's great work, An Essay on Crimes and Punishments, *appeared a year later. Arguing on the basis of utilitarian principles—the greatest good for the greatest number—he excoriated the barbaric and ineffective legal practices of his day, such as judicial torture, extreme punishment, and magisterial corruption. The effectiveness of the law, he reasoned, depended ultimately on its certainty rather than its severity. Thus, torture should be abolished and punishments made proportional to the crimes. For the same reason Beccaria became the first modern writer to advocate the abolition of capital punishment. The work proved tremendously influential, guiding legal reforms across Europe and winning champions such as Jeremy Bentham.*

From *An Essay on Crimes and Punishments*, by Cesare Beccaria Bonesana (Stanford: Academic Reprints, 1953), pp. 15–19, 47, 59–67, 95–96.

Chapter 1
Of the Origin of Punishments

Laws are the conditions under which men, naturally independent, united themselves in society. Weary of living in a continual state of war, and of enjoying a liberty, which became of little value, from the uncertainty of its duration, they sacrificed one part of it, to enjoy the rest in peace and security. The sum of all these portions of the liberty of each individual constituted the sovereignty of a nation and was deposited in the hands of the sovereign, as the lawful administrator. But it was not sufficient only to establish this deposit; it was also necessary to defend it from the usurpation of each individual, who will always endeavour to take away from the mass, not only his own portion, but to encroach on that of others. Some motives therefore, that strike the senses were necessary to prevent the despotism of each individual from plunging society into its former chaos. Such motives are the punishments established against the infractors of the laws. I say that motives of this kind are necessary; because experience shows, that the multitude adopt no established principle of conduct; and because society is prevented from approaching to that dissolution, (to which, as well as all other parts of the physical and moral world, it naturally tends,) only by motives that are the immediate objects of sense, and which being continually presented to the mind, are sufficient to counterbalance the effects of the passions of the individual which oppose the general good. Neither the power of eloquence nor the sublimest truths are sufficient to restrain, for any length of time, those passions which are excited by the lively impressions of present objects.

Chapter 2
Of the Right to Punish

Every punishment which does not arise from absolute necessity, says the great Montesquieu, is tyrannical. A proposition which may be made more general thus: every act of authority of one man over another, for which there is not an absolute necessity, is tyrannical. It is upon this then that the sovereign's right to punish crimes is founded; that is, upon the necessity of defending the public liberty, entrusted to his care, from the usurpation of individuals; and punishments are just in proportion, as the liberty, preserved by the sovereign, is sacred and valuable.

Let us consult the human heart, and there we shall find the foundation of the sovereign's right to punish, for no advantage in moral policy can be lasting which is not founded on the indelible sentiments of the heart of man. Whatever law deviates from this principle will always meet with a resistance which will destroy it in the end; for the smallest force continually applied will overcome the most violent motion communicated to bodies.

No man ever gave up his liberty merely for the good of the public. Such a chimera exists only in romances. Every individual wishes, if possible, to be exempt from the compacts that bind the rest of mankind.

The multiplication of mankind, though slow, being too great, for the means which the earth, in its natural state, offered to satisfy necessities which every day became more numerous, obliged men to separate again, and form new societies. These naturally opposed the first, and a state of war was transferred from individuals to nations.

Thus it was necessity that forced men to give up a part of their liberty. It is certain, then, that every individual would choose to put into the public stock the smallest portion possible, as much only as was sufficient to engage others to defend it. The aggregate of these, the smallest portions possible, forms the right of punishing; all that extends beyond this, is abuse, not justice.

Observe that by *justice* I understand nothing more than that bond which is necessary to keep the interest of individuals united, without which men would return to their original state of barbarity. All punishments which exceed the necessity of preserving this bond are in their nature unjust. We should be cautious how we associate with the word *justice* an idea of any thing real, such as a physical power, or a being that actually exists. I do not, by any means, speak of the justice of God, which is of another kind, and refers immediately to rewards and punishments in a life to come.

*   *   *

Chapter 12
Of the Intent of Punishments

From the foregoing considerations it is evident that the intent of punishments is not to torment a sensible being, nor to undo a crime already committed. Is it possible that torments and useless cruelty, the instrument of furious fanaticism or the impotency of tyrants, can be authorised by a political body, which, so far from being influenced by passion, should be the cool moderator of the passions of individuals? Can the groans of a tortured wretch recall the time past, or reverse the crime he has committed?

The end of punishment, therefore, is no other than to prevent the criminal from doing further injury to society, and to prevent others from committing the like offence. Such punishments, therefore, and such a mode of inflicting them, ought to be chosen, as will make the strongest and most lasting impressions on the minds of others, with the least torment to the body of the criminal.

*   *   *

Chapter 16
Of Torture

The torture of a criminal during the course of his trial is a cruelty consecrated by custom in most nations. It is used with an intent either to make him confess his crime, or to explain some contradictions into which he had been led during his examination, or discover his accomplices, or for some kind of metaphysical and incomprehensible purgation of infamy, or, finally, in order to discover other crimes of which he is not accused, but of which he may be guilty.

No man can be judged a criminal until he be found guilty nor can society take from him the public protection until it have been proved that he has violated the conditions on which it was granted. What right, then, but that of power, can authorise the punishment of a citizen so long as there remains any doubt of his guilt? This dilemma is frequent. Either he is guilty, or not guilty. If guilty, he should only suffer the punishment ordained by the laws, and torture becomes useless, as his confession is unnecessary. If he be not guilty, you torture the innocent; for, in the eye of the law, every man is innocent whose crime has not been proved. Besides, it is confounding all relations to expect that a man should be both the accuser and accused; and that pain should be the test of truth, as if truth resided in the muscles and fibres of a wretch in torture. By this method the robust will escape, and the feeble be condemned. These are the inconveniencies of this pretended test of truth, worthy only of a cannibal, and which the Romans, in many respects barbarous, and whose savage virtue has been too much admired, reserved for the slaves alone.

What is the political intention of punishments? To terrify and be an example to others. Is this intention answered by thus privately torturing the guilty and the innocent? It is doubtless of importance that no crime should remain unpunished; but it is useless to make a public example of the author of a crime hid in darkness. A crime already committed, and for which there can be no remedy, can only be punished by a political society with an intention that no hopes of impunity should induce others to commit the same. If it be true, that the number of those who from fear or virtue respect the laws is greater than of those by whom they are violated, the risk of torturing an innocent person is greater, as there is a greater probability that, *cæteris paribus,* an individual hath observed, than that he hath infringed the laws.

There is another ridiculous motive for torture, namely, *to purge a man from infamy.* Ought such an abuse to be tolerated in the eighteenth century? Can pain, which is a sensation, have any connection with a moral sentiment, a matter of opinion? Perhaps the rack may be considered as the refiner's furnace.

It is not difficult to trace this senseless law to its origin; for an absurdity, adopted by a whole nation, must have some affinity with other ideas established and respected by the same nation. This custom seems to be the offspring of religion, by which mankind, in all nations and in all ages, are so generally influenced. We are taught by our infallible church, that those stains of sin contracted through human frailty, and which have not deserved the eternal anger of the Almighty, are to be purged away in another life by an incomprehensible fire. Now infamy is a stain, and if the punishments and fire of purgatory can take away all spiritual stains, why should not the pain of torture take away those of a civil nature? I imagine, that the confession of a criminal, which in some tribunals is required as being essential to his condemnation, has a similar origin, and has been taken from the mysterious tribunal of penitence, where the confession of sins is a necessary part of the sacrament. Thus have men abused the unerring light of revelation; and, in the times of tractable ignorance, having no other, they naturally had recourse to it on every occasion, making the most remote and absurd applications. Moreover, infamy is a sentiment regulated neither by the laws nor by reason, but entirely by opinion; but torture renders the victim infamous, and therefore cannot take infamy away.

Another intention of torture is to oblige the supposed criminal to reconcile the contradictions into which he may have fallen during his examination; as if the dread of punishment, the uncertainty of his fate, the solemnity of the court, the majesty of the judge, and the ignorance of the accused, were not abundantly sufficient to account for contradictions, which are so common to men even in a state of tranquility, and which must necessarily be multiplied by the perturbation of the mind of a man entirely engaged in the thoughts of saving himself from imminent danger.

This infamous test of truth is a remaining monument of that ancient and savage legislation, in which trials by fire, by boiling water, or the uncertainty of combats, were called *judgments of God;* as if the links of that eternal chain, whose beginning is in the breast of the first cause of all things, could ever be disunited by the institutions of men. The only difference between torture and trials by fire and boiling water is, that the event of the first depends on the will of the accused, and of the second on a fact entirely physical and external: but this difference is apparent only, not real. A man on the rack, in the convulsions of torture, has it as little in his power to declare the truth, as, in former times, to prevent without fraud the effects of fire or boiling water.

Every act of the will is invariably in proportion to the force of the impression on our senses. The impression of pain, then, may increase to such a degree, that, occupying the mind entirely, it will compel the sufferer to use the shortest method of freeing himself from torment. His answer, therefore, will be an effect as necessary as that of fire or boiling water, and he will accuse himself of crimes of which he is innocent: so that the very means employed to distinguish the innocent from the guilty will most effectually destroy all difference between them.

It would be superfluous to confirm these reflections by examples of innocent persons who, from the agony of torture, have confessed themselves guilty: innumerable instances may be found in all nations, and in every age. How amazing that mankind have always neglected to draw the natural conclusion! Lives there a man who, if he has carried his thoughts ever so little beyond the necessities of life, *when he reflects on such cruelty, is not tempted to fly from society, and return to his natural state of independence?*

The result of torture, then, is a matter of calculation, and depends on the constitution, which differs in every individual, and it is in proportion to his strength and sensibility; so that to discover truth by this method, is a problem which may be better solved by a mathematician than by a judge, and may be thus stated: *The force of the muscles and the sensibility of the nerves of an innocent person being given, it is required to find the degree of pain necessary to make him confess himself guilty of a given crime.*

The examination of the accused is intended to find out the truth: but if this be discovered with so much difficulty in the air, gesture, and countenance of a man at ease, how can it appear in a countenance distorted by the convulsions of torture? Every violent action destroys those small alterations in the features which sometimes disclose the sentiments of the heart.

These truths were known to the Roman legislators, amongst whom, as I have already observed, slaves only, who were not considered as citizens, were tortured. They are known to the English a nation in which the progress of science, superiority in commerce, riches, and power, its natural consequences, together with the numerous examples of virtue and courage, leave no doubt of the excellence of its laws. They have been acknowledged in Sweden, where torture has been abolished. They are known to one of the wisest monarchs in Europe, who, having seated philosophy on the throne by his beneficent legislation, has made his subjects free, though dependent on the laws; the only freedom that reasonable men can desire in the present state of things. In short, torture has not been thought necessary in the laws of armies, composed chiefly of the dregs of mankind, where its use should seem most necessary. Strange phenomenon! that a set of men, hardened by slaughter, and familiar with blood, should teach humanity to the sons of peace.

It appears also that these truths were known, though imperfectly, even to those by whom torture has been most frequently practised; for a confession made during torture, is null, if it be not afterwards confirmed by an oath, which if the criminal refuses, he is tortured again. Some civilians and some nations permit this infamous *petitio principii* to be only three times repeated, and others leave it to the discretion of the judge; therefore, of two men equally innocent, or equally guilty, the most robust and resolute will be acquitted, and the weakest and most pusillanimous will be condemned, in consequence of the following excellent mode of reasoning. *I, the judge, must find some one guilty. Thou, who art a strong fellow, hast been able to resist the force of torment; therefore I acquit thee. Thou, being*

weaker, hast yielded to it; I therefore condemn thee. I am sensible, that the confession which was extorted from thee has no weight; but if thou dost not confirm by oath what thou hast already confessed, I will have thee tormented again.

A very strange but necessary consequence of the use of torture is, that the case of the innocent is worse than that of the guilty. With regard to the first, either he confesses the crime which he has not committed, and is condemned, or he is acquitted, and has suffered a punishment he did not deserve. On the contrary, the person who is really guilty has the most favourable side of the question; for, if he supports the torture with firmness and resolution, he is acquitted, and has gained, having exchanged a greater punishment for a less.

The law by which torture is authorised, says, *Men, be insensible to pain. Nature has indeed given you an irresistible self-love, and an unalienable right of self-preservation; but I create in you a contrary sentiment, an heroical hatred of yourselves. I command you to accuse yourselves, and to declare the truth, amidst the tearing of your flesh and the dislocation of your bones.*

*   *   *

Chapter 27
Of the Mildness of Punishments

The course of my ideas has carried me away from my subject, to the elucidation of which I now return. Crimes are more effectually prevented by the *certainty* than the *severity* of punishment. Hence in a magistrate the necessity of vigilance, and in a judge of implacability, which, that it may become an useful virtue, should be joined to a mild legislation. The certainty of a small punishment will make a stronger impression than the fear of one more severe, if attended with the hopes of escaping; for it is the nature of mankind to be terrified at the approach of the smallest inevitable evil, whilst hope, the best gift of Heaven, hath the power of dispelling the apprehension of a greater, especially if supported by examples of impunity, which weakness or avarice too frequently afford.

If punishments be very severe, men are naturally led to the perpetration of other crimes, to avoid the punishment due to the first. The countries and times most notorious for severity of punishments were always those in which the most bloody and inhuman actions and the most atrocious crimes were committed for the hand of the legislator and the assassin were directed by the same spirit of ferocity, which on the throne dictated laws of iron to slaves and savages, and in private instigated the subject to sacrifice one tyrant to make room for another.

In proportion as punishments become more cruel, the minds of men, as a fluid rises to the same height with that which surrounds it, grow hardened and insensible; and the force of the passions still continuing, in the space of an hundred years the *wheel* terrifies no more than formerly the *prison.* That a punishment may produce the effect required, it is sufficient that the *evil* it occasions should exceed the *good* expected from the crime, including in the calculation the certainty of the punishment, and the privation of the expected advantage. All severity beyond this is superfluous, and therefore tyrannical.

Men regulate their conduct by the repeated impression of evils they know, and not by those with which they are unacquainted. Let us, for example, suppose two nations, in one of which the greatest punishment is *perpetual slavery,* and in the other *the wheel:* I say, that both will inspire the same degree of terror, and that there can be no reasons for increasing the punishments of the first, which are not equally valid for augmenting those of the second to more lasting and more ingenious modes of tormenting, and so on to the most exquisite refinements of a science too well known to tyrants.

There are yet two other consequences of cruel punishments, which counteract the purpose of their institution, which was, to prevent crimes. The *first* arises from the impossibility of establishing an exact proportion between the crime and punishment; for though ingenious cruelty hath greatly multiplyed the variety of torments, yet the human frame can suffer only to a certain degree, beyond which it is impossible to proceed, be the enormity of the crime ever so great. The *second* consequence is impunity. Human nature is limited no less in evil than in good. Excessive barbarity can never be more than temporary, it being impossible that it should be supported by a permanent system of legislation; for if the laws be too cruel, they must be altered, or anarchy and impunity will succeed.

Is it possible without shuddering with horror, to read in history of the barbarous and useless torments that were cooly invented and executed by men who were called sages? Who does not tremble at the thoughts of thousands of wretches, whom their misery, either caused or tolerated by the laws, which favoured the few and outraged the many, had forced in despair to return to a state of nature, or accused of impossible crimes, the fabric of ignorance and superstition, or guilty only of having been faithful to their own principles; who, I say, can, without horror, think of their being torn to pieces, with slow and studied barbarity, by men endowed with the same passions and the same feelings? A delightful spectacle to a fanatic multitude!

REVIEW QUESTIONS

1. According to Beccaria, what is the proper basis of law in human society?
2. What is the legal purpose and function of punishment?
3. Why is torture irrational?
4. What does Beccaria's criminal theory reveal about his assumptions concerning human nature and human society?
5. What aspects of Beccaria's thought qualify as *enlightened* in the strict, historical sense of the term?

JEAN-JACQUES ROUSSEAU

FROM *The Social Contract*

Jean-Jacques Rousseau (1712–1778) was one of the most original writers of the Enlightenment. A native of Geneva, he was raised by his father, a watchmaker. At sixteen years of age, he left home and eventually settled in Paris. His first attempts to penetrate the world of philosophes and encyclopedists were not very successful. In 1750, however, he won a literary award from the Academy of Dijon for an essay that contrasted the corruption of modern civilization with the natural goodness of simple, uncivilized human beings. Rousseau eventually settled in the town of Montmorency. His years there proved to be the most fruitful of his life. In a two-year span he wrote his most significant works: La nouvelle Héloïse *(1761),* Émile *(1761), and* Le contrat social *(1762).*

In The Social Contract, *as well as his other works, Rousseau sought to balance the freedom of the individual against the needs of the collectivity. He believed the preservation of liberty depended on the creation of a new society by means of a social contract. The idea was not new, having been adopted by other enlightened thinkers from the political theory of John Locke. Rousseau's interpretation was highly original, however. Locke believed that the social contract preserved freedom; Rousseau argued that the social contract preserved equality. Under his social contract, people voluntarily relinquished certain rights and submitted to the general will, a vague entity that found expression in a set of positive laws under a virtuous legislator. These laws had absolute authority and would preserve absolute equality between people.*

From *The Social Contract*, by Jean-Jacques Rousseau, translated by Henry J. Tozer (New York: Scribner's, 1898).

Book I

I mean to inquire if, in the civil order, there can be any sure and legitimate rule of administration, men being taken as they are and laws as they might be. In this inquiry I shall endeavour always to unite what right sanctions with what is prescribed by interest, in order that justice and utility may in no case be divided.

I enter upon my task without proving the importance of the subject. I shall be asked if I am a prince or a legislator, to write on politics. I answer that I am neither, and that is why I do so. If I were a prince or a legislator, I should not waste time in saying what wants doing; I should do it, or hold my peace.

As I was born a citizen of a free State, and a member of the Sovereign, I feel that, however feeble the influence my voice can have on public affairs, the right of voting on them makes it my duty to study them: and I am happy, when I reflect upon governments, to find my inquiries always furnish me with new reasons for loving that of my own country.

CHAPTER I
SUBJECT OF THE FIRST BOOK

Man is born free; and everywhere he is in chains. One thinks himself the master of others, and still remains a greater slave than they. How did this change come about? I do not know. What can make it legitimate? That question I think I can answer.

If I took into account only force, and the effects derived from it, I should say: "As long as a people is compelled to obey, and obeys, it does well; as soon as it can shake off the yoke, and shakes it off, it does still better; for, regaining its liberty by the same right as took it away, either it is justified in resuming it, or there was no justification for those who took it away." But the social order is a sacred right which is the basis of all rights. Nevertheless, this right does not come from nature, and must therefore be founded on conventions. Before coming to that, I have to prove what I have just asserted.

CHAPTER II
THE FIRST SOCIETIES

The most ancient of all societies, and the only one that is natural, is the family: and even so the children remain attached to the father only so long as they need him for their preservation. As soon as this need ceases, the natural bond is dissolved. The children, released from the obedience they owed to the father, and the father, released from the care he owed his children, return equally to independence. If they remain united, they continue so no longer naturally, but voluntarily; and the family itself is then maintained only by convention.

This common liberty results from the nature of man. His first law is to provide for his own preservation, his first cares are those which he owes to himself; and, as soon as he reaches years of discretion, he is the sole judge of the proper means of preserving himself, and consequently becomes his own master.

The family then may be called the first model of political societies: the ruler corresponds to the father, and the people to the children; and all, being born free and equal, alienate their liberty only for their own advantage. The whole difference is that, in the family, the love of the father for his children repays him for the care he takes of them, while, in the State, the pleasure of commanding takes the place of the love which the chief cannot have for the peoples under him.

Grotius denies that all human power is established in favour of the governed, and quotes slavery as an example. His usual method of reasoning is constantly to establish right by fact. It would be possible to employ a more logical method, but none could be more favourable to tyrants.

It is then, according to Grotius, doubtful whether the human race belongs to a hundred men, or that hundred men to the human race: and, throughout his book, he seems to incline to the former alternative, which is also the view of Hobbes. On this showing, the human species is divided into so many herds of cattle, each with its ruler, who keeps guard over them for the purpose of devouring them.

As a shepherd is of a nature superior to that of his flock, the shepherds of men, i.e. their rulers, are of a nature superior to that of the peoples under them. Thus, Philo tells us, the Emperor Caligula reasoned, concluding equally well either that kings were gods, or that men were beasts.

The reasoning of Caligula agrees with that of Hobbes and Grotius. Aristotle, before any of them, had said that men are by no means equal naturally, but that some are born for slavery, and others for dominion.

Aristotle was right; but he took the effect for the cause. Nothing can be more certain than that every man born in slavery is born for slavery. Slaves lose everything in their chains, even the desire of escaping from them: they love their servitude, as the comrades of Ulysses loved their brutish condition. If then there are slaves by nature, it is because there have been slaves against nature. Force made the first slaves, and their cowardice perpetuated the condition.

I have said nothing of King Adam, or Emperor Noah, father of the three great monarchs who shared out the universe, like the children of Saturn, whom some scholars have recognized in them. I trust to getting due thanks for my moderation; for, being a direct descendant of one of these princes, perhaps of the eldest branch, how do I know that a verification of titles might not leave me the legitimate king of the human race? In any case, there can be no doubt that Adam was sovereign of the world, as Robinson Crusoe was of his island, as long as he was its only inhabitant; and this empire had the advantage that the monarch, safe on his throne, had no rebellions, wars, or conspirators to fear.

CHAPTER III
THE RIGHT OF THE STRONGEST

The strongest is never strong enough to be always the master, unless he transforms strength into right, and obedience into duty. Hence the right of the strongest, which, though to all seeming meant ironically, is really laid down as a fundamental principle. But are we never to have an explanation of this phrase? Force is a physical power, and I fail to see what moral effect it can have. To yield to force is an act of necessity, not of will—at the most, an act of prudence. In what sense can it be a duty?

Suppose for a moment that this so-called "right" exists. I maintain that the sole result is a mass of inexplicable nonsense. For, if force creates right, the effect changes with the cause: every force that is greater than the first succeeds to its right. As soon as it is possible to disobey with impunity, disobedience is legitimate; and, the strongest being always in the right, the only thing that matters is to act so as to become the strongest. But what kind of right is that which perishes when force fails? If we must obey perforce, there is no need to obey because we ought; and if we are not forced to obey, we are under no obligation to do so. Clearly, the word "right" adds nothing to force: in this connection, it means absolutely nothing.

Obey the powers that be. If this means yield to force, it is a good precept, but superfluous: I can answer for its never being violated. All power comes from God, I admit; but so does all sickness; does that mean that we are forbidden to call in the doctor? A brigand surprises me at the edge of a wood: must I not merely surrender my purse on compulsion; but, even if I could withhold it, am I in con-

science bound to give it up? For certainly the pistol he holds is also a power.

Let us then admit that force does not create right, and that we are obliged to obey only legitimate powers. In that case, my original question recurs.

CHAPTER IV
SLAVERY

Since no man has a natural authority over his fellow, and force creates no right, we must conclude that conventions form the basis of all legitimate authority among men.

If an individual, says Grotius, can alienate his liberty and make himself the slave of a master, why could not a whole people do the same and make itself subject to a king? There are in this passage plenty of ambiguous words which would need explaining; but let us confine ourselves to the word *alienate*. To alienate is to give or to sell. Now, a man who becomes the slave of another does not give himself; he sells himself, at the least for his subsistence: but for what does a people sell itself? A king is so far from furnishing his subjects with their subsistence that he gets his own only from them; and, according to Rabelais, kings do not live on nothing. Do subjects then give their persons on condition that the king takes their goods also? I fail to see what they have left to preserve.

It will be said that the despot assures his subjects civil tranquillity. Granted; but what do they gain, if the wars his ambition brings down upon them, his insatiable avidity, and the vexatious conduct of his ministers press harder on them than their own dissensions would have done? What do they gain, if the very tranquillity they enjoy is one of their miseries? Tranquillity is found also in dungeons; but is that enough to make them desirable places to live in? The Greeks imprisoned in the cave of the Cyclops lived there very tranquilly, while they were awaiting their turn to be devoured.

To say that a man gives himself gratuitously, is to say what is absurd and inconceivable; such an act is null and illegitimate, from the mere fact that he who does it is out of his mind. To say the same of a whole people is to suppose a people of madmen; and madness creates no right.

Even if each man could alienate himself, he could not alienate his children: they are born men and free; their liberty belongs to them, and no one but they has the right to dispose of it. Before they come to years of discretion, the father can, in their name, lay down conditions for their preservation and well-being, but he cannot give them irrevocably and without conditions: such a gift is contrary to the ends of nature, and exceeds the rights of paternity. It would therefore be necessary, in order to legitimize an arbitrary government, that in every generation the people should be in a position to accept or reject it; but, were this so, the government would be no longer arbitrary.

To renounce liberty is to renounce being a man, to surrender the rights of humanity and even its duties. For him who renounces everything no indemnity is possible. Such a renunciation is incompatible with man's nature; to remove all liberty from his will is to remove all morality from his acts. Finally, it is an empty and contradictory convention that sets up, on the one side, absolute authority, and, on the other, unlimited obedience. Is it not clear that we can be under no obligation to a person from whom we have the right to exact everything? Does not this condition alone, in the absence of equivalence or exchange, in itself involve the nullity of the act? For what right can my slave have against me, when all that he has belongs to me, and, his right being mine, this right of mine against myself is a phrase devoid of meaning?

Grotius and the rest find in war another origin for the so-called right of slavery. The victor having, as they hold, the right of killing the vanquished, the latter can buy back his life at the price of his liberty; and this convention is the more legitimate because it is to the advantage of both parties.

But it is clear that this supposed right to kill the conquered is by no means deducible from the state of war. Men, from the mere fact that, while they are living in their primitive independence, they have no mutual relations stable enough to constitute either the state of peace or the state of war, cannot be naturally enemies. War is constituted by a relation between things, and not between persons; and, as the state of war cannot arise out of simple personal relations, but only out of real relations, private war, or war of man with man, can exist neither in the state of nature, where there is no constant property, nor in the social state, where everything is under the authority of the laws.

Individual combats, duels, and encounters, are acts which cannot constitute a state; while the private wars, authorized by the Establishments of Louis IX, King of France, and suspended by the Peace of God, are abuses of feudalism, in itself an absurd system if ever there was one, and contrary to the principles of natural right and to all good polity.

War then is a relation, not between man and man, but between State and State, and individuals are enemies only accidentally, not as men, nor even as citizens, but as soldiers; not as members of their country, but as its defenders. Finally, each State can have for enemies only other States, and not men; for between things disparate in nature there can be no real relation.

Furthermore, this principle is in conformity with the established rules of all times and the constant practice of all civilized peoples. Declarations of war are intimations less to powers than to their subjects. The foreigner, whether king, individual, or people, who robs, kills, or detains the subjects, without declaring war on the prince, is not an enemy, but a brigand. Even in real war, a just prince, while laying hands, in the enemy's country, on all that belongs to the public, respects the lives and goods of individuals: he respects rights on which his own are founded. The object of the war being the destruction of the hostile State, the other side has a right to kill its defenders, while they are bearing arms; but as soon as they lay them down and surrender, they cease to be enemies or instruments of the enemy, and become once more merely men, whose life no one has any right to take. Sometimes it is possible to kill the State without killing a single one of its members; and war gives no right which is not necessary to the gaining of its object. These principles are not those of Grotius: they are not based on the authority of poets, but derived from the nature of reality and based on reason.

The right of conquest has no foundation other than the right of the strongest. If war does not give the conqueror the right to massacre the conquered peoples, the right to enslave them cannot be based upon a right which does not exist. No one has a right to kill an enemy except when he cannot make him a slave, and the right to enslave him cannot therefore be derived from the right to kill him. It is accordingly an unfair exchange to make him buy at the price of his liberty his life, over which the victor holds no right. Is it not clear that there is a vicious circle in founding the right of life and death on the right of slavery, and the right of slavery on the right of life and death?

Even if we assume this terrible right to kill everybody, I maintain that a slave made in war, or a conquered people, is under no obligation to a master, except to obey him as far as he is compelled to do so. By taking an equivalent for his life, the victor has not done him a favour; instead of killing him without profit, he has killed him usefully. So far then is he from acquiring over him any authority in addition to that of force, that the state of war continues to subsist between them: their mutual relation is the effect of it, and the usage of the right of war does not imply a treaty of peace. A convention has indeed been made; but this convention, so far from destroying the state of war, presupposes its continuance.

So, from whatever aspect we regard the question, the right of slavery is null and void, not only as being illegitimate, but also because it is absurd and meaningless. The words *slave* and *right* contradict each other, and are mutually exclusive. It will always be equally foolish for a man to say to a man or to a people: "I make with you a convention wholly at your expense and wholly to my advantage; I shall keep it as long as I like, and you will keep it as long as I like."

*   *   *

CHAPTER VI
THE SOCIAL COMPACT

I suppose men to have reached the point at which the obstacles in the way of their preservation in the state of nature show their power of resistance to be greater than the resources at the disposal of each individual for his maintenance in that state. That primitive condition can then subsist no longer; and the human race would perish unless it changed its manner of existence.

But, as men cannot engender new forces, but only unite and direct existing ones, they have no other means of preserving themselves than the formation, by aggregation, of a sum of forces great enough to overcome the resistance. These they have to bring into play by means of a single motive power, and cause to act in concert.

This sum of forces can arise only where several persons come together: but, as the force and liberty of each man are the chief instruments of his self-preservation, how can he pledge them without harming his own interests, and neglecting the care he owes to himself? This difficulty, in its bearing on my present subject, may be stated in the following terms:

"The problem is to find a form of association which will defend and protect with the whole common force the person and goods of each associate, and in which each, while uniting himself with all, may still obey himself alone, and remain as free as before." This is the fundamental problem of which the *Social Contract* provides the solution.

The clauses of this contract are so determined by the nature of the act that the slightest modification would make them vain and ineffective; so that, although they have perhaps never been formally set forth, they are everywhere the same and everywhere tacitly admitted and recognized, until, on the violation of the social compact, each regains his original rights and resumes his natural liberty, while losing the conventional liberty in favour of which he renounced it.

These clauses, properly understood, may be reduced to one—the total alienation of each associate, together with all his rights, to the whole community; for, in the first place, as each gives himself absolutely, the conditions are the same for all; and, this being so, no one has any interest in making them burdensome to others.

Moreover, the alienation being without reserve, the union is as perfect as it can be, and no associate has anything more to demand: for, if the individuals retained certain rights, as there would be no common superior to decide between them and the public, each, being on one point his own judge, would ask to be so on all; the state of nature would thus continue, and the association would necessarily become inoperative or tyrannical.

Finally, each man, in giving himself to all, gives himself to nobody; and as there is no associate over which he does not acquire the same right as he yields others over himself, he gains an equivalent for everything he loses, and an increase of force for the preservation of what he has.

If then we discard from the social compact what is not of its essence, we shall find that it reduces itself to the following terms:

"Each of us puts his person and all his power in common under the supreme direction of the general will, and, in our corporate capacity, we receive each member as an indivisible part of the whole."

At once, in place of the individual personality of each contracting party, this act of association creates a moral and collective body, composed of as many members as the assembly contains voters, and receiving from this act its unity, its common identity, its life, and its will. This public person, so formed by the union of all other persons, formerly took the name of *city,* and now takes that of *Republic* or *body politic;* it is called by its members *State* when passive, *Sovereign* when active, and *Power* when compared with others like itself. Those who are associated in it take collectively the name of *people,* and severally are called *citizens,* as sharing in the sovereign power, and *subjects,* as being under the laws of the State. But these terms are often confused and taken one for another: it is enough to know how to distinguish them when they are being used with precision.

CHAPTER VII
THE SOVEREIGN

This formula shows us that the act of association comprises a mutual undertaking between the public and the individuals, and that each individual, in making a contract, as we may say, with himself, is bound in a double capacity; as a member of the Sovereign he is bound to the individuals, and as a member of the State to the Sovereign. But the maxim of civil right, that no one is bound by undertakings made to himself, does not apply in this case; for there is a great difference between incurring an obligation to yourself and incurring one to a whole of which you form a part.

Attention must further be called to the fact that public deliberation, while competent to bind all the subjects to the Sovereign, because of the two different capacities in which each of them may be regarded, cannot, for the opposite reason, bind the Sovereign to itself; and that it is consequently against the nature of the body politic for the Sovereign to impose on itself a law which it cannot infringe. Being able to regard itself in only one capacity, it is in the position of an individual who makes a contract with himself; and this makes it clear that there neither is nor can be any kind of fundamental law binding on the body of the people—not even the social contract itself. This does not mean that the body politic cannot enter into undertakings with others, provided the contract is not infringed by them; for in relation to what is external to it, it becomes a simple being, an individual.

But the body politic or the Sovereign, drawing its being wholly from the sanctity of the contract, can never bind itself, even to an outsider, to do anything derogatory to the original act, for instance, to alienate any part of itself, or to submit to another Sovereign. Violation of the act by which it exists would be self-annihilation; and that which is itself nothing can create nothing.

As soon as this multitude is so united in one body, it is impossible to offend against one of the members without attacking the body, and still more to offend against the body without the members resenting it. Duty and interest therefore equally oblige the two contracting parties to give each other help; and the same men should seek to combine, in their double capacity, all the advantages dependent upon that capacity.

Again, the Sovereign, being formed wholly of the individuals who compose it, neither has nor can have any interest contrary to theirs; and consequently the sovereign power need give no guarantee to its subjects, because it is impossible for the body to wish to hurt all its members. We shall also see later on that it cannot hurt any in particular. The Sovereign, merely by virtue of what it is, is always what it should be.

This, however, is not the case with the relation of the subjects to the Sovereign, which, despite the common interest, would have no security that they would fulfil their undertakings, unless it found means to assure itself of their fidelity.

In fact, each individual, as a man, may have a particular will contrary or dissimilar to the general will which he has as a citizen. His particular interest may speak to him quite differently from the common interest: his absolute and naturally independent existence may make him look upon what he owes to the common cause as a gratuitous contribution, the loss of which will do less harm to others than the payment of it is burdensome to himself; and, regarding the moral person which constitutes the State as a *persona ficta,* because not a man, he may wish to enjoy the rights of citizenship without being ready to fulfil the duties of a subject. The continuance of such an injustice could not but prove the undoing of the body politic.

In order then that the social compact may not be an empty formula, it tacitly includes the undertaking, which alone can give force to the rest, that whoever refuses to obey the general will shall be compelled to do so by the whole body. This means nothing less than that he will be forced to be free; for this is the condition which, by giving each citizen to his country, secures him against all personal dependence. In this lies the key to the working of the political machine; this alone legitimizes civil undertakings, which, without it, would be absurd, tyrannical, and liable to the most frightful abuses.

CHAPTER VIII
THE CIVIL STATE

The passage from the state of nature to the civil state produces a very remarkable change in man, by substituting justice for instinct in his conduct, and giving his actions the morality they had formerly lacked. Then only, when the voice of duty takes the place of physical impulses and right of appetite, does man, who so far had considered only himself, find that he is forced to act on different principles, and to consult his reason before listening to his inclinations. Although, in this state, he deprives himself of some advantages which he got from nature, he gains in return others so great, his faculties are so stimulated and developed, his ideas so extended, his feelings so ennobled, and his whole soul so uplifted, that, did not the abuses of this new condition often degrade him below that which he left, he would be bound to bless continually the happy moment which took him from it for ever, and, instead of a stupid and unimaginative animal, made him an intelligent being and a man.

Let us draw up the whole account in terms easily commensurable. What man loses by the social contract is his natural liberty and an unlimited right to everything he tries to get and succeeds in getting; what he gains is civil liberty and the proprietorship of all he possesses. If we are to avoid mistake in weighing one against the other, we must clearly distinguish natural liberty, which is bounded only by the strength of the individual, from civil liberty, which is limited by the general will; and possession, which is merely the effect of force or the right of the first occupier, from property which can be founded only on a positive title.

We might, over and above all this, add, to what man acquires in the civil state, moral liberty, which alone makes him truly master of himself; for the mere impulse of appetite is slavery, while obedience to a law which we prescribe to ourselves is liberty. But I have already said too much on this head, and the philosophical meaning of the word liberty does not now concern us.

*   *   *

Book II

*   *   *

CHAPTER III
WHETHER THE GENERAL WILL IS FALLIBLE

It follows from what has gone before that the general will is always right and tends to the public advantage; but it does not follow that the deliberations of the people are always equally correct. Our will is always for our own good, but we do not always see what that is; the people is never corrupted, but it is often deceived, and on such occasions only does it seem to will what is bad.

There is often a great deal of difference between the will of all and the general will; the latter considers only the common interest, while the former takes private interest into account, and is no more than a sum of particular wills: but take away from these same wills the pluses and minuses that cancel one another, and the general will remains as the sum of the differences.

If, when the people, being furnished with adequate information, held its deliberations, the citizens had no communication one with another, the grand total of the small differences would always give the general will, and the decision would always be good. But when factions arise, and partial associations are formed at the expense of the great association, the will of each of these associations becomes general in relation to its members, while it remains particular in relation to the State; it may then be said that there are no longer as many votes as there are men, but only as many as there are associations. The differences become less numerous and give a less general result. Lastly, when one of these associations is so great as to prevail over all the rest, the result is no longer a sum of small differences, but a single difference; in this case there is no longer a general will, and the opinion which prevails is purely particular.

It is therefore essential, if the general will is to be able to express itself, that there should be no partial society within the State, and that each citizen should think only his own thoughts: which was indeed the sublime and unique system established by the great Lycurgus. But if there are partial societies, it is best to have as many as possible and to prevent them from being unequal, as was done by Solon, Numa, and Servius. These precautions are the only ones that can guarantee that the general will shall be always enlightened, and that the people shall in no way deceive itself.

*   *   *

CHAPTER IV
THE LIMITS OF THE SOVEREIGN POWER

If the State is a moral person whose life is in the union of its members, and if the most important of its cares is the care for its own preservation, it must have a universal and compelling force, in order to move and dispose each part as may be most advantageous to the whole. As nature gives each man absolute power over all his members, the social compact gives the body politic absolute power over all its members also; and it is this power which, under the direction of the general will, bears, as I have said, the name of Sovereignty.

But, besides the public person, we have to consider the private persons composing it, whose life and liberty are naturally independent of it. We are bound then to distinguish clearly between the respective rights of the citizens and the Sovereign, and between the duties the former have to fulfil as subjects, and the natural rights they should enjoy as men.

Each man alienates, I admit, by the social compact, only such part of his powers, goods, and liberty as it is important for the community to control; but it must also be granted that the Sovereign is sole judge of what is important.

Every service a citizen can render the State he ought to render as soon as the Sovereign demands it; but the Sovereign, for its part, cannot impose upon its subjects any fetters that are useless to the community, nor can it even wish to do so; for no more by the law of reason than by the law of nature can anything occur without a cause.

The undertakings which bind us to the social body are obligatory only because they are mutual; and their nature is such that in fulfilling them we cannot work for others without working for ourselves. Why is it that the general will is always in the right, and that all continually will the happiness of each one, unless it is because there is not a man who does not think of "each" as meaning him, and consider himself in voting for all? This proves that equality of rights and the idea of justice which such equality creates originate in the preference each man gives to himself, and accordingly in the very nature of man. It proves that the general will, to be really such, must be general in its object as well as its essence; that it must both come from all and apply to all; and that it loses its natural rectitude when it is directed to some particular and determinate object, because in such a case we are judging of something foreign to us, and have no true principle of equity to guide us.

Indeed, as soon as a question of particular fact or right arises on a point not previously regulated by a general convention, the matter becomes contentious. It is a case in which the individuals concerned are one party, and the public the other, but in which I can see neither the law that ought to be followed nor the judge who ought to give the decision. In such a case, it would be absurd to propose to refer the question to an express decision of the general will, which can be only the conclusion reached by one of the parties and in consequence will be, for the other party, merely an external and particular will, inclined on this occasion to injustice and subject to error. Thus, just as a particular will cannot stand for the general will, the general will, in turn, changes its nature, when its object is particular, and, as general, cannot pronounce on a man or a fact. When, for instance, the people of Athens nominated or displaced its rulers, decreed honours to one, and imposed penalties on another, and, by a multitude of particular decrees, exercised all the functions of government indiscriminately, it had in such cases no longer a general will in the strict sense; it was acting no longer as Sovereign, but as magistrate. This will seem contrary to current views; but I must be given time to expound my own.

It should be seen from the foregoing that what makes the will general is less the number of voters than the common interest uniting them; for, under this system, each necessarily submits to the conditions he imposes on others: and this admirable agreement between interest and justice gives to the common deliberations an equitable character which at once vanishes when any particular question is discussed, in the absence of a common interest to unite and identify the ruling of the judge with that of the party.

From whatever side we approach our principle, we reach the same conclusion, that the social compact sets up among the citizens an equality of such a kind, that they all bind themselves to observe the same conditions and should therefore all enjoy the same rights. Thus, from the very nature of the compact, every act of Sovereignty, i.e. every authentic act of the general will, binds or favours all the citizens equally; so that the Sovereign recognizes only the body of the nation, and draws no distinctions between those of whom it is made up. What, then, strictly speaking, is an act of Sovereignty? It is not a convention between a superior and an inferior, but a convention between the body and each of its members. It is legitimate, because based on the social contract, and equitable, because common to all; useful, because it can have no other object than the general good, and stable, because guaranteed by the public force and the supreme power. So long as the subjects have to submit only to conventions of this sort, they obey no one but their own will; and to ask how far the respective rights of the Sovereign and the citizens extend, is to ask up to what point the latter can enter into undertakings with themselves, each with all, and all with each.

We can see from this that the sovereign power, absolute, sacred, and inviolable as it is, does not and cannot exceed the limits of general conventions, and that every man may dispose at will of such goods and liberty as these conventions leave him; so that the Sovereign never has a right to lay more charges on one subject than on another, because, in that case, the question becomes particular, and ceases to be within its competency.

When these distinctions have once been admitted, it is seen to be so untrue that there is, in the social contract, any real renunciation on the part of the individuals, that the position in which they find themselves as a result of the contract is really preferable to that in which they were before. Instead of a renunciation, they have made an advantageous exchange: instead of an uncertain and precarious way of living they have got one that is better and more secure; instead of natural independence they have got liberty, instead of the power to harm others security for themselves, and instead of their strength, which others might overcome, a right which social union makes invincible. Their very life, which they have devoted to the State, is by it constantly protected; and when they risk it in the State's defence, what more are they doing than giving back what they have received from it? What are they doing that they would not do more often and with greater danger in the state of nature, in which they would inevitably have to fight battles at the peril of their lives in defence of that which is the means of their preservation? All have indeed to fight when their country needs them; but then no one has ever to fight for himself. Do we not gain something by running, on behalf of what gives us our security, only some of the risks we should have to run for ourselves, as soon as we lost it?

* * *

REVIEW QUESTIONS

1. How does Rousseau's conception of the origin of political society compare with that of Locke?
2. According to Rousseau, what is the relation between human slavery and human nature?
3. How do relations of subject and ruler come into being?
4. What is the social contract?
5. What is its relation to nature? To reason? To will?

A READING IN THE SALON OF MME GEOFFRIN (1755)   ANICET CHARLES GABRIEL LEMONNIER

Anicet Charles Gabriel Lemonnier (1743–1824) received his initial training at the School of Fine Arts in his native Rouen. Like many artists and intellectuals of his day, he was drawn to Paris, where his connections soon gained him introductions to Enlightened individuals and their patronage. The subjects of his paintings tended toward allegorical representations of classical myth and antiquity. These proved highly acceptable to the Académie Royale de Peinture, which awarded him the Prix de Rome in 1772 and granted him membership in 1789. He held a series of lucrative government pensions throughout his career. He became director of the Gobelins Manufactory in 1801 and helped to found the Musée des Beaux-Arts in his hometown of Rouen. His best-known work depicts the salon of Mme. Geoffrin, a circle of which he may have been a regular member. An imaginary reconstruction, this painting includes a number of noteworthy figures of the day, Diderot and Montesquieu among others, gathered under a bust of Voltaire. What seems to be happening in this painting? What can you tell about the nature of the gathering? What role did such salons play in the Enlightenment? What role did women play in such salons?

LADY MARY WORTLEY MONTAGU

FROM *Letters of the Right Honourable Lady Mary Wortley Montagu*

Lady Mary Wortley Montagu (1689–1762) was an English aristocrat and writer, remembered chiefly for her letters, especially those written from Turkey, where she spent time and traveled widely as wife of the British ambassador. Hers is a secular work, one of the first written by a woman about the Ottoman and Muslim worlds. Yet, its importance lies in the unique personality and voice of their author. Lady Mary was an exceptional woman in many respects. Self-educated, she taught herself Latin by reading books in her father's extensive private library. An avid writer, she composed poetry and prose from early adolescence. Strong-willed, she supplemented her own education by seeking advice from two Anglican bishops, Thomas Tenison and Gilbert Burnet. All of these qualities were singular enough and might have provided early indications of a creative personality, but her fame began with her marriage to Edward Wortley Montagu, a match her father rejected, forcing her to elope. Her will, wit, and beauty made her a valuable asset to her husband, who rose in the English government from Member of Parliament in 1715 to Lord Commissioner of the Treasury shortly thereafter, and became a prominent figure at the court of George I. When her husband was named ambassador to the Ottoman Empire in 1716, she accompanied him to Constantinople, where they remained until 1718. This voyage and her observations are recounted in a series of letters, filled with graphic detail and lively commentary. These proved an inspiration to later generations of European women travelers to the Orient, by virtue not only of her example as a traveler, but also of her claim to the particular authority of women's writing due to their ability to access private homes and female-only spaces where men were not permitted. She brought back to England far more than a broadened perspective on Muslim society and culture; she brought a technique for inoculation against smallpox that she witnessed there, known as variolation. Though Edward Jenner would later develop the safer technique of vaccination, Lady Mary's observations and advocacy made her a pioneer not only of women's writing but also of medical history.

From *Letters of the Right Honourable Lady Mary Wortley Montagu: Written during her travels in Europe, Asia and Africa, to Persons of Distinction, Men of Letters, etc., in different parts of Europe*, by Lady Mary Wortley Montagu (London: M. Cooper, 1763).

Let. XIII.
to Mr —.

VIENNA, OCT. O. S. 1716.

I DESERVE not all the reproaches you make me. If I have some time without answering your letter, it is not, that I don't know how many thanks are due to you for it; or that I am stupid enough to prefer any amusements to the pleasure of hearing from you; but after the professions of esteem you have so obligingly made me, I cannot help delaying, as long as I can, shewing you that you are mistaken. If you are sincere, when you say you expect to be extremely entertained by my letters, I ought to be mortified at the disappointment that I am sure you will receive when you hear from me; though I have done my best endeavours to find out something worth writing to you. I have seen every thing that was to be seen with a very, diligent curiosity. Here are some fine villas, particularly the late prince of Litchtenstein's; but the statues are all modern, and the pictures not of the first hands. 'Tis true, the emperor has some of great value. I was yesterday to see the repository, which they call his Treasure, where they seem to have been more diligent in amassing a great quantity of things, than in the choice of them. I spent above five hours there, and yet there were very few things that stopped me long to consider them. But the number is prodigious, being a very long gallery filled on both sides, and five large rooms. There is a vast quantity of paintings, amongst which are many fine miniatures; but the most valuable pictures, are a few of Corregio, those of Titian being at the Favorita.

THE cabinet of jewels did not appear to me so rich as I expected to see it. They shewed me here a cup, about the size of a tea dish, of one entire emerald, which they had so particular a respect for, that only the emperor has the liberty of touching it. There is a large cabinet full of curiosities of clock-work, only one of which I thought worth observing, that was a craw-fish, with all the motions so natural, that it was hard to distinguish it from the life.

THE next cabinet was a large collection of agates, some of them extremely beautiful, and of an uncommon size, and several vases of Lapis Lazuli. I was surprised to see the cabinet of medals so poorly furnished; I did not remark one of any value, and they are kept in a most ridiculous disorder. As to the antiques, very few of them deserve that name. Upon my saying they were modern, I could not forbear laughing at the answer of the profound antiquary that shewed them, that *they were ancient enough; for, to his knowledge, they had been there these forty years.* But the next cabinet diverted me yet better, being nothing else but a parcel of wax babies, and toys in ivory, very well worthy to be presented children of five years old. Two of the rooms were wholly filled with these trifles of all kinds, set in jewels, amongst which I was desired to observe a crucifix, that they assured me had spoke very wisely to the emperor Leopold. I won't trouble you with a catalogue of the rest of the lumber; but I must not forget to mention a small piece of loadstone that held up an anchor of steel too heavy for me to lift. This is what I thought most curious in the whole treasure. There are some few heads of ancient statues; but several of them are defaced by modern additions. I foresee that you will be very little satisfied with this letter, and I dare hardly ask you to be good-natured enough to charge the dulness of it on the barrenness of the subject, and to overlook the stupidity of,

Your, &c. &c.

*   *   *

Let. XXXIX.
To the Countess of —.

PERA OF CONSTANTINOPLE, MARCH 10. O. S.

I HAVE not written to you, dear sister, these many months—a great piece of self-denial. But I know not where to direct, or what part of the world you are in. I have received no letter from you since that short note of April last, in which you tell me, that you are on the point of leaving England, and promise me a direction for the place you stay in; but I have, in vain, expected it till now; and now I only learn from the gazette, that you are returned, which induces me to venture this letter to your house at London. I had rather ten of my letters should be lost, than you imagine I don't write; and I think it is hard fortune, if one in ten don't reach you. However, I am resolved to keep the copies, as testimonies of my inclination, to give you, to the utmost of my power, all the diverting part of my travels, while you are exempt from all the fatigues and inconveniences.

In the first place, then, I wish you joy of your niece; for I was brought to bed of a daughter five weeks ago. I don't mention this as one of my diverting adventures; though I must own, that it is not half so mortifying here as in England; there being as much difference, as there is between a little cold in the head, which sometimes happens here, and the consumption cough, so common in London. No body keeps their house a month for lying in; and I am not so fond of any of our customs, as to retain them when they are not necessary. I returned my visits at three weeks end; and, about four days ago, crossed the sea, which divides this place from Constantinople, to make a new one, where I had the good fortune to pick up many curiosities. I went to see the sultana Hafiten, favourite of the late emperor Mustapha, who, you know, (or perhaps you don't know) was deposed by his brother, the reigning sultan, and died a few weeks after, being poisoned, as it was generally believed. This lady was, immediately after his death, saluted with an absolute order to leave the seraglio, and chuse herself a husband among the great men at the Porte. I suppose you may imagine her overjoyed at this proposal.—Quite the contrary.—These women, who are called, and esteem themselves queens, look upon this liberty as the greatest disgrace and affront that can happen to them. She threw herself at the sultan's feet, and begged him to poniard her, rather than use his brother's widow with that contempt. She represented to him, in agonies of sorrow, that she was privileged from this misfortune, by having brought five princes into the Ottoman family; but all the boys being dead, and only one girl surviving, this excuse was not received, and she was compelled to make her choice. She chose Bekir Effendi, then secretary of state, and above four score years old, to convince the world, that she firmly intended to keep the vow she had made, of never suffering a second husband to approach her bed; and since she must honour some subject so far, as to be called his wife, she would chuse him as a mark of her gratitude, since it was he that had presented her, at the age of ten years, to, her last lord. But she never permitted him to pay her one visit; though it is now fifteen years she has been in his house, where she passes her time in uninterrupted mourning, with a constancy very little known in Christendom, especially in a widow of one and twenty, for she is now but thirty-six. She has no black eunuchs for her guard, her husband being obliged to respect her as a queen, and not to inquire at all into what is done in her apartment.

I was led into a large room, with a sofa the whole length of it, adorned with white marble pillars like a *ruelle*, covered with pale blue figured velvet, on a silver ground, with cushions of the same, where I was desired to repose, till the sultana appeared, who had contrived this manner of reception, to avoid rising up at my entrance, though she made me an inclination of her head, when I rose up to her. I was very glad to observe a lady that had been distinguished by the favour of an emperor, to whom beauties were, every day, presented from all parts of the world. But she did not seem to me, to have ever been half so beautiful as the fair Fatima I saw at Adrianople; though she had the remains of a fine face, more decayed by sorrow than time. But her dress was something so surprisingly rich, that I cannot forbear describing it to you. She wore a vest called *dualma*, which differs from a *caftan* by longer sleeves, and folding over at the bottom. It was of purple cloth, strait to her shape, and thick set, on each side, down to her feet, and round the sleeves, with pearls of the best water, of the same size as their buttons commonly are. You must not suppose, that I mean as large as those of my Lord ——, but about the bigness of a pea; and to these buttons large loops of diamonds, in the form of those gold loops, so common on birth-day coats. This habit was tied, at the waist, with two large tassels of smaller pearls, and round the arms embroidered with large diamonds. Her shift was fastened at the bottom with a great diamond, shaped like a lozenge; her girdle as broad as the broadest English ribband, entirely covered with diamonds. Round her neck she wore three chains, which reached to her knees; one of large pearl, at the bottom of which hung a fine coloured emerald, as big as a turkey-egg; another, consisting of two hundred emeralds, close joined together, of the most lively green, perfectly matched, every one as large as a half-crown piece, and as thick as three crown pieces, and another of small emeralds, perfectly round. But her ear-rings eclipsed all the rest. They were two diamonds, shaped exactly like pears, as large as a big hazle-nut. Round her *talpoche* she had four strings of pearl—the whitest and most perfect in the world, at least enough to make four necklaces, every one as large as the duchess of Marlborough's, and of the same shape, fastened with two roses, consisting of a large ruby for the middle stone, and round them twenty drops of clean diamonds to each. Besides this, her head-dress was covered with bodkins of emeralds and diamonds. She wore large diamond bracelets, and had five rings on her fingers (except Mr Pitt's) the largest I ever saw in my life. 'Tis for jewellers to compute the value of these things; but, according to the common estimation of jewels, in our part of the world, her whole dress must be worth a hundred thousand pounds sterling. This I am sure of, that no European queen has half the quantity; and the empress's jewels, though very fine would look very mean near her's. She gave me a dinner of fifty dishes of meat, which (after their fashion) were placed on the table but one at a time, and was extremely tedious. But the magnificence of her table answered very well to that of her dress. The knives were of gold, and the hafts set with diamonds. But the piece of luxury which grieved my eyes, was the table-cloth and napkins, which were all tiffany, embroidered with silk and gold, in the finest manner, in natural flowers. It was with the utmost regret that I made use of these costly napkins, which were as finely wrought as the finest handkerchiefs that ever came out of this coun-

try. You may be sure, that they were entirely spoiled before dinner was over. The sherbet (which is the liquor they drink at meals) was served in china bowls; but the covers and salvers massy gold. After dinner, water was brought in gold basons, and towels of the same kind with the napkins, which I very unwillingly wiped my hands upon, and coffee was served in china, with gold *soucoups*.[1]

THE sultana seemed in a very good humour, and talked to me with the utmost civility. I did not omit this opportunity of learning all that I possibly could of the seraglio, which is so entirely unknown amongst us. She assured me, that the story of the sultan's *throwing a handkerchief*, is altogether fabulous; and the manner, upon that occasion, no other than this: He sends the *kyslir aga*, to signify to the lady the honour he intends her. She is immediately complimented upon it, by the others, and led to the bath, where she is perfumed and dressed in the most magnificent and becoming manner. The emperor precedes his visit by a royal present, and then comes into her apartment: neither is there any such thing as her creeping in at the bed's foot. She said, that the first he made choice of was always after the first in rank, and not the mother of the eldest son, as other writers would make us believe. Sometimes the sultan diverts himself in the company of all his ladies, who stand in a circle round him. And she confessed, they were ready to die with envy and jealousy of the *happy she* that he distinguished by any appearance of preference. But this seemed to me neither better nor worse than the circles in most courts, where the glance of the monarch is watched, and every smile is waited for with impatience, and envied by those who cannot obtain it.

SHE never mentioned the sultan without tears in her eyes, yet she seemed very fond of the discourse. "My past happiness," *said she*, "appears a dream to me. Yet I cannot forget, that I was beloved by the greatest and most lovely of mankind. I was chosen from all the rest, to make all his campaigns with him; and I would not survive him, if I was not passionately fond of the princess my daughter. Yet

---

[1] Saucers.

all my tenderness for her was hardly enough to make me preserve my life. When I left him, I passed a whole twelvemonth without seeing the light. Time has softened my despair; yet I now pass some days every week in tears, devoted to the memory of my sultan." There was no affectation in these words. It was easy to see she was in a deep melancholy, though her good humour made her willing to divert me.

SHE asked me to walk in her garden, and one of her slaves immediately brought her a *pellice* of rich brocade lined with sables. I waited on her into the garden, which had nothing in it remarkable but the fountains; and from thence she shewed me all her apartments. In her bed-chamber, her toilet was displayed, consisting of two looking-glasses, the frames covered with pearls, and her night *talpoche* set with bodkins of jewels, and near it three vests of fine sables, every one of which is, at least, worth a thousand dollars (two hundred pounds English money). I don't doubt but these rich habits were purposely placed in sight, though they seemed negligently thrown on the sofa. When I took my leave of her, I was complimented with perfumes, as at the grand vizier's, and presented with a very fine embroidered handkerchief. Her slaves were to the number of thirty, besides ten little ones, the eldest not above seven years old. These were the most beautiful girls I ever saw, all richly dressed; and I observed that the sultana took a great deal of pleasure in these lovely children, which is a vast expence; for there is not a handsome girl of that age to be bought under a hundred pounds sterling. They wore little garlands of flowers, and their own hair, braided, which was all their head-dress; but their habits were all of gold stuffs. These served her coffee kneeling; brought water when she washed, &c.—'Tis a great part of the work of the older slaves to take care of these young girls, to learn them to embroider, and to serve them as carefully as if they were children of the family. Now, do you imagine I have entertained you, all this while, with a relation that has, at least, received many embellishments from my hand? This, you will say, is but too like the Arabian tales.—These embroidered napkins! and a jewel as large as a turkey's egg!—You forget, dear

sister, those very tales were written by an author of this country, and (excepting the enchantments) are a real representation of the manners here. We travellers are in very hard circumstances: If we say nothing but what has been said before us, *we are dull, and we have observed nothing*. If we tell any thing new, we are laughed at as *fabulous and romantic*, not allowing either for the difference of ranks, which affords difference of company, or more curiosity, or the change of customs, that happen every twenty years in every country. But the truth is, people judge of travellers, exactly with the same candour, good nature, and impartiality, they judge of their neighbours upon all occasions. For my part, if I live to return amongst you, I am so well acquainted with the morals of all my dear friends and acquaintances, that I am resolved to tell them nothing at all, to avoid the imputation (which their charity would certainly incline them to) of my telling too much. But I depend upon your knowing me enough, to believe whatever I seriously assert for truth; though I give you leave to be surprised at an account so new to you. But what would you say if I told you, that I have been in a haram, where the winter apartment was wainscoted with inlaid work of mother of pearl, ivory of different colours, and olive wood, exactly like the little boxes you have seen brought out of this country; and in whose rooms designed for summer, the walls are all crusted with japan china, the roofs gilt, and the floors spread with the finest Persian carpets? Yet there is nothing more true; such is the palace of my lovely friend, the fair Fatima, whom I was acquainted with at Adrianople. I went to visit her yesterday; and, if possible, she appeared to me handsomer than before. She met me at the door of her chamber, and, giving me her hand with the best grace in the world; You Christian ladies (said she, with a smile that made her as beautiful as an angel) have the reputation of inconstancy, and I did not expect, whatever goodness you expressed for me at Adrianople, that I should ever see you again. But I am now convinced that I have really the happiness of pleasing you; and, if you knew how I speak of you amongst our ladies, you would be assured, that you do me justice in making me your friend. She placed me in the corner of the sofa, and I spent the afternoon in her conversation, with the greatest pleasure in the world.—The sultana Hafiten is, what one would naturally expect to find a Turkish lady, willing to oblige, but not knowing how to go about it; and 'tis easy to see, in her manner, that she has lived excluded from the world. But Fatima has all the politeness and good breeding of a court, with an air that inspires, at once, respect and tenderness; and now, that I understand her language, I find her wit as agreeable as her beauty. She is very curious after the manners of other countries, and has not the partiality for her own, so common in little minds. A Greek that I carried with me, who had never seen her before (nor could have been admitted now, if she had not been in my train), shewed that surprise at her beauty and manners, which is unavoidable at the first sight, and said to me in Italian,—*This is no Turkish lady, she is certainly some Christian.*—Fatima guessed she spoke of her, and asked what she said. I would not have told her, thinking she would have been no better pleased with the compliment, than one of our court beauties to be told she had the air of a Turk; but the Greek lady told it to her; and she smiled, saying, *It is not the first time I have heard so: my mother was a Poloneze, taken at the siege of Caminiec; and my father used to rally me, saying, He believed his Christian wife had found some gallant; for that I had not the air of a Turkish girl.*—I assured her, that if all the Turkish ladies were like her, it was absolute necessary to confine them from public view, for the repose of mankind; and proceeded to tell her, what a noise such a face as hers would make in London or Paris. *I can't believe you,* replied she agreeably; *if beauty was so much valued in your country, as you say, they would never have suffered you to leave it.*—Perhaps, dear sister, you laugh at my vanity in repeating this compliment;

but I only do it, as I think it very well turned, and give it you as an instance of the spirit of her conversation. Her house was magnificently furnished, and very well fancied; her winter rooms being furnished with figured velvet, on gold grounds, and those for summer, with fine Indian quilting embroidered with gold. The houses of the great Turkish ladies are kept clean with as much nicety as those in Holland. This was situated in a high part of the town; and from the window of her summer apartment, we had the prospect of the sea, the islands, and the Asian mountains.—My letter is insensibly grown so long, I am ashamed of it. This is a very bad symptom. 'Tis well if I don't degenerate into a downright story-teller. It may be, our proverb, that *knowledge is no burden,* may be true, as to one's self but knowing too much, is very apt to make us troublesome to other people.

I am, &c, &c

REVIEW QUESTIONS

1. How would you characterize Lady Mary's attitude toward the non-Europeans she observed?
2. What evidence do her letters offer of a uniquely female perspective?
3. What does the range of her correspondence tell you about Lady Mary specifically and about women in the eighteenth century generally? Is such generalization justified?
4. What evidence of Enlightened principles can be found in Lady Mary's correspondence?
5. Would you consider Lady Mary a philosophe on the basis of her letters? What does she have in common with Parisian women who kept salons?
6. From Lady Mary's career and correspondence what do you learn about the public life of women in the eighteenth century?

MOSES MENDELSSOHN

"What is Enlightenment?"

Moses Mendelssohn (1729–1786) was one of the leading intellectuals of eighteenth-century Berlin. Born in Dessau, the son of a synagogue employee and Torah scribe, he wandered at age fourteen to the capital of Prussia. Without formal university training, he read broadly and established himself quickly among the leading thinkers of the German Enlightenment and the Haskalah. *For many years a close friend of playwright Gothold Lessing, he corresponded with Immanuel Kant and worked with Friedrich Nicolai. He made a name for himself as a literary critic with respected essays on Burke, Maupertuis, Pope, and Rousseau, among many others. He is, perhaps, better known today for his metaphysical writings that attempted to provide rational arguments for such topics as the immortality of the soul and the existence of God. Though a profound advocate of enlightened rationalism, he remained no less profoundly committed to his Jewish heritage, writing passionately in favor of Jewish civil rights and religious toleration, translating the Pentateuch and Psalms into German and arguing in his* Jerusalem, or on Religious Power and Judaism *(1783) that Judaism was a rational religion. He was, thus, an eclectic and original thinker of extraordinary influence and interest, both in his day and in this. The following essay, which was published in the* Berlinische Monatsschrift, *originated as a lecture, delivered in 1784.*

From *What is Enlightenment? Eighteenth-Century Answers and Twentieth-Century Questions*, by James Schmidt (Berkeley: University of California Press, 1996), pp. 53–56.

The words *enlightenment, culture,* and *education* are newcomers to our language. They currently belong only to literary discourse. The masses scarcely understand them. Does this prove that these things are also new to us? I believe not. One says of a certain people that they have no specific word for "virtue," or none for "superstition," and yet one may justly attribute a not insignificant measure of both to them.

Linguistic usage, which seems to want to create a distinction between these synonymous words, still has not had the time to establish their boundaries. Education, culture, and enlightenment are modifications of social life, the effects of the industry and efforts of men to better their social conditions.

The more the social conditions of a people are brought, through art and industry, into harmony with the destiny of man, the more education this people has.

Education is composed of culture and enlightenment. Culture appears to be more, oriented toward practical matters: (objectively) toward goodness, refinement, and beauty in the arts and social mores; (subjectively) toward facility, diligence, and dexterity in the arts and inclinations, dispositions, and habits in social mores. The more these correspond in a people with the destiny of man, the more culture will be attributed to them, just as a piece of land is said to be more cultured and cultivated, the more it is brought, through the industry of men, to the state where it produces things that are useful to men. Enlightenment, in contrast, seems to be more related to theoretical matters: to (objective) rational knowledge and to (subjective) facility in rational reflection about matters of human life, according to their importance and influence on the destiny of man.

I posit, at all times, *the destiny of man as the measure and goal of all our striving and efforts*, as a point on which we must set our eyes, if we do not wish to lose our way.

A language attains enlightenment through the sciences and attains culture through social intercourse, poetry, and eloquence. Through the former it becomes better suited for theoretical usages, through the latter for practical usages. Both together make it an educated language.

Superficial culture is called "polish" [*Politur*]. Hail the nation, whose "polish" is the consequence of culture and enlightenment, whose external splendor and elegance have a foundation of internal, genuine truth!

Enlightenment is related to culture as theory to practice, as knowledge to ethics, as criticism to virtuosity. Regarded (objectively) in and for themselves, they stand in the closest connection, although subjectively they very often are separated.

One can say: Nürnbergers have more culture, Berliners more enlightenment; the French more culture, the English more enlightenment; the Chinese much culture and little enlightenment. The Greeks had both culture and enlightenment. They were an educated nation, just as their language is an educated language. Overall, the language of a people is the best indicator of its education, of culture as well as of enlightenment, in both breadth and intensity.

Further, the destiny of man can be divided into (1) the destiny of man *as man* and (2) the destiny of man *as citizen*.

With regard to culture these two coincide; for all practical perfection has value only in relation to social life and so must correspond only to the destiny of man as a member of society. Man *as man* needs no culture: but he needs enlightenment.

Status and vocation in civil life determine each member's duties and rights, and accordingly require different abilities and skills, different inclinations, dispositions, social mores and customs, a different culture and polish. The more

these correspond, throughout all the estates, with their vocations—that is, with their respective destinies as members of society—the more culture the nation possesses.

Each individual also requires, according to his status and vocation, different theoretical insights and different skills to attain them—a different degree of enlightenment. The enlightenment that is concerned with man *as man* is universal, without distinction of status; the enlightenment of man *as citizen* changes according to status and vocation. The destiny of man remains as always the measure and goal of these efforts.

Accordingly, the enlightenment of a nation is proportional to (1) the amount of knowledge, (2) its importance—that is, its relation to the destiny (a) of man and (b) of the citizen, (3) its dissemination through all estates, (4) its accord with their vocations. Thus the degree of a people's enlightenment is determined according to an at least fourfold relationship, whose members are in part once again composed out of simpler relations of members.

The enlightenment of man can come into conflict with the enlightenment of the citizen. Certain truths that are useful to men, as men, can at times be harmful to them as citizens. The following needs to be considered here. The collision can arise between the (1) essential or (2) accidental destinies of man and the (3) essential or (4) accidental destinies of citizens.

In the absence of the essential destiny of man, man sinks to the level of the beast; without the unessential destiny he is no longer good and splendid as a creature. In the absence of the essential destiny of man as citizen, the constitution of the state ceases to exist; without the unessential destiny it no longer remains the same in some ancillary relationships.

Unfortunate is the state that must confess that for it the essential destiny of man is not in harmony with the essential destiny of its citizens, in which the enlightenment that is indispensable to man cannot be disseminated through all the estates of the realm without risking the destruction of the constitution. Here philosophy lays its hand on its mouth! Here necessity may prescribe laws, or rather forge the fetters, that are applied to mankind, to force them down, and hold them under the yoke!

However, if the unessential destiny of man comes into conflict with the essential or unessential destiny of the citizen, rules must be established according to which exceptions are made and cases of collisions decided.

If the essential destiny of man has unfortunately been brought into conflict with his unessential destiny, if certain useful and—for mankind—adorning truths may not be disseminated without destroying prevailing religious and moral tenets, the virtue-loving bearer of enlightenment will proceed with prudence and discretion and endure prejudice rather than drive away the truth that is so closely intertwined with it. Of course, this maxim has become the bulwark of hypocrisy, and we have it to thank for so many centuries of barbarism and superstition. Whenever one has desired to apprehend the crime, it sought refuge in the sanctuary. Nevertheless, the friend of mankind must defer to these considerations, even in the most enlightened times. It is difficult, but not impossible, to find the boundary that separates use from misuse.

The more noble a thing is in its perfection, says a Hebrew writer, the more ghastly it is in its decay. A rotted piece of wood is not as ugly as a decayed flower; and this is not as disgusting as a decomposed animal; and this, again, is not as gruesome as man in his decay. So it is also with culture and enlightenment. The more noble in their bloom, the more hideous in their decay and destruction.

The misuse of enlightenment weakens the moral sentiment and leads to hard-heartedness, egoism, irreligion, and anarchy. Misuse of culture produces luxury, hypocrisy, weakness, superstition, and slavery.

Where enlightenment and culture go forward in step, they are together the best shield against corruption. In their manner of destruction they are directly opposed to one another.

The education of a nation, which according to the foregoing clarification of terms is composed of culture and enlightenment, will therefore be far less subject to corruption.

An educated nation knows of no other danger than an excess of national happiness, which, like the most perfect health of the human body, can in itself be called an illness, or the transition to an illness. A nation that through education has come to the highest peak of national happiness is just for that reason in danger of collapse, because it can climb no higher.—But this leads us too far from the question at hand.

REVIEW QUESTIONS

1. What is enlightenment?
2. How does it differ from "education" and "culture," and why are these distinctions important?
3. Why does Mendelssohn introduce national distinctions into his discussion? Does he mean to suggest that enlightenment may mean different things to different peoples?
4. Why does Mendelssohn introduce the distinction between "man" and "citizen"?
5. What do you suppose Mendelssohn means by "national happiness"?

JOHN RICKMAN

FROM *Journal of Captain Cook's Last Voyage*

John Rickman was a lieutenant in the British Royal Navy, who accompanied Captain James Cook on his third and final voyage to the Pacific Ocean. The Admiralty ordered Cook's third voyage to discover the Northwest Passage. Two ships undertook the voyage: HMS Resolution, *commanded by Cook and HMS* Discovery, *commanded by Charles Clerke. Rickman served as second lieutenant in Clerke's command. They departed Plymouth in 1776, sailed to Cape Town by way of Tenerife, and from there to New Zealand. After various ports of call in the Pacific, the ships discovered the Hawaiian Archipelago before reaching the Pacific coast of North America, which they charted, passing through the Bering Strait before being stopped by ice. Returning to the Pacific, the vessels wintered in Hawaii. Landing at Kealakekua Bay during Makahiki, a harvest festival for the god Lono, they received an unexpectedly warm welcome. The atmosphere gradually changed, however, becoming tensely antagonistic and prompting Cook to sail away from Hawaii and continue his search for the Northwest Passage. When a storm damaged his ship, Cook ordered a return to Hawaii for repairs. When he landed, the conflict between his crew and the Hawaiians turned violent and Cook was killed. Once some of Cook's remains were recovered, his squadron sailed away under the command of Clerke and, after Clerke's death, returned to England in 1780 under the command of John Gore. Upon their return James King, Cook's second lieutenant on HMS* Endeavour, *completed the captain's account, which had ended with his death on 17 January 1779. The accounts of his crew were handed to the Admiralty for editing before publication. The Admiralty entrusted this task to Dr. John Douglas, Canon of St. Paul's cathedral, who received Cook's and King's journals by November 1780. To these he added the journal of the surgeon, William Anderson. The collated work appeared in June 1784 to great public interest. It was preceded, however, by the publication of several unofficial accounts, the first of which was Rickman's 1781 narrative entitled* Journal of Captain Cook's Last Voyage. *It serves to this day as an alternative to other published accounts, especially as regards the death of Cook. Of this dramatic event, it offers the first account and thus constitutes a prime source.*

From *Journal of Captain Cook's Last Voyage to the Pacific Ocean, on Discovery*, by John Rickman (London: E. Newbery, 1781)

On the 26th, being then in lat. 21.15. about six A. M. we came in sight of land, bearing from S. S. W. to N. W. very high and beautiful; we were then so much in want of provisions, that Capt. Clerke, much against his inclination, was under the necessity of substituting stock-fish in the room of beef; but we were no sooner well in with the land, than we were visited by many of the inhabitants, who came off with their canoes with all sorts of provisions which their island afforded;

and every man on board, had leave to purchase what he could for his own subsistence. This diffused a joy among the mariners that is not easy to be expressed. From a sullenness and discontent visible in every countenance the day before, all was chearfulness, mirth and jollity. Fresh provisions and kind damsels are the sailors sole delight; and when in possession of these, past hardships are instantly forgotten: even those whom the scurvy had attacked, and had rendered pale and lifeless as ghosts, brightened upon this occasion, and for the moment appeared alert. This flattering beginning, however, yielded no substantial relief. The boats that were sent to sound the shore, and to look for a harbour, went out day after day, without being able to discover so much as a safe anchorage, and we were longer in finding a harbour than in making the coast. Nothing could be more toilsome or distressing than our present situation; within sight of land, yet unable to reach it; driven out to sea, by one storm, and in danger of being wrecked on the breakers by another. At length, after having examined the leeward side of the island, Captain Cook made the signal to stand out to sea. This was on the 7th of December, when it was determined to take a long stretch, in order, if possible, to get round the S. E. extremity, and to examine the weathermost side, where we were told there was a safe harbour. In this attempt we split our main-top-mast-stay-sail, and lost sight of the Resolution. The weather continuing tempestuous for many days, heavy complaints again prevailed among the ship's company. Their sufferings, from incessant labour and scanty provisions, were grown confessedly grievous. Their grog, that had been stopped as soon as we arrived upon the coast, was again dealt out to them as usual; and it was with the kindest treatment from their officers, that the men could be kept to their duty; yet on Christmasday, when each man was allowed a pint of brandy, and free leave to enjoy himself as he liked, not a murmur was heard; they the very next day returned to business, and continued it without repining, till

The 16th of January, 1779, when, after a series of the most tempestuous weather that ever happened in that climate, the boats from both ships were sent out to examine a fine bay, where we were informed there was a harbour in which we might safely moor, and where we should be supplied with materials to refit the ships, and provisions to victual them. In the evening the boats returned with the joyful news, that they had succeeded in their search, and that the harbour promised fair to answer all that had been said of it.

On the 17th our boats were employed in towing the ships into harbour in sight of the greatest multitude of Indian spectators in canoes and on shore, that we had ever seen assembled together in any part of our voyage. It was concluded, that their number could not be less than 2 or 3000. While we were hovering upon the coast, we had often been visited by 200 canoes at a time, who came to trade, and who brought us provisions when the weather would permit; and, besides provisions, they brought us great quantities of cordage, salt, and other manufactures of the island, which the Captains purchased for the use of the ships, and without which we could not have subsisted; for during the tempestuous weather our cordage snapped rope after rope, so that our spare hands were incessantly employed, night and day, in knotting and splicing, of which there was no end.

This day, before two o'clock, P. M. we were safely moored in 17 fathom water, in company with the Resolution, which a few days before we had given over for lost. From the time of attempting to get round the island, till the 8th of January, we had never been able to get sight of her, though both ships were constantly looking out to find each other. They had suffered much in their masts and rigging, and were happy at last, as well as ourselves, to find a convenient harbour to refit. We were scarce moored, when a young man, of majestic appearance, came along side, and after an oration, and the usual ceremonies of peace had passed on both sides, he came on board, bringing with him a small barbecued hog, some ready-dressed bread-fruit, and a curious mantle of red cloth, as presents to the Captain; and in return was complimented with several axes, looking-glasses, bracelets, and other shewy articles that attracted his notice. While he was busy in admiring every thing he saw on board the Discovery, the pinnace was ordered out, and he with his attendants were taken to Capt. Cook, where he found another Chief, of a still more graceful aspect, named Kaneena. All these were received with all possible respect. In the mean time came in another Chief, named Koah, who was soon discovered to be a priest; but who, in his youth, had been a distinguished warrior. After entertaining them with music, and inviting them to partake of such refreshments as the ship afforded, and making them some handsome presents, the Captain acquainted them with his wants, by shewing them the condition of his ship, and requesting a small portion of ground to land his materials, and to erect his tents. This request was readily granted, at the same time giving the Captain to understand, that the great King was absent, that he had lately been at war with the King of the neighbouring island of Mawwhee, that he was employed in settling the terms of peace, and that in less than ten days he was expected home. That they might, notwithstanding, land whatever they thought fit; and that the ground they had occasion for should be marked out and taboo'd, that is, appropriated to their use, without any of the natives being permitted to encroach upon it. Both Captains very readily embraced the offer, and prepared to accompany their benefactors to the town near which they wished to pitch their tents. Upon their landing, several vacant plats of ground were shewn them, and, when they had made their choice, stakes were ordered to be driven at certain distances, and a line to be carried round, within which the common people were forbidden to enter, under the severest penalties. Matters being thus amicably settled, no time was lost on our part to get every thing on shore. The tents, the armourer's forge, the masts, the sails, the rigging, the water-casks, the bread, the flour, the powder, in short, every article that wanted either to be reviewed or repaired were sent on shore; and not the least interruption was given to the boats employed in the carriage, or insult offered to the persons who conducted them. On the contrary, the Chiefs offered some empty houses, that were conveniently situated near the new dock (if that may be so termed where our artificers were set to work) for the sick to lodge till their recovery. No strangers were ever more hospitably received.

On the morning after our people landed, six large double canoes were seen entering the harbour at a great rate, having not less than 30 paddles to each canoe, with upwards of 60 Indians on board, most of them naked. Seeing them on their nearer approach making towards the ships, the Captains ordered the guns to be shotted, the marines to be drawn up, and every man to be ready at his post; the Indians assembled so fast, that before noon, the ships were surrounded with more than 100 canoes, in which there were not less than 1000 Indians. They at first traded friendly, having hogs in abundance, and plenty of bread-fruit, plantains, bananoes, and whatever else the island produced; but they had not been there long, before a large stone was thrown in at the cabin-window of the Discovery, by an invisible hand. A watch was instantly set, and in less than half an hour another stone was thrown at the caulkers, as they were at work on a stage on the ship's side. The offender was seen, and in sight of the Chiefs, and the whole multitude, he was seized, brought on board, tied to the shrouds, and punished with fifty lashes. In a few minutes, such was their fright, there was not an Indian to be seen near the ships.—Like unlucky boys, when one is apprehended for some naughty trick, the rest commonly fly the place.—And in fact, these people are in many respects like children, and in none more than in this instance. Before the day closed, they all again returned to trade, and, when night approached, not a male was to be seen; but swarms of females, who came to sleep on board, though much against the will of Capt. Cook, who, upon the first arrival of the ships upon the coast, wished to have prohibited all commerce with the women of the island; but he soon found, that if that commerce was forbidden, all other trade must cease of course, for not a pig could be purchased, unless a girl was permitted to bring it to market.

There are who have blamed Capt. Cook for his severity to the Indians; but it was not to the Indians alone that he was severe in his discipline. He never suffered any fault in his own people, though ever so trivial, to escape unpunished. If they were charged with insulting an Indian, or injuring him in his property, if the fact was proved, the offender was surely punished in sight of the Indians. By this impartial distribution of justice, the Indians themselves conceived so high an idea of his wisdom, and his power too, that they paid him the same honours as they did their Et-u-a, or Good Spirit.

The caulkers, who have already been mentioned, when they came round in course to the after-part of the Resolution, found that, besides the seams that wanted closing, there were other more material defects. The rudder's eyes were almost eaten through with rust, and the bolts ready to tumble out. This was an alarming defect; and all other business was suspended till that was repaired.

Every thing went on now as smoothly as could be wished. The Chiefs, if they saw any of their own people misbehave, would themselves give information, and bring them to punishment; they were so very obliging, that, seeing us in want of wood to burn, they made an offer of a high fence, that surrounded the Morai, adjoining to the town, for a present supply.

On the 19th, being the fourth day after our arrival, several very large canoes were seen to come from the S. E. We at first thought they were the friends with whom we had traded on the other side of the island; but on their nearer approach, we found they were all armed and clothed in the military uniform, after their country manner. This gave us cause to suspect some traiterous design, but our fears were in some measure dissipated by the assurances we received from our friends on board, that they were some of the warriors that had accompanied the King in his expedition against the Eree of Maw-wee, and that they were now returning home in triumph; but, notwithstanding this assurance, it was thought prudent to be upon our guard, and the rather as the women who were on board, told us, that their people designed to attack us, and to mattee, that is, to kill us every one.

Next day, before nine in the morning, more than a thousand Indians surrounded the Discovery, insomuch that pressing their weight chiefly on one side, the ship was in danger of being over-set. The Captain ordered two great guns to be fired, in order to try what effect that would have in dispersing them. In less than three minutes, there were a thousand heads to be seen above water, so many having jumped into the sea, frighted on the sudden report of the guns; neither did a single canoe come near us all the next day. Some of the women however remained on board, who never could be prevailed on to shew themselves upon deck in the day-time; but whether from fear of their own people, or of the great guns, we never could learn. As all trade was now stopt, and nothing brought on board for our subsistence, Capt. Cook went on shore to expostulate with the Chiefs, and by some trifling presents to engage them to trade as before; threatening at the same time to lay their towns waste, if they refused to supply the ships with the provisions they stood in need of. His remonstrances had the desired effect, and next day we purchased not less than 60 large hogs, with great quantities of fruits and vegetables for the ships use.

In a few days after this, the old King Terreeoboo was seen to enter the harbour, on his return from Maw-wee. In the afternoon he visited the ship in a private manner, attended only by one canoe, in which were his wife and children. He staid on board till near ten at night, when he returned to the village Kowrowa.

The next day about noon, the King, in a large canoe, attended by two others, set out from the village, and paddled towards the ships, in great state. Their appearance was grand and magnificent. In the first canoe was Terreeoboo, and his Chiefs, dressed in their feathered cloaks and helmets, and armed with long spears and daggers. In the second, came the venerable Kaoo, the Chief of the Priests, and his brethren, with their idols displayed on red cloth. These idols were busts of a gigantic size, made of wicker-work, and curiously covered with small feathers of various colours, wrought in the same manner with their cloaks. Their eyes were made of large pearl oysters, with a black nut fixed in the centre; their mouths were set with a double row of the fangs of dogs; and together, with the rest of their features, were strangely distorted. The third canoe was filled with hogs, and various sorts of vegetables. As they went along, the Priests, in the centre canoe, sung their hymns with great solemnity; and after paddling round the ships, instead of going on board as was expected, they made towards the shore, at the beach where our men were stationed.

On their approach, the guard was instantly ordered out to receive the King; and Capt. Cook, perceiving he was going on shore, followed him, and arrived nearly at the same time. They were conducted into the tent, where they had scarce been seated, when the King rose up, and, in a very graceful manner, threw over the Captain's shoulders, the cloak he himself wore, put a feathered helmet upon his head, and a curious fan in his hand. He also spread at his feet five or six other cloaks, all exceedingly beautiful, and of great value. His attendants then brought four very large hogs, with sugar-canes, cocoa-nuts, and bread fruit. This part of the ceremony over, they all made a circle round with their images in procession, till they arrived at their Morai, where they placed their deities, and deposited their arms.

Next day both Captains, accompanied with several of their officers, went to pay the King a visit on shore. They were very respectfully received, and having dined after the Indian manner, the King rose, and clothing Capt. Cook with a mantle, such as is worn by the great Oreno in grand procession, he was conducted to the morai, or place of worship, where a garland of green plantain leaves was put upon his head, and he was seated on a kind of throne, and had the honour of exchanging names with the King, the strongest pledge of friendship these islanders can confer. He was now addressed in a long oration by a priest clothed in a vestment of party-coloured cloth, who concluded the solemnity with a choral hymn, in which he was joined by all the priests present; who had no sooner finished their song than they all fell at his feet, the King acquainting him, that this was now his building, and that he was from henceforth their Orono. From this time an Indian Priest was, by the King's order, placed at the head of his pinnace, at whose approach the Indians in their canoes, as he passed them, prostrated themselves till he was out of sight; and this they did when the Captain was alone: but the Priests had orders from the King, whenever the Captain came ashore in his pinnace, to attend him, and conduct him to his house, which the sailors now called Cook's Altar.

When all these solemnities were over, we were not a little astonished to find in this King, the same infirm, emaciated, old man, that came on board Capt. Cook when off the island of Ma-wee; and it was soon discovered, that he was then accompanied with the same persons, viz. his two younger sons, one sixteen, the other twelve, with his nephew Maiha-Macha, a man of a most savage countenance.

[When we first approached the coast of this island of O why hee, we were astonished at the sight of a mountain of a stupendous height, whose head was covered with snow. This was so rare a sight in an island between the tropics, that several of the officers and gentlemen from both ships were desirous of taking a nearer view of it; and for that purpose they requested the King's permission, and a guide to attend them, which was readily granted, and no less than ten Indians contended which should accompany them.]

On the 26th Mr. Nelson, our botanist, and four other gentlemen set out in the morning on this expedition, which they afterwards found attended with no small fatigue, and not a little danger; for after travelling two days and two nights, and experiencing the greatest fatigue and hardships; no water, no paths to direct their way; no inhabitants for many miles, and the cold excessive as they approached the mountain, which seemed covered with snow, they were glad to get back without any accident. In the course of their journey, they were directed to the cottage of an old hermit, who, they said, had formerly been a great warrior; but who, for several years past, had retired to this sequestered spot. He received them without any kind of emotion, but would accept of nothing that they offered him. He appeared by far the oldest man they had seen on the island.

On the 29th they returned to the ships, and the only advantage that accrued from their journey, was, a curious assortment of indigenous plants and some natural curiosities, collected by Mr. Nelson. During their absence every thing remained quiet at the tents, and the Indians supplied the ships with such quantities of provisions of all kinds, that orders were given to purchase no more hogs in one day than could be killed, salted, and stowed away the next day. This order was in consequence of a former order, to purchase all that could be procured for sea-stock; by which so many were brought on board, that several of them died before they could be properly disposed of.

It had been generally thought impracticable to cure the flesh of these animals in the tropical climates; and it is believed, that few trials had ever been made before those of Capt. Cook. In his first voyage in 1774, he first made the attempt, but not very successfully. But it was now become absolutely necessary, either to perfect the discovery, or relinquish the voyage.

The method we took was always to slaughter them in the afternoon, and as soon as the hair was scalded off, and the entrails removed, the carcass was divided into pieces, from four to eight pounds each, and the bones of the chine and legs taken out, and, in the large sort, the ribs also. Every piece being then carefully wiped and examined, that no bruise might escape, and all the veins cleared out, that no coagulated blood might remain, they were then handed to the salters while the flesh was still warm. After they had been well rubbed with salt, they were then placed in a heap on a stage, raised in the open air, covered with planks, and pressed with the heaviest weights we could lay on them. In this situation they lay till the next evening, when they were again well wiped and examined, and the suspicious parts taken away. They were then put into a tub of strong pickle, where they were always looked over once or twice a day, and if any piece had not taken salt, which was readily discovered by the smell, they were immediately taken out, re-examined, and the sound pieces put to fresh pickle, and the other either used immediately, or thrown away. This, however, seldom happened. After six days, they were taken out, examined for the last time, and being again lightly pressed, they were packed in barrels with a thin layer of salt between them. Some of this pork was brought to England, perfectly sweet and good.

On the 1st of February, 1779, William Watman, gunner's mate, died. His body in the afternoon was carried on shore in the pinnace, and buried, according to his own desire, in the Morai belonging to the King. The Indians who dug his grave about four feet deep, covered the bottom of it with green leaves; and when the corpse was deposited in the earth, the Chiefs who attended the funeral, put a barbecued hog at the head, and another at the feet, with a quantity of bread-fruit, plantains and bananas. More was going to be added, when Capt. Cook ordered the grave to be covered up, and a post erected to the memory of the deceased, inscribed with his name, the date of the year, day of his death, and the nation to which he belonged. From this circumstance, Capt. Cook gave this port the name of Watman's Harbour. The next day the Indians rolled large stones over his grave, and brought two barbecued hogs, plantains and bananas, cocoa-nuts, and bread-fruit, which they placed over his grave, upon a stage erected for that purpose.

We were now preparing to depart, when our Captain was presented by the King with twelve large hogs, three boats-load of bread-fruit, potatoes, sugar-cane, and cocoa-nuts; and the same present was made to Capt. Cook.

This day, Feb. 2, the King came on board, attended with twenty of his Chiefs, and gave the Captains of both ships, with their officers, an invitation to an heiva, in which many of the principal Chiefs were to be performers. Capt. Clerke excused himself from ill health; but Capt. Cook and the other Gentlemen promised to attend.

The same day the King and his Chiefs dined on board the Resolution, and were entertained with music, the whole band having orders to play all the while they sat at dinner. They were highly delighted with the music, and would not suffer the performers to rest a moment.

About four in the afternoon, the pinnaces from both ships were ordered to be in readiness to take the company ashore, with their pendants and colours displayed, to do honour to a king and people, by whom we had been so hospitably entertained. More than 200 canoes attended us to shore, where a number of Chiefs were ready to receive us, who all observed a profound silence at our landing, and conducted us to the place appointed for the entertainment. But we were much disappointed by the performers, who were far inferior to those of the Southern islands.

The only part of the performance that was tolerable, was their singing, with which the heiva or play concluded; the young princesses, the chiefs, and even the king himself joining in the chorus.

The play being ended, Capt. Cook acquainted the King that, with his permission, he would exhibit some fire-works, that, if they did not frighten, would very much astonish his people. The King very readily gave his consent; and the engineer was ordered to begin his exhibition as soon as it was dark. On the rising of the first sky-rocket, the Indians fled precipitately, and hid themselves in the houses, or wherever they could find any shelter; at first there were some thousand spectators; but in less than ten minutes there were not fifty to be seen, the King and his attendants excepted, whom the Captain and the gentlemen with the greatest difficulty persuaded to stay. When the second rose up in the air, lamentations were heard from every quarter; and when the water-rockets were played off, the King and his Chiefs were hardly to be restrained. Other fire-works it was found dangerous to exhibit, as these had already struck the spectators, the King as well as his people, with a general panic. We therefore took leave of the King and Royal family, and returned on board our respective ships. The King having been made to understand that we should sail the first fair wind, came next morning to visit the Captains of both ships, who were now preparing to sail. This being publicly known, the Indians in general expressed their concern, but particularly the young women, whose lamentations were heard from every quarter.

In the evening of the 4th of February, all hands were mustered, and none were missing.

In the morning of the 5th, we cleared the harbour, shaping our course for Maw-wee, as we had been informed by the King, that in that island there was a fine harbour and excellent water. We had not been long under sail, when the King, who had omitted to take his leave of our Captain in the morning, as not suspecting our departure so sudden, came after the ships, accompanied by the young prince, his son, in a sailing canoe, bringing with them ten large hogs, a great number of fowls, and a small turtle (a great rarity) with bread-fruit in abundance. They also brought with them great quantities of cocoa-nuts, plantains, and sugar-canes.

Besides other persons of condition who acompanied the King, there was an old priest, Kaoa, who had always shewn a particular attachment to Capt. Clerke, and who had not been unrewarded for his civility. It being rather late when they reached the ships, they staid on board but a few hours, and then all departed except the old priest and some girls, who by the King's permission were suffered to remain on board till they should arrive at some of the neighbouring isles. We were now steering with a fine breeze, but just at the close of the evening, to our great mortification, the wind died away, and a great swell succeeding, with a strong current setting right in for the shore, we were in the utmost danger of being driven upon the rocks. In the height of our distress and trouble, the old priest, who had been suffered to sleep in the great cabin, leapt overboard unseen, with a piece of silk, the Captain's property, and swam to shore.

The next day, seeing a large canoe between us and the shore, we hove-to for her coming up, and to our great surprize perceived the old King, accompanied by several of his Chiefs, having in their vessel the priest who had stolen the silk, whom the King delivered to the Captain, at the same time requesting that his fault might be forgiven. The King being told that his request was granted, unbound him, and set him at liberty; telling the Captain that, seeing him with the silk, he judged it was none of his own, and therefore ordered him to be apprehended; and had taken this method of exposing him for injuring his friend. This singular instance of Indian generosity and justice, ought not to be forgotten. It appears, however, that this old priest, who had changed names, and was proud of being called *Bretanne*, had slipt away from Mr. Bligh, master of the Resolution, to whom he had pretended to discover a much more commodious harbour, than that of Kakooa, which they had just left. As soon as they had delivered the silk, which the Captain would have had the King to accept, they departed, and had scarce reached the shore, when a heavy gale came on, with thunder, lightning, and hard rain. We wore ship, and continued working off the land all night, and soon lost sight of the Resolution, who, as well as the Discovery, continued beating about the island seven days successively, in dread every moment of being wrecked upon the coast. On the fourth day, after we had lost sight of the Resolution, the storm being a little abated, we observed her under a high part of the island, lying with her fore-top-gallant-mast down, her fore-top-sail-yard upon the cap, and the sail furled, which gave us reason to suppose that some accident had befallen her; and as we expected, so we found it. We stood down for her with a heavy gale; but it was not till next day that we could come to speak with her. Capt. Cook himself being upon deck when we came up, informed us that he had sprung his fore-mast in two different places; that the ship was leaky, and that it was with the greatest difficulty they kept her above water. He further said, that on the 7th in the morning they discovered the leak; that at that time they made thirty inches of water in three hours; and that ever since all hands had been constantly employed night and day in baling and pumping; we likewise understood, that they had split their main-top-sail, and that they were now bound to our late harbour to repair their damage. We pursued the same course; but it was not till the 11th, when we opened on the bay in which lay our port. We were very soon surrounded with our old friends, who brought us hogs, bread-fruit, plantains, bananoes, and cocoa-nuts, which they threw on board, without waiting for any recompense. We were likewise visited by the old King, the Prince, and many of the Chiefs, who came to welcome us, and who were seemingly glad of our return. About ten in the morning, both ships moored near their old birth, and presently all hands were set to work to strip the mast, and to carry it on shore to be repaired.

The next day the King came again on board, and mutual presents and mutual civilities were continued as usual: but about five in the afternoon, there came along-side a large canoe, with about 60 of their fighting men, all armed, with little or no provisions on board, and who seemed to have no good design. Our Captain observing their motions, ordered the guns to be shotted, and every man to

his post. About six, they departed, without offering the least insult; but soon after we saw, upon a high hill, a large body assembled, who were observed to be gathering stones, and laying them in heaps. At dark they were seen to disperse; but great lights and fires were kept burning all night.

In the morning of the 13th, they again assembled, and began rolling the stones from the brink of the hill, in order, as we supposed, to divert our attention, but which rather served to awaken our fears. Our Captains looking upon this as an insult, ordered the guns to be levelled, and fired among them, and in ten minutes there was not an Indian to be seen near the place.

In the afternoon, the King came on board the Resolution, and complained to Capt. Cook of our killing two of his people, intimating at the same time, that they had not the least intention of hurting us. He continued on board some hours, amusing himself with seeing the armourers at work; and when he departed, requested that they might be permitted to make him a Pahoo-a, (an instrument they use in battle when they come to close quarters) which was readily granted.

From this time forward the natives became very tumultuous and unruly, and stole every thing they could lay their hands on, with any tolerable chance of escaping. They were fired upon, but that only enraged them. One who had just stolen the armourer's tongs and an iron chisel, with both which he was making to shore, was intercepted by Capt. Cook himself, who, with a few marines, endeavoured to seize him as he was landing; but the Indians seeing his design, came rushing in a body to the water-side, among whom the fellow found means to secrete himself; and the multitude, instead of delivering him up, attacked the boats that were in pursuit of him, seized their oars, broke them, and forced our whole party to retreat.

Capt. Cook having only a few marines with him, part of those who were placed as a guard to the carpenters employed upon the mast, did not think proper to renew the attack; but returned to the tents, ordering a strict watch to be kept during the night, and his whole force to be kept under arms till the matter should be accommodated. For this purpose,

Mr. Edgar, our master, was sent with a message to the young prince, who from the beginning had behaved friendly, to acquaint him with the cause of the fray, and to demand the delinquent to be delivered up. The prince, instead of listening to his remonstrances, assumed another countenance, and Mr. Edgar was very roughly handled, and glad to make his escape with a sound beating.

The temper of the Indians was now totally changed, and they became every day more and more troublesome.

On the 14th, a vast multitude of them were seen together, making great lamentation, and moving slowly along to the beating of a drum, that scarce gave a stroke in a minute. From this circumstance, it was supposed they were burying the dead, who had been killed the day before. No violence, however, was either done or attempted this day, though the girls that were on board gave us to understand, that their countrymen only waited a favourable opportunity to attack the ships.

On the morning of the 15th, our great cutter, which was moored to the buoy, was missing from her moorings, and, upon examination, the boat's painter was found cut two fathoms from the buoy, and the remainder of the rope gone with the boat.

This gave cause to suspect that some villainy was concerting; and, in order to prevent the ill-consequences that might follow, both Captains met on board the Resolution, to consult what was best to be done on this critical occasion. The officers from both ships were present at this council, where it was resolved to seize the King, and to confine him on board till the boat should be returned.

With this view, early on the morning of the 16th, Capt. Cook, with Mr. Phillips, Lieutenant of Marines, and nine of his men, went on shore, under cover of the guns of both ships, to one side of the bay where the King resided; and Mr. King, second Lieutenant of the Resolution, who had always been stationed with a guard to protect the working party and the waterers on shore, went, as usual, to the other side. The Indians, observing our motions, and seeing the ships warping towards the towns, of which there were two, one on each side the bay, they concluded that our design was to seize their marine.

In consequence of which, most of their large war canoes took the alarm, and were making off, when our guns, loaded with grape and canister shot, drove them back; and the Captain and his guard landed without opposition. We observed, however, that their warriors were clothed in their military dress, though without arms, and that they were gathering together in a body from every direction, their Chiefs assuming a very different countenance to what they usually wore upon all former occasions. However, Capt. Cook, attended by the Lieutenant of Marines, a Serjeant, and nine privates, regardless of appearances, proceeded directly to the King's residence, where they found him seated on the ground, with about twelve of his Chiefs round him, who all prostrated themselves on seeing the Orono enter. The Captain addressed the King in the mildest terms, assuring him that no violence was intended against his person or any of his people, except against those who had been guilty of a most unprecedented act of robbery, by cutting from her moorings one of the ship's boats, without which they could neither conveniently water the ships, nor carry on the necessary communication with the shore; calling upon the King, at the same time, to give orders for the boat to be immediately restored, and inviting him, in the most friendly manner, to accompany him on board, till his orders should be carried into execution. The King protested his total ignorance of the theft; said, he was very ready to assist in discovering the thief, and should be glad to see him punished; and shewed no unwillingness himself to trust his person with the Orono, though he had lately exercised very unusual severities against his people. He was told that the tumultuous appearance of his people, and their repeated robberies, made some uncommon severities necessary; but that not the least hurt should be done to the meanest inhabitant of his island by any person belonging to the ships, without exemplary punishment; and all that was necessary for the continuance of peace was, to pledge himself for the honesty of his people. With that view, and that view only, the Captain said he came to request the King to place confidence in him, and to make his ship his residence, as the most effectual means of putting a stop to the robberies that were now daily and hourly committed and committing, by his people, both at the tents and on board the ships, and were so daring as to become insufferable. The King, upon this remonstrance, was preparing to comply, and his two sons were actually on board the pinnace to accompany the Orono, when a woman, mother to the boys, and a great favourite of the King's, came after them, and, with many tears and entreaties, besought them to come on shore and not to go on board the ships. The Chiefs, at the same time, began to take the alarm; but the good old King, not yet suspecting, or pretending not to suspect, any treachery, had made himself ready to accompany the Captain, and was actually on his way; but by this time the women and children were sent away, and the men put on their war mats, and armed themselves, and so great a body of Indians were got together, and had lined the shore, that it was impossible they could break through the multitude, who now began to behave outrageously, and to insult the guard. Capt. Cook, observing their behaviour, gave orders to the officer of marines to make way, and if any one opposed, to fire upon and instantly dispatch him. This order the Lieutenant endeavoured to carry into execution, and a lane was made for the King and his Chiefs to get to the boats; but they had scarce reached the water-side, when the word was given, that the Orono (for so they called Capt. Cook) was about to carry off their King to kill him. In an instant a number of their fighting men broke from the crowd, and with clubs and stones rushed in upon the guard, four of whom were presently dispatched. A ruffian making a stroke at Capt. Cook, was shot dead by the Captain himself, who, having a double-barreled gun, was aiming at another, when a savage came behind him, and striking him on the head with his club, felled him to the ground; and then thrust his pahooa through his body with such force, that, entering between his shoulders, the point of it came out at his breast. The quarrel now became general. The guns from the ships began to pour in their fire upon the crowd, and the musquetry from the boats; but such was their intrepidity, that, contrary to all expectation,

they stood their ground, and carried off in triumph the bodies of the dead.

Besides Capt. Cook, whose death was universally deplored, Corporal Thomas, and three privates, Hinkes, Allen, and Fadget, fell victims to their fury; and three more of the marines were desperately wounded. Lieut. Phillips, who had received a wound between the shoulders with a pahooa, shot the man dead who had wounded him, just as he was going to repeat his blow: it seemed as if it was against our Commodore that their vengeance was chiefly directed, by whose order they supposed their king was to be forced on board, and punished at his discretion. Seeing him fall, they set up a great shout, and his body was instantly surrounded by the enemy, who snatching the dagger out of each other's hands, they shewed a savage eagerness to have a share in his destruction.

Thus fell the greatest navigator that this or any other nation could boast; the account of whose death was transmitted to England by Professor Pallas, from Petersburg, long before the arrival of our journalist; and with such circumstances of agreement in the principal facts, as sufficiently prove the authenticity of both.

The Professor says, "The inhabitants shewed Capt. Cook (during his first stay) a respect that bordered on adoration; but on his second landing they grew more thievish than before; and at last, the cutter belonging to the Discovery was cut loose and carried away. The day after this happened the Captain, with his Lieutenant, and nine marines, landed. He went up to the residence of the chief Terreboo. He was received with respect; but he found a great crowd assembled with the chief. Some of them grew insolent as he made his complaints; one of them in particular indulged his grimaces in so provoking a manner, that the Captain discharged at him the shot of his fowling-piece. On which a general commotion ensued. The Lieutenant fired, and killed one dead upon the spot; but instead of dispersing, they now made a general attack, and though the marines fired one round with great effect, the crowd was not intimidated, but rushed on with such rapidity, that there was no time to load again. In the first onset Capt. Cook and four of his people were unhappily killed upon the spot; and it was with great difficulty that the Lieutenant and the remaining marines could make their retreat, most of them wounded; and it would have been almost impossible for them to have escaped, had it not been for the fire from the pinnace and long-boat, that lay at some distance from the beach. Capt. Clerke saw no possibility of revenging the loss of his gallant countryman but with great slaughter, he therefore kept upon the defensive."

—To return to our Journalist.

The dead being past recovery, the distressed situation of the living was now to be regarded. The Resolution was without her mast, and lay in a manner at the mercy of the savages, who it was every moment expected, would have cut away her moorings and drifted her on shore. It was therefore the first care of Capt. Clerke, who succeeded to the command, to order the mast to be floated away, and to get the tents and all our other baggage on board. For this purpose no time was to be lost. While many of the natives lay dead upon the beach, it was judged the properest time to take advantage of that interval of inactivity, which always succeeds any considerable exertion of Indian ferocity. Lieutenant King, who, as has been observed before, commanded the working-party on the other side the bay, and who had cultivated a friendship with the priests, whose dwellings were contiguous to the Morai, was all this while ignorant of what was going forward; but could not help being under inexpressible anxiety at seeing the extraordinary agitation by land, and hearing the firing from the ships at sea, and the boats near the shore; but at the same time had assured the priests, who were equally alarmed, that whatever might be the matter, they should be safe; was not a little startled, when just at that critical moment, two great shot from the Discovery cut a tree in the middle, under which some of them were sitting, and split a piece from a rock in a direct line to their dwellings: for Capt. Clerke being under no less concern for Lieut. King and those under his command, and having no clue, but appearances to go by, had caused the fire of the great guns to be directed to that quarter, as soon as

the natives were dispersed from the other. Our whole force was therefore collected, and, having landed under cover of our guns, we marched rapidly up the hill, with bayonets fixed, and took possession of the Morai, which stood on elevated ground, and gave us an advantage over the savages, who could not approach us from the shore, neither could they attack us from the towns, without being exposed to our fire from the ships. They made several unsuccessful attempts to dislodge us, but were repulsed with loss. After sustaining an unequal conflict for three hours, in which several of them were killed, without being able to make any impression on our small body, and without our losing a man, though several were much hurt by the stones from their slings, they at length dispersed, and left us masters of our tents and of all our other property.

Our next care was to recover the bodies of our dead. A strong party under Lieut. King, were sent out in the pinnaces and boats, with a white flag, in token of peace, to endeavour to procure them. They were met by Koah, a Chief, (with whom Mr. King was well acquainted) and of note among the savages, at the head of a vast multitude, without at first answering our signal; but Mr. King, commanding the armed boats to stop, and going himself in a small boat alone, with a white flag in his hand, had the satisfaction to be instantly understood; the men threw off their war-mats; the women returned to the beach, and Koah shewed equal confidence, by swimming off with a flag in his hand, and on entering the boat where Mr. King sat, with as much unconcern as if nothing had happened: being told that they were come to demand the body of Capt. Cook, or to declare war, if it was not instantly restored, he assured the Lieutenant, that he would go himself and procure it, begged a piece of iron of him, and joyfully swam on shore, calling out to his countrymen, that now we were all friends again; but notwithstanding this Chief's dissembled friendship, our men in the boats, who had entered into parley with the natives, were informed, that the warriors were then on the back of the hill, cutting up and dividing the bodies of the slain. While we remained in our boats, several other Chiefs came to the water-side; and one in particular, with Capt. Cook's hanger, which he drew in a vaunting manner, and brandished it over his head; others shewed themselves with the spoils taken from the dead; one having a jacket, another a shirt, a third a pair of trowsers, and so on; insulting us, as it were, with the trophies of their victory.

At this time it was thought prudent to stifle our resentment, and to reserve our vengeance till a more favourable opportunity. We were now in want of water; our sails and rigging in a shattered condition; our cordage bad, and our repairs not near finished; all therefore we had to do, was to remain upon the defensive till we were better provided.

At the close of the evening, as soon as it was dark, a canoe was heard paddling towards the Resolution, in which were two men. As it approached, both sentinels fired, but without hurting either of the men, though the balls went through the bottom of the canoe. Notwithstanding this, the canoe came close under the ship's stern; and one of the men calling out *Tinne, Tinne*, (the name Mr. King was known by) whom the Priests had always supposed to be the Orono's son, and, therefore, the Earee of the ship, this excited every one's curiosity, and orders were given to admit them on board; they were priests, and produced a piece of flesh, carefully wrapped up in a cloth, which they solemnly assured us was part of the thigh of our late Commander; that he saw it cut from the bone, but believed that all the flesh of the body was burnt; that the head and all the bones, except what belonged to the trunk, were in the possession of Terreoboo, and the other Chiefs; that what we saw, had been brought to Kaoa, the High Priest, to be made use of in some religious ceremony; and that he had sent it as a proof of the sincerity of his innocence and his friendship. Being asked, if any part of the flesh had been eaten, they expressed the utmost horror at the idea. They afterwards asked, with some apparent apprehension, when the Orono would come again, and what he would do to them on his return? The same question had been asked by others, which shews, the opinion they entertain of the spirit's power after it is separated from the body. They then desired to be set at liberty, which was granted. One of the men was the Priest who had attended

Capt. Cook, and who was ready on all occasions, to fall down and worship him. He lamented his loss with abundance of tears, and earnestly besought us to keep their coming a secret, for if it should be known, it would prove fatal to their whole fraternity. They farther informed us, that 17 of their countrymen were killed in the first action at Kowrowa, of whom five were Chiefs; and that Kaneena and his brother, our particular friends, were among the number; eight, they said, were killed at the observatory, of whom three were of the first rank. As this was the fact, the story that was given out to conceal it, may be worth relating.

On the 19th, says our journalist, the father and mother of two girls, who had concealed themselves on board the ship, came in the dead of the night, in their canoe, loaded with cocoa-nuts and breadfruit, which they had been gathering in the day for their own subsistence, as a supply for their children, lest, from what had happened, they should have been suffered to die for want; acquainting us at the same time with a treacherous design of their countrymen to cut our cables, and drift the ships ashore. They were taken on board, and detained prisoners till morning, when not an Indian was to be seen near the harbour, but such as were old and feeble, and knew not how to make their escape. The informers were tenderly treated, had presents made them, and were afterwards dismissed, at their own desire, upon a neighbouring island, with every token of kindness.—The truth is, the Priests had desired the guard-boat to attend them, lest they should have been fired at, and interrupted by the guard-boats of the other ship, by which they might have been discovered, and perhaps put to death.

Among other incidents of the present day, Feb. 16, there was one which could not be understood. Two boys were seen swimming towards the ships, singing, as they approached the ships, a mournful and plaintive song. They had each a long spear in his hand, which, on boarding the Discovery, they delivered to the Officer on the deck, and then departed. Who sent them, or for what purpose, we never could learn.

On the 17th, the different promotions took place, and according to their succession, the Officers changed ships; Capt. Clerke went on board the Resolution, and Mr. Gore, first Lieutenant of the Resolution, took the command of the Discovery.

On the 18th both ships were again warped near the shore, and a spring put upon their cables, in order to cover the boats which were sent to compleat our complement of water. On this motion crowds of inhabitants were seen to assemble, with a large black flag displayed, which we interpreted as a signal for war; but we afterwards found that it was part of their ceremony in burying their dead. Under this mistake a few guns were fired from the ships to disperse them, by which the King's nephew, Maiha Maiha, was wounded, and a poor woman lost her arm. This made a strong impression on the whole body of Indians, and we were left in quiet both this and the next day, to pursue our repairs and compleat our hold.

On the 19th they began again to be troublesome. In the morning, while the boats were loading, at the well, the stones came about the watermen like hail, some of them of more than a pound weight; one in particular was seen coming; but who threw it, no one could tell. This being attended to, a native was observed to creep out of a cavern, who, as soon as he had discharged his stone, retired back to his place of shelter. Him we marked, and returned to our ships; and it being now apparent that nothing was to be gained by fair means, orders were given to strike terror among them, by pursuing them with fire and sword. About two in the afternoon, all who were able to bear arms, as well sailors and artificers as marines, were mustered, and preparations made to sustain them, while with lighted torches they rowed on shore, and set fire to the S. E. town, pursuing the frighted inhabitants while their houses were in flames, with unrelenting fury. Many were put to death, and all driven to seek shelter where they could, scarce a house having escaped the general conflagration. In this vindictive enterprize, the cavern or hole of the crafty Indian, whose insolence had been one principal cause of the desolation that followed, was not forgotten. His cavern had been marked, as has already been observed, and on seeing our sailors approach it, such was his inveteracy, that he heaved a huge stone at the

assailants, one of whom he dangerously wounded, but was instantly dispatched by the discharge of three muskets, and a bayonet run through his body. Our vengeance being now fully executed, we returned to the ships, loaded with the spoils of the towns, consisting of bows and arrows, clubs, and arms of all kinds, which they use in battle; and having the heads of two of their fighting men, of which the courageous native was one, stuck at the bows of the pinnaces, as a terror to the enemy from ever daring again to molest us.

About four in the afternoon of the 20th, ten girls came down to the well, where the waterers were busy, with quantities of fruit, as much as they could carry, for which they would take nothing in return, only praying to be taken on board. This was denied them, as peremptory orders had been given by Capt. Clerke, forbidding the admission of any more of their women.

This day, in the morning, a Chief was seen coming down the hill, followed by a number of boys, with a white flag displayed, and carrying boughs and green branches in their hands. They came singing to the water side; but that did not prevent their receiving the fire of a party that was placed as a guard. On seeing his ensign answered by a white flag at each mizen-top-mast-head, he, accompanied with three other Chiefs, came on board, having some cocoa-nuts, plantains, and bread-fruit, as presents to the Commander, for which they would accept of nothing in return. This Chief, whose name was Eappo, came to make submission; and, as a token of his sincerity, promised to collect the bones of our deceased warrior, as he called him, and to bring them, and lay them at our feet. This was the token of the most perfect submission that a native warrior could make to his conqueror; and this was accepted on the part of our Commander. In this manner, and on these conditions, peace was to be restored.

At nine in the morning of the next day, the same old Chief returned, attended by a more numerous suit than before, having several large hogs added to his peace-offerings; and with him, likewise, he brought the bones of Capt. Cook, his back-bone, and the bones of his feet only excepted, which he promised to produce the next visit he made. On examination, the head appeared to have been scalped; the face was entirely gone; the hands had the flesh on, but scored and salted; and, as he assured the Captain, most of the flesh besides was burnt. Our Commander made signs to return the cutter, but was told it was broke up and burnt for the iron. The arms belonging to the marines, who were killed, were next demanded; but these, it was said, were carried up the country by common people, and were irrecoverable. Some presents were made to this friendly Chief, who departed well satisfied. We were now preparing to depart, when provisions of all sorts came pouring in upon us faster than we could consume them. The Chief kept his promise, and

On the 23d, Eappo and the King's son, came on board, and brought the bones of the Captain that were missing: these were all placed in due form, in a case made for the purpose, and under a triple discharge from the ships, buried in the bay. The terror of the natives on this occasion was increased, by a four pound ball being loaded by mistake, which fortunately did no other mischief than that of exciting the jealousy of the natives, that our professions of peace were not sincere; which possibly might be the case with him who loaded the gun, as the sailors in general could hardly be restrained from violence, whenever a native came within their power. Nothing more remained now to be done.

This day we had the satisfaction of getting the foremast of the Resolution shipt, which was a work of great labour, and some difficulty, as the ropes were now become rotten, and unable to sustain the purchase; however, that being at length accomplished, and the repairs compleated, so far at least as our circumstances would allow, we bent our sails in the morning; and were visited by many of our former friends, among whom was the King's youngest son, a boy of about fourteen years of age, of whom Capt. Cook was remarkably fond; and the boy, in return, was no less attached to the Captain. He came to express his sorrow for the accident that had happened, which he did by a plentiful flow of tears. He gave us to understand, that his two brothers were killed, and that his father was retired to an inaccessible place. Capt. Clerke made him

some presents that were pleasing to him, and he departed very much comforted.

About 7 in the evening, a breeze springing up in our favour, we unmoored, and soon left Karakakooa Bay, for that was the name of the bay in which we had been moored, shaping our course to the N. W. Nothing remarkable till

The 28th, when we opened upon a fine bay, in one of the Leeward Islands, called by the inhabitants O-aa-ah, where the ships came to an anchor, and where both Captains landed: they found a fine running river, but brackish towards the sea; they therefore made a very short stay. Several of the inhabitants came on board, who were so immoderately fond of iron, that they endeavoured to wrench the very ring-bolts from the hatches. Here we put ashore the family that accompanied us from O-whye, and here we purchased a few small swine; some bread-fruit and plantains, and a quantity of a root called Ta-ee, not unlike fern-root, but of an enormous size, some weighing from 60 to 70 pounds. It is a powerful anti-scorbutic, of the saccharine kind. Pounded, we made an excellent liquor from it, very pleasant, and exceedingly wholesome. We had quantities of it when we reached Kamshatska, and as good as when first purchased.

REVIEW QUESTIONS

1. How would you characterize Rickman's portrayal of the Hawaiians?
2. To what kinds of observations does Rickman devote most attention?
3. Would you describe Rickman's account as empirical or subjective? What evidence would you offer to support your answer?
4. What portrait of James Cook emerges from Rickman's account?
5. Does the death of Cook change Rickman's attitude toward the Hawaiians or his account of the voyage in any substantial way?
6. Does Rickman's account substantiate the scientific and commercial intentions of the Admiralty? If not, what purpose does the actual voyage serve?

OLAUDAH EQUIANO

FROM *The Interesting Narrative of the Life of Olaudah Equiano, or Gustavus Vassa, the African*

One of the most notable records of the slave trade, which dominated African-European relations into the nineteenth century, was the autobiography of Equiano, an ex-slave living in London. He was remarkable not only because he survived the experience of capture, transportation, and exploitation, but also because he obtained sufficient education and opportunity to record his experiences. The extract provided here describes his first encounter with white men aboard a slave ship. Freed in 1766, he toured widely, speaking and writing against the slave trade until his death sometime between 1797 and 1801.

From *The Interesting Narrative of the Life of Olaudah Equiano, or Gustavus Vassa, the African, written by himself,* edited by Werner Sollors, a Norton Critical Edition (New York: Norton, 2001), pp. 38–43.

*   *   *

The first object which saluted my eyes when I arrived on the coast was the sea, and a slave ship, which was then riding at anchor, and waiting for its cargo. These filled me with astonishment, which was soon converted into terror when I was carried on board. I was immediately handled and tossed up to see if I were sound by some of the crew; and I was now persuaded that I had gotten into a world of bad spirits, and that they were going to kill me. Their complexions too differing so much from ours, their long hair, and the language they spoke, (which was very different from any I had ever heard) united to confirm me in this belief. Indeed such were the horrors of my views and fears at the moment, that, if ten thousand worlds had been my own, I would have freely parted with them all to have exchanged my condition with that of the meanest slave in my own country. When I looked round the ship too and saw a large furnace or copper boiling, and a multitude of black people of every description chained together, every one of their countenances expressing dejection and sorrow, I no longer doubted of my fate; and, quite overpowered with horror and anguish, I fell motionless on the deck and fainted. When I recovered a little I found some black people about me, who I believed were some of those who brought me on board, and had been receiving their pay; they talked to me in order to cheer me, but all in vain. I asked them if we were not to be eaten by those white men with horrible looks, red faces, and loose hair. They told me I was not; and one of the crew brought me a small portion of spirituous liquor in a wine glass; but, being afraid of him, I would not take it out of his hand. One of the blacks therefore took it from him and gave it to me, and I took a little down my palate, which, instead of reviving me, as they thought it would, threw me into the greatest consternation at the strange feeling it produced, having never tasted any such liquor before. Soon after this the blacks who brought me on board went off, and left me abandoned to despair. I now saw myself deprived of all chance of returning to my native country, or even the least glimpse of hope of gaining the shore, which I now considered as friendly; and I even wished for my former slavery in preference to my present situation, which was filled with horrors of every kind, still heightened by my ignorance of what I was to undergo. I was not long suffered to indulge my grief; I was soon put down under the decks, and there I received such a salutation in my nostrils as I had never experienced in my life: so that, with the loathsomeness of the stench, and crying together, I became so sick and low that I was not able to eat, nor had I the least desire to taste any thing. I now wished for the last friend, death, to relieve me; but soon, to my grief, two of the white men offered me eatables; and, on my refusing to eat, one of them held me fast by the hands, and laid me across I think the windlass,[1] and tied my feet, while the other flogged me severely. I had never experienced any thing of this kind before; and although, not being used to the water, I naturally feared that element the first time I saw it, yet nevertheless, could I have got over the nettings, I would have jumped over the side, but I could not; and, besides, the crew used to watch us very closely who were not chained down to the decks, lest we should leap into the water: and I have seen some of these poor African prisoners most severely cut for attempting to do so, and hourly whipped for not eating. This indeed was often the case with myself. In a little time after, amongst the poor chained men, I found some of my own nation, which in a small degree gave ease to my mind. I inquired of these what was to be done with us; they gave me to understand we were to be carried to these white people's country to work for them. I then was a little revived, and thought, if it were no worse than working, my situation was not so desperate: but still I feared I should be put to death, the white people looked and acted, as I thought, in so savage a manner; for I had never seen among any people such instances of brutal cruelty; and this not only shewn towards us blacks, but also to some of the whites themselves. One white man in particular I saw, when we were permitted to be on deck, flogged so unmercifully with a large rope near the foremast, that he died in consequence of it; and they tossed him over

the side as they would have done a brute. This made me fear these people the more; and I expected nothing less than to be treated in the same manner. I could not help expressing my fears and apprehensions to some of my countrymen: I asked them if these people had no country, but lived in this hollow place (the ship): they told me they did not, but came from a distant one. "Then," said I, "how comes it in all our country we never heard of them?" They told me because they lived so very far off. I then asked where were their women? had they any like themselves? I was told they had: "and why," said I, "do we not see them?" they answered, because they were left behind. I asked how the vessel could go? they told me they could not tell; but that there were cloths put upon the masts by the help of the ropes I saw, and then the vessel went on; and the white men had some spell or magic they put in the water when they liked in order to stop the vessel. I was exceedingly amazed at this account, and really thought they were spirits. I therefore wished much to be from amongst them, for I expected they would sacrifice me: but my wishes were vain; for we were so quartered that it was impossible for any of us to make our escape. While we stayed on the coast I was mostly on deck; and one day, to my great astonishment, I saw one of these vessels coming in with the sails up. As soon as the whites saw it, they gave a great shout, at which we were amazed; and the more so as the vessel appeared larger by approaching nearer. At last she came to an anchor in my sight, and when the anchor was let go I and my countrymen who saw it were lost in astonishment to observe the vessel stop; and were now convinced it was done by magic. Soon after this the other ship got her boats out, and they came on board of us, and the people of both ships seemed very glad to see each other. Several of the strangers also shook hands with us black people, and made motions with their hands, signifying I suppose we were to go to their country; but we did not understand them. At last, when the ship we were in had got in all her cargo, they made ready with many fearful noises, and we were all put under deck, so that we could not see how they managed the vessel. But this disappointment was the least of my sorrow. The stench of the hold while

---

[1] An apparatus for winding rope.

we were on the coast was so intolerably loathsome, that it was dangerous to remain there for any time, and some of us had been permitted to stay on the deck for the fresh air; but now that the whole ship's cargo were confined together, it became absolutely pestilential. The closeness of the place, and the heat of the climate, added to the number in the ship, which was so crowded that each had scarcely room to turn himself, almost suffocated us. This produced copious perspirations, so that the air soon became unfit for respiration, from a variety of loathsome smells, and brought on a sickness among the slaves, of which many died, thus falling victims to the improvident avarice, as I may call it, of their purchasers. This wretched situation was again aggravated by the galling of the chains, now become insupportable; and the filth of the necessary tubs,[2] into which the children often fell, and were almost suffocated. The shrieks of the women, and the groans of the dying, rendered the whole a scene of horror almost inconceivable. Happily perhaps for myself I was soon reduced so low here that it was thought necessary to keep me almost always on deck; and from my extreme youth I was not put in fetters. In this situation I expected every hour to share the fate of my companions, some of whom were almost daily brought upon deck at the point of death, which I began to hope would soon put an end to my miseries. Often did I think many of the inhabitants of the deep much more happy than myself. I envied them the freedom they enjoyed, and as often wished I could change my condition for theirs. Every circumstance I met with served only to render my state more painful, and heighten my apprehensions, and my opinion of the cruelty of the whites. One day they had taken a number of fishes; and when they had killed and satisfied themselves with as many as they thought fit, to our astonishment who were on the deck, rather than give any of them to us to eat as we expected, they tossed the remaining fish into the sea again, although we begged and prayed for some as well as we could, but in vain; and some of my countrymen, being pressed by hunger, took an opportunity when they thought no one saw them, of trying to get a little privately; but they were discovered, and the attempt procured them some very severe floggings. One day, when we had a smooth sea and moderate wind, two of my wearied countrymen who were chained together (I was near them at the time), preferring death to such a life of misery, somehow made through the nettings and jumped into the sea: immediately another quite dejected fellow, who, on one account of his illness, was suffered to be out of irons, also followed their example; and I believe many more would very soon have done the same if they had not been prevented by the ship's crew, who were instantly alarmed. Those of us that were the most active were in a moment put down under the deck, and here was such a noise and confusion amongst the people of the ship as I never heard before, to stop her, and get the boat out to go after the slaves. However two of the wretches drowned, but they got the other, and afterwards flogged him unmercifully for thus attempting to prefer death to slavery. In this manner we continued to undergo more hardships than I can now relate, hardships which are inseparable from this accursed trade. Many a time we were near suffocation from the want of fresh air, which we were often without for whole days together. This, and the stench of the necessary tubs, carried off many. During our passage I first saw flying fishes, which surprised me very much: they used frequently to fly across the ship, and many of them fell on the deck. I also now first saw the use of the quadrant;[3] I had often with astonishment seen the mariners make observations with it, and I could not think what it meant. They at last took notice of my surprise; and one of them, willing to increase it, as well as to gratify my curiosity, made me one day look through it. The clouds appeared to me to be land, which disappeared as they passed along. This heightened my wonder; and I was now more persuaded than ever that I was in another world, and that every thing about me was magic. At last we came in sight of the island of Barbadoes,[4] at which the whites on board gave a great shout, and made

---

[2] Latrines.

[3] Instrument used to determine geographical latitude.

[4] Or Barbados, the most easterly of the Caribbean islands.

many signs of joy to us. We did not know what to think of this; but as the vessel drew nearer we plainly saw the harbour, and other ships of different kinds and sizes; and we soon anchored amongst them off Bridge Town.[5] Many merchants and planters now came on board, though it was in the evening. They put us in separate parcels, and examined us attentively. They also made us jump, and pointed to the land, signifying we were to go there. We thought by this we should be eaten by these ugly men, as they appeared to us; and, when soon after we were all put down under the deck again, there was much dread and trembling among us, and nothing but bitter cries to be heard all the night from these apprehensions, insomuch that at last the white people got some old slaves from the land to pacify us. They told us we were not to be eaten, but to work, and were soon to go on land, where we should see many of our country people. This report eased us much; and sure enough, soon after we were landed, there came to us Africans of all languages. We were conducted immediately to the merchant's yard, where we were all pent up together like so many sheep in a fold, without regard to sex or age. As every object was new to me every thing I saw filled me with surprise. What struck me first was that the houses were built with stories, and in every other respect different from those in Africa: but I was still more astonished on seeing people on horseback. I did not know what this could mean; and indeed I thought these people were full of nothing but magical arts. While I was in this astonishment one of my fellow prisoners spoke to a countryman of his about the horses, who said they were the same kind they had in their country. I understood them, though they were from a distant part of Africa, and I thought it odd I had not seen any horses there; but afterwards, when I came to converse with different Africans, I found they had many horses amongst them, and much larger than those I then saw. We were not many days in the merchant's custody before we were sold after their usual manner, which is this:—On a signal given, (as the beat of a drum) the buyers rush at once into the yard where the slaves are confined, and make choice of that parcel they like best. The noise and clamour with which this is attended, and the eagerness visible in the countenances of the buyers, serve not a little to increase the apprehensions of the terrified Africans, who may well be supposed to consider them as the ministers of that destruction to which they think themselves devoted. In this manner, without scruple, are relations and friends separated, most of them never to see each other again. I remember in the vessel in which I was brought over, in the men's apartment, there were several brothers, who, in the sale, were sold in different lots; and it was very moving on this occasion to see and hear their cries at parting. O, ye nominal Christians! might not an African ask you, learned you this from your God, who says unto you, Do unto all men as you would men should do unto you? Is it not enough that we are torn from our country and friends to toil for your luxury and lust of gain? Must every tender feeling be likewise sacrificed to your avarice? Are the dearest friends and relations, now rendered more dear by their separation from their kindred, still to be parted from each other, and thus prevented from cheering the gloom of slavery with the small comfort of being together and mingling their sufferings and sorrows? Why are parents to lose their children, brothers their sisters, or husbands their wives? Surely this is a new refinement in cruelty, which, while it has no advantage to atone for it, thus aggravates distress, and adds fresh horrors even to the wretchedness of slavery.

---

[5] Capital of Barbados.

Review Questions

1. What things capture Equiano's attention aboard the slave ship?
2. How would you characterize his reactions?
3. What is his view of his captors?
4. For whom is Equiano writing?
5. How does his writing reflect the general principles and goals of the Enlightenment?
6. Does the Enlightenment inform Equiano's view of slavery?

18 ❧ THE FRENCH REVOLUTION

The French revolutionary and Napoleonic eras, 1789–1815, launched the modern period in European history. Europe had so irrevocably changed after 1815 that contemporaries distinguished the period before 1789 as the old regime. To be sure, many features of the old regime continued into the new era, but the sentiment of sudden rupture was largely valid. In various dimensions of public life, the radical transformations of the French Revolution rendered many prerevolutionary attitudes toward society and politics obsolete. Following the abolition of feudalism, the declaration of civic equality, and the subordination of monarchy to national political sovereignty, traditional authority became irretrievable.

The areas of French society (aristocrats, civil servants, professionals, merchants, artisans, urban workers, peasants) willing to reform, if not dismantle, absolutist monarchy established the revolution's legitimacy. The wide range of grievances that had accumulated in the French provinces and cities provided the broad social base for the upheaval of 1789, just as the prevailing emphasis of eighteenth-century letters on applying reason, natural law, and social utility to public affairs offered a general intellectual framework. To understand the revolution's development, however, one must recognize that although the revolution inaugurated a new era of political rights and citizenship ideals, the specific content of "liberty, equality, fraternity" remained contested. Consequently, the freshly constituted polity of France embarked on an uncharted course of political experimentation, the prominent milestones of which (dissolution of the monarchy, regicide, radical republicanism, political terror, abolition of the slave trade, republican imperialism) subsequently defined the parameters of the modern political landscape.

The revolutionary impulses in Paris resonated throughout Europe and the world. Because France was the largest and most powerful continental state in Europe (one out of five Europeans lived in France), French politics affected all Europeans. The precedent of French constitutionalism and the Declaration of the

Rights of Man and Citizen reconfigured the domestic political cultures of not only European states but also those of colonial territories, such as Haiti, whose emancipated slaves created the new world's second republic. The level of political disputation intensified; contemporaries alternately celebrated or denounced the potential of widened political participation. Even Great Britain's stable political establishment of limited monarchy and parliamentary rule perceived French republicanism as a threat. The decision of Austria and Prussia to invade France in 1792 not only radicalized French politics but also expanded the revolutionary political arena. Napoleon's military prowess further embedded French revolutionary influence abroad with the creation of new kingdoms, the appointment of new rulers, the institution of new laws, and the transmission of constitutional politics. Hundreds of thousands of soldiers conscripted to fight in long-distance campaigns also brought home new ideas and attitudes when returning from the wars. Although the European great powers attempted to eradicate most of Napoleon's political reordering after 1815, the revolutionary challenge to traditional elites remained a permanent feature of European political life.

THOMAS JEFFERSON

The Declaration of Independence

The successful attempt of the original thirteen colonies to break their allegiance to Great Britain was an important antecedent to the French Revolution. Not only did France's financial support of the insurgent colonies precipitate the financial crisis that would compel Louis XVI to convene the Estates General but the American War of Independence also produced a political culture that celebrated principles of popular sovereignty and "unalienable" individual liberties. The Declaration of Independence, among the noblest of U.S. documents, arose out of the need to attach a preamble to a resolution by Congress, which moved in June 1776 "that these United Colonies are, and of right ought to be, free and independent States." Congress appointed a committee of five representatives to write the preamble, but one member, Thomas Jefferson (1743–1826), actually drafted the document, which was adopted by Congress on July 4, 1776.

When in the course of human events, it becomes necessary for one people to dissolve the political bands which have connected them with another, and to assume among the Powers of the earth, the separate and equal station to which the Laws of Nature and of Nature's God entitle them, a decent respect to the opinions of mankind requires that they should declare the causes which impel them to the separation.

We hold these truths to be self-evident, that all men are created equal, that they are endowed by their Creator with certain unalienable rights, that among these are Life, Liberty, and the pursuit of Happiness. That to secure these rights, Governments are instituted among Men, deriving their just powers from the consent of the governed. That whenever any Form of Government becomes destructive of these ends, it is the Right of the People to alter or to abolish it, and to institute new Government, laying its foundation on such principles and organizing its powers in such form, as to them shall seem most likely to effect their Safety and Happiness. Prudence, indeed, will dictate that Governments long established should not be changed for light and transient causes; and accordingly all experience hath shown, that mankind are more disposed to suffer, while evils are sufferable, than to right themselves by abolishing the forms to which they are accustomed. But when a long train of abuses and usurpations, pursuing invariably the same Object evinces a design to reduce them under absolute Despotism, it is their right, it is their duty, to throw off such Government, and to provide new Guards for their future security— Such has been the patient sufferance of these Colonies; and such is now the necessity which constrains them to alter their former Systems of Government. The history of the present King of Great Britain is a history of repeated injuries and usurpations, all having in direct object the establishment of an absolute Tyranny over these States. To prove this, let Facts be submitted to a candid world.

He has refused his Assent to Laws, the most wholesome and necessary for the public good.

He has forbidden his Governors to pass Laws of immediate and pressing importance, unless suspended in their operation till his Assent should be obtained; and when so suspended, he has utterly neglected to attend to them.

He has refused to pass other Laws for the accommodation of large districts of people, unless those people would relinquish the right of Representation in the Legislature, a right inestimable to them and formidable to tyrants only.

He has called together legislative bodies at places unusual, uncomfortable, and distant from the depository of their public Records, for the sole purpose of fatiguing them into compliance with his measures.

He has dissolved Representative Houses repeatedly, for opposing with manly firmness his invasions on the rights of the people.

He has refused for a long time, after such dissolutions, to cause others to be elected; whereby the Legislative powers, incapable of Annihilation, have returned to the People at large for their exercise; the State remaining in the mean time exposed to all dangers of invasion from without, and convulsions within.

He has endeavoured to prevent the population of these States; for that purpose obstructing the Laws of Naturalization of Foreigners; refusing to pass others to encourage their migrations hither, and raising the conditions of new Appropriations of Lands.

He has obstructed the Administration of Justice, by refusing his Assent to Laws for establishing Judiciary powers.

He has made Judges dependent on his Will alone, for the tenure of their offices, and the amount and payment of their salaries.

He has erected a multitude of New Offices, and sent hither swarms of Officers to harass our People, and eat out their substance.

He has kept among us, in times of peace, Standing Armies without the Consent of our legislature.

He has affected to render the Military independent of and superior to the Civil Power.

He has combined with others to subject us to a jurisdiction foreign to our constitution, and unacknowledged by our laws; giving his Assent to their Acts of pretended Legislation:

For quartering large bodies of armed troops among us:

For protecting them, by a mock Trial, from Punishment for any Murders which they should commit on the Inhabitants of these States:

For cutting off our Trade with all parts of the world:

For imposing taxes on us without our Consent:

For depriving us in many cases, of the benefits of Trial by jury:

For transporting us beyond Seas to be tried for pretended offences:

For abolishing the free System of English Laws in a neighbouring Province, establishing therein an Arbitrary government, and enlarging its Boundaries so as to render it at once an example and fit instrument for introducing the same absolute rule into these Colonies:

For taking away our Charters, abolishing our most valuable Laws, and altering fundamentally the Forms of our Governments:

For suspending our own Legislatures, and declaring themselves invested with Power to legislate for us in all cases whatsoever.

He has abdicated Government here, by declaring us out of his Protection and waging War against us.

He has plundered our seas, ravaged our Coasts, burnt our towns, and destroyed the lives of our people.

He is at this time transporting large armies of foreign mercenaries to compleat the works of death, desolation, and tyranny, already begun with circumstances of Cruelty & perfidy scarcely paralleled in the most barbarous ages, and totally unworthy the Head of a civilized nation.

He has constrained our fellow Citizens taken Captive on the high Seas to bear Arms against their Country, to become the executioners of their friends and Brethren, or to fall themselves by their Hands.

He has excited domestic insurrections amongst us, and has endeavoured to bring on the inhabitants of our frontiers, the merciless Indian Savages, whose known rule of warfare, is an undistinguished destruction of all ages, sexes, and conditions.

In every stage of these Oppressions We have Petitioned for Redress in the most humble terms: Our repeated Petitions have been answered only by repeated injury. A Prince, whose character is thus marked by every act which may define a Tyrant, is unfit to be the ruler of a free people.

Nor have We been wanting in attention to our British brethren. We have warned them from time to time of attempts by their legislature to extend an unwarrantable jurisdiction over us. We have reminded them of the circumstances of our emigration and settlement here. We have appealed to their native justice and magnanimity, and we have conjured them by the ties of our common kindred to disavow these usurpations, which, would inevitably interrupt our connections and correspondence. They too must have been deaf to the voice of justice and of consanguinity. We must, therefore, acquiesce in the necessity, which denounces our Separation, and hold them, as we hold the rest of mankind, Enemies in War, in Peace Friends.

WE, THEREFORE, the Representatives of the UNITED STATES OF AMERICA, in General Congress, Assembled, appealing to the Supreme Judge of the world for the rectitude of our intentions, do, in the Name, and by Authority of the good People of these Colonies, solemnly publish and declare, That these United Colonies are, and of Right ought to be FREE AND INDEPENDENT STATES; that they are Absolved from all Allegiance to the British Crown, and that all political connection between them and the State of Great Britain, is and ought to be totally dissolved; and that as Free and Independent States, they have full Power to levy War, conclude Peace, contract Alliances, establish Commerce, and to do all other Acts and Things which Independent States may of right do. And for the support of this Declaration, with a firm reliance on the Protection of Divine Providence, we mutually pledge to each other our Lives, our Fortunes, and our sacred Honor.

The foregoing Declaration was, by order of Congress, engrossed, and signed by the following members: ∗ ∗ ∗

REVIEW QUESTIONS

1. On what grounds does the Declaration of Independence justify a break from Great Britain?
2. Why is this document often viewed as a prominent example of the Enlightenment's political outlook?
3. Compare Locke's *Two Treatises of Government* with the American Declaration of Independence. What Lockeian influences can be detected in the declaration?

ABBÉ EMMANUEL SIEYÈS

FROM *What Is the Third Estate?*

King Louis XVI's announcement in the summer of 1788 convening the Estates General, compounded by bread riots and widespread economic hardship, heated up political debate about reform and the future of France. Because the Estates General had not met since 1614, members of the Third Estate protested against the custom that the estates meet separately and vote by order. They insisted that the estates should instead deliberate in united sessions and vote as individuals, not as corporate bodies. Equally important, the Third Estate demanded that its votes be doubled, so that it could counter the votes of the First and Second Estates. In January 1789, Abbé Emmanuel Sieyès (1748–1836), a postmaster's son who became a radical clergyman and a leader in the revolution's early stages, sought to mobilize public support for these causes with the pamphlet, What Is the Third Estate? *Its influence was pervasive and contributed to the plan to transform the Estates General into the National Constituent Assembly.*

From *A Documentary Survey of the French Revolution*, edited by John Hall Stewart (Upper Saddle River, N.J.: Prentice-Hall, 1951).

*   *   *

The plan of this book is fairly simple. We must ask ourselves three questions.

1. What is the Third Estate? *Everything.*
2. What has it been until now in the political order? *Nothing.*
3. What does it want to be? *Something.*

We are going to see whether the answers are correct. . . . We shall next examine the measures that have been tried and those that must still be taken for the Third Estate really to become something. Thus, we shall state:

4. What the Ministers have attempted and what even the privileged orders propose to do for it.
5. What ought to have been done.
6. Finally, what remains to be done in order that the Third Estate should take its rightful place.

Chapter 1
The Third Estate Is a Complete Nation

What does a nation require to survive and prosper? It needs *private* activities and *public* services.

These private activities can all be comprised within four classes of persons:

1. Since land and water provide the basic materials for human needs, the first class, in logical order, includes all the families connected with work on the land.

2. Between the initial sale of goods and the moment when they reach the consumer or user, goods acquire an increased value of a more or less compound nature through the incorporation of varying amounts of labour. In this way human industry manages to improve the gifts of nature and the value of the raw material may be multiplied twice,

or ten-fold, or a hundredfold. Such are the activities of the second class of persons.

3. Between production and consumption, as also between the various stages of production, a variety of intermediary agents intervene, to help producers as well as consumers; these are the dealers and the merchants. . . .

4. Besides these three classes of useful and industrious citizens who deal with things fit to be consumed or used, society also requires a vast number of special activities and of services directly useful or pleasant to the person. This fourth class embraces all sorts of occupations, from the most distinguished liberal and scientific professions to the lowest of menial tasks. Such are the activities which support society. But who performs them? The Third Estate. Public services can also, at present, be divided into four known categories, the army, the law, the Church and the bureaucracy. It needs no detailed analysis to show that the Third Estate everywhere constitutes nineteen-twentieths of them, except that it is loaded with all the really arduous work, all the tasks which the privileged order refuses to perform. Only the well-paid and honorific posts are filled by members of the privileged order. Are we to give them credit for this? We could do so only if the Third Estate was unable or unwilling to fill these posts. We know the answer. Nevertheless, the privileged have dared to preclude the Third Estate. "No matter how useful you are," they said, "no matter how able you are, you can go so far and no further. Honours are not for the like of you." . . .

*   *   *

It suffices to have made the point that the so-called usefulness of a privileged order to the public service is a fallacy; that, without help from this order, all the arduous tasks in the service are performed by the Third Estate; that without this order the higher posts could be infinitely better filled; that they ought to be the natural prize and reward of recognised ability and service; and that if the privileged have succeeded in usurping all well-paid and honorific posts, this is both a hateful iniquity towards the generality of citizens and an act of treason to the commonwealth.

Who is bold enough to maintain that the Third Estate does not contain within itself everything needful to constitute a complete nation? It is like a strong and robust man with one arm still in chains. If the privileged order were removed, the nation would not be something less but something more. What then is the Third Estate? All; but an "all" that is fettered and oppressed. What would it be without the privileged order? It would be all; but free and flourishing. Nothing will go well without the Third Estate; everything would go considerably better without the two others.

It is not enough to have shown that the privileged, far from being useful to the nation, can only weaken and injure it; we must prove further that the nobility is not part of our society at all; it may be a burden for the nation, but it cannot be part of it.

*   *   *

What is a nation? A body of associates living under *common laws* and represented by the same *legislative assembly*, etc.

Is it not obvious that the nobility possesses privileges and exemptions which it brazenly calls its rights and which stand distinct from the rights of the great body of citizens? Because of these special rights, the nobility does not belong to the common order, nor is it subjected to the common laws. Thus its private rights make it a people apart in the great nation. It is truly *imperium in imperio*.

As for its *political* rights, it also exercises these separately from the nation. It has its own representatives who are charged with no mandate from the People. Its deputies sit separately, and even if they sat in the same chamber as the deputies of ordinary citizens they would still constitute a different and separate representation. They are foreign to the nation first because of their origin, since they do not owe their powers to the People; and secondly because of their aim, since this consists in defending, not the general interest, but the private one.

The Third Estate then contains everything that pertains to the nation while nobody outside the Third Estate can be considered as part of the nation. What is the Third Estate? *Everything*.

*   *   *

Chapter 3
What Does the Third Estate Want to Be? *Something*

. . . The authentic requests of the Third Estate can only be adjudged through the formal demands which the great municipalities of the kingdom have addressed to the government. What do we see therein? That the People wants to become *something*, and in fact, the least thing possible. It wants to have (1) genuine representatives in the States-General, i.e., deputies *drawn from its own ranks* and competent to interpret its wishes and defend its interests. But what good would it do the Third Estate to participate in the States General if the interest opposed to its own were to preponderate there? It would simply sanction by its presence the oppression of which it would be the everlasting victim. Therefore, it most certainly cannot come and vote in the States-General unless its influence there is at least equal to that of the privileged orders. So it asks for (2) a number of representatives equal to that of the other two orders taken together. However, this equality of representation would become entirely illusory if each chamber voted separately. The Third Estate, therefore, asks for (3) the votes to be counted by heads and not by orders. Such is the whole extent of the claims which appear to have so alarmed the privileged orders; and for this reason alone have these come round to believing that the reform of abuses has become indispensable.

The Third Estate's modest aim is to possess an equal influence in the States-General to that of the privileged orders. Once again, could it ask for less? And is it not clear that if its influence is less than equal, it cannot hope to come out of its political non-existence and become *something*?

However, the great pity of it all is that the three articles which constitute the claim of the Third Estate are not enough to give it the equal influence which it cannot effectively dispense with. To grant it no more than an equal number of representatives drawn from its own ranks will be useless: for the privileged orders will continue to exercise their dominating influence in the very sanctuary of the Third Estate. . . . The more one considers this matter, the more one perceives the inadequacy of the three claims of the Third Estate. . . .

First Claim of the Third Estate: That the Representatives of the Third Estate Be Chosen Solely from among Citizens Who Really Belong to the Third Estate

We have already explained that really to belong to the Third Estate, one must either be untainted by privileges of any sort, or else relinquish them immediately and completely.

*   *   *

Second Claim of the Third Estate: That Its Deputies Be Equal in Number to Those of the Two Privileged Orders

I cannot refrain from repeating once more that the timid inadequacy of this claim is an after-effect of times gone by. The towns of the kingdom have not given enough consideration to the progress of enlightenment or even of public opinion. They would have met with no greater difficulties by demanding two votes to one; but they might even have been hastily granted the very equality which some people are so loudly opposing today.

Furthermore, when we want to decide a question of this kind, we must not simply do what is only too common, and give our personal wish or our will or custom as valid reasons. It is necessary to argue from principles. Like civil rights, political rights derive from a person's capacity as a citizen. These legal rights are identical for every person, whether his property happens to be great or small. Any citizen who satisfies all the formal requirements for an elector has the right to be represented, and the extent of his representation cannot be a fraction of the extent of some other citizen's representation. The right to be represented is single and indivisible. . . .

*   *   *

Third and Last Claim of the Third Estate: That the States-General Vote, Not by Orders, but by Heads

One can regard this question from three points of view: as apprehended by the Third Estate; as relating to the interests of the privileged classes; and in terms of sound principles. As far as the first of these is concerned, it would be pointless to add anything to what we have already said; clearly, the Third Estate considers that this claim is the necessary consequence of the two others.

The privileged classes fear the third order's possession of an influence equal to their own, and so declare it unconstitutional. This behaviour is all the more striking as they have, until this moment, enjoyed a superiority of two against one without seeing anything unconstitutional in this unjust predominance. They feel passionately that they must retain a veto on everything that might conflict with their interests. I am not going to restate the arguments by which a score of writers have combated this pretension, and the argument of "the ancient procedures." I want to make one observation only. There are, beyond any doubt, abuses in France; these abuses are profitable to some persons: but they hardly ever benefit the Third Estate, and, on the contrary, it is to the Third Estate that they do most harm. Now I ask: in such circumstances is it possible to abolish any abuse so long as those who profit therefrom retain a veto? Justice would be powerless—everything would depend entirely upon the magnanimity of the privileged classes. Would this correspond to our idea of what constitutes social order?

*   *   *

REVIEW QUESTIONS

1. What is Sieyès's tone of voice? How does it affect his argument?
2. What reasons does Sieyès provide for his claim that the Third Estate constitutes the nation?
3. What kind of political and social order does he advocate?

NATIONAL ASSEMBLY

FROM Declaration of the Rights of Man and of the Citizen

This declaration, adopted August 26, 1789, was a revolutionary clarion call to the people of France. Its subsequent impact on European political culture cannot be overestimated.

From *The Ideas That Have Influenced Civilization, in the original documents*, vol. 7, translated and edited by Oliver Joseph Thatcher (London: Roberts-Manchester, 1902), pp. 415–17.

*   *   *

The representatives of the French people, organized as a national assembly, believing that the ignorance, neglect or contempt of the rights of man are the sole causes of public calamities and of the corruption of governments, have determined to set forth in a solemn declaration, the natural, inalienable and sacred rights of man, in order that this declaration, being constantly before all the members of the social body, shall remind them continually of their rights and duties; in order that the acts of the legislative power, as well as those of the executive power, may be compared at any moment with the ends of all political institutions and may thus be more respected; in order that the grievances of the citizens, based hereafter upon simple and incontestable principles, shall tend to the maintenance of the constitution and redound to the happiness of all. Hence the National Assembly recognizes and proclaims in the presence and under the auspices of the Supreme Being the following rights of man and of the citizen:

Article 1. Men are born and remain free and equal in rights. Social distinctions can only be founded upon the general good.

2. The aim of all political association is the preservation of the natural and imprescriptible rights of man. These rights are liberty, property, security, and resistance to oppression.

3. The principle [*principe*] of all sovereignty resides essentially in the nation. No body nor individual may exercise any authority which does not proceed directly from the nation.

4. Liberty consists in being able to do everything which injures no one else; hence the exercise of the natural rights of each man has no limits except those which assure to the other members of the society the enjoyment of the same rights. These limits can only be determined by law.

5. Law can only prohibit such actions as are hurtful to society. Nothing may be prevented which is not forbidden by law, and no one may be forced to do anything not provided for by law.

6. Law is the expression of the general will. Every citizen has a right to participate personally or through his representative in its formation. It must be the same for all, whether it protects or punishes. All citizens being equal in the eyes of the law are equally eligible to all dignities and to all public positions and occupations according to their abilities and without distinction except that of their virtues and talents.

7. No person shall be accused, arrested or imprisoned except in the cases and according to the forms prescribed by law. Any one soliciting, transmitting, executing or causing to be executed any arbitrary order shall be punished. But any citizen summoned or arrested in virtue of the law shall submit without delay, as resistance constitutes an offence.

8. The law shall provide for such punishments only as are strictly and obviously necessary, and no one shall suffer punishment except it be legally inflicted in virtue of a law passed and promulgated before the commission of the offence.

9. As all persons are held innocent until they shall have been declared guilty, if arrest shall be deemed indispensable all severity not essential to the securing of the prisoner's person shall be severely repressed by law.

10. No one shall be disquieted on account of his opinions, including his religious views, provided their manifestation does not disturb the public order established by law.

11. The free communication of ideas and opinions is one of the most precious of the rights of man. Every citizen may, accordingly, speak, write and print with freedom, being responsible, however, for such abuses of this freedom as shall be defined by law.

12. The security of the rights of man and of the citizen requires public military force. These forces are, therefore, established for the good of all and not for the personal advantage of those to whom they shall be entrusted.

13. A common contribution is essential for the maintenance of the public forces and for the cost of administration. This should be equitably distributed among all the citizens in proportion to their means.

14. All the citizens have a right to decide either personally or by their representatives as to the

TENNIS COURT OATH (1792)　　　　　　　　　　　　　　　　　　　　JACQUES-LOUIS DAVID

*David's painting of the birth of the modern French nation strove not for authentic represen-
tation but rather for mythic grandeur. In depicting this disparate group of bourgeois men
committed to take an oath to transform France into a constitutional monarchy, what was
David implying about the political foundation of the new nation?*

necessity of the public contribution, to grant this freely, to know to what uses it is put, and to fix the proportion, the mode of assessment, and of collection, and the duration of the taxes.

15. Society has the right to require of every public agent an account of his administration.

16. A society in which the observance of the law is not assured nor the separation of powers defined has no constitution at all.

17. Property being an inviolable and sacred right, no one shall be deprived thereof except where public necessity, legally determined shall clearly demand it, and then only on condition that the owner shall have been previously and equitably indemnified.

REVIEW QUESTIONS

1. What similarities in issues do you see in the grievance petitions and in this declaration?
2. What are the principal differences between this declaration and the American Declaration of Independence?
3. How does this document reconcile the rights of the individual with the rights of government?
4. Which civil liberties are missing here?
5. Assess the influence of the American Declaration of Independence on the Declaration of the Rights of Man and Citizen.

SOCIETY OF THE FRIENDS OF BLACKS

FROM Address to the National Assembly in Favor of the Abolition of the Slave Trade

When the French Revolution announced a new era of human rights, the ideals of liberty and equality also affected French colonies and their extensive use of slavery. Saint Domingue, France's wealthiest Caribbean colony, worked approximately 450,000 slaves on its plantations. For this reason, the National Assembly's deputies debated the institution of slavery, a thorny issue that pitted ideals of individual liberty against the sanctity of private property. The following address of the Society of the Friends of Blacks in February 1790 captures the terms of the debate. It presented a spirited denunciation of the slave trade but did not demand an end to slavery altogether, a qualified position that evinced the powerful opposition of planters and property owners. In August 1791, responding to a new law that extended political rights merely to free blacks and mulattoes, the slaves of Saint Domingue led the first successful slave revolt in modern history. In February 1794, the National Convention, bowing to the revolution's egalitarian tenets and to the danger of losing its colonies to other European powers, emancipated slaves in all French colonies.

From *The French Revolution and Human Rights: A Brief Documentary History*, edited by Lynn Avery Hunt (New York: St. Martin's Press, 1996), pp. 107–9.

The humanity, justice, and magnanimity that have guided you in the reform of the most profoundly rooted abuses gives hope to the Society of the Friends of Blacks that you will receive with benevolence its demand in favor of that numerous portion of humankind, so cruelly oppressed for two centuries.

This Society, slandered in such cowardly and unjust fashion, only derives its mission from the humanity that induced it to defend the blacks even under the past despotism. Oh! Can there be a more respectable title in the eyes of this august Assembly which has so often avenged the rights of man in its decrees?

You have declared them, these rights; you have engraved on an immortal monument that all men are born and remain free and equal in rights; you have restored to the French people these rights that despotism had for so long despoiled; . . . you have broken the chains of feudalism that still degraded a good number of our fellow citizens; you have announced the destruction of all the stigmatizing distinctions that religious or political prejudices introduced into the great family of humankind. . . .

We are not asking you to restore to French blacks those political rights which alone, nevertheless, attest to and maintain the dignity of man; we are not even asking for their liberty. No; slander, bought no doubt with the greed of the ship-owners, ascribes that scheme to us and spreads it everywhere; they want to stir up everyone against us, provoke they want to stir up everyone against us, provoke the planters and their numerous creditors, who take alarm even at gradual emancipation. They want to alarm all the French, to whom they depict the prosperity of the colonies as inseparable from the slave trade and the perpetuity of slavery.

No, never has such an idea entered into our minds; we have said it, printed it since the beginning of our Society, and we repeat it in order to reduce to nothing this grounds of argument, blindly adopted by all the coastal cities, the grounds on which rest almost all their addresses [to the National Assembly]. The immediate emancipation of the blacks would not only be a fatal operation for the colonies; it would even be a deadly gift for the blacks, in the state of abjection and incompetence to which cupidity has reduced them. It would be to abandon to themselves and without assistance children in the cradle or mutilated and impotent beings.

It is therefore not yet time to demand that liberty; we ask only that one cease butchering thousands of blacks regularly every year in order to take hundreds of captives; we ask that one henceforth cease the prostitution, the profaning of the French name, used to authorize these thefts, these atrocious murders; we demand in a word the abolition of the slave trade. . . .

In regard to the colonists, we will demonstrate to you that if they need to recruit blacks in Africa to sustain the population of the colonies at the same level, it is because they wear out the blacks with work, whippings, and starvation; that, if they treated them with kindness and as good fathers of families, these blacks would multiply and that this population, always growing, would increase cultivation and prosperity. . . .

Have no doubt, the time when this commerce will be abolished, even in England, is not far off. It is condemned there in public opinion, even in the opinion of the ministers. . . .

If some motive might on the contrary push them [the blacks] to insurrection, might it not be the indifference of the National Assembly about their lot? Might it not be the insistence on weighing them down with chains, when one consecrates everywhere this eternal axiom: *that all men are born free and equal in rights*. So then therefore there would only be fetters and gallows for the blacks while good fortune glimmers only for the whites? Have no doubt, our happy revolution must re-electrify the blacks whom vengeance and resentment have electrified for so long, and it is not with punishments that the effect of his upheaval will be repressed. From one insurrection badly pacified will twenty others be born, of which one alone can ruin the colonists forever.

It is worthy of the first free Assembly of France to consecrate the principle of philanthropy which makes of humankind only one single family, to declare that it is horrified by this annual carnage which takes place on the coasts of Africa, that it has the intention of abolishing it one day, of mitigating the slavery that is the result, of looking for and preparing, from this moment, the means.

REVIEW QUESTIONS

1. How does the society's address propose to help blacks?
2. Why does this society not advocate the emancipation of slaves?
3. What immediate consequences does the society envision with its proposal?
4. Is the issue of slavery central or peripheral to the political vision of the French Revolution?

NATIONAL CONVENTION

FROM Levée en Masse Edict

This decree of August 23, 1793, mobilized the French nation for war, marking a new era in the modern history of warfare. Numerous setbacks of the French revolutionary army after its initial victories in 1792 compelled the government to pass a universal levy to repulse the enemy. The government's ability to conscript soldiers, requisition supplies, and organize the economy for war reveals the nationalist spirit that gripped France and provides one critical reason for success in the government's subsequent military campaigns.

From *A Documentary Survey of the French Revolution*, edited by John Hall Stewart (Upper Saddle River, N.J.: Prentice-Hall, 1951).

*   *   *

1. Henceforth, until the enemies have been driven from the territory of the Republic, the French people are in permanent requisition for army service.

The young men shall go to battle; the married men shall forge arms and transport provisions; the women shall make tents and clothes, and shall serve in the hospitals; the children shall turn old linen into lint; the old men shall repair to the public places, to stimulate the courage of the warriors and preach the unity of the Republic and hatred of kings.

2. National buildings shall be converted into barracks; public places into armament workshops; the soil of cellars shall be washed in lye to extract saltpeter therefrom.

3. Arms of caliber shall be turned over exclusively to those who march against the enemy; the service of the interior shall be carried on with fowling pieces and sabers.

4. Saddle horses are called for to complete the cavalry corps; draught horses, other than those employed in agriculture, shall haul artillery and provisions.

5. The Committee of Public Safety is charged with taking all measures necessary for establishing, without delay, a special manufacture of arms of all kinds, in harmony with the *élan* and the energy of the French people. Accordingly, it is authorized to constitute all establishments, manufactories, workshops, and factories deemed necessary for the execution of such works, as well as to requisition for such purpose, throughout the entire extent of the Republic, the artists and workmen who may contribute to their success. For such purpose a sum of 30,000,000, taken from the 498,200,000 livres in *assignats* in reserve in the "Fund of the Three Keys," shall be placed at the disposal of the Minister of War. The central establishment of said special manufacture shall be established at Paris.

6. The representatives of the people dispatched for the execution of the present law shall have similar authority in their respective *arrondissements,* acting in concert with the Committee of Public Safety; they are invested with the unlimited powers attributed to the representatives of the people with the armies.

7. No one may obtain a substitute in the service to which he is summoned. The public functionaries shall remain at their posts.

8. The levy shall be general. Unmarried citizens or childless widowers, from eighteen to twenty-five years, shall go first; they shall meet, without delay, at the chief town of their districts, where they shall practice manual exercise daily, while awaiting the hour of departure.

9. The representatives of the people shall regulate the musters and marches so as to have armed citizens arrive at the points of assembling only in so far as supplies, munitions, and all that constitutes the material part of the army exist in sufficient proportion.

10. The points of assembling shall be determined by circumstances, and designated by the representatives of the people dispatched for the execution

of the present decree, upon the advice of the generals, in co-operation with the Committee of Public Safety and the provisional Executive Council.

11. The battalion organized in each district shall be united under a banner bearing the inscription: *The French people risen against tyrants.*

12. Such battalions shall be organized according to established decrees, and their pay shall be the same as that of the battalions at the frontiers.

13. In order to collect supplies in sufficient quantity, the farmers and managers of national property shall deposit the produce of such property, in the form of grain, in the chief town of their respective districts.

14. Owners, farmers, and others possessing grain shall be required to pay, in kind, arrears of taxes, even the two-thirds of those of 1793, on the rolls which have served to effect the last payment.

*   *   *

17. The Minister of War is responsible for taking all measures necessary for the prompt execution of the present decree; a sum of 50,000,000, from the 498,200,000 *livres* in *assignats* in the "Fund of the Three Keys," shall be placed at his disposal by the National Treasury.

18. The present decree shall be conveyed to the departments by special messengers.

Review Questions

1. Which social groups and areas of the economy did this edict affect? What roles were they assigned?
2. How is this organization for war different from warfare under the old regime?
3. How does this document evoke the sense of emergency and crisis that characterized the early years of the republic?

The Haitian Declaration of Independence

On New Year's Day in 1804, the former slaves of the French colony Saint-Domingue declared their independence, the hard-won achievement of a long and bloody struggle. Starting as a slave rebellion in 1791 under the leadership of Toussaint L'Overture, the insurrection succeeded in wresting control of one-third of the island. Animated by ideals of freedom and independence, the "free citizens of color" prevailed over French and English invasions between 1793 and 1798. Napoleon also attempted to win back the lucrative colony. In 1801, he legalized slavery anew and sent 43,000 soldiers to capture the Caribbean island for France. Under the command of Jean-Jacques Dessalines, the former slaves defeated French forces at the Battle of Vertières in November 1803. Following this battle, the victors declared the island independent, renaming it Haiti. The declaration below vividly evokes the violence and high death toll of the struggle, if not also the mixed legacy of the French Revolution.

From *Slave Revolution in the Caribbean, 1789–1804: A Brief History with Documents,* translated by Laurent Dubois and John D. Garrigus (London: Macmillan, 2006), pp. 188–191.

The Commander in Chief to the People of Haiti

Citizens:

It is not enough to have expelled the barbarians who have bloodied our land for two centuries; it is not enough to have restrained those ever-evolving factions that one after another mocked the specter of liberty that France dangled before you. We must, with one last act of national authority, forever ensure liberty's reign in the country of our birth; we must take any hope of re-enslaving us away from the inhuman government that for so long kept us in the most humiliating stagnation. In the end we must live independent or die.

Independence or death . . . let these sacred words unite us and be the signal of battle and of our reunion.

Citizens, my countrymen, on this solemn day I have brought together those courageous soldiers who, as liberty lay dying, spilled their blood to save it; these generals who have guided your efforts against tyranny have not yet done enough for your happiness; the French name still haunts our land.

Everything revives the memories of the cruelties of this barbarous people: our laws, our habits, our towns, everything still carries the stamp of the French. Indeed! There are still French in our island, and you believe yourself free and independent of that republic, which, it is true, has fought all the nations, but which has never defeated those who wanted to be free.

What! Victims of our [own] credulity and indulgence for fourteen years; defeated not by French armies, but by the pathetic eloquence of their agents' proclamations; when will we tire of breathing the air that they breathe? What do we have in common with this nation of executioners? The difference between its cruelty and our patient moderation, its color and ours, the great seas that separate us, our avenging climate, all tell us plainly that they are not our brothers, that they never will be, and that if they find refuge among us, they will plot again to trouble and divide us.

Native citizens, men, women, girls, and children, let your gaze extend on all parts of this island: look there for your spouses, your husbands, your brothers, your sisters. Indeed! Look there for your children, your suckling infants, what have they become? . . . I shudder to say it . . . the prey of these vultures.

Instead of these dear victims, your alarmed gaze will see only their assassins, these tigers still dripping with their blood, whose terrible presence indicts your lack of feeling and your guilty slowness in avenging them. What are you waiting for before appeasing their spirits? Remember that you had wanted your remains to rest next to those of your fathers after you defeated tyranny; will you descend into their tombs without having avenged them? No! Their bones would reject yours.

And you, precious men, intrepid generals, who, without concern for your own pain, have revived liberty by shedding all your blood, know that you have done nothing if you do not give the nations a terrible, but just example of the vengeance that must be wrought by a people proud to have recovered its liberty and jealous to maintain it. Let us frighten all those who would dare try to take it from us again; let us begin with the French. Let them tremble when they approach our coast, if not from the memory of those cruelties they perpetrated here, then from the terrible resolution that we will have made to put to death anyone born French whose profane foot soils the land of liberty.

We have dared to be free, let us be thus by ourselves and for ourselves. Let us imitate the grown child: his own weight breaks the boundary that has become an obstacle to him. What people fought for us? What people wanted to gather the fruits of our labor? And what dishonorable absurdity to conquer in order to be enslaved. Enslaved? . . . Let us leave this description for the French; they have conquered but are no longer free.

Let us walk down another path; let us imitate those people who, extending their concern into the future and dreading to leave an example of cowardice for posterity, preferred to be exterminated rather than lose their place as one of the world's free peoples.

Let us ensure, however, that a missionary spirit does not destroy our work; let us allow our neighbors to breathe in peace; may they live quietly under the laws that they have made for themselves, and let us not, as revolutionary firebrands, declare ourselves the lawgivers of the Caribbean, nor let our glory consist in troubling the peace of the neighboring islands. Unlike that which we inhabit, theirs has not been drenched in the innocent blood of its inhabitants; they have no vengeance to claim from the authority that protects them.

Fortunate to have never known the ideals that have destroyed us, they can only have good wishes for our prosperity.

Peace to our neighbors; but let this be our cry: "Anathema to the French name! Eternal hatred of France!"

Natives of Haiti! My happy fate was to be one day the sentinel who would watch over the idol to which you sacrifice; I have watched, sometimes fighting alone, and if I have been so fortunate as to return to your hands the sacred trust you confided to me, know that it is now your task to preserve it. In fighting for your liberty, I was working for my own happiness. Before consolidating it with laws that will guarantee your free individuality, your leaders, who I have assembled here, and I, owe you the final proof of our devotion.

Generals and you, leaders, collected here close to me for the good of our land, the day has come, the day which must make our glory, our independence, eternal.

If there could exist among us a lukewarm heart, let him distance himself and tremble to take the oath which must unite us. Let us vow to ourselves, to posterity, to the entire universe, to forever renounce France, and to die rather than live under its domination; to fight until our last breath for the independence of our country.

And you, a people so long without good fortune, witness to the oath we take, remember that I counted on your constancy and courage when I threw myself into the career of liberty to fight the despotism and tyranny you had struggled against for fourteen years. Remember that I sacrificed everything to rally to your defense; family, children, fortune, and now I am rich only with your liberty; my name has become a horror to all those who want slavery. Despots and tyrants curse the day that I was born. If ever you refused or grumbled while receiving those laws that the spirit guarding your fate dictates to me for your own good, you would deserve the fate of an ungrateful people. But I reject that awful idea; you will sustain the liberty that you cherish and support the leader who commands you. Therefore, vow before me to live free and independent and to prefer death to anything that will try to place you back in chains. Swear, finally, to pursue forever the traitors and enemies of your independence.

Done at the headquarters of Gonaïves, the first day of January 1804, the first year of independence.

REVIEW QUESTIONS

1. How does this declaration characterize the French and their legacy?
2. Why the repeated use of "blood" in this document? What does this figurative language tell us about the island's social and political atmosphere?
3. How does this document envision the political future of Haiti and its neighbors?
4. What were the broader consequences of Haitian independence for South and North America?

OLYMPE DE GOUGES

FROM Declaration of the Rights of Woman

The revolution politicized millions of French men by transforming their status from subjects to citizens, but revolutionaries of all political stripes displayed extreme reluctance to incorporate women into the national political body. Heeding the new political discourse of equality, inalienable rights, and universal liberties, Olympe de Gouges (1748–1793), the self-educated daughter of a butcher, pointed out the revolutionaries' patent contradiction of applying tenets of natural law philosophy to one half of the human race but not to the other. This pamphlet, published in September 1791, documents an important discussion during the revolution over the public roles and duties of women in civil society. Olympe de Gouges engaged her critical pen over a number of issues, which led to her arrest as a counterrevolutionary and her execution in 1793.

From *Women, The Family, and Freedom: The Debate in Documents*, edited by Susan Groag Bell and Karen M. Offen (Stanford, CA: Stanford University Press, 1983), pp. 105–09.

To be decreed by the National Assembly in its last meetings or in those of the next legislature.

Preamble

The mothers, daughters, and sisters, representatives of the nation, demand to be constituted a national assembly. Considering that ignorance, disregard of or contempt for the rights of women are the only causes of public misfortune and of governmental corruption, they have resolved to set forth in a solemn declaration, the natural, inalienable and sacred rights of woman; to the end that this declaration, constantly held up to all members of society, may always remind them of their rights and duties; to the end that the acts based on women's power and those based on the power of men, being constantly measured against the goal of all political institutions, may be more respected; and so that the demands of female citizens, henceforth founded on simple and indisputable principles, may ever uphold the constitution and good morals, and may contribute to the happiness of all.

Consequently, the sex that is superior in beauty as well as in courage of maternal suffering, recognizes and declares, in the presence and under the auspices of the Supreme Being, the following rights of woman and citizen.

Article I. Woman is born free and remains equal in rights to man. Social distinctions can be founded only on general utility.

II. The goal of every political association is the preservation of the natural and irrevocable rights of Woman and Man. These rights are liberty, property, security, and especially resistance to oppression.

III. The principle of all sovereignty resides essentially in the Nation, which is none other than the union of Woman and Man; no group, no individual can exercise any authority that is not derived expressly from it.

IV. Liberty and Justice consist of rendering to persons those things that belong to them; thus, the exercise of woman's natural rights is limited only by the perpetual tyranny with which man opposes her; these limits must be changed according to the laws of nature and reason.

V. The laws of nature and of reason prohibit all acts harmful to society; whatever is not prohibited by these wise and divine laws cannot be prevented, and no one can be forced to do anything unspecified by the law.

VI. The law should be the expression of the general will: all female and male citizens must participate in its elaboration personally or through their representatives. It should be the same for all; all female and male citizens, being equal in the eyes of the law, should be equally admissible to all public offices, places, and employments, according to their capacities and with no distinctions other than those of their virtues and talents.

VII. No woman is immune; she can be accused, arrested, and detained in such cases as determined by law. Women, like men, must obey these rigorous laws.

VIII. Only punishments strictly and obviously necessary may be established by law. No one may be punished except under a law established and promulgated before the offense occurred, and which is legally applicable to women.

IX. If any woman is declared guilty, then the law must be enforced rigorously.

X. No one should be punished for their opinions. Woman has the right to mount the scaffold; she should likewise have the right to speak in public, provided that her demonstrations do not disrupt public order as established by law.

XI. Free communication of thoughts and opinions is one of the most precious rights of woman, since this liberty assures the legitimate paternity of fathers with regard to their children. Every female citizen can therefore freely say: "I am the mother of a child that belongs to you," without a barbaric prejudice forcing her to conceal the truth; she must also answer for the abuse of this liberty in cases determined by law.

XII. Guarantee of the rights of woman and female citizens requires the existence of public services. Such guarantee should be established for the advantage of everyone, not for the personal benefit of those to whom these services are entrusted.

XIII. For the maintenance of public forces and administrative expenses, the contributions of women and men shall be equal; the woman shares in all forced labor and all painful tasks, therefore she should have the same share in the distribution of positions, tasks, assignments, honors, and industry.

XIV. Female and male citizens have the right to determine the need for public taxes, either by themselves or through their representatives. Female citizens can agree to this only if they are admitted to an equal share not only in wealth but also in public administration, and by determining the proportion and extent of tax collection.

XV. The mass of women, allied for tax purposes to the mass of men, has the right to hold every public official accountable for his administration.

XVI. Any society in which the guarantee of rights is not assured, or the separation of powers determined, has no constitution. The constitution is invalid if the majority of individuals who compose the Nation have not cooperated in writing it.

XVII. The right of property is inviolable and sacred to both sexes, jointly or separately. No one can be deprived of it, since it is a true inheritance of nature except when public necessity, certified by law, clearly requires it, subject to just and prior compensation.

Postamble

Woman, wake up! The tocsin of reason is sounding throughout the Universe; know your rights. The powerful empire of nature is no longer surrounded by prejudices, fanaticism, superstition and lies. The torch of truth has dispelled all the clouds of stupidity and usurpation. Man enslaved has multiplied his forces; he has had recourse to yours in order to break his own chains. Having become free, he has become unjust toward his mate. Oh Women! Women! when will you cease to be blind? What advantages have you gained in the Revolution? A more marked scorn, a more signal disdain. During centuries of corruption, you reigned only over the weakness of men. Your empire is destroyed; what then remains for you? The proof of man's injustice. The claim of your patrimony founded on the wise decrees of nature—what have you to fear from such a splendid enterprise? The good word of the legislator at the marriage of Canaan? Do you not fear that our French legislators, who are correcting this morality, which was for such a long time appended to the realm of politics but is no longer fashionable, will again say to you, "Women, what do we have in common with you?" You must answer, "Everything!" If, in their weakness, they are obstinate in drawing this conclusion contrary to their principles, you must courageously invoke the force of reason against their vain pretensions of superiority. Unite yourselves under the banner of philosophy; deploy all the energy of your character, and soon you will see these prideful ones, your adoring servants, no longer grovelling at your feet but proud to share with you the treasures of the Supreme Being. Whatever the obstacles that are put in your way, it is in your power to overturn them; you have only to will it. Let us turn now to the frightful picture of what you have been in society; and since there is currently a question of national education, let us see if our wise legislators will think wisely about the education of women.

*   *   *

If my attempt thus to give my sex an honorable and just stability is now considered a paradox on my part, an attempt at the impossible, I must leave to men yet to come the glory of discussing this matter; but meanwhile, one can pave the way through national education, the restoration of morals, and by conjugal contracts.

MODEL FOR A SOCIAL CONTRACT BETWEEN A MAN AND A WOMAN

We, N & N, of our own free will, unite ourselves for the remainder of our lives and for the duration of our mutual inclinations, according to the following conditions: We intend and desire to pool our fortunes as community property, while nevertheless preserving the right to divide them on behalf of our own children and those we might have with someone else, mutually recognizing that our fortune belongs directly to our children, from whatever bed they might spring, and that all of them have the right to carry the name of the fathers and mothers who have acknowledged them, and we obligate ourselves to subscribe to the law that punishes the renunciation of one's own flesh and blood. We obligate ourselves equally, in case of separation, to divide our fortune, and to set apart the portion belonging to our children as indicated by the law; and in the case of perfect union, the first to die would assign half the property to their children; and if one of us should die without children, the survivor would inherit everything, unless the dying party had disposed of his half of the common wealth in favor of someone else he might deem appropriate. * * *

*   *   *

REVIEW QUESTIONS

1. Compare de Gouges's declaration with the Declaration of the Rights of Man and Citizen. Determine the parallel and divergent aspects of the two documents.

2. How does de Gouges envision women in civil society? How does this projected role differ from the social realities of eighteenth-century France?

3. What traditional institutions and mores does de Gouges criticize? What does she exhort women to do?

EDMUND BURKE AND THOMAS PAINE

Opposing Views of the Revolution

Although Edmund Burke (1730–1797), an Irish Whig member of Parliament, had supported the American cause against Great Britain in the 1770s, he denounced the French Revolution with a sustained rhetorical elegance that has few, if any, rivals. The circumstance that provoked Burke's essay was a speech in 1789 by Dr. Richard Price, who posited a close affinity between England's Glorious Revolution of 1688 and the recent French Revolution. Burke's scathing attack on the premises and principles of the French Revolution in his Reflections on the Revolution in France *(1790) incited an equally engaging rejoinder by Thomas Paine (1737–1809), a committed English democrat, whose earlier* Common Sense *had become a central political tract supporting the American Revolution. His* Rights of Man *(1791), in response to Burke, assumed the status in Britain of a primer for democratic republicanism. British government prohibited its publication and sale in vain.*

Edmund Burke

FROM *Reflections on the Revolution in France*

*   *   *

No experience has taught us that in any other course or method than that of an *hereditary crown* our liberties can be regularly perpetuated and preserved sacred as our *hereditary right*. An irregular convulsive movement may be necessary to throw

From *Reflections on the Revolution in France*, by Edmund Burke (London: J. Dodsley, 1790), pp. 34–37, 127–31.

off an irregular, convulsive disease. But the course of succession is the healthy habit of the British constitution. Was it that the legislature wanted at the act for the limitation of the crown in the Hanoverian line, drawn through the female descendants of James the First, a due sense of the inconveniences of having two or three, or possibly more, foreigners in succession to the British throne? No!—they had a due sense of the evils which might happen from such foreign rule, and more than a due sense of them. But a more decisive proof cannot be given of the full conviction of the British nation that the principles of the Revolution did not authorize them to elect kings at their pleasure, and without any attention to the ancient fundamental principles of our government, than their continuing to adopt a plan of hereditary Protestant succession in the old line, with all the dangers and all the inconveniences of its being a foreign line full before their eyes and operating with the utmost force upon their minds.

A few years ago I should be ashamed to overhead a matter so capable of supporting itself by the then unnecessary support of any argument; but this seditious, unconstitutional doctrine is now publicly taught, avowed, and printed. The dislike I feel to revolutions, the signals for which have so often been given from pulpits; the spirit of change that is gone abroad; the total contempt which prevails with you, and may come to prevail with us, of all ancient institutions when set in opposition to a present sense of convenience or to the bent of a present inclination: all these considerations make it not unadvisable, in my opinion, to call back our attention to the true principles of our own domestic laws; that you, my French friend, should begin to know, and that we should continue to cherish them. We ought not, on either side of the water, to suffer ourselves to be imposed upon by the counterfeit wares which some persons, by a double fraud, export to you in illicit bottoms as raw commodities of British growth, though wholly alien to our soil, in order afterwards to smuggle them back again into this country, manufactured after the newest Paris fashion of an improved liberty.

The people of England will not ape the fashions they have never tried, nor go back to those which they have found mischievous on trial. They look upon the legal hereditary succession of their crown as among their rights, not as among their wrongs; as a benefit, not as a grievance; as a security for their liberty, not as a badge of servitude. They look on the frame of their commonwealth, *such as it stands*, to be of inestimable value, and they conceive the undisturbed succession of the crown to be a pledge of the stability and perpetuity of all the other members of our constitution.

I shall beg leave, before I go any further, to take notice of some paltry artifices which the abettors of election, as the only lawful title to the crown, are ready to employ in order to render the support of the just principles of our constitution a task somewhat invidious. These sophisters substitute a ficti-

tious cause and feigned personages, in whose favor they suppose you engaged whenever you defend the inheritable nature of the crown. It is common with them to dispute as if they were in a conflict with some of those exploded fanatics of slavery, who formerly maintained what I believe no creature now maintains, "that the crown is held by divine hereditary and indefeasible right." These old fanatics of single arbitrary power dogmatized as if hereditary royalty was the only lawful government in the world, just as our new fanatics of popular arbitrary power maintain that a popular election is the sole lawful source of authority. The old prerogative enthusiasts, it is true, did speculate foolishly, and perhaps impiously too, as if monarchy had more of a divine sanction than any other mode of government; and as if a right to govern by inheritance were in strictness *indefeasible* in every person who should be found in the succession to a throne, and under every circumstance, which no civil or political right can be. But an absurd opinion concerning the king's hereditary right to the crown does not prejudice one that is rational and bottomed upon solid principles of law and policy. If all the absurd theories of lawyers and divines were to vitiate the objects in which they are conversant, we should have no law and no religion left in the world. But an absurd theory on one side of a question forms no justification for alleging a false fact or promulgating mischievous maxims on the other.

*   *   *

I almost venture to affirm that not one in a hundred amongst us participates in the "triumph" of the Revolution Society. If the king and queen of France, and their children, were to fall into our hands by the chance of war, in the most acrimonious of all hostilities (I deprecate such an event, I deprecate such hostility), they would be treated with another sort of triumphal entry into London. We formerly have had a king of France in that situation; you have read how he was treated by the victor in the field, and in what manner he was afterwards received in England. Four hundred years have gone over us, but I believe we are not materially changed since that period. Thanks to our sullen resistance to innovation, thanks to the cold sluggishness of our national character, we still bear the stamp of our forefathers. We have not (as I conceive) lost the generosity and dignity of thinking of the fourteenth century, nor as yet have we subtilized ourselves into savages. We are not the converts of Rousseau; we are not the disciples of Voltaire; Helvetius has made no progress amongst us. Atheists are not our preachers; madmen are not our lawgivers. We know that *we* have made no discoveries, and we think that no discoveries are to be made in morality, nor many in the great principles of government, nor in the ideas of liberty, which were understood long before we were born, altogether as well as they will be after the grace has heaped its mold upon our presumption and the silent tomb shall have imposed its law on our pert loquacity. In England we have not yet been completely embowelled of our natural entrails; we still feel within us, and we cherish and cultivate, those inbred sentiments which are the faithful guardians, the active monitors of our duty, the true supporters of all liberal and manly morals. We have not been drawn and trussed, in order that we may be filled, like stuffed birds in a museum, with chaff and rags and paltry blurred shreds of paper about the rights of men. We preserve the whole of our feelings still native and entire, unsophisticated by pedantry and infidelity. We have real hearts of flesh and blood beating in our bosoms. We fear God; we look up with awe to kings, with affection to parliaments, with duty to magistrates, with reverence to priests, and with respect to nobility. Why? Because when such ideas are brought before our minds, it is *natural* to be so affected; because all other feelings are false and spurious and tend to corrupt our minds, to vitiate our primary morals, to render us unfit for rational liberty, and, by teaching us a servile, licentious, and abandoned insolence, to be our low sport for a few holidays, to make us perfectly fit for, and justly deserving of, slavery through the whole course of our lives.

You see, Sir, that in this enlightened age I am bold enough to confess that we are generally men of untaught feelings, that, instead of casting away all our old prejudices, we cherish them to a very considerable degree, and, to take more shame to ourselves, we cherish them because they are prejudices; and the longer they have lasted and the more generally they have prevailed, the more we cherish them. We are afraid to put men to live and trade each on his own private stock of reason, because we suspect that this stock in each man is small, and that the individuals would do better to avail themselves of the general bank and capital of nations and of ages. Many of our men of speculation, instead of exploding general prejudices, employ their sagacity to discover the latent wisdom which prevails in them. If they find what they seek, and they seldom fail, they think it more wise to continue the prejudice, with the reason involved, than to cast away the coat of prejudice and to leave nothing but the naked reason; because prejudice, with its reason, has a motive to give action to that reason, and an affection which will give it permanence. Prejudice is of ready application in the emergency; it previously engages the mind in a steady course of wisdom and virtue and does not leave the man hesitating in the moment of decision skeptical, puzzled, and unresolved. Prejudice renders a man's virtue his habit, and not a series of unconnected acts. Through just prejudice, his duty becomes a part of his nature.

Your literary men and your politicians, and so do the whole clan of the enlightened among us, essentially differ in these points. They have no respect for the wisdom of others, but they pay it off by a very full measure of confidence in their own. With them it is a sufficient motive to destroy an old scheme of things because it is an old one. As to the new, they are in no sort of fear with regard to the duration of a building run up in haste, because duration is no object to those who think little or nothing has been done before their time, and who place all their hopes in discovery. They conceive, very systematically, that all things which give perpetuity are mischievous, and therefore they are at inexpiable war with all establishments. They think that government may vary like modes of dress, and with as little ill effect; that there needs no principle of attachment, except a sense of present convenience, to any constitution of the state. They always speak as if they were of opinion that there is a singular species of compact between them and their magistrates which binds the magistrate, but which has nothing reciprocal in it, but that the majesty of the people has a right to dissolve it without any reason but its will. Their attachment to their country itself is only so far as it agrees with some of their fleeting projects; it begins and ends with that scheme of polity which falls in with their momentary opinion.

These doctrines, or rather sentiments, seem prevalent with your new statesmen. But they are wholly different from those on which we have always acted in this country.

*   *   *

Thomas Paine

FROM *Rights of Man*

*   *   *

Mr. Burke talks about what he calls an hereditary crown, as if it were some production of Nature; or as if, like Time, it had a power to operate, not only independently, but in spite of man; or as if it were a thing or a subject universally consented to. Alas! it has none of those properties, but is the reverse of them all. It is a thing in imagination, the propriety of which is more than doubted, and the legality of which in a few years will be denied.

But, to arrange this matter in a clearer view than what general expressions can convey, it will be necessary to state the distinct heads under which (what is called) an hereditary crown, or, more properly speaking, an hereditary succession to the Government of a Nation, can be considered; which are,

First, The right of a particular Family to establish itself.

Secondly, The right of a Nation to establish a particular Family.

With respect to the *first* of these heads, that of a Family establishing itself with hereditary powers on its own authority, and independent of the consent of a Nation, all men will concur in calling it despotism; and it would be trespassing on their understanding to attempt to prove it.

But the *second* head, that of a Nation establishing a particular Family with *hereditary powers*, does not present itself as despotism on the first reflection; but if men will permit a second reflection to take place, and carry that reflection forward but one remove out of their own persons to that of their offspring, they will then see that hereditary succession becomes in its consequences the same despotism to others, which they reprobated for themselves. It operates to preclude the consent of the succeeding generation; and the preclusion of consent is despotism. When the person who at any time shall be in possession of a Government, or those who stand in succession to him, shall say to a Nation, I hold this power in 'contempt' of you, it signifies not on what authority he pretends to say it. It is no relief, but an aggravation to a person in slavery, to reflect that he was sold by his parent; and as that which heightens the criminality of an act cannot be produced to prove the legality of it, hereditary succession cannot be established as a legal thing.

In order to arrive at a more perfect decision on this head, it will be proper to consider the generation which undertakes to establish a Family with *hereditary powers*, apart and separate from the generations which are to follow; and also to consider the character in which the *first* generation acts with respect to succeeding generations.

The generation which first selects a person, and puts him at the head of its Government, either with the title of King, or any other distinction, acts its *own choice*, be it wise or foolish, as a free agent for itself. The person so set up is not hereditary, but selected and appointed; and the generation who sets him up, does not live under an hereditary government, but under a government of its own choice and establishment. Were the generation who sets him up, and the person so let up, to live for ever, it never could become hereditary succession; and of

From *Rights of Man,* edited by Hypatia Bradlaugh Bonner (London: Watts, 1906), pp. 60–62.

consequence, hereditary succession can only follow on the death of the first parties.

As therefore hereditary succession is out of the question with respect to the *first* generation, we have now to consider the character in which *that* generation acts with respect to the commencing generation, and to all succeeding ones.

It assumes a character, to which it has neither right nor title. It changes itself from a *Legislator* to a *Testator*, and affects to make its Will, which is to have operation after the demise of the makers, to bequeath the Government; and it not only attempts to bequeath, but to establish on the succeeding generation, a new and different form of government under which itself lived. Itself, as is already observed, lived not under an hereditary Government, but under a Government of its own choice and establishment; and it now attempts, by virtue of a will and testament, (and which it has not authority to make), to take from the commencing generation, and all future ones, the rights and free agency by which itself acted.

But, exclusive of the right which any generation has to act collectively as a testator, the objects to which it applies itself in this case, are not within the compass of any law, or of any will or testament.

The rights of men in society, are neither deviseable, nor transferable, nor annihilable, but are descendable only; and it is not in the power of any generation to intercept finally, and cut off the descent. If the present generation, or any other, are disposed to be slaves, it does not lessen the right of the succeeding generation to be free: wrongs cannot have a legal descent. When Mr. Burke attempts to maintain, that the *English Nation did at the Revolution of 1688, most solemnly renounce and abdicate their rights for themselves, and for all their posterity for ever;* he speaks a language that merits not reply, and which can only excite contempt for his prostitute principles, or pity for his ignorance.

In whatever light hereditary succession, as growing out of the will and testament of some former generation, presents itself, it is an absurdity. A cannot make a will to take from B the property of B, and give it to C; yet this is the manner in which

(what is called) hereditary succession by law operates. A certain former generation made a will, to take away the rights of the commencing generation, and all future ones, and convey those rights to a third person, who afterwards comes forward, and tells them, in Mr. Burke's language, that they have *no rights,* that their rights are already bequeathed to him, and that he will govern in *contempt* of them. From such principles, and such ignorance, Good Lord deliver the world!

But, after all, what is this metaphor called a crown, or rather what is monarchy? Is it a thing, or is it a name, or is it a fraud? Is it a thing, or is it a name, or is it a fraud? Is it "a contrivance of human wisdom," or of human craft to obtain money from a nation under specious pretences? Is it a thing necessary to a nation? If it is, in what does that necessity consist, what services does it perform, what is its business, and what are its merits? ⁎ ⁎ ⁎ It appears to be a something going much out of fashion, falling into ridicule, and rejected in some countries both as unnecessary and expensive. In America it is considered as an absurdity; and in France it has so far declined, that the goodness of the man, and the respect for his personal character, are the only things that preserve the appearance of its existence.

⁎   ⁎   ⁎

If there is any thing in monarchy which we people of America do not understand, I wish Mr. Burke would be so kind as to inform us. I see in America, a government extending over a country ten times as large as England, and conducted with regularity, for a fortieth part of the expence which government costs in England. If I ask a man in America, if he wants a King? he retorts, and asks me if I take him for an idiot? How is it that this difference happens? are we more or less wise than others? I see in America, the generality of people living in a stile of plenty unknown in monarchical countries; and I see that the principle of its government, which is that of the *equal Rights of Man*, is making a rapid progress in the world.

⁎   ⁎   ⁎

GLOIRE NATIONALE NAPOLEON (c. 1835)   FRANÇOIS GEORGIN

Lithographic prints and woodcuts popularized the French Revolution and Napoleon's empire. Inexpensive and easily vended, visual images of the revolution enabled both illiterate and rural social groups to participate in the new political culture of the revolution. What attributes of Napoleon and the French nation did the artist emphasize in this print, and what does it suggest about early nineteenth-century popular nationalism?

REVIEW QUESTIONS

1. What is Burke's position on tradition and monarchy, and what is Paine's response to it?
2. What is Burke's response to the Enlightenment and its primacy of reason?
3. How does Paine characterize the use of reason in politics?
4. How did the issue of the French Revolution have a direct bearing on British domestic politics in the 1790s?

AL-JABARTI

FROM *Chronicle of the French Occupation,* 1798

In May 1798, 400 French ships, carrying Napoleon and 36,000 men, set sail for Egypt. In an attempt to extend France's colonial empire and undermine Britain's economic dominance in the eastern Mediterranean, the French revolutionary army established control in Egypt in June 1798 after defeating the Mamluks, the military caste governing Egypt for the Ottoman Empire. In 1799 a superior British navy destroyed the French fleet in Alexandria, spurring Napoleon to return to France in the same year, leaving behind a trapped, defeated French army, which finally returned in 1801. Although brief, the French occupation of Egypt significantly changed Arab life, alerting the Arab world to the West's formidable military might and its advances in learning. Al-Jabarti, a learned Egyptian born into a family of religious scholars, captured the upheaval and suffering of the Egyptian population. In the following section Al-Jabarti cites and critiques Napoleon's announcement of French occupation.

From *Al-Jabarti's Chronicle of the French Occupation,* translated by S. Moreh (1798), pp. 24, 26–33.

*   *   *

On Monday news arrived that the French had reached Damanhūr and Rosetta, bringing about the flight of their inhabitants to Fuwwa and its surroundings. Contained in this news was mention of the French sending notices throughout the country demanding impost for the upkeep of the military. Furthermore they printed a large proclamation in Arabic, calling on the people to obey them and to raise their "Bandiera." In this proclamation were inducements, warnings, all manner of wiliness and stipulations. Some copies were sent from the provinces to Cairo and its text is:

In the name of God, the Merciful, the Compassionate. There is no god but God. He has no son, nor has He an associate in His Dominion.

On behalf of the French Republic which is based upon the foundation of liberty and equality, General Bonaparté, Commander-in-Chief of the French armies makes known to all the Egyptian people that for a long time the Şanjaqs who lorded it over Egypt have treated the French community basely and contemptuously and have persecuted its merchants with all manner of extortion and violence. Therefore the hour of punishment has now come.

Unfortunately this group of Mamluks, imported from the mountains of Circassia and Georgia have acted corruptly for ages in the fairest land that is to be found upon the face of the globe. However, the Lord of the Universe, the Almighty, has decreed the end of their power.

O ye Egyptians, they may say to you that I have not made an expedition hither for any other object than that of abolishing your religion; but this is a pure falsehood and you must not give credit to it, but tell the slanderers that I have not come to you except for the purpose of restoring your rights from the hands of the oppressors and that I more than the Mamluks, serve God—may He be praised and exalted—and revere His Prophet Muhammad and the glorious Qur'ān.

And tell them also that all people are equal in the eyes of God and the only circumstances which distinguish one from the other are reason, virtue, and knowledge. But amongst the Mamluks, what is there of reason, virtue, and knowledge, which would distinguish them from others and qualify them alone to possess every-thing which sweetens life in this world? Wherever fertile land is found it is appropriated to the Mamluks; and the handsomest female slaves, and the best horses, and the most desirable dwelling-places, all these belong to them exclusively. If the land of Egypt is a fief of the Mamluks, let them then produce the title-deed, which God conferred upon them. But the Lord of the Universe is compassionate and equitable toward mankind, and with the help of the Exalted, from this day forward no Egyptian shall be excluded from admission to eminent positions nor from acquiring high ranks, therefore the intelligent and virtuous and learned ("*ulamā*") amongst them, will regulate their affairs, and thus the state of the whole population will be rightly adjusted.

Formerly, in the lands of Egypt there were great cities, and wide canals and extensive commerce and nothing ruined all this but the avarice and the tyranny of the Mamluks.

O ye Qādis, Shaykhs and Imāms; O ye Shurbājiyya and men of circumstance tell your nation that the French are also faithful Muslims, and in confirmation of this they invaded Rome and destroyed there the Papal See, which was always exhorting the Christians to make war with Islam. And then they went to the island of Malta, from where they expelled the Knights, who claimed that God the Exalted required them to fight the Muslims. Furthermore, the French at all times have declared themselves to be the most sincere friends of the Ottoman Sultan and the enemy of his enemies, may God ever perpetuate his empire! And on the contrary the Mamluks have withheld their obeisance from the Sultan, and have not followed his orders. Indeed they never obeyed anything but their own greed!

Blessing on blessing to the Egyptians who will act in concert with us, without any delay, for their condition shall be rightly adjusted, and their rank raised. Blessing also, upon those who will abide in their habitations, not siding with either of the two hostile parties, yet when they know us better, they will hasten to us with all their hearts. But woe upon woe to those who will unite with the Mamlūks and assist them in the war against us, for they will not find the way of escape, and no trace of them shall remain.

First Article

All the villages, situated within three hours' distance from the places through which the French army passes, are required to send to the Commander-in-Chief some persons, deputed by them, to announce to the aforesaid, that they submit and that they have hoisted the French flag, which is white, blue, and red.

Second Article

Every village that shall rise against the French army, shall be burnt down.

Third Article

Every village that submits to the French army must hoist the French flag and also the flag of our friend the Ottoman Sultan, may he continue for ever.

Fourth Article

The Shaykh of each village must immediately seal all property, houses, and possessions, belonging to the Mamluks, making the most strenuous effort that not the least thing be lost.

Fifth Article

The Shaykhs, Qādis, and Imāms must remain at their posts, and every countryman shall remain peaceably in his dwelling, and also prayers shall be performed in the mosques as customary and the Egyptians, all of them shall render thanks for God's graciousness, praise be to Him and may He be exalted, in extirpating the power of the Mamlūks, saying with a loud voice, May God perpetuate the glory of the Ottoman Sultan! May God preserve the glory of the French army! May God curse the Mamluks and rightly adjust the condition of the Egyptian people.

Written in the Camp at Alexandria on the 13th of the month Messidor [the 6th year] of the founding of the French Republic, that is to say toward the end of the month Muharram in the year [1213] of the Hijra [2 July 1798].

It ends here word for word. Here is an explanation of the incoherent words and vulgar constructions which he put into this miserable letter.

His statement "In the name of God, the Merciful, the Compassionate. There is no god but God. He has no son, nor has He an associate in His Dominion." In mentioning these three sentences there is an indication that the French agree with the three religions, but at the same time they do not agree with them, nor with any religion. They are consistent with the Muslims in stating the formula "In the name of God," in denying that He has a son or an associate. They disagree with the Muslims in not mentioning the two Articles of Faith, in rejecting the mission of Muhammad, and the legal words and deeds which are necessarily recognized by religion. They agree with the Christians in most of their words and deeds, but disagree with them by not mentioning the Trinity, and denying the mission and furthermore in rejecting their beliefs, killing the priests, and destroying the churches. Then, their statement "On behalf of the French Republic, etc.," that is, this proclamation is sent from their Republic, that means their body politic, because they have no chief or sultan with whom they all agree, like others, whose function is to speak on their behalf. For when they rebelled against their sultan six years ago and killed him, the people agreed unanimously that there was not to be a single ruler but that their state, territories, laws, and administration of their affairs, should be in the hands of the intelligent and wise men among them. They appointed persons chosen by them and made them heads of the army, and below them generals and commanders of thousands, two hundreds, and tens, administrators and advisers, on condition that they were all to be equal and none superior to any other in view of the equality of creation and nature. They made this the foundation and basis of their system. This is the meaning of their statement "based upon the foundation of liberty and equality." Their term "liberty" means that they are not slaves like the Mamluks; "equality" has the aforesaid meaning. Their officials are distinguished by the cleanliness of their garments. They wear emblems on their uniforms and upon their heads. For example an Amir of ten has a large rosette of silk upon his head, like a big rose. If he is a commander of twenty-five his rosette is of two colours, and if he is a commander of a hundred his rosette is of three colours. His hat which is known as *burnayt.a* (It. *borreta*) is embroidered with gold brocade, or he may bear upon his shoulders an emblem of the same. If he has a reputation for daring and is well-known for his heroism and has been wounded several times he receives two badges on his shoulder. They follow this rule: great and small, high and low, male and female are all equal. Sometimes they break this rule according to their whims and inclinations or reasoning. Their women do not veil themselves and have no modesty; they do not care whether they uncover their private parts. Whenever a Frenchman has to perform an act of nature he does so wherever he happens to be, even in full view of people, and he goes away as he is, without washing his private parts after defecation. If he is a man of taste and refinement he wipes himself with whatever he finds, even with a paper with writing on it, otherwise he remains as he is. They have intercourse with any woman who pleases them and vice versa. Sometimes one of their women goes into a barber's shop, and invites him to shave her pubic hair. If he wishes he can take his fee in kind. It is their custom to shave both their moustaches and beard. Some of them leave the hair of their cheeks only.

They do not shave their heads nor their pubic hair. They mix their foods. Some might even put together in one dish coffee, sugar, arrack, raw eggs, limes, and so on. As for the name "Bonaparté" this is the title of their general, it is not a name. Its meaning is "the pleasant gathering," because *Bona (Būnā)* means "pleasant" and *parté* means "gathering." * * *

*   *   *

His saying *fī hādhā 'l-taraf* (hither), means "this part of the earth." His statement *wa-qūlū li 'l-muftariyīn* (but tell the slanderers) is the plural of *muftarī* (slanderer) which means liar, and how worthy of this description they are. The proof of that is his saying "I have not come to you except for the purpose of restoring your rights from the hands of the oppressors," which is the first lie he uttered and a falsehood which he invented. Then he proceeds to something even worse than that, may God cast him into perdition, with his words: "I more than the Mamluks serve God. . . ." There is no doubt that this is a derangement of his mind, and an excess of foolishness. What a worship he is speaking about, however great its intensity, *kufr* (disbelief) had dulled his heart, and prevented him from reaching the way of his salvation. There is inversion in the words which should read *innanī a'budu Allāh akthar min al-Mamālīk* (I serve God more than the Mamluks do). However, it is possible that there is no inversion, and that the meaning is "I have more troops or more money than the Mamluks" and that the accusative of specification has been omitted. So his words "I serve God" are a new sentence and a new lie.

His statement "[I] revere His Prophet" is conjoined to what goes before, as one lie joined to another, because if he respected him he would believe in him, accept his truth, and respect his nation. His statement *al-Qur'ān al-'aẓim* (the glorious Qur'ān) is joined to "His Prophet," that is, "I respect the glorious Qur'ān," and this too is a lie, because to respect the Qur'ān means to glorify it, and one glorifies it by believing in what it contains. The Qur'ān is one of the miracles of the Prophet which proves his truth, and that he is the Prophet to the end of time, and that his nation is the most noble of all nations. These people deny all that and lie in every thing they enumerate, "And many as

are the signs in the Heavens and on the Earth, yet they will pass them by, and turn aside from them."

His saying "[all people] are equal in the eyes of God" the Almighty, this is a lie and stupidity. How can this be when God has made some superior to others as is testified by the dwellers in the Heavens and on the Earth?

*   *   *

His statement *al-manāṣib al-sāmiya* (eminent positions), that means *al-murtafi'a* (elevated). This is in order to avert blame from themselves by giving high posts of authority to the low and vulgar people among them, as for example their appointment of Barṭulmān (Barthélemy) the artilleryman to the post of Katkhudā Mustaḥfiẓān. He says "and thus the state of the whole population will be rightly adjusted." Yes, that is to say, under the administration of wise and intelligent men. But they did not appoint them. The word *Muslimīn* should be *Muslimūn* in the nominative. The point of putting the word in the *naṣb* (accusative) has already been mentioned. There is another point namely: that their Islam is *naṣb* (fraud).

As for his statement "and destroyed there the Papal See," by this deed they have gone against the Christians as has already been pointed out. So those people are opposed to both Christians and Muslims, and do not hold fast to any religion. You see that they are materialists, who deny all God's attributes, the Hereafter and Resurrection, and who reject Prophethood and Messengership. They believe that the world was not created, and that the heavenly bodies and the occurrences of the Universe are influenced by the movement of the stars, and that nations appear and states decline, according to the nature of the conjunctions and the aspects of the moon. Some believe in transmigration of souls, or other fantasies. For this reason they do not slaughter ritually any animal they eat, or behead any man, before having killed them, so that the parts of his soul may not be separated and scattered, so as not to be whole in another body, and similar nonsense and erroneous beliefs. * * *

*   *   *

REVIEW QUESTIONS

1. In what ways does the French announcement accommodate Islamic culture? Is it successful?
2. What are Al-Jabarti's political, religious, and social views of the French? How are these views interconnected?
3. What made the French invasion and colonization of an Islamic culture more difficult than conquests in Europe?
4. What is the manner and method of Al-Jabarti's critique of Napoleon's announcement?

JAKOB WALTER

FROM *The Diary of a Napoleonic Foot Soldier*

The French Revolution and Napoleonic era unleashed a quarter century of war on the European continent, drawing hundreds of thousands men into the wider scope of modern warfare. Participating in campaigns from Spain to Russia, a generation of recruits endured the privations of military life in remote lands, where foraging and bivouacking proved as challenging as military engagement. Jakob Walter was one of 12,000 soldiers from Württemberg, a kingdom in southwestern Germany allied to the French cause, who served in corps commanded by Marshall Ney. Following campaigns in 1806–07 and 1809, Walter also fought in the Russian Campaign of 1812–13, serving for a time as an aide-de-camp for a major. During these campaigns, his division marched from western Germany to Moscow and back, a trek of approximately 4,400 kilometers. The following passage recounts a foot soldier's experience of Napoleon's epic and disastrous attempt to penetrate Tsarist Russia and defeat its army. Of the approximately 600,000 soldiers of the Grande Armée *that crossed into Russia, only 140,000 returned from Moscow—with even fewer crossing the border back to central Europe. The retreat from Moscow in October 1812, as depicted here, captures the tribulations of a common soldier's life.*

From *The Diary of a Napoleonic Foot Soldier*, by Jakob Watler, edited by Marc Raeff (New York: Doubleday, 1991), pp. 52–57, 71–75, 80–88.

On August 19, the entire army moved forward, and pursued the Russians with all speed. Four or five hours' farther up the river another battle started, but the enemy did not hold out long, and the march now led to Moshaisk, the so-called "Holy Valley." From Smolensk to Moshaisk the war displayed its horrible work of destruction: all the roads, fields, and woods lay as though sown with people, horses, wagons, burned villages and cities; everything looked like the complete ruin of all that lived. In particular, we saw ten dead Russians to one of our men, although every day our numbers fell off considerably. In order to pass through woods, swamps, and narrow trails, trees which formed barriers in the woods had to be removed, and wagon barricades of the enemy had to be cleared away. In such numbers were the Russians lying around that it, seemed as if they were all dead. The cities in the meantime were Dorogo-bush, Semlevo, Viasma, and Gshatsk. The march up to there, as far as it was a march, is indescribable and inconceivable for people who have not seen anything of it. The very great heat, the dust which was like a thick fog, the closed line of march in columns, and the putrid water from holes filled with dead people, and cattle brought everyone close to death; and eye pains, fatigue, thirst, and hunger tormented everybody. God! how often I remembered the bread and beer which I had enjoyed at home with such an indifferent pleasure! Now, however, I must struggle, half wild, with the dead and living. How gladly would I renounce for my whole life the warm food so common at home if I only did not lack good bread and beer now! I would not wish for more all my life. But these were empty, helpless thoughts. Yes, the thought of my brothers and sisters so far away added to my pain! Wherever I looked, I saw the soldiers with dead, half-desperate faces. Many cried out in despair, "If only my mother had not borne me!" Some demoralized men even cursed their parents and their birth.

These voices, however, raised my soul to God, and I often spoke in quietude, "God, Thou canst save me; but, if it is not Thy will, I hope that my sins will be forgiven because of my sufferings and pains and that my soul will ascend to Thee." With such thoughts I went on trustingly to meet my fate.

*   *   *

. . . Now it was October 17, and Napoleon held an army review and announced the departure for October 18, early in the morning at 3 o'clock, with the warning that whoever should delay one hour would fall into the hands of the enemies. All beer, brandy, etc., was abandoned and whatever was still intact was ordered to be burned. Napoleon himself had the Kremlin undermined and blown up. . . .

*   *   *

General Ney, about whom no one knew anything anymore, was in charge of the rear guard. He fought his way through to us. However, his forces were half gone. The march had to go on; and the striking, clubbing, and skirmishing commenced so

frightfully that the cry of murder echoed all about. The Cossacks advanced upon the army from all sides. We came toward Dubrovna, and the throng was so great that those on foot were usually beaten and cudgeled to the right and the left of the road-way at such narrow passages as marshes, rivers, and bridges here my major and I were pushed apart and lost each other again. It was not possible to recognize one another except by voice. Everyone was disguised in furs, rags, and pieces of cloth; they wore round hats and peasant caps on their heads, and many had priest's robes from the churches. It was like a world turned upside down. I had had enough of my helmet at the very beginning of the retreat. I put on a round hat, wrapped my head with silk and muslin cloths and my feet with thick woolen cloth. I had on two vests and over my doublet a thick and large Russian coat which I had taken from a Russian in exchange for my own at Smolensk on the trip into Russia; and over all this I wore my thick fur. I was so enwrapped that only my eyes had an opening out of which I could breathe. From time to time I had to break off from this opening the ice that would immediately form again from my breath.

At night in Dubrovna, when the enemy had given up their maneuvers, everyone settled down in and around the place. Every night, the fires for warming could be seen over a region four hours' long and wide, reddening the sky like red cloth. The burning villages at the side contributed most to this sight, and the shrieking, beating, and lamenting did not stop for a minute. Again and again people died, and sometimes froze to death; these were people who pressed toward the fire but were seldom permitted to get there; so they died away from the fire, and very often they were even converted into cushions in order that the living would not have to sit in the snow.

*   *   *

As we came to Orscha, it was said that we would get shoes and bread from a magazine, also oats for the horses; but this was impossible. In spite of the guards stationed around the storehouses, none of the doors could be opened, since everyone hit and shoved each other in order to get close to a door. I hurried there at first to obtain oats, but that was impossible until the guards could no longer stand their ground and the doors were sprung open. Then I climbed through a window opening, took several sacks of oats with the help of my comrades, and brought them to the camp fire. Immediately thereafter a soldier who also shared in my fire came with two loaves of bread. Now everyone's heart beat with eagerness, and everyone sprang toward the bread store. When we arrived, no one could get inside anymore, and those within could not come out because of the pressure. What was to be done? Many weak soldiers lay on the floor and were trampled down, screaming frightfully. I made for a window opening again; tore out the shutter, the wooden grating, and the window; and got five of the loaves, though they were trampled and broken. This was since Moscow the second bit of bread, for which I thanked God anew with tears.

*   *   *

While on my side march I saw lying on the ground a beautiful black bearskin with head and claws, which fugitives had had to throw away. With cries of "hurrah" I took possession of this in the hope of bringing my belongings to Germany, for I had various silver vessels from Moscow which were worth from three to four hundred florins. Besides this, I had silk goods, muslin, etc., such as I was able to take in abundance from the stalled wagons. Nevertheless, all this came to nothing. The retreat led through Kochanova, Toloczin, Krupky, Bobr, and Liecnize to Borissov. In the bustle by day and by night that hardly let me rest or sleep even a few hours in four or five nights, my horse, which was tied to my arm by a strap, was cut off and led away unnoticed. Since I was always accustomed to pulling on the strap on waking up to see whether my horse was still there, I pulled and this time felt no horse. I jumped up—and now what? I thought to myself, even if I had the whole night to spend looking, only a miracle could lead me to my horse, and the likelihood was all the more uncertain if my horse was already on the march. However, I had to do something. I ran left and right, back and forth;

and, whenever I tried to run close to a horse, my life was endangered by whipping and beating, for one could not take enough precaution against theft and robbery: usually one of those sitting by the fire had to keep watch. All at once I saw my "*Koniak*" standing before a chapel door with his strap tied to a soldier who was sleeping inside the doorway. Very softly now I in my turn cut the strap and rode toward my fire. I dared not sleep anymore, I thought, so that if my horse lover returned I could speak with him . . .

*   *   *

It was November 25, 1812, when we reached Borissov. Now the march went toward the Beresina River, where the indescribable horror of all possible plagues awaited us. On the way I met one of my countrymen, by the name of Brenner, who had served with the Light Horse Regiment. He came toward me completely wet and half frozen; and we greeted each other. Brenner said that the night before he and his horse had been caught and plundered but that he had taken to flight again and had come through a river which was not frozen. Now, he said, he was near death from freezing and starvation. This good, noble soldier had run into me not far from Smolensk with a little loaf of bread weighing about two pounds and had asked me whether I wanted a piece of bread, saying that this was his last supply. "However, because you have nothing at all, I will share it with you." He had dismounted, laid the bread on the ground, and cut it in two with his saber. "Dear, good friend," I had replied, "you treat me like a brother. I will not forget as long as I live this good deed of yours but will rather repay you many times if we live!" He had then a Russian horse, a huge dun, mounted it, and each of us had to work his way through, facing his own dangers. This second meeting, with both of us in the most miserable condition because no aid was available, caused a pang in my heart which sank in me unforgettably. Both of us were again separated, and death overtook him.

When we came nearer the Beresina River, there was a place where Napoleon ordered his pack horses to be unharnessed and where he ate. He watched his army pass by in the most wretched condition. What he may have felt in his heart is impossible to surmise. His outward appearance seemed indifferent and unconcerned over the wretchedness of his soldiers; only ambition and lost honor may have made themselves felt in his heart; and, although the French and Allies shouted into his ears many oaths and curses about his own guilty person, he was still able to listen to them unmoved. After his Guard had already disbanded and he was almost abandoned, he collected a voluntary corps at Dubrovna which was enrolled with many promises and received the name of "Holy Squadron." After a short time, however, this existed in name only, for the enemy reduced even them to nothing.

In this region we came to a half-burnt village away from the road, in which a cellar was found under a mansion. We sought for potatoes, and I also pressed down the broad stairway, although the cellar was already half filled with people. When I was at the bottom of the steps, the screaming began under my feet. Everyone crowded in, and none could get out. Here people were trampled to death and suffocated; those who wanted to stoop down for something were bowled over by those standing and had to be stepped upon. In spite of the murderous shrieking and frightful groaning, the pressure from outside increased; the poor, deathly weak men who fell had to lie there until dead under the feet of their own comrades. When I reflected on the murderous shrieking, I gave up pushing into the cellar, and I thought in cold fear: how will I get out again? I pressed flat against the wall so that it afforded me shelter and pushed myself vigorously little by little up the steps; this was almost impossible with others treading on my long coat. In the village of Sembin, where Napoleon ate, there was a burned house, under which was a low, timber-covered cellar with a small entrance from the outside. Here again, as potatoes and the like were being hunted for, suddenly the beams fell in and those who were inside and were not entirely burned up or suffocated were jumping about with burned clothes, screaming, whimpering, and freezing to death in terrible pain.

*   *   *

After a time, from about two till four o'clock in the afternoon, the Russians pressed nearer and nearer from every side, and the murdering and torturing seemed about to annihilate everyone. Although our army used a hill, on which what was left of our artillery was placed, and fired at the enemy as much as possible, the question was: what chance was there of rescue? That day we expected that everyone must be captured, killed, or thrown into the water. Everyone thought that his last hour had come, and everyone was expecting it; but, since the ridge was held by the French artillery, only cannon and howitzer balls could snatch away a part of the men. There was no hospital for the wounded; they died also of hunger, thirst, cold, and despair, uttering complaints and curses with their last breath. Also our sick, who had been conveyed to this point in wagons and consisted almost entirely of officers, were left to themselves; and only deathly white faces and stiffened hands stretched toward us.

*   *   *

When it became day again, we stood near the stream approximately a thousand paces from the two bridges, which were built of wood near each other. These bridges had the structure of sloping sawhorses suspended like trestles on shallow-sunk piles; on these lay long stringers and across them only bridge ties, which were not fastened down. However, one could not see the bridges because of the crowd of people, horses, and wagons. Everyone crowded together into a solid mass, and nowhere could one see a way out or a means of rescue. From morning till night we stood unprotected from cannonballs and grenades which the Russians hurled at us from two sides. At each blow from three to five men were struck to the ground, and yet no one was able to move a step to get out of the path of the cannonballs. Only by the filling up of the space where a cannonball made room could one make a little progress forward. All the powder wagons also stood in the crowd; many of these were ignited by the grenades, killing hundreds of people and horses standing about them.

I had a horse to ride and one to lead. The horse I led I was soon forced to let go, and I had to kneel on the one which I rode in order not to have my feet crushed off, for everything was so closely packed that in a quarter of an hour one could move only four or five steps forward. To be on foot was to lose all hope of rescue. Indeed, whoever did not have a good horse could not help falling over the horses and people lying about in masses. Everyone was screaming under the feet of the horses, and everywhere was the cry, "Shoot me or stab me to death!" The fallen horses struck off their feet many of those still standing. It was only by a miracle that anyone was saved.

In the crowd the major and I held fast to one another; and, as far as it was possible, I frequently caused my horse to rear up, whereby he came down again about one step further forward. I marveled at the intelligence with which this animal sought to save us. Then evening came, and despair steadily increased. Thousands swam into the river with horses, but no one ever came out again; thousands of others who were near the water were pushed in, and the stream was like a sheep dip where the heads of men and horses bobbed up and down and disappeared.

Finally, toward four o'clock in the evening, when it was almost dark, I came to the bridge. Here I saw only one bridge, the second having been shot away. Now it is with horror, but at that time it was with a dull, indifferent feeling, that I looked at the masses of horses and people which lay dead, piled high upon the bridge. Only "Straight ahead and in the middle!" must be the resolution. "Here in the water is your grave; beyond the bridge is the continuation of a wretched life. The decision will be made on the bridge!" Now I kept myself constantly in the middle. The major and I could aid one another; and so amid a hundred blows of sabers we came to the bridge, where not a plank was visible because of the dead men and horses; and, although on reaching the bridge the people fell in masses thirty paces to the right and to the left, we came through to the firm land.

The fact that the bridge was covered with horses and men was not due to shooting and falling alone but also to the bridge ties, which were not fastened on this structure. The horses stepped through between them with their feet and so could not help

falling, until no plank was left movable on account of the weight of the bodies. For where such a timber still could move, it was torn out of place by the falling horses, and a sort of trap was prepared for the following horse. Indeed, one must say that the weight of the dead bodies was the salvation of those riding across; for, without their load, the cannon would have caused the destruction of the bridge too soon.

*   *   *

We both hurried farther along the highway; and, being daily without bread and shelter, I thought of my friends at home and compared my misery and approaching end with my former life of plenty. I remembered a common saying at home, "A campaign is always made out to be worse than it was." With this common notion I consoled myself, thinking: "It's well that you, my beloved kindred and friends, know nothing of my condition, for it would only cause you pain, and it would be of no use to me." Yes, I thanked the Creator that only I and not my brother, too, was here. Certainly I would have lost my brother or seen him die without aid, which would have killed me as well.

I could look with indifference at the people falling by the hundreds, although the impact upon the ice bashed their heads. I could look at their rising and falling again, their dull moaning and whining, and the wringing and clenching of their hands. The ice and snow sticking in their mouths was frightful. Nevertheless, I had no feeling of pity. Only my friends were in my thoughts.

REVIEW QUESTIONS

1. How did soldiers procure food and warmth and what were the obstacles?
2. In what ways is this Russian Campaign "modern" and in what ways is it "traditional"?
3. What happens at the bridge and what does it convey about the nature of Napoleon's retreat?
4. What is the emotional tone of this soldier's narrative? What does this narrative reveal about this soldier's sensibility toward war and death?

FROM *The Code Napoleon*

The Civil Code, promulgated in 1804 and renamed the Code Napoleon *in 1807, marked a domestic triumph of the French Revolution, uniting France under one code of law that above all guaranteed civic equality and property rights. In doing so, it swept away centuries of legal privileges for the aristocracy, clergy, and government. Accompanied by commercial, criminal, penal, and civil procedure codes (1806–10), the Civil Code quickly became a legal model for modern civil society; it was widely borrowed and adapted throughout continental Europe and other regions of the world. Dubbed the "bourgeois bible," the code embodied the beliefs and values of the nineteenth-century middle classes, including their biases against women, children, and the unpropertied. The following section centers on the code's definition of women's legal status.*

From *The Code Napoleon*, translated by Bryant Barrett (London: Reed, 1811), pp. 47–50, 57–58.

Title V
Of Marriage

CHAPTER VI

OF THE RIGHTS AND RESPECTIVE DUTIES
OF HUSBAND AND WIFE

212. Husband and wife mutually owe to each other fidelity, succour, and assistance.

213. The husband owes protection to his wife, the wife obedience to her husband.

214. The wife is obliged to live with her husband, and to follow him wherever he may think proper to dwell: the husband is bound to receive her, and to furnish her with every thing necessary for the purposes of life, according to his means and condition.

215. The wife can do no act in law without the authority of her husband, even where she shall be a public trader, or not in community, or separate in property.

216. The authority of the husband is not necessary where a woman is prosecuted for criminal matters, or matters of police.

217. The wife, even not in community or separate in property, cannot give, alien, mortgage, or acquire, either gratuitously or subject to condition, without the concurrence of her husband in the acts, or his consent in writing.

218. If the husband refuses to authorize his wife to proceed at law, a judge may give authority.

219. If the husband refuse to authorize his wife to pass an act, the wife may cause her husband to be cited directly before the tribunal of first instance of the district of their common domicile, which may give or refuse the authority, after the husband shall have been heard or duly summoned to the council chamber.

220. The wife, if she is a public trader, may without the authority of her husband, bind herself in what concerns her business; and, in such case, she also binds her husband, if there is community between them. She is not reputed a public trader, if she merely retails the merchandize of her husband in his business, but only where she carries on a separate trade.

221. Where the husband has incurred a condemnation carrying afflictive or infamous punishment, although it shall only have been pronounced for contempt, the wife, even of full age, cannot, during

the continuance of the punishment, do any act in law, nor contract, until after being authorized by the judge, who may, in such case, give authority, without the husband being heard or summoned.

222. If the husband is interdicted or absent, the judge may, on cognizance of the matter, authorize the wife, either to do acts in law, or to contract.

223. No general authority, even though stipulated by a marriage contract, is valid but as to administration of the property of the wife.

224. If the husband is a minor, the authority of a judge is necessary to the wife, either to do acts in law, or to contract.

225. Nullity founded on want of authority can only be set up by the wife, by the husband, or by their heirs.

226. The wife may make a will without the authority of her husband.

CHAPTER VII
OF DISSOLUTION OF MARRIAGE

227. Marriage is dissolved,

> By the death of one of the parties;
> By divorce legally pronounced;
> By the condemnation, become definitive, of one of the parties, to a punishment carrying civil death.

CHAPTER VIII
OF SECOND MARRIAGES

228. The wife cannot contract a new marriage until ten months have elapsed since the dissolution of the preceding marriage.

Title VI
Of Divorce

CHAPTER THE FIRST
OF CAUSES OF DIVORCE

229. The husband may demand divorce for cause of adultery on the part of his wife.

230. The wife may demand divorce for cause of adultery on the part of her husband, where he shall have kept his concubine in their common house.

231. The married parties may reciprocally demand divorce for cause of excess, cruelty, or grievous injuries, by the one of them towards the other.

232. Condemnation of one of the married parties to an infamous punishment, shall be to the other party a cause of divorce.

233. The mutual and persevering consent of the parties, expressed in the manner prescribed by the law, under the conditions and after the trials the law prescribes, shall sufficiently prove that living in common is insupportable to them, and that there exists, in respect to them, a peremptory cause of divorce.

CHAPTER II
OF DIVORCE FOR CAUSE DEFINED

*   *   *

Section II

Of the Provisional Measures to Which the Demand of Divorce for Cause Defined May Give Rise

267. The provisional administration of the children shall remain with the husband plaintiff or defendant in divorce, unless it shall be otherwise ordered by the tribunal, at the request either of the mother, or of the family, or of the imperial proctor, for the greater benefit of the children.

268. The wife plaintiff or defendant in divorce, may quit the domicile of her husband during the suit, and demand an alimentary pension proportioned to the means of the husband. The tribunal shall point out the house in which the wife shall be obliged to reside, and shall fix, if that is ground for it, the alimentary pension which the husband shall be obliged to pay her.

269. The wife shall be bound to prove her residence in the house pointed out for her, as often as she shall be required so to do: in default of such

proof, the husband may refuse the alimentary provision, and, if the wife is demandant in divorce, may cause her to be declared incapable to continue her suit.

270. The wife, plaintiff or defendant in divorce, being in community of property, may, in every state of the cause, commencing from the date of the order of which mention is made in article 238, require, for the preservation of her rights, the affixing of seals upon the moveable effects in community. These seals shall not be taken off without an inventory being made with a valuation, and at the charge on the part of the husband of producing the things inventoried, or making good their value as judiciary guardian.

271. Every obligation upon the community contracted by the husband, and every alienation made by him of the immoveables belonging to the community subsequently to the date of the order of which mention is made in article 238, shall be declared null, if proved to have been made or contracted in fraud of the rights of the wife.

*   *   *

REVIEW QUESTIONS

1. What civic rights did the code accord women?
2. How did the code fix the relationship of married women to property?
3. What were the distinctions between the rights of men and women in divorce proceedings?
4. What does this law code tell us about nineteenth-century social relations between men and women?

19 ✦ THE INDUSTRIAL REVOLUTION AND NINETEENTH-CENTURY SOCIETY

The economic transition from mercantile to industrial capitalism in Britain and Europe constituted one of the momentous structural revolutions in modern civilization. Industrialization swelled the material wealth of the West, unleashing an unprecedented dynamism of sustained growth. It introduced a new scale and scope of economic activity, whose need for new markets, better infrastructure, greater capitalization, and technological innovation characterized a self-evident aspect of the modern world.

Early industrialization is commonly associated with laissez-faire political economy, a doctrine that championed free trade, private enterprise, meritocratic individualism, and the sanctity of private property. Grounded in the writings of the moral philosopher and political economist Adam Smith, it roundly attacked any interference with the "natural laws" of the marketplace, thus advocating separation of government and economy. Although Adam Smith was not the first to criticize mercantilism and advocate unrestricted trade, his treatise, by associating free trade with the "natural rights" of other individual liberties, provided the philosophical underpinnings for the political demands of Great Britain's capitalist classes, whose enfranchisement after 1832 exerted influence on state policy. By dint of the vast wealth accumulated through private enterprise, the middle classes espoused the notion that commerce and industry were the twin pillars of civil society. Liberals confidently embraced the belief that these two spheres of public life provided the material basis for progress and prosperity. Yet the new industrial economy benefited from Britain's empire, whose institution of slavery did not conform to the contractual ideals of liberalism. Moreover, nineteenth-century society adapted and thrived through imperial enterprises, offering careers and wealth in cultural settings that mixed European and indigenous customs.

Yet, in spite of England's self-proclaimed status as the "workshop of the world," industrialism clearly cut in both positive and negative directions. Con-

temporaries dubbed the new discipline of political economy the "dismal science," for the studies of Thomas Malthus and David Ricardo on population growth and wage levels suggested the implausibility of an improved general welfare. Not all agreed that laissez-faire principles were the best way to organize industrial society. Consequently, the industrialization of Europe did not follow any single model. European governments, accustomed to directing economic activity, proved reluctant to surrender to the market's "invisible hand." In contrast to England, they nurtured domestic industry with subventions and protective tariffs, mobilized state capital to assist railroad construction, promoted economic development through technical education, and oversaw the management of large-scale industrial enterprises. Moreover, European society remained predominantly rural throughout most of the nineteenth century. Hence, while one speaks of an Industrial Revolution, one must envision small handicraft workshops alongside mechanized factories and vital rural economies serving dynamic urban centers.

The onset of early industrialization also generated an extraordinary range of criticism against the premise that capitalism would benefit the majority of society. There was, for example, public outcry over the treatment of laboring women and children in the coalmines and textile mills of northern England. Robert Owen and Karl Marx are but two observers who acknowledged capitalism's material benefits but nonetheless emphasized the elemental flaws in its organization. Their concerns for the material, moral, and creative dimensions of workers' lives compelled them to offer alternative visions to the dominant principles of competition and individual self-interest. Such critical voices sharpened the debate on ethics and social justice, thus exerting force over the next century—through rational argument and political struggle—on Europe's elites to address the interests of unpropertied workers.

The transition from agricultural and handicraft economies to the new urban industrial society produced pervasive dislocation and suffering. In the countryside, the erosion of traditional authority and social stability preceded large-scale industrialization. The enclosure of common lands and the increasing demand for profitable harvests replaced the paternalistic ties that bound lords and tenant farmers with the more contractual relationship of wages and rents. Reduced to the penury of day laborers, many farmers migrated to the young industrial towns offering work. Yet squalor and grueling factory work offered little solace in the city. Unencumbered by any legal restraints, employers imposed insufferable working conditions on men, women, and children. In the 1830s, reformers likened the circumstances in English mill towns to colonial slavery and ridiculed the blind spots of bourgeois society, which fervently proselytized for slavery's abolition but could not see similar misery and exploitation in their own cities. Because of urban malnutrition, disease, alcoholism, prostitution, and theft, commentators questioned whether laissez-faire capitalism possessed a moral center. If there was one, it perhaps resided in the bourgeois home, where women were expected to

n the domestic sphere with feminine probity, maternal virtue, and wifely
rvience.

The "social question" of early industrialization inexorably took on political
ensions. The legacy of revolutionary republicanism combined with the harsh
nomic conditions of early industrial capitalism produced a new era in
social relations and political struggle. Privation in the countryside produced
machine breaking, hayrick burning, and violent confrontations with masters.
In the city, bloody interventions of governments against workers articulated
the differences of class interests between political elites and workers, who
gradually developed their own political organizations. On the continent, however, unremitting state hostility toward workers' rights produced more resolute
positions against bourgeois capitalism, most vividly expressed in the classic
pamphlet, the Manifesto of the Communist Party (1848). Influenced by the general immiseration of the 1840s and the growing concentration of capital, Karl
Marx and Friedrich Engels asserted the axiomatic existence of class struggle and
the eventual triumph of workers' socialism. The manifesto launched the political
movement of Marxist socialism, which anchored class antagonism as a central
issue in European political life.

ADAM SMITH

FROM *The Wealth of Nations*

*Adam Smith (1723–1790), a professor of logic and moral philosophy as well as the
rector of Glasgow University, wrote on moral philosophy, rhetoric, astronomy, and
the formation of languages, but his reputation rests on his work of political economy,*
An Inquiry into the Nature and Causes of the Wealth of Nations *(1776). The treatise's wide-ranging discussions on wages, profit, capital, and industry influenced
political economists for the next century, but the book's attack on mercantilism and
its corresponding advocacy of free trade heralded a new economic age. The following
selections center on the division of labor, the productive "orders" of society, the
"invisible hand" of individual interest, and the role of the state in political economy.*

From *An Inquiry into the Nature and Causes of the Wealth of Nations*, by Adam Smith,
edited by Edwin Cannan (London: Methuen and Co., 1904).

Book I

Of the Causes of Improvement in the Productive Powers of Labour, and of the Order According to Which Its Produce Is Naturally Distributed among the Different Ranks of the People

CHAPTER I
OF THE DIVISION OF LABOUR

The greatest improvement in the productive powers of labour, and the greater part of the skill, dexterity, and judgment with which it is any where directed, or applied, seem to have been the effects of the division of labour.

*   *   *

To take an example, therefore, from a very trifling manufacture; but one in which the division of labour has been very often taken notice of, the trade of the pin-maker; a workman not educated to this business (which the division of labour has rendered a distinct trade), nor acquainted with the use of the machinery employed in it (to the invention of which the same division of labour has probably given occasion), could scarce, perhaps, with his utmost industry, make one pin in a day, and certainly could not make twenty. But in the way in which this business is now carried on, not only the whole work is a peculiar trade, but it is divided into a number of branches, of which the greater part are likewise peculiar trades. One man draws out the wire, another straights it, a third cuts it, a fourth points it, a fifth grinds it at the top for receiving the head; to make the head requires two or three distinct operations; to put it on, is a peculiar business, to whiten the pins is another; it is even a trade by itself to put them into the paper; and the important business of making a pin is, in this manner, divided into about eighteen distinct operations, which, in some manufactories, are all performed by distinct hands, though in others the same man will some-times perform two or three of them. I have seen a small manufactory of this kind where ten men only were employed, and where some of them consequently performed two or three distinct operations. But though they were very poor, and therefore but indifferently accommodated with the necessary machinery, they could, when they exerted themselves, make among them about twelve pounds of pins in a day. There are in a pound upwards of four thousand pins of a middling size. Those ten persons, therefore, could make among them upwards of forty-eight thousand pins in a day. Each person, therefore, making a tenth part of forty-eight thousand pins, might be considered as making four thousand eight hundred pins in a day. But if they had all wrought separately and independently, and without any of them having been educated to this peculiar business, they certainly could not each of them have made twenty, perhaps not one pin in a day; that is, certainly, not the two hundred and fortieth, perhaps not the four thousand eight hundredth part of what they are at present capable of performing, in consequence of a proper division and combination of their different operations.

*   *   *

It is the great multiplication of the productions of all the different arts, in consequence of the division of labour, which occasions, in a well-governed society, that universal opulence which extends itself to the lowest ranks of the people. Every workman has a great quantity of his own work to dispose of beyond what he himself has occasion for; and every other workman being exactly in the same situation, he is enabled to exchange a great quantity of his own goods for a great quantity, or, what comes to the same thing, for the price of a great quantity of theirs. He supplies them abundantly with what they have occasion for, and they accommodate him as amply with what he has occasion for, and a general plenty diffuses itself through all the different ranks of the society.

*   *   *

* * * The whole annual produce of the land and labour of every country, or what comes to the same thing, the whole price of that annual produce, naturally divides itself, it has already been observed, into three parts; the rent of land, the wages of labour, and the profits of stock; and constitutes a revenue to three different orders of people; to those who live by rent, to those who live by wages, and to those who live by profit. These are the three great, original and constituent orders of every civilized society, from whose revenue that of every other order is ultimately derived.

The interest of the first of those three great orders, it appears from what has been just now said, is strictly and inseparably connected with the general interest of the society. Whatever either promotes or obstructs the one, necessarily promotes or obstructs the other. When the publick deliberates concerning any regulation of commerce or police, the proprietors of land never can mislead it, with a view to promote the interest of their own particular order; at least, if they have any tolerable knowledge of that interest. They are, indeed, too often defective in this tolerable knowledge. They are the only one of the three orders whose revenue costs them neither labour nor care, but comes to them, as it were, of its own accord, and independent of any plan or project of their own. That indolence, which is the natural effect of the ease and security of their situation, renders them too often, not only ignorant, but incapable of that application of mind which is necessary in order to foresee and understand the consequences of any publick regulation.

The interest of the second order, that of those who live by wages, is as strictly connected with the interest of the society as that of the first. The wages of the labourer, it has already been shewn, are never so high as when the demand for labour is continually rising, or when the quantity employed is every year increasing considerably. When this real wealth of the society becomes stationary, his wages are soon reduced to what is barely enough to enable him to bring up a family, or to continue the race of labourers. When the society declines, they fall even below this. The order of proprietors may, perhaps, gain more by the prosperity of the society, than

that of labourers: but there is no order that suffers so cruelly from its decline. But though the interest of the labourer is strictly connected with that of the society, he is incapable either of comprehending that interest, or of understanding its connection with his own. His condition leaves him no time to receive the necessary information, and his education and habits are commonly such as to render him unfit to judge even though he was fully informed. In the publick deliberations, therefore, his voice is little heard and less regarded, except upon some particular occasions, when his clamour is animated, set on, and supported by his employers, not for his, but their own particular purposes.

His employers constitute the third order, that of those who live by profit. It is the stock that is employed for the sake of profit, which puts into motion the greater part of the useful labour of every society. The plans and projects of the employers of stock regulate and direct all the most important operations of labour, and profit is the end proposed by all those plans and projects. But the rate of profit does not, like rent and wages, rise with the prosperity, and fall with the declension of the society. On the contrary, it is naturally low in rich, and high in poor countries, and it is always highest in the countries which are going fastest to ruin. The interest of this third order therefore, has not the same connection with the general interest of the society as that of the other two. Merchants and master manufacturers are, in this order, the two classes of people who commonly employ the largest capitals, and who by their weakness draw to themselves the greatest share of the publick consideration. As during their whole lives they are engaged in plans and projects, they have frequently more acuteness of understanding than the greater part of country gentlemen. As their thoughts, however, are commonly exercised rather about the interest of their own particular branch of business, than about that of the society, their judgment, even when given with the greatest candour (which it has not been upon every occasion) is much more to be depended upon with regard to the former of those two objects, than with regard to the latter. Their superiority over the country gentleman is, not so much in their knowledge of the publick interest, as in their having a better knowledge of their own interest than he has of his. It is by this superior knowledge of their own interest that they have frequently imposed upon his generosity, and persuaded him to give up both his own interest and that of the publick, from a very simple but honest conviction, that their interest, and not his, was the interest of the publick. The interest of the dealers, however, in any particular branch of trade or manufactures, is always in some respects different from, and even opposite to, that of the publick. To widen the market and to narrow the competition, is always the interest of the dealers. To widen the market may frequently be agreeable enough to the interest of the publick; but to narrow the competition must always be against it, and can serve only to enable the dealers, by raising their profits above what they naturally would be, to levy, for their own benefit, an absurd tax upon the rest of their fellow-citizens. The proposal of any new law or regulation of commerce which comes from this order, ought always to be listened to with great precaution, and ought never to be adopted till after having been long and carefully examined, not only with the most scrupulous, but with the most suspicious attention. It comes from an order of men, whose interest is never exactly the same with that of the publick, who have generally an interest to deceive and even to oppress the publick, and who accordingly have, upon many occasions, both deceived and oppressed it. * * *

*   *   *

But the annual revenue of every society is always precisely equal to the exchangeable value of the whole annual produce of its industry, or rather is precisely the same thing with that exchangeable value. As every individual, therefore, endeavours as much as he can both to employ his capital in the support of domestick industry, and so to direct that industry that its produce may be of the greatest value; every individual necessarily labours to render the annual revenue of the society as great as he can. He generally, indeed, neither intends to promote the publick interest, nor knows how much he is promoting it. By preferring the support of domestick to that of foreign industry, he intends only his own security; and by directing that industry in such a manner as its produce may be of the greatest value, he intends only his own gain, and he is in this, as in many other cases, led by an invisible hand to promote an end which was no part of his intention. Nor is it always the worse for the society that it was no part of it. By pursuing his own interest he frequently promotes that of the society more effectually than when he really intends to promote it. I have never known much good done by those who affected to trade for the publick good. It is an affectation, indeed, not very common among merchants, and very few words need be employed in dissuading them from it.

What is the species of domestick industry which his capital can employ, and of which the produce is likely to be of the greatest value, every individual, it is evident, can, in his local situation, judge much better than any statesman or lawgiver can do for him. The statesman, who should attempt to direct private people in what manner they ought to employ their capitals, would not only load himself with a most unnecessary attention, but assume an authority which could safely be trusted, not only to no single person, but to no council or senate whatever, and which would nowhere be so dangerous as in the hands of a man who had folly and presumption enough to fancy himself fit to exercise it.

To give the monopoly of the home-market to the produce of domestick industry, in any particular art or manufacture, is in some measure to direct private people in what manner they ought to employ their capitals, and must, in almost all cases, be either a useless or a hurtful regulation. If the produce of domestick can be brought there as cheap as that of foreign industry, the regulation is evidently useless. If it cannot, it must generally be hurtful. It is the maxim of every prudent master of a family, never to attempt to make at home what it will cost him more to make than to buy. The taylor does not attempt to make his own shoes, but buys them of the shoemaker. The shoemaker does not attempt to make his own cloaths, but employs a taylor. The farmer attempts to make neither the one nor the other, but employs those different artificers. All of them find it for their interest to employ their whole industry in a way in which they have some advantage over their neighbours, and to purchase with a part of its produce, or what is the same thing, with the price of a part of it, whatever else they have occasion for.

What is prudence in the conduct of every private family, can scarce be folly in that of a great kingdom.

*   *   *

The expence of defending the society, and that of supporting the dignity of the chief magistrate, are both laid out for the general benefit of the whole society. It is reasonable, therefore, that they should be defrayed by the general contribution of the whole society, all the different members contributing, as nearly as possible, in proportion to their respective abilities.

The expence of the administration of justice too, may, no doubt, be considered as laid out for the benefit of the whole society. There is no impropriety, therefore, in its being defrayed by the general contribution of the whole society. The persons, however, who give occasion to this expence are those who, by their injustice in one way or another, make it necessary to seek redress or protection from the courts of justice. The persons again most immediately benefited by this expence, are those whom the courts of justice either restore to their rights, or maintain in their rights. The expence of the administration of justice, therefore, may very properly be defrayed by the particular contribution of one or other, or both of those two different sets of persons, according as different occasions may require, that is, by the fees of court. It cannot be necessary to have recourse to the general contribution of the whole society, except for the conviction of those criminals who have not themselves any estate or fund sufficient for paying those fees.

Those local or provincial expences of which the benefit is local or provincial (what is laid out, for example, upon the police of a particular town or district) ought to be defrayed by a local or provincial revenue, and ought to be no burden upon the general revenue of the society. It is unjust that the whole society should contribute towards an expence of which the benefit is confined to a part of the society.

The expence of maintaining good roads and communications is, no doubt, beneficial to the whole society, and may, therefore, without any injustice, be defrayed by the general contribution of the whole society. This expence, however, is most immediately and directly beneficial to those who travel or carry goods from one place to another, and to those who consume such goods. The turnpike tolls in England, and the duties called peages in other countries, lay it altogether upon those two different sets of people, and thereby discharge the general revenue of the society from a very considerable burden.

The expence of the institutions for education and religious instruction, is likewise, no doubt, beneficial to the whole society, and may, therefore, without injustice, be defrayed by the general contribution of the whole society. This expence, however, might perhaps with equal propriety, and even with some advantage, be defrayed altogether by those who receive the immediate benefit of such education and instruction, or by the voluntary contribution of those who think they have occasion for either the one or the other.

When the institutions or publick works which are beneficial to the whole society, either cannot be maintained altogether, or are not maintained altogether by the contribution of such particular members of the society as are most immediately benefited by them, the deficiency must in most cases be made up by the general contribution of the whole society. The general revenue of the society, over and above defraying the expence of defending the society, and of supporting the dignity of the chief magistrate, must make up for the deficiency of many particular branches of revenue. * * *

*   *   *

REVIEW QUESTIONS

1. What is the organizational innovation of the pin factory? What, according to Smith, is its significance for society?
2. What are Smith's three productive orders? What political roles does he assign these orders?
3. How does Smith find businessmen's ability to serve the public good both praiseworthy and suspicious?
4. Why did Smith's metaphor of the "invisible hand" grip the minds of nineteenth-century capitalists?
5. Who, according to Smith, should maintain state costs?

Rules of a Factory in Berlin

The transition for Europeans from agricultural and artisanal labor to factory work was by no means an easy change. The task-oriented world of traditional labor clashed radically with the time-oriented, strictly routinized world of industrial capitalism. The following set of rules from a Berlin foundry and engineering works in the 1840s denotes the new demands of industrial discipline.

From *Documents of Economic European History*, vol. 1, *The Process of Industrialization, 1750–1870*, edited by Sidney Pollard and C. Holmes (New York: Arnold, 1968), pp. 534–36.

In every large works, and in the co-ordination of any large number of workmen, good order and harmony must be looked upon as the fundamentals of success, and therefore the following rules shall be strictly observed.

Every man employed in the concern named below shall receive a copy of these rules, so that no one can plead ignorance. Its acceptance shall be deemed to mean consent to submit to its regulations.

1. The normal working day begins at all seasons at 6 a.m. precisely and ends, after the usual break of half an hour for breakfast, an hour for dinner and half an hour for tea, at 7 p.m., and it shall be strictly observed.

Five minutes before the beginning of the stated hours of work until their actual commencement, a bell shall ring and indicate that every worker employed in the concern has to proceed to his place of work, in order to start as soon as the bell stops.

The doorkeeper shall lock the door punctually at 6 a.m., 8.30 a.m., 1 p.m. and 4.30 p.m.

Workers arriving 2 minutes late shall lose half an hour's wages; whoever is more than 2 minutes late may not start work until after the next break, or at least shall lose his wages until then. Any disputes about the correct time shall be settled by the clock mounted above the gatekeeper's lodge.

These rules are valid both for time- and for piece-workers, and in cases of breaches of these rules, workmen shall be fined in proportion to their earnings. The deductions from the wage shall be entered in the wage-book of the gatekeeper whose duty they are; they shall be unconditionally accepted as it will not be possible to enter into any discussions about them.

2. When the bell is rung to denote the end of the working day, every workman, both on piece- and on day-wage, shall leave his workshop and the yard, but is not allowed to make preparations for his departure before the bell rings. Every breach of this

rule shall lead to a fine of five silver groschen to the sick fund. Only those who have obtained special permission by the overseer may stay on in the workshop in order to work.—If a workman has worked beyond the closing bell, he must give his name to the gatekeeper on leaving, on pain of losing his payment for the overtime.

3. No workman, whether employed by time or piece, may leave before the end of the working day, without having first received permission from the overseer and having given his name to the gatekeeper. Omission of these two actions shall lead to a fine of ten silver groschen payable to the sick fund.

4. Repeated irregular arrival at work shall lead to dismissal. This shall also apply to those who are found idling by an official or overseer, and refuse to obey their order to resume work.

5. Entry to the firm's property by any but the designated gateway, and exit by any prohibited route, e.g. by climbing fences or walls, or by crossing the Spree, shall be punished by a fine of fifteen silver groschen to the sick fund for the first offences, and dismissal for the second.

6. No worker may leave his place of work otherwise than for reasons connected with his work.

7. All conversation with fellow-workers is prohibited; if any worker requires information about his work, he must turn to the overseer, or to the particular fellow-worker designated for the pupose.

8. Smoking in the workshops or in the yard is prohibited during working hours; anyone caught smoking shall be fined five silver groschen for the sick fund for every such offence.

9. Every worker is responsible for cleaning up his space in the workshop, and if in doubt, he is to turn to his overseer.—All tools must always be kept in good condition, and must be cleaned after use. This applies particularly to the turner, regarding his lathe.

10. Natural functions must be performed at the appropriate places, and whoever is found soiling walls, fences, squares, etc., and similarly, whoever is found washing his face and hands in the workshop and not in the places assigned for the purpose, shall be fined five silver groschen for the sick fund.

11. On completion of his piece of work, every workman must hand it over at once to his foreman or superior, in order to receive a fresh piece of work. Pattern makers must on no account hand over their patterns to the foundry without express order of their supervisors. No workman may take over work from his fellow-workman without instruction to that effect by the foreman.

12. It goes without saying that all overseers and officials of the firm shall be obeyed without question, and shall be treated with due deference. Disobedience will be punished by dismissal.

13. Immediate dismissal shall also be the fate of anyone found drunk in any of the workshops.

14. Untrue allegations against superiors or officials of the concern shall lead to stern reprimand, and may lead to dismissal. The same punishment shall be meted out to those who knowingly allow errors to slip through when supervising or stock-taking.

15. Every workman is obliged to report to his superiors any acts of dishonesty or embezzlement on the part of his fellow workmen. If he omits to do so, and it is shown after subsequent discovery of a misdemeanour that he knew about it at the time, he shall be liable to be taken to court as an accessory after the fact and the wage due to him shall be retained as punishment. Conversely, anyone denouncing a theft in such a way as to allow conviction of the thief shall receive a reward of two Thaler, and, if necessary, his name shall be kept confidential.—Further, the gatekeeper and the watchman, as well as every official, are entitled to search the baskets, parcels, aprons etc. of the women and children who are taking the dinners into the works, on their departure, as well as search any worker suspected of stealing any article whatever. ⋆ ⋆ ⋆

⋆   ⋆   ⋆

18. Advances shall be granted only to the older workers, and even to them only in exceptional circumstances. As long as he is working by the piece, the workman is entitled merely to his fixed weekly wage as subsistence pay; the extra earnings shall be paid out only on completion of the

whole piece contract. If a workman leaves before his piece contract is completed, either of his own free will, or on being dismissed as punishment, or because of illness, the partly completed work shall be valued by the general manager with the help of two overseers, and he will be paid accordingly. There is no appeal against the decision of these experts.

19. A free copy of these rules is handed to every workman, but whoever loses it and requires a new one, or cannot produce it on leaving, shall be fined 21/2 silver groschen, payable to the sick fund.

Moabit, August, 1844.

REVIEW QUESTION

1. What does the specificity of these regulati... suggest about the social realities of early factory work?
2. What areas of factory work are for newcomers the most difficult to learn? Base your answer on the rules' injunctions and monetary fines.
3. What kind of relationship is established between factory hands and their superiors?
4. How do these regulations distinguish the work experience of factories from those of agriculture, domestic service, or the traditional crafts?

THOMAS MALTHUS

FROM *An Essay on the Principle of Population*

In 1798 Thomas Malthus (1766–1834), a minister and an economist, published this essay, which challenged the Enlightenment's indomitable belief in the perfectibility of humankind. The essay raised much controversy in the early nineteenth century. It not only resigned some social groups to the inevitability of poverty but also encouraged them to abandon traditional charity. The custom of indiscriminately aiding all indigent people with satisfactory relief, argued Malthusians, only exacerbated the problem. The following passage on food supply and population increase laid the foundation for his bleak argument.

From *An Essay on the Principle of Population*, by Thomas Malthus (London: Murray, 1826).

In an inquiry concerning the improvement of society, the mode of conducting the subject which naturally presents itself, is,

1. To investigate the causes that have hitherto impeded the progress of mankind towards happiness; and,

2. To examine the probability of the total or partial removal of these causes in future.

To enter fully into this question, and to enumerate all the causes that have hitherto influenced human improvement, would be much beyond the power of an individual. The principal object of the present essay is to examine the effects of one great cause intimately united with the very nature of man; which, though it has been constantly and powerfully operating since the commencement of society, has been little noticed by the writers who have treated this subject. The facts which establish the existence of this cause have, indeed, been repeatedly stated and acknowledged; but its natural and necessary effects have been almost totally overlooked; though probably among these effects may be reckoned a very considerable portion of that vice and misery, and of that unequal distribution

POWER LOOMS IN A BRITISH COTTON FACTORY (1830)

The number of power looms in England rose from 2,400 in 1813 to 224,000 in 1850, bringing about the full mechanization of textile production. The work of spinning and weaving was now concentrated in factories, a shift that had profound consequences for urbanization and the future of industrial labor. While publicists praised the new system with words, artists illustrated the new manufacturing processes. This drawing of a cotton mill, for example, underscores the prominence of unskilled women workers, denoting a signal change in the weaving industry that excluded skilled male weavers. Yet the illustration also conveys work conditions that the viewer should question. What elements of factory life might the artist have chosen not to represent?

of the bounties of nature, which it has been the unceasing object of the enlightened philanthropist in all ages to correct.

The cause to which I allude, is the constant tendency in all animated life to increase beyond the nourishment prepared for it.

It is observed by Dr. Franklin, that there is no bound to the prolific nature of plants or animals, but what is made by their crowding and interfering with each other's means of subsistence. Were the face of the earth, he says, vacant of other plants, it might be gradually sowed and overspread with one kind only, as for instance with fennel: and were it empty of other inhabitants, it might in a few ages be replenished from one nation only, as for instance with Englishmen.

This is incontrovertibly true. Through the animal and vegetable kingdoms Nature has scattered the seeds of life abroad with the most profuse and liberal hand; but has been comparatively sparing in the room and the nourishment necessary to rear them. The germs of existence contained in this earth, if they could freely develop themselves, would fill millions of worlds in the course of a few thousand years. Necessity, that imperious, all-pervading law of nature, restrains them within the prescribed bounds. The race of plants and the race of animals shrink under this great restrictive law; and man cannot by any efforts of reason escape from it.

In plants and irrational animals, the view of the subject is simple. They are all impelled by a powerful instinct to the increase of their species; and this instinct is interrupted by no doubts about providing for their offspring. Wherever therefore there is liberty, the power of increase is exerted; and the superabundant effects are repressed afterwards by want of room and nourishment.

The effects of this check on man are more complicated. Impelled to the increase of his species by an equally powerful instinct, reason interrupts his career, and asks him whether he may not bring beings into the world, for whom he cannot provide the means of support. If he attend to this natural suggestion, the restriction too frequently produces vice. If he hear it not, the human race will be constantly endeavouring to increase beyond the means of subsistence. But as, by that law of our nature which makes food necessary to the life of man, population can never actually increase beyond the lowest nourishment capable of supporting it, a strong check on population, from the difficulty of acquiring food, must be constantly in operation. This difficulty must fall somewhere, and must necessarily be severely felt in some or other of the various forms of misery, or the fear of misery, by a large portion of mankind.

That population has this constant tendency to increase beyond the means of subsistence, and that it is kept to its necessary level by these causes, will sufficiently appear from a review of the different states of society in which man has existed. But, before we proceed to this review, the subject will, perhaps, be seen in a clearer light, if we endeavour to ascertain what would be the natural increase of population, if left to exert itself with perfect freedom; and what might be expected to be the rate of increase in the productions of the earth, under the most favourable circumstances of human industry.

*   *   *

According to a table of Euler, calculated on a mortality of 1 in 36, if the births be to the deaths in the proportion of 3 to 1, the period of doubling will be only 12 years and 4-5ths. And this proportion is not only a possible supposition, but has actually occurred for short periods in more countries than one.

*   *   *

It may safely be pronounced, therefore, that population, when unchecked, goes on doubling itself every twenty-five years, or increases in a geometrical ratio.

The rate according to which the productions of the earth may be supposed to increase, it will not be so easy to determine. Of this, however, we may be perfectly certain, that the ratio of their increase in a limited territory must be of a totally different nature from the ratio of the increase of population. A thousand millions are just as easily doubled every twenty-five years by the power of population as a thousand. But the food to support the increase from the greater number will by no means be obtained with the same facility. Man is necessarily confined in room. When acre has been added to acre till all the fertile land is occupied, the yearly increase of food must depend upon the melioration of the land already in possession. This is a fund, which, from the nature of all soils, instead of increasing, must be gradually diminishing. But population, could it be supplied with food, would go on with unexhausted vigour; and the increase of one period would furnish the power of a greater increase the next, and this without any limit.

*   *   *

It may be fairly pronounced, therefore, that, considering the present average state of the earth, the means of subsistence, under circumstances the most favourable to human industry, could not possibly be made to increase faster than in an arithmetical ratio.

The necessary effects of these two different rates of increase, when brought together, will be very striking. Let us call the population of this island eleven millions; and suppose the present produce equal to the easy support of such a number. In the first twenty-five years the population would be twenty-two millions, and the food being also doubled, the means of subsistence would be equal to this increase. In the next twenty-five years, the population would be forty-four millions, and the means of subsistence only equal to the support of thirty-three millions. In the next period the population would be eighty-eight millions, and the means of subsistence just equal to the support of half that number. And, at the conclusion of the first century, the population would be a hundred and seventy-six millions, and the means of subsistence

only equal to the support of fifty-five millions, leaving a population of a hundred and twenty-one millions totally unprovided for.

Taking the whole earth, instead of this island, emigration would of course be excluded; and, supposing the present population equal to a thousand millions, the human species would increase as the numbers, 1, 2, 4, 8, 16, 32, 64, 128, 256, and subsistence as 1, 2, 3, 4, 5, 6, 7, 8, 9. In two centuries the population would be to the means of subsistence as 256 to 9; in three centuries as 4096 to 13, and in two thousand years the difference would be almost incalculable.

In this supposition no limits whatever are placed to the produce of the earth. It may increase for ever and be greater than any assignable quantity; yet still the power of population being in every period so much superior, the increase of the human species can only be kept down to the level of the means of subsistence by the constant operation of the strong law of necessity, acting as a check upon the greater power.

*   *   *

Review Questions

1. For Malthus, how does nature check the happiness of human society?
2. What are his assumptions regarding food supply and demography? Are they valid?
3. How might this argument affect discussions on public relief of the poor?
4. How did this essay contribute to the emerging laissez-faire philosophy of the early nineteenth century?

DAVID RICARDO

"On Wages"

David Ricardo ranks with Adam Smith and Thomas Malthus as a foundational theorist of nineteenth-century political economy. Building on Malthus's belief regarding the inability of a growing population to nourish itself adequately, Ricardo saw a lawlike corollary with how the market determined wage levels according to the size of the labor force. An increased work pool, he argued, produced a surfeit of labor, which lowered the "natural price of labor" and sank wages to the level of subsistence for a worker's family. Later dubbed the "iron law of wages," this theory suggested for many contemporaries a cheerless future for waged work; for others, it also provided evidence to discredit the aims of parishes and governments to improve the lot of the working poor with welfare relief. Ricardo, however, was less pessimistic and saw benefits in unfettered markets for all social classes. Although scholars dispute whether Ricardo was the first to observe market pressures on wage levels, his Principles of Political Economy *deeply influenced economic theory during the first decades of industrialization.*

From *The Principles of Political Economy and Taxation*, by David Ricardo, edited by E.C.K. Gonner (London : George Bell and Sons, 1891), pp. 70–75.

Labour, like all other things which are purchased and sold, and which may be increased or diminished in quantity, has its natural and its market price. The natural price of labour is that price which is necessary to enable the labourers, one with another, to subsist and to perpetuate their race, without either increase or diminution.[1]

The power of the labourer to support himself, and the family which may be necessary to keep up the number of labourers, does not depend on the quantity of money which he may receive for wages, but on the quantity of food, necessaries, and conveniences become essential to him from habit, which that money will purchase. The natural price of labour, therefore, depends on the price of the food, necessaries, and conveniences required for the support of the labourer and his family. With a rise in the price of food and necessaries, the natural price of labour will rise; with the fall in their price, the natural price of labour will fall.

With the progress of society the natural price of labour, has always a tendency to rise, because one of the principal commodities by which its natural price is regulated, has a tendency to become dearer, from the greater difficulty of producing it. As, however, the improvements in agriculture, the discovery of new markets, whence provisions may be imported, may for a time counteract the tendency to a rise in the price of necessaries, and may even occasion their natural price to fall, so will the same causes produce the correspondent effects on the natural price of labour.

The natural price of all commodities, excepting raw produce and labour, has a tendency to fall,

[1] I.e., in the same position of life or comfort.

in the progress of wealth and population; for though, on one hand, they are enhanced in real value, from the rise in the natural price of the raw material of which they are made, this is more than counterbalanced by the improvements in machinery, by the better division and distribution of labour, and by the increasing skill, both in science and art, of the producers.

§ 36. The market price of labour is the price which is really paid for it, from the natural operation of the proportion of the supply to the demand; labour is dear when it is scarce, and cheap when it is plentiful. However much the market price of labour may deviate from its natural price, it has, like commodities, a tendency to conform to it.

It is when the market price of labour exceeds its natural price, that the condition of the labourer is flourishing and happy, that he has it in his power to command a greater proportion of the necessaries and enjoyments of life, and therefore to rear a healthy and numerous family. When, however, by the encouragement which high wages[2] give to the increase of population, the number of labourers is increased, wages again fall to their natural price, and indeed from a re-action sometimes fall below it.

§ 37. When the market price of labour is below its natural price, the condition of the labourers is most wretched: then poverty deprives them of those comforts which custom renders absolute necessaries. It is only after their privations have reduced their number, or the demand for labour has increased, that the market price of labour will rise to its natural price, and that the labourer will have the moderate comforts which the natural rate of wages will afford.

Notwithstanding the tendency of wages to conform to their natural rate, their market rate may, in an improving society, for an indefinite period, be constantly above it; for no sooner may

the impulse, which an increased capital gives to a new demand for labour, be obeyed, than another increase of capital be gradual and constant, the demand for labour may give a continued stimulus to an increase of people.

Capital is that part of the wealth of a country which is employed in production, and consists of food, clothing, tools, raw materials, machinery, etc., necessary to give effect to labour.

Capital may increase in quantity at the same time that its value rises. An addition may be made to the food and clothing of a country, at the same time that more labour may be required to produce the additional quantity than before; in that case not only the quantity, but the value of capital will rise.

Or capital may increase without its value increasing, and even while its value is actually diminishing; not only may an addition be made to the food and clothing of a country, but the addition may be made by the aid of machinery, without any increase, and even with an absolute diminution in the proportional quantity of labour required to produce them. The quantity of capital may increase, while neither the whole together, nor any part of it singly, will have a greater value than before, but may actually have a less.

In the first case, the natural price of labour, which always depends on the price of food, clothing, and other necessaries, will rise; in the second, it will remain stationary, or fall; but in both cases the market rate of wages will rise, for in proportion to the increase of capital will be the increase in the demand for labour; in proportion to the work to be done will be the demand for those who are to do it.

In both cases too the market price of labour will rise above its natural price; and in both cases it will have a tendency to conform to its natural price, but in the first case this agreement will be most speedily effected. The situation of the labourer will be improved, but not much improved; for the increased price of food and necessaries will absorb a large portion of his increased wages; consequently a small supply of labour, or a trifling increase in the

---

[2] In this place Ricardo uses the words "high wages," not as indicating, as in most other instance, a high proportion of the total produce, but a large quantity of necessaries, luxuries, etc.

population, will soon reduce the market price to the then increased natural price of labour.

In the second case, the condition of the labourer will be very greatly improved; he will receive increased money wages, without having to pay any increased price, and perhaps even a diminished price for the commodities which he and his family consume; and it will not be till after a great addition has been made to the population, that the market price of labour will again sink to its then low and reduced natural price.

Thus, then, with every improvement of society, with every increase in its capital, the market wages of labour will rise; but the permanence of their rise will depend on the question, whether the natural price of labour has also risen; and this again will depend on the rise in the natural price of those necessaries on which the wages of labour are expended.

It is not to be understood that the natural price of labour, estimated even in food and necessaries, is absolutely fixed and constant. It varies at different times in the same country, and very materially differs in different countries. It essentially depends on the habits and customs of the people. An English labourer would consider his wages under their natural rate, and too scanty to support a family, if they enabled him to purchase no other food than potatoes, and to live in no better habitation than a mud cabin; yet these moderate demands of nature are often deemed sufficient in countries where "man's life is cheap," and his wants easily satisfied. Many of the conveniences now enjoyed in an English cottage, would have been thought luxuries at an earlier period of our history.

From manufactured commodities always falling, and raw produce always rising, with the progress of society, such a disproportion in their relative value is at length created, that in rich countries a labourer, by the sacrifice of a very small quantity only of his food, is able to provide liberally for all his other wants.

Independently of the variations in the value of money, which necessarily affect money wages, but which we have here supposed to have no operation, as we have considered money to be uniformly of the same value, it appears then that wages are subject to a rise or fall from two causes:

1st. The supply and demand of labourers.

2ndly. The price of the commodities on which the wages of labour are expended.

Review Questions

1. How do the views of Malthus and Ricardo work together?
2. How do the views of Robert Owen (see document in this chapter) correspond to Ricardo's observations?
3. When does the price of labor flourish and when does it fall?
4. How can one interpret Ricardo's interpretation positively? When does a laborer prosper in the marketplace? How would a manufacturing economy help the living standard of laborers?

FRIEDRICH ENGELS

FROM *The Condition of the Working-Class in England in 1844*

Friedrich Engels (1820–1895), the son of a pietistic textile manufacturer from the Ruhr Valley town of Barmen, completed his apprenticeship as a textile entrepreneur in Manchester in 1842–44. Prior to this apprenticeship, Engels read critical philosophy as a student in Berlin and published articles in the opposition Cologne paper Rheinische Zeitung. *In 1842 in Cologne, Engels met Karl Marx for the first time. Manchester nurtured Engel's radical political spirit: he joined the Chartists, the movement agitating for universal suffrage and workingmen's rights; published articles in the Owenite newspaper* The New Moral World; *and wrote "Outlines of a Critique of Political Economy," which Marx published in his new Paris-based journal,* Deutsch-Französische Jahrbücher. *In 1844 Engels gathered material for a social history of England's working class, which became* The Condition of the Working-Class in England *(first published in German in 1845), a descriptive work of English industrial life that amounted to an empirical indictment of capitalism's immorality. The following passage examines Manchester, a city whose population increase of seventy thousand between 1831 and 1841 produced deplorable living conditions for the city's poor.*

From *The Condition of the Working-Class in England in 1844,* by Friedrich Engels, translated by Florence Kelley Wischnewetzky (London: George Allen and Unwin, 1892).

*   *   *

The south bank of the Irk is here very steep and between fifteen and thirty feet high. On this declivitous hillside there are planted three rows of houses, of which the lowest rise directly out of the river, while the front walls of the highest stand on the crest of the hill in Long Millgate. Among them are mills on the river, in short, the method of construction is as crowded and disorderly here as in the lower part of Long Millgate. Right and left a multitude of covered passages lead from the main street into numerous courts, and he who turns in thither gets into a filth and disgusting grime, the equal of which is not to be found—especially in the courts which lead down to the Irk, and which contain unqualifiedly the most horrible dwellings which I have yet beheld. In one of these courts there stands directly at the entrance, at the end of the covered passage, a privy without a door, so dirty that the inhabitants can pass into and out of the court only by passing through foul pools of stagnant urine and excrement. This is the first court on the Irk above Ducie Bridge—in case any one should care to look into it. Below it on the river there are several tanneries which fill the whole neighbourhood with the stench of animal putrefaction. Below Ducie Bridge the only entrance to most of the houses is by means of narrow, dirty stairs and over heaps of refuse and filth. The first court below Ducie Bridge, known as Allen's Court, was in such a state at the time of the cholera that the sanitary police ordered it evacuated, swept, and disinfected with chloride of lime. Dr. Kay gives a terrible description of the state of this court at that time. Since then, it seems to have been partially torn away and rebuilt; at least looking down from Ducie Bridge, the passer-by sees several ruined walls and heaps of débris with some newer houses. The view from this bridge, mercifully concealed from mortals of small stature by a parapet as high as a man, is characteristic for the whole district. At the bottom flows, or rather stagnates, the Irk, a narrow, coal-black, foul-smelling stream, full of débris and refuse, which it deposits on the shallower right bank. In dry weather, a long string of the most disgusting, blackish-green, slime pools are left standing on this bank, from the depths of which bubbles of miasmatic gas constantly arise and give forth a stench unendurable even on the bridge forty or fifty feet above the surface of the stream. But besides this, the stream itself is checked every few paces by high weirs, behind which slime and refuse accumulate and rot in thick masses. Above the bridge are tanneries, bonemills, and gasworks, from which all drains and refuse find their way into the Irk, which receives further the contents of all the neighbouring sewers and privies. It may be easily imagined, therefore, what sort of residue the stream deposits. Below the bridge you look upon the piles of débris, the refuse, filth, and offal from the courts on the steep left bank; here each house is packed close behind its neighbour and a piece of each is visible, all black, smoky, crumbling, ancient, with broken panes and window frames. The background is furnished by old barrack-like factory buildings. On the lower right bank stands a long row of houses and mills; the second house being a ruin without a roof, piled with débris; the third stands so low that the lowest floor is uninhabitable, and therefore without windows or doors. Here the background embraces the pauper burial-ground, the station of the Liverpool and Leeds railway, and, in the rear of this, the Workhouse, the "Poor-Law Bastille" of Manchester, which, like a citadel, looks threateningly down from behind its high walls and parapets on the hilltop, upon the working-people's quarter below.

Above Ducie Bridge, the left bank grows more flat and the right bank steeper, but the condition of the dwellings on both banks grows worse rather than better. He who turns to the left here from the main street, Long Millgate, is lost; he wanders from one court to another, turns countless corners, passes nothing but narrow, filthy nooks and alleys, until after a few minutes he has lost all clue, and knows not whither to turn. Everywhere half or wholly ruined buildings, some of them actually uninhabited, which means a great deal here; rarely a wooden or stone floor to be seen in the houses, almost uniformly broken, ill-fitting windows and doors, and a state of filth! Everywhere heaps of débris, refuse, and offal; standing pools for gutters, and a stench which alone would make it impossible for a human being in any degree civilised to live in such a district. The newly-built extension of the Leeds railway, which crosses the Irk here, has swept away some of these courts and lanes, laying others completely open to view. Immediately under the railway bridge there stands a court, the filth and horrors of which surpass all the others by far, just because it was hitherto so shut off, so secluded that the way to it could not be found without a good deal of trouble. I should never have discovered it myself, without the breaks made by the railway, though I thought I knew this whole region thoroughly. Passing along a rough bank, among stakes and washing-lines, one penetrates into this chaos of small one-storied, one-roomed huts, in most of which there is no artificial floor; kitchen, living and sleeping-room all in one. In such a hole, scarcely five feet long by six broad, I found two beds—and such bedsteads and beds!—which, with a staircase and chimney-place, exactly filled the room. In several others I found absolutely nothing, while the door stood open, and the inhabitants leaned against it. Everywhere before the doors refuse and offal; that any sort of pavement lay underneath could not be seen but only felt, here and there, with the feet. This whole collection of cattle-sheds for human beings was surrounded on two sides by houses and a factory, and on the third by the river, and besides the narrow stair up the bank, a narrow doorway alone led out into another almost equally ill-built, ill-kept labyrinth of dwellings.

A VIEW OF MANCHESTER FROM KERSAL MOOR (1852)   WILLIAM WYLD

Among the most prominent social consequences of industrialization were urbanization and mechanization. Between 1750 and 1850, the English city of Manchester swelled from twenty thousand to four hundred thousand, becoming a notorious example of overcrowding and squalor. What two ways of life are contrasted in this painting?

Enough! The whole side of the Irk is built in this way, a planless, knotted chaos of houses, more or less on the verge of uninhabitableness, whose unclean interiors fully correspond with their filthy external surroundings. And how could the people be clean with no proper opportunity for satisfying the most natural and ordinary wants? Privies are so rare here that they are either filled up every day, or are too remote for most of the inhabitants to use. How can people wash when they have only the dirty Irk water at hand, while pumps and water pipes can be found in decent parts of the city alone? In truth, it cannot be charged to the account of these helots of modern society if their dwellings are not more cleanly than the pigsties which are here and there to be seen among them. The land lords are not ashamed to let dwellings like the six or seven cellars on the quay directly below Scotland Bridge, the floors of which stand at least two feet below the low-water level of the Irk that flows not six feet away from them; or like the upper floor of the corner-house on the opposite shore directly above the bridge, where the ground floor, utterly uninhabitable, stands deprived of all fittings for doors and windows, a case by no means rare in this region, when this open ground floor is used as a privy by the whole neighbourhood for want of other facilities!

If we leave the Irk and penetrate once more on the opposite side from Long Millgate into the midst of the working-men's dwellings, we shall come into a somewhat newer quarter, which stretches from St. Michael's Church to Withy Grove and Shude Hill. Here there is somewhat better order. In place of the chaos of buildings, we find at least long straight lanes and alleys or courts, built according to a plan and usually square. But if, in the former case, every house was built according to caprice, here each lane and court is so built, without reference to the situation of the adjoining ones. The lanes run now in this direction, now in that, while every two minutes the wanderer gets into a blind alley, or, on turning a corner, finds himself back where he started from; certainly no one who has not lived a considerable time in this labyrinth can find his way through it.

If I may use the word at all in speaking of this district, the ventilation of these streets and courts is, in consequence of this confusion, quite as imperfect as in the Irk region; and if this quarter may, nevertheless, be said to have some advantage over that of the Irk, the houses being newer and the streets occasionally having gutters, nearly every house has, on the other hand, a cellar dwelling, which is rarely found in the Irk district, by reason of the greater age and more careless construction of the houses. As for the rest, the filth, débris, and offal heaps, and the pools in the streets are common to both quarters, and in the district now under discussion, another feature most injurious to the cleanliness of the inhabitants, is the multitude of pigs walking about in all the alleys, rooting into the offal heaps, or kept imprisoned in small pens. Here, as in most of the working-men's quarters of Manchester, the pork-raisers rent the courts and build pig-pens in them. In almost every court one or even several such pens may be found, into which the inhabitants of the court throw all refuse and offal, whence the swine grow fat; and the atmosphere, confined on all four sides, is utterly corrupted by putrefying animal and vegetable substances. Through this quarter, a broad and measurably decent street has been cut, Millers Street, and the background has been pretty successfully concealed. But if any one should be led by curiosity to pass through one of the numerous passages which lead into the courts, he will find this piggery repeated at every twenty paces.

Such is the Old Town of Manchester, and on re-reading my description, I am forced to admit that instead of being exaggerated, it is far from black enough to convey a true impression of the filth, ruin, and uninhabitableness, the defiance of all considerations of cleanliness, ventilation, and health which characterise the construction of this single district, containing at least twenty to thirty thousand inhabitants. And such a district exists in the heart of the second city of England, the first manufacturing city of the world. If any one wishes to see in how little space a human being can move, how little air—and *such* air!—he can breathe, how little of civilisation he may share and yet live, it is only necessary to travel hither.

*   *   *

REVIEW QUESTIONS

1. What does Engels's account of slum life tell us about the material conditions of Manchester's working class?

2. What factors contribute to the overall hazardous conditions of living in England?

3. What was Engels's purpose of writing this book for a German audience?

Evidence from the Sadler Report

The mechanized factory work of early industrialization reduced the artisanal craft of spinning and weaving to unskilled labor, which in turn ushered in a new era of exploitation. Children and women, for example, were made to work exceptionally long hours in unsafe conditions. In 1832, Michael Sadler, a Member of Parliament, chaired a committee that took testimony from a range of witnesses, young and old, to write a bill to limit children's work in textile mills. The committee amassed prodigious evidence to illuminate the cruelty of factory work, which generated public outcry. (In the same year, two other commissions investigated coal mining and urban sanitary conditions.) But the Sadler Report was criticized for its uneven selection of witnesses, its unorthodox manner of taking testimony, and its bias toward the victims. Parliament declined to consider a law on the basis of the report, yet it immediately formed a new commission whose inquiry led to the Factory Act of 1833. This landmark law forbade children under nine years to work while restricting those between the ages of nine and thirteen to nine hours and those between thirteen and eighteen to twelve hours. It furthermore banned night work for laboring children and stipulated two hours of schooling each day for them. Finally, by appointing factory inspectors to uphold these provisions, this law introduced the modern governmental supervision of factory work.

From *Parliamentary Papers,* 1831–1832, vol. XV, pp. 44, 95–97, 115, 195, 197, 339, 341–42.

JOSHUA DRAKE, CALLED IN;
AND EXAMINED.

You say you would prefer moderate labour and lower wages; are you pretty comfortable upon your present wages?—I have no wages, but two days a week at present; but when I am working at some jobs we can make a little, and at others we do very poorly.

When a child gets 3s. a week, does that go much towards its subsistence?—No, it will not keep it as it should do.

When they got 6s. or 7s. when they were pieceners, if they reduced the hours of labour, would they not get less?—They would get a halfpenny a day less, but I would rather have less wages and less work.

Do you receive any parish assistance?—No.

Why do you allow your children to go to work at those places where they are ill-treated or overworked?—Necessity compels a man that has children to let them work.

Then you would not allow your children to go to those factories under the present system, if it was not from necessity?—No.

Supposing there was a law passed to limit the hours of labour to eight hours a day, or something of that sort, of course you are aware that a manufacturer could not afford to pay them the same wager?—No, I do not suppose that they would, but at the same time I would rather have it, and I believe that it would bring me into employ: and if I lost 5d. a day from my children's work, and I got half-a-crown myself, it would be better.

How would it get you into employ?—By finding more employment at the machines, and work being more regularly spread abroad, and divided amongst the people at large. One man is now regularly turned off into the street, whilst another man is running day and night.

You mean to say, that if the manufacturers were to limit the hours of labour, they would employ more people?—Yes.

MR. MATTHEW CRABTREE, CALLED IN;
AND EXAMINED.

What age are you?—Twenty-two.

What is your occupation?—A blanket manufacturer.

Have you ever been employed in a factory?—Yes.

At what age did you first go to work in one?—Eight.

How long did you continue in that occupation?—Four years.

Will you state the hours of labour at the period when you first went to the factory, in ordinary times?—From 6 in the morning to 8 at night.

Fourteen hours?—Yes.

With what intervals for refreshment and rest?—An hour at noon.

When trade was brisk what were your hours?—From 5 in the morning to 9 in the evening.

Sixteen hours?—Yes.

With what intervals at dinner?—An hour.

How far did you live from the mill?—About two miles.

Was there any time allowed for you to get your breakfast in the mill?—No.

Did you take it before you left your home?—Generally.

During those long hours of labour could you be punctual; how did you awake?—I seldom did awake spontaneously; I was most generally awoke or lifted out of bed, sometimes asleep, by my parents.

Were you always in time?—No.

What was the consequence if you had been too late?—I was most commonly beaten.

Severely?—Very severely, I thought.

In those mills is chastisement towards the latter part of the day going on perpetually?—Perpetually.

So that you can hardly be in a mill without hearing constant crying?—Never an hour, I believe.

Do you think that if the overlooker were naturally a humane person it would be still found necessary for him to beat the children, in order to keep up their attention and vigilance at the termination of those extraordinary days of labour?—Yes; the machine turns off a regular quantity of cardings, and of course they must keep as regularly to their work the whole of the day; they must keep with the machine, and therefore however humane the slubber may be, as he must keep up with the machine or be found fault with, he spurs the children to keep up also by various means but that which he commonly resorts to is to strap them when they become drowsy.

At the time when you were beaten for not keeping up with your work, were you anxious to have done it if you possibly could?—Yes; the dread of being beaten if we could not keep up with our work was a sufficient impulse to keep us to it if we could.

When you got home at night after this labour, did you feel much fatigued?—Very much so.

Had you any time to be with your parents, and to receive instruction from them?—No.

What did you do?—All that we did when we got home was to get the little bit of supper that was provided for us and go to bed immediately. If the supper had not been ready directly, we should have gone to sleep while it was preparing.

Did you not, as a child, feel it a very grievous hardship to be roused so soon in the morning?—I did.

Were the rest of the children similarly circumstanced?—Yes, all of them; but they were not all of them so far from their work as I was.

And if you had been too late you were under the apprehension of being cruelly beaten?—I generally was beaten when I happened to be too late; and when I got up in the morning the apprehension of that was so great, that I used to run, and cry all the way as I went to the mill.

MR. JOHN HALL, CALLED IN;
AND EXAMINED.

Will you describe to the Committee the position in which the children stand to piece in a worsted mill, as it may serve to explain the number and severity of those cases of distortion which occur?—At the top of the spindle there is a fly goes across, and the child takes hold of the fly by the ball of his left hand, and he throws the left shoulder up and the right knee inward; he has the thread to get with the right hand, and he has to stoop his head down to see what he is doing; they throw the right knee inward in that way, and all the children I have seen, that bend in the right knee. I knew a family, the whole of whom were bent outwards as a family complaint, and one of those boys was sent to a worsted-mill, and first he became straight in his right knee, and then he became crooked in it the other way.

ELIZABETH BENTLEY, CALLED IN;
AND EXAMINED.

What age are you?—Twenty-three.

Where do you live?—At Leeds.

What time did you begin to work at a factory?—When I was six years old.

At whose factory did you work?—Mr. Busk's.

What kind of mill is it?—Flax-mill.

What was your business in that mill?—I was a little doffer.

What were your hours of labour in that mill?—From 5 in the morning till 9 at night, when they were thronged.

For how long a time together have you worked that excessive length of time?—For about half a year.

What were your usual hours of labour when you were not so thronged?—From 6 in the morning till 7 at night.

What time was allowed for your meals?—Forty minutes at noon.

Had you any time to get your breakfast or drinking?—No, we got it as we could.

And when your work was bad, you had hardly any time to eat it at all?—No; we were obliged to leave it or take it home, and when we did not take it, the overlooker took it, and gave it to his pigs.

Do you consider doffing a laborious employment?—Yes.

Explain what it is you had to do?—When the frames are full, they have to stop the frames, and take the flyers off, and take the full bobbins off, and carry them to the roller; and then put empty ones on, and set the frame going again.

Does that keep you constantly on your feet?—Yes, there are so many frames, and they run so quick.

Your labour is very excessive?—Yes; you have not time for any thing.

Suppose you flagged a little, or were too late, what would they do?—Strap us.

Are they in the habit of strapping those who are last in doffing?—Yes.

Constantly?—Yes.

Girls as well as boys?—Yes.

Have you ever been strapped?—Yes.

Severely?—Yes.

Could you eat your food well in that factory?—No, indeed I had not much to eat, and the little I had I could not eat it, my appetite was so poor, and being covered with dust; and it was no use to take it home, I could not eat it, and the overlooker took it, and gave it to the pigs.

You are speaking of the breakfast?—Yes.

How far had you to go for dinner?—We could not go home to dinner.

Where did you dine?—In the mill.

Did you live far from the mill?—Yes, two miles.

Had you a clock?—No, we had not.

Supposing you had not been in time enough in the morning at these mills, what would have been the consequence?—We should have been quartered.

What do you mean by that?—If we were a quarter of an hour too late, they would take off half an hour; we only got a penny an hour, and they would take a halfpenny more.

The fine was much more considerable than the loss of time?—Yes.

Were you also beaten for being too late?—No, I was never beaten myself, I have seen the boys beaten for being too late.

Were you generally there in time?—Yes; my mother has been up at 4 o'clock in the morning, and at 2 o'clock in the morning; the colliers used to go to their work about 3 or 4 o'clock, and when she heard them stirring she has got up out of her warm bed, and gone out and asked them the time; and I have sometimes been at Hunslet Car at 2 o'clock in the morning, when it was streaming down with rain, and we have had to stay till the mill was opened.

PETER SMART, CALLED IN;
AND EXAMINED.

You say you were locked up night and day?—Yes.

Do the children ever attempt to run away?—Very often.

Were they pursued and brought back again?—Yes, the overseer pursued them, and brought them back.

Did you ever attempt to run away?—Yes, I ran away twice.

And you were brought back?—Yes; and I was sent up to the master's loft, and thrashed with a whip for running away.

Were you bound to this man?—Yes, for six years.

By whom were you bound?—My mother got 15s. for the six years.

Do you know whether the children were, in point of fact, compelled to stop during the whole time for which they were engaged?—Yes, they were.

By law?—I cannot say by law; but they were compelled by the master; I never saw any law used there but the law of their own hands.

To what mill did you next go?—To Mr. Webster's, at Battus Den, within eleven miles of Dundee.

In what situation did you act there?—I acted as an overseer.

At 17 years of age?—Yes.

Did you inflict the same punishment that you yourself had experienced?—I went as an overseer; not as a slave, but as a slave-driver.

What were the hours of labour in that mill?—My master told me that I had to produce a certain quantity of yarn; the hours were at that time fourteen; I said that I was not able to produce the quantity of yarn that was required; I told him if he took the timepiece out of the mill I would produce that quantity, and after that time I found no difficulty in producing the quantity.

How long have you worked per day in order to produce the quantity your master required?—I have wrought nineteen hours.

Was this a water-mill?—Yes, water and steam both.

To what time have you worked?—I have seen the mill going till it was past 12 o'clock on the Saturday night.

So that the mill was still working on the Sabbath morning?—Yes.

Were the workmen paid by the piece, or by the day?—No, all had stated wages.

Did not that almost compel you to use great severity to the hands then under you?—Yes; I was compelled often to beat them, in order to get them to attend to their work, from their being over-wrought.

Were not the children exceedingly fatigued at that time?—Yes, exceedingly fatigued.

Were the children bound in the same way in that mill?—No; they were bound from one year's end to another, for twelve months.

Did you keep the hands locked up in the same way in that mill?—Yes, we locked up the mill; but we did not lock the bothy.

Did you find that the children were unable to pursue their labour properly to that extent?—Yes;

they have been brought to that condition, that I have gone and fetched up the doctor to them, to see what was the matter with them, and to know whether they were able to rise or not able to rise; they were not at all able to rise; we have had great difficulty in getting them up.

When that was the case, how long have they been in bed, generally speaking?—Perhaps not above four or five hours in their beds.

*   *   *

REVIEW QUESTIONS

1. What social-historical evidence can you elicit from these testimonies? How long are breaks? How long are work shifts?

2. What does the evidence suggest about the overall quality of children's lives? What is missing from their daily activities?

3. How does Peter Smart, the overseer, characterize his work and his workers?

4. What kind of punishments are inflicted?

5. What do the reforms of the Factory Act furthermore tell us about the attitudes and practices of early industrialization?

6. Can one compare the exploitation of underage workers in 1832 to contemporary labor abuses in both developed and developing countries?

ROBERT OWEN

FROM *A New View of Society*

Robert Owen (1771–1858), a highly successful manager and partner of a cotton mill in Manchester, grew disenchanted early in his life with the deplorable material and moral standards of factory workers. Resolved to direct a capitalist enterprise that could ameliorate the lives of factory workers, Owen convinced his partners to buy cotton mills in Lanarkshire, Scotland, and set up a model community, New Lanark. Workers received salubrious housing, quality goods from low-cost cooperative stores, and education for their children; in turn, Owen inculcated the moral virtues of cleanliness, order, thrift, and sobriety. Because New Lanark combined moral improvement with commercial success, Owen's communitarian project achieved international fame, and it still ranks among the most important examples of utopian socialism. In 1813, Owen delineated his views on the importance of human capital in his A New View of Society. *The following speech is included in this work.*

From *A New View of Society,* by Robert Owen (Friends of the New System, 1826).

An Address
To the Superintendants of Manufactories, and to Those Individuals Generally, Who, by Giving Employment to an Aggregated Population, May Easily Adopt the Means to Form the Sentiments and Manners of Such a Population

Like you, I am a manufacturer for pecuniary profit. But having for many years acted on principles the reverse in many respects of those in which you have been instructed, and having found my procedure beneficial to others and to myself, even in a pecuniary point of view, I am anxious to explain such valuable principles, that you and those under your influence may equally partake of their advantages.

In two Essays, already published, I have developed some of these principles, and in the following pages you will find still more of them explained, with some detail of their application to practice, under the particular local circumstances in which I undertook the direction of the New Lanark Mills and Establishment.

By those details you will find that from the commencement of my management I viewed the population, with the mechanism and every other part of the establishment, as a system composed of many parts, and which it was my duty and interest so to combine, as that every hand, as well as every spring, lever, and wheel, should effectually co-operate to produce the greatest pecuniary gain to the proprietors.

Many of you have long experienced in your manufacturing operations the advantages of substantial, well-contrived, and well-executed machinery.

Experience has also shewn you the difference of the results between mechanism which is neat, clean, well arranged, and always in a high state of repair; and that which is allowed to be dirty, in disorder, without the means of preventing unnecessary friction, and which therefore becomes, and works, much out of repair.

In the first case, the whole economy and management are good; every operation proceeds with ease, order, and success. In the last, the reverse must follow, and a scene be presented of counteraction, confusion, and dissatisfaction among all the agents and instruments interested or occupied in the general process, which cannot fail to create great loss.

If then due care as to the state of your inanimate machines can produce such beneficial results, what may not be expected if you devote equal attention to your vital machines, which are far more wonderfully constructed?

When you shall acquire a right knowledge of these, of their curious mechanism, of their self-adjusting powers; when the proper main spring shall be applied to their varied movements, you will become conscious of their real value, and you will be readily induced to turn your thoughts more frequently from your inanimate to your living machines; you will discover that the latter may be easily trained and directed to procure a large increase of pecuniary gain, while you may also derive from them high and substantial gratification.

Will you then continue to expend large sums of money to procure the best devised mechanism of wood, brass, or iron; to retain it in perfect repair; to provide the best substance for the prevention of unnecessary friction, and to save it from falling into premature decay? Will you also devote years of intense application to understand the connection of the various parts of these lifeless machines, to improve their effective powers, and to calculate with mathematical precision all their minute and combined movements? And when in these transactions you estimate time by minutes, and the money expended for the chance of increased gain by fractions, will you not afford some of your attention to consider whether a portion of your time and capital would not be more advantageously applied to improve your living machines?

From experience which cannot deceive me, I venture to assure you that your time and money, so applied, if directed by a true knowledge of the subject, would return you, not five, ten, or fifteen per cent. for your capital so expended, but often fifty, and in many cases a hundred per cent.

I have expended much time and capital upon improvements of the living machinery; and it will soon appear that the time and money so expended in the manufactory at New Lanark, even while such improvements are in progress only, and but half their beneficial effects attained, are now producing a return exceeding fifty per cent., and will shortly create profits equal to cent. per cent. on the original capital expended in them.

Indeed, after experience of the beneficial effects, from due care and attention to the mechanical implements, it became easy to a reflecting mind to conclude at once, that at least equal advantages would arise from the application of similar care and attention to the living instruments. And when it was perceived that inanimate mechanism was greatly improved by being made firm and substantial; that it was the essence of economy to keep it neat, clean, regularly supplied with the best substance to prevent unnecessary friction, and, by proper provision for the purpose, to preserve it in good repair; it was natural to conclude that the more delicate, complex, living mechanism, would be equally improved by being trained to strength and activity; and that it would also prove true economy to keep it neat and clean; to treat it with kindness, that its mental movements might not experience too much irritating friction; to endeavour by every means to make it more perfect; to supply it regularly with a sufficient quantity of wholesome food and other necessaries of life, that the body might be preserved in good working condition, and prevented from being out of repair, or falling prematurely to decay.

These anticipations are proved by experience to be just.

Since the general introduction of inanimate mechanism into British manufactories, man, with few exceptions, has been treated as a secondary and inferior machine; and far more attention has been given to perfect the raw materials of wood and metals than those of body and mind. Give but due reflection to the subject, and you will find that man, even as an instrument for the creation of wealth, may be still greatly improved.

But, my friends, a far more interesting and gratifying consideration remains. Adopt the means which ere long shall be rendered obvious to every understanding, and you may not only partially improve those living instruments, but learn how to impart to them such excellence as shall make them infinitely surpass those of the present and all former times.

Here then is an object which truly deserves your attention; and instead of devoting all your faculties to invent improved inanimate mechanism, let your thoughts be, at least in part, directed to discover how to combine the more excellent materials of body and mind, which, by a well devised experiment, will be found capable of progressive improvement.

Thus seeing with the clearness of noon-day light, thus convinced with the certainty of conviction itself, let us not perpetuate the really unnecessary evils which our present practices inflict on this large proportion of our fellow subjects. ⋆ ⋆ ⋆ But when you may have ocular demonstration, that, instead of any pecuniary loss, a well-directed attention to form the character and increase the comforts of those who are so entirely at your mercy, will essentially add to your gains, prosperity, and happiness, no reasons, except those founded on ignorance of your self-interest, can in future prevent you from bestowing your chief care on the living machines which you employ; and by so doing you will prevent an accumulation of human misery, of which it is now difficult to form an adequate conception.

That you may be convinced of this most valuable truth, which due reflection will shew you is founded on the evidence of unerring facts, is the sincere wish of

The Author.

REVIEW QUESTIONS

1. Who is Owen's intended audience? Why is Owen's analogy of workers as machines especially effective for this social group?
2. How does Owen reconcile social improvement with capitalist principles?
3. Why was Owen's argument largely dismissed by his peers as radical and unacceptable?

THE CRYSTAL PALACE (1851)

England's Great Exhibition of 1851, the first world fair, displayed over 100,000 objects from all over the world. For Prince Albert, the royal sponsor, the fair stood for the hope and welfare that industrial power would bring to the world. The prominent display of British locomotives, steam engines, luxury manufactures, and imperial splendor further called attention to England's preeminence as the "workshop of the world" and its arrival as an urbanized, industrial power. Joseph Paxton's vast exhibition hall of steel and glass, which occupied a total floor area of 990,000 square feet, was hailed as a symbol of the new era. Dubbed the Crystal Palace, the building became a prototype for industrial design in the second half of the nineteenth century. What kind of economic and political ideals might Paxton have hoped to endorse with his Crystal Palace?

ANONYMOUS

FROM *The Life & History of Captain Swing, the Kent Rick Burner, Written by Himself*

The mechanization of spinning and weaving and the introduction of threshing machines in the English countryside brought waves of machine breakings and barn burnings in the 1820s and 1830s. Although this violence is often characterized as the futile resistance to inevitable change, these uprisings are more accurately seen as highly organized, disciplined political events. Under such fictional leaders as Ned Ludd or Captain Swing, weavers, artisans, and sharecroppers organized them- selves into bands and destroyed private property that they believed had stripped them of their livelihoods and dignity. The following story, which circulated as a popular political tract in the early 1830s, compresses the major political grievances of England's agricultural workers into the life of Swing, a fictional hard-working tenant farmer driven to destitution and despair by social and political change in the early nineteenth century.

From *The Life & History of Captain Swing, the Kent Rick Burner, Written by Himself,* by Anonymous (Chubb, 1830).

I was born on the day William Pitt became Prime Minister of England. My father was one of the class of small farmers, then so numerous in England, but whom the system of large farms has now altogether extinguished in the country. My father had two sons, of whom I was the younger; and as the savings of his predecessors had rendered him wealthy in his way, he determined educating me for a profession, and sent me to a grammar school in the neighbourhood; from whence I was removed in due time to a public school, prepara- tory to my entering college. When I was about to enter college, my elder brother died,—in conse- quence of which my father changed his intention of bringing me up to a profession, and took me home to attend to the farm. As I considered my future path in life was now definitively marked out for me, I gave up my entire time and attention to acquire a thorough knowledge of agriculture, and soon became one of the best farmers in that part of the kingdom. Soon after my father died, and bequeathed to me the farm and greater part of his effects. Some time after this I became acquainted with the daughter of a neighbouring curate, * * * and after a short period I proposed marriage to her, and she became my wife. I, of course, got no fortune with her, but she had that which surpass- eth riches,—a most kind and amiable disposition; and if industry and integrity on the one side, and virtue and humility on the other, were sufficient to render our union a happy one, never was there a couple bid fairer for it than we did.

A few years passed as happily as I could wish, and three little ones added to my felicity. Although working hard all day, I at night forgot my toil and trouble when I returned to my fireside and family; and as soon as my children began to lisp, the first words I taught them to utter were the same I had myself learned when I was their age, namely, "To fear God and honour the King—to give every man his due, and behave uprightly to all." A short time after the birth of my fourth child, our old landlord died, and was succeeded by his son.

About two years after our young landlord returned home, (he had been on the Continent since the death of his father) I received a notice to quit,— the receipt of which astonished me beyond measure, as I owed no rent, and had always supported the character of being the best and most improving tenant on the estate. * * * As I found it impossible to see the lord, I called on the steward, and asked him what fault I had committed, or what crime I had been guilty of, that I should be turned out of the farm where my forefathers had lived for centuries, and which they and I had done so much to improve? "There is no fault to be found with you," replied the steward, "you have always paid your rent regularly, and conducted yourself correctly; but my lord wants your farm to make a fox-cover, and you must leave it next settling day."

"Good God!" exclaimed I, "are my wife and children to be turned out to make room for wild beasts?"—"There is no use in talking," said the steward, "your land is the best site on the estate for a fox-cover, and you must give it up."

The lord himself happened to pass by, and with tears in my eyes, I beseeched him not to turn out my family, in order to replace them with foxes. "Every man," said the lord, "*can do what he pleases with his own,*" and he walked away and left me.

*   *   *

Time, which flies equally fast whether we are miserable or happy, soon brought about the settling day, and as I found all appeals to the landlord utterly useless, I was prepared to give him possession, I had not sufficient capital to take a large farm, and small ones were not to be had, so I was obliged to dispose of my horses, black cattle, and farming machinery; and as the period I sold them was one of unusual depression, I did not receive one half their value.

As soon as my first burst of grief for the loss of my farm was over, I again applied myself to labour in my garden, (which I had taken with a cottage in the neighbourhood) and by dint of industry

and exertion supported my family, by supplying a neighbouring village with vegetables. Up to this period I had never attended a political meeting in my life, nor took any part whatever in politics; I thought our laws and legislators too good to require alteration or change; and if I hated one thing more than another, it was Radicalism, the abettors of which I considered no better than rebels and revolutionists, who wanted to destroy our glorious constitution, and cause anarchy in the country. I begun, however, now to think otherwise. I had seen all around me, my neighbours reduced from comfort to poverty, and from poverty to the poor-rates; and as, in the greater number of cases, it had arisen from no fault of their own, it occurred to me that some change was necessary; as had England been governed as it ought, those things could never have taken place. Reflections of this sort determined me to attend the great meeting at Manchester, then about to be held, and I accordingly went there. Every thing passed quietly off until noon, when, to my horror and surprise, a charge was made by the military and yeomanry on the peaceable and unarmed multitude that were assembled, and I, amongst others, was wounded by a sabre-cut in the arm. Bleeding profusely, and with my arm hanging uselessly by my side, I went into Manchester and got it dressed; I was kept awake the entire night by the pain of my wound, but consoled myself with the reflection that immediate and condign punishment would be inflicted on the lawless soldiery who had dared to massacre a peaceable multitude assembled to petition Parliament. "The King," said I, "will certainly send down a commission to have the monsters tried for their blood-thirsty outrage." What was my astonishment and indignation, in ten days after, when I saw a letter from the Secretary of State, thanking in the King's name, the military and magistrates, for massacring the people at Manchester.

I no longer wanted a proof that our country was sadly misgoverned—that a great change was necessary—and that the Reformers were the only real friends of the people.

*   *   *

[Swing is wrongfully accused of poaching and serves eighteen months in prison] When I was permitted to leave prison, I again commenced working in my garden, hoping my troubles were now over, and that, for the rest of my life, though poor, I should be allowed to rear my children peaceably and without persecution. A new and unexpected misfortune, however, arose; the parson of the parish considered his tithes not sufficiently productive, and made a claim for small tithes, which none of his predecessors had done, and demanded of me not only tithes for the current year, but also for that of the preceding one. I was unable to pay it, and was served with a law process, and, in a few weeks after, my cow sold by auction for the parson's tithes. I was now no longer able to keep my cottage and garden, and gave it up to the landlord, and rented a smaller one, having half an acre of ground attached to it. My present holding, though situated in the same parish, was two miles farther in the country than the former one, and adjoining it was a slip of uncultivated land, containing about an acre. My present landlord proposed that I should take this piece of land, in addition to what I had already; and, as an encouragement to me to do so, told me that he would not ask rent for the two first years, as during that time, he was perfectly well aware, the land would produce nothing. As I considered his proposal a fair one, I accepted it, and became his tenant for the piece of land, which I immediately set about enclosing with a ditch: having no person to assist me in making it, it was a considerable time before I had it finished: and I then commenced digging it with a spade, as I had no money to pay for getting it ploughed. In this way I fallowed it for two successive seasons; and in the beginning of the third spring I contrived, by parting with a good deal of my furniture to purchase some manure, which I carried in a basket on my head to the land: thus prepared, I sowed a crop in it, and nothing could succeed better than it did. When the time nearly came for gathering it, I was one day standing admiring it, with a gratification proportionate to the immense labour and time I had expended in bringing it about. "Although it had cost me three years labour," said I, "to grow this crop, it will nev-

ertheless amply remunerate me." I had scarcely uttered the words, when two men rode up to me, one of whom I found to be the parson, whom I had never before seen in the parish, and the other his tithe valuator. After the latter had examined the crop, the parson asked me whether I would pay in kind or money?

"How much is it parson?" asked I.—"Only the tenth of the crop," replied he; "you must be very ignorant to ask such a question."

"But," said I, "if your reverence takes the tenth of the crop, it will be three-tenths of the produce of my laud; for I have been three years bringing the land into cultivation before it could grow any thing."—"I don't understand you," said the parson; "I must have my tithe."

"Why surely," said I, "your reverence will not rob my poor little children, by taking two-tenths more than you have a right to?"—"Rob them!" roared out the parson; "I see, my good fellow, you are a Radical, but I'll make you pay me my right; you shall not defraud the church of its lawful dues."

The parson went away, and the overseers came and demanded the poor-rates; the churchwardens called for an applotment, made to repair and beautify the church, and the landlord took his rent, and I was a ruined man. My whole three years' labour went amongst them, without leaving me one shilling for myself. I was now broken in purse and spirit, and could no longer bear up against the misfortunes that had fallen upon me. I gave up my land, and as I could procure no employment, I was obliged to apply to the parish. In order to lessen the poor-rates as much as possible, the overseers and farmers met each Sunday, and every able-bodied labourer was set up to auction, and the farmer who bid most for him had him to work for him during the ensuing week. One farmer bid three shillings a week for me, and I was ordered to work for him for that sum, and four shillings that the overseer gave me, making together seven shillings a week, to support my wife, five children, and myself. At the end of a week the farmer had no further occasion for my services, and I was on the following Monday, in company with some others, yoked to a cart, and made to draw gravel to the road. "Good God!"

exclaimed I, when I found the harness upon me, "what is England reduced to, when, without any fault of my own, in the same parish that so many generations of my forefathers lived comfortable and happy, I am obliged to submit so be treated as a beast of burthen!" The work of drawing stones was so dreadfully severe, and so unlike what I had been accustomed to, that a few weeks' trial soon convinced me it would soon kill me; and I determined leaving my native parish, and seeking employment elsewhere; and with this intention I came into Kent. ✳ ✳ ✳

In Kent I found myself still worse off than at home, for I could procure no employment whatever, and as I had no claim on the poor-rates, I was in danger of starving, and felt myself compelled to return home; before, however, I could do so, my poor wife fell ill of fever, and in order to prevent her perishing from want, I was obliged to go and beg—downright hunger having conquered my reluctance to ask charity. I proceeded along the road in order to do so, and saw a fat man, dressed in black, approaching me, to whom I applied for something to prevent my wife and children dying of starvation.—"I cannot *afford* to give you any thing," replied he; "go to your parish." His manner was so repulsive, that I considered it useless to make a second application, and passed on: when I had walked a few yards, I began to think I had somewhere before seen the gentleman in black, and, after a few minutes recollection, remembered he was the Rev. Mr. Saint Paul, who had taken my cow in payment of his small tithes, and who afterwards took three-tenths of my crop for his tithe of my plot of ground: he was a pluralist; and, having five livings, seldom or never came to the parish I had lived in, except to receive his tithes, so that I did not at first recognise him. I walked on for some time longer, and not meeting any person, was obliged to return to the cottage that my wife was in, without any thing to give her; as I could not bring myself to enter the cottage and behold my wife dying for want, I sat down on the road, a little distance from the door, and soon beheld the parson returning from his walk. He had a cake in his hand, which, as he had no inclination to eat, he threw to a large pampered dog that walked beside him. The dog, having no better appetite than his master, took the cake in his mouth, played with it for a moment, then tossed it in the dirt and left it there, A little child of mine beheld the scene from the cottage door, and ran and picked the cake out of the gutter, when the parson demanded how dare she take it from his dog? "Oh, Sir!" said the little girl, "the dog will not eat it, and I wish to bring it to my poor mother, who is starving."—"Your mother and yourself ought to be in the workhouse," said the parson; "it is a shame for the parish officers to allow little naked vagabonds like you to be running about the roads."

"Can this man," thought I, "be a descendant of the Apostles, who carried nothing with them but scrip and staff, and who preached that we should consider every man as our brother, and relieve the necessities of our fellow-creatures?" Such an impression did his conduct make on me, that I got a piece of paper, and wrote a few lines, cautioning him against the consequences of his cruelty, and having signed it with my real name, "Swing," I left it at his hall-door during the night, and the following day the village rung with the report of the parson's having received a threatening notice, and that if the author could be detected, he would certainly be transported.

When writing the notice, I had not the most distant intention of making myself the instrument of punishment to the parson; it was an ebullition of the moment, called forth by my suffering, and I thought no more about it. In a few days after the serving of the notice my wife died, and I was obliged to procure a coffin from the parish to bury her; no person attended her remains to the grave but a man who helped me to carry the coffin, and my five motherless children; it was late in the afternoon when we reached the churchyard, and as the man was obliged to leave me before the grave was entirely covered in, it became quite dark ere I could finish it, and I was obliged to procure a lantern to enable me to do so. When I completed it, I beheld my five children starving and shivering with cold beside the grave of their poor mother, without the smallest prospect of obtaining any food for them before morning; and in this condition I returned towards the cottage from whence I had that day carried my wife to be buried; the idea of passing the night on the straw on which she had expired was so repugnant to me, that I determined not to do so, and as the parson's haggard was only a short distance from me, I brought my children to pass the night on some loose straw that was lying on the ground. I was too much overwhelmed with grief and misery to attend to any thing, and I forgot to extinguish the light in the lantern which was carried by one of my children; the child incautiously placed the candle close to a rick, which caught fire, and was in a few minutes in a blaze; frightened and confounded at the accident, I immediately left the place, and the next morning journeyed homewards, begging for subsistence along the road: every where I went I heard of fires and notices signed "Swing." "How happens this," thought I. "I am not the author of these burnings!—What can have caused them?" A few minutes' reflection on the history of my own life, which without any alteration may stand for that of thousands of others, enabled me to give myself a satisfactory answer. "Those fires," said I, "are caused by farmers having been turned out of their lands to make room for foxes—peaceable people assembled to petition Parliament, massacred by the military—peasants confined two years in prison for picking up a dead partridge, English labourers set up to auction like slaves, and treated as beasts of burthen,—and pluralist parsons taking a poor man's only cow for the tythe of his cabbage garden. These are the things that have caused the burnings, and not unfortunate 'Swing!'" I continued my route, reached home, and am again harnessed like a horse to a gravel cart. But I bear it with patience, under the conviction that, in a very short time, Reform or Revolution must release me from it.

REVIEW QUESTIONS

1. What change initially uprooted Swing from his prosperity, and what factors continued to cause him misfortune?
2. How had traditional authority changed in the countryside?
3. What are Swing's political sympathies at the story's beginning? How do they evolve?
4. How does this story blur the boundaries of criminality and social justice?

KARL MARX AND FRIEDRICH ENGELS

FROM *Manifesto of the Communist Party*

Published in February 1848 to proclaim the existence of a newly constituted—and minuscule—revolutionary party, the Communist Manifesto *subsequently became the most widely read political pamphlet in modern European history. The manifesto's success is grounded in its dramatic, confident presentation of a socialist blueprint for social development and political emancipation. Divided into three sections, the pamphlet outlines the class struggle between the bourgeoisie and the proletariat, the ultimate stage of history under communism, and, finally, the false promises of competing socialist doctrines. The passage below is an excerpt from the first section, which boldly lays out the economic process by which the bourgeoisie and the capitalist mode of production would falter and surrender to the next stage of history.*

From *The Marx-Engels Reader*, edited by Robert C. Tucker, 2d ed. (New York: Norton, 1978), pp. 56–62.

A spectre is haunting Europe—the spectre of Communism. All the Powers of old Europe have entered into a holy alliance to exorcise this spectre: Pope and Czar, Metternich and Guizot, French Radicals and German police-spies.

To this end, Communists of various nationalities have assembled in London, and sketched the following Manifesto, to be published in the English, French, German, Italian, Flemish and Danish languages.

*   *   *

I. Bourgeois and Proletarians

The history of all hitherto existing society is the history of class struggles.

Freeman and slave, patrician and plebeian, lord and serf, guild-master and journeyman, in a word, oppressor and oppressed, stood in constant opposition to one another, carried on an uninterrupted, now hidden, now open fight, a fight that each time ended, either in a revolutionary reconstitution of society at large, or in the common ruin of the contending classes.

In the earlier epochs of history, we find almost everywhere a complicated arrangement of society into various orders, a manifold gradation of social rank. In ancient Rome we have patricians, knights, plebeians, slaves; in the Middle Ages, feudal lords, vassals, guild-masters, journeymen, apprentices, serfs; in almost all of these classes, again, subordinate gradations.

The modern bourgeois society that has sprouted from the ruins of feudal society has not done away with clash antagonisms. It has but established new classes, new conditions of oppression, new forms of struggle in place of the old ones.

Our epoch, the epoch of the bourgeoisie, possesses, however, this distinctive feature: it has simplified the class antagonisms: Society as a whole is more and more splitting up into two great hostile camps, into two great classes directly facing each other: Bourgeoisie and Proletariat.

*   *   *

The feudal system of industry, under which industrial production was monopolised by closed guilds, now no longer sufficed for the growing wants of the new markets. The manufacturing system took its place. The guild-masters were pushed on one side by the manufacturing middle class; division of labour between the different corporate guilds vanished in the face of division of labour in each single workshop.

*   *   *

Modern industry has established the world market, for which the discovery of America paved the way. This market has given an immense development to commerce, to navigation, to communication by land. This development has, in its turn, reacted on the extension of industry; and in proportion as industry, commerce, navigation, railways extended, in the same proportion the bourgeoisie developed, increased its capital, and pushed into the background every class handed down from the Middle Ages.

*   *   *

The bourgeoisie, historically, has played a most revolutionary part.

The bourgeoisie, wherever it has got the upper hand, has put an end to all feudal, patriarchal, idyllic relations. It has pitilessly torn asunder the motley feudal ties that bound man to his "natural superiors," and has left remaining no other nexus between man and man than naked self-interest, than callous "cash payment." It has drowned the most heavenly ecstasies of religious fervour, of chivalrous enthusiasm, of philistine sentimentalism, in the icy water of egotistical calculation. It has resolved personal worth into exchange value, and in place of the numberless indefeasible chartered freedoms, has set up that single, unconscionable freedom—Free Trade. In one word, for exploitation, veiled by religious and political illusions, it has substituted naked, shameless, direct, brutal exploitation.

*   *   *

The bourgeoisie cannot exist without constantly revolutionising the instruments of production, and thereby the relations of production, and with them the whole relations of society. Conservation of the old modes of production in unaltered form, was, on the contrary, the first condition of existence for all earlier industrial classes. Constant revolutionising of production, uninterrupted disturbance of all social conditions, everlasting uncertainty and agitation distinguish the bourgeois epoch from all earlier ones. All fixed, fast-frozen relations, with their train of ancient and venerable prejudices and opinions, are swept away, all new-formed ones become antiquated before they can ossify. All that is solid melts into air, all that is holy is profaned, and man is at last compelled to face with sober senses, his real conditions of life, and his relations with his kind.

The need of a constantly expanding market for its products chases the bourgeoisie over the whole surface of the globe. It must nestle everywhere, settle everywhere, establish connexions everywhere.

* * *

The bourgeoisie, during its rule of scarce one hundred years, has created more massive and more colossal productive forces than have all preceding generations together. Subjection of Nature's forces to man, machinery, application of chemistry to industry and agriculture, steam-navigation, railways, electric telegraphs, clearing of whole continents for cultivation, canalisation of rivers, whole populations conjured out of the ground—what earlier century had even a presentiment that such productive forces slumbered in the lap of social labour?

We see then: the means of production and of exchange, on whose foundation the bourgeoisie built itself up, were generated in feudal society. At a certain stage in the development of these means of production and of exchange, the conditions under which feudal society produced and exchanged, the feudal organisation of agriculture and manufacturing industry, in one word, the feudal relations of property became no longer compatible with the already developed productive forces; they became so many fetters. They had to be burst asunder; they were burst asunder.

Into their place stepped free competition, accompanied by a social and political constitution adapted to it, and by the economical and political sway of the bourgeois class.

* * *

Modern bourgeois society with its relations of production, of exchange and of property, a society that has conjured up such gigantic means of production and of exchange, is like the sorcerer, who is no longer able to control the powers of the nether world whom he has called up by his spells. For many a decade past the history of industry and commerce is but the history of the revolt of modern productive forces against modern conditions of production, against the property relations that are the conditions for the existence of the bourgeoisie and of its rule. It is enough to mention the commercial crises that by their periodical return put on its trial, each time more threateningly, the existence of the entire bourgeois society. In these crises a great part not only of the existing products, but also of the previously created productive forces, are periodically destroyed. In these crises there breaks out an epidemic that, in all earlier epochs, would have seemed an absurdity—the epidemic of overproduction. Society suddenly finds itself put back into a state of momentary barbarism; it appears as if a famine, a universal war of devastation had cut off the supply of every means of subsistence; industry and commerce seem to be destroyed; and why? Because there is too much civilisation, too much means of subsistence, too much industry, too much commerce. The productive forces at the disposal of society no longer tend to further the development of the conditions of bourgeois property; on the contrary, they have become too powerful for these conditions, by which they are fettered, and so soon as they overcome these fetters, they bring disorder into the whole of bourgeois society, endanger the existence of bourgeois property. The conditions of bourgeois society are too narrow to comprise the wealth created by them. And how does the bourgeoisie get over these crises? On the one hand by enforced destruction of a mass of productive forces; on the other, by the conquest of new markets, and by the more thorough exploitation of the old ones. That is to say, by paving the way for more extensive and more destructive crises, and by diminishing the means whereby crises are prevented.

The weapons with which the bourgeoisie felled feudalism to the ground are now turned against the bourgeoisie itself.

But not only has the bourgeoisie forged the weapons that bring death to itself; it has also called into existence the men who are to wield those weapons— the modern working class—the proletarians.

In proportion as the bourgeoisie, i.e., capital, is developed, in the same proportion is the proletariat, the modern working class, developed—a class of labourers, who live only so long as they find work, and who find work only so long as their labour increases capital. These labourers, who must sell themselves piece-meal, are a commodity, like every other article of commerce, and are consequently exposed to all the vicissitudes of competition, to all the fluctuations of the market.

*   *   *

The proletariat goes through various stages of development. With its birth begins its struggle with the bourgeoisie. At first the contest is carried on by individual labourers, then by the workpeople of a factory, then by the operatives of one trade, in one locality, against the individual bourgeois who directly exploits them. They direct their attacks not against the bourgeois conditions of production, but against the instruments of production themselves; they destroy imported wares that compete with their labour, they smash to pieces machinery, they set factories ablaze, they seek to restore by force the vanished status of the workman of the Middle Ages.

*   *   *

But with the development of industry the proletariat not only increases in number; it becomes concentrated in greater masses, its strength grows, and it feels that strength more. The various interests and conditions of life within the ranks of the proletariat are more and more equalised, in proportion as machinery obliterates all distinctions of labour, and nearly everywhere reduces wages to the same low level. The growing competition among the bourgeois, and the resulting commercial crises, make the wages of the workers ever more fluctuating. The unceasing improvement of machinery, ever more rapidly developing, makes their livelihood more and more precarious; the collisions between individual workmen and individual bourgeois take more and more the character of collisions between two classes. Thereupon the workers begin to form combinations (Trades Unions) against the bourgeois; they club together in order to keep up the rate of wages; they found permanent associations in order to make provision beforehand for these occasional revolts. Here and there the contest breaks out into riots.

*   *   *

This organisation of the proletarians into a class, and consequently into a political party, is continually being upset again by the competition between the workers themselves. But it ever rises up again, stronger, firmer, mightier. It compels legislative recognition of particular interests of the workers, by taking advantage of the divisions among the bourgeoisie itself. Thus the ten-hours' bill in England was carried.

*   *   *

Of all the classes that stand face to face with the bourgeoisie today, the proletariat alone is a really revolutionary class. The other classes decay and finally disappear in the face of Modern Industry; the proletariat is its special and essential product.

*   *   *

All previous historical movements were movements of minorities, or in the interests of minorities. The proletarian movement is the self-conscious, independent movement of the immense majority, in the interests of the immense majority. The proletariat, the lowest stratum of our present society, cannot stir, cannot raise itself up, without the whole superincumbent strata of official society being sprung into the air.

Though not in substance, yet in form, the struggle of the proletariat with the bourgeoisie is at first a national struggle. The proletariat of each country must, of course, first of all settle matters with its own bourgeoisie.

In depicting the most general phases of the development of the proletariat, we traced the more or less veiled civil war, raging within existing society, up to the point where that war breaks out into open revolution, and where the violent overthrow of the bourgeoisie lays the foundation for the sway of the proletariat.

Hitherto, every form of society has been based, as we have already seen, on the antagonism of oppressing and oppressed classes. But in order to oppress a class, certain conditions must be assured to it under which it can, at least, continue its slavish existence. The serf, in the period of serfdom, raised himself to membership in the commune, just as the petty bourgeois, under the yoke of feudal absolutism, managed to develop into a bourgeois. The modern labourer, on the contrary, instead of rising with the progress of industry, sinks deeper and deeper below the conditions of existence of his own class. He becomes a pauper, and pauperism develops more rapidly than population and wealth. And here it becomes evident, that the bourgeoisie is unfit any longer to be the ruling class in society, and to impose its conditions of existence upon society as an over-riding law. It is unfit to rule because it is incompetent to assure an existence to its slave within his slavery, because it cannot help letting him sink into such a state, that it has to feed him, instead of being fed by him. Society can no longer live under this bourgeoisie, in other words, its existence is no longer compatible with society.

The essential condition for the existence, and for the sway of the bourgeois class, is the formation and augmentation of capital; the condition for capital is wage-labour. Wage-labour rests exclusively on competition between the labourers. The advance of industry, whose involuntary promoter is the bourgeoisie, replaces the isolation of the labourers, due to competition, by their revolutionary combination, due to association. The development of Modern Industry, therefore, cuts from under its feet the very foundation on which the bourgeoisie produces and appropriates products. What the bourgeoisie, therefore, produces, above all, is its own grave-diggers. Its fall and the victory of the proletariat are equally inevitable.

*   *   *

REVIEW QUESTIONS

1. According to Marx and Engels, what is the role of the bourgeoisie in world history?
2. How do Marx and Engels characterize the evolution of working-class political consciousness?
3. What do Marx and Engels mean by saying the bourgeoisie are their "own gravediggers"?

ELIZABETH POOLE SANFORD

FROM *Woman in Her Social and Domestic Character*

The widened separation of domestic and public spheres in the nineteenth century brought with it fundamental changes in the economic and social roles of bourgeois women. No longer expected to work in the productive sphere, middle-class married women took on domestic, motherly, and religious duties. Not surprisingly, character-ological assumptions accompanied this role of the "angel in the house." Alongside purity, delicacy, and virtue, subservience to husbands was foremost among the traits considered desirable for women. The following excerpt from Elizabeth Poole Sanford's book (1833) is an early example of the prescriptive literature aimed at middle-class women of the Victorian era.

From *Woman in Her Social and Domestic Character*, by Elizabeth Poole Sanford (Boston: Bowles, 1833).

*   *   *

Domestic comfort is the chief source of her influence, and the greatest debt society owes her; for happiness is almost an element of virtue, and nothing conduces more to improve the character of men than domestic peace. A woman may make a man's home delightful, and may thus increase his motives for virtuous exertion. She may refine and tranquillise his mind,—may turn away his anger or allay his grief. Her smile may be the happy influence to gladden his heart, and to disperse the cloud that gathers on his brow. And she will be loved in proportion as she makes those around her happy,—as she studies their tastes, and sympathises in their feelings. In social relations adaptation is therefore the true secret of her influence.

*   *   *

Domestic life is a woman's sphere, and it is there that she is most usefully as well as most appropriately employed. But society, too, feels her influence, and owes to her, in great measure, its balance and its tone. She may be here a corrective of what is wrong, a moderator of what is unruly, a restraint on what is indecorous. Her presence may be a pledge against impropriety and excess, a check on vice, and a protection to virtue.

And it is her delicacy which will secure to her such an influence, and enable her to maintain it. It is the policy of licentiousness to undermine where it cannot openly attack, and to weaken by stratagem what it may not rudely assail. But a delicate woman will be as much upon her guard against the insidious as against the direct assault, and will no more tolerate the innuendo than the avowal. She will shrink from the licentiousness which is couched in ambiguous phrase or veiled in covert allusion, and from the immorality which, though it may not offend the ear, is meant to corrupt the heart. And though a depraved taste may relish the condiments of vice, or an unscrupulous palate receive them without detection, her virtue will be too sensitive not to reject the poison, and to recoil spontaneously from the touch.

Delicacy is, indeed, the point of honor in woman. And her purity of manner will ensure to her deference, and repress, more effectually than any other influence, impropriety of every kind. A delicate woman, too, will be more loved, as well as more respected, than any other; for affection can scarcely be excited, and certainly cannot long subsist, unless it is founded on esteem.

Yet such delicacy is neither prudish nor insipid. Conversation, for instance, is one great source of a woman's influence; and it is her province, and her peculiar talent, to give zest to it. She is, and ought to be, the enlivener of society: if she restrains impropriety, she may promote cheerfulness; and it is not because her conversation is innocent that it need therefore be dull. The sentiment of woman contributes much to social interest: her feeling imparts life, and her gentleness a polish.

*   *   *

Again, to be agreeable, a woman must avoid egotism. It is no matter how superior she is, she will never be liked, if she talks chiefly of herself. The impression of her own importance can convey no pleasure to others: on the contrary, as a desire for distinction is always mutual, a sense of inferiority must be depressing.

If we would converse pleasingly, we must endeavor to set others at ease: and it is not by flattery that we can succeed in doing so, but by a courteous and kind address, which delicately avoids all needless irritation, and endeavors to infuse that good humor of which it is itself the result.

In woman this is a Christian duty. How often should they suppress their own claims rather than interfere with those of others! How often should they employ their talent in developing that of their associates, and not for its own display! How invariably should they discard pretension, and shun even the appearance of conceit; and seek to imbibe the spirit of that lovely religion, of which sympathy is the characteristic feature, and humility the pre-eminent grace!

*   *   *

It is seldom, indeed, that women are great proficients. The *chefs-d'oeuvre* of the sculptress need the polish of the master chisel; and the female pencil has never yet limned the immortal forms of beauty. The mind of woman is, perhaps, incapable of the originality and strength requisite for the sublime. Even Saint Cecilia exists only in an elegant legend, and the poetry of music, if often felt and expressed, has seldom been conceived by a female adept. But the practical talents of women are far from contemptible; and they may be both the encouragers and the imitators of genius. They should not grasp at too much, nor be content with superficial attainment; they should not merely daub a few flowers, or hammer out a few tunes, or trifle away their time in inept efforts, which at best claim only indulgence; but they should do well what they do attempt, and do it without affectation or display.

*   *   *

REVIEW QUESTIONS

1. According to Sanford, what are the character traits assigned to women? For what goals should women strive?
2. What attributes constituted the domestic sphere of women?
3. What was the ideal relationship between husband and wife? How was this ideal justified?

GEORGE ANNESLEY, VISCOUNT VALENTIA

FROM *Voyages and Travels to India, Ceylon, the Red Sea, Abyssinia, and Egypt*

In 1802–06, George Annesley (1770–1844), a British aristocrat and Member of Parliament who later became the Earl of Mountnorris, traveled extensively in India, the Middle East, and Africa at the height of the Napoleonic Wars. His three-volume travelogue provides a panoramic exposé of Britain's expanding imperial dominions and the British social classes that governed and profited from these territories. The following passage sketches the life of the European social elite in Calcutta, a constituency composed of civil and military officials as well as the merchants and clerks from the British East India Company, the private commercial enterprise that ruled Britain's Indian territories before formal governmental control in 1857. The account captures well colonial society: the markers of status, the attention to social order, and the perceived problem of "half-caste" children.

From *Voyages and Travels to India, Ceylon, the Red Sea, Abyssinia, and Egypt: In the years 1802, 1803, 1804, 1805, and 1806*, by George Annesley, Viscount Valentia (London: William Miller, 1809), pp. 238–242.

The society of Calcutta is numerous and gay; the fetes given by the Governor-General are frequent, splendid, and well arranged. The Chief Justice, the Members of Council, and Sir Henry Russel, each open their houses once a week for the reception of those who have had the pleasure of being presented to them. Independently of these, hardly a day passes, particularly during the cool season, without several large dinner parties being formed, consisting generally of thirty or forty: the convivial hospitality which prevails on these occasions would render them extremely pleasant, were they more limited; but a small and quiet party seems unknown in Calcutta. A Subscription Assembly also exists, but seems unfashionable; it is however the only place of public amusement, and I see no hopes of any other being established; for the fashionable world of Calcutta is unfortunately so divided into parties, that it is improbable any plan of public amusement could be brought forward which would not meet with opposition.

It is usual in Calcutta to rise early, in order to enjoy the cool air of the morning, which is particularly pleasant, before sun-rise. At twelve they take a hot meal, which they call tiffing, and then generally go to bed for two or three hours. The dinner hour is commonly between seven and eight, which is certainly too late in this hot climate, as it prevents an evening ride at the proper time, and keeps them up till midnight, or later. The viands are excellent, and served in great profusion, to the no small satisfaction of the birds, and beasts of prey, to whose share a considerable proportion of the remains fall; for the lower order of the Portuguese, to whom alone they would be serviceable, cannot consume the whole; and the religious prejudices of the native servants prevent them from touching any thing that is not drest by their own cast. To this circumstance is to be attributed the amazing flocks of crows and kites, which, undisturbed by man, live together in amicable society, and almost cover the houses and gardens. In their profession of seavengers, the kites and crows are assisted during the day by the adjutant bird, and at night by foxes, jackals, and hyenas, from the neighbouring jungles. The wines chiefly drank are Madeira and claret; the former, which is excellent, during the meal; the latter, afterwards. The claret being medicated for the voyage, is too strong, and has little flavour.

The usual mode of travelling is by palanquins,[1] but most gentlemen have carriages adapted to the climate, and horses, of which the breed is much improved of late years. It is universally the custom to drive out between sun-set and dinner. The mussalchees, when it grows dark, go out to meet their masters on their return, and run before them, at the rate of full eight miles an hour, and the numerous lights moving along the esplauade produce a singular and pleasing effect. It was formerly the fashion for gentlemen to dress in white jackets on all occasions, which were well suited to the country; but being thought too much an undress for public occasions, they are now laid aside for English cloth. The architecture of all the houses is Grecian, which I think by no means the best adapted to the country,

---

[1] A palanquin was a typical form of conveyance in Asia at this time. It is a long box with wooden shutters and has projecting poles so that servants can carry it on their shoulders.

as the pillars, which are generally used in the verandahs, require too great an elevation to keep out the sun, during the greater part of the morning and evening, although the heat is excessive at both those periods. In the rainy season it is still worse, as the wet beats in, and renders them totally useless. The more confined Hindoo or Gothic architecture, would surely be preferable.

On Lord Wellesley's[2] first arrival in this country, he set his face decidedly against horse-racing, and every other species of gambling, yet at the end of November, 1803, there were three day's races at a small distance from Calcutta. Very large sums were betted, and of course were lost by the inexperienced. There are a few steady and practised gamblers, who encourage every species of play among the young servants of the Company, and make a considerable profit by their imprudence. As those are marked characters, I wonder they are not sent away.

The most rapidly accumulating evil of Bengal is the increase of half-cast children. They are forming the first step to colonization, by creating a link of union between the English and the natives. In every country where this intermediate cast has been permitted to rise, it has ultimately tended to the ruin of that country. Spanish America and St. Domingo are examples of this fact. Their increase in India is beyond calculation; and though possibly there may be nothing to fear from the sloth of the Hindoos, and the rapidly declining consequence of the Mussulmauns, yet it may be justly apprehended that this tribe may hereafter become too powerful for control. Although they are not permitted to hold offices under the Company, yet they act as clerks in almost every mercantile house, and many of them are annually sent to England to receive the benefit of an European education. With numbers in their favour, with a close relationship to the natives, and without an equal proportion of that pusillanimity and indolence which is natural to them, what may not in time be dreaded from them? I have no hesitation in saying that the evil ought to be stopt; and I know no other

way of effecting this object, than by obliging every father of half-cast children, to send them to Europe, prohibiting their return in any capacity whatsoever. The expense that would thus attend upon children, would certainly operate as a check to the extension of zenanas, which are now but too common among the Europeans; and this would be a benefit to the country, no less in a moral, than in a political view.

After making these observations, I turn with much satisfaction to the brighter parts of the character of my Eastern countrymen. I can truly affirm, that they are hospitable in the highest degree, and that their generosity is unbounded. When an officer of respectability dies, in either the civil or military service, leaving a widow or children, a subscription is immediately set on foot, which in every instance has proved liberal, and not unfrequently has conferred on the parties a degree of affluence, that the life of the husband or parent could not for years have insured them. The hearts of the British in this country seem expanded by opulence: they do every thing upon a princely scale; and consequently do not save half the money that might be done with a narrower economy. The beginning, however, of a fortune being once made, it collects as rapidly as a snow ball. In seven years, or less, a capital is doubled; so that ten thousand rupees given to a child at birth, is a handsome independence by the time it arrives at the age of twenty one.

*   *   *

REVIEW QUESTIONS

1. What are the social activities of the British elite in Calcutta? Where does Annesley praise, and where does he criticize?
2. In what ways does this passage illuminate the social order of imperial India? How is the social hierarchy upheld? Are there anxieties?
3. Why is the author opposed to half-caste children? Is his comparative analysis valid?
4. After reading this account, why do you think Europeans were drawn to civil and military service in the empire? What are the attractions?

---

[2] Richard Colley Wesley, the Marquess of Wellesley, was a colonial administrator in India from 1797 to 1805, a period marked by the rapid expansion of British power.

20 ✆ THE AGE OF IDEOLOGIES: EUROPE IN THE AFTERMATH OF REVOLUTION, 1815–1848

Among the defining features of political modernity lies ideology: a coherent system of ideas in self-conscious competition with other political and socioeconomic doctrines. On the European continent, the French Revolution first opened up an ideological landscape, ranging from ultraconservative royalism on the far right to doctrines of radical democracy on the left. The organization of formal political parties was still in its infancy, but partisan choice nonetheless shaped modernity's open-ended script on citizenship. In the period between 1789 and the Revolution of 1848, the principal political ideologies of the modern era emerged: liberalism, conservatism, socialism, and democratic radicalism. The new marketplace of contesting doctrines clarified visions of sociopolitical goals and furthermore exhorted new social groups to participate in political life.

During this time period, liberalism and its ideal of constitutional rule of law stood at the center of political transformation. Since the Glorious Revolution in England, elements of a liberal social contract emerged, which earlier chapters have accented: individual liberties guaranteed by law; the sanctity of private property; unrestricted movement of individuals, ideas, and goods; and, finally, careers open to talent. Such beliefs irreparably undermined the social foundations of the Old Regime. Liberalism's emphasis on reason, social utility, and pragmatic reform, and its aversion to arbitrary rule, all converged with the Enlightenment's indomitable belief in progress. The French Revolution, however, significantly affected the course of liberalism's development. Shaped by the experience of Jacobin Terror, nineteenth-century liberals restricted the franchise to the educated and propertied, limited the authority of public government, and guarded the rights of minorities against majority rule. Overall, though, constitutional liberalism and its understanding of liberty and freedom framed the political worldview of many Europeans, whether middle class or not. In Russia, for example, liberal army officers in the 1820s plotted an insurrection (in vain) to transform Tsarist autocracy into a constitutional monarchy. Its application thus stretched from North and South America to most areas of Europe and stamped the ideological character of the revolutions that swept Europe in 1848–49.

For traditional elites, the post-Napoleonic restoration of dynastic legitimacy and aristocratic privilege framed the ideology of conservatism. Such spokesmen as Edmund Burke and Joseph de Maistre deployed history and its organic form of development to justify the "natural" hierarchy of a monarchy and its essential corollaries of religion and nobility. In the first half of the nineteenth century, conservative statesmen and rulers vigorously mobilized the power of the state and its laws to contain the spread of revolutionary ideals. In this mission they were ineffective, but conservatives nonetheless succeeded in persuading ordinary Europeans that time-honored elites provided stability and prosperity. In an age of expanded enfranchisement, conservatives held their own, persuading adherents that tradition ensured a secure future.

Democratic and socialist doctrines also widened the ideological spectrum. Moving beyond the moderate liberal social contract, democrats championed active political citizenship of all men. Some even supported women's rights, though this was still a small minority. Contemporaries dubbed many democrats "radicals" because of their preference for republics, viewing monarchy (whether absolute or constitutional) as obsolete. Many Romantic poets and writers— William Blake, Victor Hugo, and Percy Bysshe Shelley to name three—echoed the sentiment of democratic liberty in verse, prose, and song. But the struggle to enfranchise ordinary workers also took on concrete form. Emerging as one of the earliest independent working-class movements, Chartism was a national network of committees in Britain that agitated for the vote of unpropertied workers. Although unsuccessful in its immediate goals (Parliament rejected all demands), the movement alerted the nation to a mature, responsible working class, thereby laying the groundwork for subsequent reform. But this "age of ideology" also widened the conceptual boundaries of political freedom by incorporating the social and economic dimensions that conditioned political rights. Early socialist doctrine challenged the inviolability of private property and free enterprise when examining the human misery of early industrial factory work. While Pierre-Joseph Proudhon declared "property is theft," Robert Owen reorganized factory production along the principle of cooperation to ameliorate the material welfare of workers. Their emphasis on society's needs, and less so those of individuals, repositioned the ideological landscape. Karl Marx and Friedrich Engels would push socialist ideology further to the left with a systematic critique of capitalism and waged work, thus laying a foundation for various forms of socialism in the second half of the century.

Political needs and visions continued to redefine ideologies after 1848, but the basic parameters of modern political discourse had emerged, evincing both *their vices and virtues. While the revolutionary Terror of 1793–94 adumbrated the horror of political ideals to sanction murder, the fundamental concept of coherent political alternatives proved beneficial. Western civil societies remained confident that informed electorates could select and synthesize various ideological goals to effect positive change.*

MARY WOLLSTONECRAFT

FROM *A Vindication of the Rights of Woman*

Mary Wollstonecraft (1759–1797), a teacher and writer, wrote this essay as a critical response to the French Revolution. An enthusiastic supporter of the revolution, she was nonetheless angered that the National Assembly did not extend the same liberties to women as to men. Her essay, appealing to reason, utility, and natural law, exhorted both men and women to reform education for women and enable them to participate in civil society as useful members. Although scorned as a radical Francophile by her contemporaries, Wollstonecraft convincingly applied liberal reasoning to the cause of women at a critical juncture in European history.

From *A Vindication of the Rights of Woman*, by Mary Wollstonecraft (New York: Norton, 1970).

After considering the historic page, and viewing the living world with anxious solicitude, the most melancholy emotions of sorrowful indignation have depressed my spirits, and I have sighed when obliged to confess that either Nature has made a great difference between man and man, or that the civilization which has hitherto taken place in the world has been very partial. I have turned over various books written on the subject of education, and patiently observed the conduct of parents and the management of schools; but what has been the result?—a profound conviction that the neglected education of my fellow-creatures is the grand source of the misery I deplore, and that women, in particular, are rendered weak and wretched by a variety of concurring causes, originating from one hasty conclusion. The conduct and manners of women, in fact, evidently prove that their minds are not in a healthy state; for, like the flowers which are planted in too rich a soil, strength and usefulness are sacrificed to beauty; and the flaunting leaves, after having pleased a fastidious eye, fade, disregarded on the stalk, long before the season when they ought to have arrived at maturity. One cause of this barren blooming I attribute to a false system of education, gathered from the books written on this subject by men who, considering females rather as women than human creatures, have been more anxious to make them alluring mistresses than affectionate wives and rational mothers; and the understanding of the sex has been so bubbled by this specious homage, that the civilized women of the present century, with a few exceptions, are only anxious to inspire love, when they ought to cherish a nobler ambition, and by their abilities and virtues exact respect.

In a treatise, therefore, on female rights and manners, the works which have been particularly written for their improvement must not be overlooked, especially when it is asserted, in direct terms, that the minds of women are enfeebled by false refinement; that the books of instruction, written by men of genius, have had the same tendency as more frivolous productions; and that, in the true style of Mahometanism, they are treated as a kind of subordinate beings, and not as a part of the human species, when improvable reason is allowed to be the dignified distinction which raises men above the brute creation, and puts a natural sceptre in a feeble hand.

Yet, because I am a woman, I would not lead my readers to suppose that I mean violently to agitate the contested question respecting the quality or inferiority of the sex; but as the subject lies in my way, and I cannot pass it over without subjecting the main tendency of my reasoning to misconstruction, I shall stop a moment to deliver, in a few words, my opinion. In the government of the physical world it is observable that the female in point of strength is, in general, inferior to the male. This is the law of Nature; and it does not appear to be suspended or abrogated in favour of woman. A degree of physical superiority cannot, therefore, be denied, and it is a noble prerogative! But not content with this natural pre-eminence, men endeavour to sink us still lower, merely to render us alluring objects for a moment; and women, intoxicated by the adoration which men, under the influence of their senses, pay them, do not seek to obtain a durable interest in their hearts, or to become the friends of the fellow-creatures who find amusement in their society.

I am aware of an obvious inference. From every quarter have I heard exclamations against masculine women, but where are they to be found? If by this appellation men mean to inveigh against their ardour in hunting, shooting, and gaming, I shall most cordially join in the cry; but if it be against the imitation of manly virtues, or, more properly speaking, the attainment of those talents and virtues, the exercise of which ennobles the human character, and which raises females in the scale of animal being, when they are comprehensively termed mankind, all those who view them with a philosophic eye must, I should think, wish with me, that they may every day grow more and more masculine.

This discussion naturally divides the subject. I shall first consider women in the grand light of human creatures, who, in common with men, are placed on this earth to unfold their faculties; and afterwards I shall more particularly point out their peculiar designation.

I wish also to steer clear of an error which many respectable writers have fallen into; for the instruction which has hitherto been addressed to women, has rather been applicable to *ladies,* if the little indirect advice that is scattered through "Sandford and Merton" be excepted; but, addressing my sex in a firmer tone, I pay particular attention to those in the middle class, because they appear to be in the most natural state. Perhaps the seeds of false refinement, immorality, and vanity, have ever been shed by the great. Weak, artificial beings, raised above the common wants and affections of their race, in a premature unnatural manner, undermine the very foundation of virtue, and spread corruption through the whole mass of society! As a class of mankind they have the strongest claim to pity; the education of the rich tends to render them vain and helpless, and the unfolding mind is not strengthened by the practice of those duties which dignify the human character. They only live to amuse themselves, and by the same law which in Nature invariably produces certain effects, they soon only afford barren amusement.

But as I purpose taking a separate view of the different ranks of society, and of the moral character of women in each, this hint is for the present sufficient; and I have only alluded to the subject because it appears to me to be the very essence of an introduction to give a cursory account of the contents of the work it introduces.

My own sex, I hope, will excuse me, if I treat them like rational creatures, instead of flattering their *fascinating* graces, and viewing them as if they were in a state of perpetual childhood, unable to stand alone. I earnestly wish to point out in what true dignity and human happiness consists. I wish to persuade women to endeavour to acquire strength, both of mind and body, and to convince them that the soft phrases, susceptibility of heart, delicacy of sentiment, and refinement of taste, are almost synonymous with epithets of weakness, and that those beings who are only the objects of pity, and that kind of love which has been termed its sister, will soon become objects of contempt.

Dismissing, then, those pretty feminine phrases, which the men condescendingly use to soften our slavish dependence, and despising that weak elegancy of mind, exquisite sensibility, and sweet docility of manners, supposed to be the sexual characteristics of the weaker vessel, I wish to show that elegance is inferior to virtue, that the first object of laudable ambition is to obtain a character as a human being, regardless of the distinction of sex, and that secondary views should be brought to this simple touchstone.

This is a rough sketch of my plan; and should I express my conviction with the energetic emotions that I feel whenever I think of the subject, the dictates of experience and reflection will be felt by some of my readers. Animated by this important object, I shall disdain to cull my phrases or polish my style. I aim at being useful, and sincerity will render me unaffected; for wishing rather to persuade by the force of my arguments than dazzle by the elegance of my language, I shall not waste my time in rounding periods, or in fabricating the turgid bombast of artificial feelings, which, coming from the head, never reach the heart. I shall be employed about things, not words! and, anxious to render my sex more respectable members of society, I shall try to avoid that flowery diction which has slided from essays into novels, and from novels into familiar letters and conversations.

These pretty superlatives, dropping glibly from the tongue, vitiate the taste, and create a kind of sickly delicacy that turns away from simple unadorned truth; and a deluge of false sentiments and over-stretched feelings, stifling the natural emotions of the heart, render the domestic pleasures insipid, that ought to sweeten the exercise of those severe duties, which educate a rational and immortal being for a nobler field of action.

The education of women has of late been more attended to than formerly; yet they are still reckoned a frivolous sex, and ridiculed or pitied by the writers who endeavour by satire or instruction to improve them. It is acknowledged that they spend many of the first years of their lives in acquiring a smattering of accomplishments; meanwhile strength of body and mind are sacrificed to libertine notions of beauty, to the desire of establishing themselves—the only way women can rise in the world—by marriage. And this desire making mere animals of them, when they marry they act as such children may be expected to act—they dress, they paint, and nickname God's creatures. Surely these weak beings are only fit for a seraglio! Can they be expected to govern a family with judgement, or take care of the poor babes, whom they bring into the world?

If, then, it can be fairly deduced from the present conduct of the sex, from the prevalent fondness for pleasure which takes place of ambition and those nobler passions that open and enlarge the soul, that the instruction which women have hitherto received has only tended, with the constitution of civil society, to render them insignificant objects of desire—mere propagators of fools!—if it can be proved that in aiming to accomplish them, without cultivating their understandings, they are taken out of their sphere of duties, and made ridiculous and useless when the short-lived bloom of beauty is over, I presume that *rational* men will excuse me for endeavouring to persuade them to become more masculine and respectable.

Indeed the word masculine is only a bugbear; there is little reason to fear that women will acquire too much courage or fortitude, for their apparent inferiority with respect to bodily strength must render them in some degree dependent on men in the various relations of life; but why should it be increased by prejudices that give a sex to virtue, and confound simple truths with sensual reveries?

Women are, in fact, so much degraded by mistaken notions of female excellence, that I do not mean to add a paradox when I assert that this artificial weakness produces a propensity to tyrannize, and gives birth to cunning, the natural opponent of strength, which leads them to play off those contemptible infantine airs that undermine esteem even whilst they excite desire. Let men become more chaste and modest, and if women do not grow wiser in the same ratio it will be clear that they have weaker understandings. It seems scarcely necessary to say that I now speak of the sex in general. Many individuals have more sense than their male relatives; and, as nothing preponderates where there is a constant struggle for an equilibrium without it has naturally more gravity, some women govern their husbands without degrading themselves, because intellect will always govern.

REVIEW QUESTIONS

1. Why is Wollstonecraft's emphasis on education critical for her argument?
2. What are the similarities and differences between this essay and Olympe de Gouges's declaration (pp. 303–306)?
3. At which social classes was this essay aimed? What are Wollstonecraft's criticisms of the women from these classes?
4. What distinctions does Wollstonecraft make between men and women? What is her point in drawing such distinctions?

The Decembrist Revolt

During and after the Napoleonic era, the citizenship ideals of liberalism penetrated central and eastern Europe. Animated by American federalism, British constitutional monarchy, and Spain's liberal movement in 1820–23, an elite group of Russian officers and nobles attempted to overthrow the Tsarist government in December 1825: a vulnerable moment of transition following the death of Alexander I, when Nicholas I assumed the imperial crown after Constantine, his elder and more liberal-minded brother, rejected the offer of succession. The insurrection, which championed Constantine, traced its roots to the Union of Salvation, a secret society created in 1816 to link Russian society with the constitutional movements of the West. Pavel Pestel, one of the rebellion's leaders, designed a charter that advocated the emancipation of slaves, the elimination of class privilege, and the extension of political rights to men over the age of twenty. Aristocratic officers and about three thousand men, divided between northern and southern contingents, carried out the rebellion, which superior Tsarist forces swiftly defeated. The Tsar's government hanged Pavel and four other nobles, while sending many others into exile. Although the Decembrist uprising was a decisive failure in the short term, the following testimonies collected for the trials from Baron Vladimir Steingel and the officers Pavel Pastel, Pyotr Kakhovsky, and Mikhail Bestuzhev-Ryumin, suggest the degree to which western notions of political freedom circulated in Russian society. The legacy of the Decembrists lived on. They became heroes of the populist movement in the 1860s and furthermore won the admiration of such intellectuals as Leo Tolstoy.

From "Testimonies from the Decembrist Plot" from *Readings in Russian Civilization, Vol. 2: Imperial Russia, 1700–1917*, edited by Thomas Riha (Chicago: University of Chicago Press, 1964), pp. 295–300.

FROM **Pestel's Testimony**

QUESTION 6: How did the revolutionary ideas gradually develop and become implanted in men's minds? Who first conceived these ideas and continued to preach and spread them throughout the State?

ANSWER 6: This question is very difficult to answer, for it must go beyond the realm of discussion about the secret Society. However, in order to fulfill the demand of the Committee I shall try so far as I can explain it.

Political books are in the hands of everyone; political science is taught and political news spread everywhere. These teach all to discuss the activities and conduct of the Government, to praise one thing and assail another. A survey of the events of 1812, 1813, 1814, and 1815, likewise of the preceding and following periods, will show how many thrones were toppled over, how many others were established, how many kingdoms were destroyed, and how many new ones were created; how many Sovereigns were expelled, how many returned or were invited to return and were then again driven out; how many revolutions were accomplished; how many *coup d'états* carried out—all these events familiarized the minds of men with the idea of revolutions, with their possibilities, and with the favorable occasions on which to execute them. Besides that, every century has its peculiar characteristic: ours is marked by revolutionary ideas. From one end of Europe to the other the same thing is observed, from Portugal to Russia, without the exception of a single state, not even England or Turkey, those two opposites. The same spectacle is presented also in the whole of America. The spirit of reform causes mental fermentation [*faire bouillir les esprits*]. Here are the causes, I think, which gave rise to revolutionary ideas and which have implanted them in the minds of people. As to the cause of the spread of the spirit of reform through the country, it could not be ascribed to the Society, for the organization was still too small to have any popular influence.

FROM **A Letter of Kakhovsky to General Levashev**

Your Excellency,
Dear Sir!
The uprising of December 14 is a result of causes related above. I see, Your Excellency, that the Committee established by His Majesty is making a great effort to discover all the members of the secret Society. But the government will not derive any notable benefit from that. We were not trained within the Society but were already ready to work when we joined it. The origin and the root of the Society one must seek in the spirit of the time and in our state of mind. I know a few belonging to the secret Society but am inclined to think the membership is not very large. Among my many acquaintances who do not adhere to secret societies very few are opposed to my opinions. Frankly I state that among thousands of young men there are hardly a hundred who do not passionately long for freedom. These youths, striving with pure and strong love for the welfare of their Fatherland, toward true enlightenment, are growing mature.

The people have conceived a sacred truth—that they do not exist for governments, but that governments must be organized for them. This is the cause of struggle in all countries; peoples, after tasting the sweetness of enlightenment and freedom, strive toward them; and governments, surrounded by millions of bayonets, make efforts to repel these peoples back into the darkness of ignorance. But all these efforts will prove in vain; impressions once received can never be erased. Liberty, that torch of intellect and warmth of life, was always and everywhere the attribute of peoples emerged from primitive ignorance. We are unable to live like our ancestors, like barbarians or slaves.

But even our ancestors, though less educated, enjoyed civil liberty. During the time of Tsar Aleksei Mikhailovich the National Assembly, including representatives of various classes of the people, still functioned and participated in important affairs of the State. In his reign five such Assemblies were summoned. Peter I, who killed everything national in the State, also stamped out our feeble liberty. This liberty disappeared outwardly but lived within the hearts of true citizens; its advancement was slow in our country. Wise Catherine II expanded it a little; Her Majesty inquired from the Petersburg Free Economic Society concerning the value and consequences of the emancipation of peasants in Russia. This great beneficial thought lived in the heart of the Empress, whom the people loved. Who among Russians of her day and time could have read her INSTRUCTION without emotion? The INSTRUCTION alone redeems all the shortcomings of that time, characteristic of that century.

Emperor Alexander promised us much; he, it could be said, enormously stirred the minds of the people toward the sacred rights of humanity. Later he changed his principles and intentions. The people became frightened, but the seed had sprouted and the roots grew deep. So rich with various revolutions are the latter half of the past century and the events of our own time that we have no need to refer to distant ones. We are witnesses of great events. The discovery of the New World and the United States, by virtue of its form of government, have forced Europe into rivalry with her. The United States will shine as an example even to distant generations. The name of Washington, the friend and benefactor of the people, will pass from generation to generation; the memory of his devotion to the welfare of the Fatherland will stir the hearts of citizens. In France the revolution which began so auspiciously turned, alas, at the end from a lawful into a criminal one. However, not the people but the court intrigues and politics were responsible for that. The revolution in France shook all the thrones of Europe and had a greater influence upon the governments and peoples than the establishment of the United States.

The dominance of Napoleon and the war of 1813 and 1814 united all the European nations, summoned by their monarchs and fired by the call to freedom and citizenship. By what means were countless sums collected among citizens? What guided the armies? They preached freedom to us in Manifestoes, Appeals, and in Orders! We were lured and, kindly by nature, we believed, sparing neither blood nor property. Napoleon was overthrown! The Bourbons were called back to the throne of France and, submitting to circumstances, gave that brave, magnanimous nation a constitution, pledging themselves to forget the past. The Monarchs united into a Holy Alliance; congresses sprang into existence, informing the nations that they were assembled to reconcile all classes and introduce political freedom. But the aim of these congresses was soon revealed; the nations learned how greatly they had been deceived. The Monarchs thought only of how to retain their unlimited power, to support their shattered thrones, and to extinguish the last spark of freedom and enlightenment.

Offended nations began to demand what belonged to them and had been promised to them—chains and prisons became their lot! Crowns transgressed their pledges, the constitution of France was violated at its very base. Manuel, the representative of the people, was dragged from the Chamber of Deputies by gendarmes! Freedom of the press was restricted, the army of France, against its own will, was sent to destroy the lawful liberty of Spain. Forgetting the oath given by Louis XVIII, Charles X compensates *émigrés* and for that purpose burdens the people with new taxes. The government interferes with the election of deputies, and in the last elections, among the deputies only thirty-three persons were not in the service and payment of the King, the rest being sold to the Ministers. The firm, courageous Spanish people at the cost of blood rose for the liberty of their country, saved the King, the Monarchy, and the honor of the Fatherland; of their own volition the people themselves received Ferdinand as King. The King took the oath to safeguard the rights of the people. As early as the year 1812, Alexander I recognized the constitution of Spain.

Then the Alliance itself assisted France by sending her troops, and thus aided in dishonoring her army in the invasion of Spain. Ferdinand, arrested in Cadiz, was sentenced to death. He summoned Riego, swore to be once more loyal to the constitution and to expel the French troops from his territory, and begged Riego to spare his life. Honest men are apt to be trustful. Riego gave guaranty to the Cortes for the King, and he was freed. And what was the first step of Ferdinand? By his order Riego was seized, arrested, poisoned and, half-alive, that saint-martyr hero who renounced the throne offered to him, friend of the people, savior of the King's life, by the King's order is now taken through the streets of Madrid in the shameful wagon pulled by a donkey, and is hanged like a criminal. What an act! Whose heart would not shudder at it? Instead of the promised liberty the nations of Europe found themselves oppressed and their educational facilities curtailed. The prisons of Piedmont, Sardinia, Naples, and, in general, of the whole of Italy and Germany were filled with chained citizens. The lot of the people became so oppressive that they began to regret the past and to bless the memory of Napoleon the conqueror! These are the incidents which enlightened their minds and made them realize that it was impossible to make agreements with Sovereigns. . . .

The story told to Your Excellency that, in the uprising of December 14 the rebels were shouting "Long live the Constitution!" and that the people were asking "What is Constitution, the wife of His Highness the Grand Duke?" is not true. It is an amusing invention. We knew too well the meaning of a constitution and we had a word that would equally stir the hearts of all classes—LIBERTY!

*　　*　　*

The events of December are calamitous for us and, of course, must be distressing to the Emperor. Yet the events of this date should be fortunate for His Imperial Highness. After all, it was necessary sometime for the Society to begin its activities, but hardly could it have been so precipitate as in this instance. I swear to God, I wish the kind Sovereign prosperity! May God aid him in healing the wounds of our Fatherland and to become a friend and benefactor of the people. . . .

Most obedient and devoted servant of Your Excellency.

PETER KAKHOVSKY

1826
February, 24th day

FROM A Letter of A. Bestuzhev to Nicholas I

Your Imperial Highness!

Convinced that You, Sovereign, love the truth, I dare to lay before You the historical development of free thinking in Russia and in general of many ideas which constitute the moral and political basis of the events of December 14. I shall speak in full frankness, without concealing evil, without even softening expressions, for the duty of a loyal subject is to tell his Monarch the truth without any embellishment. I commence.

The beginning of the reign of Emperor Alexander was marked with bright hopes for Russia's prosperity. The gentry had recuperated, the merchant class did not object to giving credit, the army served without making trouble, scholars studied what they wished, all spoke what they thought, and everyone expected better days. Unfortunately, circumstances prevented the realization of these hopes, which aged without their fulfillment. The unsuccessful, expensive war of 1807 and others disorganized our finances, though we had not yet realized it when preparing for the national war of 1812. Finally, Napoleon invaded Russia and then only, for the first time, did the Russian people become aware of their power; only then awakened in all our hearts a feeling of independence, at first political and finally national. That is the beginning of free thinking in Russia. The government itself spoke such words as "Liberty, Emancipation!" It had itself sown the idea of abuses resulting from the unlimited power of Napoleon, and the appeal of the Russian Monarch resounded on the banks of the Rhine and the Seine. The war was still on when the soldiers, upon their return home, for the first time disseminated grumbling among the masses. "We shed blood," they would say, "and then we are again forced to sweat under feudal obligations. We freed the Fatherland from the tyrant, and now we ourselves are tyrannized over by the ruling class." The army, from generals to privates, upon its return, did nothing but discuss how good it is in foreign lands. A comparison with their own country naturally brought up the question, Why should it not be so in our own land?

At first, as long as they talked without being hindered, it was lost in the air, for thinking is like gunpowder, only dangerous when pressed. Many cherished the hope that the Emperor would grant a constitution, as he himself had stated at the opening of the Legislative Assembly in Warsaw, and the attempt of some generals to free their serfs encouraged that sentiment. But after 1817 everything changed. Those who saw evil or who wished improvement, thanks to the mass of spies were forced to whisper about it, and this was the beginning of the secret societies. Oppression by the government of deserving officers irritated men's minds. Then the military men began to talk: "Did we free Europe in order to be ourselves placed in chains? Did we grant a constitution to France in order that we dare not talk about it, and did we buy at the price of blood priority among nations in order that we might be humiliated at home?" The destructive policy toward schools and the persecution of education forced us in utter despair to begin considering some important measures. And since the grumbling of the people, caused by exhaustion and the abuses of national and civil administrations, threatened bloody revolution, the Societies intended to prevent a greater evil by a lesser one and began their activities at the first opportunity. . . .

You, Sovereign, probably already know how we, inspired by such a situation in Russia and seeing the elements ready for change, decided to bring about a *coup d'élat.* . . . Here are the plans we had for the future. We thought of creating a Senate of the oldest and wisest Russian men of the present administration, for we thought that power and ambition would always have their attraction. Then we thought of having a Chamber of Deputies composed of national representatives. . . . For enlightenment of the lower classes we wished everywhere to establish Lancasterian schools. And in order to bring about moral improvement we thought of raising the standard of the clergy by granting to them a means of livelihood. Elimination of nearly all duties, freedom from distillation and road

improvement for the state, encouragement of agriculture and general protection of industry would result in satisfying the peasants. Assurance and stability would attract to Russia many resourceful foreigners. Factories would increase with the demand for commodities, while competition would stimulate improvement, which rises along with the prosperity of the people, for the need of commodities for life and luxury is constant. . . .

Most devoted servant of
Your Imperial Highness,
ALEXANDER BESTUZHEV

[no date]

FROM A Letter of V. Steingel to Nicholas I

. . . No matter how many members there may be found of the secret Society or those who had only known of it; no matter how many may be deprived of freedom on account of it, there still remain a great many people who share those ideas and sentiments. Russia is already so educated that even shopkeepers read newspapers and newspapers report what is said in the Chamber of Deputies in Paris. Is not the first thought to occur in everyone's mind, "Why cannot we discuss our rights?" The greater number of professors, literary men, and journalists have to adhere wholeheartedly to those who wish a constitutional government, for freedom of the press is to their personal advantage. So do booksellers and merchants. Finally, all those who were in foreign countries, and some who were educated there, and all those who served or serve now in the Guard hold the same opinions. Who of the young men, even somewhat educated, have not read and have not been fascinated with the works of Pushkin, which breathe freedom? Who has not cited the fables of Denis Davydov, such as his "Head and Feet"? Perhaps among those who have the fortune to surround Your Honor, there are such. Sovereign! In order to eradicate free thinking, there is no other means than to destroy an entire generation, born and educated in the last reign. But if this is impossible, there remains one thing—to win hearts

by kindness and attract minds by decisive and evident means toward the future prosperity of the state.

Most devoted,

BARON VLADIMIR IVANOV STEINGEL

January 11th day
1826

REVIEW QUESTIONS

1. What ideals and aims do the conspirators invoke
   to justify their rebellion?

2. How do the conspirators embed their revolt
   within the larger political sweep of the American and French revolutions? How do the wars
   against Napoleon in 1812–15 bear on their conduct? How do these accounts narrate the modern history of Russia since Catherine the Great?

3. For Kakhovksy, what is the proper political role
   for nineteenth-century monarchs? How have
   kings and tsars not fulfilled this function?

4. What social classes supported this rebellion?
   What does Steingel and the others tell us about
   the degree of politicization in Russian society?

ALEXIS DE TOCQUEVILLE

FROM *Democracy in America*

*Alexis Charles Henri Clerel de Tocqueville (1805–1859) ranks as one of the brilliant
political minds of the liberal era, a politician and writer who was among the first to
compare and systematize the liberal political systems of the postrevolutionary era.
Tocqueville balanced an active career as a magistrate and legislative deputy during the
July Monarchy (1830–1848) with extensive trips to the United States and Britain.
These trips allowed him to observe the customs and manners of two political systems
that differed significantly from France's inherited tradition of centralized authority.
His* Democracy in America *(1835) and* The Old Regime and the French Revolution
*(1856) are enduring works on the relationship of individual liberty and equality to
central and federal political power. Both combine pragmatic political experience with
a detached, analytical understanding of differing political systems and their respective benefits. His observations on the civic culture of democratic politics are evinced
in the following sections on political associations and freedom of the press from*
Democracy in America.

From *The World's Greatest Classics: Democracy in America,* by Alexis de Tocqueville, translated by Henry Reeve (New York: Colonial Press, 1989), pp. 182–85, 188, 191, 196–99.

*   *   *

Political Associations in the United States

In no country in the world has the principle of association been more successfully used, or more unsparingly applied to a multitude of different objects, than in America. Besides the permanent associations which are established by law under the names of townships, cities, and counties, a vast number of others are formed and maintained by the agency of private individuals. . . .

The most natural privilege of man, next to the right of acting for himself, is that of combining his exertions with those of his fellow-creatures, and of acting in common with them. I am therefore led to conclude that the right of association is almost as inalienable as the right of personal liberty. No legislator can attack it without impairing the very foundations of society. Nevertheless, if freedom of association is a fruitful source of advantages and prosperity to some nations, it may be perverted or carried to excess by others, and a source of vigor may be changed into one of destruction. A comparison of the different methods which associations pursue, in those countries in which they are managed with discretion, as well as in those where liberty degenerates into license, may perhaps be thought useful both to governments and to parties.

The greater part of Europeans look upon an association as a weapon which is to be hastily fashioned, and immediately tried in conflict. A society is formed for discussion, but the idea of impending action prevails in the minds of those who constitute it: it is, in fact, an army; and the time given to parley serves to reckon up the strength and to inspire the troops, after which they march against the enemy. Resources which lie within the bounds of the law may suggest themselves to the persons who compose it as means, but never as the only means, of success.

Such, however, is not the manner in which the right of association is understood in the United States. In America the citizens who form the minority associate, in order, in the first place, to show their numerical strength, and so to diminish the moral authority of the majority; and, in the second place, to stimulate competition, and to discover those arguments which are most fitted to act upon the majority: for they always entertain hopes of drawing over their opponents to their own side, and of afterwards disposing of the supreme power in their name. Political associations in the United States are therefore peaceable in their intentions, and strictly legal in the means which they employ; and they assert with perfect truth, that they only aim at success by lawful expedients.

The difference which exists between the Americans and ourselves depends on several causes. In Europe there are numerous parties so diametrically opposed to the majority, that they can never hope to acquire its support, and at the same time they think that they are sufficiently strong in themselves to struggle and to defend their cause. When a party of this kind forms an association, its object is, not to conquer, but to fight. In America, the individuals who hold opinions very much opposed to those of the majority are no sort of impediment to its power; and all other parties hope to win it over to their own principles in the end. The exercise of the right of association becomes dangerous in proportion to the impossibility which excludes great parties from acquiring the majority. In a country like the United States, in which the differences of opinion are mere differences of hue, the right of association may remain unrestrained without evil consequences. The inexperience of many of the European nations in the enjoyment of liberty, leads them only to look upon freedom of association as a right of attacking the Government. The first notion which presents itself to a party, as well as to an individual, when it has acquired a consciousness of its own strength, is that of violence: the notion of persuasion arises at a later period, and is only derived from experience. The English, who are divided into parties which differ most essentially from each other, rarely abuse the right of association, because they have long been accustomed to exercise it. In France, the passion for war is so intense that there is no undertaking so mad, or so injurious to the welfare of the State, that a man does not consider himself honoured in defending it, at the risk of his life.

But perhaps the most powerful of the causes which tend to mitigate the excesses of political association in the United States is universal suffrage. In countries in which universal suffrage exists, the majority is never doubtful, because neither party can pretend to represent that portion of the community which has not voted. The associations which are formed are aware, as well as the nation at large, that they do not represent the majority. This is, indeed, a condition inseparable from their existence, for if they did represent the preponderating power, they would change the law instead of soliciting its reform. The consequence of this is that the moral influence of the Government which they attack is very much increased, and their own power is very much enfeebled.

In Europe there are few associations which do not affect to represent the majority, or which do not believe that they represent it. This belief or pretence tends greatly to increase their power, and serves admirably to legitimate their actions. For what is more excusable than violence in a righteous cause against oppression? Thus it is, in the vast labyrinth of human laws, that extreme liberty sometimes corrects the abuses of license, and that extreme democracy obviates the dangers of democratic government. In Europe, associations consider themselves in some degree the legislative and executive councils of the people, which is unable to speak for itself. In America, where they only represent a minority of the nation, they argue and they petition.

The means which the associations of Europe employ are in accordance with the end which they propose to obtain. As the principal aim of these bodies is to act, and not to debate, to fight rather than to persuade, they are naturally led to adopt a form of organization which differs from the ordinary customs of civil bodies, and which assumes the habits and the maxims of military life. They centralize the direction of their resources as much as possible, and they entrust the power of the whole party to a very small number of leaders.

The members of these associations reply to a watchword, like soldiers on duty; they profess the doctrine of passive obedience, or rather in uniting together they at once abjure the exercise of their own judgment and free will. And the tyrannical control which these societies exercise, is often far more insupportable than the authority possessed over society by the Government which they attack. Their moral force is much diminished by these excesses. They lose the sacred quality which always characterises a struggle between oppressors and the oppressed. The man who in given cases consents to obey his fellows with servility, and who submits his actions and even his opinions to their control, can have no claim to rank as a free citizen.

The Americans have also established certain forms of government for their associations, but these are invariably borrowed from the forms of the civil administration. The independence of each individual is formally recognized. As in society at large, all the members work towards the same end, but they are not obliged to follow exactly the same track. No-one abjures the exercise of his reason and his free will; rather everyone exercises that reason and that will for the benefit of a common undertaking.

*   *   *

Freedom of the Press

There are certain nations which have peculiar reasons for cherishing the freedom of the press. For in certain countries which profess to enjoy the privileges of freedom, every individual agent of the Government may violate the laws with impunity, since those whom he oppresses cannot prosecute him before the courts of justice. In this case the freedom of the press is not merely a guarantee, but the *only* guarantee of their liberty and their security which the citizens possess. If the rulers of these nations proposed to abolish the independence of the press, the people would be justified in saying: Give us the right of prosecuting your offences before ordinary tribunals, and perhaps we may then waive our right of appeal to the tribunal of public opinion.

But in the countries in which the doctrine of the sovereignty of the people ostensibly prevails, the censorship of the press is not only dangerous, it is absurd. When the right of every citizen to cooperate in the government of society is acknowledged, every citizen must be presumed to possess the power of discriminating between the different opinions of his contemporaries, and of appreciating the different facts from which inferences may be drawn. The sovereignty of the people and the freedom of the press may therefore be looked upon as inseparable institutions; the censorship of the press and universal suffrage are two things which are irreconcileably opposed, and which cannot long be retained among the institutions of the same people. Not a single individual of the twelve millions who inhabit the territory of the United States has as yet dared to propose any restrictions to the liberty of the press. . . .

In France it is not uncommonly imagined that the virulence of the press originates in the uncertain social condition, in the political excitement, and the consequent sense of general malaise which prevail in that country; and it is therefore supposed that as soon as society has resumed a certain degree of composure, the press will abandon its present vehemence. I am inclined to think that these causes explain the extraordinary ascendency it has acquired over the nation, but that they do not exercise much influence upon the tone of its language. The periodical press appears to me to be actuated by passions and propensities independent of the circumstances in which it is placed; and the present position of America corroborates this opinion.

America is perhaps, at this moment, the country of the whole world which contains the fewest germs of revolution, but the press is no less destructive in its principles than in France, and it displays the same violence without the same reasons for indignation. In America, as in France, it constitutes a singular power, so strangely composed of mingled good and evil, that it is at the same time indispensable to the existence of freedom, and nearly incompatible with the maintenance of public order. Its power is certainly much greater in France than in the United States; though nothing is more rare in the latter country than to hear of a prosecution having been instituted against it. The reason for this is perfectly simple: the Americans having once accepted the doctrine of the sovereignty of the people, apply it with perfect consistency. They never intended to establish laws for all eternity on foundations which change from day to day. There is consequently nothing criminal in an attack upon the existing laws, provided it be not attended with a violent infraction of them. They are moreover of the opinion that Courts of Justice are unable to check the abuses of the press; and that as the subtlety of human language perpetually eludes the severity of judicial analysis, offences of this nature are apt to escape the hand which attempts to apprehend them. They hold that to act with efficacy upon the press, it would be necessary to find a tribunal not only devoted to the existing order of things, but capable of surmounting the influence of public opinion, a tribunal which should conduct its proceedings without publicity, which should pronounce its decrees without assigning its motives, and punish the intentions even more than the language of the author. Whoever had the power of creating and maintaining a tribunal of this kind would be wasting his time in prosecuting the liberty of the press, for he would be the supreme master of the whole community, and he would be as free to rid himself of the authors as of their writings. In this question, therefore, there is no middle way between servitude and extreme licence. In order to enjoy the inestimable benefits which the freedom of the press ensures, it is necessary to submit to the inevitable evils which it engenders. To expect to acquire the former, and to escape the latter, is to cherish one of those illusions which commonly mislead nations in their times of sickness, when, tired with faction and exhausted by effort, they attempt to combine hostile opinions and contrary opinions upon the same soil. . . .

The influence of the press upon America is immense. It is the power which impels the circulation of political life through all the districts of that vast territory. Its eye is constantly open to detect the secret springs of political designs, and to summon the leaders of all parties to the bar of public opinion. It rallies the interests of the community round certain principles, and it draws up the creed which factions adopt. It affords a means of intercourse between parties which hear, and which address each other, without ever having been in immediate contact. When a great number of the organs of the press adopt the same line of conduct, their influence becomes irresistible; and public opinion, when it is perpetually assailed from the same side, eventually yields to the attack. In the United States each separate journal exercises but little authority: but the power of the periodical press is only second to that of the people.

* * *

REVIEW QUESTIONS

1. Why does de Tocqueville find the right of association as important as rights of personal liberty?
2. According to de Tocqueville, what role do associations play for minority views?
3. How did French and American political associations differ?
4. Why is the press, for de Tocqueville, "indispensable to the existence of freedom"?
5. Why did de Tocqueville consider the power of the press greater in France than in the United States?

JOSEPH DE MAISTRE

"Of Monarchy"

The doctrine of popular sovereignty, representative government, and rights-bearing citizenship captured the imagination of Europeans and North Americans during the Age of Revolution, dealing a severe blow to the legitimacy of monarchy. During the 1790s, Joseph de Maistre (1753–1821), a civil servant of the Duchy of Savoy who fled French occupation in 1792, penned a series of brilliant polemics castigating the principles of democracy, thus fashioning a potent defense of monarchy and Catholic social conservatism. Following the restoration of dynastic rule in 1815, his essays served as an important ideological bulwark for conservatives who decried the inexorable spread of participatory politics. The following passage comes from a tract on popular sovereignty that took aim against Jean-Jacques Rousseau, the era's most influential advocate of democratic political equality.

From *Against Rousseau: "On the State of Nature" and "On the Sovereignty of People,"* by Joseph de Maistre, translated and edited by Richard A. Lebrun (Montreal: McGill-Queen's University Press, 1996), pp. 119–25, 128, 131–34.

One can say in general that all men are born for monarchy. This is the oldest and the most universal form of government. Before the time of Theseus, there was no question of a republic in the world. Democracy above all is so rare and so transient, that we are allowed not to take it into account. Monarchical government is so natural that, without realizing it, men identify it with sovereignty; they seem to be tacitly agreed

that there is no true *sovereign* wherever there is no king. I have given several examples of this that it would be easy to multiply.

This observation is especially striking with respect to all that has been said for and against the question that was the subject of the first book of this work. The adversaries of divine origin always hold a grudge against *kings* and talk only of *kings*. They do not want to believe that the authority of kings comes from God; but it is not a question of *kingship* in particular, but of *sovereignty* in general. Yes, all sovereignty comes God; under whatever form it exists, it is not the work of man. It is one, absolute, and inviolable by its nature. So why lay the blame on kingship, as if all the inconveniences on which they call to combat this system were not the same with any kind of *government?* Once again, it is because monarchy is the *natural government*, and in ordinary discourse men confuse it with sovereignty by disregarding other governments, just as they neglect the exception when enunciating the general rule.

On this subject I will observe that the common division of governments into three kinds, monarchy, aristocracy, and democracy, rests entirely on a Greek prejudice that took hold of the schools during the Renaissance, and which we have not known how to undo. The Greeks always saw the whole world in Greece; and as the three kinds of government were well enough balanced in that small country, the statesmen of that nation imagined the general division I have just mentioned. However if we want to be accurate, logical rigour will not permit us to establish a genre on one exception, and, to express ourselves accurately, we must say: "men in general are governed by kings. However, we see nations where sovereignty belongs to several persons, and such governments can be called aristocracy or democracy, according to THE NUMBER of persons who form THE SOVEREIGN."

It is always necessary to call men back to history, which is the first master in politics, or more exactly the only master. When it is said that men are born for liberty, this is a phrase that makes no sense. If a being of a higher order undertook the *natural history* of man, surely it is in the history of facts that he would look for direction. When he knows what man is, and what he has always been, what he does and what he has always done, he would write; and undoubtedly he would dismiss as folly the idea that man is not what he must be and that his state is contrary to the laws of creation. The mere statement of this proposition is sufficient to refute it.

History is experimental politics, that is to say, the only good politics; and just as in physics a hun-

dred volumes of speculative theories disappear before a single experiment, in the same way in political science no system can be admitted if it is not the more or less probable corollary of well attested facts. If one asks what is the government most natural to man, history is there to respond: *It is monarchy.*

This form of government undoubtedly has its drawbacks, like all others; but all the declamations that fill current books on these sorts of abuses are pitiful. They are born of pride, not reason. Once it is rigorously demonstrated that nations are not made for the same form of government, that each nation has that which is best for it, and above all that "freedom . . . is not accessible to all peoples, [and] the more one ponders this principle established by Montesquieu, the more one senses its truth," we can no longer understand the meaning of these dissertations on the vices of monarchical government. If their aim is to make the unfortunate people destined to suffer these abuses feel them more vividly, this is a most barbarous pastime; if their aim is to urge men to revolt against a government made for them, it is an indescribable crime.

*   *   *

Monarchy is a *centralized* aristocracy. At all times and in all places, the aristocracy commands. Whatever form is given to governments, birth and wealth always obtain the first rank, and nowhere do they rule more harshly than where their dominion is not founded on law. But in a monarchy, the king is the centre of this aristocracy; it is true that the aristocracy rules as elsewhere; but it rules in the king's name, or if you will, the king is guided by the knowledge of the aristocracy.

*   *   *

This observation is most just; it is far from true that the king's will does everything in a monarchy. It is *supposed* to do everything, and this is the great advantage of this government; but, in fact, it only serves to centralize counsel and enlightenment. Religion, laws, customs, opinion, and class and corporate privileges restrain the sovereign and prevent him from abusing his power; it is even quite remarkable that kings are much more often accused of lacking will than of abusing it. It is always the king's council that rules.

But the *pyramidal* aristocracy that administers the state in monarchies has particular characteristics that deserve all our attention.

In all countries and under all possible governments, the highest posts will always (save exceptions) belong to the aristocracy, that is to say to nobility and wealth, most often united. Aristotle, in saying that this *must be so*, enunciated a political axiom that simple good sense and the experience of centuries do not permit us to doubt. This privilege of aristocracy is really a natural law.

Now it is one of the great advantages of monarchical government that in it the aristocracy loses, as much as the nature of things permits, all that can be offensive to the lower classes. It is important to understand the reasons for this.

1. This kind of aristocracy is legal; it is an integral part of the government, everyone knows this, and it does not awaken in anyone's mind the idea of usurpation and injustice. In republics, on the contrary, distinctions between persons exist as in monarchies, but they are harsher and more insulting because they are not the work of the law, and because popular opinion regards them as a habitual insurrection against the principle of equality recognized by the Constitution.

There was perhaps as much distinction between persons, as much arrogance, as much *aristocracy* properly speaking, in Geneva as in Vienna. But what a difference in cause and effect!

2. Since the influence of a hereditary aristocracy is inevitable (the experience of every age leaves no doubt on his point), nothing better can be imagined to deprive this influence of what it can have that might be too tiresome for the pride of the lower classes than to remove all insurmountable barriers between families in the state, and to allow none to be humiliated by a distinction that they can never enjoy.

Now this is precisely the case in a monarchy founded on good laws. There is no family whose head's merit cannot raise it from the second to the first rank, and even independently of this flatter-

ing achievement and before the family acquires through time the influence that is its due, all the posts in the state, or at least many of them, are open to merit, which take the place of hereditary distinctions for the family, and moves it toward such distinctions.

This movement of general ascension that pushes all families towards the sovereign and that constantly replenishes all the voids that are left by those that die out, this movement, I say, involves a salutary emulation, animates the flame of honour, and turns all individual ambitions towards the good of the state.

3. This order of things appears still more perfect when one reflects that the aristocracy of birth and office, already rendered very gentle by the right that belongs to every family and to every individual to enjoy the same distinctions in turn, again loses all that it could have that is too offensive for the lower classes, by the universal supremacy of the monarch before whom no citizen is more powerful than another. The man of the people, who feels insignificant when he measures himself against a great lord, measures himself against the sovereign, and the title of *subject*, which submits both to the same power and the same justice, is a kind of equality that quiets the inevitable pangs of self-esteem.

Under these last two aspects, aristocratic government cedes to monarchy. In the latter, a unique family is separated from all the others by opinion, and is considered, or can be so considered, as belonging to another nature. The greatness of this family humiliates no one, because none can be compared to it. In the first case, on the contrary, sovereignty residing on the heads of several men does not make the same impression on minds, and individuals that chance has made members of the sovereign are great enough to excite envy, but not great enough to stifle it.

*   *   *

In general, even while agreeing that all the powers reside eminently on the head of kings, the European does not believe that they have the right personally to exercise any branch of the judicial power; and, in effect, they do not get involved in it.

Abuses in this regard prove nothing; universal conscience has always protested. Here is the great character of our governments' physiognomy. Each European monarchy no doubt has its own particular traits, and, for example, it would not be surprising to find a little *Arabism* in Spain and Portugal, but all these monarchies have a family style that brings them together, and one can say of them with the greatest truth:

. . . Facies non omnibus una;
Nec diversa tamen, qualem decet esse sororum.[1]

I will certainly not deny that Christianity has modified all these governments for the better, nor that the public law of Europe has been greatly improved by this salutary law; but it also necessary to notice our common origin and the general character of the northern peoples who replaced the Roman Empire in Europe.

*   *   *

Let us divest ourselves of all prejudice and party spirit, let us renounce exaggerated ideas and all the theoretical dreams arising from the French fever, and European good sense will agree on the following propositions:

1. The king is sovereign; no one shares sovereignty with him, and all powers emanate from him.

2. His person is inviolable; no one has the right to depose or judge him.

3. He does not have the right to condemn to death, nor even to any corporal punishment. The power that punishes derives from him, and that is enough.

4. If he inflicts exile or prison in cases where reasons of state can prevent a judicial hearing, he cannot be too cautious, nor should he act without the advice of an enlightened council.

5. The king cannot judge in civil cases; the magistrates alone, in the name of the sovereign, can pronounce on property and contracts.

6. By means of certain differently composed bodies, councils, or assemblies, subjects have the right to instruct the king about their needs, to denounce abuses to him, and legally to communicate to him their *grievances* and their *very humble* remonstrances.

It is in these sacred laws, the more truly constitutional in that they are written only in men's hearts, and more particularly in the paternal communication between prince and subjects, that we find the true character of European monarchy.

Whatever the exalted and blind pride of the eighteenth century has to say, this is all that we need. These elements, combined in different ways, produce an infinity of nuances in monarchical governments. One understands, for example, that the men charged with carrying the representations or the grievances of subjects to the foot of the throne can form *bodies* or *assemblies*, that the members who compose these assemblies or bodies can vary in number and rank, and in the nature and extent of their powers; that the method of election, the frequency and duration of sessions, etc., also vary the number of these combinations: *facies non omnibus una.*[2] But you will always find this same general character, that is to say, chosen men always legally carrying to the father the complaints and wishes of the family: *nec diversa tamen.*[3]

*   *   *

How many mistakes power has committed! And how often has it ignored the means to conserve itself! Man is insatiable for power; he is infinite in his desires, and, always discontented with what he has, he loves only what he has not. People complain about the despotism of princes; they should complain about that of *man.* We are all born despots, from the most absolute monarch of Asia to the child who smothers a bird with his hand for the pleasure of seeing something in the world weaker than himself. There is no man who does not abuse power, and experience proves that the most

---

[1] "They have not all the same appearance, and yet not altogether different: as it should be with sisters." Ovid *Metamorphoses* 2:13–14. Loeb.

[2] "They have not all the same experience." Ovid *Metamorphoses* 2:13, Loeb.

[3] "And yet not altogether different." Ibid., 2:14.

abominable despots, if they come to seize the sceptre, will be precisely those who rant against despotism. But the author of nature has put limits to the abuse of power: he has willed that it destroys itself once it exceeds its natural limits. He has engraved this law everywhere, and in the physical world as in the moral world, it surrounds us and speaks to us at every moment. Look at this firearm: up to a certain point, the more you lengthen it, the more you will increase its effect. But if you pass a certain limit, you will see the effect diminish. Look at this telescope: up to a certain point, the more you increase its dimensions, the more it will produce its effect; but beyond that, invincible nature will turn against you the efforts you make to improve the instrument. This is a natural image of power. To conserve itself it must restrain itself, and it must always avoid the point where its ultimate effort leads to its last moment.

Assuredly, I do not like *popular* assemblies better than anyone else; but French madness must not disgust us with the truth and wisdom to be found in a happy mean. If there is an incontestable maxim, it is that in all seditions, insurrections, and revolutions, *the people always begin by being right, and always end by being wrong*. It is false that every nation must have its *national assembly* in the French sense; it is false that every individual must be eligible for the national council; it is even false that he can be an elector without any distinction of rank or fortune; it is false that this council should be a co-legislator; finally, it is false that it must be composed in the same way in different countries. Because these exaggerated proposals are false, does it follow that no one has the right to speak for the common good in the name of the community, and that we are prohibited from being right because the French committed a great act of madness? I do not understand this consequence. What observer would not be frightened by the actual state of minds all over Europe? Whatever the cause of such a general impulse, it exists, and it menaces all sovereignties.

Certainly, it is the duty of statesmen to seek to ward off this storm; and certainly too they will not succeed by frightened immobility or by recklessness. It is up to the wise men of all nations to reflect profoundly on the ancient laws of monarchies, the *good customs* of each nation, and the general character of European peoples. It is in these sacred sources that they will find remedies appropriate to our misfortunes, and the wise means of regeneration infinitely removed from the absurd theories and exaggerated ideas that have done us so much harm.

The first and perhaps sole source of all the evils that we suffer is contempt for the old, or, what amounts to the same thing, contempt for experience; whereas *there is nothing better than what has been proved*, as Bossuet put it very well. The laziness and vain ignorance of this century accommodates itself much better to theories that cost nothing and that flatter pride, than to the lessons of moderation and obedience that it would have to learn painfully from history. In all the sciences, but especially in politics, whose numerous and changing elements are so difficult to seize in their entirety, theory is almost always contradicted by experience. May Eternal Wisdom shine its rays on men destined to rule the destiny of others! May the peoples of Europe also close their ears to the voice of sophists, and, turning their eyes from all theoretical illusions, fix them only on these venerable laws that are rarely written, and of which it is impossible to assign either dates or authors, and which the people have not made, but which have made peoples.

These laws come from God: the rest is human!

REVIEW QUESTIONS

1. How does history serve de Maistre's argument about sovereignty?
2. What is the relationship between the monarch and the aristocracy? Why would the lower classes benefit from this relationship?
3. What affinities does this argument share with Burke's defense of monarchy (see Chapter 18)?
4. For de Maistre, what are conservatism's checks against a monarch's abuse of power?
5. Why might de Maistre's conservatism appeal to certain European readers in the 1790s and throughout the nineteenth century?

PIERRE-JOSEPH PROUDHON

FROM *What is Property?*

Pierre-Joseph Proudhon, a printer by trade, was a prodigious autodidact who engaged the key political questions facing his generation. He was among a group of writers in the 1840s to move beyond the political dimensions of equality to consider the socioeconomic circumstances that framed the potentiality of freedom. His attack on the conventional notions of justice and equality turned on the radical claim that "property was theft," which he posited as the origin of poverty and other social inequities. The following passage introduces his famous pamphlet of 1840, which captures the era's polemical tone of philosophical journalism. The essay drew wide attention— provoking a critical rejoinder from a young Karl Marx—and sparked an international discussion about alternative forms of work and production to bring about social equality. Proudhon later espoused credit unions, collective land ownership, and forms of "mutualist" production, which provided a theoretical framework for the doctrine of anarchism. In its own time, however, "What is Property?" marked the intersection of political rights with the broader issues of social equality and freedom.

From *What is Property?*, by Pierre-Joseph Proudhon, edited and translated by Donald R. Kelley and Bonnie G. Smith (Cambridge, UK: Cambridge University Press, 1994), pp. 13–16, 27–34.

If I had to answer the following question, "What is slavery?" and if I should respond in one word, "It is murder," my meaning would be understood at once. I should not need a long explanation to show that the power to deprive a man of his thought, his will, and his personality is the power of life and death. So why to this other question, "What is property?" should I not answer in the same way, "It is theft," without fearing to be misunderstood, since the second proposition is only a transformation of the first?

I undertake to discuss the very principle of our government and of our institutions—namely, property: in this I am within my right. I may be wrong in the conclusion I draw from my research, but I am within my right. I want to place the last theme of my book first, and I am still within my right.

One author teaches that property is a civil right, based on occupation and sanctioned by law; another holds that it is a natural right, arising from labour; and these doctrines, though they seem opposed, are both encouraged and applauded. I contend that neither occupation nor labour nor law can create property, which is rather an effect without a cause. Am I to be censured for this?

But complaints arise: "Property is theft!" This is the battle-cry of '93, the signal for revolutions!

Reader, be reassured that I am not an agent of discord or an instigator of sedition. I anticipate history by a few days; I reveal the truth which we try in vain to inhibit; I write the preamble of our future constitution. This apparently blasphemous proposition—"Property is theft"—would, if our assumptions permitted us to understand it, be seen as a lightning-rod against the coming thunderbolt; but too many interests and prejudices stand in the way. Unfortunately, philosophy will not change the course of events, and destiny will be fulfilled despite prophecy. In any case must not justice be done and our education be completed?

"Property is theft!" ... What a revolution in human ideas! "Proprietor" and "thief" have always been as contradictory as the beings to which they refer are antagonistic, and all languages have preserved this opposition. On what authority, then, would you attack this universal agreement and make liars of the human race? Who are you to reject the judgement of nations throughout the ages?

*   *   *

So, reader, disregard my title and character and attend only to my reasons. It is on the basis of universal agreement that I claim to correct universal error; it is to the faith in the human race that I appeal against the opinion of the human race. Have the courage to follow me; and if your will is free, your conscience is clear, and your mind able to combine two propositions to form a third, my ideas will inevitably become yours. In beginning by offering you my last word, I have wanted to warn, not defy you; for I am sure that, if you read me, you will be forced to agree. The things I speak of are so simple and so evident that you will be astonished at not having perceived them before, and you will say, "I never thought about it." Others offer you the spectacle of a genius wresting nature's secrets from her and revealing her sublime oracular messages; here you will find only a series of experiments about *justice* and *right*, a sort of verification of the weights and measures of your conscience. The operations will be conducted before your very eyes, and you alone will judge the result.

Moreover I establish no system. I merely ask an end to privilege, the abolition of slavery, the equality of rights, and the rule of law. Justice, nothing but justice, that is the sum of my argument; I leave to others the task of governing the world.

One day I asked myself: why is there so much sorrow and poverty in the world? Must people always be unhappy? I am not satisfied with the various explanations given by reformers, some blaming the general distress on the cowardice and incompetence of those in power, some on conspirators and trouble-makers, and others on ignorance and general corruption; and weary of the endless quarrels of the politicians and the press, I have wanted to investigate the matter for myself. I have consulted the masters of science, and I have read a hundred volumes of philosophy, law, political economy, and history: would to God that I lived in an age when so much reading was unnecessary. I have made every effort to obtain exact information, comparing doctrines, responding to objections, incessantly making equations and deductions, and weighing thousands of syllogisms on the scales of the most rigorous logic. In the course of this laborious effort I have collected many interesting facts, which I shall share with my friends and the public as soon as I have the leisure. But I must say, I recognised from the first that we have never understood the meaning of these common as well as sacred words: *justice, equality, liberty*; that in each case our ideas have been deeply obscure; and that this ignorance has been the sole cause both of the poverty that devours us and of all the calamities that have afflicted the human race.

*   *   *

Yes, all men believe and repeat that the equality of conditions is identical with the equality of rights, that "property" and "theft" are synonyms, that every social advantage accorded, or rather usurped under pretext of superiority of talent and service, is iniquity and robbery: all men attest these truths in their heart, I say; it remains only for them to understand them.

*   *   *

The spirit that produced the movement of '89 was a spirit of contradiction; this suffices to show that the new order of things that was substituted for the old was neither methodical nor well conceived; that, born of anger and hatred, it could not have the effect of a science based on observation and study; that its foundations, in a word, were not derived from a profound knowledge of the laws of nature and society. Thus it was seen in the so-called new institutions that the Republic was acting on the very principles that people had opposed and on all the prejudices they had intended to abolish. We congratulate ourselves, with ill-considered enthusiasm, on the glorious French Revolution, the regeneration of 1789, the great reforms that have been effected, and the change in institutions—a delusion, a delusion!

When our ideas on any subject, material, intellectual, or social, are completely transformed because of observations which we have made, I call this movement of the mind a "revolution." If there is merely a widening or modification of our ideas, this is only "progress." Thus the system of Ptolemy represented progress in astronomy, that of Copernicus was a revolution. Similarly, in 1789 there was struggle and progress, but of revolution there was none. An examination of the attempted reforms shows this.

The people, so long a victim of monarchical selfishness, hoped to deliver themselves forever by declaring that they alone were sovereign. But what was monarchy? The sovereignty of one man. What is democracy? The sovereignty of the nation, or rather of the national majority. But the sovereignty of man has always been put in the place of the sovereignty of the law, the sovereignty of will in the place of the sovereignty of reason; in one word, the passions in the place of justice. No doubt when a nation passes from the monarchical to the democratic state, there is progress, because in multiplying the sovereigns we increase the chances of substituting reason for will; but in the end there is no revolution in the government because the principle remains the same. Now, we have proof today that with the most perfect democracy we still cannot be free.[1]

Nor is that all. The people-king cannot exercise sovereignty itself; it is obliged to delegate sovereignty to agents. This is constantly reiterated by those who seek to win its favour. What does it matter whether there are five, ten, a hundred, or a thousand agents, what difference does the number and name make? It is always the government of man, the rule of will and caprice. I ask what has this pretended revolution revolutionised?

We know, too, how this sovereignty was exercised, first by the Convention, then by the Directory, then later taken over by the Consul. As for the Emperor, the strong man so much adored and mourned by the nation, he never wanted to be dependent on it; but, as if intending to defy this, he dared to demand that it be put to a vote, that is, to demand abdication of this inalienable sovereignty; and he succeeded.

But what is sovereignty? It is, they say, "the power to make laws."[2] Another absurdity, a relic of despotism. The people had long seen kings issuing their commands in this form: "for such is our pleasure"; they wished to taste in their turn the pleasure of making laws. For fifty years the nation has brought these forth in profusion—always, of course, through the agency of representatives. And the game is far from over.

The definition of sovereignty was derived from the definition of law. The law, it was said, is "the expression of the will of the sovereign," so that under a monarchy the law is the expression of the will of the king, and in a republic the law is the expression of the will of the people. Except for the difference in the number of wills, the two systems are exactly the same: both share the same error, namely, that the law is the expression of will, whereas it should be the expression of fact. Moreover they followed good leaders: they took the citizen of Geneva [Rousseau] for their prophet and the *Social Contract* for their *Koran*.

Bias and prejudice are revealed at every point of the new legislators' arguments. The people had suffered from a multitude of exclusions and privileges; their representatives made the following declaration on the people's behalf: "All men are equal by nature and before the law," an ambiguous and redundant statement. "Men are equal by nature": does this mean that they are equal in size, beauty,

---

[1] See De Tocqueville, *De la démocratie aux Etats-Unis*, and Michel Chevalier, *Lettres sur l'Amérique du Nord*. We see in Plutarch's *Life of Pericles* that in Athens honest people were obliged to conceal themselves while studying, for fear of appearing to aspire for office.

[2] "Sovereignty," according to Toullier [*Le Droit civil français suivant l'ordre du Code* (Paris, 1839; 5th edn), 1, 19], if sovereignty is anything, it is a *right*, not a *force* or a *faculty*. And what is human omnipotence?

talents, and virtue? No; what was meant, then, was political and civil equality. So it would have been enough to say: "All men are equal before the law."

But what is equality before the law? Neither the constitution of 1790, that of '93, the granted Charter [of 1814], nor the accepted Charter [1815] have been able to define it. All assume an inequality in fortune and status incompatible with even a shadow of equality in rights. . . .

*　　*　　*

The people finally legalised property. God forgive them, for they knew not what they did. For fifty years they have paid for their miserable folly. But how did the people—whose voice, they say, is the voice of God and whose conscience is infallible—how did the people come to err? How, seeking liberty and equality, have they fallen back into privilege and servitude? Always by imitating the old regime.

Formerly, the nobility and the clergy contributed towards the expenses of the state only by voluntary aid and gifts—their property could not be seized even for debt—while the commoner, overwhelmed by taxes [*tailles*] and statute labour [*corvées*], was incessantly tormented, first by the king's tax-collectors and then by those of the nobles and clergy. One whose possessions were subject to mortmain could neither bequeath nor inherit property; he was treated like the animals, whose services and offspring belong to their master by right of accession. The people wanted the conditions of ownership to be alike for all; they thought that every one should "enjoy and freely dispose of his goods, his income, and the fruit of his labour and industry." The people did not invent property; but since they did not have the same privileges in regard to it that the nobles and clergy possessed, they proclaimed the uniformity of this right. The harsher forms of property—statute-labour, mortmain, *maîtrise*, and exclusion from public office—have disappeared; the conditions of its enjoyment have been modified, but the principle still remains the same. There has been progress in the regulation of the right, but there has been no revolution.

*　　*　　*

Is the authority of man over man just?

Everyone answers, "No, the authority of man is only the authority of the law, which ought to be justice and truth." The private will counts for nothing in government, which consists first in discovering what is true and just in order to make the law, and second in supervising the execution of this law. I do not now ask whether our constitutional form of government fulfills these conditions—whether, for example, the will of the ministry never influences the declaration and interpretation of the law, or whether our deputies, in their debates, are more intent on succeeding by argument rather than by force of numbers—it is enough for me that my definition of a good government should be correct. This idea is true. Yet we see that nothing seems more just to the oriental peoples than the despotism of their sovereigns; that with the ancients and in the opinion even of the philosophers, slavery was just; that in the middle ages the nobles, the priests, and the bishops felt justified in having serfs; that Louis XIV thought that he was right when he said, "The state! I am the state"; and that Napoleon regarded it as treason to oppose his will. The idea of justice, then, as applied to sovereignty and government, has not always been what it is today; it has gone on incessantly developing and defining itself by degrees, until it has arrived at its present state. But has it reached its last stage? I think not: seeing that the last obstacle to be overcome arises from the institution of property which we have kept intact, we must, in order to finish the reform in government and consummate the revolution, attack this very institution.

Is political and civil inequality just? Some say yes; others, no. To the first I would reply that, when the people abolished all privileges of birth and caste, they probably did it because it was for their benefit; why then do they favour the privileges of fortune more than those of rank and birth? It is, they say, because political inequality is a result of property and that without property society is impossible. Thus the question just raised is reduced to a question of property. To the second I content myself with this observation: if you want to enjoy political equality, abolish property; otherwise, why do you complain?

Is property just? Everybody answers without hesitation, "Yes, property is just." I say everybody, for up to the present no one has, with full understanding of the matter, answered no. It is no easy thing to make an intelligent response to this question; only time and experience can furnish an answer. Now the solution is at hand, and it is for us to understand it. I shall try to demonstrate it.

Here is the way in which we shall proceed with this demonstration:

I. We do not dispute, we refute nobody, we contest nothing; we accept as sound all the reasons alleged in favour of property and confine ourselves to a search for its principle in order that we may then determine whether this principle is faithfully expressed by property. In fact, property being defensible on no ground except that of justice, the idea, or at least the intention, of justice must of necessity underlie all the arguments that have been made in defence of property; and as on the other hand the right of property is only exercised over those things which can be appreciated by the senses, justice, secretly objectifying itself, so to speak, must be presented as an algebraic formula. By this method of investigation, we will soon see that every imaginable argument made on behalf of property, no matter what it may be, always and necessarily leads to equality, that is, to the negation of property.

* * *

A defender of equality, I shall speak without bitterness and without anger, with the independence becoming a philosopher, and with the courage and firmness of a free man. May I, in this momentous struggle, carry into all hearts the light with which I am filled and show, by the success of my argument, that equality failed to conquer by the sword only that it might conquer by the pen!

REVIEW QUESTIONS

1. Why is property the root of most of society's ills? How is property linked to justice and political equality?
2. How does Proudhon criticize the course of the French Revolution? Why was it insufficient?
3. How does this argument envision society, government, and political participation without the institution of private property?
4. How does this argument about property affect the doctrines of liberalism and democracy? Why is the discussion of social equality troublesome for liberals and radicals?

SIMÓN BOLÍVAR

FROM "The Jamaica Letter"

Constitutional republicanism, redefined for the modern era by the United States (1787) and France (1792), found fertile soil in Latin America. Following Napoleon's invasion of Spain in 1809, an independence movement arose that sought to liberate Spanish America from its colonial status. At the head of this movement stood Simón Bolívar, the son of a wealthy Venezuelan aristocrat, who as a young man visited Europe and became conversant with rationalist and enlightened thought. Between 1809 and 1825, as a general and statesman, Bolívar organized revolutions against Spanish rule, establishing independence in territories that are now Venezuela,

*Colombia, Ecuador, Panama, Peru, and Bolivia. In recognition of Bolívar's monu-
mental contribution, these countries bestowed upon Bolívar the title of* Libertador,
*and Bolivia named itself after him. The following letter, written in exile following a
military defeat in 1815, offers Bolívar's grievances against Spain and his inspiring,
nuanced vision of independent, republican government for South America.*

From *The Liberator, Simón Bolívar*, edited by David Bushnell (New York: Alfred A. Knopf, 1970), pp. 11–19.

. . . We are a young people. We inhabit a world apart, separated by broad seas. We are young in the ways of almost all the arts and sciences, although, in a certain manner, we are old in the ways of civilized society. I look upon the present state of America as similar to that of Rome after its fall. Each part of Rome adopted a political system conforming to its interest and situation or was led by the individual ambitions of certain chiefs, dynasties, or associations. But this important difference exists: those dispersed parts later reestablished their ancient nations, subject to the changes imposed by circumstances or events. But we scarcely retain a vestige of what once was; we are, moreover, neither Indian nor European, but a species midway between the legitimate proprietors of this country and the Spanish usurpers. In short, though Americans by birth we derive our rights from Europe, and we have to assert these rights against the rights of the natives, and at the same time we must defend ourselves against the invaders. This places us in a most extraordinary and involved situation. Notwithstanding that it is a type of divination to predict the result of the political course which America is pursuing, I shall venture some conjectures which, of course, are colored by my enthusiasm and dictated by rational desires rather than by reasoned calculations.

The role of the inhabitants of the American hemisphere has for centuries been purely passive. Politically they were nonexistent. We are still in a position lower than slavery, and therefore it is more difficult for us to rise to the enjoyment of freedom. Permit me these transgressions in order to establish the issue. States are slaves because of either the nature or the misuse of their constitutions; a people is therefore enslaved when the government, by its nature or its vices, infringes on and usurps the rights of the citizen or subject. Applying these principles, we find that America was denied not only its freedom but even an active and effective tyranny. Let me explain. Under absolutism there are no recognized limits to the exercise of governmental powers. The will of the great sultan, khan, bey, and other despotic rulers is the supreme law, carried out more or less arbitrarily by the lesser pashas, khans, and satraps of Turkey and Persia, who have an organized system of oppression in which inferiors participate according to the authority vested in them. To them is entrusted the administration of civil, military, political, religious, and tax matters. But, after all is said and done, the rulers of Ispahan are Persians; the viziers of the Grand Turk are Turks; and the sultans of Tartary are Tartars. China does not bring its military leaders and scholars from the land of Genghis Khan, her conqueror, notwithstanding that the Chinese of today are the lineal descendants of those who were reduced to subjection by the ancestors of the present-day Tartars.

How different is our situation! We have been harassed by a conduct which has not only deprived us of our rights but has kept us in a sort of permanent infancy with regard to public affairs. If we could at least have managed our domestic affairs and our internal administration, we could have acquainted ourselves with the processes and mechanics of public affairs. We should also have enjoyed a personal consideration, thereby commanding a certain unconscious respect from the people, which is so necessary to preserve amidst revolutions. That is why I say we have even been deprived of an active tyranny, since we have not been permitted to exercise its functions.

Americans today, and perhaps to a greater extent than ever before, who live within the Spanish system occupy a position in society no better than that of serfs destined for labor, or at best they have no more status than that of mere consumers. Yet even this status is surrounded with galling restrictions, such as being forbidden to grow European crops, or to store products which are royal monopolies, or to establish factories of a type the Peninsula itself does not possess. To this add the exclusive trading privileges, even in articles of prime necessity, and the barriers between American provinces, designed to prevent all exchange of trade, traffic, and understanding. In short, do you wish to know what our future held?—simply the cultivation of the fields of indigo, grain, coffee, sugar cane, cacao, and cotton: cattle raising on the broad plains; hunting wild game in the jungles: digging in the earth to mine its gold—but even these limitations could never satisfy the greed of Spain. So negative was our existence that I can find nothing comparable in any other civilized society. . . .

As I have just explained, we were cut off and, as it were, removed from the world in relation to the science of government and administration of the state. We were never viceroys or governors, save in the rarest of instances; seldom archbishops and bishops; diplomats never; as military men, only subordinates: as nobles, without royal privileges. In brief, we were neither magistrates nor financiers and seldom merchants—all in flagrant contradiction to our institutions.

*   *   *

The first steps of all the new governments are marked by the establishment of juntas of the people. These juntas speedily draft rules for the calling of congresses, which produce great changes. Venezuela erected a democratic and federal government, after declaring for the rights of man. A system of checks and balances was established; and

general laws were passed granting civil liberties, such as freedom of the press and others. In short, an independent government was created. New Granada uniformly followed the political institutions and reforms introduced by Venezuela, taking as the fundamental basis of her constitution the most elaborate federal system ever to be brought into existence. . . .

*   *   *

It is harder, Montesquieu has written, to release a nation from servitude than to enslave a free nation. This truth is proven by the annals of all times, which reveal that most free nations have been put under the yoke, but very few enslaved nations have recovered their liberty. Despite the convictions of history. South Americans have made efforts to obtain liberal, even perfect, institutions, doubtless out of that instinct to aspire to the greatest possible happiness, which, common to all men, is bound to follow in civil societies founded on the principles of justice, liberty, and equality. But are we capable of maintaining in proper balance the difficult charge of a republic? Is it conceivable that a newly emancipated people can soar to the heights of liberty, and, unlike Icarus, neither have its wings melt nor fall into an abyss? Such a marvel is inconceivable and without precedent. There is no reasonable probability to bolster our hopes.

*   *   *

I do not favor American monarchies. My reasons are these: The well-understood interest of a republic is limited to the matter of its preservation, prosperity, and glory. Republicans, because they do not desire powers which represent a directly contrary viewpoint, have no reason for expanding the boundaries of their nation to the detriment of their own resources solely for the purpose of having their neighbors share a liberal constitution. They would not acquire rights or secure any advantage by conquering their neighbors unless they were to make them colonies, conquered territory, or allies, after the example of Rome. But such thought and action are directly contrary to the principles of justice which characterize republican systems; and, what is more, they are in direct opposition to the interests of their citizens, because a state, too large of itself or together with its dependencies, ultimately falls into decay. Its free government becomes a tyranny. The principles that should preserve the government are disregarded, and finally it degenerates into despotism. The distinctive feature of small republics is permanence: that of large republics varies, but always with a tendency toward empire. Almost all small republics have had long lives. Among the larger republics, only Rome lasted for several centuries, for its capital was a republic. The rest of her dominions were governed by divers laws and institutions.

The policy of a king is very different. His constant desire is to increase his possessions, wealth, and authority; and with justification, for his power grows with every acquisition, both with respect to his neighbors and his own vassals, who fear him because his power is as formidable as his empire, which he maintains by war and conquest. For these reasons I think that the Americans, being anxious for peace, science, art, commerce, and agriculture, would prefer republics to kingdoms. And, further, it seems to me that these desires conform with the aims of Europe.

We know little about the opinions prevailing in Buenos Aires, Chile, and Peru. Judging by what seeps through and by conjecture, Buenos Aires will have a central government in which the military, as a result of its internal dissensions and external wars, will have the upper hand. Such a constitutional system will necessarily degenerate into an oligarchy or a monocracy, with a variety of restrictions the exact nature of which no one can now foresee. It would be unfortunate if this situation were to follow because the people there deserve a more glorious destiny.

The Kingdom of Chile is destined, by the nature of its location, by the simple and virtuous character of its people, and by the example of its neighbors, the proud republicans of Arauco,[1] to enjoy the blessings that flow from the just and gentle laws of a republic. If any American republic is to have a long life, I am inclined to believe it will be Chile. There the spirit of liberty has never been extinguished; the vices of Europe and Asia arrived too late or not at all to corrupt the customs of that distant corner of the world. Its area is limited; and, as it is remote from other peoples, it will always remain free from contamination. Chile will not alter her laws, ways, and practices. She will preserve her uniform political and religious views. In a word, it is possible for Chile to be free.

Peru, on the contrary, contains two factors that clash with every just and liberal principle: gold and slaves. The former corrupts everything; the latter are themselves corrupt. The soul of a serf can seldom really appreciate true freedom. Either he loses his head in uprisings or his self-respect in chains. Although these remarks would be applicable to all America, I believe that they apply with greater justice to Lima, for the reasons I have given and because of the cooperation she has rendered her masters against her own brothers, those illustrious sons of Quito. Chile, and Buenos Aires. It is plain that he who aspires to obtain liberty will at least attempt to secure it. I imagine that in Lima the rich will not tolerate democracy, nor will the freed slaves and *pardos* accept aristocracy. The former will prefer the tyranny of a single man, to avoid the tumult of rebellion and to provide, at least, a peaceful system. If Peru intends to recover her independence, she has much to do.

From the foregoing, we can draw these conclusions: The American provinces are fighting for their freedom, and they will ultimately succeed. Some provinces as a matter of course will form federal and some central republics: the larger areas will inevitably establish monarchies, some of which will fare so badly that they will disintegrate in either present or future revolutions. To consolidate a great monarchy will be no easy task, but it will be utterly impossible to consolidate a great republic.

It is a grandiose idea to think of consolidating the New World into a single nation, united by pacts into a single bond. It is reasoned that, as these parts have a common origin, language, customs, and religion, they ought to have a single government to

---

[1] The Araucanian Indians of southern Chile never fell to Spanish rule. [Editor]

permit the newly formed states to unite in a confederation. But this is not possible. Actually, America is separated by climatic differences, geographic diversity, conflicting interests, and dissimilar characteristics. How beautiful it would be if the Isthmus of Panama could be for us what the Isthmus of Corinth was for the Greeks! Would to God that some day we may have the good fortune to convene there an august assembly of representatives of republics, kingdoms, and empires to deliberate upon the high interests of peace and war with the nations of the other three-quarters of the globe. This type of organization may come to pass in some happier period of our regeneration. But any other plan, such as that of Abbé St. Pierre, who in laudable delirium conceived the idea of assembling a European congress to decide the fate and interests of those nations, would be meaningless.

Among the popular and representative systems, I do not favor the federal system. It is overperfect, and it demands political virtues and talents far superior to our own. For the same reason I reject a monarchy that is part aristocracy and part democracy, although with such a government England has achieved much fortune and splendor. Since it is not possible for us to select the most perfect and complete form of government, let us avoid falling into demagogic anarchy or monocratic tyranny. These opposite extremes would only wreck us on similar reefs of misfortune and dishonor; hence, we must seek a mean between them. I say: Do not adopt the best system of government but the one that is most likely to succeed.

*   *   *

REVIEW QUESTIONS

1. What are Bolívar's grievances against Spain?
2. How does Bolívar characterize the political state of Latin America and its peoples?
3. What advice does Bolívar offer for the future of political reform in Latin America?

THE READING SOCIETY (1843)   JOHANN PETER HASENCLEVER

In this canvas, Johann Peter Hasenclever (1810–1853) depicts an early nineteenth-century reading society in Germany. These clubs provided members with an array of newspapers from throughout Europe, enabling middle-class men to inform themselves of world affairs. Contemporaries typically viewed such associations as incubators for participatory politics and liberal reforms. But here the artist gently satirizes this claim. What moods and attributes are evoked in this sedentary atmosphere? Do these newspaper readers express an urgent active citizenship or a complacent passivity? By mingling political news with the leisure activities of food, drink, and chess, what opinion is the artist conveying about this social group?

PERCY BYSSHE SHELLEY

"Feelings of a Republican on the Fall of Bonaparte," "Song to the Men of England," and "England in 1819"

Percy Bysshe Shelley (1792–1822) was a preeminent poet of English Romanticism whose idealistic sensibility toward radical democracy and social justice exemplify central strains of the Age of Revolution. Shelley was one among many Romantic poets who transformed verse into a central medium for emancipatory politics. Through friends and family, Shelley came into close contact with English radical politics, and Shelley's veneration of the common man and his philosophic meditations for a better future disclose his affinity with republicanism. The following three poems evince the power of verse to castigate Napoleon, a modern political tyrant; celebrate the common Englishman and rouse him from his political somnolence; and, finally, scorn the political order of England in 1819 after the Peterloo Massacre. The latter refers to the deaths of innocent demonstrators who had assembled on St. Peter's field outside Manchester in August 1819 to petition for suffrage and employment. In response, local authorities ordered an army cavalry to charge the peaceful protesters, killing around a dozen and injuring hundreds.

From *The Poetical Works of Percy Bysshe Shelley*, vol. III, edited by Mrs. Shelley (London: Edward Moxon, 1839), pp. 14, 186–87, 193.

Feelings of a Republican on the Fall of Bonaparte

I hated thee, fallen tyrant! I did groan
To think that a most unambitious slave,
Like thou; shouldst dance and revel on the
　　grave
Of Liberty. Thou mightst have built thy throne
5　Where it had stood even now: thou didst prefer
A frail and bloody pomp which Time has swept
In fragments towards oblivion. Massacre,
For this I prayed, would on thy sleep have
　　crept,
Treason and Slavery, Rapine, Fear, and Lust,
10　And stifled thee, their minister. I know
Too late, since thou and France are in the dust,

That Virtue owns a more eternal foe
Than Force or Fraud: old Custom, legal
　　Crime,
And bloody Faith the foulest birth of Time.

Song to the Men of England

Men of England, wherefore plough
For the lords who lay ye low?
Wherefore weave with toil and care
The rich robes your tyrants wear?

5　Wherefore feed, and clothe, and save,
From the cradle to the grave,
Those ungrateful drones who would
Drain your sweat—nay, drink your blood?

Wherefore, bees of England, forge
10 Many a weapon, chain, and scourge,
That these stingless drones may spoil
The forced produce of your toil.

Have ye leisure, comfort, calm,
Shelter, food, love's gentle balm?
15 Or what is it ye buy so dear
With your pain and with your fear?

The seed ye sow, another reaps;
The wealth ye find, another keeps;
The robes ye weave, another wears;
20 The arms ye forge, another bears.

Sow seed,—but let no tyrant reap;
Find wealth,—let no impostor heap;
Weave robes,—let not the idle wear;
Forge arms,—in your defence to bear.

25 Shrink to your cellars, holes, and cells;
In halls ye deck, another dwells.
Why shake the chains ye wrought? Ye see
The steel ye tempered glance on ye.

With plough and spade, and hoe and loom,
30 Trace your grave, and build your tomb,
And weave your winding sheet, till fair
England be your sepulchre.

England in 1819

An old, mad, blind, despised, and dying king;[1]
Princes, the dregs of their dull race, who flow
Through public scorn—mud from a muddy
    spring;
Rulers who neither see, nor feel, nor know,

---

[1] George III, King of England (1760–1820).

5 But leech-like to their fainting country cling,
Till they drop, blind in blood, without a blow;
A people starved and stabbed in the untilled
    field;
An army, which liberticide and prey
Makes as a two-edged sword to all who wield;
10 Golden and sanguine laws which tempt and
    slay;
Religion Christless, Godless—a book sealed;
A Senate—Time's worst statute unrepealed,—
Are graves, from which a glorious Phantom
    may
Burst to illumine our tempestuous day.

REVIEW QUESTIONS

1. What is Shelley's charge against Napoleon? What does he mean when stating that "Virtue" has a "more eternal foe"? What does this poem tell us about the ideological landscape of Europe in 1815?

2. What is the tone of "Song to the Men of England"? How does the poem characterize the country's political order and what is the implied course of action?

3. What social, religious, and political criticisms of English rule can you identify in "England in 1819"? How does Shelley resolve this angry poem?

4. Judging from these three poems, why was poetry a central form of political communication for liberal and democratic politics? What can verse achieve that prose cannot? What does the popularity of political verse in the early nineteenth century tell us about the age?

JOHN STUART MILL

FROM *On Liberty*

In 1859 John Stuart Mill (1806–1873) presented to Victorian society his now classic statement on individual freedom, On Liberty. *Mill, however, should not be mistaken for a typical liberal. He not only abandoned classical economic theory early in his career, advocating certain forms of government regulation, but also foresaw the moral necessity of extending the vote to workers and women. Yet he continued to harbor distrust of state authority and governments' ability to guarantee the rights of minorities. His statements on individual liberty, freedom of opinion, and limits of authority over the individual are critical to the canon of liberal political philosophy.*

From *On Liberty*, by John Stuart Mill, edited by David Spitz (New York: Norton, 1975).

Chapter I
Introductory

The subject of this Essay is not the so-called Liberty of the Will so unfortunately opposed to the misnamed doctrine of Philosophical Necessity; but Civil, or Social Liberty: the nature and limits of the power which can be legitimately exercised by society over the individual. A question seldom stated, and hardly ever discussed, in general terms, but which profoundly influences the practical controversies of the age by its latent presence, and is likely soon to make itself recognised as the vital question of the future. It is so far from being new, that, in a certain sense, it has divided mankind, almost from the remotest ages; but in the stage of progress into which the more civilised portions of the species have now entered, it presents itself under new conditions, and requires a different and more fundamental treatment.

The struggle between Liberty and Authority is the most conspicuous feature in the portions of history with which we are earliest familiar, particularly in that of Greece, Rome, and England. But in old times this contest was between subjects, or some classes of subjects, and the Government. By

liberty, was meant protection against the tyranny of the political rulers. The rulers were conceived (except in some of the popular governments of Greece) as in a necessarily antagonistic position to the people whom they ruled. They consisted of a governing One, or a governing tribe or caste, who derived their authority from inheritance or conquest, who, at all events, did not hold it at the pleasure of the governed, and whose supremacy men did not venture, perhaps did not desire, to contest, whatever precautions might be taken against its oppressive exercise. Their power was regarded as necessary, but also as highly dangerous; as a weapon which they would attempt to use against their subjects, no less than against external enemies. To prevent the weaker members of the community from being preyed upon by innumerable vultures, it was needful that there should be an animal of prey stronger than the rest, commissioned to keep them down. But as the king of the vultures would be no less bent upon preying on the flock than any of the minor harpies, it was indispensable to be in a perpetual attitude of defence against his beak and claws. The aim, therefore, of patriots was to set limits to the power which the ruler should be suffered to exercise over the community; and this limitation was what they meant by liberty. It was attempted in two ways. First, by obtaining a recognition of certain immunities, called political liberties or rights, which it was to be regarded as a breach of duty in the ruler to infringe, and which if he did infringe, specific resistance, or general rebellion, was held to be justifiable. A second, and generally a later expedient, was the establishment of constitutional checks, by which the consent of the community, or of a body of some sort, supposed to represent its interests, was made a necessary condition to some of the more important acts of the governing power. To the first of these modes of limitation, the ruling power, in most European countries, was compelled, more or less, to submit. It was not so with the second; and, to attain this, or when already in some degree possessed, to attain it more completely, became everywhere the principal object of the lovers of liberty. And so long as mankind were content to combat one enemy by another, and to be ruled by a master, on condition of being guaranteed more or less efficaciously against his tyranny, they did not carry their aspirations beyond this point.

A time, however, came, in the progress of human affairs, when men ceased to think it a necessity of nature that their governors should be an independent power, opposed in interest to themselves. It appeared to them much better that the various magistrates of the State should be their tenants or delegates, revocable at their pleasure. In that way alone, it seemed, could they have complete security that the powers of government would never be abused to their disadvantage. By degrees this new demand for elective and temporary rulers became the prominent object of the exertions of the popular party, wherever any such party existed; and superseded, to a considerable extent, the previous efforts to limit the power of rulers. As the struggle proceeded for making the ruling power emanate from the periodical choice of the ruled, some persons began to think that too much importance had been attached to the limitation of the power itself. *That* (it might seem) was a resource against rulers whose interests were habitually opposed to those of the people. What was now wanted was, that the rulers should be identified with the people; that their interest and will should be the interest and will of the nation. The nation did not need to be protected against its own will. There was no fear of its tyrannising over itself. Let the rulers be effectually responsible to it, promptly removable by it, and it could afford to trust them with power of which it could itself dictate the use to be made. Their power was but the nation's own power, concentrated, and in a form convenient for exercise. This mode of thought, or rather perhaps of feeling, was common among the last generation of European liberalism, in the Continental section of which it still apparently predominates. Those who admit any limit to what a government may do, except in the case of such governments as they think ought not to exist, stand out as brilliant exceptions among the political thinkers of the Continent. A similar tone of sentiment might by this time have been prevalent in our own country, if the circumstances which for a time encouraged it, had continued unaltered.

But, in political and philosophical theories, as well as in persons, success discloses faults and infirmities which failure might have concealed from observation. The notion, that the people have no need to limit their power over themselves, might seem axiomatic, when popular government was a thing only dreamed about, or read of as having existed at some distant period of the past. Neither was that notion necessarily disturbed by such temporary aberrations as those of the French Revolution, the worst of which were the work of a usurping few, and which, in any case, belonged, not to the permanent working of popular institutions, but to a sudden and convulsive outbreak against monarchical and aristocratic depotism. In time, however, a democratic republic came to occupy a large portion of the earth's surface, and made itself felt as one of the most powerful members of the community of nations; and elective and responsible government became subject to the observations and criticisms which wait upon a great existing fact. It was now perceived that such phrases as "self-government," and "the power of the people over themselves," do not express the true state of the case. The "people" who exercise the power are not always the same people with those over whom it is exercised; and the "self-government" spoken of is not the government of each by himself, but of each by all the rest. The will of the people, moreover, practically means the will of the most numerous or the most active *part* of the people; the majority, or those who succeed in making themselves accepted as the majority; the people, consequently, *may* desire to oppress a part of their number; and precautions are as much needed against this as against any other abuse of power. The limitation, therefore, of the power of government over individuals loses none of its importance when the holders of power are regularly accountable to the community, that is, to the strongest party therein. This view of things, recommending itself equally to the intelligence of thinkers and to the inclination of those important classes in European society to whose real or supposed interests democracy is adverse, has had no difficulty in establishing itself; and in political speculations "the tyranny of the majority" is now generally included among the evils against which society requires to be on its guard.

*   *   *

The object of this Essay is to assert one very simple principle, as entitled to govern absolutely the dealings of society with the individual in the way of compulsion and control, whether the means used be physical force in the form of legal penalties, or the moral coercion of public opinion. That principle is, that the sole end for which mankind are warranted, individually or collectively, in interfering with the liberty of action of any of their number, is self-protection. That the only purpose for which power can be rightfully exercised over any member of a civilised community, against his will, is to prevent harm to others. His own good, either physical or moral, is not a sufficient warrant. He cannot rightfully be compelled to do or forbear because it will be better for him to do so, because it will make him happier, because, in the opinions of others, to do so would be wise, or even right. These

are good reasons for remonstrating with him, or reasoning with him, or persuading him, or entreating him, but not for compelling him, or visiting him with any evil in case he do otherwise. To justify that, the conduct from which it is desired to deter him must be calculated to produce evil to some one else. The only part of the conduct of any one, for which he is amenable to society, is that which concerns others. In the part which merely concerns himself, his independence is, of right, absolute. Over himself, over his own body and mind, the individual is sovereign.

*   *   *

We have now recognised the necessity to the mental well-being of mankind (on which all their other well-being depends) of freedom of opinion, and freedom of the expression of opinion, on four distinct grounds; which we will now briefly recapitulate.

First, if any opinion is compelled to silence, that opinion may, for aught we can certainly know, be true. To deny this is to assume our own infallibility.

Secondly, though the silenced opinion be an error, it may, and very commonly does, contain a portion of truth; and since the general or prevailing opinion on any subject is rarely or never the whole truth, it is only by the collision of adverse opinions that the remainder of the truth has any chance of being supplied.

Thirdly, even if the received opinion be not only true, but the whole truth; unless it is suffered to be, and actually is, vigorously and earnestly contested, it will, by most of those who receive it, be held in the manner of a prejudice, with little comprehension or feeling of its rational grounds. And not only this, but, fourthly, the meaning of the doctrine itself will be in danger of being lost, or enfeebled, and deprived of its vital effect on the character and conduct; the dogma becoming a mere formal profession, inefficacious for good, but cumbering the ground, and preventing the growth of any real and heartfelt conviction, from reason or personal experience.

*   *   *

Chapter IV
Of the Limits to the Authority
of Society over the Individual

What, then, is the rightful limit to the sovereignty of the individual over himself? Where does the authority of society begin? How much of human life should be assigned to individuality, and how much to society?

Each will receive its proper share, if each has that which more particularly concerns it. To individuality should belong the part of life in which it is chiefly the individual that is interested; to society, the part which chiefly interests society.

Though society is not founded on a contract, and though no good purpose is answered by inventing a contract in order to deduce social obligations from it, every one who receives the protection of society owes a return for the benefit, and the fact of living in society renders it indispensable that each should be bound to observe a certain line of conduct towards the rest. This conduct consists, first, in not injuring the interests of one another; or rather certain interests, which, either by express legal provision, or by tacit understanding, ought to be considered as rights; and secondly, in each person's bearing his share (to be fixed on some equitable principle) of the labours and sacrifices incurred for defending the society or its members from injury and molestation. These conditions society is justified in enforcing, at all costs to those who endeavour to withhold fulfilment. Nor is this all that society may do. The acts of an individual may be hurtful to others, or wanting in due consideration for their welfare, without going to the length of violating any of their constituted rights. The offender may then be justly punished by opinion, though not by law. As soon as any part of a person's conduct affects prejudicially the interests of others, society has jurisdiction over it, and the question whether the general welfare will or will not be promoted by interfering with it, becomes open to discussion. But there is no room for entertaining any such question when a person's conduct affects the interests of no persons besides himself, or needs not affect them unless they like (all the persons concerned being of full age, and the ordinary amount of understanding). In all such cases, there should be perfect freedom, legal and social, to do the action and stand the consequences.

It would be a great misunderstanding of this doctrine to suppose that it is one of selfish indifference, which pretends that human beings have no business with each other's conduct in life, and that they should not concern themselves about the well-doing or well-being of one another, unless their own interest is involved. Instead of any diminution, there is need of a great increase of disinterested exertion to promote the good of others. But disinterested benevolence can find other instruments to persuade people to their good than whips and scourges, either of the literal or the metaphorical sort. I am the last person to undervalue the self-regarding virtues; they are only second in importance, if even second, to the social. It is equally the business of education to cultivate both. But even education works by conviction and persuasion as well as by compulsion, and it is by the former only that, when the period of education is passed, the self-regarding virtues should be inculcated. Human beings owe to each other help to distinguish the better from the worse, and encouragement to choose the former and avoid the latter. They should be forever stimulating each other to increased exercise of their higher faculties, and increased direction of their feelings and aims towards wise instead of foolish, elevating instead of degrading, objects and contemplations. But neither one person, nor any number of persons, is warranted in saying to another human creature of ripe years, that he shall not do with his life for his own benefit what he chooses to do with it. He is the person most interested in his own well-being: the interest which any other person, except in cases of strong personal attachment, can have in it, is trifling, compared with that which he himself has; the interest which society has in him individually (except as to his conduct to others) is fractional, and altogether indirect; while with respect to his own feelings and circumstances, the most ordinary man or woman has means of knowledge immeasurably surpassing those that can be possessed by any one else. The interference of society to overrule his judgment and purposes in what only regards himself must be grounded on general presumptions; which may be altogether wrong, and even if right, are as likely as not to be misapplied to individual cases, by persons no better acquainted with the circumstances of such cases than those are who look at them merely from without. In this department, therefore, of human affairs, Individuality has its proper field of action. In the conduct of human beings towards one another it is necessary that general rules should for the most part be observed, in order that people may know what they have to expect: but in each

person's own concerns his individual spontaneity is entitled to free exercise.

*   *   *

REVIEW QUESTIONS

1. According to Mill, what are the liberties of the individual? What is the relationship of these liberties to society?
2. What is the importance of freedom of opinion for society?
3. Why would Mill consider the "tyranny of the majority" one of the prominent ills of nineteenth-century society?

FRANCIS PLACE

The People's Charter and National Petition

As the first movement that explicitly advocated the political rights of unpropertied laborers, Chartism was a watershed in European political history. Following the Reform Act of 1832, which enfranchised the upper echelons of the bourgeoisie, radical democrats broke allegiance with liberals and sought ways to renew the call for political reform. With unions outlawed in 1834, reformers turned to the strategy of petitioning Parliament for reform. In 1838, Francis Place (1771–1854), a venerable figure in English radical politics, drew up a statement entitled the People's Charter, a set of demands presented in the National Petition submitted to Parliament in 1839. Committees throughout England and Wales circulated the charter as a petition, and collected millions of signatures. The charter was presented to Parliament in 1839 and 1842, and rejected. In 1848, with revolution rampant on the continent, Chartists organized 6 million signatures for a final petition; its submission to Parliament was demonstratively attended by 500,000 workers. England's political establishment did not bow to Chartism, but the dignity and discipline of most Chartist demonstrations commanded respect and paved the way for trade associations in 1855 and a second reform act in 1867.

From *The People's Charter and National Petition*, by Francis Place (Quigley, 1839).

Unto the Honourable the Commons of the United Kingdom of Great Britain and Ireland, in Parliament assembled, the Petition of the undersigned, their suffering Countrymen,

Humbly Sheweth,

That we, your Petitioners, dwell in a land whose merchants are noted for enterprise, whose manufacturers are very skilful, and whose workmen are proverbial for their industry.

The land itself is goodly, the soil rich, and the temperature wholesome; it is abundantly furnished with the materials of commerce and trade; it has numerous and convenient harbours; in facility of internal communication it exceeds all others.

For three-and-twenty years we have enjoyed a profound peace.

Yet, with all these elements of national prosperity, and with every disposition and capacity to take advantage of them, we find ourselves overwhelmed with public and private suffering.

We are bowed down under a load of taxes; which, notwithstanding, fall greatly short of the wants of our rulers; our traders are trembling on the verge of bankruptcy; our workmen are starving; capital brings no profit, and labour no remuneration; the home of the artificer is desolate, and the warehouse of the pawnbroker is full; the workhouse is crowded, and the manufactory is deserted.

We have looked on every side, we have searched diligently, in order to find out the causes of a distress so sore and so long continued.

We can discover none in nature, or in providence.

Heaven has dealt graciously by the people; but the foolishness of our rulers has made the goodness of God of none effect.

The energies of a mighty kingdom have been wasted in building up the power of selfish and ignorant men, and its resources squandered for their aggrandisement.

The good of a party has been advanced to the sacrifice of the good of the nation; the few have governed for the interest of the few, while the interest of the many has been neglected, or insolently and tyrannously trampled upon.

It was the fond expectation of the people that a remedy for the greater part, if not for the whole, of their grievances, would be found in the Reform Act of 1832.

They were taught to regard that Act as a wise means to a worthy end; as the machinery of an improved legislation, where the will of the masses would be at length potential.

They have been bitterly and basely deceived.

The fruit, which looked so fair to the eye, has turned to dust and ashes when gathered.

The Reform Act has effected a transfer of power from one domineering faction to another, and left the people as helpless as before.

Our slavery has been exchanged for an apprenticeship to liberty, which has aggravated the painful feeling of our social degradation, by adding to it the sickening of still deferred hope.

We come before your Honourable House to tell you, with all humility, that this state of things must not be permitted to continue, that it cannot long continue without very seriously endangering the stability of the throne, and the peace of the kingdom; that if, by God's help, and all lawful and constitutional appliances, an end can be put to it, we are fully resolved that it shall speedily come to an end.

We tell your Honourable House, that the capital of the master must no longer be deprived of its due profit; that the labour of the workman must no longer be deprived of its due reward; that the laws which make food dear, and those which, by making money scarce, make labour cheap, must be abolished; that taxation must be made to fall on property, not on industry; that the good of the many, as it is the only legitimate end, so must it be the sole study of the government.

As a preliminary essential to these and other requisite changes; as the means by which alone the interests of the people can be effectually vindicated and secured, we demand that those interests be confided to the keeping of the people.

When the State calls for defenders, when it calls for money, no consideration of poverty or ignorance can be pleaded in refusal or delay of the call.

Required as we are, universally, to support and to obey the laws, nature and reason entitle us to demand that, in the making of the laws, the universal voice shall be implicitly listened to.

We perform the duties of freemen: we must have the privileges.

We Demand Universal Suffrage.

The Suffrage, to be exempt from the corruption of the wealthy and the violence of the powerful, must be secret.

The assertion of our right necessarily involves the power of its uncontrolled exercise.

We ask for the reality of a good, not for its semblance.

We Demand the Ballot.

The connection between the representatives and the people, to be beneficial, must be intimate.

The legislative and constituent powers, for correction and for instruction, ought to be brought into frequent contact.

Errors, which are comparatively light when susceptible of a speedy popular remedy, may produce the most disastrous effect when permitted to grow inveterate through years of compulsory endurance.

To public safety, as well as public confidence, frequent elections are essential.

We Demand Annual Parliaments.

With power to choose, and freedom in choosing, the range of our choice must be unrestricted.

We are compelled by the existing law, to take for our representatives, men who are incapable of appreciating our difficulties, or who have little sympathy with them; merchants who have retired from trade, and no longer feel its harassings; proprietors of land, who are alike ignorant of its evils and their cures; lawyers, by whom the honours of the Senate are sought after only as a means of obtaining notice in the Courts.

The labours of a representative, who is sedulous in the discharge of his duty, are numerous and burdensome.

It is neither just, nor reasonable, nor safe, that they should continue to be gratuitously rendered.

We demand that, in the future election of Members of your Honourable House, the approbation of the constituency shall be the sole qualification; and that, to every representative so chosen, shall be assigned, out of the public taxes, a fair and adequate remuneration for the time which he is called upon to devote to the public service.

Finally, we would most earnestly impress on your Honourable House, that this petition has not been dictated by any idle love of change; that it springs out of no inconsiderate attachment to fanciful theories—but that it is the result of much and long deliberation, and of convictions, which the events of each succeeding year tend more and more to strengthen.

The management of this mighty kingdom has hitherto been a subject for contending factions, to try their selfish experiments upon.

We have felt the consequences, in our sorrowful experience—short glimmerings of uncertain enjoyment, swallowed up by long and dark seasons of suffering.

If the self-government of the people should not remove their distresses, it will at least remove their repinings.

Universal Suffrage will, and it alone can, bring true and lasting peace to the nation; we firmly believe that it will bring prosperity.

May it, therefore, please your Honourable House to take this our Petition into your most serious consideration; and to use your utmost endeavours, by all constitutional means, to have a law passed granting to every male of lawful age, sane mind, and unconvicted of crime, the right of voting for Members of Parliament; and directing all future elections of Members of Parliament to be in the way of secret ballot; and ordaining that the duration of Parliament so chosen shall in no case exceed one year; and abolishing all property qualifications in the Members: and providing for their due remuneration while in attendance on their Parliamentary duties.

And your Petitioners, &c.

REVIEW QUESTIONS

1. What were, according to the petition, the economic and political circumstances that occasioned this plea?

2. What are the specific points of the petition? What do these demands implicitly reveal about British political culture in the 1830s?

3. How radical were these demands? Why were they unacceptable to Parliament?

21 ∽ REVOLUTIONS AND NATION-BUILDING, 1848–1871

Nations may have long lineages, but nationalism as a doctrine is strictly a modern phenomenon. Arising as a cultural doctrine in the late eighteenth century, the sentiment of nationalism quickly became a widespread political force, constantly evolving over time and infinitely adapting to particular needs. Its impact was registered at all levels of public life. As one of the chief solvents of the Old Regime, the principle of national unity not only realigned the European state system but also radically recast political culture with a new consciousness of citizenship. Political and economic change eroded older forms of local and regional loyalties, enabling the ideal of national citizenship to embed itself as a self-evident assumption for millions of Europeans.

The cultural dominance of the French Enlightenment and its insistence on uniform standards produced a wave of cultural resistance among European writers. In contrast to the Enlightenment's search for social and artistic norms applicable to all societies, select intellectuals celebrated instead the teeming heterogeneity of European language, customs, and culture. Each culture or people, they argued, embodied a national spirit: unique manifestations of geography, climate, and language that defied qualitative comparison. Humanitas, *argued cultural nationalists, was not reducible to core characteristics but, rather, was the aggregate of humankind's cultural diversity. By honoring all cultures and nations and conferring upon them the self-evident right to develop of their own accord, early forms of cultural nationalism perceived the nation within a tolerant, cosmopolitan worldview.*

The French Revolution converted this cultural sentiment into political strength. By endowing the nation with political sovereignty and transforming subjects into citizens, the French Revolution evinced the enormous potential of nationalism to wield political and military power. Reaffirmed in flags, anthems, emblems, festivals, and dress, the words nation *and* fatherland *stirred the blood of patriots, enabling the revolutionary government to mobilize its citizenry to serve the nation-state with unprecedented engagement. Under the leadership of Napoleon, the massive revolutionary armies of citizen-soldiers stood out as a superior fighting force, compelling the great powers of Europe to adapt or perish.*

Napoleonic occupation, in turn, awakened national consciousness in other European cultures. Traditional elites initially tapped patriotism to counter Napoleon's armies but unwittingly set into motion popular movements whose ideals of national sovereignty, unified nation-states, and constitutional liberties challenged kingdoms, multinational empires, and conservative principles of social hierarchy. Emancipating peoples from the injustice of imposed foreign rule gripped the imagination of artists, writers, and poets in central and eastern Europe, who not only depicted nationalist movements as idealistic guarantors for liberty and freedom but also applied history and language to justify the legitimacy of their cause. In the first half of the nineteenth century, liberals, democrats, and nationalists formed strong bonds, for they saw a constitutional nation-state as the vehicle of progress for all social groups. The struggle to unify a people under modern principles of citizenship assumed an ethical, humanitarian character. Advocates of nationalism adopted rhetoric, imagery, and ceremonies once reserved exclusively for religions. The ideal of self-sacrifice further sanctified nationalist movements; bloodshed consecrated the nation as a higher purpose for which to die.

Nation building shaped the course of the nineteenth century, though not always in the manner envisioned by liberals. To combat nationalist agitation, the Ottoman Empire introduced Western legal reforms to solidify its sovereignty in modern times. Statesmen also reworked nationalism into a conservative mold, using patriotism and nationalist sentiment to support conservative monarchism and authoritarian government. Calculating that rural voters were inherently resistant to innovative change, conservative rulers shrewdly introduced constitutions and universal manhood suffrage to lend popular legitimacy to their conservative policies, thereby checking the reformist impulses of urban liberals. Yet nationalism did not remain the manipulative tool of conservative statesmen. Urbanization, improved communications, and the vote produced grassroots political movements that used nationalism to protect domestic industry, agitate for imperial expansion, and to brand socialists, Jews, and foreigners as pernicious influences on the nation's political body. The numerous hybrid forms of nationalisms circulating in Europe by the end of the nineteenth century contributed to the increasingly chauvinistic political culture that condoned aggressive militarism, xenophobia, and racial exclusion.

In the wake of the Industrial and French Revolutions, political consciousness underwent radical change. Traditional authority was either modified or replaced by political communities whose legitimacy and power hinged on their representation of the nation. Yet the meaning of nationalism never became fixed; it remained a protean ideology serving a wide array of political interests and social classes over the long nineteenth century (1789–1914).

JOHANN GOTTLIEB FICHTE

FROM *Addresses to the German Nation*

One of the most important ramifications of the revolutionary era was the awakening of nationalist sentiment in Europe. The origin of German national consciousness provides a good example. Following the stunning victories of France over Germany between 1802 and 1807, Napoleon redrew the map of Germany, reducing the great power status of Prussia, erecting a federation of satellite states, and creating new kingdoms. Faced with this humiliation, German rulers, statesmen, and intellectuals realized that reform from above was necessary so that the untapped energies of German citizenry could be summoned to defeat the French foe. In the occupied Prussian capital of Berlin in the winter of 1807–8, the philosopher Johann Gottlieb Fichte gave a series of lectures that called for the spiritual renewal of Germany through a program of reformed education that stressed the German nation's character and strength. His program typified the idealism and romanticism of German patriotism in this era.

From *Addresses to the German Nation*, by Johann Gottlieb Fichte, translated by R. F. Jones and G. H. Turnbull (Ashland, Ohio: Open Court, 1922).

*   *   *

Fourteenth Address

*   *   *

CONCLUSION

In the addresses which I conclude today, I have spoken aloud to you first of all, but I have had in view the whole German nation, and my intention has been to gather round me, in the room in which you are bodily present, everyone in the domain of the German language who is able to understand me. If I have succeeded in throwing into any heart which has beaten here in front of me a spark which will continue to glow there and to influence its life, it is not my intention that these hearts should remain apart and lonely; I want to gather to them from over the whole of our common soil men of similar sentiments and resolutions, and to link them together, so that at this central point a single, continuous, and unceasing flame of patriotic disposition may be kindled, which will spread over the whole soil of the fatherland to its utmost boundaries. These addresses have not been meant for the entertainment of indolent ears and eyes in the present age; on the contrary, I want to know once for all, and everyone of like disposition shall know it with me, whether there is anyone besides ourselves whose way of thinking is akin to ours. Every German who still believes himself to be a member of a nation, who thinks highly and nobly of that nation, hopes for it, ventures, endures, and suffers for it, shall at last have the uncertainty of his belief removed; he shall see clearly whether he is right or is only a fool and a dreamer; from now on he shall either pursue his way with the glad consciousness of certainty, or else firmly and vigorously renounce a fatherland here below, and find in the heavenly one his only consolation. To them, not as individuals in our everyday limited life, but as representatives of the nation, and so through their ears to the whole nation, these addresses make this appeal:

Centuries have come and gone since you were last convoked as you are to-day; in such numbers; in a cause so great, so urgent, and of such concern to all and everyone; so entirely as a nation and as Germans. Never again will the offer come to you in this way. If you now take no heed and withdraw into yourselves, if you again let these addresses go by you as if they were meant merely to tickle your ears, or if you regard them as something strange and fabulous, then no human being will ever take you into account again. Hearken now at last; reflect now at last. Go not from your place this time at least without first making a firm resolution; and let everyone who hears my voice make this resolution by himself and for himself, just as if he were alone and had to do everything alone. If very many individuals think in this way, there will soon be formed a large community which will be fused into a single close-connected force. But if, on the contrary, each one, leaving himself out, puts his hope in the rest and leaves the matter to others, then there will be no others, and all together will remain as they were before. Make it on the spot, this resolution.

*　　*　　*

To all you Germans, whatever position you may occupy in society, these addresses solemnly appeal; let every one of you, who can think, think first of all about the subject here suggested, and let each do for it what lies nearest to him individually in the position he occupies.

Your forefathers unite themselves with these addresses, and make a solemn appeal to you. Think that in my voice there are mingled the voices of your ancestors of the hoary past, who with their own bodies stemmed the onrush of Roman world-dominion, who with their blood won the independence of those mountains, plains, and rivers which under you have fallen a prey to the foreigner. They call to you: "Act for us; let the memory of us which you hand on to posterity be just as honourable and without reproach as it was when it came to you, when you took pride in it and in your descent from

us. Until now, the resistance we made has been regarded as great and wise and noble; we seemed the consecrated and the inspired in the divine world-purpose. If our race dies out with you, our honour will be turned to shame and our wisdom to foolishness. For if, indeed, the German stock is to be swallowed up in Roman civilization, it were better that it had fallen before the Rome of old than before a Rome of today. The former we resisted and conquered; by the latter you have been ground to dust. Seeing that this is so, you shall now not conquer them with temporal weapons; your spirit alone shall rise up against them and stand erect. To you has fallen the greater destiny, to found the empire of the spirit and of reason, and completely to annihilate the rule of brute physical force in the world. If you do this, then you are worthy of your descent from us."

Then, too, there mingle with these voices the spirits of your more recent forefathers, those who fell in the holy war for the freedom of belief and of religion. "Save our honour too," they cry to you. "To us it was not entirely clear what we fought for; besides the lawful resolve not to let ourselves be dictated to by external force in matters of conscience, there was another and a higher spirit driving us, which never fully revealed itself to us. To you it is revealed, this spirit, if you have the power of vision in the spiritual world; it beholds you with eyes clear and sublime. The varied and confused mixture of sensuous and spiritual motives that has hitherto ruled the world shall be displaced, and spirit alone, pure and freed from all sensuous motives, shall take the helm of human affairs. It was in order that this spirit might have freedom to develop and grow to independent existence—it was for this that we poured forth our blood. It is for you to justify and give meaning to our sacrifice, by setting this spirit to fulfil its purpose and to rule the world. If this does not come about as the final goal to which the whole previous development of our nation has been tending, then the battles we fought will turn out to be a vain and fleeting farce, and the freedom of conscience and of spirit that we won is a vain word, if from now onwards spirit and conscience are to be no more."

*   *   *

All ages, all wise and good men who have ever breathed upon this earth, all their thoughts and intuitions of something loftier, mingle with these voices and surround you and lift up imploring hands to you; even, if one may say so, providence and the divine plan in creating a race of men, a plan which exists only to be thought out by men and to be brought by men into the actual world—the divine plan, I say, solemnly appeals to you to save its honour and its existence. Whether those were right who believed that mankind must always grow better, and that thoughts of a true order and worth of man were no idle dreams, but the prophecy and pledge of the real world that is to be—whether they are to be proved right, or those who continue to slumber in an animal and vegetable existence and mock at every flight into higher worlds—to give a final and decisive judgment on this point is a work for you. The old world with its glory and its greatness, as well as its defects, has fallen by its own unworthiness and by the violence of your fathers. If there is truth in what has been expounded in these addresses, then are you of all modern peoples the one in whom the seed of human perfection most unmistakably lies, and to whom the lead in its development is committed. If you perish in this your essential nature, then there perishes together with you every hope of the whole human race for salvation from the depths of its miseries. Do not console yourselves with an opinion based on thin air and depending on the mere recurrence of cases that have already happened; do not hope that when the old civilization has fallen a new one will arise once more out of a semi-barbarous nation on the ruins of the first. In ancient times there was such a people in existence, equipped with every requirement for such a destiny and quite well known to the civilized people, who have left us their description of it; and they themselves, if they had been able to imagine their own downfall, would have been able to discover in this people the means of reconstruction. To us the whole surface of the globe is also quite well known and all the peoples that dwell thereon. But do we know a people akin to the ancestral stock of the modern world, of whom we may have the same expectation? I think that everyone who does not merely base his hopes and beliefs on idle dreaming, but investigates thoroughly and thinks, will be bound to answer this question with a NO. There is, therefore, no way out; if you go under, all humanity goes under with you, without hope of any future restoration.

This it was, gentlemen, which at the end of these addresses I wanted and was bound to impress upon you, who to me are the representatives of the nation, and through you upon the whole nation.

REVIEW QUESTIONS

1. How does Fichte define the nation? What is the significance of Fichte's stress on continuity between contemporary Germans and their forefathers?
2. What is the relationship of Fichte's nationalism to humanity?

GREECE EXPIRING ON THE RUINS OF MISSOLONGHI (1826)   EUGÈNE DELACROIX

Many nationalist movements in Europe fashioned the Greek struggle for emancipation against the Ottoman Empire in the 1820s as a romantic, epic struggle for national freedom and statehood. And in a period of reaction and censorship in Europe, artists, authors, and poets used Greek emancipation and the pan-Hellenic movement as larger metaphors for the political aspirations of liberal nationalism throughout Europe. Eugène Delacroix painted a number of allegories of Greek enslavement in the 1820s; this painting was inspired by the fall of the Greek fortress to Missolonghi Turkish forces. In personifying Greece as the female figure in the foreground, what does Delacroix imply about the nature of nation-statehood?

FRANCIS PALACKÝ

FROM *History of the Czech Nation in Bohemia and Moravia*

Although such western nations as France and England had a recognizable ancient history, many central European peoples, who formed part of larger imperial polities, did not. The assertion of historical national roots and a venerable national cultural identity was therefore the first step of the Czech national movement, which in the 1830s and 1840s strove to differentiate itself from its German and Austrian rulers. In 1836, Francis Palacký (1798–1876), a historian and journalist, published the first of his five-volume History of the Czech Nation, *a landmark study that delineated the cultural autonomy and historical mission of the Czech people. Whereas the study's first volume appeared in German, Palacký published the subsequent four in Czech, a development that typified the growing centrality of language for eastern European nationalist movements. As a politician, Francis Palacký also advocated Czech independence during the Revolution of 1848. In "A Letter to Frankfurt," he famously declared his refusal to participate in the Frankfurt Parliament of 1848, which he viewed as a pan-German diet that did not serve Slav interests. Instead, he presided over the Slav Congress in Prague in June 1848 and furthermore served as a deputy in the Austrian Reichstag, where he promoted a Habsburg federalism that offered Czechs greater autonomy within an imperial framework. Because of his scholarship and his political career, Palacký is considered one of the "fathers of the Czech nation."*

From *History of the Czech Nation in Bohemia and Moravia*, by František Palacký, edited by Jan Bažant, Nina Bažantová, and Frances Starn, in *The Czech Reader: History, Culture, Politics* (Durham, N.C. Duke University Press, 2010), pp. 133–36.

Through his aggression the German took on himself the great heritage of ancient Rome, and at this moment the mild Slav quietly advanced and settled next to him. With him a new element entered European life, no less noble, but also no less reprehensible. The main feature of t he old Slavs was the freedom and equality of all citizens, as sons of the same family. If only concord had been connected with it! Their patriarchal morality and customs would have been sufficient to secure their well-being if only they had above them some higher power to shield them from all turmoil and extraordinary disasters. The religiosity, sim-plicity, and gentleness of the Slav did not free him from stubbornness and dogmatism. He wanted neither rule nor state, but only a community, and with national unity he also refused strong ties of order and rule. While demanding that at home all keep to the same old customs, he wished everyone equal rights and Freedom. He did not recognize differences between estates, or privileges, and at the same time he did not tolerate the influence of outstanding personalities, or the quick spread of higher enlightenment. He was not eager to attack, because he was hardly able to defend himself. The more he wished simply to harvest his field in peace, the more he was subjected to the orders of foreigners. If he was not to perish definitively, the Slav had to change his habits and to accept Roman and German elements into his national life.

The main content and essential drive of all Czech-Moravian history, as we have explained, is enduring the meeting and struggle of Slav, Roman, and German cultures in the sense we discussed. Since the Czechs had no direct contact with Roman culture, but mostly through the Germans, we may say also that Czech history is based actually on their struggle with Germanic culture, the acceptance or refusal of German manners and habits by the Czechs. It is true that also other Slav tribes encountered these two elements, but it was either not so universal, vital, and penetrating, as for instance between the Poles and the Russians, or it ended long ago with an annihilation of Slav nationalities, as with the Luticians, Bodics, and other people from the Elbe region. The Czech nation alone stood up to t he Germans on equal terms; for more than a thousand years they have had the closest contacts with Germans, but they have preserved their nationality up until the present. Even though they incorporated many German features into their national life and spiritually appropriated them, they did not cease to be a Slav nation. Even today they have the same role assigned by history and geographical situation alike: to be a bridge between the German and the Slav, in general terms between the East and West in Europe.

When we interpret the history of the Czech nation we shall describe the forms that this struggle took up in our country from time immemorial. The struggle took place not only on the borders but also within the Czech lands. It was directed not only against foreigners but also local people; it was fought not only with sword and shield but also by spirit and word; by constitutions and customs, openly and discreetly, by a renowned fulmination but also by blind passion; not only toward victory or subjection but also toward appeasement. We shall show how a nation small in numbers could sometimes earn a great name, and how afterward it could decline so far as to renounce that very name. We shall see it as it was swept by tempests from east to west, which came from outside and also originated at home. From time to time it lost hope of its preservation, but it does not cease even today to hope in the future. We shall see noble rulers, true fathers of the nation; the only goal of their energetic efforts was the well-being of their nation, they were courageous leaders able to keep Czech flags victorious, and to make enemies tremble at their sight. We shall see outstanding thinkers, whose bright spirit brought light into the darkness of their age and kindled sparks of consciousness and faith in local people and abroad; they were noble patriots who were willing to forget themselves in order to bring good to their nation, devoting their time and lives to it, their entire property, all their powers. Finally, people bright and gentle, obeying the voice of their rulers and leaders, ready to invest themselves and their entire essence, when it was necessary to defend the homeland and king, religion and faith, justice and laws. But we will not conceal various obstacles that incessantly hindered the higher prosperity of homeland and nation; they came not only from foreigners and enemies, but also from local renegades, not only through open violence, but also by infidelity and treason. We shall explain how often here the low selfishness or perversity of mind of particular persons, their blindness, or the foolish passivity of a crowd, brought the community to disaster. We shall see how stupidity destroyed what could not be cleverly thwarted.

It will be comforting to look at the early, but slight flower of Slav culture, at prehistoric castles and cities, places of holy executions and prayers, defensive refuges in times of war, and centers of national industry and commerce. It is not without proud feelings that one's descendant understands that what even the greatest and most educated nations of our age want and do not always obtain, that which his Slave ancestors maintained among themselves and defended from time immemorial: namely, general freedom for all inhabitants, equality before the law, and justice, the supreme government inherited as well as elected, accountable to assemblies, free election of local offices and national delegates and other similar institutions, including jury panels that praised the safeguard of general freedom. We shall learn also how changes and corrections that were absolutely essential to the state's benefit could not be carried out here, because of fear that, together with them, feudal orders would penetrate into the country under the influence of the medieval spirit. Lordly desires always fully supported the power of the feudal system, which could sweep away and suppress all elements of old Slav constitutions that were inappropriate for them. Our nation never ceased to stand out among others with its spiritually dynamic life, partly because of its natural disposition, partly due to its enlightened leaders, and this brought to the fore new struggles and fights, stranger and nobler, but also more cruel and destructive, than Europe had seen until that time. From the three wars on spiritual matters, during which in the last half millennium all Christian nations were embroiled from bottom to top, the two first, which were caused by religious needs, started and ended in Bohemia, and they were basically Czech wars. In the first one, our nation, whose core of its existence at that time was still preserved intact, conquered almost the whole world by miraculous deeds [Hus-site Wars]. In the second war, the nation betrayed itself, and not only did it not achieve anything glorious, it almost went bankrupt [Protestant uprising of 1618]. We shall show how in these and other disasters the hand of God showed itself, it gave human beings reasons and options between good and bad: by the fruit of both, it wanted to save him.

When we look at the main changes in Czech history, we discern in it at first sight three epochs: old, middle, and new. The middle epoch is best denoted by religious struggles, entering Czech public life with the beginning of Hussitism in 1403, and ending in the year 1627 with the expatriation of all Utraquists from their homeland. In this epoch our nation reached the peak of its historical importance; what preceded must be counted to the old epoch, what followed, to the new one.

REVIEW QUESTIONS

1. How does Palacký characterize Czech community in ancient times and its relationship to German and Roman culture?
2. Why is the theme of struggle and contest critical for Czech national consciousness? What are the three historical periods of Czech national history?
3. How does Palacký commend Czech behavior and where is he critical of his national history?
4. What is Palacký's evidence for Czechs' "spiritually dynamic life" and their "historical importance"? What does Palacký mean when stating that Czechs "conquered almost the whole world by miraculous deeds"?
5. To what degree does this national narrative rewrite history? How do nationalist movements reimagine past ages and epochs?

GIUSEPPE MAZZINI

FROM *Duties of Man*

Giuseppe Mazzini (1805–1872) was one of the best-known liberal national revolutionaries of the nineteenth century. Mazzini achieved international renown for his founding of Young Italy in 1831, an organization that strove for an Italian republic and that spawned the parallel associations Young Poland, Young Germany, and Young Ireland. In 1849 Mazzini assisted Garibaldi in defending the Roman republic, and after its defeat he was compelled to flee Italy. In exile he continued his efforts as a writer for a unified Italian republic. The eventual unification of Italy during the period 1859–71 brought him little satisfaction, because it was realized under the conservative political settlement of a constitutional monarchy. His Duties of Man, *first begun in weekly installments in 1840, best characterized Mazzini's liberal-democratic humanitarian spirit, which endowed the nationalism of this period with an ethical core.*

From "Duties of Man," by Giuseppe Mazzini, translated by Ella Noyes (1870), as reprinted in *The Liberal Tradition in European Thought*, edited by David Sidorsky (New York: Putnam, 1970).

To the Italian Working Class

To you, sons and daughters of the people, I dedicate this little book, wherein I have pointed out the principles in the name and strength of which you may, if you so will, accomplish your mission in Italy; a mission of republican progress for all and of emancipation for yourselves. Let those who are specially favoured by circumstances or in understanding, and able to comprehend these principles more easily, explain and comment on them to the others, and may that spirit of love inspire them with which, as I wrote, I thought on your griefs and on your virgin aspirations towards the new life which—once the unjust inequality now stifling your faculties is overcome—you will kindle in the Italian country.

I loved you from my first years. The republican instincts of my mother taught me to seek out among my fellows the Man, not the merely rich and powerful individual; and the simple unconscious virtue of my father accustomed me to admire, rather than conceited and pretentious semi-knowledge, the silent and unnoticed virtue of self-sacrifice so often found in you. Later on I gathered from the history of our country that the true life of Italy is the life of the people, and that the slow work of the centuries has constantly tended, amid the shock of different races and the superficial transitory changes wrought by usurpations and conquests, to prepare the great democratic National Unity. . . .

DUTIES TO COUNTRY

Your first Duties—first, at least, in importance—are, as I have told you, to Humanity. You are *men* before you are *citizens* or *fathers*. If you do not embrace the whole human family in your love, if you do not confess your faith in its unity—consequent on the unity of God—and in the brotherhood of the Peoples who are appointed to reduce that unity for fact—if wherever one of your fellowmen groans, wherever the dignity of human nature is violated by falsehood or tyranny, you are not prompt, being able, to succour that wretched one, or do not feel yourself called, being able, to fight for the purpose of relieving the deceived or oppressed—you disobey your law of life, or do not comprehend the religion which will bless the future.

But what can *each* of you, with his isolated powers, *do* for the moral improvement, for the progress of Humanity? . . . God gave you this means when he gave you a Country, when, like a wise overseer of labour, who distributes the different parts of the work according to the capacity of the workmen, he divided Humanity into distinct groups upon the face of our globe, and thus planted the seeds of nations. Bad governments have disfigured the design of God, which you may see clearly marked out, as far, at least, as regards Europe, by the courses of the great rivers, by the lines of the lofty mountains, and by other geographical conditions; they have disfigured it by conquest, by greed, by jealousy of the just sovereignty of others; disfigured it so much that today there is perhaps no nation except England and France whose confines correspond to this design. They did not, and they do not, recognise any country except their own families and dynasties, the egoism of caste. But the divine design will infallibly be fulfilled. Natural divisions, the innate spontaneous tendencies of the people will replace the arbitrary divisions sanctioned by bad governments. The map of Europe will be remade. The Countries of the People will rise, defined by the voice of the free, upon the ruins of the Countries of Kings and privileged castes. Between these Countries there will be harmony and brotherhood. And then the work of Humanity for the general amelioration, for the discovery and application of the real law of life, carried on in association and distributed according to local capacities, will be accomplished by peaceful and progressive development; then each of you, strong in the affections and in the aid of many millions of men speaking the same language, endowed with the same tendencies, and educated by the same historic tradition, may hope by your personal effort to benefit the whole of Humanity.

To you, who have been born in Italy, God has allotted, as if favouring you specially, the best-defined country in Europe. In other lands, marked by more uncertain or more interrupted limits, questions may arise which the pacific vote of all will one day solve, but which have cost, and will yet perhaps cost, tears and blood; in yours, no. God has stretched round you sublime and indisputable boundaries; on one side the highest mountains of Europe, the Alps; on the other the sea, the immeasurable sea. Take a map of Europe and place one point of a pair of compasses in the north of Italy on Parma; point the other to the mouth of the Var, and describe a semicircle with it in the direction of the Alps; this point, which will fall, when the semicircle is completed, upon the mouth of the Isonzo, will have marked the frontier which God has given you. As far as this frontier your language is spoken and understood; beyond this you have no rights. Sicily, Sardinia, Corsica, and the smaller islands between them and the mainland of Italy belong undeniably to you. Brute force may for a little while contest

these frontiers with you, but they have been recognised from of old by the tacit general consent of the peoples; and the day when, rising with one accord for the final trial, you plant your tricoloured flag upon that frontier, the whole of Europe will acclaim re-risen Italy, and receive her into the community of the nations. To this final trial all your efforts must be directed.

Without Country you have neither name, token, voice, nor rights, no admission as brothers into the fellowship of the Peoples. You are the bastards of Humanity. Soldiers without a banner, Israelites among the nations, you will find neither faith nor protection; none will be sureties for you. Do not beguile yourselves with the hope of emancipation from unjust social conditions if you do not first conquer a Country for yourselves; where there is no Country there is no common agreement to which you can appeal; the egoism of self-interest rules alone, and he who has the upper hand keeps it, since there is no common safeguard for the interests of all. Do not be led away by the idea of improving your material conditions without first solving the national question. You cannot do it. Your industrial associations and mutual help societies are useful as a means of educating and disciplining yourselves; as an economic fact they will remain barren until you have an Italy. The economic problem demands, first and foremost, an increase of capital and production; and while your Country is dismembered into separate fragments—while shut off by the barrier of customs and artificial difficulties of every sort, you have only restricted markets open to you—you cannot hope for this increase. Today—do not delude yourselves—you are not the working-class of Italy; you are only fractions of that class; powerless, unequal to the great task which you propose to yourselves. Your emancipation can have no practical beginning until a National Government, understanding the signs of the times, shall, seated in Rome, formulate a Declaration of Principles to be the guide for Italian progress, and shall insert into it these words, *Labour is sacred, and is the source of the wealth of Italy.*

Do not be led astray, then, by hopes of material progress which in your present conditions can only be illusions. Your Country alone, the vast and rich Italian Country, which stretches from the Alps to the farthest limit of Sicily, can fulfil these hopes. You cannot obtain your *rights* except by obeying the commands of *Duty*. Be worthy of them, and you will have them. O my Brothers! love your Country. Our Country is our home, the home which God has given us, placing therein a numerous family which we love and are loved by, and with which we have a more intimate and quicker communion of feeling and thought than with others; a family which by its concentration upon a given spot, and by the homogeneous nature of its elements, is destined for a special kind of activity. Our Country is our field of labour; the products of our activity must go forth from it for the benefit of the whole earth; but the instruments of labour which we can use best and most effectively exist in it, and we may not reject them without being unfaithful to God's purpose and diminishing our own strength. In labouring according to true principles for our Country we are labouring for Humanity; our Country is the fulcrum of the lever which we have to wield for the common good. If we give up this fulcrum we run the risk of becoming useless to our Country and to Humanity. Before *associating* ourselves with the Nations which compose Humanity we must exist as a Nation. There can be no association except among equals; and you have no recognised collective existence.

Humanity is a great army moving to the conquest of unknown lands, against powerful and wary enemies. The Peoples are the different corps and divisions of that army. Each has a post entrusted to it; each a special operation to perform; and the common victory depends on the exactness with which the different operations are carried out. Do not disturb the order of the battle. Do not abandon the banner which God has given you. Wherever you may be, into the midst of whatever people circumstances may have driven you, fight for the liberty of that people if the moment calls for it; but fight as Italians, so that the blood which you shed may win honour and love, not for you only, but for your Country. And may the constant thought of your soul be for Italy, may all the acts of your life

be worthy of her, and may the standard beneath which you range yourselves to work for Humanity be Italy's. Do not say *I;* say *we*. Be every one of you an incarnation of your Country, and feel himself and make himself responsible for his fellow-countrymen; let each one of you learn to act in such a way that in him men shall respect and love his Country.

Your Country is one and indivisible. As the members of a family cannot rejoice at the common table if one of their number is far away, snatched from the affection of his brothers, so you should have no joy or repose as long as a portion of the territory upon which your language is spoken is separated from the Nation.

*   *   *

A Country is a fellowship of free and equal men bound together in a brotherly concord of labour towards a single end. You must make it and maintain it such. A Country is not an aggregation, it is an *association*. There is no true Country without a uniform right. There is no true Country where the uniformity of that right is violated by the existence of caste, privilege, and inequality—where the powers and faculties of a large number of individuals are suppressed or dormant—where there is no common principle accepted, recognised, and developed by all. In such a state of things there can be no Nation, no People, but only a multitude, a fortuitous agglomeration of men whom circumstances have brought together and different circumstances will separate. In the name of your love of your Country you must combat without truce the existence of every privilege, every inequality, upon the soil which has given you birth.

*   *   *

The laws made by one fraction of the citizens only can never by the nature of things and men do otherwise than reflect the thoughts and aspirations and desires of that fraction; they represent, not the whole country, but a third, a fourth part, a class, a zone of the country. The law must express the general aspiration, promote the good of all, respond to a beat of the nation's heart. The whole nation therefore should be, directly or indirectly, the legislator. By yielding this mission to a few men, you put the egoism of one class in the place of the Country, which is the union of *all* the classes.

A Country is not a mere territory; the particular territory is only its foundation. The Country is the idea which rises upon that foundation; it is the sentiment of love, the sense of fellowship which binds together all the sons of that territory. So long as a single one of your brothers is not represented by his own vote in the development of the national life—so long as a single one vegetates uneducated among the educated—so long as a single one able and willing to work languishes in poverty for want of work—you have not got a Country such as it ought to be, the Country of all and for all. *Votes,*

education, work are the three main pillars of the nation; do not rest until your hands have solidly erected them.

*   *   *

REVIEW QUESTIONS

1. How is Mazzini's nationalism related to the larger issue of humanity?
2. For Mazzini what is necessary to achieve progress in humanity?
3. How does Mazzini define a country?
4. Why might Mazzini's nationalism be termed utopian?

The Imperial Edict of the Rose Chamber

The legal frameworks of western states offered a model of reform to many modernizing governments. The reorganization of the Ottoman Empire in the mid-nineteenth century, the so-called Tanzimat, illustrates well the application of western legal principles to strengthen and reorganize Ottoman imperial rule against its gradual erosion of power and the immediate onslaught of domestic nationalist movements threatening its cohesion. The Tanzimat encompassed a series of reforms in the military, education, law, and administration, all of which attempted to apply successful European practices so that the empire could better compete against the nation-states of Europe. Central to this era of reform was the Imperial Edict of the Rose Chamber, decreed in 1839, which aimed to establish legal equality for all Ottoman subjects. Although never fully implemented, the edict marks the onset of the secularization of law, the professionalization of its bureaucracy, and a direct relationship between subject and the state.

From *The Law of the Near & Middle East: Readings, Cases, & Materials*, edited by Herbert J. Liebesny (Albany, N.Y.: State University of New York Press, 1975), pp. 46–49.

All the world knows that in the first days of the Ottoman monarchy, the glorious precepts of the Qur'an and the laws of the Empire were always honored.

The Empire in consequence increased in strength and greatness, and all its subjects, without exception, had acquired the highest degree of ease and prosperity. In the last one hundred and fifty years a succession of accidents and divers causes have brought about a disregard for the sacred code of laws and the regulations flowing therefrom, and the former strength and prosperity have changed into weakness and poverty; an empire in fact loses all its stability as soon as it ceases to observe its laws.

These considerations are ever present in our mind and, from the day of our advent to the throne the thought of the public weal, of the improvement of the state of the provinces, and of relief to the [subject] peoples has not ceased wholly to engage it. If, therefore, the geographical position of the Ottoman provinces, the fertility of the soil, the aptitude and intelligence of the inhabitants are considered, the conviction will remain that by striving to find efficacious means, the result, which with the help of God we hope to attain, can be obtained within a few years. Full of confidence, therefore, in the help of the Most High and supported by the intercession of our Prophet, we deem it right to seek through new institutions to provide the provinces composing the Ottoman Empire with the benefit of a good administration.

These institutions must be principally carried out under three heads which are:

1. Guarantees insuring to our subjects perfect security of life, honor, and fortune.
2. A regular system of assessing and levying taxes.
3. An equally regular system for the levying of troops and the duration of their service.

And in fact, are not life and honor the most precious gifts that exist? What man, however much his character may be against violence, can prevent himself from having recourse to it, and thereby injure the government and the country, if his life and honor are endangered? If, on the contrary, he enjoys in that respect perfect security, he will not depart from the ways of loyalty and all his actions will contribute to the good of the government and of his brothers.

If there is an absence of security as to one's fortune, everyone remains insensible to the voice of the Prince and the country; no one interests himself in the progress of the public good, absorbed as he is in his own troubles. If, on the contrary, the citizen keeps possession in all confidence of all his goods, then, full of ardor in his affairs, which he seeks to enlarge in order to increase his comforts, he feels daily growing and doubling in his heart not only his love for the Prince and country, but also his devotion to his native land.

These feelings become in him the source of the most praiseworthy actions.

As to the regular and fixed assessment of the taxes, it is very important that this matter be regulated; for the state which is forced to incur many expenses for the defense of its territory, cannot obtain the money necessary for its armies and other services except by means of contributions levied on its subjects. Although, thanks be to God, the inhabitants of our Empire have for some time past been delivered from the scourge of monopolies, falsely considered at other times as a source of revenue, a fatal custom still exists, although it can only have disastrous consequences; it is that of venal concessions, known under the name of "*Iltizam.*"

Under this system the civil and financial administration of a locality is delivered over to the arbitrary control of a single man; that is to say, sometimes to the iron grasp of most violent and avaricious passions, for if that contractor is not a good man, he will only look to his own advantage.

It is therefore necessary that henceforth each member of Ottoman society should be taxed for a quota determined according to his fortune and means, and that it should be impossible that anything more could be exacted from him. It is also necessary that special laws should fix and limit the expenses of our land and sea forces.

Although, as we have said, the defense of the country is an important matter, and that it is the duty of all the inhabitants to furnish soldiers for that object, it has become necessary to establish laws to regulate the contingents to be furnished by each locality according to the necessities of the time and to reduce the term of military service to four or five years. For it is at the same time doing an injustice and giving a mortal blow to agriculture and to industry to take, without consideration to the respective population of the localities, in the one more, in the other fewer men than they can furnish; it also reduces the soldiers to despair and contributes to the depopulation of the country by keeping them all their lives in the service.

In short, without several laws, the necessity for which has just been described, there can be neither strength, nor riches, nor happiness, nor tranquility for the Empire; it must, on the contrary, look for them in the existence of these new laws.

From henceforth, therefore, the cause of every accused person shall be judged publicly, as our divine law requires, after inquiry and examination, and so long as a regular judgment shall not have been pronounced, no one secretly or publicly put another to death by poison or in any other manner.

No one shall be allowed to attack the honor of any person whatever.

Each person shall possess his property of every kind and shall dispose of it in all freedom, without let or hindrance from any person whatever; thus, for example, the innocent heirs of a criminal shall not be deprived of their legal rights, and the property of the criminal shall not be confiscated. These imperial grants shall extend to all our subjects, of whatever religion or sect they may be; they shall enjoy them without exception. Perfect security is thus given to the inhabitants of our Empire in their lives, their honor, and their fortunes, as they are secured to them by the sacred text of our law.

As for the other points, as they must be settled with the assistance of enlightened opinions, our council of justice (increased by new members as shall be found necessary), to whom shall be joined, on certain days which we shall determine, our ministers and the notables of the Empire, shall assemble in order to frame laws regulating these matters concerning the security of life and fortune and the assessment of taxes. Each one in these assemblies shall freely express his ideas and give his advice.

The laws regulating the military service shall be discussed by a military council holding its meetings at the palace of the minister of war. As soon as a law shall be completed in order to be forever valid and in effect, it shall be presented to us; we shall give it our approval, which we will write at the beginning with our imperial sign-manual.

As the object of these institutions is solely to revivify religion, government, the nation, and the Empire, we engage not to do anything which is contrary thereto.

In testimony of our promise we will, after having deposited these presents in the hill containing the glorious mantle of the Prophet, in the presence of all the 'nlama' and the grandees of the Empire, make oath thereto in the name of God, and shall afterwards cause the oath to be taken by the 'nlama' and grandees of the Empire.

After that, those from among the 'nlama' or the grandees of the Empire, or any other person whatsover who shall infringe these institutions, shall undergo, without respect of rank, position, and influence, the punishment corresponding to his crime, after the latter has been fully established. A penal code shall be compiled for that purpose.

As all the public servants of the Empire receive a suitable salary, and as the salaries of those whose duties have not up to the present time been sufficiently remunerated are to be fixed, a rigorous law shall be enacted against the traffic in favoritism and offices, which the divine law disapproves and which is one of the principal causes of the decay of the Empire.

REVIEW QUESTIONS

1. What are the edict's three areas of reforms? According to this edict, why are these three spheres of law so important for the future of the state?

2. How does the decree integrate law and religion? Why does this decree enlist the support of God?

3. What does this era of reforms in the Ottoman provinces tell us about the process of modernization in the nonwestern world? What are the virtues and the drawbacks of emulating the West?

ALEXANDER II

FROM Manifesto Emancipating the Serfs

The emancipation of 22 million serfs in 1861 constitutes the most ambitious social reform of nineteenth-century Russia. Although Russia's socioeconomic structure did not undergo radical change after 1861, the abolition of serfdom inaugurated a series of judicial, military, and governmental reforms that liberalized Russian society. Extending basic civil liberties to Russians was the necessary first step in the effort to westernize Russia within the Tsarist autocratic tradition.

From *Major Problems in the History of Imperialist Russia*, edited by James Cracraft (Boston: Houghton Mifflin, 1994), pp. 340–44.

Called by Divine Providence and the sacred law of succession to Our ancestral All-Russian Throne, in response to which call We vowed in Our heart to embrace in Our Royal love and Solicitude all Our faithful of every rank and estate . . . ; investigating the condition of [those] who comprise the State, We saw that State law, while actively promoting the welfare of the higher and middle estates defining their obligations, rights, and privileges, has not equally favored the bonded people, so called because as a matter partly of old laws and partly of current custom they have been hereditarily bound to the authority of landlords, who are obliged accordingly to see to their welfare. Hitherto the rights of the lords were broad and not precisely defined in law, wherefore tradition, custom, and the lord's good will prevailed. At best this [system] produced good patriarchal relations of sincere solicitude and benevolence on the part of the lords and good-natured submission from the peasants. But owing to the decline of morals, an increase in the variety of relationships, and a lessening of the lords' direct paternal relations with their peasants, whereupon landlord rights sometimes fell into the hands of persons seeking only their own advantage; good relations weakened, and the way was opened to an arbitrariness that has been burdensome for the peasants and not conducive to their welfare, whence they have shown indifference to any improvement in their lives.

Such was perceived by Our Predecessors of worthy memory, and they took steps to improve the condition of the peasantry. But these steps were only partly successful, depending as they did on the good will and voluntary action of landlords and applicable as they were only to certain localities, as required by special circumstances or by way of experiment. . . .

We were therefore convinced that the task of improving the condition of the bonded people is a legacy to Us from Our Predecessors, and a destiny conferred upon Us in the course of events by the hand of Providence.

We began this task by an act of trust in the Russian Nobility, knowing of its great proofs of loyalty to the Throne and of its readiness to make sacrifices for the good of the Fatherland. We left it to the Nobility Itself to assemble and consider a new arrangement of peasant affairs, whereupon it was proposed to the Nobles to limit their rights over peasants and to bear the difficulties of a transformation that would entail losses to themselves. And Our trust was justified. Through its representatives in the Provincial Committees chosen by the whole Nobility of every province, the Nobility voluntarily renounced any rights to the person of the bonded ones. These Committees, after collecting the needed information, drew up proposals regarding a new order for people living in bondage and relations with lords.

* * *

Having called on God for assistance, We are resolved to complete this task.

Pursuant to these new Statutes, the bonded people are to receive in due course the full rights of free rural inhabitants.

The landlords, preserving their right of ownership of all lands belonging to them, are to grant to the peasants, in return for a certain obligation, perpetual use of their homestead as well as such quantity of plowland and other goods as is provided in the Statutes, so that they may be secure in their livelihood and fulfill their duties to the Government.

In taking advantage of this land allotment, the peasants are thereby required to fulfill the obligations to lords specified in the Statutes. In this condition, which is transitional, the peasants are temporarily obligated.

They are also to be given the right to buy their homestead; and with their lord's agreement they may acquire ownership of the plowland and other goods assigned to their perpetual use. On acquiring ownership of said land, the peasants are freed of any duties owed on it to the lord, and thus enter the well-defined estate of free peasant proprietors.

A Special Statute defines the transitional status of domestic folk, as appropriate to their duties and needs. Two years after publication of this Statute, they will receive complete freedom and certain temporary privileges.

* * *

Although these Statutes, the General, Local, and Supplementary Rules for certain special localities, for small landowners, and for peasants working in their lords' factories or industries, have been adapted as far as possible to local economic needs and practices; nevertheless, to preserve the customary order where it is mutually advantageous We leave it to the lords to reach voluntary understandings with peasants and to conclude agreements regarding the extent of the peasants' land allotments and corresponding obligations, observing therein the rules laid down for preserving the inviolability of such agreements.

As this new arrangement, given the inescapable complexity of the changes required by it, cannot be introduced at once, but rather needs time for that, meaning not less than two years: so in the course of this time, to avoid confusion, and to maintain the, public and private good, the order hitherto existing on seigneurial estates should be preserved until, on completion of the necessary preparations, the new order will begin.

* * *

Considering the inescapable difficulties involved in this transformation, We place Our hope first of all in the surpassing goodness of Divine Providence, which protects Russia.

Then do We rely on the valiant zeal for the common good of the Well-born Noble estate, to whom We cannot fail to express, on behalf of Ourselves and the whole Fatherland, well-deserved recognition of unselfish execution of Our designs. Russia will not forget that, prompted only by respect for human dignity and Christian love of neighbor, they voluntarily renounced the law of bondage and laid the basis of a new economic future for peasants. We assuredly expect that with like nobility they will exhibit the utmost care in seeing that the new Statutes are carried out in good order, and in a spirit of peace and benevolence; that every landowner will complete, on his own land, the great civic act of his entire estate; and that, having arranged the affairs of the peasants settled on his land and of his domestic folk on terms advantageous to both sides, he will thus give a good example to the rural people and an incentive to exact and conscientious fulfillment of State regulations.

Mindful of examples of the landowners' generous solicitude for the good of peasants, and of the peasants' recognition of same, We are confirmed in Our hope that mutual voluntary agreements will resolve most of the difficulties that are unavoidable when general rules are applied to the varying circumstances of individual estate lands. In this way the transition from the old order to the new will be alleviated, and mutual trust, good accord, and a unanimous aspiration for the common good will be strengthened in the future.

*   *   *

And We place Our hope in the good sense of Our people.

When word of the Government's plan to abolish the law of bondage reached peasants unprepared for it, there arose a partial misunderstanding. Some thought about freedom and forgot about obligations. But the general good sense was not disturbed in the conviction that anyone freely enjoying the goods of society correspondingly owes it to the common good to fulfill certain obligations, both by natural reason and by Christian law, according to which "every soul must be subject to the governing authorities" and "pay all of them their dues," in particular "labor, tribute, fear, and honor" * * * rights legally acquired by the landlords cannot be taken from them without a decent return or voluntary concession; and that it would be contrary to all justice to make use of the lords' land without bearing the corresponding obligations.

And now We hopefully expect that the bonded people, as a new future opens before them, will understand and accept with gratitude the important sacrifice made by the Well-born Nobility for the improvement of their lives.

They will understand that, receiving the advantages of ownership and the freedom to conduct their own affairs, they owe it to society and to themselves to realize the beneficence of the new law by a loyal, judicious, and diligent exercise of the rights granted to them. The most beneficent law cannot make people happy if they do not themselves labor to build their happiness under the protection of the law. Prosperity is acquired and increased only by hard work, the judicious use of strength and resources, strict economy, and, overall, by an honest, God-fearing life.

*   *   *

Make the sign of the cross, Orthodox people, and invoke with Us God's blessing on thy free labor, the pledge of thine own prosperity and of the public good.

Given at St. Petersburg in the year of Our Lord one thousand eight hundred sixty-one, and of Our Reign the seventh.

Alexander

REVIEW QUESTIONS

1. According to the manifesto, what social changes provoked emancipation?
2. What role does the aristocracy play in the execution of emancipation, and how realistic is this prescribed role?
3. How is religion invoked to unify Russian society in this period of change?

OTTO VON BISMARCK

FROM *The Memoirs*

Otto von Bismarck (1815–1898), a Prussian noble, served the Prussian crown as its premier statesman from 1862 to 1890. Under his aegis, Prussia united Germany, creating in 1871 the German Empire, a nation-state whose power and size significantly altered the European state system. Prussia's bid to unite Germany brought armed

conflict with Austria in 1866. Yet Prussia's military victory was only partly success-
ful, for Prussia's role as unifier could become legitimate only with popular support.
On the eve of war with Austria, Bismarck promulgated a constitution that included
a bicameral legislation and universal male suffrage, a political move that sought to
shift public opinion in favor of Prussia. The move achieved the intended effect,
enabling Bismarck to sever the once-indivisible bond between nationalism and liber-
alism. The following passage, written at the end of his life, throws light on a conserva-
tive's views of popular politics and nationalism.

From *The Memoirs*, by Otto von Bismarck, translated by A. J. Butler (New York: Fertig, 1890).

*   *   *

Looking to the necessity, in a fight against an overwhelming foreign Power, of being able, in extreme need, to use even revolutionary means, I had had no hesitation whatever in throwing into the frying-pan, by means of the circular dispatch of June 10, 1866, the most powerful ingredient known at that time to liberty-mongers, namely, universal suffrage, so as to frighten off foreign monarchies from trying to stick a finger into our national omelette. I never doubted that the German people would be strong and clever enough to free themselves from the existing suffrage as soon as they realised that it was a harmful institution. If it cannot, then my saying that Germany can ride when once it has got into the saddle was erroneous. The acceptance of universal suffrage was a weapon in the war against Austria and other foreign countries, in the war for German Unity, as well as a threat to use the last weapons in a struggle against coalitions. In a war of this sort, when it becomes a matter of life and death, one does not look at the weapons that one seizes, nor the value of what one destroys in using them: one is guided at the moment by no other thought than the issue of the war, and the preservation of one's external independence; the settling of affairs and reparation of the damage has to take place after the peace. Moreover, I still hold that the principle of universal suffrage is a just one, not only in theory but also in practice, provided always that voting be not secret, for secrecy is a quality that is indeed incompatible with the best characteristics of German blood.

The influence and the dependence on others that the practical life of man brings in its train are God-given realities which we cannot and must not ignore. If we refuse to transfer them to political life, and base that life on a faith in the secret in sight of everybody, we fall into a contradiction between public law and the realities of human life which practically leads to constant frictions, and finally to an explosion, and to which there is no theoretical solution except by way of the insanities of social-democracy, the support given to which rests on the fact that the judgment of the masses is sufficiently stultified and undeveloped to allow them, with the assistance of their own greed, to be continually caught by the rhetoric of clever and ambitious leaders.

The counterpoise to this lies in the influence of the educated classes, which would be greatly strengthened if voting were public, as for the Prussian Diet. It may be that the greater discretion of the more intelligent classes rests on the material basis of the preservation of their possessions. The other motive, the struggle for gain, is equally justifiable; but a preponderance of those who represent property is more serviceable for the security and development of the state. A state, the control of which lies in the hands of the greedy, of the *novarum rerum cupidi,* and of orators who have in a higher degree than others the capacity for deceiving the unreasoning masses, will constantly be doomed to a restlessness of development, which so ponderous a mass as the commonwealth of the state cannot follow without injury to its organism. Ponderous masses, and among these the life and development of great nations must be reckoned, can only move with caution, since the road on which they travel to an unknown future has no smooth iron rails. Every great state-commonwealth that loses the prudent and restraining influence of the propertied class, whether that influence rests on material or moral grounds, will always end by being rushed along at a speed which must shatter the coach of state, as happened in the development of the French Revolution. The element of greed has the preponderance arising from large masses which in the long run must make its way. It is in the interests of the great mass itself to wish decision to take place without dangerous acceleration of the speed of the coach of state, and without its destruction. If this should happen, however, the wheel of history will revolve again, and always in a proportionately shorter time, to dictatorship, to despotism, to absolutism, because in the end the masses yield to the need of order; if they do not recognise this need *a priori,* they always realise it eventually after manifold arguments *ad hominem;* and in order to purchase order from a dictatorship and Caesarism they cheerfully sacrifice that justifiable amount of freedom which ought to be maintained, and which the political society of Europe can endure without ill-health.

I should regard it as a serious misfortune, and as an essential weakening of our security in the future, if we in Germany are driven into the vortex of this French cycle. Absolutism would be the ideal form of government for an European political structure were not the King and his officials ever as other men are to whom it is not given to reign with superhuman wisdom, insight and justice. The most experienced and well-meaning absolute rulers are subject to human imperfections, such as overestimation of their own wisdom, the influence and eloquence of favourites, not to mention petticoat influence, legitimate and illegitimate. Monarchy and the most ideal monarch, if in his idealism he is not to be a common danger, stand in need of criticism; the thorns of criticism set him right when he runs the risk of losing his way. Joseph II is a warning example of this.

Criticism can only be exercised through the medium of a free press and parliaments in the modern sense of the term. Both correctives may easily weaken, and finally lose their efficacy if they abuse their powers. To avert this is one of the tasks of a conservative policy, which cannot be accomplished without a struggle with parliament and press. The measuring of the limits within which such a struggle must be confined, if the control of the government, which is indispensable to the country, is neither to be checked nor allowed to gain a complete power, is a question of political tact and judgment.

It is a piece of good fortune for his country if a monarch possess the judgment requisite for this—a good fortune that is temporary, it is true, like all human fortune. The possibility of establishing ministers in power who possess adequate qualifications must always be granted in the constitutional organism; but also the possibility of maintaining in office ministers who satisfy these requirements in face of occasional votes of an adverse majority and of the influence of courts and camarillas. This aim, so far as human imperfections in general allow its attainment, was approximately reached under the government of William I.

*   *   *

REVIEW QUESTIONS

1. What was Bismarck's opinion of universal suffrage?
2. What political system and balance of social forces did Bismarck advocate?
3. Why is Bismarck often viewed as a conservative revolutionary?

ERNEST RENAN

What Is a Nation?

First delivered as a lecture in 1882 at the University of Paris, this essay by Ernest Renan (1823–1892), a prolific French author on philological and historical subjects, provided a remarkably detached critique of theories that defined and legitimized European nationalisms. By dismantling the dominant explanations of nationalism of his time, Renan led the way toward viewing nations as cultural entities willed into existence by the "daily plebiscite" of believing communities. For Renan, nations had less to do with authentic historical development than with the contemporary cultural needs of social groups seeking an idealistic collective identity. For this reason Renan's argument has greatly influenced contemporary theories on nationalism.

From *What Is a Nation?*, by Ernest Renan, edited by Homi K. Bhabha, translated by Martin Thom (London: Routledge, 1990), pp. 42, 46–54.

What I propose to do today is to analyse with you an idea which, though seemingly clear, lends itself to the most dangerous misunderstandings. ＊ ＊ ＊

＊   ＊   ＊

If one were to believe some political theorists, a nation is above all a dynasty, representing an earlier conquest, one which was first of all accepted, and then forgotten by the mass of the people. According to the above-mentioned theorists, the grouping of provinces effected by a dynasty, by its wars, its marriages, and its treaties, ends with the dynasty which had established it. It is quite true that the majority of modern nations were made by a family of feudal origin, which had contracted a marriage with the soil and which was in some sense a nucleus of centralization. France's frontiers in 1789 had nothing either natural or necessary about them. The wide zone that the House of Capet had added to the narrow strip of land granted by the partition of Verdun was indeed the personal acquisition of this House. During the epoch when these acquisitions were made, there was no idea of natural frontiers, nor of the rights of nations, nor of the will of provinces. The union of England, Ireland, and Scotland was likewise a dynastic fact. Italy only tarried so long before becoming a nation because, among its numerous reigning houses, none, prior to the present century, constituted itself as the centre of [its] unity. Strangely enough, it was through the obscure island of Sardinia, a land that was scarcely Italian, that [the house of Savoy] assumed a royal title. Holland, which—through an act of heroic resolution—created itself, has nevertheless contracted an intimate marriage with the House of Orange, and it will run real dangers the day this union is compromised.

Is such a law, however, absolute? It undoubtedly is not. Switzerland and the United States, which have formed themselves, like conglomerates, by successive additions, have no dynastic basis. I shall not discuss this question in relation to France, for I would need to be able to read the secrets of the future in order to do so. Let me simply say that so loftily national had this great French royal principle been that, on the morrow of its fall, the nation was able to stand without her. Furthermore, the eighteenth century had changed everything. Man had returned, after centuries of abasement, to the spirit of antiquity, to [a sense of] respect for himself, to the idea of his own rights. The words *patrie* and citizen had recovered their former meanings. Thus it was that the boldest operation ever yet put into effect in history was brought to completion, an operation which one might compare with the attempt, in physiology, to restore to its original identity a body from which one had removed the brain and the heart.

It must therefore be admitted that a nation can exist without a dynastic principle, and even that nations which have been formed by dynasties can be separated from them without therefore ceasing to exist. The old principle, which only takes account of the right of princes, could no longer be maintained; apart from dynastic right, there is also national right. Upon what criterion, however, should one base this national right? By what sign should one know it? From what tangible fact can one derive it?

Several confidently assert that it is derived from race. The artificial divisions, resulting from feudalism, from princely marriages, from diplomatic congresses are, [these authors assert], in a state of decay. It is a population's race which remains firm and fixed. This is what constitutes a right, a legitimacy. The Germanic family, according to the theory I am expounding here, has the right to reassemble the scattered limbs of the Germanic order, even when these limbs are not asking to be joined together again. The right of the Germanic order over such-and-such a province is stronger than the right of the inhabitants of that province over themselves. There is thus created a kind of primordial right analogous to the divine right of kings: an ethnographic principle is substituted for a national one. This is a very great error, which, if it were to become dominant, would destroy European civilization. The primordial right of races is as narrow and as perilous for genuine progress as the national principle is just and legitimate.

*   *   *

The truth is that there is no pure race and that to make politics depend upon ethnographic analysis is to surrender it to a chimera. The noblest

countries, England, France, and Italy, are those where the blood is the most mixed. Is Germany an exception in this respect? Is it a purely Germanic country? This is a complete illusion. The whole of the south was once Gallic; the whole of the east, from the river Elbe on, is Slav. Even those parts which are claimed to be really pure, are they in fact so? We touch here on one of those problems in regard to which it is of the utmost importance that we equip ourselves with clear ideas and ward off misconceptions.

*   *   *

The fact of race, which was originally crucial, thus becomes increasingly less important. Human history is essentially different from zoology, and race is not everything, as it is among the rodents or the felines, and one does not have the right to go through the world fingering people's skulls, and taking them by the throat saying: "You are of our blood; you belong to us!" Aside from anthropological characteristics, there are such things as reason, justice, the true, and the beautiful, which are the same for all. Be on your guard, for this ethnographic politics is in no way a stable thing and, if today you use it against others, tomorrow you may see it turned against yourselves. Can you be sure that the Germans, who have raised the banner of ethnography so high, will not see the Slavs in their turn analyse the names of villages in Saxony and Lusatia, search for any traces of the Wiltzes or of the Obotrites, and demand recompense for the massacres and the wholesale enslavements that the Ottoss inflicted upon their ancestors? It is good for everyone to know how to forget.

*   *   *

What we have just said of race applies to language too. Language invites people to unite, but it does not force them to do so. The United States and England, Latin America and Spain, speak the same languages yet do not form single nations. Conversely, Switzerland, so well made, since she was made with the consent of her different parts, numbers three or four languages. There is something in man which is superior to language, namely, the will. The will of Switzerland to be united, in spite of the diversity of her dialects, is a fact of far greater importance than a similitude often obtained by various vexatious measures.

*   *   *

Religion cannot supply an adequate basis for the constitution of a modern nationality either. Originally, religion had to do with the very existence of the social group, which was itself an extension of the family. Religion and the rites were family rites. * * *

* * * In our own time, the situation is perfectly clear. There are no longer masses that believe in a perfectly uniform manner. Each person believes and practises in his own fashion what he is able to and as he wishes. There is no longer a state religion; one can be French, English, or German, and be either Catholic, Protestant, or orthodox Jewish, or else practise no cult at all. Religion has become an individual matter; it concerns the conscience of each person. The division of nations into Catholics and Protestants no longer exists. Religion, which, fifty-two years ago, played so substantial a part in the formation of Belgium, preserves all of its [former] importance in the inner tribunal of each; but it has ceased almost entirely to be one of the elements which serve to define the frontiers of peoples.

A community of interest is assuredly a powerful bond between men. Do interests, however, suffice to make a nation? I do not think so. Community of interest brings about trade agreements, but nationality has a sentimental side to it; it is both soul and body at once; a *Zollverein* is not a *patrie*.

*   *   *

A nation is a soul, a spiritual principle. Two things, which in truth are but one, constitute this soul or spiritual principle. One lies in the past, one in the present. One is the possession in common of a rich legacy of memories; the other is present-day consent, the desire to live together, the will to perpetuate the value of the heritage that one has received in an undivided form. Man, Gentlemen, does not improvise. The nation, like the individual,

is the culmination of a long past of endeavours, sacrifice, and devotion. Of all cults, that of the ancestors is the most legitimate, for the ancestors have made us what we are. A heroic past, great men, glory (by which I understand genuine glory), this is the social capital upon which one bases a national idea. To have common glories in the past and to have a common will in the present; to have performed great deeds together, to wish to perform still more—these are the essential conditions for being a people. One loves in proportion to the sacrifices to which one has consented, and in proportion to the ills that one has suffered. One loves the house that one has built and that one has handed down. The Spartan song—"We are what you were; we will be what you are"— is, in its simplicity, the abridged hymn of every *patrie.*

More valuable by far than common customs posts and frontiers conforming to strategic ideas is the fact of sharing, in the past, a glorious heritage and regrets, and of having, in the future, [a shared] programme to put into effect, or the fact of having suffered, enjoyed, and hoped together. These are the kinds of things that can be understood in spite of differences of race and language. I spoke just now of "having suffered together" and, indeed, suffering in common unifies more than joy does. Where national memories are concerned, griefs are of more value than triumphs, for they impose duties, and require a common effort.

A nation is therefore a large-scale solidarity, constituted by the feeling of the sacrifices that one has made in the past and of those that one is prepared to make in the future. It presupposes a past; it is summarized, however, in the present by a tangible fact, namely, consent, the clearly expressed desire to continue a common life. A nation's existence is, if you will pardon the metaphor, a daily plebiscite, just as an individual's existence is a perpetual affirmation of life. That, I know full well, is less metaphysical than divine right and less brutal than so-called historical rights. According to the ideas that I am outlining to you, a nation has no more right than a king does to say to a province: "You belong to me. I am seizing you." A province, as far as I am concerned, is its inhabitants; if anyone has the right to be consulted in such an affair, it is the inhabitant. A nation never has any real interest in annexing or holding on to a country against its will. The wish of nations is, all in all, the sole legitimate criterion, the one to which one must always return.

*   *   *

Let me sum up, Gentlemen. Man is a slave neither of his race nor his language, nor of his religion, nor of the course of rivers nor of the direction taken by mountain chains. A large aggregate of men, healthy in mind and warm of heart, creates the kind of moral conscience which we call a nation. So long as this moral consciousness gives proof of its strength by the sacrifices which demand the abdication of the individual to the advantage of the community, it is legitimate and has the right to exist. If doubts arise regarding its frontiers, consult the populations in the areas under dispute. They undoubtedly have the right to a say in the matter. This recommendation will bring a smile to the lips of the transcendants of politics, these infallible beings who spend their lives deceiving themselves and who, from the height of their superior principles, take pity upon our mundane concerns. "Consult the populations, for heaven's sake! How naive! A fine example of those wretched French ideas which claim to replace diplomacy and war by childishly simple methods." Wait a while, Gentlemen; let the reign of the transcendants pass; bear the scorn of the powerful with patience. It may be that, after many fruitless gropings, people will revert to our more modest empirical solutions. The best way of being right in the future is, in certain periods, to know how to resign oneself to being out of fashion.

REVIEW QUESTIONS

1. Which explanations for nationalism does Renan reject? Why?
2. How does Renan finally view nationalism? Does he reject that doctrine?
3. What implications does Renan's argument have for the making and unmaking of nation-states?

22 ✢ IMPERIALISM AND COLONIALISM, 1870–1914

The striking escalation of Europe's formal political control over other lands and peoples during the last half of the nineteenth century is often called the "new imperialism." The term refers to the West's renewed enthusiasm and drive for colonial empires—a calculus of political power, economic exploitation, and cultural superiority—that first began in the early modern era. England's East India Company (1600–1873) exemplified the earlier practice of private trading companies exercising monopolistic economic and military dominion over the Indian subcontinent as well as territories in Asia and Africa to control the lucrative trade in spices, silk, cotton, and tea. The introduction of Indian opium to Chinese consumers by British merchants in the early nineteenth century was another form of informal imperialism; its immoral promotion of drug addiction and disregard for Chinese law led to war in 1839. The shift from informal economic advantages to direct political control began slowly after 1850 but gathered a frenetic momentum in the 1870s with widespread European competition for new colonies. Following an Indian mutiny in 1857, Britain changed its informal economic relationship with the subcontinent by introducing direct colonial rule. Between the years 1880 and 1914, European powers radically increased their dominion in Africa, expanding their control of the continent from 10 to 90 percent. Similarly, by 1900 extensive regions of Asia had been divided up among the British, French, Dutch, Germans, and Americans. The feverish pace of colonization in this period erected unstable structures within which twentieth-century global economies, politics, and cultural exchanges would operate. Modern world history is simply inexplicable without an understanding of nineteenth-century imperialism.

Colonies assumed a new status in European culture: economically, colonies promised cheap raw materials, high yields on investments, and markets for finished goods; culturally, they provided the points of entry for the spread of Christianity and European civilization; and politically, they signified great-power status and offered a glorious, nation-uniting mission to European publics seeking solace from contentious domestic politics. Contemporaries, however, largely perceived the various justifications for imperialism as a totality: the civilizing effects of commerce and religion followed the glory of the flag. Thus arose the "friendly competition" among European nations to carve up Africa and penetrate the Far East.

Prior to the First World War, Europe almost exclusively viewed imperialism through its own interests and needs, presuming that nonwestern peoples benefited from the "civilizing mission" of the "white man's burden." Indigenous peoples, however, did not readily acquiesce in Western claims of sovereignty and successfully contested foreign governance, as in the Sudan between 1885 and 1898. Other commentators criticized European arrogance, pointing out the exploitative elements of imperialism and the crushing "black man's burden" that had accumulated from the imperialist legacy. Indeed, the Western imperial gaze saw the world as a vast space in need of transformation. In remaking the nonwestern world in its own image, the West redefined itself and its role in the world—for better or for worse.

The legacies of colonial ruling classes, imperial plantation economies, and European mass consumer markets on nonwestern manufactures forever changed indigenous societies. In creating a new set of economic, political, and social relationships between the West and the world, imperialism interpenetrated and irrevocably transformed European and nonwestern cultures. Metropole and colony, once separate entities, became fused over time into an imperial alloy, rendering the ability to return to pre-colonial conditions impossible. For this reason the multifaceted phenomenon of imperialism looms as a central element of global modernity. It not only defined the national and cultural identities of European states but also shaped colonialists' aspirations for independence and their visions of postcolonial society.

LIN TSE-HSÜ

FROM Letter to Queen Victoria

Over the course of the eighteenth and early nineteenth centuries, the British demand for tea, silk, and porcelain from China produced a vast trade imbalance, forcing Britain to purchase Chinese goods with silver. Because Chinese consumers had little desire for Western products, trading in kind proved futile. To redress the problem, British merchants turned to opium, grown in India, as a substitute for monetary payment and "opened" China to Western trade. Over time, the addictive drug took hold in Chinese society: demand soared and silver flowed back to Great Britain. In

1839, the Chinese government banned the substance and impounded over 1200 tons of opium from British export houses without compensation. Viewing this confiscation as illegal, the British government used its gunboats to enforce the restoration of trade with China, the first of two Opium Wars (1839–42; 1856–60). In 1839, Lin Tse-hsü (1785–1850), an imperial commissioner and the governor-general of the Hupeh and Hunan provinces, sent the following letter to Queen Victoria. The missive addresses the opium trade's deleterious effects on Chinese culture and society and the dubious ethics of this "free trade."

From *Chinese Repository*, Vol. 8 (February 1840), pp. 497–503.

Lin, high imperial commissioner, a president of the Board of War, viceroy of the two Keäng provinces, &c., Tang, a president of the Board of War, viceroy of the two Kwang provinces, &c., and E, a vice-president of the Board of War, lieut-governor of Kwangtung, &c., hereby conjointly address this public dispatch to the queen of England for the purpose of giving her clear and distinct information (on the state of affairs) &c.

It is only our high and mighty emperor, who alike supports and cherishes those of the Inner Land, and those from beyond the seas—who looks upon all mankind with equal benevolence—who, if a source of profit exists anywhere, diffuses it over the whole world—who, if the tree of evil takes root anywhere, plucks it up for the benefit of all nations:—who, in a word, hath implanted in his breast that heart (by which beneficent nature herself) governs the heavens and the earth! You, the queen of your honorable nation, sit upon a throne occupied through successive generations by predecessors, all of whom have been styled respectful and obedient. Looking over the public documents accompanying the tribute sent (by your predecessors) on various occasions, we find the following:—"All the people of my (i.e. the king of England's) country, arriving at the Central Land for purposes of trade, have to feel grateful to the great emperor for the most perfect justice, for the kindest treatment," and other words to that effect. Delighted did we feel that the kings of your honorable nation so clearly understood the great principles of propriety, and were so deeply grateful for the heav-

enly goodness (of our emperor):—therefore, it was that we of the heavenly dynasty nourished and cherished your people from afar, and bestowed upon them redoubled proofs of our urbanity and kindness. It is merely from these circumstances, that your country—deriving immense advantage from its commercial intercourse with us, which has endured now two hundred years—has become the rich and flourishing kingdom that it is said to be!

But, during the commercial intercourse which has existed so long, among the numerous foreign merchants resorting hither, are wheat and tares, good and bad; and of these latter are some, who, by means of introducing opium by stealth, have seduced our Chinese people, and caused every province of the land to overflow with that poison. These then know merely to advantage themselves, they care not about injuring others! This is a principle which heaven's Providence repugnates; and which mankind conjointly look upon with abhorrence! Moreover, the great emperor hearing of it, actually quivered with indignation, and especially dispatched me, the commissioner, to Canton, that in conjunction with the viceroy and lieut. governor of the province, means might be taken for its suppression!

Every native of the Inner Land who sells opium, as also all who smoke it, are alike adjudged to death. Were we then to go back and take up the crimes of the foreigners, who, by selling it for many years have induced dreadful calamity and robbed us of enormous wealth, and punish them with equal severity, our laws could not but award to them absolute annihilation! But, considering that these said foreigners did yet repent of their crime, and with a sincere heart beg for mercy; that they took 20,283 chests of opium piled up in their store-ships, and through Elliot, the superintendent of the trade of your said country, petitioned that they might be delivered up to us, when the same were all utterly destroyed, of which we, the imperial commissioner and colleagues, made a duly prepared memorial to his majesty;—considering these circumstances, we have happily received a fresh proof of the extraordinary goodness of the great emperor, inasmuch as he who voluntarily comes forward, may yet be deemed a fit subject for mercy, and his crimes be graciously remitted him. But as for him who again knowingly violates the laws, difficult indeed will it be thus to go on repeatedly pardoning! He or they shall alike be doomed to the penalties of the new statute. We presume that you, the sovereign of your honorable nation, on pouring out your heart before the altar of eternal justice, cannot but command all foreigners with the deepest respect to reverence our laws! If we only lay clearly before your eyes, what is profitable and what is destructive, you will then know that the statutes of the heavenly dynasty cannot but be obeyed with fear and trembling!

*   *   *

We have heard that in your own country opium is prohibited with the utmost strictness and severity:—this is a strong proof that you know full well how hurtful it is to mankind. Since then you do not permit it to injure your own country, you ought not to have the injurious drug transferred to another country, and above all others, how much less to the Inner Land! Of the products which China exports to your foreign countries, there is not one which is not beneficial to mankind in some shape or other. There are those which serve for food, those which are useful, and those which are calculated for re-sale;—but all are beneficial. Has China (we should like to ask) ever yet sent forth a noxious article from its soil? Not to speak of our tea and rhubarb, things which your foreign coun-tries could not exist a single day without, if we of the Central Land were to grudge you what is beneficial, and not to compassionate your wants, then wherewithal could you foreigners manage to exist? And further, as regards your woolens, camlets, and longells, were it not that you get supplied with our native raw silk, you could not get these manufactured! If China were to grudge you those things which yield a profit, how could you foreigners scheme after any profit at all? Our other articles of food, such as sugar, ginger, cinnamon, &c., and our other articles for use, such as silk piece-goods, chinaware, &c., are all so many necessaries of life to you; how can we reckon up their number! On the other hand, the things that come from your foreign countries are only calculated to make presents of, or serve for mere amusement. It is quite the same to us if we have them, or if we have them not. If then these are of no material consequence to us of the Inner Land, what difficulty would there be in prohibiting and shutting our market against them? It is only that our heavenly dynasty most freely permits you to take off her tea, silk, and other commodities, and convey them for consumption everywhere, without the slightest stint or grudge, for no other reason, but that where a profit exists, we wish that it be diffused abroad for the benefit of all the earth!

Your honorable nation takes away the products of our central land, and not only do you thereby obtain food and support for yourselves, but moreover, by re-selling these products to other countries you reap a threefold profit. Now if you would only not sell opium, this threefold profit would be secured to you: how can you possibly consent to forgo it for a drug that is hurtful to men, and an unbridled craving after gain that seems to know no bounds! Let us suppose that foreigners came from another country, and brought opium into England, and seduced the people of your country to smoke it, would not you, the sovereign of the said country, look upon such a procedure with anger, and in your just indignation endeavor to get rid of it? Now we have always heard that your highness possesses a most kind and benevolent heart, surely then you are incapable of doing or causing to be done unto another that which you should not wish another to do unto you! We have at the same time heard that your ships which come to Canton do each and every of them carry a document granted by your highness' self, on which are written these words "you shall not be permitted to carry contraband goods;" (the ship's register?) this shows that the laws of your highness are in their origin both distinct and severe, and we can only suppose that because the ships coming here have been very numerous, due attention has not been given to search and examine; and for this reason it is that we now address you this public document, that you may clearly know how stern and severe are the laws of the central dynasty, and most certainly you will cause that they be not again rashly violated!

Moreover, we have heard that in London the metropolis where you dwell, as also in Scotland, Ireland, and other such places, no opium whatever is produced. It is only in sundry parts of your colonial kingdom of Hindostan, such as Bengal, Madras, Bombay, Patna, Malwa, Benares, Malacca, and other places where the very hills are covered with the opium plant, where tanks are made for the preparing of the drug; month by month, and year by year, the volume of the poison increases, its unclean stench ascends upwards, until heaven itself grows angry, and the very gods thereat get indignant! You, the queen of the said honorable nation, ought immediately to have the plant in those parts plucked up by the very root! Cause the land there to be hoed up afresh, sow in its stead the five grains, and if any man dare again to plant in these grounds a single poppy, visit his crime with the most severe punishment. By a truly benevolent system of government such as this, will you indeed reap advantage, and do away with a source of evil. Heaven must support you, and the gods will crown you with felicity! This will get for yourself the blessing of long life, and from this will proceed the security and stability of your descendants!

In reference to the foreign merchants who come to this our central land, the food that they eat, and the dwellings that they abide in, proceed entirely from the goodness of our heavenly dynasty:—the profits which they reap, and the fortunes which they amass, have their origin only in that portion of benefit which our heavenly dynasty kindly allots them: and as these pass but little of their time in your country, and the greater part of their time in our's, it is a generally received maxim of old and of modern times, that we should conjointly admonish, and clearly make known the punishment that awaits them.

Suppose the subject of another country were to come to England to trade, he would certainly be required to comply with the laws of England, then how much more does this apply to us of the celestial empire! Now it is a fixed statute of this empire, that any native Chinese who sells opium is punishable with death, and even he who merely smokes it, must not less die. Pause and reflect for a moment: if you foreigners did not bring the opium hither, where should our Chinese people get it to re-sell? It is you foreigners who involve our simple natives in the pit of death, and are they alone to be permitted to escape alive? If so much as one of those deprive one of our people of his life, he must forfeit his life in requital for that which he has taken:—how much more does this apply to him who by means of opium destroys his fellow-men? Does the havoc which he commits stop with a single life? Therefore it is that those foreigners who now import opium into the Central Land are condemned to be beheaded and strangled by the new statute, and this explains what we said at the beginning about plucking up the tree of evil, wherever it takes root, for the benefit of all nations.

We further find that during the second month of this present year (i.e. 9th April, 1839), the superintendent of your honorable country, Elliot, viewing the law in relation to the prohibiting of opium as excessively severe, duly petitioned us, begging for "an extension of the term already limited, say five months for Hindostan and the different parts of India, and ten for England, after which they would obey and act in conformity with the new statute," and other words to the same effect. Now we, the high commissioner and colleagues, upon making a duly prepared memorial to the great emperor, have to feel grateful for his extraordinary goodness, for his redoubled compassion. Any one who within the next year and a half may by mistake bring opium to this country, if he will but voluntarily come forward, and deliver up the entire quantity, he shall be absolved from all punishment for his crime. If, however, the appointed term shall have expired, and there are still persons who continue to bring it, then such shall be accounted as knowingly violating the laws, and shall most assuredly be put to death! On no account shall we show mercy or clemency! This then may be called truly the extreme of benevolence, and the very perfection of justice!

Our celestial empire rules over ten thousand kingdoms! Most surely do we possess a measure of godlike majesty which ye cannot fathom! Still we cannot bear to slay or exterminate without previous warning, and it is for this reason that we now clearly make known to you the fixed laws of our land. If the foreign merchants of your said honorable nation desire to continue their commercial intercourse, they then must tremblingly obey our recorded statutes, they must cut off for ever the source from which the opium flows, and on no account make an experiment of our laws in their own persons! Let then your highness punish those of your subjects who may be criminal, do not

endeavor to screen or conceal them, and thus you will secure peace and quietness to your possessions, thus will you more than ever display a proper sense of respect and obedience, and thus may we unitedly enjoy the common blessings of peace and happiness. What greater joy! What more complete felicity than this!

Let your highness immediately, upon the receipt of this communication, inform us promptly of the state of matters, and of the measure you are pursuing utterly to put a stop to the opium evil. Please let your reply be speedy. Do not on any account make excuses or procrastinate. A most important communication.

REVIEW QUESTIONS

1. How does Lin perceive the power and influence of Queen Victoria? How accurate are his presumptions?
2. What are the legal grounds for Lin's argument to the British government to cease the sale of opium?
3. How does the author appeal to the honor and morality of the British crown?
4. How does this document illuminate the triangle trade route of opium between India, China, and Britain? What does this trade pattern tell us about informal imperial economies?

DAVID LIVINGSTONE

FROM Cambridge Speech of 1857

David Livingstone (1813–1873), the Scottish missionary and explorer of Africa, personified for Britain the higher cause of imperialism. Between 1840 and 1873, Livingstone traversed nearly a third of Africa, missionizing Christianity, opposing the persistent slave trade, and recording the geography and ethnographic customs of its peoples. His achievement and his self-effacing devotion to opening up Africa to commerce and Christianity provided inspiration to a nineteenth-century British public in search of a moral center to its imperialist policies in Africa. Livingstone presented this irenic speech in the same year as the Indian Mutiny, a rebellion on the subcontinent that cost thousands of lives.

From *Dr. Livingstone's Cambridge Lectures*, edited by William Monk (Cambridge: Bell, 1858).

*   *   *

My object in going into the country south of the desert was to instruct the natives in a knowledge of Christianity, but many circumstances prevented my living amongst them more than seven years, amongst which were considerations arising out of the slave system carried on by the Dutch Boers. I resolved to go into the country beyond, and soon found that, for the purposes of commerce, it was necessary to have a path to the sea. I might have gone on instructing the natives in religion, but as civilization and Christianity must go on together, I was obliged to find a path to the sea, in order that I should not sink to the level of the natives. The chief was overjoyed at the suggestion, and furnished me with twenty-seven men, and canoes, and provisions, and presents for the tribes through whose country we had to pass.

*   *   *

In a commercial point of view communication with this country is desirable. Angola is wonderfully fertile, producing every kind of tropical plant in rank luxuriance. Passing on to the valley of Quango, the stalk of the grass was as thick as a quill, and towered above my head, although I was mounted on my ox; cotton is produced in great abundance, though merely woven into common cloth; bananas and pine-apples grow in great luxuriance; but the people having no maritime communication, these advantages are almost lost. The country on the other side is not quite so fertile, but in addition to indigo, cotton, and sugarcane, produces a fibrous substance, which I am assured is stronger than flax.

The Zambesi has not been thought much of as a river by Europeans, not appearing very large at its mouth; but on going up it for about seventy miles, it is enormous. The first three hundred miles might be navigated without obstacle: then there is a rapid, and near it a coal-field of large extent. The elevated sides of the basin, which form the most important feature of the country, are far different in climate to the country nearer the sea, or even the centre. Here the grass is short, and the Angola goat, which could not live in the centre, had been seen on the east highland by Mr Moffat.

My desire is to open a path to this district, that civilization, commerce, and Christianity might find their way there. I consider that we made a great mistake, when we carried commerce into India, in being ashamed of our Christianity; as a matter of common sense and good policy, it is always best to appear in one's true character. In travelling through Africa, I might have imitated certain Portuguese, and have passed for a chief; but I never attempted anything of the sort, although endeavouring always to keep to the lessons of cleanliness rigidly instilled by my mother long ago; the consequence was that the natives respected me for that quality, though remaining dirty themselves.

I had a pass from the Portuguese consul, and on arriving at their settlement, I was asked what I was. I said, "A missionary, and a doctor too." They asked, "Are you a doctor of medicine?"—"Yes."—"Are you not a doctor of mathematics too?"—"No."—"And yet you can take longitudes and latitudes."—Then they asked me about my moustache; and I simply said I wore it, because men had moustaches to wear, and ladies had not. They could not understand either, why a sacerdote should have a wife and four children; and many a joke took place upon that subject. I used to say, "Is it not better to have children with than without a wife?" Englishmen of education always command respect, without any adventitious aid. A Portuguese governor left for Angola, giving out that he was going to keep a large establishment, and taking with him quantities of crockery, and about five hundred waistcoats; but when he arrived in Africa, he made a 'deal' of them. Educated Englishmen seldom descend to that sort of thing.

A prospect is now before us of opening Africa for commerce and the Gospel. Providence has been preparing the way, for even before I proceeded to the Central basin it had been conquered and rendered safe by a chief named Sebituane, and the language of the Bechuanas made the fashionable tongue, and that was one of the languages into which Mr Moffat had translated the Scriptures. Sebituane also discovered Lake Ngami some time previous to my explorations in that part. In going back to that country my object is to open up traffic along the banks of the Zambesi, and also to preach the Gospel. The natives of Central Africa are very desirous of trading, but their only traffic is at present in slaves, of which the poorer people have an unmitigated horror: it is therefore most desirable to encourage the former principle, and thus open a way for the consumption of free productions, and the introduction of Christianity and commerce. By encouraging the native propensity for trade, the advantages that might be derived in a commercial point of view are incalculable; nor should we lose sight of the inestimable blessings it is in our power to bestow upon the unenlightened African, by giving him the light of Christianity. Those two pioneers of civilization—Christianity and commerce—should ever be inseparable; and Englishmen should be warned by the fruits of neglecting that principle as exemplified in the result of the management of Indian affairs. By trading with Africa, also, we should at length be independent of slave-labour, and thus discountenance practices so obnoxious to every Englishman.

Though the natives are not absolutely anxious to receive the Gospel, they are open to Christian influences. Among the Bechuanas the Gospel was well received. These people think it a crime to shed a tear, but I have seen some of them weep at the recollection of their sins when God had opened their hearts to Christianity and repentance. It is true that missionaries have difficulties to encounter; but what great enterprise was ever accomplished without difficulty? It is deplorable to think that one of the noblest of our missionary societies, the Church Missionary Society, is compelled to send to Germany for missionaries, whilst other societies are amply supplied. Let this stain be wiped off. The sort of men who are wanted for missionaries are such as I see before me; men of education, standing, enterprise, zeal, and piety. It is a mistake to suppose that *any one*, as long as he is pious, will do for this office. Pioneers in every thing should be the ablest and best qualified men, not those of small ability and education. This remark especially applies to the first teachers of Christian truth in regions which may never have before been blest with the name and Gospel of Jesus Christ. In the early ages the monasteries were the schools of Europe, and the monks were not ashamed to hold the plough. The missionaries now take the place of those noble men, and we should not hesitate to give up the small luxuries of life in order to carry knowledge and truth to them that are in darkness. I hope that many of those whom I now address will embrace that honourable career. Education has been given us from above for the purpose of bringing to the benighted the knowledge of a Saviour. If you knew the satisfaction of performing such a duty, as well as the gratitude to God which the missionary must always feel, in being chosen for so noble, so sacred a calling, you would have no hesitation in embracing it.

For my own part, I have never ceased to rejoice that God has appointed me to such an office. People talk of the sacrifice I have made in spending so much of my life in Africa. Can that be called a sacrifice which is simply paid back as a small part of a great debt owing to our God, which we can never repay?—Is that a sacrifice which brings its own blest reward in healthful activity, the consciousness of doing good, peace of mind, and a bright hope of a glorious destiny hereafter?—Away with the word in such a view, and with such a thought! It is emphatically no sacrifice. Say rather it is a privilege. Anxiety, sickness, suffering, or danger, now and then, with a foregoing of the common conveniences and charities of this life, may make us pause, and cause the spirit to waver, and the soul to sink, but let this only be for a moment. All these are nothing when compared with the glory which shall hereafter be revealed in, and for, us. I never made a sacrifice. Of this we ought not to talk, when we remember the great sacrifice which HE made who left His Father's throne on high to give Himself for us.

*   *   *

REVIEW QUESTIONS

1. What was for Livingstone the relationship between commerce and missionary work?
2. What were Livingstone's perceptions of African culture?
3. Judging from this speech, how do you think Livingstone inspired a generation to enter into missionary work?

ODALISQUE WITH SLAVE (1839)   JEAN-AUGUSTE-DOMINIQUE INGRES

Over the course of the eighteenth and nineteenth centuries, literary and visual representations of the Orient became bound up in a larger colonial project of defining cultural differences between East and West. French artists particularly developed the odalisque as a genre of the imperial exotic. Odalik is the Turkish word for the slave attendant to women of the harem, but it entered into the French language as a word signifying a harem temptress. Odalisque paintings typify the West's eroticized fantasies of the Orient, which mix the sensually delightful with the tyrannical. Jean August Dominique Ingres's Odalisque with Slave, presented in 1839, is a classic example of the genre. How did this fantasy of Middle Eastern culture help define the West?

FRIEDRICH FABRI

FROM *Does Germany Need Colonies?*

The small pamphlet Does Germany Need Colonies? *by Friedrich Fabri (1824–1891), a former inspector of the Rhenish Missionary Association, was published in 1879. It was one among many publications that generated a widespread public debate in Germany regarding its need for colonies. Fabri cited overpopulation as a motivating factor, and his emphasis on Germany's "cultural mission" infused imperialism with an idealism that the general public embraced. The domestic agitation for colonial expansion by pressure groups and grass-roots associations radically affected domestic politics. Germany's decision in the 1880s to enter the race for colonial territories in Africa and Asia had, moreover, a profound impact on the European balance of power.*

From *The Imperialism Reader*, edited by Louis L. Snyder (New York: Van Nostrand, 1962), pp. 116–17.

*   *   *

Should not the German nation, so seaworthy, so industrially and commercially minded, more than other peoples geared to agricultural colonization, and possessing a rich and available supply of labor, all these to a greater extent than other modern culture-peoples, should not this nation successfully hew a new path on the road of imperialism? We are convinced beyond doubt that the colonial question has become a matter of life or death for the development of Germany. Colonies will have a salutary effect on our economic situation as well as on our entire national progress.

Here is a solution for many of the problems that face us. In this new Reich of ours there is so much bitterness, so much unfruitful, sour, and poisoned political wrangling, that the opening of a new, promising road of national effort will act as a kind of liberating influence. Our national spirit will be renewed, a gratifying thing, a great asset. A people that have been led to a high level of power can maintain its historical position only as long as it understands and proves itself to be *the bearer of a cultural mission*. At the same time, this is the only way to stability and to the growth of national welfare, the necessary foundation for a lasting expansion of power.

At one time Germany contributed only intellectual and literary activity to the tasks of our century. That era is now over. As a people we have become politically minded and powerful. But if political power becomes the primary goal of a nation, it will lead to harshness, even to barbarism. We must be ready to serve for the ideal, moral, and economic culture-tasks of our time. The French national-economist, Leroy Beaulieu, closed his words on colonization with these words: "That nation is the greatest in the world which colonizes most; if she does not achieve that rank today, she will make it tomorrow."

No one can deny that in this direction England has by far surpassed all other countries. Much has been said, even in Germany, during the last few decades about the "disintegrating power of England." Indeed, there seems to be something to it when we consider the Palmerston era and Gladstonian politics. It has been customary in our age of military power to evaluate the strength of a state in terms of its combat-ready troops. But anyone who looks at the globe and notes the steadily increasing colonial possessions of Great Britain, how she extracts strength from them, the skill with which she governs them, how the Anglo-Saxon strain occupies a dominant position in the overseas territories, he will begin to see the military argument as the reasoning of a philistine.

The fact is that England tenaciously holds on to its world-wide possessions with scarcely one-fourth the manpower of our continental military state. That is not only a great economic advantage but also a striking proof of the solid power and cultural fiber of England. Great Britain, of course, isolates herself far from the mass warfare of the continent, or only goes into action with dependable allies; hence, the insular state has suffered and will suffer no real damage. In any case, it would be wise for us Germans to learn about colonial skills from our Anglo-Saxon cousins and to begin a friendly competition with them. When the German Reich centuries ago stood at the pinnacle of the states of Europe, it was the Number One trade and sea power. If the New Germany wants to protect its newly won position of power for a long time, it must heed its *Kultur*-mission and, above all, delay no longer in the task of renewing the call for colonies.

*   *   *

REVIEW QUESTIONS

1. Why does Fabri consider the acquisition of colonies "a matter of life or death for the development of Germany"?
2. How does Fabri compare Germany's political status with that of Britain?
3. According to Fabri, what political, economic, and cultural uses will Germany derive from colonies?

RUDYARD KIPLING

"The White Man's Burden"

Rudyard Kipling (1865–1936), a prolific poet, novelist, and short-story author who won the Nobel Prize for literature in 1907, was born in Bombay to parents of high Anglo-Indian society. Schooled in England, Kipling returned to India and drew on its imperial atmosphere for his fiction and verse to great success. Alongside his literary feats, Kipling also championed the "civilizing mission" of empire throughout his life, devoutly believing in Britain's and the West's duty to educate and govern the "Sloth and heathen Folly" of the non-Western world. Composed as an exhortation to the United States to fulfill its imperial role in the Pacific, "The White Man's Burden" originally appeared in McClure's Magazine *in February 1899 during the Spanish-American War. The poem's title was immediately taken up as a slogan by imperialists.*

From *McClure's Magazine*, vol. 12 (Feb. 1899).

Take up the White Man's burden—
    Send forth the best ye breed—
Go bind your sons to exile
    To serve your captives' need;
To wait in heavy harness,
    On fluttered folk and wild—
Your new-caught, sullen peoples,
    Half-devil and half-child.

Take up the White Man's burden—
    In patience to abide,
To veil the threat of terror
    And check the show of pride;
By open speech and simple,
    An hundred times made plain,
To seek another's profit,
    And work another's gain.

Take up the White Man's burden—
    The savage wars of peace—
Fill full the mouth of Famine
    And bid the sickness cease;
And when your goal is nearest
    The end for others sought,
Watch Sloth and heathen Folly
    Bring all your hope to nought.

Take up the White Man's burden—
    No tawdry rule of kings,
But toil of serf and sweeper—
    The tale of common things.
The ports ye shall not enter,
    The roads ye shall not tread,
Go make them with your living,
    And mark them with your dead.

Take up the White Man's burden—
    And reap his old reward:
The blame of those ye better,
    The hate of those ye guard—
The cry of hosts ye humour
    (Ah, slowly!) toward the light:—
"Why brought ye us from bondage,
    "Our loved Egyptian night?"

Take up the White Man's burden—
    Ye dare not stoop to less—
Nor call too loud on Freedom
    To cloak your weariness;
By all ye cry or whisper,
    By all ye leave or do,
The silent, sullen peoples
    Shall weigh your Gods and you.

Take up the White Man's burden—
    Have done with childish days—
The lightly proffered laurel,
    The easy, ungrudged praise.
Comes now, to search your manhood
    Through all the thankless years,
Cold, edged with dear-bought wisdom,
    The judgment of your peers!

REVIEW QUESTIONS

1. What was the burden of the white man?
2. How does Kipling glorify the white man's role?
3. How are Kipling's imperial subjects characterized?
4. What were the civil and military aspects of the "white man's burden"?

The first step towards lightening

The White Man's Burden

is through teaching the virtues of cleanliness.

Pears' Soap

is a potent factor in brightening the dark corners of the earth as civilization advances, while amongst the cultured of all nations it holds the highest place—it is the ideal toilet soap.

"LIGHTENING THE WHITE MAN'S BURDEN" (1899)

Popular culture in the late nineteenth century articulated Western imperial themes in numerous ways. This 1899 soap advertisement, which plays on Kipling's "White Man's Burden," offers a clear illustration of the negative characterization of non-Western peoples in the high imperial era. Admiral George Dewey, a hero of the Spanish-American War, is featured washing with Pears' Soap; the corner illustrations and the text express the advertisement's sentiment. Alongside steamboats and commerce, soap and hygiene are characterized as new items that the West can introduce to the non-Western world. The word lighten works, then, as a racist pun. How does this advertisement help us understand how the beliefs of imperial politics became a self-evident, everyday practice?

ISMĀ'ĪL B. 'ABD AL-QĀDIR

The Siege of Khartoum (1884–85)

After 1870, when European states staked formal territorial claims during the so-called "scramble for Africa," indigenous forces also emerged that contested Western colonial administrative control. In the 1880s, for example, religious zealotry in the Sudan undermined Western sovereignty and illustrates the complexity of colonial power relations. Under the sway of Muhammad Ahmad, a holy man of a Sudanese Islamic order who proclaimed himself the Mahdi, a messianic redeemer of the Islamic faith, the Mahdiyya movement gathered a mass following that resembled earlier Islamic revivalist followings. Feeding on Sudanese resentment of Turco-Egyptian and British rule, this messianic movement declared a jihad *to re-conquer Sudanese and Egyptian territories and thereby establish unspoiled Islamic rule. This rising Mahdist army soon engaged British colonial forces, attacking and overrunning garrisons. Its siege of Khartoum in 1884–85 became world news. General Charles George Gordon, the British commander of Khartoum, defended the Sudanese city for months, and sparked a political battle in Britain between Prime Minister Gladstone, who ordered Gordon's retreat, and public opinion, which championed Gordon's insubordinate decision to defend the post. Submitting to pressure from both public opinion and Queen Victoria, Gladstone ordered Adjutant-General Garnet Wolseley and his troops to aid Gordon's trapped soldiers. Wolseley arrived days late; the city had fallen and Gordon was dead. The Mahdist regime subsequently ruled the territory until 1895, when Britain ordered General Kitchener to subjugate the Sudan, culminating in the British victory at Omduran in 1898. The following passage, written as hagiography by a devout follower of Muhammad Ahmad, throws light on the popular Sudanese perspective of its leader during the siege and the movement's blend of piety and militarism.*

From *The Life of the Sudanese Mahdi: A Historical Study of the Book of the Bliss of Him Who Seeks Guidance by the Life of the Imam the Mahdi,* edited by Haim Shaked (New Brunswick, N.J.: Transaction Books, 1979), pp. 180–85, 187–88.

The Conquest of Khartoum

When the Mahdi encamped at Abū Sa'd, he sent reinforcements to 'Abd al-Raḥmān al-Nujūmī and ordered him to tighten the siege of Gordon and the people of his government in Khartoum. The Companions carried out the order and the situation in Khartoum became very serious. The Mahdi had written to Gordon, calling him to God, to convert to Islam, and to follow the Mahdi. Also, he had written to all the notables of Khartoum, but to no avail. The siege caused a famine in Khartoum. Gordon, realizing his weakness and the failure of his tricks, ordered the removal of the poor, the disabled, the women, the weak and the slaves from the town in order to alleviate the situation of the army. They left by boats, in a most horrible condition, as if they had come out of graves, and fell on the Mahdi's camp at Abū Sa'd, begging for the necessary sustenance. The Mahdi ordered the commissioner of the Treasury to look after them, and they recuperated. When the people of Khartoum repeatedly deserted, the Mahdi wrote a proclamation to the Companions instructing them to be courteous to those who came out to him.

As for Gordon, he remained with the people of his administration and most of the notables of the town and those who had some food, hoping to attain their objective. Gordon, who was now reassured of his relief by the English, made promises to those who were with him in Khartoum. The author remarks that the English were [later] engaged at Abū Ṭulayḥ by the Companions and defeated. Their survivors reached al-Matamma and, having learned that Gordon had perished, fled to their country. The Mahdi then summoned 'Abd al-Raḥmān al-Nujūmī and the commanders who were besieging Khartoum to Abū Sa'd. There he briefed them about the manner in which to breach Khartoum, and ordered them to return to their siege positions.

On Sunday [8 Rabī II 1302/25 January 1885] the Mahdi preached to the people and roused them to the *jihād*. On Monday eve, 9 Rabī II 1302 [January 26, 1885], the Mahdi, his senior Khalifa, the other Khalifas and the Companions who were with them, crossed the river by boats and encamped at a place close to the location of the siege, near Shajarat Māḥū Bey. The Mahdi summoned all the Companions, and they gathered together in front of him. Al-Nujūrmī had previously summoned 'Abdallāh w. Jubārā, Abū Bakr w. 'Āmir and the other Companions who were besieging Khartoum from the east, at the Qaṣr Rāsikh Bey area. They all came by boat on the Nile. All the Companions gathered together in al-Nujūmī's area, for only from that area was it possible to penetrate Khartoum on foot by way of the trench. . . . When all the divisions were in the Mahdi's presence, he ordered them to assault the Turks, heedless of the trench, since God was supporting His Mahdi. Having exhorted and warned the Companions the Mahdi, with his senior Khalifa and some of the Companions, returned to Abū Sa'd by boat on that night [8–9 Rabī 11/25–26 January].

'Abd al-Raḥmān al-Nujūmī and the fighters passed the night in uttering the *tahlīl* and the *takbīr* and in prayer. Before the break of dawn the Companions attacked the trench. Despite the darkness the Turks noticed them because they were shouting the *tahlīl* and the *takbīr*, and [the Turks] poured deadly fire. Heedless, the Companions attacked the trench, penetrated the town and began slaughtering the Turks. The slaughter continued from dawn until about forenoon, when the ground became red with the blood of people and the streets were filled with corpses. Only God knows how many of the Turks and of those who joined them died. Gordon was killed in his palace, his head was cut off and hung in the market as a punishment for him and a lesson to others. A party of pashas, governors, consuls, *'umdas,* merchants and notables of the town also perished. No more than ten Companions died as martyrs. From among the people of Khartoum, only those survived who were behind locked gates or hid in the gardens near the town. They came out and swore allegiance. On the day of the conquest, the Mahdi issued a proclamation warning the Companions about the booty. He entered the town on Friday [13 Rabī II/January 30], and there he prayed the Friday prayer. He then returned to Abū Sa'd and, in Jumāda I [16 February-17 March], he moved to Omdurman and settled there.

The Expedition of Mūsā W. Muḥammad Ḥilū against the English in Abū Ṭulayḥ

When Gordon's situation had become most grave, he requested his government (*dawla*) to dispatch a large army. When this army reached Dongola, it was divided into three contingents, each equipped with military instruments and munitions and firearms which were unprecedented in the battles of the Mahdia; for example the Martini rifles which were faster and of longer range than the Remington rifles and the Sabre bayonet, etc.

*   *   *

When Muḥammad al-Khayr ʿAbdallāh learned of the arrival of the English, he sent a report to the Mahdi who was at Abū Saʿd. Muḥammad al-Khayr then announced a general mobilization for the *jihād*. All the Jaʿaliyīn and the other inhabitants of that region complied and an army, whose size only God knows, was mustered. He dispatched them to Abū Ṭulayḥ to annihilate the English contingent which was crossing the land of the Shāiqīya towards al-Matamma, before they arrived at the Nile. Muḥammad al-Khayr gave ʿAbd al-Mājid Muḥammad the command of this mission. He reached Abū Ṭulayḥ, encamped at the watering-place and sent out scouts who brought back information that the English had reached Jaqdūl, on their way to Abū Ṭulayḥ. The Companions then prepared for war. During the night, the English reached Abū Ṭulayḥ and encamped within gun-shot of the Companions. The Mahdi had dispatched Mūsā w. Ḥīlū with a large army to fight them. He reached Abū Ṭulayḥ on the morning of that night in which the English arrived. Mūsā w. Ḥīlū then roused the Companions and counselled them to concentrate the firearms in one block, the horsemen and infantry in others. But when the Companions saw the enemies of God, the English, they lost control of themselves, and all of them—including the horsemen and those who had firearms—charged in disorder. Despite the large distance between them and the unbelievers, the unbelievers poured deadly fire, and the Martini rifles had a great effect. The Companions reached the unbelievers only after many of them had died as martyrs. Nevertheless, they fought a fierce battle with the unbelievers; the Companions in support of the Religion, while the unbelievers were fighting to save their own lives. The Companions were winning the chaotic battle, having routed two of the three squares in which the unbelievers had arranged themselves and would have routed the third square had it not been for the preoccupation of some of them with the booty, which enabled the unbelievers to overcome the Companions and kill them. The English saved themselves and reached the river near al-Matamma. In this battle, a party of the Companions died as martyrs, including Mūsā w. Ḥīlū, Muḥammad w. Bilāl and others.

While the English were on their way, the Companions repeatedly engaged them in battle, but the unbelievers managed to reach al-Matamma. The Companions also encamped there. Meanwhile, most of the people of al-Matamma transferred their children and women to the east [bank] of the Nile, opposite al-Matamma, to save them from the English. Gordon, having learned that the English had moved from Dongola towards Khartoum, sent five armoured steamers, weighted with Turks and some Shāiqīya like Khashm al-Mūs, to await the English who were due at al-Matamma and to spur them on to relieve his plight. However, God caused Gordon to perish three days before their arrival. After the arrival of the English at the river, near al-Matamma, the steamers reached them, and the Turks on board joined them [on land]. They formed a large square and marched on the Companions at al-Matamma, since there was about an hour's distance between the English camp and the town. The Companions inside al-Matamma prepared for battle and fortified the town walls making embrasures and gun emplacements. As soon as the English came within range, the Companions shot at, and shelled them. In the first salvo the leader of the unbelievers, called Sir Herbert Stewart was wounded and perished. The unbelievers then withdrew to the village of al-Qalʿa, very near al-Matamma, where they set up gun emplacements. They began shelling al-Matamma and destroyed several of the Companions' gun emplacements. As they were unable to destroy the town, they withdrew to Wādī Abī Ramād.

After the battle of Abū Ṭulayḥ, the Mahdi ordered the conquest of Khartoum. As the English were confused about Gordon and had misgivings about [the fall of] Khartoum, they loaded two of the steamers with brave men and large quantities of provisions so that Gordon, were he still alive, could make use of them till—as they alleged—they would reach him. The wicked were not aware that by that time Gordon was in Hell. When the two steamers came near the ditch of Omdurman,

Ḥamdān Abū 'Anja, who at that time was on the White Nile bank near Omdurman, was assigned to prevent them from reaching Khartoum. His men fired on them, and they stopped in the middle of the river, not knowing how to save themselves. Meanwhile they were shelled from the fort of al-Muqran and they realized that Khartoum had fallen and that Gordon had perished. Only after great tribulations inflicted by Ḥamdān Abū 'Anja did they flee and return to their people.

*   *   *

After their arrival in Dongola, the English were driven by their wrath to inflict harm on the Mahdi's relatives there. They imprisoned a party of them including: Muḥammad 'Abd al-Qādir, Sharīf Sāttī 'Alī, Muḥammad Ibrāhīm, Aḥmad al-Najīb, Ḥājj Sharīfī Muḥammad Nūr, Ḥājj Sharīf Maḥmūd, and 'Abd al-Qādir 'Abd al-Karīm. They were imprisoned after their relationship to the Mahdi had been established in court. [354] The author remarks that the trial was fictitious and that the reason for it was the false claim of the unbelievers that they punished only those who were related to the Mahdi. He curses a certain [unnamed] Dongolawi who assisted the unbelievers in this matter. The English then told the Mahdi's relatives to write to the Mahdi that they would be set free only after the Mahdi released his prisoners and when they reached the English. The Mahdi's relatives complied and the English then transported them from Dongola towards their country [i.e., Egypt]. When they reached 'Anqash, about half a day's distance from Wādī Ḥalfā, the Mahdi's reply reached the English. In excerpts from the letter, which are cited by the author, the Mahdi states his refusal to accept the proposal, since the people in question had embraced Islam and preferred to stay with him.

This letter was accompanied by a letter to the Mahdi's relatives, in which the Mahdi rebuked them. When the English read the Mahdi's letter, they despaired of [obtaining] their people. They released the Mahdi's relatives, honoured them, provided riding animals and provisions, and sent them back. The Mahdi's relatives returned to Dongola and the English then returned to their country.

After the battle of Abū Ṭulayḥ and the conquest of Khartoum, the Mahdi wrote to Muḥammad al-Khayr 'Abdallāh and ordered him to go to Dongola and call on its people to follow the Mahdi and there fight the English and the Turks. Muḥammad al-Khayr commenced preparations and dispatched successive expeditions to Dongola, he himself following them. Meanwhile, he was informed of the flight of the English, [as well as] the Turks, and those townsfolk who had joined them; and that Dongola was empty of them. He reported to the Mahdi in writing and began marching to Dongola. He reached the place with his army, and called on its people to join the Mahdia. They did so without fighting.

REVIEW QUESTIONS

1. How does this account blend religious piety and religious fervor?
2. How does the author characterize the Madhi's treatment of civilians during the siege? How does the Mahdi treat "unbelievers"?
3. What attributes does the author assign the British?
4. What does this account suggest about the manner in which this movement expanded its rule over Sudanese towns and villages?
5. Is this Mahdist movement anomalous to modern times or symptomatic of it?

J. A. HOBSON

FROM *Imperialism: A Study*

Among the most trenchant and influential critiques of imperialism during its heyday stands John A. Hobson's enduring Imperialism. *Published in 1902, the study was among the first to challenge the putative economic and political advantages of formal colonial settlements and their administrations, characterizing the international phenomenon instead as the unrelenting drive for markets, resources, and economic power to benefit an elite capitalist class. The work roundly castigated imperialism. It intepreted the "fight for markets" abroad and its accompanying military and administrative expenses as a "social pathology" that was unnecessary and unproductive for domestic consumers. The following passage sketches Europe's shift from a liberal nationalism toward exploitative colonialism and imperialism.*

From *Imperialism: A Study*, by J. A. Hobson (New York: James Pott & Co., 1902), pp. 2–12.

*   *   *

The close of the third quarter of the century saw Europe fairly settled into large national States or federations of States, though in the nature of the case there can be no finality, and Italy still looks to Trieste, as Germany to Austria, for the fulfilment of her manifest destiny.

This passion and the dynastic forms it helped to mould and animate are largely attributable to the fierce prolonged resistance which peoples, both great and small, were called on to maintain against the imperial designs of Napoleon. The national spirit of England was roused by the tenseness of the struggle to a self-consciousness it had never experienced since "the spacious days of great Elizabeth." Jena made Prussia into a great nation; the Moscow campaign brought Russia into the field of European nationalities as a constant factor in politics, opening her for the first time to the full tide of Western ideas and influences.

Turning from this territorial and dynastic nationalism to the spirit of racial, linguistic, and economic solidarity which has been the underlying motive, we find a still more remarkable movement. Local particularism on the one hand, vague cosmopolitanism upon the other, yielded to a ferment of nationalist sentiment, manifesting itself among the weaker peoples not merely in a sturdy and heroic resistance against political absorption or territorial nationalism, but in a passionate revival of decaying customs, language, literature, and art; while it bred in more dominant peoples strange ambitions of national "destiny" and an attendant spirit of Chauvinism.

*   *   *

It is a debasement of this genuine nationalism, by attempts to overflow its natural banks and absorb the near or distant territory of reluctant and unassimilable peoples, that marks the passage from nationalism to a spurious colonialism on the one hand, Imperialism on the other.

Colonialism, where it consists in the migration of part of a nation to vacant or sparsely peopled foreign lands, the emigrants carrying with them full rights of citizenship in the mother country, or else establishing local self-government in close conformity with her institutions and under her final control, may be considered a genuine expansion of nationality, a territorial enlargement of the stock, language and institutions of the nation. Few colonies in history have, however, long remained in this condition when they have been remote from the mother country. Either they have severed the connection and set up for themselves as separate nationalities, or they have been kept in complete political bondage so far as all major processes of government are concerned, a condition to which the term Imperialism is at least as appropriate as colonialism. The only form of distant colony which can be regarded as a clear expansion of nationalism is the self-governing British colony in Australasia and Canada, and even in these cases local conditions may generate a separate nationalism based on a strong consolidation of colonial interests and sentiments alien from and conflicting with those of the mother nation. In other "self-governing" colonies, as in Cape Colony and Natal, where the majority of whites are not descended from British settlers, and where the presence of subject or "inferior" races in vastly preponderating numbers, and alien climatic and other natural conditions, mark out a civilisation distinct from that of the "mother country," the conflict between the colonial and the imperial ideas has long been present in the forefront of the consciousness of politicians. When Lord Rosmead spoke of the permanent presence of the imperial factor as "simply an absurdity," and Mr. Rhodes spoke of its "elimination," they were championing a "colonialism" which is more certain in the course of time to develop by inner growth into a separate "nationalism" than in the case of the Australasian and Canadian colonies, because of the wider divergence, alike of interests and radical conditions of life, from the mother nation. Our other colonies are plainly representative of the spirit of Imperialism rather than of colonialism. No considerable proportion of the population consists of British settlers living with their families in conformity with the social and political customs and laws of their native land: in most instances they form a small minority wielding political or economic sway over a majority of alien and subject people, themselves under the despotic political control of the Imperial Government or its local nominees. This, the normal condition of a British colony, is well-nigh universal in the colonies of other European countries. The "colonies" which France and Germany establish in Africa and Asia are in no real sense plantations of French and German national life beyond the seas; nowhere, not even in Algeria, do they represent true European civilisation; their political and economic structure of society is wholly alien from that of the mother country.

Colonialism, in its best sense, is a natural overflow of nationality; its test is the power of colonists to transplant the civilisation they represent to the new natural and social environment in which they find themselves. We must not be misled by names; the "colonial" party in Germany and France is identical in general aim and method with the "imperialist" party in England, and the latter is the truer title. Professor Seeley well marked the nature of Imperialism. "When a State advances beyond the limits of nationality its power becomes precarious and artificial. This is the condition of most empires, and it is the condition of our own. When a nation extends itself into other territories the chances are that it cannot destroy or completely drive out, even if it succeeds in conquering, them. When this happens it has a great and permanent difficulty to contend with, for the subject or rival nationalities cannot be properly assimilated, and remain as a permanent cause of weakness and danger."

The novelty of the recent Imperialism regarded as a policy consists chiefly in its adoption by several nations. The notion of a number of competing empires is essentially modern. The root idea of empire in the ancient and medieval world was that of a federation of States, under a hegemony, covering in general terms the entire known or recognised world, such as was held by Rome under the so-called *pax Romana*. When Roman citizens, with full civic rights, were found all over the explored world, in Africa and Asia, as well as in Gaul and Britain, Imperialism contained a genuine element of internationalism. With the fall of Rome this conception of a single empire wielding political authority over the civilised world did not disappear. On the contrary, it survived all the fluctuations of the Holy Roman Empire. Even after the definite split between the Eastern and Western sections had taken place at the close of the fourth century, the theory of a single State, divided for administrative purposes, survived. Beneath every cleavage or antagonism, and notwithstanding the severance of many independent kingdoms and provinces, this ideal unity of the empire lived. It formed the conscious avowed ideal of Charlemagne, though as a practical ambition confined to Western Europe. Rudolph of Habsburg not merely revived the idea, but laboured to realise it through Central Europe, while his descendant Charles V. gave a very real meaning to the term by gathering under the unity of his imperial rule the territories of Austria, Germany, Spain, the Netherlands, Sicily, and Naples. In later ages this dream of a European Empire animated the policy of Peter the Great, Catherine, and Napoleon. Nor is it impossible that Kaiser Wilhelm III. holds a vision of such a world-power.

Political philosophers in many ages, Vico, Macchiavelli, Dante, Kant, have speculated on an empire as the only feasible security for peace, a hierarchy of States conforming on the larger scale to the feudal order within the single State.

Thus empire was identified with internationalism. . . .

*   *   *

This early flower of humane cosmopolitanism was destined to wither before the powerful revival of nationalism which marked the next century. Even in the narrow circles of the cultured classes it easily passed from a noble and a passionate ideal to become a vapid sentimentalism, and after the brief flare of 1848 among the continental populace had been extinguished, little remained but a dim smouldering of the embers. Even the Socialism which upon the continent retains a measure of the spirit of internationalism is so tightly confined within the national limits, in its struggle with bureaucracy and capitalism, that "the international" expresses little more than a holy aspiration, and

has little opportunity of putting into practice the genuine sentiments of brotherhood which its prophets have always preached.

Thus the triumph of nationalism seems to have crushed the rising hope of internationalism. Yet it would appear that there is no essential antagonism between them. A true strong internationalism in form or spirit would rather imply the existence of powerful self-respecting nationalities which seek union on the basis of common national needs and interests. Such a historical development would be far more conformable to laws of social growth than the rise of anarchic cosmopolitanism from individual units amid the decadence of national life.

Nationalism is a plain highway to internationalism, and if it manifests divergence we may well suspect a perversion of its nature and its purpose. Such a perversion is Imperialism, in which nations trespassing beyond the limits of facile assimilation transform the wholesome stimulative rivalry of varied national types into the cut-throat struggle of competing empires.

Not only does aggressive Imperialism defeat the movement towards internationalism by fostering animosities among competing empires: its attack upon the liberties and the existence of weaker or lower races stimulates in them a corresponding excess of national self-consciousness. A nationalism that bristles with resentment and is all astrain with the passion of self-defence is only less perverted from its natural genius than the nationalism which glows with the animus of greed and self-aggrandisement at the expense of others. From this aspect aggressive Imperialism is an artificial stimulation of nationalism in peoples too foreign to be absorbed and too compact to be permanently crushed. We have welded Africanderdom into just such a strong dangerous nationalism, and we have joined with other nations in creating a resentful nationalism hitherto unknown in China. The injury to nationalism in both cases consists in converting a cohesive, pacific, internal force into an exclusive, hostile force, a perversion of the true power and use of nationality. The worst and most certain result is the retardation of internationalism. The older nationalism was primarily an inclusive sentiment; its natural relation to the same sentiment in another people was lack of sympathy, not open hostility; there was no inherent antagonism to prevent nationalities from growing and thriving side by side. Such in the main was the nationalism of the earlier nineteenth century, and the politicians of Free Trade had some foundation for their dream of a quick growth of effective, informal internationalism by peaceful, profitable intercommunication of goods and ideas among nations recognising a just harmony of interests in free peoples.

The overflow of nationalism into imperial channels quenched all such hopes. While co-existent nationalities are capable of mutual aid involving no direct antagonism of interests, co-existent empires following each its own imperial career of territorial and industrial aggrandisement are natural necessary enemies. The full nature of this antagonism on its economic side is not intelligible without a close analysis of those conditions of modern capitalist production which compel an ever keener "fight for markets," but the political antagonism is obvious.

The scramble for Africa and Asia has virtually recast the policy of all European nations, has evoked alliances which cross all natural lines of sympathy and historical association, has driven every continental nation to consume an ever-growing share of its material and human resources upon military and naval equipment, has drawn the great new power of the United States from its isolation into the full tide of competition; and, by the multitude, the magnitude, and the suddenness of the issues it throws on to the stage of politics, has become a constant agent of menace and of perturbation to the peace and progress of mankind. The new policy has exercised the most notable and formidable influence upon the conscious statecraft of the nations which indulge in it. While producing for popular consumption doctrines of national destiny and imperial missions of civilisation, contradictory in their true import, but subsidiary to one another as supports of popular Imperialism, it has evolved a calculating, greedy type of Macchiavellianism, entitled "real-politik" in Germany, where

it was made, which has remodelled the whole art of diplomacy and has erected national aggrandisement without pity or scruple as the conscious motive force of foreign policy. Earth hunger and the scramble for markets are responsible for the openly avowed repudiation of treaty obligations which Germany, Russia, and England have not scrupled to defend. The sliding scale of diplomatic language, hinterland, sphere of interest, sphere of influence, paramountcy, suzerainty, protectorate, veiled or open, leading up to acts of forcible seizure or annexation which sometimes continue to be hidden under "lease," "rectification of frontier," "concession," and the like, is the invention and expression of this cynical spirit of Imperialism. While Germany and Russia have perhaps been more open in their professed adoption of the material gain of their country as the sole criterion of public conduct, other nations have not been slow to accept the standard. Though the conduct of nations in dealing with one another has commonly been determined at all times by selfish and short-sighted considerations, the conscious, deliberate adoption of this standard at an age when the intercourse of nations and their interdependence for all essentials of human life grow ever closer is a retrograde step fraught with grave perils to the cause of civilisation.

Review Questions

1. What is the difference between colonialism and imperialism? Is Hobson opposed to all forms of colonialism? When does colonialism shade into malign imperialism?

2. When was imperialism cosmopolitan in character and why did it change? Why does Hobson characterize modern imperialism as aggressive and competitive?

3. What does Hobson mean by "internationalism" and can empire serve this doctrine?

4. Does imperialism help or hinder nationalism?

5. For Hobson, how has the "scramble for Africa and Asia" affected European civilization and statecraft?

VLADIMIR LENIN

FROM *Imperialism, the Highest Stage of Capitalism*

Imperialists' justification for formal control of colonies in the last half of the nineteenth century often carried the economic rationale of securing monopoly outlets for domestic-made goods and capital investment. Hence, although Marx never integrated imperialism into his critique of capitalism, second-generation socialists perceived capitalism in the imperial era as having entered a new phase, which witnessed the anxious attempts of banking consortiums and large-scale industrial enterprises to stake out high-yielding investments, new markets, and cheaper raw materials. In the highly influential pamphlet Imperialism, the Highest Stage of Capitalism, *first written in 1917 (and posthumously revised in the 1920s and 1930s), Lenin (1870–1924) argued that imperialism must be viewed as "parasitic or decaying capitalism." The apparent success of combining empire and capitalism, he argued, hid profound structural contradictions that brought on not only the First World War but also the imminent revolt of the colonial world from capitalist exploitation. The following passage, drawn from the pamphlet's final chapter, summarizes his principal arguments for viewing imperialism as the highest—that is, the final—stage of capitalism.*

From *Imperialism, the Highest Stage of Capitalism*, by V. I. Lenin (New York: International, 1939), pp. 123–27.

*   *   *

We have seen that the economic quintessence of imperialism is monopoly capitalism. This very fact determines its place in history, for monopoly that grew up on the basis of free competition, and precisely out of free competition, is the transition from the capitalist system to a higher social-economic order. We must take special note of the four principal forms of monopoly, or the four principal manifestations of monopoly capitalism, which are characteristic of the epoch under review.

Firstly, monopoly arose out of the concentration of production at a very advanced stage of development. This refers to the monopolist capital-ist combines, cartels, syndicates and trusts. We have seen the important part that these play in modern economic life. At the beginning of the twentieth century, monopolies acquired complete supremacy in the advanced countries. And although the first steps towards the formation of the cartels were first taken by countries enjoying the protection of high tariffs (Germany, America), Great Britain, with her system of free trade, was not far behind in revealing the same basic phenomenon, namely, the birth of monopoly out of the concentration of production.

Secondly, monopolies have accelerated the capture of the most important sources of raw materials, especially for the coal and iron industries, which are the basic and most highly cartelised industries in capitalist society. The monopoly of the most important sources of raw materials has enormously increased the power of big capital, and has sharpened the antagonism between cartelised and non-cartelised industry.

Thirdly, monopoly has sprung from the banks. The banks have developed from modest intermediary enterprises into the monopolists of finance capital. Some three or five of the biggest banks in each of the foremost capitalist countries have achieved the "personal union" of industrial and bank capital, and have concentrated in their hands the disposal of thousands upon thousands of millions which form the greater part of the capital and income of entire countries. A financial oligarchy, which throws a close net of relations of dependence over all the economic and political institutions of contemporary bourgeois society without exception—such is the most striking manifestation of this monopoly.

Fourthly, monopoly has grown out of colonial policy. To the numerous "old" motives of colonial policy, finance capital has added the struggle for the sources of raw materials, for the export of capital, for "spheres of influence," *i.e.*, for spheres for profitable deals, concessions, monopolist profits and so on; in fine, for economic territory in general. When the colonies of the European powers in Africa, for instance, comprised only one-tenth of that territory (as was the case in 1876) colonial policy was able to develop by methods other than those of monopoly—by the "free grabbing" of territories, so to speak. But when nine-tenths of Africa had been seized (approximately by 1900), when the whole world had been divided up, there was inevitably ushered in a period of colonial monopoly and, consequently, a period of particularly intense struggle for the division and the redivision of the world.

The extent to which monopolist capital has intensified all the contradictions of capitalism is generally known. It is sufficient to mention the high cost of living and the oppression of the cartels. This intensification of contradictions constitutes the most powerful driving force of the transitional period of history, which began from the time of the definite victory of world finance capital.

Monopolies, oligarchy, the striving for domination instead of the striving for liberty, the exploitation of an increasing number of small or weak nations by an extremely small group of the richest or most powerful nations—all these have given birth to those distinctive characteristics of imperialism which compel us to define it as parasitic or decaying capitalism. More and more prominently there emerges, as one of the tendencies of imperialism, the creation of the "bond-holding" (rentier) state, the usurer state, in which the bourgeoisie lives on the proceeds of capital exports and by "clipping coupons." It would be a mistake to believe that this tendency to decay precludes the possibility of the rapid growth of capitalism. It does not. In the epoch of imperialism, certain branches of industry, certain strata of the bourgeoisie and certain countries betray, to a more or less degree, one or other of these tendencies. On the whole, capitalism is growing far more rapidly than before. But this growth is not only becoming more and more uneven in general; its unevenness also manifests itself, in particular, in the decay of the countries which are richest in capital (such as England).

In regard to the rapidity of Germany's economic development, Riesser, the author of the book on the big German banks, states:

> The progress of the preceding period (1848–70), which had not been exactly slow, stood in about the same ratio to the rapidity with which the whole of Germany's national economy, and with it German banking, progressed during this period (1870–1905) as the mail coach of the Holy Roman Empire of the German nation stood to the speed of the present-day automobile . . . which in whizzing past, it must be said, often endangers not only innocent pedestrians in its path, but also the occupants of the car.

In its turn, this finance capital which has grown so rapidly is not unwilling (precisely because it has grown so quickly) to pass on to a more "tranquil" possession of colonies which have to be seized—and not only by peaceful methods—from richer nations. In the United States, economic development in the last decades has been even more rapid than in Germany, and *for this very reason* the parasitic character of modern American capitalism has stood out with particular prominence. On the other hand, a comparison of, say, the republican American bourgeoisie with the monarchist Japanese or German bourgeoisie shows that the most pronounced political distinctions diminish to an extreme degree in the epoch of imperialism—not because they are unimportant in general, but because in all these cases we are discussing a bourgeoisie which has definite features of parasitism.

The receipt of high monopoly profits by the capitalists in one of the numerous branches of industry, in one of numerous countries, etc., makes it economically possible for them to corrupt certain sections of the working class, and for a time a fairly considerable minority, and win them to the side of the bourgeoisie of a given industry or nation against all the others. The intensification of antagonisms between imperialist nations for the division of the world increases this striving. And so there is created that bond between imperialism and opportunism, which revealed itself first and most clearly in England, owing to the fact that certain features of imperialist development were observable there much earlier than in other countries.

Some writers, L. Martov, for example, try to evade the fact that there is a connection between imperialism and opportunism in the labour movement—which is particularly striking at the present time—by resorting to "official optimistic" arguments (*à la* Kautsky and Huysmans) like the following: the cause of the opponents of capitalism would be hopeless if it were precisely progressive capitalism that led to the increase of opportunism, or, if it were precisely the best paid workers who were inclined towards opportunism, etc. We must have no illusion regarding "optimism" of this kind. It is optimism in regard to opportunism; it is optimism which serves to conceal opportunism. As a matter of fact the extraordinary rapidity and the particularly revolting character of the development of opportunism is by no means a guarantee that its victory will be durable: the rapid growth of a malignant abscess on a healthy body only causes it to burst more quickly and thus to relieve the body of it. The most

dangerous people of all in this respect are those who do not wish to understand that the fight against imperialism is a sham and humbug unless it is inseparably bound up with the fight against opportunism.

From all that has been said in this book on the economic nature of imperialism, it follows that we must define it as capitalism in transition, or, more precisely, as moribund capitalism. It is very instructive in this respect to note that the bourgeois economists, in describing modern capitalism, frequently employ terms like "interlocking," "absence of isolation," etc.; "in conformity with their functions and course of development," banks are "not purely private business enterprises; they are more and more outgrowing the sphere of purely private business regulation." And this very Riesser, who uttered the words just quoted, declares with all seriousness that the "prophecy" of the Marxists concerning "socialisation" has "not come true"!

What then does this word "interlocking" express? It merely expresses the most striking feature of the process going on before our eyes. It shows that the observer counts the separate trees, but cannot see the wood. It slavishly copies the superficial, the fortuitous, the chaotic. It reveals the observer as one who is overwhelmed by the mass of raw material and is utterly incapable of appreciating its meaning and importance. Ownership of shares and relations between owners of private property "interlock in a haphazard way." But the underlying factor of this interlocking, its very base, is the changing social relations of production. When a big enterprise assumes gigantic proportions, and, on the basis of exact computation of mass data, organises according to plan the supply of primary raw materials to the extent of two-thirds, or three-fourths of all that is necessary for tens of millions of people; when the raw materials are transported to the most suitable place of production, sometimes hundreds or thousands of miles away, in a systematic and organised manner; when a single centre directs all the successive stages of work right up to the manufacture of numerous varieties of finished articles; when these products are distributed according to a single plan among tens and hundreds of millions of consumers (as in the case of the distribution of oil in America and Germany by the American "oil trust")—then it becomes evident that we have socialisation of production, and not mere "interlocking"; that private economic relations and private property relations constitute a shell which is no longer suitable for its contents, a shell which must inevitably begin to decay if its destruction be delayed by artificial means; a shell which may continue in a state of decay for a fairly long period (particularly if the cure of the opportunist abscess is protracted), but which will inevitably be removed.

REVIEW QUESTIONS

1. According to Lenin, why are monopolies a contradiction and a problem for capitalism?
2. Why does Lenin emphasize finance (as opposed to industrial) capital in his interpretation of imperialism?
3. How would imperial monopolies spur the collapse of capitalism?

EDMUND D. MOREL

FROM *The Black Man's Burden*

Alongside the dominant ideological assertion that moral responsibility obliged the West to build empires, critics of imperialism voiced their dissent. Although the most consistent denunciations came from socialists, liberals also criticized imperialism on a number of economical and political principles. Edmund D. Morel (1873–1924), a British journalist writing in the immediate aftermath of the First World War, offers here a stinging indictment of imperialism's fatal impact on Africa. Written in 1920, Morel's scathing criticism of Britain joined the postwar debate concerning the future of the colonies and the question of African self-determination.

From *The Black Man's Burden*, by Edmund D. Morel (London: National Labour Press, 1920).

*   *   *

It is with the peoples of Africa, then, that our inquiry is concerned. It is they who carry the "Black man's" burden. They have not withered away before the white man's *occupation*. Indeed, if the scope of this volume permitted, there would be no difficulty in showing that Africa has ultimately absorbed within itself every Caucasian and, for that matter, every Semitic invader too. In hewing out for himself a fixed abode in Africa, the white man has massacred the African in heaps. The African has survived, and it is well for the white settlers that he has.

In the process of imposing his political dominion over the African, the white man has carved broad and bloody avenues from one end of Africa to the other. The African has resisted, and persisted.

For three centuries the white man seized and enslaved millions of Africans and transported them, with every circumstance of ferocious cruelty, across the seas. Still the African survived and, in his land of exile, multiplied exceedingly.

But what the partial occupation of his soil by the white man has failed to do; what the mapping out of European political "spheres of influence" has failed to do; what the maxim and the rifle, the slave gang, labour in the bowels of the earth and the lash, have failed to do; what imported measles, small-pox and syphilis have failed to do; what even the oversea slave trade failed to do, the power of modern capitalistic exploitation, assisted by modern engines of destruction, may yet succeed in accomplishing.

For from the evils of the latter, scientifically applied and enforced, there is no escape for the African. Its destructive effects are not spasmodic: they are permanent. In its permanence resides its fatal consequences. It kills not the body merely, but the soul. It breaks the spirit. It attacks the African at every turn, from every point of vantage. It wrecks his polity, uproots him from the land, invades his family life, destroys his natural pursuits and occu-pations, claims his whole time, enslaves him in his own home.

Economic bondage and wage slavery, the grind-ing pressure of a life of toil, the incessant demands of industrial capitalism—these things a landless European proletariat physically endures, though hardly. * * * The recuperative forces of a temperate climate are there to arrest the ravages, which alle-viating influences in the shape of prophylactic and curative remedies will still further circumscribe. But in Africa, especially in tropical Africa, which a capitalistic imperialism threatens and has, in part, already devastated, man is incapable of reacting against unnatural conditions. In those regions man is engaged in a perpetual struggle against disease and an exhausting climate, which tells heavily upon child-bearing; and there is no scientific machinery for salving the weaker members of the community. The African of the tropics is capable of tremendous physical labours. But he cannot accommodate himself to the European system of monotonous, uninterrupted labour, with its long and regular hours, involving, moreover, as it fre-quently does, severance from natural surroundings and nostalgia, the condition of melancholy result-ing from separation from home, a malady to which the African is specially prone. Climatic conditions forbid it. When the system is forced upon him, the tropical African droops and dies.

Nor is violent physical opposition to abuse and injustice henceforth possible for the African in any part of Africa. His chances of effective resistance have been steadily dwindling with the increasing perfectibility in the killing power of modern arma-ment. Gunpowder broke the effectiveness of his resistance to the slave trade, although he continued to struggle. He has forced and, on rare occasions and in exceptional circumstances beaten, in turn the old-fashioned musket, the elephant gun, the seven-pounder, and even the repeating rifle and the gatling gun. He has been known to charge right down repeatedly, foot and horse, upon the square, swept on all sides with the pitiless and continuous hail of maxims.[1] But against the latest inventions, physical bravery, though associated with a perfect knowledge of the country, can do nothing. The African cannot face the high-explosive shell and the bomb-dropping aeroplane. He has inflicted sanguinary reverses upon picked European troops, hampered by the climate and by commissariat dif-ficulties. He cannot successfully oppose members of his own race free from these impediments, employed by his white adversaries, and trained in all the diabolical devices of scientific massacre. And although the conscripting of African armies for use in Europe or in Africa as agencies for the liquidation of the white man's quarrels must bring in its train evils from which the white man will be the first to suffer, both in Africa and in Europe; the African himself must eventually disappear in the process. Winter in Europe, or even in Northern Africa, is fatal to the tropical or sub-tropical Afri-can, while in the very nature of the case anything approaching real European control in Africa, of hordes of African soldiery armed with weapons of precision is not a feasible proposition. The Black man converted by the European into a scientifically-equipped machine for the slaughter of his kind, is certainly not more merciful than the white man similarly equipped for like purposes in dealing with unarmed communities. And the experiences of the civilian population of Belgium, East Prussia, Galicia and Poland is indicative of the sort of visi-tation involved for peaceable and powerless Afri-

---

[1] The Maxim gun was a self-powered machine gun first used in the 1880s.

can communities if the white man determines to add to his appalling catalogue of past misdeeds towards the African, the crowning wickedness of once again, as in the day of the slave trade, supplying him with the means of encompassing his own destruction.

Thus the African is really helpless against the material gods of the white man, as embodied in the trinity of imperialism, capitalistic-exploitation, and militarism. If the white man retains these gods and if he insists upon making the African worship them as assiduously as he has done himself, the African will go the way of the Red Indian, the Amerindian, the Carib, the Guanche, the aboriginal Australian, and many more. And this would be at once a crime of enormous magnitude, and a world disaster.

*　　*　　*

An endeavour will now be made to describe the nature, and the changing form, which the burden inflicted by the white man in modern times upon the black has assumed. It can only be sketched here in the broadest outline, but in such a way as will, it is hoped, explain the differing causes and motives which have inspired white activities in Africa and illustrate, by specific and notable examples, their resultant effects upon African peoples. It is important that these differing causes and motives should be understood, and that we should distinguish between them in order that we may hew our way later on through the jungle of error which impedes the pathway to reform. Diffused generalities and sweeping judgments generate confusion of thought and hamper the evolution of a constructive policy based upon clear apprehension of the problem to be solved.

The history of contact between the white and black peoples in modern times is divisible into two distinct and separate periods: the period of the slave trade and the period of invasion, political control, capitalistic exploitation, and, the latest development, militarism. Following the slave trade period and preceding the period of invasion, occurs the trade interlude which, indeed, had priority of both periods, as when the Carthagenians bartered salt and iron implements for gold dust on the West Coast. But this interlude concerns our investigations only when we pass from destructive exposure to constructive demonstration.

The first period needs recalling, in order to impress once more upon our memories the full extent of the African's claim upon us, the white imperial peoples, for tardy justice, for considerate and honest conduct.

Our examination of the second period will call for sectional treatment. The history of contact and its consequences during this period may be roughly sub-divided thus:

a. The struggle for supremacy between European invading *Settlers* and resident African peoples in those portions of Africa where the climate and other circumstances permit of Europeans rearing families of white children.

b. *Political action* by European Governments aiming at the assertion of sovereign rights over particular areas of African territory.

c. *Administrative policy,* sanctioned by European Governments, and applied by their local representatives in particular areas, subsequent to the successful assertion of sovereign rights.

These sub-divisions are, perhaps, somewhat arbitrary. The distinctiveness here given to them cannot be absolutely preserved. There is, for instance, a natural tendency for both *a* and *b* to merge into *c* as, through efflux of time, the originating cause and motive of contact is obscured by developments to which contact has given rise.

Thus racial contention for actual possession of the soil, and political action often resulting in so-called treaties of Protectorate thoroughly unintelligible to the African signees, are both landmarks upon the road leading to eventual administrative policy: *i.e.,* to direct government of the black man by the white.

*　　*　　*

It is often argued that the agricultural and arboricultural methods of the African are capable of improvement. The statement is undoubtedly true. It applies with equal force to the land of Britain. There is no difference of opinion among British agricultural experts as to the capacities for improvement in the methods of British agriculture. As for British arboriculture it is still an almost entirely neglected field of British home enterprise. We can afford to be patient with the African if he has not yet attained perfection. Why, it is only since the beginning of the 18th century that the rotation of crops has been practised in England! But the Kano farmers in Northern Nigeria have understood rotation of crops and grass manuring for at least five hundred years.

To advance such truisms as an excuse for robbing the native communities of their land, degrading farmers in their own right to the level of hired labourers urged on by the lash, and conferring monopolistic rights over the land and its fruits to private corporations, is to make truth the stalking horse of oppression and injustice. The statement of fact may be accurate. The claim put forward on the strength of it is purely predatory.

Those who urge this and kindred arguments only do so to assist the realisation of their purpose. That purpose is clear. It is to make of Africans all over Africa a servile race; to exploit African labour, and through African labour, the soil of Africa for their own exclusive benefit. They are blind to the cost in human suffering. They are indifferent to the fact that in the long run their policy must defeat its own ends. They care only for the moment, and for the objects of the moment they are prepared to sacrifice the future. But since their purpose is selfish, short-sighted and immoral it must be striven against without pause or relaxation. There can be no honest or safe compromise with these people and their policy. A great moral issue is involved. But although that issue comes first, and must come first, it is not the only issue.

For a time it may be possible for the white man to maintain a white civilisation in the colonisable, or partly colonisable, areas of the African Continent based on servile or semi-servile labour: to build up a servile State. But even there the attempt can be no more than fleeting. The days of Roman imperialism are done with for ever. Education sooner or later breaks all chains, and knowledge cannot be kept from the African. The attempt will be defeated in the north by Islam, which confers power of combination in the political sphere, and a spiritual unity which Europe has long lost in the mounting tides of her materialism. It will fail in the south through the prolificness of the African, through the practical impossibility of arresting his intellectual advance and through race admixture, which is proceeding at a much more rapid rate than most people realise. In the great tropical regions the attempt must fail in the very nature of things, if for no other reason, because it can only be enforced by employing the black man, trained in the art of modern warfare as the medium through which to coerce his unarmed brother. The former will be well content to play that part for a period more or less prolonged, but when he becomes alive to his power the whole fabric of European domination will fall to pieces in shame and ruin. From these failures the people of Europe will suffer moral and material damage of a far-reaching kind.

And the criminal folly of it! The white imperial peoples have it in their power, if their rulers will cultivate vision and statesmanship enough to thrust aside the prompting of narrow, ephemeral interests—anti-national in the truest sense—to make of Africa the home of highly-trained and prosperous peoples enriching the universe as their prosperity waxes, dwelling in plains and valleys, in forests and on plateaux made fruitful by their labours, assisted by science; a country whose inhabitants will be enterprising and intelligent, loving their land, looking to it for inspiration, cooperating faithfully in the work of the world, developing their own culture, independent, free, self-respecting, attaining to higher mental growth as the outcome of internal evolutionary processes. Why cannot the white imperial peoples, acknowledging in some measure the injuries they have inflicted upon the African, turn a new leaf in their treatment of him? For nearly two thousand years they have professed to be governed by the teachings of Christ. Can they not begin in the closing century of that era, to practise what they profess—and what their missionaries of religion teach the African? Can they not cease to regard the African as a producer of dividends for a selected few among their number, and begin to regard him as a human being with human rights? Have they made such a success of their own civilisation that they can contemplate with equanimity the forcing of all its social failures upon Africa—its hideous and devastating inequalities, its pauperisms, its senseless and destructive egoisms, its vulgar and soulless materialism? It is in their power to work such good to Africa—and such incalculable harm! Can they not make up their minds that their strength shall be used for noble ends? Africa demands at their hands, justice, and understand-

ing sympathy—not ill-informed sentiment. And when these are dealt out to her she repays a thousandfold.

*   *   *

REVIEW QUESTIONS

1. How does Morel outline the history of gradual European domination over indigenous Africans?
2. What is the extent of blame that Morel lays at Europe's door?
3. List the range of abuse and exploitation that Morel ascribes to the Western imperial powers.
4. What does Morel's criticism of Europe's exportation of industrial work habits to Africa suggest about European attitudes toward colonies?
5. Why does Morel call the preservation of colonies in Africa a criminal folly?

23 ❧ MODERN INDUSTRIES AND MASS POLITICS, 1870–1914

In the period 1870–1914, the West's prosperity as an industrial powerhouse and its maturity as a modern civil society produced an array of economic, political, and cultural challenges. Although Europe stood at the zenith of its power, its political turmoil and intellectual developments nonetheless questioned and mitigated the bourgeoisie's triumphant belief in progress and civilization.

Industrialization entered into a second, more mature stage, which produced innovative technologies and greater scales of economy. Department stores marked the arrival of mass consumer culture, with its breadth of goods and its new sales techniques. Newly invented machinery, which sewed, cut, pressed, and molded with labor-saving efficiency, allowed entrepreneurs to meet increased demands at lower prices. Employers furthermore maximized profit margins with "scientific" time-work studies, producing more efficient, rationalized regimens of work. Although hardly proportional to employers' gains, the living standards of workers rose, demonstrating capitalism's innovative abilities to adapt and prosper. But the new economic growth also brought keener competition for markets and national wealth, which sharpened political rivalries. While Britain remained the undisputed leader of the first industrial revolution, the emergence of such new leading sectors as steel, chemicals, and electrical engineering enabled German companies to achieve explosive economic expansion and thus vie with England and France for a greater share of world markets. Economic nationalism became an increasingly important component of political discussions.

The widespread introduction of universal male suffrage after 1870 launched the era of mass politics. The enfranchisement of unpropertied laborers significantly broadened the political landscape, producing a range of political views that shook the delicate equilibrium of bourgeois and aristocratic governance. Syndicalists, anarchists, socialists, communists, and democratic labor parties now competed for workers' political loyalty. In this period Marxism also ceased to be a monolithic tenet. While such socialists as Eduard Bernstein argued that socialism should revise its belief in the imminent collapse of capitalism and start to participate in parliamentary politics for incremental reform, Lenin and other radical socialists continued to embrace Marx's tenet of class struggle for new revolutionary programs.

Women also emerged as a new political constituency. No longer content with the "natural" roles of reproduction and domesticity, women contested the right arrogated by men to deny them political citizenship and control over their property and legal affairs. Awakening to new identities, women demanded the vote, the right to a higher education, and overall respect for their intelligence and ability to serve society. The failure of the political establishment to initiate change for women abetted the rise of women's associations to agitate for the vote. And when peaceful petitioning failed to produce parliamentary debates, English women resorted to civil disobedience and militancy. Hunger strikes, destruction of property, and contentious demonstrations by women scandalized Europeans and disturbed ideals of peaceful, evolutionary change. Rejecting bourgeois movements, socialist feminists advocated the economic and political mobilization of women as an important weapon for the working-class movement.

In the last third of the nineteenth century, Europe's leading intellectuals, artists, and scientists also shook the foundations of the bourgeois world, questioning the fundamental premises by which bourgeois values and norms organized society and politics. Scientific discussion of Charles Darwin's theory of natural selection threw doubt on the ordered harmony of a divine, moral universe and furthermore became susceptible to false analogies to social behavior. Philosophers attacked Judeo-Christian values of social justice as spiritually enervating and culturally debilitating. The fledgling science of psychoanalysis further challenged the bourgeoisie's belief in rational, purposive action by demonstrating that behavior was largely determined by the inner mechanisms of the unconscious. The irrational drives of crowd behavior, argued Gustave Le Bon, undermined the ability of mass politics to deliberate with logic and reason. Although the richness of European letters defies simple generalization, many of the enduring voices from this period felt increasingly detached from normative bourgeois assumptions, especially those grounded in rationality and progress.

EDUARD BERNSTEIN

FROM *Evolutionary Socialism*

At the turn of the century, Eduard Bernstein (1850–1932) was a leading member of the Social Democratic Party of Germany (SPD), Europe's largest, best-organized Marxist party. In 1899 Bernstein published Evolutionary Socialism: A Criticism and Affirmation, *which called attention to the evolutionary changes in capitalism that rendered orthodox Marxist doctrine obsolete. In the book Bernstein argued for the need to revise tactics and goals for working-class constituencies. Bernstein's treatise, which sparked an important debate among socialists, is a useful document, for it throws light not only on the revisionist political strategies of socialists but also on the changing nature of late-nineteenth-century capitalist political economy.*

From *Evolutionary Socialism: A Criticism and Affirmation*, by Eduard Bernstein, translated by Edith C. Harvey (New York: B. W. Huebsch, 1911).

*   *   *

It has been maintained in a certain quarter that the practical deductions from my treatises would be the abandonment of the conquest of political power by the proletariat organised politically and economically. That is quite an arbitrary deduction, the accuracy of which I altogether deny.

I set myself against the notion that we have to expect shortly a collapse of the bourgeois economy, and that social democracy should be induced by the prospect of such an imminent, great, social catastrophe to adapt its tactics to that assumption. That I maintain most emphatically.

The adherents of this theory of a catastrophe, base it especially on the conclusions of the *Communist Manifesto*. This is a mistake in every respect.

The theory which the *Communist Manifesto* sets forth of the evolution of modern society was correct as far as it characterised the general tendencies of that evolution. But it was mistaken in several special deductions, above all in the estimate of the *time* the evolution would take. The last has been unreservedly acknowledged by Friedrich Engels, the joint author with Marx of the *Manifesto*, in his preface to the *Class War in France*. But it is evident that if social evolution takes a much greater period of time than was assumed, it must also take upon itself *forms* and lead to forms that were not foreseen and could not be foreseen then.

Social conditions have not developed to such an acute opposition of things and classes as is depicted in the *Manifesto*. It is not only useless, it is the greatest folly to attempt to conceal this from ourselves. The number of members of the possessing classes is today not smaller but larger. The enormous increase of social wealth is not accompanied by a decreasing number of large capitalists but by an increasing number of capitalists of all degrees. The middle classes change their character but they do not disappear from the social scale.

The concentration in productive industry is not being accomplished even today in all its departments with equal thoroughness and at an equal rate. In a great many branches of production it certainly justifies the forecasts of the socialist critic of society; but in other branches it lags even today behind them. The process of concentration in agriculture proceeds still more slowly. Trade statistics show an extraordinarily elaborated graduation of enterprises in regard to size. No rung of the ladder is disappearing from it. The significant changes in the inner structure of these enterprises and their inter-relationship cannot do away with this fact.

In all advanced countries we see the privileges of the capitalist bourgeoisie yielding step by step to democratic organisations. Under the influence of this, and driven by the movement of the working classes which is daily becoming stronger, a social reaction has set in against the exploiting tendencies of capital, a counteraction which, although it still proceeds timidly and feebly, yet does exist, and is always drawing more departments of economic life under its influence. Factory legislation, the democratising of local government, and the extension of its area of work, the freeing of trade unions and systems of co-operative trading from legal restrictions, the consideration of standard conditions of labour in the work undertaken by public authorities—all these characterise this phase of the evolution.

But the more the political organisations of modern nations are democratised the more the needs and opportunities of great political catastrophes are diminished. He who holds firmly to the catastrophic theory of evolution must, with all his power, withstand and hinder the evolution described above, which, indeed, the logical defenders of that theory formerly did. But is the conquest of political power by the proletariat simply to be by a political catastrophe? Is it to be the appropriation and utilisation of the power of the State by the proletariat exclusively against the whole non-proletarian world?

He who replies in the affirmative must be reminded of two things. In 1872 Marx and Engels announced in the preface to the new edition of the *Communist Manifesto* that the Paris Commune had exhibited a proof that "the working classes cannot simply take possession of the ready-made State machine and set it in motion for their own aims." And in 1895 Friedrich Engels stated in detail in the preface to *War of the Classes* that the time of political surprises, of the "revolutions of small conscious minorities at the head of unconscious masses" was today at an end, that a collision on a large scale with the military would be the means of checking the steady growth of social democracy and of even throwing it back for a time—in short, that social democracy would flourish far better by lawful than by unlawful means and by violent revolution. And he points out in conformity with this opinion that the next task of the party should be

"to work for an uninterrupted increase of its votes" or to carry on a slow *propaganda of parliamentary activity.*

Thus Engels, who, nevertheless, as his numerical examples show, still somewhat overestimated the rate of process of the evolution! Shall we be told that he abandoned the conquest of political power by the working classes, because he wished to avoid the steady growth of social democracy secured by lawful means being interrupted by a political revolution?

If not, and if one subscribes to his conclusions, one cannot reasonably take any offence if it is declared that for a long time yet the task of social democracy is, instead of speculating on a great economic crash, "to organise the working classes politically and develop them as a democracy and to fight for all reforms in the State which are adapted to raise the working classes and transform the State in the direction of democracy."

That is what I have said in my impugned article and what I still maintain in its full import. As far as concerns the question propounded above it is equivalent to Engel's dictum, for democracy is, at any given time, as much government by the working classes as these are capable of practising according to their intellectual ripeness and the degree of social development they have attained. Engels, indeed, refers at the place just mentioned to the fact that the *Communist Manifesto* has "proclaimed the conquest of the democracy as one of the first and important tasks of the fighting proletariat."

In short, Engels is so thoroughly convinced that the tactics based on the presumption of a catastrophe have had their day, that he even considers a revision of them necessary in the Latin countries where tradition is much more favourable to them than in Germany. "If the conditions of war between nations have altered," he writes, "no less have those for the war between classes." Has this already been forgotten?

No one has questioned the necessity for the working classes to gain the control of government. The point at issue is between the theory of a social cataclysm and the question whether with the given social development in Germany and the present advanced state of its working classes in the towns and the country, a sudden catastrophe would be desirable in the interest of the social democracy. I have denied it and deny it again, because in my judgment a greater security for lasting success lies in a steady advance than in the possibilities offered by a catastrophic crash.

And as I am firmly convinced that important periods in the development of nations cannot be leapt over, I lay the greatest value on the next tasks of social democracy, on the struggle for the political rights of the working man, on the political activity of working men in town and country for the interests of their class, as well as on the work of the industrial organisation of the workers.

In this sense I wrote the sentence that the movement means everything for me and that what is *usually* called "the final aim of socialism" is nothing; and in this sense I write it down again today. Even if the word "usually" had not shown that the proposition was only to be understood conditionally, it was obvious that it *could* not express indifference concerning the final carrying out of socialist principles, but only indifference— or, as it would be better expressed, carelessness— as to the form of the final arrangement of things. I have at no time had an excessive interest in the future, beyond general principles; I have not been able to read to the end any picture of the future. My thoughts and efforts are concerned with the duties of the present and the nearest future, and I only busy myself with the perspectives beyond so far as they give me a line of conduct for suitable action now.

The conquest of political power by the working classes, the expropriation of capitalists, are no ends in themselves but only means for the accomplishment of certain aims and endeavours. As such they are demands in the programme of social democracy and are not attacked by me. Nothing can be said beforehand as to the circumstances of their accomplishment; we can only fight for their realisation. But the conquest of political power necessitates the possession of political *rights*; and the most important problem of tactics which German social democracy has at the present time to solve, appears to me to be to devise the best ways for the extension of the political and economic rights of the German working classes.

*   *   *

That which concerns me, that which forms the chief aim of this work, is, by opposing what is left of the utopian mode of thought in the socialist theory, to strengthen equally the realistic and the idealistic element in the socialist movement.

REVIEW QUESTIONS

1. According to Bernstein, in what ways was the *Communist Manifesto* incorrect?
2. What aspects of political and economic life had alleviated class conflict?
3. What is Bernstein's solution? How does it differ from orthodox Marxism?

VLADIMIR LENIN

FROM *Our Programme*

The extreme conservatism of tsarist government officials found its radical counterpart in the revolutionary doctrines of late-nineteenth-century Russian political activists. Whereas populists—the narodniki—*sought to mobilize the Russian peasantry as a revolutionary force, the emergence of an industrial working class convinced Marxist socialists that the urban proletariat would spearhead a revolution against the capitalist development being fostered by the tsarist state itself.*

Vladimir Ilich Ulyanov, better known as Lenin (1870–1924), was drawn into the Russian opposition movement after his brother was executed in 1887 for conspiring to assassinate Tsar Alexander III. In subsequent years, Lenin became one of the leading theorists of the Russian Social Democratic Workers' Party. In 1899, at the end of a period of exile in Siberia, he wrote the following statement of revolutionary principles, affirming his adherence to revolutionary Marxism and rejecting "reformist" tendencies within the international socialist movement. Four years prior to the schism between the Social Democratic Party's revolutionary Bolsheviks and the reformist Mensheviks, Lenin had already rejected cooperation with the liberal bourgeoisie and instead embraced the alternative of a "vanguard" of professional revolutionaries to lead the workers' revolution.

From *Our Programme*, by Vladimir Lenin (1899), Internet Modern History Sourcebook, www.fordham.edu/halsall/mod/1899lenin-program.html [accessed 5/17/11].

International social democracy is at present going through a period of theoretical vacillations. Up to the present the doctrines of Marx and Engels were regarded as a firm foundation of revolutionary theory—nowadays voices are raised everywhere declaring these doctrines to be inadequate and antiquated. Anyone calling himself a social-democrat and having the intention to publish a social-democratic organ, must take up a definite attitude as regards this question, which by no means concerns German social-democrats alone.

We base our faith entirely on Marx's theory; it was the first to transform socialism from a Utopia into a science, to give this science a firm foundation and to indicate the path which must be trodden in order further to develop this science and to elaborate it in all its details. It discovered the nature of present-day capitalist economy and explained the way in which the employment of workers—the purchase of labour power—the enslavement of millions of those possessing no property by a handful of capitalists, by the owners of the land, the factories, the mines, etc., is concealed. It has shown how the whole development of modern capitalism is advancing towards the large producer ousting the small one, and is creating the prerequisites which make a socialist order of society possible and necessary. It has taught us to see, under the disguise of ossified habits, political intrigues, intricate laws, cunning theories, the class struggle, the struggle between, on the one hand, the various species of the possessing classes, and, on the other hand, the mass possessing no property, the proletariat, which leads all those who possess nothing. It has made clear what is the real task of a revolutionary socialist party—not to set up projects for the transformation of society, not to preach sermons to the capitalists and their admirers about improving the position of the workers, not the instigation of conspiracies, but the organisation of the class struggle of the proletariat and the carrying on of this struggle, the final aim of which is the seizure of political power by the proletariat and the organisation of a socialist society.

We now ask: What new elements have the touting "renovators" introduced into this theory, they who have attracted so much notice in our day and have grouped themselves round the German socialist Bernstein? Nothing, nothing at all; they have not advanced by a single step the science which Marx and Engels adjured us to develop; they have not taught the proletariat any new methods of fighting; they are only marching backwards in that they adopt the fragments of antiquated theories and are preaching to the proletariat not the theory of struggle but the theory of submissiveness—submissiveness to the bitterest enemies of the proletariat, to the governments and bourgeois parties who never tire of finding new methods of persecuting socialists. Plekhanov, one of the founders and leaders of Russian social-democracy, was perfectly right when he subjected to merciless criticism the latest "Criticism" of Bernstein, whose views have now been rejected even by the representatives of the German workers at the Party Congress in Hanover [1899].

We know that on account of these words we shall be drenched with a flood of accusations; they will cry out that we want to turn the Socialist Party into a holy order of the "orthodox," who persecute the "heretics" for their aberrations from the "true dogma," for any independent opinion, etc. We know all these nonsensical phrases which have become the fashion nowadays. Yet there is no shadow of truth in them, no iota of sense. There can be no strong socialist party without a revolutionary theory which unites all socialists, from which the socialists draw their whole conviction, which they apply in their methods of fighting and working. To defend a theory of this kind, of the truth of which one is completely convinced, against unfounded attacks and against attempts to debase it, does not mean being an enemy of criticism in general. We by no means regard the theory of Marx as perfect and inviolable; on the contrary, we are convinced that this theory has only laid the foundation stones of that science on which the socialists must continue to build in every direction, unless they wish to be left behind by life. We believe that it is particularly necessary for Russian socialists to work out the Marxist theory independently, for this theory only gives general precepts, the details of which must be applied in England otherwise than in France, in France otherwise than in Germany, and in Germany otherwise than in Russia. ∗ ∗ ∗

What are the main questions which arise in applying the common programme of all social-democrats to Russia?

We have already said that the essence of this programme consists in the organisation of the class struggle of the proletariat and in carrying on this struggle, the final aim of which is the seizure of political power by the proletariat and the construction of a socialist society. The class struggle of the proletariat is divided into: the economic fight (the fight against [the] individual capitalist, or against the individual groups of capitalists by the improvement of the position of the workers) and the political fight (the fight against the Govern-

ment for the extension of the rights of the people, i.e., for democracy, and for the expansion of the political power of the proletariat). Some Russian social-democrats ∗ ∗ ∗ regard the economic fight as incomparably more important and almost go so far as to postpone the political fight to a more or less distant future. This standpoint is quite wrong. All social-democrats are unanimous in believing that it is necessary to carry on an agitation among the workers on this basis, i.e., to help the workers in their daily fight against the employers, to direct their attention to all kinds and all cases of chicanery, and in this way to make clear to them the necessity of unity. To forget the political for the economic fight would, however, mean a digression from the most important principle of international social-democracy; it would mean forgetting what the whole history of the Labour movement has taught us. Fanatical adherents of the bourgeoisie and of the government which serves it, have indeed repeatedly tried to organise purely economic unions of workers and thus to deflect them from the "politics" of socialism. It is quite possible that the Russian Government will also be clever enough to do something of the kind, as it has always endeavored to throw some largesse or other sham presents to the people in order to prevent them becoming conscious that they are oppressed and are without rights.

No economic fight can give the workers a permanent improvement of their situation, it cannot, indeed, be carried on a large scale unless the workers have the free right to call meetings, to join in unions, to have their own newspapers and to send their representatives to the National Assembly as do the workers in Germany and all European countries (with the exception of Turkey and Russia). In order, however, to obtain these rights, a political fight must be carried on. In Russia, not only the workers but all the citizens are deprived of political rights. Russia is an absolute monarchy. The Tsar alone promulgates laws, nominates officials and controls them. For this reason it seems as though in Russia the Tsar and the Tsarist Government were dependent on no class and cared for all equally. In reality, however, all the officials are chosen exclusively from the possessing class, and all are subject to the influence of the large capitalists who obtain whatever they want—the Ministers dance to the tune the large capitalists play. The Russian worker is bowed under a double yoke; he is robbed and plundered by the capitalists and the landowners, and, lest he should fight against them, he is bound hand and foot by the police, his mouth is gagged and any attempt to defend the rights of the people is followed by persecution. Any strike against a capitalist results in the military and police being let loose on the workers. Every economic fight of necessity turns into a political fight, and social-democracy must indissolubly combine the economic with the political fight into a united class struggle of the proletariat.

The first and chief aim of such a fight must be the conquest of political rights, the conquest of political freedom. Since the workers of St. Petersburg alone have succeeded, in spite of the inadequate support given them by the socialists, in obtaining concessions from the Government within a short time—the passing of a law for shortening the hours of work—the whole working class, led by a united "Russian Social-Democratic Labour Party," will be able, through obstinate fighting, to obtain incomparably more important concessions.

The Russian working class will see its way to carrying on an economic and political fight alone, even if no other class comes to its help. The workers are not alone, however, in the political fight. The fact that the people is absolutely without rights and the unbridled arbitrary rule of the officials rouses the indignation of all who have any pretensions to honesty and educations, who cannot reconcile themselves with the persecution of all free speech and all free thought; it rouses the indignation of the persecuted Poles, Finns, Jews, Russian sects, it rouses the indignation of small traders, of the industrialists, the peasants, of all who can nowhere find protection against the chicanery of the officials and the police. All these groups of the population are incapable of carrying on an obstinate political fight alone; if, however, the working class raises the banner of a fight of this kind it will be supported on all sides. Russian social-democracy will place itself at the head of all fights for the rights of the people, of all fights for democracy, and then it will be invincible.

*   *   *

REVIEW QUESTIONS

1. What tendencies within the socialist movement does Lenin reject here? Why?
2. Why, according to Lenin, must workers combine the fight for economic rights with the fight for political rights?

PETER KROPOTKIN

FROM "Anarchism: Its Philosophy and Ideal"

Written by a leading theoretician of anarchism, this pamphlet of 1896 concisely outlined the movement's rejection of the state. In place of the "dominating minorities" of governments and ruling classes, Peter Kropotkin (1842–1921) proposed organizing society through networks of voluntary associations. Anarchism, a libertarian socialism, envisioned free individuals satisfying their needs through mutual-aid societies, which promised to render superfluous all governments, armies, religions, and capitalist economies. Although anarchism focused on the positive side of unfettered individuality, it did not reject violence as a means to realize a free society. For this reason, nineteenth-century anarchists defended assassinations as moral acts benefiting humanity. Kropotkin, the son of a Russian prince, was a soldier, geographer, and government official before he left Russia to join socialist organizations in Switzerland, France, and Britain. After embracing the anarchist creed in the 1870s, he took a leading role in disseminating its ideals through numerous publications.

From "Anarchism: Its Philosophy and Ideal," by Peter Kropotkin (San Francisco: Free Society, 1898), pp. 15–17.

*   *   *

In proportion as the human mind frees itself from ideas inculcated by minorities of priests, military chiefs and judges, all striving to establish their domination, and of scientists paid to perpetuate it, a conception of society arises in which there is no longer room for those dominating minorities. A society entering into possession of the social capital accumulated by the labour of preceding generations, organizing itself so as to make use of this capital in the interests of all, and constituting itself without reconstituting the power of the ruling minorities. It comprises in its midst an infinite variety of capacities, temperaments and individual energies: it excludes none. It even calls for struggles and contentions; because we know that periods of contests, so long as they were freely fought out without the weight of constituted authority being thrown on one side of the balance, were periods when human genius took its mightiest flights and achieved the greatest aims. Acknowledging, as a fact, the equal rights of its members to the treasures accumulated in the past, it no longer recognizes a division between exploited and exploiters, governed and governors, dominated and dominators, and it seeks to establish a certain harmonious compatibility in its midst—not by subjecting all its members to an authority that is fictitiously supposed to represent society, not by crying to establish uniformity, but by urging all men to develop free initiative, free action, free association.

It seeks the most complete development of individuality combined with the highest development of voluntary association in all its aspects, in all possible degrees, for all imaginable aims; ever changing, ever modified associations which carry in themselves the elements of their durability and constantly assume new forms which answer best to the multiple aspirations of all.

A society to which pre-established forms, crystallized by law, are repugnant; which looks for harmony in an ever-changing and fugitive equilibrium between a multitude of varied forces and influences of every kind, following their own course,—these forces themselves promoting the energies which are favourable to their march towards progress, towards the liberty of developing in broad daylight and counterbalancing one another.

. . . [I]f man, since his origin, has always lived in societies, the State is but one of the forms of social life, quite recent as far as regards European societies. Men lived thousands of years before the first States were constituted; Greece and Rome existed for centuries before the Macedonian and Roman Empires were built up, and for us modern Europeans the centralized States date but from the sixteenth century. It was only then, after the defeat of the free medieval communes had been completed that the mutual insurance company between military, judicial, landlord, and capitalist authority, which we call the "State," could be fully established. . . .

We know well the means by which this association of lord, priest, merchant, judge, soldier, and king founded its domination. It was by the annihilation of all free unions: of village communities, guilds, trades unions, fraternities, and medieval cities. It was by confiscating the land of the communes and the riches of the guilds. It was by the absolute and ferocious prohibition of all kinds of free agreement between men. It was by massacre, the wheel, the gibbet, the sword, and fire that church and State established their domination, and that they succeeded henceforth to reign over an incoherent agglomeration of "subjects" who had no more direct union among themselves.

It is only recently that we began to reconquer, by struggle, by revolt, the first steps of the right of association that was freely practiced by the artisans and the tillers of the soil through the whole of the middle ages.

And, already now, Europe is covered by thousands of voluntary associations for study and teaching, for industry, commerce, science, art, literature, exploitation, resistance to exploitation, amusement, serious work, gratification and self-denial, for all that makes up the life of an active and thinking being. We see these societies rising in all nooks and corners of all domains: political, economic, artistic, intellectual. Some are as short lived as roses, some hold their own for several decades, and all strive—while maintaining the independence of each group, circle, branch, or section—to federate, to unite, across frontiers as well as among each nation; to cover all the life of civilized men with a net, meshes of which are intersected and interwoven. Their numbers can already be reckoned by tens of thousands, they comprise millions of adherents—although less than fifty years have elapsed since church and State began to tolerate a few of them—very few, indeed.

These societies already begin to encroach everywhere on the functions of the State, and strive to substitute free action of volunteers for that of a centralized State. In England we see insurance companies arise against theft; societies for coast defence, volunteer societies for land defence, which the State endeavours to get under its thumb, thereby making them instruments of domination, although their original aim was to do without the State. Were it not for church and State, free societies would have already conquered the whole of the immense domain of education. And, in spite of all difficul-

ties, they begin to invade this domain as well, and make their influence already felt.

And when we mark the progress already accomplished in that direction, in spite of and against the State, which tries by all means to maintain its supremacy of recent origin; when we see how voluntary societies invade everything and are only impeded in their development by the State, we are forced to recognize a powerful *tendency,* a latent force in modern society. And we ask ourselves this question: If five, ten, or twenty years hence—it matters little—the workers succeed by revolt in destroying the said mutual insurance societies of landlords, bankers, priests, judges, and soldiers; if the people become masters of their destiny for a few months, and lay hands on the riches they have created, and which belong to them by right—will they really begin to reconstitute that blood-sucker, the State? Or will they not rather try to organize from the simple to the complex according to mutual agreement and to the infinitely varied, ever-changing needs of each locality, in order to secure the possession of those riches for themselves, to mutually guarantee one another's life, and to produce what will be found necessary for life?

. . . It is often said that anarchists live in a world of dreams to come, and do not see the things which happen today. We see them only too well, and in their true colours, and that is what makes us carry the hatchet into the forest of prejudices that besets us.

Far from living in a world of visions and imagining men better than they are, we see them as they are; and that is why we affirm that the best of men is made essentially bad by the exercise of authority, and that the theory of the "balancing of powers" and "control of authorities" is a hypocritical formula, invented by those who have seized power, to make the "sovereign people," whom they despise, believe that the people themselves are governing. It is because we know men that we say to those who imagine that men would devour one another without those governors: "You reason like the king, who, being sent across the frontier, called out, 'What will become of my poor subjects without me?'"

Ah, if men were those superior beings that the utopians of authority like to speak to us of, if we could close our eyes to reality and live like them in a world of dreams and illusions as to the superiority of those who think themselves called to power, perhaps we also should do like them; perhaps we also should believe in the virtues of those who govern.

If the gentlemen in power were really so intelligent and so devoted to the public cause, as panegyrists of authority love to represent, what a pretty government and paternal utopia we should be able to construct! The employer would never be the tyrant of the worker; he would be the father! The factory would be a palace of delight, and never would masses of workers be doomed to physical deterioration. A judge would not have the ferocity to condemn the wife and children of the one whom he sends to prison to suffer years of hunger and misery and to die some day of anemia; never would a public prosecutor ask for the head of the accused for the unique pleasure of showing off his oratorical talent; and nowhere would we find a jailer or an executioner to do the bidding of judges who have not the courage to carry out their sentences themselves.

*   *   *

All the science of government, imagined by those who govern, is imbued with these utopias. But we know men too well to dream such dreams. We have not two measures for the virtues of the governed and those of the governors; we know that we ourselves are not without faults and that the best of us would soon be corrupted by the exercise of power. We take men for what they are worth—and that is why we hate the government of man by man, and why we work with all our might—perhaps not strong enough—to put an end to it.

But it is not enough to destroy. We must also know how to build, and it is owing to not having thought about it that the masses have always been led astray in all their revolutions. After having demolished they abandoned the care of reconstruction to the middle-class people who possessed a more or less precise conception of what they wished to realize, and who consequently reconstituted authority to their own advantage.

That is why anarchism, when it works to destroy authority in all its aspects, when it demands the abrogation of laws and the abolition of the mechanism that serves to impose them, when it refuses all hierarchical organization and preaches free agreement, at the same time strives to maintain and enlarge the precious kernel of social customs without which no human or animal society can exist. Only instead of demanding that those social customs should be maintained through the authority of a few, it demands it from the continued action of all.

*   *   *

REVIEW QUESTIONS

1. In what ways does anarchism object to the principle and practice of the state?
2. Is Kropotkin optimistic about the development of anarchism in his time?
3. How does Kropotkin respond to the charge that anarchists are dreamers?
4. How does anarchism differ from socialism?

GUSTAVE LE BON

FROM *The Crowd: A Study of the Popular Mind*

In a century that witnessed the rise of universal suffrage and the impact of mass politics on government, sociologists confronted the question whether the collective behavior of crowds differed significantly from individual action and judgment. Although not the first sociologist to address crowd psychology in modern society, Gustave Le Bon's The Crowd *(1894) garnered enormous attention for positing the provocative argument that organized crowds form an unconcious collective will that diverges from an individual's sense of reason. Adopting notions from psychology and physiology, Le Bon viewed organized masses and their herd instincts as a threat to rational government and the civic aims of participatory politics. The paradoxical dilemma loomed: if mass assemblies were a touchstone of modern democractic society, they were also a hazard.*

From *The Crowd: A Study of the Popular Mind*, by Gustave Le Bon (London: T. Fisher Unwin, 1896), pp. 25–38.

Chapter 1

GENERAL CHARACTERISTICS OF CROWDS— PSYCHOLOGICAL LAW OF THEIR MENTAL UNITY

In its ordinary sense the word "crowd" means a gathering of individuals of whatever nationality, profession, or sex, and whatever be the chances that have brought them together. From the psychological point of view the expression "crowd" assumes quite a different signification. Under certain given circumstances, and only under those circumstances, an agglomeration of men presents new characteristics very different from those of the individuals composing it. The sentiments and ideas of all the persons in the gathering take one and the same direction, and their conscious personality vanishes. A collective mind is formed, doubtless transitory, but presenting very clearly defined characteristics. The gathering has thus become what, in the absence of a better expression, I will call an organised crowd, or, if the term is considered preferable, a psychological crowd. It forms a single

being, and is subjected to the *law of the mental unity of crowds*.

It is evident that it is not by the mere fact of a number of individuals finding themselves accidentally side by side that they acquire the character of an organised crowd. A thousand individuals accidentally gathered in a public place without any determined object in no way constitute a crowd from the psychological point of view. To acquire the special characteristics of such a crowd, the influence is necessary of certain predisposing causes of which we shall have to determine the nature.

The disappearance of conscious personality and the turning of feelings and thoughts in a different direction, which are the primary characteristics of a crowd about to become organised, do not always involve the simultaneous presence of a number of individuals on one spot. Thousands of isolated individuals may acquire at certain moments, and under the influence of certain violent emotions— such, for example, as a great national event—the characteristics of a psychological crowd. It will be sufficient in that case that a mere chance should bring them together for their acts to at once assume the characteristics peculiar to the acts of a crowd. At certain moments half a dozen men might constitute a psychological crowd, which may not happen in the case of hundreds of men gathered together by accident. On the other hand, an entire nation, though there may be no visible agglomeration, may become a crowd under the action of certain influences.

A psychological crowd once constituted, it acquires certain provisional but determinable general characteristics. To these general characteristics there are adjoined particular characteristics which vary according to the elements of which the crowd is composed, and may modify its mental constitution. Psychological crowds, then, are susceptible of classification; and when we come to occupy ourselves with this matter, we shall see that a heterogeneous crowd—that is, a crowd composed of dissimilar elements—presents certain characteristics in common with homogeneous crowds—that is, with crowds composed of elements more or less akin (sects, castes, and classes)—and side by side with these common characteristics particularities which permit of the two kinds of crowds being differentiated.

But before occupying ourselves with the different categories of crowds, we must first of all examine the characteristics common to them all. We shall set to work like the naturalist, who begins by describing the general characteristics common to all the members of a family before concerning himself with the particular characteristics which allow the differentiation of the genera and species that the family includes.

*   *   *

The most striking peculiarity presented by a psychological crowd is the following: Whoever be the individuals that compose it, however like or unlike be their mode of life, their occupations, their character, or their intelligence, the fact that they have been transformed into a crowd puts them in possession of a sort of collective mind which makes them feel, think, and act in a manner quite different from that in which each individual of them would feel, think, and act were he in a state of isolation. There are certain ideas and feelings which do not come into being, or do not transform themselves into acts except in the case of individuals forming a crowd. The psychological crowd is a provisional being formed of heterogeneous elements, which for a moment are combined, exactly as the cells which constitute a living body form by their reunion a new being which displays characteristics very different from those possessed by each of the cells singly.

*   *   *

It is easy to prove how much the individual forming part of a crowd differs from the isolated individual, but it is less easy to discover the causes of this difference.

To obtain at any rate a glimpse of them it is necessary in the first place to call to mind the truth established by modern psychology, that unconscious phenomena play an altogether preponderating part not only in organic life, but also in the operations of the intelligence. The conscious life of the mind is of small importance in comparison with its unconscious life. The most subtle analyst, the most acute observer, is scarcely successful in discovering more than a very small number of the unconscious motives that determine his conduct. Our conscious acts are the outcome of an unconscious substratum created in the mind in the main by hereditary influences. This substratum consists of the innumerable common characteristics handed down from generation to generation, which constitute the genius of a race. Behind the avowed causes of our acts there undoubtedly lie secret causes that we do not avow, but behind these secret causes there are many others more secret still which we ourselves ignore. The greater part of our daily nations are the result of hidden motives which escape our observation.

It is more especially with respect to those unconscious elements which constitute the genius of a race that all the individuals belonging to it resemble each other, while it is principally in respect to the conscious elements of their character—the fruit of education, and yet more of exceptional hereditary conditions—that they differ from each other. Men the most unlike in the matter of their intelligence possess instincts, passions, and feelings that are very similar. In the case of everything that belongs to the realm of sentiment—religion, politics, morality, the affections and antipathies, etc.—the most eminent men seldom surpass the standard of the most ordinary individuals. From the intellectual point of view an abyss may exist between a great mathematician and his bootmaker, but from the point of view of character the difference is most often alight or non-existent.

It is precisely these general qualities of character, governed by forces of which we are unconscious, and possessed by the majority of the normal individuals of a race in much the same degree—it is precisely these qualities. I say, that in crowds become common property. In the collective mind the intellectual aptitudes of the individuals, and in consequence their individuality, are weakened. The heterogeneous is swamped by the homogeneous, and the unconscious qualities obtain the upper hand.

*   *   *

If the individuals of a crowd confined themselves to putting in common the ordinary qualities of which each of them has his share, there would merely result the striking of an average, and not, as we have said is actually the case, the creation of new characteristics. How is it that these new characteristics are created? This is what we are now to investigate.

Different causes determine the appearance of these characteristics peculiar to crowds, and not possessed by isolated individuals. The first is that the individual forming part of a crowd acquires solely from numerical considerations, a sentiment of invincible poser which allows him to yield to instincts which, had he been alone, he would perforce have kept under restraint. He will be the less disposed to check himself from the consideration that, a crowd being anonymous, and in consequence irresponsible, the sentiment of responsibility which always controls individuals disappears entirely.

The second cause, which is contagion, also intervenes to determine the manifestation in crowds of their special characteristics and at the same time the trend they are to take. Contagion is a phenomenon of which it is easy to establish the presence, but that it is not easy to establish the presence, but that is not easy to explain. It must be classed among those phenomena of a hypnotic order, which we shall shortly study. In a crowd every sentiment and net is contagious, and contagious to such a degree that an individual readily sacrifices his personal interest to the collective interest. This is an aptitude very contrary to his nature, and of which a man is scarcely capable, except when he makes part of a crowd.

A third cause, and by far the most important, determines in the individuals of a crowd special characteristics which are quite contrary at times to those presented by the isolated individual. I allude to that suggestibility of which, moreover, the contagion mentioned above is neither more nor less than an effect.

To understand this phenomenon it is necessary to bear in mind certain recent physiological discoveries. We know to-day that by various processes an individual may be brought into such a condition that, having entirely lost his conscious personality, he obeys all the suggestions of the operator who has deprived him of it, and commits acts in utter contradiction with his character and habits. The most careful observations seem to prove that an individual immerged for some length of time in a crowd in action soon finds himself—either in consequence of the magnetic influence given out by the crowd, or from some other cause of which we are ignorant—in a special state, which much resembles the state of fascination in which the hypnotized individual finds himself in the hands of the hypnotizer. . . .

Such also is approximately the state of the individual forming part of a psychological crowd. He is no longer conscious of his acts. In his case, as in the case of the hypnotised subjects, at the same time that certain faculties are destroyed, others may be brought to a high degree of exaltation. Under the influence of a suggestion, he will undertake the accomplishment of certain acts with irresistible impetuosity. This impetuosity is the more irresistible in the case of crowds than in that of the hypnotised subject, from the fact that, the suggestion being the same for all the individuals of the crowd, it gains in strength by reciprocity. The individualities in the crowd who might possess a personality sufficiently strong to resist the suggestion are too few in number to struggle against the current. At the utmost, they may be able to attempt a diversion by means of different suggestions. It is in this way, for instance that a happy expression, an image opportunely evoked, have occasionally deterred crowds from the most bloodthirsty acts.

We see, then, that the disappearance of the conscious personality, the conscious personality, the predominance of the unconscious personality, the turning by means of suggestion and contagion of feelings and ideas in an identical direction, the tendency to immediately transform the suggested ideas into acts; these we see, are the principal characteristics of the individual forming part of a crowd. He is no longer himself, but has become an automaton who has ceased to be guided by his will.

Moreover, by the mere fact that he forms part of an organised crowd, a man descends several rungs in the ladder of civilization. Isolated, he may be a cultivated individual: in a crowd, he is a barbarian—that is, a creature acting by instinct. He possesses the spontaneity, the violence, the ferocity, and also the enthusiasm and heroism of primitive beings, whom he further tends to resemble by the facility with which he allows himself to be impressed by words and images—which would be entirely without action on each of the isolated individuals composing the crowd—and to be induced to commit acts contrary to his most obvious interests and his best-known habits. An individual in a crowd is a grain of sand amid other grains of sand, which the wind stirs up at will.

*   *   *

It is not only by his acts that the individual in a crowd differs essentially from himself. Even before he has entirely lost his independence, his ideas and feelings have undergone a transformation, and the transformation is so profound as to change the miser into a spendthrift, the sceptic into a believer, the honest man into a criminal, and the coward into a hero. The renunciation of all its privileges which the nobility voted in a moment of enthusiasm during the celebrated night of August 4, 1789, would certainly never have been consented to by any of its members taken singly.

The conclusion to be drawn from what precedes is, that the crowd is always intellectually inferior to the isolated individual, but that, from the point of view of feelings and of the acts these feelings provoke, the crowd may, according to circumstances, be better or worse than the individual. All depends on the nature of the suggestion to which the crowd is exposed. This is the point that has been completely misunderstood by writers who have only studied crowds from the criminal point of view. Doubtless a crowd is often criminal, but also it is often heroic. It is crowds rather than isolated individuals that may be induced to run the risk of death to secure the triumph of a creed or an idea, that may be fired with enthusiasm for glory and honour, that are led on—almost without bread and without arms, as in the age of the Crusades—to deliver the tomb of Christ from the infidel, or, as in '93, to defend the fatherland. Such heroism is without doubt somewhat unconscious, but it is of such heroism that history is made. Were peoples only to be credited with the great actions performed in cold blood, the annals of the world would register but few of them.

REVIEW QUESTIONS

1. What does Le Bon mean by the "mental unity of crowds" and what are its special charateristics?
2. What are for Le Bon the pernicious effects of the "psychological crowd"?
3. What is the role of the unconscious in forming irrational mass behavior?
4. What are the implications of this argument for democratic civil society? Do you agree? What evidence can you adduce that confirms Le Bon's thesis? What evidence refutes it?

ÉDOUARD DRUMONT

FROM *Jewish France*

During the first half of the nineteenth century, European Jews won many new guarantees of legal and political equality, largely as a result of political liberalism and the growing secularization of European society. In western Europe especially, it almost seemed that centuries of anti-Semitism would be brought to an end through the quiet assimilation of Jews into mainstream national cultures. However, in the final quarter of the century, a new and virulent form of anti-Semitism emerged, threatening Jewish communities' fragile political and social gains.

In France as elsewhere, Jews became scapegoats for deep-seated cultural anxieties stimulated by the political instability of the Third Republic, as well as the massive social and economic changes generated by French industrialization. During the Dreyfus affair, French anti-Semites were rallied to the cause by Édouard Drumont (1844–1917), the editor of La Libre parole *("The Free Word"), a conservative anti-Semitic journal, and the founder of the French Anti-Semitic League. Drumont's* Jewish France, *published in 1885, enjoyed immense popularity: at least 150,000 copies were sold within two years of its first appearance, and it remained in print long into the twentieth century. As the following excerpt from his work demonstrates, Drumont's anti-Semitism took the form of an argument that "old France" was being "conquered" by an alien and parasitic Jewish culture.*

From *La France juive: Essai d'histoire contemporaine*, by Édouard Drumont (Paris: Marpon and Flammarion, 1997), translated by Cat Nilan for the present edition.

The only one who has benefitted from the Revolution [of 1789] is the Jew. Everything comes from the Jew; everything returns to the Jew.

We have here a veritable conquest, an entire nation returned to serfdom by a minute but cohesive minority, just as the Saxons were forced into serfdom by William the Conqueror's 60,000 Normans.

The methods are different, the result is the same. One can recognize all the characteristics of a conquest: an entire population working for another population, which appropriates, through a vast system of financial exploitation, all of the profits of the other. Immense Jewish fortunes, castles, Jewish townhouses, are not the fruit of any actual labor, of any production: they are the booty taken from an enslaved race by a dominant race.

It is certain, for example, that the Rothschild family, whose French branch alone possesses a declared fortune of three billion [francs], did not have that money when it arrived in France; it has invented nothing, it has discovered no mine, it has tilled no ground. It has therefore appropriated these three billion francs from the French without giving them anything in exchange.

*   *   *

All Jewish fortunes have been built up in the same manner, through an appropriation of the work of others.

*   *   *

Today, thanks to the Jew, money—to which the Christian world attached only a secondary importance and assigned only a subordinate role—has become all powerful. Capitalist power concentrated in a tiny number of hands governs at will the entire economic life of the people, enslaves their labor, and feasts on iniquitous profits acquired without labor.

These problems, familiar to all thinking Europeans, are all but unknown in France. The reason is simple. The Jew Lassalle himself has noted how slender are the intellectual foundations of the bourgeoisie, whose opinions are fabricated by the newspapers. * * *

Now, since almost all newspapers and all organs of publicity in France are in the hands of Jews or belong to them indirectly, it is not surprising that the significance and the scope of the immense anti-Semitic movement that has begun to organize itself everywhere is being carefully hidden from us.

*   *   *

In any case, it seems to me interesting and useful to describe the successive phases of this *Jewish Conquest,* to indicate how, little by little, as a result of Jewish activities, old France has been dissolved, broken up, how its unselfish, happy, loving people has been replaced by a hateful people, hungry for gold and soon to be dying of hunger.

*   *   *

Thanks to the Jews' cunning exploitation of the principles of '89, France was collapsing into dissolution. Jews had monopolized all of the public wealth, had invaded everything, except the army. The representatives of the old [French] families, whether noble or bourgeois, had divided themselves into two camps. Some gave themselves up to pleasure, and were corrupted by the Jewish prostitutes they had taken as mistresses or were ruined by the horse-sellers and money-lenders, also Jews, who aided the prostitutes. The others obeyed the attraction exercised over the Aryan race by the infinite, the Hindu Nirvana, Odin's paradise. They

became almost uninterested in contemporary life, they lost themselves in ecstasy, they barely had one foot still planted in the real world.

If the Semites could have been patient for a few years they would have achieved their goal. Jules Simon, one of the few truly wise men they count among their ranks * * *, told them exactly what they needed to do: quietly take over the earth and let the Aryans migrate up to heaven.

The Jews never wanted to listen to this message: they preferred the Semite Gambetta to the Semite Simon. * * * they believed that [Gambetta] was going to help them get rid of Christ, whom they still hated just as much as they had on the day they crucified him. Freemasonry made its contribution, Jewish journals stirred up public opinion, gold was freely distributed, police superintendents were richly paid off, although they refused to make themselves guilty of a crime up to the last minute.

What happened? * * * The Aryan—provoked, troubled, wounded in his innate feelings of nobility and generosity—felt his blood rise to his face when he saw unfortunate old [monks] dragged from their cells by the dregs of the police. He took a while to deliberate, to gather his thoughts, to reflect.

"In the name of what principle are you acting?" he asked.

"In the name of the principle of liberty," replied in unison the newspapers of Porgès, Reinach, Dreyfus, Eugène Mayer, Camille Sée, Naquet.

"And what does this principle consist of?"

"Of this: some Jew or another leaves Hamburg, Frankfurt, Vilna, or anyplace else, and he amasses a certain number of millions at the expense of the *goyim* [gentiles]. He can take his carriage out for a ride, his domicile is inviolable, unless a warrant is issued, and naturally it never is. On the other hand, a native Frenchman, a *natural Frenchman,* to use the words of Saint-Simon, gives away everything he owns to help the poor; he goes barefoot, he lives in a narrow, whitewashed cell that the servant of Rothschild's servant wouldn't want. He is the outlaw. He can be thrown out in the street like a dog."

The Aryan, roused from his slumbers, decides, not without reason, that once this so precious tolerance—talked about so much for the last hundred years—is interpreted in this way, it is better to strike back than be struck. He decides that it is more than time to wrest the country from such impatient masters. "Since the monk's rough robe is so annoying to your frock-coat, we'll give you back the yellow rag, my old Shem." Such was the upshot of [the Aryan's] meditations. It is from that moment that one can date the establishment of the first anti-Semitic—or, to be more precise, anti-Jewish—committee.

* * *

* * * The fatherland, in the sense that we at-tach to that word, has no meaning for the Semite. The Jew, to use the energetic expression of the *Israelite Alliance,* is characterized by an *inexorable universalism.*

I can see no reason for reproaching the Jews for thinking this way. What does the word "Fatherland" mean? Land of the fathers. One's feelings for the Fatherland are engraved in one's heart in the same way that a name carved in a tree is driven deeper into the bark with each passing year, so that the tree and the name eventually become one. You can't become a patriot through improvization; you are a patriot in your blood, in your marrow.

Can the Semite, a perpetual nomad, ever experience such enduring impressions?

* * * The first requirement for adopting a new fatherland, is to renounce the old one. Now, the Jew has a fatherland he never renounces: Jerusalem, the holy and mysterious city Jerusalem. In triumph or persecution, joyous or sad, it serves as a link uniting all of those children who say every year at Rosh Hashanah: "next year in Jerusalem!"

Aside from Jerusalem, every other country, whether France, or Germany, or England, is only a residence for the Jew, any old place, a social agglomeration, in the midst of which he may find himself at home, whose interests he may even find it profitable to serve for the moment, but which he joins only as a free agent, as a temporary member.

* * *

To succeed in their attack against Christian civilization, the Jews of France had to use deceit, to

lie, to disguise themselves as freethinkers. If they had said frankly: "We want to destroy that France of old, so glorious, so beautiful, and replace it with domination by a fistful of Hebrews from many lands," our fathers, less soft than ourselves, would not have let this happen. For a long time [the Jews] kept things vague, working with Freemasonry, hiding behind sonorous words: emancipation, enfranchisement, the struggle against superstition and the prejudices of another age.

* * *

* * * Among the Jews, religious persecution takes on a particularly bitter character. For them, nothing has changed: they hate Christ as much in 1885 as they hated him at the time of Tiberius Augustus, and they heap the same outrages upon him. Whipping the crucifix on Good Friday, profaning the host, besmirching sacred images: such was the great joy of the medieval Jew, and such is his great joy today. Then, he attacked the bodies of children; today, he tries to get at their souls through atheist education. Then, he bled them; today, he poisons their minds: which is worse?

* * *

Despite everything, it is difficult to escape the influence of what one hears from morning to night, from the impression of the artificial intellectual climate created by the Jewish press, and even the best sometimes are subject, despite themselves, to what we have already named the *prejudices of modernism.*

* * *

As for myself, I repeat that I claim to have done nothing more than to attempt a work of good will, to demonstrate by what an underhanded and crafty enemy France has been invaded, corrupted, and brutalized, to such a point that she has broken with her proper hands everything that once made her powerful, respected, and happy. Have I written our last will and testament? Have I laid the foundations for our rebirth? I do not know. I have done my duty, in any case, by responding with insults to the numberless insults that the Jewish press directs at Christians. In proclaiming the Truth, I have obeyed the imperious command of my conscience: *liberavi animam meam* [I have freed my soul]. ✳ ✳ ✳

✳   ✳   ✳

REVIEW QUESTIONS

1. Of what "crimes" were the Jews of France guilty, according to Drumont?
2. How did they get away with these crimes?
3. What does Drumont mean by "tolerance"? Why does he reject it?
4. What, for Drumont, are the "prejudices of modernism"?
5. Why does Drumont associate Jews with modernism?
6. After reading this excerpt, why do you think Drumont hated Jews?
7. Why do you think his arguments might have appealed to many late-nineteenth-century Europeans?

EMMELINE PANKHURST

FROM *Why We Are Militant*

In 1903, Emmeline Pankhurst (1858–1928) founded the Women's Social and Political Union, an organization that advocated militancy and direct action to promote the cause of female suffrage, which had become an international movement since the 1890s. Angered by the insouciance of the British political establishment, which remained unfazed by the massive petitions and peaceful demonstrations of suffragistes, Pankhurst's association organized hunger strikes and assaults on private property to signify the gravity of the matter. In the following speech of October 21, 1913, delivered in New York, Pankhurst justified the tactics of the Women's Social and Political Union.

From *Why We Are Militant: A Speech Delivered by Mrs. Pankhurst in New York, October 21, 1913* (London: Women's Press, 1914).

I know that in your minds there are questions like these; you are saying, "Woman Suffrage is sure to come; the emancipation of humanity is an evolutionary process, and how is it that some women, instead of trusting to that evolution, instead of educating the masses of people of their country, instead of educating their own sex to prepare them for citizenship, how is it that these militant women are using violence and upsetting the business arrangements of the country in their undue impatience to attain their end?"

Let me try to explain to you the situation.

Although we have a so-called democracy, and so called representative government there, England is the most conservative country on earth. Why, your forefathers found that out a great many years ago! If you had passed your life in England as I have, you would know that there are certain words which certainly, during the last two generations, certainly till about ten years ago, aroused a feeling of horror and fear in the minds of the mass of the people. The word revolution, for instance, was identified in England with all kind of horrible ideas. The idea of change, the idea of unsettling the established order of things was repugnant.

*   *   *

The extensions of the franchise to the men of my country have been preceded by very great violence, by something like a revolution, by something like civil war. In 1832, you know we were on the edge of a civil war and on the edge of revolution, and it was at the point of the sword—no, not at the point of the sword—it was after the practice of arson on so large a scale that half the city of Bristol was burned down in a single night, it was because more and greater violence and arson were feared that the Reform Bill of 1832 was allowed to pass into law. In 1867, John Bright urged the people of London to crowd the approaches to the Houses of Parliament in order to show their determination, and he said that if they did that no Parliament, however obdurate, could resist their just demands. Rioting went on all over the country, and as the result of that rioting, as the result of that unrest, which resulted in the pulling down of the Hyde Park railings, as a result of the fear of more rioting and violence the Reform Act of 1867 was put upon the statute books.

In 1884 came the turn of the agricultural labourer. Joseph Chamberlain, who afterwards became a very conservative person, threatened that, unless the vote was given to the agricultural labourer, he would march 100,000 men from Birmingham to know the reason why. Rioting was threatened and feared, and so the agricultural labourers got the vote.

Meanwhile, during the '80's, women, like men, were asking for the franchise. Appeals, larger and more numerous than for any other reform, were presented in support of Woman's Suffrage. Meetings of the great corporations, great town councils, and city councils, passed resolutions asking that women should have the vote. More meetings were held, and larger, for Woman Suffrage than were held for votes for men, and yet the women did not get it. Men got the vote because they were and would be violent. The women did not get it because

they were constitutional and law-abiding. Why, is it not evident to everyone that people who are patient where mis-government is concerned may go on being patient! Why should anyone trouble to help them? I take to myself some shame that through all those years, at any rate from the early '80's, when I first came into the Suffrage movement, I did not learn my political lessons.

I believed, as many women still in England believe, that women could get their way in some mysterious manner, by purely peaceful methods. We have been so accustomed, we women, to accept one standard for men and another standard for women, that we have even applied that variation of standard to the injury of our political welfare.

Having had better opportunities of education, and having had some training in politics, having in political life come so near to the "superior" being as to see that he was not altogether such a fount of wisdom as they had supposed, that he had his human weaknesses as we had, the twentieth century women began to say to themselves. "Is it not time, since our methods have failed and the men's have succeeded, that we should take a leaf out of their political book?"

We were led to that conclusion, we older women, by the advice of the young—you know there is a French proverb which says, "If youth knew; if age could," but I think that when you can bring together youth and age, as we have done, and get them to adopt the same methods and take the same point of view, then you are on the high road to success.

Well, we in Great Britain, on the eve of the General Election of 1905, a mere handful of us—why, you could almost count us on the fingers of both hands—set out on the wonderful adventure of forcing the strongest Government of modern times to give the women the vote. Only a few in number; we were not strong in influence, and we had hardly any money, and yet we quite gaily made our little banners with the words "Votes for Women" upon them, and we set out to win the enfranchisement of the women of our country.

The Suffrage movement was almost dead. The women had lost heart. You could not get a Suffrage meeting that was attended by members of the general public. We used to have about 24 adherents in the front row. We carried our resolutions and heard no more about them.

Two women changed that in a twinkling of an eye at a great Liberal demonstration in Manchester, where a Liberal leader, Sir Edward Grey, was explaining the programme to be carried out during the Liberals' next turn of office. The two women put the fateful question, "When are you going to give votes to women?" and refused to sit down until they had been answered. These two women were sent to gaol, and from that day to this the women's movement, both militant and constitutional, has never looked back. We had little more than one moribund society for Woman Suffrage in those days. Now we have nearly 50 societies for Woman Suffrage, and they are large in membership, they are rich in money, and their ranks are swelling every day that passes. That is how militancy has put back the clock of Woman Suffrage in Great Britain.

Now, some of you have said how wicked it is (the immigration commissioners told me that on Saturday afternoon), how wicked it is to attack the property of private individuals who have done us no harm. Well, you know there is a proverb which says that you cannot make omelettes without breaking eggs. I wish we could.

I want to say here and now that the only justification for violence, the only justification for damage to property, the only justification for risk to the comfort of other human beings is the fact that you have tried all other available means and have failed to secure justice, and as a law-abiding person—and I am by nature a law-abiding person, as one hating violence, hating disorder—I want to say that from the moment we began our militant agitation to this day I have felt absolutely guiltless in this matter.

I tell you that in Great Britain there is no other way. We can show intolerable grievances. The Chancellor of the Exchequer, Mr Lloyd George, who is no friend of the woman's movement, although a professed one, said a very true thing when speaking of the grievances of his own country, of Wales.

He said that there comes a time in the life of human beings suffering from intolerable grievances when the only way to maintain their self respect is to revolt against that injustice.

Well, I say the time is long past when it became necessary for women to revolt in order to maintain their self respect in Great Britain. The women who are waging this war are women who would fight, if it were only for the idea of liberty—if it were only that they might be free citizens of a free country—I myself would fight for that idea alone. But we have, in addition to this love of freedom, intolerable grievances to redress.

*　　*　　*

All my life I have tried to understand why it is that men who value their citizenship as their dearest possession seem to think citizenship ridiculous when it is to be applied to the women of their race. And I find an explanation, and it is the only one I can think of. It came to me when I was in a prison cell, remembering how I had seen men laugh at the idea of women going to prison. Why they would confess they could not bear a cell door to be shut upon themselves for a single hour without asking to be let out. A thought came to me in my prison cell, and it was this: that to men women are not human beings like themselves. Some men think we are superhuman; they put us on pedestals; they revere us; they think we are too fine and too delicate to come down into the hurly-burly of life. Other men think us sub-human; they think we are a strange species unfortunately having to exist for the perpetuation of the race. They think that we are fit for drudgery, but that in some strange way our minds are not like theirs, our love for great things is not like theirs, and so we are a sort of sub-human species.

We are neither superhuman nor are we subhuman. We are just human beings like yourselves.

*　　*　　*

When we were patient, when we believed in argument and persuasion, they said, "You don't really want it because, if you did, you would do

THE PREVENTION OF HUNGER STRIKES

In the decade prior to the First World War, the political campaign for women's suffrage reached a feverish pitch in Great Britain. Emmeline Pankhurst and followers of the Women's Social and Political Union (WSPU) embarked on a course of militant action that included damaging private property, disrupting meetings, and attempting entry into Parliament. When imprisoned and denied the status of political prisoners, WSPU women organized hunger strikes to press their case. In response, the government ordered force feedings of the prisoners, a role that cast the Liberal government of England as a cruel political hypocrite. The cartoon captures the horrific dimensions of English political life on the eve of the war. How did this cartoon criticize both the British government and the suffragist movement?

something unmistakable to show you were determined to have it." And then when we did something unmistakable they said, "You are behaving so badly that you show you are not fit for it."

Now, gentlemen, in your heart of hearts you do not believe that. You know perfectly well that there never was a thing worth having that was not worth fighting for. You know perfectly well that if the situation were reversed, if you had no constitutional rights and we had all of them, if you had the duty of paying and obeying and trying to look as pleasant, and we were the proud citizens who could decide our fate and yours, because we knew what was good for you better than you knew yourselves, you know perfectly well that you wouldn't stand it for a single day, and you would be perfectly justified in rebelling against such intolerable conditions.

Well, in Great Britain, we have tried persuasion, we have tried the plan of showing (by going upon public bodies, where they allowed us to do work they hadn't much time to do themselves) that we are capable people. We did it in the hope that we should convince them and persuade them to do the right and proper thing. But we had all our labour for our pains, and now we are fighting for our rights, and we are growing stronger and better women in the process. We are getting more fit to use our rights because we have such difficulty in getting them.

*   *   *

People have said that women could never vote, never share in the government, because government rests upon force. We have proved that is not true. Government rests not upon force; government rests upon the consent of the governed; and the weakest woman, the very poorest woman, if she withholds her consent cannot be governed.

They sent me to prison, to penal servitude for three years. I came out of prison at the end of nine days. I broke my prison bars. Four times they took me back again; four times I burst the prison door open again. And I left England openly to come and visit America, with only three or four weeks of the three years' sentence of penal servitude served. Have we not proved, then, that they cannot govern human beings who withhold their consent?

And so we are glad we have had the fighting experience, and we are glad to do all the fighting for all the women all over the world. All that we ask of you is to back us up. We ask you to show that although, perhaps, you may not mean to fight as we do, yet you understand the meaning of our fight; that you realise we are women fighting for a great idea; that we wish the betterment of the human race, and that we believe this betterment is coming through the emancipation and uplifting of women.

REVIEW QUESTIONS

1. What precedents in history does Pankhurst cite to justify her cause and tactics?
2. According to Pankhurst, what is the catalyst of political reform?
3. Why were contemporaries outraged by the idea of women's undertaking militant civil disobedience and going to prison for political beliefs?
4. Compare the positions and pleas of Wollstonecraft (Chapter 20) and Pankhurst.
5. What had changed over the course of the century?

CHARLES DARWIN

FROM *The Origin of Species*

The impact of the work of Charles Darwin (1809–1882) cannot be overestimated. The theory of natural selection not only framed the modern view of evolution but also diminished the authority of the Bible in modern thinking. Darwin's theory of how species adapted and evolved over time grew out of his five-year voyage aboard HMS Beagle *(1831–1836) as the ship's naturalist. Published in 1859,* The Origin of Species *was followed by* The Descent of Man *in 1871, which applied the theory of evolution to humans. Darwin's argument that humans descended from apes shocked a Victorian society teethed on Genesis, the biblical creation myth. The following selection comes from the conclusion of* The Origin of Species.

From *The Origin of Species*, by Charles Darwin (New York: Penguin, 1859).

*   *   *

Chapter XIV
Recapitulation and Conclusion

*   *   *

As this whole volume is one long argument, it may be convenient to the reader to have the leading facts and inferences briefly recapitulated.

That many and grave objections may be advanced against the theory of descent with modification through natural selection, I do not deny. I have endeavoured to give to them their full force. Nothing at first can appear more difficult to believe than that the more complex organs and instincts should have been perfected, not by means superior to, though analogous with, human reason, but by the accumulation of innumerable slight variations, each good for the individual possessor. Nevertheless, this difficulty, though appearing to our imagination insuperably great, cannot be considered real if we admit the following propositions, namely, that gradations in the perfection of any organ or instinct, which we may consider, either do now exist or could have existed, each good of its kind, that all organs and instincts are, in ever so slight a degree, variable, and, lastly, that there is a struggle for existence leading to the preservation of each profitable de-viation of structure or instinct. The truth of these propositions cannot, I think, be disputed.

It is, no doubt, extremely difficult even to conjecture by what gradations many structures have been perfected, more especially amongst broken and failing groups of organic beings; but we see so many strange gradations in nature, as is proclaimed by the canon, 'Natura non facit saltum,' [nature does not make a leap] that we ought to be extremely cautious in saying that any organ or instinct, or any whole being, could not have arrived at its present state by many graduated steps. There are, it must be admitted, cases of special difficulty on the theory of natural selection; and one of the most curious of these is the existence of two or three defined castes of workers or sterile females in the same community of ants; but I have attempted to show how this difficulty can be mastered.

*   *   *

As on the theory of natural selection an interminable number of intermediate forms must have

MAN IS BVT A WORM

MAN IS BUT A WORM (1881)

Charles Darwin's pathbreaking Origin of Species *(1859) was followed by his* Descent of Man *in 1871, which applied his theory of natural selection to the evolution of the human species. The implication that man descended from apes was by far the most controversial aspect of his larger argument on natural selection. Illustrating the cultural disquiet about the reconfigured relationship of humankind to the animal world, this cartoon from* Punch, *a British satirical magazine, parodied Darwin with its version of evolution, from worm to gentleman. What beliefs and social structures might Darwin's theories have threatened to undermine?*

existed, linking together all the species in each group by gradations as fine as our present varieties, it may be asked, Why do we not see these linking forms all around us? Why are not all organic beings blended together in an inextricable chaos? With respect to existing forms, we should remember that we have no right to expect (excepting in rare cases) to discover *directly* connecting links between them, but only between each and some extinct and supplanted form. Even on a wide area, which has during a long period remained continuous, and of which the climate and other conditions of life change insensibly in going from a district occupied by one species into another district occupied by a closely allied species, we have no just right to expect often to find intermediate varieties in the intermediate zone. For we have reason to believe that only a few species are undergoing change at any one period; and all changes are slowly effected. I have also shown that the intermediate varieties which will at first probably exist in the intermediate zones, will be liable to be supplanted by the allied forms on either hand; and the latter, from existing in greater numbers, will generally be modified and improved at a quicker rate than the intermediate varieties, which exist in lesser numbers; so that the intermediate varieties will, in the long run, be supplanted and exterminated.

*　　*　　*

As each species tends by its geometrical ratio of reproduction to increase inordinately in number; and as the modified descendants of each species will be enabled to increase by so much the more as they become more diversified in habits and structure, so as to be enabled to seize on many and widely different places in the economy of nature, there will be a constant tendency in natural selection to preserve the most divergent offspring of any one species. Hence during a long-continued course of modification, the slight differences, characteristic of varieties of the same species, tend to be augmented into the greater differences characteristic of species of the same genus. New and improved varieties will inevitably supplant and exterminate the older, less improved and intermediate varie-

ties; and thus species are rendered to a large extent defined and distinct objects. Dominant species belonging to the larger groups tend to give birth to new and dominant forms; so that each large group tends to become still larger, and at the same time more divergent in character. But as all groups cannot thus succeed in increasing in size, for the world would not hold them, the more dominant groups beat the less dominant. This tendency in the large groups to go on increasing in size and diverging in character, together with the almost inevitable contingency of much extinction, explains the arrangement of all the forms of life, in groups subordinate to groups, all within a few great classes, which we now see everywhere around us, and which has prevailed throughout all time. This grand fact of the grouping of all organic beings seems to me utterly inexplicable on the theory of creation.

As natural selection acts solely by accumulating slight, successive, favourable variations, it can produce no great or sudden modification; it can act only by very short and slow steps. Hence the canon of 'Natura non facit saltum,' which every fresh addition to our knowledge tends to make more strictly correct, is on this theory simply intelligible. We can plainly see why nature is prodigal in variety, though niggard in innovation. But why this should be a law of nature if each species has been independently created, no man can explain.

Many other facts are, as it seems to me, explicable on this theory. How strange it is that a bird, under the form of woodpecker, should have been created to prey on insects on the ground; that upland geese, which never or rarely swim, should have been created with webbed feet; that a thrush should have been created to dive and feed on subaquatic insects; and that a petrel should have been created with habits and structure fitting it for the life of an auk or grebe! and so on in endless other cases. But on the view of each species constantly trying to increase in number, with natural selection always ready to adapt the slowly varying descendants of each to any unoccupied or ill-occupied place in nature, these facts cease to be strange, or perhaps might even have been anticipated.

As natural selection acts by competition, it adapts the inhabitants of each country only in relation to the degree of perfection of their associates; so that we need feel no surprise at the inhabitants of any one country, although on the ordinary view supposed to have been specially created and adapted for that country, being beaten and supplanted by the naturalised productions from another land. Nor ought we to marvel if all the contrivances in nature be not, as far as we can judge, absolutely perfect; and if some of them be abhorrent to our ideas of fitness. We need not marvel at the sting of the bee causing the bee's own death; at drones being produced in such vast numbers for one single act, and being then slaughtered by their sterile sisters; at the astonishing waste of pollen by our fir-trees; at the instinctive hatred of the queen bee for her own fertile daughters; at ichneumonidae feeding within the live bodies of caterpillars; and at other such cases. The wonder indeed is, on the theory of natural selection, that more cases of the want of absolute perfection have not been observed.

*   *   *

The fact, as we have seen, that all past and present organic beings constitute one grand natural system, with group subordinate to group, and with extinct groups often falling in between recent groups, is intelligible on the theory of natural selection with its contingencies of extinction and divergence of character. On these same principles we see how it is, that the mutual affinities of the species and genera within each class are so complex and circuitous. We see why certain characters are far more serviceable than others for classification; why adaptive characters, though of paramount importance to the being, are of hardly any importance in classification; why characters derived from rudimentary parts, though of no service to the being, are often of high classificatory value; and why embryological characters are the most valuable of all. The real affinities of all organic beings are due to inheritance or community of descent. The natural system is a genealogical arrangement, in which we have to discover the lines of descent by the most permanent characters, however slight their vital importance may be.

The framework of bones being the same in the hand of a man, wing of a bat, fin of the porpoise, and leg of the horse—the same number of vertebrae forming the neck of the giraffe and of the elephant—and innumerable other such facts, at once explain themselves on the theory of descent with slow and slight successive modifications. The similarity of pattern in the wing and leg of a bat, though used for such different purposes, in the jaws and legs of a crab, in the petals, stamens, and pistils of a flower, is likewise intelligible on the view of the gradual modification of parts or organs, which were alike in the early progenitor of each class. On the principle of successive variations not always supervening at an early age, and being inherited at a corresponding not early period of life, we can clearly see why the embryos of mammals, birds, reptiles, and fishes should be so closely alike, and should be so unlike the adult forms. We may cease marvelling at the embryo of an air-breathing mammal or bird having branchial slits and arteries running in loops, like those in a fish which has to breathe the air dissolved in water, by the aid of well-developed branchiae.

*   *   *

In the distant future I see open fields for far more important researches. Psychology will be based on a new foundation, that of the necessary acquirement of each mental power and capacity by gradation. Light will be thrown on the origin of man and his history.

Authors of the highest eminence seem to be fully satisfied with the view that each species has been independently created. To my mind it accords better with what we know of the laws impressed on matter by the Creator, that the production and extinction of the past and present inhabitants of the world should have been due to secondary causes, like those determining the birth and death of the individual. When I view all beings not as special creations, but as the lineal descendants of some few beings which lived long before the first bed of the Silurian system was deposited, they seem to me to become ennobled. Judging from the past, we may safely infer that not one living species will transmit its unaltered likeness to a distant futurity. And of the species now living very few will transmit progeny of any kind to a far distant futurity; for the manner in which all organic beings are grouped, shows that the greater number of species of each genus, and all the species of many genera, have left no descendants, but have become utterly extinct. We can so far take a prophetic glance into futurity as to fortell that it will be the common and widely-spread species, belonging to the larger and dominant groups, which will ultimately prevail and procreate new and dominant species. As all the living forms of life are the lineal descendants of those which lived long before the Silurian epoch, we may feel certain that the ordinary succession by generation has never once been broken, and that no cataclysm has desolated the whole world. Hence we may look with some confidence to a secure future of equally inappreciable length. And as natural selection works solely by and for the good of each being, all corporeal and mental endowments will tend to progress towards perfection.

It is interesting to contemplate an entangled bank, clothed with many plants of many kinds, with birds singing on the bushes, with various insects flitting about, and with worms crawling through the damp earth, and to reflect that these elaborately constructed forms, so different from each other, and dependent on each other in so complex a manner, have all been produced by laws acting around us. These laws, taken in the largest sense, being Growth with Reproduction; Inheritance which is almost implied by reproduction; Variability from the indirect and direct action of the external conditions of life, and from use and disuse; a Ratio of Increase so high as to lead to a Struggle for Life, and as a consequence to Natural Selection, entailing Divergence of Character and the Extinction of less-improved forms. Thus, from the war of nature, from famine and death, the most exalted object which we are capable of conceiving, namely, the production of the higher animals, directly follows. There is grandeur in this view of life, with its several powers, having been originally breathed into a few forms or into one; and that, whilst this planet has gone cycling on according to the fixed law of gravity, from so simple a beginning endless forms most beautiful and most wonderful have been, and are being, evolved.

REVIEW QUESTIONS

1. According to Darwin, what are the driving forces of natural selection?
2. What, according to Darwin, is the relationship between heredity and environment?
3. Why is the last paragraph so successful in conveying the gist of Darwin's argument?
4. Why was the theory of natural selection so threatening to Christianity?

FRANCIS GALTON

"Eugenics: Its Definition, Scope, and Aims"

Sir Francis Galton (1822–1911), a cousin of Charles Darwin, was a British explorer, an anthropologist, and a leading figure on intelligence studies. In 1883, he coined the term eugenics, *the study of human change through genetic means, and advocated improving the human species through selective parenthood. Building on Darwin's argument of natural selection, Galton believed that mental abilities were equally inheritable and further averred that rigorous statistical investigation could demonstrate genius as an inherited trait. In so doing, he encouraged "healthy parents" to marry and reproduce often. Galton's writings spurred early twentieth-century scientists to pursue eugenics. Although conceived as a scientific doctrine of biological health to improve humankind, eugenics soon manifested racist and class prejudices. In the United States, eugenics offered a pseudoscientific basis to posit the superiority of whites over African Americans; and it further spurred state legislatures to sanction the involuntary sterilization of insane, epileptic, and mentally handicapped citizens. The worst abuse came with National Socialism, which used eugenics to mask an entirely different program of "racial hygiene." Nazis institutionalized the sterilization and killing of "asocial" cases as well as the physically and mentally handicapped into its larger genocidal policies toward Jews, Roma, and others deemed "racially inferior." The following speech was delivered to a learned society in London in 1909.*

From "Eugenics: Its Definition, Scope, and Aims," by Francis Galton, in *The American Journal of Sociology*, vol. 10, no. 1 (July 1904), pp. 1–25.

Eugenics is the science which deals with all influences that improve the inborn qualities of a race; also with those that develop them to the utmost advantage. The improvement of the inborn qualities, or stock, of some one human population, will alone be discussed here.

What is meant by improvement? What by the syllable *Eu* in Eugenics, whose English equivalent is *good*? There is considerable difference between goodness in the several qualities and in that of the character as a whole. The character depends largely on the *proportion* between qualities whose balance may be much influenced by education. We must therefore leave morals as far as possible out of the discussion, not entangling ourselves with the almost hopeless difficulties they raise as to whether a character as a whole is good or bad. Moreover, the goodness or badness of character is not absolute, but relative to the current form of civilisation. A fable will best explain what is meant. Let the scene be the Zoological Gardens in the quiet hours of the night, and suppose that, as in old fables, the animals are able to converse, and that some very wise creature who had easy access to all the cages, say a philosophic sparrow or rat, was engaged in collecting the opinions of all sorts of animals with a view of elaborating a system of absolute morality. It is needless to

enlarge on the contrariety of ideals between the beasts that prey and those they prey upon, between those of the animals that have to work hard for their food and the sedentary parasites that cling to their bodies and suck their blood, and so forth. A large number of suffrages in favour of maternal affection would be obtained, but most species of fish would repudiate it, while among the voices of birds would be heard the musical protest of the cuckoo. Though no agreement could be reached as to absolute morality, the essentials of Eugenics may be easily defined. All creatures would agree that it was better to be healthy than sick, vigorous than weak, well fitted than ill-fitted for their part in life. In short that it was better to be good rather than bad specimens of their kind, whatever that kind might be. So with men. There are a vast number of conflicting ideals of alternative characters, of incompatible civilisations; but all are wanted to give fulness and interest to life. Society would be very dull if every man resembled the highly estimable Marcus Aurelius or Adam Bede. The aim of Eugenics is to represent each class or sect by its best specimens; that done, to leave them to work out their common civilisation in their own way.

A considerable list of qualities can be easily compiled that nearly every one except "cranks" would take into account when picking out the best specimens of his class. It would include health, energy, ability, manliness and courteous disposition. Recollect that the natural differences between dogs are highly marked in all these respects, and that men are quite as variable by nature as other animals in their respective species. Special aptitudes would be assessed highly by those who possessed them, as the artistic faculties by artists, fearlessness of inquiry and veracity by scientists, religious absorption by mystics, and so on. There would be selfsacrificers, self-tormentors and other exceptional idealists, but the representatives of these would be better members of a community than the body of their electors. They would have more of those qualities that are needed in a State, more vigour, more ability, and more consistency of purpose. The community might be trusted to refuse representatives of criminals, and of others whom it rates as undesirable.

Let us for a moment suppose that the practice of Eugenics should hereafter raise the average quality of our nation to that of its better moiety at the present day and consider the gain. The general tone of domestic, social and political life would be higher. The race as a whole would be less foolish, less frivolous, less excitable and politically more provident than now. Its demagogues who "played to the gallery" would play to a more sensible gallery than at present. We should be better fitted to fulfil our vast imperial opportunities. Lastly, men of an order of ability which is now very rare, would become more frequent, because the level out of which they rose would itself have risen.

The aim of Eugenics is to bring as many influences as can be reasonably employed, to cause the useful classes in the community to contribute *more* than their proportion to the next generation.

The course of procedure that lies within the functions of a learned and active Society such as the Sociological may become, would be somewhat as follows:—

1. Dissemination of a knowledge of the laws of heredity so far as they are surely known, and promotion of their farther study. Few seem to be aware how greatly the knowledge of what may be termed the *actuarial* side of heredity has advanced in recent years. The *average* closeness of kinship in each degree now admits of exact definition and of being treated mathematically, like birth- and death-rates, and the other topics with which actuaries are concerned.

2. Historical inquiry into the rates with which the various classes of society (classified according to civic usefulness) have contributed to the population at various times, in ancient and modern nations. There is strong reason for believing that national rise and decline is closely connected with this influence. It seems to be the tendency of high civilisation to check fertility in the upper classes, through numerous causes, some of which are well known, others are inferred, and others again are wholly obscure. The latter class are apparently analogous to those which bar the fertility of most species of wild animals in zoological gardens. Out of the hundreds and thousands of species that have been tamed, very few indeed are fertile when their liberty is restricted and their struggles for livelihood are abolished; those which are so and are otherwise useful to man becoming domesticated. There is perhaps some connection between this obscure action and the disappearance of most savage races when brought into contact with high civilization, though there are other and well-known concomitant causes. But while most barbarous races disappear, some, like the negro, do not. It may therefore be expected that types of our race will be found to exist which can be highly civilised without losing fertility; nay, they may become more fertile under artificial conditions, as is the case with many domestic animals.

3. Systematic collection of facts showing the circumstances under which large and thriving families have most frequently originated; in other words, the *conditions* of Eugenics. The names of the thriving families

in England have yet to be learnt, and the conditions under which they have arisen. We cannot hope to make much advance in the science of Eugenics without a careful study of facts that are now accessible with difficulty, if at all. The definition of a thriving family, such as will pass muster for the moment at least is one in which the children have gained distinctly superior positions to those who were their class-mates in early life. Families may be considered "large" that contain not less than three adult male children. It would be no great burden to a Society including many members who had Eugenics at heart, to initiate and to preserve a large collection of such records for the use of statistical students. The committee charged with the task would have to consider very carefully the form of their circular and the persons entrusted to distribute it. The circular should be simple, and as brief as possible, consistent with asking all questions that are likely to be answered truly, and which would be important to the inquiry. They should ask, at least in the first instance, only for as much information as could be easily, and would be readily, supplied by any member of the family appealed to. The point to be ascertained is the *status* of the two parents at the time of their marriage, whence its more or less eugenic character might have been predicted, if the larger knowledge that we now hope to obtain had then existed. Some account would, of course, be wanted of their race, profession, and residence; also of their own respective parentages, and of their brothers and sisters. Finally, the reasons would be required why the children deserved to be entitled a "thriving" family, to distinguish worthy from unworthy success. This manuscript collection might hereafter develop into a "golden book" of thriving families. The Chinese, whose customs have often much sound sense, make their honours retrospective. We might learn from them to show that respect to the parents of noteworthy children, which the contributors of such valuable assets to the national wealth richly deserve. The act of systematically collecting records of thriving families would have the further advantage of familiarising the public with the fact that Eugenics had at length become a subject of serious scientific study by an energetic Society.

4. Influences affecting marriage. The remarks of Lord Bacon in his essay on Death may appropriately be quoted here. He says with the view of minimising its terrors:

"There is no passion in the mind of men so weak but it mates and masters the fear of death. Revenge triumphs over death; love slights it; honour aspireth to it; grief flyeth to it; fear pre-occupateth it."

Exactly the same kind of considerations apply to marriage. The passion of love seems so overpowering that it may be thought folly to try to direct its course. But plain facts do not confirm this view. Social influences of all kinds have immense power in the end, and they are very various. If unsuitable marriages from the Eugenic point of view were banned socially, or even regarded with the unreasonable disfavour which some attach to cousin-marriages, very few would be made. The multitude of marriage restrictions that have proved prohibitive among uncivilised people would require a volume to describe.

5. Persistence in setting forth the national importance of Eugenics. There are three stages to be passed through. *Firstly* it must be made familiar as an academic question, until its exact importance has been understood and accepted as a fact; *Secondly* it must be recognised as a subject whose practical development deserves serious consideration; and *Thirdly* it must be introduced into the national conscience, like a new religion. It has, indeed, strong claims to become an orthodox religious tenet of the future, for Eugenics cooperates with the workings of Nature by securing that humanity shall be

represented by the fittest races. What Nature does blindly, slowly, and ruthlessly, man may do providently, quickly, and kindly. As it lies within his power, so it becomes his duty to work in that direction; just as it is his duty to succour neighbours who suffer misfortune. The improvement of our stock seems to me one of the highest objects that we can reasonably attempt. We are ignorant of the ultimate destinies of humanity, but feel perfectly sure that it is as noble a work to raise its level in the sense already explained, as it would be disgraceful to abase it. I see no impossibility in Eugenics becoming a religious dogma among mankind, but its details must first be worked out sedulously in the study. Overzeal leading to hasty action would do harm, by holding our expectations of a near golden age, which will certainly be falsified and cause the science to be discredited. The first and main point is to secure the general intellectual acceptance of Eugenics as a hopeful and most important study. Then let its principles work into the heart of the nation, who will gradually give practical effect to them in ways that we may not wholly foresee.

REVIEW QUESTIONS

1. In what kinds of traits is Galton interested?
2. What are the proposed goals of eugenics?
3. How developed was eugenics as a scientific body of knowledge?
4. Can morality be separated from science? Why or why not?

THEODOR HERZL

FROM *The Jewish State*

Against the backdrop of Europe's rising tide of physical violence and political mobilization against Jews, Theodor Herzl (1860–1904) penned The Jewish State *in 1896. This landmark pamphlet redefined Zionism, the movement for a Jewish homeland, as a political question. An Austrian Jewish journalist who covered the Dreyfus affair in Paris for a Viennese newspaper, Herzl apparently became convinced that not even assimilated Jews could find a place in the nation-states of western Europe. Although not the first to propose a Jewish state in modern times, Herzl is credited with reconceptualizing Zionism as a political program of secular nationhood to be achieved through international cooperation. In 1897, after organizing the first congress of Zionists in Basel, Switzerland, he became the president of the World Zionist Organization and thereafter acted as a diplomat to convince world leaders, public opinion, and Jewish communities of Zionism's legitimacy and pragmatism. Toward this end, he also published the Zionist weekly* Die Welt. *Herzl's efforts raised Zionism to worldwide significance, generating a political impulse that contributed to Israeli national statehood in 1948.*

From *The Jewish State*, by Theodor Herzl, translated by Sylvie d'Avigdor (London: D. Nutt, 1896).

The Jewish Question

No one can deny the gravity of the situation of the Jews. Wherever they live in perceptible numbers, they are more or less persecuted. Their equality before the law, granted by statute, has become practically a dead letter. They are debarred from filling even moderately high positions, either in the army, or in any public or private capacity. And attempts are made to thrust them out of business also: "Don't buy from Jews!"

Attacks in Parliaments, in assemblies, in the press, in the pulpit, in the street, on journeys—for example, their exclusion from certain hotels—even in places of recreation, become daily more numerous. The forms of persecutions varying according to the countries and social circles in which they occur. In Russia, imposts are levied on Jewish villages; in Rumania, a few persons are put to death; in Germany, they get a good beating occasionally; in Austria, Anti-Semites exercise terrorism over all public life; in Algeria, there are travelling agitators; in Paris, the Jews are shut out of the socalled best social circles and excluded from clubs. Shades of anti-Jewish feeling are innumerable. But this is not to be an attempt to make out a doleful category of Jewish hardships.

I do not intend to arouse sympathetic emotions on our behalf. That would be a foolish, futile, and undignified proceeding. I shall content myself with putting the following questions to the Jews: Is it not true that, in countries where we live in perceptible numbers, the position of Jewish lawyers, doctors, technicians, teachers, and employees of all descriptions becomes daily more intolerable? Is it not true, that the Jewish middle classes are seriously threatened? Is it not true, that the passions of the mob are incited against our wealthy people? Is it not true, that our poor endure greater sufferings than any other proletariat? I think that this external pressure makes itself felt everywhere. In our economically upper classes it causes discomfort, in our middle classes continual and grave anxieties, in our lower classes absolute despair.

Everything tends, in fact, to one and the same conclusion, which is clearly enunciated in that classic Berlin phrase: *"Juden Raus!"* (Out with the Jews!)

I shall now put the Question in the briefest possible form: Are we to "get out" now and where to?

Or, may we yet remain? And, how long?

Let us first settle the point of staying where we are. Can we hope for better days, can we possess our souls in patience, can we wait in pious resignation till the princes and peoples of this earth are more mercifully disposed towards us? I say that we cannot hope for a change in the current of feeling. And why not? Even if we were as near to the hearts of princes as are their other subjects, they could not protect us. They would only feel popular hatred by showing us too much favor. By "too much," I really mean less than is claimed as a right by every ordinary citizen, or by every race. The nations in whose midst Jews live are all either covertly or openly AntiSemitic.

The common people have not, and indeed cannot have, any historic comprehension. They do not know that the sins of the Middle Ages are now being visited on the nations of Europe. We are what the Ghetto made us. We have attained pre-eminence in finance, because mediaeval conditions drove us to it. The same process is now being repeated. We are again being forced into finance, now it is the stock exchange, by being kept out of other branches of economic activity. Being on the stock exchange, we are consequently exposed afresh to contempt. At the same time we continue to produce an abundance of mediocre intellects who find no outlet, and this endangers our social position as much as does our increasing wealth. Educated Jews without means are now rapidly becoming Socialists. Hence we are certain to suffer very severely in the struggle between classes, because we stand in the most exposed position in the camps of both Socialists and capitalists.

*   *   *

Causes of Anti-Semitism

We shall not again touch on those causes which are a result of temperament, prejudice and narrow views, but shall here restrict ourselves to political and economical causes alone. Modern Anti-Semitism is not to be confounded with the religious persecution of the Jews of former times. It does occasionally take a religious bias in some countries, but the main current of the aggressive movement has now changed. In the principal countries where AntiSemitism prevails, it does so as a result of the emancipation of the Jews. When civilized nations awoke to the inhumanity of discriminatory legislation and enfranchised us, our enfranchisement came too late. It was no longer possible to remove our disabilities in our old homes. For we had, curiously enough, developed while in the Ghetto into a bourgeois people, and we stepped out of it only to enter into fierce competition with the middle classes. Hence, our emancipation set us suddenly within this middleclass circle, where we have a double pressure to sustain, from within and from without. The Christian bourgeoisie would not be unwilling to cast us as a sacrifice to Socialism, though that would not greatly improve matters.

At the same time, the equal rights of Jews before the law cannot be withdrawn where they have once been conceded. Not only because their withdrawal would be opposed to the spirit of our age, but also because it would immediately drive all Jews, rich and poor alike, into the ranks of subversive parties. Nothing effectual can really be done to our injury. In olden days our jewels were seized. How is our movable property to be got hold of now? It consists of printed papers which are locked up somewhere or other in the world, perhaps in the coffers of Christians. It is, of course, possible to get at shares and debentures in railways, banks and industrial undertakings of all descriptions by taxation, and where the progressive incometax is in force all our movable property can eventually be laid hold of. But all these efforts cannot be directed against Jews alone, and wherever they might nevertheless be made, severe economic crises would be their immediate consequences, which would be by no means confined to the Jews who would be the first affected. The very impossibility of getting at the Jews nourishes and embitters hatred of them. AntiSemitism increases day by day and hour by hour among the nations; indeed, it is bound to increase, because the causes of its growth continue to exist and cannot be removed. Its remote cause is our loss of the power of assimilation during the Middle Ages; its immediate cause is our excessive production of mediocre intellects, who cannot find an outlet downwards or upwards—that is to say, no wholesome outlet in either direction. When we sink, we become a revolutionary proletariat, the subordinate officers of all revolutionary parties; and at the same time, when we rise, there rises also our terrible power of the purse.

Effects of Anti-Semitism

The oppression we endure does not improve us, for we are not a whit better than ordinary people. It is true that we do not love our enemies; but he alone who can conquer himself dare reproach us with that fault. Oppression naturally creates hostility against oppressors, and our hostility aggravates the pressure. It is impossible to escape from this eternal circle.

"No!" Some soft-hearted visionaries will say: "No, it is possible! Possible by means of the ultimate perfection of humanity."

Is it necessary to point to the sentimental folly of this view? He who would found his hope for improved conditions on the ultimate perfection of humanity would indeed by relying upon a Utopia!

I referred previously to our "assimilation." I do not for a moment wish to imply that I desire such an end. Our national character is too historically famous, and, in spite of every degradation, too fine to make its annihilation desirable. We might perhaps be able to merge ourselves entirely into surrounding races, if these were to leave us in peace for a period of two generations. But they will not leave us in peace. For a little period they manage to tolerate us, and then their hostility breaks out again and again. The world is provoked somehow by our prosperity, because it has for many centuries been accustomed to consider us as the most contemptible among the poverty-stricken. In its ignorance and narrowness of heart, it fails to observe that prosperity weakens our Judaism and extinguishes our peculiarities. It is only pressure that forces us back to the parent stem; it is only hatred encompassing us that makes us strangers once more.

Thus, whether we like it or not, we are now, and shall henceforth remain, a historic group with unmistakable characteristics common to us all.

We are one people—our enemies have made us one without our consent, as repeatedly happens in history. Distress binds us together, and, thus united, we suddenly discover our strength. Yes, we are strong enough to form a State, and, indeed, a model State. We possess all human and material resources necessary for the purpose.

This is therefore the appropriate place to give an account of what has been somewhat roughly termed our "human material." But it would not be appreciated till the broad lines of the plan, on which everything depends, has first been marked out.

The Plan

The whole plan is in its essence perfectly simple, as it must necessarily be if it is to come within the comprehension of all.

Let the sovereignty be granted us over a portion of the globe large enough to satisfy the rightful requirements of a nation; the rest we shall manage for ourselves.

The creation of a new State is neither ridiculous nor impossible. We have in our day witnessed the process in connection with nations which were not largely members of the middle class, but poorer, less educated, and consequently weaker than ourselves. The Governments of all countries scourged by Anti-Semitism will be keenly interested in assisting us to obtain the sovereignty we want.

The plan, simple in design, but complicated in execution, will be carried out by two agencies: The Society of Jews and the Jewish Company.

The Society of Jews will do the preparatory work in the domains of science and politics, which the Jewish Company will afterwards apply practically.

The Jewish Company will be the liquidating agent of the business interests of departing Jews, and will organize commerce and trade in the new country.

We must not imagine the departure of the Jews to be a sudden one. It will be gradual, continuous, and will cover many decades. The poorest will go first to cultivate the soil. In accordance with a preconceived plan, they will construct roads, bridges, railways and telegraph installations; regulate rivers; and build their own dwellings; their labor will create trade, trade will create markets and markets will attract new settlers, for every man will go voluntarily, at his own expense and his own risk. The labor expended on the land will enhance its value, and the Jews will soon perceive that a new and permanent sphere of operation is opening here for that spirit of enterprise which has heretofore met only with hatred and obloquy.

If we wish to found a State today, we shall not do it in the way which would have been the only possible one a thousand years ago. It is foolish to revert to old stages of civilization, as many Zionists would like to do. Supposing, for example, we were obliged to clear a country of wild beasts, we should not set about the task in the fashion of Europeans of the fifth century. We should not take spear and lance and go out singly in pursuit of bears; we would organize a large and active hunting party, drive the animals together, and throw a melinite bomb into their midst.

If we wish to conduct building operations, we shall not plant a mass of stakes and piles on the shore of a lake, but we shall build as men build now. Indeed, we shall build in a bolder and more stately style than was ever adopted before, for we now possess means which men never yet possessed.

The emigrants standing lowest in the economic scale will be slowly followed by those of a higher grade. Those who at this moment are living in despair will go first. They will be led by the mediocre intellects which we produce so superabundantly and which are persecuted everywhere.

This pamphlet will open a general discussion on the Jewish Question, but that does not mean that there will be any voting on it. Such a result would ruin the cause from the outset, and dissidents must remember that allegiance or opposition is entirely voluntary. He who will not come with us should remain behind.

Let all who are willing to join us, fall in behind our banner and fight for our cause with voice and pen and deed.

Those Jews who agree with our idea of a State will attach themselves to the Society, which will thereby be authorized to confer and treat with Governments in the name of our people. The Society will thus be acknowledged in its relations with Governments as a State-creating power. This acknowledgment will practically create the State.

Should the Powers declare themselves willing to admit our sovereignty over a neutral piece of land, then the Society will enter into negotiations for the possession of this land. Here two territories come under consideration, Palestine and Argentine. In both countries important experiments in colonization have been made, though on the mistaken principle of a gradual infiltration of Jews. An infiltration is bound to end badly. It continues till the inevitable moment when the native population feels itself threatened, and forces the Government to stop a further influx of Jews. Immigration is consequently futile unless we have the sovereign right to continue such immigration.

The Society of Jews will treat with the present masters of the land, putting itself under the protectorate of the European Powers, if they prove friendly to the plan. We could offer the present possessors of the land enormous advantages, assume part of the public debt, build new roads for traffic, which our presence in the country would render necessary, and do many other things. The creation of our State would be beneficial to adjacent countries, because the cultivation of a strip of land increases the value of its surrounding districts in innumerable ways.

*   *   *

REVIEW QUESTIONS

1. For Herzl, what is the "Jewish Question"?
2. What is modern anti-Semitism? What does Herzl believe to be its causes and effects?
3. How does Herzl envision achieving statehood for the Jewish people?

FRIEDRICH NIETZSCHE

FROM *The Genealogy of Morals*

Over the course of his numerous writings, the German philosopher Friedrich Nietzsche (1844–1900) leveled an impressively sustained attack on Western values. Although his philosophical inquiries ranged over a wide area, his devastating criticisms of Judeo-Christian values of individual worth and social justice are probably the most disturbing of his literary corpus. Nietzsche countered his scorn for the "slave mentality" of Judeo-Christian ethics with a wholly different set of ethics that dismissed guilt and a moral conscience as corrosive to life-affirming creativity, which he called the will to power. Written in a vivid aphoristic prose and organized loosely in detached paragraphs, Nietzsche's writings were frequently misunderstood and often abused in the twentieth century. He remains among the most influential writers of the modern era.

From *The Genealogy of Morals*, by Friedrich Nietzsche, translated by J. M. Kennedy (New York: Carlton House, 1920), pp. 16–22, 25–26, 35–38.

*   *   *

9.

"But why do you talk of nobler ideals? Let us submit to the facts; that the people have triumphed—or the slaves, or the populace, or the herd, or whatever name you care to give them—if this has happened through the Jews, so be it! In that case no nation ever had a greater mission in the world's history. The 'masters' have been done away with; the morality of the vulgar man has triumphed. This triumph may also be called a blood-poisoning (it has mutually fused the races)—I do not dispute it; but there is no doubt but that this intoxication has succeeded. The 'redemption' of the human race (that is, from the masters) is progressing swimmingly; everything is obviously becoming Judaised, or Christianised, or vulgarised (what is there in the words?). It seems impossible to stop the course of this poisoning through the whole body politic of mankind—but its *tempo* and pace may from the present time be slower, more delicate, quieter, more discreet—there is time enough. In view of this context has the Church nowadays any necessary purpose? Has it, in fact, a right to live? Or could man get on without it? *Quæritur.* It seems that it fetters and retards this tendency, instead of accelerating it. Well, even that might be its utility. The Church certainly is a crude and boorish institution, that is repugnant to an intelligence with any pretence at delicacy, to a really modern taste. Should it not at any rate learn to be somewhat more subtle? It alienates nowadays, more than it allures. Which of us would, forsooth, be a freethinker if there were no Church? It is the Church which repels us, *not* its poison—apart from the Church we like the poison." This is the epilogue of a freethinker to my discourse, of an honourable animal (as he has given abundant proof), and a democrat to boot; he had up to that time listened to me, and could not endure my silence, but for me, indeed, with regard to this topic there is much on which to be silent.

10.

The revolt of the slaves in morals begins in the very principle of *resentment* becoming creative and giving birth to values—a resentment experienced by creatures who, deprived as they are of the proper outlet of action, are forced to find their compensation in an imaginary revenge. While every aristocratic morality springs from a triumphant affirmation of its own demands, the slave morality says "no" from the very outset to what is "outside itself," "different from itself," and "not itself": and this "no" is its creative deed. This volte-face of the valuing standpoint—this *inevitable* gravitation to the objective instead of back to the subjective—is typical of "resentment": the slave-morality requires as the condition of its existence an external and objective world, to employ physiological terminology, it requires objective stimuli to be capable of action at all—its action is fundamentally a reaction. The contrary is the case when we come to the aristocrat's system of values: it acts and grows spontaneously, it merely seeks its antithesis in order to pronounce a more grateful and exultant "yes" to its own self;—its negative conception, "low," "vulgar," "bad," is merely a pale late-born foil in comparison with its positive and fundamental conception (saturated as it is with life and passion), of "we aristocrats, we good ones, we beautiful ones, we happy ones."

When the aristocratic morality goes astray and commits sacrilege on reality, this is limited to that particular sphere with which it is *not* sufficiently acquainted—a sphere, in fact, from the real knowledge of which it disdainfully defends itself. It misjudges, in some cases, the sphere which it despises, the sphere of the common vulgar man and the low people: on the other hand, due weight should be given to the consideration that in any case the mood of contempt, of disdain, of superciliousness, even on the supposition that it *falsely* portrays the object of its contempt, will always be far removed from that degree of falsity which will always characterise the attacks—in effigy, of course—of the vindictive hatred and revengefulness of the weak in onslaughts on their enemies. In point of fact, there is in contempt too strong an admixture of nonchalance, of casualness, of boredom, of impatience, even of personal exultation, for it to be capable of distorting its victim into a real caricature or a real monstrosity. Attention again should be paid to the almost benevolent *nuances* which, for instance, the Greek nobility imports into all the words by which it distinguishes the common people from itself; note how continuously a kind of pity, care, and consideration imparts its honeyed *flavour*, until at last almost all the words which are applied to the vulgar man survive finally as expressions for "unhappy," "worthy of pity . . ." and how, conversely, "bad," "low," "unhappy" have never ceased to ring in the Greek ear with a tone in which "unhappy" is the predominant note: this is a heritage of the old noble aristocratic morality, which remains true to itself even in contempt. . . . The "well-born" simply *felt* themselves the "happy"; they did not have to manufacture their happiness artificially through looking at their enemies, or in cases to talk and lie themselves into happiness (as is the custom with all resentful men); and similarly, complete men as they were, exuberant with strength, and consequently *necessarily* energetic, they were too wise to dissociate happiness from action—activity becomes in their minds necessarily counted as happiness . . . all in sharp contrast to the "happiness" of the weak and the oppressed, with their festering venom and malignity, among whom happiness appears essentially as a narcotic, a deadening, a quietude, a peace, a "Sabbath," an enervation of the mind and relaxation of the limbs,—in short, a purely *passive* phenomenon. While the aristocratic man lived in confidence and openness with himself, . . . the resentful man, on the other hand, is neither sincere nor naïf, nor honest and candid with himself. His soul *squints;* his mind loves hidden crannies, tortuous paths and backdoors, everything secret appeals to him as *his* world, *his* safety, *his* balm; he is past master in silence, in not forgetting, in waiting, in provisional self-depreciation and self-abasement. A race of such *resentful* men will of necessity eventually prove more *prudent* than any aristocratic race, it will honour prudence on quite a distinct scale, as, in fact, a paramount condition of existence, while prudence among aristocratic men is apt to be tinged with a delicate flavour of luxury and refinement; so among them it plays nothing like so integral a part as that complete certainty of function of the governing *unconscious* instincts, or as indeed a certain lack of prudence, such as a vehement and valiant charge, whether against danger or the enemy, or as those ecstatic bursts of rage, love, reverence, gratitude, by which at all times noble souls have recognised each other. When the resentment of the aristocratic man manifests itself, it fulfils and exhausts itself in an immediate reaction, and consequently instills no *venom:* on the other hand, it never manifests itself at all in countless instances, when in the case of the feeble and weak it would be inevitable. An inability to take seriously for any length of time their enemies, their disasters, their *misdeeds*—that is the sign of the full strong natures who possess a superfluity of moulding plastic force, that heals completely and produces forgetfulness. . . . Such a man indeed shakes off with a shrug many a worm which would have buried itself in another; it is only in characters like these that we see the possibility (supposing, of course, that there is such a possibility in the world) of the real "*love* of one's enemies." What respect for this enemies is found, forsooth, in an aristocratic man—and such a reverence is already a bridge to love! He insists on having his enemy to himself as his distinction. He tolerates no other enemy but a man in whose character there is nothing to despise and *much* to honour! On the other hand, imagine the "enemy" as the resentful man conceives him—and it is here exactly that we see his work, his creativeness; he has conceived "the evil enemy," the "evil one," and indeed that is the root idea from which he now evolves as a contrasting and corresponding figure a "good one," himself—his very self!

*　　*　　*

12.

I cannot refrain at this juncture from uttering a sigh and one last hope. What is it precisely which I find intolerable? That which I alone cannot get rid of, which makes me choke and faint? Bad air! Bad air! That something misbegotten comes near me; that I must inhale the odour of the entrails of a misbegotten soul!—That excepted, what can one not endure in the way of need, privation, bad weather, sickness, toil, solitude? In point of fact, one manages to get over everything, born as one is to a burrowing and battling existence; one always returns once again to the light, one always lives again one's golden hour of victory—and then one stands as one was born, unbreakable, tense, ready for something more difficult, for something more distant, like a bow stretched but the tauter by every strain. But from time to time do ye grant me—assuming that "beyond good and evil" there are goddesses who can grant—one glimpse, grant me but one glimpse only, of something perfect, fully realised, happy, mighty, triumphant, of something that still gives cause for fear! A glimpse of a man that justifies the existence of man, a glimpse of an incarnate human happiness that realises and redeems, for the sake of which one may hold fast to *the belief in man!* For the position is this: in the dwarfing and levelling of the European man lurks *our* greatest peril, for it is this outlook which fatigues—we see to-day nothing which wishes to be greater, we surmise that the process is always still backwards, still backwards towards something more attentuated, more inoffensive, more cunning,

more comfortable, more mediocre, more indifferent, more Chinese, more Christian—man, there is no doubt about it, grows always "better"—the destiny of Europe lies even in this—that in losing the fear of man, we have also lost the hope in man, yea, the will to be man. The sight of man now fatigues.—What is present-day Nihilism if it is not *that?*—We are tired of *man.*

*　　*　　*

16.

Let us come to a conclusion. The two *opposing values,* "good and bad," "good and evil," have fought a dreadful thousand-year-fight in the world, and though indubitably the second value has been for a long time in the preponderance, there are not wanting places where the fortune of the fight is still undecisive. It can almost be said that in the meanwhile the fight reaches a higher and higher level, and that in the meanwhile it has become more and more intense, and always more and more psychological; so that nowadays there is perhaps no more decisive mark of the *higher nature,* of the more psychological nature, than to be in that sense self-contradictory, and to be actually still a battleground for those two opposites. The symbol of this fight, written in a writing which has remained worthy of perusal throughout the course of history up to the present time, is called "Rome against Judæa, Judæa against Rome." Hitherto there has been no greater event *than* that fight, the putting of *that* question, *that* deadly antagonism. Rome found in the Jew the incarnation of the unnatural, as though it were its diametrically opposed monstrosity, and in Rome the Jew was held to be *convicted of hatred* of the whole human race: and rightly so, in so far as it is right to link the well-being and the future of the human race to the unconditional mastery of the aristocratic values, of the Roman values. What, conversely, did the Jews feel against Rome? One can surmise it from a thousand symptoms, but it is sufficient to carry one's mind back to the Johannian Apocalypse, that most obscene of all the written outbursts, which has revenge on its conscience.

(One should also appraise at its full value the profound logic of the Christian instinct, when over this very book of hate it wrote the name of the Disciple of Love, that self-same disciple to whom it attributed that impassioned and ecstatic Gospel—therein lurks a portion of truth, however much literary forging may have been necessary for this purpose.) The Romans were the strong and aristocratic; a nation stronger and more aristocratic has never existed in the world, has never even been dreamed of; every relic of them, every inscription enraptures, granted that one can divine *what* it is that writes the inscription. The Jews, conversely, were that priestly nation of resentment *par excellence*, possessed by a unique genius for popular morals: just compare with the Jews the nations with analogous gifts, such as the Chinese or the Germans, so as to realise afterwards what is first rate, and what is fifth rate.

Which of them has been provisionally victorious, Rome or Judæa? but there is not a shadow of doubt; just consider to whom in Rome itself nowadays you bow down, as though before the quintessence of all the highest values—and not only in Rome, but almost over half the world, everywhere where man has been tamed or is about to be tamed—to *three Jews*, as we know, and *one Jewess* (to Jesus of Nazareth, to Peter the fisher, to Paul the tentmaker, and to the mother of the aforesaid Jesus, named Mary). This is very remarkable: Rome is undoubtedly defeated. At any rate there took place in the Renaissance a brilliantly sinister revival of the classical ideal, of the aristocratic valuation of all things: Rome herself, like a man waking up from a trance, stirred beneath the burden of the new Judaised Rome that had been built over her, which presented the appearance of an œcumenical synagogue and was called the "Church": but immediately Judæa triumphed again, thanks to that fundamentally popular (German and English) movement of revenge, which is called the Reformation, and taking also into account its inevitable corollary, the restoration of the Church—the restoration also of the ancient graveyard peace of classical Rome. Judæa proved yet once more victorious over the classical ideal in the French Revolution, and in a sense which was even more crucial and even more profound: the last political aristocracy that existed in Europe, that of the *French* seventeenth and eighteenth centuries, broke into pieces beneath the instincts of a resentful populace—never had the world heard a greater jubilation, a more uproarious enthusiasm: indeed, there took place in the midst of it the most monstrous and unexpected phenomenon; the ancient ideal *itself* swept before the eyes and conscience of humanity with all its life and with unheard-of splendour, and in opposition to resentment's lying war-cry of *the prerogative of the most*, in opposition to the will to lowliness, abasement, and equalisation, the will to a retrogression and twilight of humanity, there rang out once again, stronger, simpler, more penetrating than ever, the terrible and enchanting counter-war-cry of *the prerogative of the few!* Like a final sign-post to other ways, there appeared Napoleon, the most unique and violent anachronism that ever existed, and in him the incarnate problem *of the aristocratic ideal in itself*—consider well what a problem it is:—Napoleon, that synthesis of Monster and Superman.

*   *   *

REVIEW QUESTIONS

1. What are "slave morals"? Why is Nietzsche so critical of them?
2. In contrast, what does Nietzsche construe as "noble" values?
3. Is Nietzsche criticizing or endorsing the spirit of the Enlightenment?
4. What is Nietzsche's relationship with European society?
5. What does he not like about modern times?
6. Where is there room for abuse in such an argument?

SIGMUND FREUD

FROM *Five Lectures on Psychoanalysis*

Sigmund Freud (1856–1939), an Austrian doctor, is largely credited as the first scientist of psychoanalysis, a discipline that seeks to understand the mechanisms of the unconscious and to explain the role of repressed desire in determining people's actions and dysfunctions. In doing so, Freud fundamentally changed the way humankind perceived itself, thus affecting numerous disciplines of knowledge and a wide range of literary and art movements. Perhaps it is impossible to interpret twentieth-century culture without first weighing Freud's impact. Psychoanalysis arose in 1895 when Freud and Josef Breuer, a physician friend, published a case study that posited the link between hysteria and sexual malfunctions, and the need to uncover repressed memory for recovery. Freud outlined the early development of his understanding of resistance and repression in five lectures, excerpted below, presented at Clark University, Worcester, Massachusetts, in 1912.

From *Five Lectures on Psychoanalysis*, by Sigmund Freud, translated by James Strachey (London: Hogarth Press, 1976).

*   *   *

When, later on, I set about continuing on my own account the investigations that had been begun by Breuer, I soon arrived at another view of the origin of hysterical dissociation (the splitting of consciousness). A divergence of this kind, which was to be decisive for everything that followed, was inevitable, since I did not start out, like Janet, from laboratory experiments, but with therapeutic aims in mind.

I was driven forward above all by practical necessity. The cathartic procedure, as carried out by Breuer, presupposed putting the patient into a state of deep hypnosis; for it was only in a state of hypnosis that he attained a knowledge of the pathogenic connections which escaped him in his normal state. But I soon came to dislike hypnosis, for it was a temperamental and, one might almost say, a mystical ally. When I found that, in spite of all my efforts, I could not succeed in bringing more than a fraction of my patients into a hypnotic state, I determined to give up hypnosis and to make the cathartic procedure independent of it. Since I was not able at will to alter the mental state of the majority of my patients, I set about working with them in their *normal* state. At first, I must confess, this seemed a senseless and hopeless undertaking. I was set the task of learning from the patient something that I did not know and that he did not know himself. How could one hope to elicit it? But there came to my help a recollection of a most remarkable and instructive experiment which I had witnessed when I was with Bernheim at Nancy. Bernheim showed us that people whom he had put into a state of hypnotic somnambulism, and who had had all kinds of experiences while they were in that state, only *appeared* to have lost the memory of what they had experienced during somnambulism; it was possible to revive these memories in their normal state. It is true that, when he questioned them about their somnambulistic experiences, they began by maintaining that they knew nothing about them; but if he refused to give way, and insisted, and assured them that they *did* know about them, the forgotten experiences always reappeared.

So I did the same thing with my patients. When I reached a point with them at which they maintained that they knew nothing more, I assured them that they *did* know it all the same, and that they had only to say it; and I ventured to declare that the right memory would occur to them at the moment at which I laid my hand on their forehead. In that way I succeeded, without using hypnosis, in obtaining from the patients whatever was required for establishing the connection between the pathogenic scenes they had forgotten and the symptoms left over from those scenes. But it was a laborious procedure, and in the long run an exhausting one; and it was unsuited to serve as a permanent technique.

I did not abandon it, however, before the observations I made during my use of it afforded me decisive evidence. I found confirmation of the fact that the forgotten memories were not lost. They were in the patient's possession and were ready to emerge in association to what was still known by him; but there was some force that prevented them from becoming conscious and compelled them to remain unconscious. The existence of this force could be assumed with certainty, since one became aware of an effort corresponding to it if, in opposition to it, one tried to introduce the unconscious memories into the patient's consciousness. The force which was maintaining the pathological condition became apparent in the form of *resistance* on the part of the patient.

It was on this idea of resistance, then, that I based my view of the course of psychical events in hysteria. In order to effect a recovery, it had proved necessary to remove these resistances. Starting out from the mechanism of cure, it now became possible to construct quite definite ideas of the origin of the illness. The same forces which, in the form of resistance, were now offering opposition to the forgotten material's being made conscious, must formerly have brought about the forgetting and must have pushed the pathogenic experiences in question out of consciousness. I gave the name of

"*repression*" to this hypothetical process, and I considered that it was proved by the undeniable existence of resistance.

The further question could then be raised as to what these forces were and what the determinants were of the repression in which we now recognized the pathogenic mechanism of hysteria. A comparative study of the pathogenic situations which we had come to know through the cathartic procedure made it possible to answer this question. All these experiences had involved the emergence of a wishful impulse which was in sharp contrast to the subject's other wishes and which proved incompatible with the ethical and aesthetic standards of his personality. There had been a short conflict, and the end of this internal struggle was that the idea which had appeared before consciousness as the vehicle of this irreconcilable wish fell a victim to repression, was pushed out of consciousness with all its attached memories, and was forgotten. Thus the incompatibility of the wish in question with the patient's ego was the motive for the repression; the subject's ethical and other standards were the repressing forces. An acceptance of the incompatible wishful impulse or a prolongation of the conflict would have produced a high degree of unpleasure; this unpleasure was avoided by means of repression, which was thus revealed as one of the devices serving to protect the mental personality.

To take the place of a number of instances, I will relate a single one of my cases, in which the determinants and advantages of repression are sufficiently evident. For my present purpose I shall have once again to abridge the case history and omit some important underlying material. The patient was a girl, who had lost her beloved father after she had taken a share in nursing him—a situation analogous to that of Breuer's patient. Soon afterwards her elder sister married, and her new brother-in-law aroused in her a peculiar feeling of sympathy which was easily masked under a disguise of family affection. Not long afterwards her sister fell ill and died, in the absence of the patient and her mother. They were summoned in all haste without being given any definite information of the tragic event. When the girl reached the bedside of her dead sister, there came to her for a brief moment an idea that might be expressed in these words: 'Now he is free and can marry me.' We may assume with certainty that this idea, which betrayed to her consciousness the intense love for her brother-in-law of which she had not herself been conscious, was surrendered to repression a moment later, owing to the revolt of her feelings. The girl fell ill with severe hysterical symptoms; and while she was under my treatment it turned out that she had completely forgotten the scene by her sister's bedside and the odious egoistic impulse that had emerged in her. She remembered it during the treatment and reproduced the pathogenic moment with signs of the most violent emotion, and, as a result of the treatment, she became healthy once more.

Perhaps I may give you a more vivid picture of repression and of its necessary relation to resistance, by a rough analogy derived from our actual situation at the present moment. Let us suppose that in this lecture-room and among this audience, whose exemplary quiet and attentiveness I cannot sufficiently commend, there is nevertheless someone who is causing a disturbance and whose ill-mannered laughter, chattering and shuffling with his feet are distracting my attention from my task. I have to announce that I cannot proceed with my lecture; and thereupon three or four of you who are strong men stand up and, after a short struggle, put the interrupter outside the door. So now he is "repressed," and I can continue my lecture. But in order that the interruption shall not be repeated, in case the individual who has been expelled should try to enter the room once more, the gentlemen who have put my will into effect place their chairs up against the door and thus establish a "resistance" after the repression has been accomplished. If you will now translate the two localities concerned into psychical terms as the "conscious" and the "unconscious," you will have before you a fairly good picture of the process of repression.

You will now see in what it is that the difference lies between our view and Janet's. We do not derive the psychical splitting from an innate incapacity for synthesis on the part of the mental apparatus; we explain it dynamically, from the conflict of opposing mental forces and recognize it as the outcome of an active struggling on the part of the two psychical groupings against each other. But our view gives rise to a large number of fresh problems. Situations of mental conflict are, of course, exceedingly common; efforts by the ego to ward off painful memories are quite regularly to be observed without their producing the result of a mental split. The reflection cannot be escaped that further determinants must be present if the conflict is to lead to dissociation. I will also readily grant you that the hypothesis of repression leaves us not at the end but at the beginning of a psychological theory. We can only go forward step by step however, and complete knowledge must await the results of further and deeper researches.

*   *   *

To put the matter more directly. The investigation of hysterical patients and of other neurotics leads us to the conclusion that their repression of the idea to which the intolerable wish is attached has been a *failure*. It is true that they have driven it out of consciousness and out of memory and have apparently saved themselves a large amount of unpleasure. *But the repressed wishful impulse continues to exist in the unconscious.* It is on the look-out for an opportunity of being activated, and when that happens it succeeds in sending into consciousness a disguised and unrecognizable *substitute* for what had been repressed, and to this there soon become attached the same feelings of unpleasure which it was hoped had been saved by the repression. This substitute for the repressed idea—the *symptom*—is proof against further attacks from the defensive ego; and in place of the short conflict an ailment now appears which is not brought to an end by the passage of time. Alongside the indication of distortion in the symptom, we can trace in it the remains of some kind of indirect resemblance to the idea that was originally repressed. The paths along which the substitution was effected can be traced in the course of the patient's psychoanalytic treatment; and in order to bring about recovery, the symptom must be led back along the same paths and once more turned into the repressed idea. If what was repressed is brought back again into conscious mental activity—a process which presupposes the overcoming of considerable resistances—the resulting psychical conflict, which the patient had tried to avoid, can, under the physician's guidance, reach a better outcome than was offered by repression. There are a number of such opportune solutions, which may bring the conflict and the neurosis to a happy end, and which may in certain instances be combined. The patient's personality may be convinced that it has been wrong in rejecting the pathogenic wish and may be led into accepting it wholly or in part; or the wish itself may be directed to a higher and consequently unobjectionable aim (this is what we call its "sublimation"); or the rejection of the wish may be recognized as a justifiable one, but

the automatic and therefore inefficient mechanism of repression may be replaced by a condemning judgement with the help of the highest human mental functions—conscious control of the wish is attained.

*   *   *

REVIEW QUESTIONS

1. How does Freud view the pathology of hysteria and its solution?
2. What does Freud's theory of repression imply for individuals' identities and actions?
3. What were the implications of Freud's theory of the unconscious for bourgeois culture?

24 ◈ THE FIRST WORLD WAR

The assassination of Archduke Franz Ferdinand in Sarajevo in August 1914 unleashed a cataclysm of unparalleled magnitude. For four years the European combatants and their allies confronted each other in a war of global dimensions. By 1918 millions of soldiers had been killed on the battlefront, and the lives of civilians living behind the lines on the home front had been unalterably disrupted.

Europeans initially responded to the outbreak of war with jubilation and enthusiasm. Young men rushed to enlist, worried that the war—which everyone expected to be over by Christmas—would end before they could reach the front lines. But soldiers who had yearned for high drama and the chance to prove what one poet-soldier called their "untested manhood" soon discovered the sullen face of modern warfare. The new technologies of war, especially the machine gun and heavy artillery, reduced the individual soldier to insignificance, making a mockery of his bravery and leading him to fear not only the clean death brought by bullets but also the utter annihilation of being blown to bits or the long, drawn out agony of gas poisoning. For those who survived this ordeal, the Great War was a fundamental experience, forever separating them from the prewar world— and from noncombatants—and leaving deep physical and psychological scars.

Although civilians were protected from the worst horrors of the trenches, they too were deeply affected by the war. The lines between the home front and the battlefront blurred as production of armaments and munitions made civilian workers crucial to the military effort and as government-sponsored propaganda campaigns encouraged noncombatants to do their part for the war effort. Although the war brought hardships to civilians, it also brought new opportunities and even adventure, especially to young women who were suddenly freed from the restraints of prewar society.

When the war ended, Europeans were eager to believe that they had, in fact, fought "the war to end all wars." But the end of hostilities did not bring an end to the trauma and dislocation occasioned by the war. The peace settlement itself, promoted by its framers as a new, more hopeful beginning, was widely condemned as an inadequate guarantee of international security and stability.

The Trench Poets of the First World War

The outbreak of the First World War inspired a spate of poetry; one historian estimates that more than one million poems were written in 1914 alone. Like Rupert Brooke (1887–1915), many poets initially greeted the war as a release from the dreariness of civilian life. Educated at Cambridge, Brooke composed finely crafted idealistic wartime poems, especially the sonnet series "1914," which earned him lasting fame. However, as the war dragged on, soldier-poets' initial enthusiasm gave way to resignation. The British poet Wilfred Owen (1893–1918), a graduate of the University of London, condemned the older generation that had allowed the war to happen and that was now refusing to end the slaughter of "half the seed of Europe, one by one." Owen's "Dulce et decorum est," perhaps the most famous of all the First World War poems, is noteworthy not only for its antiwar sentiments but also for its stylistic innovation. Brooke died in 1915 on a hospital ship off the island of Skyros, Greece. Owen was killed in action in France one week before Armistice Day in November 1918.

Rupert Brooke*

I. PEACE

Now, God be thanked Who has matched us with
　　His hour,
　　And caught our youth, and wakened us from
　　　sleeping,
With hand made sure, clear eye, and sharpened
　　power,
　　To turn, as swimmers into cleanness leaping,
Glad from a world grown old and cold and weary,

Leave the sick hearts that honour could not
　　move,
　And half-men, and their dirty songs and dreary,
　　And all the little emptiness of love!

Oh! we, who have known shame, we have found
　　release there,
　Where there's no ill, no grief, but sleep has
　　mending,
　　Naught broken save this body, lost but breath;
Nothing to shake the laughing heart's long peace
　　there
　But only agony, and that has ending;
　　And the worst friend and enemy is but
　　Death.

*　　　*　　　*

---

* From *The Collected Poems*, by Rupert Brooke, edited by
　George E. Woodbury (New York: Lane, 1916).

V. THE SOLDIER

If I should die, think only this of me:
   That there's some corner of a foreign field
That is for ever England. There shall be
   In that rich earth a richer dust concealed;
A dust whom England bore, shaped, made aware,
    Gave, once, her flowers to love, her ways to
       roam,
A body of England's, breathing English air,
   Washed by the rivers, blest by suns of home.

And think, this heart, all evil shed away,
   A pulse in the eternal mind, no less
     Gives somewhere back the thoughts by
       England given;
Her sights and sounds; dreams happy as her day;
   And laughter, learnt of friends; and gentleness,
     In hearts at peace, under an English heaven.

*   *   *

Wilfred Owen*

"Dulce et decorum est"

Bent double, like old beggars under sacks,
Knock-kneed, coughing like hags, we cursed
   through sludge,
Till on the haunting flares we turned our backs
And towards our distant rest began to trudge.
Men marched asleep. Many had lost their boots
But limped on, blood-shod. All went lame; all
   blind;
Drunk with fatigue; deaf even to the hoots

---

* From *Poems*, by Wilfred Owen (Huebsch, 1921).

Of tired, outstripped Five-Nines that dropped
   behind.

Gas! GAS! Quick, boys!
An ecstasy of fumbling,
Fitting the clumsy helmets just in time;
But someone still was yelling out and stumbling,
And flound'ring like a man in fire or lime . . .
Dim, through the misty panes and thick green
   light,
As under a green sea, I saw him drowning.
In all my dreams, before my helpless sight,
He plunges at me, guttering, choking, drowning.
If in some smothering dreams you too could pace
Behind the wagon that we flung him in,
And watch the white eyes writhing in his face,
His hanging face, like a devil's sick of sin;
If you could hear, at every jolt, the blood
Come gargling from the froth-corrupted lungs,
Obscene as cancer, bitter as the cud
Of vile, incurable sores on innocent tongues,
My friend, you would not tell with such high zest
To children ardent for some desperate glory,
The old Lie: *Dulce et decorum est*
Pro patria mori.[1]

REVIEW QUESTIONS

1. Why does Rupert Brooke welcome war?
2. What virtues does he find in death on the battlefield?
3. How does Wilfred Owen's perception of warfare differ from Brooke's?
4. How do Owen's and Brooke's attitudes toward patriotism differ?

---

[1] "It is sweet and fitting to die for one's country." A line taken from the *Odes* of Horace (65–8 B.C.E.).

BATTLE OF VERDUN (1916)

On February 21, 1916, the German army laid siege to the fortress town of Verdun, France. The attack, although initially successful, degenerated into a long-term battle, claiming over four hundred thousand French casualties and approximately as many German. The town was never taken, and the German high command ended the campaign in July. For contemporaries and subsequent generations, the massive expense of life at the battle of Verdun, which included the use of gas and flamethrowers, epitomized the cruelty and futility of modern war. This frame is taken from front-line film footage of a French officer leading his men in a charge across No Man's Land and confronting the deadly efficiency of machine guns. How did this image of the Western Front undermine Western idealism for war and military valor?

Press Reports from the Front

In every belligerent nation, the government attempted to control the news of the war that was available to civilians. Censorship of news and correspondence home was the rule from the very beginning of the war, and as a result, families of soldiers often had only the vaguest notion of events at the front. In addition, many journalists and newspapers censored themselves, choosing to emphasize the positive, even at moments of terrible loss. The history of the war that one could read in newspapers thus often diverged remarkably from the grimmer stories that made their way back to civilians from their relatives and neighbors serving in the trenches. The following selections from French newspapers between 1914 and 1918 were collected and published in 1931 by a French magazine entitled Evolution, *under the title "Wartime Bombast (1914–1918)."*

Reprinted in *The Great War and the French People,* by Jean-Jacques Becker (Dover, N.H.: Berg, 1986), pp. 30–39.

Mobilisation, Troop Concentration and Initial Skirmishes (2–20 August 1914)

Rue des Martyrs . . . a sergeant, uncertain how to react to the ovations raised his rifle and kissed it passionately. (*Le Matin,* 7 August 1914).

My wound? It doesn't matter. . . . But make sure you tell them that all Germans are cowards and that the only problem is how to get at them. In the skirmish where I got hit, we had to shout insults at them to make them come out and fight. (*Echo de Paris,* "Story of a wounded soldier," Franc-Nohain, 15 August 1914).

I think what is happening is a very good thing. . . . I've been waiting for it these last forty years. . . . France is pulling herself together and it's my opinion she couldn't have done that without being purged by war . . . (*Petit Parisien,* statement by Monseigneur Baudrillart, 16 August 1914).

Antwerp, by contrast, is believed to be virtually impregnable. (*Le Matin,* 20 August 1914).

Morhange, Charleroi, the Retreat on the Marne (20 August–15 September 1914)

As far as our slight retreat in Lorraine is concerned, it is of no consequence. Just a minor incident. . . . I would add . . . that the enormous quantity of material we captured from the Germans bears witness to a remarkable weakening on their side. (*Petit Parisien,* LieutenantColonel Rousset, 22 August 1914).

It is impossible for this great battle [of Charleroi] to end in anything but success for us. And even if it should not give us the decisive victory that we still have every right to expect, the enemy will have been winded, crushed, a prisoner of his own losses and supply problems. (*Echo de Paris,* General Cherfils, 29 August 1914).

The wing-beat [of victory] shall carry our armies to the Rhine. . . . That will spell their complete collapse. (*Echo de Paris,* General Cherfils, 15 September 1914).

Play on, then, you blind fools, play the game of your Kaiser and of his vile brood. Play on, but at least while you do so, think about what you are doing and weep with rage. And may they think of it too, our dear soldiers, and may they double up with laughter, our good lads, as they merrily split your hides, you miserable fools. (*Petit Journal*, Jean Richepin, 25 September 1914).

My impression is that the great German army is about to retreat . . . it is only a question of days. . . . The German objective is to beat a retreat on as wide a front as possible. (*Le Matin*, dispatch from the war correspondent of *The Times*, 16 October 1914).

Like a wasp trapped in a clear crystal carafe, the vile and brutish [German] army is beating against the walls of its prison. . . . It struggles, damaging itself a little more with every vain attempt. It is wearing itself out. (*Le Matin*, 22 October 1914).

The 1915 Offensives

They all go into battle as to a fête. (*Petit Parisien*, Lieutenant-Colonel Rousset, 15 May 1915).

A sudden delirium seizes each of the men. At last we are going to emerge from our torpor! A storm of steel passes over our heads but leaves us unmoved. . . . Magic nights. (*Petit Parisien*, "Letter from the front," 17 May 1915).

Apart from about five minutes a month, the danger is minimal, even in critical situations. I don't know how I'll be able to do without this sort of life when the war is over. Casualties and death . . . that's the exception. (*Petit Parisien*, "Letter from a soldier," 22 May 1915).

Verdun (February–December 1916)

The very fact that he [the enemy] is not advancing is an outstanding success and raises immense hopes. (*Echo de Paris*, Marcel Hutin, 24 February 1916).

At the gates of Beaumont, our soldiers, who had pretended to retreat, were tremendously amused. (*Journal*, reporting the remarks of an evacuee from Verdun, 28 February 1916).

However, our losses have been great. (*Petit Parisien*, 1 March 1916).

That fact is that they [the cellars of Verdun] were relatively comfortable—central heating and electricity, if you please—and that we were not too bored in them. (*Petit Journal*, 1 March 1916).

The Russian Front (1914–1917)

He [the Cossack] has no trouble in running several Hungarians through at one go, as many as will fit on the shaft of his lance, then he flings the whole skewer away. (*Le Matin*, Halberine-Kaminsky, 5 October 1914)

The "decisive defeat" at Warsaw with which the Russian armies have this time opened up unlimited prospects to the West must seem disastrous to the Hohenzollern Empire. Let us watch now as hour by hour our allies continue their great thrust towards the Oder, towards Breslau, towards Berlin. (*Petit Parisien*, 26 October 1914).

The Russian army is admirably equipped with everything it needs for modern battle. (*Le Matin*, 8 February 1915).

The distress of our men was moving. They fell to their knees before their officers and implored them: "Let us fight with stones, with sticks, if need be with our fists." (*Le Matin*, statement by Madame Motelev, a Russian nurse, 14 May 1916).

Russia will fight to the death. . . . There will be no quitters among the Allies. (*Echo de Paris*, statement by Lloyd George, 30 September 1916).

If there is an upsurge in Russia, it is an upsurge in favour of total war. (*Echo de Paris*, J. Herbette, 11 January 1917).

The Russian Revolution (1917–1918)

Russia has been liberated. . . . If her people are in revolt . . . it is not to shirk the harsh duties of war, but on the contrary to acquit themselves with even more nobility and self-sacrifice. . . . Long live liberated Russia, which tomorrow will be Russia the liberator. (*Journal*, C. Humbert, 17 March 1917).

"How did the men at the front receive the theories of those few socialists who preached a separate peace?"

"Nobody worried about them, because no one took that poisonous propaganda seriously." (*Journal*, statement by General Filatier, Paul Erio, 2 May 1917).

Russia will never agree to a separate peace. (*Le Matin*, declaration by Milyukov to the Soviet of Workers and Soldiers, 5 May 1917).

The [U.S.] State Department does not believe that Lenin and Trotsky can stay in power for long and is ready for their fall. Those who know Trotsky consider him a lightweight, without personal worth and quite incapable of taking on the job of an organiser. (*Petit Journal*, 27 November 1917).

The reign of Lenin and Trotsky seems to be reaching its end. . . . Lenin no longer dares to leave Smolny. . . . Lenin . . . trembles for his miserable person. . . . Their dream will not be realized. . . . The hours of Lenin and Trotsky's reign are numbered. (*Journal*, Paul Erio, 26 December 1917).

Poison Gas (1915–1918)

There is no need to be inordinately alarmed about the deadly effects of poison-gas bombs. Rest assured, they are not as bad as all that. . . . They [the bombs] are quite harmless. . . . If . . . we were to tot up all the victims of poison gas and compare their numbers with all the others, we should not pay them any further attention. (*Le Matin*, André Lefebvre, 27 April 1915)

Our soldiers don't give a b— for poison gases. (*Echo de Paris*, 16 December 1916).

The German Artillery

The Germans aim low and poorly; as for their shells, 80 per cent of them do not burst. (*Journal*, 19 August 1914).

Like them, their heavy artillery is nothing but bluff. Their shells have very little effect . . . and all the noise . . . just comes from firing into the blue.

(*Le Matin*, "Letter from the front," 15 September 1914).

Anyway, our troops laugh at machineguns now. . . . Nobody pays the slightest attention to them. (*Petit Parisien*, L. Montel, 11 October 1914).

Combatants and Casualties

Our brave young lads [though injured] are far from beaten. They laugh, joke and beg to be allowed back to the firing line. (*Le Matin*, 19 August 1914).

Not at all, they said to me, we're not all that bothered, the danger is not nearly as great as you think. (*Petit Journal*, 26 October 1914).

The longer the war goes on, the less dreadful I find it. (*Echo de Paris*, "Letter from the front," 31 October 1914).

It's nothing to speak of, I'll be disabled, that's all. (*Le Matin*, remark attributed to a badly wounded soldier, 19 April 1915).

But at least they [those killed by bayoneting] will have died a beautiful death, in noble battle. . . . With cold steel, we shall rediscover poetry . . . epic and chivalrous jousting. (*Echo de Paris*, Hébrard de Villeneuve, 10 July 1915).

REVIEW QUESTIONS

1. What sentiments were expressed at the beginning of the war?
2. How do you think the public reacted when their initial hopes for a quick victory were disappointed?
3. How might the relentless optimism of such press reports have been received by the troops themselves, after the hundreds of thousands of casualties at Verdun or the Somme?
4. How did the French press portray their enemies, or their allies on the Eastern Front?
5. How might the news-reading public have reacted to this kind of nationalist enthusiasm in 1918, at the end of the war?

ERNST JÜNGER

FROM *The Storm of Steel: From the Diary of a German Storm-Troop Officer on the Western Front*

The German author Ernst Jünger (1895–1998) was so eager for adventure that he ran away from home and joined the French Foreign Legion at the age of eighteen. Still only nineteen when the First World War broke out, Jünger volunteered immediately and served with considerable distinction as an officer. The Storm of Steel, Jünger's autobiographical account of his life in the trenches, was published in 1920 and is still recognized as one of the great wartime memoirs.

The following excerpt from The Storm of Steel *provides a description of the German soldier's experience during the futile but extremely deadly First Battle of the Somme in 1916. In an attempt to relieve the French line during the German assault on Verdun, British and French troops first bombarded the German line north of the Somme River with heavy artillery and then launched an all-out assault. In the course of this battle 650,000 Germans were killed or wounded; French and British casualties totaled 195,000 and 420,000, respectively.*

From *The Storm of Steel: From the Diary of a German Storm-Troop Officer on the Western Front*, by Ernst Jünger, translated by Basil Creighton (London: Chatto and Windus, 1929).

*   *   *

In the evening we sat up a long while drinking coffee that two Frenchwomen made for us in a neighboring house. It was the strongest drink we could procure. We knew that we were on the verge this time of a battle such as the world had never seen. Soon our excited talk rose to a pitch that would have rejoiced the hearts of any freebooters, or of Frederick's Grenadiers. A few days later there were very few of that party still alive.

Guillemont

On the 23d of August we were transported in lorries to Le Mesnil. Our spirits were excellent, though we knew we were going to be put in where the battle of the Somme was at its worst. Chaff and laughter went from lorry to lorry. We marched from Le Mesnil at dusk to Sailly-Saillisel, and here the battalion dumped packs in a large meadow and paraded in battle order.

Artillery fire of a hitherto unimagined intensity rolled and thundered on our front. Thousands of twitching flashes turned the western horizon into a sea of flowers. All the while the wounded came trailing back with white, dejected faces, huddled into the ditches by the gun and ammunition columns that rattled past.

A man in a steel helmet reported to me as guide to conduct my platoon to the renowned Combles, where for the time we were to be in reserve. Sitting with him at the side of the road, I asked him, naturally enough, what it was like in the line. In reply I heard a monotonous tale of crouching all day in shell holes with no one on either flank and no trenches communicating with the rear, of unceasing attacks, of dead bodies littering the ground, of maddening thirst, of wounded and dying, and of a lot besides. The face half-framed by the steel rim of the helmet was unmoved; the voice accompanied by the sound of battle droned on, and the impression they made on me was one of unearthly solemnity. One could see that the man had been through horror to the limit of despair and there had learned to despise it. Nothing was left but supreme and superhuman indifference.

"Where you fall, there you lie. No one can help you. No one knows whether he will come back alive. They attack every day, but they can't get through. Everybody knows it is life and death."

One can fight such with fellows. We marched on along a broad paved road that showed up in the moonlight as a white band on the dark fields. In front of us the artillery fire rose to a higher and higher pitch. *Lasciate ogni speranza!*[1]

Soon we had the first shells on one side of the road and the other. Talk died down and at last ceased. Everyone listened—with that peculiar intentness that concentrates all thought and sensation in the ear—for the long-drawn howl of the approaching shell. Our nerves had a particularly severe test passing Frégicourt, a little hamlet near Combles cemetery, under continuous fire.

As far as we could see in the darkness, Combles was utterly shot to bits. The damage seemed to be recent, judging from the amount of timber among the ruins and the contents of the houses slung over the road. We climbed over numerous heaps of débris—rather hurriedly, owing to a few shrapnel shells—and reached our quarters. They were in a large, shot-riddled house. Here I established myself with three sections. The other two occupied the cellar of a ruin opposite.

At 4 A.M. we were aroused from our rest on the fragments of bed we had collected, in order to receive steel helmets. It was also the occasion of discovering a sack of coffee beans in a corner of the cellar; whereupon there followed a great brewing of coffee.

---

[1] "Abandon all hope!" These words are written on the gate of Hell in Dante Alighieri's *Inferno*.

After breakfast I went out to have a look round. Heavy artillery had turned a peaceful little billeting town into a scene of desolation in the course of a day or two. Whole houses had been flattened by single direct hits or blown up so that the interiors of the rooms hung over the chaos like the scenes on a stage. A sickly scent of dead bodies rose from many of the ruins, for many civilians had been caught in the bombardment and buried beneath the wreckage of their homes. A little girl lay dead in a pool of blood on the threshold of one of the doorways.

*   *   *

In the course of the afternoon the firing increased to such a degree that single explosions were no longer audible. There was nothing but one terrific tornado of noise. From seven onward the square and the houses round were shelled at intervals of half a minute with fifteen-centimeter shells. There were many duds among them, which all the same made the houses rock. We sat all this while in our cellar, round a table, on armchairs covered in silk, with our heads propped on our hands, and counted the seconds between the explosions. Our jests became less frequent, till at last the foolhardiest of us fell silent, and at eight o'clock two direct hits brought down the next house.

From nine to ten the shelling was frantic. The earth rocked and the sky boiled like a gigantic cauldron.

Hundreds of heavy batteries were concentrated on and round Combles. Innumerable shells came howling and hurtling over us. Thick smoke, ominously lit up by Very lights, veiled everything. Head and ears ached violently, and we could only make ourselves understood by shouting a word at a time. The power of logical thought and the force of gravity seemed alike to be suspended. One had the sense of something as unescapable and as unconditionally fated as a catastrophe of nature. An N. C. O. of No. 3 platoon went mad.

At ten this carnival of hell gradually calmed down and passed into a steady drum fire. It was still certainly impossible to distinguish one shell from another.

* * *

At last we reached the front line. It was held by men cowering close in the shell holes, and their dead voices trembled with joy when they heard that we were the relief. A Bavarian sergeant major briefly handed over the sector and the Very-light pistol.

My platoon front formed the right wing of the position held by the regiment. It consisted of a shallow sunken road which had been pounded by shells. It was a few hundred meters left of Guillemont and a rather shorter distance right of Bois-de-Trônes. We were parted from the troops on our right, the Seventy-sixth Regiment of Infantry, by a space about five hundred meters wide. This space was shelled so violently that no troops could maintain themselves there.

The Bavarian sergeant major had vanished of a sudden, and I stood alone, the Very-light pistol in my hand, in the midst of an uncanny sea of shell holes over which lay a white mist whose swaths gave it an even more oppressive and mysterious appearance. A persistent, unpleasant smell came from behind. I was left in no doubt that it came from a gigantic corpse far gone in decay. * * *

When day dawned we were astonished to see, by degrees, what a sight surrounded us.

The sunken road now appeared as nothing but a series of enormous shell holes filled with pieces of uniform, weapons, and dead bodies. The ground all round, as far as the eye could see, was plowed by shells. You could search in vain for one wretched blade of grass. This churned-up battlefield was ghastly. Among the living lay the dead. As we dug ourselves in we found them in layers stacked one upon the top of another. One company after another had been shoved into the drum fire and steadily annihilated. The corpses were covered with the masses of soil turned up by the shells, and the next company advanced in the place of the fallen.

The sunken road and the ground behind were full of German dead; the ground in front, of English. Arms, legs, and heads stuck out stark above the lips of the craters. In front of our miserable defenses there were torn-off limbs and corpses over many of which cloaks and ground sheets had been thrown to hide the fixed stare of their distorted features. In spite of the heat no one thought for a moment of covering them with soil.

The village of Guillemont was distinguished from the landscape around it only because the shell holes there were of a whiter color by reason of the houses which had been ground to powder. Guillemont railway station lay in front of us. It was smashed to bits like a child's plaything. Delville Wood, reduced to matchwood, was farther behind.

* * *

It was the days at Guillemont that first made me aware of the overwhelming effects on the war of material. We had to adapt ourselves to an entirely new phase of war. The communications between the troops and the staff, between the artillery and the liaison officers, were utterly crippled by the terrific fire. Dispatch carriers failed to get through the hail of metal, and telephone wires were no sooner laid than they were shot into pieces. Even light-signaling was put out of action by the clouds of smoke and dust that hung over the field of battle. There was a zone of a kilometer behind the front line where explosives held absolute sway.

Even the regimental staff only knew exactly where we had been and how the line ran when we came back after three days and told them. Under such circumstances accuracy of artillery fire was out of the question. We were also entirely in the dark about the English line, though often, without our knowing it, it was only a few meters from us. Sometimes a Tommy, feeling his way from one shell hole to another like an ant along a track in the sand, landed in one that we occupied, and *vice versa,* for our front line consisted merely of isolated and unconnected bits that were easily mistaken.

Once seen, the landscape is an unforgettable one. In this neighborhood of villages, meadows, woods, and fields there was literally not a bush or a tiniest blade of grass to be seen. Every hand's-breadth of ground had been churned up again and again; trees had been uprooted, smashed, and ground to touchwood, the houses blown to bits and turned to dust; hills had been leveled and the arable land made a desert.

And yet the strangest thing of all was not the horror of the landscape in itself, but the fact that these scenes, such as the world had never known before, were fashioned by men who intended them to be a decisive end to the war. Thus all the frightfulness that the mind of man could devise was brought into the field; and there, where lately had been the idyllic picture of rural peace, there was as faithful a picture of the soul of scientific war. In earlier wars, certainly, towns and villages had been burned, but what was that compared with this sea of craters dug out by machines? For even in this fantastic desert there was the sameness of the machine-made article. A shell hole strewn with bully tins, broken weapons, fragments of uniform, and dud shells, with one or two dead bodies on its edge—this was the never-changing scene that surrounded each one of all these hundreds of thousands of men. And it seemed that man, on this landscape he had himself created, became different, more mysterious and hardy and callous than in any previous battle. The spirit and the tempo of the fighting altered, and after the battle of the Somme the war had its own peculiar impress that distinguished it from all other wars. After this battle the German soldier wore the steel helmet, and in his features there were chiseled the lines of an energy stretched to the utmost pitch, lines that future generations will perhaps find as fascinating and imposing as those of many heads of classical or Renaissance times.

For I cannot too often repeat, a battle was no longer an episode that spent itself in blood and fire; it was a condition of things that dug itself in remorselessly week after week and even month after month. What was a man's life in this wilderness whose vapor was laden with the stench of thousands upon thousands of decaying bodies? Death lay in ambush for each one in every shell hole, merciless, and making one merciless in turn. Chivalry here took a final farewell. It had to yield to the heightened intensity of war, just as all fine and personal feeling has to yield when machinery gets the upper hand. The Europe of today appeared here for the first time on the field of battle. . . .

*   *   *

REVIEW QUESTIONS

1. What impact did the British bombardment have on the battle zone that Jünger describes?
2. What effect does the bombardment seem to have had on the psyches of individual soldiers?
3. How does the kind of warfare described here differ from that of the past?
4. In what sense is this warfare a product of "the Europe of today"?

VERA BRITTAIN

FROM *Testament of Youth*

Despite an eminently respectable "provincial young ladyhood," the British author Vera Brittain (1893–1970) rebelled early against the constraints imposed by age, class, and sex. Brittain insisted on pursuing her education, despite her parents' protests, and attended Sommerville, a college for women affiliated with Oxford. She experienced the outbreak of the First World War as "an infuriating personal interruption rather than a world-wide catastrophe," but this attitude changed dramati-

cally after her fiancé, her brother, and her best male friends enlisted and then died, one by one. Frustrated by her inability to become a soldier and share the hardships of her male peers, she chose the nearest thing: service as a Voluntary Aid Detachment nurse. After a period of training in England, she attended wounded soldiers on the island of Malta and on the Western Front. The following excerpts from Brittain's widely read memoir, Testament of Youth, *demonstrate the various ways in which the lives of ordinary individuals were disrupted and transformed during the course of the war.*

From *Testament of Youth: An Autobiographical Study of the Years 1900–1925*, by Vera Brittain (London: V. Gollancz, 1933).

*   *   *

Nurse's Training

On Sunday morning, June 27th, 1915, I began my nursing at the Devonshire Hospital. * * *

From our house above the town I ran eagerly downhill to my first morning's work, not knowing, fortunately for myself, that my servitude would last for nearly four years. The hospital had originally been used as a riding-school, but a certain Duke of Devonshire, with exemplary concern for the welfare of the sick but none whatever for the feet of the nursing staff, had caused it to be converted to its present charitable purpose. The main part of the building consisted of a huge dome, with two stone corridors running one above the other round its quarter-mile circumference. The nurses were not allowed to cross its diameter, which contained an inner circle reserved for convalescent patients, so that everything forgotten or newly required meant a run round the circumference. * * *

My hours there ran from 7.45 a.m. until 1 p.m., and again from 5.0 p.m. until 9.15 p.m.—a longer day, as I afterwards discovered, than that normally required in many Army hospitals. No doubt the staff was not unwilling to make the utmost use of so enthusiastic and unsophisticated a probationer. Meals, for all of which I was expected to go home, were not included in these hours. As our house was nearly half a mile from the hospital on the slope of a steep hill, I never completely overcame the aching of my back and the soreness of my feet through-

out the time that I worked there, and felt perpetually as if I had just returned from a series of long route marches.

I never minded these aches and pains, which appeared to me solely as satisfactory tributes to my love for Roland. What did profoundly trouble and humiliate me was my colossal ignorance of the simplest domestic operations. Among other "facts of life," my expensive education had omitted to teach me the prosaic but important essentials of egg-boiling, and the Oxford cookery classes had triumphantly failed to repair the omission. I imagined that I had to bring the saucepan to the boil, then turn off the gas and allow the egg to lie for three minutes in the cooling water. The remarks of a lance-corporal to whom I presented an egg "boiled" in this fashion led me to make shamefaced inquiries of my superiors, from whom I learnt, in those first few days, how numerous and devastating were the errors that it was possible to commit in carrying out the most ordinary functions of everyday life. To me, for whom meals had hitherto appeared as though by clockwork and the routine of a house had seemed to be worked by some invisible mechanism, the complications of sheer existence were nothing short of a revelation.

Despite my culinary shortcomings, the men appeared to like me; none of them were very ill, and no doubt my youth, my naïve eagerness and the clean freshness of my new uniform meant more to them than any amount of common sense and efficiency. Perhaps, too, the warm and profoundly surprising comfort that I derived from their presence produced a tenderness which was able to communicate back to them, in turn, something of their own rich consolation.

Throughout my two decades of life, I had never looked upon the nude body of an adult male; I had never even seen a naked boy-child since the nursery days when, at the age of four or five, I used to share my evening baths with Edward. I had therefore expected, when I first started nursing, to be overcome with nervousness and embarrassment, but, to my infinite relief, I was conscious of neither. Towards the men I came to feel an almost adoring gratitude for their simple and natural acceptance of my ministrations. Short of actually going to bed with them, there was hardly an intimate service that I did not perform for one or another in the course of four years, and I still have reason to be thankful for the knowledge of masculine functioning which the care of them gave me, and for my early release from the sex-inhibitions that even to-day—thanks to the Victorian tradition which up to 1914 dictated that a young woman should know nothing of men but their faces and their clothes until marriage pitchforked her into an incompletely visualised and highly disconcerting intimacy—beset many of my female contemporaries, both married and single.

In the early days of the War the majority of soldier patients belonged to a first-rate physical type which neither wounds nor sickness, unless mortal, could permanently impair, and from the constant handling of their lean, muscular bodies, I came to understand the essential cleanliness, the innate nobility, of sexual love on its physical side. Although there was much to shock in Army hospital service, much to terrify, much, even, to disgust, this day-by-day contact with male anatomy was never part of the shame. Since it was always Roland whom I was nursing by proxy, my attitude towards him imperceptibly changed; it became less romantic and more realistic, and thus a new depth was added to my love.

In addition to the patients, I managed to extract approval from most of the nurses—no doubt because, my one desire being to emulate Roland's endurance, I seized with avidity upon all the unpleasant tasks of which they were only too glad to be relieved, and took a masochistic delight in emptying bed-pans, washing greasy cups and spoons, and disposing of odoriferous dressings in the sink-room. The Matron described as "a slave-driver" by one of the elegant lady V.A.D.s who intermittently trotted in to "help" in the evenings after the bulk of the work was done—treated me with especial kindness, and often let me out through her private gate in order to save me a few yards of the interminable miles upon my feet.

My particular brand of enthusiasm, the nurses told me later, was rare among the local V.A.D.s, most of whom came to the hospital expecting to hold the patients' hands and smooth their pillows while the regular nurses fetched and carried everything that looked or smelt disagreeable. Probably this was true, for my diary records of one Buxton girl a month later: "Nancy thinks she would like to take up Red Cross work but does not want to go where she would have to dust wards and clean up as she does not think she would like that."

*   *   *

At the Western Front

Only a day or two afterwards I was leaving quarters to go back to my ward, when I had to wait to let a large contingent of troops march past me along the main road that ran through our camp. They were swinging rapidly towards Camiers, and though the sight of soldiers marching was now too familiar to arouse curiosity, an unusual quality of bold vigour in their swift stride caused me to stare at them with puzzled interest.

They looked larger than ordinary men; their tall, straight figures were in vivid contrast to the under-sized armies of pale recruits to which we had grown accustomed. At first I thought their spruce, clean uniforms were those of officers, yet obviously they could not be officers, for there were too many of them; they seemed, as it were, Tommies in heaven. Had yet another regiment been conjured out of our depleted Dominions? I wondered, watching them move with such rhythm, such dignity, such serene consciousness of self-respect. But I knew the colonial troops so well, and these were different; they were assured where the Australians were aggressive, self-possessed where the New Zealanders were turbulent.

Then I heard an excited exclamation from a group of Sisters behind me.

"Look! Look! Here are the Americans!"

I pressed forward with the others to watch the United States physically entering the War, so godlike, so magnificent, so splendidly unimpaired in comparison with the tired, nerve-racked men of the British Army. So these were our deliverers at last, marching up the road to Camiers in the spring sunshine! There seemed to be hundreds of them, and in the fearless swagger of their proud strength they looked a formidable bulwark against the peril looming from Amiens.

Somehow the necessity of packing up in a hurry, the ignominious flight to the coast so long imagined, seemed to move further away. An uncontrollable emotion seized me—as such emotions often seized us in those days of insufficient sleep; my eyeballs pricked, my throat ached, and a mist swam over the confident Americans going to the front. The coming of relief made me realise all at once how long and how intolerable had been the tension, and with the knowledge that we were not, after all, defeated, I found myself beginning to cry.

*   *   *

War's End

When the sound of victorious guns burst over London at 11 a.m. on November 11th, 1918, the men and women who looked incredulously into each other's faces did not cry jubilantly: "We've won the War!" They only said "The War is over."

From Millbank I heard the maroons crash with terrifying clearness, and, like a sleeper who is determined to go on dreaming after being told to wake up, I went on automatically washing the dressing bowls in the annex outside my hut. Deeply buried beneath my consciousness there stirred the vague memory of a letter that I had written Roland in those legendary days when I was still at Oxford and could spend my Sundays in thinking of him while the organ echoed grandly through New College Chapel. It had been a warm May evening, when all the city was sweet with the scent of wallflowers and lilac, and I had walked back to Micklem Hall after hearing an Occasional Oratorio by Handel, which described the mustering of troops for battle, the lament for the fallen and the triumphant return of the victors.

"As I listened," I told him, "to the organ swelling forth into a final triumphant burst in the song of victory, after the solemn and mournful dirge over the dead, I thought with what mockery and irony the jubilant celebrations which we hail the coming of peace will fall upon the ears of those to whom their best will never return, upon whose sorrow victory is built, who have paid with their mourning for the others' joy. I wonder if I shall be one of those who take happy part in the triumph—or if I shall listen to the merriment with a heart that breaks and ears that try to keep out the mirthful sounds."

And as I dried the bowls, I thought: "It's come too late for me. Somehow I knew, even at Oxford, that it would. Why couldn't it have ended rationally, as it might have ended, in 1916, instead of all that trumpet-blowing against a negotiated peace, and the ferocious talk of secure civilians about marching to Berlin? It's come five months too late—or is it three years? It might have ended last June, and let Edward, at least, be saved! Only five months—it's such a little time, when Roland died nearly three years ago."

But on Armistice Day not even a lonely survivor drowning in black waves of memory could be left alone with her thoughts. A moment after the guns had subsided into sudden, palpitating silence, the other V.A.D. from my ward dashed excitedly into the annex.

"Brittain! Brittain! Did you hear the maroons? It's over—it's all over! Do let's come out and see what's happening!" Mechanically, I followed her into the road, as I stood there, stupidly rigid, long after the triumphant explosions from Westminster had turned into a distant crescendo of shouting, I saw a taxicab turn swiftly in from the Embankment toward the hospital. The next moment there was a cry for doctors and nurses from passers-by, for in rounding the corner the taxi had knocked down a small elderly woman who in listening, like myself, to the wild noise of a world released from nightmare, had failed to observe its approach.

As I hurried to her side I realised that she was all but dead and already past speech. Like Victor in the mortuary chapel, she seemed to have shrunk to the dimensions of a child with the sharp features of age, but on the tiny chalk-white face an expression of shocked surprise still lingered, and she stared hard at me as Geoffrey had stared at his orderly in those last moments of conscious silence beside the Scarpe. Had she been thinking, I wondered, when the taxi struck her, of her sons at the front, now safe? The next moment a medical officer and some orderlies came up, and I went back to my ward.

But I remembered her at intervals throughout that afternoon, during which, with a half-masochistic notion of "seeing the sights," I made a circular tour to Kensington by way of the intoxicated West End. With aching persistence my thoughts went back to the dead and the strange irony of their fates—to Roland, gifted, ardent, ambitious, who had died without glory in the conscientious performance of a routine job; to Victor and Geoffrey, gentle and diffident, who, conquering nature by resolution, had each gone down bravely in a big "show"; and finally to Edward, musical, serene, a lover of peace, who had fought courageously through so many battles and at last had been killed while leading a vital counter-attack in one of the few decisive actions of the War. As I struggled through the waving, shrieking crowds in Piccadilly and Regent Street on the overloaded top of a 'bus, some witty enthusiast for contemporary history symbolically turned upside down the signboard "Seven Kings."

Late that evening, when supper was over, a group of elated V.A.D.s who were anxious to walk through Westminster and Whitehall to Buckingham Palace prevailed upon me to join them. Outside the Admiralty a crazy group of convalescent Tommies were collecting specimens of different uniforms and bundling their wearers into flag-strewn taxis; with a shout they seized two of my companions and disappeared into the clamorous crowd, waving flags and shaking rattles. Wherever we went a burst of enthusiastic cheering greeted our Red Cross uniform, and complete strangers adorned with wound stripes rushed up and shook me warmly by the hand. After the long, long blackness, it seemed like a fairy-tale to see the street lamps shining through the chill November gloom.

I detached myself from the others and walked slowly up Whitehall, with my heart sinking in a sudden cold dismay. Already this was a different world from the one that I had known during four life-long years, a world in which people would be light-hearted and forgetful, in which themselves and their careers and their amusements would blot out political ideals and great national issues. And in that brightly lit, alien world I should have no part. All those with whom I had really been intimate were gone; not one remained to share with me the heights and the depths of my memories. As the years went by and youth departed and remembrance grew dim, a deeper and ever deeper darkness would cover the young men who were once my contemporaries.

For the first time I realised, with all that full realisation meant, how completely everything that had hitherto made up my life had vanished with Edward and Roland, with Victor and Geoffrey. The War was over; a new age was beginning; but the dead were dead and would never return.

REVIEW QUESTIONS

1. How did Brittain's experiences as a nurse change her attitude toward human sexuality?
2. Why did she so willingly accept the hard and sometimes unpleasant work nursing entailed?
3. How does Brittain describe the newly arrived American troops?
4. In a letter to her fiancé, Brittain expressed the fear that the war would put "a barrier of indescribable experience between men and the women whom they loved." Do you think this concern was valid?

FROM **The Versailles Treaty**

Toward the end of the war, the American president Woodrow Wilson began to lobby for a "peace without victory" and proposed a set of Fourteen Points as the basis for eventual peace negotiations. Wilson envisioned a just settlement that would permanently eradicate recourse to armed conflict by striking at the root causes of all wars and not simply at the incidental factors that had precipitated this particular war. He called for an end to the arms races and secret diplomacy of the prewar era, and he proposed that the new international order be based on the principles of democracy, international free trade, and the right of ethnic minorities to self-determination, all of which would be guaranteed by a league of nations. When the new German government sued for peace in late 1918, it did so in the hope that the peace settlement would be negotiated on the basis of Wilson's proposals. However, Germany was not allowed to send representatives to the Versailles Conference, and the representatives of the European Allies—Georges Clemenceau for France, David Lloyd George for Britain, and Vittorio Orlando for Italy—produced a rather different treaty from that suggested by the Fourteen Points. Despite Wilson's very active role in the framing of the settlement, the Versailles Treaty of 1919 was not ratified by the U.S. Congress, and the United States never joined Wilson's cherished League of Nations.

From The Versailles Treaty, World War I Document Archive Web page, http://wwi.lib.byu.edu/index.php/Peace_Treaty_of_Versailles.

*   *   *

The Covenant of the League of Nations

The HIGH CONTRACTING PARTIES, In order to promote international cooperation and to achieve international peace and security

by the acceptance of obligations not to resort to war by the prescription of open, just and honourable relations between nations

by the firm establishment of the understandings of international law as the actual rule of conduct among Governments, and

by the maintenance of justice and a scrupulous respect for all treaty obligations in the dealings of organised peoples with one another

Agree to this Covenant of the League of Nations.

*   *   *

ARTICLE 8

The Members of the League recognise that the maintenance of peace requires the reduction of national armaments to the lowest point consistent with national safety and the enforcement by common action of international obligations. The Council, taking account of the geographical situation and circumstances of each State, shall formulate plans for such reduction for the consideration and action of the several Governments. Such plans shall be subject to reconsideration and revision at least every ten years.

*   *   *

ARTICLE 10

The Members of the League undertake to respect and preserve as against external aggression the territorial integrity and existing political independence of all Members of the League. * * *

ARTICLE 11

Any war or threat of war, whether immediately affecting any of the Members of the League or not, is hereby declared a matter of concern to the whole League, and the League shall take any action that may be deemed wise and effectual to safeguard the peace of nations. ∗ ∗ ∗

ARTICLE 12

The Members of the League agree that if there should arise between them any dispute likely to lead to a rupture, they will submit the matter either to arbitration or to inquiry by the Council, and they agree in no case to resort to war until three months after the award by the arbitrators or the report by the Council.

∗   ∗   ∗

ARTICLE 16

Should any Member of the League resort to war in disregard of its covenants ∗ ∗ ∗, it shall ipso facto be deemed to have committed an act of war against all other Members of the League, which hereby undertake immediately to subject it to the severance of all trade or financial relations, the prohibition of all intercourse between their nationals and the nationals of the covenant-breaking State, and the prevention of all financial, commercial, or personal intercourse between the nationals of the covenant-breaking State and the nationals of any other State, whether a Member of the League or not. ∗ ∗ ∗ Any Member of the League which has violated any covenant of the League may be declared to be no longer a Member of the League by a vote of the Council concurred in by the Representatives of all the other Members of the League represented thereon.

∗   ∗   ∗

ARTICLE 18

Every treaty or international engagement entered into hereafter by any Member of the League shall be forthwith registered with the Secretariat and shall as soon as possible be published by it. No such treaty or international engagement shall be binding until so registered.

∗   ∗   ∗

ARTICLE 22

To those colonies and territories which as a consequence of the late war have ceased to be under the sovereignty of the States which formerly governed them and which are inhabited by peoples not yet able to stand by themselves under the strenuous conditions of the modern world, there should be applied the principle that the well-being and development of such peoples form a sacred trust of civilisation and that securities for the performance of this trust should be embodied in this Covenant. The best method of giving practical effect to this principle is that the tutelage of such peoples should be entrusted to advanced nations who by reason of their resources, their experience or their geographical position can best undertake this responsibility, and who are willing to accept it, and that this tutelage should be exercised by them as Mandatories on behalf of the League. The character of the mandate must differ according to the stage of the development of the people, the geographical situation of the territory, its economic conditions, and other similar circumstances. Certain communities formerly belonging to the Turkish Empire have reached a stage of development where their existence as independent nations can be provisionally recognised subject to the rendering of administrative advice and assistance by a Mandatory until such time as they are able to stand alone. The wishes of these communities must be a principal consideration in the selection of the Mandatory. Other peoples, especially those of Central Africa, are at such a stage that the Mandatory must be responsible for the administration of the territory under conditions which will guarantee freedom of conscience and religion, subject only to the maintenance of public order and morals, the prohibition of abuses such as the slave trade, the arms traffic, and the liquor traffic, and the prevention of the establishment of fortifications or military and naval bases and of military training of the natives for other than police purposes and the defence of territory, and will also secure equal opportunities for the trade and commerce of other Members of the League. There are territories, such as South-West Africa and certain of the South Pacific Islands, which, owing to the sparseness of their population, or their small size, or their remoteness from the centres of civilisation, or their geographical contiguity to the territory of the Mandatory, and other circumstances, can be best administered under the laws of the Mandatory as integral portions of its territory, subject to the safeguards above mentioned in the interests of the indigenous population. In every case of mandate, the Mandatory shall render to the Council an annual report in reference to the territory committed to its charge. * * *

ARTICLE 23

* * * The Members of the League: (a) will endeavour to secure and maintain fair and humane conditions of labour for men, women, and children, both in their own countries and in all countries to which their commercial and industrial relations extend, and for that purpose will establish and maintain the necessary international organisations; (b) undertake to secure just treatment of the native inhabitants of territories under their control; (c) will entrust the League with the general supervision over the execution of agreements with regard to the traffic in women and children, and the traffic in opium and other dangerous drugs; (d) will entrust the League with the general supervision of the trade in arms and ammunition with the countries in which the control of this traffic is necessary in the common interest; (e) will make provision to secure and maintain freedom of communications and of transit and equitable treatment for the commerce of all Members of the League. In this connection, the special necessities of the regions devastated during the war of 1914–1918 shall be borne in mind; (f) will endeavour to take steps in

matters of international concern for the prevention and control of disease.

*   *   *

ARTICLE 42

Germany is forbidden to maintain or construct any fortifications either on the left bank of the Rhine or on the right bank to the west of a line drawn 50 kilometres to the East of the Rhine.

ARTICLE 43

In the area defined above the maintenance and the assembly of armed forces, either permanently or temporarily, and military maneuvers of any kind, as well as the upkeep of all permanent works for mobilization, are in the same way forbidden.

ARTICLE 44

In case Germany violates in any manner whatever the provisions of Articles 42 and 43, she shall be regarded as committing a hostile act against the Powers signatory of the present Treaty and as calculated to disturb the peace of the world.

ARTICLE 45

As compensation for the destruction of the coalmines in the north of France and as part payment towards the total reparation due from Germany for the damage resulting from the war, Germany cedes to France in full and absolute possession, with exclusive rights of exploitation, unencumbered and free from all debts and charges of any kind, the coal-mines situated in the Saar Basin. * * *

*   *   *

ARTICLE 49

* * * At the end of fifteen years from the coming into force of the present Treaty the inhabitants of the [Saar Basin] shall be called upon to indicate

the sovereignty under which they desire to be placed.

*   *   *

ARTICLE 51

The territories [of Alsace and Lorraine] which were ceded to Germany in accordance with the Preliminaries of Peace signed at Versailles on February 26, 1871, and the Treaty of Frankfort of May 10, 1871, are restored to French sovereignty as from the date of the Armistice of November 11, 1918. * * *

*   *   *

ARTICLE 80

Germany acknowledges and will respect strictly the independence of Austria * * * ; she agrees that this independence shall be inalienable, except with the consent of the Council of the League of Nations.

ARTICLE 81

Germany * * * recognises the complete independence of the Czecho-Slovak State. * * *

*   *   *

ARTICLE 84

German nationals habitually resident in any of the territories recognised as forming part of the Czecho-Slovak State will obtain Czecho-Slovak nationality ipso facto and lose their German nationality.

*   *   *

ARTICLE 87

Germany, in conformity with the action already taken by the Allied and Associated Powers, recognises the complete independence of Poland. * * *

*   *   *

ARTICLE 102

The Principal Allied and Associated Powers undertake to establish the town of Danzig, together with the rest of the territory described in Article 100, as a Free City. It will be placed under the protection of the League of Nations.

*   *   *

ARTICLE 116

Germany acknowledges and agrees to respect as permanent and inalienable the independence of all the territories which were part of the former Russian Empire on August 1, 1914.

* * * Germany accepts definitely the abrogation of the Brest-Litovsk Treaties and of all other treaties, conventions, and agreements entered into by her with the Maximalist Government in Russia.

*   *   *

ARTICLE 119

Germany renounces in favour of the Principal Allied and Associated Powers all her rights and titles over her oversea possessions.

*   *   *

ARTICLE 160

* * * The total number of effectives in the Army of the States constituting Germany must not exceed one hundred thousand men, including officers and establishments of depots. The Army shall be devoted exclusively to the maintenance of order within the territory and to the control of the frontiers.

The total effective strength of officers, including the personnel of staffs, whatever their composition, must not exceed four thousand. * * *

*   *   *

ARTICLE 168

The manufacture of arms, munitions, or any war material, shall only be carried out in factories or works the location of which shall be communicated to and approved by the Governments of the Principal Allied and Associated Powers, and the number of which they retain the right to restrict. ✷ ✷ ✷

✷   ✷   ✷

ARTICLE 173

Universal compulsory military service shall be abolished in Germany.

The German Army may only be constituted and recruited by means of voluntary enlistment.

✷   ✷   ✷

ARTICLE 181

✷ ✷ ✷ The German naval forces in commission must not exceed:

6 battleships of the Deutschland or Lothringen type, 6 light cruisers, 12 destroyers, 12 torpedo boats. ✷ ✷ ✷

No submarines are to be included.

All other warships, except where there is provision to the contrary in the present Treaty, must be placed in reserve or devoted to commercial purposes.

✷   ✷   ✷

ARTICLE 198

The armed forces of Germany must not include any military or naval air forces. ✷ ✷ ✷

✷   ✷   ✷

ARTICLE 227

The Allied and Associated Powers publicly arraign William II of Hohenzollern, formerly German Emperor, for a supreme offence against international morality and the sanctity of treaties. ✷ ✷ ✷

✷   ✷   ✷

ARTICLE 231

The Allied and Associated Governments affirm and Germany accepts the responsibility of Germany and her allies for causing all the loss and damage to which the Allied and Associated Governments and their nationals have been subjected as a consequence of the war imposed upon them by the aggression of Germany and her allies. ✷ ✷ ✷

ARTICLE 232

The Allied and Associated Governments recognise that the resources of Germany are not adequate, after taking into account permanent diminutions of such resources which will result from other provisions of the present Treaty, to make complete reparation for all such loss and damage.

The Allied and Associated Governments, however, require, and Germany undertakes, that she will make compensation for all damage done to the civilian population of the Allied and Associated Powers and to their property during the period of the belligerency of each as an Allied or Associated Power against Germany. ✷ ✷ ✷

ARTICLE 233

The amount of the above damage for which compensation is to be made by Germany shall be determined by an Inter-Allied Commission. ✷ ✷ ✷

✷   ✷   ✷

Organisation of Labour

Whereas the League of Nations has for its object the establishment of universal peace, and such a peace can be established only if it is based upon social justice;

And whereas conditions of labour exist involving such injustice, hardship, and privation to large numbers of people as to produce unrest so great that the peace and harmony of the world are imperilled; and an improvement of those conditions is urgently required; * * *

Whereas also the failure of any nation to adopt humane conditions of labour is an obstacle in the way of other nations which desire to improve the conditions in their own countries;

The HIGH CONTRACTING PARTIES, moved by sentiments of justice and humanity as well as by the desire to secure the permanent peace of the world, agree to the following:

ARTICLE 387

A permanent organisation is hereby established for the promotion of the objects set forth in the Preamble. * * *

*   *   *

ARTICLE 427

[The HIGH CONTRACTING PARTIES] recognise that differences of climate, habits, and customs, of economic opportunity and industrial tradition, make strict uniformity in the conditions of labour difficult of immediate attainment. But, holding as they do, that labour should not be regarded merely as an article of commerce, they think that there are methods and principles for regulating labour conditions which all industrial communities should endeavour to apply, so far as their special circumstances will permit.

Among these methods and principles, the following seem to the High Contracting Parties to be of special and urgent importance:

First. The guiding principle above enunciated that labour should not be regarded merely as a commodity or article of commerce.

Second. The right of association for all lawful purposes by the employed as well as by the employers.

Third. The payment to the employed of a wage adequate to maintain a reasonable standard of life as this is understood in their time and country.

Fourth. The adoption of an eight hours day or a forty-eight hours week as the standard to be aimed at where it has not already been attained.

Fifth. The adoption of a weekly rest of at least twenty-four hours, which should include Sunday wherever practicable.

Sixth. The abolition of child labour and the imposition of such limitations on the labour of young persons as shall permit the continuation of their education and assure their proper physical development.

Seventh. The principle that men and women should receive equal remuneration for work of equal value.

Eighth. The standard set by law in each country with respect to the conditions of labour should have due regard to the equitable economic treatment of all workers lawfully resident therein.

Ninth. Each State should make provision for a system of inspection in which women should take part, in order to ensure the enforcement of the laws and regulations for the protection of the employed. * * *

ARTICLE 428

As a guarantee for the execution of the present Treaty by Germany, the German territory situated to the west of the Rhine, together with the bridgeheads, will be occupied by Allied and Associated troops for a period of fifteen years from the coming into force of the present Treaty.

*   *   *

ARTICLE 430

In case either during the occupation or after the expiration of the fifteen years referred to above the Reparation Commission finds that Germany refuses to observe the whole or part of her obligations under the present Treaty with regard to reparation, the whole or part of the areas specified in Article 429 will be reoccupied immediately by the Allied and Associated forces.

ARTICLE 431

If before the expiration of the period of fifteen years Germany complies with all the undertakings resulting from the present Treaty, the occupying forces will be withdrawn immediately.

*   *   *

ARTICLE 434

Germany undertakes to recognise the full force of the Treaties of Peace and Additional Conventions which may be concluded by the Allied and Associated Powers with the Powers who fought on the side of Germany and to recognise whatever dispositions may be made concerning the territories of the former Austro-Hungarian Monarchy, of the Kingdom of Bulgaria and of the Ottoman Empire, and to recognise the new States within their frontiers as there laid down.

REVIEW QUESTIONS

1. What guarantees of permanent international peace are incorporated into this treaty?
2. Assuming that all of the clauses in this treaty were to be enforced, does it provide the basis for a lasting peace?
3. Is this a "peace without victory"?
4. How do you think Germans responded to this treaty?
5. To what extent are the rights and liberties of disenfranchised minorities—whether ethnic minorities in eastern Europe, colonial subjects, or the world's laborers—guaranteed by this treaty?

War Propaganda

Poster art was a leading form of propaganda used by all belligerents in the First World War to enlist men, sell war bonds, and sustain morale on the home front. Posters also demonized the enemy and glorified the sacrifices of soldiers the better to rationalize the unprecedented loss of life and national wealth. The following posters, from a wide range of combatant nations during the war, share a common desire to link the war effort to a highly gendered set of obligations and allegiances. Why would nationalism resort to such gendered images in a time of crisis? What does this tell us about the way that myths of national belonging are created and sustained in times of urgency?

E. V. KEALY, 1915
Britain

ARTIST UNKNOWN, C. 1914
Russia

HOWARD CHANDLER CHRISTY, 1917
Britain

CHARLES STAFFORD DUNCAN, 1918
United States

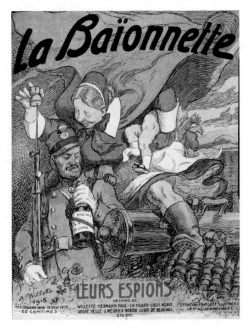

ADOLPHE LEON WILLETTE, 1915
France

25 ❧ TURMOIL BETWEEN THE WARS

The Great War was not only physically devastating but it also did considerable psychological and spiritual damage. During the war, the trauma of trench warfare sometimes pushed soldiers over the edge of sanity into madness, a condition euphemistically known as shell shock. In the aftermath of the war, it almost seemed as if European society as a whole was suffering from a nervous breakdown of monumental proportions. Peace, so long desired, did not bring the security and prosperity for which so many yearned. Instead, the European nations lurched from one crisis to the next during the 1920s and 1930s, and another episode of international warfare erupted at the end of these two short decades of uneasy peace.

The crisis of "total" war produced conditions conducive to the rise of totalitarianism, a distinctively modern form of authoritarian government. In Russia, the initial stages of the Soviet revolution generated hopes for the creation of a modern communist utopia, hopes shared both by Russian revolutionaries and by many progressives outside of Russia. However, Stalin's rise to power and his imposition of a Communist Party dictatorship put an end to this dream. Stalin's authoritarianism of the left was paralleled by fascist movements in eastern and central Europe. Mussolini's fascism and Hitler's Nazism shared many elements of traditional right-wing ideology, but they also sought to incorporate elements of left-wing theory and practice, producing a revolutionism of the right. Many Europeans, disillusioned with liberalism and democracy, greeted charismatic dictatorship as a new and attractive political option.

The tendency to look to extremist political movements for solutions to social problems was greatly reinforced by the economic crisis brought on by the Great Depression of the 1930s. Throughout Europe, the Depression caused a dramatic polarization of the political spectrum and a realignment of political allegiances. The greatest losers were the centrist parties still committed to liberalism and parliamentary democracy.

In response to the dislocations of the era, many intellectuals subjected traditional orthodoxies to ruthless scrutiny. Philosophers, scientists, and artists all puzzled over the purpose of human existence in a cosmos that seemed bereft of transcendent meaning, and many wondered whether God was dead, or at least unwilling to intervene in human affairs. The pointless carnage of the war had crushed the optimism of Belle Époque culture. That Europeans had allowed such a cataclysm to occur at all suggested that irrational impulses played an important role in human behavior and that progress was not so inevitable as nineteenth-century positivists had thought. Technological and scientific advances, though impressive, brought new dangers—including devastating increases in the destructiveness of military weapons—and they did not provide answers to human beings' deepest yearnings for spiritual knowledge and sustenance.

N. N. SUKHANOV

FROM *The Russian Revolution 1917*

Nikolai Nikolayevich Himmer (1882–1940), known more widely as Sukhanov, was a well-known journalist who commented frequently on political and economic affairs in St. Petersburg (Petrograd). A firsthand observer of the outbreak of revolution in the Russian capital in 1917, he was not affiliated with any political party at the time. By temperament, however, his allegiances were on the left—he was well connected throughout the socialist movement, he had worked closely with Maxim Gorky before the revolution, and he counted Alexander Kerensky among his friends.

Sukhanov's account of the first meeting of the reconstituted Petrograd Soviet on February 27, 1917 captures something of the euphoria of these first days of revolution. The first meeting of the Soviet took place in the Tauride Palace, the seat of the Russian Duma. It was attended by fifty deputies—mostly intellectuals from the various socialist party organizations in the capital and a few unaffiliated militants—and approximately two hundred onlookers. Few workers attended this meeting, and none were elected to serve on the executive committee. In spite of this, however, the deputies showed their enthusiasm for the popular resistance in the capital to the forces of the tsar's police force and unanimously resolved to call themselves the Petrograd Soviet of Workers' and Soldiers' Deputies.

The Petrograd Soviet had first convened during the failed revolution of 1905, and its reappearance in 1917 was a marker of the new movement's radical potential. Not yet controlled by the Bolsheviks, the Soviet was seen by many at the time as the only legitimate voice of the Russian people and a necessary complement to the more elite and liberal center of power being created simultaneously by Kerensky and his partners in the provisional government. Ultimately, this "dual" power structure—an elite movement instigated by former Duma politicians and a popular movement that brought together radicals, socialists, and elements from the military's rank and file—would prove unworkable. Threatened both from the right—in the Kornilov affair—and eventually also from the left by the Bolsheviks, the provisional government's power-haring experiment with the Petrograd Soviet lasted only until October, when the Bolshevik coup brought to power a new group led by Lenin and Trotsky.

From *The Russian Revolution 1917, a Personal Record*, by N. N. Sukhanov, edited, abridged, and translated by Joel Carmichael (Princeton, N.J.: Princeton University Press, 1984), pp. 58–64.

*   *   *

I elbowed my way through the crowd from the Catherine Hall to the rooms occupied by the Soviet.

The hall was filling up. Sokolov was running around giving orders and seating the deputies. In an authoritative way, without, however, any discernible justification, he was explaining to those present what sort of vote they had, whether consulting or deciding,[1] and who had no voice at all. In particular he explained to me that I had a vote—I don't remember now what kind. But of course these judicial decisions of the future senator had not the slightest practical significance.

I ran into Tikhonov, and we took places at the table at a respectful distance from its head, which was occupied by official personages, the deputies Chkheidze and Skobelev, members of the self-appointed Ex. Com., Gvozdev, Kapelinsky of the Cooperative movement,[2] and Grinevich, one of the leaders of the Petersburg Mensheviks.

B. O. Bogdanov, the most active member of the Ex. Com., was missing for some reason; I think he only turned up a day later. Nearby at the table towered the massive figure of Steklov,[3] more reminiscent of a bearded central-Russian smallholder than an Odessa Jew.

Also there at the head of the table, pestering all and sundry with something or other, was Khrustalev-Nosar, the former chairman and leader (together with Trotsky) of the Soviet in 1905. Sokolov was bustling about there too; at 9 o'clock precisely he opened the session of the Soviet with a resolution to elect the Praesidium . . . Kerensky turned up for a short time.

I no longer felt any longing for the centres of the movement; I had no feeling of being cut off from the living process. I was in the very crucible of great events, the laboratory of the revolution.

*   *   *

At the moment the meeting opened around 250 deputies were there. But new groups kept pouring into the hall, God knows with what mandates or intentions.

---

[1] A 'consulting' vote or voice merely gave one the right to express his opinion without participating in the voting. [Editor]

[2] A broad democratic movement completely independent of the Government, created to organize the so-called consumers' unions in an attempt to dispense with middlemen in retail commerce, thus substantially lowering prices of consumer commodities. Started in Russia in the [1860s], and developed vigorously after 1905. It also had cultural aims, and was strongly supported by workers, peasants, and liberals.

Before the First World War it comprised more than two million members. [Editor]

[3] Steklov (Nakhamkes), Yurii Mikhailovich (1873–1937): active revolutionary from the beginning of the nineties in Odessa. Outside all factions for a long time. Joined the Bolsheviks after the October insurrection and for a long time was the editor of the official *Izvestiya* (News). [Editor]

What ought to be the agenda for this plenipotentiary assembly of the representatives of the democracy in the decisive hour of the revolution? Under any circumstances it was plainly impossible to make the *political* problem the first item, and force the task of forming the revolutionary Government. What with the general vagueness of the situation and the above-mentioned temper of the right wing of the Tauride Palace, this problem could only be put on the agenda with one object—to decide it out of hand by proclaiming the Soviet the supreme state power. Under these conditions it was up to others to place the question of power on the agenda—to the advocates of an immediate dictatorship of the Soviet, who might have been the Bolsheviks headed by Shlyapnikov, or the SRs led by Alexandrovich.

In any case both these groups were weak and unprepared, without initiative and incapable of taking their bearings in the situation. Neither introduced the question. Meanwhile circumstances themselves introduced some absolutely unpostponable business concerning the technique of revolution itself.

The people I talked to incidentally about the agenda were of course right: the movement would be crushed without emergency *economic* measures—organizing the provisioning of the capital, taking immediate steps to defend the city and stop anarchy, and mobilizing the forces of the local garrison and the working-class population to repel a possible attack on Petersburg—that is, without the strategic defence of the revolution. Whatever the ultimate form of government, only the Soviet could achieve this "technique" of the revolution.

As for the strategic measures, defensive and offensive, they were being handled by the Military Commission, the kernel and majority of which in those hours was composed of Soviet elements. To carry strategy into the general meeting of the Soviet was absurd. But it was vital to do something else—place under Soviet control the activities of the Military Commission, which was established—topographically—in the right wing of the Palace.

Naturally, the Duma deputies Chkheidze, Kerensky, and Skobelev were nominated to the Praesidium and elected immediately without opposition. Besides the chairman and his two colleagues four secretaries were elected—Gvozdev, Sokolov, Grinevich, and the worker Pankov, a Left Menshevik. If I'm not mistaken Kerensky declaimed a few meaningless phrases that were supposed to be a hymn to the people's revolution, and immediately vanished into the right wing, not to appear again in the Soviet.

I don't remember what happened to the future permanent chairman of the Soviet, Chkheidze. Skobelev was left to take the chair; in the midst of the hurly-burly and the general excitement he had neither a general plan of action nor control of the meeting itself, which proceeded noisily and quite chaotically. But this by no means prevented the Soviet from performing at this very first session its basic task, vital to the revolution—that of concentrating into one centre all the ideological and organizational strength of the Petersburg democracy, with undisputed authority and a capacity for rapid and decisive action.

Immediately after the formation of the Praesidium the customary demands for "order" rang out from various sides. The chairman, wishing to end formalities, put forward for confirmation the already functioning Credentials Committee, headed by Gvozdev, but it was not in the least surprising that business was interrupted at this point by the soldiers, who demanded the floor to make their reports. The demand was enthusiastically supported, and the scene that followed was worthy of enthusiasm.

Standing on stools, their rifles in their hands, agitated and stuttering, straining all their powers to give a connected account of the messages entrusted to them, with their thoughts concentrated on the narrative itself, in unaccustomed and half-fantastic surroundings, without thinking and perhaps quite unaware of the whole significance of the facts they were reporting, in simple, rugged language that infinitely strengthened the effect of the absence of emphasis—one after another the soldiers' delegates told of what had been happening in their companies. Their stories were artless, and repeated each other almost word for word. The audience listened as children listen to a wonderful, enthralling fairy-tale they know by heart, holding their breaths, with craning necks and unseeing eyes.

'We're from the Volhynian Regiment . . . the Pavlovsky . . . the Lithuanian . . . the Keksholm . . . the Sappers . . . the Chasseurs . . . the Finnish . . . the Grenadiers . . .'

The name of each of the magnificent regiments that had launched the revolution was met with a storm of applause.

'We had a meeting . . .' 'We've been told to say . . .' 'The officers hid . . .' 'To join the Soviet of Workers' Deputies . . .' 'They told us to say that we refuse to serve against the people any more, we're going to join with our brother workers, all united, to defend the people's cause . . . We would lay down our lives for that.' 'Our general meeting told us to greet you . . .' 'Long live the revolution!' the delegate would add in a voice already completely extinguished by the throbbing roar of the meeting.

Dreadful rifles, hateful greatcoats, strange words! Theoretically all this had been known, well known, known since that morning. But in practice no one had understood or digested the events that had turned everything topsy-turvy . . .

It was then and there proposed, and approved with storms of applause, to fuse together the revolutionary army and the proletariat of the capital and create a united organization to be called from then on the 'Soviet of Workers' and Soldiers' Deputies . . .'

But a great many regiments were still not with us. Were they hesitating, consciously neutral, or ready to fight the 'enemy within'?

The situation was still critical. There was the possibility of bloody skirmishes between the organized regiments and their officers. The revolution might still be captured with bare hands.

*   *   *

Frankorussky, the 'Supply Man,' finally got the floor, and having given a short sketch of the supply position in Petersburg and all the possible consequences of hunger amongst the masses, proposed that a Supply Commission be elected, ordered to set to work at once, and given adequate powers. There was of course no debate on this. The Commission was elected at once from the Socialist supply specialists headed by V. G. Grohman. Having waited for this moment, all those elected immediately withdrew in order to work.

Meanwhile M. A. Braunstein, who had apparently been elected to the Supply Commission, came up to me and urged me to take the floor at once with a resolution on the defence of the city. I didn't see the slightest advantage in coming forward and suggested that I merely second his motion. He got the floor and very successfully, with the full attention and sympathy of the meeting, described the state of affairs.

Braunstein proposed that directives be given the city districts through the delegates present for every factory to appoint a militia (100 men out of every thousand), for district committees to be formed, and for plenipotentiary Commissars to be appointed in each district to restore order and direct the struggle against anarchy and pogroms.[4] I spoke in support of his resolution, after informing the meeting of the activities of the Military Commission and warning them of the danger of confusing functions and powers. The resolution was accepted in principle, but there was still no machinery to put it into practice; there were neither boundaries between the districts (were they to be the future Soviet and municipal wards or the old police divisions?) nor assembly points, nor volunteer Commissars . . .

In connexion with the defence of the city there naturally cropped up a proposal for a proclamation to the populace in the name of the Soviet. In general, supplying the capital, and as far as possible the provinces, with information and elementary directives to the populace was the most pressing task of the moment, even though it was relatively simple

---

[4] Braunstein, by the way, was the first of us to use this word Commissar, which was later so needlessly misused.

and required no special attention from the meeting. One of my neighbours proposed the election of a Literary Commission to be entrusted with the immediate composition of an appeal to be presented to the Soviet later for confirmation.

But this organizational work, which had already taken up about an hour, was interrupted again. A young soldier burst through the flimsy barrier at the doors and rushed to the centre of the hall. Without asking for the floor or waiting for permission to speak he raised his rifle above his head and shook it, choking and gasping as he shouted the joyful news:

'Comrades and brothers, I bring you brotherly greetings from all the lower ranks of the entire Semyonovsky regiment of Life Guards. All of us to the last man are determined to join the people against the accursed autocracy, and we swear to serve the people's cause to the last drop of our blood!'

In his emotion, bordering on frenzy, the youthful delegate of the mutinous Semyonovskys, who had plainly attended a school of party propaganda, was really, in these banal phrases and stereotyped terminology, pouring out his soul, overflowing with the majestic impressions of the day and consciousness that the longed-for victory had been achieved. In the meeting, disturbed in the midst of current business, there gushed forth once again a torrent of romantic enthusiasm. No one stopped the Semyonovsky from finishing his lengthy speech, accompanied by thunderous applause. The importance of this news was obvious to everyone: the Semyonovsky Regiment had been one of the most trustworthy pillars of Tsarism. There was not a man in the room who was not familiar with the 'glorious' traditions of the 'Semyonovsky boys' and in particular did not remember their Moscow exploits in 1905.[5] All that was over. In a flash the stinking fog was dispersed by the light of this new and blinding sun.

It appeared that there were delegates from the newly insurgent regiments in the hall. They had not ventured to ask for the floor but now came forward after the Semyonovsky had opened the way for them. Once again the assembly heard tales of a whole series of army units—one of the Cossack regiments, I think an armoured division, an electro-technical battalion, a machine-gun regiment—the terrible enemies of the people just a short while before and from now on a firmly united band of friends of the revolution. The revolution was growing and increasing in strength with every moment.

Elections continued for the Literary Commission. Sokolov, Peshekhonov, Steklov, Grinevich, and I were elected. No objections were raised: there were no factional struggles or party candidates. Moreover, no directives at all were given to the Commission, and it was clear to everyone that the proclamation would be published in the form in which they submitted it. Thus was accomplished the Soviet's first act of any political significance.

*   *   *

---

[5] The Semyonovskys were notorious for their part in the brutal suppression of the Moscow uprising in 1905. [Editor]

REVIEW QUESTIONS

1. What does Sukhanov's account reveal about the intentions and priorities of those who participated in the formation of the Petrograd Soviet?
2. Whom did the Soviet claim to speak for?
3. What was the significance of the support the Soviet's deputies received from soldiers?
4. Why was one of the first acts of the Soviet the election of a Literary Commission?
5. Was the Petrograd Soviet taking the initiative in the February Revolution? Or was it responding to events that were not fully within its control?

PETROGRAD SOVIET OF WORKERS' AND SOLDIERS' DEPUTIES

Order Number One, 1 March 1917

Once the provisional government and the Petrograd Soviet were created—and oper-ating from the left and right wings of the Tauride Palace—the primary goal of the new revolutionary authority in St. Petersburg was to reestablish order in the streets and to convince the soldiers who had mutinied against their officers to return to their barracks. The violence at the end of February had taken everybody by surprise, and it was imperative for the new government to establish itself as a legitimate authority. Many of the soldiers were afraid that they would be punished for their acts of disobedience, however, and they would not comply without guarantees of immunity. Suspicious of the provisional government, which they feared would take the side of their officers, the soldiers turned to the Petrograd Soviet. The Soviet readily complied with their demands, issuing Order Number One, which replaced the authority of the army's officer corps with a system of soldiers' committees that would operate on a democratic principle.

The historian William Henry Chamberlin described the creation of this order in the following terms: "On the night of the 14th, in one of the rooms of the crowded, noisy, smoke-filled Tauride Palace the radical lawyer, N. D. Sokolov, suddenly elevated by the Revolution to the post of a Soviet leader, sat at a writing desk, sur-rounded by a throng of soldiers. First one soldier, then another threw out suggestions, all of which Sokolov obediently wrote down. When the suggestions were exhausted the paper received the heading: 'Order Number One.' When the monarchist Shulgin read the contents of this extraordinary document he exclaimed to himself, 'This is the end of the army'; and this view was widely shared in conservative military circles."[1] Another historian, Orlando Figes, has written, "This crucial document . . . did more than anything else to destroy the discipline of the army, and thus in a sense brought the Bolsheviks to power."[2]

From *The Russian Revolution, 1917–1921*, by William Henry Chamberlin (Princeton, N.J.: Princeton University Press, 1987, first published in 1935 by Macmillan), vol. 1, pp. 429–30.

March 1, 1917

To the garrison of the Petrograd District. To all the soldiers of the Guard, army, artillery and fleet for immediate and precise execution, and to the workers of Petrograd for information.

The Soviet of Workers' and Soldiers' Deputies has decided:

1. In all companies, battalions, regiments, depots, batteries, squadrons and separate branches of military service of every kind and on warships immediately choose com-

---

[1] William Henry Chamberlin, *The Russian Revolution, 1917–1921* (Princeton, N.J.: Princeton University Press, 1987), vol. 1, p. 86.

[2] Orlando Figes, *A People's Tragedy: The Russian Revolution, 1891–1924* (New York: Penguin, 1996), pp. 330–31.

mittees from the elected representatives of the soldiers and sailors of the above mentioned military units.

2. In all military units which have still not elected their representatives in the Soviet of Workers' Deputies elect one representative to a company, who should appear with written credentials in the building of the State Duma at ten o'clock on the morning of March 2.

3. In all its political demonstrations a military unit is subordinated to the Soviet of Workers' and Soldiers' Deputies and its committees.

4. The orders of the military commission of the State Duma are to be fulfilled only in those cases which do not contradict the orders and decisions of the Soviet of Workers' and Soldiers' Deputies.

5. Arms of all kinds, as rifles, machineguns, armored automobiles and others must be at the disposition and under the control of the company and battalion committees and are not in any case to be given out to officers, even upon their demand.

6. In the ranks and in fulfilling service duties soldiers must observe the strictest military discipline; but outside of service, in their political, civil, and private life soldiers cannot be discriminated against as regards those rights which all citizens enjoy. Standing at attention and compulsory saluting outside of service are especially abolished.

7. In the same way the addressing of officers with titles: Your Excellency, Your Honor, etc. is abolished and is replaced by the forms of address: Mr. General, Mr. Colonel, etc.

Rude treatment of soldiers of all ranks, and especially addressing them as "thou" is forbidden; and soldiers are bound to bring to the attention of the company committees any violation of this rule and any misunderstandings between officers and soldiers.

This order is to be read in all companies, battalions, regiments, marine units, batteries and other front and rear military units.

REVIEW QUESTIONS

1. What authority did Order Number One require all military units to recognize?

2. In what way was the Duma's power over the military curtailed by Order Number One?

3. In what way did this document recognize the rights of citizenship possessed by the rank and file in the military?

4. How did these rights of citizenship challenge the conventional definition of military discipline?

5. What kinds of difficulties might officers at the front have faced in the aftermath of Order Number One?

OCTOBER (1927)   SERGEI EISENSTEIN

The reconstruction of history through film often treads the fine line between art and politi-
cal persuasion. Created in 1927 for the tenth anniversary of the Bolshevik Revolution,
Sergei Eisenstein's October *depicted the Bolshevik storming of the Winter Palace on October 25,*
1917 as a spectacular expression of popular will and revolutionary valor. In reality, the
event had little dramatic flair; the Winter Palace, the seat of Aleksandr Kerensky's provi-
sional government, was guarded by only a handful of cadets who offered little or no resis-
tance. How might this film have influenced Soviet citizens' perception and memory of the
October Revolution?

ALEXANDRA KOLLONTAI

FROM *The Autobiography of a Sexually Emancipated Communist Woman*

Alexandra Kollontai (1872–1952) grew up in an educated, affluent, and fairly liberal Russian family. She married young, but left her husband and son to study political economy in Switzerland, where she became actively involved in socialist organizing. Originally a Menshevik, Kollontai became a Bolshevik in 1915, largely because of the Bolshevik opposition to the war, and entered into a friendly correspondence with Lenin.

After the October Revolution, Kollontai was named People's Commissar of Social Welfare, becoming the only woman to hold a cabinet post in the new Bolshevik government. As director of the Women's Bureau (Zhenotdel), she agitated in favor of economic liberty for working women and state welfare benefits for mothers. Her advocacy of women's rights and free love was not universally popular, and in the years following the revolution she found herself increasingly at odds with the Communist Party leadership. In 1922, Kollontai was assigned a diplomatic post in Norway—a gentle form of exile—and she spent much of the rest of her life outside of Russia. In memoirs written in 1926, she recounted the heady early days of the revolution, when a total transformation of Russian society still seemed possible.

From *The Autobiography of a Sexually Emancipated Communist Woman*, by Alexandra Kollontai, translated by Salvator Attanasio (New York: Herder and Herder, 1971).

*   *   *

When one recalls the first months of the Workers' Government, months which were so rich in *magnificent illusions,*[1] plans, ardent initiatives to improve life, to organize the world anew, months of the real romanticism of the Revolution, one would in fact like to write about all else save about one's self. I occupied the post of Minister of Social Welfare from October of 1917 *to March of 1918*. It was not without opposition that I was received by the former officials of the Ministry. Most of them sabotaged us openly and simply did not show up for work. But precisely this office could not interrupt its work, come what may, since in itself it was an extraordinarily complicated operation. It included the whole welfare program for the war-disabled, hence for hundreds of thousands of crippled soldiers and officers, the pension system in general, foundling homes, homes for the aged, orphanages, hospitals for the needy, the work-shops making artificial limbs, the administration of playing-card factories (the manufacture of playing cards was a State monopoly), *the educational system,* clinical hospitals for women. In addition a whole series of educational

---

[1] By 1926, it was already necessary to be cautious about how one described one's involvement in the revolution, and Kollontai censored her own writing. Italics indicate passages in the original manuscript that were not included in the published version of her memoirs.

institutes for young girls were also under the direction of this Ministry. One can easily imagine the enormous demands these tasks made upon a small group of people who, at the same time, were novices in State administration. In a clear awareness of these difficulties *I formed,* immediately, an auxiliary council in which experts such as physicians, jurists, pedagogues were represented alongside the workers and the minor officials of the Ministry. The sacrifice, the energy with which the minor employees bore the burden of this difficult task was truly exemplary. It was not only a matter of keeping the work of the Ministry going, but also of initiating reforms and improvements. New, fresh forces replaced the sabotaging officers of the old regime. A new life stirred in the offices of the formerly highly conservative Ministry. Days of grueling work! And at night the sessions of the councils of the People's Commissar (of the cabinet) under Lenin's chairmanship. A small, modest room and only one secretary who recorded the resolutions which changed Russia's life to its bottommost foundations.

*   *   *

My main work as People's Commissar consisted in the following: by decree to improve the situation of the war-disabled, to abolish religious instruction in the schools for young girls which were under the Ministry (this was still before the general separation of Church and State), and to transfer priests to the civil service, to introduce the right of self-administration for pupils in the schools for girls, to reorganize the former orphanages into government Children's Homes (*no distinction was to be made between orphaned children and those who still had fathers and mothers*), to set up the first hostels for the needy and street-urchins, to convene a committee, composed *only* of doctors, which was to be commissioned *to elaborate* the free public health system for the whole country. In my opinion the most important accomplishment of the People's Commissariat, however, was the legal foundation of a Central Office for Maternity and Infant Welfare. The draft of the bill relating to this Central Office was signed by me in January of 1918. A second decree followed in which *I* changed all mater-

nity hospitals into free Homes for Maternity and Infant Care, in order thereby to set the groundwork for a comprehensive government system of pre-natal care. I was greatly assisted in coping with these tasks by Dr. Korolef. We also planned a "Pre-Natal Care Palace," a model home with an exhibition room in which courses for mothers would be held *and, among many other things,* model day nurseries were also to be established. We were just about completing preparations for such a facility in the building of a girls' boarding school at which formerly young girls of the nobility had been educated and which was still under the direction of a countess, when a fire destroyed our work, which had barely begun! Had the fire been set deliberately? . . . I was dragged out of bed in the middle of the night. I rushed to the scene of the fire; the beautiful exhibition room was totally ruined, as were all the other rooms. Only the huge name-plate "Pre-Natal Care Palace" still hung over the entrance door.

My efforts to nationalize maternity and infant care set off a new wave of insane attacks against me. All kinds of lies were related about the "nationalization of women," *about my legislative proposals which assertedly ordained that little girls of 12 were to become mothers.* A special fury gripped the religious followers of the old regime when, *on my own authority (the cabinet later criticized me for this action),* I transformed the famous Alexander Nevsky monastery into a home for war-invalids. The monks resisted and a shooting fray ensued. The press again raised a loud hue and cry against *me.* The Church organized street demonstrations *against my action* and also pronounced "anathema" against me. . . .

I received countless threatening letters, but I never requested military protection. I always went out alone, unarmed and without any kind of a bodyguard. In fact I never gave a thought to any kind of danger, being all too engrossed in matters of an utterly different character. In February of 1918 a first State delegation of the Soviets was sent to Sweden *in order to clarify different economic and political questions.* As Peoples' Commissar I headed this delegation. But our vessel was shipwrecked; we were saved by landing on the Aland Islands which belonged to Finland. At this very time the struggle between the Whites and the Reds in the country had reached its most crucial moment and the German Army was also making ready to wage war against Finland.

*   *   *

Now began a *dark time* of my life which I cannot treat of here since the events are still too fresh in my mind. *But the day will also come when I will give an account of them.*

There were differences of opinion in the Party. I resigned from my post as People's Commissar *on the ground of total disagreement with the current policy. Little by little I was also relieved of all my other tasks. I again gave lectures and espoused my ideas on "the new woman" and "the new morality."* The Revolution was in full swing. The struggle was becoming increasingly irreconcilable and bloodier, *much of what was happening did not fit in with my outlook.* But after all there was still the unfinished task, women's liberation. Women, of course, had received all rights but in practice, of course, they still lived under the old yoke: without authority in family life, enslaved by a thousand menial household chores, bearing the whole burden of maternity, even the material cares, because many women now found life alone as a result of the war and other circumstances.

*   *   *

A flood of new work was waiting for me. The question now was one of drawing women into the people's kitchens and of educating them to devote their energies to children's homes and day-care centers, the school system, household reforms, and still many other pressing matters. The main thrust of all this activity was to implement, in fact, equal rights for women as a labor unit in the national economy and as a citizen in the political sphere and, of course, with the special proviso: maternity was to be appraised as a social function and therefore protected and provided for by the State.

*   *   *

A serious illness tore me away from the exciting work for months. Hardly having recovered—at that time I was in Moscow—I took over the direction of the Coordinating Office for Work among Women and again a new period of intensive, grueling work began. A communist women's *newspaper* was founded, conferences and congresses of women workers were convoked. The foundation was laid for work with the women of the East (Mohammedans). Two world conferences of communist women took place in Moscow. The law liberalizing abortion was put through and a number of regulations of benefit to women were introduced by our Coordinating Office and legally confirmed. *At this time I had to do more writing and speaking than ever before. . . .* Our work received wholehearted support from Lenin. And Trotsky, although he was overburdened with military tasks, unfailingly and gladly appeared at our conferences. Energetic, gifted women, two of whom are no longer alive, sacrificially devoted all their energies to the work of the Coordinating Office.

At the eighth Soviet Congress, as a member of the Soviet executive (*now there were already several women on this body*), I proposed a motion that the Soviets in all areas contribute to the creation of a consciousness of the struggle for equal rights for women and, accordingly, to involve them in State and communal work. I managed to push the motion through and to get it accepted but not without resistance. It was a great, an enduring victory.

A heated debate flared up when I published my thesis on the new morality. *For our Soviet marriage law, separated from the Church to be sure, is not essentially more progressive than the same laws that after all exist in other progressive democratic countries.* * * * [A]lthough the illegitimate child *was* placed on a legal par with the legitimate child, in practice a great deal of hypocrisy and injustice still exists in this area. When one speaks of the "immorality" which the Bolsheviks purportedly propagated, it suffices to submit our marriage laws to a close scrutiny to note that in the divorce question we are on a par with North America whereas in the question of the illegitimate child we have *not yet even* progressed as far as the Norwegians.

The most radical wing of the Party was formed around this question. My theses, my *sexual and moral* views, were bitterly fought *by many Party comrades of both sexes: as were still other differences of opinion in the Party regarding political guiding principles.* Personal and family cares were added thereto and thus months in 1922 went by without fruitful work. Then in the autumn of 1922 came my official appointment to the legation of the Russian Soviet representation in Norway. I really believed that this appointment would be purely formal and that therefore in Norway I would find time to devote to myself, to my literary activity. Things turned out quite differently. With the day of my entry into office in Norway I also entered upon a wholly new course of work in my life which drew upon all my energies to the highest degree.

*   *   *

REVIEW QUESTIONS

1. What kind of work did Kollontai do as People's Commissar of Social Welfare?
2. What does her work tell you about the social welfare policies of the revolutionary government?
3. Who opposed Kollontai's efforts in favor of women's liberation? Why?

Daily Life under Stalin

Josef Stalin ruled the Soviet Union unchallenged from 1928 until his death in 1953. It was during this period that the institutions of Soviet rule that would last until the 1990s were largely created. From Lenin, Stalin had inherited the one-party state, and his goal was to use this state to build a socialist nation in Russia. Socialism, in theory, meant the abolition of private property and the establishment of an economy in which the state would replace the market as the primary mechanism for the distribution of goods and resources. In practice, Stalinism meant an abrupt and brutal transformation of a largely peasant society into a modern industrial nation, unified by a common Soviet culture. The early years of his rule, 1928–1931, were years of extraordinary change, as the first Five-Year Plan of industrial development was announced, and private property in agriculture was abolished. Millions of rural Russians were forced to adapt to a new kind of collective agricultural production organized by local kolkhoz, *or cooperatives. In order to feed the urban populations that were conscripted into the building of the Soviet Union's industrial infrastructure, the state simply confiscated the grain produced in the countryside, leaving very little for those who had actually grown the crops. Historians estimate that as many as 5 million people died in the ensuing famines in Ukraine in 1931–32.*

In recent decades, the history of Stalin's revolution has been rewritten as historians have found new documentation on the effects of Stalinism on ordinary people in the Soviet Union. The following three documents show the effects of Stalin's revolution in the countryside: the first two give a glimpse of the opinions of industrial work-

ers and rural farmers during the first Five-Year Plan, and the third indicates the efforts—not always successful—of Stalin's officials to remake Russian culture by controlling the sources of information and its circulation.

From *Stalinism as a Way of Life: A Narrative in Documents,* edited by Lewis Siegelbaum and Andrei Sokolov (New Haven: Yale University Press, 2000), pp. 44–46, 52–53, 64–65.

Letter to Stalin and Kalinin [ostensibly] from Workers at Red Putilovets Factory, Leningrad, March 1930. * * * Typed Copy.

[*Translator's note:* Much of the spelling, punctuation, capitalization, usage, and syntax in this letter is that of a person with little education. To convey the meaning of the text fully, these characteristics are reflected only minimally here.]

To the Secretary and to the Head of the VTsIK (Vsesoiuznyi Tsentral'nyi Ispolnitel'nyi Komitet [All-Union central executive committee] Stalin and Kalinin.

We, the workers of the Red Putilovets Plant, fifty in number, have discussed and have decided that we once and for all protest against the terors [*sic*] and persecutions of the peasants and the one who you deprive of the vote and consider them kulaks. We all as one, members of the VKPb [Vsesoiuznaia Kommunisticheskaia Partitia (bol'shevikov), All-Union Communist Party of the Soviet Union] have a tie with the countryside, to us write our fathers and brothers how they're deprived of the vote and are not asked if they are agreed to be on the kolkhoz or not, but right off the bat their property is taken away by the careerists, and they're driven into prisons the shame of Soviet power, as capitalists do not do as you do in a free country, you throw into prison those who worked from morning till late night, the toilers who've put their whole life into their home and into their farm. You've called them kulaks only because they slept on their fist [the literal meaning of *kulak*] not having a pillow to themselves in their home, [*sic*] You regard those as kulaks who made their farm prosper and gave income to the state. You drove them

into cellars and want them to rot alive, these fathers and brothers of ours, and posted their grandson with a rifle to guard them like wild animals. We're indignant against this, for what have we fought, for what have we shed blood when we did not expect this, that our worker-peasant reign would torment our fathers and brothers so. Why then do we need the VKP since it makes life impossible for all of us?

They kill, throw people into prison, and take all that we have gained with hands hardened by toil. We demand an order be given immediately to the local organizations and stop the teror [*sic*] in our free country, pay attention what they're saying, all the Leningrad workers they're leaving the party only because nowadays everyone's being persecuted. No one has a liking for Soviet authority, but consider you torturers of the Russian people. Why do we have to do the five-year plan so thoroughly when we've become poor after such wealth as we have in Russia even if you take only sugar that they used to feed the pigs with, and now you can't buy it even if you have the money, and also our children are starving and we have absolutely nothing to feed them with. We want Comrade Trotsky to be right and Comrade Bukharin and other comrades, but you squeeze everyone tighter and tighter, you want to complete the five-year plan in four years. You like it that the Komsomol members shout, but they are really dumbbells and sheep who don't understand anything, and you must pay attention to all of the proletariat and peasantry now this is why they send you a thousand curses and consider you violators and not rulers of the Russian people. You've robbed all the capitalists and you have your hands on small-time property owners and on the peasants. You're sending millions of toilers before their time to the next world at the same time you are writing that we are a nation of free laborers. We didn't know that poor peasants would be shown so much respect. It seems like it would be better if everyone was a poor peasant and beggars. You can't get nothing from a poor peasant, a poor peasant is a loafer and that's just why he's poor he is used to getting everything from others for nothing. You are now collecting scrap metal and rags. Doesn't that mean that you're begging alms from workers? But what you ought to do is give to him. Where is the wealth that we inherited from the capitalists? Even the poor peasants, they are gasping, specially in the country they don't look a lump of sugar in the eye, why the hell a five-year plan when they don't let you live here and now, who have we built the damn five-year plan for. You are destroying millions of people. It's become ridiculous you forced registering of old men workers for the Party, and who doesn't join up you threaten to fire. * * *

One day I was talking with an elderly worker he openly declared how we now have a time of persecution of everybody they don't let you live out your days peacefully. There's a fact no one can deny. * * *

Letter to *Pravda* on Collectivization in Lower Volga Krai, 1930. * * * Typed Copy.

In one village I went to an exhibition. Before looking at the exhibits we had to go to a big meeting. Speeches are given: a spokesman for the RIK [Raionnyi Ispolnitel'nyi Komitet, district executive committee], the agronomist, the supervisor of the reading room [izbach], the chairman of the ural soviet [sel'sovet] and its secretary. The RIK spokesman and the agronomist talk about successes of the state together with lavish praise of collective kolkhoz cultivation of the land and its advantages over private cultivation and so on. The members of the rural soviet speak about the achievements of that village. After finishing his speech while others were speaking, the RIK spokesman started composing a resolution about the desirability of organizing a land society. Having finished composing, he reads that the land society is going to promote the idea of

contributing to a loan for industrialization in each peasant household; during the current year he wants to organize two large-scale collectives, etc. He finishes reading. Then he asks the peasants to speak from the floor, those in favor and those against. Everyone remains silent, no one says a word. The supervisor of the reading room gets up, repeats the question, again there is silence. The RIK spokesman says, "So, everyone's agreed?" Laughter in the crowd. Here you have an irrefutable picture of the self-inspired kolkhoz movement. Precisely this type of information is given to the press about the kolkhoz movement and the party acts upon it, a great amount of it is fake documentation invented and composed by those party members who pursue the personal goal of advancing themselves, and the peasant's silence results from unwillingness and fears of being accused of espionage, of exile, of being put in prison, fines, having to suffer confiscation, and having to pay various burdensome taxes.

Then a look at the exhibits. An example of the judging process: representing horticulture are apple trees two or three years old, some belonging to a private peasant and others from a kolkhoz. The chairman, an agronomist, having looked over the kolkhoz apple trees along with the judging committee, goes up to the peasant and says, "Although these apple trees both in the roots and in the crown are better than the kolkhoz ones, we should give precedence to the kolkhoz because of our class distinctions." Laughter again in the crowd. As a result the first prize goes to the kolkhoz, and the peasant gets a certificate of merit. Peasant experts understood this fake judging and how the local authorities, using agronomists, aim to show agricultural achievement in their village and to show that such achievements supposedly occur not because of peasant experts but because of the activities of the local authorities. In point of fact no one made even the slightest effort to look into any aspect of the middle-sized peasant farm economy, nor was anyone willing to do more than compile official charts, and therefore exhibitions in many villages did not take place. The sentence dished out by the agronomist judging the apple trees is nothing more than subtle mockery of the party's class line. So this is what all educated people working in the Soviet Union survive on, and their slogan, like that of the peasants, is to own something. On account of this peasants say that former landowners sit in our central offices and hold power, taking vengeance on us for land and estates taken from them. * * *

Letter from W. M. Kovalchuk on Flight from Collective Farms in North Caucausus Krai, 1932. * * * Typed Copy.

I write not as one who gives in to difficulties, not as an enemy of Soviet power, but as a man who fought for it.

In Chamlyk Raion there is one kolkhoz, second in size in the krai, that fulfills a three hundred thousand-pood state grain procurement, but the trouble is this socialist farm is melting like the spring snow, people are fleeing the kolkhoz for who knows where. At the kolkhoz they took all the grain away and left a little field corn for the people to live on. All this is the result of the kolkhoz's unavoidable disintegration, and what disgrace that is!

The kolkhoz plants wheat and lives on corn. Everyone's mood is almost anti-Soviet. Dear comrades, now you go and take any one of us, set in front us only field corn without any grease, dress us in rags, shoes without soles, and force us to work on the steppe when the temperature is twenty-five degrees below zero; wouldn't any of you become a deviant and curse all and everything?

Here is one example. At the stanitsa, we have some thirteen thousand hectares of land; before the revolution there were twelve thousand people, and now there are eight thousand. There has been a decrease in people, the rest don't have the strength to do the harvesting; as a result thousands of hectares of various crops are rotting on the steppe, overgrown with weeds.

The people have become pretty malicious, they look disapprovingly at the Communists, the Communist cell has lost its authority. Members of the party also. Now we have to meet contract requirements for delivery of hens, this also intensifies anger among the peasants. Out of people fighting for Soviet power they are now making people who are against Soviet power because every last kernel of grain has been taken from them and they have nothing to chew on. Every night seven to ten households abandon the stanitsa. This on account of the good life. I've permitted myself to express my opinion as one comrade to another, to the masses I speak differently, the way Soviet authority talks.

Memorandum of N. Malstev to Ya. Rudzutak and Ye. Yaroslavsky on Purge of Libraries, 16 October 1932. * * * Typed Original.

Libraries have been purged of pernicious and outdated literature by NKPros [Narodnyi Komissariat Provescheniia, People's Commissariat of Education] without adequate instructions and control. The only instructions from Glavpol[it]prosvet [Glavnoe upravlenie politicheskogo proveshchevniia, chief directorate of political education], dated 29 March 1930, present no defined order for book inspection and removal and are filled with ambiguities and obviously incorrect and harmful directives that could not serve as a practical guide for conducting a purge. Therefore in some oblasts (Moscow and Leningrad) instructions solely for those oblasts appeared; more often than not, in view of the difficulty of this undertaking and the risks involved the matter was allowed to take its own course, whatever happened would happen, and responsibility could be placed on those who actually carried out the work.

And what happened was very bad. At a meeting of those who conducted the purges, it came to light that more than 60 percent of all book holdings have been withdrawn. There are libraries in which the portion of books withdrawn reached 80 or 90 percent. Correspondance from very different corners of the USSR indicates that the classics of philosophy, science, belles-lettres, and even revolutionary Marxism have been removed: Marx, Engels, Lenin, Stalin, Tolstoy, Turgenev, Goncharov,

Dickens, Hugo, resolutions of party congresses, reports of congresses of soviets, Sechenov, Timirazev, Khvolson, Ivan Pavlov. The names of these "withdrawn" authors alone indicate criminal activity in the way the purge was conducted.

It is difficult to explain all this by lack of sophistication and stupidity in those carrying out the purge. It is one thing that in certain instances Lenin's books were withdrawn, for instance, because they were listed under the last name Il'in, or Marx's "Communist Manifesto" with Riazanov's foreword, but in many other instances this explanation breaks down.

Lists of works recommended for removal produced by purging committees in Moscow and Leningrad drawn up by "authoritative" and "educated" people give directions that in the provinces could lead to nothing else. Under "Philosophy" the Leningrad instructions propose that "idealistic philosophy should be removed entirely from circulation" (leaving only Kant's and Hegel's works). The works of bourgeois sociologists Spencer, Tarde, M. Kovalevsky, and Simmel are being withdrawn, as are Bukharin's *Istmat* [*Istoricheskii materializm*, historical materialism], Deborin, Kornilov, from the section of antireligious literature Kautsky's *Foundations of Christianity* and the titles of ninety books that I personally am unacquainted with but which include many surnames of Communists. From the "Social and Political" section Kautsky's *The Economic Doctrines of Karl Marx*, Luxemburg's *Accumulation of Capital*, Rosenberg's *Commentaries on Das Kapital*, Sabsovich, Borian's *State Control in the Soviet Union and in Western Europe*, Yaroslavsky, volumes 2 and 4, Nevsky, Kerzhentsev, Bogdanov's *Lessons in Political Economy*, Hilferding, Tugan-Baranovsky.

✳ ✳ ✳ The lists for belles-lettres was drawn up in a completely arbitrary way. Why withdraw Hamsun, Dickens, Hauptmann, Zlatovratsky, Potapenko, Rostand, Oscar Wilde, Fet, Hugo, Sudermann, even Lunacharsky, Balmont, A. K. Tolstoy, and many, many others who by the humblest and most general assessment are on a higher level and less pernicious than the hundreds of junky kinds of belles-lettres that Gosizdat [Gosudarst-

vennoe izdatel'stvo, state publishing firm] puts out even now?

A kind of sadistic guardianship of the reader results from all this. The main instructions of Glavpolitprosvet are more restrained and balanced. But even according to them, "all prerevolutionary literature" concerned with upbringing and education, all prerevolutionary mathematics textbooks, all anthologies of Russian literature, collections of pieces for recitation, oral public reading and narration "should be removed from local public libraries and transferred to central and pedagogical libraries." ✳ ✳ ✳

This is a really terrible peril to all this because of the quite unacceptable and unregulated way in which the books were removed. What is the "central" library that is supposed to make the final decision about the fate of a book withdrawn, whether to throw it out or sell it? ✳ ✳ ✳ This decision has been left to the discretion of the local authorities. The Moscow Oblast Library created such centers in twenty-three spots. Glavpolitprosvet instructions propose that "all books deemed properly withdrawn—once two copies have been deposited in the archives and a selection made of those having potential value for research and specialized libraries—are to be sold unbound to factories for recycling into paper."

According to the Glavpolitprosvet instructions, two copies of a huge number of books of great value are supposed to be kept in the "archives" of a library. ✳ ✳ ✳ Except for books "worthy of being actively promoted to the reading masses," all other books not subject to the purge and removal process are to be put into these repositories. These books should be "kept separate from the main core [of books] in a special room or on separate shelves or in separate cabinets. Free access to them should not occur, catalogue cards for them are to be removed from the general catalogue and maintained separately for reference purposes." The only possible meaning is that, after the official purge, readers can only use permitted books made available to them by a librarian at the latter's discretion, for there is no way for them even to know what else the library has (the catalogue cards having been withdrawn).

All the instructions put great emphasis on the urgency of this work and the need to speed it up. Books were hauled to the Moscow Oblast Library by the truckload during the night; any organized receiving of them was out of the question. To tell what is what in such a mass of books is utterly impossible. An easy solution was sought and found: sell the books. The Oblast Library got itself a pretty good source of income out of the purge. The result? Secondhand book dealers all had books with uncanceled library identification stamps. This bacchanalia of stupidity was followed by a bacchanalia of stealing, for you couldn't have created a more irresponsible atmosphere for the bad element among library workers than by letting books with library identification stamps appear on the secondhand book market legally. ＊ ＊ ＊

Therefore I propose:

1. To put forward a proposal ＊ ＊ ＊ to stop immediately the purging, transportation, and reselling of books from all libraries.

2. To create ＊ ＊ ＊ a commission to unmask the real culprits of criminal purging activity and to develop measures to liquidate the harmful consequences of this activity.

REVIEW QUESTIONS

1. Are the criticisms of Stalinist policies that are evident in these documents aimed at the goals of the revolution itself or at the ways the representatives of the Soviet state are going about achieving these revolutionary goals? What is the significance of this distinction for the authors of these critiques?

2. What is the attitude of the Leningrad workers in the first document toward the rural peasantry? What does this tell you about the relationship between urban workers and rural peasants in the first decade of the Soviet Union's history?

3. What does the second document reveal about attitudes in the countryside toward the Soviet policy of favoring collective farms?

4. What does the third document reveal about the effects of the collectivization program on agricultural production and the condition of the peasantry?

5. What does the fourth document, on the purging of libraries, reveal about the wider cultural goals of the Stalinist revolution?

BENITO MUSSOLINI

FROM "Born of a Need for Action"

Fascism emerged during the 1920s as a response to the unsettled political, economic, and social climate of the postwar period. Although it was a global phenomenon, it enjoyed its greatest successes in Germany and Italy.

As the first fascist head of state, Benito Mussolini (1883–1945) was an inspiration to other would-be dictators throughout the 1920s. Mussolini began his political career as a socialist journalist, but his ardent support for Italian participation in the First World War caused him to be expelled from the Socialist Party. In the chaos of the immediate postwar years in Italy, Mussolini created his own Fascist Party, encouraging his followers to silence political opponents through the use of violence.

The Italian ruling elite, confronted with widespread strike activity and the threat of a communist takeover, handed over the reins of government to Mussolini in 1922, after he demonstrated the strength of the fascist movement with a march on Rome. Many Italians welcomed this development, seeing Mussolini as a great leader—Duce— whose forceful rule would bring order, prosperity, and a renewal of national strength and pride. In 1932, ten years after his seizure of power, Mussolini wrote an article on fascism for an Italian encyclopedia, setting down in writing for the first time the ideological premises of the movement.

From *The Estate of Benito Mussolini*, translated by Jane Soames (London: Hogarth Press, 1933).

*   *   *

Fascism was not the nursling of a doctrine worked out beforehand with detailed elaboration; it was born of the need for action and it was itself from the beginning practical rather than theoretical; it was not merely another political party but, even in the first two years, in opposition to all political parties as such, and itself a living movement.

*   *   *

The years which preceded the march to Rome were years of great difficulty, during which the necessity for action did not permit of research or any complete elaboration of doctrine. The battle had to be fought in the towns and villages. There was much discussion, but—what was more important and more sacred—men died. They knew how to die. Doctrine, beautifully defined and carefully elucidated, with headlines and paragraphs, might be lacking; but there was to take its place something more decisive—Faith.

*   *   *

Fascism is now a completely individual thing, not only as a regime but as a doctrine. And this means that to-day Fascism, exercising its critical sense upon itself and upon others, has formed its own distinct and peculiar point of view, to which it can refer and upon which, therefore, it can act in the face of all problems, practical or intellectual, which confront the world.

And above all, Fascism, the more it considers and observes the future and the development of humanity quite apart from political considerations of the moment, believes neither in the possibility nor the utility of perpetual peace. It thus repudiates the doctrine of Pacifism—born of a renunciation of the struggle and an act of cowardice in the face of sacrifice. War alone brings up to its highest tension all human energy and puts the stamp of nobility upon the peoples who have the courage to meet it. All other trials are substitutes, which never really put men into the position where they have to make the great decision—the alternative of life or death. Thus a doctrine which is founded upon this harmful postulate of peace is hostile to Fascism.

*   *   *

* * * Fascism [is] the complete opposite of * * * so-called scientific and Marxian Socialism, the materialist conception of history; according to which the history of human civilization can be explained simply through the conflict of interests among the various social groups and by the change and development in the means and instruments of production. That the changes in the economic field—new discoveries of raw materials, new methods of working them, and the inventions of science—have their importance no one can deny; but that these factors are sufficient to explain the history of humanity excluding all others is an absurd delusion. Fascism, now and always, believes in holiness and in heroism; that is to say, in actions influenced by no economic motive, direct or indirect.

*   *   *

* * * Fascism repudiates the conception of "economic" happiness, to be realized by Socialism and, as it were, at a given moment in economic evolution to assure to everyone the maximum of well-being. Fascism denies the materialist conception of happiness as a possibility, * * * : that is to say, Fascism denies the validity of the equation, well-being=happiness, which would reduce men to the level of animals, caring for one thing only—to be fat and well-fed—and would thus degrade humanity to a purely physical existence.

After Socialism, Fascism combats the whole complex system of democratic ideology, and repudiates it, whether in its theoretical premises or in its practical application. Fascism denies that the majority, by the simple fact that it is a majority, can direct human society; it denies that numbers alone can govern by means of a periodical consultation, and it affirms the immutable, beneficial and fruitful inequality of mankind, which can never be permanently levelled through the mere operation of a mechanical process such as universal suffrage.

*   *   *

* * * Fascism denies, in democracy, the absurd conventional untruth of political equality dressed out in the garb of collective irresponsibility, and the myth of "happiness" and indefinite progress. But, if democracy may be conceived in diverse forms—that is to say, taking democracy to mean a state of society in which the populace are not reduced to impotence in the State—Fascism may write itself down as "an organized, centralized and authoritative democracy."

*   *   *

A party which entirely governs a nation is a fact entirely new to history, there are no possible references or parallels. Fascism uses in its construction whatever elements in the Liberal, Social or Democratic doctrines still have a living value * * *

*   *   *

* * * If the nineteenth century was a century of individualism (Liberalism always signifying individualism) it may be expected that this will be the century of collectivism, and hence the century of the State.

*   *   *

The foundation of Fascism is the conception of the State, its character, its duty, and its aim. Fascism conceives of the State as an absolute, in comparison with which all individuals or groups are relative, only to be conceived of in their relation to the State. * * * In 1929, at the first five-yearly assembly of the Fascist regime, I said:

"For us Fascists, the State is not merely a guardian, preoccupied solely with the duty of assuring the personal safety of the citizens; nor is it an organization with purely material aims, such as to guarantee a certain level of well-being and peaceful conditions of life; for a mere council of administration would be sufficient to realize such objects. Nor is it a purely political creation, divorced from all contact with the complex material reality which makes up the life of the individual and the life of the people as a whole. The State, as conceived of and as created by Fascism, is a spiritual and moral fact in itself, since its political, juridical and economic organization of the nation is a concrete thing: and such an organization must be in its origins and development a manifestation of the spirit. The State is the guarantor of security both internal and external, but it is also the custodian and transmitter of the spirit of the people, as it has grown up through the centuries in language, in customs and in faith. And the State is not only a living reality of the present, it is also linked with the past and above all with the future, and thus transcending the brief limits of individual life, it represents the immanent spirit of the nation. The forms in which States express themselves may change, but the necessity for such forms is eternal. It is the State which educates its citizens in civic virtue, gives them a consciousness of their mission and welds them into unity; harmonizing their various interests through justice, and transmitting to future generations the mental conquests of science, of art, of law and the solidarity of humanity. It leads men from primitive tribal life to that highest expression of human power which is Empire: it links up through the centuries the names of those of its members who have died for its existence and in obedience to its laws, it holds up the memory of the leaders who have increased its territory and the geniuses who have illumined it with glory as an example to be followed by future generations. When the conception of the State declines, and disunifying and centrifugal tendencies prevail, whether of individuals or of particular groups, the nations where such phenomena appear are in their decline."

*   *   *

* * * The Fascist State is unique, and an original creation. It is not reactionary, but revolutionary, in that it anticipates the solution of the universal political problems which elsewhere have to be settled in the political field by the rivalry of parties, the excessive power of the Parliamentary regime and the irresponsibility of political assemblies; while it meets the problems of the economic field by a system of syndicalism which is continually increasing in importance, as much in the sphere of labour as of industry: and in the moral field enforces order, discipline, and obedience to that which is the determined moral code of the country. Fascism desires the State to be a strong and organic body, at the same time reposing upon broad and popular support. The Fascist State has drawn into itself even the economic activities of the nation, and, through the corporative social and educational institutions created by it, its influence reaches every aspect of the national life and includes, framed in their respective organizations, all the political, economic and spiritual forces of the nation. A State which reposes upon the support of millions of individuals who recognize its authority, are continually conscious of its power and are ready at once to serve it, is not the old tyrannical State of the medieval lord nor has it anything in common with the absolute governments either before or after 1789. The individual in the Fascist State is not annulled but rather multiplied, just in the same way that a soldier in a regiment is not diminished but rather increased by the number of his comrades. The Fascist State organizes the nation, but leaves a sufficient margin of liberty to the individual; the latter is deprived of all useless and possibly harmful freedom, but retains what is essential; the deciding power in this question cannot be the individual, but the State alone.

*   *   *

Review Questions

1. Why did Mussolini reject pacifism?
2. What implications do his comments about war have for the policies of the fascist state?
3. Which aspects of socialism and democracy does Mussolini reject? Which does he retain?
4. What exactly does Mussolini mean when he defines the fascist state as "an organized, centralized and authoritative democracy"?
5. What role does the individual play in this state?

ADOLF HITLER

FROM *Mein Kampf*

German Nazism shared many of the tenets of Italian fascism. Like Mussolini, Adolf Hitler (1889–1945) rejected democracy as bankrupt and promoted an authoritarian politics based on the "leadership principle." Hitler was also an ardent militarist who believed that war was a crucial test of a nation's vigor. Germany's defeat in 1918 was not the result of military failure, he insisted, but rather the product of the diseased condition of German society in general. This corruption and weakness was caused by the diabolical machinations of the Jewish people, whom Hitler portrayed as a degenerate "race" engaged in an international conspiracy designed to destroy the "national principle" binding the German people together as a "master race." In response to this threat, Hitler offered himself as the leader—Führer—of a revitalized, militantly nationalist Germany purged of all those who would weaken or diminish the racial purity of the German people.

Hitler was jailed for nine months after a failed coup d'état, the Beer Hall Putsch of 1923. During his imprisonment, he wrote Mein Kampf *("My Struggle"), a massive, rambling political memoir detailing the political agenda of the Nazi Party. Many of the political arguments presented in* Mein Kampf *parallel those underpinning Italian fascism. What distinguishes Hitler's thought is his obsessive preoccupation with racial "hygiene" as the basis of national strength.*

From *Mein Kampf*, by Adolf Hitler, translated by Alvin Johnson (New York: Reynal and Hitchcock, 1940).

*   *   *

What we have to fight for is the security of the existence and the increase of our race and our people, the nourishment of its children and the preservation of the purity of the blood, the freedom and independence of the fatherland in order to enable our people to mature for the fulfillment of the mission which the Creator of the universe has allotted also to them.

*   *   *

A further example for the half-heartedness and the weakness of the leading authority in pre-War Germany in the most important vital questions of the nation can be the following: Parallel with the political and moral infection of the people went a no less terrible poisoning of the health of the national body. Syphilis began to spread more and more, especially in the great cities. * * *

*   *   *

The cause * * * lies primarily in our prostitution of love. Even if the result of this were not this terrible disease, yet it would still be of deepest danger for the people, for the moral devastation which this depravity brings with it are sufficient to destroy a people slowly but surely. The Judaization of our spiritual life and the mammonization of our mating impulse sooner or later befouls our entire new generation, for instead of vigorous children of natural feeling, only the miserable specimens of financial expedience come forth. For this becomes more and more the basis and the only prerequisite for our marriages. Love, however, finds an outlet somewhere else.

Naturally, one can also here mock Nature for a certain time, but the revenge will not fail to appear, it only will appear later, or rather, it is often recognized too late by the people.

* * *

The sin against the blood and the degradation of the race are the hereditary sin of this world and the end of a mankind surrendering to them.

* * *

Prostitution is a disgrace to mankind, but one cannot abolish it by moral lectures, pious intentions, etc., but its limitation and its final elimination warrant the abolition of quite a number of preliminary conditions. But the first is and remains the creation of the possibility of early marriage, according to human nature, above all for the man; because the woman is here only the passive part, anyhow.

* * *

Marriage also cannot be an end in itself, but has to serve the one greater aim, the propagation and preservation of the species and the race. Only this is its meaning and its task.

* * *

* * * Education and training have to eliminate quite a series of evils about which one hardly cares at all today. Above all, in our present-day education a balance between intellectual instruction and physical training has to take place. What today calls itself a *gymnasium* is an insult to the Greek example. With our education one has entirely forgotten that in the long run a healthy mind is able to dwell only in a healthy body. Especially when, with a few exceptions, one looks at the great masses of the people, this principle receives absolute validity.

In pre-War Germany there was a time when one no longer cared for this truth. One simply went on sinning against the body, and one thought that

in the one-sided training of the 'mind' one possessed a safe guaranty for the greatness of the nation. A mistake which began to avenge itself much sooner than one thought. It is no accident that the bolshevistic wave found nowhere a better ground than in those places where a population, degenerated by hunger and constant undernourishment, lives: in Central Germany, Saxony, and the Ruhr district. In all these districts, however, a serious resistance on the part of the so-called "intelligentsia" to this Jewish disease hardly takes place any longer for the simple reason that the intelligentsia itself is physically completely degenerated, though less by reasons of distress than by reasons of education. The exclusively intellectual attitude of our education of the higher classes makes them unable—in a time where not the mind but the fist decides—even to preserve themselves, let alone to hold their ground. In physical deficiencies there lies not infrequently the first cause of personal cowardice.

The exceeding stress on a purely intellectual training and the neglect of physical training favor also in much too early youth the formation of sexual conceptions. The boy who, by sports and gymnastics, is brought to an ironlike inurement succumbs less to the need of sensual gratification than the stay-at-home who is fed exclusively on intellectual food. A reasonable education, however, must take this into consideration. Further, it must not forget that on the part of the healthy young man the expectations of the woman will be different than on the part of a prematurely corrupted weakling.

Thus the entire education has to be directed towards employing the free time of the boy for the useful training of his body. He has no right to loaf about idly in these years, to make streets and movie theaters insecure, but after his daily work he has to steel and harden his young body so that life will not find him too soft some day. To get this under way and also to carry it out, to guide and to lead is the task of the education of youth, and not the exclusive infiltration of so-called wisdom. It has also to do away with the conception that the treatment of the body were the concern of each individual. There is no liberty to sin at the expense of posterity and, with it, of the race.

*   *   *

It is a half measure to allow incurably ill people the permanent possibility of contaminating the other healthy ones. But this corresponds entirely to a humaneness which, in order not to hurt one individual, lets hundreds of others perish. The demand that for defective people the propagation of an equally defective offspring be made impossible is a demand of clearest reason and in its planful execution it means the most humane act of mankind. It will spare undeserved suffering to millions of unfortunates, but in the future it will lead to an increasing improvement of health on the whole. The determination to proceed in this direction will also put up a dam against the further spreading of venereal diseases. For here, if necessary, one will have to proceed to the pitiless isolation of incurably diseased people; a barbaric measure for one who was unfortunate enough to be stricken with it, but a blessing for the contemporaries and for posterity. The temporary pain of a century may and will redeem millenniums from suffering.

*   *   *

Any crossing between two beings of not quite the same high standard produces a medium between the standards of the parents. That means: the young one will probably be on a higher level than the racially lower parent, but not as high as the higher one. Consequently, it will succumb later on in the fight against the higher level. But such a mating contradicts Nature's will to breed life as a whole towards a higher level.

*   *   *

Just as little as Nature desires a mating between weaker individuals and stronger ones, far less she desires the mixing of a higher race with a lower one, as in this case her entire work of higher breeding, which has perhaps taken hundreds of thousands of years, would tumble at one blow.

Historical experience offers countless proofs of this. It shows with terrible clarity that with any mixing of the blood of the Aryan with lower races the result was the end of the culture-bearer. North America, the population of which consists for the greatest part of Germanic elements—which mix only very little with the lower, colored races— displays a humanity and a culture different from those of Central and South America, where chiefly the Romanic immigrants have sometimes mixed with the aborigines on a large scale. By this example alone one may clearly and distinctly recognize the influence of the race mixture. The Germanic of the North American continent, who has remained pure and less intermixed, has become the master of that continent, he will remain so until he, too, falls victim to the shame of blood-mixing.

*   *   *

Everything that today we admire on this earth—science and art, technique and inventions— is only the creative product of a few peoples and perhaps originally of *one* race. On them now depends also the existence of this entire culture. If they perish, then the beauty of this earth sinks into the grave with them.

*   *   *

All great cultures of the past perished only because the originally creative race died off through blood-poisoning.

*   *   *

He who wants to live should fight, therefore, and he who does not want to battle in this world of eternal struggle does not deserve to be alive.

*   *   *

What we see before us of human culture today, the results of art, science, and techniques, is almost exclusively the creative product of the Aryan.

*   *   *

If one were to divide mankind into three groups: culture-founders, culture-bearers, and culture-destroyers, then, as representative of the first kind, only the Aryan would come in question. It is from him that the foundation and the walls of all human creations originate, and only the external form and color depend on the characteristics of the various peoples involved. He furnishes the gigantic building-stones and also the plans for all human progress, and only the execution corresponds to the character of the people and races in the various instances.

*   *   *

But if it is ascertained that a people receives, takes in, and works over the essential basic elements of its culture from other races, and if then, when a further external influence is lacking, it stiffens again and again, then one can perhaps call such a race a *"culture-bearing"* one but never a *"culture-creating"* one.

*   *   *

The Jew forms the strongest contrast to the Aryan. Hardly in any people of the world is the instinct of self-preservation more strongly developed than in the so-called "chosen people." The fact of the existence of this race alone may be looked upon as the best proof of this. Where is the people that in the past two thousand years has been exposed to so small changes of the inner disposition, of character, etc., as the Jewish people? Which people finally has experienced greater changes than this one—and yet has always come forth the same from the most colossal catastrophes of mankind? What an infinitely persistent will for life, for preserving the race do these facts disclose!

Also the intellectual abilities were schooled in the course of centuries. Today the Jew is looked upon as "clever," and in a certain sense he has been so at all times. But his reason is not the result of his own development, but that of object lessons from without.

*   *   *

As now the Jew (for reasons which will immediately become evident from the following) was never in the possession of a culture of his own, the bases for his spiritual activity have always been furnished by others. At all times his intellect has developed through the culture that surrounds him.

*   *   *

In the Jewish people, the will to sacrifice oneself does not go beyond the bare instinct of self-preservation of the individual. The seemingly great feeling of belonging together is rooted in a very primitive herd instinct, as it shows itself in a similar way in many other living beings in this world. Thereby the fact is remarkable that in all these cases a common herd instinct leads to mutual support only as long as a common danger makes this seem useful or unavoidable. The same pack of wolves that jointly falls upon its booty dissolves when its hunger abates.

*   *   *

The Jew remains united only if forced by a common danger or is attracted by a common booty; if both reasons are no longer evident, then the qualities of the crassest egoism come into their own, and, in a moment, the united people becomes a horde of rats, fighting bloodily among themselves.

If the Jews were alone in this world, they would suffocate as much in dirt and filth, as they would carry on a detestable struggle to cheat and to ruin each other, although the complete lack of the will to sacrifice, expressed in their cowardice, would also in this instance make the fight a comedy.

Thus it is fundamentally wrong to conclude, merely from the fact of their standing together in a fight, or, more rightly expressed, in their exploiting their fellow human beings, that the Jews have a certain idealistic will to sacrifice themselves.

*   *   *

* * * The Jewish people, with all its apparent intellectual qualities, is nevertheless without any true culture, especially without a culture of its own. For the sham culture which the Jew possesses today is the property of other peoples, and is mostly spoiled in his hands.

*   *   *

No, the Jew possesses no culture-creating energy whatsoever, as the idealism, without which there can never exist a genuine development of man towards a higher level, does not and never did exist in him. His intellect, therefore, will never have a constructive effect, but only a destructive one. ✳ ✳ ✳

✳   ✳   ✳

The Jews were always a people with definite racial qualities and never a religion, only their progress made them probably look very early for a means which could divert disagreeable attention from their person. But what would have been more useful and at the same time more harmless than the "purloining" of the appearance of being a religious community? For here, too, everything is purloined, or rather, stolen. But resulting from his own original nature the Jew cannot possess a religious institution for the very reason that he lacks all idealism in any form and that he also does not recognize any belief in the hereafter.

✳   ✳   ✳

The State is a means to an end. Its end is the preservation and the promotion of a community of physically and psychically equal living beings. This very preservation comprises first the racial stock and thereby it permits the free development of all the forces slumbering in this race. Again and again a part of them will primarily serve the preservation of the physical life and only another part will serve the promotion of a further mental development. But

actually the one always creates the presumption for the other.

States that do not serve this purpose are faulty specimens, even miscarriages.

✳   ✳   ✳

Thus the highest purpose of the folkish State is the care for the preservation of those racial primal elements which, supplying culture, create the beauty and dignity of a higher humanity. We, as Aryans, are therefore able to imagine a State only to be the living organism of a nationality which not only safeguards the preservation of that nationality, but which, by a further training of its spiritual and ideal abilities, leads it to the highest freedom.

✳   ✳   ✳

REVIEW QUESTIONS

1. What were the greatest threats to the racial purity of Germans, according to Hitler?
2. What solutions did he propose?
3. What were the fundamental goals of education in the Nazi state?
4. In what sense did Jews pose a threat to Aryans?
5. On what evidence did Hitler base his arguments?

FRITZ STERN

FROM *Five Germanys I Have Known*

Fritz Stern was born in 1926 in what is now Wroclaw, a large city in western Poland. At the time of his birth, Wroclaw was part of the German Empire and was known as Breslau. He came from a family of assimilated Jews that had converted to Lutheranism a generation before his birth. His father was a doctor and a veteran of the German army in the First World War, and his mother was an educator. In 1938, because of their Jewish roots, the Stern family was forced to emigrate from Germany to the

United States. He became a noted professor of German history at Columbia University, and he was particularly well known for his work on the origins of National Socialism in Germany. In the selections below, Stern describes the experiences of his family as the Nazi regime consolidated its hold on German society after Hitler came to power in 1933. He describes the tensions in his family between their Jewish roots and their Christian faith as well as the difficult subject of emigration, which was increasingly debated in Jewish families in Germany after 1933. Stern's father had more opportunities than most families because of his professional qualifications. Many countries had placed strict limits on the number of refugees that they would accept, and it was often difficult to get permission to settle abroad.

From *Five Germanys I Have Known*, by Fritz Stern (New York: Farrar, Strauss and Giroux, 2006), pp. 98, 109–13.

Before 1933, I didn't even know about my Jewish roots. But then, at some point very shortly after Hitler's accession to power, in one of my verbal fights with my sister, I dredged up some anti-Semitic epithet and threw it at her. Instantly, I was summoned to my father's study, a rare event in itself. I wish I could remember exactly what he said to me, but I know I left his study aware of our Jewish origins and ashamed of having abused my sister in that manner, my father's severe reprimand serving simultaneously as an astounding revelation. The full significance of this dawned on me only in the following weeks. My earlier fear of Nazis had come merely from my associating them with violence and power. After all, even a child could intuit that just about any decent person could fall victim to that violence: one didn't have to be Jewish. Now I saw it differently. Barely seven years old, I began to be at least partially, blessedly enlightened. I began to have some sense of who I was—and, gradually, of who I was not.

*   *   *

* * * [O]ur close-knit family, with its inevitable tensions and a perhaps excessive amount of sibling conflict, was roiled by my sister's wish to attend confirmation class and be confirmed. Toni was fifteen at the time, with strong religious yearnings, and the only tradition she knew was Christian, though I don't think she had gone to church regularly. Normally this would have been a private matter, but on this issue, given the political conditions, the line between private and public was difficult to draw. Her wish to be confirmed brought home to us the very real (if limited) conflict between the Christian churches and the Nazi regime, which early on had decreed that the former must abide by the non-Aryan paragraphs of the Civil Service Law. This Nazi command to discriminate against Christians of Jewish descent was a key issue in the intermittent struggles between the regime and the Protestant churches, which were divided on how to respond to the National Socialists in any case. Official Protestantism had been hostile to the Weimar Republic, and many of its clergy were beset by deep-seated anti-Semitism, virulently enhanced by hatred of Weimar's "godless culture." Even before Hitler's rise to power, the Protestant churches had among them groups who called themselves "German Christians," dedicated to an extreme *völkisch* faith, clamoring for the elimination of the Old Testament from the teachings of the Church and forbidding any acknowledgment of the Judaic origins of Christianity. (This patently absurd doctrine had already arisen among some Protestant theologians in the late nineteenth century.) With Hitler in power, the German Christians' self-definition said it all: they now called themselves "the SA of Jesus Christ." Hitler hoped that the German Christians could capture the entire Protestant establishment. That effort failed, and other pastors recognized that despite features they might admire in Nazism, there were issues of theology and church autonomy that could not be compromised.

The conflict between the Nazi regime and a significant number of other Protestant pastors came into the open when Martin Niemöller, a pastor in the affluent Berlin suburb of Dahlem, founded an Emergency Union of Protestant Pastors, a forerunner of what was later called the Confessing Church. Members of the latter, which was particularly strong in Silesia, refused to abide by the non-Aryan proscription. (An oft-repeated parable was told at the time: a Breslau pastor opens his Sunday sermon by asking all non-Aryans to leave; he repeats the demand thrice, at which point the figure on the Cross disappears. These antiregime stories had a kind of momentary anesthetizing effect; they were a refuge into never-never land.) The struggle between pastors such as Niemöller and the Nazis grew more intense as the 1930s progressed. Niemöller himself, with his own ambivalent feelings about Jews and the place of the church in the state, was incarcerated in Dachau and Buchenwald until the end of the war. Thousands of Catholic priests and Protestant pastors were jailed in those years, and their stand lent hope to critics of the regime.

My mother, responding to and strongly seconding my sister's wishes, found a member of the Confessing Church, Pastor Schröter, who eagerly welcomed Toni to his confirmation class. (In fact, before the first meeting of the class and before her arrival, he told the group that a non-Aryan would be joining them, to which one responded, "Then we have to be especially nice to her.") My parents attended Toni's confirmation, but I rebelled and refused to go, despite my family's entreaties. And yet I was impressed that Pastor Schröter had been repeatedly arrested for his open defiance of the regime's orders; he even taunted the Gestapo men who listened to his sermons. I had a child's thrill at learning that Schröter communicated with next-cell prisoners by knocking on the wall in Morse code. These vivid stories bolstered my admiration for dissenters and resisters—an admiration I never lost.

*　　*　　*

The main topic in 1935 wasn't religion—it was emigration. My parents' intention had been clear from that summer in Paris, and they continued to explore—and were encouraged to explore—all possible avenues. An inquiry was made concerning the United States; the indirect reply came in March 1934 from the Emergency Committee in Aid of Displaced Foreign Physicians: "We have Dr. Stern's credentials on file and his name has been brought to the attention of medical institutions in this country." If an opportunity were to arise, the committee would notify him at once; if he wanted to immigrate to practice medicine, he would have to come in under the German immigration quota and pass the requisite examinations.

The United States seemed very remote. It was hard enough to resolve leaving your home, your language, your German past. My father hoped for a clinical position in Europe, or in a country closer to Europe than America. Negotiations were carried on by another emergency committee to assist German scholars, headed by Fritz Demuth and located in Zurich. The next likely prospect, explored by Demuth, was a professorship in Tehran. Jadassohn, whose ailing wife depended on my father's epistolary advice, had moved to Zurich and was supervising these efforts. In July, he wrote that my father's old teacher Erich Frank, now in Istanbul, had told him about his contractual arrangements there; it was information that could serve as a basis for negotiations with Tehran. He was reassuring that "from the point of view of climate, T. is good, with the exception of water." A later letter acknowledged that hygienically Tehran was rather sad, but "the roads excellent." My father took out the atlas, showed me a map of Persia, and pointed to the mountains near Tehran. Onkel Pu continued, in his necessarily telegraphic, gnomic way. "We understand perfectly how difficult the decision is for you, but no one can take it for you." I gathered that my father wasn't pursuing this possibility with all the energy that might have been necessary. In September, Jadassohn wrote again: "I am not the least bit sorry that T. is out. Following my principle, I never spoke for or against it, but I was convinced that it isn't for you."

The next major possibility focused on Ankara. The great Turkish modernizer-dictator Kemal Ataturk had decided early on to profit from Hitler's expulsionary policies and had invited leading German émigrés to positions in Turkey. Istanbul had not only an astounding circle of German economists but also great physicians, including Erich Frank and my father's old friend Rudolf Nissen, who hoped to facilitate our move to Ankara. In the end those negotiations collapsed as well. Some thought was given to posts in Pisa and in Shanghai.

Emigration was the central topic not only for my father but for many of his colleagues. And there was a steady exodus of friends and associates to all sorts of destinations. So I owe my first impressions of the vastness of the world to the terrors we were trying to leave behind. When acknowledging such a dubious gift of fate, or indeed any other unlikely, ironically burdened blessing, my father and I would invoke the Nazi slogan that we saw at construction sites or at other mundane wonders: *Das verdanken wir dem Führer*! (We owe that to the Führer!)

America, long known as the land of unlimited opportunities, was now dubbed by refugees the land of "unpaid opportunities." But after the disappointments with Tunisia, Persia, and Turkey, and a brief interlude of serious negotiations with the Prince of Liechtenstein about running some government sanitarium there, thoughts of emigrating to the United States intensified. In January 1936, Florence Willstätter, Richard's American sister-in-law, sent us an affidavit. Jadassohn, too, offered help, noting that "besides New York there are other cities in the U.S. which are not so overcrowded." He also wrote about contacts in Palestine—an option that was also discussed, the more so as the Nazi government, eager to get rid of Jews, made extra concessions for emigration there.

The government, which still contained some "conservatives," most notably Hjalmar Schacht as minister of economics, tried to balance the demands of its most radical elements, who wanted a final onslaught on Jewish life and property, with the conservatives' warning that Jews remained important in the German economy and that open violence would have unpleasant repercussions abroad. (The specter of world Jewry's revenge!) In May 1935, the Central Association of German Citizens of Jewish Faith estimated that 450,000 "full"—that is, unconverted—Jews remained in Germany as well as 50,000 converted ones. In September of that year, at the annual party rally—that master pageant brilliantly captured in Leni Riefenstahl's film *Triumph of the Will*—the regime opted for a "legal solution" to the problem of these half-million Jewish Germans, announcing the infamous Nürnberg decrees, which excluded Jews and non-Aryans from German citizenship, assigning them the status of "state subjects." The Nürnberg laws were a further shock, and the definition of who exactly was Jewish continued to bedevil the regime and its potential victims for years: another law "for the protection of German blood and honor" proscribed all sexual relations between Jews and Aryans; violations involving "racial defilement" were severely punished, and Jewish households were forbidden to employ any Aryan German woman younger than forty-five years of age. (The largest number of denunciations made to the Gestapo in subsequent years involved charges of "racial defilement." These, when proven, punished the Jews involved far more harshly than their Aryan partners.)

Both the intent and reception of the Nürnberg laws were complex. The regime wanted to satisfy radical anti-Jewish demands while discouraging individual acts of violence, such as had occurred before. And it certainly intended to rob Jews of their rights as citizens, casting them out of the German national community. Also, now that Hindenburg was safely dead, the thousands of Jewish war veterans were no longer exempt.

The prohibition of sexual relations between Aryan and Jew not only outlawed intermarriage but also gave official sanction to the vulgar slur that Jewish men had an innate compulsion to seduce German women. This had been a commonplace of popular German anti-Semitism even before the Nazis came to power; it was the obscene staple of Julius Streicher's pornographic weekly *Der Stürmer*, with its disgusting caricatures and lurid stories. *Der Stürmer* had its own display cases on many street corners, often close to schools.

So the new laws made the definition of Jewish and non-Aryan both more urgent and more difficult. Within a few years, life or death was to depend on the fine distinction, newly introduced, as to who was a half or quarter Jew. And the need to prove pure Aryan ancestry became a full-time German industry. To criticize, let alone to mock; this new requirement would have implied insufficient faith in the Führer and in the validity of racial determinism.

REVIEW QUESTIONS

1. Did young Fritz Stern consider himself to be Jewish? What were the particular pressures faced by families that had converted to Christianity? What is his perception of the ways that Christian churches had reacted to the Nazi government?
2. What possibilities did the Stern family have for emigration? What was the attitude of the German authorities toward the emigration of Jews in 1938?
3. Stern places particular emphasis on the effects of the Nürnberg laws of 1935. What were their effects for Jewish families or for families like his that had converted to Christianity?

GEORGE ORWELL

FROM *The Road to Wigan Pier*

Europeans had hoped that the end of the First World War would signal a renewed prosperity: instead they experienced one economic crisis after another in the 1920s and 1930s. A feverish period of economic revival began in 1925, but it was brought to a precipitous halt by the crash of the U.S. stock market in 1929. Although the global economy was gradually stabilized during the middle to late 1930s, the Depression did not truly come to an end until a new world war—and a tremendous increase in the production of armaments—kicked the economies of the industrialized nations back into high gear.

The United States and Germany endured the greatest hardships during the Depression, but all of the industrialized nations of western Europe suffered from high rates of unemployment and the demoralization caused by economic collapse. In the mid-1930s, George Orwell (pseudonym of Eric Arthur Blair, 1903–1950), was asked by the Left Book Club to travel through northern England and write a report on workers' conditions for the book club's members. Already known to progressive readers as the author of Down and Out in Paris and London *(1933), a sympathetic account of life among the transient poor, Orwell was an unorthodox socialist whose perceptions of workers were strongly shaped by his rejection of the prejudices of the "shabby-genteel" lower middle class into which he had been born. In* The Road to Wigan Pier *(1937), Orwell describes the lives of unemployed workers living "on the dole," the welfare benefits provided by the British government.*

From *The Road to Wigan Pier*, by George Orwell (New York: Harcourt, Brace, 1958), pp. 76–77, 79–82, 85–90.

*   *   *

When you see the unemployment figures quoted at two millions, it is fatally easy to take this as meaning that two million people are out of work and the rest of the population is comparatively comfortable. I admit that till recently I was in the habit of doing so myself. I used to calculate that if you put the registered unemployed at round about two millions and threw in the destitute and those who for one reason and another were not registered, you might take the number of underfed people in England (for *everyone* on the dole or thereabouts is underfed) as being, at the very most, five millions.

This is an enormous under-estimate, because, in the first place, the only people shown on unemployment figures are those actually drawing the dole—that is, in general, heads of families. An unemployed man's dependants do not figure on the list unless they too are drawing a separate allowance. A Labour Exchange officer told me that to get at the real number of people *living on* (not drawing) the dole, you have got to multiply the official figures by something over three. This alone brings the number of unemployed to round about six millions. But in addition there are great numbers of people who are in work but who, from a financial point of view, might equally well be unemployed, because they are not drawing anything that can be described as a living wage. Allow for these and their dependants, throw in as before the old-age pensioners, the destitute and other nondescripts, and you get an *underfed* population of well over ten millions. * * *

Take the figures for Wigan, which is typical enough of the industrial and mining districts. The number of insured workers is round about 36,000 (26,000 men and 10,000 women). Of these, the number unemployed at the beginning of 1936 was about 10,000. But this was in winter when the mines are working full time; in summer it would probably be 12,000. Multiply by three, as above, and you get 30,000 or 36,000. The total population of Wigan is a little under 87,000; so that at any moment more than one person in three out of the whole population—not merely the registered workers—is either drawing or living on the dole. Those ten or twelve thousand unemployed contain a steady core of from four to five thousand miners who have been continuously unemployed for the past seven years. And Wigan is not especially badly off as industrial towns go. Even in Sheffield, which has been doing well for the last year or so because of wars and rumours of war, the proportion of unemployment is about the same—one in three of registered workers unemployed.

*   *   *

Nevertheless, in spite of the frightful extent of unemployment, it is a fact that poverty—extreme poverty—is less in evidence in the industrial North than it is in London. Everything is poorer and shabbier, there are fewer motor-cars and fewer well-dressed people; but also there are fewer people who are obviously destitute. Even in a town the size of Liverpool or Manchester you are struck by the fewness of the beggars. London is a sort of whirlpool which draws derelict people towards it, and it is so vast that life there is solitary and anonymous. Until you break the law nobody will take any notice of you, and you can go to pieces as you could not possibly do in a place where you had neighbours who knew you. But in the industrial towns the old communal way of life has not yet broken up, tradition is still strong and almost everyone has a family—potentially, therefore, a home. In a town of 50,000 or 100,000 inhabitants there is no casual and as it were unaccounted-for population; nobody sleeping in the streets, for instance. Moreover, there is just this to be said for the unemployment regulations, that they do not discourage people from marrying. A man and wife on twenty-three shillings a week are not far from the starvation line, but they can make a home of sorts; they are vastly better off than a single man on fifteen shillings.

*   *   *

But there is no doubt about the deadening, debilitating effect of unemployment upon everybody, married or single, and upon men more than upon women.

*   *   *

Take a miner, for instance, who has worked in the pit since childhood and has been trained to be a miner and nothing else. How the devil is he to fill up the empty days? It is absurd to say that he ought to be looking for work. There is no work to look for, and everybody knows it. You can't go on looking for work every day for seven years.

*   *   *

I first became aware of the unemployment problem in 1928. * * * At that time nobody cared to admit that unemployment was inevitable, because this meant admitting that it would probably continue. The middle classes were still talking about "lazy idle loafers on the dole" and saying that "these men could all find work if they wanted to," and naturally these opinions percolated to the working class themselves. I remember the shock of astonishment it gave me, when I first mingled with tramps and beggars, to find that a fair proportion, perhaps a quarter, of these beings whom I had been taught to regard as cynical parasites, were decent young miners and cotton-workers gazing at their destiny with the same sort of dumb amazement as an animal in a trap. They simply could not understand what was happening to them. They had been brought up to work, and behold! it seemed as if they were never going to have the chance of working again. In their circumstances it was inevitable, at first, that they should be haunted by a feeling of personal degradation. That was the attitude towards unemployment in those days: it was a disaster which happened to *you* as an individual and for which *you* were to blame.

When a quarter of a million miners are unemployed, it is part of the order of things that Alf Smith, a miner living in the back streets of Newcastle, should be out of work. Alf Smith is merely one of the quarter million, a statistical unit.

*   *   *

When people live on the dole for years at a time they grow used to it, and drawing the dole, though it remains unpleasant, ceases to be shameful. * * * The people have at any rate grasped that unemployment is a thing they cannot help. It is not only Alf Smith who is out of work now; Bert Jones is out of work as well, and both of them have been "out" for years. It makes a great deal of difference when things are the same for everybody.

*   *   *

But they don't necessarily lower their standards by cutting out luxuries and concentrating on necessities; more often it is the other way about—the more natural way, if you come to think of it. Hence the fact that in a decade of unparalleled depression, the consumption of all cheap luxuries has increased. The two things that have probably made the greatest difference of all are the movies and the mass-production of cheap smart clothes since the war. The youth who leaves school at fourteen and gets a blind-alley job is out of work at twenty, probably for life; but for two pounds ten on the hire-purchase system he can buy himself a suit which, for a little while and at a little distance, looks as though it had been tailored in Savile Row. The girl can look like a fashion plate at an even lower price. You may have three halfpence in your pocket and not a prospect in the world, and only the corner of a leaky bedroom to go home to; but in your new clothes you can stand on the street corner, indulging in a private daydream of yourself as Clark Gable or Greta Garbo, which compensates you for a great deal. And even at home there is generally a cup of tea going—a "nice cup of tea"—and Father, who has been out of work since 1929, is temporarily happy because he has a sure tip for the Cesarewitch.

Trade since the war has had to adjust itself to meet the demands of underpaid, underfed people, with the result that a luxury is nowadays almost always cheaper than a necessity. One pair of plain solid shoes costs as much as two ultra-smart pairs. For the price of one square meal you can get two pounds of cheap sweets. You can't get much meat for threepence, but you can get a lot of fish-and-chips. Milk costs threepence a pint and even "mild" beer costs fourpence, but aspirins are seven a penny and you can wring forty cups of tea out of a quarter-pound packet. And above all there is gambling, the cheapest of all luxuries. Even people on the verge of starvation can buy a few days' hope ("Something to live for," as they call it) by having a penny on a sweepstake.

*   *   *

Of course the post-war development of cheap luxuries has been a very fortunate thing for our rulers. It is quite likely that fish and chips, art-silk stockings, tinned salmon, cut-price chocolate (five two-ounce bars for sixpence), the movies, the radio, strong tea and the Football Pools have between them averted revolution. Therefore we are sometimes told that the whole thing is an astute manœuvre by the governing class—a sort of "bread and circuses" business—to hold the unemployed down. What I have seen of our governing class does not convince me that they have that much intelligence. The thing has happened, but by an unconscious process—the quite natural interaction between the manufacturer's need for a market and the need of half-starved people for cheap palliatives.

*   *   *

Review Questions

1. Why, according to Orwell, was extreme poverty less common in the north of England than in the south?
2. What impact did long-term unemployment have on workers in northern England?
3. Why were the poor addicted to cheap luxuries?

Sigmund Freud

FROM *Civilization and Its Discontents*

The interwar years witnessed a generalized collapse of confidence in the values and practices promoted by nineteenth-century liberalism. Many Europeans rejected the principles of parliamentary democracy, individualism, and reason in favor of authoritarianism, collectivism, and the reign of instinct. Writing in the late 1920s, Sigmund Freud asked himself, "How has it happened that so many people have come to take up this strange attitude of hostility to civilization?" Freud was puzzled and disturbed by the rise of irrationalist political movements, and he sought psychological explanations for the seething discontent with civilized society expressed by so many Europeans during this period. While Freud's earlier writings had focused on the expression—and repression—of the sexual instinct, Civilization and Its Discontents *(1930) dealt with what Freud identified as a countervailing aggressive instinct.*

Freud's own perspective on civilization revealed a deep pessimism about human nature. Although he conceived of modern European society as marking a high point in human cultural development, he argued that Western "civilization" could only be realized and maintained through the painful repression of the individual's instinctual sexual and aggressive drives. When instinct was successfully sublimated—redirected into socially beneficial ends—it produced art, literature, science, industry, and stable government. On the other hand, no amount of human progress could ever compensate the individual for the loss of the spontaneous expression of these primordial impulses.

From *Civilization and Its Discontents*, by Sigmund Freud, translated by James Strachey (New York: Norton, 1961), pp. 55–59.

*　　*　　*

* * * Sexual love is a relationship between two individuals in which a third can only be superfluous or disturbing, whereas civilization depends on relationships between a considerable number of individuals. When a love-relationship is at its height there is no room left for any interest in the environment; a pair of lovers are sufficient to themselves, and do not even need the child they have in common to make them happy. * * *

So far, we can quite well imagine a cultural community consisting of double individuals like this, who, libidinally satisfied in themselves, are connected with one another through the bonds of common work and common interests. If this were so, civilization would not have to withdraw any energy from sexuality. But this desirable state of things does not, and never did, exist. Reality shows us that civilization is not content with the ties we have so far allowed it. It aims at binding the members of the community together in a libidinal way as well and employs every means to that end. It favours every path by which strong identifications can be established between the members of the community, and it summons up aim-inhibited libido on the largest scale so as to strengthen the communal bond by relations of friendship. In order for these aims to be fulfilled, a restriction upon sexual life is unavoidable. But we are unable to understand what the necessity is which forces civilization along this path and which causes its antagonism to sexuality. There must be some disturbing factor which we have not yet discovered.

The clue may be supplied by one of the ideal demands, as we have called them, of civilized society. It runs: "Thou shalt love thy neighbour as thyself." It is known throughout the world and is undoubtedly older than Christianity, which puts it forward as its proudest claim. Yet it is certainly not very old; even in historical times it was still strange to mankind. Let us adopt a naïve attitude towards it, as though we were hearing it for the first time; we shall be unable then to suppress a feeling of surprise and bewilderment. Why should we do it? What good will it do us? But, above all, how shall we achieve it? How can it be possible? My love is something valuable to me which I ought not to throw away without reflection. It imposes duties on me for whose fulfilment I must be ready to make sacrifices. If I love someone, he must deserve it in some way. (I leave out of account the use he may be to me, and also his possible significance for me as a sexual object, for neither of these two kinds of relationship comes into question where the precept to love my neighbour is concerned.) He deserves it if he is so like me in important ways that I can love myself in him; and he deserves it if he is so much more perfect than myself that I can love my ideal of my own self in him. Again, I have to love him if he is my friend's son, since the pain my friend would feel if any harm came to him would be my pain too—I should have to share it. But if he is a stranger to me and if he cannot attract me by any worth of his own or any significance that he may already have acquired for my emotional life, it will be hard for me to love him. Indeed, I should be wrong to do so, for my love is valued by all my own people as a sign of my preferring them, and it is an injustice to them if I put a stranger on a par with them. But if I am to love him (with this universal love) merely because he, too, is an inhabitant of this earth, like an insect, an earthworm or a grass-snake, then I fear that only a small modicum of my love will fall to his share—not by any possibility as much as, by the judgement of my reason, I am enti-tled to retain for myself. What is the point of a pre-cept enunciated with so much solemnity if its fulfilment cannot be recommended as reasonable?

On closer inspection, I find still further diffi-culties. Not merely is this stranger in general unworthy of my love; I must honestly confess that he has more claim to my hostility and even my hatred. He seems not to have the least trace of love for me and shows me not the slightest consider-ation. If it will do him any good he has no hesita-tion in injuring me, nor does he ask himself whether the amount of advantage he gains bears any proportion to the extent of the harm he does to me. Indeed, he need not even obtain an advantage; if he can satisfy any sort of desire by it, he thinks nothing of jeering at me, insulting me, slandering me and showing his superior power; and the more secure he feels and the more helpless I am, the more certainly I can expect him to behave like this to me. If he behaves differently, if he shows me con-sideration and forbearance as a stranger, I am ready to treat him in the same way, in any case and quite apart from any precept. Indeed, if this gran-diose commandment had run "Love thy neighbour as thy neighbour loves thee," I should not take exception to it. And there is a second command-ment, which seems to me even more incompre-hensible and arouses still stronger opposition in me. It is "Love thine enemies." If I think it over, however, I see that I am wrong in treating it as a greater imposition. At bottom it is the same thing.

I think I can now hear a dignified voice admon-ishing me: "It is precisely because your neighbour

is not worthy of love, and is on the contrary your enemy, that you should love him as yourself." ⁂

Now it is very probable that my neighbour, when he is enjoined to love me as himself, will answer exactly as I have done and will repel me for the same reasons. I hope he will not have the same objective grounds for doing so, but he will have the same idea as I have.

*   *   *

The element of truth behind all this, which people are so ready to disavow, is that men are not gentle creatures who want to be loved, and who at the most can defend themselves if they are attacked; they are, on the contrary, creatures among whose instinctual endowments is to be reckoned a power-ful share of aggressiveness. As a result, their neigh-bour is for them not only a potential helper or sexual object, but also someone who tempts them to satisfy their aggressiveness on him, to exploit his capacity for work without compensation, to use him sexually without his consent, to seize his pos-sessions, to humiliate him, to cause him pain, to torture and to kill him. *Homo homini lupus.*[1] Who, in the face of all his experience of life and of history, will have the courage to dispute this asser-tion? As a rule this cruel aggressiveness waits for some provocation or puts itself at the service of some other purpose, whose goal might also have been reached by milder measures. In circum-stances that are favourable to it, when the mental counter-forces which ordinarily inhibit it are out of action, it also manifests itself spontaneously and reveals man as a savage beast to whom consider-ation towards his own kind is something alien. Anyone who calls to mind the atrocities commit-ted during the racial migrations or the invasions of the Huns, or by the people known as Mongols under Jenghiz Khan and Tamerlane, or at the cap-ture of Jerusalem by the pious Crusaders, or even, indeed, the horrors of the recent World War—anyone who calls these things to mind will have to bow humbly before the truth of this view.

---

[1] "Man is a wolf to man."

The existence of this inclination to aggression, which we can detect in ourselves and justly assume to be present in others, is the factor which disturbs our relations with our neighbour and which forces civilization into such a high expenditure [of energy]. In consequence of this primary mutual hostility of human beings, civilized society is perpetually threatened with disintegration. The interest of work in common would not hold it together; instinctual passions are stronger than reasonable interests. Civilization has to use its utmost efforts in order to set limits to man's aggressive instincts and to hold the manifestations of them in check by psychical reaction-formations. Hence, therefore, the use of methods intended to incite people into identifications and aim-inhibited relationships of love, hence the restriction upon sexual life, and hence too the ideal's commandment to love one's neighbour as oneself—a commandment which is really justified by the fact that nothing else runs so strongly counter to the original nature of man. In spite of every effort, these endeavours of civilization have not so far achieved very much. It hopes to prevent the crudest excesses of brutal violence by itself assuming the right to use violence against criminals, but the law is not able to lay hold of the more cautious and refined manifestations of human aggressiveness. The time comes when each one of us has to give up as illusions the expectations which, in his youth, he pinned upon his fellow-men, and when he may learn how much difficulty and pain has been added to his life by their ill-will.

*   *   *

REVIEW QUESTIONS

1. Why is it so difficult to love one's neighbor as oneself?
2. Why is this commandment a necessary requirement of civilized society?
3. What is human nature like, according to Freud?
4. What specific historical events and developments might be explained by Freud's theory of aggression?

26 ❧ THE SECOND WORLD WAR

The Great War had been disastrous, but its outbreak could be blamed on the errors of political leaders and military planners who had allowed diplomatic arrangements and mobilization timetables to take on a life of their own. That a second world war could occur so soon after the first suggested that periodic outbreaks of global warfare were perhaps essential elements in the functioning of modern industrial societies. Similarly, this second failure of the nations of the world to avoid armed conflict suggested that human beings were incapable of controlling their innate aggressiveness and learning from their past mistakes. The Second World War was a total war whose worst horrors—the Holocaust and the bombing of major urban areas—resulted in the slaughter of civilians on a scale hitherto unimagined. Once again, the war made painfully clear the astounding degree of devastation that might occur when humans directed the technologies of industry toward destructive ends.

Yet if the Second World War was dishearteningly destructive it was not so absurd as the First World War had been. In 1914, the outbreak of war seemed almost arbitrary, and even the War Guilt Clause of the Versailles Treaty could not dispel the postwar conviction that the war had been the fault of no one and everyone. In 1939, on the other hand, the outbreak of war took the form of an overt act of aggression by Germany. Many attempts had been made to appease Hitler, but all diplomatic negotiations had failed in the face of his determination to go to war. During the Great War, the military leadership's adoption of a strategy of attrition had stripped the individual soldier's death of meaning, depriving military service of all heroism. During the Second World War, the German army's lightning-war strategy returned the elements of speed and mobility to warfare. Military engagements once again reached decisive conclusions, producing clear winners and losers.

However, from the start, the Second World War was most clearly distinguished from the First World War by its ideological component. To both soldiers and civilians, this new conflict presented itself as a struggle not merely between competing nations but between two fundamentally opposed political and social philosophies, between fascism and antifascism. On the personal level this meant that the war presented clear choices, even if these choices often took the form of extremely difficult ethical decisions. On both sides, government propaganda fanned the flames of political passions, producing a strong sense of conviction among fascists and antifascists alike. At the same time, the increasingly manifest viciousness and brutality of the fascist regimes generated intense opposition both within Germany and Italy and in the territories the two states occupied. Participants in resistance movements experienced an acute sense of human agency: having committed themselves to the antifascist cause, they engaged in actions that exposed them to the risk of imprisonment, torture, and execution.

The defeat of the Axis powers—Germany, Italy, and Japan—seemed like a triumph for the principles of democracy, tolerance, and individual liberty. After the war, the world's nations renewed their commitment to international governance through the creation of the United Nations, but many people continued to fear that the twentieth century was doomed to experience yet another global cataclysm, especially as growing tensions between the Soviet Union and the United States developed into an ominously tense Cold War. At the same time, peoples who lived under European colonial regimes in Africa and Asia were ultimately disappointed in their hopes that a postwar settlement would bring reform or national independence for their societies. Any optimism generated by the return of peace was quickly overshadowed by the emergence of a bipolar system of international relations: The world's two superpowers, armed to the teeth with devastating weapons of destruction, insisted that the rest of the world choose sides.

The Atlantic Charter and Third World Nationalism

The Atlantic Charter was the product of a meeting between Winston Churchill and Franklin D. Roosevelt in August 1941. Churchill, the prime minister of Britain, had already been at war with Hitler's armies for almost two years. Meanwhile, Hitler had just invaded the Soviet Union in the east, and the Japanese were preparing their surprise attack on Pearl Harbor, which would bring the United States into the war four months later. In this tense atmosphere, Churchill and Roosevelt met in secret in Placentia Bay, Newfoundland, to issue the Atlantic Charter. Subsequently adopted by the Declaration by the United Nations (January 1, 1942), the charter was a declaration of common aims between Britain and the United States. The two nations avowed their commitment to the principles of national self-determination, freedom of trade and commerce, international cooperation to improve standards of living and economic justice throughout the world, and a pledge to work toward international peace and disarmament. During the postwar period, U.S. support for the United Nations and the rebuilding of Europe reflected the continued power of these goals.

Many people living under European colonial regimes in Asia and Africa assumed that the Atlantic Charter would lead to the end of colonialism and national independence for their countries after the defeat of Germany and Japan. At a minimum they expected that colonial governments that denied basic citizenship rights to colonial subjects would be reformed. This was especially true in French colonies such as Algeria and Indochina, because the Vichy government in France had collaborated extensively with the Nazis during the war. In Indochina, for example, nationalists were disappointed when the United States did not support their cause of independence from the French, and angry that the new French government in 1944 did not promise to reform the colonial system. Ho Chi Minh (1890–1969), who became a communist and an anticolonial militant in the years after World War I while working as a laborer in France and Britain, led the Vietnamese nationalist movement for almost thirty years. In the speech reproduced here, he tried to portray those who supported French colonialism as being on the side of the Axis powers— Japan, Italy, and Germany—and he placed the struggle of Vietnamese nationalism on the same side as the United States, Britain, China, and Russia, allied during the war years.

The Atlantic Charter*

On 14 August 1941, President Roosevelt and Prime Minister Churchill, at the conclusion of their mid-ocean conference made the following joint declaration of "certain common principles in the national policies of their respective countries on which they base their hopes for a better future of the world."

FIRST, their countries seek no aggrandizement, territorial or other;

SECOND, they desire to see no territorial changes that do not accord with the freely expressed wishes of the people concerned;

THIRD, they respect the right of all peoples to choose the form of government under which they

live; and the wish to see sovereign rights and self government restored to those who have been forcibly deprived of them;

FOURTH, they will endeavor, with due respect for their existing obligations to further the enjoyment by all States, great or small, victor or vanquished, of access, on equal terms, to the trade and to the raw materials of the world which are needed for their economic prosperity;

FIFTH, they desire to bring about the fullest collaboration between all nations in the economic field with the object of securing, for all, improved labor standards, economic advancement and social security;

SIXTH, after the final destruction of the Nazi tyranny, they hope to see established a peace which will afford to all nations the means of dwelling in safety within their own boundaries, and which will afford

---

* From *The Atlantic Charter*, edited by Douglas Brinkley and David R. Facey-Crowther (New York: St. Martin's Press, 1994), pp. xvii–xviii.

assurance that all the men in all the lands may live out their lives in freedom from fear and want;

SEVENTH, such a peace should enable all men to traverse the high seas and oceans without hindrance;

EIGHTH, they believe that all of the nations of the world, for realistic as well as spiritual reasons, must come to the abandonment of the use of force. Since no future peace can be maintained if land, sea or air armaments continue to be employed by nations which threaten, or may threaten, aggression outside of their frontiers, they believe, pending the establishment of a wider and permanent system of general security, that the disarmament of such nations is essential. They will likewise aid and encourage all other practicable measures which will lighten for peace-loving peoples the crushing burden of armaments.

By *Franklin D. Roosevelt*
Winston Churchill

Ho Chi Minh's Speech Delivered in the First Days of the Resistance War in South Viet-Nam (November 1945)*

Compatriots!

During the Second World War, the French colonialists twice sold out our country to the Japanese. Thus they betrayed the allied nations, and helped the Japanese to cause the latter many losses.

Meanwhile they also betrayed our people, exposing us to the destruction of bombs and bullets. In this way, the French colonialists withdrew of their own accord from the Allied ranks and tore up the treaties they had earlier compelled us to sign.

Notwithstanding the French colonialists' treachery, our people as a whole are determined to side with the allies and oppose the invaders. When the Japanese surrendered, our entire people single-mindedly changed our country into a Democratic

---

* Reprinted from *On Revolution: Selected Writings*, by Ho Chi Minh, edited by Bernard B. Fall (New York: Frederick A. Praeger, 1967), pp. 158–59.

Republic and elected a provisional Government which is to prepare for a national congress and draw up our draft Constitution. Not only is our act in line with the Atlantic and San Francisco Charters, etc., solemnly proclaimed by the Allies, but it entirely conforms with the glorious principles upheld by the French people: Liberty, Equality, and Fraternity.

It is thus clear that in the past the colonialists betrayed the Allies and our country, and surrendered to the Japanese. At present, in the shadow of the British and Indian troops, and behind the Japanese soldiers, they are attacking the South of our country.

They have sabotaged the peace that China, the United States, Britain, and Russia won at the cost of scores of millions of lives. They have run counter to the promises concerning democracy and liberty that the allied powers have proclaimed. They have of their own accord sabotaged their fathers' principles of liberty and equality. In consequence, it is for a just cause, for justice of the world, and for Viet Nam's land and people that our compatriots throughout the country have risen to struggle, and are firmly determined to maintain their independence. We do not hate the French people and France. We are energetically fighting slavery, and the ruthless policy of the French colonialists. We only safeguard our own against the French invaders. Hence we are not alone. The countries which love peace and democracy, and the weaker nations all over the world, all sympathize with us. With the unity of the whole people within the country, and having many sympathizers abroad, we are sure of total victory.

The French colonialists have behaved lawlessly in the South for almost one-and-a-half months. Our southern compatriots have sacrificed their lives in a most valiant struggle. Public opinion in the great countries—China, the United States, Russia, and Britain—has supported our just cause.

Compatriots throughout the country! Those in the South will do their utmost to resist the enemy. Those in the Center and the North will endeavor to help their southern compatriots and be on the alert.

The French colonialists should know that the Vietnamese people do not want bloodshed, that they love peace. But we are determined to sacrifice even millions of combatants and fight a long-term war of resistance in order to safeguard Viet-Nam's independence and free her children from slavery. We are sure that our war of resistance will be victorious.

Let the whole country be determined in the war of resistance!

Long live independent Viet-Nam!

REVIEW QUESTIONS

1. Why did Churchill and Roosevelt choose this moment to reaffirm their commitment to national self-determination and international cooperation to ensure economic development?

2. Do you think they both intended that this commitment would extend to people in Asia and Africa living under the colonial authority of European powers?

3. Why would Ho Chi Minh choose to express his support for the Allied powers in 1945?

4. What is Ho Chi Minh's opinion of France's revolutionary republican tradition?

5. Why does Ho Chi Minh emphasize the nationalist side of his political program, rather than his commitment to socialism? Is there a tension between these two allegiances?

PRIMO LEVI

Survival in Auschwitz

In December 1943, Primo Levi (1919–1987) was a twenty-four-year-old former chemistry student attempting to connect with a partisan group in the mountains north of Turin. Captured by the Facist Militia, Levi admitted he was Jewish. The Italians handed him over to the Germans and he was deported to Auschwitz in Poland, the largest of the Nazi concentration camps. Auschwitz was in reality a complex of three different camps—an extermination camp at Birkenau, a slavelabor camp called Buna, and a prison camp for political prisoners. Almost 1.5 million people were killed at Auschwitz by the Nazis; 90 percent of this number were Jews.

Levi noted in the preface of his book that it was his "good fortune to be deported to Auschwitz only in 1944, that is after the German Government had decided, owing to the growing scarcity of labour, to lengthen the average life-span of the prisoners destined for elimination; it conceded noticeable improvements in the camp routine and temporarily suspended killings at the whim of individuals." Levi was held in Auschwitz for over a year, much of it working for the rubber factory in Buna run by the German company IG Farben. He managed to stay behind when the camp was abandoned in the face of advances by the Russian army in the spring of 1945. Forced to go east to escape the continuing war, he spent an additional year struggling to return home as a refugee. His two-volume memoir of these experiences has been translated into English as Survival in Auschwitz *(first published in Italy in 1947 as* Se questo è un uomo*) and* The Reawakening (La tregua, 1963). *After returning to*

MAP OF *EINSATZGRUPPEN* MASSACRES (1941–1942)

Barbed wire, disease-ridden barracks, malnourished prisoners, gas chambers, and crematoria are the principal images of the Holocaust inflicted on Jews and other Europeans by the racial genocide of Nazi Germany. Yet before such death camps as Auschwitz and Treblinka were put into full operation, approximately 1.2 million Jews were killed with rifles by mobile killing units in 1941–42. Four select groups, composed of approximately one thousand SS and auxiliary police units, swept behind the advancing German army in its invasion of the Soviet Union in August 1941 to carry out the first massive wave of racial and political murder, primarily of Russian Jews and Soviet partisans. Typically, victims were rounded up, forced to dig a mass grave, and then executed with rifles at the gravesite. This map of eastern central Europe, which constituted the cultural center of European Jewry, locates the principal sites of massacres by the mobile killing units. What does this map convey about the geographic breadth of Nazi genocide before the death camps were put into operation?

Italy, Levi worked as a manager in a Turin chemical factory, simultaneously pursuing a career as a writer. He died in 1987, an apparent suicide.

Levi's autobiographical writings are remarkable for their ability to document the inverted moral universe of camp life, the irrational rules that all prisoners had to master to ensure their survival for another day. Throughout his experience he never lost his powers of observation—this was perhaps a vestige of his scientific training. Some might be horrified at his suggestion that we look at the Lager *(the German word for camps) as an enormous biological and social experiment, but Levi manages to suggest that we can learn from even the most unfathomable of horrors. The first section begins with the arrival of the deportees' train at Auschwitz after several days' journey in winter without heat, food, water, or sanitary facilities. Levi notes that there were forty-five people in his wagon when they arrived at the camp, and only four returned to their homes after the war. His, he says, was "by far the most fortunate wagon."*

From *Survival in Auschwitz: The Nazi Assault on Humanity*, by Primo Levi, translated by Stuart Woolf (New York: Collier, 1993), pp. 19–20, 27–28, 33–35, 42–43, 87–89.

The door opened with a crash, and the dark echoed with outlandish orders in that curt, barbaric barking of Germans in command which seems to give vent to millennial anger. A vast platform appeared before us, lit up by reflectors. A little beyond it, a row of lorries. Then everything was silent again. Someone translated: we had to climb down with our luggage and deposit it alongside the train. In a moment the platform was swarming with shadows. But we were afraid to break that silence: everyone busied himself with his luggage, searched for someone else, called to somebody, but timidly, in a whisper.

A dozen SS men stood around, legs akimbo, with an indifferent air. At a certain moment they moved among us, and in a subdued tone of voice, with faces of stone, began to interrogate us rapidly, one by one, in bad Italian. They did not interrogate everybody, only a few: "How old? Healthy or ill?" And on the basis of the reply they pointed in two different directions.

Everything was silent as an aquarium, or as in certain dream sequences. We had expected something more apocalyptic: they seemed simple police agents. It was disconcerting and disarming. Someone dared ask for his luggage: they replied, "luggage afterwards." Someone else did not want to

leave his wife: they said, "together again afterwards." Many mothers did not want to be separated with their children: they said "good, good, stay with child." They behaved with the calm assurance of people doing their normal duty of every day. But Renzo stayed an instant too long to say good-bye to Francesca, his fiancée, and with a single blow they knocked him to the ground. It was their everyday duty.

In less than ten minutes all the fit men had been collected together in a group. What happened to the others, to the women, to the children, to the old men, we could establish neither then nor later: the night swallowed them up, purely and simply. Today, however, we know that in that rapid and summary choice each one of us had been judged capable or not of working usefully for the Reich; we know that of our convoy no more than ninety-six men and twenty-nine women entered the respective camps of Monowitz-Buna and Birkenau, and that of all the others, more than five hundred in number, not one was living two days later. We also know that not even this tenuous principle of discrimination between fit and unfit was always followed, and that later the simpler method was often adopted of merely opening both the doors of the wagon without warning or instructions to the new arrivals. Those who by chance climbed down on one side of the convoy entered the camp; the others went to the gas chamber.

On the Bottom

Häftling[1]: I have learnt that I am Häftling. My number is 174517; we have been baptized, we will carry the tattoo on our left arm until we die.

The operation was slightly painful and extraordinarily rapid: they placed us all in a row, and one by one, according to the alphabetical order of our names, we filed past a skilful official, armed with a sort of pointed tool with a very short needle. It seems that this is the real, true initiation: only by "showing one's number" can one get bread and soup. Several days passed, and not a few cuffs and punches, before we became used to showing our number promptly enough not to disorder the daily operation of food-distribution: weeks and months were needed to learn its sound in the German language. And for many days, while the habits of freedom still led me to look for the time on my wristwatch, my new name ironically appeared instead, a number tattooed in bluish characters under the skin.

Only much later, and slowly, a few of us learnt something of the funereal science of the numbers of Auschwitz, which epitomize the stages of destruction of European Judaism. To the old hands of the camp, the numbers told everything: the period of entry into the camp, the convoy of which formed a part, and consequently the nationality. Everyone will treat with respect the numbers from 30,000 to 80,000: there are only a few hundred left and they represented the few survivals from the Polish ghettos. It is as well to watch out in commercial dealings with a 116,000 or a 117,000: they now number only about forty, but they represent the Greeks of Salonica, so take care that they do not pull the wool over your eyes. As for the high numbers they carry an essentially comic air about them, like the words "freshman" or "conscript" in ordinary life. The typical high number is a corpulent,

docile and stupid fellow: he can be convinced that leather shoes are distributed at the infirmary to all those with delicate feet, and can be persuaded to run there and leave his bowl of soup "in your custody."

* * *

We had soon learned that the guests of the Lager are divided into three categories: the criminals, the politicals and the Jews. All are clothed in stripes, all are Häftlinge, but the criminals wear a green triangle next to the number sewn on the jacket; the politicals wear a red triangle; and the Jews, who form the large majority, wear the Jewish star, red and yellow. SS men exist but are few and outside the camp, and are seen relatively infrequently. Our effective masters in practice are the green triangles, who have a free hand over us, as well as those of the other two categories who are ready to help them—and they are not few.

And we have learnt other things, more or less quickly, according to our intelligence: to reply "*Jawohl*," never to ask questions, always to pretend to understand. We have learnt the value of food; now we also diligently scrape the bottom of the bowl after the ration and we hold it under our chins when we eat bread so as not to lose the crumbs. We, too, know that it is not the same thing to be given a ladleful of soup from the top or from the bottom of the vat, and we are already able to judge, according to the capacity of the various vats, what is the most suitable place to try and reach in the queue when we line up.

We have learnt that everything is useful; the wire to tie up our shoes, the rags to wrap around our feet, waste paper to (illegally) pad out our jacket against the cold. We have learnt, on the other hand, that everything can be stolen, in fact is automatically stolen as soon as attention is relaxed; and to avoid this, we had to learn the art of sleeping with our head on a bundle made up of our jacket and containing all our belongings, from the bowl to the shoes.

* * *

In addition, there are innumerable circumstances, normally irrelevant, which here become

---

[1] Prisoner.

problems. When one's nails grow long, they have to be shortened, which can only be done with one's teeth (for the toenails, the friction of the shoes is sufficient); if a button comes off, one has to tie it on with a piece of wire; if one goes to the latrine or the washroom, everything has to be carried along, always and everywhere, and while one washes one's face, the bundle of clothes has to be held tightly between one's knees: in any other manner it will be stolen in that second. If a shoe hurts, one has to go in the evening to the ceremony of the changing of the shoes: this tests the skill of the individual who, in the middle of the incredible crowd, has to be able to choose at an eye's glance one (not a pair, one) shoe, which fits. Because once the choice is made, there can be no second change.

And do not think that shoes form a factor of secondary importance in the life of the Lager. Death begins with the shoes; for most of us, they show themselves to be instruments of torture, which after a few hours of marching cause painful sores which become fatally infected. Whoever has them is forced to walk as if he was dragging a convict's chain (this explains the strange gait of the army which returns every evening on parade); he arrives last everywhere, and everywhere he receives blows. He cannot escape if they run after him; his feet swell and the more they swell, the more the friction with the wood and the cloth of the shoes becomes insupportable. Then only the hospital is left: but to enter the hospital with a diagnosis of "*dicke Füsse*" (swollen feet) is extremely dangerous, because it is well known to all, and especially to the SS, that here there is no cure for that complaint.

[Null Achtzehn]

He is Null Achtzehn. He is not called anything except that, Zero Eighteen, the last three figures of his entry number; as if everyone was aware that only a man is worthy of a name, and that Null Achtzehn is no longer a man. I think that even he has forgotten his name, certainly he acts as if this was so. When he speaks, when he looks around, he gives the impression of being empty inside, noth-ing more than an involucre, like the slough of certain insects which one finds on the banks of swamps, held by a thread to the stones and shaken by the wind.

Null Achtzehn is very young, which is a grave danger. Not only because boys support exhaustion and fasting worse than adults, but even more because a long training is needed to survive here in the struggle of each one against all, a training that young people rarely have. Null Achtzehn is not even particularly weak, but all avoid working with him. He is indifferent to the point of not even troubling to avoid tiredness and blows or to search for food. He carries out all the orders that he is given, and it is foreseeable that when they send him to his death he will go with the same total indifference.

He has not even the rudimentary astuteness of a draughthorse, which stops pulling a little before it reaches exhaustion: he pulls or carries or pushes as long as his strength allows him, then he gives way at once, without a word of warning, without lifting his sad, opaque eyes from the ground. He made me think of the sledge-dogs in London's books, who slave until the last breath and die on the track.

But as all the rest of us try by every possible means to avoid work, Null Achtzehn is the one who works more than all. It is because of this, and because he is a dangerous companion, that no one wants to work with him; and as, on the other hand, no one wants to work with me, because I am weak and clumsy, it often happens that we find ourselves paired together.

The Drowned and the Saved

*   *   *

We can perhaps ask ourselves if is necessary or good to retain any memory of this exceptional human state. To this question we feel that we have to reply in the affirmative. We are in fact convinced that no human experience is without meaning or unworthy of analysis, and that fundamental values, even if they are not positive, can be deduced from this particular world which we are describing. We would also like to consider that the Lager was preeminently a gigantic biological and social experiment.

Thousands of individuals, differing in age, condition, origin, language, culture and customs, are enclosed within barbed wire: there they live a regular, controlled life which is identical for all and inadequate to all needs, and which is more rigorous than any experimenter could have set up to establish what is essential and what adventitious to the conduct of the human animal in the struggle for life.

We do not believe in the most obvious and facile deduction: that man is fundamentally brutal, egoistic and stupid in his conduct once every civilized institution is taken away, and that the Häftling is consequently nothing but a man without inhibitions. We believe, rather, that the only conclusion to be drawn is that in the face of driving necessity and physical disability many social habits and instincts are reduced to silence.

But another fact seems to us worthy of attention: there comes to light the existence of two particularly well differentiated categories among men—the saved and the drowned. Other pairs of opposites (the good and the bad, the wise and the foolish, the cowards and the courageous, the unlucky and the fortunate) are considerably less distinct, they seem less essential, and above all they allow for more numerous and complex intermediary gradations.

This division is much less evident in ordinary life; for there it rarely happens that a man loses himself. A man is normally not alone, and in his rise or fall is tied the destinies of his neighbours; so that it is exceptional for anyone to acquire unlimited power, or to fall by a succession of defeats into utter ruin. Moreover, everyone is normally in possession of such spiritual, physical and even financial resources that the probabilities of shipwreck, of total inadequacy in the face of life, are relatively small. And one must take into account a definite cushioning effect exercised both by the law, and by the moral sense which constitutes a selfimposed law; for a country is considered the more civilized the more the wisdom and efficiency of its laws hinder a weak man from becoming too weak or a powerful man too powerful.

But in the Lager things are different: here the struggle to survive is without respite, because everyone is desperately and ferociously alone. If some [prisoner] vacillates, he will find no one to extend a helping hand; on the contrary, someone will knock him aside, because it is in no one's interest that there will be one more "muselman"[2] dragging himself to work every day; and if someone, by a miracle of savage patience and cunning, finds a new method of avoiding the hardest work, a new art which yields him an ounce of bread, he will try to keep his method secret, and he will be esteemed and respected for this, and will derive from it an exclusive, personal benefit; he will become stronger and so will be feared, and who is feared is ipso facto, a candidate for survival.

In history and in life one sometimes seems to glimpse a ferocious law which states: "to he that has will be given; from he that has not, will be taken away." In the Lager, where man is alone and where the struggle for life is reduced to its primordial mechanism, this unjust law is openly in force, is recognized by all. With the adaptable, the strong and astute individuals, even the leaders willingly keep contact, sometimes even friendly contact, because they hope later to perhaps derive some benefit. But with the muselmans, the men in decay, it is not even worth speaking, because one knows already that they will complain and will speak about what they used to eat at home. Even less worthwhile is it to make friends with them, because they have no distinguished acquaintances in the camp, they do not gain any extra rations, they do not work in profitable Kommandos, and they know no secret method of organizing. And in any case, one knows that they are only here on a visit, that in a few weeks nothing will remain of them but a handful of ashes in some nearby field and a crossed-out number on a register. Although engulfed and

---

[2] This word "*Muselmann*," I do not know why, was used by the old ones of the camp to describe the weak, the inept, those doomed to selection.

swept along without rest by the innumerable crowd of those similar to them, they suffer and drag themselves along in an opaque intimate solitude, and in solitude they die or disappear, without leaving a trace in anyone's memory.

REVIEW QUESTIONS

1. Levi notes the cursory or even arbitrary nature of the selection process that decided whether new arrivals at the camp would be killed or put to work, and elsewhere he notes that the rubber factory at Buna never produced a single piece of rubber. Why did the camp authorities insist on rules and procedures to select laborers, when they obviously didn't care if these procedures were followed carefully, or if the prisoners were actually fit enough to do productive labor?

2. What was the purpose of the camp practice of numbering prisoners?

3. What was the significance of the various hierarchies that Levi identifies within camp society?

4. Why does Levi describe the camp as a "struggle of each one against all"?

5. Who are the "drowned" and the "saved"?

FROM *Trials of War Criminals before the Nuremberg Military Tribunals*

Although many postwar philosophers emphasized the moral ambiguities of human action and the relativism of all moral and ethical systems, these postmodern approaches were counterbalanced by a desire to reaffirm the existence of clear lines between good and evil, right and wrong. Survivors sought to ensure that all of humanity would know about the murder of millions of concentration camp inmates, and they called for a judgment on those who had committed crimes against humanity.

Beginning in 1945, many surviving members of the Nazi leadership were put on trial in the city of Nuremberg. The "doctors' trial," which began in December 1946, involved the prosecution of twenty-three German doctors and administrators who had used concentration camp inmates as unwilling subjects in a variety of gruesome and often pointless experiments, including intentional infection with contagious diseases such as malaria and spotted fever, experimental surgery, and exposure to extreme cold, mustard gas, and various poisons. On December 6, 1946, Brigadier General Telford Taylor presented the opening statement for the prosecution, detailing both the specific crimes committed by the defendants and the broader significance of their trial.

From *Trials of War Criminals before the Nuremberg Military Tribunals under Control Council Law No. 10. Nuremberg, October 1946–April 1949* (Washington, D.C.: U.S. Government Printing Office, 1949–53).

Opening Statement of the Prosecution by Brigadier General Telford Taylor, 9 December 1946

The defendants in this case are charged with murders, tortures, and other atrocities committed in the name of medical science. The victims of these crimes are numbered in the hundreds of thousands. A handful only are still alive; a few of the survivors will appear in this courtroom. But most of these miserable victims were slaughtered outright or died in the course of the tortures to which they were subjected.

For the most part they are nameless dead. To their murderers, these wretched people were not individuals at all. They came in wholesale lots and were treated worse than animals. They were 200 Jews in good physical condition, 50 gypsies, 500 tubercular Poles, or 1,000 Russians. The victims of these crimes are numbered among the anonymous millions who met death at the hands of the Nazis and whose fate is a hideous blot on the page of modern history.

*   *   *

The mere punishment of the defendants, or even of thousands of others equally guilty, can never redress the terrible injuries which the Nazis visited on these unfortunate peoples. For them it is far more important that these incredible events be established by clear and public proof, so that no one can ever doubt that they were fact and not fable; and that this Court, as the agent of the United States and as the voice of humanity, stamp these acts, and the ideas which engendered them, as barbarous and criminal.

We have still other responsibilities here. The defendants in the dock are charged with murder, but this is no mere murder trial. We cannot rest content when we have shown that crimes were committed and that certain persons committed them. To kill, to maim, and to torture is criminal under all modern systems of law. These defendants did not kill in hot blood, nor for personal enrichment. Some of them may be sadists who killed and tortured for sport, but they are not all perverts. They are not ignorant men. Most of them are trained physicians and some of them are distinguished scientists. Yet these defendants, all of whom were fully able to comprehend the nature of their acts, and most of whom were exceptionally qualified to form a moral and professional judgment in this respect, are responsible for wholesale murder and unspeakably cruel tortures. It is our deep obligation to all peoples of the world to show why and how these things happened. It is incumbent upon us to set forth with conspicuous clarity the ideas and motives which moved these defendants to treat their fellow men as less than beasts.

*   *   *

To the German people we owe a special responsibility in these proceedings. Under the leadership of the Nazis and their war lords, the German nation spread death and devastation throughout Europe. This the Germans now know. So, too, do they know the consequences to Germany: defeat, ruin, prostration, and utter demoralization. Most German children will never, as long as they live, see an undamaged German city.

*   *   *

This case, and others which will be tried in this building, offer a signal opportunity to lay before the German people the true cause of their present misery. The walls and towers and churches of Nuremberg were, indeed, reduced to rubble by Allied bombs, but in a deeper sense Nuremberg had been destroyed a decade earlier, when it became the seat of the annual Nazi Party rallies, a focal point for the moral disintegration in Germany. * * *

*   *   *

That murder should be punished goes without the saying, but the full performance of our task requires more than the just sentencing of these defendants. Their crimes were the inevitable result of the sinister doctrines which they espoused, and these same doctrines sealed the fate of Germany, shattered Europe, and left the world in ferment.

Wherever those doctrines may emerge and prevail, the same terrible consequences will follow. That is why a bold and lucid consummation of these proceedings is of vital importance to all nations. That is why the United States has constituted this Tribunal.

*   *   *

Before taking up these experiments one by one, let us look at them as a whole. Are they a heterogeneous list of horrors, or is there a common denominator for the whole group?

A sort of rough pattern is apparent on the face of the indictment. Experiments concerning high altitude, the effect of cold, and the potability of processed sea water have an obvious relation to aeronautical and naval combat and rescue problems. The mustard gas and phosphorous burn experiments, as well as those relating to the healing value of sulfanilamide for wounds, can be related to air raid and battlefield medical problems. It is well known that malaria, epidemic jaundice, and typhus were among the principal diseases which had to be combated by the German Armed Forces and by German authorities in occupied territories.

To some degree, the therapeutic pattern outlined above is undoubtedly a valid one, and explains why the Wehrmacht, and especially the German Air Force, participated in these experiments. Fanatically bent upon conquest, utterly ruthless as to the means or instruments to be used in achieving victory, and callous to the sufferings of people whom they regarded as inferior, the German militarists were willing to gather whatever scientific fruit these experiments might yield.

But our proof will show that a quite different and even more sinister objective runs like a red thread through these hideous researches. We will show that in some instances the true object of these experiments was not how to rescue or to cure, but how to destroy and kill. The sterilization experiments were, it is clear, purely destructive in purpose. The prisoners at Buchenwald who

were shot with poisoned bullets were not guinea pigs to test an antidote for the poison; their murderers really wanted to know how quickly the poison would kill.

*   *   *

The 20 physicians in the dock range from leaders of German scientific medicine, with excellent international reputations, down to the dregs of the German medical profession. All of them have in common a callous lack of consideration and human regard for, and an unprincipled willingness to abuse their power over the poor, unfortunate, defenseless creatures who had been deprived of their rights by a ruthless and criminal government. All of them violated the Hippocratic commandments which they had solemnly sworn to uphold and abide by, including the fundamental principles never to do harm. * * *

*   *   *

I intend to pass very briefly over matters of medical ethics, such as the conditions under which a physician may lawfully perform a medical experiment upon a person who has voluntarily subjected himself to it, or whether experiments may lawfully be performed upon criminals who have been condemned to death. This case does not present such problems. No refined questions confront us here.

None of the victims of the atrocities perpetrated by these defendants were volunteers, and this is true regardless of what these unfortunate people may have said or signed before their tortures began. Most of the victims had not been condemned to death, and those who had been were not criminals, unless it be a crime to be a Jew, or a Pole, or a gypsy, or a Russian prisoner of war.

Whatever book or treatise on medical ethics we may examine, and whatever expert on forensic medicine we may question, will say that it is a fundamental and inescapable obligation of every physician under any known system of law not to perform a dangerous experiment without the subject's consent. In the tyranny that was Nazi Germany, no one could give such a consent to the medical agents of the State; everyone lived in fear and acted under duress. I fervently hope that none of us here in the courtroom will have to suffer in silence while it is said on the part of these defendants that the wretched and helpless people whom they froze and drowned and burned and poisoned were volunteers.

* * *

This case is one of the simplest and clearest of those that will be tried in this building. It is also one of the most important. It is true that the defendants in the box were not among the highest leaders of the Third Reich. They are not the war lords who assembled and drove the German military machine, nor the industrial barons who made the parts, nor the Nazi politicians who debased and brutalized the minds of the German people. But this case, perhaps more than any other we will try, epitomizes Nazi thought and the Nazi way of life, because these defendants pursue the savage promises of Nazi thought so far. The things that these defendants did, like so many other things that happened under the Third Reich, were the result of the noxious merger of German militarism and Nazi racial objectives.

* * *

Germany surrendered herself to this foul conjunction of evil forces. The nation fell victim to the Nazi scourge because its leaders lacked the wisdom to foresee the consequences and the courage to stand firm in the face of threats. Their failure was the inevitable outcome of that sinister undercurrent of German philosophy which preaches the supreme importance of the state and the complete subordination of the individual. A nation in which the individual means nothing will find few leaders courageous and able enough to serve its best interests.

* * *

The Nazis have, to a certain extent, succeeded in convincing the peoples of the world that the Nazi system, although ruthless, was absolutely efficient; that although savage, it was completely scientific; that although entirely devoid of humanity, it was highly systematic—that "it got things done." The evidence which this Tribunal will hear will explode this myth. The Nazi methods of investigation were inefficient and unscientific, and their techniques of research were unsystematic.

These experiments revealed nothing which civilized medicine can use. It was, indeed, ascertained that phenol or gasoline injected intravenously will kill a man inexpensively and within 60 seconds. * * * There is no doubt that a number of these new methods may be useful to criminals everywhere and there is no doubt that they may be useful to a criminal state.

* * *

Apart from these deadly fruits, the experiments were not only criminal but a scientific failure. * * * The moral shortcomings of the defendants and the precipitous ease with which they decided to commit murder in quest of "scientific results," dulled also that scientific hesitancy, that thorough thinking-through, that responsible weighing of every single step which alone can insure scientifically valid results. Even if they had merely been forced to pay as little as two dollars for human experimental subjects, such as American investigators may have to pay for a cat, they might have thought twice before wasting unnecessary numbers, and thought of simpler and better ways to solve their problems. The fact that these investigators had free and unrestricted access to human beings to be experimented upon misled them to the dangerous and fallacious conclusion that the results would thus be better and more quickly obtainable than if they had gone through the labor of preparation, thinking, and meticulous preinvestigation.

* * *

In short, this conspiracy was a ghastly failure as well as a hideous crime. The creeping paralysis of Nazi superstition spread through the German medical profession and, just as it destroyed character and morals, it dulled the mind.

Guilt for the oppressions and crimes of the Third Reich is widespread, but it is the guilt of the leaders that is deepest and most culpable. Who could German medicine look to to keep the profession true to its traditions and protect it from the ravaging inroads of Nazi pseudo-science? This was the supreme responsibility of the leaders of German medicine. ＊ ＊ ＊ That is why their guilt is greater than that of any of the other defendants in the dock. They are the men who utterly failed their country and their profession, who showed neither courage nor wisdom nor the vestiges of moral character. It is their failure, together with the failure of the leaders of Germany in other walks of life, that debauched Germany and led to her defeat. It is because of them and others like them that we all live in a stricken world.

REVIEW QUESTIONS

1. Why, according to General Taylor, was it so important that the defendants be tried for their crimes?
2. Other than punishing specific guilty individuals, what purpose was being served by these trials?
3. To what extent is Taylor's statement an indictment of Nazi science in general?
4. How does Taylor's indictment of Nazi medical experiments on human subjects differ from Primo Levi's suggestion that the Lager be seen as a "gigantic biological and social experiment"?
5. Do you agree with Taylor's suggestion that it is necessary to distinguish between the "guilt of leaders" and the guilt of others, and that the former are more culpable? What potential problems might such an idea have caused in the postwar period?

TADATAKA KURIBAYASHI

FROM *A Child's Experience: My Experience of the Atomic Bomb*

On August 6, 1945, an atomic bomb was dropped on the Japanese city of Hiroshima, killing 66,000 people outright. On August 9, another bomb was dropped on Nagasaki, killing 39,000. In the following weeks and months, many more died as a result of radiation exposure and of injuries sustained at the time of the explosions.

The decision to drop the newly developed atomic bomb on Japan continues to generate heated debate among philosophers, historians, and the general public. Those who defend this particular deployment of nuclear weapons argue that it brought a more rapid end to the war, thereby saving the lives of countless American soldiers and Japanese civilians. Others counter that the Japanese government was already on the verge of surrender and that the targeting of civilian populations for military ends is, in any case, indefensible. Evaluation of this event is further complicated by the fact that the decision to use the atomic bomb was made in the context of emerging Cold War hostilities. Truman was eager to end the war with Japan and keep the Soviet Union out of the Asian theater, and he may also have wished to provide Stalin with a graphic demonstration of the enhanced military might of the United States.

During the war years, Allied propaganda supplied Americans and Europeans with highly stereotyped and racist caricatures of the Japanese. In the postwar period, this dehumanized image was challenged by movies and books documenting the tragic consequences of the use of nuclear weapons. In the 1960s, Tadataka Kuribayashi recounted his own experience of the bombing of Hiroshima. In early 1945, Kuribayashi had been attending school in Hiroshima. In April of that year, he was evacuated to the nearby peasant village of Tsutsuga, along with eighteen other children.

From *A Child's Experience: My Experience of the Atomic Bomb,* by Tadataka Kuribayashi, www.cooper.edu/humanities/core/hss3/t_kuribayashi.html [accessed 5/20/11].

The Fatal Day (6 August)

The weather was fine in the village on the morning of the 6 August, which was more than one month after the parents-visiting day. In the precincts of a shrine adjacent to the school, we boys in the 6th grade were undergoing training in the Morse signals. Cool breeze blew under ginkgo trees, and the cicadas seemed to be singing the joys of summer. Suddenly I felt something warm on my left cheek and turned back. It seemed like a strong reflection from a mirror. Then a roaring sound shook the whole village. While I was wondering what had happened, a column of clouds appeared above the mountains in the south. That was not an ordinary cloud but of a superb pink color. Gradually it assumed the shape of a mushroom and rose to the sky.

When I returned to the temple, the matron said she had felt a strong tremor even in the temple. As time passed, the fine sky gradually became dark, and in the late afternoon, a lot of cinders of paper and other things fell down from the sky. First a rumor said that an arsenal had exploded, but I later heard that a fire engine from an adjacent village had gone to Hiroshima City for rescue, but because of the strong fire, could not go beyond Yokogawa and returned. Thus, though I was small, I felt something unusual had happened. However, I didn't even imagine that the big city of Hiroshima had instantaneously become a sheet of fire.

Soon I heard that many people with severe burns had returned to the village. All of these people were from the village and were working in Hiroshima. Since then, there was no communication from the parents. After more than a week, a teacher told us that there had been an important announcement and that Japan had lost the war, but now I cannot remember sorrow or anxiety at that time. We might have been too young to have any direct emotion about the big change for the nation. Even though the war ended, we couldn't do anything. No one came to fetch us, and everyone lived anxiously from day to day.

At the beginning of September, I received a wrinkled-up postcard. Though my mother's name was mentioned, the handwriting with a pencil, some parts of which were blurred, was not my mother's. The card simply said, "I am in the reception center in Miyajima. Come here immediately." and a simple map of the place was shown. I wondered why my mother had not written it herself, but was glad to know where she was. However, the date on the card showed that many days had passed since it had been written. Next day, I, accompanied by Mr. Yamakawa, left for Miyajima. That was the 2 September.

I looked at the town of Hiroshima while I proceeded from Yokogawa to Koi. It was a field of charred ruins. The city streetcar which just began to run between Koami-cho and Koi had numerous flies on the ceiling. It was a strange sight. We took a boat from Miyajima-guchi. I saw the old big torii (Shinto shrine archway) and the beautiful Itsukushima Shrine, but they just looked a faded landscape painting to me. I wanted to go to the reception center and see the face of my mother as soon as possible. I was so eager to see her that I felt the boat was extremely slow. Soon we arrived at the center, which was a big building to the north of the shrine. When I stood at the entrance, I felt some kind of anxiety, which was an emotion difficult to express.

Attending on Mother

I looked for Mother with my teacher. It was a big room with tens of tatami mats, and the spaces between A-bomb survivors lying on futon (bed-clothes) produced a forlorn atmosphere. We took one round, but couldn't find her. While I took the second round, looking into the face of each person, I was astonished to find Mother, lying on her face and exhausted. She was a small person, but she looked even smaller. Suppressing the tremor of my voice, I called her quietly. There was no answer. I called her again. Then she noticed and slightly raised her head. She saw the teacher behind me, and took out some bills to give to him. He refused to receive them, and left there after a short while saying that he had business at the school.

When Mother told me about the death of Father, I was not so surprised. I might have been somewhat ready to hear the news. Deprived of a flush of hope, I imagined my father being burnt to death in agony. My heart was wrung. We didn't know if my elder brother, who had gone abroad to war was dead or alive. I naturally had a dark prospect about our future, but resolved firmly to continue to live with my mother no matter how poor we would be. Mother told me to take the cloth off her back. I found brown burns all over her back. Because of the burns, she couldn't lie on her back. Why does my mother, as innocent as a person could be, have to be tortured like this? I could not suppress the anger I felt. From that day, I took care of her for 2 nights and 3 days. However, the only medicine provided was mercurochrome. We were even short of cresol. When Mother arrived at the center, she was fine and even washed other people's clothes, but when I got there she couldn't even move her body.

She was engaged in building-demolition work near the Tsurumi Bridge when she was exposed to the flash. She couldn't do anything for Mrs. Takai, who was immediately burned to death in front of her, and climbed the Hijiyama Hill in a hurry with her back burned. From the hill, she looked at the city, which was a hell on earth. With other people, she was first accommodated in the reception center in Ninoshima, and moved to Miyajima. The terrible gas which entered to the depth of her body gradually damaged her bones and organs. She had completely lost her appetite.

Remorse

No one had disposed of my mother's urine, so her lower body gave out a stench. Her stool was not like that of a human being. Its color and smell were like those of internal organs that had been melted and had become a sticky liquid. I felt that the only way to give humaneness back to her was to clean the chamber pot often. Though I was eager to care for her, I became negligent once. On the second night at the center, I heard Mother's small voice calling me, but I was so sleepy that I pretended as though I didn't hear her. She called me twice, but didn't say anything more. Whenever I remember this, there is a sharp pain in my heart.

At the camp, simple food such as salty soup with one dumpling was served three times. No boiled rice was served. We were allowed to drink as many cups of soup as we liked, and I had three or four more cups of soup. My mother smiled wryly. At that time, she was too weak to speak. I saw the front of a big torii, gateway to a Shinto shrine, from the window of the lavatory. Looking at the B-29 bomber which sometimes came flying, I shouted to myself "Idiot!" It was all the resistance I, as a boy, could offer. And I sometimes cried secretly in the lavatory.

Death of Mother

At lunch-time on 4 September, the third day, Mother started to writhe in pain. Her unusual action completely upset me. All I could do was to absentmindedly look at my suffering Mother. After suffering for 30 minutes, she regained her calmness. However, it was the last calmness, the sign of the end of life. I continued calling her name, clinging to her body. Tears welled up in the eyes of my speechless mother and tears rolled down her cheek. I wondered if the tears were from the sorrow of eternal parting between mother and child or from an anxiety about my future. I shall never forget the tears of my Mother I saw on that day.

I continued crying even after a white cloth was placed over Mother's face. Some irritated people reproached me, saying "Be quiet!" Shouldn't I feel sorry for the death of my most precious mother? My tears seemed to have forgotten to stop until evening.

Return to Tsutsuga Village

There was a middle-aged man who happened to come to the camp as an attendant. He was kind enough to offer to take charge of me, probably in pity of me who had been left an orphan. I answered I would decide after consulting with my teacher at the Saihoji Temple where I had been evacuated. He decided to take me there. Wrapping my mother's personal belongings, I had rice ball made for lunch. The man and I left Miyajima Island, leaving what had to be done including the burial of my dead mother to the officials at the camp.

Arriving at the Miyajima-guchi streetcar station, I found a streetcar already there. The streetcar was about to leave the station. I had a return ticket but the man did not have one and bought his own ticket. He hurried to the platform after he had his ticket punched. I tried to follow him, but a man at the gate told me that the ticket I had was for a train, not for a streetcar and showed me the way to the railway station. I started walking toward the station at once, never thinking of anything. There is no way of knowing if the man left for Hiroshima by streetcar or returned to Miyajima. The fact that the one ticket I had served as the turning point of my fate still makes me think of the mysteriousness of fate.

The train I got on took me close to Tsutsuga Village; from Miyajima-guchi to Yokogawa and from Yokogawa to Kabe to Aki-imuro. I felt relieved when I was picked up by a truck driver at Aki-imuro who took me to Kake. An old man who shared the ride had a water bottle and gave me some water. The water tasted so good and I felt the water coursing down through my bowels. The old man was returning to Tsutsuga Village and I asked him to take me there.

It was very far from Kake to Tsutsuga. The road along a river seemed to be endless. I tottered after several persons while half sleeping late at night. When I reached Tsutsuga Village, I noticed there were no other people except the old man who had given me water. We walked for another 40 minutes and finally reached the front of the Saihoji Temple at dawn. At that time I felt undescribably happy. I expressed my thanks and said farewell to the old man. I entered the main hall of the temple. I thought I had to report to my teacher that I had returned, but I decided to do so later in the morning because I did not want to wake him up. I stole into a mosquito net, under which some children were sleeping, carrying my bedclothes and lay down. In the morning, my teacher was very surprised to learn that I had returned. I had never experienced such a long trip.

Left Alone

I resumed my life at the temple. An increasing number of children were leaving the temple together with their parent or sibling or relative who came there to take them home. However, traffic was completely paralyzed due to a heavy flood caused by an unprecedented typhoon which hit the prefecture. So, there was no choice but to walk all the way to Hiroshima.

Children who had homes to return to were happy. Most of the children had lost either a parent or other family members. It was only I that had lost both parents and had no relatives. I had nowhere to go except an orphanage where I was taken care of. In spite of sheer unhappiness, I, as a child, did not think so seriously of it.

In the end, only three children including myself stayed behind at the temple. The temple was too big for the three of us. I heard that the relatives of Yoshihiro Inoue and Yoko Minematsu would come to the temple later for some reason. Then, it was decided that children including those living in neighboring villages who had no home to return would be accommodated in a temple at Togouchi adjacent to Tsutsuga. I was hurriedly crossing a mountain pass when it began to get dark on 3 October. There was no one to be seen and everything was ominously still and silent.

I, an 11-year-old boy, only thought of running out of the weird trees, not being afraid of my future life which would bring me loneliness and starvation. Frequently frightened at the sound of my footsteps, I kept running, only wishing I could reach the village as soon as possible.

*   *   *

REVIEW QUESTIONS

1. What does this account tell you about the Japanese experience in the Second World War?
2. To what extent might the testimony of survivors like Kuribayashi influence historical interpretations of the use of atomic weapons?
3. How should historians approach the analysis of events heavily charged with moral significance, such as the Holocaust and the deployment of nuclear weapons?
4. How do the bombings of Hiroshima and Nagasaki differ from the Holocaust?

FROM Charter of the United Nations

Before the atomic bomb brought the war in the Pacific to a dramatic close, a new international peacekeeping organization was already being organized to replace the League of Nations. On June 26, 1945, the United Nations was established by a formal charter drawn up at an international congress held in San Francisco. Vested with the authority to maintain and deploy peacekeeping forces, the United Nations was intended to be a more effective agency for world peace than its predecessor had been. And, although the United Nations was not able to solve the many problems generated by the Cold War, it nevertheless served as an important arena for the negotiation of conflicts between member nations. The preamble and first chapter of the United Nations Charter set out the primary goals of the organization.

From Charter of the United Nations, United Nations Web page, www.un.org/ [accessed 5/20/11].

Preamble

WE THE PEOPLES OF THE UNITED NATIONS DETERMINED

to save succeeding generations from the scourge of war, which twice in our lifetime has brought untold sorrow to mankind, and

to reaffirm faith in fundamental human rights, in the dignity and worth of the human person, in the equal rights of men and women and of nations large and small, and

to establish conditions under which justice and respect for the obligations arising from treaties and other sources of international law can be maintained, and

to promote social progress and better standards of life in larger freedom,

AND FOR THESE ENDS

to practice tolerance and live together in peace with one another as good neighbours, and

to unite our strength to maintain international peace and security, and

to ensure, by the acceptance of principles and the institution of methods, that armed force shall not be used, save in the common interest, and

to employ international machinery for the promotion of the economic and social advancement of all peoples,

HAVE RESOLVED TO COMBINE OUR EFFORTS TO ACCOMPLISH THESE AIMS

Accordingly, our respective Governments, through representatives assembled in the city of San Francisco, who have exhibited their full powers found to be in good and due form, have agreed to the present Charter of the United Nations and do hereby establish an international organization to be known as the United Nations.

ARTICLE 1

The Purposes of the United Nations are:

1. To maintain international peace and security, and to that end: to take effective collective measures for the prevention and removal of threats to the peace, and for the suppression of acts of aggression or other breaches of the peace, and to bring about by peaceful means, and in conformity with the principles of justice and international law, adjustment or settlement of international disputes or situations which might lead to a breach of the peace;

2. To develop friendly relations among nations based on respect for the principle of equal rights and self-determination of peoples, and to take other appropriate measures to strengthen universal peace;

3. To achieve international co-operation in solving international problems of an economic, social, cul-

tural, or humanitarian character, and in promoting and encouraging respect for human rights and for fundamental freedoms for all without distinction as to race, sex, language, or religion; and

4. To be a centre for harmonizing the actions of nations in the attainment of these common ends.

ARTICLE 2

The Organization and its Members, in pursuit of the Purposes stated in Article 1, shall act in accordance with the following Principles.

1. The Organization is based on the principle of the sovereign equality of all its Members.

2. All Members, in order to ensure to all of them the rights and benefits resulting from membership, shall fulfill in good faith the obligations assumed by them in accordance with the present Charter.

3. All Members shall settle their international disputes by peaceful means in such a manner that international peace and security, and justice, are not endangered.

4. All Members shall refrain in their international relations from the threat or use of force against the territorial integrity or political independence of any state, or in any other manner inconsistent with the Purposes of the United Nations.

*   *   *

REVIEW QUESTIONS

1. How does this preamble compare with the Covenant of the League of Nations from the Versailles Treaty (pp. 517–523)?

2. To what extent was the United Nations statement of goals formulated as a response to the Second World War experience?

Aerial Bombardment

Aerial bombardment of cities and their civilian populations began in the First World War, but in the Second World War it became a routine strategy of every belligerent power. Beginning with the massive bombings of Polish towns and cities in 1939 and the destruction of Rotterdam and Coventry in 1940 during the German invasion of the Netherlands and the Battle of Britain, the practice soon became general. In May 1942, the British Royal Air Force launched a raid on Cologne that employed over 1,000 aircraft, dropping more than 2,000 tons of explosives on the city. Before the war ended similar attacks were carried out in Essen, Bremen, Hamburg, Kassel, Darmstadt, Pforzheim, Swinemunde, and Dresden. In many of these attacks the casualties were counted in the tens of thousands. The most extreme example in Europe may have been the July 1943 bombing of Hamburg, which had already been a frequent target of Allied bombing since 1940. During eight days and seven nights of repeated bombing raids a firestorm was created that generated winds of up to 150 mph and temperatures reaching 1,500 degrees Fahrenheit. Some estimates put the number of casualties as high as 45,000, most of whom died from lack of oxygen as the air was sucked out of their underground shelters. Eight square miles of the city were completely incinerated. Even this event was overshadowed by the destruction of central Tokyo by U.S. planes dropping conventional incendiary bombs in February 1945, when over 100,000 people were killed. The war in the Pacific ended with Japan's surrender soon after U.S. president Harry Truman ordered nuclear bombs dropped on Hiroshima and Nagasaki on August 6 and 9, 1945. Over 100,000 were killed outright by the blasts at Hiroshima and Nagasaki, with tens of thousands more dying in subsequent months of burns and radiation exposure. The targeting of civilian populations on such a massive scale was the culmination of the doctrine of total war, *in which the entire capacities of a nation were mobilized at times of conflict, a mobilization that effectively dismantled older distinctions between the front line and nonmilitarized zones.*

WARSAW, 1939

ST. PAUL'S CATHEDRAL, LONDON, January 23, 1941

THE BOMBING OF DRESDEN (1945)   WALTER HAHN

COLOGNE, GERMANY, March 7, 1945

HAMBURG, GERMANY, August 1943

ROUEN, FRANCE, c. May 30, 1945

NAGASAKI, JAPAN, August 1945

HIROSHIMA, JAPAN, 1945

585

27 ⚬ THE COLD WAR WORLD: GLOBAL POLITICS, ECONOMIC RECOVERY, AND CULTURAL CHANGE

At the beginning of the twentieth century, the European great powers dominated the world, both materially and—at least in the opinion of Europeans—culturally. Even after the First World War, European power seemed only slightly diminished, especially when the newest contender for world power status, the United States, chose to retreat again into isolationism after the war.

After the Second World War, the world was a dramatically different place. A second great cataclysm had left much of Europe in ruins, and the former great powers found themselves confronted with the enormous task of reconstructing what they themselves had destroyed. The new bipolar balance of world power, pitting the United States against the Soviet Union, decreased the global power and prestige of individual European nations, drawing them into the orbits of the two competing superpowers. Europe was divided in two by an "Iron Curtain," and the cultures, economies, and political systems of the two Europes were deeply marked by the new realities of the Cold War.

European dominance had ended, but the Western European nations soon rallied, achieving general levels of prosperity, technological sophistication, and democratic participation never before experienced in their histories. American economic aid reinvigorated Western European economies, greatly increasing the material well-being of ordinary people. Cradle-to-grave social welfare programs provided education, medical care, and guarantees that no citizen would be deprived of the minimum necessities of life. The appurtenances of consumer culture—radios, cars, televisions, dishwashers, seaside vacations—became available to the majority of Western Europeans.

The economic "miracle" did not come to Eastern Europe, always under-developed by Western standards. Eastern Europe's poverty and technological backwardness were only reinforced by the domination of the powerful Soviet Union. Communist regimes throughout Eastern Europe retained their hold on power not through popular support but through the threat of Soviet invasion. Communist heads of state were forced to follow the dictates of economic and military planners in Moscow, often to the detriment of their own citizens. The death of Stalin in 1953 brought some easing of repression, and standards of living did improve, if more gradually and less opulently than in the West. But Stalin's successors continued to rule Eastern Europe with a firm hand, stifling dissent and emphasizing heavy industrial and military production at the expense of consumer goods. When the Soviet bloc collapsed in the late 1980s, bringing a surprisingly sudden end to the Cold War, Eastern Europe remained burdened with the bitter legacy of economic underdevelopment and political immaturity.

In both the East and the West, postwar culture was unsettled and complex. The war had demonstrated the moral bankruptcy of fascism (even if nostalgia for militarism, nationalism, and racial cleansing lingered in the hearts of many), but no other alternative ideologies won unqualified support. For many, the simple joys of life were enough. After the hardships of the war, consumerism and leisure culture offered a welcome respite from ideology. On the other hand, intellectuals struggled to come to terms with the implications of wartime genocide, economic and political globalization, and the Americanization of European culture. Although the Cold War left many feeling powerless in the face of impersonal forces such as superpower politics and the threat of nuclear annihilation, others drew renewed hope from the anticolonial struggles of Third World peoples and the protests of civil rights activists around the world.

WINSTON CHURCHILL

FROM "The Sinews of Peace"

During the Second World War, long-standing tensions between the Soviet Union and the other Allied states were set aside in favor of a unified war effort. However, even before the war had ended, mutual suspicions were revived, especially as Allied leaders began to negotiate postwar territorial settlements. The United States and Great Britain promoted the creation of capitalist democracies throughout Europe, whereas Stalin sought to establish communist satellite states in the East.

One of the defining moments of the emerging Cold War came on March 5, 1946, when Winston Churchill (1874–1965), who had been voted out of office as prime minister by war-weary Britons that year, gave a speech at Westminster College in Fulton, Missouri, attended by the U.S. president Harry S Truman. In this speech, entitled "The Sinews of Peace," Churchill called on Americans and Western Europeans to maintain a unified front against the Soviet threat.

From *The Sinews of Peace,* vol. 7, edited by R. R. James (New York: Chelsea House, 1946).

*   *   *

A shadow has fallen upon the scenes so lately lighted by the Allied victory. Nobody knows what Soviet Russia and its Communist international organisation intends to do in the immediate future, or what are the limits, if any, to their expansive and proselytising tendencies. I have a strong admiration and regard for the valiant Russian people and for my wartime comrade, Marshal Stalin. There is deep sympathy and goodwill in Britain—and I doubt not here also—towards the peoples of all the Russias and a resolve to persevere through many differences and rebuffs in establishing lasting friendships. We understand the Russian need to be secure on her western frontiers by the removal of all possibility of German aggression. We welcome Russia to her rightful place among the leading nations of the world. We welcome her flag upon the seas. Above all, we welcome constant, frequent and growing contacts between the Russian people and our own people on both sides of the Atlantic. It is my duty however, for I am sure you would wish me to state the facts as I see them to you, to place before you certain facts about the present position in Europe.

From Stettin in the Baltic to Trieste in the Adriatic, an iron curtain has descended across the Continent. Behind that line lie all the capitals of the ancient states of Central and Eastern Europe. Warsaw, Berlin, Prague, Vienna, Budapest, Belgrade, Bucharest and Sofia, all these famous cities and the populations around them lie in what I must call the Soviet sphere, and all are subject in one form or another, not only to Soviet influence but to a very high and, in many cases, increasing measure of control from Moscow. Athens alone—Greece with its immortal glories—is free to decide its future at an election under British, American and French observation. The Russian-dominated Polish Government has been encouraged to make enormous and wrongful inroads upon Germany, and mass expulsions of millions of Germans on a scale grievous and undreamed-of are now taking place. The Communist parties, which were very small in all these Eastern States of Europe, have been raised to preeminence and power far beyond their numbers and are seeking everywhere to obtain totalitarian control. Police governments are prevailing in nearly every case, and so far, except in Czechoslovakia, there is no true democracy.

*   *   *

The safety of the world requires a new unity in Europe, from which no nation should be permanently outcast. It is from the quarrels of the strong parent races in Europe that the world wars we have witnessed, or which occurred in former times, have sprung. Twice in our own lifetime we have seen the United States, against their wishes and their traditions, against arguments, the force of which it is impossible not to comprehend, drawn by irresistible forces, into these wars in time to secure the victory of the good cause, but only after frightful slaughter and devastation had occurred. Twice the United States has had to send several millions of its young men across the Atlantic to find the war; but now war can find any nation, wherever it may dwell between dusk and dawn. Surely we should work with conscious purpose for a grand pacification of

Europe, within the structure of the United Nations and in accordance with its Charter. That I feel is an open cause of policy of very great importance.

*   *   *

From what I have seen of our Russian friends and Allies during the war, I am convinced that there is nothing they admire so much as strength, and there is nothing for which they have less respect than for weakness, especially military weakness. For that reason the old doctrine of a balance of power is unsound. We cannot afford, if we can help it, to work on narrow margins, offering temptations to a trial of strength. If the Western Democracies stand together in strict adherence to the principles of the United Nations Charter, their influence for furthering those principles will be immense and no one is likely to molest them. If

however they become divided or falter in their duty and if these all-important years are allowed to slip away then indeed catastrophe may overwhelm us all.

*   *   *

REVIEW QUESTIONS

1. What was the Iron Curtain? Where was it?
2. What policies was Churchill promoting in this speech?
3. What specific response do you think he hoped to elicit from his U.S. audience?
4. To what extent were his remarks shaped by the existence of nuclear weapons? By the U.S. tradition of isolationism?

NIKITA KHRUSHCHEV

FROM "On the Cult of Personality and Its Consequences"

Stalin's death in 1953 was followed by an intense struggle for power within the Soviet leadership. At midnight on the night of February 25, 1956, the victor of this contest, first secretary Nikita Khrushchev (1894–1971), gave a "secret speech" to the twentieth congress of the Communist Party. In blunt language, Khrushchev denounced Stalin's authoritarianism as a deviation from the Marxist-Leninist principles of the Bolshevik revolution. Later that year, Khrushchev reestablished friendly relations with Yugoslavia's independent communist leader, Josip Broz Tito, demonstrating a new willingness on the part of the Soviet state to tolerate "different roads to Socialism." When he became premier in 1958, Khrushchev rejected the inevitability of war with noncommunist states, cultivating a foreign policy based on "peaceful coexistence."

As a loyal communist, Khrushchev remained committed to single-party rule, the planned economy, and state censorship, but his de-Stalinization campaign produced a notable thaw within the Soviet Union. Many political prisoners were released, and many of those who had died or been imprisoned during Stalin's reign of terror were exonerated of any crimes. Greater intellectual freedom was granted to artists, while ordinary Soviet citizens, who had long suffered as a result of Stalin's single-minded focus on the development of heavy industry, benefited from a redirection of the economy toward greater production of consumer goods.

From *The Stalin Dictatorship: Khrushchev's "Secret Speech" and Other Documents*, edited by T. H. Rigby (Sydney: Sydney University Press, 1968), pp. 23–25, 29–32, 36–37, 52–53, 58–62, 65, 84.

Comrades! In the report of the Central Committee of the party at the 20th Congress, in a number of speeches by delegates to the Congress, as well as before this during plenary sessions of the CPSU Central Committee, quite a lot has been said about the cult of the individual and about its harmful consequences.

After Stalin's death the Central Committee of the party began to implement a policy of explaining concisely and consistently that it is impermissible and foreign to the spirit of Marxism-Leninism to elevate one person, to transform him into a superman possessing supernatural characteristics akin to those of a god. Such a man supposedly knows everything, sees everything, thinks for everyone, can do anything, and is infallible in his behaviour.

This kind of belief about a man, namely about Stalin, was cultivated among us for many years.

*   *   *

The great modesty of the genius of the revolution, Vladimir Ilyich Lenin, is known. Lenin always stressed the role of the people as the creator of history, the directing and organizational role of the party as a living and creative organism, and also the role of the Central Committee.

Marxism does not negate the role of the leaders of the workers' class in directing the revolutionary liberation movement.

While ascribing great importance to the role of the leaders and organizers of the masses, Lenin at the same time mercilessly stigmatized every manifestation of the cult of the individual, inexorably combated views which are foreign to Marxism, about the "hero" and the "crowd," and countered all efforts to oppose the "hero" to the masses and to the people.

*   *   *

In addition to the great accomplishments of V. I. Lenin for the victory of the working class and of the working peasants, for the victory of our party and for the application of the ideas of scientific communism to life, his acute mind expressed itself also, in the fact that he detected in Stalin in time those negative characteristics which resulted later in grave consequences.

*   *   *

Stalin acted not through persuasion, explanation, and patient co-operation with people, but by imposing his concepts and demanding absolute submission to his opinion. Whoever opposed this concept or tried to prove his viewpoint, and the correctness of his position, was doomed to removal from the leading collective and to subsequent moral and physical annihilation. This was especially true during the period following the 17th Party Congress [in 1934], when many prominent party leaders and rank-and-file party workers, honest and dedicated to the cause of communism, fell victim to Stalin's despotism.

*   *   *

It was precisely during this period (1935–1937–1938) that the practice of mass repression through the government apparatus was born, first against the enemies of Leninism—Trotskyites, Zinovievites, Bukharinites, long since politically defeated by the party, and subsequently also against many honest communists, against those party cadres who had borne the heavy load of the Civil War and the first and most difficult years of industrialization and collectivization, who actively fought against the Trotskyites and the rightists for the Leninist party line.

Stalin originated the concept "enemy of the people." This term automatically rendered it unnecessary that the ideological errors of a man or men engaged in a controversy be proven; this term made possible the employment of the most cruel repression, violating all norms of revolutionary legality, against anyone who in any way disagreed with Stalin, against those who were only suspected of hostile intent, against those who had bad reputations. This concept, "enemy of the people," actually eliminated the possibility of any kind of ideological struggle or the making of one's views known on this or that issue, even those of a practical character. In the main, and in actuality, the only proof of guilt used, against all norms of current legal science, was the "confession" of the accused himself; and, as subsequent probing proved, "confessions" were acquired through physical pressures against the accused.

*   *   *

[Stalin] discarded the Leninist method of convincing and educating; he abandoned the method of ideological struggle for that of administrative violence, mass repressions, and terror. He acted on an increasingly larger scale and more stubbornly through punitive organs, at the same time often violating all existing norms of morality and of Soviet laws.

Arbitrary behavior by one person encouraged and permitted arbitrariness in others. Mass arrests and deportations of many thousands of people, execution without trial and without normal investigation created conditions of insecurity, fear and even desperation.

This, of course, did not contribute toward unity of the party ranks and of all strata of working people, but on the contrary brought about the annihilation and expulsion from the party of workers who were loyal but inconvenient to Stalin.

*   *   *

Were our party's sacred Leninist principles observed after the death of Vladimir Ilyich?

Whereas during the first few years after Lenin's death party congresses and Central Committee plenums took place more or less regularly, later, when Stalin began increasingly to abuse his power, these principles were crudely violated. This was especially evident during the last 15 years of his life. Was it a normal situation when over 13 years elapsed between the 18th and 19th Party Congresses, years during which our party and our country experienced so many important events? These events demanded categorically that the party pass resolutions pertaining to the country's defense during the Patriotic War and to peacetime construction after the war. Even after the end of the war a congress was not convened for over 7 years.

*   *   *

In practice Stalin ignored the norms of party life and trampled on the Leninist principle of collective party leadership.

Stalin's arbitrariness *vis-à-vis* the party and its Central Committee became fully evident after the 17th Party Congress which took place in 1934.

*   *   *

It has been established that of the 139 members and candidates of the Party's Central Committee who were elected at the 17th Congress, 98 persons, i.e. 70 percent, were arrested and shot (mostly in 1937–1938). (*Indignation in the hall.*)

*   *   *

The power accumulated in the hands of one person, Stalin, led to serious consequences during the Great Patriotic War.

When we look at many of our novels, films and historical "scientific studies," the role of Stalin in the Patriotic War appears to be entirely improbable. Stalin had foreseen everything. The Soviet Army, on the basis of a strategic plan prepared by Stalin long before, used the tactics of so-called "active defense," i.e., tactics which, as we know, allowed the Germans to come up to Moscow and Stalingrad. Using such tactics the Soviet Army, supposedly thanks only to Stalin's genius, turned to the offensive and subdued the enemy. The epic victory gained through the armed might of the Land of the Soviets, through our heroic people is ascribed in this type of novel, film and "scientific study" as being completely due to the strategic genius of Stalin.

*   *   *

During the war and after the war Stalin put forward the thesis that the tragedy which our nation experienced in the first part of the war was the result of the "unexpected" attack of the Germans against the Soviet Union. But, Comrades, this is completely untrue. As soon as Hitler came to power in Germany he assigned himself the task of liquidating communism. The fascists were saying this openly; they did not hide their plans. In order to attain this aggressive end all sorts of pacts and blocs were created, such as the famous Berlin-Rome-Tokyo axis. Many facts from the pre-war period clearly showed that Hitler was going all out to begin a war against the Soviet state and that he had concentrated large armed units, together with armored units, near the Soviet borders.

Documents which have now been published show that by April 3, 1941, Churchill, through his ambassador to the U.S.S.R., Cripps, personally warned Stalin that the Germans had begun regrouping their armed units with the intent of attacking the Soviet Union. It is self-evident that Churchill did not do this at all because of his friendly feeling toward the Soviet nation. He had in this his own imperialistic goals—to bring Germany and the U.S.S.R. into a bloody war and thereby to strengthen the position of the British Empire. Just the same, Churchill affirmed in his writings that he sought to "warn Stalin and call his attention to the danger which threatened him." Churchill stressed this repeatedly in his dispatches of April 18 and in the following days. However, Stalin took no heed of these warnings. What is more, Stalin ordered that no credence be given to information of this sort, in order not to provoke the initiation of military operations.

*   *   *

When there developed an exceptionally serious situation for our army in 1942 in the Kharkov region, we correctly decided to drop an operation whose objective had been to encircle Kharkov, because the real situation at that time would have threatened our army with fatal consequences if this operation had been proceeded with.

We communicated this to Stalin, stating that the situation demanded changes in operational plans in order to prevent the enemy from liquidating a sizable concentration of our army.

Contrary to common sense, Stalin rejected our suggestion and issued the order to continue the operation aimed at the encirclement of Kharkov, despite the fact that at this time many army concentrations were themselves actually threatened with encirclement and liquidation.

*   *   *

And what was the result of this? The worst that we had expected. The Germans surrounded our army concentrations and consequently we lost hundreds of thousands of our soldiers. This is Stalin's military "genius"; this what it cost us. (*Movement in the hall.*)

*   *   *

In the same vein, let us take, for instance, our historical and military films and some works of literature; they make us feel sick. Their true objective is the propagation of the theme of praising Stalin as a military genius. Let us recall the film, "The Fall of Berlin." Here only Stalin acts; he issues orders in the hall in which there are many empty chairs and only one man approaches him and reports something to him—that is Poskrebyshev, his loyal shieldbearer. (*Laughter in the hall.*)

And where is the military command? Where is the Political Bureau? Where is the Government? What are they doing and with what are they engaged? There is nothing about them in the film. Stalin acts for everybody; he does not reckon with anyone, he asks no one for advice. Everything is shown to the nation in this false light. Why? In order to surround Stalin with glory, contrary to the facts and contrary to historical truth.

*   *   *

Not Stalin, but the party as a whole, the Soviet Government, our heroic army, its talented leaders and brave soldiers, the whole Soviet nation—these are the ones who assured the victory in the Great Patriotic War. (*Tempestuous and prolonged applause.*)

*   *   *

Comrades, let us reach for some other facts. The Soviet Union is justly considered as a model of a multi-national state because we have in practice assured the equality and friendship of all nations which live in our great fatherland.

All the more monstrous are the acts whose initiator was Stalin and which represent crude violations of the basic Leninist principles of the nationality policy of the Soviet state. We refer to the mass deportations from their native places of whole nations, together with all communists and komsomol members without any exception; this deportation action was not dictated by any military considerations.

Thus, as early as the end of 1943, when there occurred a permanent breakthrough at the fronts of the Great Patriotic War benefiting the Soviet Union, a decision was taken and carried out concerning the deportation of all the Karachai from the lands on which they lived. In the same period, at the end of December 1943, the same lot befell the whole population of the Kalmyk Autonomous Republic. In March 1944 all the Chechen and Ingush peoples were deported and the Chechen-Ingush Autonomous Republic was liquidated. In April 1944, all Balkars were deported to faraway places from the territory of the Kabardino-Balkar Autonomous Republic and the Republic itself was renamed the Karbardin Autonomous Republic. The Ukrainians avoided meeting this fate only because there were too many of them and there was no place to which to deport them. Otherwise, he would have deported them also. (*Laughter and animation in the hall.*)

*   *   *

The willfulness of Stalin showed itself not only in decisions concerning the internal life of the country but also in the international relations of the Soviet Union.

The July plenary session of the Central Committee studied in detail the reasons for the development of conflict with Yugoslavia. It was a shameful role which Stalin played here. The "Yugoslav affair" contained no problems which could not have been solved through party discussions among comrades. There was no significant basis for the development of this "affair"; it was completely possible to have prevented the rupture of relations with that country. This does not mean, however, that the Yugoslav leaders did not make mistakes or did not have shortcomings. But these mistakes and shortcomings were magnified in a monstrous manner by Stalin, which resulted in a break of relations with a friendly country.

*   *   *

Comrades! The 20th Congress of the Communist Party of the Soviet Union has manifested with a new strength the unshakable unity of our party, its cohesiveness around the Central Committee, its resolute will to accomplish the great task of building communism. (*Tumultuous applause.*) And the fact that we present in all their ramifications the basic problems of overcoming the cult of the individual which is alien to Marxism-Leninism, as well as the problem of liquidating its burdensome consequences, is evidence of the great moral and political strength of our party. (*Prolonged applause.*)

We are absolutely certain that our party, armed with the historical resolutions of the 20th Congress, will lead the Soviet people along the Leninist path to new successes, to new victories. (*Tumultuous, prolonged applause.*)

Long live the victorious banner of our party—Leninism! (*Tumultuous, prolonged applause ending in ovation. All rise.*)

REVIEW QUESTIONS

1. What was the cult of personality?
2. In what sense was Stalin's style of rule a violation of Marxist-Leninist theory, according to Khrushchev?
3. What specific errors is Stalin accused of in this speech?
4. What do these accusations tell you about Khrushchev's intentions as the new leader of the Soviet Union?

French Students and Workers Unite in Protest

In the Soviet bloc, the brief easing in state repression initiated by Khrushchev came to an end with his abrupt fall from power in 1964. Under Leonid Brezhnev, the Soviet political leadership returned to more traditional policies, although Stalinism was not revived. When the Czechoslovakian leadership sought to loosen its ties to the Soviet Union in 1968, tanks and Soviet troops soon put an end to the Prague Spring.

During this same period, the centrist governments and white-collar bureaucrats of Western Europe cooperated to produce unprecedentedly prosperous economies. Yet affluence and political stability generated their own frustrations: young people, especially, rejected the stodgy conformity of their elders, calling for a radical recasting of social, political, and economic relations. De-Stalinization in the East had stimulated the revival of Socialist and Communist parties in the West, and this inspired a new generation of radical activists operating outside of the established left-wing parties. In 1968, French students in Paris followed the lead of their Czechoslovakian counterparts, engaging in violent protests against the stifling traditionalism of the universities and against the conservatism of Charles de Gaulle's government. They were eventually joined by as many as 10 million striking workers, bringing France to a virtual standstill in mid-1968.

From *Writing on the Wall, France 1968: A Documentary Anthology,* by Vladimir Fisera (New York: St. Martin's Press, 1978), pp. 133–34, 138–39.

Your Struggle Is Our Struggle!

We are occupying the faculties, you are occupying the factories. Aren't we fighting for the same thing? Higher education only contains 10 per cent workers' children. Are we fighting so that there will be more of them, for a democratic university reform? That would be a good thing, but it's not the most important. These workers' children would just become like other students. We are not aiming for a worker's son to be a manager. We want to wipe out segregation between workers and management.

There are students who are unable to find jobs on leaving university. Are we fighting so that they'll find jobs, for a decent graduate employment policy? It would be a good thing, but it is not vital. Psychology or sociology graduates will become the selectors, the planners and psychotechnicians who will try to organise your working conditions; mathematics graduates will become engineers, perfecting maximum-productivity machines to make your life even more unbearable. Why are we, students who are products of a middle-class life, criticising capitalist society? The son of a worker who becomes a student leaves his own class. For the son of a middle-class family, it could be his opportunity to see his class in its true light, to question the role he is destined for in society and the organisation of our society. We refuse to become scholars who are out of touch with real life. We refuse to be used for the benefit of the ruling class. We want to destroy the separation that exists between those who organise and think and those who execute their decisions. We want to form a classless society; your cause is the same as ours.

You are asking for a minimum wage of 1,000 francs in the Paris area, retirement at sixty, a 40-hour week for 48 hours' pay.

STUDENT UPRISING IN PARIS (MAY 1968)

In May 1968, sparked by the government's announcement that it was closing a French university in Nanterre, students at the Sorbonne University in Paris protested with street demonstrations, which quickly broadened into political protests against the French state. The protests escalated into a national crisis after thousands of workers went on strike to support the students' grievances. Although government officials sought to deny the magnitude and significance of the May protests, such photos as this one were instrumental in eliciting popular support by communicating the revolutionary mood of Paris to a national audience. With the student protests following revolts in communist Europe and colonial Africa in the 1950s and 1960s, why did this image of Paris shock the French nation in 1968?

These are long-standing and just demands: nevertheless, they seem to be out of context with our aims. Yet you have gone on to occupy factories, take your managers as hostages, strike without warning. These forms of struggle have been made possible by perseverence and lengthy action in various enterprises, and because of the recent student battles.

These struggles are even more radical than our official aims, because they go further than simply seeking improvements for the worker within the capitalist system, they imply the destruction of the system. They are political in the true sense of the word: you are fighting not to change the Prime Minister, but so that your boss no longer retains his power in business or society. The form that your struggle has taken offers us students the model for true socialist activity: the appropriation of the means of production and of the decision-making power by the workers.

Our struggles converge. We must destroy everything that seeks to alienate us (everyday habits, the press, etc.). We must combine our occupations in the faculties and factories.

Long live the unification of our struggles!

The Workers' Red Flag Is Flying over Renault: Down with the Anti-Popular Gaullist Régime

For ten years the working class has gradually fought to gain unity in each factory; to defend in each company its working conditions, which are systematically attacked by the big capitalists. Workers' fights have succeeded in containing the bosses' offensive, but the division of the workers' forces and the policy of class collaboration which has become the rule *even at the level of the confederate leadership of the CGT*[1] have prevented the mass struggles from bringing about the downfall of the anti-popular régime of unemployment and poverty.

For a month now the progressive students who reject the bourgeois university, who want to be on the side of the people struggling against the bosses' régime, have put their full strength into the battle.

By their tenacity, their resolution, their desire to link their struggle with that of the working class, which is the main force in the struggle against the big capitalist bosses and the government, the mass of progressive students has been able to strike a resounding blow against Gaullism. The workers have understood this: the progressive current in the student movement reflects the desire of the people to fight, its desire to get rid of Gaullism. The progressive students' determination has reminded the workers that only forceful action pays off. The class-collaborating unions which have encouraged the workers to demonstrate peacefully and with dignity only in order to receive alms, the unions which have sabotaged the mass struggles at Caen, at La Rhodia in Lyon, at Schwarz-Haumont, at Alluvac, at Alès in the ceramics industry, at Dassault, at Renault, *can today no longer resist the drive of the working masses.*

The battle flag has passed into the hands of the proletariat. The leaders of the CGT have first of all attacked the students' progressive movement in a disgusting way, using the same phrases as the government is using. Then, when the workers demonstrated their desire to intervene in force to take the lead in the battle against capitalism and its régime, the CGT and PCF[2] leaderships called for a strike with petty-bourgeois, academic slogans. But the workers understood, and put all their strength into the battle.

The government wishes to quell the revolt; Pompidou has just said so. The government is panic-stricken. The repression of the workers and the progressive students, the repression of the real communists who are fighting for popular victory, will change nothing. People's hatred of the class enemy will increase tenfold. A tremendous force is rising today. *The people will win!*

---

[1] *Confédération Générale du Travail* (General Confederation of Labor), a communist labor union.

[2] *Parti Communiste Français* ("French Communist Party").

Against unemployment, starvation wages, fiend-ish work rates. Against police and bosses' repression. Freedom for the people!

REVIEW QUESTIONS

1. In what sense was the workers' struggle also the students' struggle?

2. What specific reforms were students and work-ers seeking?
3. What were their broader goals?
4. Why did radical workers at Renault reject the leadership of the General Confederation of Labor and the French Communist Party?
5. Why did they seek to ally their movement with that of the student protesters?

VÁCLAV HAVEL

FROM *The Power of the Powerless*

Václav Havel (born 1936), a playwright and poet, was one of the participants in a political dissident movement in Czechoslovakia that became known as Charter 77. The Charter, issued in Prague on New Year's Day in 1977, was a declaration and defense of human and civil rights in Czechoslovakia, and a challenge to the Czech government to lift its censorship and persecution of those who disagreed with the regime. For his Charter activities, Havel was jailed for four months in 1977 and again from 1979 to 1983, when he was released because of very poor health. He remained under close surveillance by the Czech security police until the fall of communism in Eastern Europe. In November 1989, Havel emerged as a leader of a new group that had organized to push for democratic reforms, the Civic Forum. When this group succeeded in brokering the transfer of power from the discredited communist regime in Czechoslovakia's "Velvet Revolution," Havel was named interim president in December 1989. In July 1990 he was reelected president in a democratic election. He resigned from the presidency in protest when the Czechoslovakian union was dissolved in 1992, but in 1993, Havel was reelected president of the Czech Republic, an office he held until February 2003.

Along with fellow Charter activists Rudolf Battek, Václav Benda, and Václav Cerny, Havel succeeded in giving a theoretical foundation to movements of dissent in Eastern Europe in the 1970s and 1980s. Central to the Charter's work of dissent was its defense of a free arena for public expression and political association. Their success can be gauged by the important echoes of Charter 77 that can be found, for example, in the work of Solidarity activists in Poland, who readily acknowledged the influence of the Czech dissidents. In his famous essay The Power of the Powerless, *Havel explores the function of ideology in daily life in Czechoslovakia and looks for ways to challenge its embrace.*

From *The Power of the Powerless*, by Václav Havel et al. (Armonk, N.Y.: Palach Press, 1985), pp. 27–29, 35–37, 39, 78–79.

The manager of a fruit and vegetable shop places in his window, among the onions and carrots, the slogan: "Workers of the World, Unite!" Why does he do it? What is he trying to communicate to the world? Is his enthusiasm so great that he feels an irrepressible impulse to acquaint the public with his ideals? Has he really given more than a moment's thought to how such a unification might occur and what it would mean?

I think it can safely be assumed that the overwhelming majority of shopkeepers never think about the slogans they put in their windows, nor do they use them to express their real opinions. That poster was delivered to our greengrocer from the enterprise headquarters along with the onions and carrots. He put them all into the window simply because it has been done that way for years, because everyone does it, and because that is the way it has to be. If he were to refuse, there could be trouble. He could be reproached for not having the proper "decoration" in his window; someone might even accuse him of disloyalty. He does it because these things must be done if one is to get along in life. It is one of the thousands of details that guarantee him a relatively tranquil life "in harmony with society," as they say.

Obviously the greengrocer is indifferent to the semantic content of the slogan on exhibit; he does not put the slogan in his window from any personal desire to acquaint the public with the ideal it expresses. This, of course, does not mean that his action has no motive or significance at all, or that the slogan communicates a subliminal but very definite message. Verbally, it might be expressed this way: "I, the greengrocer XY, live here and I know what I must do. I behave in the manner expected of me. I can be depended upon and am beyond reproach. I am obedient and therefore I have the right to be left in peace." This message, of course, has an addressee: it is directed above, to the greengrocer's superior, and at the same time it is a shield that protects the greengrocer from potential informers. The slogan's real meaning, therefore, is rooted firmly in the greengrocer's existence. It reflects his vital interests. But what are those vital interests?

Let us take note: if the greengrocer had been instructed to display the slogan, "I am afraid and therefore unquestioningly obedient," he would not be nearly as indifferent to its semantics, even though the statement would reflect the truth. The greengrocer would be embarrassed and ashamed to put such an unequivocal statement of his own degradation in the shop window, and quite naturally so, for he is a human being and thus has a sense of his own dignity. To overcome this complication, his expression of loyalty must take the form of a sign which, at least on its textual surface, indicates a level of disinterested conviction. It must allow the greengrocer to say "What's wrong with the workers of the world uniting?" Thus the sign helps the greengrocer to conceal from himself the low foundations of his obedience, at the same time concealing the low foundations of power. It hides them behind the façade of something high. And that something is *ideology.*

Ideology is a specious way of relating to the world. It offers human beings the illusion of an identity, of dignity, and of morality while making it easier for them to *part* with them. As the repository of something "supra-personal" and objective, it enables people to deceive their conscience and conceal their true position and their inglorious *modus vivendi*, both from the world and from themselves. It is a very pragmatic, but at the same time an apparently dignified, way of legitimizing what is above, below, and on either side. It is directed towards people and towards God. It is a veil behind which human beings can hide their own "fallen existence," their trivialization, and their adaptation to the status quo. It is an excuse that everyone can use, from the greengrocer, who conceals his fear of losing his job behind an alleged interest in the unification of the workers of the world, to the highest functionary, whose interest in staying in power can be cloaked in phrases about service to the working class. The primary excusatory function of ideology, therefore, is to provide people, both as victims and pillars of the post-totalitarian system, with the illusion that the system is in harmony with the human order and the order of the universe.

*   *   *

Why in fact did our greengrocer have to put his loyalty on display in the shop window? Had he not already displayed it sufficiently in various internal or semipublic ways? At trade-union meetings, after all, he had always voted as he should. He had always taken part in various competitions. He voted in elections like a good citizen. He had even signed the "anti-Charter." Why on top of all that, should he have to declare his loyalty publicly? After all, the people who walk past his window will certainly not stop to read that, in the greengrocer's opinion, the workers of the world ought to unite. The fact of the matter is, they don't read the slogan at all, and it can be fairly assumed they don't even see it. If you were to ask a woman who had stopped in front of his shop what she saw in the window, she could certainly tell you whether or not they had tomatoes today, but it is highly unlikely that she noticed the slogan at all, let alone what it said.

It seems senseless to require the greengrocer to declare his loyalty publicly. But it makes sense nevertheless. People ignore his slogan, but they do so because such slogans are also found in other shop windows, on lamp posts, bulletin boards, in apartment windows, and on buildings; they are everywhere, in fact. They form part of the panorama of everyday life. Of course, while they ignore the details, people are very aware of that panorama as a whole. And what else is the greengrocer's slogan but a small component in that huge backdrop to daily life?

The greengrocer had to put the slogan in his window, therefore, not in the hope that someone might read it or be persuaded by it, but to contribute, along with thousands of other slogans, to the panorama that everyone is very much aware of. This panorama, of course, has a subliminal meaning as well: it reminds people where they are living and what is expected of them. It tells them what everybody else is doing, and indicates to them what they must do as well, if they don't want to be excluded, to fall into isolation, alienate themselves from society, break the rules of the game, and risk the loss of their peace and tranquility and security.

If an entire district town is plastered with slogans that no one reads, it is on the one hand a message from the district secretary to the regional secretary, but it is also something more: a small example of the principle of social *auto-totality* at work. Part of the essence of the post-totalitarian system is that it draws everyone into its sphere of power, not so they may realize themselves as human beings, but so they may surrender their human identity in favour of the identity of the system, that is, so they may become agents of the system's general automatism and servants of its self-determined goals, so they may participate in the common responsibility for it, so they may be pulled into and ensnared by it, like Faust with Mephistopheles. More than this: so they may create through their involvement a general norm and, thus, bring pressure to bear on their fellow citizens. And further: so they may learn to be comfortable with their involvement, to identify with it as though it were something natural and inevitable and ultimately, so they may—with no external urging—come to treat any non-involvement as an abnormality, as arrogance, as an attack on themselves, as a form of dropping out of society. By pulling everyone into its power structure, the post-totalitarian system makes everyone instruments of a mutual totality, the autototality of society.

*   *   *

Let us now imagine that one day something in our greengrocer snaps and he stops putting up the slogans merely to ingratiate himself. He stops voting in elections he knows are a farce. He begins to say what he really thinks at political meetings. And he even finds the strength in himself to express solidarity with those for whom his conscience commands him to support. In this revolt the greengrocer steps out of living within the lie. He rejects the ritual and breaks the rules of the game. He discovers once more his suppressed identity and dignity. He gives his freedom a concrete significance. His revolt is an attempt to *live within the truth*.

The bill is not long in coming. He will be relieved of his post as manager of the shop and transferred to the warehouse. His pay will be reduced. His hopes for a holiday in Bulgaria will evaporate. His children's access to higher education will be threatened. His superiors will harass him and his fellow workers will wonder about him. Most of those who apply these sanctions, however, will not do so from any authentic inner conviction but simply under pressure from conditions, the same conditions that once pressured the greengrocer to display the official slogans. They will persecute the greengrocer either because it is expected of them, or to demonstrate their loyalty, or simply as part of the general panorama, to which belongs an awareness that this is how situations of this sort are dealt with, that this, in fact, is how things are always done, particularly if one is not to become suspect oneself. The executors, therefore, behave essentially like everyone else, to a greater or lesser degree: as components of the posttotalitarian system, as agents of its automatism, as petty instruments of the social auto-totality.

*   *   *

If the basic job of the "dissident movements" is to serve truth, that is to serve the real aims of life, and if that necessarily develops into a defense of the individual and his or her right to a free and truthful life (that is, a defence of human rights and a struggle to see the laws respected) then another stage of this approach, perhaps the most mature stage so far, is what Václav Benda has called the development of parallel structures.

*   *   *

What are these structures? Ivan Jirous was the first in Czechoslovakia to formulate and apply in practice the concept of a "second culture." Although at first he was thinking chiefly of non-conformist rock music and only certain literary, artistic or performance events close to the sensibilities of those non-conformist musical groups, the term "second culture" very rapidly came to be used for the whole area of independent and repressed culture, that is, not only for art and its various currents but also for the humanities, the social sciences and philosophical thought. This

"second culture," quite naturally, has created elementary organizational forms: *samizdat* editions of books and magazines, private performances and concerts, seminars, exhibitions and so on. (In Poland all of this is vastly more developed: there are independent publishing houses and many more periodicals, even political periodicals; they have means of proliferation other than carbon copies, and so on. In the Soviet Union, *samizdat* has a longer tradition and clearly its forms are quite different.) Culture, therefore, is a sphere in which the "parallel structures" can be observed in their most highly developed form. Benda, of course, gives thought to potential or embryonic forms of such structures in other spheres as well: from a parallel information network to parallel forms of education (private universities), parallel trade unions, parallel foreign contacts, to a kind of hypothesis on a parallel economy. On the basis of these parallel structures, he then develops the notion of a "parallel *polis*" or state or, rather, he sees the rudiments of such a *polis* in these structures.

*   *   *

These parallel structures, it may be said, represent the most articulated expressions so far of "living within the truth." One of the most important tasks the "dissident movements" have set themselves is to support and develop them. Once again, it confirms the fact that all attempts by society to resist the pressure of the system have their essential beginnings in the pre-political area. For what else are parallel structures than an area where a different life can be lived, a life that is in harmony with its own aims and which in turn structures itself in harmony with those aims? What else are those initial attempts at social self-organization than the efforts of a certain part of society to live—as a society—within the truth, to rid itself of the selfsustaining aspects of totalitarianism and, thus, to extricate itself radically from its involvement in the post-totalitarian system. What else is it but a nonviolent attempt by people to negate the system within themselves and to establish their lives on a new basis, that of their own proper identity?

REVIEW QUESTIONS

1. Why does Havel begin his analysis of what he calls the "post-totalitarian system" with the example of the political slogan in the greengrocer's shop, rather than, say, with a discussion of the power of state institutions in communist Czechoslovakia?

2. How does Havel define ideology? What is the function of ideology in the society he describes?

3. What does he mean by "auto-totality"? How is it different from the more overt forms of coercion used by the Soviet state during the Stalinist period?

4. In what way did what Havel calls "living within the truth" constitute a challenge to the status quo in Czechoslovakia in the 1970s and 1980s?

5. Is there any way in which Havel's argument about the constraints of ideology and social conformity can be applied to other forms of society besides the late-twentieth-century Eastern European socialist states that are his focus here?

MIKHAIL GORBACHEV

FROM "On Restructuring the Party's Personnel Policy"

The Polish reform movement's eventual triumph in the late 1980s would have been unimaginable if it had not been for the dramatic changes taking place in the Soviet Union. After the ouster of Khrushchev in 1964, the aging Soviet political bureaucracy had returned to business as usual, under the leadership of Leonid Brezhnev. This ended when Mikhail Gorbachev (born 1931), the youngest member of the Politburo, was elected general secretary of the Communist Party in 1985, a position he held until the collapse of the Soviet Union in 1991. Beginning in 1987, Gorbachev initiated an extensive reform campaign, intended to revitalize the Soviet economy through increased democracy, greater "openness" (glasnost) and a substantial "restructuring" (perestroika) of the political and economic institutions of the Soviet state. At the same time, he encouraged reform movements within other Eastern European states, allowing organizations such as Solidarity in Poland and Civic Forum in Czechoslovakia to emerge as powerful and influential forces for change.

Although Gorbachev embraced democratization and economic modernization, he was not ready to relinquish state control over the Soviet economy. Restructuring introduced limited free-market mechanisms, but it also upheld the fundamental premise of the state-planned economy. In an important speech to the Communist Party Central Committee in January 1987, Gorbachev laid out his critiques of the existing Soviet system and his plans for reforming that system.

From *Speeches and Writings*, by Mikhail Gorbachev (New York: Pergamon Press, 1986).

Restructuring Is an Objective Necessity

Our Plenary Meeting is taking place in the year of the 70th anniversary of the Great October Socialist Revolution. Almost seven decades ago the Leninist Party raised over the country the victorious banner of Socialist revolution, of struggle for Socialism, freedom, equality, social justice and progress and against oppression and exploitation, poverty and the subjugation of minority nationalities.

For the first time in world history, the working man and his interests and needs were made the focal point of state policy. The Soviet Union achieved truly epoch-making successes in political, economic, social, cultural and intellectual development as it built Socialist society. Under the leadership of the Party, the Soviet people built Socialism, won the victory over Nazism in the Great Patriotic War, rehabilitated and strengthened the national economy and made their homeland a mighty power.

Our achievements are immense and indubitable and the Soviet people rightfully take pride in their successes. They constitute a firm base for the fulfilment of our current programmes and our plans for the future. But the Party must see life in its entirety and complexity. No accomplishments, not even the most impressive, should obscure either contradictions in societal development or our mistakes and failings.

*   *   *

A need for change was coming to a head in the economy and other fields—but it was not realized through the political and practical work of the Party and the State.

What was the reason for that complex and controversial situation?

The main cause—and the Politburo considers it necessary to say so with utmost frankness at the Plenary Meeting—was that the CPSU Central Committee and the leadership of the country failed, primarily for subjective reasons, to see in time and in full the need for change and the danger of the intensification of crisis phenomena in society, and to formulate a clear policy for overcoming them and making better use of the opportunities intrinsic to the Socialist system.

*   *   *

In fact, a whole system of weakening the economic tools of government emerged and a mechanism of retarding socio-economic development and hindering progressive change developed, which made it possible to tap and use the advantages of Socialism. That retarding process was rooted in serious shortcomings in the functioning of the institutions of Socialist democracy, outdated political and theoretical concepts, that often did not correspond to reality, and conservative managerial machinery.

All this adversely affected development in many spheres in the life of society. Take material production: the growth rates of the national income in the past three five-year plan periods dropped by more than half. Most plan targets have not been met since the early 1970s. The economy as a whole became cumbersome and relatively unreceptive to innovation. The quality of a considerable part of the output no longer met current requirements, and imbalances in production became aggravated.

*   *   *

Having successfully resolved the question of employment and provided basic social guarantees, at the same time we failed to realize in full the potential of Socialism to improve housing conditions, food supply, transport, health care and education, and to solve a number of other vital problems.

There were violations of the most important principle of Socialism—distribution according to work. Efforts to control unearned income were indecisive. The policy of material and moral incentive to work efficiently was inconsistent. Large, unjustified bonuses and various additional incentives were paid and figure-padding for profit was allowed to take place. Parasitic sentiments grew stronger and the mentality of "wage levelling" began to take hold, and that hit workers who could work better and wanted to work better, while making life easier for the idle.

The violation of the organic relationship between the measure of work and measure of consumption not only perverts the attitude to work, holding back the growth of productivity, but leads to distortion of the principle of social justice—and that is a question of great political importance.

Elements of social corrosion that emerged in the past few years had a negative effect on society's morale and inconspicuously eroded the lofty moral values which have always been characteristic of our people and of which we are proud—ideological dedication, labour enthusiasm and Soviet patriotism.

As an inevitable consequence of all this, interest in the affairs of society slackened, manifestations of callousness and scepticism appeared and the role of moral incentive to work declined. The stratum of people, some of them young people, whose ultimate goal in life was material wellbeing and gain by any means, grew wider. Their cynical stand acquired more and more aggressive forms, poisoning the mentality of those around them and triggering a wave of consumerism. The spread of alcohol and drug abuse and a rise in crime became indicators of the decline of social mores.

Disregard for laws, report-padding, bribe-taking and the encouragement of toadyism and sycophancy had a deleterious influence on the moral atmosphere in society.

Real care for people, for the conditions of their life and work and for social wellbeing were often replaced with political flirtation—the mass distribution of awards, titles and prizes. An atmosphere of permissiveness was taking shape, and exactingness, discipline and responsibility were declining.

Serious shortcomings in ideological and political education were in many cases disguised with ostentatious activities and campaigns and celebrations of numerous jubilees at the centre and in the provinces. The world of day-to-day realities and that of make-believe wellbeing were increasingly parting ways.

The ideology and mentality of stagnation had their effect on culture, literature and the arts. Criteria in appraising artistic creative work were debased. As a consequence, quite a few mediocre, faceless works appeared, which did not give anything to the mind or the heart, along with works which raised serious social and moral problems and reflected true to life conflicts. Stereotypes from capitalist mass culture, with its propagation of vulgarity, primitive tastes and spiritual callousness, began to infiltrate Soviet society to a larger extent.

* * *

The situation in the Party was also influenced by the fact that in a number of cases the Party bodies did not attach proper attention to strict compliance with the Leninist principles and norms of Party life. This made itself especially manifest, perhaps, in breaches of the principle of collective leadership. What I mean is the weakening of the role of Party meetings and elective bodies, which denied Communists the opportunity to contribute energetically to the discussion of vital issues and, in the analysis, actually to influence the atmosphere in work collectives and in society as a whole.

The principle of equality between Communists was often violated. Many Party members in senior executive positions were beyond control or criticism, which resulted in failures in work and serious breaches of Party ethics.

We cannot overlook the just indignation of working people at the conduct of senior officials in whom trust and authority had been vested and who were called upon to stand guard over the interests of the state and its citizens, and who themselves abused their authority, suppressed criticism and sought personal gain, some even becoming accomplices in—if not organizers of—criminal activities.

* * *

It was in this situation that the question of accelerating the socio-economic development of the country—the question of restructuring—was raised. The case in point is actually a radical turn, comprising measures of a revolutionary character. When we talk about restructuring and associated processes of profound democratization, we mean truly revolutionary and comprehensive transformations in society.

We need to make this decisive turn because we simply do not have the choice of any other way. We must not retreat and do not have anywhere to retreat to.

*   *   *

The main purport of our strategy is to combine the achievements of the scientific and technological revolution with a plan-based economy and set the entire potential of Socialism going again.

Restructuring is reliance on the creative endeavour of the masses, all-round extension of democracy and Socialist self-government, encouragement of initiative and self-organized activities, better discipline and order, greater openness, criticism and self-criticism in all fields of public life, and high respect for the value and dignity of the individual.

Restructuring means the ever greater role of intensive growth factors in Soviet economic development, reinstatement and enhancement of Leninist principles of democratic centralism in the management of the national economy, employment of cost benefit methods of management everywhere, renunciation of the domineering style of management and administration by decree, conversion of all units of the economy to the principles of full-scale economic accountability and new forms of organizing labour and production, and every kind of incentive for innovation and Socialist enterprise.

Restructuring means a decisive turn to science, the businesslike partnership of science and practice for the sake of the highest possible end-results, the ability to ground any undertaking on sound scientific basis, readiness and keen desire on the part of scientists to assist the Party's policy of revitalizing society, and concern for the development of science and research personnel and for their active engagement in the process of change.

Restructuring means the priority development of the social sphere, increasingly satisfying the Soviet people's requirements for adequate working and living conditions, recreational facilities, education and medical services. It means unfailing concern for raising the intellectual and cultural standards of every person and of society as a whole: it is the ability to combine decision making on the major, cardinal problems of public life with that on the current issues of immediate interest to the people.

Restructuring means vigorously ridding society of any deviations from Socialist morals, consistently enforcing the principles of social justice, harmony between words and deeds, indivisibility of rights and duties, promotion of conscientious, high quality work, and overcoming pay-levelling and consumerism.

The final aim of the restructuring effort is, I believe, clear: it is to effect a thorough going change in all aspects of public life, to give Socialism the most advanced forms of social organization, and to bring out the humane nature of our system in all decisive aspects—economic, social, political and moral—to the fullest possible degree.

This is, comrades, the task we have in motion. The restructuring effort is unfolding along the entire front. It is acquiring a new quality, not only gaining in scope but also penetrating the deepest fibres of life.

*   *   *

To Deepen Socialist Democratism and Develop Self-government by the People

We now understand better than ever before the profundity of Lenin's thought about the vital, inner link between Socialism and democracy.

The entire historical experience of our country has convincingly demonstrated that the Socialist System has in practice ensured citizens' political and socio-economic rights and personal freedoms, demonstrated the advantages of Soviet democracy and given each person confidence in the morrow.

But in conditions of restructuring, when the task of intensifying the human factor has become so urgent, we must return once again to Lenin's approach to the question of the maximum democratism of the Socialist system under which people feel that they are their own masters and creators.

"We must be guided by experience, we must allow complete freedom to the creative faculties of the masses," Vladimir Lenin said.

Indeed, democracy, the essence of which is the power of the man of labour, is the form of realizing his extensive political and civil rights, his interest in transformations and practical participation in their implementation.

A simple and lucid thought is becoming increasingly entrenched in social consciousness: a house can be put in order only by a person who feels that he owns this house. This truth is correct not only in the wordly sense but also in the socio-political one.

This truth must be undeviatingly applied in practice. I repeat, in practice. Otherwise the human factor will be ineffectual.

It is only through the consistent development of the democratic forms inherent in Socialism, through a broadening of self-government, that our advancement in production, science and technology, literature, culture and the arts, in all areas of social life, is possible. It is only this way that ensures conscientious discipline. The restructuring itself is possible only through democracy and due to democracy. It is only this way that it is possible to give scope to Socialism's most powerful creative force—free labour and free thought in a free country.

Therefore the further democratization of Soviet society is becoming the Party's urgent task. Herein, properly speaking, lies the essence of the course of the April Plenum, of the 27th Congress of the CPSU for deepening Socialist self-government by the people. The point at issue is, certainly, not any break up of our political system. We should make use of all its potentialities with maximum effectiveness, fill the work of the Party, the Soviets and the government bodies, public organizations and work

collectives with deep democratic contents, breathe new life into all cells of the social organism.

This process is already under way in the country. The life of the Party organizations is becoming more full-blooded. Criticism and self-criticism are broadening. The mass media have begun working more actively. The Soviet people can sense the salutary effect of openness, which is becoming a norm of society's life.

The congresses of the creative unions proceeded in an atmosphere of principledness and criticism. New public organizations are being set up. The All-Union Organization of War and Labour Veterans has come into being. The Soviet Cultural Fund has been set up. Work is under way to set up women's councils. All these facts indicate the growing participation of the working people in social affairs and in the administration of the country.

*   *   *

We wish to turn our country into a model of a highly developed state, into a society with the most advanced economy, the broadest democracy, the most humane and lofty ethics, where the working man will feel that he is master, will enjoy all the benefits of material and spiritual culture, where the future of his children will be secure, where he will have everything that is necessary for a full and interesting life. And even sceptics would be forced to say: yes, the Bolsheviks can accomplish anything. Yes, truth is on their side. Yes, Socialism is a system serving man, working for his benefit, in his social and economic interests, for his spiritual elevation.

REVIEW QUESTIONS

1. Why, according to Gorbachev, was restructuring an objective necessity?
2. What social, political, and economic forms would this restructuring take?
3. Why was it crucial that social, political, and economic reform go hand in hand?

4. What elements of free-market capitalism were included in Gorbachev's economic restructuring?

5. In what ways did Gorbachev remain a traditional communist in his economic thinking?

SIMONE DE BEAUVOIR

FROM *The Second Sex*

During the twentieth century, the traditional divisions between the experiences of men and women started to blur. New technologies decreased the premium once placed on men's greater physical strength, making it possible for women to do jobs once reserved only for men. At the same time, female fertility decreased substantially: as improved health conditions allowed more children to survive to adulthood, couples increasingly sought to have fewer children. New birth-control technologies made this increasingly easy. Whereas reproductive and child-rearing duties had once played a predominant role in most women's adult lives, motherhood now became only one aspect of a more varied lifetime experience.

However, if the material conditions of women's lives had changed significantly, attitudes toward women had not. If anything, the immediate postwar period saw a resurrection of traditional models of femininity and masculinity. On the other hand, the popularization of existentialist philosophy, which argued that every individual has the responsibility to be an active agent, to create the self through "engagement" with other human beings, helped to fuel a growing resistance to "objectification"— entrapment in the limiting conceptual categories of outside society—whether on the basis of race, gender, or class. In 1949 the French novelist and existential philosopher Simone de Beauvoir (1908–1986) published The Second Sex, *an extended philosophical essay that called on women to reject socially imposed models of appropriate feminine identity and to become authentic individuals in their own right. The Second Sex was initially greeted with outrage and howls of derision, but the revival of feminism in the 1960s brought de Beauvoir a new, more sympathetic audience, and her arguments exercised a strong influence over the U.S. and European women's movements.*

From *The Second Sex*, by Simone de Beauvoir (Paris: Gallimard, 1997), translated by Cat Nilan for the current edition.

If being female is not a sufficient definition of woman, if we also refuse to explain her through "the eternal feminine," and if we nevertheless admit (if only provisionally), that there are women on this planet, then we are forced to ask ourselves the question: what is a woman?

Simply stating the problem suggests one immediate response. It is significant that I ask this question. A man would never think of writing a book about the peculiar position that males occupy in the ranks of humanity. If I want to define myself, I am first obligated to declare: "I am a woman." That truth constitutes the foundation upon which all other affirmations will be based. A man never begins by declaring himself an individual of a certain sex: that he is a man goes without saying. It is only as a formality that "male" and "female" appear as symmetrical terms in town hall records and identification papers. The relationship between the sexes is not that of two electrical poles: the man represents both the positive and the neutral to such an extent that in French one says "*les hommes*" ("men") to designate all human beings. * * * Woman is so strongly associated with the negative that her every trait is imputed to her as a limitation, without reciprocity. It annoys me when, during the course of an abstract discussion, a man says: "You think such and such a thing because you are a woman." I know that my only defense is to reply: "I believe it because it is true," eliminating in that manner my own subjectivity. It's out of the question to answer: "And you think the contrary because you are a man," because it is understood that the fact of being a man is not a peculiarity. A man is in the right in being a man; it is the woman who is in the wrong. In practice, just as the ancients identified an absolute vertical against which the oblique was defined, there is an absolute human type that is masculine. Woman has ovaries, a uterus; these are the peculiarities that enclose her in her subjectivity. It is often said that she thinks with her glands. Man arrogantly forgets that his own anatomy also includes hormones, testicles. He experiences his body as being in a direct and normal relationship with the world, which he believes he apprehends objectively, whereas he considers the body of a woman to be weighted down by all of its specificities: an obstacle, a prison. * * * Humanity is male and man defines woman not in and of herself but relative to him; she is not considered an autonomous being. * * * And she is nothing other

than what man decides; thus she is called "the sex," meaning that she appears to the male, in essence, as a sexuated being. For him, she is sex, and therefore she is so absolutely. She is defined and differentiated in relation to man and not he in relation to her; she is the inessential as compared with the essential. He is the Subject, he is the Absolute: she is the Other.

The category of the *Other* is as old as consciousness itself. * * * No collectivity ever defines itself as the One without immediately positing an Other in opposition to it. If three travelers happen to be gathered together by chance in the same cabin, that is enough to make all other travelers vaguely hostile "others." For the villager, all of the people who do not belong to his village are suspect "others"; for the native of one country, the inhabitants of other countries are "foreigners." Jews are "others" to the antisemite; Blacks are "others" to American racists; indigenous peoples are "others" to the colonizers; proletarians are "others" to the propertied classes. * * *

But the other consciousness opposes to this claim a reciprocal claim: when he travels, the native is shocked to discover that the natives of neighboring countries regard him in his turn as a foreigner. Between villages, clans, nations, and classes there are wars, potlatches, markets, treaties, and conflicts that deprive the idea of the Other of its absolute sense and reveal its relativity. Willingly or not, individuals and groups are forced to recognize the reciprocity of their relations. How then has it happened that between the sexes that reciprocity has not been admitted, that one of the terms has affirmed itself as the only essential one, denying all relativity in relation to its corollary, defining it as pure otherness? Why don't women contest male sovereignty? No subject spontaneously admits, from the first, that it is the inessential. It is not the Other who by defining himself as Other defines the One: he is posited as Other by the One posing himself as One. But in order for the return from Other to One not to happen, it is necessary that he submit to this foreign point of view. Where does woman's submission come from?

*   *   *

* * * The parallel established by Bebel between women and the proletariat is the most apt: like women, proletarians are not a minority and they have never constituted a separate collectivity. Nevertheless, in the absence of a *single* event, it is a historical development that explains their existence as a class and which accounts for the distribution of *these* individuals in that class. There have not always been proletarians; there have always been women. Women are women through their physiology. However far one goes back into history, women have always been subordinated to man. Their dependency is not the consequence of an event or a development; it did not *happen*. It is in part because otherness escapes the accidental character of a historical fact in this case that it appears here as an absolute. Something that happened over time can be undone at another time. The Blacks of Haiti, among others, have proved this. On the other hand, it would appear that a natural condition defies change. In truth, nature is no more an immutable given than historical reality. If woman reveals herself as the inessential that never returns to the essential, it is because she herself does not set that reversal into motion. Proletarians say "We." Blacks too. Positing themselves as subjects they change the bourgeoisie and Whites into "others." * * * Women do not say "we." Men say "women" and women use this word to designate themselves, but they do not posit themselves authentically as Subject. Proletarians made a revolution in Russia, the Blacks in Haiti, the Indochinese are fighting in Indochina. Women's action has never been anything more than a symbolic disturbance. They have won only what men were willing to concede to them. They have taken nothing: they have merely received.

*   *   *

There are deep analogies between the situation of women and that of Blacks. Today both are emancipating themselves from the same paternalism and the former master class wishes to keep them in "their place," that is to say, the place it has chosen for them. In both cases, that master class lavishes more or less sincere praise on the virtues of the "good Black," childish, happy-go-lucky, his soul slumbering, and on "the real woman," who is frivolous, puerile, irresponsible, submissive to man. In both cases, it derives its argument from the situation it has in fact created. George Bernard Shaw's witticism is well known: "The white American," he said, in essence, "relegates the Black to the rank of shoeshine boy and he concludes from this that the Black is good for nothing but shining shoes." This vicious circle is found in all analogous circumstances; when an individual, or a group of individuals, is held in a situation of inferiority, the fact is that he *is* inferior. But we must be clear about what we mean by *to be*. It is in bad faith to give it a substantial meaning, when it should be read in the dynamic, Hegelian sense: *to be* is to have become, it is to have been made that which one appears to be. Yes, as a whole women today *are* inferior to men, which is to say that their situation is offered them fewer opportunities. The problem is determining whether or not this state of affairs should continue.

Many men hope that it will; not all of them have disarmed themselves yet. The conservative bourgeoisie continues to see women's emancipation as a menace to its morality and its interests. Certain males fear feminine competition. Just the other day, a male student declared in the *Hebdo-Latin*: "Every female student who takes a position as a doctor or a lawyer *steals* a place from us." He certainly doesn't have any questions about his rights over this world. But it is not only economic concerns that are at play here. One of the benefits that oppression guarantees to the oppressors is that the humblest among them feels himself *superior*: a "poor White" in the Southern United States consoles himself by saying that he is not a "dirty Negro," and more affluent Whites skillfully exploit this pride. In the same way, the most mediocre of males believes himself a demigod compared with women.

REVIEW QUESTIONS

1. What *is* a woman, according to de Beauvoir?
2. How has woman become an "Other"?
3. How can she become a "Self"?

4. In what ways are the conditions of blacks, Jews, workers, and women similar? In what ways are they different?
5. Why do you think de Beauvoir chose to make these particular comparisons?

28 ☛ A WORLD WITHOUT WALLS: GLOBALIZATION AND THE WEST

At the beginning of recorded human history, the entire population of the world probably consisted of fewer than 10 million people. Ten thousand years later, the world population is rapidly approaching 7 billion. Human ingenuity has made possible the production of enough food and material goods to sustain this enormous population, but this achievement puts serious strains on the environment and creates intense competition for limited resources.

Innovations in transportation and communication have made it possible for people around the world to have far more intimate and informed relations with each other than ever before. Earth's surface remains subdivided by national boundaries, but the problems confronting humanity are, increasingly, international problems that can be solved only through global cooperation. From a historical perspective, it is already clear that human history has become world history and that even the most isolated regions are no longer insulated from the general trend toward global integration.

One of the most important factors in the emerging history of the contemporary world is the deep divide separating developed and developing nations. Most of the inhabitants of affluent and technologically advanced regions such as Japan, the United States, and Western Europe enjoy extremely high standards of living and can expect to live long and healthy lives. The four-fifths of Earth's people who live in developing regions (sometimes called the Third World) regularly suffer from a lack of basic necessities, including adequate food, clean drinking water, and a bare minimum of health care.

The reasons for this dramatic disparity in the distribution of wealth are complex, but they are closely linked to the historical processes of colonization and decolonization. During the late nineteenth century, imperialist powers acquired colonies in the hopes of procuring raw materials, cheap labor, and national gran-

*deur. The builders of empire were largely uninterested in modernizing the econo-
mies or political systems of their colonies, and they often destroyed indigenous
industries and governments at the same time that they crushed expressions of
cultural resistance. After the Second World War, most of these colonies regained
their independence, as a result of either more or less voluntary withdrawal on the
part of the colonizers or violent conflict.*

*The newly independent states of Africa and Asia faced substantial chal-
lenges, not the least of which were the international tensions generated by the
Cold War. When the Soviet Union and the United States sought allies in the
Third World, both superpowers tended to support dictators friendly to their strategic aims, thereby discouraging the emergence of independent democracies. In
addition, most former colonies were strongly disadvantaged in the economic
arena by technological backwardness, a legacy of colonial rule. The developed
nations have been slow to come to the aid of struggling Third World nations, and
the political instability produced by desperate poverty and often violent competition for land and resources continues to threaten global peace and prosperity.*

*In the 1990s, all of these historical tensions converged as the world entered a
new phase of instability. The collapse of communism in Eastern Europe and the
Soviet Union brought greater political freedoms to many millions of people, but
this sudden transformation also produced prolonged political crisis in many
areas, leading to the violent breakup of Yugoslavia, the splitting of Czechoslovakia into two ethnically distinct nations, the war in Chechnya, and the ever-
present threat of renewed ethnic violence throughout the former communist
world. In this uncertain context, the international bodies that had their origins
in the Cold War—NATO, the United Nations, the European Union—struggled to
redefine their roles, often with only marginal success. In the former Yugoslavia
and in Rwanda, over a million people were killed in genocidal conflicts, as the
rest of the "civilized" world watched. The major powers in Europe and the United
States were helpless to coordinate a coherent response or to stop the killing, in
spite of fifty years of international treaties and legal decisions designed to prevent
a recurrence of the Holocaust in the aftermath of World War II.*

*Al Qaeda's September 11, 2001 attacks on New York and Washington thus
came at a moment when Europeans and Americans were less sure than ever
about how best to confront the problems facing the world at the dawn of the
twenty-first century. The Bush administration's response—a doctrine of preemp-
tive war—was a major revision of decades of American policy that committed
the United States to unilateral action in the face of perceived threats. In the
buildup to the second Iraq war in 2003, it was difficult for many in the United
States to avoid thinking in terms of a global clash of civilizations—East versus
West. However such simplistic formulations obscure the complex past that
underlies the history of terrorism in the Middle East, its relationship to Islamic
traditions, and more recent events in the region.*

These immediate crises, as serious as they are, might only be a part of a larger set of problems facing the world today. As developing regions struggle to come to terms with the legacies of colonialism and superpower conflict, they are also called on to participate in forging global solutions to global problems. Uncontrolled population growth, the exploitation and mismanagement of natural resources, and unregulated industrial and commercial development pose serious dangers to the survival of all humanity. Similarly, the transfer of people, capital, and consumer goods and land, air, and water pollution can no longer be contained within national boundaries. While individual identity remains deeply rooted in local cultural traditions, the future history of humanity may hinge on our ability to develop a model of global citizenship that balances the rights of the individual with the responsibilities of all human beings to both the local and the global communities.

MAHATMA GANDHI

FROM *The Essential Writings*

The Indian struggle for independence from Great Britain can be traced back to the early nineteenth century, but it first became a mass movement after the First World War. Indian nationalists supported India's participation in the war on the Allied side, but they were angered by Britain's failure to reward this service with a greater degree of self-government. Under the charismatic leadership of Mahatma ("Great Soul") Gandhi (1869–1948), the Indian independence movement became a model for other colonial independence struggles.

Having trained as a lawyer in Britain, the young Mohandas Gandhi worked for many years among the East Indian community of South Africa, where he experienced the effects of racial discrimination in the acute form of apartheid. As he struggled to maintain his human dignity in a system that looked on him as nothing more than a common laborer, he drew sustenance from the Hindu religious traditions of India, building his "soul force" through a commitment to truth, love, and ascetic practices (such as vegetarianism, sexual abstinence, and manual labor). When he returned to India in 1913, Gandhi became active in the Indian National Congress and directed the fledgling independence movement toward adopting a strategy of peaceful noncooperation. At the same time, he also lobbied for economic self-sufficiency. Taking as his symbol the spinning wheel, he argued that the spiritual and material poverty of the Indian masses could be alleviated through the revival of indigenous traditions of small-scale, low-tech textile production.

From *The Essential Writings of Mahatma Gandhi*, edited by Raghavan Iyer (Oxford: Oxford University Press, 1991).

FROM **The Doctrine of the Sword**

In this age of the rule of brute force, it is almost impossible for anyone to believe that anyone else could possibly reject the law of the final supremacy of brute force. And so I receive anonymous letters advising me that I must not interfere with the progress of non-co-operation even though popular violence may break out. Others come to me and assuming that secretly I must be plotting violence, inquire when the happy moment for declaring open violence will arrive. They assure me that the English will never yield to anything but violence secret or open. Yet others, I am informed, believe that I am the most rascally person living in India because I never give out my real intention and that they have not a shadow of a doubt that I believe in violence just as much as most people do.

Such being the hold that the doctrine of the sword has on the majority of mankind, and as success of non-co-operation depends principally on absence of violence during its pendency and as my views in this matter affect the conduct of a large number of people, I am anxious to state them as clearly as possible.

I do believe that where there is only a choice between cowardice and violence I would advise violence. Thus when my eldest son asked me what he should have done, had he been present when I was almost fatally assaulted in 1908, whether he should have run away and seen me killed or whether he should have used his physical force which he could and wanted to use, and defended me, I told him that it was his duty to defend me even by using violence. Hence it was that I took part in the Boer War, the so-called Zulu rebellion and the late War. Hence also do I advocate training in arms for those who believe in the method of violence. I would rather have India resort to arms in order to defend her honour than that she should in a cowardly manner become or remain a helpless witness to her own dishonour.

But I believe that non-violence is infinitely superior to violence, forgiveness is more manly than punishment. *Kshama virasya bhushanam.*

"Forgiveness adorns a soldier." But abstinence is forgiveness only when there is the power to punish; it is meaningless when it pretends to proceed from a helpless creature. A mouse hardly forgives a cat when it allows itself to be torn to pieces by her. I, therefore, appreciate the sentiment of those who cry out for the condign punishment of General Dyer and his ilk. They would tear him to pieces if they could. But I do not believe India to be helpless. I do not believe myself to be a helpless creature. Only I want to use India's and my strength for a better purpose.

Let me not be misunderstood. Strength does not come from physical capacity. It comes from an indomitable will. An average Zulu is any way more than a match for an average Englishman in bodily capacity. But he flees from an English boy, because he fears the boy's revolver or those who will use it for him. He fears death and is nerveless in spite of his burly figure. We in India may in a moment realize that one hundred thousand Englishmen need not frighten three hundred million human beings. A definite forgiveness would therefore mean a definite recognition of our strength. With enlightened forgiveness must come a mighty wave of strength in us, which would make it impossible for a Dyer and a Frank Johnson to heap affront upon India's devoted head. It matters little to me that for the moment I do not drive my point home. We feel too downtrodden not to be angry and revengeful. But I must not refrain from saying that India can gain more by waiving the right of punishment. We have better work to do, a better mission to deliver to the world.

I am not a visionary. I claim to be a practical idealist. The religion of non-violence is not meant merely for the ⋆ ⋆ ⋆ saints. It is meant for the common people as well. Non-violence is the law of our species as violence is the law of the brute. The spirit lies dormant in the brute and he knows no law but that of physical might. The dignity of man requires obedience to a higher law—to the strength of the spirit.

I have therefore ventured to place before India the ancient law of self-sacrifice. ⋆⋆⋆

Non-violence in its dynamic condition means conscious suffering. It does not mean meek submission to the will of the evil-doer, but it means the putting of one's whole soul against the will of the tyrant. Working under this law of our being, it is possible for a single individual to defy the whole might of an unjust empire to save his honour, his religion, his soul and lay the foundation for that empire's fall or its regeneration.

And so I am not pleading for India to practise non-violence because it is weak. I want her to practise non-violence being conscious of her strength and power. No training in arms is required for realization of her strength. We seem to need it because we seem to think that we are but a lump of flesh. I want India to recognize that she has a soul that cannot perish and that can rise triumphant above every physical weakness and defy the physical combination of a whole world. What is the meaning of Rama, a mere human being, with his host of monkeys, pitting himself against the insolent strength of ten-headed Ravana surrounded in supposed safety by the raging waters on all sides of Lanka? Does it not mean the conquest of physical might by spiritual strength? However, being a practical man, I do not wait till India recognizes the practicability of the spiritual life in the political world. India considers herself to be powerless and paralysed before the machine-guns, the tanks and the aeroplanes of the English. And she takes up non-co-operation out of her weakness. It must still serve the same purpose, namely, bring her delivery from the crushing weight of British injustice if a sufficient number of people practise it.

* * * I invite even the school of violence to give this peaceful non-co-operation a trial. It will not fail through its inherent weakness. It may fail because of poverty of response. Then will be the time for real danger. The high-souled men, who are unable to suffer national humiliation any longer, will want to vent their wrath. They will take to violence. So far as I know, they must perish without delivering themselves or their country from the wrong. If India takes up the doctrine of the sword, she may gain momentary victory. Then India will cease to be the pride of my heart. I am wedded to India because I owe my all to her. I believe absolutely that she has a mission for the world. She is not to copy Europe blindly. India's acceptance of the doctrine of the sword will be the hour of my trial. I hope I shall not be found wanting. My religion has no geographical limits. If I have a living faith in it, it will transcend my love for India herself. My life is dedicated to service of India through the religion of non-violence which I believe to be the root of Hinduism.

Meanwhile I urge those who distrust me, not to disturb the even working of the struggle that has just commenced, by inciting to violence in the belief that I want violence. I detest secrecy as a sin. Let them give non-violent non-co-operation a trial and they will find that I had no mental reservation whatsoever.

FROM **Non-Violence — The Greatest Force**

*   *   *

The cry for peace will be a cry in the wilderness, so long as the spirit of non-violence does not dominate millions of men and women.

An armed conflict between nations horrifies us. But the economic war is no better than an armed conflict. This is like a surgical operation. An economic war is prolonged torture. And its ravages are no less terrible than those depicted in the literature on war properly so called. We think nothing of the other because we are used to its deadly effects.

Many of us in India shudder to see blood spilled. Many of us resent cow-slaughter, but we think nothing of the slow torture through which by our greed we put our people and cattle. But because we are used to this lingering death, we think no more about it.

The movement against war is sound. I pray for its success. But I cannot help the gnawing fear that the movement will fail, if it does not touch the root of all evil—man's greed.

Will America, England and the other great nations of the West continue to exploit the so-called weaker or uncivilized races and hope to attain peace that the whole world is pining for? Or

GANDHI AT SPINNING WHEEL   MARGARET BOURKE-WHITE

Mahatma Gandhi's strategy of achieving independence for India through boycotts and nonparticipation in civil institutions marks a high point in nonviolent political struggles in the twentieth century. A cornerstone of Gandhi's political program was his assertion that when Indians could break their economic dependence on British manufacturers (of textiles, for example), Indian political independence could be achieved. How does this photograph of Gandhi capture the philosophy and program of his politics?

will Americans continue to prey upon one another, have commercial rivalries and yet expect to dictate peace to the world?

Not till the spirit is changed can the form be altered. The form is merely an expression of the spirit within. We may succeed in seemingly altering the form but the alteration will be a mere make-believe if the spirit within remains unalterable. A whited sepulchre still conceals beneath it the rotting flesh and bone.

Far be it from me to discount or under-rate the great effort that is being made in the West to kill the war-spirit. Mine is merely a word of caution as from a fellow-seeker who has been striving in his own humble manner after the same thing, maybe in a different way, no doubt on a much smaller scale. But if the experiment demonstrably succeeds on the smaller field and, if those who are working on the larger field have not overtaken me, it will at least pave the way for a similar experiment on a large field.

I observe in the limited field in which I find myself, that unless I can reach the hearts of men and women, I am able to do nothing. I observe further that so long as the spirit of hate persists in some shape or other, it is impossible to establish peace or to gain our freedom by peaceful effort. We cannot love one another, if we hate Englishmen. We cannot love the Japanese and hate Englishmen.

We must either let the Law of Love rule us through and through or not at all. Love among ourselves based on hatred of others breaks down under the slightest pressure. The fact is such love is never real love. It is an armed peace. And so it will be in this great movement in the West against war. War will only be stopped when the conscience of mankind has become sufficiently elevated to recognize the undisputed supremacy of the Law of Love in all the walks of life. Some say this will never come to pass. I shall retain the faith till the end of my earthly existence that it shall come to pass.

REVIEW QUESTIONS

1. Why must the strategy of nonviolence proceed from a position of strength, according to Gandhi?
2. In what ways were Indians strong, according to Gandhi?
3. What does Gandhi mean by "economic war"?
4. How can human beings bring an end to *all* wars?
5. Why do you think the strategy of passive resistance to oppression was so popular among many participants in the independence and civil rights movements of the mid–twentieth century?

FRANTZ FANON

FROM *The Wretched of the Earth*

Gandhi's strategy of peaceful resistance had a profound impact on other twentieth-century movements for social change. Yet many independence activists rejected this approach, arguing that the imperial powers would never relinquish their control over colonial holdings without violence. Instead, these activists looked for inspiration to the armed struggles led by Ho Chi Minh in Vietnam and Fidel Castro in Cuba.

Militant anti-imperialists recognized that resistance movements could never outgun the colonizers, but they were convinced that sustained guerilla warfare would eventually convince the imperial powers that the costs of maintaining control over a colony were simply too high.

For Frantz Fanon (1925–1961), violence was not simply a tactic in anti-imperial conflicts: it also served an important role in the psychological decolonization of subject peoples. Born in the French colony of Martinique, Fanon trained as a psychiatrist in Martinique and France before becoming an active participant in the Algerian independence movement of the 1950s. Fanon argued that the physical and psychological violence of the colonial system had traumatized colonized peoples, generating individual and communal mental illness. Violent resistance to imperialism would permit subject peoples to purge this trauma and to build a new and independent community based on their shared experience of retaliation. In The Wretched of the Earth, *published in 1961 shortly before his untimely death from cancer, Fanon analyzed anti-imperial violence as a pathological response to a pathological system and as a necessary therapy for the social maladies generated by colonialism.*

From *The Wretched of the Earth*, by Frantz Fanon, translated by Constance Farrington (New York: Grove/Atlantic, 1963), pp. 83–84, 88–90, 96–98, 102.

*   *   *

The existence of an armed struggle shows that the people are decided to trust to violent methods only. He of whom *they* have never stopped saying that the only language he understands is that of force, decides to give utterance by force. In fact, as always, the settler has shown him the way he should take if he is to become free. The argument the native chooses has been furnished by the settler, and by an ironic turning of the tables it is the native who now affirms that the colonialist understands nothing but force. The colonial regime owes its legitimacy to force and at no time tries to hide this aspect of things. Every statue, whether of Faidherbe or of Lyautey, of Bugeaud or of Sergeant Blandan—all these conquistadors perched on colonial soil do not cease from proclaiming one and the same thing: "We are here by the force of bayonets. . . ."

*   *   *

The violence of the colonial regime and the counter-violence of the native balance each other and respond to each other in an extraordinary reciprocal homogeneity. This reign of violence will be the more terrible in proportion to the size of the implantation from the mother country. The development of violence among the colonized people will be proportionate to the violence exercised by the threatened colonial regime. In the first phase of this insurrectional period, the home governments are the slaves of the settlers, and these settlers seek to intimidate the natives and their home governments at one and the same time. They use the same methods against both of them. The assassination of the Mayor of Evian, in its method and motivation, is identifiable with the assassination of Ali Boumendjel. For the settlers, the alternative is not between *Algérie algérienne* and *Algérie française* but between an independent Algeria and a colonial Algeria, and anything else is mere talk or attempts at treason. The settler's logic is implacable and one is only staggered by the counter-logic visible in the behavior of the native insofar as one has not clearly understood beforehand the mechanisms of the settler's ideas. From the moment that the native has chosen the methods of counter-violence, police reprisals automatically call forth reprisals on the side of the nationalists. However, the results are not equivalent, for machine-gunning from airplanes and bombardments from the fleet go far beyond in horror and magnitude any answer the natives can make. This recurring terror de-mystifies once and for all the most estranged members of the colonized race. They find out on the spot that all the piles of speeches on the equality of human beings do not hide the commonplace fact that the seven Frenchmen killed or wounded at the Col de Sakamody kindles the indignation of all civilized consciences, whereas the sack of the douars of Guergour and of the dechras of Djerah and the massacre of whole populations—which had merely called forth the Sakamody ambush as a reprisal— all this is of not the slightest importance. Terror, counter-terror, violence, counter-violence: that is what observers bitterly record when they describe the circle of hate, which is so tenacious and so evident in Algeria.

In all armed struggles, there exists what we might call the point of no return. Almost always it is marked off by a huge and all-inclusive repression which engulfs all sectors of the colonized people. This point was reached in Algeria in 1955 with the 12,000 victims of Phillippeville. * * *

*   *   *

Then it became clear to everybody, including even the settlers, that "things couldn't go on as before." Yet the colonized people do not chalk up the reckoning. They record the huge gaps made in their ranks as a sort of necessary evil. Since they have decided to reply by violence, they therefore are ready to take all its consequences. They only insist in return that no reckoning should be kept, either, for the others. To the saying "All natives are the same" the colonized person replies, "All settlers are the same."

*   *   *

The appearance of the settler has meant in the terms of syncretism the death of the aboriginal society, cultural lethargy, and the petrification of individuals. For the native, life can only spring up again out of the rotting corpse of the settler. This then is the correspondence, term by term, between the two trains of reasoning.

But it so happens that for the colonized people this violence, because it constitutes their only work, invests their characters with positive and creative qualities. The practice of violence binds them together as a whole, since each individual forms a violent link in the great chain, a part of the great organism of violence which has surged upward in reaction to the settler's violence in the beginning. The groups recognize each other and the future nation is already indivisible. The armed struggle mobilizes the people; that is to say, it throws them in one way and in one direction.

The mobilization of the masses, when it arises out of the war of liberation, introduces into each man's consciousness the ideas of a common cause, of a national destiny, and of a collective history. In the same way the second phase, that of the building-up of the nation, is helped on by the existence of this cement which has been mixed with blood and anger. Thus we come to a fuller appreciation of the originality of the words used in these underdeveloped countries. During the colonial period the people are called upon to fight against oppression; after national liberation, they are called upon to fight against poverty, illiteracy, and underdevelopment. The struggle, they say, goes on. The people realize that life is an unending contest.

We have said that the native's violence unifies the people. By its very structure, colonialism is separatist and regionalist. Colonialism does not simply state the existence of tribes; it also reinforces it and separates them. The colonial system encourages chieftaincies and keeps alive the old Marabout confraternities. Violence is in action all-inclusive and national. It follows that it is closely involved in the liquidation of regionalism and of tribalism. Thus the national parties show no pity at all toward the caids and the customary chiefs. Their destruction is the preliminary to the unification of the people.

At the level of individuals, violence is a cleansing force. It frees the native from his inferiority complex and from his despair and inaction; it makes him fearless and restores his self-respect. Even if the armed struggle has been symbolic and the nation is demobilized through a rapid movement of decolonization, the people have the time to see that the liberation has been the business of each and all and that the leader has no special merit.

*   *   *

Today, national independence and the growth of national feeling in underdeveloped regions take on totally new aspects. In these regions, with the exception of certain spectacular advances, the different countries show the same absence of infrastructure. The mass of the people struggle against the same poverty, flounder about making the same gestures and with their shrunken bellies outline what has been called the geography of hunger. It is an underdeveloped world, a world inhuman in its poverty; but also it is a world without doctors, without engineers, and without administrators. Confronting this world, the European nations sprawl, ostentatiously opulent. This European opulence is literally scandalous, for it has been founded on slavery, it has been nourished with the blood of slaves and it comes directly from the soil and from the subsoil of that underdeveloped world. The well-being and the progress of Europe have been built up with the sweat and the dead bodies of Negroes, Arabs, Indians, and the yellow races. We have decided not to overlook this any longer. When a colonialist country, embarrassed by the claims for independence made by a colony, proclaims to the nationalist leaders: "If you wish for independence, take it, and go back to the Middle Ages," the newly independent people tend to acquiesce and to accept the challenge; in fact you may see colonialism withdrawing its capital and its technicians and setting up around the young State the apparatus of economic pressure. The apotheosis of independence is transformed into the curse of independence, and the colonial power through its immense resources of coercion condemns the young nation to regression. In plain words, the colonial power says: "Since you want independence, take it and starve." The nationalist leaders have no other choice but to turn

to their people and ask from them a gigantic effort. A regime of austerity is imposed on these starving men; a disproportionate amount of work is required from their atrophied muscles. An autarkic regime is set up and each state, with the miserable resources it as in hand, tries to find an answer to the nation's great hunger and poverty. We see the mobilization of a people which toils to exhaustion in front of a suspicious and bloated Europe.

*   *   *

* * * The imperialist states would make a great mistake and commit an unspeakable injustice if they contented themselves with withdrawing from our soil the military cohorts, and the administrative and managerial services whose function it was to discover the wealth of the country, to extract it and to send it off to the mother countries. We are not blinded by the moral reparation of national independence; nor are we fed by it. The wealth of the imperial countries is our wealth too. On the universal plane this affirmation, you may be sure, should on no account be taken to signify that we feel ourselves affected by the creations of Western arts or techniques. For in a very concrete way Europe has stuffed herself inordinately with the gold and raw materials of the colonial countries: Latin America, China, and Africa. From all these continents, under whose eyes Europe today raises up her tower of opulence, there has flowed out for centuries toward that same Europe diamonds and oil, silk and cotton, wood and exotic products. Europe is literally the creation of the Third World. The wealth which smothers her is that which was stolen from the underdeveloped peoples. The ports of Holland, the docks of Bordeaux and Liverpool were specialized in the Negro slave trade, and owe their renown to millions of deported slaves. So when we hear the head of a European state declare with his hand on his heart that he must come to the aid of the poor underdeveloped peoples, we do not tremble with gratitude. Quite the contrary; we say to ourselves: "It's a just reparation which will be paid to us."

*   *   *

REVIEW QUESTIONS

1. In what ways did colonial regimes breed violence?
2. What did Fanon believe were the positive benefits of anti-imperial violence for the community? For the individual?
3. According to Fanon, how did Europe compare with its former colonies?
4. In what sense is the wealth of Europe the "creation of the Third World"?

STANLEY HOFFMANN

FROM "Obstinate or Obsolete? The Fate of the Nation-State and the Case of Western Europe"

Stanley Hoffmann (1928–2015), for many years a professor of politics and history at Harvard University, was born in Vienna and became a French citizen as a young man while pursuing his education in Paris. He founded Harvard's Center for European Studies in 1968. In this essay, written in 1966, he considers the progress made since the end of World War II in the process of European integration. He argues that the optimism of the immediate postwar years, in which a new unity and sense of purpose could be found in an integrated Europe that would be free of the destructive nationalisms of the past, had dissipated. Europe was still a continent of nation-states, pursuing different goals from one another, and unlikely to move further toward political integration. Pay special attention to his analysis of the French and German positions, and the different way that they interpreted the power and influence exercised by the United States and the Soviet Union over Europe.

From "Obstinate or Obsolete? The Fate of the Nation-State and the Case of Western Europe," by Stanley Hoffman, *Daedalus*, 95 (3): pp. 862–915.

If there was one part of the world in which men of good will thought that the nation-state could be superseded, it was Western Europe. One of France's most subtle commentators on international politics has recently reminded us of E. H. Carr's bold prediction of 1945: 'we shall not see again a Europe of twenty, and a world of more than sixty indepen-dent sovereign states'. Statesmen have invented original schemes for moving Western Europe 'beyond the nation-state', and political scientists have studied their efforts with a care from which emotional involvement was not missing. The conditions seemed ideal. On the one hand, nationalism seemed at its lowest ebb; on the other, an adequate formula and method for building a substitute had apparently been devised. Twenty years after the end of World War II—a period as long as the whole interwar era—observers have had to revise their judgments. The most optimistic put their hope in the chances the future may still harbor, rather than in the propelling power of the present; the less optimistic ones, like myself, try simply to understand what went wrong.

My own conclusion is sad and simple. The nation-state is still here, and the new Jerusalem has been postponed. * * *

*   *   *

Western Europe in the postwar years has been characterized by three features which have affected all of its nations. But each of those features has nevertheless affected each of the six nations in a different way because of the deep differences that have continued to divide the Six.

1. The first feature—the most hopeful one from the viewpoint of the unifiers—was the temporary demise of nationalism. In the defeated countries—Germany and Italy—nationalism had become associated with the regimes that had led the nations into war, defeat, and destruction. The collapse of two national ideologies that had been bellicose, aggressive, and imperialistic brought about an almost total discredit for nationalism in every guise . . .

However, the demise of nationalism affected differently the various nations of the half-continent. On the one hand, there were significant differences in national consciousness. If nationalism was low, patriotic sentiment was extremely high in liberated France. The circumstances in which the hated Nazis were expelled and the domestic collaborators purged amounted to what I have called elsewhere a rediscovery of the French political community by the French: the nation seemed to have redeemed its 'cohesion and distinctiveness'. On the contrary, in Germany especially, the destruction of nationalism seemed to have been accompanied by a drop in national consciousness as well: what was distinctive was guilt and shame; what had been only too cohesive was being torn apart not by internal politi-

cal cleavages, but by partition, zones of occupation, regional parochialisms blessed by the victors. The French national backbone had been straightened by the ordeal, although the pain had been too strong to tempt the French to flex nationalistic muscles; the German national backbone appeared to have been broken along with the strutting jaw and clenched fist of Nazi nationalism. Italy was in slightly better shape than Germany, in part because of its Resistance movements, but its story was closer to the German than to the French.

*   *   *

2. The second feature common to all the West European national institutions, yet affecting them differently, was the 'political collapse of Europe'. Europe did not merely lose power and wealth: such losses can be repaired, as the aftermath of World War I had shown. Europe, previously the heart of the international system, the locus of the world organization, the fount of international law, fell under what de Gaulle has called 'the two hegemonies'. The phrase is, obviously, inaccurate and insulting: one of those hegemonies took a highly imperial form, and thus discouraged and prevented the creation in Eastern Europe of any regional entity capable of overcoming the prewar national rivalries. Nothing is to be gained; however, by denying that US hegemony has been a basic fact of life. American domination has indeed had the kinds of 'domination effects' any hegemony produces: the transfer of decision-making in vital matters from the dominated to the dominator breeds a kind of paternalism in the latter, and irresponsibility (either in the form of abdication or in the form of scapegoatism) in the former. But the consequences of hegemony vary according to its nature. The peculiar nature of this domination has also had unique consequences—better and worse than in the classical cases. One may dominate because one wants to and can; but one may also dominate because one must and does: by one's weight and under the pressures of a compelling situation. This has been America's experience: its hegemony was 'situational', not deliberate.

The effects have been better than usual, insofar as such hegemony restricted itself to areas in which European nations had become either impotent or incapable of recovery by self-reliance. It left the dominated with a considerable freedom of maneuver, and indeed prodded them into recovery, power recuperation, and regional unity; it favored both individual and collective emancipation. But the effects have been worse precisely because this laxity meant that each party could react to *this* common feature of the national situations (that is, American hegemony) according to the distinctive *other* features of his national situation, features left intact by the weight and acts of the US, by contrast with the USSR. American domination was only one part of the picture. Hence the following paradox: both America's prodding and the individual and collective impotence of Western European nations, now reduced to the condition of clients and stakes, ought logically to have pushed them into unity-for-emancipation—the kind of process Soviet policy discouraged in the other half of Europe. But the very margin of autonomy left to each West European nation by the US gave it an array of choices: between accepting and rejecting dependence, between unity as a weapon for emancipation and unity as merely a way to make dependence more comfortable. It would have been a miracle if all the nations had made the same choice; the diversity of national situations has ultimately prevailed. To define one's position toward the US was the common imperative, but each one has defined it in his own way.

*   *   *

3. The divisions and contradictions, described above were sharpened by the third common feature, which emerged in the mid-1950s and whose effects have developed progressively since: the nuclear stalemate between the superpowers. The impact of the 'balance of terror' on the Western alliance has been analyzed so often and well that nothing needs to be added here; but what is needed is a brief explanation of how the two splits already discussed have been worsened by Europe's gradual discov-

ery of the uncertainties of America's nuclear protection (now that the US could be devastated too), and how some new splits appeared. For to the extent to which the stalemate has loosened up a previously very tight situation—tight because of the threat from the East and the ties to the US—it has altogether sharpened previous differences in national situations *and* increased the number of alternatives made available to elites and statesmen. Greater indeterminacy has meant greater confusion.

First, the split between French 'resistance' and German 'resignation' has become deeper. The dominant political elites in Germany have interpreted the new national situation created by the balance of terror as merely adding urgency to their previous calculation of interest. The nuclear stalemate was, given Germany's position, deemed to increase the danger for the West: the US was relatively less strong, the Soviet Union stronger, that is, more of a threat. . . . If America's monopoly was broken, if America's guarantee was weakened thereby, what was needed in a world that was not willing to let Germany rearm with nuclear weapons, in a continent that could not really develop a nuclear force of its own capable of replacing America's and of matching Russia's—was a German policy so respectful of America's main concerns, and also so vigilant with respect to the Soviet Union, that the US would both feel obligated to keep its mantle of protection over Germany and not be tempted into negotiating a detente at Germany's expense. German docility would be the condition for, and counterpart of, American entanglement . . .

In France, on the contrary, the balance of terror reinforced the attitude of resistance: what had always been a goal—emancipation—but had in fact been no more than a hope, given the thickness of the iron curtain, the simple rigidity of the superpowers' policies in the days of Mr. Dulles, and Europe's inability to affect the course of events, now became a possibility; for the giants' stalemate meant increased security for the less great (however much they might complain about the decrease of American protection and use it as a pretext, their lament coexisted with a heightened feeling of protection against war in general). What the Germans saw as a liability was an opportunity to the French. Germany's situation, its low national consciousness, incited most German leaders to choose what might be called a 'minimizing' interpretation of the new situation; France's situation, its high national consciousness and, after 1958, the doctrine of its leader, incited French political elites to choose a 'maximizing' interpretation. The increasing costs of the use of force made this use by the superpowers less likely, American protection less certain but also less essential, Europe's recovery of not merely wealth but power more desirable and possible— possible since the quest for power could be pushed without excessive risk of sanctions by the two giants, desirable since power, while transformed, remains the moving force and *ultima ratio* of world politics.

*   *   *

We must come now to the balance sheet of the 'European experiment'. The most visible aspect is the survival of the nations. To be sure, they survive transformed: first, swept by the advent of the 'age of mass consumption', caught in an apparently inexorable process of industrialization, urbanization, and democratization, they become more alike in social structure, in economic and social policies, even in physical appearance; there is a spectacular break between a past which so many monuments bring to constant memory, and a rationalized future that puts these nations closer to the problems of America's industrial society than to the issues of their own history. Second, these similarities are promoted by the Common Market itself: it is of no mean consequence that the prospect of a collapse of the Market should have brought anguish to various interest groups, some of which had fought its establishment: the transnational linkages of businessmen and farmers are part of the transformation. Third, none of the Western European nations is a world power any longer in the traditional sense, that is, in the sense either of having physical establishments backed by military might

in various parts of the globe, or of possessing in Europe armed forces superior to those of any non-European power.

And yet they survive as nations. Let us go back to the criteria of integration listed above. On foreign and defense policies, not only has no power been transferred to common European organs, but France has actually taken power away from NATO, and, as shown in part two, differences in the calculations of the national interest have, if anything, broadened ever since the advent of the balance of terror. As for intra-European communications, research shows that the indubitably solid economic network of EEC has not been complemented by a network of social and cultural communications; the links between some of those societies and the US are stronger than the links among them. Indeed, even in the realm of economic relations, the Common Market for goods has not been completed by a system of pan-West European enterprises: enterprises that find themselves unable to compete with rivals within EEC often associate themselves with American firms rather than merge with such rivals. Finally, views about external issues, far from becoming more compatible, appear to reflect as well as to support the divergent definitions of the national interest by the statesmen. French elite opinion puts Europe ahead of the North Atlantic partnership, deems bipolarity obsolete, is overwhelmingly indifferent or even hostile to the US, and is still highly suspicious of Germany; only a minority comes out in favor of a genuine political federation of Western Europe and thinks that US and French interests coincide. German elite opinion puts the North Atlantic entente ahead of Europe, believes that the world is still bipolar, is overwhelmingly favorable to the US, deems US and German interests in agreement, is either favorably inclined toward France or at least not hostile, and shows a majority in favor of a European federation. There is no common European outlook. Nor is there a common 'project', a common conception of either Europe's role in world affairs or Europe's possible contribution to the solution of the problems characteristic of all industrial societies.

REVIEW QUESTIONS

1. Why does Hoffmann say that the conditions were good in Western Europe after World War II to look for alternatives to the nation-state? Does he believe that the nation-state is obsolete? Why or why not?

2. He identifies three historical developments after World War II that affected the many European nations in different ways, making integration more difficult. What were these developments?

3. What are the effects of Soviet and U.S. power in Europe after World War II, according to Hoffman? Did U.S. policy encourage European integration?

4. Hoffman places special emphasis on the nuclear arms race as having been an obstacle to European integration. How was the possibility of nuclear confrontation between the U.S. and the Soviet Union seen differently in France and Germany?

MARK MAZOWER

FROM *Dark Continent: Europe's Twentieth Century*

Mark Mazower was born in Britain in 1958 and is a professor of history at Columbia University. He has written widely on European history in the twentieth century, and is a specialist in Greek and Balkan history. This excerpt is from his 1998 book Dark Continent: Europe's Twentieth Century, *in which he argued that the survival of democratic regimes in twentieth-century Europe may have been due more to chance and contingent circumstances than to any intrinsic association between democratic values and European identities.*

From "Epilogue: Making Europe," from *Dark Continent: Europe's Twentieth Century*, by Mark Mazower (New York: Random House, 2000), pp. 395–98.

"Democracy has won," wrote Zbigniew Brzezinski in 1990. "The free market has won. But what in the wake of this great ideological victory is today the substance of our beliefs?" As the euphoria which greeted the end of the Cold War gave way to gloomy misgivings, Francis Fukuyama saw communism's collapse ushering in the end of history and the dawning of a more prosaic and less heroic era. Others foresaw instead the rebirth of history's demons—nationalism, fascism and racial and religious struggle. They talked about "the return of history" and drew grim parallels—as Sarajevo hit the headlines—between 1992 and the eve of the First World War.

In fact, history had neither left Europe nor returned to it. But with the end of the Cold War, Europe's place in history changed. Europe is once again undivided, but it no longer occupies the central role in world affairs which it held before the Cold War began. Understanding where we stand today thus requires not only seeing how the present resembles the past, but how it differs from it as well. Sometimes it is easier to dream the old dreams—even when they are nightmares—than to wake up to unfamiliar realities.

"With the passing of the centuries," two French historians concluded in 1992, "Europe discovers that beyond the differences of its tongues and customs, its people partake of a common culture . . . Europe is becoming conscious of the existence of a European identity." Made with unfortunate timing in the year civil war broke out in Yugoslavia, this bold claim has a respectable pedigree. In 1936, another year of civil war, the British historian H. A. L. Fisher asserted that Europe was unified by a civilization which was "distinct . . . all pervading and preponderant," resting upon "an inheritance of thought and achievement and religious aspiration." And a few years later, in *The Limits and Divisions of European History*, the émigré Polish scholar Oskar Hàlecki pleaded for the fundamental unity of the continent at the very moment his country formed part of the Communist bloc.

It is as though one response to the bloody struggles of this century has been to deny their internecine character: one side is made to stand for the true Europe—*l'Europe européenne* in the striking phrase of Gonzague de Reynold—while the others are written off as usurpers or barbarians. The intellectual tradition which identifies Europe with the cause of liberty and freedom goes back many centuries. But if we face the fact that liberal democracy failed between the wars, and if we admit that communism and fascism also formed part of the continent's political heritage, then it is hard to deny that what has shaped Europe in this century is not a gradual-convergence of thought and feeling, but on the contrary a series of violent clashes between antagonistic New Orders. If we search for Europe not as a geographical expression, but as what Federico Chabod called "an historic and moral individuality," we find that for much of the century it did not exist.

What was new in Europe's history was not the existence of conflict, but rather its scale. Compared with the great dynastic empires of the past—the long centuries of Byzantine, Habsburg and Ottoman rule—the utopian experiments of twentieth-century ideologies came and went with striking speed: yet their struggle brought new levels of violence into European life, militarizing society, strengthening the state and g millions of people with the help of modern bureaucracies and technologies. In the 1870–71 Franco-Prussian War the death-toll was 184,000; in the First World War it was above eight million, and more than forty million Europeans—half of them civilians—died in the Second World War. The depth of these wounds was directly proportionate to the grandeur of the ambitions held by the various protagonists, each of whom aspired to remake Europe—inside and out—more thoroughly than ever before. It is not surprising if today Europe is suffering from ideological exhaustion, and if politics has become a distinctly unvisionary activity. As Austria's former chancellor Franz Vranitsky once supposedly remarked: "Anyone with visions needs to see a doctor."

This disillusionment colours the strange post-1989 triumph of democracy in Europe. Seventy years earlier, the consolidation of democracy across the continent after the First World War fitted liberal dreams of a new world order: Europe seemed destined to become the model for mankind. Through the League of Nations the new states of eastern Europe would learn the habits of democracy from the more advanced and mature states of the West, while through colonies and mandates, the great imperial powers would spread democracy more widely. The defeat of communism in Europe in 1989 carried no such global implications, and no such evangelical dreams. Democracy suits Europeans today partly because it is associated with the triumph of capitalism and partly because it involves less commitment or intrusion into their lives than any of the alternatives. Europeans accept democracy because they no longer believe in politics. It is for this reason that we find both high levels of support for democracy in cross-national opinion polls and high rates of political apathy. In contemporary Europe, democracy allows racist parties of the Right to coexist with more active protection of human rights than ever before. It encompasses both the grass-roots politics of Switzerland and near-dictatorship in post-communist Croatia.

The real victor in 1989 was not democracy but capitalism, and Europe as a whole now faces the task which western Europe has confronted since the 1930s, of establishing a workable relationship between the two. The inter-war depression revealed that democracy might not survive a major crisis of capitalism, and in fact democracy's eventual triumph over communism would have been unimaginable without the reworked social contract which followed the Second World War. The ending of full employment and the onset of welfare retrenchment make this achievement harder than ever to sustain, especially in societies characterized by ageing populations. The globalization of financial markets makes it increasingly difficult for nation-states to preserve autonomy of action, yet markets—as a series of panics and crashes demonstrates—generate their own irrationalities and social tensions. The globalization of labour, too, challenges prevailing definitions of national citizenship, culture and tradition. Whether Europe can chart a course between the individualism of American capitalism and the authoritarianism of East Asia, pre serving its own blend of social solidarity and political freedom, remains to be seen. But the end of the Cold War means that there is no longer an opponent against whom democrats can define what they stand for in pursuit of this goal. The old political signposts have been uprooted, leaving most people without a clear sense of direction.

This sense of *fin de siècle* disorientation is largely a European problem which reflects the specific historical experience of Europe this century,

and the carnage that followed its once-fervent faith in utopias. A self-belief rooted in Christianity, capitalism, the Enlightenment and massive technological superiority encouraged Europeans to see themselves over a long period as a civilizational model for the globe. Their trust in Europe's world mission was already evident in the seventeenth and eighteenth centuries and reached its apogee in the era of imperialism. Hitler was in many ways its culminating figure and through the Nazi New Order came closer to its realization than anyone else. Now that the Cold War has ended, Europe is once more undivided, and this makes its loss of belief in the pre-eminence of its civilization and values all the more obvious. Many of the newly freed states of the former Soviet empire cannot wait to join "Europe." Yet what that "Europe" is, and where it stands in the world, seem less and less clear.

REVIEW QUESTIONS

1. What leads Mazower to question the relationship between Europe and "the cause of liberty and freedom"?

2. What does the history of Europe in the twentieth century tell us about the relationship between democracy and capitalism, according to Mazower?

3. Why does Mazower question the need for Europeans to claim a common identity at the dawn of the twenty-first century, in the wake of decolonization and the end of the Cold War?

OLIVIER ROY

FROM *Globalized Islam: The Search for a New Ummah*

Olivier Roy is a professor at EHESS, the School of Advanced Studies in Social Sciences in Paris, France. He specializes in the study of Islamic political movements, especially in Afghanistan and Iran. His books include The Failure of Political Islam *and (with Mariam Abou Zahab)* Islamist Networks: The Afghan-Pakistan Connection. *This excerpt comes from his book* Globalized Islam *(2004), which focuses on the ways that globalization, westernization, and the experience of living as a minority has shaped the relationship between Muslims and Islam in the contemporary world. In this passage, he asks the question "What is Bin Laden's strategy?"*

From *Globalized Islam: The Search for a New Ummah*, by Olivier Roy (New York: Columbia University Press, 2004), pp. 55–57.

Osama Bin Laden has no strategy in the true sense of the word. Nothing was organised for the day after 9/11: no other attacks or assassinations, no upheavals in Egypt, Saudi Arabia or Algeria. Some elements suggest coherence in Osama Bin Laden's long-term outlook. The assassination of Commander Ahmed Shah Massoud, an anti-Taliban Afghan leader, on 9 September 2001 was planned months before (the two killers had been waiting for weeks to meet him). Taliban and Al Qaeda troops had been massed on the northern front since June 2001; for the first time fighters from the Islamic Movement of Uzbekistan (IMU) joined an anti-Massoud mobilisation, a sign that this was seen as the final battle. But no real battle happened, as if the troops had been waiting for something: the collapse of the United Front of Afghanistan in the wake of its leader's death. Massoud's assassination nevertheless came too late—just days before the first US military officers entered the Panjshir Valley. Obviously, however, Osama Bin Laden had wanted to clean up Afghanistan before an unavoidable US attack. He knew the United States would retaliate on Afghan territory and he was expecting the offensive. For Bin Laden the references were Vietnam, the Soviet defeat in Afghanistan, and the US withdrawals from Lebanon in 1984 and Somalia ten years later. He was convinced that the United States would not stand a long war and that in any case a protracted war would stir up plenty of turmoil and even uprisings in Pakistan, Saudi Arabia and Egypt—with no need to organise them. The US position would be unsustainable. In short, he was banking on a war of attrition that would destabilise the power of the United States and its allies in the region (the Saudis first, although I do not think that the Saudi regime was the primary target). In this sense, his aim has been inadvertently achieved in Iraq.

Bin Laden made two critical mistakes. First, he did not realise that the Afghan population was fed up with the Taliban and that the Pashtun tribesmen who have been supporting the Taliban (principally over issues of law and order, conservative Islam and Pashtun supremacy) were not willing to lose their lives and property for an uncertain worldwide *jihad* against the US hyperpower. The international agenda of Osama Bin Laden simply had no appeal in Afghanistan. He probably did not expect the sudden collapse of his Taliban allies or the thirst for revenge of the non-Pashtuns (ethnic issues were always logically downplayed by Bin Laden, who renounced his ethnic and national backgrounds to fight for a universal cause). Second, he overestimated the reaction of the 'Arab in the street'. Osama Bin Laden did not grasp that the genuine anti-Americanism of the 'average' Arab had never led to a sustainable political mobilisation, and that if such mobilisation ever did happen it would be over Palestine and Iraq—that is, over Arab and not Islamic issues.

In this sense Al Qaeda terrorism is totally different from that of the 'usual' terrorists in the Middle East and elsewhere. Iran-sponsored terrorism in the 1980s, as well as attacks by the Irish Republican Army (IRA) or Tamil Tigers, fitted into a political strategy: Iran wanted to bring about the end of Western support for Iraq and the departure of Western forces from Lebanon, while the IRA and Tamil Tigers wanted to achieve independence (which was also the aim of the Jewish underground movement Irgun Zvai Leumi in Palestine in the 1940s). Palestinian suicide bombers want an end to the Israeli occupation of Gaza and the West Bank (although some would also like to see the end of Israel, which is another issue). Whatever the means, there is room for negotiation. The IRA, the PLO, the Tamil Tigers and even the Basque separatist group ETA are seen as legitimate political actors to the extent they will potentially cease terrorist actions. But with Bin Laden there is no room for negotiation. His aim is simply to destroy Babylon.

In this sense the historical continuity of which Osama Bin Laden is part has nothing to do with the Islamic tradition of *jihad*. Notwithstanding the debate on what the word really means, it is clear that *jihad*, as an armed struggle, has always been instrumentalised for political and strategic purposes, by state actors or would-be state actors. Bin Laden's *jihad* has more to do with the ethos of a modern Western terrorist, as we have seen above. For the sake and pleasure of Allah (*reza*), for the sake of self-achievement (in death), for escaping a corrupt world . . . There is a strange mix of deep personal pessimism and collective millenarianist optimism among this type of terrorists: they do not trust the people they are fighting for (they are also indifferent to killing Muslims), they are sure to die, and as political scientist Farhad Khosrokhavar pointed out in the case of the Iranian martyrs of the Iran–Iraq War, they know that, even if they succeed, in the future society will not match the ideals for which they are fighting.[1] It is reminiscent of the Russian socialist revolutionaries of the end of the nineteenth century, and the idea that a spectacular attack at the heart of the power will suddenly show the alienated masses that their time has come and they will rise up. As Lenin put it, this is a childish view. Osama Bin Laden has lived in a pre-Leninist world.

But what are the repercussions of these facts? First, there is no basis for negotiation with Osama Bin Laden: his fight, as we have seen, is not directly linked to the various conflicts in the Middle East. These conflicts will certainly provide Al Qaeda with new volunteers, and solving them will not necessarily dry up the pool from which Al Qaeda recruits, because this pool has more to do with the West than with the Middle East. The second consequence is that Al Qaeda is not a strategic threat but a security problem. The war on terrorism is a metaphor, not a real policy.

REVIEW QUESTIONS

1. Why does Roy suggest that Osama Bin Laden "has no strategy"?
2. According to Roy, what makes Bin Laden's terrorism different from the terrorism of what he refers to as the "usual terrorists in the Middle East and elsewhere"?
3. What conclusions does Roy draw from his analysis of Bin Laden's goals?

---

[1] Farhad Khosrokhavar, *L'islamisme et la mort. Le martyre révolutionnaire en Iran*, Paris: Harmattan, 1995.

The Greek Debt Crisis

In 2009, shortly after the global financial crisis of 2008, the Greek government announced that its debts were much greater than previously reported. Banks responded by charging the Greek government much higher interest to borrow the money it needed for normal operating expenses, and by 2010 Greece was nearly bankrupt. The Greek economy went into a free fall; in July 2015 unemployment was 28%.

Under such conditions, governments sometimes choose to devalue their currency, because inflation can give a short-term boost to the economy. Since Greece was a member of the Eurozone, however, this option was not available to them. Greece shares its currency, the euro, with 18 other European nations. The European Union faced a choice—either reduce Greek debt by making their creditors take a "haircut," or arrange for a bailout with funds from other European countries. The only other option was "Grexit"—a Greek exit from the Eurozone. No country that had joined the Eurozone had ever left, and the consequences of such a step were uncertain. Some feared that it might be catastrophic for Europe as a whole.

Between 2010 and 2015, the so-called troika—the International Monetary Fund, the European Central Bank, and the European Commission—negotiated with successive Greek governments to establish the terms for three international bailouts. In each case, the troika demanded a strict "austerity" policy before the bailout funds could be dispersed: deep cuts in government spending, tax reforms, and international oversight. This position was popular among Europe's wealthier countries, especially Germany.

The latest such negotiations culminated in July 2015, when a Greek government headed by the left-wing Syriza party negotiated once more for a third bailout. Syriza argued that the austerity package of spending cuts doomed Greece to years of hardship, and a loss of national sovereignty. Germans, led by Chancellor Angela Merkel and finance minister Wolfgang Schäuble, felt that debt forgiveness would be rewarding the Greek government for its improvident spending and refusal to reform.

These two documents describe the positions on both sides of the debate. The Thessaloniki Program is a manifesto from the Greek Coalition of the Radical Left (SYRIZA) from 2014, before they took power from the previous government headed by Antonis Samaras in January 2015. It points out that Germany benefited from debt reduction after World War II, and it recalls the forced loan that the Nazi government imposed on Greece after invading in 1941. The second is an editorial by Alan Posener, a British-German journalist who examines the German perspective on the crisis, and German resentment at being compared to Nazis.

Syriza: The Thessaloniki Programme

THE CONTEXT OF NEGOTIATION

We demand immediate parliamentary elections and a strong negotiation mandate with the goal to:

Write-off the greater part of public debt's nominal value so that it becomes sustainable in the context of a European Debt Conference. It happened for Germany in 1953. It can also happen for the South of Europe and Greece.

Include a "growth clause" in the repayment of the remaining part so that it is growth-financed and not budget-financed.

Include a significant grace period ("moratorium") in debt servicing to save funds for growth.

Exclude public investment from the restrictions of the Stability and Growth Pact.

A European New Deal of public investment financed by the European Investment Bank.

Quantitative easing by the European Central Bank with direct purchases of sovereign bonds.

Finally, we declare once again that the issue of the Nazi Occupation forced loan from the Bank of Greece is open for us. Our partners know it. It will become the country's official position from our first days in power.

On the basis of this plan, we will fight and secure a socially viable solution to Greece's debt problem so that our country is able to pay off the remaining debt from the creation of new wealth and not from primary surpluses, which deprive society of income.

With that plan, we will lead with security the country to recovery and productive reconstruction by:

Immediately increasing public investment by at least €4 billion.

Gradually reversing all the Memorandum injustices.

Gradually restoring salaries and pensions so as to increase consumption and demand.

Providing small and medium-sized enterprises with incentives for employment, and subsidizing the energy cost of industry in exchange for an employment and environmental clause.

Investing in knowledge, research, and new technology in order to have young scientists, who have been massively emigrating over the last years, back home.

Rebuilding the welfare state, restoring the rule of law and creating a meritocratic state.

We are ready to negotiate and we are working towards building the broadest possible alliances in Europe.

The present Samaras government is once again ready to accept the decisions of the creditors. The only alliance which it cares to build is with the German government.

This is our difference and this is, at the end, the dilemma:

European negotiation by a SYRIZA government, or acceptance of the creditors' terms on Greece by the Samaras government.

*   *   *

The Bailout Crisis: Germany's View of How Greece Fell From Grace

Alan Posener

Did he or didn't he? Last week, the biggest media story in Germany was whether or not Yanis Varoufakis had flipped us the finger. After a video of the Greek finance minister "showing the stinkfinger" (as Germans put it) was screened on a talk show, a satirist claimed he had doctored the video and that the finger-flip was a fake. A day later he recanted.

Experts pored over the "Varoufake" video like JFK conspiracy buffs over the Zapruder footage. No matter that the video dates from 2013 and has no bearing on today's politics—the "Varoufake" story

---

From "The Thessaloniki Programme," *Syriza* (Sept. 2014).

From "The bailout crisis: Germany's view of how Greece fell from grace," by Alan Posener, *The Guardian* (21 March 2015).

eclipsed riots in Frankfurt and terrorism in Tunis. For Germany, Greece is more than a pesky problem on the periphery of Europe. It's an obsession.

One can understand the Greeks' obsession with Germany, which the Syriza government blames for austerity policies that have brought the country to its knees. But Germany has built a firewall round its banks to protect them from the fallout from a "Grexit".

Its position—that Greece must honour the terms of its bailout—has the backing of most other EU members and EU institutions. It could regard the antics of an inexperienced government faced with the harsh realities of life in the eurozone with equanimity. This is, in fact, the attitude that Germany's finance minister, Wolfgang Schäuble, has maintained.

Germans admire Schäuble for keeping his cool. Greek caricatures portraying him as a Nazi have caused outrage. Germans also resent Greek demands for reparations for the brutal occupation in the second world war, and hints that they might confiscate German property to enforce payment. The Greeks do have a point, and Germany is willing to negotiate. But using Germany's past to blackmail Angela Merkel's government in totally unrelated negotiations is not a good idea. For decades, Germany's bad conscience has been exploited by its European friends. But there is a growing—and dangerous—feeling here that enough is enough.

Ironically, back in the 1990s, Helmut Kohl gave up the deutschmark and accepted the euro in order to reassure the French that Germany would not become Europe's hegemon. In return, members of the euro club were supposed to abide by strict rules to ensure the common currency did not become like, well, the franc, lira or drachma. And now to have the past dredged up and flung in Germany's face by a country that lied its way into the eurozone, refused to reform while it was rolling in cheap money courtesy of the common currency, can't or won't collect taxes properly, has been bailed out repeatedly and still doesn't accept the rules—this could well be the final straw. The Greeks can congratulate themselves on a self-fulfilling prophecy the oracle at Delphi would have been proud of: nationalism is rearing its ugly head in Germany again.

Indeed, the rise of populism at home is a main reason Merkel cannot climb down. On the right, the anti-euro, anti-immigrant and vaguely anti-American party Alternative für Deutschland will probably get into the Bundestag in 2017. On the left, a campaign against the free trade agreement between the EU and the US is gaining momentum. On the streets, people have demonstrated in Dresden against "Islamisation" and the "lying press" and rioted in Frankfurt against the European Central Bank and capitalism in general. Squeezed by radicals on left and right, the pro-Europe centre may not hold.

The situation in the rest of Europe is even worse. Cave in to the Greeks, government officials mutter, and the next thing you know the Spanish will elect the populists of Podemos, the Irish will go for Sinn Féin and both will demand handouts, to be paid for by you-know-who. France's Marine Le Pen will have more arguments for leaving the eurozone or even the EU. And let's not even mention Britain. Meanwhile, Vladimir Putin tears up treaties, tramples on his neighbours' sovereignty and threatens the EU's eastern flank, and Islamic State kills people just across the Mediterranean.

When Athens threatens to turn to Russia, open its borders and let immigrants from Syria into Europe, or even wave Isis fighters through, it is not only behaving irrationally—you don't threaten the people you want money from, unless you're a gangster. It is destroying the glue that holds Europe together: trust.

Germans' attitudes toward politics are informed by their history and based on Kantian ethics: ends never justify means. Rules, therefore, must never be broken, even if they are self-defeating. This is alien to Anglo-Saxon policymakers, who follow the utilitarian precepts of Jeremy Bentham and John Stuart Mill. And it is alien, of course, to southern European politicians, for whom political expediency will always trump principles. In the euro crisis, Germany has repeatedly seen the rules bent, broken, changed and broken again. The EU needs to understand that this is intensely worrying to most Germans.

At the deepest level, however, German exasperation with the Greeks is rooted in fear. At the end of this century, Germany will have fewer than 60 million inhabitants, 25 million fewer than today. By 2050 the demographic great powers of Europe will be Turkey, France and Britain (in that order).

Germany, a country with an ageing, shrinking, underqualified and poorly paid workforce, a country fixated on hammering metal rather than tapping touch-screens and addicted to unsustainably high exports, could find itself in an economic crisis sooner rather than later.

For the German elite at least, European integration is the answer. Germany feels that it needs to establish an economically stable, rule-based and politically united Europe while it still has the power to do so. Greece's antics thus awaken the angst that dares not speak its name.

What to do? The Greeks have made their point. Many Germans inside and outside the government realise that austerity must be eased. They accept that Germany has benefited from the same set of euro rules that drove Greece into bankruptcy, and that Greece needs help.

What the Greeks ought to do now is to help Germany help them by going short on the rhe-toric . . . and producing realistic plans for reform. Their politicians are no longer playing primarily to a Greek audience. Europe is watching.

REVIEW QUESTIONS

1. The Syriza manifesto is aimed at the Greek electorate prior to the elections of January 2015. How does it explain what it will do in the next round of negotiations with European leaders? What charges does it make against the Samaras government?

2. Posener also describes the Greek debt crisis as a question that has implications for German electoral politics. What are the pressures that Angela Merkel and Wolfgang Schäuble feel from their own voters as they negotiate with Greece about a bailout?

3. What does this clash of interests and electoral politics say about the prospects of European integration? Do people in Greece and Germany still think of themselves as primarily Greek and German, before they think of themselves as Europeans?

Credits

Photo Credits

Page 57: Erich Lessing/Art Resource, NY; **p. 63:** Erich Lessing/Art Resource, NY; **p. 87:** Foto Marburg/Art Resource, NY; **p. 101:** Erich Lessing/Art Resource, NY; **Page 116:** The Granger Collection, New York; **p. 127 (top):** Art Gallery of New South Wales; **p. 127 (middle):** Bettmann/Corbis; **p. 127 (bottom):** Art Gallery of New South Wales; **p. 137:** The Gallery Collection/Corbis; **p. 164:** Mary Evans Picture Library/age footstock; **p. 169:** Gianni Dagli Orti/The Art Archive at Art Resource, NY; **p. 197 (1 & 2):** Bettmann/Corbis; **p. 197 (3 & 4):** Heritage Images/Corbis; **p. 215:** The Granger Collection, New York; **p. 226:** The Granger Collection, New York; **p. 259:** The Gallery Collection/Corbis; **p. 296:** RMN-Grand Palais/Art Resource, NY; **p. 311:** Imagerie d'Epinal 2001; **p. 334:** Art Resource, NY; **p. 342:** The Royal Collection Trust/© Her Majesty Queen Elizabeth II 2015; **p. 351:** © Victoria & Albert Museum, London; **p. 393:** akg-images/Newscom; **p. 409:** Erich Lessing/Art Resource, NY; **p. 437:** © Harvard Art Museum/Art Resource, NY; **p. 441:** North Wind Pictures; **p. 479:** From the book *Spectacle of Women* by Lisa Tickner; **p. 482:** Punch Limited; **p. 505:** Hulton-Deutsch Collection/Corbis Premium Collection; **p. 524 (left):** Daniel Deme/epa/Corbis; **p. 524 (right):** Swim Ink 2, LLC/Corbis; **p. 525 (top):** Swim Ink 2, LLC/Corbis; **p. 525 (bottom left):** Swim Ink 2, LLC/Corbis; **p. 525 (bottom right):** Stapleton Collection/Corbis; **p. 534:** Heritage Images/Getty Images; **p. 582 (left):** Julien Bryan/AP Photo; **p. 582 (right):** Corbis; **p. 583 (top):** Deutsche Fotothek/picture alliance/ZB/Newscom; **p. 583 (bottom):** Corbis; **p. 584 (top):** The Granger Collection, New York; **p. 584 (bottom):** Hulton-Deutsch/Hulton-Deutsch Collection/Corbis; **p. 585 (top):** Underwood & Underwood/Corbis; **p. 585 (bottom):** Hulton-Deutsch/Hulton-Deutsch Collection/Corbis; **p. 595:** Hulton-Deutsch Collection/Corbis; **p. 615:** AP Photo.

Text Credits

Leon B. Alberti: Reprinted by permission of Waveland Press, Inc., from *The Family in Renaissance Florence, Book Three: I Libri Della Famiglia*, translated by Renée Neu Watkins. Long Grove, IL: Waveland Press, Inc., 1994. All rights reserved.

Jean Bodin: From *On Sovereignty*, pp. 46–50. Copyright © Cambridge University Press 1992. Reprinted with the permission of Cambridge University Press.

Cesare Beccaria Bonesana: From *An Essay on Crimes and Punishments*, by Cesare Beccaria Bonesana. Stanford: Academic Reprints, 1953, pp. 15–19, 47, 59–67, 95–96. Reprinted by permission of Branden Books.

John Calvin: *Theological Treatises* From *John Calvin*, by G. R. Potter and M. Greengrass. London: Edward Arnold, 1983.

Catherine the Great: "Proposals for a New Code of Law," from *Documents of Catherine the Great: The Correspondence with Voltaire and the Instruction of 1767 in the English Text of 1768*, translated by W. F. Reddaway. Copyright © 1931 Cambridge University Press. Reprinted with permission from Cambridge University Press.

Geoffrey Chaucer: From *The Canterbury Tales: Nine Tales and the General Prologue: A Norton Critical Edition*, by Geoffrey Chaucer, edited by V. A. Kolve and Glending Olson, pp. 192–207. Copyright © 1989 by W. W. Norton & Company. Used by permission of W. W. Norton & Company, Inc.

Christopher Columbus: "The First Voyage of Christopher Columbus," from *Selected Documents Illustrating the Four Voyages of Columbus, Vol. 1*, edited and translated by Cecil Jane, The Hakluyt Society, 1930. Reprinted by permission of David Higham Associates, Ltd.

Bartolomeo de Giano: From "A Letter on the Cruelty of the Turks," by Bartolomeo de Giano, trans. W. L. North. *Patrologia Graeca*, Vol. 158, edited by J. P. Migne. Venice: Bibliotheca S. Michele, 2004, 1055–1068. Reprinted with permission.

Olympe de Gouges: "Declaration of the Rights of Woman," from *Women, the Family and Freedom: The Debate in Documents, Volume 1, 1750–1880*, by Susan Groag Bell and Karen M. Offen, eds. Copyright © 1983 by the Board of Trustees of the Leland Stanford Junior University. All rights reserved. Used with permission of Stanford University Press, www.sup.org.

Joseph de Maistre: From *Against Rousseau: "On the State of Nature" and "On the Sovereignty of People,"* by Joseph de Maistre, translated and edited by Richard A. Lebrun. Montreal: McGill-Queen's University Press, 1996, pp. 119–125, 128, 131–134.

Michel de Montaigne: pp. 132–135 and 150–159 from *The Complete Essays of Montaigne* translated by Donald Frame. Copyright © 1958 by the Board of Trustees of the Leland Stanford Junior University. All rights reserved. Used with the permission of Stanford University Press, www.sup.org.

Christine de Pizan: from *The Book of the City of Ladies* by Christine de Pizan, translated by Earl Jeffrey Richards. Copyright © 1982, 1998 by Persea Books. Reprinted by permission of Persea Books, Inc., New York.

Laurent Dubois and John D. Garrigus (trans.): "The Haitian Declaration of Independence," from *Slave Revolution in the Caribbean, 1789–1804: A Brief History with Documents,* translated by Laurent Dubois and John D. Garrigus. London: Macmillan, 2006, pp. 188–191. Reprinted with permission.

Desiderius Erasmus: "Cyclops, or the Gospel Bearer," from Craig R. Thompson, *Erasmus: Ten Colloquies, 1st Edition.* Copyright © 1957, pages 120–129. Reprinted by permission of Pearson Education, Inc., Upper Saddle River, N.J.

Olaudah Equiano: From *The Interesting Narrative of Olaudah Equiano, or Gustvus Vassa the African, Written by Himself: Norton Critical Edition,* edited by Werner Sollors. Copyright © 2001 by W. W. Norton & Company, Inc. Used by permission of W. W. Norton & Company, Inc.

Frantz Fanon: From *The Wretched of the Earth,* translated by Constance Farrington, pp. 83–84, 88–90, 92–94, 96–98, 102. Copyright © 1963 by *Présence Africaine.* Used by permission of Grove/Atlantic, Inc.

Vladimir Fisera: From *Writing on the Wall, France 1968: A Documentary Anthology,* by Vladimir Fisera. Copyright © 1978 Vladimir Fisera. Reproduced with permission of Palgrave Macmillan.

Sigmund Freud: From *Civilization and Its Discontents,* by Sigmund Freud, translated by James Strachey, pp. 55–59. Copyright © 1961 by James Strachey, renewed 1989 by Alix Strachey. Used by permission of W. W. Norton & Company, Inc. "Five Lectures on Psychoanalysis," by Sigmund Freud. © Copyrights, The Institute of Psycho-Analysis and The Hogarth Press for permission to quote from *The Standard Edition of the Complete Psychological Works of Sigmund Freud,* translated and edited by James Strachey. Reprinted by permission of The Random House Group Ltd.

Galileo Galilei: From *Discoveries and Opinions of Galileo,* by Galileo Galilei, translated by Stillman Drake. Copyright © 1957 by Stillman Drake. Used by permission of Doubleday, a division of Random House, Inc.

Mahatma Gandhi: "The Doctrine of the Sword" and "Nonviolence, The Greatest Force," from *The Essential Writings of Mahatma Gandhi,* pp. 236–242. Reprinted by permission of the Navajivan Trust.

Adolf Hitler: Excerpt from *Mein Kampf,* by Adolf Hitler, published by Pimlico. Copyright © 1939, 1943 by Houghton Mifflin Company. Reprinted by permission of Houghton Mifflin Harcourt Publishing Company. All rights reserved. Reprinted by permission of The Random House Group Ltd.

Stanley Hoffmann: From "Obstinate or Obsolete? The Fate of the Nation-State and the Case of Western Europe," *Daedalus,* 95 (3), p. 862–915. MIT Press Journals. Reprinted with permission.

Lynn Hunt: "Address to the National Assembly in Favor of the Abolition of the Slave Trade," from *The French Revolution and Human Rights: A Brief Documentary History,* edited and translated by Lynn Hunt. Copyright © 1996 by Bedford/St. Martin's. Reproduced by permission of Bedford/St. Martin's.

Ernst Jünger: From *The Storm of Steel: From the Diary of a German Storm-Troop Officer on the Western Front,* translated by Basil Creighton, published by Chatto & Windus, pp. 83–91, 98–100. Reprinted by permission of The Random House Group Ltd.

Nikita Khrushchev: "On the Cult of Personality and Its Consequences," by Nikita Khrushchev. From *The Stalin Dictatorship: Khrushchev's "Secret Speech" and Other Documents,* edited by T. H. Rigby. Sydney: Sydney University Press, 1968. Reprinted by Permission of Sydney University Press.

Tadataka Kuribayashi: "A Child's Experience: My Experience of the Atomic Bomb," by Tadataka Kuribayashi, www.csi.ad.jp/ABOMB, from A-Bomb WWW Museum.

Vladimir Lenin: From "Our Programme," by Vladimir Lenin (1899), Marxists Internet Archive, http://marxists.org/archive/lenin/works/1899/articles/index.htm. From *Imperialism, The Highest Stage of Capitalism,* pp. 123–127. Reprinted by permission of International Publishers Co., New York.

Primo Levi: "The Journey," "On the Bottom," "[Null Achtzehn]," and "The Drowned and the Saved," from *If This Is A Man (Survival in Auschwitz)* by Primo Levi, translated by Stuart Woolf. Copyright © 1959 by Orion Press, Inc., © 1958 by Giulio Einaudi editore S.P.A. Used by permission of Viking Penguin, a division of Penguin Group (USA) Inc.

Herbert J. Liebesny (ed.): "Legal Reform in the Ottoman Empire: The Imperial Edict of the Rose Chamber," from *The Law of the Near & Middle East: Readings, Cases, & Materials,* edited by Herbert J. Liebesny. Albany, N.Y.: State University of New York Press, 1975, pp. 46–49. Reprinted by permission of the State University of New York Press.

Sebastian Lotzer: "The Twelve Articles of the Peasants of Swabia," from *The Revolution of 1525: The German Peasants' War from a New Perspective,* edited and translated by Peter Blickle, Thomas A. Brady, Jr., and H. C. Erik Midelfort, pp. 195–201. Copyright © 1981 The Johns Hopkins University Press. Reprinted with permission of The Johns Hopkins University Press.

Martin Luther: "Preface," pp. 2–9, from *The Large Catechism of Martin Luther,* by Martin Luther, translated by

Robert Fischer. Copyright © 1959 Fortress Press. Used by permission of Augsburg Fortress Publishers.

Niccolò Machiavelli: Excerpts from pp. 31–32, 44–50, *The Prince: A Norton Critical Edition, Second Edition* by Niccolò Machiavelli, translated by Robert M. Adams. Copyright © 1992, 1977 by W. W. Norton & Company, Inc. Used by permission of W. W. Norton & Company, Inc.

Karl Marx and Friedrich Engels: from *The Marx-Engels Reader*, edited by Robert C. Tucker. 2nd Ed.; New York: W. W. Norton, 1978, pp. 56–62.

Mark Mazower: "Epilogue: Making Europe," from *Dark Continent: Europe's Twentieth Century*, by Mark Mazower. Copyright © 1998 by Mark Mazower. Used by permission of Alfred A. Knopf, a division of Random House, Inc.

Moses Mendelssohn: From *What Is Enlightenment?: Eighteenth-Century Answers and Twentieth-Century Questions*, translated and edited by James Schmidt. Berkeley, Calif.: University of California Press, 1996, pp. 53–56. Published by the University of California Press. Reprinted by permission of the publisher.

Giovanni Michiel: pp. 72–76, 78–79 from *The Pursuit of Power: Venetian Ambassadors' Reports*, edited and translated by James Davis. English translation copyright © 1970 by James C. Davis. Reprinted by permission of HarperCollins Publishers.

Ho Chi Minh: "Speech Delivered in the First Days of the Resistance War in South Vietnam," from *Ho Chi Minh: On Revolution*, edited and with an introduction by Bernard B. Fall, pp. 158–159. Reprinted by permission.

Sir Thomas More: Excerpts from pp. 30–33, 40–42, 50–51, 64, *Utopia: A Norton Critical Edition, Second Edition* by Sir Thomas More, translated by Robert M. Adams. Copyright © 1992, 1975 by W. W. Norton & Company, Inc. Used by permission of W. W. Norton & Company, Inc.

Benito Mussolini: "Born of a Need for Action," from *The Political and Social Doctrine of Fascism*, by Benito Mussolini, translated by Jane Soames, published by The Hogarth Press. Reprinted by permission of The Random House Group Ltd.

George Orwell: Excerpts from *The Road to Wigan Pier*, by George Orwell. Copyright © 1958 and renewed 1986 by the Estate of Sonia B. Orwell, reprinted by permission of Houghton Mifflin Harcourt Publishing Company. Copyright © George Orwell, 1937, by permission of Bill Hamilton as the Literary Executor of the Estate of the Late Sonia Brownell Orwell and Secker & Warburg Ltd.

František Palacký: From "History of the Czech Nation in Bohemia and Moravia," edited by Jan Bažant, Nina Bažantová, and Frances Starn, in *The Czech Reader: History, Culture, Politics*, pp. 133–136. Copyright © 2010 Jan Bazant. All rights reserved. Republished by

permission of the copyright holder and the publisher. www.dukeupress.edu.

Blaise Pascal: From *Pensées* by Blaise Pascal, translated with an introduction by A. J. Krailsheimer. Penguin Classics, 1966. Copyright © A. J. Krailsheimer, 1966. Reproduced by permission of Penguin Books Ltd.

Giovanni Pico: "Oration on the Dignity of Man," from *Reflections on the Philosophy of the History of Mankind*, by Johann Gottfried Herder, edited by Frank Edward Manuel. Copyright © 1968 by The University of Chicago. Reprinted by permission of the University of Chicago Press.

Sidney Pollard and Colin Holmes (eds.): "Rules of a Factory in Berlin," from *Documents of Economic European History, Volume 1: The Process of Industrialization, 1750–1870*, edited by Sidney Pollard and C. Holmes. Copyright © 1968 Edward Arnold and Company Ltd. Reproduced with permission of Palgrave Macmillan.

Alan Posener: From "The bailout crisis: Germany's view of how Greece fell from grace," Alan Posener, *The Guardian*. 21 March 2015. Reprinted with permission.

Pierre-Joseph Proudhon: From *What is Property?*, by Pierre-Joseph Proudhon, edited and translated by Donald R. Kelley and Bonnie G. Smith, pp. 13–16, 27–34. Copyright © 1994 Cambridge University Press. Reprinted with permission from Cambridge University Press.

Ernest Renan: "What is a Nation?," by Ernest Renan, translated by Martin Thom, *Nation and Narration*, edited by Homi K. Bhabha. Copyright © 1990 by Routledge. Reproduced by permission of Taylor & Francis Books UK.

Thomas Riha (ed.): "Testimonies from the Decembrist Plot," from *Readings in Russian Civilization, Vol. 2: Imperial Russia, 1700–1917* (1964), pp. 295–300. Edited by Thomas Riha. University of Chicago Press. Reprinted with permission.

Oliver Roy: "What is Bin Laden's Strategy," from *Globalized Islam: The Search for a New Ummah*. Copyright © 2004 Columbia University Press. Reprinted with permission of the publisher.

St. Teresa of Ávila: From *The Life of Teresa of Jesus: The Autobiography of Teresa Avila*, translated by E. Allison Peters. New York: Bantam Doubleday Dell, 1991. Reprinted by permission of the publisher.

Haim Shaked (ed.): From *The Life of the Sudanese Mahdi: A Historical Study of the Book of the Bliss of Him Who Seeks Guidance by the Life of the Imam the Mahdi*, by Ismāʻīl b. ʻAbd al-Qādir, edited by Haim Shaked. New Brunswick, N.J.: Transaction Books, 1979, pp. 180–185, 187–188. Reprinted by permission of Transaction Publishers.

Lewis Siegelbaum and Andrei Sokolov (eds.): "Daily Life Under Stalin," from *Stalinism As A Way of Life: A Narrative in Documents*, pp. 44–46, 52–53, 64–65.

Copyright © 2004 by Yale University. Reprinted by permission of Yale University Press.

Louis L. Snyder (ed.): "Does Germany Need Colonies?," by Friedrich Fabri, from *The Imperialism Reader*, edited by Louis L. Snyder. New York: Van Nostrand, 1962, pp. 116–117.

Fritz Stern: From *Five Germanys I Have Known*, by Fritz Stern. New York: Farrar, Straus and Giroux, 2006, pp. 98, 109–113. Reprinted with the permission of Farrar, Straus and Giroux, LLC.

John Hall Stewart (ed.): "What is the Third Estate?," by Abbé Emmanuel Sieyès, and "Levée en Masse Edict," from *A Documentary Survey of the French Revolution, 1st Edition*, edited by John Hall Stewart. Copyright ©

1951. Reprinted by permission of Pearson Education, Inc., Upper Saddle River, N.J.

N. N. Sukhanov: *The Russian Revolution, 1917*, pp. 58–64. Copyright © 1984 Princeton University Press. Reprinted by permission of Princeton University Press.

Syriza Staff: From "The Thessaloniki Programme," *Syriza*, September 2014.

Every effort has been made to contact the copyright holder of each of the selections. Rights holders of any selections not credited should contact Permissions Department, W. W. Norton & Company, Inc., 500 Fifth Avenue, New York, NY, 10110, in order for a correction to be made in the next reprinting of our work.